A Genealogical History of
Robert Adams
of
Newbury, Mass.
and
His Descendants
1635–1900

Compiled and Edited by

Andrew N. Adams

Author of the *History of Fair Haven, Vt.*, and of the *History of the Adams Family of Braintree and Quincy, Mass.*; Member of the New England Historic Genealogical Society; great, great grandson of Dea. James Adams, an original settler of old Londonderry (now Derry), N.H.; formerly Member of the Senate of Vermont, and Genealogist of the Adams Families of New England.

WITH ILLUSTRATIONS

HERITAGE BOOKS
2020

HERITAGE BOOKS
AN IMPRINT OF HERITAGE BOOKS, INC.

Books, CDs, and more—Worldwide

For our listing of thousands of titles see our website
at
www.HeritageBooks.com

A Facsimile Reprint
Published 2020 by
HERITAGE BOOKS, INC.
Publishing Division
5810 Ruatan Street
Berwyn Heights, Md. 20740

Originally published by the author:
The Tuttle Co., Printers
Rutland, Vt.
1900

— Publisher's Notice —

The hand-penciled notes in the margins of the text have been preserved to the best of our ability. We make no claim as to their accuracy, but offer them as a possible enhancement to the documentation contained within.

In reprints such as this, it is often not possible to remove blemishes from the original. We feel the contents of this book warrant its reissue despite these blemishes and hope you will agree and read it with pleasure.

International Standard Book Number
Paperbound: 978-0-7884-2145-7

LIST OF ILLUSTRATIONS.

Adams Homestead (See Page 7),	Frontispiece
Andrew N. Adams,	1
Amy Adams,	92
Matthew McKelvey and wife, Nancy,	102
Mary Adams Wilson,	123
Henry Sewall Adams,	129
Capt. John Quincy Adams,	131
John Calvin Adams,	178
Dr. Daniel S. Adams,	186
Mary Electa Adams,	197
Henry Proctor Adams,	198
Dr. John Glennings C. Adams,	199
Le Roy F. Adams,	226
Ethan Lovell and wife, Martha McKelvey,	228
Hon. Leonard Bates and wife,	230
John McKelvey and wife, Jane R. H., and son, Ralph H.,	240
Mary A. Barnes,	261
Capt. John G. B. Adams,	289
Amelia Ann Weston,	292
Helen Bellows Fisk,	297
James Henry Adams,	353
Dr. John Franklin Adams,	358
Dr. Ezra Herbert Adams,	360
Willis Adams Marean,	384
Matthew T. McKelvey and family,	397
Rev. Clarence F. Swift, D. D., and family,	399
John Jay McKelvey and wife, Mary,	402
Children of John Jay McKelvey and wife, Mary,	406
Alice Rowland McKelvey Milne and children,	417
James E. Melville Milne,	420

EXPLANATION.

Numbers occurring in the margin on the left of any name re-occur in brackets following when the name again occurs as a parent in the next or succeeding generation.

Thus, the marginal number refers forward to descendants, and the bracket number backward to ancestors.

TO THE READER.

You are asked to bear in mind that these are the records of only one branch or line of the great Adams Family of New England. There are other branches, both larger and smaller— notably that of Henry Adams of Braintree and Quincy, Mass., whose history was published by the author two years ago (1898), in a volume of 1250 pages, also "William of Ipswich," "John of Plymouth," "George of Watertown," as well as several other first-comers in Massachusetts, Connecticut, Maine, and New Hampshire. The author has compiled extensive lists of all these families, which could be published for the benefit of others, if there were sufficient interest among the living descendants to warrant the labor and expense.

This book was begun many years ago when few of the original records had been printed, and it has been carried forward under many difficulties and discouragements, and is now completed only through the solicitation and encouragement of a few interested friends. If it prove to be full of errors, omissions, misstatements, it will not be surprising, for a large part of the material has been obtained only by persistent importunity and correspondence, wearying to the patience and kindness of the good friends who were interested and willing to help. In not a few instances whole families have failed, or neglected, or positively refused to lend any assistance.

Unhistoric and misleading statements have been published for truths, which have raised false expectations on the part of many people. On account of this, the book will prove a disappointment; but such as it is—being an honest effort to give useful and correct knowledge, the author submits it to public criticism, hoping it may prove useful and afford pleasure through many generations.

To the many friends who have rendered valuable assistance, and who have waited long and patiently for the completion of the work — some of whom are no longer alive — I wish here to make acknowledgment of my obligations, and among these I call

TO THE READER.

to mind, and will name, Mrs. Elizabeth Reno of Brighton, Pa., Mrs. Fanny L. Freeman of Syracuse, N. Y., Mrs. Helen B. Fisk of Logansport, Ind., Mrs. Amelia R. Weston of Georgetown, Mass., Mrs. Susan E. H. Camden of Parkersburg, W. Va., Mrs. John Q. Adams of Hampden, Mass., Mrs. Charlotte E. Osgood of No. Andover, Mass., Mrs. Anna B. Boynton of W. Newbury, Mass., Miss Harriet N. Adams of Sutton, N. H., Miss Agnes M. Adams of St. Clair, Mich., Miss Ida H. Adams of Boston, Mass., Miss Annie A. Clarke of Portland, Me., Miss Alice A. Priest, and her cousin, Miss Mabel C. Williard of Shenandoah, Ia., John McKelvey of Sandusky, O., Le Roy F. Adams of Brattleboro, Vt., Edwin P. Adams of Marlboro, Vt., Mark Trafton Adams of Boston, Mass., John Collins Adams of New London, N. H., Daniel D. Adams and Stephen P. Hale of Newbury, Mass., Oliver W. Adams of Holyoke, Mass., Raymond M. D. Adams of Byfield, Mass., D. M. Wilson of Worcester, Mass., Stephen A. Tyrrell of Hill, N. H., Dr. Ezra Herbert Adams of Toronto, Ont., James Henry Adams of Hanover, Ont., and others whose kindness is duly appreciated, and whose labor will live to benefit and help thousands in the ages to come.

A. N. ADAMS.

Fair Haven, Vt., July, 1900.

ANDREW N. ADAMS

THE DESCENDANTS OF ROBERT ADAMS
OF NEWBURY, MASS.

Born in England in 1602, Robert Adams came first to Ipswich in Massachusetts Bay in A. D. 1635, bringing with him his wife Eleanor (Wilmot?) and his first two children. He was a tailor by trade, resided in Salem in 1638-9 and removed to Newbury in 1640, where he acquired a large farm and valuable property, and died October 12, 1682, aged 81 years. His will was made at Newbury, March 7, 1680-1, and probated Nov. 27, 1682. His wife Eleanor died June 12, 1677, and he married 2nd, Feb. 6, 1678, Sarah (Glover) Short, the widow of Henry Short. She died in Newbury, Oct. 24, 1697.

He is believed by many to have come from Devonshire, and to have been a son of Robert and Elizabeth Sharlon or Sharland, connected with the Ap Adam pedigree, and through that connection to have been a cousin of Henry Adams of Braintree—(afterward Quincy, Mass.), the ancestor of the presidents, John and John Quincy Adams. This famous Welsh pedigree, beginning with Ap Adam in the time of Edward the First, about the close of the 13th century, and changing to the name of ADAMS in the eighth generation, runs through thirteen generations down to Nicholas, who married and had no issue. To this pedigree has been appended by a later hand, according to competent judges, a brother of Nicholas, named John, who married Margaret Squier, and had Richard, who married and had Robert, the father of Robert of Newbury. There is no evidence whatever to sustain this pleasing belief. His origin is not positively known.

Dr. James Savage, in his Geneological Dictionary of all the earliest or first-comers in New England (1860), says: "Robert

Adams, tailor, in Salem, 1638, by one tradition came from Devonshire, by another of *equal value* was from Holderness, County of York." According to Joshua Coffin, the historian of Newbury (1845), Robert Adams "was two or three years in Ipswich, and had before coming over, two children, John and Joanna, and at Salem, Abraham, born 1639; he removed to Newbury 1640, and had Isaac, 1648, and youngest Archelaus." He is believed to have resided within a few rods of the spot where his descendants, Col. Daniel Adams and Robert Adams, afterward lived. Mr. Coffin was mistaken in naming Archelaus among his sons. The Archelaus who has been classed as such, was a son of Lieut. John Adams, who was a son of "William of Ipswich." That he was equally mistaken in assuming that Robert Adams came from Devonshire, there is fair ground for belief.

If coming from Holderness it is not impossible that he was of Scotch origin and blood. There is a tradition among some of the descendants that he was a Scotchman.

The shears with which Robert Adams wrought and which he brought with him from England—a large pair, hand-made—are now in the possession of his descendant, Stephen P. Hale of Newbury, *later owned by Mary A. Rolfe of Newbury.*
The will of Robert Adams alludes to and confirms an agreement made with his loving wife, Sarah, before marriage,—gives her "my great chest and the highest chair in the room wherein we live," both of which she is to restore at her death, or if she shall marry again, "also all the money I have," she not to be accountable to any one, and "to enjoy the parlor wholly for one year." To his eldest son, John, he gives 20£ to be paid by his executors within twelve months after his decease; to his son Isaac he bequeaths 5£ yearly during life "in English corn, pork, beef, and such like, also my wearing apparel, and the bed in the north garret and all the furniture belonging to it, and the least, brass pot and pot hooks, etc." To Jacob he gives the house he lives in and the land adjoining to it as now fenced in, and the meadow on the neck or south side of Newbury River. To his daughter Hannah he gives 20£ to be paid within one year; to Joanna, or her children, the bed and furniture belonging to it in the parlor, and the biggest brass pot, and the chest and chair

previously mentioned when they are returned, to have them when 18 years of age or when she marries; to daughter Elizabeth, wife of Edward Phelps, he gives one cow; to daughter Joanna, wife of Launcelot Granger, one cow; to daughter Mary, wife of Jeremiah Goodrich, one cow. To the three sons of Abraham, then born—Robert, Abraham, Isaac—he gives each a gun, and to the two older each a sword. All the rest of his effects he gives to Abraham.

He provides that his lands shall go to Robert, the eldest son of Abraham, also the great brass kettle, table, and irons and spit; Abraham and his son Robert to be joint executors, but Abraham to have power to act alone till Robert should become of age. "And though I appoint Robert Adams my heir after his father, Mary, the wife of said Abraham, is not to be debarred of any just claim if left a widow." Further, to Joanna Granger he bequeaths his pewter tankard and a pewter bowl, and to Mary, daughter of Abraham, a box with lock and key and six diaper knapkins." If Robert come into possession of the lands by reversion he is to give to either of his two brothers "now in being"—Abraham and Isaac—20£ a piece. His loving friends, Mr. John Woodbridge and Mr. Nichols Noyes, were to be overseers of the will, and to them, each one, was bequeathed one of his best wethers.

Signed and sealed March 7, 1680. *Will proved 28, 9mo; 168 A few rods on left, from path between Uncle Dan's and Mrs. Chas. Adams.*

Inventory taken Nov. 3, 1682 by Tristram Coffin and Caleb Moody.

Orchard, dwelling-house, barn, etc. 80 acres upland, 60 acres meadow and freehold, 600.
Livestock, 94.
Furniture etc. 222.
Total 916£1

ROBERT ADAMS.

Children of ROBERT ADAMS and his wife Eleanor; res. Newbury, Mass.

 i. JOHN[2], b. in England, date unknown. He is said to have come to America with his father, and it has been supposed that he married a Miss Woodman, and was the father of Archelaus of Salisbury; but the probate records show that Archelaus of Salisbury was the son of Lieut. John, and grandson of "William of Ipswich."

  He appears to have been living in 1680, when his father's will was made, and yet is passed over with a simple bequest of 20 lbs, no wife or children being alluded to, from which it may fairly be inferred that he was unmarried, and left, no issue. Records were kept, and handed down of all the children of Sergt. Abraham, and of Jacob, the only sons apparently who married and left descendants.

1. ii. JOANNA[2], b. in England, about 1633–4; m. Jan. 4, 1654, Launcelot Granger, b. in England. They removed to Suffield. Conn., where he d. 3 Sept., 1689.

×2. iii. SERGT. ABRAHAM[2], b. in Salem, Mass., 1639; m. Nov. 10, 1670, Mary Pettengill, dau. of Richard and Joanna (Ingersoll) Pettengill, b. July 6, 1652; d. 19 Sept., 1705, age 53.

  He was a corporal in the militia 1685–1693, and became sergeant in 1703. He d. in Newbury, in Aug., 1714, aged 75. [*]

---

* Soon after Sergt. Abraham's death, viz.: on the 17th day of Sept., 1714, in the 13th year of Her Majesty's reign (Queen Anne) the children entered into and made the following

Agreement:—We, the subscribers, children of our honored father, Abraham Adams, late of Newbury, deceased, do mutually agree upon and make the following division of said estate to and among ourselves, in full settlement thereof.

Imprimis; Robert Adams, eldest son, is to enjoy all ye lands and buildings thereon in Newbury, called ye homestead, which lands were given by our honored grandfather, Robert Adams, late of Newbury, in his last will and testament, and all ye lands lately laid out to ye freehold right of our said grandfather on ye lower common in said town, and ye part of ye wood lott belonging to said freehold and ye land thereunto belonging, and all land yt shall be laid out in Newbury to said right with all other profits and privileges belonging to said freehold, or yt shall hereafter redound thereto, and ye Tow-combs in ye garret of ye dwelling house for the 20 shillings given him in his father's will, to be ye said Robert's—the eldest son, paying to his two brothers, Abraham and Isaac, 20 lbs apiece according to ye will of his said grandfather,—and all other payments appointed to him to make.

Item, Abraham is to enjoy for his part of said estate all ye land on which he dwells which was purchased of Mr. Samuel Sewall Esq with all profits and privileges ytunto belonging, and one-sixth part in all ye land in Haverhill except one-half of what was purchased of Peasley which is allotted for Isaac, and yt according to quantity and quality, and 24 lbs personal estate, which he has already received to his satisfaction,—the said Abraham engaging himself, and his heirs, executors and administrators to pay all debts due from said estate, and to receive all debts due to ye same.

Item; Isaac Adams is to enjoy for his part ye piece of meadow or marsh land of Jackman's at Kent's Island in Newbury, and one-half of ye tract of land

3.	iv.	ELIZABETH², b. in Newbury, about 1641-2; m. Edward Phelps, and removed to Andover, Mass., where he d. 3 Oct., 1689.
4.	v.	MARY², b. in Newbury, about 1643-5; m. Nov. 15. 1660, Jeremiah Goodrich.
	vi.	ISAAC², b. in Newbury, 1647-8; d. unm. after 1680.
	vii.	JACOB², b. in Newbury, Apr. 23. 1649; d. 12 Aug., 1649.
5.	viii.	HANNAH², b. in Newbury, June 25, 1650; m. Feb. 10, 1682, Wm- Wareham. *had dau. Joanna by Joseph Mayo Oct. 12,*
6.	ix.	JACOB², b. in Newbury, Sept. 13, 1651; m. Apr. 7, 1677, Anna Allen [Ellen?], dau. of Nicholas Allen of Dorchester, Mass. She was b. Jan. 3, 1658.

He removed, probably, about 1681-2, to Suffield (now Connecticut), where he was one of the most prominent and influential of the early settlers. He was often chosen to important offices, was a member of the General Court of the colony, then held in Boston, 1711 to 1714, and again in 1717. He d. in Boston, suddenly, in Nov. 1717, while in attendance upon his duties as a member of the General Court from Suffield.

He acquired a large property, and was greatly esteemed. His will, dated Nov. 20, 1717, is recorded both in Boston, and at Northampton, which was the county seat of Hampshire county—to which Suffield then belonged.

---

in quantity and quality bought of Peasley att Haverhill on ye southerly side, and 35 lbs. 14 shillings personal estate, in hand received to his full satisfaction, and one-sixth part of land in Haverhill.

Item; John Adams is to enjoy for his portion of said estate, 94 lbs. personal estate, in hand received to his full satisfaction, and one-sixth part of land att Haverhill, except one-half of what was purchased of Peasley.

Item; Matthew Adams is to have and hold for his part of said estate ye rate lott lying on ye upper woods, one-quarter part of ye marsh on Plum Island in quantity and quality, and one-sixth of ye land att Haverhill, except one-half of what was purchased of Peasley and 24 lbs. in moveables * * * *

Item; Israel Adams is to hold etc * * ye two acres and a half of land and orchard which Matthew Adams dwelt on, at the date hereof, bought of John Poor, and one-half quarter of ye marsh land at Plum Island, and ye land lately laid out in the lower Common and ye rate-right with ye land belonging to it, and 29 lbs. 19 shillings in personal estate, in hand received to his full satisfaction, and one-sixth of ye land att Haverhill except etc; and 2 shillings rate-right purchased of Coffin etc. * * * *

Item; Richard Adams is to have, hold and enjoy for his part, ye tract of land purchased of Henry Lunt, and ye lott lying on ye flatts by Merrimac river, both freehold and rate-part, and one-fourth and half-fourth of marsh at Plum Island, and one-half of ye wood lott belonging to the rate right etc * * * ye piece of marsh land bought of Mr. Titcomb at Salisbury, and one-eighth of land at Haverhill except, etc.=and 24 lbs. in personal estate.

Item; Mary Thurlow is to have 5 lbs. in hand with what she formerly received.

Item; Sarah Adams to have 80 lbs. and as money out of movable part about 40 lbs. in full.

Item; Dorothy Adams to have 80 lbs. personal estate and about 18 lbs. additional.

Signed by Robert, Abraham, Isaac, John, Matthew, Israel and Richard Adams, and Mary Thurlow, Sarah Adams, and Dorothy Adams.

Children of JOANNA², (1634) [1] (Robert¹) and Launcelot Granger; res. Suffield, Conn.

   i. JOHN GRANGER, b. in Newbury, Mass., Jan. 15, 1654-5; m. Feb. 9, 1678, Martha Poor, dau. of Daniel and Mary (Farnum) Poor of Andover, Mass.; b. Nov. 4, 1654; d. 4 Dec., 1723. He d. at Andover, Mass., 5 April, 1725 [6 Dec., 1682 ?].
  ii. THOMAS GRANGER, b. in Newbury; m. Nov. 14, 1683, Mindwell Taylor, dau. of Stephen and Elizabeth (Newell) Taylor, b. Nov. 5, 1663; res. Suffield, Conn. He d. March, 1729-30.
 iii. GEORGE GRANGER, b. in Newbury, Nov. 28, 1658; m. April 26, 1693, Lydia Younglove, dau. of Rev. John Younglove, the first minister of Suffield, Conn.; res. Simsbury, Conn.
  iv. ROBERT GRANGER, b. in Newbury. He was shot by the Indians at Brookfield, Mass., 8 Aug., 1709. See Hist. of Brookfield.
   v. MARY GRANGER, b. in Newbury ; m. John Burbank, Jr. of Suffield. He d. 25 March, 1729. She d. in Suffield, 21 Dec. 1629.
  vi. ELIZABETH GRANGER, b. in Newbury, March 13, 1662; m. July 16, 1684, Vicary Sikes, son of Richard and Phebe Sikes of Springfield, Mass.; b. March 3, 1649; d. 25 April, 1708. She d. 20 March, 1692.
 vii. DOROTHY GRANGER, b. in Newbury, Feb. 17, 163-4; m. April, 1689, Dr. Robert Olds of Suffield. He d. 16 Jan., 1727-8. She was his 2d wife.
viii. REBECCA GRANGER, b. in Newbury ; m. March 4, 1686; Joseph Woolcott, son of John Woolcott of Ipswich, Mass.; b. Feb. 2, 1663-4. She d. at No. Brookfield, Mass., 27 July, 1693. She was murdered by the Indians at Brookfield, with two of her children, 27 July, 1693.
  ix. SAMUEL GRANGER, b. in Newbury, July 26, 1668 ; m. March 16, 1700, Esther Hanchett, dau. of Dea. John Hanchett ; b. Aug. 1, 1678 ; d. 20 May, 1721 ; res. Suffield, Conn. He d. 22 April, 1721.
   x. HANNAH GRANGER b. m. Thomas Taylor, son of Stephen and Elizabeth Taylor of Windsor, Conn. She d. 9 Sept., 1729.
  xi. ABRAHAM GRANGER, b. in Newbury, April 17, 1673; m. (1) 1706, Hannah Hanchett, dau. of Dea. John and Ether (Prichet) Hanchett of Suffield ; she d. 7 June, 1726. He m. (2) Hannah ——.

Children of SERGT. ABRAHAM², (1639) [2] (Robert¹) and Mary (Pettengill) Adams; res. Newbury, Mass.

7.   i. MARY³, b. in Newbury, Jan. 16, 1672; m. about 1694-5, George Thurlow (or Thorley), son of Thomas and Judith (March) Thurlow, b. March 12 1670 ; d. 17 Jan., 1714.

[Handwritten note at top: The house built in 1812 by Deacon ... changes a Canandaigua, N.Y. was sold in 1920 to the Cong. Board of Ministerial Relief to be used as a home for Cong. ministers and wives. Jefferson gave Mr. G. Adams this house on his return from ...]

8. ii. ROBERT[3], b. in Newbury, May 12, 1674; m. Aug., 1695, Rebecca Knight, dau. of John and Rebecca (Noyes) Knight, b. April 27, 1674. He was a yeoman, res. Newbury, near Newburyport. He d. 3 Feb., 1769. His will, made Oct. 1, 1765, was proved Aug. 25, 1769. In it he mentions his son John as unm., his grand dau. Sarah, wife of Nathaniel Atkinson, his dau. Mary Merrill, grand dau. Mary Creasy, grandsons Jacob and Zebulon, and sons Abraham and Robert.

9. iii. CAPT. ABRAHAM[3], b. in Newbury, May 2, 1676; m. Dec., 1703, Anne Longfellow, dau. of Wm. and Anne (Sewall) Longfellow. Wm. Longfellow came from England, and was ancestor of the poet Henry Wadsworth Longfellow. His wife Anne was dau. of Henry and Jane (Dummer) Sewall, and sister of the Hon. Chief Justice Samuel Sewall. Anne Longfellow Adams d. in Byfield, 24 Feb., 1758, aged 74 years.

Abraham began life as a sailor, and became a sea-captain. He made numerous voyages to the W. Indies and to England. His father gave him a farm above the falls in Byfield, now "Highfields," and he built there the house shown as it now appears in the frontispiece, the home of Mr. Geo. W. Adams. "In it are the original deeds of the estate and two chairs which were brought to her new home by the bride. Many other relics—desks, tables, spinning wheels, chairs, warming pans, china, pewter, a tall clock, a sword, used in the battle of Bunker hill, the diary of Josiah Adams, silhouettes of colonial men and maids, are among the treasures of the house." Capt Abraham became a successful farmer, and d. in Byfield, 8 April, 1763, aged 86.

10. iv. ISAAC[3], b. in Newbury, Feb. 26, 1678-9; m. [pub. Feb. 24, 1707] Hannah Spofford, dau. of Samuel and Sarah (Burpee) Spofford of Rowley, Mass.; b. Feb. 12, 1684; d. in Boxford, 3 Sept. 1775, aged 96 years.

He began life as a weaver, but became a farmer. He resided in Rowley, and died there. His will was made Jan 24, 1737, proved Mar. 27, 1738. He had purchased a farm in Boxford in 1716, to which his widow removed after his death.

11. v. SARAH[3], b. in Newbury, Apr. 15, 1681; m. Jan. 28, 1714-5, John Hutchinson of Andover, Mass.

She settled in Andover and died there.

12. vi. JOHN[3], b. in Newbury, Mar. 7, 1684; m. (1) Jan. 22, 1707, Elizabeth Noyes; she d. childless, 23 Dec., 1708; m. (2) Nov. 17, 1713, Sarah Pearson; she d. 10 Dec., 1754-6.

He was a farmer; res. Rowley, now Georgetown, Mass., on the north side of Pentucket Pond. He d. 8 May, 1750; his will was made Nov. 25, 1746, and mentions wife Sarah, dau. Sarah Hazen, dau. Elizabeth Hardy, and children Hannah and John.

X13. vii. DR. MATTHEW[3], b. in Newbury, May 25, 1686; m. Apr. 4, 1707, Sarah Knight, prob. dau. of John and Rebecca (Noyes) Knight; b. Feb. 25, 1679; d. 29 Oct., 1778.

He is said to have been at first a cordwainer, then a farmer in Byfield Parish, and to have been the first practicing physician in W. Newbury after 1726. He d. 15 [24?] Nov., 1755; his will was made Aug. 3, 1753, and proved Dec. 8, 1755, *lived on Crane Neck Hill*

viii. ISRAEL³, b. in Newbury, Dec. 25, 1688; m. Oct. 15, 1714, Rebecca Atkinson; she m. 2nd, Oct. 10, 1716, Joseph Hilton of Exeter, N. H. He d. in Waltham, Mass., 12 Dec., 1714; no issue.

ix. DOROTHY³, b. in Newbury, Oct. 25, 1691; was unm. 1715.

14. x. RICHARD³, b. in Newbury, Nov. 22, 1693; m. Dec. 12, 1717, Susanna Pike, prob. dau. of John and Lydia (Little) Pike, b. Apr. 3, 1697; d. 17 Oct., 1754.

He was a husbandman in Newbury, and d. in Newburyport, 2 Nov., 1777-8, age 84 years. His will was made Aug. 2, 1770, proved Nov. 2, 1778. He names his dau. Mary, grandson Nathaniel, son of Enoch, granddau. Hannah, the dau. of Daniel, late of Newburyport, and sons John, Moses, Edmund and Richard.

Children of ELIZABETH², [3] (Robert¹) and Edward Phelps; res. Andover, Mass.

Savage says, "besides others, they had
i. JOHN PHELPS, b. in Newbury, Mass., Dec. 15, 1657.
He was killed by the Indians at Scarboro, Me., 29 June, 1677.
ii. EDWARD PHELPS, JR.
m. Mar. 9, 1682, Ruth Andrews, and had Edward and Bathsheba.

Children of MARY², (1643-5) [4] (Robert¹) and Jeremiah Goodrich; res. Newbury, Mass.

i. MARY GOODRICH, b. Nov. 21, 1663; m. Apr. 21, 1684, Arthur Thresher; res. Newbury, Mass.
ii. WILLIAM GOODRICH, b. Aug. 2, 1665.
iii. JEREMIAH GOODRICH, JR., b. May, 1666-7.
iv. DEA. PHILIP GOODRICH, b. Nov. 23, 1669; m. Apr, 16, 1700, Mehitable Woodman.
He was an early settler in Lunenburg, Mass., and d. there 10 Jan., 1729.
v. ELIZABETH GOODRICH, b. Feb. 27, 1679; m. Oct. 10, 1710, John Cooper.
vi. HANNAH GOODRICH, b. Nov. 15, 1681; m. 1703, Nath'l Pettengill; b. Jan. 21, 1676.
vii. JOHN GOODRICH, b. May 26, 1685; m. Hannah Brown.

Child of HANNAH[3], (1650) [5] (Robert[1]) and William Wareham; res. Newbury, Mass.

    i. PAUL WAREHAM, b. Oct. 2, 1683.

Joanna, b. Oct 12, 1678, named in her grand-father's will. She m. Joseph Lunt, now 1st Daniel Lunt.

Children of JACOB[2], (1651) [6] (Robert[1]) and Anna (Allen) Adams; res. Suffield, Conn.

15.   i.   DOROTHY[3], b. in Newbury, June 25, 1679 ; m. Jan. 12, 1698, Richard Austin ; b. 1666 ; d. 29 Oct., 1733, age 67 years. She d. 26 June, 1772.
16.   ii.   REBECCA[3], b. in Newbury, Aug. 26, 1680; m. Dec. 29, 1714, John Harmon ; res. Suffield, Conn.
17.   iii.   SERGT. JACOB[3], b. in Suffield, Conn., about 1681-2; m. Dec. 24, 1702, Mercy Gillett.
        He was an active and leading citizen of Suffield, and was chosen in 1705 "to make speeches and lead votes on prudential matters." He d. in Suffield, 28 Oct., 1756.
18.   iv.   DANIEL[3], b. in Suffield, about 1682-3 ; m. Dec. 24, 1712, Mary Sikes. She d. 20 Mar., 1756 ; res. Suffield, Conn.
19.   v.   ELIZABETH[3], b. in Suffield, Aug. 10, 1686; [m. Dec. 29, 1719, Daniel Warner of Sunderland, Mass.?]. A son Daniel Warner; m. at Stafford, Conn., 1791, Anna Pember.
20.   vi.   LIEUT ABRAHAM[3], b. in Suffield, Nov. 10, 1687; m. (1) Apr. 7, 1713, Joanna Norton of Suffield ; she d. 3 Sept., 1726. m. (2) July 25, 1733, Anna Hayden, dau. of Samuel and Anna (Holcomb) Hayden of Windsor, Conn.; b. May 2, 1700. He d. in Suffield, 12 Feb. 1769.
        A "Lieut. Abraham" of Suffield was one of a Committee, Nov. 4, 1745, to decide the location of the meeting-house in Wilbraham, Mass., and was awarded 4 Lbs for his services.
   vii.   JOHN[3], b. in Suffield; d. 9 Nov., 1690.
21.   viii.   JOHN[3], b. in Suffield June 18, 1694; m. (1) July 26, 1722, Abigail Roe or Rowe, dau. of Peter and Sarah (Remington) Rowe. m. (2) July 12, 1732, Martha Winchell ; res. Suffield, Conn.

[Fourth Generation.

Children of MARY³, (1672) [7] (Sergt. Abraham², Robert¹) and George Thurlow; res. Newbury, Mass.

 i. JUDITH THURLOW, b. in Newbury, Sept. 6, 1696; probably d. unm.
 ii. MARY THURLOW, b. in Newbury, Apr. 11, 1699; m. Jan. 19, 1738. Rev. Joseph Secombe.
 iii. THOMAS THURLOW, b. in Newbury, Dec. 11, 1701; m. Mar. 12, 1723, Joanna Pike, a sister of Susanna who m. Richard Adams, son of Sergt. Abraham². He d. 28 Aug., 1789.
 iv. GEORGE THURLOW, b. in Newbury, June 5, 1707; m. May 25, 1726, Elizabeth Hale.

Children of ROBERT³, (1674) [8] (Sergt. Abraham², Robert¹) and Rebecca (Knight) Adams; res. Long-Barn Farm, so-called, Newbury, Mass.

22. i. ABRAHAM⁴, b. in Newbury, July 8, 1696; m. Dec. 16, 1716, Abigail Pierce, dau. of Benjamin and Lydia (Frost) Pierce; b. Jan. 26, 1702; was living 1771. He was a farmer in Newbury, Mass. His will was proved May 31, 1773.
23. ii. REBECCA⁴, b. in Newbury, Jan. 28, 1698; m. Dec. 22, 1721, Dea. Joseph Morse, 3d son of Ens. Anthony and Sarah (Pike) Morse of Newbury; b. Apr. 3, 1694. She d. before 1765, and he m. 2nd, Mary Jackman.
24. iii. MARY⁴, b. in Newbury, Mar. 5, 1700; m. Nov. 23, 1724, James Merrill, son of Abel, son of Nathaniel of Newbury. They removed to Falmouth, Me., 1739. He made his will Apr. 6, 1753; it was proved Oct. 2, 1757.
25. iv. ROBERT⁴, b. in Newbury, Nov. 20, 1702; m. Oct. 29, 1725, Anne Jaques, dau. of Stephen Jaques of Newbury; she d. 14 Sept., [or 17 Oct., ?] 1778.
  He was a farmer in "auld Newbury," and d. there 5 Mar., 1773. His will was made Aug. 9, 1770, and proved Mar. 31, 1773. [*]
  Mrs. Deborah (Adams) Pike, wife of Rev. John Pike, D. D. of Rowley, Mass., and great granddaughter of Robert and Anne, says in a letter to the author, that her mother, Polly, her grandfather, Capt. Israel, and her great grandfather, Robert, as well as she herself, were all born on "the long-barn farm" in Newbury. "My

---

*The tomb-stone of Robert (1702) in the old cemetery above Newburyport, has this inscription:

  "For near——12——years
  This man an asthma had:
   Above ——10——years
  He was not in a bed:
   He to murmur
  Was never heard by won,
   But waited patient
  Till his change did come."

Fourth Generation.] OF NEWBURY, MASS. 11

     great grandfather Robert built the house—now (1892) in good condition,—for his two sons, Capt. Israel and Liphe, but the *long barn* was taken down in my childhood (1815-1840) and a new one built by my father."
  v. JACOB⁴, b. in Newbury, Nov. 10, 1704 ; d. young.
26. vi. JOHN⁴, b. in Newbury, Nov. 2, 1705 ; m. Nov. 2, 1730, Elizabeth Morse, dau. of Benjamin and Susanna Morse of Newbury, Mass.; b. 1706.
     He was a farmer and cordwainer, in Newbury ; removed to Falmouth, Me., in Apr., 1753. He purchased 4 acres of land in Falmouth, May 15, 1747, on the N. E. of Pesumpscott river, of George and Mary Tuck, and is said in the deed to be of Newbury. He was there in Apr., 1753, etc. [Vol. 27, p. 291], when he made a deed of land in Falmouth, near his residence, to James Merrill, calling him his brother. He made a deed Feb. 28, 1776, to his son Benjamin [Bk. 8, p. 430]. His will was made before Feb., 1776, and he d. after 1782, and before June, 1787. Mary Lombard (afterward Mary Huston) testified in June, 1787, that John was deceased.
27. vii. JACOB⁴, b. in Newbury, Dec. 22, 1713; m. Aug. 31, 1742, Mary Hills. Administration was granted on his estate in Newbury, July 1, 1745.
  viii. DOROTHY⁴, b. in Newbury, Jan. 12, 1718. She is said to have d. before 1765.

Children of CAPT. ABRAHAM³, (1676) [9] (Sergt. Abraham², Robert¹) and Anne (Longfellow) Adams ;. res. Newbury-Byfield, Mass.

28. i. ANNE⁴, b. in Newbury, Apr. 29, 1705; m. Dec. 11, 1727, Robert Stuart, son of Ebenezer and Elizab. (Johnson) Stuart of Rowley, Mass.; b. Nov. 26, 1701 ; d. near the close of the Revolutionary war. They set. in Kingston, N. H., where she d., 1787. Their first home, in the woods of Kingston, afterward Newton, N. H., was a log cabin. He had been an employee of Gov. Dummer at Rowley. He was a Baptist, and helped to organize the first Baptist church in New Hampshire at Newton, in 1755. He built a church of logs called "Stuart's Church," and supported the preaching, refusing to pay the town minister's tax, for which an unsuccessful attempt was made to arrest him.
29. ii. WILLIAM⁴, b. in Newbury, May 8, 1706 ; m. Apr. 22, 1728, Elizabeth Noyes, dau. of John and Mary (Thurlo) Noyes of Newbury, b. Jan. 16, 1708 ; d. 1787 ; adm. on her est. granted May 8, 1787.
     He set. in that part of Rowley which is now Georgetown, Mass., and built a house long after occupied by his son-in-law, Benja. Adams Jr., on land which his father, Capt. Abraham had purchased as early as 1721-2. The house was burned in 1800. He was one of the original founders of the church in Georgetown in 1732, then the 2nd parish in Rowley. He was a farmer, and d. in the winter 1765-6. His will was made May 9, 1765, proved

Mar. 24, 1766, and makes mention of his brother Abraham, and the nine children.

iii. MARY⁴, b. in Newbury, Sept. 26, 1707; m. Sept. 30, 1728, Thomas Poor of Andover, Mass.; res. Andover, Mass.; d. without issue.

iv. STEPHEN⁴, bapt. at Byfield, Apr. 16, 1712; d. young.

30. v. SARAH⁴, b. in Newbury, Sept. 29, 1713; bapt. Oct. 6; m. Sept. 29, 1735, Dea. Samuel Somerby of Newburyport, Mass.; res. Rowley. Mass.

31. vi. ABRAHAM⁴, b. in Newbury, Aug. 24, 1715; m. (1) Nov. 18, 1737, Mary Coleman of Newbury; she d. of fever at the birth of triplets, May 6, 1752, age 35 years; the children d. the same day. m. (2) Jan. 29, 1760, Sarah Foster.

He was a tanner in Methuen, 1742–1747, but resided the most of his life in Rowley, now So. Georgetown, on what was the Shute place, Nelson Street. His mind became unsound and he hung himself in the entry of his house, 18 Sept., 1771, age 56 years.

32. vii. SAMUEL⁴, b. in Newbury, bapt. at Byfield, June 6, 1717; m. Nov. 26, 1747, Mary (Jewett) Brown of Rowley. He succeeded to the homestead, Newbury-Byfield (Highfields), and is described as a shrewd business man, who acquired a large property.

He went with four of his sons as soldiers in the war of the Revolution, and his house was a rendezvous for all the patriots.

He d. 8 May, 1791, age 73 years. His widow d. 17 Nov., 1812, at the age of ninety.

33. viii. REV. JOSEPH⁴, b. in Newbury, May 8, 1719; m. [pub. Nov. 29, 1746] widow Mary Greenleaf of Newbury. He graduated from Harv. Col. in 1742, and became "a zealous new-light preacher," his converts organizing a church in Newburyport.

He set. in Stratham, N. H., in June, 1756, and d. there 24 Feb., 1785, age 65.

34. ix. REV. BENJAMIN⁴ [also called "Mr."] (twin), b. May 8, 1719; m. (1) May 15, 1748, Elizabeth Payson, dau. of Rev. Mr. Payson of Rowley; she d. 23 Dec., 1753; m. (2) Rebecca Nichols of Amherst, N. H.

He graduated from Harv. College in 1738, became first a teacher, then a minister, ordained at Lynn, Mass., Nov. 5, 1755, now Lynnfield, where he d., it is said, in his pulpit, 4 May, 1777, age 57.

35. x. CAPTAIN NATHAN⁴, b. in Newbury, June 17, 1721; m. Feb. 17, 1757, Mary Trumbull of Charlestown, Mass.

He was a carpenter; set. in Charlestown, where he was an innkeeper, and his house was burned by the British in 1775. He served as a captain in the French war.

36. xi. HENRY⁴, b. in Newbury, Nov. 18, 1722; m. (1) Nov. 20, 1746, Sarah Emery of Newbury; she d. 7 Feb. 1764, aged 37; m. (2) Mar. 2, 1767-8, Catherine Gerrish; she m. 2nd, Dec. 4, 1777, Benja. Poor.

He was a farmer, near his father, at Newbury-Byfield; d. 15 Oct., 1773, age 51.

Fourth Generation.] OF NEWBURY, MASS. 13

Children of ISAAC³ (1679) [10] (Sergt. Abraham², Robert¹) and Hannah (Spofford) Adams; res. Rowley, Mass.

38. i. HANNAH⁴, b. in Rowley, June 15, 1709; m. [pub. Jan. 15, 1731], David Burbank of Bradford, Mass.; res. Bradford; she d. 20 Aug., 1744.

39. ii. SAMUEL⁴, b. in Rowley, Feb. 9 [bapt. 18th], 1710-1; m. June 28, 1732, in Bradford, Mary Burbank, given also as Sarah Burbank; res. Rowley, Mass. He d. 18 Dec., 1736, and his widow m. [pub. Jan. 4, 1738] Benja. Scott.

40. iii. CAPT. ISAAC⁴, b. in Rowley, May 25, 1713; m. Apr. 1, 1743, Mary or Mercy Wood, dau. of Dr. David Wood; b. 1720; d. ~~1794~~ June 10, a7 He set. in Boxford, Mass., in 1738; was commissioned as captain of the 2nd Co. of militia of Boxford, Sept. 1, 1762; was selectman for 14 years; represented the town in the General Court in 1783, and the three years following, also in 1778. He d. on his home farm 20 Mar., 1797, age 83 years.

41. iv. ISRAEL⁴, b. in Rowley, Apr. 25, 1716; m. Oct. 16, 1740, Deborah Searle of Rowley; she d. in Georgetown, Mass., Oct., 1789. Bapt. church record says buried the last day of the month; yeoman; res. Rowley, Mass. He made his will Apr. 21, 1784. He d. in Jan., 1789; will was proved May 8, 1799.

42. v. DAVID⁴, b. in Rowley, June 15, 1720; m. Sept. 29, 1742, Hannah Jackson. He d. of consumption 18 May, 1751; res. Byfield parish, Rowley, Mass.

vi. ABIGAIL⁴, b. in Rowley, June 28, 1722; d. 24 Nov. 1737.

vii. MARY⁴, b. in Rowley, Oct. 12, 1724; d. young.

Child of SARAH³, (1681) [11] (Sergt. Abraham², Robert¹) [later, Sarah Hutchinson]; res. Newbury and Andover, Mass.

43. i. ISRAEL⁴, b. in Newbury, Feb. 24, 1707-8; m. Mar. 20, 1733, Tabitha Farnum of Andover, Mass. She d. in Rindge, N. H.; 18 Feb., 1804, age 97.

He was called "Benoni" in early life; became a cordwainer in Andover; was a soldier in the French and Indian war; removed and settled in Rindge, N. H., about 1772, where he d. 16 Oct., 1789, age about 82 or 83.

This account of the birth of Israel is received by the author from an old record in the possession of Mrs. Julia A. M. Spofford of West Boxford, Mass., one of the descendants. It has been published in *The Essex Antiquarian*, Vol. II., No. 2, (February, 1898).

Its correctness is disputed, and another account is given of Israel's ancestry, by John M. Adams of West Lebanon, Columbia Co., N. Y. He claims that Israel was the son of Abraham Olney Adams and his wife Hannah La Grasse, dau. of Donald La Grasse of Drumlanrig, Scotland, that he was b. in Quincy, Mass., in 1706, removed to Keene, N. H., and thence to Andover and Littleton, Mass., finally to Rindge, N. H., where he d. 16 Oct., 1789. age 83 years ; that he married (1) in 1726 Mercy Holdridge of Stonington, Conn. ; m. (2) Mar. 20, 1733, Tabitha Farnum, and m. (3) Polly White of Providence, R. I.

Abraham Olney Adams, according to this account, was b. near Charlestown, Mass., Jan. 11, 1680, and was son of Stephen Olney Adams, who was b. in Tenterden, Kent Co., Eng., Apr. 18, 1620 ; m. twice, (1) in Maidstone, Eng., May 1, 1645, to Lydia Hartwell ; she d. in Maidstone, 1650.

Stephen Olney was an officer in Cromwell's army, and was wounded at the battle of Worcester, Sept. 3, 1651. Fleeing to America to save his life he settled near Charlestown, Mass., and m. (2) 1678, Priscilla Durrie, who was the mother of Abraham Olney and others. She d. in 1718, age 98 years.

The only child of Israel by his first wife, Mercy Holdridge, it is stated, was Stephen, b. in Rowley, June 6, 1727. See Stephen, No. 96, where this account is further discussed.

Children of JOHN[3], (1684) [12] (Sergt. Abraham[2], Robert[1]) and Sarah (Pearson) Adams; res. Rowley, Mass.

44.   i.   SARAH[4], b. in Rowley, Oct. 11, 1714 ; m. Oct. 13, 1737, Jeremiah Hazen, son of John and Sarah (Nelson) Hazen, b. Feb. 29, 1715 ; d. in Rowley, of smallpox, 5 June, 1779.

45.   ii.   ELIZABETH[4], b. in Rowley, June 18, 1717; m. Mar. 21, 1742–3, Reuben Hardy of Bradford, Mass. She survived him, and d. in Bradford, 19 Aug., 1792.

     iii.   MEHITABLE[4], b. in Rowley, June 21, 1719 ; d. June, 1736.

46.   iv.   JOHN[4], b. in Rowley, Apr. 12, 1721 ; m. (1) Aug. 3, 1748, Sarah or Mary Brocklebank ; m. (2) June 10, 1755, Elizabeth Kilborn of Rowley ; m. (3) Sept. 18, 1764, Mrs. Meribah Stickney, dau. of Jonathan and Rebecca (Hardy) Tenney and widow of Samuel Stickney of Bradford, Mass. She was b. in Bradford, Mass., Mar. 4, 1727 ; m. 1st, Oct. 11, 1743, Samuel Stickney, who d. 31 Oct., 1755. She d. in New London, N. H., 21 July, 1803.

John Adams set. in New London, N. H., about 1780, and d. 28 Sept., 1803. His will was proved Oct. 23, 1803.

     v.   MARY[4], b. in Rowley, Feb. 11, 1722; bapt. in Byfield, Feb. 17 ; d. 6 Aug., 1736.

     vi.   BENJAMIN[4], b. in Rowley, Dec. 8, 1724. He was not mentioned in his father's will, and probably died before Nov., 1746.

     vii.   HANNAH[4], b. in Rowley, Aug. 11, 1727. Did she m. John Woodman,—pub. Dec. 12, 1751 ?

     viii.   MOSES[4], b. in Rowley, Nov. 7, 1730 ; d. 26 July, 1736.

Children of DR. MATTHEW³, (1686) [13] (Sergt. Abraham², Robert¹) and Sarah (Knight) Adams; res. Crane Neck Hill) West Newbury, Mass.

 i. MATTHEW⁴, b. in West Newbury, Jan. 19, 1707 ; d. 27 Jan., 1707.

47. ii. MATTHEW⁴, b. in West Newbury, Mar. 19, 1709 ; m. (1) May 2, 1734, Sarah Bartlett. m. (2) May 17, 1744, Hannah Rawlins, dau. of Benjamin and Hannah (Annis) Rawlins, b. May 22, 1726; d. 3 July, 1782 ; res. W. Newbury, Mass. He d. 2 Jan., 1765 [?].

48. iii. SARAH⁴, b. in West Newbury, Sept. 5, 1711 ; m. June 5, 173—, Joseph Bartlett. She d. in W. Newbury, 16 Feb., 1745.

49. iv. ABRAHAM⁴, b. in West Newbury, May 10, 1713 ; m. Mar. 14, 1738, Mary Adams, dau. of Richard and Susanna (Pike) Adams, b. Oct. 8, 1718 ; d. 29 July, 1789.
  He was called "Abraham 3d ;" d. 29 May, 1795, age 82 years.

50. v. JUDITH⁴, b. in West Newbury, Apr. 2, 1716 ; m. Mar. 18, 1736, Capt. Edmund Little, son of Enoch and Elizabeth (Worth) Little, b. Sept. 5, 1715 ; d. 29 Aug., 1803. She d. 7 Sept., 1784.

 vi. EUNICE⁴, b. in West Newbury, Apr. 7, 1719.

 vii. JOSEPH⁴, b. in West Newbury ; bapt. at Byfield, July 29, 17——

 viii. ELIZABETH⁴, b. in West Newbury, Apr. 28, 1728.

Children of RICHARD³, (1693) [14] (Sergt. Abraham², Robert¹) and Susanna (Pike) Adams; res. Newbury, Mass.

 i. MARY⁴, b. in Newbury, Oct. 8, 1718 ; m. Mar. 14, 1738, Abraham Adams, son of Dr. Matthew and Sarah (Knight) Adams. She d. Aug., 1789, age 71 years.

 ii. JOHN⁴, b. in Newbury, Sept. 9, 1720 ; d. 20 Mar., 1723.

51. iii. HANNAH⁴, b. in Newbury, Nov. 16, 1722; m. Apr. 20, 1742-3, Capt. Daniel Chute, son of James and Mary (Thurston) Chute (James³, James², Lionel¹) b. in Byfield, May 6, 1722. She d. 28 April, 1792 [1812?].

52. iv. ENOCH⁴, b. in Newbury, Sept. 24, 1724 ; m. July 28, 1747, Sarah Jackman. She d. Nov., 1773.
  He was a cordwainer ; res. Newbury-Byfield, Mass., and d. suddenly 27 July, 1749, age 24 yrs. 10 mos.

53. v. RICHARD⁴, b. in Newbury, Nov. 2, 1726 ; m. Jan. 21, 1755, Sarah Noyes ; she d. 31 Jan., 1821.
  He was a farmer ; res. Newburyport, Mass.; d. 6 Nov., 1788, age 62 years.

 vi. SUSANNA⁴, b. in Newbury, Aug. 5, 1729 ; d. 19 June, 1745.

54. vii. JOHN⁴, b. in Newbury, July 30, 1732 ; m. Dec. 22, 1761, Elizabeth Thorla or Thorlow. She d. 4 Sept., 1820, in her 82nd year ; res. Newbury, Mass. He d. 2 Sept., 1811, age 79 years.

55. viii. DANIEL[4], b. in Newbury, Sept. 13, 1734; m. Oct. 26, 1758, Edna Noyes; she m. 2nd, May 4, 1777, John Noyes, Jr. He d. in Newbury, 1 Dec., 1759, age 25 yrs. 2 mos.
56. ix. MOSES[4], b. in Newbury, June 17, 1737; m. Feb. 6, 1770, Ruth Palmer. He d. in Newbury, 16 Sept., 1817, age 80 yrs. 8 mos.
57. x. DEA. EDMUND[4], b. in Newbury, Oct. 24, 1740; m. (1) Nov. 22, 1764, Hannah Thurston. She d. 14 Sept., 1807, age 66 years; m. (2) about 1811, Mrs. Betsey Kimball of Hampstead, N. H.

He removed to Derry, N. H., where he settled on the farm long belonging in the family of Dea. James Adams, a Scotch-Irish first comer, and ancestor of the author of this work, situated about one mile east of Derry street. He d. there 18 Jan., 1825, age 84 years.

Children of DOROTHY[3], (1679) [15] (Jacob[2], Robert[1]) and Capt. Richard Austin; res. Suffield, Conn.

  i. RICHARD AUSTIN, JR., b. Oct. 9, 1699.
  ii. DOROTHY AUSTIN, b. July 26, 1801.
  iii. JACOB AUSTIN, b. June 1, 1804.
  iv. EBENEZER AUSTIN, b. Apr. 22, 1806.
  v. ANNA AUSTIN, b. Jan. 16, 1808-9.
  vi. JOSEPH AUSTIN, b. Jan. 26, 1810-11.
  vii. REBECCA AUSTIN, b. Apr. 16, 1813.
  viii. MOSES AUSTIN, b. Apr. 25, 1816.
  ix. ELIAS AUSTIN, b. Apr. 14, 1818.

Children of REBECCA[3], (1680) [16] (Jacob[2], Robert[1]) and John Harmon; res. Suffield, Conn.

  i. REBECCA HARMON, b. Apr. 14 1717; m. Nov. 11, 1735, Dudley Remington, son of Dea. Joseph and Eliza (Dudley) Remington. She d. 29 Jan., 1783.
  ii. HANNAH HARMON, b. Feb. 8, 1779.
  iii. SARAH HARMON, b. Mar. 12, 1721.

Children of SERGT. JACOB[3], (1681) [17] (Jacob[2], Robert[1]) and Mercy (Gillett) Adams; res. Suffield, Conn.

58. i. JACOB[4], b. in Suffield, Nov. 15, 1703; m. Apr. 25, 1729, Elizabeth Warner of Enfield, Conn.; d. Dec. 1771; res. Suffield, Conn. He d. 24 Sept., 1768.
  ii. JOHN[4], b. in Suffield, Aug. 18, 1705; d. 25 Aug., 1706-7.

Fourth Generation.] OF NEWBURY, MASS. 17

59. iii. JOHN[4], b. in Suffield, Jan. 25, 1706; m. July 12, 1733, **Martha** Winchell, called "John of Suffield," by Hinman. She d. 22 Nov., 1760.
60. iv. MERCY[4], b. in Suffield, Feb. 19, 1708-9. Did she m. Thomas Savary? [*]
61. v. AGNES[4], b. in Suffield, Feb. 4, 1710; m. May 16, 1732, Nathaniel Austin.
    vi. JONATHAN[4], b. in Suffield, Nov. 9, 1713.
    vii. ELIZABETH[4], b. in Suffield, June 15, 1715; m. July 4, 1743, Samuel Lane, son of Samuel Lane, b. Sept. 27, 1712; d. 1750. [†]
    viii. MARY[4], b. in Suffield, Feb. 17, 1716.
62. ix. BENJAMIN[4], b. in Suffield, Oct. 7, 1718; [m. Oct. 19, 1767, Deborah Baion?]. He d. 29 Apr., 1779.
63. x. RACHEL[4], b. in Suffield, Sept. 4, 1725; m. (1) ———, 1743, Posthumous Sikes; m. (2) ———, 1758, Jove Hopkins.

Children of DANIEL[3], (1683) [**18**] (Jacob[2], Robert[1]) and Mary (Sikes) Adams; res. Suffield, Conn.

64. i. ZEBULON[4], b. in Suffield, Sept. 27, 1713; m. (1) June 17, 1742, Bertha King, dau. of Daniel King. She d. 22 Jan., 1761, age 40 years; no issue; m. (2) Jan. 24, 1762, Sarah [Susan?] Pengilly. She d. Sept., 1816; m. (3) ———, Lucy Bacon. He d. in Suffield, 25 Dec., 1795.
    ii. GIDEON[4], b. in Suffield, Mar. 26, 1716; d. at sea, 6 Aug., 1734.
    iii. MARY[4], b. in Suffield, July 19, 1719; d. 4 May, 1741.
    iv. STEPHEN[4], b. in Suffield, Feb. 21, 1721; d. 10 May, 1737,
65. v. ELIZABETH[4], b. in Suffield, Apr. 2, 1724; m. Oct. 13, 1745, Simon Kendall, son of Joshua and Susanna (Harrington) Kendall, b. Dec. 16, 1724; d. 13 Nov., 1769. She d. 12 Dec., 1791.
66. vi. DANIEL JR.[4], b. in Suffield, Apr. 30, 1726; m. July 6, 1747, Rebecca Kendall, dau. of Joshua and Susanna (Harrington) Kendall, b. June 24, 1727.

Children of LIEUT. ABRAHAM[3], (1687) [**20**] (Jacob[2], Robert[1]) and Joanna (Norton) Adams; res. Suffield, Conn.

    i. ABRAHAM[4], b. in Suffield, Feb. 19, 1715.
        He was living in Oct., 1726, when, upon the death of his mother, the father was appointed guardian of the four children, Abraham, Joseph, Joanna and Freegrace.

---

* A Mercy of Suffield, m. at Sheffield, Mass., Mar. 3, 1743, Ethan David Clark.

† She survived him and was his executrix.

[An Abraham was of Crum Elbow, Dutchess Co., N. Y., and purchased land in the Great Division, Nine Partner's Tract, in July, 1746, and he was probably at Sheffield, Mass., in 1755.]

 ii. REV. JOSEPH[4], b. in Suffield, Jan. 24, 1718-9. He was a member of Yale College in 1738.

 iii. JOANNA[4], b. in Suffield, Aug. 23, 1720.

67. iv. FREEGRACE[4], b. in Suffield, Nov. 14–19, 1723 ; m. Apr. 4, 1753, Anna Kent, dau. of Samuel and Abiah (Dwight) Kent, b. Oct. 2, 1730; d. 8 Sept., 1807, age 77.

  He removed, and set. in Marlboro, Vt., about 1774, and d. there in Aug., 1815, age 92 years.

 v. SILENCE[4], b. in Suffield, Aug., 22, 1726 ; d. same day.

 vi. MOURNFUL[4] (twin), b. in Suffield, Aug. 22, 1726. She d. 5 Sept. 1726, two days after her mother.

Children of LIEUT. ABRAHAM[3], (1687) and Anne (Hayden) Adams.

68. vii. ANNA[4], b. in Suffield, May 27, 1734 ; probably m. (1) Feb. 8, 1759, Elijah Leonard, 2nd son of Abel (Benjamin[2], John[1]) and Esther (Austin) Leonard, b. in Conway, Mass., Apr. 14, 1733 ; m. (2) ———, Russell Leonard, cousin of Elijah. She d. in Conway, 1833, age 99 years.

69. viii. SAMUEL[4], b. in Suffield, Sept. 4, 1736 ; m. (1) Nov. 9 1767, Dorcas Frost ; she d. 26 Jan., 1778, in her 33d year ; m. (2) Feb. 18, 1779, Elizabeth Purchase. She d. in Westhaven, Vt., 27 Sept., 1820.

  He followed his sons to Westhaven, Vt., and d. there 24 Mar., 1811.

Children of JOHN[3], (1694) [21] (Jacob[2], Robert[1]) and Abigail (Rowe) Adams; res. Suffield, Conn.

70. i. MOSES[4], b. in Suffield, July 8, 1722-3; m. Oct. 30, 1746, Mehitable Sikes ; she d. 27 Apr., 1813, age 93. He d. in Suffield, 18 Oct., 1809, age 87 years.

71. ii. CAPT. SIMEON[4], b. in Suffield, Nov. [4?] 20, 1724 ; m. Jan. [8 ?] 28, 1765-6, Susanna Underwood, dau. of Jonathan Underwood, b. in Westfield, Mass., Sept. 22, 1747 ; d. in Marlboro, Vt., 14 Sept., 1845, age 98 years.

  He was a soldier in the French war; was twice taken a captive, and carried to Canada, but was exchanged and returned.

  He purchased a farm in Marlboro, Vt., in 1783, of Joseph Pease of Suffield, and probably removed to Marlboro about this time. He is called "Captain Simeon," and there is a tradition that Susanna drove British officers out of her house during the Revolution. He d. in Marlboro, 1 Aug., 1803, age 79 years.

iii. ANNA[4], b. in Suffield, June 8, 1727.

72. iv. LIEUT. JOEL[4], b. in Suffield, Dec. 20, 1729 ; m. July 16, 1761, Elizabeth Fowler ; she d. at 90 years of age.

He was a soldier in the French war, and was wounded in the battle at Lake George, 1755. He held a Lieutenant's commission under the English crown. He is said to have manumited his slaves that they might participate in the war for independence. He settled in Marlboro, Vt. His will was probated, Mar., 1820. He left his property to his wife, his sons Job, Bildad, and Joel Jr., and to his daughters Lucina Hale, Elizabeth Otis, and Sarah Winchester; Joel Jr. was named as executor.

v. LUCY[4], b. in Suffield, May 31, 1731.

Children of ABRAHAM⁴, (1696) [**22**] (Robert³, Sergt. Abraham², Robert¹) and Abigail (Pierce) Adams; res. Newbury, Mass.

73.   i. ROBERT⁵, b. in Newbury, Nov. 25, 1717; m. Sept. 7, 1738, Love Jaques, dau. of Henry and Mary (Coffin) Jaques. He d. 24 Aug., 1785. His will was made July 25, 1785, proved Sept. 26, 1785.

74.   ii. LYDIA⁵, b. in Newbury, Oct. 31, 1719; m. Jan. 3, 1738, Eliphalet Jaques, son of Henry and Mary (Coffin) Jaques, b. 1714; d. 24 June, 1804. She d. 7 June, 1798.

      iii. ABIGAIL⁵, b. in Newbury, Nov. 11, 1721; d. unm. 1758, age 36 years.

75.   iv. BENJAMIN⁵, b. in Newbury, Apr. 13, 1723 [Apr. 20, 1724?]; m. (1) Aug. 6, 1747, Abigail Kendrick, dau. of Capt. John Kendrick of Newton, Mass., b. Mar. 14, 1726; m. (2) Jan. 23, 1755, Sarah Burrage.

        He was a book binder; settled in Boston about 1745, where he d. 1778.

76.   v. MARY⁵, b. in Newbury, Aug. 26, 1727. [Did she m. ——— Creasy? See will of Robert³.]

77.   vi. CHARLES⁵, b. in Newbury, Nov. 4, 1729; m. (1) Jan. 25, 1753, Rebecca Adams, dau. of Robert and Ann (Jaques) Adams, b. Jan. 25, 1730; d., 1758; m. (2) Dec. 18, 1760, Mary Hills, dau. of Smith and Mary (Sawyer) Hills, b. July 31, 1735; d. 26 Dec., 1805. He d. in the midst of a thunder storm, 9 Jan., 1802, age 72 yrs. and 2 mos.

78.   vii. MEHITABLE⁵, b. in Newbury, Nov. 5, 1734; m. June 11, 1763, John Knight, son of Joseph and Rebecca (Noyes) Knight, b. Mar. 12, 1726.

     viii. DANIEL⁵, b. in Newbury, Mar. 31, 1739; d. unm.

79.   ix. ELIZABETH⁵, b. in Newbury, July 15, 1741; m. Dec. 17, 1761, Jacob Freeze.

80.   x. SARAH⁵, b. in Newbury, Aug. 7, 1743; m. 1774, Isaac Adams, an Englishman.

Children of REBECCA⁴, (1698) [**23**] (Robert³, Sergt. Abraham², Robert¹) and Dea. Joseph Morse; res. Newbury, Mass.

81.   i. DEA. ANTHONY MORSE, b. Sept. 22, 1722; m. (1) [pub. at Falmouth, Me., Feb. 26, 1744], Hannah Merrill; m. (2) Susan (Wallace) Jones.

        He was a farmer, weaver, and doctor, of versatile ability; was a deacon for 40 years. He removed to Falmouth, Me., where he d. in 1806, age 84 years.

      ii. REBECCA MORSE, b. Sept. 12, 1724.

     iii. JOSEPH MORSE, b, June 24, 1727.

Fifth Generation.] OF NEWBURY, MASS. 21

  iv. SARAH MORSE, b. Feb. 18, 1729-30.
  v. MARY MORSE, b. Mar. 13, 1731-2.
82. vi. ELIPHALET MORSE, b. July 29, 1733 ; m. (1) Mar. 9, 1757, Abigail Pettengill ; m. (2) Mar. 12, 1761, Anna Rolfe.
   He was a member of the First Church in Newbury, Mass.; removed to Bradford, N. H., after 1776.
  vii. ELIZABETH MORSE, b. Dec. 21, 1734.

Children of MARY⁴, (1700) [24] (Robert³, Sergt. Abraham², Robert¹) and James Merrill; res. Falmouth, Me.

83. i. ISRAEL MERRILL, b. in Newbury, about 1725-6 ; m. [pub. at Falmouth, Aug. 20, 1743] Abigail Cawley or Cauley of Falmouth, Me. He d. at N. Yarmouth, Me., before Apr., 1753.
  ii. DEA. HUMPHREY MERRILL, b. in Newbury ; m. (1) [pub. Aug. 29, 1741], Betsey Merrill, dau. of Moses³, of N. Yarmouth, (Daniel², Nathaniel¹) ; m. (2) June 18, 1783, Mrs. Mary (Noyes) Weare, dau. of Nathan Noyes, and widow of Joseph Weare. She d. in Falmouth, before 1825.
  iii. REBECCA MERRILL, b. in Newbury; m. before 1753, John Cauly. He was a soldier in Capt. Samuel Noyes' Co.,—enlisted from Falmouth, May 15, 1775 ; d. 21 Sept., 1775.
  iv. PRISCILLA MERRILL, b. in Newbury.
  v. ADAMS MERRILL, b. in Stratham, N. H.; m. [pub. Nov. 19, 1757], Elizabeth Titcomb of Falmouth, Me.
  vi. MAJ. JAMES MERRILL, b. in Stratham, 1728 ; m. Jan. 24, 1754, Abigail Brackett [*], b. May 21, 1727 ; d. 6 Nov., 1806.
   He was a soldier of the Revolution and a prominent man in Falmouth; d. 16 Nov., 1806.
84. vii. LIEUT. JOSHUA MERRILL, b. in Stratham ; m. [pub. at Falmouth, Nov. 1, 1755] Mary Winslow, dau. of Nathan and Charity (Hall) Winslow, b. in Falmouth, 1739; d. 1832. She m. 2nd, Greenfield Pote; was reputed to be "the handsomest girl in Cumberland county."
   He enlisted as a soldier in Capt. Samuel Noyes' Co., Col. Edmund Phinney's Reg., and was 2nd Lieutenant. He d. in Falmouth, 1782.
85. viii. MARY MERRILL, b. in Stratham ; m. [pub. Sept. 29, 1750], Capt. Samuel Noyes, b. Mar. 15, 1725.
   He raised a company in Falmouth, for the war, which included his own son and many of his kindred.
  ix. DOROTHY MERRILL, b. in Stratham ; m. [pub. May 25, 1753], John Blake of Falmouth, Me.

---

* Maj. James Merrill is reported as having married (1) Mary R. Adams ; m. (2) Abigail Adams.

x. SUSANNA MERRILL, b. in Falmouth, Me.; m. [pub. June 22, 1761], Moses Adams, son of John and Elizabeth (Morse) Adams.

xi. SILAS MERRILL, b. in Falmouth ; m. (1) Susanna Knight ; m. (2) Hannah Matthews.
He was a soldier in Capt. Noyes' Co. from Falmouth, Me.

Children of ROBERT⁴, (1702) [25] (Robert³, Sergt. Abraham², Robert¹) and Anne (Jaques) Adams; res. Newbury, Mass.

i. ISRAEL⁵, b. in Newbury, July 19, 1726 ; d. Mar., 1730.

ii. REBECCA⁵, b. in Newbury, Jan. 25. 1730 ; m. Jan. 25, 1753, Charles Adams, son of Abraham and Abigail (Pierce) Adams. She d. without issue, in 1758, age 28 years.

iii. EUNICE⁵, b. in Newbury, Jan. 12, 1732 ; d. unm.

86. —iv. CAPT. ISRAEL⁵, b. in Newbury, Mar. 22, 1735 ; m. Nov. 11, 1779, Deborah Jaques ; she d. 20 May, 1837, age 99 yrs. and 23 dys. He d. 4 Jan., 1812, age 77 years.

87. v. LIPHE⁵, b. in Newbury, May 8, 1736 ; m. May 14, 1775, Mary Boynton of Newbury ; she d. 7 Feb., 1822. He d. 20 Sept., 1801, age 65 yrs., 4 mos.

vi. SARAH⁵, b. in Newbury, May 23, 1739 ; d. 9 Jan., 1778, age 38–9.

88. vii. CAPT. SILAS⁵, b. in Newbury, Feb. 8 [16?], 1741; m. Sept. 3 [8?], 1779, Lucy Underwood of Portsmouth, N. H. She m. 2nd, Daniel Do'dge, and d. 12 Sept., 1844, age 74 years.
He was a cordwainer, also a soldier in the Revolution. He enlisted and went to Lexington, Apr. 19, 1775, probably in Capt. Jacob Gerrish's Company; was commissioned as Lieutenant, June 27, 1775, and became Captain of a company of men from Newbury, Danville, Rowley, and Middleton in 1777. He was called out in Apr., 1777, to re-enforce Gen. Michael Farley in Rhode Island. He d. 19 Feb. [15 Nov.], 1800, age 59 yrs., 9 mos.

89. viii. ANNA⁵, b. in Newbury, Mar. 14, 1745 ; m. Apr. 28, 1767, John Knapp, son of Nathaniel and Sarah (Hart) Knapp (Isaac³, John², William¹), b. in Newburyport, Oct. 3, 1744 ; d. Feb., 1797. She d. 29 Sept., 1778.

90. ix. ROBERT⁵, b. in Newbury, July 24, 1750 ; m. July 12, 1774, Eunice Little, dau. of Capt. Edmund and Judith (Adams) Little ; she m. 2nd, Sept. 18, 1788, Bradstreet Tyler, and settled in Boxford, Mass.
He was a cordwainer and weaver in Newbury, and d. 3 Dec., 1776, age 26 years.

Children of JOHN[4], (1705) [**26**] (Robert[3], Sergt. Abraham[2], Robert[1]) and Elizabeth (Morse) Adams; res. Newbury, Mass., and Falmouth, Me.

91. i. SUSANNA[5], b. in Newbury, Sept. 6, 1731; m. at Falmouth, Aug. 17, 1754, Nathaniel Thompson, son of Joseph Thompson.

Joseph Thompson and wife were admitted to the First Church in Falmouth from the church in Newbury in 1746. Nathaniel Thompson and wife Susanna sign many deeds in Falmouth down to a period as late as June, 1803. He was a mariner and had two brothers, Joseph and Edward.

92. ii. JANE[5], b. in Newbury, May 13, 1733; m. at Falmouth, Nov. 2, 1754, Joseph Graves.

He went from Lynn, Mass., to Falmouth; had four brothers, Samuel, Johnson, John, and Crispus, the first three going with him to Falmouth, and later settling in Topsham, Me. He was selectman in Falmouth, 1770, and a grantee with his brother Samuel in Mar., 1758, of one-half of 1000 acres to be laid out near the Cathanee river.

93. iii. CAPT. JOSHUA[5], b. in Newbury, Feb. 5, 1735; m. [pub. Sept. 4, 1774], Mrs. Anne (Deering) Fullerton, widow of Wm. Fullerton of Portsmouth, N. H., b. Mar. 3, 1744. [*].

A Joshua, from Falmouth, enlisted at Bradford, Mass., as a private in Capt. Wm. Hudson Bullard's Co., Col. Ichabod Alden's Reg., also Col. John Brooks' Reg.—served from Feb. 10, 1777 to Oct. 12, when he is reported to have died—was called "Capt. Joshua of New Casco"—(a part of Falmouth) in 1774, and was deceased July 11, 1787.

94. iv. CORPORAL MOSES[5], b. in Newbury, Nov. 5, 1737; m. [pub. at Falmouth, June 22, 1761], Susanna Merrill, dau. of James and Mary (Adams) Merrill (his cousin).

He was a Corporal in Capt. Samuel Noyes' Co., Col. Phinney's 31st Reg., enlisted from Falmouth, May 5, 1775, and marched to headquarters July 13.

Nov. 30, 1813, Moses Adams of Falmouth, gent., conveyed 50 acres of land in Falmouth to his son "Moses, Jr.," it being the whole of that part of my home farm on which I now dwell, which lies to the south-east side of the town road and the county road.

In Dec., 1813, he is called a yeoman of Falmouth, and deeds to his son Isaac, yeoman of Falmouth, "50 acres or the whole of that part of the home farm on which I now dwell, which lies on the north-west side of the county road, bounded on the south-west by land of my son Moses, Jr., and land of Nathan Merrill, and on the south-east by the road," referring to deed made by his honored father, John Adams, Sept. 14, 1774.

---

* She had by Wm. Fullerton, 3 children; 1. Elizabeth, who m. Elias Merrill; 2, Hannah, m. Elliot Deering, and 3, Miriam, who m. Daniel Poor.

95. v. BENJAMIN[5], b. in Newbury, Jan. [or June?], 25, 1745 ; m. (1) (probably) Miriam Watson, dau. of John and Tabitha (Whitney) Watson; m. (2) in Gorham, Me., Nov. 26, 1778, Elizabeth Frost of Gorham ; she was living, 1791.

He was a resident in Falmouth, a cordwainer, July 5, 1782, and sold land in Falmouth—"that part commonly called New Casco"— to James Merrill, the deed being signed both by John Adams and Elizabeth, his wife, and by Benjamin and Elizabeth.

Aug 2, 1787, he was " of Gorham," and was the administrator of the estate of Joshua Adams, "late of Falmouth," deeding the east half of the 100-acre lot, "No. 15," in No. Yarmouth, which Joshua Adams had purchased in company with John True [*], on the 17th of June, 1771, and which was sold at public auction July 11, 1787.

In 1792 he was a licensed retailer in Gorham. He was taxed in Gorham in 1799, and d. in Portland, June, 1805, age 60 years—said to have been " late of Gorham."

---

* This [John True was son of John and Mary (Brown) True, and was b. in Salisbury, Mass., Oct. 14, 1737. His wife was Dorothy Adams of Falmouth ; they were published June 4, 1760, both in No. Yarmouth, where he resided, and in Falmouth. [May she not have been a sister of Corp. Moses and Benjamin, younger than Moses, older than Benjamin?] Their children were as follows :

1. RUTH TRUE, b. in No. Yarmouth, June 29, 1761 ; d. in Litchfield, Me., Mar. 8, 1820 ; m. 1793, James Brooks. He d. in Litchfield, Apr. 21, 1825, age 58 years.
2. MOLLY TRUE, b. in No. Yarmouth, Dec. 29, 1762; m. Jan. 29, 1790, John Worthley, Jr., son of John and Martha (Bailey) Worthley, b. Dec. 9, 1760 ; d. at Phillips, Me.
3. BETTY TRUE, b. in No. Yarmouth, Dec. 1, 1764.
4. JOHN TRUE, b. in No. Yarmouth, Nov. 25, 1766; set. in Haverhill, Mass. ; d. without issue.
5. DANIEL TRUE, b. in No. Yarmouth, July 18, 1768 ; d. in Litchfield, Mass., Mar. 10, 1830 ; m. (1) in Topsham, Me., Nov. 24, 1794, Rebecca Graves, dau. of Joseph and Jane (Adams) Graves, b. Sept. 2, 1769 ; d. in No. Yarmouth, May 2, 1808 ; m. (2) Aug. 14, 1808, Mrs. Sally (West) True, dau. of Wm. Blay and Patience (Hammon) West, and widow of John True, b, Jan. 27, 1773 ; d. 4 Jan., 1851.
6. JOSHUA MORSE TRUE, b. in No. Yarmouth, May 13, 1770 ; d. in Turner, Me., Feb. 5, 1846 ; m. Sept. 1, 1796, Lucy Page, b. Apr. 15, 1771 ; d. in Greene, Me., Feb. 26, 1829.
7. JANE TRUE, b. in No. Yarmouth, Oct. 4, 1772, d. in Phillips, Me., June 17, 1855 ; m. Mar. 18, 1798, Asa Worthley, son of John and Martha (Bailey) Worthley, b. May 17, 1771 ; d. in Avon, Me., Nov. 5, 1888.
8. MIRRIAM TRUE, bapt. at No. Yarmouth, Aug. 6, 1795.
9. DOLLY TRUE, b. 1777; d. in No. Yarmouth, July 11, 1811 ; m. Feb. 12, 1799, Capt. Richmond Loring, 3rd son of Bezaleel and Elizabeth (Mason) Loring, b. Feb. 1, 1775 ; d. May 12, 1857.
10. SALLY TRUE, b. 1779 ; d. in No. Yarmouth, Nov. 16, 1844 ; m. Jan. 24, 1805, Amos Storer, b. Nov. 2, 1780 ; d. Dec. 22, 1843.
11. ADAMS TRUE, b. 1781 ; d. in Augusta, Me., Mar., 1856 ; m. Jan. 25, 1808, Rebecca Johnson, dau. of Jasper and Rebecca (Ross) Johnson, b. in Freeport, Me., Dec. 12, 1785 ; d. in No. Yarmouth, Feb. 7, 1863.
12. MOSES TRUE, b. in No. Yarmouth, June 7, 1787.

[Fifth Generation.] OF NEWBURY, MASS. 25

Children of JACOB⁴, (1713) [27] (Robert³, Sergt. Abraham²,
Robert¹) and Mary (Hills) Adams; res. Newbury, Mass.

    i. JACOB, JR.⁵, b. in Newbury, Feb. 12, 1743.
    ii. ZEBULON⁵, b. in Newbury, Nov. 19, 1744.

Children of ANNE⁴, (1705) [28] (Capt. Abraham³, Sergt.
Abraham², Robert¹) and Robert Stuart; res. Newton, N. H.

    i. SAMUEL STUART, b. Nov. 3, 1728. *m. Grace, dau. of Richard ?* He died and left two children, Samuel (prob. of Bristol, Vt.), and Abigail, who m. Benj. Brown of Deerfield, N. H. */previous to Aug. 31, 1781/*
    ii. AN INFANT.
    iii. SARAH STUART, b. Oct. 16, 1732; m. *Daniel* Chase of Newbury, Mass. *was widow in 1781 when her father's w--*
    iv. AN INFANT. *was ma--*
    v. ANNE STUART, b. Oct. 31, 1736; m. *Bernard* Hoyt. *lived up country*
    vi. MARY STUART, b. Mar. 11, 1739; m. *Sam'l* Chase of Litchfield, N. H.
    vii. ELIZABETH STUART, b. Mar. 10, 1741; m. Stephen Currier of South Hampton, N. H.
    viii. CAPT. ROBERT STUART, JR., b. Sept. 30, 1743; m. Mar. 1, 1770, Ruth Currier, dau. of Richard Currier of Amesbury, Mass., b. Nov. 2, 1749; d. 21 June, 1833.
        An officer in the Revolution, d. 27 June, 1819.
    ix. STEPHEN STUART, b. Dec. 25, 1745; m. *Sally* Peaslee, and set. in Kingston, N. H. *had children Moses and James who settled in Me--Stephen, Eben, Anne, Abigail, Elizabeth*
    x. EBEN STUART, b. 1748; d. early.

(margin notes: Thos Sam'l m. Hannah Brown dau of Dan'l Brown and Ruth Whittier had 9 children)

Children of WILLIAM⁴, (1706) [29] (Capt. Abraham³, Sergt.
Abraham², Robert¹) and Elizabeth (Noyes) Adams; res. Rowley
(Georgetown), Mass.

96.   i. STEPHEN⁵, b. in Rowley, Feb. 27, 1728–9; m. 1760, Susanna Dorman, dau. of Jacob and Mercy Dorman of Topsfield, Mass. Her birth is recorded in Topsfield as Sept. 15, 1740, but no more is given. She is said to have died 15 Oct., 1804.
        According to a letter written by Mrs. Hannah P. Lane of E. Sangerfield, Me., a grand-daughter of Stephen, in Oct., 1891, Stephen resided in Rowley and Topsfield, Mass., "until after about half of his children were born, then he removed his family to Henniker, N. H., where he was one of the first settlers of that town."

From Duncan Stuart Family.

L. W. Coggswell, in his History of Henniker (1880), says, "Stephen Adams, son of William and Betty (Noyes), came to town soon after the incorporation, and settled in the north-east part,"— "a large man, jovial, willful, obstinate; had six children born in Rowley, others in Henniker. He died 11 Jan., 1811. She d. 15 Oct., 1804."

Mr. John M. Adams of W. Lebanon, N. Y., a grandson of Jacob Adams, and great grandson of Stephen, claims that Stephen, who married Susanna Dorman, was not the son of William (1706), but was a son of Israel Adams and Mercy Holdridge, son of Abraham Olney and Hannah (La Grasse) Adams. The account given by Mr. Adams, while it has some marks of plausibility, is yet quite indefinite, and more or less vague, derived from data "kept on fly leaves of old books and margins," "disconnected and difficult to copy."

There are no records confirming them to be found in any of the towns and counties of Massachusetts,—a thing which is certainly most remarkable, where records were kept to a greater or less extent.

Mrs. Lane's father was Enoch, the youngest of the eleven children of Stephen and Susanna, born in Henniker, Jan. 5, 1783, and he was living at a time sufficiently early to be able to know surely who his parents were and he was accustomed to converse with his children upon the subject. Alluding to the claim of Mr. John M. Adams, Mrs. Lane says, under date of Sept. 9, 1891, "It does not agree with what my father used to tell me of his family."

The birth of Stephen, son of William, is given in the Rowley records as Feb. 27, 1729. Mr. Adams makes it June 6, 1727, and it may well be that there was another Stephen, born, not in Rowley, but in some other place, who did *not* marry Susanna Dorman.

Whatever may have been the exact truth may never be clearly established, and it has been deemed advisable, in the circumstances, to give the records as they appear in this connection.

 ii. ELIZABETH⁵, b. in Rowley, Apr. 17, 1731, bapt. at Byfield, Apr. 25, as "Eliza;" d. in Rowley, unm. Her estate was administered Nov. 2, 1789.

 iii. ANNE⁵, b. in Rowley, Nov. 3, 1733; m. Capt. Timothy Jackman of Rowley, Mass.

97. iv. CAPT. BENJAMIN⁵, b. in Rowley, Nov. 20, 1735; m. Mary Harriman, dau. of John Harriman, Esq. She d. at Beaver Falls, Pa., in 1818.

He was known as "lawyer Ben. Adams," because of his frequent connection with litigation, also as "Capt. Mirabeau," because of a fancied resemblance to that noted Frenchman.

He was a military man, enlisted as a private at the breaking out of the Revolution, Apr. 19, 1775, serving several days at Cambridge. He was in a return of service in Dec., 1775, and was commissioned as Captain of a company in Col. Jedediah Huntington's Regiment, Feb. 3, 1776. He served in Col. Johnson's Regiment from Aug. 18 to Nov. 30, 1777, when he was discharged.

He was engaged in the battle of Stillwater; his company taking a cannon from the British and losing it, then re-taking it the same day. After the establishment of independence, he was a member of the Massachusetts Legislature, in 1778-9, and 1780. In 1790, he removed to western Pennsylvania—Washington county—and died at the house of his son-in-law, Chas. Wheeler, 23 Dec., 1817.

 v. MOLLY[5], b. in Rowley, July 13, 1738. She d. at the alms-house, unm., 18 Jan., 1822.

 vi. SUSANNA[5], b. in Rowley, Sept., 1740 ; d. unm., July, 1802.

98. vii. SARAH[5], b. in Rowley, Sept. 3, 1743 ; m. Oct. 12, 1769, Daniel Ayer, son of William and Sarah (Little) Ayer, b. Jan. 28, 1743 ; d. in Plaistow, N. H., 6 June, 1805.

 viii. DR. SAMUEL[5], b. in Rowley, ———.

He practiced medicine in Abington, Mass., and appears to have died there, Feb. 4, 1779, "Sarah" is mentioned as "wife of the late Dr. Adams of Abington." She also was deceased, and her heirs were Samuel Barstow and Job House, also David Jenkins, one of the children of Esther House.

 ix. JUDITH[5], b. in Rowley, ———; m. Dec. 7, 1772, Benjamin Adams, son of Matthew and Hannah (Rawlins) Adams; she d. 14 Nov., 1823. He d. 25 Feb., 1819.

Children of ABRAHAM[4], (1715)[31] (Capt. Abraham[3], Sergt. Abraham[2], Robert[1]) and Mary (Coleman) Adams; res. New Rowley (Georgetown), Mass.

 i. MARY[5], b. in New Rowley, Nov. 12, 1738 ; m. Mar. 25, 1760, Benjamin Jaques.

99. ii. REV. PHINEAS[5], b. in New Rowley, Mar. 3, 1742-3 ; m. May 9, 1771, Mrs. Priscilla Perkins, b. June 10, 1742.

He graduated from Harvard College in 1762, received a call to Haverhill, Mass., Mar. 2, 1769, and was settled and ordained there Jan. 9, 1771 ; "was a man of amiable disposition, sound sense, excellent understanding, and extensive reading." He is said to have purchased a chaise in 1796, when there were only two in the town. He d. in Haverhill, 15 Nov., 1801.

100. iii. CAPT. BENJAMIN[5], b. in New Rowley, Mar. 1, 1746-7 ; m. (1) Dec. 4, 1770, Sarah or Sally Spofford, dau. of Elijah and Lucy (Peabody) Spofford of Georgetown, b. Sept. 21, 1751 ; d. 4 Nov., 1776 ; m. (2) May 21, 1778, Betsey Woodman, dau. of Samuel and Mary Woodman of Bradford, Mass., b. Oct. 11, 1747 ; d. 11 Jan. 1816.

He was a tanner, and was known as "Tanner Adams," of Georgetown. He occupied the "Temperance House," which was the first house painted white in Georgetown, and considered "a rather aristocratic mansion."

He made his will Feb. 23, 1808; d. 10 Jan., 1821, age 75 years. His will was proved Mar. 6, 1821; mentions wife Betsey, daughter Sally, and sons Benjamin, Samuel, Jesse, and son Joseph, to whom the others were to pay $600 per year.

iv. JOSEPH⁵, b. in New Rowley, Feb. 14, 1748-9; d. while in college, 5 Jan., 1768.

v. JESSE⁵, b. in New Rowley, Apr. 28, 1750; administration of his estate June 6, 1791.

Child of ABRAHAM⁴, (1715) and Sarah (Foster) Adams.

101.   vi. POLLY⁵ [or Sally], b. in New Rowley, Oct. 5, 1761; m. [pub. Sept. 23, 1786], Benjamin Spofford, son of Lieut. Abel Spofford of Rowley, Mass., b. July 25, 1750, d. 19 Feb., 1836. He m. 2nd, Nov. 14, 1792, Mrs. Lydia (Warren) Wood of Boxford, Mass. She d. 6 Sept., 1839, age 95.

Children of SAMUEL⁴, (1717) [32] (Capt. Abraham³, Sergt. Abraham², Robert¹) and Mary Jewett (Brown) Adams; res. Newbury-Byfield, Mass.

i. JOSEPH⁵, b. in Newbury-Byfield, Sept. 28, 1748. He was a poet, and blind; was provided for in his father's will; d. unm., 6 Oct., 1815.

ii. MARY⁵, b. in Newbury-Byfield, July 15, 1750; d. unm., 27 Oct., 1771.

iii. SAMUEL⁵, b. in Newbury-Byfield, Oct. 27, 1752; m. Elizabeth Woodman.

He was a soldier in the Revolution; settled afterward in Derry, N. H., where he d. 12 Jan., 1822, age 69 years. As his brother David inherited his property, it is inferred that he had no children.

102.   iv. ELDER DAVID⁵, b. in Newbury-Byfield, Dec. 10, 1754, bapt. Dec. 15; m. Sept. 22, 1778, Mary Woodman, b. Nov. 9, 1752; d. 19 Sept., 1816.

He was a soldier in the Revolution; enlisted Apr. 24, 1775, and served 18 days in Capt. Jacob Gerrish's Co., Col. Moses Little's Regiment, also 2 months in Capt. Silas Adams' Co., Col. Titcomb's Regiment, June 29, 1777.

He settled in Derry, N. H., in 1782, and d. there 24 Jan., 1838, age 83.

v. ADJ. JOSIAH⁵, b. in Newbury-Byfield, Apr. 3, 1757, bapt. Apr. 10. He enlisted as a private in Capt. Jacob Gerrish's Co., Col. Moses Little's Reg., May 1, 1775, and served three months and 8 days. He was in service at Winter Hill, near Boston in Jan. 1778; was Adjutant in Col. Jacob Gerrish's Reg. in Apr., 1778, and served 3 months and 3 days He served as clerk and quarter-master in Col. Little's Regiment, and became a Lieutenant in the militia; d, unm., 5 Jan., 1852, age 94.

103. vi. CAPT. STEPHEN[5], b. in Newbury-Byfield, May 5, 1760; m. (1) Dec. 25, 1782-3, Sarah Adams, dau. of Rev. Benja. and Rebecca (Nichols) Adams of Lynn; she d. 20 Sept., 1800; m. (2) May 5, 1801-2, Rebecca Adams, elder sister of Sarah; she d. 9 April, 1837.

He was only 16 years old when he enlisted, but stood 6 ft. 4 in. high—the tallest man in Byfield; was in the battle of Trenton; became Captain in the militia. He d. in Newburyport, 8 Feb., 1838.

vii. JANE[5], b. in Newbury-Byfield,—bapt. Apr. 24, 1763; d. unm., 28 Feb., 1838.

Children of REV. JOSEPH[4], (1719) [33] (Capt. Abraham[3], Sergt. Abraham[2], Robert[1]) and Mary (Greenleaf) Adams; res. Stratham, N. H.

104. i. MARY[5], b. in Exeter, N. H., about 1747-8; m. (1) Daniel Hoyt, b. Dec. 25, 1750. He d. 9 May, 1797; m. (2) —— Waterhouse, res. Stratham, N. H.

105. ii. JOSEPH[5], b. in ——, May 11, 1750; m. Dec. 31, 1775, Mary Fosdick; she d, at 94 years of age.

He was a cabinet-maker in Exeter, N. H., in 1783; removed to Roxbury, Mass., in 1801, where he d. 22 Nov., 1849, age 99 years. His will was proved at Dedham, Mass., Dec. 28, 1849. He gave his mansion house to his wife, the increase of his real estate in Roxbury and Boston to his sons John, George, and Joseph Thornton, saying that Benjamin and Charles Frederick were in no need; and he made a bequest to his grand-daughter Elizabeth Cartwright Adams.

iii. INFANT.

106. iv. DR. CALEB GREENLEAF[5], b. in Exeter, Jan. 8, 1752; m. Dec. 8, 1774, Mary Folsom, dau. of Gen. Nath'l and Mary (Smith) Folsom of Portsmouth, b. Aug. 21, 1751; she m. 2nd, Gov. John Taylor Gilman, and d. 15 Oct., 1812.

He was appointed Surgeon in Col. Enoch Poor's 3rd N. H. Reg., May 20, 1775, and served 2 months 17 days.

Apr. 17, 1779, he purchased a house and lot on the south side of Court St., in Exeter, of his father-in-law, Nath'l Folsom, who became the administrator of his estate; an inventory was made Sept. 1, 1785.

107. v. LIEUT. JOHN[5], b. in Exeter, 1758; m. Jan. 11, 1788, Anne Folsom, dau. of Col. John and his 2nd wife, Martha Wiggins, b. June 6, 1762; d. about 1835.

He was a 1st Lieutenant in the 1st Continental Reg., and drew a pension as a soldier of the Revolution; a member of the Society of the Cincinnati. He d. 28 Aug., 1847, age 89 years.

vi. NATHAN[5], b. in Exeter, 1760. He d. unm., 1826, "a little over 60 years old."

Child of REV. BENJAMIN⁴, (1719) [**34**] (Capt. Abraham³, Sergt. Abraham², Robert¹) and Elizabeth (Payson) Adams; res. Lynn (now Lynnfield), Mass.

    i. NATHANIEL⁵, b. prob., in Newbury, Mass., Feb. 12, 1749; was probably a soldier in the Revolution.

Children of REV. BENJAMIN⁴, (1719) and Rebecca (Nichols) Adams.

    ii. REBECCA⁵, b. in Lynnfield, July 22, 1757; m. May 5, 1801, Capt. Stephen Adams, son of Samuel and Mary (Jewett) Adams of Byfield. She d. 9 Apr., 1837.

108   iii. DR. BENJAMIN⁵, b. in Lynnfield, Sept. 7, 1758; m. Mar. 9, 1788, Lois Orne of Salem. Dr. Benja. was probably the drummer from Lynn in Capt. Nath'l Bancroft's Co.; served Apr. 19, 1775, for 2 days.

    He practiced medicine first in Amherst, N. H.; returned to Lynnfield where he remained, and d. 16 Jan., 1811. His will, made July 28, 1810, was proved Apr. 16, 1811; it mentions only one dau., Lois.

    iv. ELIZABETH⁵, b. in Lynnfield, Mar. 22, 1760; m. Joseph Bullard of Springfield, Mass. She d. ———.

    v. SARAH⁵, b. in Lynnfield, Dec. 31, 1761; m. Dec. 25, 1783, Capt. Stephen Adams, son of Samuel and Mary (Jewett) Adams (1st wife); she d. in Newbury, 20 Sept., 1800. He m. 2nd, her sister Rebecca, and d. 8. Feb., 1838.

    vi. ANNE⁵, b. in Lynnfield, June 12, 1766; m. Aug. 8, 1784, Nathan Porter of Beverly. [The Beverly record says "Nancy" Adams.]

    Nathan Porter was son of Samuel and Sarah (Skinner) Porter, b Mar. 1, 1742; d. 1789.

109.   vii. JOSEPH⁵, b. in Lynnfield, Apr. 11, 1769; m. [pub. Mar. 21, 1795], Mary Webb, dau. of Josiah and Martha Webb of Marblehead; res. Danvers, Mass.; she d. 11 Oct., 1843, age 71. He d. 20 Nov., 1821, age 51 years.

    viii. NATHAN⁵ (twin), b. in Lynnfield, Apr. 11, 1769; m. May 16, 1796, Hannah McCarthy.

    He was a tanner, merchant, and auctioneer; res. Charlestown, Mass. He d. 11 Sept., 1830; no issue.

Children of CAPT. NATHAN⁴, (1721) [**35**] (Capt. Abraham³, Sergt. Abraham², Robert¹) and Mary (Trumbull) Adams; res. Charlestown, Mass.

    i. NATHAN⁵, b. in Charlestown, Dec. 4, 1757; d. young.

Fifth Generation.] OF NEWBURY, MASS. 31

110.   ii.   NATHAN⁵, b. in Charlestown, Jan. 2, 1761 ; m. Feb. 1788, Mary Pierce of Lunenburg, Mass.; she d. in Pomfret, Conn., Aug , 1832.

He removed in 1793, from Lunenburg, Mass., to Shirley, Mass., thence to Cavendish, Vt., in 1800, and from Cavendish to Pomfret, Conn., in 1807. He d. in Pomfret, 13 Dec., 1844.

iii.   JOSEPH⁵, b. in Charlestown, Oct. 2, 1762.

Child buried Dec. 11, 1764

Children of HENRY⁴, (1722) [36] (Capt. Abraham³, Sergt. Abraham², Robert¹) and Sarah (Emery) Adams; res. Newbury, Mass.

   i.   ANNE⁵, b. in Newbury, Apr. 2, 1747 ; d. 15 Oct., 1773, seven hours after her father.

   ii.   JOHN⁵, b. in Newbury, Oct. 4, 1748 ; m. Mary ———— ; she m. 2nd, —— — Hidden.

He was a saddler and harness-maker in Newburyport, Mass.; administration on his estate was granted to his brother Enoch, June 26, 1777 ; probably no issue.

111.   iii.   ENOCH⁵, b. in Newbury, July 11, 1752 ; m. (1) Aug. 6, 1778, Sally Bragg; she d. 9 July, 1801 ; m. (2) Jan. 30, 1803, Lydia Moody.

He was a tanner and currier ; removed from Andover, Mass., to Andover, Oxford Co., Me., where he was a manufacturer of morocco wallets, a surveyor, and a large land-owner. He d. in Andover, Me., 19 Aug., 1819.

112.   iv.   NATHAN⁵, b. in Newbury, May 1, 1755 ; m. Johanna Batchelder of Danvers, Mass., prob. dau. of Dea. Ebenezer Batchelder of So. Kingston, N. H., b. Oct. 7, 1760.

He was a clock-maker by trade ; may have been the soldier, aged 20 years, who enlisted from Newbury as a drummer in Capt. Gerrish's Company, Col. Little's Reg., serving from Apr. 24 to Sept. 5, 1775, and again for six weeks, beginning Mar., 1777. He settled in Wiscasset, Me.

113.   v.   SARAH⁵, b. in Newbury, Feb. 1, 1757; m. June 3, 1780, Samuel Northen of Rowley, Mass., bapt. July 10, 1757 ; d. 30 Dec., 1824. She d. Apr., 1839.

   vi.   PAUL⁵, b. in Newbury, Mar. 23, 1763.

He is said to have been a sadler in Haverhill, Mass., in 1783, and to have d. in Chester, N. H., 22 Feb., 1848, age 85 years.

   vii.   MEHITABLE⁵, b. in Newbury, June 12, 1764 ; m. Dec. 24, 1795, Joseph Peters of Andover, Mass.

Children of SAMUEL⁴, (1710–11) [39] (Isaac⁴, Sergt. Abraham², Robert¹) and Sarah (Burbank) Adams; res. E. Bradford (Groveland), Mass.

   i.   SARAH⁵, b. ———, bapt. in Byfield Parish, Dec. 23, 1733.

114. ii. COL. SAMUEL⁵, b. ——, bapt. in Byfield, May 16, 1736 ; m. Sept. 15, 1764, Mary Stickney, dau. of Samuel and Miribah (Tenney) Stickney, b. June 30, 1744 ; d. 3 Jan., 1802.
   He was a cordwainer, and is described as "an eccentric man." He purchased a farm in E. Bradford (Groveland) in 1760—owned at this time by George H. Adams, son of Moses and Sarah (Colby) Adams—on which he settled, and died there 29 Mar., 1814.

Children of CAPT. ISAAC⁴, (1713) [40] (Isaac³, Sergt. Abraham², Robert¹) and Mercy (Wood) Adams; res. Boxford, Mass., and Rindge, N. H.

   i. DARIUS⁵, b. in Boxford, Apr. 29, 1744. He was a soldier in the Revolution ; d. unm.
   ii. ISAAC⁵, b. in Boxford, June 12, 1745, *June 2, 1745 Boxford record*
   He settled in Rindge, N. H., in 1772, and enlisted in the war, Apr. 23, 1775, and was killed at the battle of Bunker Hill, June 17, 1775. His gun and bayonet are preserved by Thomas A. Adams, Gorham, N. H.
115. iii. MARY⁵ (twin), b. in Boxford, June 12, 1745 ; m. [pub. June 24, 1767], William Porter, son of Moses and Mary (Chadwick) Porter of Boxford, Mass., b. Apr. 27, 1744. He d. 26 July, 1822.
116. iv. CAPT. DAVID⁵, b. in Boxford, June 20, 1747 ; m. May 5, 1773 Phebe Spofford, dau. of Dea. Abner and Sarah (Coleman) Spofford of Byfield, b. Jan. 6, 1757 ; d. 17 Feb., 1822, age 71 years.
   He set. in Rindge, N. H., 1772-3 ; was a soldier in the Revolution, and afterward a captain of the militia ; served as constable in 1786 ; d. 17 Nov., 1831.
117. v. CAPT. SAMUEL⁵, b. in Boxford, Aug. [11 ?] 22, 1750 ; m. July 9, 1773, Lucy Spofford, dau. of Col. Eliphalet and Lucy (Peabody) Spofford of Boxford, Mass., b. Sept. 18, 1753 ; d. 23 Feb., 1813.
   He removed with his father to Rindge, N. H., in 1772-3, and to Jaffrey, N. H., in 1778. He served as a soldier in Capt. Brown's Company in 1777, and was stationed at Ticonderoga. He became a Captain in the militia; built the first meeting-house in Jaffrey, N. H. He d. in Jaffrey, of typhus fever, 21 Feb., 1813, and was buried in the same grave with his wife.
   vi. THOMAS⁵, b. in Boxford, Oct. 7, 1752.
   He was a private soldier from Boxford, enlisted Apr. 19, 1775, under Capt. John Cushing, Col. Samuel Johnson's Reg.; served 5 days; d. in Rindge, N. H., unm.
   vii. DANIEL⁵, b. in Boxford, May 5, 1754.
   He was a private in Capt. John Cushing's Co., Col. Samuel Johnson's Reg., Apr. 19, 1775, 4 days. He also served under Gen. Stark in 1777, in Capt. Stone's Company; was, perhaps, Lieut. in Col. Nichols' Reg. He d. unm., about 1800.

[Fifth Generation.] OF NEWBURY, MASS.

- viii. MERCY⁵, b. in Boxford, Oct. 6, 1756 *(16) Boxford*; m. May 15, 1791, John Tyler of Boxford.
- ix. JACOB⁵, b. in Boxford, Feb. 15, 1759.
  He is said to have set. in New Hampshire, where he married and had children, but no trace of him has been found.
- x. ISRAEL⁵, b. in Boxford, Feb. 7, 1761 ; m. Jan. 14, 1807–8, Lucinda Baxter of Rindge, N. H.; she d. in Rindge, 1 Mar., 1864, age 90 years ; farmer in Boxford, selectman, 1799, 1800, and 1803 ; d. 30 Apr., 1834 ; no issue.

Children of ISRAEL⁴, (1716) [41] (Isaac³, Sergt. Abraham², Robert¹) and Deborah (Searle) Adams; res. W. Rowley (Georgetown), Mass.

- i. ABIGAIL⁵, b. in W. Rowley, Jan. 31, 1743–4 ; d. young.
- 118. ii. ISRAEL⁵, JR., b. in W. Rowley, Apr. 15, 1748; m. (1) [pub. Feb. 8, 1770], Elizabeth Searle ; she d. 16 Oct., 1804 ; m. (2) Feb. 8, 1807, Anna Ober Bodwell. [*]
  He was a soldier in the Revolution, and acted as a spy for Gen. Washington. He is said to have resided in Georgetown, north of Pentucket Pond, and for that reason was called "Pond Israel."
  He was a resident of Methuen, Mass., and removed thence to Sanbornton, N. H., in 1799, where he drove the first chaise in the town. He removed to Hill, N. H., and d. 18 July, 1818, age 70 years.
- iii. ABIGAIL⁵, b. in W. Rowley, Sept. 2, 1750 ; m. before 1784, ——— Goodwin.
- iv. MARY⁵, b. in W. Rowley, Sept. 23, 1753 ; was living unm., 1784.
- v. ELIZABETH⁵, b. in W. Rowley, Feb. 23, 1759, was bapt. Mar. 4, 1759 ; d. 8 May, 1779.

Children of DAVID⁴, (1720) [42] (Isaac³, Sergt. Abraham², Robert¹) and Hannah (Jackson) Adams; res. W. Rowley (Georgetown), Mass.

- i. HANNAH⁵, b. in W. Rowley, Nov. 29, 1746, was bapt. at Byfield, Dec. 15, 1746 ; d. 4 Apr., 1840.
- ii. MARY⁵, b. in W. Rowley, bapt. at Byfield, June 29, 1748.
- iii. DAVID⁵, b. in W. Rowley, bapt. Sept. 17, 1749 ; d. 7 Aug., 1750.

---

* One authority says he m. 2nd [pub. Mar. 23, 1790], Hannah Kimball—probably incorrect.

Children of ISRAEL⁴, (1707) [43] (Sarah³, Sergt. Abraham², Robert¹) and Tabitha (Farnum) Adams; res. Andover, Mass., and Rindge, N. H.

119.   i. ISRAEL⁵, b. in Andover, Jan. 26, 1733-4 ; m. Oct. 11 [Nov. 20 ?], 1760, Elizabeth Stevens; she d. 9 Nov., 1809, age 71 years. He set. in Rindge, N. H., in 1772, and d. 15 May, 1809.

120.   ii. CAPT. JOHN⁵, b. in Andover, July 3, 1735 ; m. (1) Sept. 15 [Nov. 23 ?], 1758, Hannah Osgood, dau. of Peter Osgood ; she d. 22 Oct., 1770, age 56 years ; m. (2) June 24, 1773, Hannah Thurston of Rowley, Mass., b. Jan. 4, 1744; d. 22 Jan., 1775 ; m. (3) May 21, 1776, Mary Holt ; she d. 9 Nov., 1829, age 89 years.

He was a cordwainer, and a soldier in the French war, served at Cape Breton and Ticonderoga; also served in the Revolution at Cambridge, and at Saratoga. He was commissioned as a First Lieutenant, in Capt Nathaniel Lovejoy's Company, Col. Samuel Johnson's Regiment in Apr., 1775, and became a Captain of militia. He was a deacon in the church at No. Andover, and was termed "John Adams, gentleman." He d. in No. Andover, Mass., 27 June. 1813. [*]

  iii. ELIZABETH⁵, b. in Andover, Dec. 24, 1737; m. Nov. 29, 1759, Michael Carleton.
  iv. JOSHUA⁵, b. in Andover, Nov. 9, 1739 ; d. 7 Dec., 1757.

121.   v. DAVID⁵, b. in Andover, May 2, 1742 ; m. (1) May 1, 1766, Abiah Ordway of Methuen, Mass., b. Mar. 7, 1744 ; d. 29 July, 1776; m. (2) about 1778, Martha Marsh, b. Jan. 12, 1743; d. 9 Apr., 1812.

He was a cordwainer in Dracut and Methuen, Mass.; d. in Londonderry, N. H., 19 Apr., 1815, age 73 years.

  vi. SARAH⁵, b. in Andover, July 26, 1744 ; d. 30 Aug., 1746.
  vii. TWIN, with Sarah ; d. young.

Children of SARAH⁴ (1714) [44] (John³, Sergt. Abraham², Robert¹) and Jeremiah Hazen; res. Rowley, Mass.

  i. SARAH HAZEN, b. in Rowley, July 23, 1738 ; m. Nov. 28, 1760, Jeremiah Chaplin.
  ii. MOSES HAZEN, b. Dec. 9, 1743 ; m. Rebecca ———.
  iii. SARAH HAZEN, b. Mar. 17, 1748-9 ; d. 9 Feb., 1778.
  iv. JANE HAZEN, b. June 17, 1753.

Child of ELIZABETH⁴, (1717) [45] (John³, Sergt. Abraham², Robert¹) and Reuben Hardy; res. Bradford, Mass.

  i. ISRAEL HARDY, b. in Bradford, Sept. 2, 1756.
    [There may have been other children, but no record is found.]

---

* The births of Israel and John are given in the records of both Andover and Littleton, Mass.

Fifth Generation.]   OF NEWBURY, MASS.   35

Children of JOHN⁴, (1721) **[46]** (John³, Sergt. Abraham², Robert¹) and Sarah (Brocklebank) Adams; res. W. Rowley, Mass. and New London, N. H.

122.   i.   CORP. JOHN⁵, b. in W. Rowley, Sept. 9, 1749; m. Mar. 4, 1777 [pub. Dec. 22, 1776], Mollie Brocklebank of W. Rowley. She d. 27 July, 1840, age 82 years.
He was a corporal in the Revolution. He settled in New London, N. H., and d. 15 Mar., 1821, age 73 years. His will was made at New London, Dec. 27, 1814; proved Apr. 13, 1821.

123.   ii.   BENJAMIN⁵, b. in W. Rowley, Feb. 19, 1751; m. June 24, 1775, Mary Burpee; d. 1826.
He rem. 1799, and set. in Tunbridge, Vt., where he d. Oct., 1825.

124.   iii.   SARAH⁵, b. in W. Rowley, Mar. 23, 1753; m. [pub. Dec. 12, 1776], James Brocklebank of W. Rowley.
James and Sarah signed a receipt, Nov. 23, 1804, for a legacy from her father.   *Int. pub. Oct. 8, 1774*

125.   iv.   LOIS⁵, b. in W. Rowley, Nov. 15, 1754; m. Nov. 15, 1774, Daniel Perkins of Boxford.
Receipts for legacies from estate of John Adams were given by Enos, Daniel and Sarah Perkins, and one from Nathan and Lois Smith, dated at Bridgewater, N. H., Sept. 27, 1809.

Children of JOHN⁴, (1721), and Elizabeth (Kilborn) Adams.

v.   ELIZABETH⁵, b. in W. Rowley, Jan. 29, 1756; m. [pub. July 23, 1775] Israel Adams, son of Matthew and Hannah (Rawlins) Adams, who gave a receipt to the executor of John Adams' est. signed "Israel 3d."

vi.   JANE⁵, b. in W. Rowley, May 25, 1757; m. Dec. 13, 1781, John Sawyer Blaisdell of Newbury, Mass. He d. 7 Jan., 1832.

126.   vii.   SOLOMON⁵, b. in W. Rowley, Mar. 4, 1759; m. (1) [pub. Aug. 28, 1779], Molly Bancroft; m. [2] Mary Sargent.
He was a soldier in the Revolution. He served in the army 5 mos. and 12 days., from July to Dec., 1780, and drew a pension. Set. in New London, N. H., 1780; d. 18 Mar., 1834.

viii.   JEDEDIAH⁵, b. in W. Rowley, Jan. 18, 1761; d. 31 Oct., 1765.

127.   ix.   MARY⁵, b. in W. Rowley, Nov. 23, 1763; m. [pub. June 2, 1783], Silas Plumer of Haverhill.

Children of JOHN⁴, (1721) and Maribah (Stickney) Adams.

128.   x.   MOSES⁵, b. in W. Rowley, July 21, 1765; m. (1) [pub. Feb. 6, 1790] Dolly Perley of Boxford; she d. 19 Jan., 1799; m. (2) Hannah Flanders; she d. 4 Oct., 1840; res. New London, N. H.; d. 24 Mar., 1858.

129. xi. JONATHAN[5], b. in W. Rowley, Sept. 27, 1767; m. (1) Phoebe Brocklebank, b. July 3, 1769, d. 27 Feb. 1807; m. (2) May, 1808. Abigail Weymouth. b. Feb. 29, 1776, d. in W. Hartford, Vt., 6 Feb., 1864. He set. in Tunbridge, Vt., and d. 28 Feb., 1842.

Children of MATTHEW[4], (1709) [47] (Dr. Matthew[3], Sergt. Abraham[2], Robert[1]) and Hannah (Rawlins) Adams; res. Crane Neck Hill, W. Newbury, Mass.

    i. SARAH[5], b. in W. Newbury, Apr. 1, 1745; m. Dec. 1, 1767, Parker Jacques, Jr.

130. ii. ISRAEL 3D[5], b. in W. Newbury, Sept. 14, 1746; m. [pub. July 30, 1775] Elizabeth Adams, dau. of John and Elizabeth (Kilborn) Adams; she d. Oct. or Nov., 1788, age about 32 yrs. and 10 mos.
He set. in Henniker, N. H.; d. 16 Nov., 1835, age 89 yrs., 1 mo., and 22 days.

131. iii. JOHN[5], b. in W. Newbury, Sept. 14, 1749. m. (1) Mar. 24, 1773, Judith Follensby; she d. in Hempstead, N. H., in 1786; no issue; m. (2) Hannah Moor.
He set. in Hempstead, N. H., and rem. 1788 to Sutton, N. H., where he d. 8 May, 1830, age 81 years.

X 132. iv. BENJAMIN[5], b. in W. Newbury, Aug. 20, 1752; m. Dec. 7, 1772, Judith Adams, dau. of William and Elizabeth (Noyes) Adams; she d. 14 Nov., 1823.
To distinguish him from others he was called "Newtown Ben," that being the nickname for that part of Newbury where he resided. He settled in New Rowley, now Georgetown, Mass., in 1793, but sold out in Nov., 1800, his house having been burned, and rem. to New London, N. H., where he d. 25 Feb., 1819.

133. v. JOSEPH[5], b. in W. Newbury, Mar. 22, 1755; m. Jan. 6, 1774, Mary Carleton.
He was a yeoman, and is said to have resided in Plaistow, N. H., in 1787. He d. 24 Mar. 1820. His will was made Sept. 13, 1819; proved May 2, 1820.

    vi. ELIZABETH[5], b. in W. Newbury, Aug. 4, 1759; [m. Apr. 7, 1791, Maj. John Rowe of Gloucester, Mass.?]

    vii. MARTHA[5], b. in W. Newbury; d. unm.

Children of ABRAHAM[4], (1713) [49] (Dr. Matthew[3], Sergt. Abraham[2], Robert[1]) and Mary (Adams) Adams; res. Newbury, Mass.

    i. PRUDENCE[5], b. in Newbury, Nov. 1, 1738 ; m. Apr. 17, 1760, John Brickett ; she d. before 1796.

Fifth Generation.] OF NEWBURY, MASS. 37

  ii. HANNAH⁵, b. in Newbury, Mar. 17, 1741; d. unm. 2 Mar., 1778.

134. iii. CAPT. STEPHEN⁵, b. in Newbury, Feb. 5, 1742; m. Dec. 8, 1761, Sarah Bartlett; she d. 17 Oct., 1826.
   He was probably a private in Capt. Silas Adams' Co., June, 1777 —serving 2 months. He was a farmer in West Newbury; and his estate was administered Nov. 25, 1793.

  iv. JOSEPH⁵, b. in Newbury, Oct. 28, 1743; m. Feb. 22, 1770, Abigail Thurlow, dau. of George and Elizabeth (Hale) Thurlow, b. Apr. 27, 1746. He is believed to have died without issue.

  v. SUSANNA⁵, b. in Newbury, July 30, 1746; m. Mar. 15, 1768, Stephen Dole, son of Richard and Sarah (Emery) Dole, b. July 7, 1740; d. 27 July, 1814, age 73 years. She d. in W. Newbury, 25 Mar., 1828, age 82 years.

135. vi. ABRAHAM⁵, b. in Newbury, May 13, 1748; m. Nov. 18, 1768, Mary Bricket of Newbury.
   He is called "Abraham 4th," in the record of his marriage at West Newbury. He was a farmer and blacksmith and removed to Boscowen, N. H., in 1793.

  vii. ENOCH⁵, b. in Newbury, Jan., 1750; d. in W. Newbury, 20 Aug., 1776.

  viii. MARY⁵, b. in Newbury, Jan., 1752; m. Nov. 24, 1778, Jonathan Ilsley; res. Newbury, Mass.

  ix. DAVID⁵, b. in Newbury, June 24, 1754; d. 20 Sept., 1806.

136. x. SARAH⁵, b. in Newbury, Mar. 2, 1756; m. May 1, 1777, Benja. Plummer, Jr.; she d. 22 Jan., 1812, age 56 years. He d. 19 Oct., 1817, age 66 years.

  xi. LYDIA⁵, b. in Newbury, Jan. 28, 1758; d. Mar., 1793.

137. xii. DANIEL⁵, b. in Newbury, Apr. 27, 1760; m. May 25, 1779, Hannah Poor; she m. 2nd, Silas Moulton of Newbury. He was a farmer; d. 19 July, 1782.

Children of JUDITH⁴, (1716) [50] (Dr. Matthew³, Sergt. Abraham², Robert¹) and Capt. Edmund Little; res. Newbury, Mass.

  i. ELIZABETH LITTLE, b. Mar. 23, 1738; m. Dec. 7, 1763, Abraham Day, son of Abraham and Mary (Bailey) Day. She d. 5 Mar., 1777.

  ii. JOSEPH LITTLE, b. May 4, 1741; m. (1) Apr. 28, 1762, Elizabeth Merrill; she d. 27 Oct., 1763; m. (2) Nov. 11, 1766, Mary Johnson, dau. of Rev. Wm. Johnson; she d. 18 June, 1829. He d. 4 Apr., 1823.

  iii. JOHN LITTLE, b. Sept. 13, 1743; m. Apr. 25, 1765, Ruth Hale, dau. of Ezekiel Hale; she d. 1 June, 1829, age 83 years; res. W. Newbury, Mass. He d. 28 Feb., 1825.

- iv. JUDITH LITTLE, b. Aug. 21, 1746; m. (1) July 12, 1774, Abraham Adams, son of Robert and Love (Jaques) Adams; he d. 4 Apr., 1801; m. (2) Capt. Joseph Noyes. She d. 1825; no issue.
- v. ENOCH LITTLE, b. June 1, 1748; m., Mary Hale, a half-sister of Ruth Hale; she d. 8 Aug., 1820, age 69 years. He d. 15 Aug., 1820.
- vi. SARAH LITTLE, b. May 9, 1750; m. Mar. 31, 1770, Samuel Thurlow of W. Newbury. She d. Feb., 1825.
- vii. MARY LITTLE (twin), b. May 9, 1750; m. 1771, John Merrill; he d. 21 May, 1821. She d. 18 Jan., 1828.
- viii. EUNICE LITTLE, b. July, 1753; m. (1) July 12, 1774, Robert Adams, son of Robert and Anne (Jaques) Adams, b. July 24, 1750; d. 3 Dec., 1776; m. (2) Sept. 18, 1788, Dea. Bradstreet Tyler, and rem. to Boxford, Mass. She d. about 1796.
- ix. PRUDENCE LITTLE, b. May 4, 1755; d. young.
- x. HANNAH LITTLE, b. July 18, 1757; m. Capt. Samuel Dole, son of John and Sarah Dole, b. Nov. 14, 1749; he d. 15 Apr., 1805. She d. 6 Apr., 1843.

Children of HANNAH[4], (1722) [51] (Richard[3], Sergt. Abram[2], Robert[1]) and Capt. David Chute; res. Rowley, Mass.

- i. JUDITH CHUTE, b. Jan. 20, 1743; m. Daniel Thurston.
- ii. JAMES CHUTE, b. Jan. 6, 1745; d. 25 Jan, 1749.
- iii. DAVID CHUTE, b. Dec. 28, 1747; d. 25 Jan., 1749.
- iv. SUSANNA CHUTE, b. Jan., 1749; d. 20 Jan., 1749.
- v. JAMES CHUTE, b. Feb. 16, 1751; m. June 13, 1775, Mehitable Thurston, dau. of Richard Thurston of Rowley; she d. 18 Oct., 1819. He d. in Madison, Ind., 28 Apr., 1825.
- vi. DAVID CHUTE, b. Jan., 1753; d. 20 May, 1756.
- vii. DAVID CHUTE, b. Jan. 25, 1754; d. 12 Aug., 1760.
- viii. DAVID CHUTE, b. Aug. 19, 1756; m. 1793, Ruth Searle; she d. Mar., 1847. He d. in Newbury, Sept., 1843.
- ix. RICHARD CHUTE, b. Aug. 4, 1758; d. 3 Aug., 1760.
- x. DANIEL CHUTE, b. Sept. 28, 1760; m. 1790, Polly Stimpson of Reading; she d. 9 Oct., 1851, age 91½ years. He d. in Reading, Mass., Mar., 1843.
- xi. MARY CHUTE, b. Dec. 8, 1762; m. Dea. Benja. Coleman; he d. in 1846, age 94 years. She d. 1849.
- xii. HANNAH CHUTE, b. Apr., 1762; m. July 17, 1792, Rev. Ariel Parish of Lebanon, Conn.

Children of ENOCH⁴, (1724) [52] (Richard³, Sergt. Abraham², Robert¹), and Sarah (Jackman) Adams; res. Newbury, Mass.

    i. LIEUT. NATHANIEL⁵, b. in Newbury, June 20, 1748; m. Nov. 9, 1784, Mary Pearson.

        He was probably a soldier, and served as a sergeant in Capt. Gerrish's company, Col. Moses Little's regiment, from Apr. 24, 1775, for 3 mos. and 14 days. He may have been in Capt. Josiah French's company, Col. Edw. Wigglesworth's regiment, drawing pay for travel from Albany to his home, Jan. 30, 1777. He was styled "gentleman," and in 1784 was called "Lieutenant." He d. 11 Oct., 1828, age 80 years; no issue.

    ii. SUSANNA⁵, b. in Newbury, Nov. 27, 1749; d. young.

Children of RICHARD⁴, (1726) [53] (Richard³, Sergt. Abraham², Robert¹) and Sarah (Noyes) Adams; res. Newbury, Mass.

138.   i. ENOCH⁵, b. in Newbury, Nov. 29, 1755; m. May 11, 1781, Elizabeth Russell of Newbury, b. June 27, 1759; d. Aug., 1802.

        He was a soldier in Capt. Gerrish's company from Newbury, in Apr., 1775. He set. in Salisbury, N. H., and drew a pension. He d. 27 Feb., 1842, age 87 years.

139.   ii. PAUL⁵, b. in Newbury, Apr. 12, 1758; m. (1) Apr. 30, 1785, Hannah Ilsley of Newbury; m (2) Feb. 28, 1803, Hannah G. Keniston.

        He was a farmer, blacksmith, miller and Quaker; d. 9 Sept., 1833.

140.   iii. DANIEL⁵, b. in Newbury, Nov. 15, 1760; m. (1) Nov. 26, 1788, Edna Noyes; she d. 14 Feb., 1799, age 40 years; m. (2) [pub. May 1, 1800] Sarah Pierce of Newburyport; she d. 1 Jan., 1849, age 88 yrs., 8 mos.

        He was a farmer and cordwainer, and became a miller about 1789; res. Newbury, Mass.; d. 2 Aug., 1846, age 86 years.

141.   iv. SARAH⁵, b. in Newbury, May 2, 1763; m. Dec. 26, 1799, Samuel Blake.

142.   v. SIMEON⁵, b. in Newbury, Aug. 27, 1765; m. Apr. 13, 1790, Sarah Little, dau. of Dr. Stephen Little of Portsmouth, N. H., a Surgeon in the British navy. She was a woman of great refinement and energy of character; she d. 20 Feb., 1857.

        He was a soldier at the time of the Shay rebellion; removed to Limerick, Me., where he created an excellent farm, with good buildings, and much fruit; was a consistant Christian and an uncompromising friend of Temperance. He was a lover of music, and performed on the violincello. He d. 27 Aug., 1834.

143.   vi. HANNAH⁵, b. in Newbury, Sept. 7, 1768; m. (1) Feb. 19, 1796, Paul Thurlow; m. (2) Dec. 18, 1838, George Adams, son of John and Elizabeth (Thurlow) Adams (his 2nd wife).

    vii. ELIZABETH⁵, b. in Newbury, Apr. 17, 1770; m. Oct. 27, 1792, George Adams, son of John and Elizabeth (Thurlow) Adams. She d. 28 Mar., 1838.

144. viii. ASA[5], b. in Newbury, Oct. 14, 1772; m. July 1, 1795, Dorothy Morse, prob. dau. of Eliphalet and Ann (Rolfe) Morse of Bradford, N. H., b. Feb. 25, 1776, and called "Dolly."
He is said to have been "of Norwich, Vt." He d. 16 May, 1801.
145. ix. EBENEZER[5], b. in Newbury, July 19, 1776; m. Sept. 18, 1795, Edna Adams, dau. of Moses and Ruth (Palmer) Adams.

Children of JOHN[4], (1732) [54] (Richard[3], Sergt. Abraham[2], Robert[1]) and Elizabeth (Thurlow) Adams; res. Newbury, Mass.

i. MOODY[5], b. in Newbury, Sept. 8, 1762. He was drowned at sea, 27 Apr., 1790.

ii. JESSE[5], b. in Newbury, Jan. 1764. He was lost at sea with his brother, 27 Apr., 1790.

146. iii. ELIZABETH[5], b. in Newbury, May 19, 1766-7; m. Feb. 19, 1789, Paul Thurlow; he d. 30 Nov., 1795, age 21 years. She d. 9 Oct., 1795.

147. iv. GEORGE[5], b. in Newbury, Sept. 23, 1768; m. (1) Oct. 27, 1792, Elizabeth Adams, dau. of Richard and Sarah (Noyes) Adams; she d. 28 Mar., 1838; m. (2) Dec. 18, 1838, Hannah (Adams) Thurlow, dau. of Richard and Sarah (Noyes) Adams, and widow of Paul Thurlow.
He was a farmer in Newbury; d. 31 Mar., 1850, age 81 years.

148. v. SIMON[5], b. in Newbury, May 24, 1770; m. Oct. 19, 1799, Sarah Lunt; she d. 13 Apr., 1817. He d. 25 Sept., 1836.

vi. SUSANNA[5], b. in Newbury, Feb. 21, 1772; m. June 29, 1809, David Longfellow of Newbury, Mass. She d. in Winthrop, Me., 17 July, 1843.

vii. DR. FREEBORN[5], b. in Newbury, Sept. 30, 1774; m. in Newberry, S. C., Judith Finch. He d. in Newberry, S. C., Oct., 1812, leaving two daughters and one son.

viii. DR. ISAAC[5], b. in Newbury, Feb. 15, 1777.
He graduated from Harvard College in 1798, and d. unm. 4 June, 1807, age 31 years.

149. ix. JOHN[5], b. in Newbury, Nov. 13, 1778; m. June 22, 1800, Margaret Lunt; she d. 22 Oct., 1860, age 79 years. He d. 16 Jan., 1862.

x. GREEN[5], b. in Newbury, Nov. 11, 1781.
He went away to the West; was believed to be alive in 1820, but nothing further is known of him.

Child of DANIEL[4], (1734) [55] (Richard[3], Sergt. Abraham[2], Robert[1]) and Edna (Noyes) Adams; res. Newbury, Mass.

i. HANNAH[5], b. in Newbury, Aug. 17, 1759; m. Feb. 5, 1789, Paul Lunt of Newbury, Mass.

Children of MOSES[4], (1737) **[56]** (Richard[3], Sergt. Abraham[2], Robert[1]) and Ruth (Palmer) Adams; res. Newbury, Mass.

    i. ELIZABETH[5], b. in Newbury, Aug. 31, 1761 ; d. unm.

150. ii. RUTH[5], b. in Newbury, Mar. 24, 1763 ; m. Mar. 25, 1783, Joseph Thurlow, son of John and Ruth (Stevens) Thurlow, b. Jan. 2, 1757. He m. 2nd, Hannah Chase, and d. 8 Aug., 1837. She d. 22 Apr., 1789.

    iii. HANNAH[5], b. in Newbury, Nov. 6, 1764; m. Oct. 19, 1797, Joseph Russell, Jr.

    iv. SUSANNA[5], b. in Newbury, Aug. 1, 1766 ; m. Oct. 29, 1800, Jona. Merritt, Jr.

    v. EUNICE[5], b. in Newbury, Aug. 21, 1768 ; m. Feb. 24, 1814, Nathan Longfellow, son of Samuel and Rebecca (Chase) Longfellow, b. Dec. 26, 1773. He m. 1st, Anna Downer, who d. 2 May, 1813. Eunice was his 2nd wife, and had no children. He d. 26 Oct., 1840.

151. vi. MOSES[5], b. in Newbury, Oct. 10, 1770 ; m. (1) May 16, 1793, Phoebe Jewett of Rowley ; m. (2) Dec. 24, 1811, Marcia Lee Lunt. He was a yeoman ; res. Newbury, Mass.

152. vii. EZRA[5], b. in Newbury, Jan. 31, 1773 ; m. Jan. 14, 1796, Betsey Adams, dau. of Capt. Stephen and Sarah (Bartlett) Adams; she d. 2 Apr., 1818, almost 43 years.
        He was a farmer ; retired and set. in Lowell, Mass ; d. Aug., 1856, age 84 years.

    viii. DUDLEY[5], b. in Newbury, Mar. 14, 1775 ; d. 3 Oct., 1778.

    ix. EDNA[5], b. in Newbury, Sept. 20, 1778 ; m. Sept. 18, 1795, Ebenezer Adams, son of Richard and Sarah (Noyes) Adams.

    x. DUDLEY[5], b. in Newbury, Aug. 10, 1781 ; d. unm. 29 Dec., 1852.

    xi. ZILPHA[5], b. in Newbury, June 8, 1786 ; d. 11 Aug., 1809.

Children of DEA. EDMUND[4], (1740) **[57]** (Richard[3], Sergt. Abraham[2], Robert[1]) and Hannah (Thurston) Adams; res. Derry. N. H.

153. i. ENSIGN JAMES[5], b. in Newbury, May 5, 1765 ; m. in Derry, Jan. 24, 1793, Anna Griffin. He d. in Derry, 1 May, 1853, age 88 years.

    ii. JANE[5], b. in Newbury, June 2, 1767 ; d. young.

    iii. AMOS[5], b. in Newbury, May 10, 1768. He was killed in a saw-mill, 13 Mar., 1813, unm.

    iv. PATIENCE[5], b. in Newbury, July 16, 1770 ; m. 1794, John Moore. She d. 20 July, 1806.

154. v. JANE[5], b. in Newbury, Feb. 13, 1773 ; m. Dec. 31, 1794, Daniel Marsh of Walpole, N. H. ; he was b. in Londonderry, N. H., enlisted when 16 years of age in the war of the Revolution, but was

refused. He set. in Walpole, 1791 ; d. 9 Aug., 1857. She d. in Walpole, N. H., 24 Sept., 1859.

vi. HANNAH[5], b. in Newbury, Feb. 8, 1775 ; d. 5, June, 1795.

155. vii. EDMUND[5], b. in Newbury, Apr. 3 [May 14], 1777; m. 1808, Elizabeth Carr ; she d. 2 May, 1858. He d. 8 Sept., 1858.

viii. RICHARD[5], b. in Newbury, Nov. 14, 1779 ; d. young.

ix. BENJAMIN[5], b. in Newbury, May 31, 1782 ; d. in Havana, Cuba, 2 Sept., 1811, unm.

x. JACOB[5], b. in Newbury. Jan. 14, 1785.
He founded the Adams Female Academy of Derry, and d. there unm. 10 Aug., 1822.

Child of DEA. EDMUND[4], (1740) and Betsey (Kimball) Adams.

xi. SUSAN[5], b. in Derry, about 1811 ; m. 1831, ——- Pepper, a lawyer.

Children of JACOB[4], (1703) [58] (Sergt. Jacob[3], Jacob[2], Robbert[1]) and Elizabeth (Warner) Adams; res. Suffield, Conn.

i. DORCAS[5], b. in Suffield, Oct. 11, 1731.

ii. ZADOC[5], b. in Suffield, Nov. 28, 1733 ; d. 4 May, 1737.

156. iii. ZADOC[5], b. in Suffield, May 2, 1736; m. Ruth Bush of Westfield, Mass., b. 1742: d. 20 Feb., 1825, age 80 years. He d. 31 Oct., 1806, age 70 years.

iv. ASHBEL[5], b. in Suffield, Mar. 22, 1739.
He probably married and had a son Israel[6], who m. at Westhaven, Vt., Dorcas Adams, dau. of Samuel and Elizabeth (Purchase) Adams, b. Jan. 30, 1788, removing to Ohio.

v. ELIZABETH[5], b. in Suffield, June 17, 1747.

Children of JOHN[4], (1706) [59] (Sergt. Jacob[3], Jacob[2], Robert[1]) and Martha (Winchell) Adams; res. Suffield, Conn.

i. MARTHA[5], b. in Suffield, May 19, 1734; d. 22 Nov., 1760 [1741 ?].

ii. ABIA[5], b. in Suffield, Feb. 28, 1735.

iii. HANNAH[5], b. in Suffield, Jan. 17, 1737-8.

iv. MARY[5], b. in Suffield, Mar. 28, 1740.

v. JOHN[5], b. in Suffield, Sept. 13, 1741 ; d. young.

vi. JOHN[5], b. in Suffield, Oct. 12, 1744 ; m. Abigail Allen. He d. 15 Sept., 1776, leaving one child, Abigail[6], b. Mar. 27, 1776.

vii. JOSEPH WINCHELL[5], b. in Suffield, May 17, 1748.

Children of BENJAMIN⁴, (1718) [62] (Sergt. Jacob³, Jacob², Robert¹) and Deborah (Baion) Adams; res. Suffield, Conn.

    i. MERCY⁵, b. in Suffield, May 28, 1768; d. 21 May, 1775.
    ii. NANCY⁵, b. in Suffield, Oct. 3, 1769.
    iii. BENJAMIN⁵, b. in Suffield, July 3, 1772.
    iv. MERCY⁵, b. in Suffield, Apr. 9, 1776.
    v. PHINEAS⁵, b. in Suffield, Apr. 9, 1779.

        There are, probably, descendants of this family living, but no records have been preserved, and nothing appears to be known of them among descendants in Suffield or elsewhere of the name and kindred.

Children of ZEBULON⁴, (1713) [64] (Daniel³, Jacob², Robert¹) and Susanna (Pengilly) Adams; res. Suffield, Conn.

    i. SUSANNA⁵, b. in Suffield, Feb. 8, 1763; m. Jan. 17, 1787, Capt. Asahel Adams, son of Zadoc and Ruth (Bush) Adams, who d. in Norwich, Vt., 8 Sept., 1802. She d. in Norwich, Vt., 25 Oct., 1802.
157.   ii. ZEBULON⁵, JR., b. in Suffield, July 21, 1765; m. Apr. 15, 1790, Lucy Ball; she d. 15 May, 1816, age 52 yrs. 4 mos. He d. 15 Aug., 1827, age 62 years.
    iii. STEPHEN⁵, b. in Suffield, Apr. 6, 1768-9; m. Mar. 26, 1794, Abigail Ball, b. Nov., 1770; d. 28 Feb., 1861. He d. in Suffield, 29, Oct., 1830, age 62 years, leaving his property to his sister's son, Roswell Adams 2nd.

Children of ELIZABETH⁴, (1724) [65] (Daniel³, Jacob², Robert¹) and Simon Kendall; res. Suffield, Conn.

    i. ELIZABETH KENDALL, b. Mar. 12, 1747; m. 1765, Robert Granger, Jr.
    ii. MARY KENDALL, b. Apr. 27, 1749; m. 1767, Gideon King.
    iii. ELIAKIM KENDALL, b. June 21, 1751.
    iv. SIMON KENDALL, b. Oct. 6, 1754; m. Jan. 14, 1777, Theoda Bronson; she d. 18 July, 1817. He d. 6 Nov., 1818.
    v. AMOS KENDALL, b. Mar. 21, 1757.
    vi. LUCY KENDALL, b. Sept. 29, 1759.
    vii. DAVID KENDALL, b. Nov. 10, 1761; d. 24 June, 1762.
    viii. BETHINA KENDALL, b. May 3, 1763.
    ix. OLIVE KENDALL, b. Sept. 18, 1765; d. 27 Sept., 1775.
    x. JOSHUA KENDALL, b. Dec. 10, 1767.

Children of **DANIEL**⁴, (1726) [**66**] (Daniel³, Jacob², Robert¹) and Rebecca (Kendall) Adams; res. Suffield, Conn.

    i. MARY⁵, b. in Suffield, May 19, 1748.
    ii. REBECCA⁵, b. in Suffield, Apr. 25, 1751.
    iii. SUSANNA⁵, b. in Suffield, Apr. 5, 1753.
    iv. CAPT. GIDEON⁵, b. in Suffield, Jan. 19, 1754; m. Rhoda Hanchett; she d. in Rome, N. Y., about 1854, age 92 years. [*]
        He was a soldier in the Revolution, and probably a Corporal in Capt. Edw. Griswold's Co., Col. Belden's Reg., at Peekskill, N. Y., Apr. 7 to May 4, 1777. He received a pension at 80 years of age. He removed to Stephentown, Rensselaer Co., N. Y., and then in 1802 to Westmoreland, Oneida Co., N. Y. He d. at Verona, Oneida Co., in the spring of 1833-6.
    v. ELIJAH⁵, b. in Suffield, Oct. 26, 1760.
    vi. HULDAH⁵, b. in Suffield, Jan. 22, 1763.

Children of FREEGRACE⁴, (1723) [**67**] (Lieut. Abraham³, Jacob², Robert¹) and Anna (Kent) Adams; res. Suffield, Conn.

    i. JULIANA⁵, b. in Suffield, July 5, 1753; m. Ezekiel Rice.
    ii. LOUISA⁵, b. in Suffield, Dec. 7, 1754; d. 23 Apr., 1755.
159.   iii. ELIPHALET⁵, b. in Suffield, Jan. 29, 1756; m, Dec. 20, 1778, Patience Rice, dau. of Phineas Rice, b. Sept. 28, 1753; d. at Acton, Ont., 4 June, 1832.
        He was a soldier in the Revolution—served under Gen. Stark; was at the evacuation of Boston, and the surrender of Gen. Burgoyne. He settled in Cambridge, Washington Co., N. Y., where his house and household goods were burned, and he removed about 1798 to Stoke, in Lower Canada, where 16 families received a crown grant of 1600 acres of land. He removed thence in 1829, to Esquesing, Halton Co., Ont., where his three sons, Rufus, Ezra, and Zenas had become settlers. He d. at Acton (Adamsville), Halton Co., Ont., 2 July, 1844.
    iv. EZEKIEL⁵, b. in Suffield, Nov. 29, 1757; m. Sally Rice.
        He settled in Cambridge, Washington Co., N. Y.
        An Ezekiel Adams, probably, a son of the above, b. Dec. 18, 1806, d. 30 Apr., 1879, m. in Cambridge, Jan. 29, 1829, Jemima Rice, dau. of Daniel Rice, and granddaughter of Thomas and Thankful (Eldridge) Rice; she was b. Nov. 28, 1810; married 2nd Nov. 9, 1881, Hon. Samuel North, and died 12 July, 1885, without issue.

---

* A Gideon Adams was published at Suffield, Jan, 24, 1778, to Theoda Kent. No other Gideon has been found in Suffield.

160.	v.	LOVISA[5], b. in Suffield, Dec. 18-20, 1759 ; m. Dec. 27, 1778, Ichabod King, son of Capt. Joseph and Hannah (Devotion) King of Marlboro, Vt., b. in Suffield, May 14, 1756; d. in Marlboro, 18 Dec., 1834. She d. in Marlboro, 31 Dec., 1834. Mr. King was a soldier in the Revolution—a private in the 2nd Connecticut Regiment, May 10 to Dec. 10, 1775, and from Dec., 1775, to Jan., 1777, in the 22nd Reg. of the Continental army. He represented the town of Marlboro in the legislature of Vermont in 1798, and again in 1800.
	vi.	FREEGRACE[5], b. in Suffield, Nov. 22, 1761; d. 27 Mar., 1762.
161.	vii.	ANNA[5], b. in Suffield, Mar. 21, 1763; m. about 1801, William Nye (his 2d wife) ; res. Halifax, Vt.
162.	viii.	FREEGRACE[5], JR., b. in Suffield, Apr. 1, 1765 ; m. Susanna Halliday ; she was b. Feb. 25, 1768; d. 19 Sept., 1851. He rem. with his father to Marlboro, Vt., took the Freeman's oath at Marlboro in 1788, and became a prominent and influential citizen. He d. in Marlboro, 23 July, 1824, age 69 years.
163.	ix.	TEMPERANCE[5], b. in Suffield, April 2, 1768; m. 1794, Jonathan Kellogg, son of Martin and Phillis (Kent) Kellogg. He d. 22 Sept., 1799. She d. before Nov. 16, 1812.
164.	x.	JEMIMA[5], b. in Suffield, May 2, 1770; m. Nov. 5, 1809, William Alverson of Halifax, Vt., b. in Smithfield, R. I., June 8, 1769, d. in Halifax, 29 May, 1839. She d. in Whitewater, Wis., 19 Apr. 1855.

Children of ANNA[4], (1734) [**68**] (Lieut. Abraham[3], Jacob[2], Robert[1]) and Elijah Leonard; res. Conway, Mass.

    i. ROGER LEONARD, b. in Conway, Mar. 15, 1760; m. Jane Clark. He d. in Conway, Mass.

    ii. AUGUSTUS LEONARD, b. Nov. 24. 1761; d. 27 May, 1765.

    iii. HAYDEN LEONARD.

    iv. AUGUSTUS LEONARD ; m. Cynthia Spencer ; she d. in Conway, 27 Aug., 1853.

    He was lost in the war of 1812.

    v. ELIJAH LEONARD, JR., b. in Springfield, Mass., Dec. 4, 1766 ; m. Abigail Hayden, dau. of Dr. Moses Hayden of Conway.

    He was a skillful architect in Boston, assisting on the plans for Fanueil Hall and the Old South Church ; he d. in Dorchester and was buried on Boston Common.

    [While the author does not claim that the connection of this family is proved or established, he is yet firmly pursuaded that it is correct.]

46 ROBERT ADAMS [Fifth Generation.

Children of SAMUEL⁴, (1736) [**69**] (Lieut. Abraham³, Jacob², Robert¹) and Dorcas (Frost) Adams; res. Suffield, Conn., and Westhaven, Vt.

165. i. ABRAHAM⁵, b. in Suffield, Mar. 2, 1769 ; m. Louisa Spurr of Hampton, N. Y.
        He rem. with his brother Samuel and set. in Fair Haven [now Westhaven], Vt, in 1792; he d. in Benson, Vt.

  ii. ANNE⁵, b. in Suffield, Oct. 12, 1770 ; m. Nov. 24, 1798, Zadoc Adams, son of Zadoc and Ruth (Bush) Adams ; he d. 25 Oct., 1844. She d. 30 Apr., 1847.

  iii. SOPHIA⁵, b. in Suffield, July 24, 1772 ; d. 14 Oct., 1778.

  iv. SAMUEL⁵, b. in Suffield, May 18, 1774 ; m. Rebecca Ames of Rutland, Vt.; children all deceased.

  v. LUCINDA⁵, b. in Suffield, Mar. 1, 1776 ; m. Joseph Davidson, and removed to the West.

Children of SAMUEL⁴, (1736) and Elizabeth (Purchase) Adams.

  vi. ELI⁵, b. in Suffield, Jan. 28, 1780 ; d. in Westhaven, Vt., unm., 5 Sept., 1809.

166. vii. ELIZABETH⁵, b. in Suffield, June 18, 1782 ; m. (1) Jan. 1, 1804, Samuel Kenyon, b. in Chesterfield, N. H., Aug. 25, 1777 ; d. 1815 ; m. (2) Aug. 24, 1824, Col. Isaac Cutler of Fair Haven, Vt. He was b. in Brookfield, Mass., Jan. 4, 1753, and m. 1st, Susanna Watson, who d. 21 Feb., 1824, age 68 years. He had been a soldier in the Revolution ; was a hotel-keeper, and a justice of the peace. He removed to Westhaven in 1827, and d. Nov., 1832. She d. 13 Feb., 1876.

167. viii. HORACE⁵, b. in Suffield, Aug. 1, 1784 ; m. Feb. 9, 1812, Orra Billings, dau. of Ebenezer Billings, granddaughter of Rev. Edward Billings. the first settled minister of Greenfield, Mass.; she d. 16 June, 1857. He d. in Westhaven, 28 Mar., 1866.

  ix. DORCAS⁵, b. in Suffield, Jan. 30, 1788; m. at Westhaven, Vt., Israel Adams, said to have been a cousin of Zadoc, who married Anne, above—probably a son of Ashbel (1739). They removed to Marietta, O., and no trace of them has been found.

Children of MOSES⁴, (1722) [**70**] (John³, Jacob², Robert¹) and Mehitable (Sikes) Adams; res. Suffield, Conn.

168. i. SETH⁵, b. in Suffield, Feb. 18, 1746-7 ; m. (1) Sept. 7, 1770, Elizabeth Lane; she d. 4 Dec., 1773 ; m. (2) —— Fairman ; m. (3) Lydia Taylor.

He was a soldier of the Revolution ; settled in Agawam, Mass. ; d. in Troy, Pa , 18 Nov., 1835.

ii. TRYPHENA⁵, b. in Suffield, Nov. 7, 1748 ; m. John Lane ; they set. in Stockbridge, Mass.

iii. JOHN⁵, b. in Suffield, Oct. 22, 1750. He was a soldier and died in the army. of sickness, at the time Sir Henry Clinton took possession of New York. He left a wife and one child.

iv. ABIGAIL⁵, b. in Suffield, Jan. 29, 1752 ; m. Jan. 15, 1798, Charles Granger, son of Benja. Granger, b. Mar. 7, 1730-1; d. 31 Jan., 1813. He m. 1st, Abigail Hanchett, and had 4 children. He was a wagoner from Suffield to Lexington in Apr., 1775. Abigail was a 2nd wife, and d. without issue 10 Apr., 1823.

v. MOSES⁵, JR., b. in Suffield, Dec. 27, 1754 ; m. Dec. 18, 1777, Roxana Kent of W. Springfield, Mass. He set. in Norwich, Mass., and removed to Ohio about 1804.

vi. LUCY⁵, b. in Suffield, Jan. 22, 1757 ; m. Charles Lane.

169. vii. THADDEUS⁵, b. in Suffield, May 10, 1759 ; m. Polly Plumb of Middletown. Conn. ; she d. 1847, age 84 years. They set. in Norwich, Mass., about 1806, where he d. 27 Sept., 1839.

170. viii. JONATHAN⁵, b. in Suffield, Feb. 7, 1762; m. Apr. 19, 1792, Eunice Allen ; she d. 6 Jan., 1841, age 84 years. He set. near his father in Suffield, and d. 16 Nov., 1814.

Children of CAPT. SIMEON⁴, (1724) [71] (John³, Jacob², Robert¹) and Susanna (Underwood) Adams ; res. Suffield, Conn.

i. HANNAH⁵, b. in Suffield, Nov. 23, 1766-7; d. 20 [27 ?] Nov., 1770-1.

171. ii. CAPT. OLIVER⁵, b. in Suffield, Apr. 3, 1769 ; m. Aug., 1791, Lucy Miller, dau. of David and Anna Miller, b. Oct. 13, 1766 ; d. 17 Nov., 1834.

He settled in Marlboro, Vt., in 1777, but removed to Hinsdale, N. H., in 1815, going thither barefooted and negotiating for the 300-acre farm then known as " the White Tavern." This he kept open as a public house until 1831, and it was a noted and popular resort. It is now known as Elmwood Farm, and is owned by a grandson, Wm. Bradley Adams. The house is still painted white. Capt Oliver d. 28 Jan., 1828.

172. iii. CAPT. SIMEON⁵, b. in Suffield, Jan. 8, 1776 ; m. Aug., 1797, Lucy Mather, dau. of Maj. Timothy Mather, b. Feb. 26, 1780 ; d. 31 Mar., 1860. He set. in Marlboro, Vt., in 1777, and d. there 13 Dec., 1846.

iv. DAVID⁵, b. in Suffield, June 9, 1773 ; m. Jan., 1799.

173. v. HANNAH⁵, b. in Suffield, Oct. 10, 1775; m. Aug., 1796, Josiah Britton, b. 1773; d. 2 Jan., 1844, age 73 years. She d. in Hubbardston, Mass.

48 ROBERT ADAMS [Fifth Generation.

174. vi. SUSANNA[5], b. in Suffield, July 11, 1778 ; m. (1) Nov. 12, 1797, Nathan Halliday ; m. (2) Mr. Babbitt.
Mr. Halliday was a tanner by trade, in Marlboro, Vt., and Richmond, N. H. He started to remove to the West with his family in 1815, driving a team to Buffalo, N. Y., where he embarked on a vessel on Lake Erie, but was driven back by a storm. He sickened and died at Buffalo, and his widow returned to Vermont. She d. in Rutland, Mass., 29 Dec., 1875.

vii. RUFUS[5], b. in Suffield, Mar. 28, 1785.

Children of LIEUT. JOEL[4], (1729) [72] (John[3], Jacob[2], Robert[1]) and Elizabeth (Fowler) Adams; res. Suffield, Conn.

i. LUCINA[5], b. in Suffield, Mar. 31, 1762; m. ——— Hale; set. in Milan, O.

175. ii. ELIZABETH[5], b. in Suffield, Oct. 13, 1763 ; m. Aug. 31, 1786, Arunah Otis, son of Stephen and Lucy (Chandler) Otis, b. in Colchester, Conn., Jan. 6, 1763.
He was a soldier in the Revolution ; enlisted at 18 years of age, and assisted to lay a cable across the Hudson at W. Point, 1781. He set. in Rutland, Jeff. Co., N. Y., in 1805 ; was a farmer and blacksmith, and d. 15 Feb., 1833. She d. in Rutland, N. Y., 4 Feb., 1830, age 66 yrs. 4 mos.

176. iii. JOB[5], b. in Suffield, Apr. 3, 1765 ; m. Candace ———. He set. in Marlboro, Vt., and rem. thence to Antwerp, Jeff. Co., N. Y.

177. iv. BILDAD[5] (twin), b. in Suffield, Apr. 3, 1765 ; m. (1) Mary Haynes ; she came with her parents in 1815 to Huron Co., O.; she was a teacher ; d. in Milan, Erie Co., O., 7 Sept., 1822 ; m. (2) Mrs. Esther Harper.
He rem. from Marlboro, Vt., with his parents about 1786, settling in 1815, in Milan, Greenfield township, Huron Co., O.; was a member of the first board of County Commissioners, helping to organize the county—the western end of the "Western Reserve," known as "the Fire Lands." He served as a cavalryman in the war of 1812-14, and d. in Milan in the fall of 1826.

178. v. JOEL[5], JR., b. in Suffield, 1767 ; m. Priscilla Kimball.
He was a soldier in the Revolution, serving in Bradley's Battalion, Wordsworth's Brigade. He rem. from Marlboro, Vt., to Ellisburg, Jeff. Co., N. Y., and thence to Erie Co., O., before 1830 ; d. in Birmingham, O., in 1843, age 76 years.

179. vi. SARAH[5], b. in Suffield, May 17, 1768; m. Asa Winchester; he d. 25 Oct., 1831; set. in Marlboro, Vt., where she d. 9 Feb., 1847.

Sixth Generation.] OF NEWBURY, MASS. 49

Children of ROBERT⁵, (1717) [73] (Abraham⁴, Robert³, Sergt. Abraham², Robert¹) and Love (Jaques) Adams; res. "The Farms," Newbury, Mass.

  i. JOSEPH⁶, b. in Newbury, 1738 ; m. Feb. 22, 1768, Elizabeth Atkinson. He d. 30 May, 1790. His will was made Mar. 27, 1790, proved June 25, 1790; no heirs are mentioned.

180. ii. HENRY⁶, b. in Newbury, Feb. 15, 1741; m. (1) Dec. [pub. Nov. 7], 1767, Sarah Dole ; she d. 2 Mar., 1784 ; m. (2) Nov. 30, 1786, Sarah Pulsifer of Ipswich, Mass ; m. (3) May 3, 1799, Hannah Severance of Kingston, N. H., b. July 3, 1769 ; d. 23 Mar., 1851. He d. 30 Aug., 1837, age 96 yrs. 6 mos. 15 days.

  iii. ABRAHAM⁶, b. in Newbury, Oct. 2, 1746 ; m. July 12, 1774, Judith Little, dau. of Capt. Edmund Little ; she m. 2nd, Capt. Joseph Noyes, and d. 1825.
   He was a blacksmith in Newburyport, Mass.; d. 4 Apr., 1801 ; will was proved May 6, 1801 ; no issue.

181. iv. MOLLY⁶, b. in Newbury, May 10, 1750 ; m. Jan., 1767-8 Anthony Morse, Jr., son of Anthony and Martha (Morrill) Morse, b. in Salisbury, Mass., Mar. 31, 1746; d. 1794. She d. Feb., 1838, age 87 yrs. 9 mos.

  v. ABIGAIL⁶, b. in Newbury, June 27, 1753 ; d. unm. before 1785.

182. vi. DANIEL⁶, b. in Newbury, Nov. 24, 1756 ; m. (1) Dec. 25, 1777; Elizabeth Colley of Marblehead, Mass., b. Sept. 4, 1758 ; d. 28 Sept., 1783 ; m. (2) Jan. 14, 1787, Mary Lord of Ipswich, Mass.; she d. at the house of her dau., Mrs. Hannah Poor. He d. 21 Mar., 1843, age 85 yrs. 4 mos. ⟨Jan. 1849⟩

Children of LYDIA⁵, (1719) [74] (Abraham⁴, Robert³, Sergt. Abraham², Robert¹) and Eliphalet Jaques; res. Newbury, Mass.

  i. HENRY JAQUES, b. Mar. 9, 1738 ; m. Sarah Knight, and d. 13 Jan., 1792.
  ii. DAVID JAQUES, b. Sept. 22. 1739 ; d. 18 Dec., 1760.
  iii. EDMUND JAQUES, b. June 23, 1740 ; d. 7 Feb., 1742.
  iv. LYDIA JAQUES, b. Nov. 19, 1742; d. 30 Mar., 1776.
  v. ELIPHALET JAQUES, b. Sept. 14, 1744 ; d. 23 Sept., 1750.
  vi. EDMUND JAQUES, b. Sept. 16, 1746 ; d. 30 Jan., 1748.
  vii. ENOCH JAQUES, b. May 10, 1748 ; m. Mary Hale, and d. 30 Jan., 1809.
  viii. EUNICE JAQUES, b. Mar. 31, 1750 ; m. Samuel Pearson ; d. 10 Sept., 1836.
  ix. SALLY JAQUES, b. Feb. 14, 1752 ; d. unm. 16 Aug., 1775.
  x. PARKER JAQUES, b. Mar. 11, 1754 ; m. Nancy Newman, and d. 13 May, 1848.

xi. MEHITABLE JAQUES, b. Apr. 17, 1756; m. Richard Smith, and d. 23 Apr., 1810.

xii. POLLY JAQUES, b. May 9, 1758 ; d. 14 Jan., 1760.

xiii. ELIPHALET JAQUES, b. Mar. 19, 1761 ; d. 9 Aug., 1761.

Children of BENJAMIN[5], (1723) [75] (Abraham[4], Robert[3], Sergt. Abraham[2], Robert[1]) and Abigail (Kendrick) Adams; res. Boston Mass.

183. i. BENJAMIN[6], JR., b. in Newbury, 1784 ; m. 1778 Sarah Pond.
    He must have descendants living in or near Boston, but all attempts to find them have proved fruitless.

184. ii. ABRAHAM[6], b. in Boston, Mass., 1750 ; m. Mary Blackman, dau. of John and Abigail (How) Blackman of Dorchester, Mass., b. May 24, 1751.
    He was a leather-dresser in Newbury St., Boston ; d. 6 June, 1806. His will was made June 6, and proved June 23, 1806.

iii. ABIGAIL[6], b. in Boston, 1752; is reported to have d. 21 Mar., 1855.

185. iv. CALEB[6], b. in Boston, May 9, 1754-5 ; m. Hannah Blackman, sister of Mary; she was b. Oct. 21, 1759.

Children of BENJAMIN[5], (1723) and Sarah (Burrage) Adams.

186. v. DANIEL[6], b. in Boston, 1756-7.
    He was a hatter. A Daniel b. in 1756, resided in Hopkinton and Barre, Mass., and d. in Putney, Vt., in 1838, who may have been this Daniel, but no knowledge or clue exists among the many descendants to prove his identity with this Daniel.

187. vi. SAMUEL[6], b. in Boston, June 7, 1759; m. May 31, 1781, Catherine Fenno.
    He was a wire-worker on Ann street, Boston, and known as "rat trap Adams"; d. in Boston, 31 Mar., 1796, age 36 yrs. 9 mos.

188. vii. ISAAC[6], b. in Boston, Aug. 11, 1761 ; m. (1) Aug. 9, 1788, Abigail Blackman, sister of Mary and Hannah, b. in Dorchester, Aug. 9, 1768 ; d. 9 Aug., 1819 ; m. (2) Sept. 11, 1820, Sally Newman of Boston, b. Oct. 19, 1775.
    He was a soldier at 15 years of age, drafted into the army, and was a prisoner in Dartmour prison, where he learned to write, etc.

viii. EUNICE[6] b in Boston, Dec. 12, 1763.

Children of CHARLES[5], (1729) [**77**] (Abraham[4], Robert[3], Sergt. Abraham[2], Robert[1]) and Mary (Hills) Adams; res. Newbury, Mass.

  i. INFANT, b. in Newbury, Oct 22, 1761; d. same day.

189. ii. JACOB[6], b. in Newbury, July 17, 1764; m. (1) Oct. 22, 1789, Elizabeth Hidden, b. Mar. 30, 1762; d. 26 July, 1817, age 55 years ; m. (2) Dec. 10, 1817, Hannah Bartlett, dau. of Nathaniel and Hannah (Hills) Bartlett, b. Dec., 1773 ; d. 23 Aug., 1832.
   He was a teamster; res. Newbury, Mass., d. 28 Oct., 1850, age 86 years.

190. iii. AMOS[6], b. in Newbury, Apr. 25, 1768 ; m. Nov. 3, 1799, Sally Whitney, of St. Johns, N. B., b. Nov. 10, 1776; d. 8 Sept., 1853.
   He was a ship-builder ; set. in St. Johns, N. B., 1791 ; d. 13 Nov., 1827, at St. Johns, N. B.

191. iv. SMITH[6], b. in Newbury, Feb. 22, 1771; m. Oct. 5, 1794, Hannah Bray, dau. of Aaron and Hannah (Davis) Bray, b. Mar. 26, 1771 ; d. 29 Dec., 1841. He was a cooper ; res. Newbury; d. 10 Mar., 1831.

192. v. REBECCA[6], b. in Newbury, Feb. 1, 1775 ; m. Nov. 24, 1797, Samuel Davis, son of Aaron and Mary (Knapp) Davis ; b. Oct. 18, 1766 ; d. 5 Jan., 1836. She d. 23 Apr., 1848.

193. vi. MARY[6], b. in Newbury, Mar. 28, 1778 ; m. Apr. 29, 1866, Robert Morse, son of Anthony and Molly (Adams) Morse, b. Mar. 16, 1783 ; d. 10 Jan., 1836; rem. to Boston, 1820. She d. 18 Nov., 1855.

194. vii. MARTHA[6], b. in Newbury, Jan. 17, 1782 ; m. (1) Nov. 11, 1805, Obadiah Short, son of Richard and Judith (Lunt) Short, b. 1778 ; d. 20 Nov., 1805, nine days after marriage; m. (2) Nov. 18, 1810, Edmund Smith, son of Richard and Mehitable (Jaques) Smith, b. Aug. 31, 1785; d. 14 June, 1849. Mr. Smith m. 2nd, Oct. 12, 1849, Mrs. Mary (Huse) Moody. She d. 29 Sept., 1846.

Children of MEHITABLE,[5] (1734) [**78**] (Abraham[4], Robert[3], Sergt. Abraham[2], Robert[1]) and John Knight; res. Newbury, Mass.

  i. ELIZABETH KNIGHT, b. Apr. 15, 1764; m. Mar. 28, 1886, Oliver Martin.

  ii. REBECCA KNIGHT, b. Nov. 5, 1765 ; m. Aug. 14, 1783, Moses Rogers.

  iii. ABIGAIL KNIGHT, b. Feb. 20, 1767; m. Feb. 6, 1794, Nehemiah Emerson.

  iv. SARAH KNIGHT, b. Dec. 2. 1768 ; m. ——— Howard.

  v. ADAMS KNIGHT. b. June 26, 1771 ; m. Nov. 6, 1798, Alice Little, b. Dec. 8, 1768 ; d. 22 Nov., 1851. He d. 10 Oct., 1848, age 78 yrs. 8 mos.

  vi. JOHN KNIGHT, b. Dec. 8, 1774; m. Jan. 12, 1809, Mary Jaques.

  vii. MEHITABLE KNIGHT, b. Apr. 12, 1777 ; d. 16 Sept., 1778.

Children of SARAH⁵, (1743) [**80**] (Abraham⁴, Robert³, Sergt. Abraham², Robert¹) and Isaac Adams; res. Newburyport, Mass.

    i. ELEANOR ADAMS, b. May 26, 1779; m. Moses Hale.
    ii. THOMAS ADAMS, b. July 23, 1784; m. (1) June 21, 1805, Mary Leach; m. (2) Oct. 18, 1813, Sarah Saunders.

Children of DEA. ANTHONY MORSE, (1722) [**81**] and his wife Hannah Merrill; res. Falmouth, Me.

195.   i. JOSEPH MORSE, b. in Falmouth, Feb. 29, 1745; m. Hannah Hunt, dau. of Ephraim Hunt. He set. in Brunswick, Me.; was a cordwainer; d. 10 Feb., 1817.
196.   ii. JOHN MORSE, b. in Falmouth, Aug. 13, 1746; m. (1) 1769, Sarah Sanders; she d. 1805; m. (2) Leonice Riggs. He d. 12 June, 1826; res. Gray, Me.
    iii. MARK MORSE, b. in Falmouth; m. Sarah Switcher, res. Gray, Me.; d. age about 70 years; a dau. Hannah m. Chas. McDaniels; another m. John Russell.
    iv. ANTHONY MORSE, b. in Falmouth; m. Susanna Elliot; res. Brunswick, Me.; d. age about 68 years; had James, Anthony, Adams.
    v. MARY MORSE; m. Jona. Sawyer; res. Gloucester, Mass.
    vi. ANN MORSE; m. Wm. Greeley; res. Gray, Me.
    vii. HANNAH MORSE; m. Richard Colby; res. Gray, Me.
    viii. ELIPHALET MORSE; m. Sally Riggs; res. Portland, Me.; d. age about 35 years.
    ix. SARAH MORSE; m. Joshua Weeks; res. Gray, Me.
    x. REBECCA MORSE; m. James Riggs; res. Falmouth, Me.
    xi. PATIENCE MORSE; m. James Moses; res. Falmouth, Me.
    xii. LUCY MORSE; d. unm.
197.   xiii. EPHRAIM MORSE, b. about 1770; m. Rachel Noyes; she d. 1847. He was a ship-wright; res. in or near Portland, Me.; d. at about 72 years of age.

Children of ELIPHALET MORSE, (1733) [**82**] and Abigail Pettengill; res. Newbury, Mass., and Bradford, N. H.

    i. MARY MORSE, b. in Newbury, Nov. 12, 1758; m. Bartlett Creassey.
    ii. SARAH MORSE, b. in Newbury, June 18, 1760; d. young.

Sixth Generation.] OF NEWBURY, MASS. 53

Children of ELIPHALET MORSE, (1733) and Anna Rolfe.
- iii. JOSEPH MORSE, b. Apr. 16, 1763; m. Judith Short; res. Bradford, N. H.
- iv. JONATHAN MORSE, b. 1765; m. 1791, Mary Clark; d. at Bradford, N. H., 27 Apr., 1847.
- v. APPHIA MORSE, b. in Norwich, Vt., July, 1767.
- vi. SARAH MORSE, b. in Norwich, Jan 3, 1770; m. Isaiah Short. She d. at Bradford, N. H., 11 Dec., 1835.
- vii. ANNE MORSE, b. in Norwich, Oct. 1, 1773.
- viii. DOLLY MORSE. b. in Norwich, Feb. 25, 1775; m. July 1, 1795, Asa Adams, son of Richard and Sarah (Noyes) Adams, said to be of Norwich, Vt.

Children of ISRAEL MERRILL (1725) [83] and Abigail Cauley; res. Falmouth, Me.
- i. ISRAEL MERRILL, bapt. 1744.
- ii. NICHOLAS MERRILL.
- iii. ABIA MERRILL.
- iv. LEVI MERRILL.

Children of LIEUT. JOSHUA MERRILL, [84] and Mary Winslow; res. Falmouth, Me.
- i. COL. JAMES MERRILL, b. in Falmouth; m. Hannah Hall, b. 1757; d. in Portland, 1825, age 68 years.
- ii. CAPT. JOSHUA MERRILL, b. Feb. 2, 1758; m. Dec. 16, 1783, Molly Thompson, dau. of Joseph and Sarah Thompson, b. in Falmouth, July 30, 1762. He was a mariner, deacon and selectman; res. Falmouth; d, 10 Nov., 1837, age 79 years.
- iii. ELIAS MERRILL, b. in Falmouth; m. [pub. Mar. 11, 1784] Elizabeth Fullerton, dau. of Wm. and Anne (Deering) Fullerton of Portsmouth, N. H.
  He was for many years Register of Deeds for Cumberland Co.; d. 1823, age 65 years.
- iv. ELEANOR MERRILL, b. in Falmouth, May, 1759; m. Apr., 1777, Seward Porter of Weymouth, Mass.
- v. CHARITY MERRILL, b. in Falmouth; m. Josiah Noyes; res. in Falmouth.
- vi. SALOME MERRILL, b. in Falmouth; m. James Merrill (cousin).
- vii. HEZEKIAH MERRILL. b. in Falmouth, Feb. 22, 1768; m. 1790, at Freeport, Me., Charlotte Pote, dau. of Capt. Greenfield and Jane (Grant) Pote, b. 1773.
  He was a shipwright; res. Freeport, Me.

- viii. DORCAS MERRILL, b. in Falmouth; m. Capt. Wm. Pote, son of Capt. Greenfield and Jane (Grant) Pote of Freeport, Me.; d. in Freeport, Me.
- ix. SAMUEL MERRILL, b. in Falmouth; d. in infancy.
- x. SYBIL MERRILL, b. in Falmouth, Feb. 21, 1779; m. Aug., 1794, Abia Chamberlain, son of Nath'l and Eleanor (Whitman) Chamberlain, b. in Pembroke. Mass., Nov. 3, 1768; d. at Cape Elizabeth, Me., 22 Nov., 1856. She d. in Scarborough, Me., 17 Jan., 1841.

Child of MARY MERRILL ( ) [85] and Capt. Samuel Noyes; res. Falmouth, Me.

- i. SAMUEL NOYES, JR., b. June 25, 1752; m. Jan. 27, 1780, Lydia Barton. Their children were :
  1. John, b. Jan. 30, 1781.
  2. Dorcas, b. Oct. 13, 1782.
  3. Amos, b. Dec. 31, 1784.
  4. Ruth, b. Sept. 25, 1787.
  5. Reuben, b. Aug. 15, 1789.
  6. Eunice, b Dec. 17, 1791.
  7. Nathaniel, b. Aug. 14, 1793.
  8. Elizabeth, b. Apr. 22, 1795.
  9. Susan; m. Moses Adams, son of James and Hannah (Weymouth) Adams.

Children of CAPT. ISRAEL[5], (1735) [86] (Robert[4], Robert[3], Sergt. Abraham[2], Robert[1]), and Deborah (Jaques) Adams; res. Newbury, Mass.

- i. POLLY[6], b. in Newbury, Aug. 27, 1782; m. April 20, 1813, Col. Daniel Adams, son of Daniel and Mary (Lord) Adams. He d. 16 Oct., 1866. She d. 21 Sept., 1863.

Children of LIPHE[5], (1736) [87] (Robert[4], Robert[3], Sergt. Abraham[2], Robert[1]) and Mary (Boynton) Adams; res. Newbury, Mass.

- i. EUNICE[6], b. in Newbury, Aug. 3, 1775; d. unm., 20 Oct., 1848.
- ii. ANNA[6], b. in Newbury, Dec. 4, 1776; d. 4 Sept., 1778.
- 198. iii. SARAH[6], b. in Newbury, Dec. 10, 1777; m. Feb. 18, 1795, Moses Kent of Newburyport, blockmaker, son of Moses, d. Oct., 1831, age 58 years. The parents and four of their children died between 1828 and 1833. She d. 31 Oct., 1830.

[Sixth Generation.]   OF NEWBURY, MASS.   55

199. iv. ROBERT⁶, b. in Newbury, May 20, 1787; m. (1) June 12, 1808, Hannah Little, b. Oct. 9, 1789; d. 26 March, 1841; m. (2) Aug. 10, 1843, Sarah Poor. He d. 2 Aug., 1855, age 68 years.

Children of CAPT. SILAS⁵, (1741) [88] (Robert⁴, Robert³, Sergt. Abraham², Robert¹) and Lucy (Underwood) Adams; res. Newbury, Mass.

200. i. ANNA⁶, b. in Newbury. July 25, 1780; m. Jan. 1, 1800, Dea. Ezra Hale, son of Ezra⁵ and Anna (Knight) Hale. He was son of Benjamin⁴, John³, John², Thomas¹. He was town clerk of Newbury for a period of 37 years—between 1804 and 1844. He was b. in Newbury Sept. 23, 1771; d. 6 Nov. 1846. She d. 21 Apr., 1862.
201. ii. LUCY⁶, b. in Newbury, Oct. 23, 1785; m. Nov. 24, 1807, Thomas Cook, who d. in Dec., 1859. She d. 31 Jan., 1859.
202. iii. CHARLOTTE⁶, b. in Newbury, Dec. 31, 1787; m. Feb. 19, 1808, James Johnson. She d. 20 Nov., 1876.

Children of ANNA⁵, (1745) [89] (Robert⁴, Robert³, Sergt. Abraham², Robert¹) and John Knapp; res. Newburyport, Mass.
   i. JOHN KNAPP, JR., b. June 9, 1769; m. Oct. 11, 1794, Mary Davis, who d. 11 Oct., 1814. He d. 10 March, 1814.
   ii. ANNA KNAPP, b. Oct. 9, 1771; m. Nov. 8, 1795, Thomas Cross, b. Jan. 28, 1771.
   iii. REBECCA KNAPP, b. Jan. 21, 1774; d. 7 July, 1797.
   iv. SILAS KNAPP, b. Aug. 24, 1776.

Child of ROBERT⁵, (1750) [90] (Robert⁴, Robert³, Sergt. Abraham², Robert¹), and Eunice (Little) Adams; res. Newbury, Mass.
   i. ROBERT⁶, b. in Newbury, Aug. 14, 1775; m. Oct. 10, 1799, Susanna Little. She m. 2d, 1806, John Coker. He d. 19 Aug., 1801, age 26 years.
        Will made Aug. 11, 1801; proved Oct. 7, 1801. He was of "Newburyport," and had one child "Eunice."

Children of JANE⁵, (1733) [92] (John⁴, Robert³, Sergt. Abraham², Robert¹) and Joseph Graves; res. Falmouth and Topsham, Me.

203. i. JOSHUA GRAVES, b. in Topsham, Sept. 6, 1767; m. Mehitable Hutchinson, dau. of Samuel and Betsey (Johnson) Hutchinson, b. Apr. 2, 1779. He set. in Wayne, Me.; d. 18 Nov., 1855.

ii. REBECCA GRAVES, b. in Topsham, Sept. 2, 1769; m. Nov. 24, 1796, at Topsham, Daniel True (1st wife), son of John and Dorothy (Adams) True. She d. in N. Yarmouth, Me., 2 May, 1808.
iii. JOSEPH GRAVES, b. in Topsham ; m. Nov. 19, 1795, at Topsham, Cynthia West, dau. of Wm. Blay and Patience (Hammond) West, of Wayne and Bangor, Me.
204. iv. SAMUEL GRAVES, b. in Topsham ; m. Catherine Sutherland.
205. v. NATHANIEL GRAVES, b. in Topsham, Dec. 16, 1772 ; m. Dec. 16, 1800, at Litchfield, Me., Abigal (Palmer) Dingley.
He set. in Guilford, Piscataqnis Co., Me.
206. vi. MOSES GRAVES, b. in Topsham, Jan. 5, 1778; m. Martha Mallett. He d. in Topsham, 5 Jan., 1855.
vii. ANNA GRAVES, b. in Topsham ; m. Chas. Gowell of Bowdoin. She d. in Topsham.
viii. JOANNA GRAVES, b. in Topsham. She d. in Topsham, unm.

Child of CAPT. JOSHUA[5], (1735) [93] (John[4], Robert[3], Sergt. Abraham[2], Robert[1]) and Anne Deering (Fullerton) Adams; res. (New Casco) Portland, Me.

207. i. JOSEPH[6], b. in New Casco, about 1775 ; m. Feb. 15, 1798, at Windham, Me., by Peter T. Smith, J. P., Sarah Lewis, an adopted dau. of Archelaus Lewis of Westbrook, Me. He d. before Sept. 23, 1841, when she was his widow, living in Westbrook, and made a conveyance of all her interest in Cumberland Co., inherited from her father, to Archelaus Lewis, then living—[Westbrook was set off from Falmouth in 1814]; she d. in Portland, 2 Jan., 1844, age 64 years.

Children of CORP. MOSES[5], (1737) [94] (John[4], Robert[3], Sergt. Abraham[2], Robert[1]) and Susanna (Merrill) Adams; res. Falmouth, Cumberland Co., Me.

208. i. JAMES[6], b. in Falmouth, 1765 ; m. Hannah Weymouth of Gray, Me.; she d. 28 Oct., 1810. He d. in Portland, Me., 27 Apr., 1843, age 78 years.
209. ii. ISRAEL[6], b. in Falmouth ; m. Sept. 20, 1792, Elizabeth Swett of Falmouth. He d. in Falmouth.
iii. SABRINA[6], b. in Falmouth ; m. —— Haskell of No. Yarmouth, Me.
210. iv. ISAAC[6], b. in Falmouth, Aug. 10, 1774; m. Priscilla Skillings, dau. of Simeon Skillings of Cape Elizabeth, Me. ; b. Jan. 9, 1789; d. in Falmouth, 21 Aug., 1867, age 78 yrs. 7 mos. 12 days. He d. in Falmouth, 11 Mar., 1852, age 77 years.

211. v. MOSES⁶, JR., b. in Falmouth, Apr. 16. 1776; m. Sarah Skillings, b. 1772 (sister of Priscilla); she d. in Portland, 4 Feb., 1852, age 80 years He d. in Deering, Me., 26 Nov., 1859.

He was a yeoman in Falmouth, Dec. 2, 1813, at which time he, together with Sarah, his wife, deeded land in Falmouth—"that part of the home farm that formerly belonged to my father, Moses Adams, which he lately sold to me"—to Moses Merrill, Jr., of Falmouth. In 1831 and again in 1851 he was "of Portland," and had his residence on South Street, in a homestead purchased of Thomas M. Haskell.

Children of BENJAMIN⁵, (1745) [95] John⁴, Robert³, Sergt. Abraham², Robert¹) and Miriam (Watson) Adams; res. Falmouth and Gorham, Me.

212. i. JOSHUA⁶, b. in Falmouth, Oct., 1766-7, bapt. in the First Parish Church, Oct. 10, 1766.7; m. [pub. June 17, 1792, at Gorham] Sarah or Sally Plumer, dau. of Aaron and Lydia (Libby) Plumer, b. in Scarboro, Me., Mar. 9, 1771; d. Aug., 1838.

He was a shoemaker; set first in Limington, Me.; rem. about 1796 to Wales, Me., where he d. in 1848.

213. ii. SAMUEL⁶, b. in Falmouth, Feb. 20-8, 1769; bapt. Mar. 19; m. (1) Mar. 27-8, 1791-2, at Falmouth, Mary Allen, dau. of —— and Dorcas (Neal) Allen [*]; b. Sept. 7, 1769; m. (2) Mrs. Sarah Smith of Gray, Me., widow of Hon. John Smith; m. (3) before 1821, Mary Field of Falmouth, dau. of Benjamin Field.

He set. in Limington, Me., soon after his first marriage, and rem. thence three or four years later to Gray, Me. He was injured in early life, and disabled for doing hard labor, and became a market and milk-man. In Apr., 1823, he was a yeoman in Gray, and, together with Stephen Field and wife of Falmouth, he and his wife Mary conveyed all their rights in the homestead of Benjamin Field, late of Falmouth, to Zaccheus Lumbert of Falmouth. In May, 1834, he was a yeoman in Falmouth, and conveyed to his son, Samuel, the land in Falmouth which he had purchased of George Black in Dec., 1824, reserving the use of the same to himself and wife during their natural lives. He d. in Falmouth.

  iii. BETTY⁶, b. in Falmouth; bapt. Nov. 4, 1770; d. young.

214. iv. CAPT. JACOB⁶, b. in Falmouth; bapt. Apr. 26, 1772; m. Oct. 12, 1794, at Portland, Me., Dorcas Davis, b. 1775.

"The schooner 'Charles,' Capt. Jacob Adams, bound from Boston to Portland, on the evening of July 12, 1807, ran on the reef at Richmond's Island, in Casco Bay, in the fog, and was totally lost. Of twenty-two persons aboard, mostly passengers, sixteen perished,

---

* Dorcas (Neal) Allen m. 2nd Jedediah Dow, and was the grandmother of Hon. Neal Dow.

among whom were the captain and his wife. The place where the vessel struck is now known as Adams' Head. This accident cast a great gloom over the city. The body of Mrs. Adams was never found. but Capt. Adams was buried in the old Eastern Cemetery."

    v. DAVID[6], b. in Falmouth; bapt. Nov. 28, 1773; m. Mary ———. She d. 8 Sept., 1813. He d. 2 Nov., 1800.

    vi. BETTY[6], b. in Falmouth; bapt. Jan. 22, 1775; m. ——— Stout.

215.   vii. BENJAMIN WATSON[6], b. in Portland, Me., Mar. 9, 1778; m. Aug. 25, 1805, at Windham, Me., Elizabeth Varney, dau. of Elijah and Sarah Varney of Windham, Me., b. 1783; d. 13 June, 1856. She m. 2d, Joseph Neal, and had three children, two of whom were Benjamin A. Neal. b. May 13, 1826, and Betsey. b. Mar., 1828.

        He was "of Falmouth" in Jan., 1805, and purchased land in Gray, Me.

        In 1809, he had removed to Wales, Me., and sold his land in Gray.

        July 27, 1807, Benjamin Adams and Elizabeth of Windham, sell to Sarah Varney (her mother), one-tenth of two-thirds of the real estate of Elijah Varney, late of Windham, being that part which fell to me, the said Elizabeth, as heir to the estate of said Elijah, my honored father. * * *

        Jan. 20, 1817, Elizabeth Adams of Wales, County of Lincoln, widow, sells to Thomas Varney, of Windham, yeoman, land in Windham which my father, Elijah Varney, died seized of, by which I mean to convey all the remainder of my tenth part except two-thirds which I sold my mother, Sarah Varney, previous to Feb. 10, 1813.

    viii. NATHANIEL[6].

Children of STEPHEN[5], (1728) [96] (William[4], Capt. Abraham[3], Sergt. Abraham[2], Robert[1]) and Susanna (Dorman) Adams; res. Henniker, N. H.

216.   i. JACOB[6], b. in Rowley or Topsfield, Mass., Feb. 23, 1761; m. Dec. 19, 1790, Lydia Hall, dau. of Noah and Lydia Hall, b. May 24, 1768. She d. in New Lebanon, N. Y., 22 Oct., 1844, age 77 years.

        He was a soldier in the Revolution; rem. to Hancock, Berkshire Co., Mass., where he d. 25 Mar., 1841.

    ii. AMELIA[6], b. in Topsfield, May 26, 1762. She joined the Shakers; res. Enfield, N. H.

    iii. JULIANA[6], b. in Topsfield, Sept. 1, 1764; res. Enfield, N. H.; d. 13 Aug., 1812.

    iv. HENRY[6], b. in Topsfield, Sept. 3, 1766. He became a Shaker; res. Enfield, N. H.

    v. SUSANNA[6], b. in Topsfield, March 28, 1769; d. 10 Nov., 1776.

    vi. DAVID[6], b. in Topsfield, Nov. 5, 1771; d. in Topsfield, 10 Nov., 1771.

Sixth Generation.] OF NEWBURY, MASS. 59

217. vii. DAVID⁶, b. in Topsfield, Nov. 8, 1772; m. (1) about 1806, Thankful W. Miller of Ackworth, N. H.; m. (2) Lovina George. [Page ?]
He set. in Orange, Vt., prob. in Henniker, N, H., 1799-1806; d. in Orange, Vt., Feb., 1858.

viii. ELIJAH⁶, b. in Topsfield or Bradford, Dec. 9, 1774, d. 9 June, 1775.

218. ix. ISRAEL⁶, b. prob. in Henniker, N. H., Jan. 25, 1776; m. Feb. 12, 1811, Betsey Sargent.
He rem. to New Orleans about 1820, leaving his wife.

219. x. SUSANNA⁶, b. in Henniker, Oct. 17, 1779; m. Dec. 4, 1803, Barzilla Hayward, eldest son of Isaiah and Sarah (Bartlett) Hayward (and the sixth generation from Thomas, the first comer); b. in Bridgewater, Mass., Nov. 26, 1778. He removed to Grantham, N. H., 1800; d. 28 Nov., 1828. She d. in Grantham, N. H., 6 Feb., 1827.

220. xi. ENOCH⁶, b. in Henniker, Jan. 5, 1783; m. Nov. 27, 1810, Eunice Whidden of Canterbury, N. H. She d. 5 Mar., 1855-6.
He rem. to Sangerfield and thence to Amestown, Me., where he d. 8 Aug., 1860.

Children of CAPT. BENJAMIN⁵, (1735) [**97**] (William⁴, Capt. Abraham³, Sergt. Abraham², Robert¹) and Mary (Harriman) Adams; res. New Rowley (Georgetown), Mass.

i. MARTHA⁶, b. in Rowley, Apr. 1, 1760, d. 10 Dec., 1766.

ii. MARY⁶, b. in Rowley, Nov. 29, 1761, d. 7 Dec., 1766.

221. iii. KATHARINE⁶, b. in Rowley, Nov. 19, 1764; m. about 1783, Rev. Samuel Wheeler. He was b. in 1726; d. in 1785; was a chaplain in the Continental Army. She d. in Clarksburg, W. Va., 10 Oct,. 1856.

222. iv. DR. SAMUEL⁶, b. in Rowley, Sept. 5, 1767; m. Aug. 12, 1785.6, Elizabeth Plumer, eldest dau. of Nathaniel Plumer of Newburyport; b. in Bradford, Mass., Mar. 24, 1769. She d. at the homestead, Beaver, Pa., 25 Feb., 1842.
He studied medicine with Dr. J. Manning of Ipswich, and removed soon after his marriage to western Pennsylvania, where he spent an active and useful life.
The Plumers' had removed to a place named Chartiers, near Pittsburg, Pa., and Dr. Adams followed soon, taking with him his slave servants and a heavily built carriage. After eleven years in Alleghany County, he removed and settled in Beaver township, Beaver Co., on Beaver Creek, seven miles above its mouth, where he took up a large farm, erected houses and mills, practiced his profession, became a minister in the Methodist church, and at last died on the 6th of March, 1832, greatly honored and revered. He had an extensive acquaintance, his practice and preaching covering many miles around, and his ample home served both as a hospital and as a place of worship and entertainment. His wife is

described as a woman of rare charms, beautiful in person and character, inclined to rational thought and Quaker habits, most efficient in many ways as the mother of a large family, enduring heroicly and nobly the hardships of a pioneer life in a new country, far from her childhood home and loved scenes.

223.   v. PATTY[6], b. in Rowley, Aug. 5, 1770; m. Feb. 4, 1796, Samuel Plumer; b. Oct. 6, 1772 ; d. 31 Oct., 1820; res. Franklin, Venango Co., Pa. She d. 2 Oct., 1847.

Children of SARAH[5], (1793) [**98**] (William[4], Capt. Abraham[3], Sergt. Abraham[2], Robert[1]) and Daniel Ayer; res. Plaistow, N. H.

   i. SARAH AYER[6], b. Oct. 9, 1771 ; m. David Gile, b. in Plaistow, July 13, 1770, d. 21 May, 1843. She d. 23 Aug., 1803.
  ii. SAMUEL AYER, b. Dec. 13, 177–; m. Mary Chase of Haverhill, Mass. A dau., Sarah Ann, was b. Sept. 8, 1806. He d. 1847.
 iii. DANIEL AYER, JR., b. Oct. 29, 1782 ; m. Feb. 22, 1806, Anna Day. He d. 5 Feb., 1844. Their children were:
       1. Darius, b. May 4, 1807.
       2. Malinda, b. Oct. 29, 1808.
       3. Oliver, b. Aug. 2, 1810.

Children of REV. PHINEAS[5], (1742–3) [**99**] (Abraham[4], Capt. Abraham[3], Sergt. Abraham[2], Robert[1]) and Priscilla (Perkins) Adams; res. Haverhill, Mass.

   i. PRISCILLA[6], b. in Haverhill, June 10, 1772.
  ii. PHINEAS[6], JR., b. in Haverhill, Oct. 7, 1773.
       He is reported to have settled in Boston, but no record has been found.

Children of CAPT. BENJAMIN[5], (1746) [**100**] Abraham[4], Capt. Abraham[3], Sergt. Abraham[2], Robert[1]) and Sarah (Spofford) Adams; res. New Rowley (Georgetown), Mass.

   i. JOSEPH[6], b. in New Rowley, Apr. 20, 1771 ; m. Judith Lane of Rowley, Mass. ; she d. a widow.
       He was a tanner by trade ; occupied the "Wallingford House" in Boxford, Mass., and d. of consumption 19 Nov., 1812; had a dau. who d. in infancy.

224. ii. BENJAMIN[6], b. in New Rowley, June 14, 1773; m. May 17, 1798, Lois Perley of Boxford, Mass. ; she d. 22 Jan., 1842, age 70 years.
       He was a resident of Georgetown, Mass., and d. 2 Jan., 1852, age 78 years.
 iii. ABRAHAM[6], b. in New Rowley, July 20, 1776. He was a student in Atchinson Academy, and d. 20 Aug., 1791.

Sixth Generation.] OF NEWBURY, MASS. 61

Children of CAPT. BENJAMIN⁵, (1746) and Betsey (Woodman) Adams.

 iv. SALLY⁶, b. in New Rowley, June 1, 1780; m. Mar. 26, 1818, Maj. Paul Nelson, son of Soloman and Elizabeth (Mighill) Nelson of Rowley, b. Apr. 16, 1775 ; d. 22 Nov. 1857. She d. without issue 25 Nov., 1856, age 76 years.

 v. HON. SAMUEL⁶, b. in New Rowley, May 23, 1784 ; m. [pub. June 12, 1818] Nancy or Ann Wheelwright, dau. of Capt. Wheelwright of Newbury ; she m. 2nd a cousin of same name.

  He graduated from Harvard College in 1806, was principal of Dummer Academy at Byfield, a teacher in Newburyport, a justice of the peace and representative from Rowley in the General Court, also a senator. He d. 23 Oct., 1821 ; no issue.

 vi. JESSE⁶, b. in New Rowley, July 6, 1789. He rem. to Baltimore, Md., but returned to Rowley, where he d. of consumption, unm., 10 Feb., 1816, age 26 years.

Children of POLLY⁵, (1761) [101] (Abraham⁴, Capt. Abraham³, Sergt. Abraham², Robert¹) and Benjamin Spofford; res. Boxford, Mass.

 i. SALLY SPOFFORD, b. Dec. 31, 1786. m. Dec. 23, 1807, Phineas Barnes of Boxford, Mass. They set. in Waltham, Mass.

 ii. MARY A. SPOFFORD, b. Jan. 4, 1789; m., Dec. 31, 1828, Nathaniel C. Nelson of Groton, Mass.; b. Feb. 17, 1767 ; d. 19 Mar., 1853. They set. in Georgetown, Mass. She d. 15 Jan., 1856.

Children of ELDER DAVID⁵, (1754) [102] (Samuel⁴, Capt. Abraham³, Sergt. Abraham², Robert¹) and Mary (Woodman) Adams; res. Derry, N. H.

225. i. COL. SAMUEL⁶, b. in Newbury, Mass., Apr. 20, 1779 ; m. Dec. 31, 1816, Sarah Fitz, a sister of the Rev. Daniel Fitz, who was for forty years pastor of the Congregational Church in Ipswich, Mass.; she d. 24 Apr., 1878, age 84 years.

  He was a man of character and note, a representative in the Legislature, 1830 ; d. in Derry, 12 Sept., 1861, age 82 years.

 ii. MARY⁶, b. in Newbury, Mar. 29, 1781; d. unm., 12 Apr., 1838.

 iii. DAVID⁶, b. in Derry, Nov. 4, 1782 ; d. 4 Mar., 1805.

 iv. JOHN WOODMAN⁶, b. in Derry, Aug. 22. 1785 ; d. unm., in Cincinnati, O.

226. v. HANNAH[6], b. in Derry, Aug. 20-8, 1788; m. (1) Dec. 27, 1810, Robert McGraw; he d. 28 Nov., 1817; m. (2) Jan. 19, 1819, William Parker of Goffstown, N. H.; he d. 9 Aug., 1839. She d. 26 Feb., 1869.
227. vi. BETSEY[6], b. in Derry, Dec. 12. 1792; m. Dec. 16, 1813, Charles Redfield, son of Ambrose Redfield. He rem. in 1840 to Williamsburg, N. Y., and later to Adrian, Mich., where he d. 7 July, 1846, age 61 years. She d. in Adrian, Mich., 27 Sept., 1877.
228. vii. SALLY[6], b. in Derry, Feb. 29, 1795; m. Hon. David Steele of Goffstown, N. H. She d. 5 Mar., 1888.

Children of CAPT. STEPHEN[5], (1760) [**103**] (Samuel[4], Capt. Abraham[3], Sergt. Abraham[2], Robert[1]) and Sarah (Adams) Adams; res. Newburyport, Mass.

    i. POLLY[6], b. in Newbury, Apr. 15, 1785; d. unm., 1859.
229. ii. COL. GIBBINS[6], b. in Newbury, Jan. 14, 1787; m. Sept. 20-5, 1817, Elizabeth Adams, dau. of David and Elizabeth (Colley) Adams. She d. 30 Jan. 1859.
       He was an officer of the Massachusetts militia; d. 28 Oct., 1862.
    iii. SAMUEL[6], b. in Newbury, Oct. 7, 1788; d. unm., 17 Aug., 1842.
    iv. MARIA[6], b. in Newbury, May 25, 1790; d. 1793.
230. v. STEPHEN[6], b. in Newbury, Apr. 9, 1792; m. Jan. 15, 1722, Mary Ann Longfellow, dau. of Nathan and Anna (Downer) Longfellow, b. Apr. 13, 1802, d. 16 Oct., 1874. He d. in Byfield, Mass., 8 July, 1874.
231. vi. MARIA[6], b. in Newbury, July 18, 1794; m. Nov., 1818, Col. Josiah Titcomb, son of Caleb and Judith (Bricket) Titcomb of Byfield, b. Feb. 27, 1788, d. 1 Apr., 1856. She d. 15 Nov., 1878.
    vii. SALLY[6], b. in Newbury, July 11, 1796; d. unm., 1850.
232. viii. SEWALL[6], b. in Newbury, Apr. 21, 1798; m. Dec. 7, 1820, Sarah Ilsley, b. Jan. 7, 1802, d. 13 Feb., 1860, age 58 years. He d. 25 March, 1835, age 37 years.

Child of MARY[5], (1747-8) [**104**] (Rev. Joseph[4], Capt. Abraham[3], Sergt. Abraham[2], Robert[1]) and Daniel Hoyt; res. Stratham, N. H.

    i. BENJAMIN HOYT, b. Dec. 3, 1774; m. Jane ——; res. Stratham.

Sixth Generation.] OF NEWBURY, MASS. 63

Children of JOSEPH[5], (1750) [105] (Rev. Joseph[4], Capt. Abraham[3], Sergt. Abraham[2], Robert[1]) and Mary (Fosdick) Adams; res. Roxbury, Mass.

233.   i. THOMAS FOSDICK[6], b. in Exeter, N. H., Nov. 8, 1776; m. (1) in 1795, an English lady, and went abroad; she d. with heirs; m. (2) Susan Fenton of Philadelphia; res. Roxbury, Mass. He d. 22 Dec., 1811.

ii. JOSEPH[6], b. in Exeter, May 11, 1779; d. 5 Oct., 1795.

234.   iii. BENJAMIN[6], b. in Exeter, May 13, 1781; m. April 4, 1818, Louisa Ann Walter, dau. of Lynde Walter of Boston.

He was a merchant in Boston in business with his brother Caleb, and later with brother Charles Frederick. He d. in Boston 13 Nov., 1858. His will was made Oct. 21, 1858, and proved Nov. 29. To his wife, Louisa Ann - with whom he had passed the happiest part of his life—he left his mansion house in Pemberton square, together with his interest in a club stable, his horses, carriages, and certain other estate. The residue of his personal property he left to his friend Stephen P. Fuller, and his sons-in-law, Samuel H. Russell and Robert C. Winthrop, Jr., as trustees for his four daughters, viz.: Louisa A. Russell, Caroline Walter Oxnard, Helen Curtis Everett, and Frances Pickering Winthrop. [Vol. 156, p. 215, Probate Records.]

iv. HENRY[6], b. in Roxbury, Mar. 29, 1783; d. 9 Aug., 1795.

235.   v. JOHN[6], b. in Roxbury, Dec. 2, 1786; m. Mar 17, 1829, Eliza Hatch, second dau. of Asa and Martha Hatch of Boston, b. Jan. 13, 1797; d. at Deer Park, L. I., 29 May, 1876; res. Lowell, Mass.; He d. 17 Mar., 1859.

vi. CALEB[6], b. in Roxbury, Jan. 3, 1787.

He was a well-known merchant in Boston, and d. there unm., 4 Dec., 1828. See his will, made July 28, 1827, proved Dec. 15, 1828. [Vol. 126, p. 591.]

He gives to his father and mother, $4,000; to his brother Benjamin, $2,000; to his brother George, $6,000; to his brother Charles F., $6,000; to his brother Joseph Thornton, $6,000; to his nephew, Henry F., $2,000; and to his niece, Elizabeth Cartwright Adams, $2,000, and also $500—the interest only to be paid to her till she should be 20 years of age, when she would receive the principal.

To his brothers, Benjamin, George and Charles F., he gives $8,000 in trust, the interest to be used for the benefit of his brother John and sister Mary during life, and on the death of John and Mary the principal to be divided equally to Louisa Ann and Caroline, daughters of his brother Benjamin, and Charles F., Jr., and Emeline Matilda, the son and daughter of his brother Charles. The residue to go to Charles F. Benjamin, George and Charles F. were appointed executors Dec. 15, 1828.

vii. MARY[6], b. in Roxbury, May 11, 1789; d. unm., 3 Jan., 1828.

236. viii. GEORGE⁶, b. in Roxbury, Sept. 10, 1792; m. Sept. 29, 1836, Mary Ann Leach, dau. of Thomas and Mary (Buckmer) Leach, b. Sept. 28, 1811; d. in Brookline, 19 Nov., 1891. He d. in Brookline, Mass., 21 Dec., 1868.

    His will was made at Brookline, Dec. 10, 1850, proved Jan. 25, 1869. His brother Benjamin was named executor. One-third of his estate he gave to his wife, and the residue to his children, Mary Isabell, Helen Isadore, Emma Frances and George Henry.

237. ix. CHARLES FREDERICK⁶, b. in Roxbury, 1794; m. (1) Oct. 31, 1822, Caroline H. Walter, a sister of Louisa Ann Walter above; m. (2) Sept. 4, 1844, Anna DeHone of Boston. He d. in Roxbury, 3 Apr., 1862, age 68 years.

    His will was made May 6, 1861, and proved May 5, 1862 [Vol. 160, p. 311]. He gave to his dau. Emily Matilda $2,000 in trust till Jan. 1, 1865, the interest of which was to be paid to his neice, Elizabeth Cartwright Adams, semi-annually. To his brother George, in trust for the four children of George, he gave four shares of the par value of $1,000 each of the Amoskeag Manufacturing Co. He gave to Anna Debon Blake, dau. of Edward Blake, Esq., who was named for his late wife, $500, and to Susan Bodel Shober, "dau. of my friend, Samuel S. Shober," $1,000. Emily Matilda was made executrix.

    The *Boston Transcript* of Apr. 4, 1862, mentions the sudden death from heart disease of Charles Frederick Adams, as a well-known merchant, partner in the firm of Adams, Homer & Co.; Chestnut St., and distinguished for his excellence of character and probity.

238. x. JOSEPH THORNTON⁶, b. in Roxbury; m. Susan Pierce Jarvis, dau. of Dr. Leonard and Clarissa (Draper) Jarvis, who rem. from Boston to Claremont, N. H.; she was born in 1809.

    He was a graduate from Harvard College in 1820; was representative of Boston 1830-31, 1833, 1836; d. 17 June, 1865. His will was made at Claremont, Apr. 18, 1862, proved at Newport, N. H.

Children of DR. CALEB G⁵, (1752) [**106**] Rev. Joseph⁴, Capt. Abraham³, Sergt. Abraham², Robert¹) and Mary (Folsom) Adams; res. Exeter, N. H.

    i. DOLLY⁶, b. in Exeter, Jan. 7, 1776; she d. 30 Jan., 1810.

    ii. NATHANIEL FOLSOM⁶, b. in Exeter, Mar. 19, 1782; m. Eliza Burley.

    June 18. 1817, Mark Walker, one of the creditors of the estate of Nathaniel F. Adams, late of the State of Ohio, but formerly of Exeter, N. H., gentleman, deceased, prayed that letters of administration might be granted to him, and the same were granted Aug. 18, 1817.

Children of LIEUT. JOHN⁵, (1758) [**107**] (Rev. Joseph⁴, Capt. Abraham³, Sergt. Abraham², Robert¹) and Ann (Folsom) Adams; res. Stratham, N. H.

  i. SARAH⁶, b. in Stratham, Sept. 11, 1788; d. 29 Aug., 1806.

239. ii. REV. JOHN FOLSOM⁶, b. in Stratham. May 23, 1790-1; m. (1) Feb. 24, 1818, Mary Lane, dau. of Jabez Lane, b. in Stratham, Apr. 10. 1789; d. 1 Mar., 1866; m. (2) July 25, 1867, Sarah W. (Treadwell) Lock.

   He was a minister of the M. E. Church; began preaching in the N. E. Conference in 1812, and became presiding elder in 1840; was a representative in the N. H. Legislature from Stratham in 1849-50, and from Greenland later. He d. in Greenland, 11 June, 1881, age 91 years.

  iii. MARY ANN⁶, b. in Stratham, May 7, 1792-3; d. unm., 1891.

  iv. JOSEPH⁶, b. in Stratham, Apr. 26, 1794. He was a teacher in Boston and in Virginia. He d. in Stratham, unm., 1841.

  v. CALEB⁶, b. in Stratham, June 26, 1796; d. 6 Mar., 1809.

240. vi. DAVID⁶, b. in Stratham, Apr. 30, 1798; m. 1821, Martha Sheriff; she d. Aug., 1867.

   He was a cabinet maker in Bangor, Me., and d. there 23 Nov., 1841.

241. vii. BENJAMIN F.⁶, b. in Stratham, Nov. 27, 1799; m. Malinda Sanborn.

   He was a cabinet maker in Bangor, Me.; d. in Stratham, 1875.

  viii. MARTHA⁶, b. in Stratham, Aug. 10, 1801; m. Freeman Harvey of Barnet, Vt. He d. Nov., 1840. She d. at Marengo, Ill., 25 Nov., 1840, leaving no issue.

242. ix. NATHAN⁶, b. in Stratham, Sept. 23, 1803; m. Oct. 21, 1857, Martha Marston, dau. of Charles and Elizabeth (Pierce) Marston, of Greenland, N. H.; b. June 17, 1833.

   He is a farmer on the homestead in Stratham, 1899.

243. x. ELIZA⁶, b. in Stratham, Aug. 7, 1805; m. Oct. 23, 1839, Capt. Caleb Wiggin of Stratham. He was b. Jan. 8, 1796; m. 2nd, June 13, 1848, Amelia Robinson. She d. Aug., 1892. He d. 10 Aug., 1887. Eliza d. 28 Feb., 1848.

244. xi. REV. CHARLES⁶, D. D., b. in Stratham, Jan. 24, 1808; m. July 29, 1833, Sarah Emery Porter, dau. of Rev. Huntington Porter of Rye, N. H. She d. in Evansville, Ill., 17 Sept., 1891. He was graduated from Bowdoin College in 1833.

Children of DR. BENJAMIN⁵, (1758) [**108**] (Rev. Benjamin⁴, Capt. Abraham³, Sergt. Abraham², Robert¹) and Lois (Orne) Adams; res. Lynnfield, Mass.

i. EDWARD AUGUSTUS⁶, b. in Lynnfield, Mar. 24, 1794; d. 8 March, 1796.
ii. EDWARD AUGUSTUS⁶, b. in Lynnfield, Jan. 31, 1797; d. 14 Feb., 1797.
iii. DELIA AUGUSTA⁶, b. in Lynnfield, June 13, 1804; d. 30 May, 1805.
iv. LOIS⁶, b. in Lynnfield, bapt. Oct. 6, 1805; mentioned in her father's will.
v. BENJAMIN PERKINS⁶, b. in Lynnfield, Nov. 7, 1809; d. 13 Nov., 1809.

Children of JOSEPH⁵, (1770) [109] (Benjamin⁴, Capt. Abraham³, Sergt. Abraham², Robert¹) and Mary (Webb) Adams; res. Danvers, Mass.

245. i. MARTHA WEBB⁶, b. in Danvers, Apr. 5, 1796; m. Allen Newhall of Hingham, Mass., b. Dec. 7, 1793, d. 4 Aug., 1848. She d. in Hingham, 22 Feb., 1878, age 82 years.
246. ii. JOSEPH⁶, JR., b. in Danvers, July 27, 1800; m. Frances H. Straw of Haverhill, Mass., b. Mar. 26, 1800; d 23 Jan., 1868.
He was a shoe-manufacturer in Lynn, Mass.
247. iii. LOUISA NICHOLS⁶, b. in Danvers, Aug. 25, 1804; m. Sept. 18, 1826, Joseph Clapp, Jr., of Dorchester, Mass., b. July 6, 1801; d. 10 Dec., 1879. She d. 6 Oct., 1880.
248. iv. MARY ANN⁶, b. in Salem, Mass., Dec. 6, 1807; m. Oliver Hunt Bowman of Milton, Mass., b. 1809, d. 13 Aug., 1854. She d. in Dorchester, Mass., 12 July, 1889.
249. v. BENJAMIN WEBB⁶, b. in Salem, June 25, 1809; m. May 2, 1829, Jane Baker Ford of Dorchester, Mass., b. Sept. 14, 1809; d. 11 March, 1880. He d. in Danvers, Mass., 18 Dec., 1882.
vi. FANNY ALMIRA⁶, b. in Salem, Jan. 11, 1813; m. July 30, 1835, Elijah French, son of Edward and Abigail French, b. in Sharon, Mass., Mar. 9, 1809; d. in Dorchester, 26 Dec., 1884.

Children of NATHAN⁵, (1761) [110] (Capt. Nathan⁴, Capt. Abraham³, Sergt. Abraham², Robert¹) and Mary (Pierce) Adams; res. Shirley, Mass., and Pomfret (Abington Parish), Conn.

i. MARY B⁶, b. in Lunenburg, Mass., Aug., 1790; d. unm. in Lunenburg, Dec., 1847.
250. ii. JOHN BREED⁶, b. in Lunenburg, Mass., May, 1793; m. April, 1824, Adeline Preston of Ashford, Conn.; d. 16 Apr., 1850.
He rem. to Connecticut 1804; set. in Ashford, (now Eastford), in 1820; teacher and merchant; d. in Eastford, 23 Oct., 1862.

Sixth Generation.]   OF NEWBURY, MASS.   67

    iii. SUSAN⁶, b. in Shirley, Mass., Sept., 1794; m. Roswell Eastman; she d. 1870; no issue.
    iv. EBENEZER⁶, b. in Shirley, May, 1797; d. July, 1797.
    v. BETSEY⁶, b. in Shirley, June 17, 1798; d. 28 Aug., 1890, age 92 years; unm.
    vi. NANCY⁶, b. in Cavendish, Vt., Apr. 19, 1801; d. unm., 5 Feb., 1869.
251. vii. SALLY⁶, b. in Cavendish. Oct., 1803; m. Joseph A. Dresser of Pomfret, Conn. She d. in Putnam, Conn., Aug., 1858.
252. viii. CAPT. GEORGE⁶, b. in Pomfret, Conn., Nov. 12, 1807; m. May, 1835, Lucy M. Prescott of Ashford, Conn., b. Feb. 11, 1816. He d. in Eastford, Conn., 2 June, 1889.
    ix. WILLIAM LEWIS⁶, b. in Pomfret, Oct. 16, 1809; d. in Abington, Conn., 5 April, 1836.

Children of ENOCH⁵, (1752) [111] (Henry⁴, Capt. Abraham³, Sergt. Abraham², Robert¹) and Sally (Bragg) Adams; res. Andover, Mass., and Andover, Oxford Co., Me.

253. i. ENOCH⁶, JR., b. in Andover, Mass., June 22, 1779; m. Mar. 26, 1807, Lucy Strickland, dau. of Rev. John Strickland of Andover, Me.
        He was a farmer in Andover, Me., d. there 26 Feb., 1849.
254. ii. COL. JOHN EMERY⁶, b. in Andover, Mass., Dec. 5, 1780; m. (1) Jan. 5, 1805, Sarah Moody, dau. of Ebenezer Moody, b. 1787, d. 1835; m. (2) [pub. Mar. 26, 1836], Sophia Jones, who d. about 1873.
        He was a farmer and lumberman; rem. from Andover, Me., to Cleveland, O., in 1826, and later to Solon, Ia., where he d. Oct., 1840.
255. iii. SARAH⁶, b. in Andover, Mass., Nov. 17, 1782; m. James H. Withington of Dorchester, Mass., b. 1784, d. 29 July, 1837, age 53; res. Peru, Me. She d. 8 Aug., 1830.
    iv. DOLLY⁶, b. in Andover, Mass., Nov. 17, 1784; m. John Farrington of Andover, Me. He d. 4 Mar., 1840. She d. 24 Mar., 1842.
256. v. DR. JOSEPH⁶, b. in Andover, Mass., Apr. 4, 1788; m. Mar. 26, 1812, Betsey Farnum, dau. of David and Dorcas (Wheeler) Farnum of Rumford, Me. She m. 2nd Jeremiah Hall of Rumford, and d. 29 Nov., 1865.
        He studied medicine with Dr. Warren Mann of Hallowell, Me., and began the practice of his profession in Rumford, Me. He removed to Iowa in 1836; was the inventor of a current water-wheel which he was engaged in erecting on the Iowa river at Iowa City when he contracted the typhoid fever of which he died 5 Aug., 1840.
    vi. HENRY⁶, b. in Andover, Mass., Aug. 15, 1790, d. 9 Dec., 1817.
257. vii. MOSES⁶, b. in Andover, Me., June 17, 1793; m. Dorcas Farnum, dau. of David and Dorcas (Wheeler) Farnum, b. Sept. 12, 1799. She m. 2nd Bradbury Richardson, and d. 20 Jan., 1873.

He was a mill-wright in Andover, Me., d. in Ohio in the fall of 1833.

258. viii. MARY⁶, b. in Andover, Me., May 30, 1796 ; m. Oct. 28, 1819, Capt. Adam Willis of Hanover, Me. He d. 13 May, 1874. She d. 15 Apr., 1881.'

ix. SAMUEL⁶, b. in Andover, Me., Sept. 7, 1798, d. 26 July, 1802.

259. x. WILLIAM⁶, b. in Andover, Me., March 23, 1801; m. (1) Betsey Crockett of Norway, Me. She d. 11 July, 1861 ; m. (2) June 6, 1863, Mrs. Delia C. Chase of Boston, Mass.
He was a farmer in Andover, Me., d. 20 July, 1882.

Children of NATHAN⁶, (1755) [112] (Henry⁴, Capt. Abraham³, Sergt. Abraham², Robert¹) and Johanna (Batchelder) Adams; res. Edgecomb, Me.

i. ELIZABETH⁶, b. in Andover, Mass., Aug. 18, 1786 ; m. Jerry Smith of Pittston, Me.

260. ii. JULIA⁶, b. in 1801 ; m. July 4, 1824, James Stinson of Wiscasset, Me., d. 28 Jan., 1855, age 60 years ; res. Wiscasset, Me. She d. 19 July, 1890, age 90 years.

iii. MARY⁶ ; m. Mark Hall of Damariscotta, Me.; rem. to California.

261. iv. PAMELIA⁶ ; m. 1813, Spencer Greenleaf of Wiscasset, Me.

v. JEFFERSON⁶; m. in Masssachusetts, d. in California.

vi. SAMUEL⁶.
A sea-captain ; killed on a foreign coast.

vii. JOSEPH⁶.
Seaman ; d. abroad.

viii. SARAH⁶ ; m. Thomas Jackson ; res. Whitefield, Lincoln Co., Me.

Children of SARAH⁵, (1757) [113] (Henry⁴, Capt. Abraham³, Sergt. Abraham², Robert¹) and Samuel Northend; res. Rowley, Mass.

i. ELIZABETH NORTHEND, b. April 1, 1781 ; m. John Kent.
She had one daughter, Caroline Kent, who married Thomas Merrill. Elizabeth d. 24 Sept., 1856.

ii. SAMUEL NORTHEND, b. 1783 ; d. 1802.

iii. JOHN NORTHEND, b. May 18, 1785; m. (1) Anna Titcomb ; she d. 7 Feb., 1848, aged 58 years ; m. (2) Nov. 20, 1856, Mrs. Ruhamah Stevens.
He was a selectman in Newbury, 1828 and 1833, and represented the town in the Legislature, 1833. He was the father of Wm. D. Northend, lawyer of Salem, Mass. He d. 20 Mar., 1865.

Child of COL. SAMUEL[6], (1736) [114] (Samuel[4], Isaac[3], Sergt. Abraham[2], Robert[1]) and Mary (Stickney) Adams; res. E. Bradford (Groveland), Mass.

262. i. SAMUEL[6], JR., b. in E. Bradford, Sept. 12, 1768; m. (1) Aug. 23, 1793, Margaret Harriman of Rowley, Mass. She became insane and ran away, and was drowned in the Artichoke river, W. Newbury, 21 June, 1809 ; m. (2) Dec. 30, 1831, Mary Savory, dau. of Chas and Hannah Savory of Georgetown, Mass.; b. July 27, 1780; d. 27 Feb., 1841.

He was a farmer on the homestead in Groveland. He made his will June 18, 1825, proved Sept. 27 ; d. 27 July, 1825.

Children of MARY[5], (1745) [115] (Capt. Isaac[4], Isaac[3], Sergt. Abraham[2], Robert[1]) and William Porter; res. Boxford, Mass.

    i. HANNAH PORTER, b. Jan. 26, 1769; m. Zechariah Bacon.
    ii. WILLIAM PORTER, b. Mar. 26, 1770 ; m. Lettice Wallace ; res. Haverhill, N. H., and Danville, Vt. ; d. in Danville, Vt.
    iii. JAMES PORTER, b. Aug. 28, 1771 ; m. Margaret Tilton.
    iv. AARON PORTER, b. June 7, 1773; m. Nov. 2, 1807, Rebecca Blanchard ; res. Danville, Vt.
    v. MARY PORTER, b. June 3, 1775; m. Amos Carlton ; res. St. Johnsbury, Vt.
    vi. SARAH PORTER, b. Apr. 22, 1777 ; m. John Osgood: res. Haverhill, N. H.
    vii. ISAAC ADAMS PORTER, b. May 22, 1779; m. (1) Catherine Buel ; m. (2) May, 1816, Mary Norman; m. (3) in 1818, at Concord, N. H.
    viii. ELIZABETH PORTER, b. Nov. 29, 1782.
    ix. PARMELIA PORTER, b. Feb. 5, 1785 ; m. Luther Clark; res. Danville, Vt.

Children of CAPT. DAVID[6], (1747) [116] (Capt. Isaac[4], Jr., Isaac[3], Sergt. Abraham[2], Robert[1]) and Phebe (Spofford) Adams; res. Rowley, Mass., and Rindge, N. H.

    i. SALLY[6], b. in Rindge, Aug. 18, 1774, d. unm., 11 Aug., 1850.
    ii. ISAAC[6], b. in Rindge, Jan. 8, 1776, d. 18 Jan., 1776.
263. iii. PHEBE[6], b. in Rindge, Feb. 21, 1777 ; m. May 1, 1802-3, Henry Hale, son of Col. Nathan and Abigail (Grout) Hale. He d. 2 June, 1861, age 81 years ; res. Chelsea, Vt., where she d. 17 Jan., 1815.
264. iv. MERCY[6], b. in Rindge, Mar. 24, 1779; m. Mar. 29, 1805, James Stevens, son of Lieut. James and Elizabeth (Lacey) Stevens of Jaffrey, N. H., b. Aug. 11, 1779, d. 5 Feb., 1857. She d. 9 Feb., 1860.

	v.	DAVID[6], b. in Rindge, Oct. 12, 1780, d. 13 Sept., 1781.
265.	vi.	DAVID[6], b. in Rindge, Mar. 11, 1782; m. (1) 1812, Silence Sawin of Templeton, Mass., b. in Natick, Mass., Nov. 8, 1785, d. 14 Mar., 1835, age 50 years; m. (2) Sept. 7, 1836, Zerviah (Morse) Clark, dau. of Adam and Lydia (Bacon) Morse, and widow of Warren Clark. He was a farmer on the homestead in Rindge, N. H., d. 19 Aug., 1852.
266.	vii.	MOODY[6], b. in Rindge, March 25, 1784; m. Jan. 18, 1814, Betsey Batchelder, dau. of Samuel Batchelder of New Ipswich, b. Jan. 16, 1789, d. 26 Aug., 1858, age 69 years. He set. in New Ipswich, N. H., and d. Feb., 1868, age 84 years.
	viii.	ISAAC[6], b. in Rindge, July 14, 1788, d. 18 July, 1788.
267.	ix.	NAOMI[6] (twin), b. in Rindge, July 14, 1788; m. Feb. 2, 1809, Isaac Spofford, son of Moody and Huldah (Spofford) Spofford, b. in Georgetown, Mass., Dec. 5, 1781; res. Brighton, Mass. She d. 5 Nov., 1854.
	x.	JOHN SPOFFORD[6], b. in Rindge, May 8, 1791; d. in Rindge, unm., 19 Feb., 1852.
268.	xi.	ISAAC[6], b. in Rindge, Aug. 18, 1793; m. (1) Mar. 27, 1823, Sophia Spofford, dau. of Jacob and Mary (Tenney) Spofford; b. Nov. 12, 1793; d. 21 Dec., 1833; m. (2) Apr. 2, 1834, Sarah J. Searle of Rowley, Mass. She d. in Reading, Mass., 16 Oct., 1877, age 72 years. He set. in W. Boxford, Mass., in 1822, and d. 31 July, 1876.

Children of CAPT. SAMUEL[5], (1750) [117] (Capt. Isaac[4], Isaac[3], Sergt. Abraham[2],˙Robert[1]) and Lucy (Spofford) Adams; res. Rindge and Jaffrey, N. H.

269.	i.	ELIPHALET[6], b. in Rindge, Feb. 10, 1775; m. Jan. 13, [18?] 1805, Mary Washburn, b. Apr. 29, 1770. He set. in Pictou, Ont., where he was a successful builder and dealer in lumber.
270.	ii.	ISAAC[6], b. in Rindge, Nov. 18, 1776; m. (1) 1800, Deborah Twitchell, who was drowned in the Androscogin River in 1803; m. (2) 1803, Olive Wight of Dublin, N. H. She was of Scotch-Irish descent. She d. 22 Mar., 1856, age 79 years. He set. in Gilead, Me., about 1800, and d. 12 Nov., 1848.
	iii.	SALLY[6], b. in Jaffrey, Jan. 12 [June 28?], 1779; m. Jacob Georstine; res. Northport, Ont. She d. 1854.
271.	iv.	SAMUEL[6], b. in Jaffrey, Aug. 16, 1782; m. (1) 1815, Sally Wright of Jaffrey, N. H. She d. 14 Aug., 1837, age 47 years; m. (2) 1841, Eliza Larned of Dublin, N. H. She d. 1890. He set. in Watertown, N. Y.; d. 18 Dec., 1854.
272.	v.	LUCY[6], b. in Jaffrey, Jan. 23, 1785; m. 1804, Lieut. Artemas Lawrence, son of Benjamin and Rebecca (Wood) Lawrence. He d. in Jaffrey, 15 May, 1841. She d. 4 June, 1852.

Sixth Generation.] OF NEWBURY, MASS. 71

273. vi. MARY⁶ [Polly?], b. in Jaffrey, Jan. 5, 1787; m. (1) Jan. 23, 1810, Perley Putnam Burnham, b. Jan. 5, 1782; d. 8 Dec., 1820; m. (2) July 20, 1828, Joseph G. Swan, b. Mar. 23, 1800; d. 31 Jan., 1866; res. Gilead, Me. She d. 8 Mar., 1873.

vii. ISRAEL⁶, b. in Jaffrey, Jan. 27, 1790; m. Dec. 24, 1821, Harriet Putnam, dau. of Col. Juthro and Mary (Holton) Putnam, b. in Danvers, Mass., May 22, 1789; d. 2 Nov., 1863.
He was a merchant in Danvers, Mass., and d. 8 Feb., 1857; no issue.

274. viii. JACOB⁶, b. in Jaffrey, Sept. 21, 1791; m. Sept. 21, 1816, Jemima Van Skiver. She d. 29 Nov., 1831.
He set. in Consecon, Canada, in 1810, and d. 21 Dec., 1866.

275. ix. ELIZABETH⁶, b. in Jaffrey, Mar. 24, 1794; m. Mar. 8, 1830, Eliphaz Chapman. She d. in Bethel, Me., 15 Oct., 1847, and he m. 2nd, Salome Burnham, by whom he had children, and d. in Gilead, Me., 9 July, 1844, age 69 years.

x. DAVID⁶, b. in Jaffrey, Aug. 9, 1796; m. Mary Kemp, who d. in Illinois.
He set. in Watertown, N. Y.; was perhaps a soldier in 1812, and was drowned in the Ohio River, Oct., 1847.

xi. LOUISA⁶, b. in Jaffrey, Mar. 3, 1799.

276. xii. JONATHAN⁶, b. in Jaffrey, Oct. 8, 1801; m. Oct. 6, 1824, Hannah Adams, dau. of Daniel and Phoebe (Britton) Adams, b. Feb. 13, 1804; d. in Woodstock, Vt., 4 Feb., 1890.
This birth is given in the History of Jaffrey, N. H., and in the Spofford Genealogy.
He was a blacksmith; set. first in Peterboro, N. H.; rem. thence to Chester, Vt., where he d. 19 June, 1843, and was buried in Springfield, Vt.

Children of ISRAEL⁵, JR., (1748) [118] (Israel⁴, Isaac³, Sergt. Abraham², Robert¹) and Elizabeth (Searle) Adams; res. Hill, N. H.

i. BETSEY⁶; d. suddenly, Nov., 1804.

ii. RUTH⁶, bapt. in Byfield, Mass., May 19, 1771; d. 23 July, 1806.

iii. ISAAC⁶, b. in Rowley, Mass., bapt. Nov. 21, 1773.
He was a book-maker in Portland, Me.; representative 1807-1811 Mass. Legislature; a rep. and editor of *Portland Press;* d. unm. 5 July, 1834, age 60 years.

iv. HANNAH⁶, bapt. in Byfield, Mass., Aug. 27, 1775; m. Nov. 1, 1798, John Currey [?].

277. v. DEBORAH⁶, bapt. in Byfield, Aug. 25, 1782; m. Solomon Winchester at Portland, Me.; rem. to Baltimore, and d. 1858. He d. 1826.

vi. JOHN⁶, b. in Rowley, Mass., Feb. 21, 1784.

278. vii. JOSEPH SEARLE[6], b. in Rowley, Mass., Mar. 28, 1785; m. Hannah Wells, dau. of Peter Wells of Bridgewater, N. H.; res. Hebron and Hill, N. H.
He rem. to Framingham, Mass., 1855, and d. there 12 Dec., 1867.

Children of ISRAEL[5], JR., (1748) and Anna (Ober) Adams.

viii. ELIZA[6]; d. in Boston, unm., about 1856.
279. ix. CHARLES[6], b. in Hill, Feb. 15, 1812; m. Mar. 8, 1838, Melinda Emerson, dau. of Ebenezer and Mary (Blake) Emerson; b. in Bridgewater, N. H., Apr. 22, 1816; res. Bridgewater and Londonderry, N. H. He d. 7 Sept., 1885, age 73 years.
280. x. GEORGE W.[6], b. in Hill, Nov. 26, 1815; m. (1) 1844, Louisa M. Tandy; d. 26 Nov., 1873; m. (2) May 2, 1881, Mary Cass Carr.
He set. in Haverhill, Mass., in 1844; d. 13 Mar., 1899, age 84 yrs. 3 mos.
xi. RUTH[6], b. in Hill: d. soon.

Children of ISRAEL[5], (1733) [**119**] (Israel[4], Sarah[4], Sergt. Abraham[2], Robert[1]) and Elizabeth (Stevens) Adams; res. Rindge, N. H.

i. ELIZABETH[6], b. in Andover, Mass., Nov. 4, 1761; d. in Rindge, unm., 28 Sept., 1835.
ii. JOSHUA[6], b. in Andover, Aug. 24, 1763.
He is supposed to have been killed at the battle of Plattsburg, Sept., 1814.
iii. SAMUEL[6], b. in Andover, Nov. 7, 1765; d. in Rindge, unm., 5 Mar., 1852.
281. iv. ISRAEL[6], 3D, b. in Andover, Jan. 13, 1768; m. Aug. 28, 1796, Sally Adams, dau. of Nathaniel Adams of Ashburnham, Mass. She d. 4 May, 1838, age 67.
He was a farmer on the homestead in Rindge; was selectman, etc. He d. 16 Sept., 1856.
v. ESTHER[6], b. in Andover, May 26, 1770; d. unm., 26 May, 1822.
vi. SARAH[6], b. in Rindge, 1773; d. unm., 21 Nov., 1823.
vii. DANIEL[6], b. in Rindge, 1778.
He set. in Rodman, Jefferson Co., N. Y.; was a farmer and d. unm., 1871.
viii. HANNAH[6], b. in Rindge, 1784; d. unm., 19 Jan., 1852.

Children of CAPT. JOHN[5], (1735) [120] (Israel[4], Sarah[3], Sergt. Abraham[2], Robert[1]) and Hannah (Osgood) Adams; res. No. Andover, Mass.

    i. HANNAH[6], b. in No. Andover, July 26, 1760 ; d. 30 Aug., 1863.
    ii. SARAH[6], b. in No. Andover, July, 1762; d. 2 Sept., 1763.

282.   iii. LIEUT. AND MAJOR JOHN[6], b. in No. Andover, Feb. 26, 1766 ; m. Dec. 8, 1789, Dorcas Falkner; she d. 23 Sept., 1837, age 71 years.
        He was a farmer in Andover, a Brigade Major in the State militia and served at the time of Shay's rebellion. He was commissioned as Captain in 1793 and called "John Adams, Jr., Gentleman." He d. 28 Sept., 1839, age 73 years.

    iv. DR. ISAAC[6], b. in No. Andover, Apr. 25, 1767.
        He was a student at Harvard College, class of 1789, but did not graduate. He became a physician and practiced his profession in Newburyport, Mass., but afterward engaged in trade, and made several voyages as master of a vessel, removing finally to Michigan.

Child of CAPT. JOHN[5], (1735) and Hannah (Thurston) Adams.

    v. JOSEPH[6], b. in No. Andover, May, 1774; d. 22 June, 1776.

Children of DAVID[5], (1742) [121] (Israel[4], Sarah[3], Sergt. Abraham[2], Robert[1]) and Abiah (Ordway) Adams; res. Methuen, Mass.

    i. SARAH[6], b. in Dracut, Mass., May 19, 1767 ; d. 13 Nov., 1801.
    ii. JAMES[6], b. in Dracut, Nov. 19, 1768 ; d. 13 Feb., 1790.
    iii. DAVID[6], b. in Dracut, Apr. 6, 1771 ; d. 21 Jan., 1813.
    iv. ABIAH BROWN[6], b. in Dracut, Sept. 8, 1773 ; d. 13 Feb., 1790.

283.   v. DANIEL[6], b. in Dracut, Oct. 17, 1775 ; m. Oct. 24, 1805, Sophia Kimball, dau. of Moses and Rebecca Kimball, b. Apr. 12, 1780 ; d. 24 Nov., 1868 ; res. Boxford, Mass. He d. 2 Mar., 1828, age 52 years.

Children of DAVID[5], (1742) and Martha (Marsh) Adams.

284.   vi. CAPT. JOHN MARSH[6], b. in Methuen, Jan. 18, 1779 ; m. about 1814, Mary Jackson. She d. in Monroe, Mich., about 1872, age 88 years.
        He probably set. in Londonderry, N. H.; d. 25 Apr., 1815. His will was proved May 18, 1815. His widow rem. to Le Roy, N. Y., and thence to Monroe, Mich.

    vii. POLLY[6], b. in Methuen, Nov. 24, 1781.

285. viii. ROBERT⁶, b. in Methuen, Nov. 13, 1783; m. about 1808, Sarah or Sally Jackson, dau. of Samuel Jackson, b. July 6, 1789; d. 4 Feb., 1863.
> He rem. from Londonderry in 1834 to Genesee Co., N. Y.; thence to Niagara Co. in 1836; to Erie Co., 1841, and to Richmond, Ashtabula Co., O., in 1845; d. 14 Feb., 1864–5.

ix. MARTHA⁶, b. in Methuen; m. Amos Kendall; res. Methuen, Mass.

Children of CORP. JOHN⁵, JR., (1749) [**122**] (John⁴, John³, Sergt. Abraham², Robert¹) and Molly (Brocklebank) Adams; res. New London, N. H.

i. BETSEY⁶, b. in Rowley, Mass., Aug. 23, 1778; d. 8 Jan., 1850, unm.
ii. HEPZIBAH⁶, b. in Rowley, Feb. 21, 1780; d. in New London, unm.
iii. PATTY⁶, b. in Rowley, Feb. 19, 1782; m. Daniel Bickford.
> A son, Dr. Hezekiah Bickford is said to have lived and died in Massachusetts.

286. iv. JENNY⁶, b in Rowley, Apr. 8, 1784; m. Nov., 1807, Robert Colburn. She d. in Springfield, N. H., 12 Dec., 1833.
287. v. HEZEKIAH⁶, b. in New London, June 20, 1786; m. 1812, Peggy Stinson. She d. in Vermillion, Dakota, 1876; res. New London, N. H. He d. in Andover, N. H., Jan., 1847.
288. vi. POLLY⁶, b. in New London, Aug. 29, 1799; m. Nov. 16, 1823, Seth Freeman Sargent, b. June 16, 1799; d. 21 Apr., 1886. She d. in Nebraska, 30 June, 1873.
vii. IRENE⁶, d. unm.
viii. THOMAS⁶, d. unm.

Children of BENJAMIN⁵, (1751) [**123**] (John⁴, John³, Sergt. Abraham², Robert¹) and Mary (Burpee) Adams; res. Tunbridge, Vt.

289. i. ASA⁶, b. in Rowley, Mass., [?] Mar., 1781; m. Dec. 4, 1817, Sophronia Hutchinson. He d. in Tunbridge, Dec., 1870.
290. ii. POLLY⁶, b. in Rowley, [?] Jan. 4, 1784; m. July 29, 1810, Moses Hackett, b. in Goffstown, N. H., July 30, 1783. He d. July, 1825. She d. in Strafford, Vt., 28 July, 1860.
291. iii. BENJAMIN⁶, b. in Gilmanton, N. H., 1787; m. 1806, Susan Hutchinson. She d. June, 1876.
> He settled in Fayston, Vt., in 1841; rem. to Duxbury, Vt., in Apr., 1843, and d. Feb., 1876.

292. iv. SALLY⁶, b. in Tunbridge; m. George Hackett.

Children of SOLOMON⁵, (1759) [126] (John⁴, John³, Sergt. Abraham², Robert¹) and Molly (Bancroft) Adams; res. New London, N. H.

293. i. SOLOMON⁶, JR., b. in Rowley, Mass., Feb. 23, 1780; m. Mary Collins, dau. of Joseph Collins of Springfield, N. H., d. 1879, age 86 years.
He set. in Springfield, N. H.; rem. 1824 to New London, N. H., d. 22 June, 1851, age 71 years.
ii. MARY⁶, b. in Rowley; m. (1) David Barnard of Enfield, N. H.; m. (2) David Goodrich of Enfield; res. Springfield, N. H.; no issue.
iii. SUSAN⁶, b. in Rowley; d. in New London, N. H., unm.
iv. ABIGAIL⁶, b. in New London, N. H.; m. John Hayes; grandson in Manchester. She d. in Nebraska.
v.   ELIZA⁶, b. in New London; d. unm.
294. vi. EMILY,⁶ b. in New London, 1794; m. Apr. 6, 1818, Ezekiel Sargent. She d. 27 Nov., 1864.
295. vii. PETER⁶, b. in New London, 1800; m. 1841, Jamima Whittier of Newport, N. H. She m. after his death and rem. to Vermont; res. Canaan, N. H. He d. in Canaan.

Children of SOLOMON⁵, (1759) and Mary (Sargent) Adams.

296. viii. DANIEL NOYES⁶, b. in New London, Sept. 12, 1803; m. (1) 1832, Eliza Williams, dau. of Joseph Williams of Sunnapee, N. H., d. 1851; m. (2) 1852, Calista A. Richardson of Springfield, N. H., d. 1860; m. (3) Mrs. Sophia Pierce Webster of Claremont, N. H.
He was a merchant; set. in Springfield, N. H. 1823, and d. 8 July, 1886.
ix. ZEBEDEE⁶, b. in New London; d. unm. in Springfield, N. H.
x.   AUGUSTINE⁶, b. in New London; d. unm. in Springfield.
297. xi. LOIS⁶, b. in New London; married Gilman Sawyer of Springfield, N. H., b. in Hampstead, N. H., Apr. 24, 1806; d. in Manchester, 3 June, 1875. He m. 2nd, Elvira Blood. She d. of consumption.
xii. CHLOE⁶, b. in New London, 1815; d. unm., 27 June, 1851, age 36 years.

Children of MOSES⁵, (1765) [128] (John⁴, John³, Sergt. Abraham², Robert¹) and Dolly (Perley) Adams; res. New London, N. H.

i.   ANNA⁶, b. in New London, Jan. 27, 1791; d. unm., 19 Mar., 1813.
298. ii. MOSES⁶, JR., b. in New London, Aug. 22, 1792; m. 1819, Betsey Stinson, b. Feb. 22, 1802, d. Apr., 1876.

He was a farmer; rem. to Grafton, N. H., 1866; d. at Brockton, Mass., 18 Dec., 1868.

299. iii. HON. CYRUS[6], b. in New London, July 7, 1795 ; m. May 11, 1820, Nancy Stinson, d. 4 Oct., 1863.

He was a saddler, etc.; res. Grafton, N. H.; member of Legislature and Senate of New Hampshire ; d. 4 Dec., 1865.

Children of MOSES[5], (1765) and Hannah (Flanders) Adams.

300. iv. HANNAH[6], b. in New London, Mar. 20, 1803 ; m. Benjamin Perley of Springfield, N. H., b. 1802, d. 14 May, 1868. Mr. Perley m. 2nd, Mrs. Eliza (Gage) Collins and had two children, viz.: Augusta, who m. Edwin F. Messer, and Abby, who m. George Tilton ; res. New London, N. H. She d. 8 July, 1841.

v. BELINDA[6], b. in New London, Jan. 18, 1808 ; d. 10 Aug., 1810.

vi. MYRA[6], b. in New London, Aug. 17, 1811 ; d. unm., 11 Nov., 1885.

Children of JONATHAN[5], (1767) [129] (John[4], John[3], Sergt. Abraham[2], Robert[1]) and Phebe (Brocklebank) Adams; res. Tunbridge, Vt.

301. i. REBECCA[6], b. in Tunbridge, July 29, 1789 ; m. May 8, 1808, Thomas Brocklebank, b. Jan. 14, 1778; d. 27 Apr., 1865; res. Plainfield, N. H. She d. 2 Sept., 1858.

302. ii. RAPSIMA[6], b. in Tunbridge, Dec. 16, 1792 ; m. Jan. 26, 1817, James Brocklebank, b. Nov. 9, 1794; d. 28 Oct., 1859; res. Plainfield, N. H. She d. 29 Sept., 1879.

iii. JOHN[6], b. in Tunbridge, Sept. 8, 1796 ; d. unm. near Cincinnati, O., 24 Oct., 1822.

303. iv. MOSES[6], b. in Tunbridge, Aug. 23, 1799 ; m. Dec. 31, 1822, Mary Folsom, dau. of Rev. Peter and Hannah (Weymouth) Folsom, b. Nov. 24, 1803 ; d. 31 Dec., 1872. He d. 9 Aug., 1849.

304. v. SETH[6], b. in Tunbridge, July 16, 1803 ; m. Nov. 18, 1827, Huldah Folsom, dau. of Peter and Hannah (Weymouth) Folsom, b. Feb. 5, 1809 ; d. 1 July, 1871.

He was a carpenter ; res. Tunbridge, Vt.; d. 18 Mar., 1892.

305. vi. JONATHAN TENNEY[6], b. in Tunbridge, Oct. 6, 1805 ; m. (1) Mar. 27, 1826, Elizabeth Rackley ; d. 1827 ; m. (2) Jan., 1828, Hannah Rackley ; d. Aug., 1841 ; m. (3) 1844, Diadama Warren, of Covington, N. Y.; d. 21 Sept., 1870.

He rem. 1830 to Pembroke, Genesee Co., N. Y., and thence 1863 to Shelby. Ocean Co., Mich.; d. 9 May, 1872.

Sixth Generation.]   OF NEWBURY, MASS.   77

Child of JONATHAN⁵, (1767) and Abagail (Weymouth) Adams.

306. vii. GEORGE W⁶, b. in Tunbridge, Feb. 19, 1809 ; m. Feb. 12, 1832, Eliza M. Haskell ; d. 28 Mar., 1885. He d. in Royalton, Vt., 12 Dec., 1869.

Children of ISRAEL⁵ 3D, (1746) [130] (Matthew⁴, Dr. Matthew³, Sergt. Abraham², Robert¹) and Elizabeth (Adams) Adams; res. Henniker, N. H.

    i. JOHN⁶, b. in Newbury, Mass. ; d. in Portsmouth, N. H., in the War of 1812.
307. ii. ISRAEL⁶, b. in Newbury, Feb. 11, 1780 ; m. (1) July 27, 1800, Charity Bailey, b. in Rowley, Mass., Aug. 7, 1781 ; d. 23 Jan., 1803, age 26 yrs. 5 mos. 16 days ; m. (2) Sept. 15, 1808, Rhoda Harthorn, dau. of Dea. Ebenezer and Rhoda Harthorn, b. Aug. 12, 1778; d. 9 July, 1850, age 71 yrs. 10 mos. 29 days ; m. (3) Jan. 13, 1850, Lucy Dame, b. Mar. 9, 1797. She d. 3 Sept., 1866.
    He was a military officer and commanded a company in 1812. He was a selectman in Goshen, N. H., in 1827, and one of the founders of the Methodist Church. He d. in Goshen, 29 Jan., 1865.

Children of JOHN⁵, (1749) [131] (Matthew⁴, Dr. Matthew³, Sergt. Abraham², Robert¹) and Judith (Follensby) Adams; res. Newbury, Mass.

308. i. JOHN⁶, b. in Newbury, May 15, 1776 ; m. (1) July 4, 1798, Sarah Kimball, dau. of Caleb and Sarah (Sawyer) Kimball of Hampstead, N. H., b. in Hampstead, Oct. 23, 1775 ; d. 17 Oct., 1839; m. (2) 1842, Martha (Cotting) Bean, dau. of Benjamin and Abigail Cotting. She d. 27 July, 1865.
    He was a prominent and influential citizen of Sutton, N. H., was justice of the peace and selectman in 1817, 1824–5. Was known as "Squire Adams." He d. 5 Apr., 1864.
    ii. JOSEPH⁶, b. in Newbury, 1783 ; d. in Sutton, N. H., unm., 10 Dec., 1838, age 55 years.
309. iii. HENRY⁶, b. in Newbury, July 23, 1787 ; m. 1815, Betsey Maxom, b. June 16, 1792 ; d. 31 Dec, 1840, age 48 years ; res. Sutton, N. H. He d. 27 Sept., 1836, age 49 years.

Children of BENJAMIN⁵, (1752) [132] (Matthew⁴, Dr. Matthew³, Sergt. Abraham², Robert¹) and Judith (Adams) Adams; res. New London, N. H.

ROBERT ADAMS [Sixth Generation.

×310. i. BENJAMIN⁶, b. in W. Newbury, Mass., Sept. 1, 1773 ; m. Sept. 15, 1796, Susanna Goodhue of Newburyport, Mass., b. Mar. 12, 1774 ; d. 30 Dec., 1822.
He was a carpenter ; res. Boston ; rem. West and d.

311. ii. JUDITH⁶, b. in W. Newbury, Feb. 12, 1775 ; m. Apr. 12, 1799, David Hopson ; d. 23 Apr., 1854 ; res. Springfield, N. H. She d. 30 May, 1858.

iii. SALLY⁶, b. in W. Newbury, Jan. 1, 1777 ; d. 26 Sept., 1778.

312. iv. MATTHEW⁶, b. in W. Newbury, Dec. 17, 1778 ; m. (1) 1801, Rebecca Dow of Newport, N. H., b. Sept. 23, 1776 ; d. 24 May, 1805 ; m. (2) Sept. 24, 1805, Hannah Cheney, b. Nov. 25, 1783 ; d. 1858, age 75 years; res. Newbury, N. H. He d. 10 Sept., 1828.

313. v. ELIZABETH⁶, b. in W. Newbury, Sept. 10, 1780 ; m. Apr. 29, 1811, Joseph Kelly, b. Jan. 9, 1780 ; d. 14 Oct., 1814 ; res. New London, N. H. She d. 4 Feb., 1830.

314. vi. MARY⁶, b. in Newburyport, May 21, 1782 ; m. Apr., 1801, Levi Harvey of New London, N. H., b. Feb. 22, 1774 ; d. 5 Feb., 1857. She d. in New London, N. H.

vii. WILLIAM⁶, b. in Newburyport. Dec. 12, 1784 ; d. 6 May, 1785.

viii. HANNAH R.⁶, b. in Newburyport, Aug. 18, 1786 ; d. unm. 27 July, 1829.

315. ix. REV. THEOPHILUS B.⁶, b. in Beverly, Mass., Feb. 18, 1789 ; m. (1) Jemima Knowlton, dau. of Robert Knowlton of New London, N. H., b. Feb. 17, 1787 ; d. 28 Jan., 1819 ; m. (2) June 2, 1819, Lydia Bagley.
He was a Baptist, soldier 1812 ; wounded and taken prisoner ; d. in Ackworth, N. H., 15 Aug., 1831.

x. APHIA⁶, b. in Beverly, Apr. 26, 1791 ; d. 19 July, 1793.

316. xi. JEREMIAH⁶ b. in Beverly, Apr. 15, 1793 ; m. Mar. 2, 1813, Sarah Wardwell of Salisbury, N. H., b. Feb. 11, 1783 ; d. 31 Mar., 1855.
He was a farmer ; res. New London, N. H. ; d. 22 Aug., 1832.

Children of JOSEPH⁵, (1755) [133] (Matthew⁴, Dr. Matthew³, Sergt. Abraham², Robert¹) and Mary (Carleton) Adams ; res. Plaistow or Londonderry, N. H.

i. MOSES⁶.
ii. PARKER⁶.
iii. JAMES⁶.
iv. BETSEY⁶.
v. SARAH⁶, [b. 1771 ; d. 28 Aug., 1775.?]
vi. MARY⁶, m. —— Johnson.
vii. HANNAH⁶, m. —— Johnson.

Children of CAPT. STEPHEN⁵, (1742) [134] (Abraham⁴, Dr. Matthew³, Sergt. Abraham², Robert¹) and Sarah (Bartlett) Adams; res. W. Newbury, Mass.

- i. DAVID⁶, b. in W. Newbury, July 12, 1762 ; m. Mar. 1, 1798, Lydia Wheeler.
  A farmer ; rem. to Walpole, N. H., 1799, and d. before 1827.
- ii. SARAH BARTLETT⁶, b. in W. Newbury, Dec. 19, 1764; d. unm.
- iii. CALEB⁶, b. in W. Newbury, Sept. 5, 1767 ; d. young.
- iv. JUDITH⁶, b. in W. Newbury, Apr. 9, 1770 ; d. 19 Oct., 1793.
- v. BETSEY⁶, b. in W. Newbury, June 28, 1775 ; m. Jan. 14, 1796, Ezra Adams, son of Moses and Ruth (Palmer) Adams. He d. Aug , 1856. She d. 2 Apr., 1818.
- vi. ENOCH⁶, b. in W. Newbury, Mar. 3, 1778; d. 7 Dec., 1779.
- vii. HANNAH⁶. b. in W. Newbury, Nov. 27, 1780 ; d. unm.
- viii. STEPHEN⁶, b. in W. Newbury, June 3, 1782, d. young.
- ix. STEPHEN⁶, b. in W. Newbury, June 3, 1784 ; m. Jan. 27, 1813-4, Mary Jaques.

Children of ABRAHAM⁵, (1748) [135] (Abraham⁴, Dr. Matthew³, Sergt. Abraham², Robert¹) and Mary (Bricket) Adams; res. Newbury, Mass., and Boscawen, N. H.

- i. SUSANNA⁶, b. in Newbury, Dec. 24, 1768; m. at W. Newbury, Feb. 12, 1786, Thos. Worthen.
- ii. JOSEPH⁶, b. in Newbury, May 1, 1779 ; prob. m. Judith ———, and had John⁷, b. May 20, 1800.
- iii. HANNAH⁶ (twin), b. in Newbury, May 1, 1779.
- 317. iv. CAPT. TAPPAN⁶, b. in Newbury, Oct. 13, 1786 ; m. Sept. 22, 1805, Betsey Morse, dau. of Moses and Sarah Morse, b. Dec. 19, 1781, d. 1874.
  He was a sea-captian, resided on "Knowlton Hill," about one mile from Penacook village ; was in the East India trade, and was "lost at sea" with his vessel.
- 318. v. ABRAHAM B.⁶, ; m. Sarah Elliott.

Enoch Elliott, b. in Boscawen, Feb. 17, 1810-12.
Charles Wm. Adams, son of Wm. and Hannah Adams, was b. in Boscawen, Feb. 16, 1801.
A John Adams m. in Boscawen, Apr. 20, 1848, Mary P. Webster.
May 5, 1846, Moses Moody m. Phebe Adams.
May 15, 1847, Wm. Elkins m. Rose Ann Adams.

Children of SARAH[5], (1756) [136] (Abraham[4], Dr. Matthew[3], Sergt. Abraham[2], Robert[1]) and Benjamin Plumer; res. Newbury, Mass.

 i. ENOCH PLUMER, b. Oct. 24, 1777; m. Mehitable Thurston, dau. of John and Eunice Thurston. He d. 8 May, 1860.
 ii. WILLIAM PLUMER, b. Aug. 11, 1781; d. unm. in New York, 1821.
 iii. DANIEL PLUMER, b. Apr. 28, 1783; d. 27 Dec., 1862, unm.

Child of DANIEL[5], (1760) [137] (Abraham[4], Dr. Matthew[3], Sergt. Abraham[2], Robert[1]) and Hannah (Poor) Adams; res. Newbury, Mass.

 i. ENOCH[6], b. in Newbury, Mass., Dec. 12, 1779.
  He was drowned in a well in 1822.

Children of ENOCH[5], (1755) [138] (Richard[4], Richard[3], Sergt. Abraham[2], Robert[1]) and Elizabeth (Russell) Adams; res. Salisbury, N. H.

 i. RUSSELL[6], b. in Newbury, Mass., Jan. 20, 1782; d. 21 Oct., 1788.
 ii. RICHARD[6], b. in Salisbury, N. H., Aug. 21, 1783; d. Nov. 1788.
319. iii. ELI[6], b. in Salisbury, Sept. 29, 1784; m. 1824, Abigail True; res. Salisbury, N. H. He d. 17 July, 1832.
320. iv. JUDITH[6], b. in Salisbury, Jan. 2, 1787; m. 1808, Enoch Eastman of Boscowen, N. H.; res. Webster, N. H. He d. 29 Sept., 1865, age 96 yrs. 6 mos. She d. 9 Sept., 1874.
321. v. RUSSELL[6], b. in Salisbury, May 12, 1788; m. Susan Fifield, dau. of Obadiah P. Fifield; res. Hill, N. H. He d. 19 Nov., 1859. She d. 27 Sept., 1856.
322. vi. RICHARD[6], b. in Salisbury, July 29, 1790; m. Dec. 28, 1813, Sarah Dunbar, dau. of Abel and Sarah (Howard) Dunbar; res. Hill, N. H. He d. 26 Mar., 1859. She d. 25 Dec., 1870.
323. vii. ELIZABETH[6], b. in Salisbury, May 3, 1792; m. Oct. 1, 1810, James Young; res. Ackworth, N. H. She d. 24 July, 1865.
324. viii. PHEBE[6], b. in Salisbury, July 2, 1795; m. Jesse Livingston. She d. 18 Dec., 1877.
325. ix. DORCAS[6], b. in Salisbury, July 19, 1797; m. David S. Woodward, a hotel keeper. He was b. July 11, 1796, and d. in Hill, N. H., 18 Jan., 1892; res. Franklin, N. H. She. d. in Hill, 10 Mar., 1877.

Children of PAUL⁵, (1758) [139] (Richard⁴, Richard³, Sergt. Abraham², Robert¹) and Hannah (Ilsley) Adams; res. Newbury, Mass.

  i. JERUSHA⁶, b. in Newbury, Feb. 25, 1787; d. 5 Apr., 1863.
  ii. RUTH⁶, b. in Newbury, June 8, 1793; d. unm. 15 May, 1870.
  iii. HANNAH⁶, b. in Newbury, Mar. 8, 1795; d. unm. 14 May, 1870.
326. iv. JANE⁶, b. in Newbury, June 10, 1797; m. 1827, Abraham Granger, son of Luther and Ruth (Goodwell) Granger of Middlefield, Mass.; b. in Chester, Mass., April 19, 1799; d. in Hinsdale, Mass., 23 May, 1836. She d. in W. Worthington, Mass., 16 Jan., 1884.
  v. CAROLINE⁶, b. in Newbury, May 24, 1799; d. unm. 8 Feb., 1830.
327. vi. ASA⁶, b. in Newbury, July 21, 1801; m. Nov. 20, 1826, Nancy Little. She. d. 16 Oct., 1882. He d. 20 Oct., 1885.

Children of PAUL⁵, (1758) and Hannah G. (Keniston) Adams.

  vii. JOHN JONES⁶, b. in Newbury, Oct. 1, 1805; m. Nov., 1832, Lucy Ilsley; she d. Nov., 1888; no issue. He d. 15 Apr., 1874.
328. viii. MARY⁶, b. in Newbury, March 7, 1807; m. 1831, Capt. Geo. W. Dennis, who came from Baltimore, Md.; res. Newburyport, Mass. He d. in Newburyport, Mass., in 1867. She d. in Astoria, Ore., Feb., 1881.
329. ix. SENECA⁶, b. in Newbury, Dec. 25, 1808; m. July, 1839, Sarah B. Rolfe, dau. of Moses Rolfe. She d. 10 May, 1894, age 84 yrs. 7 mos. He was taken out of his burning dwelling house and died a week later, 21 Sept., 1862.
330. x. REBECCA⁶, b. in Newbury, July 22, 1812; m. Nov., 1832, Benjamin C. Perkins. She d. Oct., 1895.
  xi. PAUL⁶, JR., b. in Newbury, Nov. 7, 1814; m. Nov. 27, 1838, Harriet N. Lanford; no issue. He was lost at sea.
331. xii. THOMAS HALL⁶, b. in Newbury, Feb. 10, 1817; m. Dec. 2, 1838, Mary J. Jennings. She d. 5 Sept., 1888, age 71 years. He d. 15 July, 1875, age 58 yrs. 5 mos.

Children of DANIEL⁵, (1760) [140] (Richard⁴, Richard³, Sergt. Abraham², Robert¹) and Edna (Noyes) Adams; res. Newbury, Mass.

  i. SYLVIA⁶, b. in Newbury, Nov. 12, 1789; d. 25 Oct., 1816.
  ii. MOODY⁶, b. in Newbury, June 17, 1791; deaf and dumb; d. unm. 4 Feb., 1884.

iii. GILES[6], b. in Newbury, Dec. 30, 1792 ; drowned 13 Nov., 1819.
iv. ELEANOR[6] (twin), b. in Newbury, Dec. 30, 1792 ; m. April 21, 1832, Capt. Jeremiah Jewett ; his 2nd wife ; no issue ; res. Byfield, Mass. She d. in Georgetown.
v. SARAH[6], b. in Newbury, Nov. 25, 1794 ; d. unm. 12 Mar., 1880 ; age 85 yrs. 3 mos.
vi. AARON[6]. b. in Newbury, Sept. 15, 1796 ; drowned 13 Nov., 1819.
vii. EDNA[6], b. in Newbury, Nov. 13, 1798 ; d. 26 Nov., 1878 ; age 80 years.

Child of DANIEL[5], (1760) and Sarah (Pierce) Adams.
viii. ABIGAIL[6], b. in Newbury, Nov. 24, 1803; m. Jan., 1830, Tallock Brownbeck. She d. in Newbury, Mass.

Children of SARAH[5],(1763)[141] (Richard[4], Richard[3], Sergt. Abraham[2], Robert[1]) and Samuel Blake ; res. Lynn, Mass.
i. AMOS BLAKE.
ii. SAMUEL BLAKE.
iii. ABIGAIL BLAKE, m. —— — Wallace.
iv. DOLLY BLAKE, m. Col. Nathaniel Harris of Ipswich, Mass.
v. ELSIE BLAKE.

Children of SIMEON[5], (1765) [142] (Richard[4], Richard[3], Sergt. Abraham[2], Robert[1]) and Sarah (Little) Adams; res. Limerick, York Co., Me.

332. i. CLARISSA[6], b. in Limerick, Jan. 27, 1791; m. Dec. 7, 1813, Ebenezer Cleaves Bradbury, son of Samuel and Abigail (Cleaves) Bradbury, b. June 2, 1788. She d. in New Limerick, Me., 11 June, 1871.
ii. SIMEON[6], b. in Limerick, Mar. 18, 1793 ; d. 1 Aug., 1895.
333. iii. DR. CLEMENT JACKSON[6], b. in Limerick, Mar. 10, 1795 ; m. July 3, 1821, Hannah Osgood, dau. of James and Abigail (Evans) Osgood; b. Aug. 12, 1799 ; d. 20 Aug., 1832.

He studied medicine with Dr. Alex. Ramsey of Fryeburg, Me.; practiced his profession at Limington and Bridgton, Me.; "was a genial, courteous gentleman"; d. in Bridgton, 4 (10 ?) Oct., 1853.

334. iv. SIMEON[6], b. in Limerick, July 21, 1797 ; m. Mar. 13, 1825, Caroline L. Fluent, dau. of Richard Fluent, b. July 4, 1804 ; d. 5 Jan., 1851. He settled in Corinna, Me., in 1824, and d. 11 April, 1883.
v. SARAH[6], b. in Limerick, Dec. 15, 1800 ; m. Lot Wiggan. She d. 4 Dec., 1846 ; no issue.

vi. EBENEZER⁶, b. in Limerick, Mar. 11, 1802 ; m. Lydia Hobson of W. Buxton, Me.; res. W. Buxton, Me.; she d. 8 Mar., 1896. He d. 30 Nov., 1890 ; no issue.

335. vii. DR. STEPHEN⁶, b. in Limerick, Mar. 31, 1804 ; m. Mar. 27, 1831, Mrs. Mary L. (Hobbs) Marston. She d. 15 Dec., 1878.
He graduated from the Maine Medical College in 1829. Settled in W. Newfield ; d. 6 Nov., 1898 ; age 94 yrs. 7 mos. 6 days.

336. viii. MARY⁶, b. in Limerick, July 17, 1807 ; m. Sept. 8, 1835, Dea. John Evans, son of John and Mary (Hill) Evans, b. July 1, 1809 ; d. 5 April, 1880 ; res. Fryeburg, Me. She d. 20 May, 1893, age 86 years.

ix. ELIZABETH⁶, b. in Limerick, Dec. 23, 1810 ; m. Jan. 23, 1846, Moses Noyes Adams, son of Ebenezer and Edna (Adams) Adams, b. Nov. 25, 1807, living 1898 ; res. Grape Island, Mass. She d. 18 Aug., 1879.

x. LUCRETIA⁶, b. in Limerick, Jan. 2, 1813 ; d. 7 Dec., 1873, unm.

xi. REBECCA⁶, b. in Limerick, Feb. 23, 1815 ; d. 15 July, 1838.

Children of HANNAH⁵, (1768) [**143**] (Richard⁴, Richard³, Sergt. Abraham², Robert¹) and Paul Thurlow; res. Newbury, Mass.

i. PHEBE THURLOW, b. Aug. 15, 1797; m. June 13, 1811, Michael Wormstead, of Newbury, Mass. He d. 18 Mar., 1850. She d. 12 Jan., 1887.

ii. DOLLY THURLOW, b. Dec. 20, 1798; m. (1) Nov. 14, 1819, Moses Tappan. He d. at sea, 1824; m. (2) Oct. 24, 1830, Henry S. Trivet. He d. 30 Aug., 1875. She d. 31 Dec., 1878.

iii. SALLY THURLOW, b. May 23, 1800 ; m. Nov. 7, 1819, Benj. Thurlow (cousin). He d. 23 Feb., 1868. She d. 29 Sept., 1868.

iv. SUSANNAH THURLOW, b. Sept. 4, 1802 ; m. Mar. 19, 1823, Phineas George. She d. 13 Nov., 1892.

v. PATIENCE THURLOW, b. Feb. 4, 1804 ; m. Nov. 23, 1820, Josiah P. Noyes. She d. 3 Oct., 1843.

vi. PAUL THURLOW, b. June 25, 1805 ; d. 1 July, 1806.

vii. PAULINA THURLOW, b. Mar. 21, 1809 ; m. Thomas Greenwood of Ipswich, Mass. She d. 1893.

viii. ZACCHEUS PIKE THURLOW, b. June 26, 1811 ; m. June 19, 1831, Mary Noyes ; she d. 27 Dec., 1893 ; living 1898 ; res. Merrimac, Mass.

Children of ASA⁵, (1772) [**144**] (Richard⁴, Richard³, Sergt. Abraham², Robert¹) and Dorothy (Morse) Adams; res. Newbury, Mass.

84   ROBERT ADAMS   [Sixth Generation.

337.   i.   RICHARD⁶, b. in Newbury, Jan. 23, 1796 ; m. April 30, 1821, Abigail Little; she d. 30 Oct., 1865, age 68 years.
             He was a carpenter in Newbury, Mass.; d. 28 Dec., 1857.
        ii. DOLLY⁶, b. in Newbury, 1800; d. 12 Apr., 1803.

Children of EBENEZER⁵, (1776) [145] (Richard⁴, Richard³, Sergt. Abraham², Robert¹) and Edna (Adams) Adams; res. Newbury, Mass.

338.   i.   LOIS⁶, b. in Newbury, Apr. 10, 1799 ; m. Jan. 22, 1839, Harrison Dearborn ; d. 1863. She d. 6 Nov., 1877.
339.   ii.   NATHAN⁶, b. in Newbury, Jan. 26, 1801; m. Apr. 6, 1826, Lovisa Knowles. He d. 28 Sept. 188–.
340.   iii. ELIZA⁶, b. in Newbury, Oct. 23, 1803 ; m. Dec. 30, 1822, Ebenezer Little.
        iv.   CATHERINE⁶, b. in Newbury, Sept. 9, 1805; d. 15 June, 1810.
341.   v.   MOSES NOYES⁶, b. in Newbury, Nov. 25, 1807 ; m. Jan. 23, 1846, Elizabeth Adams, his cousin, dau. of Simeon and Sarah (Little) Adams; d. 18 Aug., 1879.
              Farmer; res. High St., Newbury, Mass.; living 1898. d. Oct. 6. 1906.
        vi.   ISAAC W.⁶,   b. in Newbury, 1810; d. 23 Sept., 1827.
        vii. CATHERINE⁶, b. in Newbury, Jan. 26, 1812 ; d. 3 Dec., 1822.
342.   viii. PHILLIP D.⁶, b. in Newbury, Oct. 13, 1814; m. Dec. 30, 1841, Ruth Coffin ; res. Newburyport, Mass.; living 1898. died Feb. 25. 1913.
        ix.   EBEN⁶, b. in Newbury, Jan. 26, 1817; m. Dec. 4, 1845, Eliza Ilsley Adams, dau. of Sewall and Sarah (Ilsley) Adams, b. May 20, 1825 ; d. 27 Oct., 1880 ; res. Newbury. He d. 18 June, 1873, age 56 years; no issue.
343.   x.   CHARLES W.⁶, b. in Newbury, Sept. 20, 1818; m. Apr. 29, 1864, Mary Elizabeth Adams, dau. of Stephen and Mary Ann (Longfellow) Adams, b. Feb. 11, 1837. He d. 5 Feb., 1892.
        xi.   ALBERT⁶, b. in Newbury, Oct. 8, 1820 ; d. 22 Sept., 1822.

Children of ELIZABETH⁵, (1766) [146] (John⁴, Richard³, Sergt. Abraham², Robert¹) and Paul Thurlow; res. Newbury, Mass.

        i.   JESSE THURLOW, b. July 7, 1789 ; m. Nov. 27, 1813, Eunice Knight Disney. She d. 17 Dec., 1875.
        ii. MOODY THURLOW, b. June 13, 1791 ; m. (1) Mar. 28, 1815, Ann Little ; she d. 15 Oct., 1863; m. (2) 1865, Eliza Pickett; she d. 26 Mar. ——— He d. 21 Sept., 1869.

Sixth Generation.] OF NEWBURY, MASS. 85

 iii. ELIZABETH THURLOW, b. Jan. 23, 1793; m. Dec. 16, 1821, Joseph Griffith; he d. Apr., 1875. She d. 20 Mar., 1847.
 iv. HANNAH THURLOW, b. Oct. 13, 1794; m. Oct. 9, 1814, Mayo Gerrish; he d. 12 June, 1871. She d. 12 Dec., 1869.

Children of GEORGE[5], (1768) [**147**] (John[4], Richard[3], Sergt. Abraham[2], Robert[1]) and Elizabeth (Adams) Adams; res. Newbury, Mass.

344. i. GEORGE[6], b. in Newbury, May 5, 1793; m. Dec. 22, 1823, Judith Dole, dau. of Enoch and Molly (Plumer) Dole, b. Jan. 21, 1794; d. 9 Dec., 1851, age 58 years; res. Newbury. He d. 16 Jan., 1870, age 76 years.
 ii. MOODY[6], b. in Newbury, Jan. 4, 1795; drowned 1 Sept., 1798.
345. iii. NANCY[6], b. in Newbury, Nov. 11, 1796; m. Josiah B. Tilton of Deerfield, N. H., son of Samuel and Deborah (Batchelder) Tilton, b. May 28, 1799; res. Deerfield, N. H. She d. 5 June, 1875.
 iv. ISANNA[6], b. in Newbury, Apr. 18, 1800; m. Joseph Tappan, Jr.; no issue; res. Newburyport, Mass. She d. 3 July, 1885.
346. v. MOODY[6], b. in Newbury, Dec. 27, 1802; m. May 10, 1832, Eliza Adams, dau. of Ezra and Betsey (Adams) Adams; she d. 19 Mar., 1881; res. Derry, N. H.; set. there about 1840. He d. 5 Sept., 1848.
347. vi. FREEBORN[6], b. in Newbury, June 14, 1806; m. Nov. 27, 1828, Ruth Adams, dau. of Ezra and Betsey (Adams) Adams; she d. 23 Aug., 1890; set. in Somerville, Mass., 1851. He d. 2 Dec., 1891, age 85 yrs. 5 mos.
 vii. ELIZA[6], b. in Newbury, Oct. 31, 1810; d. 20 Nov., 1810.

Children of SIMON[5], (1770) [**148**] (John[4], Richard[3], Sergt. Abraham[2], Robert[1]) and Sarah (Lunt) Adams; res. Newbury, Mass.
 i. JOANNA[6], b. in Newbury, Aug. 5, 1800; m. Feb. 2, 1836, John Adams, son of James Adams of Derry, N. H.; his 2nd wife; res. Derry, N. H. She d. 3 July, 1876; no issue.
348. ii. ISAAC[6], b. in Newbury, Mar. 28, 1807; m. (1) April 7, 1835, Hannah H. Plumer, d. 21 July, 1836, age 23 years; m. (2) 1839, Hannah Kent, d. June, 1858, age 48 years; res. Newbury, Mass. He d. 2 Dec., 1855.
349. iii. JESSE[6], b. in Newbury, Aug. 11, 1812; m. (1) Jan. 7, 1836, Elizabeth Kent; d. 19 Mar., 1843, age 28 years; m. (2) Oct. 18, 1849, Sarah Ann Knapp; d. 15 June, 1859, aged 41 years; res. Newbury, Mass. He d. 15 May, 1888.

[handwritten note: Elizabeth Kent was dau. of Jacob and Mary (Noyes) Kent.]

[handwritten note next to 348: dau. of Jacob and Mary (Noyes) Kent]

[handwritten note: no. 360]

Children of JOHN⁵, (1778) [149] (John⁴, Richard³, Sergt. Abraham², Robert¹) and Margaret (Lunt) Adams; res. Newbury, Mass.

350. i. WILLIAM⁶, b. in Newbury, Jan. 30, 1801; m. May 2, 1843, Mary Osgood, d. in Newburyport, Mass. He d. 6 June, 1877. *(Oct. 15, 1878)*

351. ii. MARGARET⁶, b. in Newbury, Aug. 20, 1803; m. Nov. 25, 1823, Elisha Bean, d. 12 Jan., 1887. She d. 19 Nov., 1885.

352. iii. ELVIRA⁶, b. in Newbury, April 10, 1810; m. Dec. 6, 1831, Moses Plumer, d. 4 Jan., 1850, aged 46 years. She d. 5 June, 1866. *son of Capt. Jeremiah Plumer*

353. iv. JOHN COFFIN⁶, b. in Newbury, May 23, 1812; m. June 23, 1838, Sarah J. Noyes, b. Aug. 21, 1814; d. 11 May, 1875. He d. in Newbury, Mass., 18 Feb., 1871-2. *dau. of John and Sarah (Knight) Noyes.*

v. FREDERICK⁶, b. in Newbury, Mar. 14, 1815; d. 17 Mar., 1817.

vi. SARAH ANN⁶, b. in Newbury, Jan. 11, 1820; d. 20 Feb., 1844.

vii. CHARLES⁶, b. in Newbury, May 18, 1824; m. (1) Nov. 12, 1862, Elizabeth Lunt, d. 2 Mar., 1863; m. (2) June 10, 1867, Hannah Small; living in Newbury; no issue. He d. 30 April, 1888. *his cousin* *(Brookin)*

d. May 29, 1899 aged 70 yrs. 9 mos.
A son b. Feb. 12, 1870 d. the same day

Children of RUTH⁵, (1763) [150] (Moses⁴, Richard³, Sergt. Abraham², Robert¹) and Joseph Thurlow; res. Newbury, Mass.

i. JOSEPH THURLOW, b. July 6, 1783; m. Jan. 21, 1810, Sarah Titcomb; res. Newburyport, Mass. He d. 22 Jan., 1841.

ii. STEPHEN THURLOW, m. ——— Watson. He d. soon after marriage.

Children of MOSES⁵, (1770) [151] (Moses⁴, Richard³, Sergt. Abraham², Robert¹) and Phebe (Jewett) Adams; res. Newbury, Mass.

354. i. PHEBE JEWETT⁶, b. in Newbury, Mar. 19, 1794; m. Dec. 22, 1811, Col. Benjamin Jackman Tenney, son of Oilver and Judith (Jackman) Tenney, b. in Rowley, Mass., Nov. 3, 1788; d. 2 May, 1840. She d. 7 Jan., 1841-2.

355. ii. CAPT. RICHARD⁶, b. in Newbury, Mar. 19, 1795; m. May 3, 1818, Mary Cook; she d. 21 May, 1886. He d. 29 Jan., 1857.

iii. MOSES⁶, b. in Newbury, Feb. 12, 1797; d. 5 Apr., 1805.

iv. HARRIET⁶, b. in Newbury, Feb. 26, 1798; m. (1) Dec. 29, 1820 Joseph Adams, son of David and Elizabeth (Colley) Adams; he d. 6 Apr., 1841; m. (2) Mar. 22, 1855, Thomas Johnson of Rowley, Mass. She d. 20 Aug., 1875.

v. SARAH⁶, b, in Newbury, Mar. 8, 1801; d. 17 Dec., 1821.

vi. MARY⁶, b. in Newbury, Feb. 22, 1803; d. 29 June, 1849.

356. vii. MOSES[6], b. in Newbury, Oct. 3, 1804-5 ; m. Nov. 18, 1832, Sarah H. Elwell, b. July 16, 1810 ; d. 8 Feb., 1871.
He was a shipwright in W. Gloucester, Mass. He d. 15 June, 1878.

Children of MOSES[5], (1770) and Marcia Lee (Lunt) Adams.

357. viii. JOHN POPKIN[6], b. in Newbury, Aug. 31, 1812 ; m. Eugenia Daniels. He d. in New York.
ix. ZILPAH[6], b. in Newbury, May 1, 1814 ; m. Roger Newton Pierce.
x. WASHINGTON[6], b. in Newbury, Feb. 7, 1816 ; m. June 20, 1846, Susan Boyd Claflin ; she d. 22 Feb., 1886.
He was a grocer in Newburyport, Mass. He d. 15 July, 1885 ; no issue.
358. xi. WOODBRIDGE[6], b. in Newbury, Feb. 26, 1819; m. Aug. 12, 1841, Mary Peabody, dau. of Ezekiel and Polly (Goodhue) Peabody of Ipswich, Mass., b. Aug. 8, 1817; living 1898. He d. in Boston, Mass., 11 Dec., 1849, buried in Ipswich, Mass.
xii. SARAH J.[6], b. in Newbury, Sept. 2, 1823 ; d. 14 Jan., 1841.

Children of EZRA[5], (1773) [152] (Moses[4], Richard[3], Sergt. Abraham[2], Robert[1]) and Betsey (Adams) Adams; res. W. Newbury, Mass.

359. i. MIRA[6], b. in W. Newbury, Sept. 16, 1797; m. Mar. 12, 1823, Leonard S. Wood. She d. 7 Sept., 1868.
ii. JUDITH[6], b. in W. Newbury, Apr. 12, 1801 ; d. unm. in Lowell, Mass., 26 Apr., 1877.
iii. JOSEPH[6], b. in W. Newbury, July 17, 1803 ; m. 1833, Catherine Swan, dau. of Maj. Edward Swan of Gardiner, Me.
He graduated from Bowdoin College in 1825 ; studied law in Hallowell, Me., and practiced his profession in Pittston, Me., till 1835, when he rem. to Gardiner. He was the cashier of the Gardiner National Bank from 1840 to 1849, when he went to California. Returning he became treasurer of Gardiner Savings Bank, cashier, etc. He d. in Gardiner, 26 Apr., 1879.
iv. RUTH[6], b. in W. Newbury, Nov. 24, 1805 ; m. Nov. 27, 1828, Freeborn Adams, son of George and Elizabeth (Adams) Adams. She d. 23 Aug., 1890 ; res. Somerville, Mass.
v. ELIZA[6], b. in W. Newbury, Nov. 24, 1808; m. May 10, 1832, Moody Adams, son of George and Elizabeth (Adams) Adams. She d. 19 Mar., 1881 ; res. Derry, N. H.
vi. MARY[6], b. W. Newbury, July 16, 1810; d. unm. in Lowell, Mass., Feb., 1879.

vii. ZILPAH⁶, b. in W. Newbury, May 22, 1812; m. Apr., 1836, Edmund Adams, son of Ens. James and Anna (Griffin) Adams (2nd wife) of Derry, N. H. She d. in Derry, N. H.

viii. ISAAC⁶, b. in W. Newbury, Sept. 21, 1815; d. 22 Oct., 1815.

Children of ENS. JAMES⁵, (1765) [153] (Dea. Edmund⁴, Richard³, Sergt. Abraham², Robert¹) and Anna (Griffin) Adams; res. Derry, N. H.

360. i. JOHN⁶, b. in Derry, Oct. 17, 1793; m. (1) 1817, Betsey Corning; d. 26 Dec., 1834; m. (2) Feb. 2, 1836, Joanna Adams, dau. of Simon and Sarah (Lunt) Adams, of Newbury; d. 3 July, 1876, age 75 yrs. 11 mos. He d. in Derry, 28 May, 1872.

361. ii. BENJAMIN⁶, b. in Derry, Oct. 13, 1795; m. June 21, 1831, Mehitable Hoyt. He d. in Derry, 19 Mar., 1883.

362. iii. DAVID⁶, b. in Derry, Oct. 19, 1797; m. (1) Mar. 7, 1824, Polly Corning; m. (2) Sept., 1839, Adelia Maria Griffis, dau. of Jasper and Elizabeth (Simmons) Griffis, b. Jan. 25, 1808; d. 3 June, 1852.
He rem. to Lockport, N. Y., 1817, and d. 30 Jan., 1868.

iv. HANNAH⁶, b. in Derry, May 26, 1799; m. Dec. 6, 1843, John Hunkins. She d. 19 Nov., 1872; no issue.

363. v. EDMUND⁶, b. in Derry, Feb. 4, 1802; m. (1) Oct. 16, 1828, Jane Marsh; d. 10 June, 1833; m. (2) Apr., 1836, Zilpah Adams, dau. of Ezra and Betsey Adams of Newbury, Mass. He d. 10 Dec., 1868.

vi. MARY⁶, b. in Derry, July 12, 1805; m. June, 1835, Calvin Pepper. She d. in Chicago, Ill., May, 1836; no issue.

vii. SARAH⁶, b. in Derry, July 13, 1808; d. in infancy.

viii. SARAH⁶, b. in Derry, June 7, 1814; m. Aug. 2, 1839, Ira G. Bean. She d. 2 Dec., 1872; no issue.

364. ix. REBECCA P.⁶, b. in Derry, Jan. 6, 1816; m. Apr. 30, 1839, Ezra Hale of Newburyport, Mass., son of Ezra and Anna Hale (2nd wife), b. Mar. 30, 1804; res. Rowley, Mass.; living 1898.

Children of JANE⁵, (1773) [154] (Dea. Edmund⁴, Richard³, Sergt. Abraham², Robert¹) and Daniel Marsh; res. Walpole, N. H.

i. EDMUND MARSH, b. May 19, 1797; m. Oct. 9, 1823, Isabella Hosmer.

ii. HANNAH MARSH, b. Feb. 10, 1799; d. 13 June, 1831.

iii. ELIZA MARSH, b. July 5, 1801; m. Nov. 11, 1840, Henry P. Foster of Walpole, N. H., b. 1799; d. 18 Aug., 1861. She d. 10 Dec., 1881.

Sixth Generation] OF NEWBURY, MASS.

iv. SARAH MARSH, b. Oct. 6, 1803 ; d. 4 June. 1868.
v. JANE MARSH, b. Dec. 4, 1805 ; m. Oct. 16, 1828, Edmund Adams, son of Ens. James Adams of Derry, N. H. She d. 10 June, 1838.
vi. DANIEL MARSH, b. Aug. 26, 1808 ; d. unm. 21 July, 1872.
vii. AMOS MARSH, b. Oct. 16, 1810 ; d. 9 Oct., 1815.
viii. BENJAMIN MARSH, b. Sept. 18, 1812 ; d. 29 Dec., 1812.
ix. FARNHAM MARSH, b. May 21, 1815 ; m. July 19, 1863, Judith B. Moulthrop.
x. KATHERINE MARSH, b. Sept. 9, 1817 ; m. Oct. 15, 1848, Geo. Joslyn of Surry, N. H. He d. 28 Sept., 1877.

Children of EDMUND⁵, (1777) [155] (Dea. Edmund⁴, Richard³, Sergt. Abraham², Robert¹) and Elizabeth (Carr) Adams; res. Derry, N. H.

i. HANNAH⁶, b. in Derry, Feb. 24, 1809 ; d. unm.
ii. JOHN⁶, b. in Derry, Dec. 19, 1810 ; d. unm. 13 Aug., 1856.
iii. MARY⁶, b. in Derry, Oct. 10, 1812; d. unm.
iv. ELIZA⁶, b. in Derry, Jan. 15, 1815 ; d. unm.
v. MARGARET⁶, b. in Derry, July 8, 1817 ; d. unm.
vi. EDMUND⁶, b. in Derry, Nov. 22, 1819 ; d. unm.
365. vii. BENJAMIN⁶, b. in Derry, July 10, 1824 ; m. Dec. 15, 1885, Katie J. Foster.
viii. AMOS⁶, b. in Derry, Feb. 13, 1829 ; d. 21 Aug., 1856.

Children of ZADOC⁵, (1736) [156] (Jacob⁴, Sergt. Jacob³, Jacob², Robert¹) and Ruth (Bush) Adams; res. Suffield, Conn.

i. RACHEL⁶, b. in Suffield, 1761 ; d. 9 Sept., 1802, age 41 years.
366. ii. CAPT. ASAHEL⁶, b. in Suffield, 1762-3 ; m. Jan. 17, 1787, Susanna Adams, dau. of Zebulon and Susanna (Pingelley) Adams ; d. in Norwich, Vt., 25 Oct., 1802. He d. in Norwich, Vt., 8 Sept., 1802, age 41 years.
367. iii. NOADIAH⁶, b. in Suffield, Nov. 28, 1763 ; m. 1791, Mary Bedortha ; d. 17 Feb., 1859, age 88 years. He d. 28 April, 1832, age 68 years.
368. iv. ZADOC⁶, JR., b. in Suffield, 1765-6 ; m. Nov. 24, 1798, Anne Adams, dau. of Samuel and Dorcas (Frost) Adams, b. Oct. 12, 1770 ; she d. 30 April, 1847. He d. 25 Oct., 1844, aged 78 yrs. 9 mos.
369. v. DORCAS⁶, b. in Suffield, 1769 ; m. April 10, 1794, Edwin Bement. She d. 30 Jan., 1852, age 83 years.
370. vi. EBENEZER⁶, b. in Suffield, 1771 ; m. Lydia Owen ; she d. 24 Oct., 1818. He d. 10 Jan., 1819, age 48 years.

371. vii. RUTH⁶, b. in Suffield, 1774; m. May 10, 1797, Josiah King. He m. 2d Thankful Parmalee, and d. 14 Jan., 1824, age 50 years. She d. 15 April, 1800, age 26 years.
372. viii. ARAH⁶, b. in Suffield, 1775; m. (1) Elizabeth Gray; m. (2) Charlotte Avery; she d. in Stratford, Conn., 8 July, 1856, age 78 years. He d. 22 Nov., 1826, age 51 years. Arah was a carpenter; res. Suffield.
373. ix. ORPHA⁶, b. 1780; m. Nov. 27, 1800, Zepheniah Snow. She d. 1 Nov., 1842, age 62 years.

Children of ZEBULON⁵, JR., (1765) [157] (Zebulon⁴, Daniel³, Jacob², Robert¹) and Lucy (Ball) Adams; res. Suffield, Conn.

374. i. CALVIN⁶, b. in Suffield, Aug. (2?) 12. 1790-1; m. about 1815, Lucy King, dau. of Lieut. Eliphalet King, who was a soldier in the French War; she d. 20 Jan., 1856, age 65 years. He resided in Suffield, and d. 20 Feb., 1863.
  ii. ZEBINA⁶, b. in Suffield, Aug. 19, 1794-5; m. Mary King, dau. of Seth King; she d. 1 Feb., 1874; no issue. He d. in Suffield, 6 June, 1876.
375. iii. HARRIET⁶, b. in Suffield, July 4, 1800-1; m. 1819, Ashbel Dewey, son of Solomon and Ésther Dewey, b. in Westfield, Mass., June 19, 1795.
  He was an elder in the church of Later Day Saints; rem. to Nauvoo, Ill., in 1846, and was on his way to Salt Lake City, Utah, when he died at Omaha, Neb., 6 Oct., 1846. She d. 15 May, 1871.
376. iv. SUSANNA⁶, b. in Suffield, May 15, (19 ?) 1803; m. Mar. 3, 1831, Oren Kendall, son of Joshua Kendall, b. Oct. 10, 1798; d. 7 Jan., 1859. She d. 8 June, 1885.
377. v. EMILY⁶, b. in Suffield, Mar. 3, 1806; m. 1828-9, Julius King, son of Jonah King, b. Nov. 16, 1804; d. 10 Sept., 1861. She d. 16 Mar., 1881.

Children of CAPT. GIDEON⁵, (1754) [158] (Daniel⁴, Daniel³, Jacob², Robert¹) and Rhoda (Hanchett) Adams; res. Suffield, Conn., and Oneida Co., N. Y.

378. i. CALVIN⁶, b. in Suffield, Oct. 16, 1780; m. Dec. 28, 1801, Martha Stilman, dau. of Amos and Sarah (Clinton) Stilman of Watertown, Conn., b. Apr. 3, 1781; d. 15 Nov., 1836.
  They set. in Verona, Oneida Co., N. Y., 1802-3; he d. in Verona, 8 Mar., 1868.

Sixth Generation.] OF NEWBURY, MASS. 91

379. ii. CHARLOTTE[6], b. in Suffield, Oct. 2, 1782; m. Sept. 17, 1801, Seth S. Sedgwick, son of Titus and Amney (Sackett) Sedgwick. She d. in Verona, N. Y., 23 Dec., 1862.

380. iii. RHODA[6], b. in Stephentown, N. Y., July 7, 1786; m. Jan. 27, 1805, Clark Smith, son of Amos Smith of Woodbury, Conn., b. in Woodbury, July 3, 1784; d. 29 July, 1864.
 They set. in Busti, Chautauqua Co., N. Y., soon after marriage, and she d. 3 Feb., 1867.

381. iv. ABBY[6], b. in Stephentown, June, 1787; m. 1807, Chester Loomis, who d. 1851.
 They set. in Cicero, Onondaga Co., N. Y., in 1823, where she d. 24 Jan., 1860, age 72 years.

382. v. HORACE[6], b. in Stephentown, Oct. 16, 1790; m. (1) Jan. 1, 1814, Sally Wylie, b. Aug. 1, 1793; d. 19 Nov., 1820; m. (2) Feb. 11, 1821, Mary Lyndon, b. Apr. 21, 1799; d. 17 Nov., 1835; m. (3) Apr. 20, 1837, Susanna Lawton Peckham, b. Nov. 15, 1789; d. 13 Mar., 1875.
 He set. in Rome, N. Y., in 1835; was a contractor and builder; d. in Rome, 6 Dec., 1857.

383. vi. REBECCA[6], b. in Stephentown, Apr. 1, 1797; m. Oct. 14, 1819, Jotham G. Goodspeed, b. in Madison Co., N. Y., Apr. 17, 1800; d. in Shiawassa, Mich., 8 Nov., 1865. She d. at So. Lyons, Mich., 15 Aug., 1887, age 92 years.

384. vii. HARVEY[6], b. in Stephentown, Dec. 14, 1799; m. 1821, Deborah Fields, dau. of John and Silence (Lincoln) Fields, b. 1798; d. 13 Oct., 1860.
 They rem. from Central Square, Oswego Co., N. Y., in 1854, to Brooklyn, Jackson Co., Mich. He d. 20 Nov., 1872.

viii. INFANT; d. young.

Children of ELIPHALET[5], (1756) [159] (Freegrace[4], Lieut. Abraham[3], Jacob[2], Robert[1]) and Patience (Rice) Adams; res. Cambridge, N. Y.

385. i. ELIPHALET[6], JR., b. in Cambridge, Oct. 20, 1779; m. Narcissa Ward.
 He removed with his parents about 1798, to Stoke, Richmond Co., P. Q., where he married, and where he d. 22 Jan., 1832. His widow rem. with her children to Esquesing, Halton Co., Ont.

386. ii. PHEBE[6], b. in Cambridge, May 31, 1781; m. Feb. 17, 1805, at Acton, Ont., Joseph H. Kilborn, b. in Litchfield Co., Conn., Feb. 15, 1771; d. 15 Nov., 1814. She d. at Okemos, Ingraham Co., Mich., 22 Jan., 1864.

387. iii. RUFUS⁶, b. in Cambridge, June 11, 1783; m. Maria Hubbard of Montpelier, Vt.; she d. in Hamilton, Ont., 1867.
  He was a millwright; set. in Esquesing, Ont., and with his brother Ezra built mills in the village of Adamsville, now Acton, on the Grand Trunk Railway, 14 miles from Guelph. He d. in Acton, 6 May, 1856.

iv. VINCENT⁶, b. in Cambridge, Mar. 11, 1785.
  He was drowned in the St. Francis river, Canada, by the upsetting of a boat.

v. LUCINDA⁶, b. in Cambridge, Jan 11, 1787.
  Drowned with her brother Vincent.

388. vi. REV. EZRA⁶, b. in Cambridge, July 17, 1788; m. (1) June 12-20, 1814, Isa Proctor; she d. 29 Sept., 1832; m. (2) Aug. 8, 1833, Amy (Edmunds) Curtis, wid. of John G. Curtis; she d. 23 April, 1864; m. (3) Betsey (Edmunds) Griffin, sister of Amy and widow of Smith Griffin.
  He was a minister in the Wesleyan Meth. Church in Canada ; d. Drayton, Ont., 1 Dec., 1871.

vii. ELECTA⁶, b. probably in Cambridge, May 31, 1790; m. about 1845, Thomas Ebbage, a retired sea captain, who d. 29 May, 1860; no issue.

389. viii. REV. ZENAS⁶, b. in Cambridge, April 7, 1792; m. June 19, 1826, at Upper Gilmanton, N. H., Ruth Fellows, dau. or Jacob Fellows, b. in Plymouth, N. H., April 7, 1800; d. at Brockville, Ont., 4 Dec. 1864.
  He was a Wesleyan Methodist, d. in Acton, 17 Nov., 1847.

ix. ZARA⁶, b. Feb. 17, 1794; d. 17 Oct., 1796.
x. WILLIAM⁶, b. Mar. 11, 1796; d. 16 Oct., 1796.
xi. PHINEAS RICE⁶, b. Sept. 15, 1798; d. in Acton, Ont., unm., 21 April, 1830.

Children of LOVISA⁵, (1759) [**160**] (Freegrace⁴, Lieut. Abraham³, Jacob², Robert¹) and Ichabod King; res. Marlboro, Vt.

390. i. ICHABOD KING, JR., b. Feb. 27, 1780; m. (1) Jan. 4, 1807, Clarissa Howard, dau. of Jonathan and Sarah (Mather) Howard, b. Sept. 29, 1781; d. 7 Mar., 1832; m. (2) Feb. 27, 1833, Sally Hatch, dau. of James and Esther (Tucker) Hatch, b. in Halifax, Vt., Mar. 10, 1790; d. in Jacksonville, Vt., 30 June, 1885. He d. in W. Brattleboro, Vt., 9. Sept., 1862; was buried in Marlboro, Vt.

ii. LOVISA KING, b. Mar. 23, 1782; d. unm. 11 July, 1847.

391. iii. JUSTIN KING⁶, b. Mar. 7, 1784; m. (1) ———— ————; she d. 5 Nov. 1819; m. (2) Ann ————; she d. Aug. 9, 1883; m. (3) Aug. 2, 1835, Elizabeth Hunt, "late from Boston and half-niece of 1st wife."
  He settled in Boston in 1805, but removed to Cincinnati, O., in 1815, where he continued, and d. 20 Mar., 1852.

AMY ADAMS.

Sixth Generation.]   OF NEWBURY, MASS.   93

  iv. JOSEPH KING, b. June 9, 1786 ; d. 23 Jan., 1789.
  v. IRA KING, b. Sept. 7, 1788; d. at Marlboro, Vt., unm., 6 July, 1860.
  vi. POLLY KING, b. Oct. 10, 1791 ; m. Jan. 19, 1815, Levi Howard, son of Jonathan and Sarah (Mather) Howard, b. June 5, 1784, d. 4 July, 1862. She d. 27 June, 1865; no issue.
392. vii. HANNAH KING, b. Nov. 6, 1793 ; m. Dec. 26, 1820, Emory Powers, son of Josiah and Susanna (Parks) Powers, b. in Marlboro, Vt., April 23, 1796, d. in New York, 9 June, 1863 ; buried in Ludlow, Vt. She d. in Ludlow, Vt., 25 June, 1867.
393. viii. ANNA KING, b. Feb. 8, 1796 ; m. Feb. 18, 1821, Joseph Angel Hamilton, son of John and Amy (Angel) Hamilton, b. July 15, 1796, d. 6 Nov., 1828 ; res. Marlboro, Vt. She d. 31 Jan., 1847.
394. ix. LUCINDA KING, b. Dec. 29, 1798 ; m. Jan. 20, 1828, Rufus Caldwell, son of John and Elizabeth (Swan) Caldwell of Northfield, Mass., b. Oct. 15, 1797; d. 17 Jan., 1849 ; res. Northfield, (West) Mass. She d. 16 Feb., 1889.
395. x. JOSEPH KING, b. Aug. 26, 1803 ; m. (1) June 10, 1827, Sarah Childs, dau. of Jonathan and Abiah (Larrabee) Childs, b. in Cambridge. Vt., June 22, 1802 ; d. in Marlboro, Vt., 7 Nov., 1840 ; m. (2) April 4, 1843, Chloe White, dau. of Joseph and Hannah (Hazeltine) White, b. in Dover, Vt., Mar. 16, 1804 ; d. in Marlboro, Vt., 12 Aug., 1877 ; res Marlboro, Vt. He d. in W. Brattleboro, Vt., 22 April, 1882.

Children of ANNA[5], (1863) [**161**] (Freegrace[4], Lieut. Abraham[3], Jacob[2], Robert[1]) and William Nye ; res. Halifax, Vt.

396. i. ANNA NYE, b. Oct. 31, 1802; m. Jan. 4, 1820, David Niles of Halifax ; b. in Stonington, Conn., Mar. 21, 1793 ; d. in Halifax, 16 Feb., 1870. She d. in Halifax, 22 Apr., 1880.
  ii. JEMIMA NYE, b. May 22, 1809 ; m. Charles Brown; res. Smithfield, Pa.

Children of FREEGRACE[5], JR., (1765) [**162**] (Freegrace[4], Lieut. Abraham[3],|Jacob[2], Robert[1]) and Susanna (Halliday) Adams ; res. Marlboro, Vt.

397. i. CAPT. MILTON[6], b. in Marlboro, Aug. 6, 1792 ; m. July 4, 1815, Lodice Mather, dau. of Erastus Mather, b. Mar. 25, 1794 ; d. 20 Mar., 1844. He d. in Springfield, Mass., 14 Apr., 1880.
398. ii. MARTIN[6], b. in Marlboro, Apr. 1, 1794 ; m. Feb. 29, 1824, Anna W. Elmer, dau. of Ozias and Anna Wright (Smith) Elmer of Hinsdale, N. H. ; she d. 30 Aug., 1882, age 78 yrs. and 1 week. He d. 9 Aug., 1858.

ROBERT ADAMS [Sixth Generation.

- iii. SUSANNA⁶, b. in Marlboro, May 2, 1796 ; m. Mar. 21, 1816, Rufus Mixer, of Brattleboro, Vt. She d. 1 Oct., 1842.
- 399. iv. ELIHU⁶, b. in Marlboro, June 4, 1798 ; m. Nov. 13, 1828, Sophia Wait of Whateley, Mass., b. Mar. 27, 1798 ; d, 15 Oct., 1891 ; res. Chicopee and Springfield, Mass. He d. 2 Dec., 1878.
    He was a prominent man, alderman of the city, and for a score of years high sheriff and jailor of Hampden Co.
- 400. v. HENRY⁶, b. in Marlboro, Aug. 14, 1800 ; m. Jan. 10, 1826, Asenath Pratt, dau. of Emerson Pratt; she d. 23 Feb., 1853. He d. 24 July, 1841.
- 401. vi. LEPHA⁶, b. in Marlboro, Oct. 23, 1802 ; m. Aug. 27, 1823, Francis C. Munn ; res. Chicopee, Mass. She d. 3 Nov., 1875.
- 402. vii. EZEKIEL⁶, b. in Marlboro, Mar. 17, 1805 ; m. (1) Janette Wait of Whateley, Mass. ; m. (2) Lydia Colton of Longmeadow, Mass. He d. 4 Feb., 1878.
- 403. viii. HORACE⁶, b. in Marlboro, June 3, 1807 ; m. Mary Love of Troy, N. Y. ; she d. 10 July, 1895; res. Chicopee, Mass. He d. 3 June, 1866. April 1, 1867, Mary of Chicopee was appointed guardian of Dwight, Minor son of Horace, late of Chicopee.
- 404. ix. ANN⁶, b. in Marlboro, Feb. 19, 1810 ; m. Alonzo Wait of Whateley, b. Aug. 4, 1807 ; d. 10 Jan., 1892 ; res. Chicopee, Mass., for 50 years. She d. 26 Jan., 1858.

Children of TEMPERANCE⁵, (1768) [163] (Freegrace⁴, Lieut. Abraham³, Jacob², Robert¹) and Jonathan Kellogg; res. Suffield, Conn.

- i. SALLY KELLOGG, b. Saturday, April 4, 1795.
- ii. CYNTHIA KELLOGG, b. Tuesday, Aug. 23, 1797.
- iii. TEMPERANCE KELLOGG, b. Wednesday, Feb. 27, 1799.

Children of JEMIMA⁵, (1770) [164] (Freegrace⁴, Lieut. Abraham³, Jacob², Robert¹) and William Alverson ; res. Halifax, Vt.

- 405. i. WILLIAM ALVERSON, b. Jan. 3, 1811 ; m. Aug. 31, 1835, at Woodford, Vt., Eliza Pierce, b. in Cortland, N. Y., Dec. 15, 1809; d. in Clinton, Ia., 4 Nov., 1889. He d. in Clinton, Ia., 13 Dec., 1869, and was buried in Whitewater, Wis.
- 406. ii. JEMIMA ALVERSON, b. May 9, 1812 ; m. (1) Jonathan Niles, son of Samuel and Freedom (Hale) Niles, b. Dec. 21, 1807, d. 16 June, 1838 ; m. (2) May 28, 1845, at Brattleboro, Vt., Julius Robbins, son of Nathan and Nancy (Bangs) Robbins, b. in Deerfield, Mass., May 14, 1814 ; d. 2 April, 1882 ; res. Halifax, Vt., and Deerfield, Mass. She d. in Deerfield, Mass., 21 May, 1891.

iii. FRANK ALVERSON, b. Jan. 8, 1816.
    He rem. to California at an early day, and d. unm. at San Francisco.

Children of ABRAHAM⁵, (1769) [165] (Samuel⁴, Lieut. Abraham³, Jacob², Robert¹) and Louisa (Spurr) Adams ; res. Benson, Vt.

i. DAVID⁶, b. in Benson, Sept. 21, 1797; m. Catherine Gibbs, dau. of Aaron and Hannah (Maynard) Gibbs, b. July 16, 1797, d. 23 July, 1876. He d. in Benson, 23 Mar., 1880; no issue.

407. ii. SOPHIA⁶, b. in Benson, Sept. 28, 1799 ; m. Jonas Gibbs, son of Aaron and Hannah (Maynard) Gibbs. He m. 2nd Martha A. Tracheret, and d. 17 Oct., 1884, age 85 yrs. 8 mos. She d. in Benson, 29 Mar., 1868.

iii. MATILDA⁶, b. in Benson, July 4, 1802; m. Feb. 2, 1849, Jacob Winter (his 2nd wife) ; he d. 18 July, 1868, age 82 years; res. Ticonderoga, N. Y. She d. in Benson, 23 Oct., 1890 ; no issue.

408. iv. MALINDA⁶ (twin), b. in Benson, July 4, 1802 ; m. Peter Corbett, a Scotchman from Putnam, N. Y., b. Mar. 8, 1798.
    They rem. about 1853, to Greenbush, Wis., where she d. 18 Mar., 1879.

409. v. LOVISA⁶, b. in Benson, Sept. 30, 1805 ; m. (1) 1829, James LeBarron, son of David and Martha (Chatfield) Le Barron, b. Oct. 10, 1783 ; d. 25 Feb., 1837 ; m. (2) Dec. 12, 1841, Richard Grinnell, son of Levi and Hannah (Woodstock) Grinnell, b. Jan. 10, 1813, d. 30 Aug., 1875. She d. in Benson, 24 Feb., 1849.

410. vi. ABRAHAM⁶, JR., b. in Benson, Dec. 18, 1808 ; m. 1838, Merinda E. Bartlett, dau. of Hooker Bartlett, a soldier of 1812, and son of a soldier of the Revolution; she was b. Sept. 4, 1816; was living in 1893.
    He removed from Benson to Forest, Wis., in 1845, and set. in Fond du Lac, Wis.; was a prominent Methodist. He d. 8 Oct., 1868.

411. vii. ELI⁶, b. in Benson, Nov. 20, 1810; m. Sophia Parsons of Castleton, Vt.
    He rem. to Greenbush, Wis. He d. in Fond du Lac, Wis.

viii. CHLOE⁶, b. in Benson, Aug. 10, 1812 ; d. young.

412. ix. CHLOE ANGELINE⁶, b. in Benson, Sept. 12, 1816 ; m. Sept. 24, 1840, James Higgins, son of Daniel and Hannah (Le Barron) Higgins, b. in Le Roy, N. Y., July 21, 1813 ; d. 5 Apr., 1869. She d. 20 Feb., 1867.

x. ANGELINE⁶, b. in Benson, Sept. 14, 1818 ; d. young.

413.   xi.   WILLIAM SPURR⁶, b. in Benson, June 16, 1819; m. Sept. 12, 1849, Martha E. Peck, dau. of Worcester and Sarah E. Peck of Castleton, Vt., b. Feb. 8, 1821; d. 8 Feb., 1893.
He rem. to Wisconsin, settling on a farm in Forest, Calumet Co., surrounded by Indians. He sold his place in 1865, and set. in Empire, Fond du Lac Co., where he was living in 1895.

Children of ELIZABETH⁵, (1782) [166] (Samuel⁴, Lieut. Abraham³, Jacob², Robert¹) and Samuel Kenyon; res. Benson and Westhaven, Vt.

414.   i.   BETSEY MARIA KENYON, b. Sept. 9, 1804; m. about 1825, Joyce Billings; he d. about 1875; res. Westhaven. She d. about 1881.
415.   ii.   ORRA EMMA KENYON, b. Sept. 16, 1810; m. Nov. 29, 1829, John W. Gregg, b. in Benson, Jan. 27, 1808; d. in Occoquan, Va., 26 Jan., 1900; res. Occoquan, Va.
416.   iii.   DORCAS DIADEMIA KENYON, b. Feb. 7, 1813; m. Feb. 1, 1835, Hon. Nathaniel Fish, son of Stephen Fish, of Fair Haven, Vt., b. in Fair Haven, May 1, 1813.
He was a man of much original ability; was prominent in the affairs of town and state, member of the House of Representatives from Westhaven 1853-4, and of the Senate of Vermont, 1863-4; he d. in Benson, 1 Mar., 1881, and was buried in Fair Haven. She d. in Benson, 16 Oct., 1890, and was buried in Fair Haven.

Children of HORACE⁵, (1754) [167] (Samuel⁴, Lieut. Abraham³, Jacob², Robert¹) and Ora (Billings) Adams; res. West Haven, Vt.

417.   i.   LUCY BILLINGS⁶, b. in West Haven, Feb. 28, 1813; m. Oct. 25, 1835, Jonathan Smead, Jr., b. April, 1812; d. 21 Jan., 1866. She d. in Greenfield, Mass., 1 Dec., 1866.
418.   ii.   FANNY⁶, b. in West Haven, Sept. 15, 1814; m. April 7, 1839, Youmans Merritt, who was b. and d. in Shoreham, Vt. She d. in Shoreham, Vt., 28 Jan., 1889.
       iii.   JULIA⁶, b. in West Haven, April 7, 1816; d. unm. Nov., 1879.
419.   iv.   SAMUEL⁶, b. in West Haven, June 3, 1818; m. (1) Sept. 18, 1839, Mary Ann Goodrich, dau. of Chauncey Goodrich, b. in Fair Haven, Vt., Dec. 9, 1817; d. 11 June, 1853; m. (2) July 6, 1854, Aurelia W. Larrabee, dau of Benjamin Larrabee of Shoreham, Vt.; she d. 1860; m. (3) April 27, 1864, Mrs. Angeline (Ray) Hill, widow of Chauncey Hill; she d. 28 June, 1886.
He was a farmer in West Haven, d. 20 Aug., 1889.

Sixth Generation.] OF NEWBURY, MASS. 97

420. v. ESTHER JOYCE⁶, b. in West Haven, Dec. 19, 1820; m. May 7, 1837, William Forbes, son of James Forbes, b. Aug. 11, 1811 ; d. 16 Jan., 1865. She survives, 1899 ; res. Troy, N. Y.
421. vi. REBECCA W.⁶, b. in West Haven, Jan. 20, 1824 ; m. Dec. 28, 1843, Levi N. Goodrich, son of Chauncey Goodrich of Fair Haven, Vt., b. Sept. 9, 1820; res. Concord, Mich.
      vii. HENRY⁶, b. in West Haven, Feb. 4, 1826; d. June, 1826.
      viii. EMILY BILLINGS⁶, b. in West Haven, Dec. 19, 1828 ; d. unm. 8 Oct., 1849.

Child of SETH⁵, (1746-7) [168] (Moses⁴, John³, Jacob², Robert¹) and Elizabeth (Lane) Adams; res. Agawam, Mass.

422. i. SETH⁶, JR., b. in West Springfield, Mass., Feb. 7, 1772 ; m. (1) Mar. 6, 1801, Polly Bush, b. Apr. 6, 1781 ; d. 21 Nov., 1803; m. (2) April 4, 1811, Tabitha Warriner, b. Feb., 1785, d. 9 Dec., 1841.
      He made his will April 20, 1833 ; proved Nov., 1833 ; d. in Agawam, Mass., 12 June, 1833.

Children of SETH⁵, (1746-7) and ―――― (Fairman) Adams.

423. ii. LEVI⁶, b. in W. Springfield about 1774-5 ; m. Desdemonia Munger, eldest dau. of Daniel Munger ; she d. in Warsaw, N. Y., 28 April, 1857, age 81 years. He d. in W. Springfield, May, 1812, age 38 years.
424. iii. ELIZABETH⁶, b. in W. Sprinfield, 1778 ; m. Julius Appleton ; he d. 1848, age 64 years ; res. Springfield, Mass. She d. 1853, age 75 years.
425. iv. LUCY⁶, b. in W. Springfield, Aug. 31, 1779 ; m. Jan. 8, 1800, Jotham Wright, b. Jan. 3, 1775; d. 5 Sept., 1875 ; res. Enfield (now Thompsonville,) Conn. She d. 21 Aug., 1854.
426. v. GAIUS⁶, b. in W. Springfield, Jan. 18, 1781; m. Mar. 22, 1808, Cynthia Kent, b. Oct. 7, 1785 ; d. 20 Oct., 1862.
      He set. in Springfield, Bradford Co., Pa., in 1808, d. Aug.; 1857.
      vi. PERSIS⁶, b. in W. Springfield; m. ―――― Brown ; res. and d. in Longmeadow, Mass.
427. vii. ENOS⁶, b. in W. Springfield, Oct. 7, 1785 ; m. Jan. 1, 1809, Sarah Ann Dickinson, dau. of Dr. Benjamin and Sarah (Ashley) Dickinson, b. in Whateley, Mass., Aug. 22, 1788 ; d. in Bennington, Vt., 17 Aug., 1860.
      He set. in Rowe, Mass., rem. to Heath, Mass., and thence in 1834, to Bennington, Vt. He was a tanner and currier, and shoemaker ; later a manufacturer; d. 24 May, 1857.

(7)

Children of SETH[5], (1747) and Lydia (Taylor) Adams; res. West Springfield, Mass.

428. viii. JERE[6], b. in W. Springfield, May 25, 1793 ; m. July 6, 1816, Cynthia Decker, b. Oct. 1, 1796 ; d. in Troy, Pa., 14 July, 1870.
He was a tanner and currier, having learned the business with his brother Enos in Heath, Mass. He rem. and set. in Athens, Pa., in 1815, d. 20 Jan., 1867, in Waverly, N. Y., and was buried in Troy, Pa.

ix. LEWIS[6], b. in W. Springfield, d, unm. in Suffield, Conn., age 18 years.

429. x. JOEL[6], b in W. Springfield, April 25, 1801 ; m. 1829, Fidelia Crandall of Cooperstown, N. Y., b. Oct. 29, 1807 ; d. 29 April, 1854.
He set. in Lawrenceville, Tioga Co., Pa., in 1831. Was in tanning, boot and shoe, and saddlery business for 50 years. He learned his trade with his brother Enos in Heath, Mass.; rem. West in 1815-6. He d. 8 Aug., 1882.

xi. LUCINDA[6], b. in W. Springfield ; d. young—after Lewis.

Children of THADDEUS[5], (1759) [169] (Moses[4], John[3], Jacob[2], Robert[1]) and Polly (Plumb) Adams; res. Norwich, Mass.

i. SALLY[6], b. in Suffield, Conn., Aug. 6, 1783 ; m. Elihu Chapin of Norwich, Mass.
They rem. to the West.

430. ii. POLLY[6], b. in Suffield, Mar. 11, 1785; m. Alvin Barnum ; res. Northampton, Mass.

431. iii. WAIT[6], b. in Suffield, Dec. 22, 1786 ; m. (1) Jan. 28, 1813, Olive Cole ; m. (2) Sally Chapman of Westfield, Mass. He d. in Chester, Mass., 15 Feb., 1879.

432. iv. MEHITABLE[6], b. in Suffield, Feb. 17, 1789-90 ; m. Feb. 6, 1812, James Cook of Norwich, Mass., b. Sept. 9, 1787 ; d. June, 1855. She d. in Westfield, Mass., Apr., 1886, age 96 years.

433. v. THADDEUS[6], JR., b. in Suffield, Oct. 22, 1792 ; m. Aug. 20, 1816, Percy Bosworth of Montgomery, Mass. ; she d. 23 June, 1869. He d. in Norwich, 20 Oct., 1842.

vi. ALFRED[6], b. in Suffield, June 22, 1794 ; m. Harriet Shurtliff of Montgomery, Mass.

vii. MINERVA[6], b. in Suffield, Oct. 11, 1797.

viii. RHODA[6], b. in Suffield, Aug. 22, 1799 ; m. Allen Lewis of Westfield, Mass. She d. in Westfield, 12 Aug., 1868, age 69 years; had one dau., who d. early.

434. ix. MARTIN[6], b. in Suffield, Sept. 14, 1802 ; m. Apr. 12, 1827, Sally Brown, b. 1797, d. Mar., 1844.
He was a farmer ; res. Norwich, Mass.; d. 11 Nov., 1853, age 51 years.

Sixth Generation.]   OF NEWBURY, MASS.   99

435.   x. HARRIET[6], b. in Suffield, May 25, 1804; m. Apr. 30, 1835, Alpheus Beach of Agawam, Mass.; res. Norwich, Mass. She d. 9 Aug., 1899, age 95 years.
436. xi. HIRAM[6], b. in Norwich, Mass., Aug. 20, 1808 ; m. Armeluna Dibble of Agawam, Mass.

Children of JONATHAN[5], (1762) [170] (Moses[4], John[3], Jacob[2], Robert[1]) and Eunice (Allen) Adams; res. Agawam, Mass.

437.   i. EUNICE[6], b. in Suffield, Conn., Feb. 3, 1793; m. 1818, Harvey Wright of Suffield ; he d. in Maine, Broome Co., N. Y., Aug., 1872. She d. 6 June, 1820.
      ii. LUTHER[6], b. in Suffield, Oct. 19, 1794; d. unm. 12 May, 1869, age 74 years.
438. iii. MIRIAM[6], b. in Suffield, Mar. 10, 1798 ; m. Oct. 24, 1824, Geo. J. Hubbard. She d. 10 Oct., 1851.

Children of CAPT. OLIVER[5] (1769) [171] (Simeon[4], John[3], Jacob[2], Robert[1]) and Lucy (Miller) Adams; res. Marlboro, Vt., and Hinsdale, N. H,

439.   i. LUCY[6], b. in Marlboro, Jan. 22, 1792 ; m. Oct. 31, 1814-15, Rufus Mather, son of Phineas and Huldah (Taylor) Mather, b. Oct. 22, 1788; d. 10 Feb., 1872. She d. at Feeding Hills, Mass., 1 Mar., 1859.
440. ii. ABRAHAM[6], b. in Marlboro, Oct. 5, 1793-4; m. July 13, 1816, Beda Mather, dau. of Phineas Mather, b. in Marlboro, Oct. 27, 1798; d. 6 Mar., 1873
           He was a farmer in Marlboro, Vt.; rem. to Middleport (Royalton Township), Niagara Co., N. Y., and d. there 27 Mar., 1842.
441. iii. POLLY[6], b. in Marlboro, Nov. 19, 1795-6; m. Feb. 20, 1820, Gad Mather, brother of Rufus Mather, b. Sept. 6, 1793; d. 21 April, 1841 ; res. Middleport, N. Y. She d. 29 Nov., 1850.
442. iv. SUSANNA[6], b. in Marlboro, Jan. 16-20, 1798 ; m. Jan. 23, 1820, Archibald Robinson ; res. Middleport, N. Y.
443.   v. OLIVER[6], JR., b. in Marlboro, April 6, 1799-1800; m. (1) Mar. 21, 1824, at Hinsdale, Electa Elmer, dau. of Hezekiah and Tabitha (Wright) Elmer, b. Dec. 3, 1799 ; d. 19 Aug., 1824 ; m. (2) Dec., 1826, Fannie Stearns, dau. of Walter Clapp and Tryphena (Shattuck) Stearns, b. Dec. 3, 1797 ; d. 14 Aug., 1867. He set. in Hinsdale, N. H., in 1815 ; d. 22 Feb., 1876.

444. vi.   ANNA⁶, b. in Marlboro, Jan. 30, 1801-2 ; m. Jan. 25, 1819, Ora Barrett, son of Philip Barrett, b. April 9, 1797 ; d. 16 Sept., 1845 ; res. Hinsdale, N. H., d. 18 Sept., 1848.
445. vii. SALLY⁶, b. in Marlboro, Oct. 8, 1803-4 ; m. 1821, Harry Thomas. She d. 12 Nov., 1884.
      viii. BRADLEY⁶, b. in Marlboro, Aug. 3, 1807 ; d. unm. 19 June, 1830, of consumption ; was a great worker.

Children of CAPT. SIMEON⁵, (1771) [172] (Simeon⁴, John³, Jacob², Robert¹) and Lucy (Mather) Adams; res. Marlboro, Vt.

446. i.   CAPT. IRA⁶, b. in Marlboro, Feb. 23, 1798 ; m. Apr. 25, 1821, Lucy Houghton, dau. of Capt. Nahum Houghton, b. July 9, 1797 ; d. 18 Apr., 1878 ; res. on the farm and old tavern stand of Samuel Whitney in Marlboro. He d. 17 Apr., 1889.
447. ii.   PHILENA⁶, b. in Marlboro, March 3, 1800 ; m. Feb. 27, 1822, Dr. Chester A. Olds, b. Oct. 24, 1798 ; d. 21 July, 1862. She d. in Cincinnati, O., 8 Nov., 1877.
448. iii. SIMEON⁶, b. in Marlboro, Mar. 24, 1803 ; m. Nov. 26, 1828, Mary Ann W. Sargent, b. in Brattleboro, Vt., May 13, 1805. He d. in Marlboro, 12 Apr., 1885.
449. iv.   LUCY⁶, b. in Marlboro, Mar. 8, 1805 ; m. Apr. 27, 1825, Bradley Houghton. She d. in Marlboro, 14 May, 1831.
450. v.   CLARK⁶, b. in Marlboro, Apr. 27, 1807 ; m. May 4, 1845, Beulah D. Hill. He d. in Marlboro, 29 May, 1872.
      vi.   HANNAH⁶, b. in Marlboro, June 23, 1809 ; m. Haines E. Baker of Putney, Vt, She d. 28 Feb., 1841.
451. vii. TIMOTHY MATHER⁶, b. in Marlboro, Oct. 18, 1811 ; m. (1) Feb. 9, 1842, Harriet P. Winchester, b. Aug. 23, 1820; d. 22 Nov., 1856 ; m. (2) Dec. 15, 1857, Amaretta Whitney, b. July 15, 1829; d. 1 Feb., 1888 ; res. on the old homestead, Marlboro, Vt. He d. 22 May, 1885.
      viii. LOUISA⁶, b. in Marlboro, Nov. 16, 1813 ; d. unm. 23 Apr., 1887.
452. ix.   LUCIUS F.⁶, b. in Marlboro, June 18, 1816 ; m. March 20, 1845, Clarinda Winchester, dau. of Carley P. and Patty (Bassett) Winchester. He d. 2 May, 1881.
453. x.   SAMUEL NEWELL⁶, b. in Marlboro, Jan. 27, 1819 ; m. March 9, 1847, at Circleville, O., Cornelia H. Rogers, dau. of Samuel and Juliette Hollister, b. Nov. 20, 1828, d. at St. Paul, Minn., 29 Apr., 1874, age 47 years. He d. in Winona, Minn., 24 Feb., 1869, age 49 years.
454. xi.   MINERVA⁶, b. in Marlboro, May 15, 1821 ; m. Lyman N. Olds, son of Joseph Olds of Circleville, O. She d. in Circleville, 27 May, 1847.

Children of HANNAH⁵, (1775) [173] (Capt. Simeon⁴, John³, Jacob², Robert¹) and Josiah Brittan; res. Hubbardston, Mass.

    i. WILLIAM BRITTAN, b. Sept., 1798; d. 14 Apr., 1817.

455. ii. SUSAN BRITTAN, b. Aug. 23, 1801; m. Apr. 17, 1823, Col. Calvin G. Howe of Rutland, Mass. She d. in Burlington, Vt., 14 Feb., 1879.

456. iii. JOSIAH BRITTAN, JR., b. 1806; m. Sarah Maria ———. He d. in Worcester, Mass., 30 Apr., 1863.

    iv. HANNAH BRITTAN, b. Mar., 1810; d. 16 Sept., 1811.

    v. LYMAN WHITNEY BRITTAN, b. in Barre, Mass.

457. vi. SIMEON ADAMS BRITTAN, b. in Barre, July 15, 1812; m. Margaret N. Ball; she d. 9 Dec., 1888, age 67 years. He d. in Rutland, Mass., 7 July, 1887, age 75 years.

Children of SUSANNA⁵, (1778) [**174**] (Capt. Simeon⁴, John³, Jacob², Robert¹) and Nathan Halladay.

    i. RHODA HALLADAY, b. Oct. 14, 1798; d. in Buffalo, N. Y., about 1815-7.

    ii. HENRY HALLADAY, b. Oct. 11, 1800; d. 1 Aug., 1803.

458. iii. ALMIRA HALLADAY, b. March 14, 1803; m. Stephen White of Coleraine, Mass. She d. at Stamford, Vt.

459. iv. HENRY ADAMS HALLADAY, b. March 2, 1805; m. 1832, Caroline Stearns. He d. at Troy, N. Y., 18 Mar., 1890.

460. v. WILLARD NATHAN HALLADAY, b. 1808; m. Sabra ———. He d. at Hartwellville, Vt., 25 Aug., 1867.

461. vi. SUSAN HALLADAY, b. Dec. 17, 1810; m. (1) ——— White; m. (2) at Searsburg, Vt., Aug. 10. 1845, Daniel Read Wheeler of Rutland, Mass.; he d. at Rutland, Mass., 8 May, 1899, age 81 years. She is living (1899).

    vii. LUCIUS HALLADAY, b. probably in 1812; d. at Buffalo, N. Y., about 1815-7.

Children of ELIZABETH⁵, (1763) [**175**] (Lieut. Joel⁴, John³, Jacob², Robert¹) and Arunah Otis; res. Rutland, Jefferson Co., N. Y.

    i. ELIZABETH OTIS, b. May 28, 1787; m. April 11, 1811, Benjamin Wilcox; rem. to Streetsboro, Portage Co., O. She d. 7 Mar., 1862.

    ii. LUCY OTIS, b. April 28, 1789; m. Oct. 28, 1807, James Woodward. res. Rutland, N. Y. She d. 28 April, 1863.

    iii. MERCY OTIS, b. May 11, 1791; m. Oct. 9, 1806, Solomon Willard; res. Pamelia, Jefferson Co., N. Y. She d. 2 April, 1858, age 68 yrs. 10 mos. 18 days.

102   ROBERT ADAMS   [Sixth Generation.

iv. FANNY OTIS, b. Aug. 6, 1793.; m. 1813, Edward Winslow.
v. WEALTHY OTIS, b. Aug. 13, 1795; m. Jan. 1, 1818, Alden Adams, son of Joel Jr. and Priscilla (Kimball) Adams; set. in Antwerp and Sacketts Harbor, N. Y. She d. 28 May, 1880.
vi. RUBY OTIS, b, May 1, 1798; m. Mar. 4, 1821, Sterling Graves; res. Antwerp, N. Y. She d. 5 May, 1859.
vii. JOEL A. OTIS, b. Dec. 18, 1803; m. Aug. 12, 1827, Malina Wood, dau. of John Wood, b. July 14, 1805; she d. 4 Oct., 1869, age 64 years. He d. 11 Mar., 1887.
viii. ARUNAH OTIS, JR., b. Jan. 11, 1807; d. 19 Aug., 1839.

Children of JOB[5], (1765) [**176**] (Lieut. Joel[4], John[3], Jacob[2], Robert[1]) and ———— Adams; res. Suffield, Conn., and Marlboro, Vt.

462.
i. GEORGE[6], b. in Marlboro, Mar. 29, 1790; m. (1) Polly Woodward; d. 30 Sept., 1826; was buried in Antwerp, N. Y.; m. (2) about 1827, Polly Edgerton, b. 1790; she d. in Theresa, N. Y., 21 Jan., 1874, age 84 yrs. 2 mos. 9 days.

He rem. to Rutland, or Ellisburg, Jefferson Co., N. Y., about 1810, thence to Antwerp, N. Y., 1822-3, and to Theresa, N. Y., 1847; d. in Theresa, 29 Aug., 1849.

ii. ELIAS[6], b. in Antwerp, N. Y.; rem. West in 1840.
iii. JOB[6], b. in Antwerp, N. Y.

Children of BILDAD[5], (1765) [**177**] (Lieut. Joel[4], John[3], Jacob[2], Robert[1]) and Mary (Haynes) Adams; res. Marlboro, Vt.

i. MARIA[6], b. in Marlboro, Aug. 27, 1794; d. 17 July, 1801, being kicked by a horse.
ii. POLLY[6], b. in Marlboro, Nov. 15, 1795; d. unm. in Greenfield, O.
iii. JOHN[6], b. in Marlboro, Dec. 25, 1796.

He was a soldier in the War of 1812-14; d. in Greenfield, O., 1818, age 22 years.

463.
iv. NANCY[6], b. in Marlboro, July 30, 1798; m. Mar. 27, 1818, Matthew McKelvey.

She rem. with her parents in 1815, and settled in what is now Greenfield, Huron Co., O., where she taught the first school of Huron County (Peru). She d. in Blanchard, Hardin Co., 27 Jan., 1842.

Matthew McKelvey was son of William and Mary (Toppings) McKelvey, b. in Westmoreland Co., Pa., Jan. 30, 1794; was a soldier in the War of 1812-14; set. in Huron Co., O., in 1815; d. 18 Mar., 1853.

MATTHEW MCKELVEY AND WIFE, NANCY.

From photographs of portraits painted in oil, in the city of Sandusky. Being the first portraits painted in that city.

v. BILDAD⁶, b. in Marlboro, Apr. 18, 1800 ; d. in Milan, O., in 1828, unm.

vi. MARIA⁶, b. in Marlboro, Dec. 25, 1801 ; d. 13 Mar,, 1803.

464. vii. CANDACE⁶, b. in Marlboro, Sept. 1, 1803 ; m. Dec. 31, 1826, at Milon, O., Lewis Andrews, son of Eli and Lois (Chittenden) Andrews, b. in Tompkins Co., N. Y., Nov. 14, 1799 ; d. in Branch Co., Mich., 17 Oct., 1884. She d. 28 May, 1883.

465. viii. HORACE HALE⁶, b. in Marlboro, May 21, 1805 ; m. at Milan, O., Lorania G. Kinney ; she d. 15 Aug., 1850. He d. 12 Apr., 1847.

ix. SARAH⁶, b. in Marlboro, Feb. 17, 1807 ; m. Gilbert F. Morden. She res. in Canada ; had one child, and d. young.

x. EMILY⁶, b. in Marlboro, Nov. 1, 1809 ; m. Dec. 2, 1830, Luther Kinney, son of Elijah and Lucretia (Colvin) Kinney, b. June 29, 1807 ; d. in Lawton, Mich., 9 Feb., 1882. She d. in Lawton, Mich., 31 Dec., 1888; no issue.

They rem. from Huron Co., O., in 1840 to Michigan and settled near Benton, Barrick Co.

xi. SUSANNA⁶ [Lucina ?], b. in Marlboro, Aug. 27, 1811 ; m. Jan. 1, 1832, Dr. Charles H. Leggett of Huron, Erie Co., O.

They were both drowned while crossing the Huron river in a row-boat, May 29, 1832 ; no issue.

Children of JOEL⁵, JR., (1767) [178] (Lieut. Joel⁴, John³, Jacob², Robert¹) and Priscilla (Kimball) Adams; res. Marlboro, Vt., and Ellisburg, Jefferson Co., N. Y.

466. i. ALDEN⁶, b. in Marlboro, Aug. 21, 1796 ; m. Jan. 1, 1818. Wealthy Otis of Rutland, N. Y.; she d. in Carthage, Jefferson Co., N. Y., 28 May, 1880, age 84 years. He d. at Adams Centre, Jefferson Co , N. Y., 3 Apr., 1868, age 71 years.

ii. BETSEY⁶, b. in Marlboro, Dec. 21, 1798 ; d. 29 Aug., 1800.

iii. ELLIOT⁶, b. in Marlboro, July 24, 1801.

He res. at one time in Prairie du Chien, Wis., but rem. and d. at Crow Wing, Minn., about 1858, unm.

iv. RUEL⁶, b. in Marlboro, Dec. 26, 1803 ; d. 17 June, 1804.

467. v. BETSEY⁶, b. in Marlboro, Nov. 11, 1805 ; m. Dec. 28, 1825, Davi Heald, b. Oct. 1, 1801, d. 8 May, 1872 ; res Bellville, Jefferson Co. N. Y. She d. 14 Sept., 1881.

vi. LURA⁶, b. in Marlboro, Aug. 4, 1808 ; d. unm. at Forestville, Delaware Co., Ia., 1871.

468. vii. JOEL⁶, b. in Marlboro, Aug. 15. 1811 ; m. Eveline Adams.

He was a soldier in the war with Mexico ; returned from the war, but did not live with his wife ; it has been said he married again. He d. at Port Hope, Ont., about 186 ?.

Children of SARAH[6], (1768) [179] (Lieut. Joel[4], John[3], Jacob[2], Robert[1]) and Asa Winchester; res. Marlborough, Vt.

 i. GARDNER WINCHESTER, b. Jan. 6, 1791 ; d. in Marlboro, Vt., unm., 21 May, 1830.
 ii. CLARK WINCHESTER, b. Jan. 11, 1793 ; d. 26 Apr., 1795.
469. iii. MARTIN WINCHESTER, b. Mar. 6, 1795 ; m. Clarissa Hillard ; res. Marlborough, Vt. He d. 1856.
 iv. LUCINA WINCHESTER, b. Dec. 2, 1797 ; m. Dolphus Pratt. She d. in Marlboro, 7 Dec., 1820 ; one dau., Lucina, m. Wm. Thomas of No. Stamford, Vt.
470. v. SARAH WINCHESTER, b. Apr. 11, 1800 m. Lovell Clark. They set. in Denmark, Lewis Co., N. Y. She d. in Carthage, N. Y., 1880.
471. vi. CLARK ADAMS WINCHESTER, b. Dec. 31, 1802 ; m. (1) Mar. 22, 1831, Louisa Thayer, b. Apr. 7, 1808 ; d. Jan., 1847 ; m. (2) Aug. 31, 1847, Hannah Tucker, b. Oct. 19, 1819 ; living 1899 ; no issue. He d. in Marlborough, 12 Feb., 1888.
472. vii. LUCY WINCHESTER, b. May 12, 1805 ; m. Geo. Higley ; he d. in Marlboro. She d. in Marlboro.
 viii. ASA FRANKLIN WINCHESTER, b. Apr. 9, 1808 ; m. Clarissa Willis ; set. in New Jersey.

Seventh Generation.] OF NEWBURY, MASS. 105

Children of HENRY⁶, (1741) [180] (Robert⁵, Abraham⁴, Robert³, Sergt. Abraham², Robert¹) and Sarah (Dole) Adams; res. Newbury, Mass.

473. i. ALICE⁷, b. in Newbury, May 22, 1768 ; m. Apr. 25, 1799, Enoch Boynton, son of Enoch and Abigail (Tarring) Boynton, b. Dec. 5, 1772; d. 27 Jan., 1859. She d. 20 Dec., 1811.

ii. JUDITH⁷, b. in Newbury, Feb. 3, 1770 ; d. 3 June, 1793.

474. iii. PHEBE⁷, b. in Newbury, Sept. 2, 1772 ; m. May 7, 1795, Nathaniel Currier of Newbury ; d. 4 Oct., 1830, age 70 years. She d. 7 April, 1848, age 75 yrs. 7 mos. 5 days.

475. iv. HENRY⁷, b. in Newbury, Dec. 21, 1774 ; m. Dec. 27, 1798, Sarah Jaques Pearson ; she d. 11 Dec., 1814.
He was a carpenter in Newburyport, Mass.; d. 13 Dec., 1813, age 39 years.

v. SARAH⁷, b. in Newbury, Feb. 13, 1776 ; m. Jan. 13, 1795, Dudley Brown of Kensington, N. H.

vi. POLLY⁷, b. in Newbury, Jan. 6, 1778 ; m. Oct. 4, 1817, Ziba Merritt.

476. vii. ESTHER⁷, b. in Newbury, July 22, 1779; m. July 19, 1797, Moses Goodwin. She d. 30 Apr., 1866.

viii. JOHN⁷, b. in Newbury, Aug. 10, 1781 ; d. young.

477. ix. JOSEPH⁷, b. in Newbury, Aug. 12, 1783 ; m. (1) Dec. 14, 1807, Rachel Boynton, called "crazy Rachel"; she d. 5 Nov., 1851, age 75 years; m. (2) Feb. 21, 1852, Nancy E. Goodwin ; she d. 10 Aug., 1875, age 64 years. He d. 14 Dec., 1863, age 80 years.

Children of HENRY⁶, (1741) and Sarah (Pulsifer) Adams.

x. ANNA⁷, b. in Newbury, Sept. 7, 1787 ; d. 26 Oct., 1788.

xi. POLLY⁷, b. in Newbury, Jan. 6, 1788 ; bapt. in Ipswich, May 24, 1789.

478. xii. ABRAHAM⁷, b. in Newbury, Sept. 8, 1791 ; bapt. in Ipswich, June 3, 1792; m. Aug. 29, 1815, Dorothy Everett of New London ; she d. 12 Nov., 1862, age 57 years. He d. 25 Oct., 1863, age 72 years.

479. xiii. HANNAH⁷, b. in Newbury, Feb. 25, 1800 ; m. June 16, 1831, Ebenezer Plumer. She d. 28 Nov., 1857.

480. xiv. LYDIA S.⁷, b. in Newbury, Oct. 18, 1802 ; m. June 18, 1819, Henry Lander. She d. 18 Nov., 1881.

Children of MOLLY[6], (1750) [181] (Robert[5], Abraham[4], Robert[3], Sergt. Abraham[2], Robert[1]) and Anthony Morse, Jr.; res. Newbury, Mass.

 i. MOLLY MORSE, b. June 14, 1770; m. David Kimball of Cape Ann, Mass.
 ii. HANNAH MORSE, b. Apr. 29, 1774; m. Richard [Joseph?] Smith of Newburyport, Mass.
 iii. FANNY MORSE, b. June 20, 1777; d. soon.
 iv. FANNY MORSE, b. May 14, 1779; m. Capt. Moses Short of Boston, a master mariner.
 v. ROBERT MORSE[7], b. Mar. 14, 1781; d. 15 May, 1783.
 vi. ROBERT MORSE, b. Mar. 13, 1783; m. Apr. 20, 1806, Mary Adams, dau. of Charles and Mary (Hills) Adams.
  He set. in Boston, Mass., in 1820.
 vii. MOSES MORSE, b. June 6, 1785; d. unm. 21 Oct., 1809.
 viii. NABBY A. MORSE, b. 1787.

Children of DANIEL[6], (1756) [182] (Robert[5], Abraham[4], Robert[3], Sergt. Abraham[2], Robert[1]) and Elizabeth (Colley) Adams; res. Newbury, Mass.

482. i. LOVE[7], b. in Newbury, Apr. 12, 1777-8; m. Jan. 27, 1801, Stephen Pettengill, son of Henry and Sarah (Cheever) Pettengill. He m. 2nd, Sarah Curtis of Marblehead, and d. Feb., 1847. She d. Aug., 1813. [*]
 ii. ELIZABETH[7], b. in Newbury, Nov. 17, 1879; d. young.

Children of DANIEL[6], (1756) and Mary (Lord) Adams.

483. iii. COL. DANIEL[7], b. in Newbury, Nov. 11, 1787; m. Apr. 20, 1813' Polly Adams, dau. of Capt. Israel and Deborah (Jaques) Adams; she d. 21 Sept., 1863. He d. 16 Oct., 1866, age 79 years.
 iv. ELIZABETH[7], b. in Newbury, Jan. 7, 1791; m. Sept. 25, 1817, Col. Gibbins Adams, son of Capt. Stephen and Sarah (Adams) Adams. She d. 29 June, 1859, age 68 years.
484. v. MARY[7], b. in Newbury, Jan. 24, 1795; m. Apr. 27, 1819, Gilman Sargent; res. Portland, Me. She d. 3 Jan., 1835, and he m. again.
485. vi. JOSEPH[7], b. in Newbury, Sept. 7, 1797; d. Dec., 1798.
 vii. JOSEPH[7], b. in Newbury, Dec. 9, 1799; m. Dec. 29, 1820, Harriet Adams, dau. of Moses and Phebe (Jewett) Adams; she m. 2nd, Mar. 22, 1855, Thos. Johnson of Rowley, Mass., and d. 20 Aug, 1875. He d. 6 Apr., 1841, age 41 years.

*Henry Pettengill was a son of Stephen[4], Nathaniel[3], Matthew[2], Richard[1].

486. viii. HANNAH LORD⁷, b. in Newbury, May 15, 1807; m. Apr. 24, 1832, George J. Poor, son of Paul Poor. He was b. May 20, 1801; m. 2nd, June 10, 1852, Susan Bond Jones, and d. 4 May, 1879. She d. in Rowley, Jan., 1849. *mistake, should be Mary, wife of Dan'l (182) who died Jan. 1849.*

Children of ABRAHAM⁶, (1750) [184] (Benjamin⁵, Abraham⁴, Robert³, Sergt. Abraham², Robert¹) and Mary (Blackman) Adams; res. Boston, Mass.

    i. SUSANNA⁷, b. in Boston; m. George H. Leach; he d. in Boston, 20 May, 1880.
    ii. ABRAHAM⁷, b. in Boston.
    iii. THOMAS⁷, b. in Boston.
    iv. POLLY⁷, b. in Boston; m. William Hogg; he d. 18 May, 1878. On the 25th of May, his widow, Mary, petitioned to be appointed administratrix. There appears to have been one son, Richard Hogg.
    v. EMMA⁷, b. in Boston.
    vi. MARY⁷, b. in Boston.
    vii. SALLY CROWELL⁷, b. in Boston.

    Many efforts have been put forth to find some descendant of this family, but with no result.

Children of CALEB⁶, (1754) [185] (Benjamin⁵, Abraham⁴, Robert³, Sergt. Abraham², Robert¹) and Hannah (Blackman) Adams; res. Boston, Mass.

487. i. ISAAC⁷, b. prob. in Boston about 1788-90; m. Oct. 30, 1822, Mary Stowell of Worcester, Mass.
    He was a saddler and harness-maker, and had a shop on Ann street in Boston.
488. ii. SUSAN⁷, b. in Boston, Dec. 10, 1791; m. May 5, 1810, Benjamin Longley, b. in Littleton, Mass., May 26, 1788; d. in Boston, 23 Mar., 1832. She d. in Boston, 27 Nov., 1847.
    iii. LUCY⁷, b. in Boston; d. unm.

Children of SAMUEL⁶, (1759) [187] (Benjamin⁵, Abraham⁴, Robert³, Sergt. Abraham², Robert¹) and Catherine (Fenno) Adams; res. Boston, Mass.

    i. BENJAMIN F.⁷, b. in Newbury, Mass., May 6, 1782; m. Elizabeth Deuilis. [?]

ii. CATHERINE⁷, b. in Newbury, Nov. 7, 1783 ; d. 3 Feb., 1784.
iii. CATHERINE NOYES⁷, b. in Newbury, July 29, 1785 ; m. July 26, 1806, William Fenno.
iv. NANCY⁷, b. in Newbury, July 19, 1787 ; d. 3 Feb., 1788.
v. JOHN FENNO⁷, b. in Newbury, Feb. 22, 1789; m. June 6, 1811, Sarah Towne ; res. Boston.
vi. SAMUEL⁷, b. in Newbury, July 10, 1791 ; d. at sea.
vii. ELIZABETH⁷, b. in Newbury, Jan. 2, 1795 ; d. 2 Oct., 1795.
viii. HARRIET⁷, b. in Newbury, Dec. 16, 1796 ; m. John Motley. She d. in Mobile, Ala.

Children of ISAAC⁶, (1761) **[188]** (Benjamin⁵, Abraham⁴, Robert³, Sergt. Abraham², Robert¹) and Abigail (Blackman) Adams ; res. Boston, Mass.

  i. BENJAMIN⁷, b. in Boston, Dec. 15, 1790 ; was drowned 17 May, 1797.

489. ii. AARON⁷, b. in Boston, July 17, 1793 ; m. May 22, 1814, Hannah Prince, b. June 30, 1795 ; d 12 Nov., 1843.
   He was an editor and printer ; res. Newburyport, Mass.; d. 19 Apr., 1827.

  iii. HARRIET⁷, b. in Boston, Sept. 23, 1795 ; m. Benjamin Harrington of West Cambridge, Mass. She d. 23 June, 1836.
  iv. GEORGE⁷, b. in Boston, Dec. 14, 1797 ; d. same day.
  v. EMELINE⁷, b. in Boston, Sept. 30, 1799 ; d. 14 Dec., 1799.

490. vi. SARAH WELCH⁷, b. in Boston, Oct. 29, 1800 ; m. 1822, Wm. P. Codman, b. in Boston, 1798 ; d. in Brentwood, L. I., 1878.
   She was a wid. with her dau., in Cambridge, Mass., and furnished some of the data here given. She d. 25 Mar., 1894.

  vii. MARY⁷, b. in Boston, Sept. 6, 1803 ; d. unm. 25 Mar., 1828.
491. viii. CAROLINE KEZIA⁷, b. in Boston, Sept. 7, 1804 ; m. Thomas Blake Hall, b. 1805 ; d. in Quincy, Mass., 1876. She d. about 1890.
492. ix. BENJAMIN⁷, b. in Boston, Jan. 18, 1807 ; m. (1) July 3, 1829, Ann Belcher Leonard of Milton, Mass., b. 1808 ; d. 22 Jan., 1849, age 41 years ; m. (2) 1855, Martha Hadley of Boston, b. 1823.
   He was a book-binder; res. Boston, Mass.; d, 10 Sept., 1878.
   Benjamin⁷ made his will Aug. 20, 1878, which was probated Oct. 14, 1878. He makes bequests to his son Benjamin of Milford, and to his grandson, Charles W., son of Webster Adams ; gives his furniture in his house at No. 8 Parkman street to his wife Martha, and all his tools and machinery in his shop at No. 37 Cornhill to his son, Albert H., on condition that he pay to the widow four dollars per week during her life, otherwise the same to be sold, and a division made.

493. x. ABRAHAM DODDRIDGE[7], b. in Boston, Nov. 28, 1810; m. Mary Jane Thurston, dau. of Caleb and Mary (Gilman) Thurston, b. in Exeter, N. H., Apr. 26, 1800; d. in Townsend, Mass., 18 Mar., 1882, age 81 yrs. 10 mos. 24 days.
   He was a shoe-maker in Charlestown, Mass., and a farmer in Townsend Harbor, Mass.; d. 17 Sept., 1876, age 65 yrs. 3 mos.
xi. ELIZABETH[7], b. in Boston, May 8, 1812; m. Silas Mason of Gardner, Me. She d. 5 Oct., 1848; twin sons d. the same day.

Children of JACOB[6], (1764) [**189**] (Charles[5], Abraham[4], Robert[3], Sergt. Abraham[2], Robert[1]) and Elizabeth (Hidden) Adams; res. Newbury, Mass.

i. ELIZABETH[7], b. Nov. 26, 1793; d. 23 Sept., 1794, age 9 mos. 27 days.
ii. MARY E.[7], b. June 2, 1806; d. 10 Sept., 1806.

Children of AMOS[6], (1768) [**190**] (Charles[5], Abraham[4], Robert[3], Sergt. Abraham[2], Robert[1]) and Sally (Whitney) Adams; res. St. John, N. B.

i. MARY[7], b. Aug. 21, 1800, d. unm. 2 May, 1869.
ii. CHARLES[7], b. Mar. 9, 1802; m. (1) Nov. 24, 1839, Almira Leavitt; m. (2) Sept. 15, 1847, Mary S. Chipman. He d. 1849, age 47 years.
iii. ELIZA[7], b. Oct. 22, 1805; m. Aug. 24, 1836, Thomas Hardenbrook; no issue.
iv. JANE[7], b. Sept. 30, 1808; m. May 17, 1835, Capt. Thomas Leavitt; no issue.
v. GEORGE SMITH[7], b. Apr. 13, 1810; d. 1873.
vi. SARAH[7], b. Jan. 15, 1812; m. Apr. 24, 1834, Capt. Edward W. Higgins. She d. 1848; no issue.
vii. EMILY SOPHIA[7], b. Oct. 9, 1813; m. Sept. 3, 1849, Michael McCarthy; no issue.
viii. WILLIAM HENRY[7], b. Aug. 7, 1815; m. June 4, 1846, Julia A. Smith.
   He was a hardware merchant, and d. 14 Dec., 1864.
ix. JOHN AUGUSTUS[7], b. May 7, 1818-9; m. Aug. 29, 1862, Cecilia Rainsford; one child, who d. young.

Children of SMITH[6], (1771) [**191**] (Charles[5], Abraham[4], Robert[3], Sergt. Abraham[2], Robert[1]) and Hannah (Bray) Adams; res. Newbury, Mass.

494. i. AARON BRAY¹, b. in Newbury, Oct. 24, 1796 ; m. (1) May 14, 1837, Mrs. Betsey (Brown) Clark, wid. of Philip Clark, b. Apr. 7, 1793, d. 13 May, 1840; m. (2) June 20, 1841, Mrs. Mary M. (Dutton) Cheever, dau. of Benja. and Sarah (Currier) Dutton, b. Mar. 18, 1806 ; d. 18 May, 1892.

He was a merchant in Newburyport; d. 5 May, 1869.

495. ii. HANNAH¹, b. in Newbury, Nov. 4, 1798 ; m. June 23, 1821, Seward Lee, a sea-captain, b. Feb. 15, 1795 ; d. 22 Apr., 1871. She d. 10 July, 1854.

496. iii. MARY H.¹, b. in Newbury, Nov. 2, 1800 ; m. (1) Apr. 7, 1836, Wm. Coker, a ship carpenter, b. Dec. 28, 1794 ; d. 21 April 1851 ; m. (2) June 11, 1855, Capt. Seward Lee (2nd wife). She d. 5 Feb., 1886.

497. iv. WILLIAM B.¹, b. in Newbury, June 16, 1803 ; m. (1) June 16, 1825, Martha Morse, dau. of Merrill and Hannah (Currier) Morse, b. Dec. 29, 1805 ; d. 5 Nov., 1825 ; m. (2) Dec. 3, 1826, Ann Atkinson Stanwood, dau. of Thomas and Elizabeth (Rhodes) Stanwood, b. May 13, 1797 ; d. 7 Jan., 1879.

He was a cooper in Newburyport, Mass,. and d. 13 Dec., 1849.

498. v. CHARLES¹, b. in Newbury, Oct. 21, 1805 ; m. Nov. 26, 1826, Sarah Noyes, dau. of Wadleigh and Hannah (Savory) Noyes, b. June 16, 1803 ; d. 24 Nov., 1894.

He was a cooper, and d. in Newburyport, 15 Aug., 1877.

499. vi. ALMIRA¹, b. in Newbury, Aug. 7, 1808; m. May 15, 1837 ; Capt. Eleazer P. Short, b. Aug. 28, 1807 ; d. 7 Aug., 1870. She d. 7 Aug., 1873.

500. vii. SMITH¹, b. in Newbury, June 26, 1811 ; m. (1) Nov. 30, 1837, Eliza. Jane Hoague, dau. of Dudley and Sarah (Newton) Hoague, b. Nov. 1, 1811 ; d. 12 Nov., 1858, age 47 years ; m. (2) Nov. 7, 1859, Mrs. Emma (Currier) Post, dau. of Edmund and Emma (Gould) Currier, b. Mar. 25, 1806 ; d. 21 Oct., 1846, age 90 yrs. 6 mos.

He was a cooper in Newburyport. He d. 11 Jan., 1898, age 86 yrs. 6 mos.

Children of REBECCA⁶, (1775) [192] (Charles⁵, Abraham⁴, Robert³, Sergt. Abraham², Robert¹) and Samuel Davis ; res. Newbury, Mass.

i. AMOS A. DAVIS, b. Sept. 3, 1798 ; was a peddler ; d. unm. 27 Feb. 1838.

ii. WILLIAM K. DAVIS, b. Sept. 24, 1800; m. Dec. 15, 1840, Mrs. Ruth (Somerby) Growther, and d. 12 May, 1879.

iii. CHARLES A. DAVIS, b. Sept. 2, 1803 ; m. June 2, 1832, Mary W. Hooker.

iv. OBADIAH S. DAVIS, b. June 27, 1806 ; m. Aug. 28, 1843, Mary J. Andrews. He d. 12 April, 1857.

Seventh Generation.] OF NEWBURY, MASS.

 v. SAMUEL DAVIS, b. Sept. 20, 1809; m. Sept. 24, 1843, Ellen Humphreys. He was a rope-maker, and d. 2 April, 1864.
 vi. REBECCA K. DAVIS, b. April 22, 1812; d. unm.
 vii. BELINDA H. DAVIS, b. Jan. 30, 1815; m. March 28, 1831, Ebenezer B. Robbins, son of John and Elizabeth (Bray) Robbins. She d. 30 Sept., 1876.

Children of MARY⁶, (1778) [**193**] (Charles⁵, Abraham⁴, Robert³, Sergt. Abraham², Robert¹) and Robert Morse; res. Newburyport, Mass.

 i. MARY MORSE, b. May 26, 1807; d. 17 Feb., 1824.
 ii. ROBERT MORSE, b. May 18, 1809; d. 24 March, 1816.
 iii. MOSES MORSE, b. Oct. 6, 1810; d. 10 June, 1812.
 iv. CATHARINE DAVENPORT MORSE, b. July 27, 1812; m. May 24, 1837, Anthony Hanson of Dover. N. H.; and d. 13 Mar., 1872.
 v. MOSES MORSE, b. Mar. 2, 1815; d. 20 Jan., 1821.
 vi. ROBERT MORSE, b. Dec. 13, 1816; m. (1) Nov. 18, 1846, Abby C. Dow, b. Nov. 18, 1826, d. 16 Jan., 1862; m. (2) Dec. 23, 1868, Minerva E. Battell, b. Oct. 10, 1843, d. 22 Oct., 1869. He was a flour merchant, and d. 10 April, 1870.
 vii. CHARLES ANTHONY MORSE, b. in Boston, Oct. 15, 1822; m. Sept. 30, 1856, Mary Elizabeth Wells, dau. of John and Hannah (Wells) Wells, b. Feb. 11, 1831; res. 10 Franklin st., Cambridgeport, Mass.
He is a wire-worker of the firm of "Morss & Wythe."

Children of MARTHA⁶, (1782) [**194**] (Charles⁵, Abraham⁴, Robert³, Sergt. Abraham², Robert¹) and Edmund Smith; res. Newburyport, Mass.

 i. MARTHA SMITH, b. April 11, 1812; m. June 6, 1833, David G. Watts, a mason by trade, b. Nov. 25, 1809; d. 27 Feb., 1849. She d. 20 Feb., 1887.
 ii. MARY ANN SMITH, b. Sept. 20, 1814; m. June 1, 1842, Daniel Johnson, b. Nov. 14, 1817. She d. 24 Jan., 1880.
 iii. EDMUND SMITH, ESQ., b. Aug. 19, 1816; m, Nov. 30, 1837, Abigail S. Hoague. He d. 28 Feb., 1884, age 67 yrs. 6 mos.

Children of JOSEPH MORSE, (1745) [**195**] and Hannah Hunt; res. Brunswick, Cumberland Co., Me.

 i. JOHN MORSE, b. in Portland, Me., Jan. 23, 1773; m. May 5, 1798, Ann Lunt; res. Brunswick, Me. He d. 13 Feb., 1808.

ii. HANNAH MORSE, b. Oct. (Nov.?) 12, 1775 ; m. John Combs of Brunswick, Me. She d. 20 May, 1838.
iii. EPHRAIM MORSE, b. Nov. 10, 1777 ; m. Sarah Stanwood.
iv. ANNE B. MORSE (Nancy?), b. Oct. 23 (Nov. 8?), 1779 ; m. Abner Melcher.
v. MARTHA MORSE, b. Sept. 23, 1781 ; m. Daniel Allen ; res. Freeport, Me. She d. 23 Nov., 1847.
vi. JOSEPH B. MORSE, b. Jan. 13, 1783-4 ; m. Lucy Sylvester.
vii. ANTHONY MORSE, b. Mar. 13, 1785-6 ; d. unm. 31 July, 1807.
viii. MARY MORSE, b. April 30, (Mar?) 1787-8 ; d. 1807-8.
ix. SUSAN B. MORSE, b. July 30, 1790 ; m. Geo. Minot.
x. SARAH MORSE (twin), b. July 30, 1790 ; m. Abner Melcher ; d. 23 Nov., 1843 ; res. Illinois.
xi. BENJAMIN R. MORSE, b. May 17 1793 ; m. (1) L. Melcher ; m. (2) Clarissa (Hunt) Prescott.
xii. ELIPHALET MORSE, b. Dec. 26, 1796 ; d. young.

Children of JOHN MORSE, (1746) [**196**] and Sarah Sanders ; res. Gray, Cumberland Co., Me.

i. JOHN MORSE, JR., b. June 25, 1770 ; m. 1796, Rebecca Young. He d. 12 June, 1826.
ii. ENOCH MORSE, b. July 3, 1772 ; m. Eunice Russell ; res. Gray, Me.
iii. SARAH MORSE, b. Sept. 26, 1774 ; m. Nathaniel Russell ; res. Oxford, me.
iv. ANTHONY MORSE, b. Aug. 9, 1775. He was drowned.
v. DAVID MORSE, b. April 18, 1778 ; m. Mary Rider ; res. Gray, Me.
vi. HANNAH MORSE, b. Oct. 13, 1779 ; m. Calvin Shaw.
vii. SUSAN MORSE, b. April 28, 1781 ; m. Enoch Frost.
viii. ABIGAIL MORSE, m. Samuel Rider ; res. Portland, Me.
ix. JOSEPH MORSE, b. Mar. 21, 1787 ; m. 1810, Abigail Knight.
x. BENJAMIN MORSE, b. 1791 ; m. (1) 1819, Margaret Sherman ; m. (2) Jan. 9, 1823, Lucy Rogers.
xi. MARY MORSE, b. Aug. 1, 1793.

Children of EPHRAIM MORSE, (1770) [**197**] and Rachel Noyes ; res. Portland, Me.

i. NATHANIEL MORSE, b. Aug. 28, 1792 ; m. Elizabeth Cobb ; res. Westbrook, Me.
ii. NANCY MORSE, b. Aug. 22, 1794 ; m. Samuel Long ; res. Falmouth, Me.

- iii. STEPHEN MORSE, b. Aug. 2, 1796; m. (1) Mary Sanger; m. (2) Sarah N. Thomas.
  He was a master mariner; res. Portland, Me.
- iv. MARGARET MORSE, b. Mar. 2, 1800; m. (1) Simon Shute; m. (2) Joshua Pennell. }
- v. MARY MORSE, b. Jan. 7, 1802; m. Michael Dodd; res. Boston, Mass.
- vi. EPHRAIM MORSE, b. Nov. 13, 1804; m. Mary Gifford; res. Portland, Me.
- vii. JANE MORSE, b. Feb. 13, 1806; m. John Barbour; res. Portland, Me.
- viii. SUSAN MORSE, b. Nov. 30, 1808; m. Robert Knight; res. Falmouth, Me.
- ix. LUCY MORSE, b. Jan. 31, 1811; m. Jesse M. Hartshorn.

Children of SARAH⁵, (1777) [198] (Liphe⁵, Robert⁴, Robert³, Sergt. Abraham², Robert¹) and Moses Kent; res. Kent's Island, Newbury, Mass.
- i. CAPT. MOSES KENT, b. 1797; d. 30 May, 1828.
- ii. MARY ANN KENT, b. 1798-9; d. [15 Sept., 1831] or 9 Nov., 1828, age 30 years; m. John Pearson.
- iii. JOHN KENT, m. Caroline ——, and d. 24 Mar., 1833.
- iv. HENRY S. KENT, set. in Boston, and rem. to California.

Children of ROBERT⁶, (1787) [199] (Liphe⁵, Robert⁴, Robert³, Sergt. Abraham², Robert¹) and Hannah (Little) Adams; res. Newbury, Mass.
- i. MARY LITTLE⁷, b. in Newbury, Nov. 7, 1808; d. 22 Oct., 1809.
- 501. ii. MARY⁷, b. in Newbury, Nov. 7, 1810; m. May 5, 1831, Gideon R. Lucy. She d. 10 Feb., 1836.
- iii. LIPHE⁷, b. in Newbury, Sept. 2, 1815; d. 4 Apr., 1838.

Children of ANNA⁶, (1780) [200] (Capt. Silas⁵, Robert⁴, Robert³, Sergt. Abraham², Robert¹) and Dea. Ezra Hale; res. Newbury, Mass.
- i. ANNA HALE, b. Nov. 6, 1800; d. 7 Nov., 1801.
- ii. ANNA HALE, b. Sept. 4, 1802; m. Nov. 27, 1827, Charles Courier, a sail maker of Newburyport, Mass.; he d. 8 May, 1868. She d. 17 May, 1882.

iii. EZRA HALE, JR., b. Mar. 30, 1804; m. (1) May 5, 1829, Almira Perkins; m. (2) Apr. 30, 1839, Rebecca P. Adams, dau. of Ens. James Adams of Derry, N. H.
He set. in Rowley, Mass., and d. in 1890, age 85 years.
iv. SILAS ADAMS HALE, b. Nov. 25, 1805.
He was lost at sea, Dec. 11, 1825.
v. LUCY HALE, b. Sept. 14, 1807; d. same day.
vi. DANIEL KNIGHT HALE, b. Sept. 9, 1808; m. Apr. 29, 1838, Elizabeth Colley Pettengill, dau. of Stephen and Love (Adams) Pettengill, b. Oct. 1, 1812. He d. 6 Oct., 1870.
vii. LUCY HALE, b. Dec. 17, 1810; m. June 10, 1835, Stephen Kimball; his 1st wife. She d. 6 Jan. 1837.
viii. ADELINE HALE, b. Dec. 24, 1812; m. Sept. 27, 1836, James B. Knight. She d. about 1882.
ix. GEO. WASHINGTON HALE, b. June 10, 1815; m. Oct. 17, 1841, Anne Titcomb. He d. 2 Nov., 1891.
x. ALMIRA HALE, b. Aug. 2, 1817; m. Oct. 13, 1838, Stephen Kimball; his second wife; he d. 1 Apr., 1899. She d. 1 Apr., 1899, and both were buried the same day.
xi. CHARLES HENRY HALE, b. Apr. 1, 1820; m. May 5, 1846, Sarah Jane Adams, dau. of Sewall Adams. He d. 6 June, 1897.
xii. SARAH JANE HALE, b. May 5, 1823.
xiii. SALOME HALE, b. Jan. 16, 1827; m. Nov. 14, 1850, Wm. T. Colby. She d. Sept., 1869.

Children of LUCY⁶, (1785) [201] (Capt. Silas⁵, Robert⁴, Robert³, Sergt. Abraham², Robert¹) and Thomas Cook; res. Newburyport, Mass.

i. THOMAS COOK, JR., b. July 10, 1808; m. Sarah Colby, and d. 1869.
ii. SARAH D. COOK, d. unm., age about 74 years.
iii. SILAS COOK, b. Apr. 1, 1824; d. unm. about 1892.

Children of CHARLOTTE⁶, (1787) [202] (Capt. Silas⁵, Robert⁴, Robert³, Sergt. Abraham², Robert¹) and James Johnson; res. Newburyport, Mass.

i. JOSEPH JOHNSON, b. Nov. 25, 1808.
ii. JOSHUA JOHNSON, b. July 21, 1810.
iii. ADELINE JOHNSON, b. Jan. 13, 1814.
iv. LUCY A. JOHNSON, b. Jan. 10, 1816; d. 25 June, 1816.
v. LUCY A. JOHNSON, b. April 22, 1817.

vi. ALMIRA JOHNSON, b. Mar. 6, 1819 ; d. 9 Jan., 1892.
vii. BENJAMIN N. JOHNSON, b. Mar. 3, 1822.
viii. MARY B. JOHNSON, b. Jan. 7, 1823.
ix. PHILIP B. JOHNSON, b. Oct. 1, 1824.
x. SEWALL JOHNSON, b. April 29, 1829.
xi. JULIA MELISSA JOHNSON, b. Jan. 10, 1834.

Children of JOSHUA GRAVES, (1767) [**203**] and Mehitable Hutchinson; res. Wayne, Kennebec Co., Me.
i. REBECCA GRAVES.
ii. CHARLES GRAVES.
iii. JOSHUA GRAVES.
iv. JANE GRAVES.
v. OSGOOD GRAVES.
vi. MEHITABLE GRAVES.
vii. CLARISSA GRAVES.
viii. SEWALL GRAVES.
ix. SAMUEL H. GRAVES.

Children of SAMUEL GRAVES, (   ) [**204**] and Catherine Sutherland; res. Topsham, Me.
i. ALEXANDER GRAVES, m. Sarah Jaques of Bowdoinham, Me.; res. Topsham, Me.
ii. PATIENCE GRAVES.

Children of NATHANIEL GRAVES, (1772) [**205**] and Abigail Palmer Dingley; res. Guilford, Piscataquis Co., Me.
i. NATHANIEL GRAVES.
ii. STILLMAN GRAVES.
iii. ALFRED GRAVES.
iv. PRUDENCE GRAVES.
v. HARRIET GRAVES.
vi. MARTHA GRAVES.

Children of MOSES GRAVES, (1778) [**206**] and Martha Mallet; res. Topsham, Sagadaho Co., Me.
i. ADAMS TRUE GRAVES, b. April 21, 1804; m. Katharine Hathorn and had :
1. Cyrus Edwin, b. Sept. 19, 1837, living in Florida, unm.

2. Angelia Catharine, b. Feb. 27, 1839; m. 1857, Chas. Cook of Milton, Mass., and d. in Dorchester, Mass., 1881.
3. Bernice Mallett, b. Oct. 9, 1843 ; m. Nov. 27, 1866, Emery C. Mallett ; res. Topsham, Me.

ii. DEBORAH GRAVES, b. Sept. 18, 1807 ; m. Dec. 25, 1830, Asa Merrill Wood of Bowdoinham ; set. in Gardiner, Me., and d. 7 Aug., 1892.
iii. MOSES ADAMS GRAVES, b. June 7, 1810 ; m. Ann Sawyer of Topsham, Me.
iv. CAROLINE GRAVES, b. May 20, 1813 ; d. unm. Aug., 1876.
v. COLLAMER M. GRAVES, b. April 1, 1816 ; d. Dec., 1816.
vi. ALFRED COLLAMER GRAVES, b. Mar. 29, 1818 ; m. June 17, 1856, Susan B. Jack; res. Topsham, Me. Children were:
1. Edgar Henry, b. Dec. 10, 1858; d. 22 Jan., 1879.
2. Albert Moses, b. Dec. 2, 1860 ; m. Maria Fairbox.
3. Cora Estelle, b. Aug. 18, 1864 ; d. 23 Dec., 1884.
4. Alfred C., d. Feb., 1884.
vii. JOSEPH WM. GRAVES, b. Sept. 11, 1820; m. Ann C. Berry of Topsham, Me., and has one son, Frank L., in Boston.
viii. DR. STOCKBRIDGE P. GRAVES, b. April 6, 1826 ; m. Mar. 27, 1854, F. Ellen Graves, dau. of David Graves of Bowdoinham, Me.; res. Saco, Me. Children :
1. Martha Ella, b. Nov. 9, 1855 ; m. Chas. Nickerson ; res. Garden City, Minn.
2. Dr. Roscoe S., b. Nov. 5, 1858; m. (1) Kate Tarbox ; m. (2) Maud Andrews.
3. Fred Payne, b. Jan. 25, 1866.

Children of JOSEPH⁶, ( ) [207] (Capt. Joshua⁵, John⁴, Robert³, Sergt. Abraham², Robert¹) and Sarah (Lewis) Adams; res. Portland, Cumberland Co., Me.

i. SUSAN⁷, b. in Falmouth, 1800 ; d. in Gorham, Me., 13 Mar., 1855, aged 55 years.
ii. MARY⁷, b. 1801 ; d. unm. in Portland, 23 Dec., 1877, age 76 years.

Children of JAMES⁶, (1765) [208] (Moses⁵, John⁴, Robert³, Sergt. Abraham², Robert¹) and Hannah (Weymonth) Adams; res. Falmouth, Me.

Seventh Generation.] OF NEWBURY, MASS.

502. i. MOSES[7], b. in Falmouth, April 17, 1805 ; m. (1) Susan Noyes, dau. of Samuel, Jr. and Lydia (Barton) Noyes, and granddau. of Capt. Samuel and Mary (Merrill) Noyes ; m. (2) in Falmouth, Hannah Titcomb, dau. of Nathan and Susan Titcomb of N. Yarmouth, Me., b. in Falmouth, 1798 ; d. in Portland, 13 April, 1874, age 75 years. He d. in Portland, Me., 17 April, 1867.
503. ii. MARY[7], b. in Falmouth ; m. Mar. 11, 1832, at Portland, Cotton Murray of Cumberland, Me. ; res. Cumberland, Me.
504. iii. HARRIET A.[7], b. in Falmouth ; m. June 24, 1832, at Portland, Abel Grover, b. 1808 ; d. in Deering, Me., 28 April, 1880, age 72 years ; res. Portland, Me. He d. 24 June, 1882.

Children of ISRAEL[6], ( ) [209] (Moses[5], John[4], Robert[3], Sergt. Abraham[2], Robert[1]) and Elizabeth (Swett) Adams ; res. Falmouth, Cumberland Co., Me.

505. i. JOHN[7], b. in Falmouth, May 25, 1794 ; m. (1) Apr., 1830, Mary Noyes, b. in Falmouth, 1808 ; d. in Portland, Me., Dec., 1836 ; m. (2) May 6, 1838, Mrs. Charlotte (Blanchard) Pratt, wid. of Asa Pratt, b. on Long Island, Portland, Aug. 25, 1810 ; d. in Elmira, Ill., 28 Nov., 1809 ; res. Falmouth, Me. He d. in Elmira, Ill., 20 Jan., 1879-80.
      ii. BENJAMIN[7], b. in Falmouth ; d. unm. in Freeport, Me.
506. iii. HANNAH SWETT[7], b. in Falmouth, June 16, 1799 ; m. Nov. 2, 1819, Tristam Gilman Prince, son of Thomas and Hannah (Prince) Prince of No. Yarmouth, Me., b. Aug. 13, 1792. She d. 19 Feb., 1875.
      iv. MARY PETTENGILL[7], b. in Falmouth ; m. George Hall of Falmouth, Me. ; no issue.
507. v. LOUISA SEWALL[7], b. in Falmouth, 1807 ; m. July 19, 1835, Daniel Carr of Portland, Me. She d. in Portland, 13 Mar., 1848, age 41 years.
      vi. ARETHUSA[7], b. in Falmouth ; d. unm.
      vii. EUNICE[7], b. in Falmouth ; d. young.
      viii. BRADLEY[7]. He was killed in an accident on the G. T. R. R. in 1874, aged about 60 years ; unm.

Children of ISAAC[6], (1774) [210] (Moses[5], John[4], Robert[3], Sergt. Abraham[2], Robert[1]) and Priscilla (Skilling) Adams ; res. Falmouth, Cumberland Co., Me.

      i. RUTH NOYES[7], b. in Falmouth, Oct. 7, 1809 ; m. Mar. 7, 1854, at Portland, Charles A. Bradley, son of Parson Caleb and Sarah (Crocker) Bradley, b. 1813 ; d. in Deering, Me., 28 May, 1895, age 82 yrs. 5 mos. ; res. Westbrook, Cumberland Co., Me. He d. in Deering, Me., about 1875 ; no issue.

	ii.	MARY SUSAN¹, b. in Falmouth, Apr. 27, 1812. This record was given in the records from Portland, but her dau. reports that she was b. in 1828.
	iii.	ISAAC DEERING¹, b. in Falmouth, Mar. 17, 1815; d. in Falmouth, 11 Mar., 1817.
508.	iv.	DOROTHY MERRILL¹, b. in Falmouth, May 10, 1817; m. Mar. 30, 1841, Sewall B. Dunham of Falmouth. She d. in Falmouth, 2 July, 1883, age 64 years.
	v.	LUCY ANN SKILLING¹, b. in Falmouth, July 29, 1819; m. Dec. 11 [16?], 1858, at Falmouth, Nathaniel Atkins, Jr., of Westbrook, Me., b. 1814; d. in Deering, Me., 1 Apr., 1885, age 71 years; no issue; res. Morrill's Corner, Me.
509.	vi.	BENJAMIN WHITING¹, b. in Falmouth, Dec. 2, 1824; m. Dec. 28, 1850, at Falmouth, Sarah Barton Colley, dau. of Joseph and Ann (Noyes) Colley, b. in Falmouth, Nov. 23, 1830; d. in Cumberland, Me., 11 June, 1881; age 56 yrs. 7 mos. He is living, 1900, at Cumberland Junction, Me.
	vii.	EDWIN ROBERT¹, b. in Falmouth, Mar. 29, 1827; d. in Falmouth, 4 July, 1880, age 53 years; unm.
510.	viii.	MARY SUSAN¹, b. in Falmouth, Apr. 27, 1828; m. Nov. 27, 1846, Robert Noyes, son of James Noyes, b. in Falmouth, Jan. 8, 1799; d. 7 Dec., 1869. She d. 27 Nov., 1898, age 70 years.
	ix.	BRADLEY JEWETT¹, b. in Falmouth, July 17, 1830; m. Apr., 1865, at Bradley's Corner, Westbrook, Me., Sarah Pettengill Dunbar, dau. of Peter and Hannah (Jackson) Dunbar, b. in Falmouth, Feb. 16, 1836; no issue. Both are living, 1900, in Falmouth.
	x.	ANGELINA KIMBALL¹, b. in Falmouth, Nov. 15, 1832; d. in Falmouth, unm., 13 Sept., 1858.

Children of MOSES⁴, JR., (1776) [211] (Moses⁵, John⁴, Robert³, Sergt. Abraham², Robert¹) and Sarah (Skilling) Adams; res. Falmouth, Me.

511.	i.	SILAS MERRILL¹, b. in Falmouth, Apr. 1809; m. [pub. at Portland, Apr. 5, 1834–5] Olive Elizabeth Moulton, dau. of Elias and Mary (Skilling) Moulton, b. in Scarboro, Me., Sept. 24, 1812; d. in Deering, Me., 29 Sept., 1888, age 76 years. He was a merchant in Portland, Me., 1851–55, and in Boston, Mass., 1757; retired to a farm in Deering, Me.
512.	ii.	MOSES WOODMAN¹, b. in Falmouth, Dec. 21, 1811; m. at Portland, Aug. 29, 1835, Frances Emeline Cutter, b. in Medford, Mass., May 22, 1811; d. in Munson, Ill., 17 Aug., 1867; res. Munson, La Salle Co., Ill. He d. in Chicago, 4 Feb., 1900.

513. iii. MARTHA PREBLE[7], b. in Falmouth, June 4, 1815; m. Dec. 28, 1841, Samuel Fabyan Haggett, son of Samuel F. and Sally (Skilling) Haggett, b. in Portland in 1818; d. in Portland, 14 Sept., 1885, age 67 years. She d. in Portland, 20 Aug., 1894, age 79 yrs. 2 mos. 16 days.

514. iv. MARY ANN D.[7], b. in Falmouth, Feb. 14, 1818; m. in Portland, Aug. 27, 1837, Capt. Wm. W. Parker, son of Wm. Parker of Worcester, Mass. He was a sea captain, b. Feb. 14, 1813; d. at Amboy, China, 13 Dec., 1862. She d. in E. Boston, Mass., 4 Oct., 1880.

Children of JOSHUA[6], (1766–7) [212] (Benjamin[5], John[4], Robert[3], Sergt. Abraham[2], Robert[1]) and Sarah (Plumer) Adams; res. Wales, Androscoggin Co., Me.

515. i. BENJAMIN[7], b. in Limington, Me., Apr. 8, 1793; m. 1814, Margaret Clark. He d. 11 March, 1843.

516. ii. AARON[7], b. in Limington, Jan. 9, 1795; m. (1) Jan. 16, 1825, Hannah Phillips, b. Aug. 14, 1804; d. 16 Sept., 1830; m. (2) May 10, 1832, Eliza Jove, dau. of Elijah and Mary (Herrick) Jove, b. Nov. 30, 1804; d. 13 May, 1877.
He was a resident of Monmouth, Me., for many years; d. Mar., 1871.

517. iii. CHARLES M.[7], b. in Wales, Me., Dec. 9, 1796; m. 1820, Hannah McDonald; res. Dixmont, Penobscot Co., Me.

iv. DAVID[7], b. in Wales, May 11, 1799; d. 11 July, 1808.

518. v. JOSHUA[7], JR., b. in Wales, Apr. 16, 1801; m. (1) at Farmington, Me., Oct. 13, 1825, Abigail Frost Mosher; she d. 16 Dec., 1857; m. (2) 1861, Mary Jane Pierson; she d. in Wilton, Me., 1885.
He was a tanner by trade, and later a manufacturer; prominent in reform and education, and in the Congregational church. He d. in Wilton, Me., 19 Dec., 1881-2.

519. vi. MIRIAM W.[7], b. in Wales, June 1, 1803; m. Dec. 3, 1828, James F Smith, son of Nath'l and Mary (Parsons) Smith, b. Apr. 6, 1796; d. 6 Apr., 1843; res. Monmouth, Me. She d. in Pembroke, N. H., 20 June, 1886.

520. vii. LYDIA[7], b. in Wales, Sept. 29, 1806; m. Dec. 25, 1827, James Owen, son of Hugh and Mary (McFarland) Owen, b. in Lisbon, Me. Sept. 25, 1804; d. 4 Oct., 1869. She d. in Fairfield, Me., 1 Apr., 1886.

521. viii. JACOB[7], b. in Wales, April 3, 1808; m. at Bridgewater, Me., Mar. 31, 1831, Eliza Bridges of Bridgton, Me. He d. in Wales, 1 Sept., 1838.

522. ix. SARAH[7], b. in Wales, Apr. 18, 1810; m. 1837, Cyrus K. Foss. She d. in Washington, D. C., 1885.

523. x. DAVID P.[7], b. in Wales, Apr. 25, 1812; m. 1833, Adeline Lothrop. He d. in Wales, 13 Dec., 1835, and the widow and children rem. to Wisconsin and died there.
  xi. JANE G.[7], b. in Wales, Oct. 10, 1815; d. 28 July, 1818.

Children of SAMUEL[6], (1769) [213] (Benjamin[5], John[4], Robert[3], Sergt. Abraham[2], Robert[1]) and Mary (Allen) Adams; res. Falmouth, Me.

  i. ROBERT[7], b. in Limington; m. Nov. 18, 1792.
      He was a mariner, and unm.; was lost on the privateer Dash, 21 Jan. 1815.
524. ii. ISAAC[7], b. in Limington, Nov. 23-8, 1794; m. (1) Sarah Smith, dau. of Hon. John Smith of Lewiston, b. 1802; d. 27 Jan., 1846; m. (2) Jan. 10, 1847, at Portland, Elvira Allen. He d. in Gray, Me.; 24 Aug., 1872 [Sept., 1871?]
  iii. DAVID[7], b. Jan. 4. 1797; d. 2 Nov., 1800.
525. iv. KATHERINE JANE[7], b. in Gray, Me., July 9, 1799; m. Dec. 2, 1819, Joseph Allen, b. Feb. 24, 1798; d. 25 Sept., 1854; res. Gray, Me. She d. 3 Aug., 1876.
526. v. ABIGAIL[7], b. in Gray, July 14, 1802; m. John Hamilton. She d. in Garland, Me.
527. vi. SILAS HALL[7], b. in Gray, Apr. 28, 1804; m. May 13, 1832, Hannah Smith, dau. of Hon. John and Sarah (Staples) Smith, b. Oct. 7, 1805; d. in Worcester, Mass., 22 Dec., 1899, age 94 years. He d. in Worcester, 9 Sept., 1880.
528. vii. SAMUEL[7], JR., b. in Gray, Feb. 7, 1807; m. Eliza Black of Falmouth. He d. in Falmouth, 3 May, 1877.
529. viii. ISAIAH[7], b. in Gray, Nov. 20, 1811; m. July 22, 1841, at New Gloucester, Me., Sarah J. Dwinall, dau. of Aaron and Celia (Cushman) Dwinall, b. in Lisbon, Me., June 23, 1819; she d. in Merrimac, Mass., 12 Mar., 1889; res. Gray, Me. He d. 2 July, 1855.

Children of CAPT. JACOB[6], (1772) [214] (Benjamin[5], John[4], Robert[3], Sergt. Abraham[2], Robert[1]) and Dorcas (Davis) Adams; res. Portland, Me.

530. i. SALLY[7], b. in Portland, Jan. 18, 1795; m. June 17, 1818, Matthew Cobb, son of Isaac Cobb, b. in Windham, Me., June 4, 1796; d. in Portland, 6 Mar., 1865. She d. in Portland, 27 Feb., 1870.
531. ii. MIRIAM[7], b. in Portland; m. June 13, 1816, Nathaniel Roberts, b. 1796; d. in Portland, 17 Aug., 1869. She d. in Portland, 29 Oct., 1859.

    iii. WILLIAM⁷, b. in Portland.
    iv. GEORGE⁷, b. in Portland.
    v. SON⁷, b. in Portland.
        The three latter were brought up by their uncle, Benja. W. Adams, at Windham, Me. They all went to sea and d. young.

Child of BENJAMIN WATSON⁶, (1778) [215] (Benjamin⁵, John⁴, Robert³, Sergt. Abraham², Robert¹) and Elizabeth (Varney) Adams; res. Windham, Cumberland Co., Me.

532.   i. JOHN WATSON⁷, b. in Windham, Aug. 24, 1806 ; m. Nov. 11, 1827, Lydia Simpson Morrison; she d. 16 July, 1869. He d. in Buckfield, Me., 17 Jan., 1892 ; cabinet-maker; res. Kent's Hill and Monmouth, Me.

Children of JACOB⁶, (1761) [216] (Stephen⁵, William⁴, Capt. Abraham³, Sergt. Abraham², Robert¹) and Lydia (Hall) Adams; res. Hancock, Mass.

    i. SUSAN AMELIA⁷, b. in Hancock, Sept. 19, 1792 ; m. —— Forbes; res. Broadalbin, Fulton Co., N. Y.; rem. to Virginia.
533.   ii. JOHN HALL⁷, b. in Hancock, Feb. 10, 1796 ; m, Jan. 1, 1830, Abbey Everts, dau. of Eli and Susan (Merriam) Everts, b. in Richmond, Mass., Oct. 7, 1799 ; d. in New Lebanon, N. Y., 22 Nov., 1884. He set. in New Lebanon, Columbia Co., N. Y., d. 17 Nov., 1884.
        He was a millwright and machinist, and a freethinker.
    iii. HANNAH⁷, b. in Hancock, 1798; d. unm. among the Shakers.
    iv. HENRY⁷, b. in Hancock, 1801 ; d. among the Shakers.
    v. GEORGE⁷, b. in Hancock, 1804; d. among the Shakers.

Children of DAVID⁶, (1772) [217] (Stephen⁵, William⁴, Capt. Abraham³, Sergt. Abraham², Robert¹) and Thankful (Miller) Adams; res. Orange, Vt.

534.   i. STEPHEN⁷, b. in Orange, Oct. 4, 1807 ; m. Feb., 1837, Mrs. Nancy (Livermore) Rockwood, dau. of Salem and Anna Livermore, and wid. of Moses Rockwood of Grafton, Vt., b. Oct. 13, 1800 ; d. 27 Dec., 1875. He d. in Paxton, Mass., 4 Nov., 1846.

535. ii. DAVID⁷, b. in Orange, Oct. 28, 1809 ; m. Laura Clark of Barre, Vt. He d. in Barre, Vt., spring of 1847, and his widow rem. to Leicester, Mass., where she m. 2nd Nelson Hare, and 3d Eli Rigglesworth.

Children of DAVID⁶, (1772) and Lovina (George) Adams.

536. iii. MOSES⁷, b. in Orange, Dec. 14, 1814 ; m. Dec. 14, 1841, Emiline King, dau. of George King, b. June, 1821. He d. in Dakota City, Ia., 1893.
iv. EUNICE⁷, b. in Orange ; d. 30 Aug., 1816.
537. v. SUSANNA⁷, b. in Orange, October 30, 1816 ; m. Sept. 30, 1846, Henry Graff; he d. 17 Aug., 1889. She d. in Leicester, 15 May, 1882.
vi. MARIA⁷, b. in Orange, Oct. 16, 1818 ; d. 30 May, 1825.
538. vii. JOHN Q.⁷, b. in Orange, Oct. 16, 1820 ; m. Mar. 22, 1847, Eliza J. Wood, dau. of Alvin and Betsey (Prentiss) Wood of Plainfield, N. H.; she m. 2nd 1894, Samuel J. Darling of Groton, Vt. He set. in Groton, Vt., in 1852 ; rem. 1878 to Rutland, Ia., and d. there 26 May, 1887.
viii. SAMUEL⁷, b. in Orange, Mar. 1, 1823.
Reported as blind, married and divorced ; res. Eden, Vt.
ix. BETSEY⁷, b. in Orange, Dec. 18, 1825 ; d. young.
539. x. JUDITH⁷, b. in Orange, Oct. 16, 1828 ; m. May 22, 1847, Frank G. Lufkin, son of Isaac and Lucy Lufkin, b. in Royalston, Mass.; he rem. to Groton, Mass., and m. 2d time. She d. in Worcester, Mass.

Children of ISRAEL⁶, (1776) [218] (Stephen⁵, William⁴, Capt. Abraham³, Sergt. Abraham², Robert¹) and Betsey (Sargent) Adams; res. Henniker, N. H. and New Orleans, La.

540. i. ISRAEL⁷, b. in Henniker, 1815 ; m. Mar. 3, 1837, Maggie McDonald; res. New Orleans, La.
541. ii. JOHN⁷, b. in Henniker, 1817 ; m. at New Orleans, Mary Jones.

Children of SUSANNA⁶, (1779) [219] (Stephen⁵, William⁴, Capt. Abraham³, Sergt. Abraham², Robert¹) and Barzillai Hayward; res. Grantham, N. H.

i. ALBERT HAYWARD, b. in Grantham, 1807.
He settled in Troy, N. Y., in 1834, where he engaged in the hardware business, and died 25 Feb., 1892.
ii. AZRA HAYWARD, b. in Grantham, 1809. He married and had several children ; set. in Akron, O., and d. there 1842.

MARY ADAMS WILSON.

542. iii. SUSAN HAYWARD, b. in Grantham, Dec. 20, 1814 ; m. 1832-4, Nathaniel T. Cofran ; set. in Goshen, N. H.; he d. in Goshen, 12 Nov., 1877, age 70 years. She d. in Newport, N. H., 1892.

Children of ENOCH⁶, (1783) [220] (Stephen⁵, William⁴, Capt. Abraham³, Sergt. Abraham², Robert¹) and Eunice (Whidden) Adams; res. Sangerfield and Amestown, Me.

543. i. HANNAH PARSONS⁷, b. in Sangerfield, July 6, 1814; m. Nov. 3, 1836, Benjamin Lane ; he d. 24 Jan., 1884 ; res. E. Sangerville, Me. She d. 25 Jan., 1896.
544. ii. SUSANNA⁷, b. in Sangerfield, June 1, 1816 ; m Nov. 17, 1839, Enos G. Flanders ; res. E. Sangerfield, Me. She d. 3 Mar., 1897.
      iii. JOHN⁷, b. in Sangerfield, July 7, 1818 ; d. 28 Sept., 1821.
      iv. ELIZABETH⁷, b. in Sangerfield, June 7, 1821 ; m. Nov. 14, 1850, Dr. J. G. Springall of England. She d. 17 Sept., 1852 ; no issue.
      v. JULIA⁷, b. in Sangerfield, Dec. 21, 1823 ; d. 29 Mar., 1846.

Child of KATHERINE⁶, (1764-6) [221] (Capt. Benjamin⁵, William⁴, Capt. Abraham³, Sergt. Abraham², Robert¹) and Rev. Samuel Wheeler; res. Washington, Washington Co., Pa.

545. i. REV. CHARLES WHEELER, D. D., L. L. D., b. April 8, 1784 ; m. Mar. 12, 1813, Charity Anna Nelson, dau. of Samuel and Anna Nelson ; she was b. in Massachusetts, Jan. 1, 1791; d. in Pruntytown, W. Va., 23 Mar., 1865.

He was ordained at Washington, Pa., Oct. 15, 1814, and settled there in the Baptist ministry, remaining for twenty-four years. He removed to Pruntytown, W. Va., in 1840, and there founded the Baptist church, and also Rector College, of which he became president. He died in Pruntytown, 11 Jan., 1851, in his 67th year, much beloved and tenderly remembered by all his students.

Children of DR. SAMUEL⁶, (1767) [222] Capt. Benjamin⁵, William⁴, Capt. Abraham³, Sergt. Abraham², Robert¹) and Elizabeth (Plumer) Adams; res. Beaver Falls, Beaver Co., Pa.

546. i. MARY⁷, b. in Bradford, Mass., Dec. 30, 1785 ; m. about 1806, James Wilson, a merchant of Beaver, Pa.; he d. 6 April, 1857.

He was son of Robert Wilson of Galgoon Park, b. in County Antrim, near Belfast, Ire., in 1775, and settled in Beaver, Pa., in 1796.

She was characterized by a strong mind, and an active poetic talent; numerous specimens of her composition are preserved. She was a devoted adherent of the M. E. Church, removing in 1831 to Weston, Va. (now W. Va.) She d. there 2 Dec., 1880, greatly beloved.

547. ii. DR. MILO[7], b. in Westmoreland Co., Pa., Jan. 31, 1790-1; m. (1) 1818, Maria Johnson, who d. in April, 1823; m. (2) July 15, 1826, Cynthia B. Darragh, dau. of Robert and Deborah Darragh of Beaver, b. Feb. 24, 1807; d. in Beaver, 25 Oct., 1895.

He was at one time sheriff of Beaver Co., Pa. He studied medicine with Dr. Philip Mowry of Pittsburg; res. Beaver, Pa., d. 18 Aug., 1846.

548. iii. SOPHRONIA[7], b. in Alleghany Co., Pa., Oct. 13, 1791-2; m. May 10, 1825, John T. Miller; he d. July, 1866. They removed to Ohio, 1857. She d. in Springfield, O., 26 Oct., 1859.

iv. CLARINDA[7], b. in Alleghany Co., May 27, 1795; m. Jonathan Beatty.

They removed to Indiana, where she died soon after her marriage, 30 Nov., 1818, leaving a child, Washington Beatty, who grew to manhood and disappeared.

v. JULIETTE[7], b. in Alleghany Co., April 7, 1797.

She was a teacher in Uniontown, Pa., d. unm. 8 Sept., 1829.

vi. MILTON B.[7], b. in Alleghany Co., Aug. 3, 1799.

He was owner of the land on which the city of Jackson, Mich., is built; d. in Rochester, Pa., unm. 20 Nov., 1871.

vii. DR. SOCRATES[7], b. in Beaver, Pa., Mar. 24, 1801; m. Nancy Ingraham. He removed to Maumee, O., and d. soon after at Beardstown, Ill., 2 Aug., 1831; she d. 4 Aug., 1831, and both were buried the same day in one grave.

549. viii. ELVIRA W.[7], b. in Beaver, April, 1804; m. July 9, 1822. Hon. John Dickey, son of Robert Dickey, b. June 23, 1794.

He was appointed U. S. Marshal 1852-3, in the district of western Pennsylvania; was sheriff of his county, State senator, and member of Congress for two terms. He was a man of great influence as a Democratic leader; d. in Sharon, Pa., 14 Mar., 1853; res. Sharon, Mercer Co., Pa. She d. 22 Feb., 1873.

550. ix. ELIZABETH P.[7], b. in Beaver, Feb. 18, 1807; m. Jan. 22, 1828, Ele W. Beall, b. in Frederick Co., Va., Feb. 9, 1802; res. Beaver, Pa. She d. 29 Oct., 1881.

x. A DAUGHTER, b. 1808; d. young.

551. xi. SAMUEL PLUMER[7], b. in Beaver, April 16, 1812; m. Mar. 21, 1837, Ellen B. Barker, dau. of Abner Barker of Pittsburg, Pa. She was living 1894.

He built mills at Beaver Falls; enlisted in 1861 and served in an Ohio regiment; d. at Salem, O., 31 Aug., 1865, buried in New Brighton, Pa.

Seventh Generation.] OF NEWBURY, MASS. 125

Children of PATTY⁶, (1770) [223] (Capt. Benjamin⁵, William⁴, Capt. Abraham³, Sergt. Abraham², Robert¹) and Samuel Plumer; res. Franklin, Venango Co., Pa.

    i. WALKER PLUMER, b. in Alleghany Co., Pa., Nov. 24, 1796; d. in Franklin, unm. 1859.

552.   ii. MARY HARRIMAN PLUMER, b. in Jackson township, Venango Co., Pa., Jan. 20, 1799; m. Jan. 13, 1818, John McCalmont, son of John McCalmont, b. in Armagh Co., Ire., Jan. 11, 1750; came to America 1766, and served in the Continental Army through the Revolution. She d. in Franklin, Pa., 3 Sept., 1848.

    iii. HON. ARNOLD PLUMER, b. in Venango Co., June 5, 1801; m. Feb. 6, 1827, Margaret McClellan.

        He was elected a Member of Congress in 1830 and 1840; was twice appointed U. S. Marshal for the western district of Pennsylvania, and became the treasurer of the State in 1848; d. in Franklin, 28 April, 1869.

    iv. HON. BENJAMIN ADAMS PLUMER, b. in Venango Co., Sept. 24, 1803; m. May 8, 1831, Eliza Power, dau. of George Power, the first white settler of Franklin.

        He was treasurer of his county, 1836-8, and postmaster at Franklin during the same time. He was appointed by the Governor Associate Judge of the court of Venango Co., in 1843, re-appointed in 1848, and elected by the people in 1851; continuing in the office until his death. He was a colonel of the militia, and an enterprising and prominent merchant in Franklin; d. 22 Mar., 1856.

    v. SAMUEL F. PLUMER, b. in Venango Co., July 16, 1806; m. July 23, 1840, Sarah Power. He d. in Franklin, Pa., 2 Dec., 1861, greatly respected.

    vi. PATTY ADAMS PLUMER, b. in Venango Co., Mar. 19, 1809; m. Feb. 21, 1839, Prof. George W. Clarke of Alleghany College, Meadville, Pa. She d. at Akron, O., 28 May, 1859.

    vii. HANNAH W. PLUMER, b. in Alleghany Co., May 21, 1811; m. Sept. 1, 1831, Rev. John Robinson. She d. at the residence of her only son in Staten Island, N. Y., 16 Dec., 1886.

Children of BENJAMIN⁶, (1773) [224] (Capt. Benjamin⁵, Abraham⁴, Capt. Abraham³, Sergt. Abraham², Robert¹) and Lois (Perley) Adams; res. Georgetown, formerly New Rowley, Mass.

553.   i. ABRAHAM⁷, b. in New Rowley, April 25, 1800; m. [pub. Dec. 6, 1834] Ruth Ann Lofty; she d. in Cambridge, Mass., 29 Dec., 1896, age 83 yrs. 4 mos. 25 days. He was drowned 8 Aug., 1849.

554.   ii. LOUISA⁷, b. in New Rowley, Sept. 27, 1801; m. Nov. 26, 1823, Col. John Kimball, son of Benjamin and Mary (Coffin) Kimball of Rowley, b. Feb. 11, 1797; d. 4 Dec., 1857; res. Georgetown. She d. 29 Nov., 1891.

iii. HETTY PERLEY⁷, b. in New Rowley, Aug. 5, 1804 ; m. April 8, 1829, John A. Lovering ; he d. 4 July, 1881. She d. 12 Mar., 1830 ; no issue.

555. iv. BENJAMIN PERLEY⁷, b. in New Rowley, Sept. 5, 1806 ; m. (1) Mary Ann Cummings ; had a dau. Catherine C., who d.; m. (2) June, 1841, Abby Leach Stimson, b. 1807 ; d. 1872.
He was a merchant in Topsfield, Mass., was a member of the Mass. Legislature, 1853 ; d. 10 July, 1875.

556. v. CHARLES HENRY⁷, b. in New Rowley, May 17, 1809 ; m. May 27, 1833, Eliza Moore of Topsfield, who d. 23 May, 1891.
He set. in Georgetown ; rem. 1852 to Danvers, Mass. ; was deputy sheriff. He d. 1 June, 1877.

vi. SAMUEL⁷, b. in New Rowley, June 17, 1811 ; m. Dec. 25, 1848, Elizabeth Ann Gould ; no issue.
He was a merchant ; res. Topsfield, Mass.

557. vii. GEORGE WASHINGTON⁷, b. in New Rowley, Feb. 8, 1815, or Jan. 26, 1816 ; m. Mar. 11, 1855, Sarah J. Perley.
He is described as "courtly, polite, urbane"; res. So. Georgetown, Mass. He d. 3 Jan., 1897.

558. viii. SARAH SPOFFORD⁷, b. in New Rowley, Feb. 11, 1821 ; m. Oct. 22, 1846, Chas. S. Piper of Wolfboro, N. H. ; he d. 25 Feb., 1891. She d. 25 Feb., 1891 ; res. Somerville, Mass.

Children of COL. SAMUEL⁶, (1779) [**225**] (Elder David⁵, Samuel⁴, Capt. Abraham³, Sergt. Abraham², Robert¹) and Sarah (Fitz) Adams ; res. Derry, N. H.

i. MARY WOODMAN⁷, b. in Derry, Oct. 23, 1817 ; d. 9 Nov., 1818.

559. ii. CAROLINE SAWYER⁷, b. in Derry, Aug. 25, 1819 ; m. (1) Mar. 9, 1838, Albert S. Nesmith of New York ; m. (2) 1875, Oliver Perkins of Wakefield, Mass. She d. Aug., 1884.

560. iii. LOUISA⁷, b. in Derry, Feb. 17, 1822 ; m. July 7, 1847, Rev. Charles S. Porter of Boston. She d. 7 July, 1879.

561. iv. GEORGE FITZ⁷, b. in Derry, June 29, 1824 ; m. Jan. 29, 1846, Elizabeth W. Whitney of Nashua, N. H. ; res. Derry, N. H.

Children of HANNAH⁶, (1788) [**226**] (Elder David⁵, Samuel⁴, Capt. Abraham³, Sergt. Abraham², Robert¹) and William Parker ; res. Goffstown, N. H.

i. HANNAH A. PARKER, b. in Goffstown ; d. 1896.

ii. JOHN M. PARKER, b. in Goffstown ; res. Goffstown.

iii. DAVID A. PARKER, b. in Goffstown ; d. 1895.

Children of BETSEY⁶, (1792) [**227**] (Elder David⁵, Samuel⁴, Capt. Abraham³, Sergt. Abraham², Robert¹) and Charles Redfield; res. Adrian, Mich.

- i. MARY ANNE REDFIELD, b. May 1, 1815; m. Sept. 28, 1835, Wm. E. Kimball. She d. 21 Oct., 1837.
- ii. CHARLES REDFIELD, JR., b. Jan. 15, 1817; m. Aug. 10, 1845, Sarah A. H. Gaylord; res. Adrian, Mich.
- iii. SARAH ELIZABETH REDFIELD, b. Jan. 1, 1820; m. Nov. 22, 1841, Wm. E. Kimball (2nd wife); res. Adrian, Mich. She d. 1898.
- iv. JANE LOUISA REDFIELD, b. Dec. 2, 1825; m. Mar., 1850, Nelson M. Howard; res. Toledo, O.
- v. SUSAN P. REDFIELD, b. Dec. 21, 1827; m. Apr. 17, 1847, W. Huntington Smith; res. Adrian, Mich.

Children of SALLY⁶, (1795) [**228**] (Elder David⁵, Samuel⁴, Capt. Abraham³, Sergt. Abraham², Robert¹) and Hon. David Steele: res. Goffstown, N. H.

- i. MARY STEELE, m. James English.
- ii. MARTHA STEELE.
- iii. JAMES STEELE; res. Chicago, Ill.

Child of COL. GIBBINS⁶, (1787) [**229**] (Capt. Stephen⁵, Samuel⁴, Capt. Abraham³, Sergt. Abraham², Robert¹) and Elizabeth (Adams) Adams; res. Newbury-Byfield, Mass.

562. i. GEORGE WILLIAM⁷, b. in Newbury, April 20, 1818; m. Nov. 14, 1848, Mary Tyler Thurlow, dau. of William and Mary (Coker) Thurlow, b. Feb. 13, 1822, living 1900. He d. in Newbury-Byfield, Mass., 27 Jan., 1859.

Children of STEPHEN⁶, (1792) [**230**] (Capt. Stephen⁵, Samuel⁴, Capt. Abraham³, Sergt. Abraham², Robert¹) and Mary Ann (Longfellow) Adams; res. Newbury-Byfield, Mass.

563. i. ADELINE⁷, b. in Newbury, Aug. 27, 1823; m. (1) Sept. 22, 1852, Benjamin Huse; he d. 5 Feb., 1853; m (2) June 1, 1857, Isaac W. Wheelright; he d. 14 July, 1895. She d. in Newbury-Byfield, 20 Jan., 1896.

128 ROBERT ADAMS [Seventh Generation.

564. ii. ALBERT S.[7], b. in Newbury, July 9, 1825 ; m. Dec. 19, 1850, Abigail M. Dummer. *who died May 11, 1908* He was a machinist and carpenter; res. Lawrence, Amesbury, and later Hyde Park, Mass.; was Representative for Amesbury, 1879 ; became superintendent of Water Works at Hyde Park, 1884 ; d. 15 Dec., 1898, age 73 years.

    iii. EDWIN H.[7], b. in Newbury, May 10, 1828; d. 19 July, 1829.

565. iv. CAROLINE L,[7] b. in Newbury, June 9, 1831 ; m. Mar. 14, 1856, Fred W. Blake. She d. 20 Oct., 1896.

    v. JOSEPH EDWIN[7], b. in Newbury, Dec. 5, 1833 ; d. 8 May, 1864.

    vi. MARY E.[7], b. in Newbury, Feb. 11, 1837 ; m. April 29, 1864, Charles Wm. Adams, son of Ebenezer and Edna (Adams) Adams, b. Sept. 20, 1818 ; d. 5 Feb., 1892; res. Newbury Farms, Mass.

566. vii. LEONARD[7], b. in Newbury, Oct. 6, 1840 ; m. May 14, 1868, Adeline E. Wallis, dau. of Denison and Mary E. Wallis of Hamilton, Mass., b. 1849. *d. Feb. 7, 1919.* *d. Oct. 26, 1934* He is a farmer in Newbury-Byfield, Mass.

    viii. MARTHA[7], b. in Newbury, Sept. 20, 1842 ; d. 10 Mar., 1862.

Children of MARIA[6], (1794) [231] (Capt. Stephen[5], Samuel[4], Capt. Abraham[3], Sergt. Abraham[2], Robert[1]) and Col. Josiah Titcomb; res. Newbury-Byfield, Mass.

    i. CHARLES WM. TITCOMB, b. Feb. 10, 1821 ; m. Mar. 16, 1845, Phebe Jane Pearson ; living 1898. He d. 7 Oct., 1893.

    ii. ANN MARIA TITCOMB, b. May 22, 1823 ; m. April 17, 1845, Paul Titcomb; he d. 27 Jan., 1894. She is living 1898.

    iii. JOHN ADAMS TITCOMB, b. Aug. 21, 1827; m. Elizabeth Hervey; res. 1898 in Groveland, Mass.

    iv. INFANT SON, b. Sept. 28, 1829 ; d. 10 Oct., 1829.

    v. SARAH JANE TITCOMB, b. Dec. 27, 1832; m. Aug., 1868, Philip A. Rogers. She d. 25 Feb., 1885.

    vi. EMILY TITCOMB, b. July 9, 1836 ; d. 3 Feb., 1839.

Children of SEWALL[6], (1798) [232] (Capt. Stephen[5], Samuel[4], Capt. Abraham[3], Sergt. Abraham[2], Robert[1]) and Sarah (Ilsley) Adams; res. Derry, N. H.

567. i. SARAH JANE[7], b. in Derry, Feb. 18, 1823 ; m. May 5, 1846, Charles Henry Hale, b. April 1, 1820 ; d. 6 June, 1897 ; res. 6 Allen St., Newburyport, Mass.

HENRY SEWALL ADAMS.

Seventh Generation.] OF NEWBURY, MASS.

ii. ELIZA ILSLEY⁷, b. in Derry, May 20, 1825 ; m. (1) Dec. 4, 1845, Eben Adams, son of Ebenezer and Edna Adams, b. Jan. 26, 1817 ; d. 18 June, 1873 ; m. (2) Jan. 12, 1875, George Edw. Adams, son of George and Judith (Dole) Adams. She d. 27 Oct., 1880.

iii. HENRY SEWALL⁷, b. in Derry, June 8, 1827 ; d. 19 May, 1831.

568. iv. JAMES AUGUSTUS⁷, b. in Derry. Oct. 22, 1830; m. (1) Oct. 28, 1853, Hannah I. Adams, dau. of Asa and Nancy (Little) Adams, b. June 8, 1827 ; d. 28 April, 1863; m. (2) Sept. 3, 1865, Harriet Augusta Coffin, b. June 20, 1831; res. Newburyport, Mass. *d. Aug. 10, 1906.*

569. v. HENRY SEWALL⁷, b. in Derry, Aug. 3, 1831 ; m. Aug. 19, 1853, Hannah M. Little, dau. of Stephen W. and Hannah M. (Russell) Little, b. Jan. 1, 1835.

He was a resident of Newburyport from 1846 to 1853 ; was appointed an employee in the Boston postoffice in 1853, and has been the treasurer since 1863.

570. vi. CAPT. JOHN QUINCY⁷, b. in Derry, Sept. 18, 1834 ; m. Dec. 3, 1862, Hattie A. Forsyth of Chelsea, Mass.

Educated in the public schools, he became a clerk in the Boston postoffice in 1855. During the Civil War he was commissioned 1st Lieutenant of the 4th unattached company, M. V. M., which enlisted May 3, 1864, for three months, and afterwards served four years with rank of captain on the staff of Brig. Gen. Isaac S. Burrill, 1st. Brigade, M. V. M. He was a member of the Chelsea Common Council, 1866-1869, of the Board of Alderman 1869-1871, and of the Board of Education 1874-1886. In 1892 he was appointed superintendent of the Somerville postoffice, and transferred back to the Boston office in 1897, as assistant to the superintendent of the delivery division. He is a member of the Star of Bethlehem Lodge, F. A. M., of the Shekinah R. A. Chapter, and of the Palistine Commandery, K. T.

Children of THOMAS FOSDICK⁶, (1776) [233] (Joseph⁵, Rev. Joseph⁴, Capt. Abraham³, Sergt. Abraham², Robert¹) and Susan (Fenton) Adams; res. Roxbury, Mass.

i. HENRY F.⁷, b. in Roxbury, 1807; d. unm., 1830.

ii. ELIZABETH CARTWRIGHT⁷, b. in Roxbury, 1811. She d. in Roxbury, 9 Mar., 1862, aged 51 years, unm.; was named in the will of her uncle Caleb in July, 1827, and received a bequest of twenty-five hundred dollars, also named in the will of her uncle Chas. Frederick in 1861.

Children of BENJAMIN⁶, (1781) [234] (Joseph⁵, Rev. Joseph⁴, Capt. Abraham³, Sergt. Abraham², Robert¹) and Louisa Ann (Walter) Adams; res. Boston, Mass.

- i. LOUISA ANN⁷, b. in Boston; m. Samuel Hammond Russell; res. 1900, Boston, Mass.
- ii. CAROLINE WALTER⁷, b. in Boston; m. George Dearborn Oxnard. She d. in Boston, 7 May, 1898 ; no issue.
- iii. ———, Omited by request.
- iv. FRANCES PICKERING⁷, b. in Boston, May 10, 1835 ; m. Oct 15, 1857, Hon. Robert C. Winthrop, Jr. She d. in Rome, Italy, 23 April, 1860 ; no issue.

Children of JOHN⁶, (1785-6) [235] (Joseph⁵, Rev. Joseph⁴, Capt. Abraham³, Sergt. Abraham², Robert¹) and Elizabeth (Hatch) Adams; res. Lowell, Mass.

- 571. i. MARY E.⁷, b. in Lowell, Jan. 21, 1830 ; m. March 5, 1863, Wm. H. Bartlett, fourth son of Dr. John S. and Martha Bartlett of New York City ; res. 108 W. 98 Street, New York City.
- 572. ii. GEORGE W.⁷, b. in Lowell, Jan. 3, 1832 ; m. Dec. 24, 1857, Emily E. Butters of Dracat, Mass., dau. of George and Martha (Spiller) Butters. He d. in Lowell, 18 Sept., 1890, age 59 years.
- 573. iii. CAROLINE CATHWRIGHT⁷, b. in Lowell, July 5, 1833 ; m. Sept. 14, 1859, Wm. H. Bartlett of N. Y. (his 1st wife). She d. in Lowell, 19 Nov., 1861.
- iv. MARIA THERESA⁷, b. in Lowell, Aug. 3, 1835 ; d. in Roxbury, Mass., 13 Sept., 1838.
- 574. v. JOHN HANCOCK⁷, b. in Lowell, May 26, 1837 ; m. (1) 1863, Emma Davis of Tewkesbury, Mass., b. 1847 ; m. (2) Sept. 3, 1888, Mrs. Maria Gotham, a native of England ; res. 1899, Lowell, Mass.
- 575. vi. MARIA THERESA⁷, b. in Lowell, Aug. 17, 1842 ; m. Aug. 17, 1862, at Lowell, Edw. G. Tuckerman, son of Edw. G. and Ann Eliza Tuckerman of Boston ; res. New York City.

Children of GEORGE⁶, (1792) [236] (Joseph⁵, Rev. Joseph⁴, Capt. Abraham³, Sergt. Abraham², Robert¹) and Mary Anne (Leach) Adams; res. Brookline, Mass.

- i. MARY ISABELLE⁷, b. in Roxbury, Mass., Sept. 4, 1837 ; d. unm. 30 Sept., 1864.
- ii. HELEN ISADORE⁷, b. in Boston, Mar. 14, 1839 ; living 1899, unm. in Brookline, Mass.

CAPT. JOHN QUINCY ADAMS.

Seventh Generation.] OF NEWBURY, MASS. 131

576. iii. GEORGE HENRY[1], b. in Boston, April 15, 1843 ; m. (1) May 6, 1893, Marion R. Wildes, dau. of Moses and Emeline A. (Heath) Wildes, b. Dec. 2, 1854; d. 23 Feb., 1896 ; m. (2) Oct. 26, 1898, Sarah Leeds Macomber, dau. of William Macomber of Newton Center.
He enlisted in 1862 as a member of Co. C, 44th Massachusetts Reg. of Vols ; res. No. 7 St. Albans Hall, Richmond Court, Brookline, Mass.

iv. EMMA FRANCES, b. in Boston, Nov. 13, 1844 ; m. Oct. 11, 1871, William West of Philadelphia, a soldier in the Civil War, member of G. A. R. and of the Loyal Legion, b. 1839; d. 1889. She d. 19 Dec., 1883.

v. CORNELIA GERTRUDE[7], b. in Boston, Aug. 18, 1846 ; d. 26 June, 1849.

Children of CHARLES FREDERICK[6], (1794) [**237**] (Joseph[5], Rev. Joseph[4], Capt. Abraham[3], Sergt. Abraham[2], Robert[1]) and Caroline H. (Walter) Adams; res. Boston, Mass.

i. EMELINE MATILDA[7], b. in Boston, Oct. 4, 1823 ; m. Caleb N. Curtis. He d. about 1889.

ii. DR. HORACE WALTER[7], b. in Boston.
He graduated from Harvard College in 1849, received degree of M. D., 1853, and d. 1861.

iii. CAROLINE WALTER[7], b. in Boston ; d. young.

iv. CHARLES FREDERICK[7], JR., b. in Boston, Feb. 3, 1824.
He graduated from Harvard College in 1843. Studied law in the Harvard Law School and with Chas. G. Loring. Esq., went to California for his health in 1849; returned, and d. 30 Dec., 1856, age 32 years.

Children of JOSEPH THORNTON[6], (   ) [**238**] (Joseph[5], Rev. Joseph[4], Capt. Abraham[3], Sergt. Abraham[2], Robert[1]) and Sarah Pierce (Jarvis) Adams; res. Boston, Mass., and Claremont, N. H.

i. DR. JEFFREY THORNTON[7], b. in Boston, 1831.
He was appointed an assistant surgeon in the U. S. Navy in Dec., 1861 ; resigned in Mar., 1863 ; gave up work in 1864, and d. at Claremont, N. H., 17 June, 1865; will proved July 26, 1865.

ii. LEONARD JARVIS[7], b. in Boston. He d. 25 June, 1862 ; will proved at Newport, N. H., June 25, 1862.

iii. SUSAN JARVIS[7], b. in Boston ; d. 1868.

iv. ELLEN GRACE DERBY[7], b. in Boston ; m. Capt. Andrew Dunlap, of U. S. N.; res. Washington, D. C.

Children of REV. JOHN FOLSOM⁶, (1790-1) [**239**] (Lieut. John⁵, Rev. Joseph⁴, Capt. Abraham³, Sergt. Abraham², Robert¹) and and Mary (Lane) Adams; res. Stratham, N. H.

    i. SALLY⁷, b. in Stratham, 1817 ; d. young.

    ii. REV. JOSEPH AUGUSTUS⁷, b. in So. New Market, N. H., Mar. 18, 1818 ; m. 1843. Sophia A. Metcalf, dau. of Rev. Alfred and Ann (Poor) Metcalf ; she d. about 1897.
        He was a Methodist minister, and the first principal of the New Hampshire Conference Seminary at Tilton, N. H. He rem. to California and d. in 1860 ; no issue.

    iii. LAURA LIVERMORE⁷, b. in Livermore, Me., June 14, 1820 ; m. (1) June, 1845, Rev. Isaac W. Huntley ; he d. Nov., 1853 ; no issue ; m. (2) Sept. 5, 1860, Rev. Franklin Furber. She d. in Milton, Mass., 21 Dec., 1887; no issue.

    iv. AMY MARY⁷, b. in Barre, Vt., Aug. 8, 1822 ; d. unm., Feb., 1861.

577.   v. LUCY HEDDING⁷, b. in Lynn, Mass., Jan. 7, 1826 ; m. 1856, Samuel Augustus Hatch of Greenland, N. H.; he d. about 1889. She d. in Greenland, N. H., 11 June, 1875.

578.   vi. JOHN WILLIAM⁷, b. in Stratham, June 20, 1828 ; m. (1) Mar., 1856, Charlotte Ann Wiggins ; she d. 1864 ; m. (2) Sept. 5, 1866, at Portland, Me., Sarah F. Waterhouse.
        He was superintendent of schools in Stratham, N. H., in 1849 ; rem. to Portland, Me., where he assisted in building the street railway, and in organizing the Portland Horticultural Society, of which he was secretary. Removing to Springfield, Mass., he became a director in and treasurer of the Hampden Co. Agricultural Society, and is the proprietor with his son and son-in-law of the North Main Street Nursery. He was the Representative of Springfield in the general court for 1892-93.

Children of DAVID⁶, (1798) [**240**] (Lieut. John⁵, Rev. Joseph⁴, Capt. Abraham³, Sergt. Abraham², Robert¹) and Martha (Sheriff) Adams; res. Bangor, Me.

579.   i. MARTHA ANNA⁷, b. in Exeter, N. H., July 1, 1822 ; m. Aug. 10, 1840, Bradstret Moody ; he d. Sept., 1880. They settled in Newton, Mass., in 1860. She d. Dec., 1896.

580.   ii. MARY ANN⁷, b. in Exeter, May 20, 1825 ; m. Sept., 1849, Abbo Roby Davis; he was b. Mar. 7, 1823, d. 31 Dec., 1884; res. Chelsea, Mass., 1894.

581.   iii. ABIGAIL CHAPMAN⁷, b. in Exeter, Dec. 20, 1828 ; m. (1) Aug. 12, 1850, Chas. Henry Draper; he d. in Cambridge, Mass., 17 July, 186— ; m. (2) Geo. Marston. She d. 17 July, 1866.

    iv. JOHN F.⁷, b. in Exeter, June 8, 1831 ; d. unm. 80 Oct., 1861.

Children of BENJAMIN F.⁶, (1799) [**241**] (Lieut. John⁵, Rev. Joseph⁴, Capt. Abraham³, Sergt. Abraham², Robert¹) and Malinda (Sanborn) Adams; res. Bangor, Me.

 i. JOHN Q.⁷, d. young.
 ii. CHARLES HENRY⁷, d. young.
 iii. CHARLES⁷, d. young.
 iv. SARAH ELIZABETH⁷, d. young.
 v. ANN CAROLINE⁷, d. aged 19 years.
 vi. MARY ELIZA⁷, m. Alex. Warfield of Bangor, Me.
 vii. NATHANIEL FREDERICK⁷, d. aged 19 years.
 viii. ELIZA MATILDA⁷, m. ——— Stark.

Children of NATHAN⁶, (1803) [**242**] (Lieut. John⁵, Rev. Joseph⁴, Capt. Abraham³, Sergt. Abraham², Robert¹) and Martha (Marston) Adams; res. Stratham, N. H.

 i. GEORGE W.⁷, b. in Stratham, Jan. 23, 1858; d. 17 Sept., 1861.
 ii. MARTHA ETTA⁷, b. in Stratham, Oct. 24, 1862; d. 27 July, 1864.

Children of ELIZA⁶, (1805) [**243**] (Lieut. John⁵, Rev. Joseph⁴, Capt. Abraham³, Sergt. Abraham², Robert¹) and Capt. Caleb Wiggin.

 i. MARY CAROLINE WIGGIN, b. April 11, 1841 ; res. Newburyport, Mass.; unm.
 ii. ANNE ELIZA WIGGIN, b. Oct. 31, 1843 ; res. Newburyport, Mass.; unm.
 iii. CALEB WHITMORE WIGGIN, b. June 28, 1846 ; d. 25 Nov., 1846.

Children of REV. CHARLES⁶, D. D., (1808) [**244**] (Lieut. John⁵, Rev. Joseph⁴, Capt. Abraham³, Sergt. Abraham², Robert¹, and Sarah Emery (Porter) Adams; res. Rye, N. H.

582. i. SARAH PORTER⁷, b. in Rye, Aug. 25, 1834; m. William A. Barnes, res. Piedmont, Clallam Co., Wash.
583. ii. COL. CHARLES HENRY⁷, b. in Newbury, Vt., April 24, 1836 ; m. June 10, 1861, Elvira Hamilton.
  He was Assistant Adjutant General of Illinois; was Captain of Co. B., 10th Illinois Inf., in April, 1861 ; became Major and Lieut.-Colonel in May ; was Lieut.-Col. of the 1st Regiment of Illinois Lt. Artillery from Oct., 1861, till he was honorably discharged ; Nov., 1864, he acted as Inspector and Chief of Artillery on Gen. Grant's Staff, Army of Tenn.; res. Washington, D. C., 1898.

584. iii. CHARLOTTE A.⁷, b. ⁑in ⁑Newbury, Sept. 15, 1837; m. Nov. 6, 1860, Jacob Hayner; res. Bell Brook, Ohio.

iv. MARY ELIZABETH⁷, b. in Lynn, Mass., Dec. 7, 1840; d. unm. at Roxbury, Mass., April, 1896.

v. EDWARD HUNTINGTON⁷, b. in Wilbraham, Mass., Dec. 21, 1842.
He enlisted in the army, and was corporal in Co. B, 10th Illinois Infantry; April to Oct., 1861, was Lieut. of Battery H, 1st Illinois Lt. Artillery, Oct. 1861, to July, 1863; was killed in action at Jackson, Miss., 10 July, 1863.

585. vi. CAPT. GEORGE HUNTINGTON⁷, b. in Boston, Jan. 14, 1846; m. April 27, 1877, Augusta Holmes, dau. of Artemas H. Holmes of New York.
He served in the army 1863 to 1866; was breveted Major; graduated from the Law School of Harvard University in 1872, and was admitted to the bar in New York in 1874, practicing his profession in New York in co-partnership with Mr. H. Huntley.
In May, 1877, he formed a partnership with Artemas H. Holmes, under the firm name of Holmes & Adams. He was assistant district attorney in 1884, and one of the board of managers of the Harvard Club in 1895-97; was associated with Frederick H. Allen in the firm of Adams & Allen on Wall Street. He died suddenly at the Flower Hospital, 8 April, 1900.

vii. FRANK⁷, b. in Lowell, Mass., Sept. 25, 1849; d. at Omaha, Neb., 6 April, 1865.

Children of MARTHA WEBB⁶, (1796) **[245]** (Joseph⁵, Benjamin⁴, Capt. Abraham³, Sergt. Abraham², Robert¹) and Allen Newhall; res. Hingham, Mass.

i. MARGARET NEWHALL, b. in Lynn, Mass., June 19, 1818; m. (1) Benjamin Guild; m. (2) —— Newcomb. She d. in Quincy, Mass., 1867.

ii. JOSEPH ADAMS NEWHALL, b. in Lynn, June 12, 1822; m. (1) Feb. 4. 1846, Lucy Ann Lincoln, dau. of Marshall and Lucy (Stodder) Lincoln, b. April 15, 1822; d. 3 Sept., 1850; m. (2) 1851, Elizabeth W. Lincoln, b. April 10, 1828, sister of Lucy Ann; res. Hingham, Mass.; no issue.

iii. HENRY ALLEN NEWHALL, b. in Lynn, Jan. 12, 1826; d. in Dorchester, 4 Aug., 1828.

iv. HARRIET MILLER NEWHALL, b. in Dorchester, Mass., April 1, 1831; m. Timothy Sprague of Hingham, Mass., son of Luther Spague, b. May 10, 1830 (Harriet M., his first wife). She d. in Hingham, 29 April, 1886.

v. MARTHA FRANCES NEWHALL, b. in Dorchester, Mass., Aug. 3, 1834; m. Nov. 29, 1854, Waterman T. Burrill of Hingham.

vi. GEORGE ALLEN NEWHALL, b. in Dorchester, Mass., Jan. 18, 1838 ; m. May 12, 1858, Mary A. Studley, dau. of Benjamin G. and Miriam (Burrill) Studley, b. Oct. 1, 1838 ; res. Hingham, Mass.

Children of JOSEPH⁶, JR., (1800) [246] (Joseph⁵, Rev. Benjamin⁴, Capt. Abraham³, Sergt. Abraham², Robert¹) and Frances H. (Straw) Adams; res. Lynn, Mass.

    i. JOHN QUINCY⁷, b. in Lynn, Nov. 2, 1825 ; d. unm. 10 Feb. 1860.
    ii. JOSEPH WARREN⁷, b. in Lynn, April 16, 1828.
        He is a shoe manufacturer in Sangers, Mass.; unm.
586. iii. FRANCES MARIA⁷, b. in Lynn, Jan. 26, 1832 ; m. 1852, Daniel W. Foster, son of Nehemiah and Susan M. Foster, b. 1831, and is deceased ; res. Lynn, Mass.
587. iv. MARY ELLEN⁷, b. in Lynn, May 3, 1835 ; m. June 10, 1858, George F. Breed ; he d. in Brandon, Vt., 20 Aug., 1890 ; res. 1895, Clinton, Mass.
588. v. REUBEN JOHNSON⁷, b. in Lynn, Mar. 19, 1839 ; m. Jane Knowlton of Swampscot, Mass.
        In insane asylum, Danvers.
    vi. CHARLES EDWARD⁷, b. in Lynn, Oct. 24, 1842 ; d. 18 Sept., 1865.

Children of LOUISA NICHOLS⁶, (1804) [247] (Joseph⁵, Benjamin⁴, Capt. Abraham³, Sergt. Abraham², Robert¹) and Joseph Clapp, Jr. ; res. Dorchester, Mass.

    i. LOUISA ANN CLAPP, b. Aug. 13, 1827 ; d. unm. 19 Apr., 1886.
    ii. JOSEPH WARREN CLAPP, b. Sept. 13, 1830 ; m. (1) Sept. 12, 1861, Martha Ingalls ; m. (2) Mrs. Mary Hopkins, sister of Martha Ingalls ; res. Hazel, N. C.
    iii. MARIA ALMIRA CLAPP, b. Jan. 28, 1833 ; d. unm., 19 Jan., 1885.
    iv. CORNELIUS CLAPP, b. Dec. 30, 1834 ; m. Ruth Burbank. He was killed on the railroad, 8 May, 1875.
    v. MARY ELLEN CLAPP, b. Aug. 21, 1839 ; m. Nov. 20, 1861, Albert Kimball of Gardner, Me.; res. Lynn. Mass.

Children of MARY ANN⁶, (1807) [248] (Joseph⁵, Rev. Benjamin⁴, Capt. Abraham³, Sergt. Abraham², Robert¹) and Oliver Hunt Bowman ; res. Milton, Mass.

    i. OLIVER HUNT BOWMAN, JR., b. in Milton. April 13, 1829 ; m. April 23, 1850, Eunice Jones.
    ii. CHARLES RICE BOWMAN, b. in Boston, Aug. 24, 1831 ; d. unm. 27 March, 1873.

136   ROBERT ADAMS   [Seventh Generation.

  iii. ALMIRA BOWMAN, b. Feb. 21, 1834; m. April 13, 1851, Wm. Madden of Stoughton, Mass. She d. 27 April, 1875.
  iv. MARY ANN BOWMAN, b. Nov. 14, 1837; d. 31 July, 1840.
  v. WILLIAM HENRY BOWMAN, b. in Milton, Aug. 27, 1840; m. Feb. 6, 1863, Elizabeth Packard of Dorchester, Mass.
  vi. MARY ANN BOWMAN, b. in Milton, Feb. 28, 1843; m. Aug. 11, 1868, Frank E. Willis of Sudbury, Mass.; res. Dorchester, Mass.
  vii. HARRISON GRAY BOWMAN, b. in Milton, Sept. 18, 1845; m. June 2, 1868, Mary J. Wade.
  viii. GEO. DAY BOWMAN, b. in Milton, Mar. 21, 1848; m. Oct. 11, 1890, Mary Louisa Monroe.

Children of BENJAMIN WEBB⁶, (1809) [249] (Joseph⁵, Rev. Benjamin⁴, Capt. Abraham³, Sergt. Abraham², Robert¹) and Jane Baker (Ford) Adams; res. Danvers, Mass.

  i. JOSEPH⁷, b. in Danvers, April 10, 1830; d. 7 June, 1830.
  ii. MARY JANE⁷, b. in Danvers, April 15, 1831; d. 10 Sept., 1854.
591. iii. GEO. BENJAMIN⁷, b. in Danvers, Oct. 23, 1832; m. June 14, 1857, Abby Dobber of Marblehead, Mass.; res. Roxbury, Mass.
592. iv. JOSEPH NICHOLS⁷, b. in Danvers, Nov. 16, 1834; m. Oct. 17, 1857, Susan Jane Fairfield; res. Roslindale, Mass.
  v. ELIJAH FRENCH⁷, b. in Danvers, Oct. 15, 1836; d. 17 Sept., 1863.
  vi. HENRY⁷, b. in Danvers, Aug., 1838; d. 24 Sept., 1838.
593. vii. HELEN ISADORA⁷, b. in Danvers, Mar. 9, 1842; m. 1863, Alonzo Collins of Laconia, N. H.; res. Lakeport, N. H.
  viii. ELIZABETH FORD⁷, b. in Danvers, Dec. 12, 1843; m. Nov., 1859; Orin Buck of Hyannis, Mass. She has an adopted dau. Ora, who m. one Desilia, a Portuguese. He d. about 1896.
  ix. REBECCA FESSENDEN⁷, b. in Danvers, Sept. 11, 1846; d. 27 Sept., 1847.
  x. IDA SELINA⁷, b. in Danvers, April 23, 1853; d. 9 Mar., 1856.

Children of JOHN BREED⁶, (1793) [250] (Nathan⁵, Capt. Nathan⁴, Capt. Abraham³, Sergt. Abraham², Robert¹) and Adeline (Preston) Adams; res. Ashford, now Eastford, Conn.

594. i. JOHN QUINCY⁷, b. in Ashford, Mar. 22, 1826; m. April 27, 1847, Sarah Catharine Clark of Towshend, Mass.; she d. 31 Dec., 1878. He settled in Boston; rem. to Brooklyn, N. Y., about 1850, where he d. 6 Dec., 1870.
595. ii. NATHAN PRESTON⁷, b. in Ashford, Dec. 30, 1828; m. Dec. 24, 1849, Julia J. Pasco of Stafford, Conn. He set. in Rockville, Conn; rem. to Broad Brook (E. Windsor), Conn., where he d. 18 June, 1871.

Seventh Generation.] OF NEWBURY, MASS. 137

596.   iii.   MARY ADELINE⁷, b. in Ashford, Dec. 3, 1834; m. Mar. 9, 1858, Andrew Lamphere of Eastford, Conn., son of Solomon and Charlotte (Huntington) Lamphere, b. Dec. 25, 1829, (in Ashford, Conn.) They rem. 1881, from Eastford to Abington, Conn.

598.   iv.   JAMES ERWIN⁷, b. in Ashford, Aug. 15, 1830; m. (1) Nov., 1863, Mary Harvey; she d. July, 1864; m. (2) Nov., 1873, Hannah Williams of Brooklyn, N. Y.
         He was a member of the 15th Mass. Reg., and was wounded at Balls Bluff, Va., Oct., 1861, disabling him for service. He set. in Brooklyn, N. Y., 131 Macon St.

       v.   HENRY HARRISON⁷, b. in Ashford, Dec. 4, 1843.
         He enlisted at Hartford, Conn., Aug., 1862, in Co. G, 16th Reg. Conn. Vols.; was in the battle of Antietem, Sept. 17, 1862, at Fredericksburg and Suffold in 1863; was taken prisoner April 20, 1864, and imprisoned at Andersonville, S. C., from May 4 to Sept. 10; rem. to Charleston and Florence. S. C., in Oct., where he d. 20 Oct., 1864.

Children of SALLY⁶, (1803) **[251]** (Nathan⁵, Capt. Nathan⁴, Capt. Abraham³, Sergt. Abraham², Robert¹) and Joseph A. Dresser; res. Pomfret, Conn.

       i.   WILLIAM LEWIS DRESSER, b. in Pomfret; d. in Ashford, age 8 years.
      ii.   EMILY DRESSER, b. in Pomfret; m. Sumner Webber. She d. in Fiskdale, Mass., Aug., 1872.

Children of CAPT. GEORGE⁶, (1807) **[252]** (Nathan⁵, Capt. Nathan⁴, Capt. Abraham³, Sergt. Abraham², Robert¹) and Lucy M. (Prescott) Adams; res. Ashford, now Eastford, Conn.

       i.   HENRY PRESTON⁷, b. in Ashford, Feb. 4, 1836; d. 5 April, 1842.
      ii.   WILLIAM LEWIS⁷, b. in Ashford, Sept. 8, 1837.
         He was a teacher; enlisted 1862 in Co. D, 18th Connecticut Vols.; was killed at Piedmont, W. Va., 5 June, 1864.
     iii.   MARY ANNA⁷, b. in Ashford, Jan. 26, 1839; m. Oct. 24, 1864, Wm. H. Latham; d. 29 April, 1896; they set. 1868 in Providence, R. I. She d. 13 July, 1896; no issue.

598.   iv.   GEORGE AUGUSTUS⁷, b. in Ashford, April 5, 1841; m. (1) Aug. 8, 1867, Ruth A. Miller, dau. of John Miller; m. (2) Aug., 1888, Mary Brady.
         He is a grocer in Providence, R. I.

599.   v.   ELIZABETH B.⁷, b. in Eastford, Dec. 11, 1844; m. Dec., 1866, James E. Latham; res. Providence, R. I.

600.   vi.   EVELYN AMELIA⁷, b. in Eastford, April 18, 1850; m. Nov. 23, 1870, Samuel G. Pellet; res. Providence, R. I.

Children of ENOCH[6], (1779) [253] (Enoch[5], Henry[4], Capt. Abraham[3], Sergt. Abraham[2], Robert[1]) and Lucy (Strickland) Adams; res. Andover, Oxford Co., Me.

- i. SALLY BRAGG[7], b. in Andover, Aug. 19, 1808; d. 14 Feb., 1809.
- ii. ENOCH MILTON[7], b. in Andover, Jan. 12, 1810 ; d. April, 1811.
- 601. iii. WILLIAM[7], b. in Andover, Oct. 7, 1811 ; m. May 15, 1838, Lucinda Hall, dau. of Jeremiah Hall of Rumford, Me., b. Mar. 4, 1818 ; d. 29 Mar., 1882.
  He was a farmer ; d. in Andover, 18 May, 1879.
- iv. JOHN WESLEY[7], b. in Andover, Feb. 9, 1814; m. 1840, Euphrasia Blodgett. He d. July, 1871 ; no issue.
- 602. v. JULIA[7], b. in Andover, Sept. 2, 1816; m. Mar. 3, 1834, David B. Sawyer, son of Barnabas and Sarah Sawyer, b. in Otisfield, Me., Feb. 20, 1807 ; d. 24 April, 1864. She rem. to Wis., where she still resides, 1899.
- 603. vi. EMILY[7], b. in Andover, Dec. 27, 1817; m. Mar. 22, 1842, Nelson Frickett, son of Wm. Frickett, b. in Durham, Me., June 28, 1815 ; d. 10 Mar., 1871 ; res. Wilson's Mills, Me., where she d. 14 April, 1851.
- 604. vii. HARRIET[7] (twin), b. in Andover, Dec. 27, 1817; m. 1838, Simeon Shurtleff, son of Alsah and Annie (Shaw) Shurtleff, b. in Paris, Me., Sept. 2, 1810 ; d. in Portland, Me., 13 Oct., 1892 ; res. Wilson's Mills, Me. She d. in Portland, Me., 4 Mar., 1844.
- 605. viii. ALMIRA[7], b. in Andover, May 15, 1824 ; m. 1851, John A. Bolster. She d. 11 Mar., 1879.
- 506. ix. MARY[7], b. in Andover, July 12, 1826 ; m. Aug. 31, 1856, John Stone Lovejoy, son of Stephen and Pamelia (Bragg) Lovejoy, b. in Andover, Dec. 4, 1823 ; d. 5 Aug., 1893 ; res. Andover, Me.; living 1899.
- 607. x. DR. ENOCH[7], b. in Andover, May 21, 1829 ; m July 1, 1851, May H. Case, dau. of Wm. Case of Lubec, Me., b. July 20, 1829.
  He grad. from Harvard Medical College in 1851, and set. in Litchfield, Me.; was surgeon of the 14th Maine Reg., 1861 to 1864 ; d. 23 Jan., 1900.
- xi. DOLLY FARRINGTON[7], b. in Andover, May 31, 1831 ; d. 19 May, 1845.

Children of COL. JOHN EMERY[6], (1780) [254] (Enoch[5], Henry[4], Capt. Abraham[3], Sergt. Abraham[2], Robert[1]) and Sarah (Moody) Adams; res. Andover, Me., and Cleveland, Ohio.

- 608. i. JOHN EMERY[7], b. in Andover, Dec. 22, 1805; m. Jan. 18, 1828, Belinda Bell, b. Mar. 10, 1811 ; living 1899.
  He was a farmer and settled in Warrensville. Cuyahoga Co., O., in 1826, d. there 9 Mar., 1890.

ii. SARAH MOODY⁷, b. in Andover, Feb. 9, 1808; m. Henry Church, a rope-maker ᵃⁿᵈ died soon after marriage in 1828; no issue.

609. iii. LYDIA BARTLETT⁷, b. in Andover, Nov. 15, 1809; m. P. Clark Brown, a builder. She d. in Johnson Co., Iowa, about 1840.

610. iv. EBENEZER MOODY⁷, b. in Andover, Sept. 7, 1811; m. (1) April 9, 1836, Sally Gleason, b. July 10, 1810; d. 22 April, 1837; m. (2) 1842, Henrietta Lyon, b. May 10, 1819; living 1899.

Mr. Adams was a pioneer farmer, one of the earliest settlers in Solon, Johnson Co., Iowa, where he d. on the 9th of January, 1900' age almost 90 years. In 1826, when but 15 years of age, he removed with his father's family to Cleveland, Ohio, and thence in 1838 to Iowa, by way of the Ohio and Mississippi rivers. He went to California in 1849, returning in 1850, and while acquiring wealth by his industry and good judgment, attained a wide and enviable reputation for his high character and upright life.

611. v. ENOCH⁷, b. in Andover, Sept., 1813; m. Feb. 26, 1840, Lorinda Auter, dau. of Aaron° and Sarah (Haymaker) Auter, b. Nov. 14, 1818; living 1899.

He was a merchant tailor; settled in Cuyahoga Falls, Ohio, in 1841, removed in 1862 to Akron, Ohio, and thence to Cleveland in 1878, where he d. 25 Nov., 1887. He is described as an upright, honorable man, and an early, staunch and fearless advocate of the anti-slavery cause.

612. vi. MOSES⁷, b. in Andover, Nov., 1815; m. Jan. 9, 1857, Sarah J. Keisler.

He settled in Solon, Ia., in 1838-9; was a steadfast Republican, a friend of temperance, kind and generous-hearted. He d. in Solon, 23 Mar., 1899, leaving a beautiful home and valuable estate.

613. vii. FRANCIS CUSHMAN⁷, b. in Andover, Sept. 18, 1820; m. 1854, Elizabeth Edwards, b. in Cornwall Co., Eng., Nov. 9, 1829; d. in Chicago, Ill., 30 June, 1897.

He settled in Iowa City, Ia., d. 25 Feb., 1883.

614. viii. MATILDA⁷, b. in Cleveland, O., July, 1826; m. Daniel F. McCune of Solon, Ia., ; he. d. Feb., 1876. She d. 6 July, 1863.

615. ix. JAMES MONROE⁷, b. in Cleveland, Oct. 29, 1828; m. July, 1855, Sophia Dudley, dau. of Wm. M. Dudley of Erie Co., N. Y., b. 1832; res. Solon, Iowa.

Children of SARAH⁶, (1782) [255] (Enoch⁵, Henry⁴, Capt. Abraham³, Sergt. Abraham², Robert¹) and James H. Withington; res. Peru, Oxford Co., Me.

i. JAMES H. WITHINGTON, JR.; m. Alfreda Bosworth of Solon, Me.

He was a graduate of Colby College, and a teacher in Hallowell, Me., and Philadelphia, Pa., d. 3 June, 1877.

ii. SARAH WITHINGTON, d. unm.

iii. MARY WITHINGTON, (twin), d. unm.

Children of DR. JOSEPH⁶, (1788) **[256]** (Enoch⁵, Henry⁴, Capt. Abraham³, Sergt. Abraham², Robert¹) and Betsey (Farnum) Adams; res. Rumford, Oxford Co., Me.

616.   i. DAVID FARNHAM⁷, b. in Standish, Me., Mar. 4, 1813; m. April 22, 1834, Dorcas Virgin Glines.

            He was a farmer and a merchant in Caribou, Me.; was educated at Wesleyan Seminary, Kent's Hill, Me.; d. 23 Jan., 1882.

617. ii. ERASMUS DARWIN⁷, b. in Sumner, Me., Dec. 31, 1814; m. Aug. 5, 1841, Catherine Sturgis, dau. of Hon. John Sturgis of Sturgis, Mich., b. in Brownstown, Wayne Co., Mich., July 24, 1821; d. at McAlister, Ind. Ter., 24 Jan., 1899.

            He was educated at Kent's Hill, Me., and was a successful teacher; removed west in 1836; worked for two years at his trade as a cabinet-maker in Cleveland, O., then was a teacher in St. Louis; Mo., and Monmouth, Ill. In 1846 he settled in what is now Cedar Falls, Black Hawk Co., Ia., then an unbroken wilderness, frequented by Indians; he and his brother-in-law, Wm. Sturgis, being the first white settlers. He subsequently resided in Newtonia, Mo., Clearwater, Kan., and Prescott, Arizona. He settled in McAlister, Ind. Ter., in 1892, where he now resides at the advanced age of 85 years. He is known as "Squire Adams," an early friend of temperance and the anti-slavery cause.

618. iii. MARIA BARTLETT⁷, b. in Rumford, Me., Mar. 26, 1817; m. June 18, 1839, Dr. David H. Goodno, a druggist, who d. 5 Feb., 1893.

            She was educated at Wesleyan Seminary; res. in Hallowell, Me. and Washington, D. C., and d. 11 July, 1848.

619. iv. WARREN MANN⁷, b. in Rumford, June 12, 1819; m. Dec. 5, 1844, Adrian Washburn, dau. of James and Clarissa (Thomas) Washburn of Hartford, Me.

            He is a blacksmith and farmer; res. Rumford Falls, Me.

      v. MABEL WAIT⁷, b. in Rumford, July 13, 1821; d. 9 Sept., 1822.

620. vi. DR. HENRY MILGROVE⁷, b. in Rumford, July 23, 1823; m. (1) June 10, 1850, Cordelia Hill of Waterville, Me.; m. (2) Dec. 25, 1866, Lettie E. Hill.

            He graduated from Bowdoin Medical College in 1849, and settled in Hallowell, Me.; removed in 1855 to Cedar Falls, Ia., and thence in 1880 to Pukweana, Brale Co., So. Dak.

621. vii. MARTHA HALL⁷, b. in Rumford, Aug. 29, 1825; m. Oct. 26, 1848, Hon. Wm. W. Bolster, son of Gen. Alvan and Cynthia (Wheeler) Bolster, b. July 6, 1823. She d. 20 Aug., 1866, and he m. 2d Aug. 17, 1868, Florence Josephine Reed of Auburn, Me.

      viii. MARK TRAFTON⁷, b. in Rumford, Aug. 19, 1835; m. Jan. 2, 1865, Emily Louisa Wardwell, dau. of Jeremiah and Janette (Burnham) Wardwell of Rumford, Me.

            He was educated at Hallowell Academy, and located as a furniture merchant in Boston, Mass.; no issue.

Children of MOSES⁶, (1793) [257] (Enoch⁵, Henry⁴, Capt. Abraham³, Sergt. Abraham², Robert¹) and Dorcas (Farnham) Adams; res. Andover, Oxford Co., Me.

622.   i. ADAM WILLIS⁷, b. in Andover, Sept. 18, 1818; m. Aug. 11, 1844, Ann M. Bean. He settled in Haverhill, Mass.; d. 2 July, 1889.

    ii. ELIAS BARTLETT⁷, b. in Andover, Sept. 13, 1823; d. unm. 1884.

623.   iii. AUGUSTUS HALL⁷, b. in Andover, Nov. 6, 1827; m. (1) April 8, 1855, Mary A. Harrington; she d. Jan., 1868; m. (2) Jan. 29, 1869, Malinda Augusta Smith. She d. 6 June, 1899.

He settled in Haverhill, Mass., in 1851; has been a merchant in Boston of shoe-findings, and a dealer in real estate in Haverhill; was an old-time Republican; a director of the Pautucket Savings Bank; an Odd Fellow, and an earnest Unitarian. He died at his home in Haverhill, 8 April, 1900, greatly respected.

Children of MARY⁶, (1796) (258] (Enoch⁵, Henry⁴, Capt. Abraham³. Sergt. Abraham², Robert¹) and Capt. Adam Willis; res. Hanover, Oxford Co., Me.

  i. WILLIAM A WILLIS, b. Sept. 16, 1822; m. (1) Feb, 17, 1850, E—— E. Hibbard; she d. 17 Feb., 1875; m. (2) Jan. 11, 1876, Mrs. N. G. Folsom.
He is a farmer in Dummer, N. H.

  ii. ASENATH HOWARD WILLIS, b. May 17, 1825; m. Oct. 15, 1848, Dr. Chas. Russell; res. No. Fayette, Me.

  iii. JOHN E. WILLIS, b. Apr. 7, 1827; m. Mar. 28, 1849, L. Wight; she d. 12 May, 1884.
He was sheriff of Coos Co., N. H.; also an officer in the Union Army; was killed on the railroad, 20 Jan. 1877; res. Gorham, N. H.

  iv. ETHAN WILLIS, b. Dec. 7, 1829; m. Mar. 25, 1852, Selvina Wight of Gilead, Me.
He is an architect and builder; res. W. Paris, Me.

  v. THOMAS W. WILLIS, b. Dec. 12, 1833; m. July 3, 1858, Julia L. Smith of Newry, Me.; res. Caribou, Me.

Children of WILLIAM⁶, (1801) [259] (Enoch⁵, Henry⁴, Capt. Abraham³, Sergt. Abraham², Robert¹) and Betsey (Crocket) Adams; res. Andover, Mass.

  i. BETSEY C.⁷, b. in Andover, July 17, 1825; m. Francis Dresser, a merchant; res. Andover, Me. She d. 17 Apr., 1859.

  ii. WILLIAM⁷, b. in Andover, June 10, 1827.
He went to California; found a nugget of gold worth $1600; was murdered 13 Mar., 1851.

624. iii. JOHN QUINCY[1], b. in Andover, Feb. 28, 1829; m. Mar. 29, 1856, Susan E. McIntire of Hollis, Me.
He was a farmer in Andover; d. 7 Nov., 1881.

iv. LEWIS BENNET[7], b. in Andover, July 31, 1836; d. 19 May, 1842.

Children of JULIA[6], (1801) [260] (Nathan[5], Henry[4], Capt. Abraham[3], Sergt. Abraham[2], Robert[1]) and James Stinson; res. Wiscasset, Me.

    i. DAVID GILMORE STINSON, b. Mar. 25, 1825; m. Dec. 27, 1859, Helen S. Page. He d. 9 Jan., 1876.

    ii. JAMES HENRY STINSON, b. Mar. 18, 1829; d. 4 Nov., 1864.

    iii. SAMUEL ADAMS STINSON, b. Nov. 22, 1830; m. [pub. Oct. 27, 1856], Lucretia B. Page of Hallowell, Me. He d. 18 Feb., 1865.

    iv. FREDERICK T. STINSON, b. May 30, 1835; d. 4 June, 1842.

Children of SAMUEL[6], JR., (1768) [262] (Col. Samuel[5], Samuel[4], Isaac[3], Sergt. Abraham[2], Robert[1]) and Margaret (Harriman) Adams; res. E. Bradford (Groveland), Mass.

625. i. ISAAC[7], b. in East Bradford, Dec. 14, 1793; m. July, 1817, Margaret Bishop of Salem, Mass., b. 1798, d. Oct., 1874. He d. in Groveland, Mass., 8 Nov., 1862.

626. ii. MARY[7], b. in East Bradford, Mar. 16, 1795; m. 1822, Aaron L. Clark of Ipswich, Mass.; he d. in Georgetown, Mass., 1845. She d. in Georgetown, 1861.

627. iii. SALLY[7], b. in East Bradford, Oct. 14, 1798; m. June 10, 1823, Jacob Dresser of Boxford, Mass. and Albany, Me. Jacob Dresser m. 2nd Aug. 5, 1840, Sophia Hale of Turner, Me.; he d. 16 Dec., 1854, age 62 yrs. 9 mos. She d. in Albany, Me., 29 Mar., 1839.

628. iv. ENOCH[7], b. in East Bradford, May 27, 1799; m. 1825, Mary A. Willey; she d. 22 Dec., 1886, age 80 years.
He was a shoemaker; d. in Georgetown, Mass., 4 Sept., 1863.

629. v. SAMUEL[7], b. in East Bradford, July 6, 1802; m. Sept. 20, 1824, Sally B. Clark of Ipswich, Mass.; b. Sept. 26, 1804; d. 26 Jan., 1885. He set. in Haverhill, Mass., in 1833, d. 25 May, 1851.

630. vi. HANNAH[7], b. in East Bradford, Dec. 2, 1805; m. Dec. 9, 1828, Stephen Horr of Waterford, Me., b. Feb. 1, 1798; he d. 13 July, 1874; res. No. Waterford, Me. She d. 7 Jan., 1852.

Child of SAMUEL[6], JR., (1768) and Mary (Savory) Adams

631. vii. MOSES[7], b. in Groveland, Mass., Oct. 13, 1810; m. Jan. 14, 1830, Sarah Colby of Newburyport, dau. of Enoch and Sally Colby; she d. 21 Jan., 1887.
He was a farmer and veterinary in Groveland, Mass.; was killed by a railroad engine, 15 Jan., 1876.

Children of PHEBE⁶, (1777) [263] (Capt. David⁵, Isaac⁴, Jr., Isaac³, Sergt. Abraham², Robert¹) and Henry Hale; res. Chelsea, Vt.

    i. POLLY HALE, b. in Rowley, Mass., Aug. 3, 1803; m. Feb. 5, 1829, Dr. Hiram Bliss; res. Waldoboro, Me.
    ii. HENRY HALE, b. in Windsor, Vt., Apr. 22, 1805; d. 6 Dec., 1807.
    iii. MARK HALE, b. Aug. 20, 1806; midshipman in U. S. N.
    iv. A SON, b. Jan. 26, 1808; d. same day.
    v. TWIN, b. in Chelsea, Vt., Dec. 28, 1808; d. same day.
    vi. TWIN, b. in Chelsea, Vt., Dec. 28, 1808; d. same day.
    vii. LOUISA HALE, b. in Chelsea, Jan. 6, 1810; m. June, 1830, Rev. Elihu Scott of Hampton, N. H.
    viii. PHEBE HALE, b. in Chelsea, May 23, 1811; m. Stephen Vincent, and d. in Chelsea, 5 May, 1856.
    ix. A DAUGHTER (twin with Phebe), d. same day.
    x. THOMAS HALE, b. in Chelsea, Jan. 18, 1813; m. Sarah Ballou Potter, was a graduate of the University of Vermont 1852, and editor of the Vermont Journal at Windsor, Vt. He d. in Keene, N. H.
    xi. COL. HARRY HALE, b. in Chelsea, June 21, 1814; m. Nov. 28, 1855, Mary Elizabeth Fletcher, dau. of Parish Fletcher of Bridport, Vt. He graduated from the University of Vermont in 1840 with Henry J. Raymond; was Secretary of Civil and Military Affairs to Gov. Chas. Paine, 1841-43, and a lawyer in Minneapolis, Minn. He d. in St. Paul, Minn., 7 Dec., 1890.

Children of MERCY⁶, (1779) [264] (Capt. David⁵, Isaac⁴, Jr., Isaac³, Sergt. Abraham², Robert¹) and James Stevens; res. East Jaffrey, N. H.

    i. SALLY STEVENS, b. Apr. 15, 1806; d. unm. 22 Aug., 1879.
    ii. WM. PEABODY STEVENS, b. Mar. 19, 1807; m. June 21, 1850, Mary Elizabeth Stratton of Jaffrey, N. H. He d. 19 June, 1882.
    iii. CHARLES STEVENS, b. Jan. 4, 1816; d. unm. 11 Aug., 1886.

Children of DAVID⁶, (1782) [265] (Capt. David⁵, Capt. Isaac⁴, Jr., Isaac³, Sergt. Abraham², Robert¹) and Silence (Sawin) Adams; res. Rindge, N. H.

632.   i. SILENCE JONES⁷, b. in Rindge, Oct. 21, 1813; m. June 4, 1831, Julius C. Sherwin; he d. in New Ipswich, N. H. She d. in Natick, Mass., 31 Jan., 1884.

ROBERT ADAMS [Seventh Generation.

633.
 ii. EDWIN SPOFFORD⁷, b. in Rindge, Oct. 29, 1815; m. (1) June 12, 1844, Cynthia Ann Whitbeck of Castleton, N. Y.; she d. 10 June, 1883; m. (2) Aug. 3, 1864, Frances F. Colby.
   He was a teacher in Dover, N. H.; Principal of the Grammar School in Brooklyn, N. Y., and d. in Brooklyn, 31 Jan., 1878.
 iii. CATHERINE SAWIN⁷, b. in Rindge, Apr. 11, 1819; living unm. in Keene, N. H.
 iv. MARY JONES⁷, b. in Rindge, Nov. 6, 1820; d. in Natick, Mass., 26 Feb., 1897.
 v. DAVID WOOD⁷, b. in Rindge, Feb. 1, 1823; m. Sept. 3, 1865, Martha Shattuck of Groton, Mass.
   He set. in Groton, Mass.; rem. to Nashua, N. H.; d. in Carlisle, Mass., 18 Sept., 1867; no issue.

634.
 vi. HON. MOSES SAWIN⁷, b. in Rindge, Oct. 19, 1826; m. 1856, Lizzie Damon of Springfield, Mass.
   He served one and one-half years in the army; practiced law in Wichita, Sedgwick Co., Kan.; became a Judge of the court in Fremont Co., Kan.; rem. to Canon City, Col.

Children of MOODY⁶, (1784) [266] (Capt. David⁵, Capt. Isaac⁴, Jr., Isaac³, Sergt. Abraham², Robert¹) and Betsey (Batchelder) Adams; res. New Ipswich, N. H.

 i. ELIZABETH WOODBURY⁷. b. in New Ipswich, Sept. 18, 1815.
   She was in an asylum at Concord for 17 years, and d. unm. 29 Oct., 1885.
 ii. WILLIAM MOODY⁷, b. in New Ipswich, Feb. 9, 1818; d. 3 Oct., 1826.
 iii. MYRA JANE⁷, b. in New Ipswich, Sept. 9, 1823; d. 12 Oct., 1826.
 iv. MYRA JANE⁷, b. in New Ipswich, Feb. 18, 1828; m. Jan. 8, 1852, Geo. Boyden.
   They settled in Washington, D. C. in 1861, where she d. 30 Mar., 1890, age 62 years.
 v. WILLIAM MOODY⁷, b. in New Ipswich, June 18, 1830; d. 30 Oct., 1830.

Children of NAOMI⁶, (1788) [267] (Capt. David⁵, Capt. Isaac⁴, Jr., Isaac³, Sergt. Abraham², Robert¹) and Isaac Spofford; res. Brighton, Mass.

 i. EDWIN COLEMAN SPOFFORD, d. young.
 ii. LEWIS TENNY SPOFFORD, d. young.
 iii. SARAH HALE SPOFFORD, d. at 22 years of age.
 iv. LEWIS EDWIN SPOFFORD, d. at 21 years of age.
 v. PHEBE ADAMS SPOFFORD, m ——— Morse of Roxbury, Mass.
 vi. LUCINDA BAXTER SPOFFORD, d. at 15 years of age.

Seventh Generation.] OF NEWBURY, MASS. 145

Children of ISAAC⁶, (1793) [268] (Capt. David⁵, Capt. Isaac⁴, Jr., Isaac³, Sergt. Abraham², Robert¹) and Sophia (Spofford) Adams; res. West Boxford, Mass.

  i. CHARLES ISRAEL⁷, b. in West Boxford, Dec. 21, 1823.
    He graduated from Dartmouth College, 1852, and from Howard Law School, 1857; became a member of the Suffolk Bar, and d. unm. in West Boxford, 8 Mar., 1862.

635. ii. MARY PARKER⁷, b. in West Boxford, Sept. 24, 1826; m. June 20, 1860, Horace L. Peckham of Townshend, Mass.; he is deceased She set. in Malden, Mass.; res. Townshend, Mass.

  iii. CHANDLER BRAMAN⁷, b. in W. Boxford, July 21, 1829.
    He graduated from Union College in 1855; was a civil engineer and d. at Monticello, Minn.; unm. 17 Nov., 1861-2.

Children of ISAAC⁶, (1793) and Sarah J. (Searle) Adams.

  iv. SARAH SOPHIA⁷, b. in West Boxford, Oct. 5, 1834.
    She was a successful teacher for more than 25 years; d. unm. at Gowanda, Cattaraugus Co., N. Y., 3 Oct., 1881.

636. v. ISAAC MILTON⁷, b. in W. Boxford, Feb. 24, 1841; m. Nov. 26, 1873, Emeline Twitchell of Boston. He set. in Fargo, No. Dak., May, 1882; rem. to Minneapolis, Aug., 1896.

637. vi. STEPHEN SEARLE⁷, b. in W. Boxford, Nov. 8, 1842; m. Mar., 1773, Hannah Goodell of Marshfield, Erie Co., N. Y, He set. in Sioux City, Ia., d. July, 1895.

Children of ELIPHALET⁶, (1775) [269] (Capt. Samuel⁵, Capt. Isaac⁴, Jr., Isaac³, Sergt. Abraham², Robert¹) and Mary (Washburn) Adams; res. Picton, Ont.

  i. LUCY⁷, b. in Picton, April 22, 1806; m. Abraham Steele and had four children, all of whom are deceased.

  ii. DANIEL⁷, b. in Picton, Oct. 2, 1807; d. 8 June, 1817.

  iii. SARAH⁷, b. in Picton, Oct. 6, 1809; m. John Murray.

  iv. HANNAH⁷, b. in Picton, Sept. 16, 1811; m. William Vance. She d. 9 Dec., 1893.

  v. MARY ANN⁷, b. in Picton, Aug. 4, 1813; m. Lewis Munaker.

  vi. ELIZA⁷, b. in Picton, May 21, 1815; m. Thomas McCready.

Children of ISAAC⁶, (1776) [**270**] (Capt. Samuel⁵, Capt. Isaac⁴, Jr., Isaac³, Sergt. Abraham², Robert¹) and Deborah (Twitchell) Adams; res. Gilead, Oxford Co., Me.

 i. ELIPHALET⁷, b. in Gilead, Feb., 1801; d. 1803.

 ii. INFANT⁷, drowned with the mother in the Androscoggin river, 1802.

Children of ISAAC⁶, (1776) and Olive (Wight) Adams.

638. iii. ELIPHALET⁷, b. in Gilead, Me., Feb. 23, 1804; m. Dec. 22, 1828, Mary Peabody; she d. 26 Aug., 1872. He d. in Gilead, 3 May, 1878.

 iv. DARIUS⁷, b. in Gilead, April 1, 1805.
  He graduated from Bowdoin College, 1830, studied law and was admitted to the bar; set. in Rockton, Winnebago Co., Ill., and became a farmer; d. unm. Nov , 1880.

639. v. PROF. SAMUEL⁷, b. in Gilead, Dec. 19, 1806; m. Sept. 15, 1836, Mary Jane Moulton, dau. of Dr. Jotham Moulton of Bucksport, Me., b. Sept. 20, 1810; d. 11 Oct., 1887.
  Her sister Lucy S., m. Samuel Adams of Castine, Me.
  Dr. Adams received his early education in the common schools of Maine and in Gorham Academy, entering Bowdoin College at Brunswick in 1827. He graduated with honor in 1831, and became principal of the high school at Bucksport, Me. Having begun the study of medicine at Palmyra, N. Y., he returned to Maine and continued his studies with Dr. Jotham Moulton of Bucksport, also attended medical lectures at the College and received the degree of M. D. in 1836. He acted as tutor of modern languages in the College, and began to practice medicine in Brunswick. He removed to Jacksonville in 1838, and became professor of Chemistry, Mineralogy and Geology in Illinois College, spending the remainder of his life as a teacher and writer in connection with the College, and attaining a most honored and extensive reputation. Several able papers were contributed by him in 1871-75 to the Biblical Repository and the New Englander in review of Darwin, Comte and Spencer. He was a lover of art and science, and is spoken of with the highest esteem by all his students. He d. at Jacksonville, 28 Apr., 1877.

640. vi. DEBORAH⁷, b. in Gilead, Mar. 23, 1808; m. April 28, 1835, Thomas Peabody; he d. in Sheridan township, Davise Co., Mo., 19 July, 1870. She d. in Gilead, Me., 11 Sept., 1854.

 vii. LUCY⁷, b. in Gilead, June 9, 1810; m. Sept., 1841, Rev. Sylvanus Robbins, M. D., of Webster City, Iowa. She d. in Gilead, 22 June, 1882.

641. viii. APHIA⁷, b. in Gilead, Oct. 3, 1811; m. April 3, 1837, Caleb S. Peabody, b. Oct. 9, 1808; d. 10 Oct., 1888. She died in Gorham, Me., 3d Nov., 1851.

642. ix. ISAAC[7], b. in Gilead, July 23, 1813 ; m. Oct., 1845, Lucia K. Bartlett of Bethel, Me. ; she d. soon after her dau., 1864.
   He was a merchant; set. in Rockton, Winnebago Co., Ill., and d. 15 April, 1883.

643. x. DEA. ISRAEL[7], b. in Gilead, May 26, 1815 ; m. Dec. 2, 1843, Betsey E. Stearns of Bethel, Me. He settled in Bethel, Me.; rem. about 1870 to Manhattan, Riley Co., Kan.

644. xi. OLIVE[7], b. in Gilead, Oct. 31, 1818 ; m. Feb. 21, 1843, David Blake of Bethel, Me.; he d. 8 Aug., 1856. She was a widow on the home farm, Gilead, Me.; d. 27 Mar., 1895.

Children of SAMUEL[6], (1782) [271] (Capt. Samuel[5], Capt. Isaac[4], Jr., Isaac[3], Sergt. Abraham[2], Robert[1]) and Sarah or Sally (Wright) Adams; res. Watertown, Jefferson Co., N. Y.

   i. JOHN WRIGHT[7], b. in Jaffrey, N. H., Nov. 5, 1816; [m. 1846, Barrintha Gowdy, b. 1826; d.;]1895 ; res. Watertown, N. Y.; d. without issue, 1884.

645. ii. ISRAEL[7], b. in Rodman, N. Y., Nov. 12, 1818 ; m. Jan. 23, 1857, Harriet A. Boynton, dau. of Jona. Boynton, who rem. from Bennington, Vt., to Rodman in 1809 ; she was b. in 1826. He d. in Watertown, 16 Feb., 1896.

   iii. ARTEMAS L.[7], b. in Rodman, Jan., 1821 ; m. (1) 1854, Delilah Hill ; d. 1861 ; m. (2) Mary J. Adams; res. Watertown, N. Y.

   iv. LUCY A.[7], b. in Rodman, Sept. 3, 1822 ; m. 1868, Pierson K. Thurston; he d. in 1869. She d. in Watertown, 20 Jan., 1870.

   v. CAROLINE ELIZABETH[7], b. in Rodman, July 21, 1826 ; m. Feb. 12, 1865, Henry Andrews; he d. 1896. She d. 1871 ; no issue.

Child of SAMUEL[6], (1782) and Eliza (Larned) Adams.

   vi. SARAH E.[7], b. in Watertown, Aug. 31, 1843 ; d. 7 Sept., 1845.

Children of LUCY[6], (1785) [272] (Capt. Samuel[5], Capt. Isaac[4], Jr., Isaac[3], Sergt. Abraham[2], Robert[1]) and Lieut. Artemas Lawrence; res. Jaffrey, N. H.

   i. LUCY LAWRENCE, b. Apr. 8, 1805 ; m. —— Barrett ; res. Jamestown, N. Y.

   ii. MARY ANN LAWRENCE, b. Sept. 23, 1811 ; m. —— Fenton ; res. Jamestown, N. Y.

Children of MARY⁶, (1787) [**273**] (Capt. Samuel⁵, Capt. Isaac⁴, Jr., Isaac³, Sergt. Abraham², Robert¹) and Perley Putnam Burnham; res., Gilead, Me.

    i. CHARLES BURNHAM. b. Oct. 30, 1810; d. unm. at Gilead, 1 June, 1848.
    ii. MARY BURNHAM, b. Feb. 28, 1812; m. about 1848, Dean Lunt of Peru, Me; he d. Mar., 1883. She d. 5 Oct., 1887; no issue.
    iii. PERLEY P. BURNHAM, b. Apr. 10, 1814; d. unm. at Gilead, 29 Sept., 1874.
    iv. PINCKNEY BURNHAM (twin), b. Apr. 10, 1814; m. (1) Sept. 10, 1839, Lydia Cross; she d. without issue; m. (2) Feb. 22, 1845, Betsey M. Austin of Peru, Me.; m. (3) Apr. 7, 1864, Nancy E. Walker; res. Bethel, Me. He d. 1 Dec., 1893.
    v. GEO. BURNHAM, b. Feb. 2, 1816; m. Jan. 27, 1842, Florilla A. Burbank of Gilead, Me.
646. vi. BETSEY ADAMS BURNHAM, b. Dec. 20, 1817; m. Jan. 4, 1842, Valentine L. Stiles, b. Aug. 24, 1818; d. 10 Jan. 1875; res. Gorham, Me. She d. 5 Nov., 1891.
    vii. LUCY ANN BURNHAM, b. Jan. 20, 1819; m. 1848, James L. Dillaway of Boston; he d. at Bethel, Me., 7 Apr., 1883. She d. in Bethel, Me., 15 Jan., 1882.

Children of JACOB⁶, (1791) [**274**] (Capt. Samuel⁵, Capt. Isaac⁴, Jr., Isaac³, Sergt. Abraham², Robert¹) and Jemima Van Skiver) Adams; res. (Glenvia) Picton, Ont.

    i. ELIZA⁷, b. in (Glenvia) Picton, Dec. 25, 1817; m. Geo. Jones of Hiller township, Prince Edward Co., Ont. She d. about 1845.
    ii. MARY⁷, b. in Picton, Jan. 8, 1820; m. Wm. Johnson of Consecon, Ont. She d. about 1875.
    iii. LUCY⁷, b. in Picton, Nov. 29, 1821; m. Aug. 22, 1849, Wm. B. Blakely of Cherry Valley; living 1898.
    iv. DANIEL⁷, b. in Picton, Nov. 11, 1823; m. at Auburn, N. Y. He d. in Auburn a few years ago.
    v. CHRISTIANA⁷, b. in Picton, Feb. 21, 1826; d. unm. about 1867.
    vi. ISABELLA⁷, b. in Picton, June 16, 1828; m. Daniel Howe of Hillers, Ont.; deceased.

Child of ELIZABETH⁶, (1794) [**275**] (Capt. Samuel⁵, Capt. Isaac⁴, Jr., Isaac³, Sergt. Abraham², Robert¹) and Eliphaz Chapman; res. Gilead, Me.

    i. LUCY ELIZABETH⁷, b. in Gilead, Oct. 31, 1831; m. Dec. 19, 1853, Jos. G. Rounds; he d. in Malden, Mass., July, 1892. She d. in Malden, Oct., 1894.
    They rem. from Winthrop, Me., to Malden, Mass.

Seventh Generation.] OF NEWBURY, MASS. 149

Children of JONATHAN⁶, (1801) [276] (Capt. Samuel⁵, Capt. Isaac⁴, Jr., Isaac³, Sergt. Abraham², Robert¹) and Hannah (Adams) Adams; res. Chester, Vt.

    i. SAMUEL SWAN⁷, b. in Jaffrey, N. H., Sept. 18, 1826; d. in California, 8 Sept., 1850.

    ii. GEORGE SPOFFORD⁷, b. in Jaffrey, Oct. 2, 1827, d. in Chester, Vt., 25 Feb., 1839.

647. iii. ENOS HOLMES⁷, b. in Jaffrey, Dec. 31, 1829 ; m. (1) Mar. 17, 1857, Clemintine Ward of Chester, Vt., b. May 7, 1838 ; m. (2) Sept. 4, 1870, Lizzie Albee of Springfield, Vt., b. June 19, 1834. He rem. from Chester to Lowell, Mass., 1845.

648. iv. DARIUS⁷, b. in Jaffrey, 1831; m. May 8, 1854, Gracie A. Huey of Springfield, Vt. He d. in Lowell, Mass., 14 Dec., 1869, and widow m. Joseph Smart of Ascutneyville, Vt.

    v. HARRIET MARIA⁷, b. in Oct. 7, 1834 ; m. Nov. 30, 1854, George L. Cutler of Springfield, Vt. She d. 6 July, 1874.

649. vi. CHARLES ANDERSON⁷, b. June 17, 1837 ; m. May 5, 1855, Annette Sawyer, dau. of Samuel and Dorothy Sawyer of Lowell, Mass. He enlisted in June, 1862, in Co. H, 33d Mass. Reg. He d. at Lookout Mountain, 28 Oct., 1863.

650. vii. ELLEN LOUISA⁷, b. in Chester, Oct. 26, 1839 ; m. Nov. 9, 1878, Rev. J. F. Simmons ; res. Woodstock, Vt.

651. viii. GEORGE DANIEL⁷, b. in Chester, Sept. 28, 1843 ; m. Sept. 8, 1869, Dora Hussey of Billerica, Mass., dau. of Christopher C. and Lydia (Coffin) Hussey of Nantucket, Mass.; res. Wellesley Hills, Mass.

Children of DEBORAH⁶, (1782) [277] (Israel⁵, Jr., Israel⁴, Isaac³, Sergt. Abraham², Robert¹) and Solomon Winchester; res. Wiscassett, Me.

    i. THOMAS WELD WINCHESTER, d. 1858.

    ii. MARY ELIZABETH WINCHESTER, m. (1) John T. Brown of Baltimore, Md.; m. (2) June, 1847, Coleman S. Adams, son of Joseph Searle and Hannah (Wells) Adams. She d. 2 Oct., 1856.

    iii. MARTHA S. WINCHESTER, d. unm. in Baltimore, Md., 1872.

Child of JOSEPH SEARLE⁶, (1785) [278] (Israel⁵, Jr., Israel⁴, Isaac³, Sergt. Abraham², Robert¹) and Hannah (Wells) Adams; res. Hill, N. H., and Framingham, Mass.

652. i. COLEMAN SEARLE⁷, b. in Hebron, N. H., May 6, 1826 ; m. (1) June, 1847, Mary Elizabeth Winchester ; she d. 2 Oct., 1856 ; m. (2) June, 1859, Abby W. Whitney, b. June, 1829; d. 24 Mar., 1879.

    He studied medicine and law; rem. to Boston, and thence to Framingham, Mass., where he d. 24 Aug., 1885.

Children of CHARLES⁶, (1812) [**279**] (Israel⁵, Jr., Israel⁴, Isaac³, Sergt. Abraham², Robert¹) and Melinda (Emerson) Adams; res. Londonderry, N. H.

653.   i. JOSEPH⁷, b. in Bridgewater, N. H., Oct. 21, 1838; m. June 28, 1868, Georgiana Kelly of W. Rumney, N. H., dau. of Moses and Aurilla Kelly, b. Mar. 9, 1849. He d. 27 Oct., 1870.
      ii. EBEN E.⁷, b. in Hebron, N. H., Nov. 10, 1840; d. 27 Sept., 1848.
      iii. CHARLES WESLEY⁷, b. in Hebron, Mar. 18, 1844; d. 6 June, 1864.
654.   iv. ISRAEL GILMAN⁷, b. in Hebron, April 5, 1846; m. May 28, 1871, Ruby Anna Elliot, dau. of Daniel Elliot of Rumney, N. H., b. Sept. 11, 1848; res. Londonderry, N, H.
      v. OCENIA⁷, b. in Hebron, Oct. 30, 1849; d. 21 Oct., 1850.
      vi. MARY ANN⁷, b. in Hebron, Aug. 16, 1852; d. 22 Sept., 1863.
      vii. EBEN GEORGE⁷, b. in Hebron, Oct. 23, 1854; d. 2 Apr., 1856.
      viii. OCENIA M.⁷, b. in Hebron, June 13, 1858; d. 6 Sept., 1863.

Children of GEORGE W.⁶, (1815) [**280**] (Israel⁵, Jr., Israel⁴, Isaac³, Sergt. Abraham², Robert¹) and Louisa M. (Tandy) Adams; res. Haverhill, Mass.

655.   i. JOHN QUINCY⁷, b. in Haverhill, Feb. 17, 1844; m. Dec. 13, 1875, Eleanor Ella Hunkins; res. Haverhill, Mass. *d. July 8, 1931*
656.   ii. REV. FRANK E.⁷, b. in Haverhill, Nov. 29, 1847; m. (1) 1876, Mary E. Parker, dau. of Haven and Elizabeth Parker of Hill, N. H.; she d. 16 Aug., 1889; m. (2) July, 1893, Mrs. Elizabeth M. Knott of Port Dover, Ont.
He is a Universalist clergyman.
      iii. CHARLES H.⁷, b. in Haverhill, July 4, 1851. *unm.*
He graduated at the New Hampton Institute, 1871, and at the Boston University Law School, 1874, with the degree of L. L. D.; unm.; res. Haverhill, Mass,
      iv. GEORGE M.⁷, b. in Haverhill, Dec. 7, 1858; m. about 1885, Sarah Herron of Cheyenne, Wyo.; she d. 1887; res. La Plata Junc., La Plata Co., Col.

Children of ISRAEL⁶ 3D, (1768) [**281**] (Israel⁵, Israel⁴, Sarah³, Sergt. Abraham², Robert¹) and Sally (Adams) Adams; res. Rindge, N. H.

657.   i. SYBIL⁷, b. in Rindge, Jan. 7, 1797; m. June 1, 1826, Ebenezer Stratton; he d. 5 Jan., 1864. She d. in Jaffrey, N. H., 16 Aug., 1870.

Seventh Generation.] OF NEWBURY, MASS. 151

  ii. SUSAN⁷, b. in Rindge, Dec. 24, 1798; m. (1) July 5, 1827, Martin Smith, son of David Smith; he rem. to Pawlet, Vt., where he d. leaving a son, Martin A. Smith of Pittsford, Vt.; m. (2) Adin Green of Middletown, Vt.; he d. Nov., 1860, leaving a son, Albert A. Green, b. June 16, 1844. She d. in Middletown, Vt., 13 Oct., 1886.

  iii. CLARISSA⁷, b. in Rindge, Jan. 10, 1802 ; d. unm. in Jaffrey, N. H., 13 Aug., 1869.

  iv. ISRAEL⁷, b. in Rindge, Mar. 12, 1804; d. 1 Aug., 1809.

658. v. ALBERT⁷, b. in Rindge, May 4, 1807 ; m. May 26, 1836, Mary Pollard of Winchendon, N. H., dau. of Levi and Rhoda Pollard; she d. 29 Oct., 1884.
    He was a farmer in Rindge, N. H., d. 13 May, 1875.

  vi. ISRAEL⁷, b. in Rindge, Jan. 16, 1810; d. 1 Apr., 1810.

659. vii. ARAD⁷, b. in Rindge, Apr. 26, 1812 ; m. May 9, 1839, Ruba Hall, b. Dec. 7, 1815.
    He was a merchant in Rindge and Jaffrey, N. H., for 20 years, and was a director of Monadnock Bank. He d. in Jaffrey, 25 July, 1877.

660. viii. LOUISA⁷, b. in Rindge, Jan. 22, 1815; m. (1) 1844, Marshall Adams Hale, son of Moses and Ruth (Towne) Hale, b. July 11, 1822 ; he d. 18 July, 1852; m. (2) Mar. 16, 1856, John Platts, son of Asa Platts of Charlestown, Mass.

Children of LIEUT. AND MAJ. JOHN⁶, (1766) [282] Capt. John⁵, Israel⁴, Sarah³, Sergt. Abraham², Robert¹) and Dorcas (Falkner) Adams; res. No. Andover, Mass.

661. i. COL. JOSEPH HENRY⁷, b. in No. Andover, Mar. 21, 1790 ; m. about 1816-7, Sarah Brown White.
    He settled in Boston, where he became Lieut.-Colonel of the Independent Corps of Cadets ; president of the Ocean Ins. Co., and was elected in 1842 president of the N. E. Mutual Marine Insurance Co., which positions he held until his death, 1 July, 1861.

662. ii. HANNAH⁷, b. in North Andover, Dec. 18, 1791; m. May 4, 1813, Daniel Appleton, Jr., Esq., of Haverhill and Boston, b. in Haverhill, Dec. 10, 1785, rem. to New York in 1825 ; founded the famous Appleton Publishing House, and published his first work in 1831, his son William H. being his chief assistant. He d. in New York, 27 Mar., 1849. Hannah d. 28 May, 1859.

  iii. MARY HOLT⁷, b. in No. Andover, Nov. 4, 1793 ; m. Aug. 14, 1838, Nathaniel Lord, Jr., of Ipswich, Mass. She d. without issue.

663. iv. CHARLOTTE⁷, b. in No. Andover, May 29, 1796 ; m. July 14, 1821, Lieut. Isaac Osgood ; he d. 2 Sept., 1834 ; res. No. Andover, Mass. She d. 27 July, 1871.

 v. ISAAC⁷, b. in No. Andover, Oct. 27, 1798 ; d. 27 Oct., 1801.
 vi. MARTHA⁷, b. in No. Andover, May 28, 1801 ; m. Sept. 30, 1829, Rev. John Chauncey of Charlton, Mass. She d. in Schenectady, N. Y., 25 July, 1875.
 vii. LOUISA⁷, b. in No. Andover, Dec. 28, 1803 ; m. Dec. 7, 1825, Jonathan Leavitt.
 viii. SARAH ANN⁷, b. in North Andover, Feb. 2, 1806 ; m. Nov. 9, 1834, Rev. Asa D. Smith, D. D., b. in Amherst, N. H., Sept. 21, 1809 ; d. in Hanover, N. H., 16 Aug., 1877. She d. in Hanover, N. H., 24 Sept., 1882.
 ix. EMELINE OSGOOD⁷, b. in No. Andover, Jan. 31, 1808 ; d. 21 Mar., 1811.
 x. JOHN OSGOOD⁷, b. in Andover, Sept. 3, 1811 ; d. 1 Jan., 1832.

Children of DANIEL⁶, (1775) [**283**] (David⁵, Israel⁴, Sarah³, Sergt. Abraham², Robert¹) and Sophia (Kimball) Adams; res. W. Boxford, Mass.

 i. EDWIN S.⁷, b. in Boxford, Sept. 14, 1806 ; m. (1) Jan. 13, 1842, Elvira Chase, dau. of James and Hannah (Kimball) Chase, b. 1809 ; d. 2 July, 1879 ; m. (2) about 1880, Mrs. Amanda (Fowler) Davis ; she d. March, 1887, a week later than he died. He d. in West Boxford, Mass., Mar., 1887 ; no issue.
664. ii. JULIA MARIA⁷, b. in Boxford, Jan. 14, 1809 ; m. Feb. 1, 1844, Leverett Winslow Spofford, b. Nov. 11, 1809.

Child of CAPT. JOHN MARSH⁶, (1779) [**284**] (David⁵, Israel⁴, Sarah³, Sergt. Abraham², Robert¹) and Mary (Jackson) Adams; res. Londonderry, N. H.

 i. JOHN MARSH⁷, JR., b. in Londonderry, Sept. 18, 1815 ; m. 1841, Mary Ann Flanders ; living 1895.
 He rem. soon after marriage, 1841, to Le Roy, Genesee Co., N.Y., and thence to Toronto, Ont. In 1866, he settled in Monroe, Mich., where he was a hardware merchant, and where he d. 26 June, 1883, age 67 years ; no issue.

Children of ROBERT⁶, (1783) [**285**] (David⁵, Israel⁴, Sarah³, Sergt. Abraham², Robert¹) and Sally (Jackson) Adams; res. Londonderry, N. H., and Ashtabula, Co., O.

665. i. SAMUEL JACKSON⁷, b. in Londonderry, Mar. 16, 1810 ; m. (1) at Cassewaga, Pa., Jan. 17, 1835, Phebe E. Stevens; m. (2) Polly James ; res. Richmond, O. He d. 16 July, 1862.

666. ii. BENJAMIN FRANKLIN[7], b. in Londonderry, Oct. 2, 1811; m. Apr. 7, 1834, Hannah Greeley, dau. of Gilbert Greeley; she m. 2nd Granville Hill of Hudson, N. H., and res. later at Nashau, N. H. He d. at Le Roy, N. Y., 10 Oct., 1848.

iii. DAVID[7], b. in Londonderry, May 4, 1813; d. 14 May, 1815.

667. iv. CLARISSA JANE[7], b. in Londonderry, May 12, 1816; m. Alonzo Helmer. She d. 2 Sept., 1869.

668. v. PRESCOTT JONES[7], b. in Londonderry, Oct. 6, 1817; m. Jan. 3, 1843, Artemesia Whitford; she d. 20 Nov., 1892; res. Leonidas, Mich. He d. 19 Apr., 1899.

vi. MARGARET E.[7], b. in Londonderry, Nov. 2, 1821; m. Dec. 12, 1849, Loring Houghton; he d. 23 Dec., 1891; res. Richmond, O.; no issue.

vii. DAVID JACKSON[7], b. in Londonderry, Nov. 24, 1823; m. May 13, 1850, Mary Maxwell Smith, dau. of Samuel Smith, b. in Cazenovia, N. Y., Jan. 19, 1824. He set. in Warren, O. in 1875; living 1900; no issue.

viii. MARTHA MARIA[7], b. in Londonderry, Dec. 19, 1825; d. 12 May, 1841.

xi. NANCY[7], b. in Londonderry, Sept. 29, 1827; d. 11 Apr., 1843.

Children of JENNY[6], (1784) [286] (John[5], Jr., John[4], John[3], Sergt. Abraham[2], Robert[1]) and Robert Colburn; res. Springfield, N. H.

i. BETSEY COLBURN. b. in Wheelock, Vt., Sept. 16, 1809; d. unm. in New London, N. H., 17 Aug., 1872.

ii. ASA COLBURN, b. in Wheelock, Mar. 7, 1811; d. 28 Jan., 1893; res. White River Junction, Vt.

iii. JOHN ADAMS COLBURN, b. in Wheelock, Oct. 7, 1812; res. Pennacook, N. H., 1891.

iv. CYRUS COLBURN, b. in New London, N. H., Aug. 31, 1814.

v. JOHANNA COLBURN, b. in New London, Oct. 7, 1816.

vi. CHARLES COLBURN, b. in Springfield, N. H., Feb. 18, 1819; d. in Fall River, Mass., 24 Jan., 1891.

vii. MARY JANE COLBURN, b. in Springfield, Nov. 13, 1821; rem. to Wisconsin.

viii. IRENA A. COLBURN, b. in Springfield, Mar. 30, 1823; d. 24 Mar., 1846.

ix. HARRIET A. COLBURN, b. in Springfield, Apr. 9, 1826; m.; but no issue.

Children of HEZEKIAH⁶, (1786) [**287**] (John⁵, John⁴, John³, Sergt. Abraham², Robert¹) and Peggy (Stinson) Adams; res. New London, N. H.

669. i. MARY J.⁷, b. in New London, Jan. 27, 1814 ; m. Feb. 10, 1837, Simeon B. Drake, b. June 6, 1806 ; d. 8 Jan., 1873.
670. ii. NANCY S.⁷, b. in New London, May 24, 1815 ; m. (1) 1832, Allen Haskins, b. 1809 ; d. 1845 ; m. (2) Sept., 1847, David Cooper, b. June 14, 1799 ; d. 26 June, 1885; P. O., Sutton, N. H.

Children of POLLY⁶, (1799) [**288**] (Corp. John⁵, Jr., John⁴, John³, Sergt. Abraham², Robert¹) and Seth Freeman Sargent; res. New London, N. H.

  i. RANSOM SARGENT, b. Aug. 7, 1824 ; d. 10 Aug., 1825.
671. ii. CYRILLA SARGENT, b. Aug. 24, 1826 ; m. Geo. W. F. Hayes ; res. New London, N. H. She d. 7 Sept., 1886.
  iii. RANSOM F. SARGENT, b. Mar. 16, 1837.

Children of ASA⁶, (1781) [**289**] (Benjamin⁵, John⁴, John³, Sergt. Abraham², Robert¹) and Sophronia (Hutchinson) Adams; res. North Tunbridge, Vt.

672. i. AZRO⁷, b. in Tunbridge, Feb. 6, 1822 ; m. May 4, 1851, Mary C. Hawes of Concord, N. H. ; res. Chelsea ; P. O., No. Tunbridge, Vt.
  ii. CAROLINE E.⁷, b. in Tunbridge, June 1, 1824 ; m. June 1, 1848, Harvey Noyes. She d. 16 Sept., 1890 ; res. No. Tunbridge, Vt. ; no issue.
  iii. TWIN SISTERS, b. Aug. 7, 1826 ; d. next day.
  iv. SARAH M.⁷, b. in Tunbridge, June 5, 1828 ; m. Nov. 26, 1863, James Pressey ; res. No. Tunbridge, Vt. ; no issue.
  v. SUSAN H.⁷, b. in Tunbridge, Oct. 20, 1830 ; d. 7 Oct., 1833.

Children of BENJAMIN⁶, (1787) [**291**] (Benjamin⁵, John⁴, John³, Sergt. Abraham², Robert¹) and Susan (Hutchinson) Adams; res. Tunbridge and Duxbury, Vt.

  i. BENJAMIN H.⁷, b. in Tunbridge, Nov. 17, 1810 ; m. Nov. 4, 1837, Melvina M. Cushman, b. Dec. 10, 1808 ; she m. 2d Nathaniel Stockwell of Waitsfield, Vt.
  He studied law, and was admitted to the bar of Orange Co., Vt., June 15, 1836; rem. Jan., 1839 to Waitsfield, Vt., where he d. 13

Oct., 1849; "a rare man, gifted, eloquent, persuasive, genial, generous to a fault, the best advocate I ever saw or heard," was said by one who knew him.

He was a soldier in the War of 1812, and was drawing a pension at time of death.

674. ii. SUSAN⁷, b. in Tunbridge, 1823; m. 1847, Park Avery; res. Moretown, Vt.

Children of SOLOMON⁶, JR., (1780) [293] (Solomon⁵, John⁴, John³, Sergt. Abraham², Robert¹) and Mary (Collins) Adams; res. Springfield and New London, N. H.

675. i. MARY E.⁷, b. in Springfield, May 29, 1814; m. Oct. 24, 1834-5, Ija Gay of New London; he d. 27 Sept., 1888, age 81 yrs. 8 mos. She d. May 1895, age 81 years.

ii. MIRANDA SMITH⁷, b. in Springfield, Oct., 19, 1816; unm.; res. New London, N. H.

676. iii. DENNIS H.⁷, b. in Springfield, Nov. 16, 1819-20; m. (1) Sept. 13, 1850, Betsey A. Everett, b. in New London, Nov. 27, 1833; d. in Sutton, N. H., 14 Sept., 1864; m. (2) Dec. 16, 1865, Betsey A. Clough Upton of Wilmot, b. Mar. 1, 1842; d. in Pennacook, N. H., 17 May, 1889.
He set. in New London, 1824; rem. to Sutton, N. H., 1857.

677. iv. JOSEPH COLLINS⁷, b. in New London, July 31, 1824; m. Nov. 29, 1857, Ann Elizabeth Wiggins of Springfield, N. H.; res. New London, N, H. He d. 18 Oct., 1899.

678. v. NORMAN B.⁷, b. in New London, Dec. 22, 1828; m. Nov. 6, 1852, Hannah A. J. Sargent of Dumbarton, N. H.; she m. 2nd April 20, 1872, Solon Cooper; res. New London, N. H. He d. 6 May, 1889, age 60 yrs. 4 mos. 14 days.

Children of EMILY⁶, [1794) [294] (Solomon⁵, John⁴, John³, Sergt. Abraham², Robert¹) and Ezekiel Sargent; res. New London, N. H.

i. W. H. H. SARGENT, b. May 2, 1819.

ii. EMILY MARIA SARGENT, b. Mar. 18, 1821.

iii. EDWARD RULLIVEN SARGENT, b. Mar. 18, 1823.

iv. JULIA A. SARGENT, b. Apr. 13, 1825.

v. LOUIS ADAM SARGENT, b. July 12, 1829.

vi. ANDREW J. SARGENT, b. Nov. 12, 1833.

Children of PETER⁶, (1800) [**295**] (Solomon⁵, John⁴, John³, Sergt. Abraham², Robert¹) and Jemima (Whittier) Adams; res. New London, N. H.

  i. SYLVESTER⁷, b. in New London ; d. age 2 years.
  ii. JEMIMA⁷, b. in New London about 1823; d. in W. Springfield, 1847, age 24 years.
679. iii. SYLVANUS⁷, b. in New London, Jan. 27, 1825 ; m. (1) about 1847, Martha S. Hoyt ; m. (2) Harriet E. Flagg ; m. (3) Aldena D. Matthews ; res. W. Rumney, N. H.
  iv. ROXALIA⁷, b. in New London, 1827 ; d. 1833.
  v. RUTH⁷, b. in New London, 1829 ; m. Chester Preston. She d. 1855-6; no issue.
680. vi. JOHN Q.⁷, b. in Orange, Nov. 22, 1830 ; m. (1) ——— ; m. (2) Amanda Farmer, b. Jan. 8, 1837 ; d. 1863. He d. 1863.
  vii. NAOMI⁷, b. in Orange, 1832 ; m. (1) ———Stevens ; m. (2) Justin Colburn. She d. 1890.
  viii. ELIZABETH⁷, b. 1834 ; m. Frank Dunton. She d. 1890.
  ix. ADELINE⁷, b. in Orange, 1836 ; d. 1855.
  x. DANIEL⁷, b. in Orange, 1837 ; d. 1863.

Children of DANIEL NOYES⁶, (1803) [**296**] (Solomon⁵, John⁴, John³, Sergt. Abraham², Robert¹) and Eliza (Williams) Adams; res. West Springfield, N. H.

  i. SUSAN AUGUSTA⁷, b. in Springfield, N. H., 1833 ; m. Nov. 20, 1862, Rev. Lucian H. Adams of Derry, N. H., son of Edmund and Jane (Marsh) Adams, a missionary in Asia. She d. in Turkey, 18 Nov., 1866.
681. ii. DANIEL HAMILTON⁷, b. in Springfield, 1836 ; m. (1) Orinda T. Kingsley of Springfield ; m. (2) Ada Stacey of Providence, R. I. He was a merchant and the postmaster in W. Springfield, and d. 9 May, 1891.
  iii. EMILY ELIZA⁷, b. in Springfield, Mar. 13, 1840 ; m. Daniel P. Quimby. She d. Dec., 1874-5 ; no issue.

Children of DANIEL NOYES⁶, (1803) and Calista A. (Richardson) Adams.

682. iv. HELEN FRANCES⁷, b. in Springfield, Oct. 16, 1855 ; m. 1875, Waldo S. Chase. She d. Nov., 1883.
  v. JENNIE JOSEPHINE⁷, b. in Springfield, July 23, 1868; m. 1884, Rev. Lorin Webster, a son of Mrs. Sophia (Pierce) Webster; she was the 3d wife of Daniel Noyes Adams.

Children of LOIS⁶, (   ) [297] (Solomon⁵, John⁴, John³, Sergt. Abraham², Robert¹) and Gilbert Sawyer; res. Springfield, N. H.

683.   i.   GEORGE W. SAWYER, m. Jan. 3, 1863, Nancy Ann Ryder; res. Manchester, N. H.; d. 1884.
       ii. EMILY SAWYER. She d. at 17 years of age.

Children of MOSES⁶, JR., (1792) [298] (Moses⁵, John⁴, John³, Sergt. Abraham², Robert¹) and Betsey (Stinson) Adams; res. New London, N. H.

684.   i.   ANNA⁷, b. in New London, Oct. 4, 1820; m. Mar. 30, 1840, Martin Packard of Brockton, Mass.; he d. 26 Mar., 1894. She d. Sept., 1894.
685.   ii. DOLLY P.⁷, b. in New London, Nov. 22, 1825; m. Dec. 31, 1851, Asa Tribon of Brockton, Mass. She d. 6 Dec., 1894.
       iii. SARAH⁷, b. in New London, Oct. 15, 1833; d. in infancy.
686.   iv. MARY E.⁷, b. in New London, June 25, 1838; m. Jan. 12, 1866, David N. Chandler of Grafton, N. H. She d. 8 Dec., 1893.

Child of HON. CYRUS⁶, (1795) [299] (Moses⁵, John⁴, John³, Sergt. Abraham², Robert¹) and Nancy (Stinson) Adams; res. Grafton, N. H.

687.   i.   NANCY ALBINA⁷, b. in Grafton, Apr. 9, 1827; m. Feb. 20, 1851, Peter Kimball of Boscowen, N. H., son of Benjamin H. and Mary (Kilborn) Kimball, b. Mar. 25, 1817; d. 21 Mar., 1881; res. Grafton, N. H.

Children of HANNAH⁶, (1803) [300] (Moses⁵, John⁴, John³, Sergt. Abraham², Robert¹) and Benjamin Perley; res. Springfield, N. H.

       i.   CYRUS A. PERLEY; d. age 2 years.
       ii. ——— ———
       iii. HANNAH ADELPHIA PERLEY; m. Erastus Rollins; res. Frontariza, Mexico, in 1892

Children of RAPSIMA⁷, (1792) [**302**] (Jonathan⁵, John⁴, John³, Sergt. Abraham², Robert¹) and James Brocklebank; res. Plainfield, N. H.

    i. PARMELIA C. BROCKLEBANK; b. July 29, 1817; m. Mar. 23, 1846, Edson G. Baldwin ; res. Plainfield, N. H.
    ii. MOSES A. BROCKLEBANK, b. Mar. 24, 1819; m. Mar., 1844, Sophronia Wheeler ; res. Canaan, N. H.
    iii. MIRANDA BROCKLEBARK, b. Feb. 24, 1821 ; m. June 7, 1847, Stephen G. Bliss ; res. Hartford, Vt.
    iv. AMY W. BROCKLEBANK, b. June 28, 1823 ; m. in Wisconsin, and d. there 2 May, 1863.
    v. CYRUS A. BROCKLEBANK, d. unm. 26 May, 1854,
    vi. SARAH J. BROCKLEBANK, b. Oct. 2, 1824; m. and res. in Boston; d. 25 Feb., 1876.
    vii. MARY A. BROCKLEBANK, b. Mar. 2, 1832; m. Martin Chapman ; res. Meriden, N. H.
    viii. D. FRANKLIN BROCKLEBANK, b. Sept. 21, 1834; m. Jan. 24, 1864, Hattie Chapman ; res. Fitchburg, Mass.
    ix. LAURA L. BROCKLEBANK, b. May 19, 1837 ; m. Rev. A. R. B. Perkins, and d. in Raynham, Mass., 28 Dec., 1891.

Children of MOSES⁶, (1799) [**303**] (Jonathan⁵, John⁴, John³, Sergt. Abraham², Robert¹) and Mary (Folsom) Adams; res. Tunbridge, Vt.

688.   i. JOHN LEWIS⁷, b. in Tunbridge, Oct. 16, 1826 ; m. (1) July 9, 1851, Frances A. Broughton ; she d. 1859 ; m. (2) June 16, 1862, Mrs. Eliza Estee.
    He was a news correspondent in various localities. He d. in Burlington, Ia., 31 Aug. 1878.
689.   ii. MARTHA⁷, b. in Tunbridge, Jan. 11, 1833 ; m. (1) June 15, 1852, Henry Morse Sanborn, b. Jan. 10, 1833 ; he d. in Andersonville Prison, 11 Oct., 1864 ; m. (2) Nov. 3, 1868, John F. Bennett of Tunbridge, Vt.; res. Tunbridge, Vt.

Children of SETH⁶, (1803) [**304**] (Jonathan⁵, John⁴, John³, Sergt. Abraham², Robert¹) and Huldah (Folsom) Adams; res. Tunbridge, Vt.

    i. HANNAH⁷, b. in Tunbridge, Mar. 29, 1832 ; d. 6 Sept., 1834.
690.   ii. LUNA⁷, b. in Tunbridge, Jan. 30, 1836 ; m. Feb. 22, 1860, Alvah J. Dutton, son of John Dutton of W. Randolph, Vt. She is a widow ; res. W. Randolph, Vt.

691. iii. ARTHUR C.⁷, b. in Tunbridge, Feb. 5, 1842 ; m. Apr. 18, 1865, Rosa Lee, dau. of Michael and Mary (Cunningham) Lee, b. Dec. 25, 1839 ; res. Tunbridge, Vt.

Children of JONATHAN TENNY⁶, (1805) [305] (Jonathan⁵, John⁴, John³, Sergt. Abraham², Robert¹) and Hannah (Rackley) Adams; res. Pembroke, N. Y., and Shelby, Mich.

692. i. GEORGE WEYMOUTH⁷, b. in Tunbridge, Vt., June 8, 1828 ; m. Nov. 1, 1853, Anna Eliza Anderson, dau. of David and Harriet (Cleveland) Anderson.
He is a millwright; res. Corfu, Genesse Co., N. Y.

693 ii. DANIEL⁷, b. in Tunbridge, Sept. 5, 1830; m. Feb. 12, 1857, Julia M. Cummings, b. Dec. 31, 1839.
He removed to New York state with his parents in 1830, then to Fairfax Co., Va., and thence to Ovid, Branch Co., Mich. He was a carpenter and builder, and erected the first frame house in Denver, Col., in 1858 ; returned to Michigan in 1860, settling in Otto, Ocena Co., in 1864. He d. 14 July, 1891, a member of the Free Baptist Church.

694. iii. JOHN S.⁷, b. in Pembroke, N. Y., Sept. 5, 1831; m. 1855-6, Anna Maria Reynolds of Ovid, Mich.
He was a soldier ; enlisted in the fall of 1862 in the 5th Michigan Cavalry, and served in all the engagements of his regiment until he was captured at Trevilians, Va., June'11, 1864, and sent to Andersonville and Libby ; returning to Michigan in broken health. He d. near Hart, Oceana Co., 23 Oct., 1875, age 44 years.

iv. ELIZABETH JENETTE⁷, b. in Pembroke, June 19, 1834 ; m. Feb. 1, 1866, Dr. William E. Lewis ; res. Boston, Mass.; no issue.

695. v. JOSEPH S.⁷, b. in Pembroke, Feb. 28, 1836 ; m. 1861, Elizabeth Churchill of Batavia, N. Y. ; res. Scottsville, Mich.

696. vi. NATHAN⁷, b. in Pembroke, Mar. 9, 1838-9 ; m. Oct. 23, 1865, Emily C. Parson of Coldwater, Mich.
He was a soldier in the 11th Michigan regiment ; res. Shelby, Mich.

697. vii. HANNAH LORETTA⁷, b. in Darien, N. Y., Jan. 25, 1841 ; m. 1864, John Randall of Shelby, Mich. She d. Jan., 1893 ; res. Shelby, Mich.

Children of JONATHAN TENNY⁶, (1805) and Diadama (Warren) Adams.

698. vii. PHEBE ANN⁷, b. in Darien, N. Y., 1845 ; m. Nov. 6, 1866, Rev. Ambrose Bears of the Menonite Church ; res. Shelby, Mich. She d. 20 May, 1875.

160   ROBERT ADAMS   [Seventh Generation.

 ix. SETH⁷, b. in Darien, Feb. 23, 1847 ; d. 27 Aug., 1848.

699. x. HARRIET ELIZA⁷, b. in Darien, Nov. 22, 1849 ; m. June 1, 1868, Lawrence Colburn ; res. Shelby, Mich.

Children of GEORGE W.⁶, (1809) [306] (Jonathan⁵, John⁴, John³, Sergt. Abraham², Robert¹) and Eliza M. (Haskell) Adams; res. Tunbridge, Vt.

 i. ABIGAIL W.⁷, b. in Tunbridge, Aug. 27, 1833; d. 28 Nov., 1834.

 ii. REV. DAVID H.⁷, b. in Tunbridge, Aug. 25, 1835; m. (1) Aug. 17, 1865, Harriet S. Morey ; she d. 24 Dec., 1889 ; m. (2) June 5, 1894, Mrs. Arianna Merrill of Worcester, Mass.
  He graduated from Middlebury College, 1860 ; from New Hampton Theo. School, 1864, and set. as pastor of Free Baptist Church, Gonic, N. H.; rem. to Hampton, N. H., in June, 1895 ; no issue.

 iii. CYRUS A.⁷, b. in Tunbridge, Feb. 5, 1837 ; m. May 24, 1865, Ellen M. Gage.
  He was a member of the Brigade Band of the 2d Vermont Regiment ; d. in Huntington, Pa., 19 Sept., 1888; one child d. in infancy.

700. iv. GEORGE S.⁷, b. in Tunbridge, Mar. 26, 1841 ; m. Mar. 19, 1868, Bell J. West ; res. Chelsea, Vt.

 v. JOHN Q.⁷, b. in Tunbridge, Jan. 9, 1845 ; d. 18 Apr., 1864.

701. vi. FRANK A.⁷, b. in Tunbridge, Jan. 4, 1847 ; m. Jan. 31,1872, Carrie E. Davis ; res. Hanover, N. H.; P. O., Etna, N. H.

Children of ISRAEL⁶, (1780) 307] (Israel⁵, 3d, Matthew⁴, Dr. Matthew³, Sergt. Abraham², Robert¹) and Charity (Bailey) Adams; res. Henniker and Goshen, N. H.

702. i. CHARITY⁷, b. in Rowley, Mass., Feb. 29, 1801 ; m. (1) Feb. 5, 1829, Seth Franklin Currier of Hopkinton, N. H.; he died Aug., 1833 ; m. (2) John Palfrey. She d. in Nashua, N. H., 11 June, 1853.

703. ii. ISRAEL⁷, b. in Henniker, N. H., Dec. 4, 1802; m. (1) July 2, 1826, at Deerfield, N. Y., Sally Cross of Deerfield; she d. 2 June, 1832 ; m. (2) April 8, 1833, Lois Lillie ; res. Hornellsville, N. Y.

704. iii. ELIZABETH⁷, b. in Henniker, Aug. 17, 1804 ; m. Dec. 28, 1825, Dea. Timothy Morse, son of Rev. Timothy and Sally (Farmer) Morse, b. Sept. 11, 1795 ; d. in Lowell, Mass., 21 Nov., 1847 ; res. Hopkinton, N. H., and Lowell, Mass. She d. 5 June, 1877.

705. iv. THOMAS BAILEY⁷, b. in Henniker, May 27, 1806 ; m. Apr. 2, 1834, Mary Perry of Henniker, N. H.; res. Bradford, N. H. He d. in Hillsboro, N. H., 1897.

 v. GEORGE W.⁷, b. in Henniker, Dec. 4, 1807 ; d. same day.

Seventh Generation.] OF NEWBURY, MASS. 161

Children of ISRAEL[6], (1780) and Rhoda (Harthorn) Adams.

706. vi. EBENEZER H.[7], b. in Henniker, Sept. 10, 1809 ; m. (1) Apr. 3, 1838, Charlotte Purrington ; b. in Henniker, Nov. 5, 1814 ; d. in Goshen, N. H., 30 May, 1846 ; m. (2) Apr. 6, 1847, Mercy Purrington of Goshen, N. H.; she d. 4 Nov., 1848 ; m. (3) Feb. 12, 1849, Belinda Cutts of Newbury, N. H.
   He rem. to New London, N. H., in Apr., 1849 ; returned to Goshen in Jan.,1865 ; d. 10 Aug., 1877.

   vii. RHODA HOWE[7], b. in Henniker, Oct. 30, 1810 ; d. 4 Nov. following.

707. viii. AMANDA[7], b. in Henniker, Sept. 25, 1811; m. Apr. 7, 1833, Rev. Azel P. Brigham, son of Thomas Brigham, b. in Enosburg, Vt., April 7, 1809.
   He was educated at Redfield Academy, Kent's Hill, Me., and was a member of the N. E. M. E, Conference for twelve years ; he d. in Hanover, N. H., 28 Sept., 1843. She d. 16 Aug., 1848.

708. ix. AUGUSTA[7] (twin), b. in Henniker, Sept. 25, 1811 ; m. Sept. 13, 1841, Rev. Richard M. Smith, son of Luke and Sally (Fisher) Smith, b. in Georgetown, Me., Aug. 25, 1814.
   He was a teacher in Richmond Co., Ky., for six years after his marriage ; then was set. in Canton, Scituate and Bridgewater, Mass.; he d. 7 June, 1872. She d. in Providence, 8 Dec., 1896.

709. x. CHRISTOPHER C[7]., b. in Henniker, June 21, 1813 ; m. Sarah Ann Franklin.
   He removed to Hornellsville, N, Y., before marriage ; was in Hartsville (Purdy Creek P. O.) Steuben Co., N. Y., in 1878.

710. xi. JOHN[7], b. in Henniker, Dec. 3, 1815 ; m. (1) Mar. 27, 1840, Mary Moon ; she d. Dec., 1842 ; m. (2) Sept. 28, 1842, Nancy Davis, dau. of Oliver and Relief (Heath) Davis of Ackworth, N. H., res. Hornellsville, N. Y.; d. 28 Sept., 1843.

   xii. CASSANDRA[7], b. in Henniker, July 25, 1817 ; m. Sept. 30, 1851, Nathaniel W. Dudley, son of Jacob Dudley, b. in 'Andover, N. H., Jan. 7, 1807 ; d. in Lebanon, N. H., 29 Mar., 1879 ; she was his 3d wife. She d. in Lebanon, N. H., 23 Jan., 1881 ; no issue.

   xiii. AARON[7], b. in Henniker, May 21, 1819 ; d. 23 May, 1819 ; age 27 hours.

   xiv. MOSES[7] (twin), b. in Henniker, May 21, 1819 ; d. 22 May ; age 9 hours.

   xv. ROANA CUTLER[7], b. in Henniker, July 27, 1820 ; d. in Nashua, N. H., 18 Sept., 1838 ; age 18 years.

(11)

Children of JOHN⁶, (1776) [308] (John⁵, Matthew⁴, Dr. Matthew³, Sergt. Abraham², Robert¹) and Sarah (Kimball) Adams; res. Sutton, N. H.

711.   1. JUDITH FOLLANSBEE⁷, b. in Sutton, Nov. 19, 1799; m. 1820, Moses D. Wadleigh, son of Moses D. and Elizabeth (Dow) Wadleigh, b. Sept. 21, 1794; d. in Bradford, N. H., 8 July, 1850-1. She d. in Manchester, N. H., 4 Aug., 1853.

712.   ii. BENJAMIN F.⁷, b. in Sutton, Aug. 10, 1801; m. (1) 1824, Betsey Sargent of Warner, N. H., dau. of Asa Sargent; she d. 1829; m. (2) Oct. 11, 1832, Nancy N. White of Bow, N. H., b. Nov. 23, 1809; d. 7 Apr., 1869.
   He was a clothier by trade; was in business in Bradford, N. H. for 12 years; then settled on a farm in Sutton; was a representative in the legislature in 1858, and esteemed as an able man; d. in Sutton, 13 Apr., 1869.

713. iii. JOHN⁷, b. in Sutton, Oct. 26, 1803; m. Dec. 15, 1831, Mary Elizabeth Horton, dau. of Stephen and Margaret (McCoy) Horton of Milton, Mass., b. Nov. 11, 1812; d. suddenly 2 Jan., 1899, age 86 years.
   He located in Milton, Mass., where he was a stone-cutter and had charge of the Milton Railway Company; returned to Sutton in 1846, and occupied a farm, which he sold in Dec., 1864, taking up his abode in Warner village. He d. 26 July, 1865.

714. iv. SUSAN KIMBALL⁷, b. in Sutton, Jan. 15, 1807; m. Apr. 15, 1829, John Andrews, son of Nathan and Hannah (Gregg) Andrews, b. Mar. 3, 1804; d. in Bradford, N. H., 1 Jan., 1870. She d. in Melrose, Mass., 13 Sept., 1877.

715.   v. ELIZA JANE⁷, b. in Sutton, Jan. 22, 1809; m. Apr., 14, 1831, David A. Bunton, b. in Goffstown, N. H., Oct. 18, 1805, set. in Manchester, N. H., in Mar., 1837; became a director of the Manchester and Lowell R. R.; represented Manchester in the Legislature in 1842 and 43; was alderman in 1847 and 1865, and mayor in 1861 and 62. He d. 10 July, 1890.

716. vi. GEORGE W.⁷, b. in Sutton, Jan. 24, 1813; m. Oct. 15, 1840, Nancy C. Bean of Warner; she d. 19 Dec., 1896.
   He set. in Manchester, in 1846; was a grocer; d. 5 July, 1897.

     vii. HARRIET N.⁷, b. in Sutton, Sept. 3, 1815.
   She was a teacher in 1837-39; became a dress-maker in Manchester, and invented a chart for dress-cutting; she removed to her native town in 1883, and tho' in her 85th year, has materially assisted in supplying this record.

Children of HENRY⁶, (1787) [309] (John⁵, Matthew⁴, Dr. Matthew³, Sergt. Abraham², Robert¹) and Betsey (Maxom) Adams; res. Sutton, N. H.

        i. WARREN ALBERN⁷, b. in Sutton, July 27, 1815; d. in Sutton unm., 9 July, 1891.

ii. JUDITH⁷, b. in Sutton, Apr. 21, 1817; m. Feb. 22, 1838, Aldin Youngman of Lempster, N. H. She d. in Lempster, 30 Apr., 1892; had four children.
iii. JOHN Q⁷, b. in Sutton, May 14, 1819; d. 11 Apr., 1826.
iv. LINDSLEY⁷, b. in Sutton, May 18, 1821; m. Katie Meadley.
He was a dentist and d. suddenly in Oakland, Cal.; no issue
v. URSULA MARIA⁷, b. in Sutton, Oct. 1, 1823; d. in Bradford, N. H., 22 Sept., 1841.
vi. MARANTHA⁷, b. in Sutton, Jan. 19, 1825–6; d. in Lempster, N. H., 18 Oct., 1844.
vii. JOHN⁷, b. in Sutton, Dec. 14, 1827; d. Jan., 1849–50.
717. viii. HORTENSIA⁷, b. in Sutton, Apr. 20, 1830; m. Oct. 6, 1865, Alonzo Nelson, son of Adelbert W. Nelson; he d. 17 Aug., 1877. She d. 13 July, 1889.
718. ix. ADELAIDE⁷, b. in Sutton, Aug. 6, 1833; m. Feb. 11, 1857, David W. Bagley; he d. 20 Nov., 1898. She d. 25 Apr., 1896.
719. x. JOSEPH HENRY⁷, b. in Sutton, July 11, 1836; m. Aug. 24, 1862, Judith Sargent Currier, b. Jan. 17, 1832; res. Hopkinton and Contoocuck, N. H.

Children of BENJAMIN⁶, (1773) [310] (Benjamin⁵, Matthew⁴, Dr. Matthew³, Sergt. Abraham², Robert¹) and Susana (Goodhue) Adams; res. Newburyport and Boston, Mass.

i. SUSANNA⁷, b. in Newburyport, Oct. 3, 1797.
ii. SARAH⁷, b. in Newburyport, Aug. 15, 1799; d. same day.
iii. CAPT. SAMUEL GOODHUE⁷, b. in Newburyport, July 22, 1800; m. Sept. 5, 1822, Eliza Gordon.
He was a carpenter, and set. in Boston about 1811; was appointed on the police, May 26, 1854, and became Captain; was retired June 3, 1859; d. 3 June, 1859.
iv. PAUL⁷, b. in Newburyport, June 9, 1802; d. in 2 days.
v. SILAS⁷ (twin), b. in Newburyport, June 9, 1802; d. in 2 days.
vi. BENJAMIN⁷, b. in Newburyport, June 23, 1803.
vii. JOHN BODILY⁷, b. in Newburyport, Apr. 11, 1805.
viii. JOSEPH MITCHELL⁷, b. in Newburyport, Feb. 11, 1807.
ix. JAMES FOSTER⁷, b. in Newburyport, Dec. 8, 1808; d. 29 Dec., 1809.
x. ANDREW A.⁷, b. in Newburyport, Sept. 10, 1810; d. April, 1811.
xi. ELIZABETH⁷, b. in Newburyport, Feb. 7, 1812.
xii. THOMAS⁷, b. in Newburyport, Oct. 23, 1814.
xiii. CHARLES⁷, b. in Newburyport, Aug. 16, 1817; is reported to have m. twice; rem. to the west and never heard from. *m. Lucy Helen Ever removed to Helena. Brigadier-general in Confederate Army. His daughter Kate was second wife of Capt. Arthur Keller, father of Helen Adams Keller.*

Children of JUDITH⁶. (1775) [311] (Benjamin⁵, Matthew⁴, Dr. Matthew³, Sergt. Abraham², Robert¹) and David Hopson; res. Springfield, N. H.

    i. BENJAMIN HOPSON, b. Apr. 3, 1800; d. 6 Aug., 1800.
    ii. HANNAH R. HOPSON, b. Jan. 7, 1803; d. May, 1883.
    iii. DAVID HOPSON, b. July 20, 1817; d. 25 July, 1817.

Child of MATTHEW⁶, (1778) [312] (Benjamin⁵, Matthew⁴, Dr. Matthew³, Sergt. Abraham², Robert¹) and Rebecca (Dow) Adams; res. Newbury, N. H.

    i. BENJAMIN⁷, b. in Newbury, July 10, 1803. He d. in Woburn, Mass., 27 Aug., 1880.

Children of MATTHEW⁶, (1778) and Hannah (Cheney) Adams.

    ii. REBECCA⁷, b. in Newbury, May 25, 1806; m. Nov. 21, 1837, Joel Harriman. She d. in Newbury, 15 Mar., 1841; no surviving issue.

720.   iii. THOMAS JEFFERSON⁷, b. in Newbury, Nov. 29, 1807; m. Nov. 24, 1830, Rachel Rowe of Newbury, N. H.; res. Bradford, N. H. He d. 22 Feb., 1869, age 61 years.

721.   iv. JOHN LANGDON⁷ (twin), b. in Newbury, Nov. 29, 1807; m. June 12, 1832, Jane Felch of Newbury, N. H.; she d. 8 June, 1855. He d. in Franklin Falls, N. H., 25 Apr., 1886.

722.   v. ENOCH CHENEY⁷, b. in Newbury, Aug. 9, 1809; m. Nov. 26, 1846, Mrs. Elizabeth Bean (Eaton) Nourse of Hopkinton, N. H.
        He was gored by a bull and d. in New London, N. H., 9 July, 1880, age 71 years.

    vi. WILLIAM A.⁷, b. in Newbury, June 11, 1811.
        He was a successful teacher; d. unm., in Newbury, N. H., 3 July, 1836.

    vii. HANNAH C.⁷, b. in Newbury, Mar. 20, 1813; m. May 2, 1837, Squire Chase. She d. in Newbury, N. H.

    viii. JUDITH A.⁷, b. in Newbury, Dec. 23, 1814; m. Apr. 12, 1836, Ira Gilingham. She d. in Newbury, N. H.

    ix. SUSAN C⁷ (twin), b, in Newbury, Dec. 23, 1814; m. Nov. 12, 1845, James Madison Hoyt of Newbury, N. H., b. in Bradford, Sept. 20, 1814. She d. in Bradford, N. H.; no issue.

    x. HARRIET⁷, b. in Newbury, Mar. 5, 1817; m. Feb. 15, 1839, Reuben Johnson. She d. in Claremont, N. H.

    xi. LUCINDA⁷, b. in Newbury, Aug 19, 1819; m. Oct. 20, 1842, Albert Brown. She d. in Bradford, N. H.

xii. EMELINE⁷, b. in Newbury, April 22, 1821; m. Aug. 24, 1841, John Collins. She d. in Manchester, N. H., 1865; no issue.
xiii. ADELINE⁷, b. in Newbury, July 17, 1824; m. April 23, 1850, Moses Smythe. She d. in Bradford, N. H., 16 Sept, 1854.

Children of ELIZABETH⁶, (1780) [313] (Benjamin⁵, Matthew⁴, Dr. Matthew³, Sergt. Abraham², Robert¹) and Joseph Kelly; res. New London, N. H.

i. APHIA KELLY, b. Nov. 19, 1812; m. Joshua Colby; res. Merrimac, Mass.
ii. JUDITH A. KELLY, b. Feb. 10, 1814; d. 14 Feb., 1814.

Children of MARY⁶, (1782) [314] (Benjamin⁵, Matthew⁴, Dr. Matthew³, Sergt. Abraham², Robert¹) and Levi Harvey; res. New London, N. H.

i. GEO. W. HARVEY, b. Sept. 30, 1801; d. 1838.
ii. ELIZA HARVEY, b. Jan 2, 1803.
iii. JOHN L. HARVEY, b. April 22, 1805.
    Was a policeman in Boston, Mass.
iv. SARAH HARVEY, b. May 5, 1807.
v. RUTH W. HARVEY, b. Feb. 18, 1809; d. 18 Oct., 1832.
vi. JAMES M. HARVEY, b. Jan. 15, 1811; d. 13 Feb., 1811.
vii. PIERCE HARVEY, b. Dec. 17, 1811.
viii. WM. H. H. HARVEY, b. Dec. 22, 1813; d. 5 Nov., 1821.
ix. STEPHEN D. HARVEY, b. Dec. 15, 1815.
x. MARY A. HARVEY, b. Feb. 3, 1818.
xi. CALISTA HARVEY, b. Feb. 5, 1821; d. 29 June, 1822.
xii. RUFUS L. HARVEY, b. Oct. 25, 1823; d. 14 April, 1852.

Children of REV. THEOPHILUS B.⁶, (1789) [315] (Benjamin⁵, Matthew⁴, Dr. Matthew³, Sergt. Abraham², Robert¹) and Jemima (Knowlton) Adams; res. Ackworth, N. H.

i. JEREMIAH⁷, b. in Newburyport, Mass., Aug. 27, 1807; m. Emily Currier, dau. of John Currier of Unity, N. H. He d. in Nashua, N. H., July, 1854; no issue.
ii. LOUISA⁷, b. in Newburyport, Mar. 27, 1800; m. Asa Sargent of Ackworth, N. H. She d. of consumption soon after her marriage; no issue.
723. iii. REBECCA⁷, b. in Newburyport, Dec. 8, 1811; m. Ephraim Collins of Salisbury, N. H.

724. iv. THEOPHILUS B.¹, JR., b. in New London, N. H., April 23, 1814 ; m. Dec. 7, 1837, Fanny Currier, dau. of John Currier of Unity, N. H., b. April, 1816 ; living 1898. He set. in Nashua, N. H., 1845, d. April, 1896.
725. v. JOSEPH M⁷, b. in New London, Feb. 21, 1816 ; m. Abigail A. Weed. He d. in Cambridge, Mass., 31 June, 18—.
    vi. ALPHEUS⁷, b. in New London, Nov. 1, 1818. He was lost at sea.

Children of REV. THEOPHILAS B.⁶, (1789) and Lydia (Bagley) Adams.

    vii. JEMIMA⁷, b. in New London, Dec. 15, 1820 ; d. unm.
    viii. DOROTHY⁷, b. in New London, Dec. 17, 1821 ; m. Geo. Putnam of Newport, N. H.
726. ix. HARRISON H.⁷, b. in Ackworth, N. H., Aug. 31, 1823 ; m. Feb, 21, 1848, Lydia Ann Osgood of Amesbury ; set. in Newburyport, 1848. He d. in Newburyport, Mass., 4 Oct., 1877.
    x. JUDITH⁷, b. in Ackworth, Dec., 1824 ; d. unm.
    xi. CARVER PARKER⁷, b. in Ackworth, Aug. 27, 1826.
        He is said to have married twice, but no one is ready to supply a record ; many efforts to obtain it have failed ; resides Seabrook, N. H. He d. in Salisbury, Mass., 28 Sept., 1856.
    xii. LOUISA⁷, b. in Ackworth, April 26, 1828 ; d. in Salisbury, Mass., 28 Sept., 1856.
    xiii. JOHN B⁷., b. in Ackworth, Dec., 1829 ; d. Sept., 1831.

Children of JEREMIAH⁶, (1793) [316] (Benjamin⁵, Matthew⁴, Dr. Matthew³ Sergt. Abraham², Robert¹) and Sarah (Wardwell) Adams ; res. New London, N. H.

    i. MARY L⁷, b. in New London, Oct. 16, 1813 ; d. 10 Mar., 1836.
    ii. HANNAH R.⁷, b. in New London, Dec. 12, 1815 ; m. Sept. 8, 1854, Joseph Bartlett of Dorchester, N. H. They set. in Goffstown, N. H., where he d. 1877, age 67 years. She removed to Bedford, N. H., 1883, and d. 22 Feb., 1895; no issue.
727. iii. BENJAMIN F.⁷, b. in New London, June 24, 1818 ; m. 1839, Lucinda Allen of Milford, Mass. ; b. Oct. 12, 1817 ; d. in Jamestown, Mercer Co., Pa., 7 Oct., 1861. He resided several years in Milford, Mass. ; rem. and set. in Royalton, Crawford Co., Pa., 1855 ; d. 18 Feb., 1873.
    iv. SARAH⁷, b. in New London, May 12, 1820 ; d. 19 April, 1830.
    v. URSULA⁷, b. in New London, Jan. 16, 1823 ; d. 21 Aug., 1825.

Seventh Generation.] OF NEWBURY, MASS. 167

vi. URSULA C.⁷, b. in New London, July 18, 1825 ; m. Oct. 8, 1851, Charles P. Clement of Boscawen, N. H. She set. in Bedford, N. H., in 1876 ; rem. from Manchester ; no issue.

vii. ANDREW J.⁷, b. in New London, Mar. 18, 1828; d. 13 Sept,, 1828.

Child of CAPT. TAPPAN⁶, (1786) [317] (Abraham⁵, Abraham⁴, Dr. Matthew³, Sergt. Abraham², Robert¹) and Betsey (Morse) Adams; res. Boscawen, N. H.

728 i. MARY⁷, b. in Boscawen, 1806 ; m. Feb. 6, 1827, Luke Shepard. She d. in Boscawen, 20 Jan., 1834, age 28 years.

Child of ABRAHAM B.⁶, (   ) [318] (Abraham⁵, Abraham⁴, Dr. Matthew³, Sergt. Abraham², Robert¹) and Sarah (Elliot) Adams; res. Boscawen, N. H.

i. ENOCH ELLIOT⁷, b. in Boscawen, Feb. 17, 1810-12.
There were probably others, but the author has been unable to find them.

Children of ELI⁶, (1784) [319] (Enoch⁵, Richard⁴, Richard³, Sergt. Abraham², Robert¹) and Abigail (True) Adams; res. Salisbury, N. H.

i. ALVIN⁷, b. in Salisbury, 1825 ; m. Mar. 1845, Mrs. Phebe Flanders. He d. May, 1845 ; was killed by his team running away.

729. ii. FRANCIS⁷, b. in Salisbury about 1826 ; m. Mrs. Lydia Colby of Whitefield, N. H.; res. Warner, N. H.; rem. to Manchester, N. H., and d. there.

Children of JUDITH⁶, (1787) [320] (Enoch⁵, Richard⁴, Richard³, Sergt. Abraham², Robert¹) and Enoch Eastman; res. Webster, N. H.

i. ENOCH EASTMAN, b. May 26, 1809 ; m. Sophronia Colby of Weare, N. H.
He set. in Salisbury, N. H.; d. of consumption.

ii. BETSEY EASTMAN; b. July 25, 1810 ; m. Samuel Morse of Franklin, N. H.; he d. of consumption in the spring of 1875. She d. 3 Nov., 1870.

iii. DANIEL EASTMAN, b. July 17, 1812.

iv. TIMOTHY EASTMAN, b. Nov. 21, 1814 ; m. Arvilla Stevens of Salisbury, N. H. He d. Jan.. 1891; res. Salisbury, N. H.

v. JUDITH EASTMAN, b. Sept. 27, 1816 ; d. unm., 1 Oct., 1891.

ROBERT ADAMS [Seventh Generation.

- vi. MOSES EASTMAN, b. Sept. 22, 1819; d. 3 May, 1868.
- vii. DORCAS A. EASTMAN, b. June 7, 1823; d. 19 Oct., 1825.
- viii. DORCAS A. EASTMAN, b. April 13, 1825; living unm., 1898; res. Webster, N. H.

Children of RUSSELL⁴, (1788) [321] (Enoch⁵, Richard⁴ Richard³, Sergt. Abraham², Robert¹) and Susan (Fifield) Adams; res. Hill, N. H.

- i. EMELINE⁷, b. in Hill, Nov. 23, 1813; d. 18 Nov., 1818.
- 730. ii. GILSON⁷, b. in Hill, June 15, 1815; m. (1) Apr. 15, 1845, Harriet N. Jones; she d. 12 Jan., 1853; m. (2) 1855, Abbie H. Quincy of Denmark, Me.; she d. 13 Sept., 1864; m. (3) Mar., 1865, Martha Gammage. He set. in Sweden, Me., and d. 26 Mar., 1881.
- 731. iii. HARRISON⁷, b. in Hill, June 6, 1817; m. Nov. 7, 1843, Margaret Morse, dau. of Dea. John and Nancy (Gliddon) Morse of Haverhill, Mass.; b. May 7, 1823; d. 12 Sept., 1883; res. Haverhill, Mass., and Hill, N. H.; d. 17 Feb., 1882.
- iv. DANIEL⁷, b. in Hill, Feb. 3-5, 1819. He d. in Hill, unm., 15 Apr., 1868.
- 732. v. JAMES R.⁷, b. in Hill, Jan. 26, 1821; m. Emily Young of Ackworth, N. H., dau. of James and Elizabeth (Adams) Young. He set. in Hill, N. H.; d. 8 May, 1889.
- 733. vi. ENOCH⁷, b. in Hill, Feb. 24, 1823; m. Sept. 25, 1856, Sylvia A. Babcock, daughter of Ebenezer and Sylvia (Jennings) Babcock, b. in 1827; res. Belmont, N. H.; living 1898.
- 734. vii. OBADIAH F.⁷, b. in Hill, Nov. 29, 1824; m. Louisa Burke of Madison, N. H. He set. in Jamaica Plain, Mass.; d. 14 Mar., 1894.
- viii. EMELINE S.⁷, b. in Hill, Jan. 26, 1830; d. 19 Jan., 1843.

Children of RICHARD⁶, (1790) [322] (Enoch⁵, Richard⁴, Richard³, Sergt. Abraham², Robert¹) and Sarah (Dunbar) Adams; res. Hill, N. H.

- i. URSULA⁷, b. in Salisbury, N. H., Aug. 16, 1814; d. 1827.
- ii. SIMEON⁷, b. in Hill, Sept. 13, 1815; d. Oct., 1817.
- 735. iii. EMILY⁷, b. in Hill, Oct. 12, 1817; m. 1844, Joseph B. Spiller; he d. 21 May, 1880; res. Haverhill, Mass. She d. in W. Roxbury, Mass., 12 Nov., 1896.
- iv. RICHARD F.⁷, b. in Hill, Apr. 15, 1819; d. Mar., 1835.
- 736. v. DORCAS⁷, b. in Hill, Feb. 1, 1821; m. (1) June 19, 1842, Jonas Tyrrell, son of Samuel Tyrrell of Bridgewater, N. H.; m. (2) 1885, Isaiah Fowler; d. 1888. She is living 1899.
- vi. SARAH H.⁷, b. in Hill, Nov. 2, 1822; d. 1885.

737. vii. ELIZABETH⁷, b. in Hill, Aug. 11, 1824; m. Jan., 1844, Daniel Tyrrell, bro. of Jonas ; a shoe-maker, b. Apr. 28, 1821 ; res. Hill Center, N. H.

738. viii. HENRY⁷, b. in Hill, Jan. 16, 1826 ; m. (1) Aug., 1862, Sarah True Judkins, dau. of Moses and Sarah (True) Judkins, b. in Unity, N. H., Aug., 1841 ; d. in Sacramento, Cal., 9 Oct., 1883 ; m. (2) Aug. 12, 1877, Edith S. Spiller of Salem, Mass.; she d. 13 July, 1883 ; m. (3) Oct. 13, 1888, Louisa Brown.

 He rem. to California in 1844, and was engaged in mining until 1870, when he settled in Stockton, and became Superintendent of the Stockton Gas Co., and a prominent citizen. He d. suddenly 19 Jan., 1893.

739. ix. PHEBE JANE⁷, b. in Hill, Apr. 2, 1827; m. Feb. 10, 1857, Daniel Lovering; he d. 9 Apr., 1897 ; res. Sanbornton, N. H. She d. 11 July, 1898.

x. SUSAN ABIGAIL⁷, b. in Hill, Aug. 4, 1829 ; d. Dec., 1840.

740. xi. STEPHEN C.⁷, b. in Hill, Mar. 9, 1831 ; m. Jan. 17, 1853, Elizabeth B. Currier.

 He set. in Haverhill, Mass.; enlisted in the 35th Regiment of Massachusetts Vols.; was wounded in the battle of Antietam, and d. 25 Sept., 1862, after the amputation of his leg.

xii. ENOCH G.⁷, b. in Hill, June 8, 1833 ; m. 1858, Ellen Tucker ; she d. 1892. He d. in Franklin, N. H., 1889 ; no issue.

Children of ELIZABETH⁶, (1792) [**323**] (Enoch⁵, Richard⁴, Richard³, Sergt. Abraham², Robert¹) and James Young; res. Ackworth, N. H.

i. CYNTHIA YOUNG, b. May 5, 1811 ; m. William Stevens ; res. Ackworth, N. H.

ii. ELIZABETH YOUNG, b. Sept. 14, 1812; m. Joseph G. Smith.

iii. DANIEL YOUNG, b. July 14, 1814 ; m. Laura Mason; res. Hill, N. H. He d. 11 Sept., 1870.

iv. PHEBE YOUNG, b. Aug. 14, 1816 ; unm.

v. MILTON YOUNG, b. Sept. 8, 1818 ; m. Jane Avery.
He set. in Jamaica Plain, Mass.

vi. JERUSHA JUDITH YOUNG, b. Mar. 26, 1821 ; m. Milton Mason ; res. Hill, N. H. She d. 17 Jan., 1883.

vii. JAMES ADAMS YOUNG, b. Mar. 15, 1823; res. Jamaica Plain, Mass.

viii. EMILY YOUNG, b. Feb. 15, 1825 ; m. James R. Adams (cousin), son of Russell and Susan (Fifield) Adams; res. Hill, N. H.

170   ROBERT ADAMS   [Seventh Generation.

- ix. GEORGE W. YOUNG, b. Jan. 7, 1827 ; res. Ackworth, N. H.
- x. SARAH ANN YOUNG, b. Jan. 27, 1829 ; m. Gilman Livingston (cousin), son of Jesse and Phebe (Adams) Livingston ; res. W. Unity, N. H.
- xi. THOMAS YOUNG, b. Mar. 19, 1831, unm.

Children of PHEBE⁶, (1795) [**324**] (Enoch⁵, Richard⁴, Richard³, Sergt. Abraham², Robert¹) and Jesse Livingston ; res. Hill, N H.

- i. BENJAMIN LIVINGSTON, b. Jan.,1811 ; m. Almeda Scribner.
- ii. PHEBE LIVINGSTON, d. unm.
- iii. GILMAN LIVINGSTON, b. Mar. 31, 1823; m. Sarah A. Young, dau. of James and Elizabeth (Adams) Young ; both living 1898 ; res. W. Unity, N. H.
- iv. ROSANA LIVINGSTON, m. Daniel Quimby.
- v. MELINDA LIVINGSTON, d. unm.
- vi. JACKSON LIVINGSTON, m. ―― Lord ; res. Iowa.
- vii. SAMUEL LIVINGSTON, m. Rebecca Carleton ; res. Faribault, Minn.
- viii. SYLBIA LIVINGSTON, m. Ephraim Lord.

Children of DORCAS⁶, (1797) [**325**] (Enoch⁵, Richard⁴, Richard³, Sergt. Abraham², Robert¹) and Daniel S. Woodward ; res. Hill, N. H.

- i. ELIZABETH WOODWARD, b. Sept. 2, 1828 ; m. Sept. 3, 1854, John Pollard ; res. Malden, Mass. She d. 22 Dec., 1876 ; no issue.
- ii. HANNAH S. WOODWARD, b. Nov. 1, 1830 ; m. Aug. 16, 1869, Perley B. Dickinson ; res. Hill Centre, N. H.; one child Filmore V., b. Jan. 7, 1871.
- iii. PHEBE L. WOODWARD, b. Jan. 7, 1832 ; m. George Howe, who d. in West Roxbury, Vt., 14 May, 1874, from wounds received in the army ; 1 child, Nellie F., b. May 29, 1860, who m. June 22, 1878, Wallace E. Smith. Phebe L. d. in Hill, 21 Apr., 1897.
- iv. DANIEL R. WOODWARD, b. April 10, 1833 ; m. at Lowell, Mass., Jan. 30, 1854, Laura D. Davis.
   He is a stone carver ; res. Franklin, N. H.
- v. STEPHEN WOODWARD, b. Aug. 22, 1834 ; m. June 9, 1856, Nancy Morrill.
   He is a mechanic ; res. Franklin Falls, N. H.
- vi. ALVIN A. WOODWARD, b. May 22, 1836 ; m. June 18, 1859, Ellen M. Marden ; res. Hill, N. H.

vii. DORCAS WOODWARD, b. Feb. 22, 1838 ; m. July 4, 1859, Edwin E Clark.

viii. DIANA A. WOODWARD, b. Sept. 22, 1839 ; m. (1) Mar. 1, 1860, Benjamin Morrill; he d. 4 July, 1860 ; m (2) Aug. 27, 1865, Wm. H. Roberts ; res. Northfield, N. H.

ix. PAULINA WOODWARD, b. Sept. 7, 1842 ; d. 8 Oct., 1844.

x. FRANK R. WOODWARD, b. Feb. 9, 1845 ; m. (1) 1865, Lydia L. Gordon ; m. (2) Mar. 29, 1886, Ella E. Hilpert ; res. Hill, N. H.

Children of JANE[6], [1797) [326] (Paul[5], Richard[4], Richard[3], Sergt. Abraham[2], Robert[1]) and Abraham Granger ; res. Worthington, Mass.

i. REBECCA S. GRANGER, b. Jan. 12, 1828 ; m. July 2, 1865, Russell Tower of Worthington, Mass.; res. W. Worthington, Mass.

ii. PAUL L. GRANGER, b. Nov. 24, 1830 ; m. Mar. 14, 1855, Laura M. Ballou of Peru, Mass.; res. Florence, Mass.

iii. RUTH A. GRANGER, b. Oct. 23, 1833 ; m. Dec. 12, 1855, Franklin J. Robinson of Worthington, Mass.; he d. 5 Nov., 1886.

iv. ABRAHAM W. GRANGER, b. April 15, 1836; m. Nov. 10, 1874, Rachel J. Tucker of Peru, Mass.; res. W. Worthington, Mass. He d. 24 Nov., 1898.

Children of ASA[6], (1801) [327] (Paul[5], Richard[4], Richard[3], Sergt. Abraham[2], Robert[1]) and Nancy (Little) Adams; res. Newbury, Mass.

i. HANNAH ILSLEY[7], b. in Newbury, June 8, 1827 ; m. Oct. 28, 1853, James Augustus Adams, son of Sewall and Sarah (Ilsley) Adams. She d. 28 Apr., 1861.

ii. LUCRETIA LITTLE[7], b. in Newbury, Feb. 16, 1829 ; d. unm. 30 Apr., 1865.

iii. SILAS[7] (twin), b. in Newbury, Feb. 16, 1829. He was killed 26 Jan., 1890.

741. iv. PAUL[7], b. in Newbury, Oct. 22, 1830 ; m. (1) Nov. 11, 1852, Mary J. Tenney, dau. of Daniel S. and Caroline (Little) Tenney ; b. Apr. 30, 1834, (divorced) ; m. (2) Martha R. Russell; d. dept. 12, 1926 He is a druggist ; res. Newburyport, Mass. d. Aug. 2. 1921

742. v. HAZEN MICHAEL[7], b. in Newbury, Aug. 18, 1832 ; m. Sept., 1856, Lucy A. Ilsley ; res. Newburyport, Mass. d., 1920

743. vi. NANCY[7], b. in Newbury, Aug. 15, 1835 ; m. Dec. 27, 1855, Richard Knight ; res. Newburyport, Mass., since 1882.

vii. ASA[7], b. in Newbury, Nov. 26, 1836 ; d. 26 June, 1837.

744. viii. ASA[7], b. in Newbury, July 4, 1838; m. July 11, 1859, Eliza A. Tenney. He d. in Newburyport, Mass., 15 Sept., 1875.
745. ix. JOSEPH LITTLE[7], b. in Newbury, July 14, 1842; m. Jan. 10, 1882, Elizabeth A. Woods. *d. July 6. 1922.*
He is a carpenter; res. Newburyport, Mass.
d. July 14. 1930

Children of MARY[6], (1807) [328] (Paul[5], Richard[4], Richard[3], Sergt. Abraham[2], Robert[1]) and Capt. George W. Dennis; res. Newburyport, Mass.

    i. GEORGE FOX DENNIS; d. at 18 or 19 years of age.
    ii. HENRY THOMAS DENNIS; d. unm., 1880.
    iii. MARY ADAMS DENNIS, b. 1835; d. at 18 or 19 years of age.
    iv. LUCY EMILY DENNIS, b. about 1839; m. Jos. C. Davis of Astoria, Ore.; res. Astoria, Ore.
    v. HARRIET ADAMS DENNIS, b. Nov. 9, 1840; m. Sept. 10, 1862, Moses Young; res. Newbury, Mass.
    vi. PAUL ADAMS DENNIS; d. at 14 years of age.
    vii. JOHN JACOB DENNIS; drowned when 11 years old.
    viii. GEORGIANA STEWART DENNIS; d. young.

Children of SENECA[6], (1808) [329] (Paul[5], Richard[4], Richard[3], Sergt. Abraham[2], Robert[1]) and Sarah B. (Rolfe) Adams; res. Newbury, Mass.

    i. JOHN ROLFE[7], b. in Newbury, June 20, 1842; d. 7 Sept., 1862.
746.   ii. MOSES CYRUS[7], b. in Newbury, Feb. 29, 1844; m. Feb. 5, 1871, Mary Dodge. *d. Aug. 19. 1920.*
He has been a conductor of the street railway.
    iii. CAROLINE ELIZABETH[7], b. in Newbury, Nov. 23, 1846; d. 25 Oct., 1862.

Children of REBECCA B.[6], (1812) [330] (Paul[5], Richard[4], Richard[3], Sergt. Abraham[2], Robert[1]) and Benjamin C. Perkins; s. Newbury, Mass.

    i. CAROLINE PERKINS, b. Oct. 7, 1832; d. unm. 4 Apr., 1894.
    ii. SALOME PERKINS, b, Feb. 15, 1834; m. Sept. 8, 1864, James N. Frost; res. Newburyport, Mass.
    iii. BENJAMIN F. PERKINS, b. Mar. 15, 1835; m. Nov. 16, 1856, Lois Edna Dearborn; res. Newbury, Mass.
    iv. MARY ANN PERKINS, b, Mar. 23, 1836; m. Nov. 24, 1863, Ralph Atwood. She is a deaf mute; res. Columbus, O.

[Seventh Generation.] OF NEWBURY, MASS.

 v. PAUL ADAMS PERKINS, b. Mar. 22, 1838 ; d. 2 Apr., 1838.
 vi. PAUL ADAMS PERKINS, b. Nov. 14, 1839 ; d. 19 Sept., 1840.
 vii. PAUL ADAMS PERKINS, b. May 11, 1841 ; m. Oct. 27, 1864, Hannah C. Cilley ; res. Newbury, Mass.
 viii. JOSEPH PERKINS, b. Jan. 30, 1843 ; m. (1) Mar. 6, 1866, Lucy Dennis (his cousin) ; m. (2) Jan. 1, 1878, Mrs. Idelia J. Goodwin. He d. 20 Apr., 1882.
 ix. LEWIS CONVERSE PERKINS, b. June 23, 1850 ; d. 26 Oct., 1864.

Children of THOMAS HALL⁶, (1817) [**331**] (Paul⁵, Richard⁴, Richard³, Sergt. Abraham², Robert¹) and Mary J. (Jennings) Adams; res. Rowley, Mass.

747. i. LUCY JANE⁷, b. in Newbury, Mass., June 26, 1843 ; m. March 30, 1862, Charles W. Rogers, son of Eben P. Rogers, b. Feb. 3, 1839 ; a miller by trade ; res. Ipswich, Mass.
748. ii. EDWIN HALL⁷, b. in Newbury, Sept. 28, 1849 ; m. (1) Sept. 28, 1871, Olive Abbie Howe ; she d. 7 Aug., 1878 ; m. (2) May 17, 1882, Ina Jane Saunders.
He is a boot and shoe dealer ; res. Rowley, Mass.

Children of CLARISSA⁶, (1791) [**332**] (Simeon⁵, Richard⁴, Richard³, Sergt. Abraham², Robert¹) and Ebenezer Cleaves Bradbury; res. New Limrick, Me.

 i. HALL JACKSON BRADBURY, b. Oct. 13, 1815.
 ii. TRYPHOSA CLEAVES BRADBURY, b. June 3, 1817.
 iii. CLEMENT ADAMS BRADBURY, b. Mar. 18, 1819.
 iv. CHRISTOPHER COLUMBUS BRADBURY, b. Apr. 18, 1821.
 v. EBENEZER BRADBURY, b. Feb. 28, 1823.
 vi. STEPHEN LITTLE ADAMS BRADBURY, b. Mar. 27, 1827.
 vii. SIMON ADAMS BRADBURY, b. Mar. 10, 1829.
 viii. CHARLES FREEMAN BRADBURY, b. July 31, 1832.
 ix. DANIEL WEBSTER BRADBURY, b. Aug. 18, 1835.

Children of DR. CLEMENT JACKSON⁶, (1795) [**333**] (Simeon⁵, Richard⁴, Richard³, Sergt. Abraham², Robert¹) and Hannah (Osgood) Adams; res. Limington and Bridgton, Me.

 i. EDWARD LEWIS O.⁷, b. in Limington, April 8, 1822 ; d. 16 Dec., 1825.
 ii. SARAH JANE⁷, b. in Limington, Jan. 28, 1825 ; d. 8 Feb., 1825.

749. iii. EDWARD LEWIS OSGOOD⁷, b. in Limington, July 27, 1827 ; m. Jan. 21, 1854, Lydia Jane Walker, dau. of Benjamin Walker of Bridgton, Me.

He began to learn the business of printing, but abandoned it, and went into trade with his brother Charles of Bridgton. Later he removed to Portland, and became deputy sheriff and jailor, also U. S. collector of Internal Revenue. He engaged in insurance in 1870 ; d. 13 July, 1895.

iv. CHARLES CARROLL⁷, b. in Limington, Sept. 7, 1829 ; d. unm. 4 May, 1859.

750. v. SUSAN OSGOOD⁷, b. in Limington, Jan. 27, 1832 ; m. Dec. 21, 1860, Alonzo B. Walker of Portland, Me.

vi. JAMES RILEY⁷, b. in Limington, Nov. 16, 1834 ; d. 30 Jan., 1869.

Children of SIMEON⁶, (1797) [**334**] (Simeon⁵, Simeon⁴, Richard⁴, Richard³, Sergt. Abraham², Robert¹) and Caroline (Fluent) Adams ; res. Corinna, Penobscot Co., Me.

i. GEORGE WALTER⁷, b. in Corinna, Oct. 25, 1827 ; m. 1882, Rose M. Short.

He is a lumber-surveyor ; set. 1854, at No. 707 Stockton St., San Francisco, Cal.

751. ii. CAROLINE MARGARET⁷, b. in Corinna, June 21, 1829 ; m. (1) Sept. 6, 1848, Wm. Tibbetts of Palmyra, Me., son of Nicholas Tibbets of Wolfboro, N. H., b. Oct. 21, 1824 ; d. 16 Mar., 1856 ; m. (2) 1860, Capt. William P. Sanford, son of Caleb Sanford, b. in So. Dartmouth, Mass., Sept. 11, 1819 ; d. 15 Mar., 1876 ; res. Portland, Me.

752. iii. MARY ELIZABETH⁷, b. in Corinna, Nov. 3, 1832 ; m. Mar. 15, 1853, Stephen S. Wedgwood of Corinna, Me.; res. Newport, Me.

753. iv. JOHN QUINCY⁷, b. in Corinna, Mar. 10, 1835 ; m. Jan. 23, 1857, Helen M. Burgess, b. Dec. 14, 1836.

He set. in Palmyra in 1872 ; P. O., Newport, Me.

754. v. ELLEN LUCRETIA⁷, b. in Corinna, Sept. 30, 1839 ; m. July 21, 1856, George W. Pillsbury. She d. in Palmyra, Me., 10 Aug., 1862.

Children of DR. STEPHEN⁶, (1804) [**335**] (Simeon⁵, Richard⁴, Richard³, Sergt. Abraham², Robert¹) and Mary L. Hobbs (Marston) Adams ; res. W. Newfield, Me.

i. CLEMENT JACKSON⁷, b. in W. Newfield, Dec. 9, 1833 ; m. June 6, 1869, Sarah Jane Dorman of Newfield.

He was a produce merchant ; res. Newfield, Me.; d. 9 Apr., 1899.

Seventh Generation.] OF NEWBURY, MASS.

ii. STEPHEN LITTLE⁷, b. in W. Newfield, Jan. 28, 1837 ; m. (1) Caroline Perkins ; m. (2) Love Lord.
He is a produce merchant; res. Newfield, Me.

iii. REBECCA LITTLE⁷, b. in W. Newfield, Aug. 26, 1840 ; m. Dec. 25, 1862, Dr. Noah Sanborn of Tamworth, N. H.
He graduated from the Dartmouth Medical College; became a surgeon in the army ; practiced for a time in Maine, and set. in 1872 in Bayonne, N. J., where he was an honored and successful physician until his death, which occurred Sept. 6, 1894 ; res. Bayonne, N. J.; no issue.

iv. CHARLES QUINCY⁷, b. in W. Newfield, July 27, 1848 ; d. 14 Sept., 1849.

Children of MARY⁶, (1807) [**336**] (Simeon⁵, Richard⁴, Richard³, Sergt. Abraham², Robert¹) and Dea. John Evans; res. Fryeburg, Me.

755. i. DR. SIMEON ADAMS EVANS, b. April 14, 1837 ; m. (1) Jan. 1, 1866, Louisa H. Ilsley of Fryeburg ; b. May 21, 1836 ; d. at Hopkinton, N. H., 22 Sept., 1868 ; m. (2) June 8, 1871, Susan A. Hill, dau. of Col. John and Elizabeth (Eastman) Hill.
He was graduated from Bowdoin College in 1860 ; studied in the Maine Medical College in 1861 ; became hospital steward of the 13th Maine regiment in Nov., 1861, serving with Gen. Butler at Ship Island ; later he was assistant surgeon of the 14th Maine regiment, Col. T. W. Porter, and served till Jan., 1865. Completing his medical studies at Brunswick, he settled in practice at Hopkington, N. H., removing in 1870 to Conway, N. H. He is U. S. medical examiner.

ii. JOHN HILL EVANS, b. May 5, 1840 ; d. 25 June, 1842.

756. iii. MARY LITTLE EVANS, b. April 18, 1842 ; m. Oct. 2, 1872, Joseph T. Laird.
She was preceptress of Dexter Academy in Maine, and of a young ladies seminary at Freehold, N. J.

iv. SARAH LUCRETIA EVANS, b. July 24, 1846 ; d. 5 Feb., 1847.

757. v. CLINTON BUSWELL EVANS, b. Aug. 3, 1848; m. June 3, 1886, Emma Rose Townsend, dau. of Capt. Wm. Townshend of the British army.
He graduated from Dartmouth College in 1873, and was for ten years an associate editor of the *Springfield Republican*; removed to Chicago in 1883, and became the financial editor of the *Chicago Tribune*. He established the financial journal, *The Economist*, in 1888.

vi. **CLARA ELIZABETH EVANS**, b. Nov. 24, 1850 ; d. 25 July, 1855.

'Children of RICHARD⁶, (1796) [**337**] (Asa⁵, Richard⁴, Richard³, Sergt. Abraham², Robert¹) and Abigail (Little) Adams; res. Newbury, Mass.

758. i. GILES AARON⁷, b. in Newbury, Mar. 31, 1822; m. Jan. 13, 1848, Sarah E. Jackman; she d. 5 Mar., 1895.
He is a carpenter; res. Newburyport, Mass.

759. ii. MARY LITTLE⁷, b. in Newbury, Sept. 20, 1823; m. Apr. 28, 1847, Joseph Noyes Rolfe.; she d. Dec. 1893.

760. iii. ASA⁷, b. in Newbury, Nov. 1, 1824; m. July 2, 1857, Mary C. Coleman.
He was a farmer on the homestead, Newbury, Mass. He d. 7-8 June, 1898.

iv. CALVIN⁷, b. in Newbury, May 23, 1827; d. 16 June, 1831.

v. RUFUS⁷, b. in Newbury, Mar. 31, 1829; m. Oct. 26, 1855, Eunice Short Goodwin. *She d. May 24, 1923*
He is a builder; was a representative, 1861-64; res. Newburyport, Mass.; no issue.

761. vi. ELIZABETH NOYES⁷, b. in Newbury, Feb. 24, 1831; m. Sept. 16, 1860, Anthony Knapp; res. Newburyport, Mass.

vii. ANNIE ROLFE⁷, b. in Newbury, June 14, 1832; d. unm. Jan., 1898.

762. viii. MARGARET EMERY⁷, b. in Newbury, Sept. 3, 1833; m. July 1, 1857, Geo. Washington Knight, son of John Knight. She d. 30 Sept., 1872.

ix. RICHARD CALVIN⁷, b. in Newbury, Dec. 14, 1835; d. 29 May, 1836.

763. x. SUSAN PIKE⁷, b. in Newbury, Sept. 24, 1838; m. Mar. 10, 1859, Col. Charles L. Ayer; she d. 22 Feb., 1891.

xi. RICHARD⁷, b. in Newbury, July 23, 1842; d. 2 Sept., 1842.

Children of LOIS⁶, (1799) [**338**] (Ebenezer⁵, Richard⁴, Richard³, Sergt. Abraham², Robert¹) and Harrison Dearborn; res. Newbury, Mass.

i. LOIS EDNA DEARBORN, b. in Newbury, Feb., 1841; m. Benjamin F. Perkins. Jr. She d. 1887.

ii. EBEN HARRISON DEARBORN, b. in Newbury, 1845; res. Newbury, Mass.; unm.

Children of NATHAN⁶, (1801) [**339**] (Ebenezer⁵, Richard⁴, Richard³, Sergt. Abraham², Robert¹) and Louisa (Knowles) Adams; res. Newbury, Mass.

764. i. ISAAC WATTS⁷, b. in Newbury, Dec. 14, 1827; m. (1) Jan. 4, 1857, Elizabeth T. Chase; she d. 7 May, 1859, age 35 yrs. 1 mo.; m. (2) May 11, 1862, Ann Maria Goodwin, dau. of William and Eliza

Seventh Generation.] OF NEWBURY, MASS. 177

(Knight) Goodwin, b. Aug. 31, 1828 ; she d. 11 Feb., 1896, age 67 yrs. 5 mos.; res. West Newbury, Mass. He d. 23 June, 1894, age 66 yrs. 6 mos. 9 days.

 ii. ALBERT F.⁷, b. in Newbury, Mar. 21, 1829 ; res. Newbury, Mass.; unm.

765. iii. CAPT. DENNIS⁷, b. in Newbury, June 1, 1830 ; m. Nov. 7, 1858, *d. May* Mary M. Jaques, b. in Pike Co., Ill., Oct. 28, 1839.

   He is a farmer; rem. to Illinois, 1855, and thence, in Nov., 1858, to Judson, Sulivan Co., Mo. He served as Captain of Co. C, 66th Reg. of Missouri Vols., and as Lieut. in Co. I, 44th Missouri Reg.; was in the battle at Franklin, Tenn., Nov. 30, 1864 ; was wounded by the bursting of a shell at the seige of Ft. Spanish, Ala., and was mustered out Aug. 15, 1865.

766. iv. GREEN⁷, b. in Newbury, Dec. 18, 1831 ; m. Mar. 6, 1863, Emily Stewart ; res. Newbury, Mass. *d. Oct. 4, 1907*

767. v. LOUISA⁷, b. in Newbury, Jan. 12, 1833 ; m. June 15, 1854, Capt. Edwin Janvrin ; he d. 9 Oct., 1882. *Louisa d. Nov. 21, 1905*

768. vi. CAROLINE⁷, b. in Newbury, Aug. 8, 1835 ; m. June 26, 1855, Charles Ordway. *d. June 1902*

 vii. MOSES⁷, b. in Newbury, Feb. 14, 1837 ; d. 16 Aug., 1868.

 viii. ADELAIDE⁷, b. in Newbury, Jan. 21, 1840 ; d. 15 May, 1844.

 ix. NATHAN L.⁷, b. in Newbury, Jan. 23, 1841 ; living unm. in W. Newbury, Mass. *d. Mar. 27, 1908*

 x. CHARLES M.⁷, b. in Newbury, Dec. 27, 1842 ; d. 21 May, 1844.

769. xi. ADELAIDE⁷, b. in Newbury, Apr. 15, 1844 ; m. June 6, 1869, Stephen S. Huse ; res. Newton Junc., N. H.

Children of ELIZA⁶, (1803) [340] (Ebenezer⁵, Richard⁴, Richard³, Sergt. Abraham², Robert¹) and Ebenezer Little; res. Newbury, Mass.

 1. CATHARINE A. LITTLE, b. Sept. 16, 1823; m. Mar. 21, 1850, Edward H. Little, son of Henry and Phebe (Little) Little.

 ii. DANIEL NOYCE LITTLE, b. Jan. 15, 1826 ; d. 10 Jan., 1831.

 iii. GEORGE F. LITTLE, b. July 6, 1828 ; d. 26 Jan., 1831.

 iv. SARAH NOYCE LITTLE, b. Aug. 7, 1830 ; d. 4 Mar., 1847.

 v. GEORGE F. LITTLE, b. Mar. 24, 1832; m. (1) Feb. 2, 1854, Alice Little, dau. of Henry and Phebe (Little) Little; she d. 25 Feb., 1889 ; m. (2) Apr., 1891, Mary Dodge Story, b. 1839 ; res. Newbury, Mass.

 vi. EDNA A. LITTLE, b. June 2, 1834 ; d. 2 June, 1839.

 vii. ABIGAIL N. LITTLE (twin), b. June 2, 1834 ; d. 9 June, 1834.

 viii. DANIEL NOYES LITTLE, b. Mar. 8, 1836; d. 8, Mar., 1858.

(12)

ix. EBENEZER LITTLE, JR., b. Sept. 29, 1841; m. Apr. 9, 1863, Lucy Abby Greenleaf, dau. of Daniel and Lucy (Pettengill) Greenleaf, b. Apr. 11, 1845; res. Newbury, Mass.

x. SARAH ELIZA LITTLE, b. Feb. 1, 1853; m. June 10, 1873, Edwin C. Little, son of Rev. Elbridge G. Little.

Children of MOSES NOYES⁶, (1807) [**341**] (Ebenezer⁵, Richard⁴, Richard³, Sergt. Abraham², Robert¹) and Elizabeth (Adams) Adams; res. Newbury, Mass.

    i. MOSES N.⁷, b. in Newbury, Nov. 1, 1846; m. Dec. 23, 1877, Florence Jacques. He was drowned 25 Nov., 1878; no issue. *Florence d. Jan. 19, 19*

    ii. ELIZABETH⁷, b. in Newbury, June 3, 1848; res. Newbury, Mass., living unm. *d. June 21, 1936*

    iii. WALTER SCOTT⁷, b. in Newbury, Feb. 10, 1851. He was a farmer in Newbury; d. unm., 1898.

    iv. MARY R.⁷, b. in Newbury, May 18, 1854; d. 20 Mar., 1855.

Children of PHILIP D.⁶, (1814) [**342**] (Ebenezer⁵, Richard⁴, Richard³, Sergt. Abraham², Robert¹) and Ruth (Coffin) Adams; res. Newbury, Mass.

770. i. PHILIP TYLER⁷, b. in Newbury, July 5, 1842; m. Nov. 10, 1873, Emma Wright. *died June 22, 1910* He is an engineer; res. Essex, Mass.

771. ii. JOHN CALVIN⁷, b. in Newbury, Mar. 16, 1844; m. Dec. 25, 1864, Hattie S. Davis. *She d. Apr. 11, 1923.*
He is a veteran station agent of the Boston & Maine R. R., at Marblehead, Mass., having been employed in the railroad service for 30 years, and having charge of four different station houses on the same site; he had the reputation at one time of being the swiftest skater in Essex county; is a Mason and member of Winslow Lewis Commandery, Salem, Mass.

772. iii. MARTHA BELL⁷, b. in Newbury, Aug. 1, 1846; m. Oct. 23, 1867, Caldwell Bowlen, a grocer; b. in Truro, N. S.; d. 17 Apr., 1879. She d. 30 Jan., 1899.

773. iv. CHARLES ALBERT⁷, b. in Newbury, June 27, 1848; m. 1874, Susan E. Sanborn; res. Newburyport, Mass. *d. Aug. 23, 1927*

    v. FRANK DODDRIDGE⁷, b. in Newbury, Feb. 7, 1852; m. Apr. 20, 1893, Carrie Amanda Wiley; res. Newburyport, Mass.; no issue. *d. Nov. 25, 1928*

    vi. MARY ALLEN⁷, b. in Newbury, Jan. 26, 1854; d. 2 Sept., 1868.

    vii. HELEN FRANCES⁷, b. in Newbury, Nov. 12, 1856; res. Newburyport, Mass.; unm. *d. Mar. 1930.*

JOHN CALVIN ADAMS.

Children of CHARLES W.[5] (1818) [343] (Ebenezer[5], Richard[4], Richard[3], Sergt. Abraham[2] Robert[1]) and Mary Elizabeth (Adams) Adams; res. Newbury, Mass. *d. Nov. 26, 1923*

    i. MARY EDNA[7], b. in Newbury, Sept. 28, 1866; m. Sept. 28, 1892, Harry De B. Page of Chatham, N. J.; res. Chatham, Morris Co., N. J.; no issue. *d. May 23, 1923*

    ii. ELIZA ILSLEY[7], b. in Newbury, Feb. 2, 1872; res. Newbury, Mass.; unm. *d. Dec. 29, 1936*

11. A son born Nov. 9, 1867 d. Dec. 1867.

Children of GEORGE[6], (1793) [344] (George[5], John[4], Richard[3], Sergt. Abraham[2], Robert[1]) and Judith (Dole) Adams; res. Newbury, Mass.

774.   i. GEORGE EDWARD[7], b. in Newbury, June 1, 1824; m. (1) Sept. 14, 1851, Susan B. Folsom; she d. 4 July 1874; m. (2) Jan. 12, 1875, Eliza Ilsley Adams, widow of Eben Adams and dau. of Sewall and Sarah (Isley) Adams; she d. 27 Oct., 1880; m. (3) Dec. 21, 1885, Sarah A. Wills. *who d. June 25, 1912* He was a farmer in "Newbury Farms," and highly esteemed; he d. suddenly 29 Dec., 1899.

    ii. DANIEL DOLE[7], b. in Newbury, April 22, 1830; m. Sept. 20, 1865, Eveline K. Taylor of Landaff, N. H., dau. of John and Caroline (Stevens) Taylor, b. Sept. 21, 1833; no issue; res. Newbury, Mass., a retired farmer. *died July 28, 1920 Eveline K. T. d. Aug. 12, 1925*

Children of NANCY[6], (1796) [345] (George[5], John[4], Richard[3], Sergt. Abraham[2], Robert[1]) and Josiah B. Tilton; res. Deerfield, N. H.

    i. GEO. ADAMS TILTON, b. Aug. 4, 1824; m. Ann Lord Manning of Newbury. He d. in Deerfield, N. H.

    ii. JOHN MOODY TILTON, b. Dec. 8, 1826; was drowned at about 20 years of age.

    iii. HARRISON JOSIAH TILTON, b. March 27, 1830; m. (1) Kate Robinson. He d. in Medford, Mass.

    iv. WASHINGTON VAN BUREN TILTON, b. Sept. 25, 1832; m. (1) Susan Veasey, dau. of Benning W. Veasey.
        He was a teacher; res. Deerfield, N. H.

    v. ALBERT FOLSOM TILTON, b. April 8, 1835; m. Emma E. Manning (sister of Ann); res. Needham, Mass.

    vi. ELIZABETH NANCY TILTON, b. June 6, 1838; m. (1) ——— Bolton; m. (2) Hannah Ackerman of Exeter, N. H.; res. Durham, N. H.

Children of MOODY⁶, (1802) [**346**] (George⁵, John⁴, Richard³, Sergt. Abraham², Robert¹) and Eliza (Adams) Adams; res. Derry, N. H.

    i. ANDREW M.⁷, b. in Deerfield, N. H., Apr. 24, 1833; d. in Derry, unm., 6 Feb., 1856, age 22 yrs. 10 days.

    ii. MARY ELIZABETH⁷, b. in Deerfield, Sept. 1, 1835; d. 16 Feb., 1849.

775. iii. ZILPAH⁷, b. in Deerfield, Feb. 11, 1840; m. Nov. 7, 1867, James J. Thomas; he d. in Boston; res. Boston. She d. 20 Oct., 1868.

776. iv. EZRA⁷, b. in Derry, N. H., July 4, 1842; m. May 3, 1868, Fanny M. Russell of Salem, Mass.; res. Worcester, Mass.

    v. ABBY C.⁷, b. in Derry, Apr, 6, 1845; m. Jan. 9, 1869, Hartley W. Brown, a policeman of Providence, R. I.

    vi. FRANK PIERCE⁷, b. in Derry, Feb. 18, 1848; m. Nellie Leonard. He is a railroad engineer; res. Campello, Plymouth Co., Mass.

Children of FREEBORN⁶, (1806) [**347**] (George⁵, John⁴, Richard³, Sergt. Abraham², Robert¹) and Ruth (Adams) Adams; res. Somerville, Mass.

    i. FREEBORN⁷, JR., b. in Newbury, Mass., Dec. 21, 1829; m. April 9, 1851, Rebecca Poole, dau. of Galen and Harriet Poole, b. April 19, 1829; res. So. Boston, Mass. He d. 20 Sept., 1899; no issue.

777. ii. SARAH LITTLE⁷, b. in Newbury, July 12, 1831; m. June 15, 1853, Geo. Henry Thurston, b. in So. Boston, May 25, 1831; res. Lexington, Mass.

778. iii. GARDINER⁷, b. in Newbury, July 29, 1833; m. April 22, 1855, Frances Melvina Leeds, dau. of Warren and Mary J. (Alden) Leeds; she d. 6 Feb., 1880; res. Chelsea, Mass.

779. iv. CHARLES⁷, b. in Dorchester, Mass., June 4, 1841; m. Sept. 16, 1862, Mary Ellen Leeds (sister of Melvina), b. April 14, 1841; res. Somerville, Mass.

    v. MARY ELIZABETH⁷, b. in So. Boston, July 22, 1851; d. 5 Aug., 1851.

Children of ISAAC⁶, (1807) [**348**] (Simon⁵, John⁴, Richard³, Sergt. Abraham², Robert¹) and Hannah (Kent) Adams; res. Newbury, Mass.

    i. A SON, b. in Newbury, Oct. 26, 1840; d. 26 Nov., 1840.

780. ii. WARREN⁷, b. in Newbury, July 31, 1842; m. 1873, Jane Withum [*d. June 13, 1908*]; res. Newburyport, Mass. [*d. Dec. 22, 1918*]

Seventh Generation.] OF NEWBURY, MASS 181

Children of JESSE⁶, (1812) [349] (Simon⁵, John⁴, Richard³, Sergt. Abraham², Robert¹) and Elizabeth (Kent) Adams; res. Newbury, Mass.

781.   i. SIMON AUGUSTUS⁷ *Burton*, b. in Newbury, Oct. 1, 1836; m. Dec. 15, 1866, Elizabeth Brown, dau. of True Brown, Esq. *and Deborah Jaq* He is a farmer; res. Newbury, Mass. *died Nov. 30, 1903*
   ii. SARAH ELIZABETH⁷, b. in Newbury, Dec. 5, 1838. Deaf and dumb; unm. *died Jan. 27, 1909*
   educated in district school, Newbury Farm

Children of JESSE⁶ (1812) and Sarah Ann (Knapp) Adams.
   iii. EMMA JANE⁷, b. in Newbury, April 15, 1851; m. Sept. 20, 1879, Frank Higgins; 1 child, d. in infancy. She d. 8 Dec., 1880. *Frank Hig*
   iv. ISAAC KNAPP⁷, b. in Newbury, June 7, 1856; d. 12 Oct., 1856. *drowned*

Arthur Preston b. May 27, 1880 at Carra
d. Feb 12, 1881

Child of WILLIAM⁶, (1801) [350] (John⁵, John⁴, Richard³, *Falls,* Sergt. Abraham², Robert¹) and Mary (Osgood) Adams; res. *June 13* Newbury, Mass.

d. Apr 24, 1940
782.   i. CHARLES WILLIAM⁷, b. in Newbury, Oct. 14, 1847; m. Mar. 14, 1871, *m* Virginia Fairfield; res. Newburyport, Mass. Machinist. *d. Jan. 23, 1918*

Children of MARGARET⁶, (1803) [351] (John⁵, John⁴, Richard³, Sergt. Abraham², Robert¹) and Elisha Bean; res. Newbury, Mass.
   i. ELISHA BEAN, JR., b. July 3, 1825; m. June 28, 1848, Louisa Noyes; res. Newbury, Mass. *Elisha d. Apr. 1, 1915 Louisa d*
   ii. JOHN ADAMS BEAN, b. Dec. 27, 1835; m. (1) Dec. 9, 1858, Jane *Feb 10,* Fuller; she d. 25 Nov., 1863; m. (2) Aug. 10, 1865, Hannah Chase; res. Newburyport, Mass. *John A. d. May 17, 1906*

Child of ELVIRA⁶, (1810) [352] (John⁵, John⁴, Richard³, Sergt. Abraham², Robert¹) and Moses Plumer; res. Newbury, Mass.
   i. JEREMIAH PLUMER, b. Oct. 8, 1835; d. 20 Apr., 1874.

Children of JOHN COFFIN⁶, (1812) [353] (John⁵, John⁴, Richard³, Sergt. Abraham², Robert¹) and Sarah Jane (Noyes) Adams; res. Newbury, Mass.

ROBERT ADAMS   [Seventh Generation.

783. i. LEWIS AUSTIN⁷, b. in Newbury, Jan. 3, 1839; m. May 5, 1868, *d. Sept. 26, 1926.* Emily M. Hutchinson, dau. of Ira and Mary A. (Hobson) Hutchinson; she d. 28 Oct., 1889; res. Rowley, Mass.

784. ii. MARGARET COFFIN⁷, b. in Newbury, Nov. 29, 1840; m. Apr. 30, 1869, Daniel Adams Brown; res. Newbury, Mass. *d. Jan. 13, 1931*

w. of True iii. JUSTIN NOYES⁷, b. in Newbury, Sept. 18, 1842; m. Jan. 1, 1882, *of Deborah* Louisa Still; res. Beatrice, Humbolt Co., Cal.; no issue. *d. Oct. 22, 1907*

(nis) Brown iv. SARAH ANN⁷, b. in Newbury, Aug. 16, 1844; res. Rowley, Mass.; *b. Apr. 25, 1839* unm. *d. Apr. 1, 1932.*

d. Oct. 20, 1901 v. MARY JANE⁷, b. in Newbury, Nov. 21, 1846; d. 16 Oct., 1865.

vi. CATHARINE NOYES⁷, b. in Newbury, Apr. 4, 1849; m. Aug. 13, *d. Mar. 30, 1932* 1881, Benjamin Proctor Mighill, son of Nathaniel and Maria (Proctor) Mighill, b. June/7, 1845; res. Rowley, Mass.; no issue.

June 12, 1925
785. vii. JAMES KNIGHT⁷, b. in Newbury, Oct. 14, 1851; m. Jan. 28, 1870, Lizzie A. Goodwin, *dau. of Sam'l and Nancy (Russell) Gooden* He is a farmer; res. Newbury, Mass. *He d. Nov. 4, 1937*

viii. JOHN NOYES⁷, b. in Newbury, Apr., 12, 1854; unm. res. Beatrice, Cal.; *d. Oct. 27, 1936, in San Francisco, Cal.*

ix. FRANK HALE⁷, b. in Newbury, Oct. 30, 1857; d. unm. 20 Oct., 1888.

x. MABEL ASHTON⁷, b. in Newbury, May 12, 1860; d. 26 Sept., 1863.

Children of PHEBE JEWETT⁶, (1794) [354] (Moses⁵, Moses⁴, Richard³, Sergt. Abraham², Robert¹) and Col. Benjamin J. Tenney; res. Newbury, Mass.

    i. ALBERT GORHAM TENNEY, b. July 2, 1814.
       He graduated from Bowdoin College in 1835; set. in Brunswick, Me.

    ii. PHEBE JEWETT TENNEY, b. Aug. 29, 1817; m. Andrew Bartlett; res. Plymouth, Mass.

    iii. MOSES OLIVER TENNEY, m. Deborah H. ——; res. Rowley, Mass.

    iv. GEO. BENJAMIN TENNEY, b. Aug. 10, 1827; res. Brunswick, Me.

    v. CHARLES HENRY TENNEY, b. Sept. 15, 1830; m. Feb. 13, 1855, Eliza Ann Philbrick; she d. 18 Sept., 1862, and he m. 2nd, Mary (Bacon) Bariston [?] He d. in Lynn, Mass., 1898.

    vi. MARY ELIZABETH TENNEY, b. June 12, 1832; d. 22 June, 1834.

Children of CAPT. RICHARD⁶, (1795) [355] (Moses⁵, Moses⁴, Richard³, Sergt. Abraham², Robert¹) and Mary (Cook) Adams; res. Newbury, Mass.

    i. SARAH⁷, b. in Newbury, Jan. 30, 1819; d. 5 Feb., 1838.

Louisa (Still) widow of Justin N.
m. (2) Walter Church, Sept. 2, 1914 **Died**
" (3) Theodore F. Wise...

Seventh Generation.] OF NEWBURY, MASS. 183

786. ii. DAVID JEWETT⁷, b. in Newbury, Sept. 18, 1820; m. Sarah Chase Pettengill ; res. Newburyport, Mass. He d. 10 Sept., 1882.
787. iii. RICHARD⁷, b. in Newburyport, June 10, 1822; m. (1) 1843, Lydia Moody, dau. of Henry and Miriam (Foster) Moody, b. in Salisbury, Feb. 14, 1824 ; d. in Charlestown, Mass., 4 Jan., 1880 ; m. (2) June 7, 1881, Mrs. Emma F. (Sewall) Phelps, b. Nov., 1847; living at 41 Bartlett St., Charlestown.
He was a cabinet-maker ; res. Charlestown, Mass.; d. in July, 1899.
788. iv. JOHN Q.⁷, b. in Newbury, Jan. 27, 1824 ; m. Eliza Ann Hager. *d. May 10.*
He was a market-man in Newburyport; d. 20 Mar., 1894.
789. v. EDWIN⁷, b. in Newbury, Nov. 16, 1825 ; m. (1) 1853, Louisa J. Murphy ; she d. 8 July, 1863, age 38 years ; m. (2) Feb., 1864, Hannah *d. Dec. 15* Jane Young. He d. in Newburyport, 5 Dec., 1889.
vi. XENOPHON⁷, b. in Newbury, Nov. 28, 1827 ; d. 25 Feb., 1836.
vii. CHARLES EDWARD⁷, b. in Newbury, Oct. 4, 1829 ; d. 30 June, 1871.
viii. MARY FRANCES⁷, b. in Newbury, Sept. 17, 1831 ; d. 7 Apr., 1855.
ix. WILLIAM EDWARDS⁷, b. in Newbury, Aug. 17, 1833 ; m. Frances Ann Disney ; she d. in Concord, N. H., 19 Sept., 1899. He d. 17 May, 1863 ; no issue.
x. MARY ELLEN⁷ b. in Newbury, Aug. 28, 1835 ; d. 13 Nov., 1860.
790. xi. XENOPHON⁷, b. in Newbury, Apr. 26, 1838 ; m. June 28, 1860, Sarah H. Knight. *d. Apr. 4, 1914*
He is a market-man; res. Newburyport, Mass.
791. xii. MOSES COOK⁷, b. in Newbury, June 3, 1840 ; m. Oct. 6, 1861, Lizzie J. Disney *She d. June 6, 1923.*
He is a grocer in Newburyport, Mass.
xiii. BENJAMIN TENNEY⁷, b. in Newbury, Sept. 8, 1842 ; d. unm. 18 Nov., 1876.

Children of MOSES⁶, (1804) [**356**] (Moses⁵, Moses⁴, Richard³, Sergt. Abraham², Robert¹) and Sarah H. (Elwell) Adams; res. W. Gloucester, Mass.

i. SARAH E⁷, b. in W. Gloucester, May 10, 1833 ; m. Jan. 9, 1852, Joshua Bray. She d. 20 Apr., 1855.
ii. MARY W.⁷, b. in W. Gloucester, Jan. 2, 1836 ; d. 14 June, 1836.
792. iii. MOSES⁷, b. in W. Gloucester, Sept. 12, 1837 ; m. Oct. 5, 1859, Ellen Mears, dau. of Henry and Abigail Mears of Essex ; b. May 24, 1837. He set in Essex, Mass., in 1857; d. 16 July, 1894.
iv. MARY A.⁷, b. in W. Gloucester, April 25, 1840 ; m. Henry Bray ; res. in Lynn. She d. 8 Mar., 1870.
v. GEORGE H.⁷, b. in W. Gloucester, May 14, 1843 ; m. July 5, 1868, Lucy E. Poland, of Essex. He d. 24 Apr., 1871 ; no issue.

vi. PHEBE E.[7], b. in W. Gloucester, Dec. 28, 1848 ; m. Parksey Osgood; dau. Cora m. H. E. Marshall, 125 Milk Street, Boston. Phebe E. d. 29 May, 1875 ; res. Eagle Street, E. Boston.

Children of JOHN POPKIN[6], (1812) [357] (Moses[5], Moses[4], Richard[3], Sergt. Abraham[2], Robert[1]) and Eugenia (Daniels) Adams; res. New York City.

 i. MARCIA[7], living unm.
 ii. LIZZIE[7], m. Com. Fred W. Wise of the U. S. Navy ; res. Washington, D. C.

Children of WOODBRIDGE[6], (1819) [358] (Moses[5], Moses[4], Richard[3], Sergt. Abraham[2], Robert[1]) and Mary (Peabody) Adams; res. Ipswich, Mass.

 i. SARAH[7], b. in Ipswich, Nov. 21, 1842 ; res. Ipswich, Mass.; unm.
793. ii. MARY P.[7], b. in Ipswich, Dec. 13, 1844; m. James G. Robinson; res. Providence, R. I.
794. iii. JOHN PEABODY[7], b. in Ipswich, Sept. 10, 1847 ; m. Oct. 26, [Sept. 10?] 1876, Helen M. Todd, dau. of Ezekiel R. and Jane N. (Adams) Todd. *John P. d. Feb 23, 1916. Helen M. d. Nov 22, 1933* He is a watch-maker in Boston ; res. Auburndale, Mass.
 iv. GEORGE W.[7], b. in Ipswich, Aug. 1, 1849 ; d. 22 Nov., 1854.

Children of MIRA[6], (1797) [359] (Ezra[5], Moses[4], Richard[3], Sergt. Abraham[2], Robert[1]) and Leonard S. Wood; res. Salem, Mass.

 i. JOSEPH WOOD, b. in Groveland, Mass., June 5, 1823 ; m. Peace Buffum of Salem, Mass.
 ii. BETSEY WOOD, b. in Groveland, 1824 ; d. in Salem in 1847.
 iii. MIRA ANN WOOD, b. in Groveland, 1826 ; d. in Salem, 1847.
 iv. LEONARD WOOD, b. in Groveland, 1827 ; d. in Newburyport, 1843.
 v. SARAH JANE WOOD, b. Mar. 23, 1830 ; m. James Monroe Prime of Salem, Mass. Both d. in Creighton, Neb.
 vi. MARY PEPPER WOOD, b. Jan. 22, 1832 ; m. Philip G. Skinner of Salem, Mass.; res. Green Cove Springs, Fla.
 vii. LOUISIA MATILDA WOOD, b. July 8, 1836 ; m 1856, Edward F. Danforth of Salem, Mass.; res. Beverly, Mass.
 viii. CHARLOTTE ADAMS WOOD, b. 1841 ; m. Robert Rowley of Salem, Mass.; res. Middleton, Mass.

Seventh Generation.] OF NEWBURY, MASS. 185

Children of JOHN[6], (1793) [360] (Ens. James[5], Edmund[4], Richard[3], Sergt. Abraham[2], Robert[1]) and Betsey (Corning) Adams; res. (Wilson's Crossing), Londonderry, N. H.

795. i. JAMES[7], b. in Londonderry, Dec. 26, 1817 ; m. Nov. 8, 1854, Lois Ann Hall; she d. 4 May, 1884. He d. 27 June, 1875.
796. ii. CHARLES[7], b. in Londonderry, Aug. 13, 1819 ; m. June 5, 1842-3, Mary Hall, b. Mar. 24, 1819 ; d. 17 Apr., 1894
          He was an undertaker ; res. Derry, N. H.; living 1899.
797. iii. HORACE[7], b. in Londonderry, June 8, 1821 ; m. (1) 1856, Margaret Richardson ; she d. 4 Sept., 1859 ; m. (2) about 1860, Lucy Ann (Farwell) Anderson, widow of John Anderson.
          He is a farmer in Hempstead, N. H.
798. iv. ELIZA[7], b. in Londonderry, Aug. 31, 1823 ; m. Dec. 26, 1848, James Pettengill, b. in Londonderry, N. H., Dec. 25, 1818 ; res. Amherst, N. H.
799. v. NATHAN[7], b. in Londonderry, July 22, 1825 ; m. Nov. 20, 1845, Jane E. Boyce.
          He was a farmer in Bedford, N. H.; d. 30 Jan., 1897.
      vi. CLARISSA[7], b. in Londonderry, July 28, 1828 ; d. 27 July, 1830.
      vii. OTIS[7], b. in Londonderry, June 9, 1830 ; m. Nov. 26, 1862, Sarah F. Webster ; res. Wilson's Crossing, Londonderry, N. H.; no issue.

Children of BENJAMIN[6], (1795) [361] (Ens. James[5], Dea. Edmund[4], Richard[3], Sergt. Abraham[2], Robert[1]) and Mehitable (Hoyt) Adams; res Derry, N. H.

      i.   JOHN[7], b. in Derry, Oct. 5, 1833 ; d. 3 Apr., 1834.
      ii. MARY[7], b. in Derry, Nov. 25, 1835 ; d. unm. 20 Jan., 1874.
      iii. WILLIAM[7], b. in Derry, Oct. 9, 1838 ; d. 8 Oct., 1841.
      iv. ALBERT[7], b. in Derry, Apr. 27, 1841 ; d. 9 Sept., 1862.
      v.   JAMES[7], b. in Derry, Aug. 19, 1843 ; d. 9 Aug., 1864.
800. vi. JANE[7], b. in Derry, Nov. 21, 1845 ; m. June 12, 1877, W. Preston Melvin ; res. the old homestead, east of Derry village, where Dea. James Adams from Ulster settled in 1722.

Child of DAVID[6], (1797) [362] (Ens. James[5], Dea. Edmund[4], Richard[3], Sergt. Abraham[2], Robert[1]) and Polly (Corning) Adams; res. Derry, N. H.

      i. DARIUS S.[7], b. in Derry, Aug. 15, 1833 ; m. Apr. 30, 1863, Elizabeth Griffis, dau. of Peter and Margaret (Croy) Griffis.
         He is a farmer ; res. Warren's Corner, Niagara Co., N. Y.; no issue.

Children of DAVID⁶, (1797) and Adelia Maria (Griffis) Adams.

801.   ii. ANNA ELIZABETH⁷, b. in Lockport, N. Y., Oct. 9, 1844 ; m. Nov. 7, 1871, Myron D. Tracey of Lockport; res. Warren's Corner, N.Y.
       iii. DR. DANIEL S.⁷, b. in Lockport, May 3, 1846 ; m. Nov. 17, 1870, Cora A. Fox, dau. of Andrew F. and Margaret A. Fox of Auburn, N. H., b. Aug. 31, 1850 ; d. 22 Feb., 1898.
            He was educated at Avon, N. Y., and Columbia College, N. Y.; set. in Manchester, N. H., in the practice of his profession, 1872, no issue.

Children of EDMUND⁶, (1802) [363] (Ens. James⁵, Dea. Edmund⁴, Richard³, Sergt. Abraham², Robert¹) and Jane (Marsh) Adams; res. Derry, N. H.

802.   i. REV. LUCIEN HARPER⁷, b. in Derry, July 28, 1829 ; m. (1) Nov. 20, 1862, Augusta S. Adams, dau. of Daniel Noyes and Eliza (Williams) Adams of Springfield, N. H., b. Sept. 16, 1833 ; d. in Turkey, Asia, 18 Nov., 1866 ; m. (2) Oct. 11, 1867, N. Dora Francis of Newington, Conn., b. Dec. 29, 1840 ; d. in Turkey, Mar., 1891.
          He was graduated from Dartmouth College, 28 July, 1859, and from Andover Theological Seminary, 1861 ; was settled in the ministry at Petersham. Mass.; ordained Oct. 28, 1862. He went to Asia Minor as a missionary of the A. B. F. M. in 1864, and retired in 1895; res. Derry, N. H.
       ii. GEORGE WASHINGTON⁷, b. in Derry, Apr. 5, 1830 ; d. 5 Apr., 1831.
803.   iii. DANIEL MARSH⁷, b. in Derry, Jan. 22, 1833 ; m. (1) Aug. 5, 1856, Helen A. True ; she d. in Kansas, 10 Oct., 1863 ; m. (2) Jan. 7, 1867, Olive A. Thomas, dau. of Chester and Thankful Sophia Thomas of Topeka, Kan., b. May 2, 1847 ; d. 13 June, 1879.
            He was a pay-master in the service of the United States, 1862 till 1867 ; set. in Topeka, Kan., and established the First National Bank of Lawrence, Kan., d. in Topeka, 13 June, 1879.

Children of REBECCA P.⁶, (1816) [364] (Ens. James⁵, Dea. Edmund⁴, Richard³, Sergt. Abraham², Robert¹) and Ezra Hale ; res. Rowley, Mass.

       i. EZRA HALE ; d. at years of age.
       ii. LEWIS H. HALE, b. Jan. 31, 1843 ; m. Abbie Shannon of Hampstead, N. H.; res. Haverhill, Mass.; living 1898.
       iii. EZRA HALE, JR., b. Feb. 1, 1846 ; m. Margaret Miller ; res. Somerville, Mass.

DR. DANIEL S. ADAMS.

Seventh Generation.] OF NEWBURY, MASS. 187

 iv. FRANCIS E. HALE, b. Mar. 8, 1847; m. Julia Bourne; res. Merrimac, Mass. *d.*

 v. ANNA M. HALE, b. Apr. 19, 1850; res. Rowley, Mass.; unm. *d.*

 vi. JAMES O. HALE, b. July 21, 1852; m. Abby Pearson; res. Byfield, Mass.

 vii. THADDEUS HALE, b. Aug., 1854; m. Mary Rogers; res. Rowley, Mass. *d. Apr. 1917.*

 viii. EMILY A. HALE, b. June 1, 1858; res. Rowley, Mass.; unm.

 ix. CHARLES ALBERT HALE, b. about 1860; d. unm. about 1888. *d. May 3, 1935.*

Child of BENJAMIN⁶, (1824) [365] (Edmund⁵, Edmund⁴, Richard³, Sergt. Abraham², Robert¹) and Katie (Foster) Adams; res. Derry, N. H.

 i. BENJAMIN FOSTER⁷, b. in Derry, N. H., Sept. 9, 1884.

Children of CAPT. ASAHEL⁶, (1762) [366] (Zadoc⁵, Jacob⁴, Sergt. Jacob³, Jacob², Robert¹) and Susanna (Adams) Adams; res. Norwich, Vt.

804. i. ROSWELL⁷, 2ND, b. in Norwich, Apr. 5, 1794; m. Mar. 19, [5?] 1819, Lucy Sikes, dau. of David and Lucy (Sikes) Sikes, b. Jan. 12, 1794, d. 4 Jan., 1861, age 67 years.

  Upon the death of his parents at Norwich, Vt., in the autumn of 1802, he returned with his uncles, his mother's brothers, Zebulon, Jr., and Stephen, to Suffield, Conn., and made his home with his uncle Stephen, who was without offspring. He d. in Suffield, 15 Oct. [27 Sept.], 1853.

 ii. RHODOLPHUS⁷, b. in Norwich, May 12, 1798. He d. at Norwich, a few days after his mother, 31 Oct., 1802.

Children of NOADIAH⁶, (1764) [367] (Zadoc⁵, Jacob⁴, Sergt. Jabob³, Jacob², Robert¹) and Mary (Bedortha) Adams; res. Suffield, Conn.

805. i. ALVIN⁷, b. in Suffield, Apr. 19, 1792; m. Jan. 1, 1817, Hannah Ainsworth, b. Sept. 29, 1793; d. 29 Mar., 1830; res. Agawam, Mass. He d. 11 Feb., 1834.

806. ii. HARVEY⁷, b. in Suffield, Dec. 11, 1793; m. (1) Oct. 28, 1819, Mary Porter of W. Springfield, Mass.; she d. in Agawam, 4 May, 1858, age 62 years; m. (2) Betsey (Button) Allen, widow of Joseph Allen. He d. in Springfield, Mass., 19 July, 1882, age 88 years.

807.   iii.   LUCIUS⁷, b. in Suffield, Dec. 31, 1795 ; m. Julia Norton of Bennington, Vt. He d. at Northampton, Mass., 6 Nov., 1825, age 30 years.
       iv.   BETSEY⁷, b. in Suffield, Feb. 5, 1798 ; d. unm., 23 Oct., 1872, age 74 years.
       v.   NOADIAH⁷, b. in Suffield, Mar. 17, 1800 ; d. unm. Oct., 1893.
       vi.   JOSEPH BEDORTHA⁷, b. in Suffield, Aug. 9, 1803 ; d. unm. 9 Apr., 1831, age 28 years.

Children of ZADOC⁶, JR., (1765) [**368**] (Zadoc⁵, Jacob⁴, Sergt. Jacob³, Jacob², Robert¹) and Anne (Adams) Adams; res. Suffield, Conn.

808.   i.   DIANTHE⁷, b. in Suffield, Oct. 7, 1790 ; m. Calvin Sikes.
       ii.   ARABELLA⁷, b. in Suffield, July 31, 1792; d. unm. 15 Apr., 1852, age 59 years.
       iii. CHARLOTTE⁷, b. in Suffield, Feb. 1, 1795 ; m. John Gunn.
       iv.   THEODORE⁷, b. in Suffield, July 8, 1797. He m. and d. soon thereafter ; no issue.
       v.   MATILDA⁷, b. in Suffield, Dec. 28, 1799 ; d. unm. 2 Mar., 1867.
       vi.   LUCINDA⁷, b. in Suffield, Dec. 26, 1800 ; d. unm.
       vii. ASAHEL⁷, b. in Suffield, July 5, 1803 ; m. (1) Apr. 11, 1832, Mrs. Phebe (Granger) Heath, widow of Henry Heath; she d. 1850; m. (2) ―― Kingsbury ; res. Stafford, Conn.
       viii. CLARISSA⁷, b. in Suffield, Sept. 9, 1805 ; d. 19 Oct., 1806.
       ix.   HENRY WILLIAM⁷, b. in Suffield, Jan. 13, 1809 ; d. unm.
       x.   MARY ANN⁷, b. in Suffield, Jan. 12, 1812 ; d. unm.
       xi.   GAMALIEL⁷, b. in Suffield, May 21, 1814. He d. in Virginia unm. ―"an undutiful son."

Children of DORCAS⁶, (1769) [**369**] (Zadoc⁵, Jacob⁴, Sergt. Jacob³, Jacob², Robert¹) and Edmund Bement; res. Suffield, Conn.

       i.   EDWIN BEMENT, b. July 14, 1797 ; m. Sept., 1828, Almira (Adams) Sikes, dau. of Ebenezer and Lydia (Owen) Adams, and widow of Zenas Sikes. He d. 23 Jan., 1878.
       ii.   THOMAS BEMENT ; m. ―― Leonard.
       iii. MARY S. BEMENT, b. Feb. 18, 1803 ; m. Feb. 28, 1827, Otis Pierce.
       iv.   HARRIET BEMENT ; m. Benjamin Woodworth.
       v.   HENRY BEMENT.

Children of EBENEZER⁶, (1771) [**370**] (Zadoc⁵) Jacob⁴, Sergt. Jacob³, Jacob², Robert¹) and Lydia (Owen) Adams; res. Suffield, Conn.

Seventh Generation.] OF NEWBURY, MASS. 189

809. i. ALMIRA⁷, b. in Suffield, Apr. 7, 1796; m. (1) about 1816, Zenas Sikes; he was killed, Feb., 1825-6; m. (2) Sept., 1828, Edwin Bement, son of Edmund and Dorcas (Adams) Bement, b. July 14, 1797; d. 23 Jan., 1878. She d. in Suffield, 21 Oct., 1877.
810. ii. JARVIS⁷, b. in Suffield, 1798; m. Feb. 6. 1826, Hannah (Denslow) Williams. He d. in Hartford, Conn., 6 June, 1852, age 54 years.
811. iii. RUTH⁷, b. in Suffield, Nov. 23, 1799; m. Dec. 9, 1821, Stoddard Parker, son of John and Love (Billings) Parker. She d. in Springfield, Mass., 9 Dec., 1891.
812. iv. LYDIA⁷, b. in Suffield about 1802-3; m. David Tyler; res. Agawam, Mass.
813. v. CYNTHIA⁷, b. in Suffield, Dec. 3, 1805; m. Dec. 16, 1829, Oren Parker, son of John and Love (Billings) Parker, b. July 2, 1803; d. 13 Feb., 1872. She d. 30 Sept., 1872.
814. vi. NEWTON SKINNER⁷, b. in Suffield, May 16, 1808; m. in N. Y., Catherine Bundle. He d. in Suffield, Mar., 1835.
815. vii. HANNAH⁷, b. in Suffield, Nov. 5, 1810; m. (1) Nov. 8, 1832, Cornelius R. Doremus, b. June 2, 1811; d. 8 Mar., 1840; m. (2) John Van Delinda, son of Ralph Van Delinda, b. Dec. 6, 1806; d. 2 June, 1876. She d. 23 Dec., 1891.
.viii. SOPHRONIA⁷, b. in Suffield, Sept. 26, 1813; m. (1) Dec. 17, 1831, Andrew McKnight; he d. 4 Aug., 1839; m. Nov. 8, 1840, Thos. McKnight, bro. of Andrew; he d. 1 May, 1841; m. (3) Apr. 4, 1861, Wm. L. Wilson; he d. 28 Dec., 1895. She was living in Thompsonville, Conn., 1899, and assisted in this record.
ix. MINER⁷, b. in Suffield, Feb. 10, 1818; m. Dec. 4, 1835, Mary S. Root of Palmer, Mass. He res. in Bondville; d. in Palmer, and was buried there; had a daughter who d. young.

Child of RUTH⁶, (1774) [371] (Zadoc⁵, Jacob⁴, Sergt. Jacob³, Jacob², Robert¹) and Josiah King; res. Suffield, Conn.

i. ALMIRA KING, b. Oct. 5, 1797; m. Benjamin Richardson.

Children of ARAH⁶, (1775) [372] (Zadoc⁵, Jacob⁴, Sergt. Jacob³, Jacob², Robert¹) and Elizabeth (Gray) Adams; res. Suffield, Conn.

816. i. EDWARD⁷, b. in Suffield, 1801; m. (1) Oct. 1, 1822, Sally Worthington, b. 1800; d. 26 Apr., 1843, age 43 years; m. (2) Jan. 21, 1845, Mrs. Julia A. Webster; she d. 22 Apr., 1850, age 45 years; m. (3) Mar. 12, 1858, Mrs. Luvan Topliff; she d. in Monson, Mass., 17 Dec., 1874, age 66 years.

Edward Adams learned the trade of a wagon-maker, and worked with David Smith of Springfield, Mass. He set. in So. Wilbraham, Mass. (now Hampden), and established there the first wagon-shop of the town—still occupied by his son. He d. 6 Oct., 1872, age 71 years; administration of his estate was granted Nov. 6, 1872.

817. ii. ELIZA[7], b. in Suffield, Feb. 18, 1804; m. Dec. 18, 1828, Roderick Fuller of Somers, Conn.; he d. in Westfield, 10 Sept., 1859. She d. 23 Aug., 1871; res. Westfield, Mass.

iii. NATHANIEL[7], b. in Suffield, 1806; m. Apr. 5, 1826, Anne Woodworth; res. on the river road, Suffield, Conn. He d. 13 Feb., 1850, no issue.

818. iv. JOHN[7], b. in Suffield, 1809; m. Sept. 7, 1831, Betsey Snow, dau. of Arthur and Olinela (Sharlon) Snow, b. in Chester, Conn., 1812; d. in Meriden, 1874; res. Suffield, Conn. He d. Apr., 1861, age 52 years.

Children of ORPHA[6], (1780) [373] (Zadoc[5], Jacob[4], Sergt. Jacob[3], Jacob[2], Robert[1]) and Zepheniah Snow; res. Suffield, Conn.

i. WARREN SNOW, b. in Suffield, Mar 10, 1801.
He is reported to have removed to Vermont, and to have died near Boston, unm.

818½. ii. RHODOLPHUS SNOW, b. in Suffield, June 14, 1803; m. Aug. 17, 1829, Mary Ann King, dau. of Jarvah King, b. in Suffield, Oct. 6, 1807; d. 16 Apr., 1858, age 51 years; res. Suffield. He d. 16 Mar., 1871.

iii. LURA SNOW, b. in Suffield, Sept. 30, 1806; m. Edward Lester of Suffield; he d in Meriden, Conn.

iv. ORVILLE SNOW, b. in Suffield; m. Clarissa Woodworth, dau. of Geo. Woodworth of Suffield; no issue.

Children of CALVIN[6], (1791) [374] (Zebulon[5], Jr., Zebulon[4], Daniel[3], Jacob[2], Robert[1]) and Lucy (King) Adams; res. Suffield, Conn.

i. CALVIN LYMAN[7], b. in Suffield, May 22, 1816; res. Suffield; d. unm. 18 June, 1896.

819. ii. LOUIS K.[7], b. in Suffield, Oct. 2, 1822; m. Jan. 9, 1853, Sophronia Parker, dau. of Oren and Cynthia (Adams) Parker, b. Dec. 2, 1830; d. 26 Oct., 1886.
He rem. to California in 1849, remaining three years; returning in 1853, he rem. to the west in 1883, and is now [1898] Postmaster at Shoshone, Idaho, and Chairman of the Republican Committee of Lincoln County.

Children of HARRIET[6], (1801) [**375**] (Zebulon[5], Jr., Zebulon[4], Daniel[3], Jacob[2], Robert[1]) Ashbel Dewey; res. Westfield, Mass.

820.   i.   MARIA LUCY DEWEY, b. in Westfield, Aug. 3, 1823; m. Jan. 9, 1846, John Mills Woolley, b. in Newton, Chester Co., Pa., Nov. 20, 1822; rem. to Nauvoo, Ill., in 1845, and to Salt Lake City, Utah, in 1847; was a missionary and a Bishop of the Mormon Church, and d. 18 Aug., 1864. She is living, 1899, at 324 E. Fourth St., So. Salt Lake City, Utah.

821.   ii. ALBERT CORNING DEWEY, b. in Westfield, Nov. 5, 1825; m. (1) May 21, 1846, Maria Loomis, b. in Russell, Mass., Sept. 22, 1828; m. (2) Feb. 11, 1856, Sarah Burton, b. in England, Sept. 21, 1825; m. (3) July 12, 1867, Elizabeth Ann Wright, b. in New Jersey, Dec. 1, 1832; res. Salt Lake City, Utah, and Gray, Bingham Co., Idaho.

822.   iii. BENJAMIN FRANKLIN DEWEY, b. in Westfield, May 5, 1829, m. (1) at San Bernardino, Cal., May 3, 1855, Eliza Smithson; m. (2) at Salt Lake City, Oct. 5, 1869, Diza Paralle Russell, b. May 9, 1848; d. 22 July, 1895; res. White Hills, Mohan Co., Arizona.

823.   iv. JOHN HENRY DEWEY, b. in Westfield, Feb. 7, 1832; m. July 29, 1855, Ann Lamoreaux, b. Apr. 8, 1834; res. Salt Lake City, Utah.

Children of SUSANNA[6], (1803 [**376**] (Zebulon[5], Jr., Zebulon[4], Daniel[3], Jacob[2], Robert[1]) and Oren Kendall; res. Suffield, Conn.

i.   ADELINE A. KENDALL, b. Dec. 15, 1831; m. Feb. 2, 1852, Charles Brewster; he d. 17 Dec., 1882; res. Suffield, Conn.; postoffice, Thomsonville, Conn.

ii. ANNETTE O. KENDALL, b. Jan. 20, 1837; d. in Suffield, 22 May, 1860.

Children of EMILY[6], (1806) [**377**] (Zebulon[5], Jr., Zebulon[4], Daniel[3], Jacob[2], Robert[1]) and Julius King; res. Suffield (Mapleton), Conn.

i.   JANE ELIZA KING, b. Sept. 18, 1830; m. Nov. 23, 1848, Julius F. Sikes, son of Zenas and Almira (Adams) Sikes; res. Suffield (Mapleton), Conn.; living 1898.

ii. HESDEN J. KING, b. July 9, 1832; m. Jan., 1859, Helen Pomeroy. He set. in Elizabeth, N. J., and d. 4 Dec., 1886.

Children of CALVIN⁶, (1780) [**378**] (Capt. Gideon⁵, Daniel⁴, Daniel³, Jacob², Robert¹) and Martha (Stillman) Adams; res. Verona, Oneida Co., N. Y.

824.   i. SILAS WILMOT⁷, b. in Verona, Sept. 3, 1803; m. Lydia Bidwell of Verona, N. Y.; b. Nov. 12, 1806; res. Verona, N. Y.; 7 children; res. Galesville, Wis. He d. 16 Aug., 1871.
825.   ii. ELIZA ANGELINE⁷, b. in Verona, Jan. 28, 1806; m. Sept. 19, 1827, Chester Ives. Bidwell, brother of Lydia, b. Jan. 4, 1799; d. 2 Jan., 1869; res. Galesville, Trempealeau, Co., Wis. She d. 23 Apr., 1899, age 93 years.
826.   iii. GIDEON⁷, b. in Verona, March 6, 1808; m. Orinda Haskins of Onondaga Co., N. Y.; she d. at Butte, Mont., 24 Sept., 1882. He set. in Mauston, Juneau Co., Wis., 1870; d. 30 Oct., 1877.
827.   iv. SARAH CLINTON⁷, b. in Verona, June 10, 1813; m. 1835, Wm. S. Wilder, b. Nov. 8, 1813; d. 14 Jan., 1870; 7 children. She d. 25 Mar., 1882.

Children of CHARLOTTE⁶, (1782) [**379**] (Capt. Gideon⁵, Daniel⁴, Daniel³, Jacob², Robert¹) and Seth Sackett Sedgwick; res. Verona, Oneida Co., N. Y.

  i. HIEL SEDGWICK, b. in Verona, Aug. 5, 1802.
  ii. IRENE SEDGWICK, b. Nov. 5, 1803; m. Feb. 12, 1826, Henry Nobles, who d. at No. West, Ohio, 11 Aug., 1850. She d. 1868.
  iii. ABIGAIL SEDGWICK, b. April 24, 1805; m. Aug., 1823, George Cadwell. She d. in Verona, 22 Feb., 1876.
  iv. SARAH A. SEDGWICK, b. Nov. 22, 1806; m. Feb. 28, 1830, Lovewell Johnson, son of Hon. Lovewell Johnson; he d. 28 Feb., 1845. She d. 10 May, 1886.
  v. TERRISA SEDGWICK, b. Sept. 17, 1808; m. Nov., 1826, Roswell Gates. She d. Feb., 1837.
  vi. STEPHEN SEDGWICK, b. May 25, 1810; m. Sept., 1832, Marianna Easton, b. in New Haven, N. Y., Oct. 9, 1817; d. in Bainbridge, Mich., 29 Nov., 1887. He d. 12 Apr., 1873.
  vii. NEWTON SEDGWICK, b. Mar. 1, 1812; m. July, 1833, Dorcas ———, and d. Jan., 1834.
  viii. JULIA SEDGWICK, b. Nov. 22, 1813; d. Oct., 1837.
  ix. HARVEY SEDGWICK, b. Oct. 14, 1815; m. Philinda Cross. He d. at Popsippi, Wis., 7 Apr., 1374.
  x. MARY SEDGWICK, b. May 25, 1817; died at Palermo, N. Y., Aug., 1856.
  xi. CHESTER SEDGWICK, b. Dec. 3, 1820; m. Sept., 1843, Elmina Hoyt. He d. at W. Monroe, N. Y., Mar., 1881.

Seventh Generation.] OF NEWBURY, MASS. 193

xii. CALVIN C. SEDGWICK, b. June 27, 1822; m. April, 1842, Harriet N. Webb; res. Sandusky, Wis.
xiii. INFANT, b. Aug. 30, 1824; d. 7 Sept., 1824.

Children of RHODA⁶, (1786) [**380**] (Capt. Gideon⁵, Daniel⁴, Daniel³, Jacob², Robert¹) and Clark Smith; res. Busti, Chautauqua Co., N. Y.

i. OLIVER P. SMITH, b. in Westmoreland, N. Y., Mar. 26, 1806.
ii. RANSOM JEWETT SMITH, b. in Westmoreland, July 26, 1809; m. (1) 1840, Lucinda Davis; d. 1841; m. (2) Aug. 4, 1846, Agnes Gray Baxter, b. in Scotland; she d. 3 June, 1889. He d. in Busti, N. Y., 16 Apr., 1876.
iii. EZRA H. SMITH, b. July 26, 1811. He rem. to Kansas, and d. 26 July, 1862.
iv. LOVISA O. SMITH, b. May 18, 1813; m. Hiram Smith, b. in Shelby, Orleans Co., N. Y., Aug. 20, 1814, and d. at Olean, N. Y., 14 Sept., 1888. They res. in Jamestown, N. Y. She d. 23 Apr., 1874.
v. SHELDON SMITH, b. July 26, 1816; m. (1) Amelia Thompson; she d. in Detroit, Mich., 12 Sept., 1859; m. (2) Sarah Fowler, b. at Rockford, Ill., Oct. 27, 1829; living 1898, Los Gatos, Cal.
He was an architect of marked ability in Detroit, Mich. He designed many of the public buildings in Michigan, and was a man of classic and refined taste. He d. in Detroit, 28 May, 1869.
vi. MAJOR HARVEY A. SMITH, b. Jan. 13, 1819; m. (1) Mary Broadhead; she d. Nov., 1852; m. (2) Mary L. Gurley.
He was an editor, poet and lawyer; d. during the civil war.
vii. JULIUS C. SMITH, b. Aug. 5, 1822; m. May 19, 1847, Mary E. Robertson; she d. 12 Dec., 1886; res. Bradford, McKean Co., Pa. He is living, 1898, the only surviving child of Rhoda Adams Smith.

Children of ABBY⁶, (1787) [**381**] (Capt. Gideon⁵, Daniel⁴, Daniel³, Jacob², Robert¹) and Chester Loomis; res. Cicero, Onondaga Co., N. Y.

i. FANNY LOOMIS, b. in Cicero, Dec. 12, 1809; m. Feb. 21, 1832, Jefferson Freeman; he d. 1867; res. Syracuse, N. Y.
She was living in 1899, a woman of great vitality and strength of character, intellectually brilliant, a poetic writer and leader of thought and society.
ii. EMMA A. LOOMIS, b. Aug. 9, 1811; m. Sept. 11, 1834, Nathaniel Cornell; she d. in Iowa, 15 Apr., 1891.

iii. MARCEMUS A. LOOMIS, b. Feb. 3, 1814 ; m. Dec. 25, 1847, Elizabath Brown ; living, Onondaga Valley, N. Y.
iv. MARIA L. LOOMIS, b. Nov. 12, 1816 ; m. Dec. 25, 1852, Thomas Varney. She d. in Oakland, Cal., 30 Mar., 1888.
v. ALVIRA LOOMIS, b. June 13, 1818 ; m. Feb., 1840, James Raleigh. She d. June, 1845.
vi. CHAUNCEY C. LOOMIS, b. Oct. 9, 1820 ; m. 1850, Lucy Ostrander ; res. Clay, N. Y. He d. 1869.
vii. SOPHIA LOOMIS, b. May 21, 1822 ; m. 1843, John M. Field.
viii. HARRIET A. LOOMIS, b. Nov. 19, 1823 ; living 1895, unm.
ix. ROSETTA LOOMIS, b. June 1, 1825 ; d. 16 Dec., 1846.
x. MARY J. LOOMIS, b. May 1, 1827 ; m. 1848, Chauncey N. Adams ; He d. 1888. She d. 21 July, 1892.
xi. ADDISON J. LOOMIS, b. Dec. 3, 1831 ; m. Caroline Loomis ; res. Cicero, N. Y.
xii. HENRY H. LOOMIS, b. Apr. 20, 1833 ; m. 1854, Clara Merriam ; res. Syracuse, N. Y.

Children of HORACE⁶, (1790) [382] (Capt. Gideon⁵, Daniel⁴, Daniel³, Jacob², Robert¹) and Sally (Wylie) Adams; res. Rome, N. Y.

828. i. ELIZA ANGELINE⁷, b. in Rome, Nov. 26, 1814 ; m. Jan. 6, 1841, Philander Soper, son of Philander Soper, b. in Rome, N. Y., Nov. 14, 1815 ; d. 18 Oct. 1894. He m. 2nd, Feb. 28, 1856, Sarah Elizabeth Holcomb ; she d. 6 May, 1862 ; one dau. He m. 3rd, Jan. 1, 1864, Lydia Hazen Knight ; she d. 28 July, 1894. Eliza Angeline d. 17 Mar., 1855.
ii. HORACE WYLIE⁷, b. in Rome, Nov. 2, 1816 ; m. Feb. 22, 1844, Caroline S. Peckham ; she d. 11 May, 1888. He d. 15 Nov., 1862 ; no issue.
829. iii. WINFRED SCOTT⁷, b. in Rome, May 14, 1819 ; m. Dec. 15, 1840, Elouisa Miller. He d. in Phelps, N. Y., 17 Apr., 1893.

Children of HORACE⁶, (1790) and Mary (Lyndon) Adams.
iv. DANFORD⁷, b. in Rome, Apr. 7, 1822 ; d. 23 Mar., 1823.
830. v. SARAH⁷, b. in Rome, Nov. 4, 1823 ; m. Mar. 12, 1846, Joshua R. Lawton, son of Joshua R. and Phebe Lawton, b. in Conn., 1823 ; d. 6 Mar., 1885 ; set. in Pittsfield, Mass.
831. vi. ROBY⁷, b. in Rome, Aug. 6, 1825 ; m. Jan. 5, 1848, Charles Stanton Lawton, son of Joshua R. and Phebe Lawton, b. in Conn., Oct. 8, 1823 ; d. in Pittsfield, Mass., 15 June, 1866; set. in Chicago, Ill.

Seventh Generation.] OF NEWBURY, MASS. 195

832. vii. CLINTON[7], b. in Rome, Mar. 30, 1828 ; m. Mary Savery ; res. Valley Mills, Madison Co., N. Y.
833. viii. HENRY L.[7], b. in Rome, Apr. 26, 1830; m. Mar. 18, 1857, Mary A. Noble ; res. Rome, N. Y.
834. ix. AMANDA[7], b. in Rome, Jan. 20, 1833 ; m. Sept. 1865, Wm. Baker ; res. Saticoy, Ventura Co., Cal. She d. 4 Apr., 1897.
    x. CALEB MILLER[7], b. in Rome, Sept. 8, 1835; m. Feb. 9, 1859, Emma L. Stebbins ; res. Phelps, Ontario Co., N. Y.; no issue.

Children of REBECCA[6], (1796) [383] (Capt. Gideon[5], Daniel[4], Daniel[3], Jacob[2], Robert[1]) and Jothan G. Goodspeed; res. Bancroft, Shiawassie Co., Mich.

    i. CALVIN GOODSPEED, b. in Hastings, N. Y., Jan. 11, 1821; m. (1) Rosabella Hadley ; m. (2) Sarah Chambers. He d. in Willamstown, Mich., 7 Feb., 1895.
    ii. ELIJAH F. GOODSPEED, b. Jan. 13, 1823; m. 1848, Eliza M. Beall. He d. in California.
    iii. SARAH ANN GOODSPEED, b. Dec. 25, 1826 ; d. 1831.
    iv. OSCAR J. GOODSPEED, b. Oct. 30, 1831 ; m. Feb. 17, 1858, Mary Letts of So. Lyon, Mich ; res. So. Lyon, Mich.
    v. CHAS. HARVEY GOODSPEED, b. Feb. 22, 1833; m. May 24, 1858, Helen L. Adams, dau. of Harvey and Deborah (Field) Adams, b. Dec. 3, 1835 ; res. Bancroft, Mich.
    vi. SARAH ANTOINETTE GOODSPEED, b. Jan. 14, 1836 ; m. (1) Nov. 14, 1862, Gilbert Fay ; m. (2) Nov. 17, 1865, De Forest F. Burnett; res. Lansing, Mich.
    vii. AURELIA GOODSPEED, b. Oct. 4, 1843 ; m. Sept. 20, 1867, Albert E. Letts ; res. So. Lyon, Oakland Co., Mich.

Children of HARVEY[6], (1799) [384] (Capt. Gideon[5], Daniel[4], Daniel[3], Jacob[2], Robert[1]) and Deborah (Field) Adams; res. Brooklyn, Jackson Co., Mich.

835. i. AMANDA E.[7], b. in Verona, N. Y., April 19, 1823 ; m. Nov. 8, 1841, Geo. Spencer; res. Fergus, Saginaw Co., Mich.
    ii. HARVEY F.[7], b. in Verona, Feb. 5, 1825 ; m. 1848, Frances —— of Cleveland, Ohio ; res. Soldiers Home, Sanduski, Ohio ; no issue.
836. iii. RHODA[7], b. in Verona, Oct. 10, 1827 ; m. 1846, Henry Lincoln ; res. Bancroft, Mich. She d. 26 April, 1855.
837. iv. GEO. HADLEY[7], b. in Penn Yan, N. Y., Jan. 28, 1850 ; m. Sept. 15, 1854, Mary E. Higgins, dau. of Capt. Jesse Higgins of Hallowell, Me., b. 1830; d. in Brooklyn, N. Y.
    He resided in Indianapolis, Ind., 1857–1869, then removed to New York City, where he is a publisher of maps.

196   ROBERT ADAMS   [Seventh Generation.

838. v. MARY J.⁷, b. in Central Square, Nov. 30, 1832 ; m. Jan., 1856, Albert Fay, ; he d. 1864; res. Fergus, Mich.
839. vi. HELEN L,⁷, b. in Central Square, Nov. 19, (Dec. 6?), 1836 ; m. May 19 or 24, 1858, Chas. H. Goodspeed, son of Jotham G. and Rebecca (Adams) Goodspeed, b. Feb. 22, 1833 ; res. Bancroft, Mich.
    vii. JOHN Q.⁷, b. in Central Square, Nov. 6, 1839 ; m. 1859, Emma Matthewson ; res. Owosso, Mich.
He was a soldier in the civil war.

Children of ELIPHALET⁶, JR., (1779) [385] (Eliphalet⁵, Freegrace⁴, Lieut. Abraham³, Jacob² Robert¹) and Narcissa (Ward) Adams; res. Stoke, Richmond Co., P. Q.

    i. LUCINDA⁷, b. in Stoke, May 12, 1808 ; m. —— Livereaux ; res. in Lower Canada.
840. ii. LEWIS ALANSON⁷, b. in Stoke, May 4, 1810 ; m. Nov. 7, 1836, Elizabeth Fawcett.
        They set. in Drayton, Wellington Co., Ont., 1832. He d. 28 Mar., 1880.
    iii. RANSOM⁷, b. in Stoke, Feb. 4, 1812 ; d. at Acton, Ont., unm., 10 May, 1881.
841. iv. EZRA⁷, b. in Stoke, April 10, 1814 ; m. Sept. 14, 1843, Jerusha Worden of Acton, Ont. ; she d. 23 Feb., 1885. He d. 1 Mar., 1895.
842. v. MARTHA⁷, b. in Stoke, Feb. 13, 1818 ; m. Henry Calute ; res. Acton and Sarnia, Ont.
    vi. ZENAS⁷, b. in Stoke, May 13, 1820 ; d. at Drayton, Ont., unm.
843. vii. WELLINGTON⁷, b. in Stoke, April 15, 1822 ; m. Mar. 26, 1851, Ellen Clemenshaw ; she d. 12 Sept., 1887; res. Minto, Ont. He d. 30 Apr., 1862.

Children of PHEBE⁶, (1781) [386] (Eliphalet⁵, Freegrace⁴, Lieut. Abraham³, Jacob², Robert¹) and Joseph H. Kilborn; res. Acton, Ont.

    i. WILLIAM VINCENT KILBORN, b. Oct. 28, 1806 ; drowned in the St. Francis river, 4 May, 1829.
    ii. JOSEPH HENRY KILBORN, b. May 8, 1809 ; m. (1) Mar. 18, 1832, Susan Hughes.
    iii. CAROLINE CORDELIA KILBORN, b. Dec. 17, 1811 ; m. Jan. 20, 1839, Freeman Bray.
    iv. CLARISSA MARIA KILBORN, b. Nov. 6, 1814; d. 18 Mar., 1815.

MARY ELECTA ADAMS.

Children of RUFUS⁶, (1783) [**387**] (Eliphalet⁵, Freegrace⁴, Lieut. Abraham³, Jacob², Robert¹) and Maria (Hubbard) Adams; res. Acton, Halton Co., Ont.

843½. i. EMELINE MARIA⁷, b. in Westbury, Que., May 29, 1822 ; m. Rev. Francis Coleman, b. 1813; living in Hamilton, Ont., 1900. She d. at Acton, Ont., 23 June, 1858, age 38 years.
ii. MARY ELECTA⁷, b. in Westbury, Nov. 10, 1823.
"She was a woman of exceptional ability, education and influence. She began teaching at an early age, and was a prominent figure in educational circles in Canada, her efforts being especially directed to the higher education of women. She taught in various towns, mostly women's academies, until she became principal of the Wesleyan Female College in Hamilton, Ont., where she remained for many years. She spent two years in Italy studying languages, and returned to open her own school for young women at Coburg, Ont., known as 'Brookhurst.' Later she became principal of Ontario Ladies' College, Whitby, Ont., where she spent eleven years. Her work was characterized by broad principles and lofty ideals. She was a woman of unusual beauty and most commanding presence, and was especially gifted as an artist and writer." [*] She d. 5 Nov., 1898.
iii. LUCIUS RUFUS⁷, b. Oct. 11, 1825.
He entered the ministry of the Wesleyan Methodist Church, and settled at Mitchell, Perth Co., Ont., where he d. in the first year of his ministry, 24 Aug., 1854, age 28 years.
ii. JOHN QUINCY⁷, b. June 19, 1827 ; d. 6 May, 1849.
v. AUGUSTA MINERVA⁷, b. Oct. 1, 1830.
Living, unm.; res. Morley, Alberta, N. W. Ter.
vi. CLARISSA ELVIRA⁷, b. Dec. 16, 1832 ; d. 1 Dec., 1833.

---

*REFRESHMENT.

Hast thou had hours when life seemed empty all,
And waste the garden thou wert set to till,
Like tide-swept sands that only white and still,
Unanswering lay beneath the Heaven's gray pall?
No ripening fruit to answer to His call,
Discouragement hath waited on the will ;
And did some human voice that brought a thrill
Out of the silence, on the hearing fall ;
'I could not rest till I had come to see
And tell you how your life hath blessed my own ?'
Burst a cool spring ; the heart, refreshed and free,
Went on its way under a smiling sun.
If ever this had happened unto thee,
Thou knowest a joy that's next to God's ' Well done.' "

Children of REV. EZRA⁶, (1788) [388] (Eliphalet⁵, Freegrace⁴, Lieut. Abraham³, Jacob², Robert¹) and Isa (Proctor) Adams; res. Acton and Drayton, Ont.

845. i. BETSEY ALMIRA⁷, b. in Frederickburg, U. C., Oct. 16, 1815 ; m. July 5. 1832, Rev. Thomas Hurlburt ; he d. at Mauctontin Island, Ont., 14 Apr., 1873. She d. in Toronto, Ont., Dec., 1863.

846. ii. HENRY PROCTOR⁷, b. near Lundy's Lane, Ont., Mar. 12, 1822; m. (1) Jan. 24, 1844, Huldah Griffin, dau. of Mrs. Betsey (Edmunds) Griffin ; she d. 15 Aug., 1856 ; m. (2) Emily Griffin, sister of Huldah Griffin; she d. 20 Apr., 1873 ; m. (3) Dec. 28, 1874, Elizabeth Cass.

He set. in Acton, Ont., in 1836, and there learned his trade as a miller, remaining till 1844 ; was in Westport, Mo., 1847-1850 ; set. in Hanover, Ont., in 1855, where he built mills and did an extensive business, building up the village. He was prominent as a Mason, school trustee, and superintendent of the Sunday School of the M. E. Church. He rem. to Bruce, N. Dakota, in 1881, and d. 2 Jan., 1882 ; was buried at Cavalier, N. Dak.

847. iii. DR. WILLIAM CASE, b. near Lundy's Lane, Oct. 18, 1823 ; m. Oct. 20, 1857, Matilda Osman, dau. of John Osman, Esq., of Seneca Falls, N. Y.

He graduated as a surgeon dentist from Victoria College, and began the practice of his profession in Toronto, Ont., in 1852, when there were only three other dentists in the city. He was the first to make use of nitrous oxide or laughing gas in Canada ; was one of the founders of the first Dental College in Toronto, and became a professor in it ; was a pioneer and leader in introducing vulcanized rubber plates and platinum in the manufacture of artificial teeth. He was an earnest and devoted leader in the M. E. Church, and highly esteemed by his friends. He d. in Toronto, 16 Jan., 1899.

848. iv. JANE MARIA⁷, b. in Acton, Ont., July 22, 1826 ; m. about 1852, Archibald McCallum, a teacher ; res. Toronto, Ont.; had one son who d. young. She d. of quick consumption.

849. v. ELIZA ROXANA⁷, b. in Acton, May 4, 1828 ; m. Mar. 21, 1846, Rev. Matthew Swann, son of Francis and Margaret Swann, b. Apr. 11, 1822 ; educated in Upper Canada College ; res. Fergus, Ont.

850. vi. GEORGE WASHINGTON⁷, b. in Acton, July 4, 1830 ; m. Aug. 23, 1852, Isabella Jane Lowes, b. in Cavan, Ont., Sept. 12, 1833 ; res. Grand Rapids, Mich.

vii. JOHN⁷, b. in Acton, Sept. 22, 1832 ; d. 6 Nov., 1832.

Children of REV. EZRA⁶, (1788) and Amy Edmunds (Curtis) Adams.

851. viii. ELECTA ANN⁷, b. in Maneytown, Ont., Sept. 10, 1834 ; m. Rev. James E. Dyer ; res. Toronto, Ont. She d. 2 July, 1897.

HENRY PROCTOR ADAMS.

DR. JOHN GLENNINGS C. ADAMS.

852.   ix.   SARAH ROWENA[1], b. in Brockville, Ont., Dec. 28, 1835 ; m. Rev. Thomas Culbert.
853.   x.   DR. JOHN GLENNINGS CURTIS[1], L. D. S., b. in Acton, Ont., Mar. 16, 1839 ; m. Dec. 18, 1861, Sarah Ann Fawcett, dau. of John Fawcett of Dayton, Ont., b. in Trafalgar, Halton Co., Ont., Jan. 14, 1845 ; d. in Toronto, Ont., 28 Oct., 1896.

A woman of great benevolence and virtue.

Dr. Adams is one of the foremost men of Toronto ; a man of great and noble virtue, spending his life and labor and possessions to benefit and help his fellow-men. For twenty-five years he has carried on and maintained the only free Dental Hospital for the poor in Toronto, and the importance of his work of reform among the school children of Toronto, and other places, will only be fully realized and appreciated when he has passed away. He is a prominent and influential official of the Avenue Road Methodist Church of Toronto.

Children of REV. ZENAS[6], (1792) [**389**] (Eliphalet[5], Freegrace[4], Lieut. Abraham[3], Jacob[2], Robert[1]) and Ruth (Fellows) Adams; res. Acton, Halton Co., Ont.

854.   i.   CHARLES FREDERICK[7], b. in Salisbury. Mass., Aug. 16, 1827 ; m. at Marmington, Ont., June 15, 1855, Ann Maywood, b. in Hull, Ont., Mar. 18, 1835 ; d. at E. Tawas, Mich., 23 Oct., 1892.

He was a carpenter in Millbank, Ont.; rem. in 1859 to Illinois, and thence in 1863, to Saginaw City, Mich. He set. in E. Tawas, Mich., in July, 1864 ; enlisted in the 15th Michigan Regiment in Oct.; served under Gen. Sherman ; was honorably discharged May 30, 1865.

855.   ii.   MARY[7], b. in Weymouth, Mass., Nov. 7, 1828 ; m. at Acton, Ont., Sept. 21, 1849, Rev. William Glass, a Methodist clergyman. She was educated in the Burlington Ladies' Academy at Hamilton, Ont., and became a teacher ; res. St. Clair, Mich.

       iii. CHARLOTTE[7], b. in Acton, Ont , May 17, 1830.

She prepared herself as a teacher in the Toronto Normal School, 1852–54, when she went with her cousins, Rev. Mr. and Mrs. Hulburt, as a missionary among the Indians at Rossville, Hudson Bay Ter., where she labored for four years. For several years thereafter she taught among the Indians near Sarnia, Ont., and in the Islands of Georgian Bay, and was greatly esteemed by them. She d. at the home of her cousins, Rev. Mr. and Mrs. Dyer, at St. Johns, near London, Ont., 26 Mar., 1867.

       iv.   WILBUR F.[7], b. in Acton, Aug. 11, 1831 ; d. 17 Aug., 1832.
       v.   ESTHER[7], b. in Acton, Dec. 28, 1832 ; d. 13 May, 1851.
856.   vi.   WILBUR FISK[7], b. in Acton, Mar. 14, 1834 ; m. Sept. 30, 1857, Nancy Christie, dau. of Robert Christie of Trowbridge, Ont., b. Apr. 16, 1836.

He was educated in the Normal School at Toronto, and was a successful teacher for a number of years. He set. at Owen Sound, Ont., and became a photographer ; rem. to St. Clair, Mich., and d. there 8 Aug., 1886.

vii. JOSEPH FELLOWS[7], b. in Acton, Mar. 3, 1836.

He was a student in the Normal School at Toronto, and in 1860 entered Baldwin University at Berea, O. In 1861 he joined a company for the war, but the company was not accepted ; he enlisted again from Illinois, in 1864, and was assigned to service on the U. S. S. Valley City in the North Atlantic blockading squadron—helping in the rescue of Lieut. Cushing on the Roanoke river ; he set. later in St. Clair, Mich., where he still resides ; unm.

857. viii. LUCINDA RUTH[7], b. in Acton, Mar. 7, 1838 ; m. at Hamilton, Ont., June 4, 1867, Rev. Thos. Lottridge Wilkinson, son of Rev. John Wilkinson, of the New Connection Methodist Church of Canada, b. Sept. 26, 1836.

She was educated as a teacher at Toronto and Hamilton, Ont.; res. 1899, Hanover, Ont.

858. ix. HARRIET ELECTA[7], b. in Acton, Dec. 22, 1839; m. Dec. 27, 1859, Rev. Daniel Stewart Kenney; b. in Ontario; rem. to Iasco Co., Mich., in 1862 ; enlisted 1864 in the U. S. Navy with his brother-in-law, Joseph Fellows Adams ; after his discharge he rem. with his family to Boyd Co., Ky., and later to Nebraska and Kansas ; he was ordained an elder in the M. E. Church in Crawford Co., Ark.

She was a teacher ; d. in Seward Co., Neb., 17 Sept., 1871.

x. AGNES MARIA[7], b. in Acton, Jan. 20, 1842.

She was educated at Wesleyan Female College, Dundas, and Hamilton, Ont., and at the Normal School, Toronto, and was a successful teacher for many years; res. St. Clair, Mich.; unm.

859. xi. ABIGAIL LUCRETIA[7], b. in Acton, Nov. 1, 1844 ; m. Oct. 25, 1871, Rev. Daniel S. Kenney (his 2d wife); res. Van Buren, Crawford Co., Ark.

Children of ICHABOD KING[6], JR., (1780) [**390**] (Lovisa[5], Freegrace[4], Lieut. Abraham[3], Jacob[2], Robert[1]) and Clarissa Howard; res. Marlboro, Vt.

860. i. LAURA KING, b. in Marlboro, Vt., Apr. 16, 1808; m. June 22, 1834, Marlboro, Vt., Josiah Powers, son of Josiah and Susanna (Parks) Powers, b. in Marlboro, Vt., Apr. 28, 1806 ; d. in West Brattleboro, Vt., 8 Jan., 1882 ; buried in Marlboro, Vt. She d. in Marlboro, Vt., 1 Sept., 1887.

ii. LEVI KING, b. in Marlboro, Vt., June 20, 1811 ; d. 22 Nov., 1812, Marlboro, Vt.

861. iii. LEVI KING, b. in Marlboro, Vt., May 28, 1814; m. Jan. 31, 1849, at Tolu, Ky., Mary Elizabeth Hicklin, dau. of Avery Madison and Lucinda (Knight) Hicklin, b. in Golconda, Ill., Oct. 9, 1830. He d. in Livingston Co., Ky., 26 Oct., 1882 ; res. Carrsville, Ky.

Seventh Generation.] OF NEWBURY, MASS. 201

iv. CARLOS KING, b. in Marlboro, Vt., Aug. 4, 1816 ; m. Mar. 15, 1859, Burlington, Ia., Mrs. Susan Spencer Alexander, dau. of Frederick and Sophia D. (Spencer) Spencer, b. in London, Eng., Oct. 31, 1818 ; res. Burlington, Ia.; no issue.

862. v. HOLLIS KING, b. in Marlboro, Vt., Nov. 13, 1818 ; m. June 13, 1850, at Wardsboro, Vt., Jane Elizabeth Derby, dau. of Joel and Frances Mackey (Howe) Derby, b. in Hinsdale, N. H., Sept. 11, 1833. He d. in Marlboro, Vt., 28 Oct., 1863.

vi. DAVID KING, b. in Marlboro, Vt., Jan. 30, 1821.
He rem. to California, and has not been heard from since 1863.

863. vii. CLARA KING, b. in Marlboro, Vt., Dec. 29, 1823 ; m. Sept. 18, 1846, at Troy, N. Y., Josiah Powers (his 2nd wife) see 860, i.; she d. in W. Brattleboro, Vt., 25 Feb., 1895 ; buried in Marlboro, Vt.

Children of JUSTIN KING⁶, (1784) [**391**] (Lovisa⁵, Freegrace⁴, Lieut. Abraham³, Jacob², Robert¹) rnd Ann Cook ; res. Boston, Mass., and Cincinnati, O.

i. ANN KING, b. in Boston, Mass.; d. in Cincinnati, O., 5 Feb., 1817.

863¼. ii. ELIZABETH KING, b. in Boston, Nov. 1, 1812 ; m. Dec. 23, 1827, Cincinnati, O., Newton Thomas Procter, son of Abram Procter, b. in Mason Co., Ky., April 26, 1803 ; d. in Whitcomb, Ind., 4 Apr., 1862. She d. at Whitcomb, Franklin Co., Ind., 7 Feb., 1891.

iii. ALICE KING, b. in Boston, Mar. 3, 1815 ; d. 6 Oct., 1821, Cincinnati, O.

863½. iv. CHARLES COOK KING, b. in Cincinnati, O., May 18, 1816 ; m. (1) Mar. 3, 1839, Martha Chumley, dau. of Frank and Martha Chumley, b. in Tenn., Apr. 4, 1820, ; d. 10 Sept., 1859 ; m. (2) 1871, St. Louis, Mo., Mrs. Catherine (Baumann) Hubbell, b. in Philadelphia, Pa., 1839. He d. in Cincinnati, O., 3 June, 1880.

v. MARY KING, b. in Cincinnati, Jan., 1818 ; d. in Cincinnati, O., about 1877, unm ; buried at Mt. Carmel, Ind.

vi. ANN KING, b. in Cincinnati, Aug. 25, 1819 ; d. 4 Aug., 1820.

Children of JUSTIN KING⁶, (1784) and Ann Moss.

vii. SON, b. in Cincinnati, O., Feb. 2, 1821 ; d. in Cincinnati, O., 5 Dec., 1821.

viii. SON, b. and d. in Cincinnati, O., Apr., 1823.

ix. DANIEL E. KING; b. in Cincinnati, O.; d. in Covington Ky., 1860.

Children of HANNAH KING⁶, (1793) [**392**] (Lovisa⁵, Freegrace⁴, Lieut. Abraham³, Jacob², Robert¹) and Emory Powers; res. Ludlow, Vt.

i. A DAUGHTER, b. in Marlboro, Vt.; d. age 3 weeks.

      ii. WESLEY EMORY POWERS, b. in Marlboro, Mar. 29, 1822; d. in Keene, N. H., 8 Sept., 1836.

864. iii. ELLIS KING POWERS, b. in Marlboro, May 6, 1824 ; m. Nov. 27, 1872, at Chesterfield, N. J., Caroline Bullock, dau. of Wm. Wood and Mary Ivins (Davis) Bullock, b. in Chesterfield, N. J., July 10, 1844. He d. in New York City, 29 Nov., 1888 ; bur. in Ludlow, Vt.

865. iv. HANNAH MARANDA POWERS, b. in Marlboro, Nov. 1, 1825 ; m. May 3, 1848, at Wardsboro, Vt., Ira Willard Gale, son of Ebenezer and Polly (Chamberlin) Gale, b. in Windham, Vt., July 27, 1818; res. Ludlow, Vt.

      v. HOLLIS LYMAN POWERS, b. in Marlboro, Oct. 6, 1827.
           He was a successful hotel-keeper in New York City, and d. there unm. 5 Feb., 1886 ; buried in Ludlow, Vt.

      vi. A DAUGHTER, who died in infancy.

      vii. LUCINA LOVISA POWERS, b. in Marlboro, July 16, 1831 ; d. in Wardsboro, Vt., 6 July, 1849.

      viii. LUCINDA CORDELIA POWERS, b. in Marlboro, June 23, 1833 ; d. in Marlboro, Vt., 30 Jan., 1839.

Children of ANNA KING[6], (1796) [**393**] (Lovisa[5], Freegrace[4], Lieut. Abraham[3], Jacob[2], Robert[1]) and Joseph Angel Hamilton; res. Halifax, Vt., and Marlboro, Vt.

866. i. JOSEPH HENRY HAMILTON, b. in Halifax, Vt., June 19, 1824 ; m. (1) Feb. 28, 1852, Marlboro, Vt., Abbie Adams Mather, dau. of Timothy and Harriet (Winslow) Mather, b. in Marlboro, Vt., June 5, 1831 ; d. in Marlboro, Vt., 5 Apr., 1859 ; m. (2) Dec. 31, 1861, Marlboro, Vt., Abbie Cross, dau. of Peter and Dorcas (Wild) Cross, b. in Bradford, Vt., Jan. 15, 1826 ; d. in West Brattleboro, Vt., 12 Feb., 1899 ; buried in Marlboro, Vt.; res. W. Brattleboro, Vt.

867. ii. JULIA ANNA HAMILTON, b. in Marlboro, May 21, 1826 ; m. May 21, 1849, Marlboro, Vt., Laban Jones, son of Laban and Hannah (Dean) Jones, b. in Dover, Vt., Dec. 8, 1825 ; d. in Dover, 2 Dec., 1885. She d. in Dover, Vt., 21 July, 1878.

      iii. LUCINDA AMY HAMILTON, b. in Marlboro, Aug. 11, 1828 ; m. Sept. 8, 1859, at Springfield, Mass., Preston Fay Perry, b. in Dover, Vt., Nov. 18, 1821 ; d. in Brattleboro, Vt., 16 Sept., 1887. She d. in W. Brattleboro, 11 Nov., 1883 ; no issue.

Children of LUCINDA KING[6], (1798) [**394**] (Lovisa[5], Freegrace[4], Lieut. Abraham[3], Jacob[2], Robert[1]) and Rufus Caldwell; res. West Northfield, Mass.

868. i. RUFUS KING CALDWELL, b. in West Northfield, Apr. 2, 1829 ; m. (1) Dec. 5, 1860, Gill, Mass., Almeda Harriet Bascom, dau. of Henry and Rhoda (Munn) Bascom, b. in Greenfield, Mass., Dec. 23, 1827 ; d. in W. Northfield, Mass., 3 Jan., 1885 ; m. (2) Sept. 27,

Seventh Generation.] OF NEWBURY, MASS. 203

        1893, Springfield, Mass., Mrs. Martha Amanda Sexton King, dau. of Oliver and Mary (Cooley) Sexton, b. in Springfield, Mass., Aug. 13, 1836 ; res. W. Northfield, Mass.

869.   ii. HARRIET LUCINDA CALDWELL, b. in W. Northfield, Jan. 16, 1831 ; m. Jan. 31, 1854, W. Northfield, Dr. Elijah Pierce Burton, son of Timothy and Mary (Pierce) Burton, b. in So. Windham, Vt., Jan. 8, 1826 ; res. Corydon, Iowa.

870.   iii. HANNAH MARIA CALDWELL, b. in W. Northfield, Feb. 19, 1833 ; m. at Chicago, Ill., Sept. 18, 1856, Henry Baxter Parker, son of Henry and' Matilda (Perry) Parker, b. in Millbury, Mass., Nov. 30, 1831 ; d. in Northfield, 21 Nov., 1897; buried in W. Northfield. She d. in Northfield, 20 Jan., 1899 ; buried in W. Northfield, Mass.

871.   iv. SUSAN MANDANA CALDWELL, b. in W. Northfield, Mass., May 28, 1835 ; m. June 25, 1857, W. Northfield, Dwight Solomon Priest, son of Nathan and Mary (Gunn) Priest, b. in W. Northfield, Mass., Aug. 28, 1832 ; res. Northfield, Mass., and Shenandoah, Ia. She d. in Chicago, Ill., 8 Feb., 1893 ; buried in W. Northfield, Mass.

872.   v. JULIA ANN CALDWELL, b. in W. Northfield, Mass., Nov. 28, 1837 ; m. Dec. 19, 1859, New York City, Charles Thomas Willard, son of Oliver and Sarah Jones (Harvey) Willard, b. in Wardsboro, Vt., May 8, 1837 ; d. in Philadelphia, Pa., 10 Aug., 1866. She d. in New Haven, Conn., 5 Feb., 1899 ; buried in W. Northfield, Mass.; res. Philadelphia, Pa., and New Haven, Conn.

873.   vi. JOHN WESLEY CALDWELL, b. in W. Northfield, Mass., Apr. 17, 1841 ; m. Oct. 2, 1866, Jane Ann Ferris, dau. of Elijah and Phebe (Mackey) Ferris, b. in Newburg, N. Y., Jan. 22, 1830. He d. in New York City, 14 May, 1894 ; buried in W. Northfield, Mass.; res. New York City.

Children of JOSEPH KING^6, (1803) [**395**] (Lovisa^5, Freegrace^4, Lieut. Abraham^3, Jacob,^{2} Robert^1) and Sarah Childs; res. Marlboro, Vt.

874.   i. JOSEPH MERRITT KING, b. in Marlboro, Vt., May 2, 1828 ; m. April 15, 1885, Guthrie Center, Ia., Mrs. Frances Amine (Taylor) Raymond, dau. of William Henry and Effie Frances (Fitch) Taylor, b. in Milan, O., June 13, 1847 ; res. Red Oak, Ia.

875.   ii. JUSTIN LEAVITT KING. b. in Marlboro, Vt., Dec. 5, 1829 ; m.* Nov. 21, 1861, Athol, Mass., Martha Twichell, dau. of Capt. Benjamin Marshall and Asenath (Lovering) Twichell, b. in Athol, Mass., April 22, 1838 ; res. W. Brattleboro, Vt.

      iii. ALONZO KING, b. in Marlboro, Vt., Aug. 17, 1831 ; d. in Marlboro, 2 April, 1836.

876.   iv. SARAH ELVIRA KING, b. in Marlboro, Vt., Aug. 26, 1833 ; m. Jan. 7, 1862, at Marlboro, Vt., James Edward Priest, son of Nathan and Mary (Gunn) Priest, b. in W. Northfield, Mass., Aug. 11, 1829 ; d. in W. Northfield, 23 Dec., 1875 ; res. W. Brattleboro, Vt.

v. MARY EMELINE KING, b. in Marlboro, Vt., Feb. 15, 1836; d. in Marlboro, Vt., 5 April, 1839.

Children of JOSEPH KING⁶, (1803) and Chloe White.

vi. MARY AUGUSTA KING, b. in Marlboro, Vt., Feb. 4, 1844; m. Aug. 2, 1882, Upton, Mass., Newcomb Spencer, son of David and Adaline (Corbitt) Spencer, b. in Wilmington, Vt., Sept. 3, 1848; no issue; res. Halifax, Vt.

vii. HERBERT AUGUSTUS KING, b. in Marlboro, Vt., Oct. 19, 1845; d. unm. at Marlboro, Vt., 16 Sept., 1879; res. Upton, Mass.

viii. DELEVAN DUANE KING, b. in Marlboro, Vt., July 3, 1849; d. in Marlboro, Vt., 16 Sept., 1849.

Children of ANNA NYE, (1802) [**396**] (Anna⁵, Freegrace⁴, Lieut. Abraham³, Jacob², Robert¹) and David Niles; res. Halifax, Vt.

i. WILLIAM NILES, b. in Halifax, Vt., Feb. 16. 1821; m. Apr. 11, 1858, Prudence B. Rice; she d. 5 Feb., 1859. He d. in Halifax, 1 Feb., 1896.

ii. ANNIS NILES, b. in Halifax, Vt., Nov. 2, 1823; m. Mar. 11, 1847, Thomas Smith of Halifax. She d. in Halifax, 18 May, 1897.

iii. HORACE LEAVITT NILES, b. Mar. 6, 1829; d. in Halifax, 4 Sept., 1846.

iv. EMELINE NILES, b. in Halifax, Vt., Apr. 7, 1836; m. Dec. 7, 1856, O. Chester Thurber of Halifax; he d. 31 Mar., 1896; res. W. Halifax, Vt., 1900.

v. OLIVE NILES, b. in Halifax, Vt., Feb. 22, 1838; m. Nov. 21, 1855, J. Wm. Plumb of Halifax. She d. 30 Dec., 1856.

Children of CAPT. MILTON⁶, (1792) [**397**] (Freegrace⁵, Jr., Freegrace⁴, Lieut. Abraham³, Jacob², Robert¹) and Lodice (Mather) Adams; res. Springfield, Mass.

877. i. FREDERICK AUGUSTUS L.⁷, b. in Marlboro, Vt., Mar. 31, 1816; m. July 21, 1840, Adeline Ashley, dau. of Enoch Ashley of W. Springfield, Mass.; she d. Nov., 1889. He d. in Springfield, Mass., 19 Oct., 1852.

ii. EMELINE⁷, b. in Marlboro, Vt., Dec. 30, 1818; d. 9 Mar., 1835, age 17 years.

878. iii. PHILENA⁷, b. in Marlboro, Vt., May 18, 1821; m. Edwin L. Drake of Castleton, Vt.; he m. a second time, and d. in Bethlehem, Pa. She d. 28 Mar., 1855, age 32 years.

Seventh Generation.] OF NEWBURY, MASS. 205

879.   iv. OLIVE MATHER[7], b. in Marlboro, Dec. 11, 1823 ; m May 19, 1846, James S. Bryant of Chicopee Falls, Mass. She d. 10 Oct., 1860.
880,   v. EMELINE, b. in Chicopee Falls, Mass., May 30, 1838; m. Mar. 8, 1867, David Kellogg, b. July 31; 1829 ; res. Springfield, Mass.

Children of MARTIN[6], (1794) [398] (Freegrace[5], Jr., Freegrace[4], Lieut. Abraham[3], Jacob[2], Robert[1]) and Anna W. (Elmore) Adams; res. Hinsdale, N. H.

881.   i. ANNE CORDELIA[7], b. in Hinsdale, Apr. 1, 1830; m. Oct., 1851, Frank B. Cadwell. He enlisted in 1862 in the 1st Regt. Massachusetts Cavalry, was taken sick and d. in the hospital at Washington, D. C., soon after enlisting, age 36 years.
       ii. MARTIN MARCELLUS[7], b. in Salem, N. Y., Oct., 1831.
            He was a teacher and hotel-keeper ; unm. ; d. in Springfield, Mass., Dec., 1878.

Children of ELIHU[6], (1798) [399] (Freegrace[5], Jr., Freegrace[4], Lieut. Adams[3], Jacob[2], Robert[1]) Sophia (Wait) Adams; res; (Chicopee) Springfield, Mass.

       i.   ANTOINETTE S.[7], b. in Hinsdale, N. H., Sept. 8, 1829; d. 3 Apr., 1831.
       ii. DAVID F.[7], b. Nov. 14, 1831 ; d. 22 Sept., 1832.
       iii. JAMES F.[7], b. June 5, 1833 ; d. 9 Jan., 1834.
       iv. MARY JANE[7], b. Oct. 16, 1834 ; d. 16 Mar., 1835.
       v.   JENETTE[7], b. July 21, 1836 ; d. 21 Sept., 1837.
       vi. JANE ANTOINETTE[7], b. June 10, 1838 ; d. 23 Mar., 1842.
       vii. HARRISON T.[7], b. July 24, 1840 ; d. 6 Apr., 1842.
       viii. HARRISON THEODORE[7], b. Apr. 28, 1844 ; d. 27 Jan., 1846.
882.   ix. KATE SOPHIA[7], b. May 11, 1847 ; m. Nov. 14, 1867, John W. Trafton ; res. W. Somerville, Mass.

Children of LEPHA[6], (1802) [401] (Freegrace[5], Jr., Freegrace[4], Lieut. Abraham[3], Jacob[2], Robert[1]) and Francis C. Munn; res. Chickopee Falls, Mass.

       i.   CHARLES HENRY MUNN, b. Mar. 3, 1824 ; m. Jane Harris of Dracut, deceased ; res. Lowell, Mass.   He d. 1863.
       ii. HENRIETTA MUNN, b. Sept. 7, 1825 ; m. Thomas Patterson; res. Chicopee Falls, Mass.
       iii. HARRIET S. MUNN, b. July 28, 1827 ; m. Gordon S. Deming of Fayettville, N. C.; res. Fayetteville, N. C. She d. 13 July, 1879.

- iv. FRANCIS D. MUNN, b. Feb. 12, 1829 ; m. (1) Feb. 12, 1850, Mary U. Harris of Dracut; m. (2) June 29, 1881, Emily F. Wilkins of Middleton, Mass.; res. Lowell, Mass.
- v. FREDERICK MUNN, b. Nov. 14, 1830 ; m. (1) Oct. 25, 1854, Hannah Sargent of Lowell, Mass.; m. (2) Jan. 8, 1878, Mrs. Emeline Hardy of Lowell, Mass.; res. Lowell, Mass.
- vi. HELEN MUNN, b. Mar. 18, 1833 ; d. at Chicopee Falls, 28 July, 1838.
- vii. GEORGE M. MUNN, b. Mar. 3, 1835 ; m. (1) Sarah A. Leslie of Lowell ; m. (2) Sarah A. Ellis of Medfield ; res. Fitchburg, Mass.
- viii. EUGENE MUNN, b. June 8, 1838 ; d. unm. 15 Apr., 1883.
- ix. HORACE E. MUNN, b. Dec. 20, 1842.
  He is a merchant at Chicopee Falls, Mass.; unm.

Children of HORACE⁶, (1807) [403] (Freegrace⁵, Jr., Freegrace⁴, Lieut. Abraham³, Jacob², Robert¹) and Mary (Love) Adams; res. Chicopee, Mass.

- i. HELEN M.⁷, b. probably in Chicopee about 1843 ; d. 25 Nov., 1868, age about 25 years.
- ii. ATERISTA M.⁷, m. June 27, 1870, Samuel W. Parshley ; b. Apr. 14, 1822 ; res. Chicopee, Mass. She d. 1 Mar., 1893 ; no issue.
- iii. DWIGHT⁷, d. aged about 28 years.

Children of ANN⁶, (1810) [404] (Freegrace⁵, Jr., Freegrace⁴, Lieut. Abraham³, Jacob², Robert¹) and Alonzo Waite; res. Chicopee, Mass.

Mrs. Miller says there were four children, two of whom died in infancy ; another was married in 1859 to Wm. Whealley of Syracuse, N. Y.; d. 26 June, 1861. Beyond this she can give no information except of herself, viz.:

SUSANNA JANE WAITE, b. Apr., 15, 1850; m. Oct., 1874, Col. Watson J. Miller of New Haven ; res. Shelton, Conn.

Children of WILLIAM ALVERSON, (1811) [405] and Eliza Pierce; res. Woodford, Vt.

- i. HENRIETT ALVERSON, b. July 16, 1837 ; d. in Woodford, Vt., 7 Feb., 1838.
- ii. ADELBERT ALVERSON, b. June 25, 1839 ; d. in Woodford, Vt., 10 Feb., 1840.
- iii. GEORGE FAXON ALVERSON, b. Jan. 7, 1841.
  Nothing known of him.

883.   iv.   ADELAIDE FINETTE ALVERSON, b. Jan. 16, 1843 ; m. Dec. 8, 1859, at Waukesha Wis , Chas. Henry Lee, son of Geo. and Sarah (Rose) Lee, b. Feb. 25, 1836, in Elyria, O ; res. Clinton, Iowa.
884.   v.   EMELINE ELIZA ALVERSON, b. Jan. 25, 1845 ; m. Sept. 10, 1866, at Whitewater, Wis., John Taylor, son of John and Anna (Sheppard) Taylor, b. Nov. 18, 1832 ; res. 1900, Clinton, Ia.
885.   vi.   LAURA VINETT ALVERSON, b. May 17, 1847; m. (1) Oct. 15, 1865, at Fort Atkinson, Wis., Henry Dake. son of Martin Dake, b. in Whitewater, Wis., July 24, 1845 ; d. in Chicago, Ill.; m. (2) Mar. 23, 1874, at Clinton, Ia., Chas. Fales, son of Joseph Thomas Fales, b. in Dubuque, Ia.; res. Clinton, Iowa.

Children of JEMIMA ALVERSON, (1812) [406] and Jonathan Niles.

886.   i.   LORETTE NILES, b. in Halifax, Vt., Sept. 17, 1836 ; m. April 30, 1854, at Deerfield, Mass., Geo. Henry Gilbert, son of Isaac and Mary Ann (Foster) Gilbert, b. in Hartford, Conn., Nov. 26, 1829. She d. in Hartford, Conn., 17 Sept., 1874.
ii.   ADDISON NILES, b. in Halifax, Mar. 1, 1838 ; m. July 18, 1869, at Southbury, Conn., Lucy Jane Judson, dau. of Ransom and Lucy (Tuttle) Judson, b. May 25, 1834, in Woodbury, Conn. He d. in Southbury, Conn., 27 Aug., 1869 ; no issue.

Children of JEMIMA ALVERSON, (1812) and Julius Robbins.

i.   EMMA AUGUSTA ROBBINS, b. in Deerfield, Mass., Nov. 15, 1846; res. Deerfield, Mass.; unm.
ii.   DELIA ROBBINS, b. in Deerfield, Nov. 11, 1852 ; m. June 25, 1879, James Buchanan Foster, son of Wm. and Harriet M. (Nudd) Foster, b. in Meriden, Conn., Oct., 1856 ; res. Deerfield, Mass. Children :
   1.   Edith Harriet, b. Aug. 5, 1879 ; d. 6 Oct., 1879.
   2.   Howard, b. Mar. 24, 1884 ; d. 31 Mar., 1884.

Children of SOPHIA^6, (1799) [407] (Abraham^5, Samuel^4, Lieut. Abraham^3, Jacob^2, Robert^1) and Jonas Gibbs; res. Benson, Vt.

i.   HARRIET GIBBS, b. in Benson, Sept. 16, 1825 ; m. June 12, 1842, Alphonso Higgins, son of Dan. She d. 22 June, 1890, age 65 years.
ii.   MARYETTE GIBBS, b. in Benson, Aug. 13, 1828 ; m. Judah Carter of Benson; he d. 14 Feb., 1894, age 71 years. She is living, 1897.
iii.   GEORGE H. GIBBS, b. in Benson, Nov., 1831 ; m. Martha Goodrich. He d. 1 May, 1864.

- iv. CHARLOTTE GIBBS, b. in Benson, Jan. 13, 1834 ; m. Martin Jackman ; res. Fair Haven, Vt.
- v. ALMON J. GIBBS, b. in Benson, Dec. 18, 1835 ; m. Dec. 16, 1858, Sarah A. Proctor, dau. of Jonathan Nelson Proctor of Fair Haven, Vt.; she d. in Oct., 1899. He set. in Fair Haven, Vt.
- vi. CHLOE GIBBS, b. in Benson, July 7, 1838 ; m. Byron A. Carter (brother of Judah) ; he d. 26 Jan., 1896.

Children of MALINDA⁶, (1802) [408] (Abraham⁵, Samuel⁴, Lieut. Abraham³, Jacob², Robert¹) and Peter Corbett; res. Benson, Vt., and Greenbush, Wis.

- i. SYLVESTER CORBETT, b. in Benson, Aug. 18, 1824; m. Mary Kellogg.
- ii. JAMES M. CORBETT, b. in Benson, Apr. 11, 1826; m. Cinderella Barrager.
- iii. WILLIAM HENRY CORBETT, b. in Benson, Mar. 21, 1828 ; m. Levina Diadamia Pettet.
- iv. JOHN CORBETT, b. in Benson, May 29, 1830.
- v. SILAS CORBETT, b. in Benson, Mar. 6, 1832 ; d. in infancy.
- vi. SARAH ANNA CORBETT, b. in Benson, Mar. 13, 1834 ; m. Charles Barrager; living, 1897, in Crete, Neb.
- vii. MARY JANE CORBETT, b. in Benson, July 5, 1836 ; m. Joshua Rouse of Whitehall, N. Y.
- viii. JEROME B. CORBETT, b. in Benson, Nov. 5, 1838 ; m. Apr. 27, 1867, Helen Louisa Grinnell. He d. 19 Feb., 1879.
- ix. CHARLES ADAMS CORBETT, b. in Benson, Nov. 21, 1840 ; m. Mary Jane Lewis ; res. Greenbush, Wis.
- x. LESTER MONROE CORBETT, b. in Benson, Apr. 1, 1843 ; m. Ann Pettet.
- xi. ALEXANDER B. CORBETT, b. in Benson, Feb. 6, 1846 ; m. Helen Fussellneaux.

Children of LOVISA⁶, (1805) [409] (Abraham⁵, Samuel⁴, Lieut. Abraham³, Jacob², Robert¹) and James Le Barron; res. Benson, Vt.

- i. JAMES DECATUR LE BARRON, b. in Benson, May 24, 1830 ; d. 16 Aug., 1840.
- ii. SAMUEL A. LE BARRON, b. in Benson, July 18, 1832 ; d. 28 June, 1836.
- iii. DANIEL WILLIAM LE BARRON, b. in Benson ; d. 12 Oct., 1842.
- iv. MARTHA M. LE BARRON, b. in Benson, July 21, 1834 ; m. Henry Kellogg; he d. Oct., 1895. She d. in Ripon, Wis., 7 Dec., 1859.

v. DAVID ADAMS LE BARRON, b. in Benson, Mar. 1, 1836; m. Helen Kellogg. He d. in Ripon, Wis., 14 Nov., 1864.

Children of LOVISA⁶, (1805) and Richard Grinnell.

  i. MARY E. GRINNELL, b. in Benson, Dec. 11, 1842; m. Oct. 30, 1878, Luther W. Brown ; res. Benson, Vt.

  ii. ETHALINDA GRINNELL, b. in Benson, Nov., 1846, d. in 17 days.

  iii. HELEN LOVISA GRINNELL, b. in Benson, July 17, 1848 ; m. (1) Apr. 27, 1867, Jerome B. Corbett, son of Peter and Malinda (Adams) Corbett; he d. 19 Feb., 1879 ; m. (2) Oct. 19, 1880, Chas. R. Winchester of Benson ; res. Benson, Vt.

Children of ABRAHAM⁶, JR., (1808) [410] (Abraham⁵, Samuel⁴, Lieut. Abraham³, Jacob², Robert¹) and Miranda E. (Bartlett) Adams; res. Forest, Calumet Co., Wis.

887. i. SAMUEL A.⁷, b. in Benson, Vt., Mar. 10, 1839 ; m. 1861, Minnie Heath ; res. Loyal, Clark Co., Wis.

888. ii. EMILY E.⁷, b. in Benson, Nov. 25, 1840; m. 1862; David Rogers ; res. Loyal, Wis.

  iii. MORTIMER⁷, b. in Benson, Nov. 1, 1842.
      He enlisted in Co. A, 10th Wis. Vols.; d. in hospital at Cincinnati, O., 27 May, 1862.

889. iv. EMEROY C.⁷, b. in Benson, Feb. 7, 1845 ; m. 1866, Henry D. Ransier ; res. Menomonie, Wis.

  v. HELEN S.⁷, b. in Fond du Lac, Wis., Sept. 22, 1847 ; m. 1866, William Keyes. She d. 1871.

890. vi. NOBLE D.⁷, b. in Fond du Lac, Feb. 12, 1850 ; m. 1881, Agnes Carter ; res. Mukwanago, Waukesha Co., Wis.

891. vii. DAVID Q.⁷, b. in Fond du Lac, May 23, 1852 ; m. 1883, Laura Baker ; res. St. Paul, Minn.

892. viii. FRANKIE E.⁷, b. in Food du Lac, Feb. 8, 1855 ; m. 1877, Charles A. George.; res. Menomonie, Dunn Co., Wis.

  ix. EUGENE C.⁷, b. in Fon du Lac, Jan. 16, 1857 ; res. Gettysburg, Potter Co., So. Dak.; unm.

893. x. ERNEST C.⁷, b. in Fond du Lac, Dec. 20, 1859 ; m. 1886, Ella Hart ; res. Gettysburg, So. Dak.

894. xi. W. DELISLE⁷, b. in Fond du Lac, Nov. 16, 1861 ; m. 1894, Mabel E. Irvine ; res. Menomonie. Wis.
      He is a dealer in agricultural implements.

Children of ELI[6], (1810) [411] (Abraham[5], Samuel[4], Lieut. Abraham[3], Jacob[2], Robert[1]) and Sophie (Parsons) Adams; res. Greenbush, Wis.

    i. DR. JAMES[7], m Mary Lamb of Greenbush.
        He practiced law and medicine, and had one child ; d. in Oconto, Wis.
    ii. FRANCES[7], m. Dr. John Starr. She d. in Chicago, Ill; no issue.
    iii. ROLLIN[7].
        He went off to work in the north woods of Wisconsin, and has never been heard from.
    iv. CLARK[7].
        He went away and was never heard from.

Children of CHLOE ANGELINE[6], (1816) [412] (Abraham[5], Samuel[4], Lieut. Abraham[3], Jacob[2], Robert[1]) and James Higgins; res. Benson, Vt.

    i. ORLIN H. HIGGINS, b. in Benson, Feb. 14, 1841; d. in Chicago, Ill., 4 Nov., 1862.
    ii. SELUCIA H. HIGGINS, b. in Benson, July 31, 1842 ; m. Oct. 15, 1858, Chandler B. Gibbs of Hubbardton, Vt.; res. Reading, Vt.
    iii. MARTHA S. HIGGINS, b. in Benson, Apr. 22, 1844 ; d. 4 May, 1869.
    iv. SARAH M. HIGGINS, b. in Benson, Oct. 11, 1845 ; living 1897, in Benson ; unm.
    v. DANIEL HIGGINS, b. in Benson, Sept. 4, 1847 ; m. Oct. 17, 1876, Elizabeth McLaughlin of Putnam, N. Y. ; set. in Ticonderoga, N. Y.
    vi. TEMPERANCE HIGGINS, b. in Benson, Aug. 7, 1849 ; d. 19 Nov., 1866.
    vii. JAMES M. HIGGINS, b. in Benson, Mar. 19, 1853 ; d. 5 Apr., 1869.

Children of WILLIAM SPURR[6], (1819) [413] (Abraham[5], Samuel[4], Lieut. Abraham[3], Jacob[2], Robert[1]) and Martha E. (Peck) Adams; res. Empire, Fond du Lac Co., Wis.

895.   i. ALMIRA S.[7], b. in Forest township, Wis., Sept. 28, 1850 ; m. Dec. 25, 1879, Jerry W. Briggs, b. Apr. 11, 1849. They set. in Nebraska, 1880 ; rem. to Oakfield, Wis., 1883.
896.   ii. WILSON M.[7], b. in Forest, June 27, 1852 ; m. Sept. 21, 1880, Adeline E. White, b. July 1, 1857.
        He set. in Greenbush, Wis., 1881 ; rem. July, 1887, to Upson, Iron, Co., Wis. He is a grocer.

Seventh Generation.] OF NEWBURY, MASS. 211

897. iii. DAYTON A.[7], b. in Forest, Sept. 4, 1855; m. Nov. 24, 1880, Josephine Thayer.
    He set. in Stevens Point, Wis., 1887; rem. 1893, to Empire, Wis.
898. iv. WILBUR C.[7], b. in Forest, Aug. 2, 1855; m. Apr. 10, 1875, Emeline Hopkins, b. Feb. 17, 1855.
    He set. in Empire, Wis., 1878; rem. to Eden, Fond du Lac Co., Wis., 1893.
899. v. ELLSWORTH C.[7], b. in Forest, Nov. 6, 1861; m. Sept. 28, 1889, Mrs. Laura D. Palmer, b. Feb. 2, 1865.
    He set. in Clear Lake, Wis.; rem. 1891 to Joel, Polk Co., Wis.

Children of ORRA EMMA KENYON, (1810) [415] and John W. Gregg; res. Occoquan, Va.

  i. HENRY O. GREGG, b. in West Haven, Vt., Aug. 6, 1830; d. Mar. 1831.
  ii. MYRON E. GREGG, b. in West Haven, Oct. 30, 1833; m. at Washington, D. C., Nov. 23, 1867; res. Tarpon Springs, Fla.
  iii. MARY E. GREGG, b. in Mexico, N. Y., Apr. 25, 1837; m. Mar. 22, 1855, George Storer of Glens Falls, N. Y.; res. Washington, D. C.
  iv. LAURA E. GREGG, b. in Glens Falls. N. Y., Aug. 26, 1839; m. (1) Thos. Bohannon; killed in the civil war, 26 May, 1864; m. (2) Oct. 19, 1869, M. E. Selecman; res. Occoquan, Va.
  v. JOHN W. GREGG, JR., b. in Kingsbury, N. Y., Aug. 16, 1843; m. at Washington, D. C., Nov. 20, 1872.
  vi. FRANK GREGG, b. in Glens Falls, Aug. 25, 1854; d. Jan., 1856.

Children of DORCAS DIADEMIA KENYON, (1813) [416] and Hon. Nathaniel Fish; res. West Haven, Vt.

  i. DR. NEWELL S. FISH, b. in West Haven, Sept. 20, 1835; m. at Shabbona, Ill., 1865, Elizabeth Corey.
    He practiced medicine for 15 years, and d. at Pawpaw, Ill., 13 Sept., 1877.
  ii. SAMUEL ADAMS FISH, b. in West Haven, Aug. 21, 1837; m. Oct. 19, 1864, Hannah J. Field. He d. in West Haven, 30 Dec., 1870.
  iii. CHLOE E. FISH, b. in West Haven, Apr. 11, 1845; d. 13 Apr., 1867.
  iv. MATTIE J. FISH, b in West Haven, Sept. 6, 1849; m, Mar. 31, 1880, Charles M King, son of Moseley King of Benson, Vt.; res. Benson, Vt. Children:
    1. Candace D. King, b. Aug. 24, 1881.
    2. Carl F. King, b. Mar. 23, 1885.

Children of LUCY BILLINGS⁶, (1813) [417] (Horace⁵, Samuel⁴, Lieut. Abraham³, Jacob², Robert¹) and Jonathan Smead, Jr.; res. Greenfield, Mass.

 i. JONATHAN HENRY SMEAD, b. Dec. 28, 1839; m. Dec. 18, 1869, Sarah Newton; res. New Bedford, Mass.
 ii. HORACE ADAMS SMEAD, b. Feb. 6, 1842; m. 1868, Anna J. Fisher; res. Greenfield, Mass.
 iii. SARAH PYNCHON SMEAD, b. Dec. 16, 1844; a teacher; unm.; res. Greenfield, Mass.
 iv. EDWIN BILLINGS SMEAD, b. Jan. 19, 1849; m. Oct. 30, 1878, Rose Whitney.
  He is Principal of Agricultural School in Hartford, Conn.
 v. CHAS. SAMUEL SMEAD, b. Jan. 16, 1851; d. 21 Apr., 1873.

Children of FANNY⁶, (1814) [418] (Horace⁵, Samuel⁴, Lieut. Abraham³, Jacob², Robert¹) and Youmans Merritt; res. Shoreham, Vt.

 i. MARY C. MERRITT, b. Nov. 8, 1844; living 1897, in Shoreham, unm.
 ii. KENT W. MERRITT, b. Apr. 24, 1851; m. Mar. 9, 1880, Eva Wait; res. Shoreham, Vt.

Children of SAMUEL⁶, (1818) [419] (Horace⁵, Samuel⁴, Lieut. Abraham³, Jacob², Robert¹) and Mary Ann (Goodrich) Adams; res. West Haven, Vt.

900. i. FRANCES ELIZA⁷, b. in West Haven, Jan. 22, 1841; m. Nov. 9, 1868, Orson C. Martin of Shoreham, Vt.; b. June 7, 1842.
901. ii. HENRY J.⁷, b. in West Haven, Jan. 3, 1843; m. Mar. 3, 1869, Hannah L. Martin, dau. of Isaac and Temperance (Higgins) Martin; b. in Benson, Vt., Sept. 9, 1847.
  He is a farmer; res. West Haven, Vt.
 iii. GEORGE S.⁷, b. in West Haven, Oct. 2, 1844; m. Mar. 29, 1875, Marcia Field, dau. of Rodney and Harriet (Capron) Field of West Haven; no issue; res. West Haven, Vt.

Children of ESTHER JOYCE⁶, (1820) [420] (Horace⁵, Samuel⁴, Lieut. Abraham³, Jacob², Robert¹) and William Forbes; res. Fort Edward, N. Y.

 i. LYDIA LUCINA FORBES, b. Apr. 28, 1838; d. 28 May, 1845.
 ii. LUCY S. FORBES, b. Oct. 12, 1842; d. unm. 20 Feb. 1895.

Seventh Generation.] OF NEWBURY, MASS. 213

  iii. ELLEN L. FORBES, b. July 25, 1846 ; m. May 4, 1886, Henry Clay Bascom ; he d. 13 Dec., 1896; res. Lansingburgh, N. Y.
902. iv. EMILY A. FORBES, b. Sept. 25, 1851 ; m. Oct. 1, 1873, Richard W. Kempshall ; res. Peoria, Ill.

Children of REBECCA W.⁶, (1824) [421] (Horace⁵, Samuel⁴, Lieut. Abraham³, Jacob², Robert¹) and Levi N. Goodrich; res. Concord, Mich.

  i. FANNY ELVIRA GOODRICH, b. July 14, 1845 ; d. 23 Oct., 1869.
903. ii. EMILY ORRA GOODRICH, b. May 27, 1848 ; m. Feb. 6, 1879, Herbert S. Read ; res. Concord, Mich.
904. iii. FLOYD IRWIN GOODRICH, b. Dec. 16, 1854; m. Mar. 7, 1877, Ida A. Marsh ; res. Concord, Mich.
905. iv. ELIZABETH MARIA GOODRICH; b. Sept. 16, 1856 ; m. June 15, 1887, Wm. J. Grills ; res. Concord, Mich.
  v. ALMA LOUISA GOODRICH, b. May 3, 1862.

Children of SETH⁶, JR., (1772) [422] (Seth⁵, Moses⁴, John³, Jacob², Robert¹) and Polly (Bush) Adams; res. West Springfield, Mass.

  i. MARY⁷, b. in W. Springfield, June 26, 1801 ; m. (1) Matthew Winters; m.(2) —— Ellis. She d. at Dundee, Yates Co., N. Y.; no issue.
  ii. ELIZA⁷, b. in W. Springfield, Sept. 25, 1803 ; d. 12 May, 1824.

Children of SETH⁶, JR., (1772) and Tabitha (Warriner) Adams.

906. iii. RALPH⁷, b. in W. Springfield, Dec. 20, 1812 ; m. Mar. 26, 1840, Frances A. Leonard, b. Aug. 23, 1820 ; d. in Cleveland, O., 31 May, 1837.
   He was executor of his father's will in 1883.
  iv. PHILANCE⁷, b. in W. Springfield, May 33, 1814 ; d. 10 Apr., 1824.

Children of LEVI⁶, (1774) [423] (Seth⁵, Moses⁴, John³, Jacob², Robert¹) Desdemonia (Munger) Adams; res. W. Springfield (Agawam), Mass.

  i. HIRAM⁷, b. in W. Springfield about 1802 ; drowned at three or four years of age.

214   ROBERT ADAMS   [Seventh Generation.

    ii. BENJAMIN FRANKLIN⁷, b. in W. Springfield, Dec. 2, 1803 ; m. Mahala ———.
        He was a machinist ; d. in Monson, Mass., 5 Aug., 1853. He had two sons who d. young.
    iii. MINOR⁷, b. in W. Springfield about 1804; d. in Marlboro, Conn., unm., 26 Feb., 1842.
907. iv. DESDEMONIA⁷, b. in W. Springfield, Dec. 16, 1805 ; m. Jan. 1, 1826, Daniel U. Lee; he d. 24 Oct., 1872. She is living at Highland, Oakland Co., Mich., 1899.
    v. ALVIRA⁷, b. in W. Springfield, 1807 ; m. Hezekiah Griswold. She d. in Enfield, Conn.; is said to have had two children who died young.
    vi. LORIN⁷, b. in W. Springfield, Oct. 7, 1809.
        He became permanently deaf consequent upon swimming in the Connecticut river ; settled and resided with his brother, Hiram E., at Warsaw, N. Y., and d. there unm. 14 Apr., 1874, age 65 years.
908. vii. HIRAM E.⁷, b. in Enfield, Conn , Mar. 1, 1811; m. (1) May 12, 1842, Marrietta Hodge, dau. of Ichabod Hodge, b. Apr. 4, 1822 ; d. 4 Aug., 1845 ; m. (2) Sylvinia Hodge, sister of Marrietta, b. Apr. 16, 1812, and living 1899. He d. in Warsaw, N. Y., 2 Jan., 1886, age 75 years.
909. viii. ELIZABETH WORTHINGTON⁷, b. in Enfield, April 8, 1813 ; m. Oct. 9, 1837, Chauncey C. Buxton of Warsaw, N. Y.; he d. 13 Feb., 1889. She moved from Warsaw to Angelica, N. Y., in 1888 ; d. in Buffalo, N. Y., 21 Mar., 1898, age 84 years.

    Children of LUCY⁶, (1779) [425] (Seth⁵, Moses⁴, John³, Jacob², Robert¹) and Jotham Wright; res. Enfield, Conn.
    i. SALLY WRIGHT, b. Aug. 31, 1801 ; d. 22 Sept., 1801.
    ii. DOROTHY WRIGHT, b. Sept. 17, 1803 ; m. Sterling R. Aans. She d. 24 Nov., 1874.
    iii. WILLIAM WRIGHT, b. Mar. 10, 1805 ; m. Abigail Simons.
        He was a soldier in the 10th Conn. Regt., and d. at Fortress Monroe, 27 June, 1864.
    iv. HENRY CORBIN WRIGHT, b. June 11, 1807 ; d. unm.
    v. CLARISSA WRIGHT, b. Dec. 12, 1809 ; m. Jan. 13, 1831, Jabez King. Jr., b. Nov. 22, 1802; d. 17 Aug., 1850. She d. 24 Nov., 1874.
    vi. LOUISA WRIGHT, b. Nov. 1, 1811 ; m. Edward Chipman.
    vii. SAMUEL WRIGHT, b. May 16, 1814; m. Rosetta J. Chaffee. He d. 14 Mar., 1849.

    Children of GAIUS⁶, (1781) [426] (Seth⁵, Moses⁴, John³, Jacob², Robert¹) and Cynthia (Kent) Adams; res. Springfield, Bradford Co., Pa.

Seventh Generation.] OF NEWBURY, MASS.

910. i. HENRY LEWIS[7], b. in Springfield, Mar. 10, 1809; m. Jan. 9, 1832, Lucy Sherman; she d. 27 July, 1891. He d. at Columbia Cross Roads, Pa., 5 Mar., 1891.
911. ii. JAMES KENT[7], b. in Springfield, Feb. 6, 1811; m. (1) May 2, 1834, Malinda Potter; she d. 1848; m. (2) Aug. 14, 1850, Eliza Mosher; she d. 19 Apr., 1882. He set. in Troy, Pa., in 1831; d. 8 Feb., 1896.
iii. BELA KENT[7], b. in Springfield, Aug. 20, 1813; m. (1) Sept. 8, 1820, Mary Cooley; m. (2) May, 1872, Louisa Wattles. He set. in Rome, Bradford Co., Pa., after 1872.
iv. CYNTHIA KENT[7], b. in Springfield, Feb. 4, 1815; d. 24 Jan., 1847.
912. v. HARRIET[7], b. in Springfield, May 29, 1818; m. Sept. 3, 1843, Sidney Struble; res. Ionia, Mich.
vi. MARGARET[7], b. in Springfield, Sept. 10, 1820; d. unm. 29 May, 1895.
913. vii. JOEL[7], b. in Springfield, Jan. 10, 1824; m. Oct. 13 [22?], 1851, Joanna Strange, b. Nov. 10, 1830; d. 6 Dec., 1893.
He was a farmer; rem. 1884, from Springfield to Troy, Pa.
914. viii. LUCRETIA[7], b. in Springfield, Apr. 26, 1826; m. Mar. 4, 1846, Ambrose Brown, b. Mar. 4, 1823; d. 13 Feb., 1863. She d. in Springfield, Pa., 27 Mar., 1894.
915. ix. JERE[7], b. in Springfield, Apr. 25, 1831; m. Dec. 4, 1866, Maria Scott, d. 1898; res. Agawam, Mass.

Children of ENOS[6], (1785) [427] (Seth[5], Moses[4], John[3], Jacob[2], Robert[1]) and Sarah Ann (Dickinson) Adams; res. Bennington, Vt.

916. i. BENJAMIN DICKINSON[7], b. in Rowe, Mass., Sept. 27, 1809; m. (1) Sarah Ann Getchell (divorced); m. (2) Jan. 25, 1852, Lydia Ann Wardsworth; she d. 21 Jan., 1867, age 49 years. He d. in Bennington, Vt., 16 Feb., 1862.
ii. ENOS[7], b. in Heath, Mass., Mar. 25, 1816; m. 1846, Sarah Ann Sayders, dau. of Jacob and Nancy Sayders of Bennington, Vt.
He was a manufacturer; res. Bennington, Vt.; d. 1898; no issue.
917. iii. JULIA ANN[7], b. in Heath, May 5, 1817; m. Sireno Pierson Peck, son of Lanson and Sarah Peck; he d. 5 July, 1859, age 42 years. She d. in Bennington, Vt., 6 July, 1861.
918. iv. LAURIETTE ASHLEY[7], b. in Heath, Apr. 27, 1821; m. Sireno Pierson Peck (1st wife). She d. in Bennington, 24 July, 1851.

Children of JERE[6], (1793) [428] (Seth[5], Moses[4], John[3], Jacob[2], Robert[1]) and Cyntha (Decker) Adams; res. Athens, Bradford Co., Pa.

919. i. NELSON[7], b. in Athens, May 15, 1817; m. May 13, 1838, Mary Wilbor. He d. in Troy, Pa., 12, July, 1892.

ii. MARY ANN[7], b. in Athens, Sept. 28, 1819; d. in Troy, Pa., 12 Nov. 1845.
920. iii. LUCINDA MARIA[7], b. in Athens, Oct. 5, 1821; m. Feb. 18, 1840, at Troy, Pa., Frederick Orwan. She d. in Troy, 8 Dec., 1845.
iv. SETH[7], b. in Athens, July 14, 1823; d. 1 Nov., 1823.
v. JULIA ELIZABETH[7], b. in Athens, Sept. 26, 1825; m. 1846, in Troy, Pa., Dr. Thomas Parsons. She d. 31 Dec., 1847.
vi. JOHN QUINCY[7], b. in Athens, Mar. 25, 1829; d. in Troy, 27 Jan., 1845.
vii. LYNDIA TAYLOR[7], b. in Troy, Pa., Feb. 19, 1835; d. 10 Nov., 1845.

Children of JOEL[6], (1801) [**429**] (Seth[5], Moses[4], John[3], Jacob[2], Robert[1]) and Fidelia (Crandall) Adams; res. Lawrenceville, Tioga Co., Pa.

921. i. CLARISSA JANE[7], b. in Lawrenceville, Aug. 27, 1829; m. May 4, 1848, Rev. Ransom Marean, a Baptist clergyman, b. in Maine, Broome Co., N. Y., Apr. 27, 1817, whose ancestors moved in 1800 from Massachusetts to Broome Co., N. Y.

He entered Madison University, Hamilton, N. Y., in 1841, when he was 24 years of age, and entered upon the work of the ministry at his graduation, continuing until he was 70 years old, his last pastorate being of 27 years duration at So. Livonia, Livingston Co , N. Y., when he retired and settled in Rochester, N. Y., where he still lives (1899). He was three times married. By his first wife, a Miss Page, he had two sons, one of whom died in infancy, the other, named Charles A., was a soldier at 18 years of age, and died in the service of his country after suffering many months imprisonment at Andersonville and Florence. Clarissa Jane Adams was the second wife, and d. 24 Oct., 1863.

ii. EMILY[7], b. in Lawrenceville, Aug. 15, 1830, res. on homestead, Lawrenceville, Pa.; unm.
922. iii. MARTHA[7], b. in Lawrenceville, Dec. 4, 1831; m. June 8, 1857, John Wildman Winder, son of Thomas and Hannah Winder; a photographer, b. May 26, 1828, ; res. 1899, New Orleans, La. She d. at Uvalde, Tex., 8. Jan., 1883.
iv. SETH[7], b. in Lawrenceville, Mar. 9, 1833, ; d. 23 Sept., 1834.
923. v. MARIA[7], b. in Lawrenceville, Oct. 6, 1835; m. June 8, 1858, Simeon Anson Goodwin; He d. 1880.
924. vi. CHARLOTTE[7], b. in Lawrenceville, Mar. 6, 1836; m. Feb. 24, 1864, Ward H. Merchant, b. Apr. 6, 1838; res. Lawrenceville, Pa.
925. vii. ENOS SETH[7], b. in Lawrenceville, Oct. 21, 1837; m. 1861, Hannah J. Nicholson, b. in Cincinnati, Mar. 25, 1843; d. 23 Sept., 1894; res. Cincinnati, O.; rem. to Mexico.
926. viii. FIDELIA[7], b. in Lawrenceville, June 25, 1840; m. Aug. 17, 1868, James Edwin Sweetland, son of Anson Sweetland, b. June 27,

Seventh Generation.] OF NEWBURY, MASS. 217

    1845 ; d. Sept., 1893 ; res. Hazelhurst, McKean Co., Pa. She d. 10 Nov., 1897.

927. ix. ELBERT J.⁷, b. in Lawrenceville, Apr. 3, 1844 ; m. (1) Feb., 1868, Mary E. Simms of Jacksonville, Ill.; she d. 10 Oct., 1870 ; m. (2) Dec. 5, 1871, Susan C. Cassell of Jacksonville, Ill.; she d. 12 Nov., 1888. He d. at Helena, Mont., 26 Jan., 1892.

928. x. LUCY⁷, b. in Lawrenceville, Feb 11, 1845 ; m. June 10, 1863, Wesley C. Chapin, son of Joselyn Chapin of Livonia, N. Y.; res. Whitehall, Ill.

  xi. MARY⁷, b. in Lawrenceville, Jan. 19, 1846 ; d. 4 Nov., 1851.

Children of POLLY⁶, (1785) **(430]** (Thaddeus⁵, Moses⁴, John³, Jacob², Robert¹) and Alvin Barnum; res. Northampton, Mass.

 i. CAROLINE BARNUM ; m. Julius Clapp.
 ii. EMELINE BARNUM; m. Martin B. Graves.

Child of WAIT⁶, (1786) **[431]** (Thaddeus⁵, Moses⁴, John³, Jacob², Robert¹) and Olive (Cole) Adams; res. Chester, Mass.

 1. ANSEL⁷, was killed by fall of a tree.

Children of WAIT⁶, (1786) and Sally (Chapman) Adams.

 ii. SOPHIA⁷, m Theodore Johnson of Chester Hill, Mass. She d. 15 Feb., 1879.
 iii. SILAS⁷, b. 1836 ; d. in Northampton, Mass., Sept., 1863, age 27 years.
 iv. MARY⁷.

Children of MEHITABLE⁶, (1790) **[432]** (Thaddeus⁵, Moses⁴, John³, Jacob², Robert¹) and James Cook; res. Westfield, Mass.

 i. HARRIET COOK, b. Jan. 11, 1813 ; d. 28 Nov., 1855.
 ii. LUCY B. COOK, b. July 11, 1815 ; d. July, 1893.
 iii. JAMES COOK, b. Aug. 21, 1818 ; m. Sept. 22, 1857, Nancy Atwater, widow of Jeremiah Atwater. He was living, 1899.
 iv. CATHARINE M. COOK, b. Feb. 28, 1829 ; d. 23 Mar., 1829.
 v. JANE M. COOK, b. July 2, 1830 ; d. 14 May, 1849.

Children of THADDEUS⁶, JR., (1792) **[433]** (Thaddeus⁵, Moses⁴, John³, Jacob², Robert¹) and Percy (Bosworth) Adams; res. Norwich, Mass.

929. i. GAMALIEL KING⁷, b. in Norwich, Feb. 21, 1817 ; m. Jan. 25, 1847, Lucina M. Barton of West Hampton, Mass.; she d. 25 Apr., 1887. He was living in East Hampton, Mass. in 1898.

ii. JOSEPH E.⁷, b. in Norwich, Nov. 17, 1818.
He enlisted in the Mexican War, and afterward 'set. in Texas, where he married and had several children, one of whom was James Robert ; he m. Jan. 23, 1898, Fanny May Bowman, dau. of J. H. Bowman of Plano, Collin Co., Tex. Joseph E. d. 22 Oct., 1880, age 61 years.

930. iii. ALFRED⁷, b. in Norwich, Dec, 22, 1820; m. Nov. 1, 1848, Maria Davis of Northampton, Mass.; she d. 1899.
He was a railroad conductor on the Connecticut River R. R. for many years; res. Springfield, Mass.

iv. RAYMOND⁷, b. in Norwich, May 10, 1824 ; d. at about 12 years of age.

v. ORPHA AUGUSTA⁷, b. in Norwich, Jan. 23, 1829 ; 'd. 13 Nov., 1831.

931. vi. ELIZA ANN⁷, b. in Norwich. Dec. 19, 1830 ; m. about 1850-51, Leander Brigham, a broom-maker of Montague, Mass. ; b. in Suffield, Conn., Mar. 23, 1823 ; d. 19 June, 1888.

Children of MARTIN⁶, (1802) [**434**] (Thaddeus⁵, Moses⁴, John³, Jacob², Robert¹) and Sally (Brown) Adams; res. Norwich, Mass.

i. ASHLEY⁷, b. in Norwich, Sept., 1833.
He was a boot-maker; enlisted in the 8th Missouri Reg.; is now a member of the National Military Hospital, Leavenworth, Kan., crippled with rheumatism.

ii. HORACE⁷, b. in Norwich, Sept., 1844-5.
He was a machinist ; d. unm. 15 Feb., 1867.

932. iii. MARIETTE⁷, b. in Norwich, Apr. 30, 1837 ; m. Jan. 1, 1857, Leander L. Rhodes ; he d. 24 Apr., 1896 ; res. West Hampton, Mass.

iv. WALTER F.⁷, b. in Norwich, May 8, 1840; m. May 24, 1871, Anna J. Dingman.
He is a farmer in Norwich ; no issue.

v. SARAH⁷, b. in Norwich, Mar. 4, 1844.
She was an employee of Button Factory at East Hampton, Mass.; d. 14 May, 1880.

Child of HARRIET⁶, (1804) [**435**] (Thaddeus⁵, Moses⁴, John³, Jacob², Robert¹) and Alpheus Beach ; res. Agawam, Mass.

i. MINERVA BEACH, m. James D. Beach of Norwich, Mass.

Children of HIRAM⁵, (1808) **[436]** (Thaddeus⁵, Moses⁴, John³, Jacob², Robert¹) and Armeluna (Dibble) Adams; res. Norwich, Mass.

    i. GEORGE⁷.
    ii. JUSTIN⁷.
    iii. TIRZEY⁷, m. ——— Loomis, a son of Perley Loomis, in Westfield, Mass.

Child of EUNICE⁶, (1793) **[437]** (Jonathan⁵, Moses⁴, John³, Jacob², Robert¹) and Harvey Wright; res. Suffield, Conn.

    i. JENETTE SEARLE WRIGHT, b. Feb. 27, 1819; m. Oct., 1836, William D. Curtis; he d. in Broome Co., N. Y., 11 June, 1853; res. Suffield, Conn.

Children of MIRIAM⁶, (1798) **[438]** (Jonathan⁵, Moses⁴, John³, Jacob², Robert¹) and Geo. J. Hubbard; res. Agawam, Mass.

    i. GEO. J. HUBBARD, JR., b. Nov. 27, 1824; d. 23 Sept., 1847.
    ii. MARIA HUBBARD, b. Nov. 27, 1826; m. Nov. 25-7, 1847, Appleton S. Manley.
    iii. JANE T. HUBBARD, b. Oct. 12, 1828; m. Oct. 12, 1847, Charles Osgood; she d. 13 June, 1864.
    iv. SHERMAN W. HUBBARD, b. July 11, 1831; living, unm.
    v. JOSEPH G. HUBBARD, b. Apr. 28, 1833; m. Elizabeth Manley. He d. in Suffield.
    vi. JAMES W. HUBBARD, b. Feb. 14, 1834; d. young.
    vii. JOHN L. HUBBARD, b. Apr. 20, 1835-6; m. Apr. 10, 1878, Sarah M. Atwater of Suffield, Conn; farmer; res. Agawam, Mass.
    viii. JAMES W. HUBBARD, b. Feb. 14, 1837; d. June, 1840.
    ix. NEWTON K. HUBBARD, b. Dec. 13, 1839; m. Lizzie Clayton; res. Fargo, N. Dak.

Children of LUCY⁶, (1792) **[439]** (Capt. Oliver⁵, Capt. Simeon⁴, John³, Jacob², Robert¹) and Rufus Mather; res. Marlboro, Vt.

    i. HENRY T. MATHER, b. Mar. 16, 1816; m. Oct. 12, 1842, Lucy Ingraham; he d. 30 Apr., 1854.
    ii. LUCY M. MATHER, b. June 5, 1820; m. Oct. 16, 1837, Aaron Bragg of W. Springfield, Mass.; she d. 14 Nov., 1890.
    iii. FRANKLIN MATHER, b. Nov. 20, 1823; d. 12 May, 1824.

220   ROBERT ADAMS   [Seventh Generation.

iv. ELIZA J. MATHER, b. May 25, 1825; m. May 19, 1845, John Taylor of Feeding Hills, Mass.; he d. 30 Nov., 1869. She res. 1898, on the homestead at Feeding Hills.
v. HULDAH MATHER, b. Dec. 27, 1827; m. July 31, 1849, Benjamin O. Tyler of Philadelphia, Pa. She d. 12 July, 1865.
vi. ANNA A. MATHER, b. Aug. 3, 1830; m. Apr. 13, 1853, Erastus E. White. They rem. and set. in Owosso, Mich.

Children of ABRAHAM⁶, (1794) [440] (Capt. Oliver⁵, Simeon⁴, John³, Jacob², Robert¹) and Beda (Mather) Adams; res. Royalton, Niagara Co., N. Y.

933.   i. PHINEAS M.⁷, b. in Marlboro, Vt., July 19, 1817; m. (1) Sept. 8, 1838, Olive Austin, b. Jan. 6, 1816; she d. in Pana, Ill.
He rem. to Pana, Ill., in 1860, and later to Dallas, Texas, where he married again, and died.

ii. MARY E.⁷, b. in Marlboro, July 11, 1819; d. unm. 11 Sept., 1842.

934.   iii. HULDAH TAYLOR⁷, b. in Marlboro, Mar. 12. 1821 ; m. July 13, 1842, Lorin King, son of David and Electa (McKee) King, from Pelham, Mass., b. June 12, 1819; d. 16 Jan., 1885. She d. 15 Jan., 188-.

iv. LUCY MILLER⁷, b. in Marlboro, Mar. 23, 1823; d. unm. of consumption, 3 May, 1853.

935.   v. RUFUS⁷, b. in Marlboro, Oct. 20, 1824; m. Feb. 7, 1855, Caretta Kimball, b. in Enosburg, Vt., Dec. 18, 1829. They set. in Pana, Christian Co., Ill.

vi. SON, b. in Marlboro, Sept. 20, 1826 ; d. same day.

vii. ESTHER HULL⁷, b. in Marlboro, Oct. 6, 1827; d. 22 Oct., 1854.

936.   viii. HANNAH JANE⁷, b. in Marlboro, Oct. 30, 1829 ; m. Jan. 1, 1852, Henry S. Harrington, son of Henry Harrington of W. Lebanon, Columbia Co., N. Y., b. in 1826 ; living 1900 ; res. Orangeport, Niagara Co., N. Y.

937.   ix. OLIVER L.⁷, b. in Marlboro, Jan. 12, 1831-2 ; m. Oct. 17, 1857, Mary Elizabeth Storer, b. Aug. 12, 1833; res. Ransomville, Niagara Co., N. Y. He d. 1 Nov., 1897.

938.   x. LUCIUS F.⁷, b. in Royalton, N. Y., Apr. 15, 1835 ; m. (1) June 25, 1862, Eliza Gott; she d. 8 Jan., 1868; m. (2) July 15, 1870, Sophia Merritt, b. Mar. 11, 1839 ; res. Lockport, N. Y.

939.   xi. CHARLES F.⁷, b. in Royalton, N. Y., Sept. 1, 1838; m. Sept. 14, 1865, Sarah Caroline Brown, b. in Royalton, N. Y., May 11, 1842.
He is a stock-dealer in Chicago ; res. Morgan Park, Ill.

940.   xii. GAD MATHER⁷, b. in Royalton, N. Y., Apr. 2, 1840; m. Feb. 6, 1864, Josephine Benson, b. Nov. 12, 1840 ; res. 1900, Buffalo, N. Y.

Seventh Generation.] OF NEWBURY, MASS. 221

Children of POLLY⁶, (1795) [**441**] (Capt. Oliver⁵, Simeon⁴, John³, Jacob², Robert¹) and Gad Mather; res. Middleport (Royalton Township), Niagara Co., N. Y.

 i. LOVINA MATHER, b. 1821 ; d. 29 Dec., 1842, age 21 years.
 ii. LUCINA MATHER, b. about 1823-4; m. Ira Gale of Middleport, N. Y.; rem. to Michigan.
 iii. AMANDA MATHER, b. 1826 ; d. 10 Oct., 1852, age 26 years. She m. Robert Burrill and had a dau. who m. Charles Bennett.
 iv. POLLY MATHER, b. 1827; d. 18 Mar., 1848, age 21 years.
 v. ANGELINE MATHER, b. 1834; d. 3 Oct., 1860, age 26 years.
 vi. SARAH MATHER, b. 1836. She d. 25 Jan., 1862, age 26 years.

Children of SUSANNA⁶, (1798) [**442**] (Capt. Oliver⁵, Simeon⁴, John³, Jacob², Robert¹) and Archibald Robinson; res. Middleport, N. Y.

 i. OLIVER ROBINSON.
 ii. SOPHIA ROBINSON.
 iii. HIRAM ROBINSON.

Children of OLIVER⁶, JR., (1800) [**443**] (Capt. Oliver⁵, Simeon⁴, John³, Jacob², Robert¹) and Fanny (Stearns) Adams; res. Hinsdale, N. H.

 i. LUCY ANNA⁷, b. in Hinsdale, Sept. 25, 1827 ; d. unm. 27 May, 1863.
941. ii. SARAH BAGG⁷, b. in Hinsdale, Sept. 20, 1829; m. June 2, 1852, Wilson Harris ; set. in Cleveland, O., 1873.
942. iii. WILLIAM BRADLEY⁷, b. in Hinsdale, Feb. 4, 1831; m. Feb. 3, 1860, Polly Ann Winchester, dau. of Antipass and Lovis (Kelsey) Winchester of Marlboro, Vt.; b. Nov. 14, 1834; d. June, 1897; res. Hinsdale, N. H
943. iv. HENRY⁷, b. in Hinsdale, Nov. 14, 1832 ; m. (1) Dec. 29, 1858, Helen M. Hastings of Chesterfield, N. H.; she d. 7 Feb., 1867 ; m. (2) Mar. 28, 1868, Eva S. Pettee of Hubbardton, Vt.; she d. 5 May, 1882. He rem. 1883 to Columbus, Neb.; returned to Vermont 1890, and d. in So. Hebron, N. Y., 4 Jan., 1892.
 v. OLIVER MILLER⁷, b. in Hinsdale, Aug. 28, 1834; res. Napa City, Cal.; unm.
  He was a member of the Chicago Mercantile Battery, and was wounded at Memphis.
944. vi. CAROLINE FRANCES⁷, b. in Hinsdale, Mar. 11, 1836 ; m. July 26, 1860, Solon N. Alexander; b. Feb. 17, 1833 ; d. 17 Jan., 1899 ; res. Bellows Falls, Vt.

- vii. LUTHERA THERESA[7], b. in Hinsdale, Dec. 9, 1838; m. May 18, 1859, Rev. O. H. Jasper, D. D., of Tilton, N. H.; he d. 1893-4; res. Tilton, N. H.; living 1897; no issue.
- viii. HANNAH AUGUSTA[7], b. in Hinsdale, Aug. 31, 1840; res. with Mrs. Fisk, Springfield, Mass.; unm.

945.
- ix. EMELINE GRATIA[7]. b. in Hinsdale, May 10, 1842; m. Aug. 27, 1862, Noyes Wilson Fisk, son of Thomas T. Fisk of Hinsdale; b. May 15, 1839. He was a private in Co. H, 46th Mass. Reg. of Vols.; res. Springfield, Mass.

Children of ANNA[6], (1802) [**444**] (Capt. Oliver[5], Simeon[4], John[3], Jacob[2], Robert[1]) and Ora Barrett; res. Hinsdale, N. H.

- i. LUCY N. BARRETT, b. Nov. 2, 1820; m. 1837, Lyndan Flynn Doolittle. She d. in Hinsdale, N. H., 6 Oct., 1845.
- ii. LOCKHART BARRETT, b. Oct. 29, 1822; m. Nov. 28, 1843. Mila A. Hines; res. Brattleboro, Vt.
  They have two children, a dau. and a son.
- iii. POLLY A. BARRETT, b. Feb. 11, 1824; d. in Hinsdale, 9 Jan., 1825.
- iv. ALVIN T. BARRETT, b. June 7, 1826; m. (1) 1849, Julia Scott; m. (2) Caroline Scott, both daus. of Elijah and Louisa (Robinson) Scott. He rem. to Brattleboro, Vt., and d. 28 Apr., 1865.
- v. OLIVER A. BARRETT, b. Mar. 16, 1828; d. in Hinsdale, 22 Oct., 1844.
- vi. HENRY W. BARRETT, b. July 2, 1830; d. in Hinsdale, 26 June, 1848.
- vii. GEORGE L. BARRETT, b. Mar. 1, 1835; m. 1860, Francis Goodenough; res. Springfield, Mass.; d. 3 Aug., 1870.
- viii. DWIGHT M. BARRETT, b. Aug. 7, 1839; d. in Brattleboro, Vt., Aug., 1857.
- ix. HARRIET S. BARRETT, b. Oct. 26, 1839; m. Nov. 3, 1857, J. Albert Taylor; res. Brattleboro, Vt.; two children deceased.

Children of SALLY[6], (1804) [**445**] (Capt. Oliver[5], Simeon[4], John[3], Jacob[2], Robert[1]) and Harry Thomas; res. Marlboro, Vt.

- i. HENRY ADAMS THOMAS, b. Apr. 1, 1822; res. Hudson, Lenawee Co., Mich.
- ii. SARAH A. THOMAS, b. May 17, 1824; m. June 16, 1847, Gideon Strong; res. Lincoln, Ill.
- iii. WILLIAM THOMAS, b. Feb. 8, 1826; m. Ann Smith; res. Guilford, Vt.
- iv. CHARLOTTE S. THOMAS, b. Mar. 28, 1828; m. Dan. Warren of Marlboro, Vt.

v. BRADLEY A. THOMAS, b. Jan. 26, 1831.
vi. ZEPHENIA THOMAS, b. Sept. 17, 1833; d. 23 Sept., 1842.
vii. LUCY A. THOMAS, b. July 18, 1834-5; m. May 14, 1858, Chas. H. Denison; settled in Springfield, Mass., about 1878.
viii. GEO. M. THOMAS, b. May 24, 1838; m. (1) Susan Richmond; m. (2) Louisa Thayer, widow of Frank Stockwell; P. O., W. Brattleboro, Vt.
ix. ROSWELL A. THOMAS, b. Sept. 4, 1841; m. Harriet Maria Whitney, dau. of Emery S. and Sarepth (Hale) Whitney, b. Dec. 10, 1839; res. Mt. Pulaski, Ill. He d. in Lincoln, Ill., 25 Mar., 1884; no issue.
x. ANNA L. THOMAS, b. Oct. 14, 1844; m. Geo. Ames; res. Marlboro, Vt.

Children of CAPT. IRA^6, (1798) [**446**] (Capt. Simeon^5, Simeon^4, John^3, Jacob^2, Robert^1) and Lucy (Houghton) Adams; res. Marlboro, Vt.

946. i. SIMEON HOUGHTON^7, b. in Marlboro, Feb. 5, 1822; m. (1) Jan. 1, 1846, Louisa Baker of W. Springfield, Mass.; she d. 9 Feb., 1847. Her infant dau. d. 14 Feb., 1847, age 12 days; m. (2) May 10, 1848, Lucinda Ethel Knight, dau. of Benjamin Knight. He d. 1899; res. West Marlboro, Vt.
ii. ANNETTE^7, b. in Marlboro, May 21, 1823; d. 10 May, 1833.
iii. IRA^7, b. in Marlboro, Nov. 10, 1824; d. 5 Aug., 1825.
947. iv. IRA^7, JR., b. in Marlboro, May 31, 1826; m. Feb. 14, 1849, Eliza Winchester, dau. of Martin Winchester of Marlboro, Vt.; res. Marlboro, Vt. He d. 12 Aug., 1899.
v. CHARLES^7, b. in Marlboro, Nov. 28, 1827; d. 6 May, 1833.
vi. WILLIAM H.^{7}, b. in Marlboro, July 19, 1829; d. 17 Aug., 1830.
vii. LUCY^7, b. in Marlboro, Jan. 24, 1833; m. (1) Jan. 15, 1849, Franklin Harris, son of Oliver Harris of Wilmington, Vt.; m. (2) Delphi W. Yeaw, of E. Dover, Vt.; res. E. Dover, Vt.
948. viii. CHARLES MORTON^7, b. in Marlboro, Aug. 3, 1835; m. Oct. 6, 1857, Marilla Lucinda Howe of Dover, Vt., dau. of Lambert and Lucinda Howe; she m. 2nd, Wm. W. Barney of Guilford, Vt.; b. Feb. 13, 1837. He d. 20 Dec., 1874.
949. ix. ANNETTE MINERVA^7, b. in Marlboro, May 21, 1837; m. Oct. 17, 1857, Daniel Green Leonard, son of Elder Daniel Leonard of W. Dover, Vt., b. in W. Dover, Sept. 21, 1833; d. in Wilmington, 13 Aug., 1892; res. Wilmington, Vt., since 1891.
x. GEORGE HENRY^7, b. in Marlboro, May 5, 1840; m. (1) Rosie Mather of Marlboro, Vt.; m. (2) Alice Leonard of Wardsboro, Vt.; res. W. Dover, Vt.
He is living and has sons, Clifton and Carl, but no records can be obtained.

Children of PHILENA[6], (1800) [447] (Capt. Simeon[5], Simeon[4], John[3], Jacob[2], Robert[1]) and Dr. Chester A. Olds; res. Circleville, O.

    i. LUCY MATHER OLDS, b. Dec. 22, 1822; d. 4 Jan., 1847.

950.   ii. LYMAN WHITNEY OLDS, b. Nov. 3, 1824; m. Aug. 8, 1848, Sarah M. Curry of Brownsville, Pa.

        He was b. in Newfane, Vt., and rem. to Circleville, O., in 1845; thence to Lythopolis, O., and in 1853 to Muscatine, Iowa, where he was a prominent merchant and banker, an influential and much respected citizen; he d. 19 Apr., 1895.

  iii. MARY JANE OLDS, b. Oct. 25, 1826; d. 18 Jan., 1829.

  iv. SARAH JANE OLDS, b. Jan. 8, 1829; m. —— Olds, a cousin.

  v. CHESTER OLDS, b. Feb. 10, 1831; d. 17 July, 1832.

  vi. CHESTER ADAMS OLDS, b. Mar. 22, 1833.

  vii. HENRY CLINTON OLDS, b. May 16, 1835; living unm., 1900.

  viii. ROSALTHE OLDS, b. Dec. 30, 1837; m. Thomas R. Patterson; res. Cincinnati, O.; no issue.

  ix. JOSEPH EDWIN OLDS, b. Sept. 28, 1840; d. Aug., 1864.

  x. FREDERICK H. OLDS, b. Mar. 1, 1846; d. 6 Oct., 1847.

Children of SIMEON[6], (1803) [448] (Capt. Simeon[5], Simeon[4], John[3], Jacob[2], Robert[1]) and Mary Ann W. (Sargent) Adams; res. Marlboro, Vt.

951.   i. SARAH[7], b. in Marlboro, May 15, 1832; m. Cotton Mather Houghton; he d. in Guilford, Vt. She d. 15 July, 1856.

952.   ii. HENRY[7], b. in Marlboro, Dec. 27, 1833; m. (1) Oct. 6, 1857, Lucy Ann Winchester, dau. of Clark Adams and Louisa (Thayer) Winchester, b. Oct. 17, 1833; d. 9 Sept., 1870; m. (2) Nov. 12, 1872, Ellen L. Fowler, dau. of Jerome Thompson, and widow of LeRoy Fowler, b. June 24, 1847; res. Marlboro, Vt.

953.   iii. HANNAH[7], b. in Marlboro, Feb. 15, 1836; m. Mar. 16, 1859, David Mather, son of Capt. Daniel and Almira (Miller) Mather, b. Mar. 6, 1836; res. Marlboro, Vt.

954.   iv. LUCY[7], b. in Marlboro, Jan. 10, 1838; m. Oct. 7, 1857, George C. Higley, son of George and Lucy (Winchester) Higley, b. Apr. 5, 1835; res. Marlboro, Vt.

955.   v. LUTHER[7], b. in Marlboro, Mar. 26, 1840; m. Dec. 12, 1860, Susan Emeline Winchester, dau. of Clark A. and Louisa (Thayer) Winchester, b. Dec. 29, 1839; res. W. Halifax, Vt. He d. 30 May, 1893.

956.   vi. MARY ANN[7], b. in Marlboro, July 8, 1842; m. Feb. 10, 1864, Elliot J. Higley, son of George and Lucy (Winchester) Higley, b. Nov. 24, 1841; res. Guilford, Vt.

Seventh Generation.] OF NEWBURY, MASS.

957. vii. SIMEON[1], b. in Marlboro, July 15, 1844 ; m. Dec. 31, 1867, Mrs. Mary Jane (Squir) Fulton ; res. W. Rindge, N. H.
   viii. SAMUEL[7], b. in Marlboro, Aug. 24, 1846 ; res. Clay Center, Clay Co., Kan.; unm,
958. ix. DAVID[7], b. in Marlboro, Oct. 14, 1850 ; m. Nov. 29, 1867, Louisa Jenette Adams. dau. of Simeon H. and Lucinda E. (Knight) Adams, b. July 29, 1849 ; res. Marlboro, Vt.

Children of CLARK[5], (1807) [450] (Capt. Simeon[6], Simeon[4], John[3], Jacob[2], Robert[1]) and Beulah D. (Hill) Adams; res. Newfane, Vt.

   i. CLARK HIRAM[7], b. in Newfane, July 2, 1848.
      He rem. to Star, Greenwood Co., Kan, 1877 ; is a farmer ; unm.; present res. Miltonvale, Cloud Co., Kan.
   ii. STELLA B.[7], b. in Newfane, Oct. 21, 1851 ; m. Apr. 2, 1868, George Washburn ; res. Somerville, Mass.
   iii. CYRUS F.[7], b. in Newfane, May 3, 1857 ; d. 22 Sept., 1881.

Children of TIMOTHY MATHER[6], (1811) [451] (Capt. Simeon[5], Simeon[4], John[3], Jacob[2], Robert[1]) and Harriet P. (Winchester) Adams; res. Marlboro, Vt.

959. i. HENRY LE ROY[7], b. in Marlboro, Nov. 15, 1842 ; m. Mar. 2, 1871, Ellen M. Dunklee; she m. 2nd Willard Higley of Marlboro, Vt. He d. 15 Apr., 1880.
   ii. ROSALTHA MINERVA[7], b. in Marlboro, May 21, 1846 ; d. 10 Oct., 1860.
   iii. INFANT SON, b. May 11, 1855; d. 25 June, 1855.

Children of TIMOTHY MATHER[6], (1811) and Amaretta (Whitney) Adams.

   iv. HUGH MATHER[7], b. in Marlboro, Dec. 24, 1858 ; m. Feb. 15, 1883, Flora I. Lynde ; no issue.
   v. JOHN GILBERT[7], b. in Marlboro, Apr. 25, 1860 ; d. 22 Aug., 1861.
   vi. HARRIET WINCHESTER[7], b. in Marlboro, Sept. 5, 1862 ; d. 15 Sept., 1884.

Children of LUCIUS FRANKLIN[6], (1816) [452] (Capt. Simeon[5], Simeon[4], John[3], Jacob[2], Robert[1]) and Clarinda (Winchester) Adams; res. Marlboro, Vt.

960. i. LE ROY F.[7], b. in Marlboro, Apr. 23, 1846; m. Oct. 28, 1872, Ella Crosby, dau. of Edward and Betsey L. (Jones) Crosby, b. July 7, 1857; he set. in Brattleboro, 1870.
961. ii. LOREN M.[7], b. in Marlboro, Aug. 9, 1847; m. Mar. 3, 1881, Cora M. Jillson, dau. of Lewis Jillson and Sarah E. Chase of Whitingham, Vt.; he set. in Guilford, Vt., 1896.
962. iii. LUCIUS W.[7], b. in Marlboro, Sept. 19, 1859; m. Oct. 20, 1889, Ola E. Clough; res. Brattleboro, Vt., 1888.
963. iv. NELLIE J.[7], b. in Marlboro, Jan. 24, 1854; m. Oct. 5, 1876, Charles H. Smith; res. So. Minneapolis, Minn.

Children of SAMUEL NEWELL[6], (1819) [453] (Capt. Simeon[5], Simeon[4], John[3], Jacob[2], Robert[1]) and Cornelia H. (Rogers) Adams; res. Circleville, O.

  i. JULIETTE ROGERS[7], b. Apr. 17, 1848; m. Sept. 28, 1869, at La Cross, Wis., Radcliff A. Shumaker.
  ii. LUCY MATHER[7], b. Sept. 20, 1851; m. (1) Sept. 1, 1885, at Saratoga, Dak., Frank Pomeroy; he d. 18 June, 1891; m. (2) Jan. 7, 1892, Nehemiah Hulett; he d. 25 July, 1892.
  iii. CLARA NEWELL[7], b. Oct. 20 1853; m. Nov. 3, 1875, William H. Shumaker of Owatonna, Wis.

Child of MINERVA[6], (1821) [454] (Capt. Simeon[5], Simeon[4], John[3], Jacob[2], Robert[1]) and Lyman N. Olds; res. Circleville, O.

  i. EDWARD M. OLDS.

Children of SUSAN BRITTAN, (1801) [455] and Col. Calvin G. Howe; res. Rutland, Mass.

  i. WILLIAM HOWE, b. in Rutland, April 29, 1824; res. Worcester, Mass., formerly of Burlington, Vt.
  ii. CHARLES P. HOWE, b. in Rutland, Sept. 20, 1825; d. 7 Oct., 1865.
  iii. SIMEON BRITTAN HOWE, b. in Rutland, Mar. 2, 1841; d. at Denver, Col., 10 Nov., 1898.

Children of ALMIRA HALLADAY, (1803) [458] and Stephen White; res. Coleraine, Mass.

  i. SUSAN AMELIA WHITE, b. 1834; m. Rev. A. W. Goodnow. She d. at Wilmington, Vt, 1873.

LE ROY F. ADAMS.

Seventh Generation.] OF NEWBURY, MASS. 227

  ii. JAMES LEWIS WHITE, b. Feb. 24, 1838; res. Bridgeport, Conn.
  iii. WM. LYMAN WHITE, b. Mar. 31, 1840; res. North Adams, Mass,
  iv. HANNAH ALMIRA WHITE, b. 1842; d. at Stamford, Vt., 1860. [?]
  v. ALBERT LAWSON WHITE, b. May 27, 1845; m. Addie Smith ; res. Springfield, Mass.

Children of HENRY ADAMS HALLADAY, (1805) [459] and Caroline Stearns; res. Troy, N. Y.

  i. HORATIO HENRY HALLADAY, b. in Halifax, Vt., Aug. 11, 1834; m. Nellie Perham ; res. Troy, N. Y.
  ii. LUCIUS W. HALLADAY.
  iii. WILLIAM HALLADAY.
  iv. CARRIE HALLADAY, b. 1845 ; m. 1867, Irving Hayner ; res. Troy, N. Y.

Children of WILLARD NATHAN HALLADAY, (1808) [460] and Sabra L. ———.

  i. ELLEN M. HALLADAY, b. Mar. 17, 1831 ; m. Apr. 21, 1861, Elliot B. Fuller; res. Hartwellville, Vt.
  ii. JOSEPHINE C. HALLADAY, b. Feb. 26, 1837; m. (1) June 12, 1855, Ezra Canedy ; m. (2) ——— Allard; res. Bennington, Vt.
  iii. NATHAN W. HALLADAY, b. Feb. 11, 1840 ; d. Mar., 1848.
  iv. SUSAN L. HALLADAY, b. Apr. 4, 1842 ; m. Dec. 28, 1862, Lewis G. Evans ; res. Bennington, Vt.
  v. FRANCELIA E. HALLADAY, b. July 1, 1844 ; m. L. Evans; res. Bennington, Vt.
  vi. ALBERT H. HALLADAY, b. Mar. 7, 1848.

Children of SUSAN HALLADAY, (1810) [461] and Daniel Read Wheeler; res. Rutland, Mass.

  i. DANIEL MERRICK WHEELER, b. July 3, 1846 ; m. Nov. 19, 1868. Arvilla Jane Putnam, b. in Whitingham, Vt., Jan. 10, 1848.
  He is a civil engineer, and a member of the State Board of Railroad Commissioners ; res. Worcester, Mass. Children :
    1. Ethel Arvilla Wheeler, b. in Worcester, Oct. 14, 1869 ; m. Jan. 28, 1891, Henry R. Chase of Minneapolis, Minn.
    2. Milton Merrick Wheeler, b. in Worcester, Nov. 30, 1870 ; m. Nov. 10, 1898, Jessie McLarren of Argyle, N. S.
    He is a civil engineer ; res. Worcester, Mass.
    3. Ralph Morton Wheeler, b. in Worcester, June 13, 1872 ; d. 20 June, 1872.

  4. Inez Viola Wheeler, b. in Worcester, Aug. 22, 1874; m. Jan. 31, 1894, Edmund Raymond Kinsey, C. E., of St. Louis, Mo.
  5. Abbie Wheeler, b. in Rutland, Mass., June 8, 1880; d. at Winslow, Ark., 19 Aug., 1881.
  6. Clara Susan Wheeler, b. in Winslow, Ark., June 25, 1882.
  7. Grace Leola Wheeler, b. in Winona, Minn., Nov. 23, 1891.
 ii. INFANT DAUGHTER.
 iii. WALTER ADAMS WHEELER, b. Aug. 14, 1850; m. (1) Aug. 26, 1872, Emma F. Newell, dau. of Nahum Newell of Holden, Mass.; she d. 5 Nov., 1885; m. (2) June 9, 1887, Mrs. Mary A. (Wedge) King, dau. of Newell and Sarah A. Wedge of Sutton, Mass.; res. Rutland, Mass. Children of Emma F.:
  1. Herbert Walter Wheeler, b. Oct. 3, 1873.
  2. Arthur Merrick Wheeler, b. July 19, 1876; d. 19 Feb., 1878.
  3. Arthur Clifford Wheeler, b. June 2, 1879.
  4. Chester Adams Wheeler, b. Dec. 15, 1884.
  Children of Mary A.:
  5. Merrick Wedge Wheeler, b. May 28, 1888; d. 2 Nov., 1889.
  6. Merrill Halladay Wheeler, b. Jan 22, 1891.
 iv. ABBIE ALMIRA WHEELER, b. June 15, 1855; m. July 28, 1874, Ellis Patterson of Boston, Mass.; res. Jamaica Plain, Boston. Children:
  1. Ellis Patterson, b. Sept. 24, 1875. He is a graduate of Harvard University; a veterinary in Worcester, Mass.
  2. Sidney Patterson, b. Jan. 9, 1878. He is a graduate of Harvard University, and a teacher in Worcester, Mass.
  3. Caro Patterson, b. July 2, 1880; d. 14 Oct., 1880.
  4. Abbot Patterson, b. Mar. 16, 1884.

Child of GEORGE⁶, (1790) [462] (Job⁵, Joel⁴, John³, Jacob², Robert¹) and Polly (Woodward) Adams; res. Antwerp and Theresa, N. Y.

 i. JANE⁷, b. in Rutland, N. Y., July 10, 1821; m. —— Hall.

Children of GEORGE⁶, (1790) and Polly (Edgerton) Adams.

964. ii. ELIAS⁷, b. in Antwerp, N. Y., Sept. 5, 1828; m. Sept. 15, 1859, Cornelia Elizabeth Hall, dau. of Asa and Elizabeth (Merrick) Hall. He set. in Theresa, Jeff. Co., N. Y., in 1847, and d. there 22 Sept., 1891.
 iii. ELIZA⁷, b. in Antwerp, May 2, 1830; d. in Theresa unm., 28 Sept., 1876; buried in Antwerp, N. Y.

ETHAN LOVELL AND WIFE, MARTHA McKELVEY.

Seventh Generation.] OF NEWBURY, MASS. 229

Children of NANCY⁶, (1798) [463] (Bildad⁵, Joel⁴, John³, Jacob², Robert¹) and Matthew McKelvey; res. Greenfield, Huron Co., O.

    i. ELIZABETH McKELVEY, b. Feb. 12, 1819; d. in Plymouth, O., 10 Jan., 1834; unm.
    ii. MIRIAM McKELVEY, b. June 9, 1821; d. 25 June, 1822.
    iii. MARY McKELVEY (twin), b. June 9, 1821; d. in Plymouth, O., 23 July, 1842.
    iv. SARAH McKELVEY, b. May 5, 1823; d. in Blanchard, O., 23 July, 1841.
    v. NANCY McKELVEY, b. in Sandusky, Nov. 8, 1824; d. in Blanchard, 19 July, 1841.
    vi. GEORGE McKELVEY, b. in Plymouth, June 28, 1826; d. in Plymouth, O., 18 Sept., 1827.
    vii. JANE McKELVEY, b. in Plymouth, June 9, 1828; d. in Blanchard, 21 July, 1841.
    viii. MARTHA McKELVEY, b. in Plymouth, Mar. 31, 1831; m. Dec. 30, 1854, at No. Fairfield, O., Ethan Lovell, son of David and Mary (Chilcott) Lovell, b. June 17, 1819; d. 29 Apr., 1898; res. "Fine View Home Farm," Greenfield, O.
965.   ix. MATTHEW McKELVEY, b. in Plymouth, Feb. 25, 1833; m. May 2, 1858, Mary Woolsey, dau. of David and Katurah (Bloomer) Woolsley of Sandusky, O.

        Matthew McKelvey was a merchant in Sandusky for a number of years from 1853; afterwards he became interested in vineyards and the publication of a newspaper; wrote poetry and several practical books, "The Soldier's Story," and others. He is now a resident of Tiffin, O., and proprietor of a printing office.

966.   x. JOHN McKELVEY, b. in Plymouth, Feb. 8, 1835; m. June 26, 1861, Jane Rowland Huntington; res. Sandusky, O.

        He is a large land owner, and an active citizen of Sandusky, being identified with several extensive industries, and president of a number of railroad corporations.

Children of CANDACE⁶, (1803) [464] (Bildad⁵, Joel⁴, John³, Jacob², Robert¹) and Lewis Andrews; res. Milan, Erie Co., O.

967.   i. LOUISA ANDREWS, b. in Milan, O., Sept. 8, 1827; m. (1) Jan. 1, 1846, Orin Downs; d. in Cleveland, O., 13 Aug., 1850; m. (2) about 1853, John Eaton. She d. 11 Sept., 1885.
968.   ii. EDWIN ANDREWS, b. in Milan, Dec. 19, 1828; m. Nov. 4, 1855, Lydia Olmstead; she d. Nov., 1897; res. Sphinx Corners, Berrien Co., Mich.

969. iii. EMILY ANDREWS, b. in Milan, Nov. 26, 1830; m. Oct. 9, 1853, Curtis Printiss; he d. 16 Jan., 1896. She rem. with her parents to Branch Co., Mich., in 1849.

970. iv. LUCINA ANDREWS, b. in Vermillion, O., May 7, 1833; m. (1) Oct. 7, 1855, Abraham Phillips; m. (2) Oct. 8, 1864, John Newcomb of Coldwater, Mich.; he d. 27 Oct., 1870; res. Union City, Mich.

v. GEORGE ANDREWS, b. in Vermillion, Apr. 29, 1835.
He went away from home before the civil war, and has never been heard from,

vi. MARY ANDREWS, b. in Berlin, O., Nov. 28, 1889; m. July 15. 1885, John Brancher; res. Branch Co., Mich.; no issue.

Children of HORACE HALE[6], (1805) [465] (Bildad[5], Joel[4], John[3], Jacob[2], Robert[1]) and Lorania G. (Kinney) Adams; res. Green Creek, Sandusky Co., O.

971. i. FRANKLIN B.[7], b. in Sandusky Co., O., Jan. 11, 1828; m. (1) Oct. 23, 1850, Lucinda Fletcher, dau. of Thomas and Barbara (Ulery) Fletcher of Porter township, Van Buren Co., Mich., b. Apr. 12, 1830; d. in Lawton, Mich, 10 May, 1879; m. (2) Mar. 15, 1881, Anna Fletcher, dau. of Elijah and Eliza Fletcher, b. Feb. 20, 1856; res. Lawton.

ii. PHEBE[7], b. in Sandusky Co., Aug. 27, 1830; d. 1833.

972. iii. URI M.[7], b. in Sandusky Co., Nov. 2, 1832; m. Apr. 19, 1865, Jane McKain, dau. of Thomas and Jane (Morrow) McKain, b. Jan. 2, 1842.
He rem. with his parents in 1837, to Porter township, Van Buren Co., Mich., and is the owner of a fine farm near Lawton, Mich.

973. iv. SARAH LUCINA[7], b. in Sandusky Co., Aug. 23, 1835; m. Dec. 3, 1856, Dorry Fletcher, son of Thomas and Barbara (Ulery) Fletcher, b. Aug. 14, 1828; res. Lawton, Mich.

974. v. EMILY LORANIA[7], b. in Porter, Van Buren Co., Mich., Apr. 10, 1839; m. Feb. 22, 1866, Isaac Leonard Bates, son of Jarius and Zurina Sophia*(Phelps) Bates, b. near Syracuse, N. Y., July 12, 1835. He was a soldier, 2d Lieut. of Co. C., 3rd Michigan Cavalry; enlisted Sept. 17, 1861; discharged Oct. 5, 1865; res. 1866-1869, in Porter, Mich.; 1869-1886, Schoolcraft, Mich., and then set. in Garden Prairie (Andover P. O.), Brown Co., So. Dak.

975. vi. MARY CALISTA[7], b. in Van Buren Co., Mich., Mar. 20, 1842; m. Dec. 25, 1866, D. F. Smith, b. in Wentworth Co., Ont. She was educated at Hillsdale College, Mich. They rem. from Burlington, Ont., to Burlington, Iowa, and thence to Chicago, Ill.

HON. LEONARD BATES AND WIFE, EMILY ADAMS.

Seventh Generation.] OF NEWBURY, MASS. 231

Children of ALDEN[6], (1796) [466] (Joel[5], Jr., Joel[4], John[3], Jacob[2], Robert[1]) and Wealthy (Otis) Adams; res. Antwerp, Jefferson Co., N. Y.

976.   i.   HORACE HALE[7], b. in Edinburgh, N. Y., Mar. 20, 1819 ; m. Sept. 15, 1842, Lucy Willard of Pamelia, Jefferson Co., N. Y.; she d. in Carthage, 6 Jan., 1881, age 63 years. He set. in Antwerp, N. Y.; d. 4 Jan., 1889, age 69 years.
         He was known as an upright, honest man ; a democrat in politics, and was several times a supervisor of his town, and a member of the State Assembly.

977.   ii.   LUCY MARIA[7], b. in Antwerp, N. Y., Mar. 25, 1829; m. (1) Mar. 28, 1849, Henry Stebbins of Antwerp, N. Y.; m. (2) James Guthrie ; res. at The Colonial, 6325 Monroe Ave., Chicago, Ill.

Children of BETSEY[6], (1805) [467] (Joel[5], Jr., Lieut. Joel[4], John[3], Jacob[2], Robert[1]) and David Heald; res. Birmingham, Erie Co., O.

978.   i.   GEORGE HEALD, b. May 12, 1827 ; m. May 18, 1850, Maria Shaffer of Birmingham, O.; res. Birmingham, Erie Co., O.
979.   ii.   CLARK HEALD, b. Feb 12, 1830 ; m. 1866, Catherine Gilmore.
980.   iii.   CHARLES S. HEALD, b. Apr. 3, 1833 ; m. 1862, Emily Middleton. He d. 6 Mar., 1880.
981.   iv.   ALONZO K. HEALD, b. in Birmingham, July 24, 1835 ; m. Apr. 7, 1860, Julia Heath, b. in Russia, Loraine Co., O., Feb. 10, 1837. He set. in Iowa in 1856, and is a merchant in Farley, Dubuque Co., Iowa.
982.   v.   AMOS S. HEALD, b. in Birmingham, Mar. 24, 1839 ; m. (1) 1867, Amanda Brown ; she d. 1872 ; m. (2) 1890, Mrs. Charlotte Frisbie.
      vi.   ASA HEALD, b. in Birmingham, Mar. 28, 1842 ; d. young.
983.   vii.   FRANK A. HEALD, b. in Birmingham, May 16, 1844 ; m. (1) Rachel German ; she d. 1875 ; m. (2) Aramantha Needham.

Children of MARTIN WINCHESTER, (1795) [469] (Sarah[5], Lieut. Joel[4], John[3], Jacob[2], Robert[1]) and Clarissa Hilliard; res. Marlboro, Vt.

      i.   BETSEY WINCHESTER, b. Jan. 21, 1819 ; m. 1844, Fred Mather.; res. Colerain, Mass.
      ii.   CYRUS MATHER WINCHESTER, b. Jan. 9, 1822 ; m. Nancy Hall.
      iii.   HORACE HALE WINCHESTER, b. April 15, 1824 ; m. Mary Forken. He d. in Gibbon, Neb.

ROBERT ADAMS   [Seventh Generation.

    iv. ELIZA WINCHESTER, b. May 23, 1826; m. Feb. 14, 1849, Ira Adams, Jr., son of Capt. Ira and Lucy (Houghton) Adams; res. Marlboro, Vt.
    v. GEORGE WINCHESTER, b. Mar. 1, 1832; m. Jennette Higley; He d. in Marlboro, Vt., 1894.
    vi. HIRAM CLARK WINCHESTER, b. Aug. 20 1835; m. Mary Higley; res. W. Brattleboro, Vt.

Children of SARAH WINCHESTER⁶, (1800) [470] and Lovell Clark; res. Denmark, Lewis Co., N. Y.

    i. LUCINA O. CLARK, b. 1831; m. Jackson Tomblin; res. Antwerp, N. Y.
    ii. LUCY A. CLARK, b. 1836; m. John Gillette; res. Carthage, N. Y.
    iii. ASA WINCHESTER CLARK, d. at 27 years of age.
    iv. ELVIRA P. CLARK, b. 1844; m. John J. Perham; res. Watertown, N. Y.

Children of CLARK ADAMS WINCHESTER. (1802) [471] and Louisa Thayer; res. Marlboro, Vt.

    i. SARAH E. WINCHESTER, b. Sept. 30, 1831; d. 10 Feb., 1832.
    ii. LUCY ANN WINCHESTER, b. Oct. 17, 1833; m. Oct. 6, 1857, Henry Adams, son of Simeon and Mary Ann W. (Sargent) Adams. She d. 9 Sept., 1870.
    iii. JENETTE WINCHESTER, b. Oct. 30, 1835; d. 14 Jan., 1839.
    iv. MARY E. WINCHESTER, b. May 3, 1838; d. 17 Feb., 1839.
    v. SUSAN E. WINCHESTER, b. Dec. 29, 1839; m. Dec. 12, 1860, Luther Adams, son of Simeon and Mary Ann W. (Sargent) Adams; res. Wilmington, Vt.
    vi. LOUISA J. WINCHESTER, b. Sept. 11, 1842; d. 22 Mar., 1864.
    vii. EVERTON WELLS WINCHESTER. b. Feb. 9, 1845; m. (1) Dec. 12, 1865, Eliza Houghton, dau. of Bradley Houghton.; m. (2) Samantha Falkner.
    viii. INFANT, b. Jan. 4, 1847; d. 6 Jan., 1847.

Children of LUCY WINCHESTER, (1805) [472] and George Higley; res. Marlboro, Vt.

    i. LUCINDA HIGLEY, b. Apr. 16, 1830; d. 1836.
    ii. SARAH WINCHESTER HIGLEY, b. Feb. 16, 1833, ; m. Jan. 15, 1858, Alfred Stevens; res. New York State.

Seventh Generation.] OF NEWBURY, MASS. 233

  iii. GEORGE CLARK HIGLEY, b. April 5, 1835; m. Oct. 6, 1857, Lucy Adams, dau. of Simeon and Mary Ann (Sargent) Adams; res. Marlboro, Vt.
  iv. LUCY JENETTE HIGLEY, b. July 24, 1838; m. July 20, 1858, Bradley Houghton, Sr. She d. 27 Jan., 1864.
  v. JOHN ELLIOT HIGLEY, b. Nov. 24, 1841; m. Feb., 1864, Mary Ann Adams, dau. of Simeon and Mary Ann (Sargent) Adams; res. Guilford, Vt.

Children of ALICE⁷, (1768) [473] (Henry⁶, Robert⁵, Abraham⁴, Robert³, Sergt. Abraham², Robert¹) and Enoch Boynton · res. West Newbury, Mass.

  i. ABIGAIL LEE BOYNTON, b. Aug. 19, 1800; d. 4 Nov., 1831.
  ii. SARAH DOLE BOYNTON, b. Feb. 14, 1802; d. 1861.
  iii. ENOCH TARRING BOYNTON, b. May 1, 1804; d. 18 June, 1826.
  iv. ADDING BOYNTON, b. May 27, 1806; m. Dec. 5, 1833, Roxana Stevens of N. Brookfield, Mass., and they had two daughters, now deceased. He d. 27 Aug., 1882.
  v. ISABELLA BOYNTON, b. Jan. 11, 1809; d. 11 Jan., 1810.

Children of PHEBE⁷, (1772) [474] (Henry⁶, Robert⁵, Abraham⁴, Robert³, Sergt. Abraham², Robert¹) and Nathaniel Currier; res. Newbury, Mass.

  i. PHEBE CURRIER, b. Aug. 26, 1795; m. (1) Mar. 15, 1818, Aaron Cheever; m. (2) Oct. 16, 1831, Joseph H. Jewett; d. in New Orleans, 23 Aug., 1855, age 70 years. She d. 18 Aug., 1865, age 70 years.
  ii. NATHANIEL CURRIER, b. Nov. 23, 1796; m. Elizabeth Churchill of Yarmouth, N. S.; she d. in San Francisco, Cal. He d. in Newburyport, 6 June, 1866, age 69 yrs. 7 mos.
  iii. ALICE CURRIER, b. Aug. 3, 1799; m. Jan. 17, 1822, Robert Gurney, b. Dec. 18, 1799; d. in Portsmouth, N. H., 12 Dec., 1878. She d. in Portsmouth, N. H., 10 Oct., 1879, age 80 yrs. 2 mo. 7 days.

984.   iv. CHARLES CURRIER, b. Aug. 22, 1800; m. Nov. 29, 1827; Anna Hale of Newbury, Mass., dau. of Ezra and Anna (Adams) Hale, b. in Newbury, Sept. 4, 1802; d. 17 May, 1882.   He d. 8 May, 1868, age 67 yrs. 8 mos. 16 days.

v. AMOS CURRIER, b. Jan. 9, 1802; m. Apr. 13, 1824, Jane W. Gurney, dau. of Nathaniel and Martha (Hastings) Gurney, b. Nov. 1. 1805; d. 27 May, 1879.   He d. 29 Sept., 1846, age 44 yrs. 8 mos. 20 days.

vi. HARRIET CURRIER, b. Nov. 8, 1803; d. 17 Oct., 1804.

vii. SUSANNA MARY CURRIER, b. Feb. 6, 1805; m. Mar. 31, 1825, Richard Fowler, son of Capt. Samuel and Mollie (Blaisdell) Fowler of Salisbury, Mass., b. May 2, 1802; d. 26 Apr., 1881.   She d. 8 Feb., 1875, age 70 years.

viii. GEORGE CURRIER, b. Dec. 14, 1806; m. Dec. 25, 1831, Almira Wells of Newbury, dau. of Samuel and Elizabeth (Swazey) Wells of Exeter, N. H., b. Nov. 23, 1807; d. 27 Aug., 1857. He d. 18 May, 1863, age 58 yrs. 5 mos. 4 days.

ix. HARRIET CURRIER, b. Nov. 28, 1808; m. Sept. 27, 1827, Henry Stockman, son of John and Sarah (Sleeper) Stockman, b. Feb. 3, 1803; d. 19 Mar., 1883.   She d. 16 Mar., 1863, age 54 yrs. 3 mos. 18 days.

x. JOANNA CURRIER, b. Oct. 3, 1811; m. July 28, 1831, Moses Stockman, bro. of Henry, b. Oct. 28, 1807; d. 23 Sept., 1879.   She d. 6 June, 1843, age 31 yrs. 8 mos. 3 days.

xi. HENRY ADAMS CURRIER, b. Apr. 1, 1814; d. 19 Oct., 1832.

Children of HENRY[7], (1774) [475] (Henry[6], Robert[5], Abraham[4], Robert[3], Sergt. Abraham[2], Robert[1]) and Sarah J. (Pearson) Adams; res. Newburyport, Mass.

i. SAMUEL P.[8], b. in Newburyport, Nov. 19, 1799; d. 30 July, 1822.

ii. CLARISSA[8], b. in Newburyport, Feb. 24, 1802; m. Nov. 8, 1821, Wade Ilsley (his 1st wife). She d. 4 Apr., 1825; no surviving issue.

iii. PHILIP[8], b. in Newburyport, Mar. 3, 1804; d. 14 Sept., 1804.

985.   iv. PHILIP[8], b. in Newburyport, July 13, 1805; m. Mary Goodwin; dau. of Samuel and Elizabeth (Knight) Goodwin of Newburyport; she d. in Shelbyville, Ky., 1888, age 80 years.

He set. in Shelbyville, Ky., and d. in Florence, Texas, 1895, age 90 years.

v. EDWARD[8], b. in Newburyport, Nov. 4, 1807; d. 24 May, 1808.

vi. CAROLINE ELIZABETH[8], b. in Newburyport, Aug. 2, 1811.

vii. SARAH[8], b. in Newburyport, Feb. 24, 1814; d. 6 Mar., 1826.

Children of ESTHER⁷, (1779) [476] (Henry⁶, Robert⁵, Abraham⁴, Robert³, Sergt. Abraham², Robert¹) and Moses Goodwin; res. Newbury, Mass.

    i. MOSES GOODWIN, b. June 26, 1798.
    ii. MOSES GOODWIN, b. Dec. 2, 1799; m. Naomi Walker. He d. 20 Aug., 1880; no issue.
    iii. HANNAH WOODWELL GOODWIN, b. June 28, 1801; d. 17 Sept., 1839.
    iv. JOHN GOODWIN, b. Apr. 10, 1803; d. 22 Aug., 1838; unm.
    v. LYDIA GOODWIN, b. Jan. 10, 1805; d. 7 Apr., 1845; unm.
    vi. MARY GOODWIN, b. May 18, 1810; m. John Poor. She d. 7 Apr., 1894.
    vii. A SON, "still born." Feb. 10, 1814.
    viii. SYLVIA GOODWIN, b. Aug. 13, 1819; d. 3 Apr., 1854.

Children of JOSEPH⁷, (1783) [477] (Henry⁶, Robert⁵, Abraham⁴, Robert³, Sergt. Abraham², Robert¹) and Rachel (Boynton) Adams; res. Newbury, Mass.

986.   i. JOEL⁸, b. in Newbury, Oct. 31, 1810; m. July, 1832, Irene Felch; she d. 13 Oct., 1869. He d. Oct., 1872.
987.   ii. OBED⁸, b in Newbury, July 12, 1810; m. [pub. Oct. 27] Nov., 1844, Laura A. Lakeman of Ipswich; she d. 18 June, 1864; res. Ipswich, Mass. He d. 27 Sept., 1848.
    iii. SETH⁸, b. in Newbury, May 5, 1819; d. young.

Child of JOSEPH⁷, (1783) and Nancy E. (Goodwin) Adams.

988.   iv. NANCY JENNIE⁸, b. in Newbury, Feb. 10 1854; m. Aug. 27, 1874, Edward Osgood; res. Newburyport, Mass.

Children of ABRAHAM⁷, (1791) [478] (Henry⁶, Robert⁵, Abraham⁴, Robert³, Sergt. Abraham², Robert¹) and Dolly (Everett) Adams; res. Newbury, Mass.

    i. THURZA⁸, b. in Newbury, July 12, 1819; d. 24 July, 1819.
989.   ii. CHARLES⁸, b. in Newbury, July 24, 1821; m. (1) Mar. 19, 1844, Adelaide Clement; d. 16 Dec., 1849, age 28 yrs. 9 mos. 18 days; m. (2) June 6, 1851, Matilda P. Woodcock; she d. 9 Dec., 1898, age 77 yrs. 8 mos. 9 days. He d. 9 June, 1868.
990.   iii. HARRIET⁸, b. in Newbury, Nov. 30, 1822; m. Apr. 15, 1843, Daniel D. Nealey of Exeter, N. H. She d. 30 Dec., 1857.

iv. ROZELLA[8], b. in Newbury, Sept. 20, 1824; d. 25 Dec., 1824.
v. WASHINGTON[8], b. in Newbury, April 10, 1830; d. unm. 5 Mar., 1862.
vi. MARTHA[8], b. in Newbury, May 6, 1832; m. June 2, 1859, Wm. Poor; no issue; res. Newburyport, Mass.

Children of HANNAH[7], (1800) [**479**] (Henry[6], Robert[5], Abraham[4], Robert[3], Sergt. Abraham[2], Robert[1]), and Ebenezer Plumer; res. Newbury, Mass.

i. SARAH PLUMER, b. Sept., 1832; m. George Adams; she d. 1858; no issue.
ii. EBEN PLUMER (twin), b. Sept., 1832; d. young.

Children of LYDIA S.[7], (1802) [**480**] (Henry[6], Robert[5], Abraham[4], Robert[3], Sergt. Abraham[2], Robert[1]) and Henry Lander; res. Newbury, Mass.

i. HENRY A. LANDER, b. Sept. 23, 1820; m. June 4, 1848, Ann P. Clark. He d. 19 July, 1892.
ii. CHARLES W. LANDER, b. Oct., 1822; d. 1865.
iii. HANNAH W. LANDER, b. Oct. 17, 1824; m. Apr., 1848, Samuel W. Green. She d. June, 1895.
iv. AUGUSTA C. LANDER, b. Feb., 1827; m. John J. Noyes.
v. MARY C. LANDER, b. Nov., 1835; m. Sept. 15, 1864, Andrew J. Haynes.
vi. ELLEN L. LANDER, b. Feb., 1838; m. May, 1863, Geo. W. Williams.

Children of ROBERT MORSE, (1783) [**481**] and Mary Adams; res. Newburyport and Boston, Mass.

i. MARY MORSE, b. in Newburyport, May 26, 1807; d. 17 Feb., 1824.
ii. ROBERT MORSE, b. in Newburyport, May 18, 1809; d. 24 May, 1816.
iii. MOSES MORSE, b. in Newburyport, Oct. 6, 1810; d. 10 June, 1812.
iv. CATHARINE DAVENPORT MORSE, b. in Newburyport, July 27, 1812; m. May 24, 1837, Anthony Hanson of Dover, N. H.
v. MOSES MORSE, b. in Newburyport, Mar. 2, 1815; d. 20 June, 1821.
vi. ROBERT MORSE, b. in Newburyport, Dec. 13, 1816; m. (1) Nov. 18, 1846; Abby C. Dore; m. (2) Minerva E. Bartlett. He d. 13 Apr., 1870.

Eighth Generation.] OF NEWBURY, MASS. 237

vii. CHAS. ANTHONY MORSS, b. in Boston, Oct. 15, 1822; m. Sept. 30, 1836, Mary Elizabeth Wells, dau. of John and Hannah (Wells) Wells, b. Feb. 11, 1831; res. Boston, Mass. Children:
1. Charles Anthony, Jr., b. July 13, 1857; m. Martha Houghton Reed.
2. Robert, b. Nov. 16, 1860; d. 16 Feb., 1863.
3. John Wells, b. Dec. 15, 1862.
4. Everett, b. Mar. 6, 1865; m. Ethel Carlton Reed.
5. Henry Adams, b. Aug. 30, 1871.

Children of LOVE⁷, (1777) [482] (Daniel⁶, Robert⁵, Abraham⁴, Robert³, Sergt. Abraham², Robert¹) and Stephen Pettengill; res. Newbury, Mass.

991.   i. HENRY PETTENGILL, b. Dec. 2, 1801; m. Apr., 1825, Abigail Palmer Dole, dau. of Ralph and Martha Friend (Palmer) Dole of Rowley (Georgetown), b. Mar. 19, 1805; d. 31 Dec., 1873, age 68 yrs. 9 mos. 12 days; res. Georgetown, Mass. He d. 6 Jan., 1894, age 93 yrs. 1 mo. 4 days.

   ii. STEPHEN PETTENGILL, b. Sept. 13, 1803.
       He was a sailor's mate, and d. at Savannah, Ga., of yellow fever in 1825, age 22 years.

992. iii. ELIZABETH COLLY PETTINGILL, b. Oct. 1, 1812; m. Apr. 29, 1838, Daniel Knight Hale, son of Ezra and Anna (Adams) Hale, b. Sept. 9, 1808, d. 6 Oct., 1870; res. Newbury, Mass. She d. 3 Apr., 1896.

Child of COL. DANIEL⁷, (1787) [483] (Daniel⁶, Robert⁵, Abraham⁴, Robert³, Sergt. Abraham,² Robert¹) and Polly (Adams) Adams; res. Rowley, Mass.

   i. DEBORAH⁸, b. in Rowley, Aug. 20, 1814; m. Aug. 11, 1841, Rev. John Pike, D. D., son of Capt. Richard and Mary (Boardman) Pike, b. in Newburyport, July 3, 1813; d. in Rowley, 20 Sept., 1899. He was graduated from Bowdoin in 1833, and from Andover Theological Seminary in 1837; preached in N. Falmouth, Mass., till 1840, then was the esteemed pastor in Rowley for 28 years. Becoming blind in later life, he yet continued his pulpit work, preaching nearly every Sunday, with the assistance of his gifted wife, to the inmates of the House of Correction at Ipswich, until his wife's demise at their home in Rowley, 30 Dec., 1893; no issue.

Child of MARY⁷, (1795) [484] (Daniel⁶, Robert⁵, Abraham⁴, Robert³, Sergt. Abraham², Robert¹) and Gilman Sargent; res. Portland, Me.

    i. RUFUS SARGENT.
        Removed to the west and lost track of.

Children of JOSEPH⁷, (1799) [485] (Daniel⁶, Robert⁵, Abraham⁴, Robert³, Sergt. Abraham², Robert¹) and Harriet (Adams) Adams; res. Newbury, Mass.

    i. DANIEL PALMER⁸, b. in Newbury, Apr. 27, 1823; m. June 26‘ 1851, Caroline Elizabeth Ackley of New York; 1 child, Harriet, died age 1 year. He d. 23 Dec., 1854.

993.   ii. JANE N⁸., b. in Newbury, Mar. 15, 1828; m. Feb. 1, 1849, Ezekiel R. Todd; he d. 1867. She d. 17 Feb., 1868; res. Rowley, Mass.

    iii. MARY L.⁸, b. in Newbury, Dec., 1831; d. 14 Mar., 1853.

994.   iv. CALEB CUSHING⁸, b. in Newbury, Mar. 23, 1833; m. Nov. 27, 1857, Sarah F. Jewett.
        He was a jeweler, and settled in Brooklyn, N. Y., in 1852, where he d. suddenly 13 Dec., 1893, much lamented.

995.   v. JOSEPH WEBSTER⁸, b. in Newbury, Sept. 3, 1835; m. Nov. 26, 1857, Mary P. Cook, dau. of Mr. Charles Cook; res. Newbury, Mass. *d. Aug 3. 1924.*

996.   vi. HON. JOHN POPKIN⁸, b. in Newbury, Apr. 21, 1837; m. Oct. 22, 1878, Grace Chapman, dau. of James Holmes and Jane Forrister (Hamilton) Chapman of Kent, Eng., b. in New York City, Dec. 4, 1848.
        He settled in Brooklyn, N. Y., in 1865, and became Commissioner of Public Works. He was educated at Dummer Academy; studied law with Hon. Caleb Cushing in Newburyport, and was admitted to the bar in that city. He was president of the Y. M. Christian Association of Brooklyn for two years, and was a prominent man. He d. suddenly 2 July, 1895, age 56 years.

Child of HANNAH LORD⁷, (1807) [486] (Daniel⁶, Robert⁵, Abraham⁴, Robert³, Sergt. Abraham², Robert¹) and George J. Poor; res. Rowley, Mass.

    i. FRANCIS POOR, b, Apr., 1835; d. 26 Apr., 1872.

Children of ISAAC⁷, (1788–9) [487] (Caleb⁶, Benjamin⁵, Abraham⁴, Robert³, Sergt. Abraham², Robert¹) and Mary (Stowell) Adams; res. Boston, Mass.

i. SUSAN⁸; d. young.
ii. SUSAN⁸; d. young.
iii. JOHN STOWELL⁸, b. probably in Boston; m. Harriet ———; he made his will Mar. 4, 1882; it was proved June 29, 1898.

>He names his wife "Harriet" and her heirs, and if she dies before him, his friend Geo. L. Stafford of Boston is to be his executor.

Children of SUSAN⁷, (1791) [**488**] (Caleb⁶, Benjamin⁵, Abraham⁴, Robert³, Sergt. Abraham², Robert¹) and Benjamin Longley; res. Boston, Mass.

>There are said to have been 12 children, three of whom were living in 1899; one of these, Mrs. Arthur Warren, 134 Greenway Ave., Roxbury, Mass., does not answer inquiries. Another, Mrs. Mary M. Eaton, 16 Pleasant St., Cambridgeport, Mass., says in letter of Nov. 20, 1899, "I can tell you very little. My father d. Mar. 23, 1832; I was b. Oct. 3, 1820; m. 1844, to Daniel Hobbs; he d. Dec., 1865; I m. 1874, Jacob Eaton; he d. July 17, 1894."

Children of AARON⁷, (1793) [**489**] (Isaac⁶, Benjamin⁵, Abraham⁴, Robert³, Sergt. Abraham², Robert¹) and Hannah (Prince) Adams; res. Newburyport, and Boston, Mass.

997. i. MARY AUGUSTA⁸, b. in Newburyport, May 12, 1815; m. John Henry Dennis, son of Henry and Catherine (Wales) Dennis, b. in Baltimore, Md., May 24, 1813; d. 27 June, 1869. He was a house painter, and only bro. of Capt. Geo. W. Dennis; came to Newburyport on a sailing vessel, and found there, unexpectedly, his brother. She d. 1896.

ii. ANNA BOARDMAN⁸, b. in Boston, Mass., May 30, 1817; m. William H. Worden. She is a widow in the Old Ladies' Home, 1898; no issue.

998. iii. ELIZA THERESA⁸, b. in Boston, July 6, 1819; m. Jan. 23, 1842, George Washington Somerby, a sea captain; he d. in Boston. 27 Feb., 1845.

999. iv. MARTHA AGNES⁸, b. in Boston, Oct. 5, 1821; m. June 7, 1846, Samuel Merrill, son of John and Margaret Merrill, b. in Hillsboro, N. H., Dec. 25, 1824; d. in Boston, 22 Mar., 1851.

Children of SARAH WELCH⁷, (1800) [**490**] (Isaac⁶, Benjamin⁵, Abraham⁴, Robert³, Sergt. Abraham², Robert¹) and William P. Codman; res. Boston, Mass.

i. SARAH ANN CODMAN, b. in Boston, Aug. 10, 1823; m. Jan. 12, 1842, Geo. B. Nightingale of Quincy, Mass.; he d. 4 Dec., 1857.
ii. CAROLINE H. CODMAN, b. in Boston, 1825 ; d. 1831.
iii. WILLIAM LYMAN CODMAN, b. in Boston, 1827 ; d. 1829.
iv. CHARLES ALFRED CODMAN (twin), b. in Boston, 1827 ; m. 1851, C. A. Jennings of Chelsea, Mass.
v. MARY ELIZABETH CODMAN, b. in Boston, 1830 ; d. 1831.
vi. MARY MELVINA CODMAN, b. in Boston, 1834 ; m. Nov. 23, 1859, Nathan Cheney of Athol, Mass; he d. 23 Nov., 1871; res. Cambridge, Mass., 1894.

Children of CAROLINE KEZIA[7], (1804) [**491**] (Isaac[6], Benjamin[5], Abraham[4], Robert[3], Sergt. Abraham[2], Robert[1]) and Thomas Blake Hall; res. Quincy, Mass.

i. EDWIN BLAKE HALL, b. in Quincy, Apr., 1832 ; m. 1852, Caroline Kent.
He was an engineer for many years at Bloomington, Ill.
ii. CAROLINE MASON HALL, b. in Quincy, 1835; m. Benjamin Taylor of Orleans, Mass. She d. in Charlestown, Mass., in 1891.

Children of BENJAMIN[7], (1807) [**492**] (Isaac[6], Benjamin[5], Abraham[4], Robert[3], Sergt. Abraham[2] Robert[1]) and Ann Belcher (Leonard) Adams; res. Boston, Mass.

1000. i. BENJAMIN[8], b. in Boston, Oct. 30, 1830 ; m. (1) Sept. 1, 1850, Ann Stone Walker of Upton, Mass.; she d. 19 July, 1869 ; m. (2) Apr. 1, 1872, Eliza Johnson Gay of Stoughton, Mass., widow of Geo. H. Shepard, b. Mar. 12, 1845.
He is agent of Adams' Express Co., at Milford, Mass.
ii. MELVIN[8], b. in Boston, 1832 ; d. 1853; unm.]
1001. iii. WEBSTER[8], b. in Boston, May, 1834 ; m. Emily Blanchard. He d. in Chelsea, Mass., 13 Nov., 1871.
iv. HORACE[8], b. in Boston, 1836; m. Delia Page. He d. in Chelsea, Mass., 20 Aug., 1860; no issue.
v. ALBERT[8], b. in Boston, 1838 ; d. 1842.
vi. HOWARD[8] (twin), b. in Boston, 1838 ; d. 28 Feb., 1842; buried in same grave as Albert.
vii. ALBERT HOWARD[8], b. in Boston, Oct., 1842 ; m. Clara Dobson [Gray?] ; divorced. He is a book-binder ; no issue.

JOHN McKELVEY AND WIFE, JANE ROWLAND HUNTINGTON, AND THEIR YOUNGEST SON, RALPH HUNTINGTON.

Eighth Generation.] OF NEWBURY, MASS. 241

Children of ABRAHAM DODDRIDGE⁷, (1810) [493] (Isaac⁶, Benjamin⁵, Abraham⁴, Robert³, Sergt. Abraham², Robert¹) and Mary Jane (Thurston) Adams; res. Townsend Harbor, Mass.

1002. i. FRANCIS DODDRIDGE⁸, b. in Quincy, Mass., Oct. 1835; m. (1) 1857, Mary Jane Arnold of Charlestown, Mass., dau. of Asia Arnold of Charlestown; m. (2) Dec. 1, 1875, Sarah Elizabeth Davis, dau. of John S. and Charlotte (Caldwell) Davis, b. in Barnardston, Mass., June 15, 1840; d. 9 Feb., 1889.

        He was a cooper; enlisted and served three years in the army; was a prisoner at Libby, Salisbury and Bell Island; he d. in Townsend, Mass., 23 Mar., 1884.

1003. ii. WILLIAM RUSSELL⁸, b. in Boston, May 10, 1838; m. Dec. 23, 1868, Lavinia J. Phillips, dau. of Joshua B. and Mary Jane (Goodwin) Phillips, b. in Lynn, Mass., Oct. 10, 1847.

        He was a sole-leather cutter in Haverhill, Mass.; enlisted at San Francisco, Cal., 1862, in the 3rd Veteran Infantry; served on the Plains for four years, was wounded twice, and was discharged at Salt Lake in 1866.

  iii. ISAAC⁸, b. in Charlestown, Mass., 1840; d. 1843.

Children of AARON BRAY⁷, (1796) [494] (Smith⁶, Charles⁵, Abraham⁴, Robert³, Sergt. Abraham², Robert¹) and Mary M. Dutton (Cheever) Adams; res. Newburyport, Mass.

  i. AARON BRAY⁸, JR., b. in Newburyport, June 27, 1842; m. Sept. 22, 1887, Sarah Carrie Nelson, dau. of John B. Nelson; res. Newburyport, Mass. *d. July 17, 1943 aged 92 yrs. 1.*
  ii. GEORGE PETTINGILL⁸, b. in Newburyport, Apr. 5, 1845; m. Nov. 8, 1883, Georgia A. Bailey. He rem. west.

Children of HANNAH⁷, (1798) [495] (Smith⁶, Charles⁵, Abraham⁴, Robert³, Sergt. Abraham², Robert¹) and Capt. Seward Lee; res. Newburyport, Mass.

  i. MARY ANN LEE, b. Feb. 7, 1833; m. Jan. 15, 1854, Joseph Haslam of Salem, Mass.; he d. at Salem, 13 Feb., 1870, age 39 years. She d. 26 June, 1867.
  ii. GEORGE SMITH LEE, b. Apr. 31, 1835; d. 22 Jan., 1841.
  iii. ELIZABETH A. LEE, b. Sept. 13, 1841; d. 15 Feb., 1842.
  iv. HANNAH ELLEN LEE, b. Oct. 8, 1844; m. Nov. 25, 1866, George E. Peterson. She d. Aug., 1893.

(16)

Children of MARY H.[7], (1800) [**496**] (Smith[6], Charles[5], Abraham[4], Robert[3], Sergt. Abraham[2], Robert[1]) and William Coker; res. Newburyport, Mass.

    i. HARRIET PEARSON COKER, b. Jan. 26, 1837; m. July 4, 1870, Micajah B. Mansfield, of Salem, Mass., son of William Mansfield and Sarah B. Dailey; he d. 28 Dec., 1871, age 35 yrs. 5 mos.

    ii. EDWARD C. COKER, b. Oct. 7, 1838; m. Apr. 10, 1868, Mary A. F. Ellis.

Children of WILLIAM BRAY[7], (1803) [**497**] (Smith[6], Charles[5], Abraham[4], Robert[3], Sergt. Abraham[2], Robert[1]) and Ann Atkinson (Stanwood) Adams; res. Newburyport, Mass.

    i. WILLIAM HENRY[8], b. in Newburyport, Nov. 1, 1827. He was a line-maker, and d. unm. 19 May, 1875.

    ii. MARTHA ANN[8], b. in Newburyport, Aug. 7, 1829; m. Sept. 4, 1851, James E. Kimball, son of Edward and Emiline (Huse) Kimball, b. Aug. 28, 1828; res. Newburyport, Mass.

    iii. ELIZABETH STANNARD[8], b. in Newburyport, July 13, 1833; d. 13 Mar., 1856; unm.

Children of CHARLES[7], (1805) [**498**] (Smith[6], Charles[5], Abraham[4], Robert[3], Sergt. Abraham[2], Robert[1]) and Sarah (Noyes) Adams; res. Newburyport, Mass.

1004   i. SMITH[8], b. in Newburyport, Apr. 22, 1828; m. (1) Oct. 16, 1848, Mary Sanders Stevens, dau. of Capt. Moses and Phimelia (Sanders) Stevens of Bangor, Me., b. Mar. 23, 1829; m. (2) Sept. 6, 1864, Ellen Jane Wilson of Milltown, Me., dau. of James and Catherine Wilson, b. Mar. 11, 1836.
He is a clock-maker; set. in Milltown, Oct., 1866. He collated and published the records of his family and others.

    ii. HANNAH SAVORY[8], b. in Newburyport, May 25, 1830; burned Jan. 24, 1833, and d. 3 Mar., 1833.

1005   iii. SARAH ELIZABETH[8], b. in Newburyport, Feb. 16, 1832; m. Nov. 7, 1853, Thomas Jefferson Spinney of Portsmouth, N. H., son of Samuel and Sybil (Bunker) Spinney of York, Me., b. Jan. 30, 1830; d. 6 Mar., 1878. She d. 4 June, 1860, leaving an infant child.

    iv. CHARLES AARON[8], b. in Newburyport, May 3, 1834; d. unm.

    v. HARRIET DUTTON[8], b. in Newburyport, Nov. 6, 1836; d. 27 Apr., 1862; unm.

[Eighth Generation.] OF NEWBURY, MASS.

  vi. ESTHER LEE[8], b. in Newburyport, Jan. 10, 1841 ; m. Sept. 6, 1866, William R. D. Mansfield, son of Wm. and Sarah B. (Dailey) Mansfield of Salem, Mass., b. July 1, 1822; d. 18 Nov., 1890 ; res. Salem, Mass.; no issue.

1006. vii. MARY SWETT[8], b. in Newburyport, Apr., 29, 1843 ; m. Feb. 27, 1868, Joseph Haslam, steam-boiler maker from Manchester, Eng., b. Feb. 9, 1831 ; d. 13 Feb., 1870 ; res. Newburyport, Mass.

  viii. DANIEL WEBSTER[8], b. in Newburyport, May 27, 1845 ; m. Mar. 16, 1869, Miriam W. Spinney, dau. of Joseph and Lydia (Warner) Spinney of Portsmouth, N. H., b. Mar. 21, 1846 ; res. Portsmouth, N. H.; no issue.

1007. ix. AMOS HENRY[8], b. in Newburyport, Sept. 19, 1849 ; m. Sept. 25, 1870, Cynthia C. Dunn, dau. of Edward and Eliza M. (Blaisdell) Dunn of Franklin, Me., b. June 26, 1850.
    He was a book-keeper and salesman; res. Newburyport, Mass. He d. 28 June, 1896, age 46 yrs. 9 mos.

Children of ALMIRA[7], (1808) [**499**] (Smith[6], Charles[5], Abraham[4], Robert[3], Sergt. Abraham[2], Robert[1]) and Capt. Eleazer P. Short; res. Newburyport, Mass.

  i. WILLIAM WHEELER SHORT, b. Sept. 20, 1839; d. 21 Jan., 1840.
  ii. ANN WHEELER SHORT, b. Feb. 12, 1841; m. May 8, 1862, Ira F. Harriman.
  iii. ELEAZER M. SHORT, b. Mar. 12, 1844.
  iv. HARRIET P. SHORT, b. Sept. 12, 1846.
  v. JAMES K. SHORT, b. Feb. 7, 1850 ; m. June 2, 1880, Florence L. Bricket, and d. in Haverhill, Mass., 9 Oct., 1885.
  vi. SAMUEL P. SHORT, b. Nov. 1, 1852 ; d. 15 Sept., 1853.

Children of SMITH[7], (1811) [**500**] (Smith[6], Charles[5], Abraham[4], Robert[3], Sergt. Abraham[2], Robert[1]) and Elizabeth Jane (Hoague) Adams; res. Newburyport, Mass.

  i. ELIZABETH SMITH[8], b. in Newburyport, July 15, 1840 ; d. 29 Aug., 1840.
  ii. A SON, who d. at birth.

Child of MARY[7], (1810) [**501**] (Robert[6], Liphe[5], Robert[4], Robert[3], Sergt. Abraham[2], Robert[1]) and Gideon R. Lucy; res. Newburyport, Mass.

  i. GEORGE LUCY, b. Jan. 9, 1834 ; m. (1) Mar. 23, 1858, Eliza A. Hill; m. (2) Dec. 15, 1881, Mrs. Elvira Hodgdon; res. Newburyport, Mass.

Children of MOSES⁷, (1805) [502] (James⁶, Moses⁵, John⁴, Robert³, Sergt. Abraham², Robert¹) and Susan (Noyes) Adams; res. Falmouth, and Portland, Me.

  i. EUNICE⁸, b. in Falmouth, Me., July 25, 1827 ; d. in Portland, Me., 6 Sept., 1841, age 1⅓ yrs. 2 mos.
1008. ii. HANNAH WEYMOUTH⁸, b. in Falmouth, Oct. 2, 1828; m. Aug. 11, 1853, at Portland, John H. Riggs, son of John L. and Catherine S. Riggs, b. in Portland, June 10, 1826 ; d. 1865. She d. in Portland.
1009. iii. JAMES A.⁸, b. in Falmouth, July 1, 1831 ; m. Apr. 19, 1859, at Portland, Clarissa Ann Robinson, dau. of James and Susan (Barbour) Robinson, b. in Lewiston, Me., Nov. 8, 1833 ; res. Woodford's, 43 High St., Portland, Me. He d. 10 Aug., 1891.
  iv. RUTH⁸, b. in Falmouth ; d. in infancy.

Children of MOSES⁷ (1805) and Hannah (Titcomb) Adams.

1010. v. SUSAN NOYES⁸, b. in Falmouth, Apr. 7, 1837 ; m. Sept. 9, 1855, at Portland, Francis A. DeBremon. She d. in New York State.
1011. vi. CHARLES HENRY⁸, b. in Portland, Me., Jan. 29, 1839 ; m. Aug. 1, 1865, at Portland, Helen Pierce Skillings, dau. of Noyes and Diana (Berry) Skillings, b. in Boston, Mass., April 17, 1838 ; res. Portland, Me.

Children of MARY⁷, ( ) [503] (James⁶, Moses⁵, John⁴, Robert³, Sergt. Abraham², Robert¹) and Cotton Murray; res. Cumberland, Cumberland Co., Me.

  i. ANGELINE MURRAY, d. in Cumberland, unm., 21 Aug., 1899.
  ii. MARY JANE MURRAY, m. —— Russell, a soldier who died in the Civil War. She d. in Cumberland, Me.; no issue.

Children of HARRIET A.⁷, ( ) [504] (James⁶, Moses⁵, John⁴, Robert³, Sergt. Abraham², Robert¹) and Abel Grover; res. Portland, Cumberland Co., Me.

  i. INFANT, b. Apr. 2, 1833 ; d. in infancy.
  ii. SAMUEL A. GROVER, b. May 17, 1834 ; d. in Portland, 17 Sept., 1841.
  iii. LEMUEL O. GROVER, b. Oct. 27, 1836 ; d. in Portland, 14 Sept., 1837.
  iv. LEMUEL O. GROVER, b. Oct. 24, 1838 ; d. in Portland, 28 Oct., 1838.

Eighth Generation.] OF NEWBURY, MASS. 245

 v. INFANT, b. July 9, 1842; d. in Portland, 18 Sept., 1842.
 vi. GEORGIANA T. GROVER, b. Dec. 9, 1843 ; d. in Gorham, Me., about 1863.

Children of JOHN⁷, (1794) [505] (Israel⁶, Moses⁵, John⁴, Robert³, Sergt. Abraham², Robert¹) and Mary (Noyes) Adams; res. Falmouth, Cumberland Co., Me.

1012. i. BENJAMIN BRADLEY⁸, b. in Freeport, Me., Mar. 1, 1831 ; m. July 3, 1856, in Henry Co., Ill., Elizabeth Ann Welch, dau. of Nehemiah and Dolly Welch, b. in Groton, Vt., May 25, 1840 ; d. at Minonk, 20 Aug., 1864 ; res. Minonk, Woodford Co., Ill., and Kearney, Neb.
 ii. SARAH LOUISA⁸, b. in Freeport, Dec. 11, 1833 ; m. [pub. in Portland, May 30, 1854] Alvin A. Pride of Windham, Me.; he is deceased ; res. La Rose, Marshall Co., Ill.
 iii. JOHN QUINCY⁸, b. in Freeport, Jan. 27, 1835, res. La Rose, Ill.; unm.

Children of JOHN⁷, (1794) and Catherine B. (Pratt) Adams.

 iv. ELIZABETH ELLEN⁸, b. in Falmouth, Feb. 10, 1839; d. in Elmira, Ill. 7 Oct., 1861.
 v. HANNAH ROSINA⁸, b. in Falmouth, Aug. 24, 1840; m. Dec. 15, 1862, George Moses Adams, son of Silas Merrill and Olive E. (Moulton) Adams; res. (Deering dist.), Portland, Me.
1013. vi. DANIEL SEWALL⁸, b. in Falmouth, Mar. 11, 1842 ; m. Oct. 3, 1865, at Minonk, Ill., Martha Brittan Welch, dau. of Nehemiah and Dolly Welch, b. in Groton, Vt., June 10, 1844 ; res. Cornwallis, Benton Co., Ore., since Feb., 1894.
 vii. ASA PRATT⁸, b. in Falmouth, June 13, 1844 ; m. Jan. 27, 1871, at Osceola, Ill, Mary Perkins ; no issue ; res. Osceola, Stark Co., Ill.
 viii. MARY NOYES⁸, b. in Falmouth, May 19, 1847; m. (1) June 14, 1870, Webster Hudson of Elmira, Ill.; m. (2) about 1891, Ambrose Fuller ; res. Elmira, Stark Co., Ill.; no issue.
 ix. ADELAIDE⁸, b. in Falmouth, Aug. 23, 1849 ; d. 15 Jan.,'1850.
1014. x. HATTIE EUNICE⁸, b. in Falmouth, Aug. 2, 1851 ; m. Jan 1, 1879, at Elmira, Ill., Howard Early ; res. Kewanee, Henry Co., Ill.

Children of HANNAH SWETT⁷, (1799) [506] (Israel⁶, Moses⁵, John⁴, Robert³, Sergt. Abraham², Robert¹) and Tristam Gilman Prince ; res. Portland, Me.

246   ROBERT ADAMS   [Eighth Generation.

1015. i. JULIA B. PRINCE, b. June 9, 1821 ; m. Dec. 10, 1840, at Portland, Harrison G. Cole of Bangor, Me.
   ii. SARAH E. PRINCE, b. Dec. 16, 1823 ; d. in Portland, 22 June, 1826.
   iii. LOUISA S. PRINCE, b. Apr. 11, 1825 ; d. in Portland, 6 July, 1826.
   iv. IRENE C. L. PRINCE, b. Nov. 2, 1826 ; m. Jan. 23, 1853, George H. Bailey, son of Henry and Louisa (Davis) Bailey. She d. 3 Dec., 1854.
   v. CHARLES G. PRINCE, b. June 3, 1830; d. in Portland, 20 Aug., 1831.
   vi. MARTHA W. PRINCE, b. July 17, 1832; d. in Portland, 20 May, 1834.
1016. vii. HENRY G. PRINCE, b. May 27, 1835 ; m. Jan. 2, 1868, Sarah G. Frazier ; res. Oakland, Cal.
1017. viii. ELLEN R. PRINCE, b. June 12, 1837 ; m. May 3, 1865, Chas. L. Bugbee of San Francisco, Cal.; he d. 3 Jan., 1880. She d. in Oakland, Cal., 28 Feb., 1880.
1018. ix. EDWARD B. PRINCE, b. May 27, 1841 ; m. Aug. 22, 1864, Florence A. Knight, dau. of Thomas E. and Dorcas (Bradford) Knight of Cape Elizabeth, Me.

Children of LOUISA SEWALL[7], (1807) [507] (Israel[6], Moses[5], John[4], Robert[3], Sergt. Abraham[2], Robert[1]) and Daniel Carr; res. Portland, Cumberland Co., Me.
   i. DANIEL B. CARR, b. July 24, 1839 ; d. 31 July, 1839.
   ii. LOUISA B. CARR, b. Sept. 19, 1841 ; d. young.
   iii. ANNAH GILMAN CARR, b. May 26, 1843; d. young.

Children of MARY SUSAN[7], (1828) [508] (Isaac[6], Moses[5], John[4], Robert[3], Sergt. Abraham[2], Robert[1]) and Robert Noyes; res. Falmouth, Me.
   i. INFANT.
   ii. CHARLES D. NOYES.
   iii. WHITING ALONZO NOYES.
   iv. MARY ANNA NOYES, living (Roxbury), Boston ; unm.

Children of DOROTHY MERRILL[7], (1817) [509] (Isaac[6], Moses[5], John[4], Robert[3], Sergt. Abraham[2], Robert[1]) and Sewall B. Dunham; res. Falmouth, Cumberland Co., Me.
   i. JOSEPH F. DUNHAM, b. Jan., 1842 ; d. 16 Feb., 1843, age 13 mos.
   ii. ISAAC D. DUNHAM, b. Oct., 1844 ; m. Georgiana Morris Libby; she m. 2d Chas. H. Dunham, cousin of Isaac D. He d. 26 July, 1881, leaving several children.

Children of BENJAMIN WHITING[7], (1824) [**510**] (Isaac[6], Moses[5], John[4], Robert[3], Sergt. Abraham[2], Robert[1]) and Sarah Barton (Colley) Adams; res. Cumberland Junc., Cumberland Co., Me.

   i. JULIETTA[8], b. in Falmouth, Me., Nov. 21, 1851 ; living in Cumberland, Me., unm. 1900.

1019. ii. GEORGE WILLIAM[8], b. in Falmouth, Aug. 25, 1853 ; m. Aug. 15, 1874, at Cumberland, Eudora Hannah Barton, dau. of Capt. Winthrop and Mary H. (Newcomb) Barton of Saccarappa, Me., b. Feb. 4, 1856 ; res. Cumberland, Me.

   iii. ELLA FLORENCE[8], b. in Falmouth, Apr. 5, 1856; res. Cumberland, Me.; unm.

   iv. ERIXENE CHASE[8], b. in Falmouth, Feb. 22, 1858 ; m. June 30, 1892, at Dover, N. H., Anson F. Tilton, a printer ; res. Northwood Ridge, N. H.; no issue.

   v. ANGELINA KIMBALL[8], b. in Falmouth, July 4, 1861 ; res. (Deering dist.), Portland, Me., 1900 ; unm.

   vi. FRANCES ELLEN[8], b. in Yarmouth, Me., May 4, 1863; d. in Yarmouth, 24 Nov., 1866.

   vii. CHARLES EDWARD[8], b. in Cumberland, Me., Dec. 5, 1870; m. Aug., 1996, at Berwick, Me., Hattie Johnson, dau. of William and ——— (Hurd) Johnson of Springvale, Me.; no issue.

   viii. HENRY GILBERT[8], b. in Cumberland, Jan. 8, 1873. He is a railroad station agent, Cumberland ; unm.

Child of SILAS MERRILL[7], (1809) [**511**] (Moses[6], Jr., Moses[5], John[4], Robert[3], Sergt. Abraham[2], Robert[1]) and Olive Elizabeth (Moulton) Adams; res. Deering, Cumberland Co., Me.

1020. i. GEORGE MOSES[8], b. in Portland, Me., Sept. 29, 1834 ; m. at Elmira, Ill., Dec. 15, 1862, Hannah Rosina Adams, dau. of John and Charlotte B. (Pratt) Adams, b. in Falmouth, Me., Aug. 24, 1840.

   He was a farmer ; d. 10 Aug., 1892 ; res. (Deering), Portland, Me.

Children of MOSES WOODMAN[7], (1811) [**512**] (Moses[6], Jr., Moses[5], John[4], Robert[3], Sergt. Abraham[2], Robert[1]) and Frances Emeline (Cutter) Adams; res. Portland, Cumberland Co., Me.

   i. [WM.?] FRANCIS CUTTER[8], b. in Portland, Me., Nov. 7, 1836 ; He was a member of Co. L, 14th Illinois Cavalry Regt.; was a prisoner in five southern prisons ; present res. Chicago, Ill.; unm.

ii. SARAH MARIA[8], b. in Portland, June 18, 1838; m. at Munson, Ill., Aug. 24, 1862, Asa Smith, who was a soldier in Co. A, 124th Illinois Volunteers, and d. on Dauphin Island, Mobile Bay, in one of the last battles of the war; no issue. She is a widow in Stuart, Neb.

iii. MOSES ANDREW[8], b. in Portland, Sept. 16, 1840; res. Chicago, Ill.; unm.

1021. iv. ELLA ELETHEA[8], b. in Portland, Apr. 19, 1842; m. (1) Sept. 10, 186-, Lorenzo Warren Eldridge of Atkinson, Ill., formerly of Chatauqua, N. Y.; he d. in Chicago, 16 Aug., 1870; m. (2) Albert Henry Simonton (divorced Sept., 1882); res. Chicago, Ill.

v. EDWARD SILAS[8], b. in Portland, June 18, 1844; m. but had no issue; he d. in Seattle, Wash., 19 May, 1898.

1022. vi. MARY FRANCES[8], b. in Portland, Oct. 1, 1846; m. Apr. 5, 1869, Henry Boyce of Salem, Mass.

vii. CHARLOTTE LOUISA[8], b. in Munson, Ill., m. Sept. 1, 1897, Joseph A. Miller of Stuart, Neb.

Children of MARTHA PREBLE[7], (1815) [513] (Moses[6], Jr., Moses[5], John[4], Robert[3], Sergt. Abraham[2], Robert[1]) and Samuel Fabyan Haggett, Jr.; res. Portland, Cumberland Co., Me.

i. MARY ELIZABETH HAGGETT, b. Nov. 2, 1844; d. in Portland, 8 May, 1877; unm.

ii. SAMUEL FABYAN HAGGETT, b. Sept. 9, 1846; d. in Portland, 9 Oct., 1883; unm.

1023. iii. FRANCES ALLEN HAGGETT, b. May 25, 1849; m. at Portland, June 19, 1873, Charles P. Waldron, son of Americus P. and Ann Maria (Mason) Waldron, b. in Portland, Mar. 3, 1845, a ticket agent; res. Portland, Me.

Children of MARY ANN D.[7], (1818) [514] (Moses[6], Jr., Moses[5], John[4], Robert[3], Sergt. Abraham[2], Robert[1]) and Capt. William W. Parker; res. Portland, Me.

1024. i. SARAH FRANCES PARKER, b. Apr. 14, 1839; m. Dec. 5, 1858, Samuel K. Worthen; res. Bristol, N. H.

ii. WILLIAM SILAS PARKER, b. Feb. 3, 1841; d. 2 Apr., 1850.

iii. MOSES ADAMS PARKER, b. Oct. 12, 1845; m. July 2, 1878, Mate N. Wilbur of Skowhegan, Me.; no issue; res. Skowhegan, Me.

iv. ELLEN AUGUSTA PARKER, b. July 31, 1848; d. 15 Dec., 1849.

v. ANNIE MARIA PARKER, b. Feb. 23, 1851; m. Mar. 2, 1870, Geo. P. Hayden of Charlestown, Mass.; had one daughter. She d. 26 Aug., 1871.

vi. SILAS WILLIAM PARKER, b. Oct. 4, 1852; m. (1) 1873, Sarah H. Steele of Paducah, Ky.; she d. 9 Nov., 1874; m. (2) Dec. 25, 1885, Nellie M. Prescott of Haverhill, Mass.; she d. 22 Dec., 1893.

1025. vii. DR. FRANK HOWARD PARKER, b. July 3, 1855; m. Jan. 15, 1885, Marion E. King of E. Boston.
He graduated 1891 from College of Physicians and Surgeons; has been a resident of Malden, Mass., since 1885.

Children of BENJAMIN[7], (1793) [515] (Joshua[6], Benjamin[5], John[4], Robert[3], Sergt. Abraham[2], Robert[1]) and Margaret (Clark) Adams; res. Wales, Androscoggin Co., Me.

    i. JANE[8], b. in Wales, Nov. 15, 1814; m. —— Collamore.
   ii. JOSHUA[8]. b. in Wales; m. —— Higgins.
  iii. BENJAMIN[8], b. in Wales.
   iv. CHARLES[8], b. in Wales.
    v. JOHN[8], b. in Wales.

Children of AARON[7], (1795) [516] (Joshua[6], Benjamin[5], John[4], Robert[3], Sergt. Abraham[2], Robert[1]) and Hannah (Phillips) Adams; res. Monmouth, Kennebec Co., Me.

    i. ELIZA[8], b. in Wales, Me., Sept. 21, 1825; d. unm. in Monmouth, 16 Aug., 1848,

1026. ii. WILLIAM P.[8] b. in Wales, Mar. 24, 1827; m. Dec. 28, 1852, Sarah E. T. Thompson of Wolfboro, N. H.; res. Wolfboro, N. H. He d. 13 Jan., 1900.

  iii. HANNAH P.[8], b. in Wales, June 22, 1830; d. 25 Sept., 1830.

Children of AARON[7], (1795) and Eliza (Jove) Adams.

   iv. HANNAH P.[8], b. in Wales, Nov. 5, 1832; d. unm. 27 Nov., 1881.
    v. MARY A.[8], b. in Wales, Aug 30, 1834; m. Dec. 10, 1868, Rufus A. Brainerd; he d. 3 Oct., 1895; res. Hallowell, Me.; no issue.

1027. vi. GEORGE N.[8], b. in Wales, Apr. 17, 1836; m. Feb. 14, 1864, Elizabeth B. Foss of Biddeford, Me. He settled in Wheeling, Me., in 1868, and d. there 17 Nov., 1888.

1028. vii. SARAH A.[8], b. in Wales, Mar. 31, 1838; m. Mar. 6, 1867, Geo. W. Fogg, son of Geo. W. and Hannah (Blue) Fogg of Monmouth, Me , b. Mar. 27, 1831.

 viii. ELVIRA F.[8], b. in Wales, Oct. 17, 1841; res. Hallowell, Me.; unm.

Children of CHARLES M.[7], (1796) [517] (Joshua[6], Benjamin[5], John[4], Robert[3], Sergt. Abraham[2], Robert[1]) and Hannah (McDonald) Adams; res. Dixmont, Penobscot Co., Me.

1029. i. CHARLES HENRY[8], b. probably in Dixmont, May 4, 1822; m. 1850, Mary Garcelon Fuller of Lewiston, Me. He d. 27 Aug., 1876, age 54 years.

ii. JAMES M.[8], b. in Dixmont, 1827; m. Lizzie Stevenson. He d. in Portland, Me., 20-29 Apr., 1856; was buried in Saco, Me., and his widow m. ——— Hazeltine, and settled in Boston; no issue.

1030. iii. ALMIRA[8], b. in Dixmont; m. Dr. Byron Porter of Newport, Me.; res. Newport, Me.

1031. iv. JOHN QUINCY[8], m. Abby ———; res. Dix Island, Me.

v. MARY FRANCES[8], m. Samuel H. Crocker. She d. in Dixmont; no issue.

1032. vi. GEORGE E[8]; m. Angie Jenison Dixon; res. Dixmont, Me.

vii. ALBERT[8], m. ——— Gould. He resides in Hallowell, Me., and has a son Harry, but no record can be obtained.

1033. viii. NELLIE[8], m. 1835, E. Woodward Whittemore; his 2d wife; res. Fairfield, Me.

ix. SARAH ELIZABETH[8], res. Fairfield, Me.; unm.

Many efforts have been made to complete these records in vain.

Children of JOSHUA[7], JR., (1801) [518] (Joshua[6], Benjamin[5], John[4], Robert[3], Sergt. Abraham[2], Robert[1]) and Abigail F. (Mosher) Adams; res. Farmington and Wilton, Me.

1034. i. ESTHER ELIZABETH[8]. b. in Farmington, July 1, 1826; m. at Wilton, June 19, 1853, Corydon Batcheller, son of John and Lucinda (Stevens) Batcheller, b. in Solon, Me., Aug. 27, 1826; d. in Emporia, Kan., 17 Oct., 1880. He was a tanner at Wilton for many years; rem. to La Cross, Wis., in 1866, and engaged in business at several places; buried at La Cross; She died at LaCross, 10 Feb., 1897.

1035. ii. LIEUT. ISAAC ROGERS[8], b. in Farmington, Mar. 22, 1829; m. (1) at Farmington, Sept. 12, 1853, Louisana Maynard Hender; m. (2) at Reedfield, Me., Mar. 22, 1860, Eliza Jane Adams, dau. of John Watson and Lydia (Simpson) Adams.

He enlisted at the breaking out of the Civil War, in Co. A, 8th Maine Regt., and later became a Lieutenant in the 2d Maine Cavalry; was wounded in battle Sept. 27, and d. at Marianna, Fla., 13 Oct., 1864.

iii. JAMES HENRY[8], b. in Farmington, Feb. 21, 1831; m. at Wilton, Nov. 13, 1860, Phebe Learnard. He d. in Wilton, 24 Jan., 1857.

His widow m. 2d Col. E. T. Luce of Boston. A son of James Henry adopted the step-father's name, and is Edgar Luce, a druggist in Pueblo, Col.

1036. iv. SERGT. JOSHUA RICHMOND⁸, b. in Farmington, July 17. 1833 ; m. at Phillips, Me., Jan. 1, 1860, Melvina Susan Whitney, dau. of Benjamin and Susan (Wells) Whitney of Gray, Me.

He was a member of the 8th Maine Regt., and was wounded in the battle at Marianna, Sept. 27, 1864 ; recovered and returned home ; res. Stratton, Franklin Co., Me.

 v. CAPT. JOHN MOSHER⁸, b. in Farmington, Mar. 14, 1836 ; m. at Jacksonville, Fla., May, 1866, Mrs. May Brown.

He went to the war as a Lieutenant in the 8th Maine Regt.; was promoted to be a Captain. He entered Bowdoin College, but left for the war ; res. 1900, Jacksonville, Fla.; no issue.

 vi. CHARLES MORRIS⁸ (twin), b. in Farmington, Mar. 14, 1836; m. at Farmington, May 2, 1857, Betsey Ann Cheney.

He enlisted in the 8th Maine Regt. as a drummer; d. in New York on his way home, of chronic diarrhœa, 30 June, 1862.

 vii. GEORGE WILLIAM MOSHER⁸, b. in Farmington, Feb. 23, 1839.

He enlisted for the war, but not being accepted, accompanied as a helper of his brother, Capt. John Mosher. He was graduated from Bowdoin College and entered the Theological School at Bangor, but retired on account of ill health. He d. at La Cross, Wis., 4 Sept., 1868.

 viii. DR. ABBIE MERRILL⁸, b. in Farmington, Sept. 25, 1842.

She was a teacher in the public schools of La Cross, Wis., for a number of years after 1868 ; entered the Medical College of Syracuse University in 1881 ; was graduated in 1884, and has practiced her profession in reformatory institutions and at her home in La Cross ; is now conducting a Sanitarium for Women, and takes a leading part in the Universalist church and reform work.

Children of MIRIAM W.⁷, (1803) [519] (Joshua⁶, Benjamin⁵, Jonn⁴, Robert³, Sergt. Abraham², Robert¹) and James F. Smith; res. Monmouth, Me.

1037. i. JOHN ALDEN SMITH, b. May 19, 1830 ; m. Nov. 29, 1853, Amy Elizabeth Wiggin of Lewiston, Me.

He was a miner ; probably d. in Boulder, Col.

 ii. SARAH E. SMITH, b. Dec. 16, 1831 ; res. Wheeling, Mo.; unm.

 iii. JAMES P. SMITH, b. Aug. 30, 1833 ; d. 12 June, 1876 ; unm.

 iv. NATHANIEL M. SMITH, b. July 14, 1835 ; d. 3 Apr., 1873 ; unm.

 v. JACOB A. SMITH, b. Sept. 21, 1838 ; d. 27 Aug., 1858.

1038. vi. MARY R. SMITH, b. Dec. 1, 1840 ; m. Nov. 19, 1866, Isaac Walker, of Pembroke, N. H.; res. Pembroke, N. H.

ROBERT ADAMS [E'ghth Generation.

Children of LYDIA⁷, (1806) [520] (Joshua⁶, Benjamin⁵, John⁴, Robert³, Sergt. Abraham², Robert¹) and James Owen ; res. Fairfield, Somerset Co., Me.

    i. MARY M. OWEN, b. Oct. 28, 1828 ; unm.; res. Fairfield, Me.
       She has rendered valuable assistance in this work.
    ii. HANNAH F. OWEN, b. Nov. 28, 1830 ; m. Dec. 9, 1860, E. Woodward Whittemore of Fairfield, Me. She d. 5 Jan., 1863, leaving two children who d. in infancy.

Children of JACOB⁷, (1808) [521] (Joshua⁶, Benjamin⁵, John⁴, Robert³, Sergt. Abraham², Robert¹) and Eliza (Bridges) Adams; res. Wales, Androscoggin Co., Me.

    i. ROBERT⁸.
    ii. PRISCILLA⁸.

Children of SARAH⁷, (1810) [522] (Joshua⁶, Benjamin⁵, John⁴, Robert³, Sergt. Abraham², Robert¹) and Cyrus K. Foss.

    i. MRS. B. F. LEIGHTON ; res. 708 Mass. Ave., Washington, D. C.
    ii. MISS L. M. FOSS.
    iii F. H. FOSS ; res. Vergennes, Vt.
    iv. FRED FOSS ; deceased.

Child of DAVID P.⁷, (1812) [523] (Joshua⁶, Benjamin⁵, John⁴, Robert³, Sergt. Abraham², Robert¹) and Adeline (Lothrop) Adams; res. Wales, Androscoggin Co., Me.

    i. FRANCES⁸.

Children of ISAAC⁷, (1794) [524] (Samuel⁶, Benjamin⁵, John⁴, Robert³, Sergt. Abraham², Robert¹) and Sarah (Smith) Adams; res. Gray, Cumberland Co., Me.

1039. i. BENJAMIN⁸, b. in Gray, Jan. 15, 1820; m. (1) Aug. 25, 1844 at Gray, Abigail Hatch, dau. of Thomas Hatch; m. (2) (pub. in Portland, Sept. 9, 1864) Elizabeth B. Chamberlain ; m. (3) Nov. 28, 1872, at Portland, Mrs. Susan M. (Gardner) Stone, b. Mar. 17, 1824 ; d. in East Deering, Me., 19 Oct., 1886, age 62 yrs. 7 mos. 2 days ; m. (4) Elizabeth St. Marie of Montreal, P. Q.
      He was a furniture dealer in Portland, Me. for many years ; d. at E. Deering, 7 Feb., 1900.

Eighth Generation.] OF NEWBURY, MASS. 253

  ii. SARAH JANE⁸, b. in Gray, Nov. 17, 1821; living in Gray, unm. 1900.

1040. iii. JOHN SMITH⁸, b. in Gray, Feb. 23, 1825 ; m. [pub. Sept. 2, 1846–7, in Windham, Me.], Sarah H. Purington, b. June 17, 1830 ; d. 8 Feb., 1894. He is living in Gray, Me., 1900.

1041. iv. MARY ELIZABETH⁸, b. in Gray, July 4, 1827; m. Apr. 15, 1849, William Elder, b. Sept. 3, 1823; d. 10 Jan.. 1899. She is living in Gray, Me., 1900.

1042. v. HELEN⁸, b. in Gray, Jan. 16, 1830 ; m. Mar. 26, 1856, Stephen Huston of Gray, Me., b. Nov. 7, 1825 ; res. Gray, Me.

  vi. KATHERINE⁸, b. in Gray; d. in infancy.

1043. vii. ISAAC H.⁸, b. in Gray, July, 1835 ; m. Jan. 10, 1869, Libbie Field, dau. of Nathaniel and Maria (DeGroof) Field, b. in Springfield, O., May 26, 1853 ; res. Vale, Ore.
    He left Maine in 1859 ; crossed the plains to California with an ox-team during that summer ; rem. 1881 from Reno, Neb., to Vale, Ore.

  viii. KATHERINE ALLEN⁸, b. in Gray, Jan. 17, 1837 ; m. Silas Lowell Adams (cousin).

  ix. ABIGAIL FRANCES⁸, b. in Gray, Nov. 7, 1840 ; res. Gray, Me.; unm.

  Children of KATHERINE JANE⁷, (1799) [525] (Samuel⁶, Benjamin⁵, John⁴, Robert³, Sergt. Abraham², Robert¹) and Joseph Allen.

  i. MARY JANE ALLEN, b. Sept. 5, 1820 ; d. 27 Feb., 1821.

1044. ii. ROBERT ADAMS ALLEN, b. May 29, 1822 ; m. Sarah E. Smith, dau. of Capt. Benjamin Smith of Gray, Me., b. July 20, 1827. He is postmaster at W. Gray, Me.

  iii. DORCAS LEIGHTON ALLEN, b. Sept. 1, 1824 ; m. Oct. 11, 1847, William Berry. She d. 19 Jan., 1848.

1045. iv. SARAH ABBIE ALLEN, b. Dec. 7, 1828 ; m. Dura Lander Bailey, b. Nov. 10, 1822 ; d. 26 Dec., 1898.

  Children of ABIGAIL⁷, (1802) [526] (Samuel⁶, Benjamin⁵, John⁴, Robert³, Sergt. Abraham², Robert¹) and John Hamilton ; res. Garland, Penobscot Co., Me.

  i. SAMUEL HAMILTON, m. Harriet Skillinger of Poland, Me.; res. Garland, Me.

  ii. HANNAH FRANCES HAMILTON, m. James Stuart of Garland, Me.

iii. MARY SUSAN HAMILTON, m. (1) —— Stuart; m. (2) George Washington Adams (cousin), son of Samuel and Eliza (Black) Adams.
iv. ABIGAIL HAMILTON, m. Abel Stuart.
v. AMELIA HAMILTON.
vi. SARAH DWINAL HAMILTON.

Children of SILAS HALL[7], (1804) [527] (Samuel[6], Benjamin[5], John[4], Robert[3], Sergt. Abraham[2], Robert[1]) and Hannah (Smith) Adams: res. Gray, Cumberland Co., Me.

    i. MARY[8], b. in Gray, Mar. 24, 1834; d. 28 May, 1834.

1046. ii. LORENZO BENSON[8], b. in Gray, Apr. 17, 1836; m. at Ellsworth, Me., Apr. 2, 1864, Clara Alice Forsyth, dau. of Ebenezer and Ann (Myers) Forsyth, b. in Ellsworth, Apr. 22, 1844.

1047. iii. SILAS LOWELL[8], b. in Grays Corner, Mar. 21, 1838-9; m. Mar. 24, 1860, Katherine Allen Adams (cousin), dau. of Isaac and Sarah (Smith) Adams, b. Jan. 17, 1837. He d. in West Gray, Me., 9 July, 1897.

1048. iv. HANNAH SUSAN[8], b. in Gray, Dec. 6, 1841-2; m. Mar. 27, 1871, John Walton Gray, b. in Scotland; he was drowned in Shrewsbury river, N. J., and buried in Long Branch, 9 Apr., 1898.

1049. v. JOHN[8], b. in Gray, Oct. 21, 1844; m. Mar. 17, 1873, Eleanor J. Wheeler, dau. of Isaiah and Julia (Foster) Wheeler, of Bridgewater, Vt., b. Dec. 14, 1843.
    He was a soldier in the civil war; member of Co. K, 7th Maine Regiment; d. in Worcester, Mass., 16 May, 1886.

Children of SAMUEL[7], (1807) [528] (Samuel[6], Benjamin[5], John[4], Robert[3], Sergt. Abraham[2], Robert[1]) and Eliza (Black) Adams; res. Falmouth, Me.

1050. i. JOSHUA[8], b. in Falmouth; m. Maria A. Brown; res. 27 Brattle St., Portland, Me.

1051. ii. ANDREW JACKSON[8], b. in Falmouth; m. (1) Jan. 19, 1854, in Falmouth, Me., Cordelia J. Sweet; m. (2) Dec. 16, 1865, in Portland, Mary J. Murdock; res. Falmouth, Me.

    iii. GEORGE WASHINGTON[8], b. in Falmouth; m. Mary Susan Hamilton (cousin), dau. of John and Abigail (Adams) Hamilton.
    iv. ISAIAH.
    v. MARY ELIZABETH.

Children of ISAIAH[7], (1811) [**529**] (Samuel[5], Benjamin[6], John[4], Robert[3], Sergt. Abraham[2], Robert[1]) and Sarah J. (Dwinal) Adams; res. Gray, Cumberland Co., Me.

    i. CHARLES DANIEL[8], b. in Gray, May 18, 1842; m. Jan., 1869, Georgia Straw of Newfield, Me.; res. Reading, Mass.; no issue.
    ii. SAMUEL F.[8], b. in Gray, Aug. 30, 1843.
        He removed to the west, 1860; unm.
1052.   iii. CELIA ANNA[8], b. in Gray, Mar. 12, 1851; m. Nov. 30, 1871, Daniel M. Means of Freeport, Me., son of Clark and Elizabeth Nye (Porter) Means, b. Feb. 2, 1843; res. Merrimac, Mass.
    iv. AARON ISAIAH[8], b. in Gray, July 22, 1855; res. Cripple Creek, Col.; unm.

Children of SALLY[7], (1795) [**530**] (Capt. Jacob[6], Benjamin[5], John[4], Robert[3], Sergt. Abraham[2], Robert[1]) and Matthew Cobb; res. Portland, Me.

1053.   i. CAPT. JACOB ADAMS COBB, b. Dec. 28, 1818; m. Dec. 16, 1841, Sarah Matilda Hyde of Brooklyn, N. Y.
        He was a sea-captain for many years, sailing from New York. He d. in Brooklyn, N. Y., 10 Oct., 1865.
    ii. HIRAM COBB, b. July 9, 1822; he d. unm. in So. Boston, Mass., 17 Nov., 1845.
    iii. MARY ANN COBB, b. April 19, 1827; living in 1900 in Portland, Me.; unm.
    iv. FRANCES ELLEN COBB, b. Sept. 10, 1832; d. in Portland, Me., 25 Sept., 1832.
1054.   v. CYNTHIA MARIA COBB, b. Dec. 9, 1834; m. Apr. 10-13, 1862, at Brooklyn, N. Y., Daniel Webster Ames, son of Daniel S. and Cynthia (Blunt) Ames, b. in Norridgewock, Me., June 17, 1830; living 1900, Portland, Me.
    vi. SARAH MARIA GRIFFITH COBB, b. Jan. 26, 1836; d. in Portland, Me., 28 Sept., 1841.

Children of MIRIAM[7], ( ) [**531**] (Capt. Jacob[6], Benjamin[5], John[4], Robert[3], Sergt. Abraham[2], Robert[1]) and Nathaniel Roberts; res. Portland, Me.

1055.   i. COL. THOMAS A. ROBERTS, b. July 7, 1817; m. Apr. 3, 1842, Mary A. Frates, dau. of Antonio and Mary Frates, b. in Portland, Jan. 2, 1818; d. 17 Nov., 1878. He d. in Portland, 9 Feb., 1888.
    ii. DORCAS ROBERTS, b. Jan. 16, 1819; d. in Portland, 5 Oct., 1820.
    iii. DORCAS A. ROBERTS, b. Sept. 25, 1820; m. Jan. 4, 1846, John Bradford. She d. in Portland, Me.; no issue.

ROBERT ADAMS [Eighth Generation.

1056.
- iv. JAMES S. ROBERTS, b. Nov. 5, 1822; m. Abba A. Lord; she d. in Watertown, Mass., 10 Nov., 1889, age 67 yrs. 8 mos. 19 days. He d. in Portland, 31 Jan., 1845.
- v. GEORGE W. ROBERTS, b. Oct. 22, 1824; m. Eliza Law; res. Newark, N. J.

1057
- vi. WILLIAM H. ROBERTS, b. Nov. 11, 1826; m. Irene B. Lane; she d. in Portland, 31 Jan., 1898, age 67 yrs. 3 mos.
- vii. FRANCES E. ROBERTS, b. Sept. 22, 1828; m. Aug. 5, 1858, Thos. F. Roberts (cousin).
- viii. MARGARET S. ROBERTS, b. June 20, 1830; m. James Rackliff; She d. in Portland.
- ix. MARY M. ROBERTS, b. Aug. 23, 1832; d. in Portland.

1058.
- x. SARAH W. ROBERTS, b. Sept. 2, 1834; m. Nov. 16, 1850, Geo. A. Merry; res. Cape Elizabeth, Me.
- xi. HARRIET E. ROBERTS, b. Jan. 29, 1838; m. Aug. 17, 1853, James R. Gray.

Children of JOHN WATSON[7], (1806) [532] (Benjamin Watson[6], Benjamin[5], John[4], Robert[3], Sergt. Abraham[2], Robert[1]) and Lydia Simpson (Morrison) Adams; res. Monmouth, Kennebec Co., Me.

- i. MARY ANN[8], b. in Kent's Hill, Me., Mar. 31, 1829; d. 8 July, 1831.
- ii. ELIZA JANE[8], b. in Kent's Hill, May 4, 1830; m. (1) Mar. 22, 1859, Isaac R. Adams of Wilton, Me., a Lieutenant of the 1st Maine Cavalry, who d. of wounds in the Civil War, son of Justin, Jr., and Abigail F. (Mosher) Adams; d. July, 1872; m. (2) Silas Mitchell of Buckfield, Me.; he d. 26 Nov., 1887. She d. in Buckfield, Oxford Co., Me., 20 Mar; 1897; no issue.
- iii. MARY ANN[8], b. in Kent's Hill, Feb. 1, 1832; m. June 11, 1884, James G. Blossom, son of James E. and Austis (Wilcox) Blossom of Monmouth, Me,; res. Waltham, Mass.; no issue.
- iv. CHARLOTTE AUGUSTA[8], b. in Kent's Hill, Mar. 4, 1834; m. Oct. 1, 1887, Josiah Hutchinson of Buckfield. She d. in Waltham, Mass., 19 Mar., 1899; no issue.

1059.
- v. SARAH ELIZABETH[8], b. in Kent's Hill, Dec. 4, 1836; m. Sept. 7, 1871, Edward H. Phinney of Milford, Mass.; he d. 5 Feb., 1875; res. Waltham, Mass.
- vi. WILLIAM H. HARRISON, b. in Kent's Hill, Apr. 20, 1841; m. Mar. 1862, Ellen F. Packard of Kent's Hill; she d. 21 June, 1871.
  He was a soldier; d. near Fredericksburg, Va., 16 Apr., 1863; no issue.
- vii. EMILY J.[8], b. in Kent's Hill, Aug. 27, 1847; d. 28 Dec., 1864; unm.

Eighth Generation.] OF NEWBURY, MASS. 257

Children of JOHN HALL⁷, (1796) [533] (Jacob⁶, Stephen⁵, William⁴, Capt. Abraham³, Sergt. Abraham², Robert¹) and Abby (Everts) Adams; res. W. Lebanon, Columbia Co., N. Y.

    i. GEORGE FRANKLIN⁸, b. in New Lebanon, N. Y., Nov. 13, 1830; d. 21 Oct., 1833.
    ii. HANNAH⁸, b. in New Lebanon, Oct. 23, 1832; d. 18 July, 1833.
1060. iii. JOHN MERRIAM⁸, b. in New Lebanon, Oct. 15, 1834; m. (1) Mar. 15, 1859, Hattie A. Bigelow of Minnesota; m. (2) Feb. 1, 1884, at Minneapolis, Sarah A. Stinson; she d. in New Lebanon, 1 July, 1890; m. (3) Oct. 18, 1892, Susie E. Morrissy of Arlington, Vt.
        Farmer; res. W. Lebanon, N. Y.; was employed 1853, in the government survey west of Minnesota; became a scout and guide among the Sioux Indians; also a millwright in Minnesota; a soldier in Co. A, 1st Minn. Cavalry, and an Orderly Sergeant in Co. B, 11th Inf. Vols., and returned to New Lebanon, 1884.

Children of STEPHEN⁷, (1807) [534] (David⁶, Stephen⁵, William⁴, Capt. Abraham³, Sergt. Abraham², Robert¹) and Nancy Livermore (Rockwood) Adams; res. Paxton, Mass.

1061. i. AARON⁸, b. in Grafton, Mass., Dec. 10, 1838; m. Sept. 11, 1868, Mary C. Sigman of Kansas.
        He removed to Kansas during the free state struggle, and served as cavalryman from that State in the Civil war; res. near Salina, Saline Co., Kan.
    ii. DEXTER⁸, b. in Grafton, Apr., 1840; d. June, 1840.
1062. iii. MARIA⁸, b. in Rutland, Mass., May 14, 1841; m. Dec. 28, 1870, John L. Wheelock; res. Spencer, Mass.
1063. iv. JANE EMILY⁸, b. in Paxton, Mass., Apr. 29, 1844; m. Sept. 20, 1868, George M. Berkeley of Sublette, Ill.; res. Dixon, Ill., and Kansas; rem. to Worcester, Mass., 1893.

Children of DAVID⁷, (1809) [535] (David⁶, Stephen⁵, William⁴, Capt. Abraham³, Sergt. Abraham², Robert¹) and Laura (Clark) Adams; res. Orange and Barre, Vt.

    i. SARAH⁸, b. in Orange; m. Lewis Gates, a soldier in the 42d Mass. Regt., in the Civil War.
    ii. ANNETTE⁸.
1064. iii. GEORGE⁸, m. Aug. 31, 1862, in Leicester, Mass., Charlotte James of Leicester; she. d. 27 Aug., 1873, age 28 yrs. 8 mos. 9 days.
        He is reported to have married again, and settled in New Hampshire.

(17)

258   ROBERT ADAMS   [Eighth Generation.

Children of MOSES[7], (1814) [536] (David[6], Stephen[5], William[4], Capt. Abraham[3], Sergt. Abraham[2], Robert[1]) and Emeline (King) Adams; res. Dakota, Humbolt Co., Iowa.

  i. HON. ALBERT MARTIN[8], b. in Orange, Vt., Apr. 16, 1843; m. Dec. 9, 1876, Maggie Little of Decora, Ia.
   He enlisted Aug. 20, 1862, in Co. F., 42d Mass. Reg., for one year; was captured at Galveston, Texas, in Aug., 1863, and afterward returned home; rem. in 1864 to Avery, Humbolt Co., Ia., and enlisted in Co. F, 2d Iowa Cavalry; was taken prisoner at Nashville, Tenn., in Dec., 1864, and confined at Andersonville till Apr., 1865; was discharged July 12, 1865, and became editor and publisher of the *Humbolt Independent* in 1874; mayor of Dakota City, etc.; is a democrat; no issue.

1065. ii. CHARLES WOOD[8], b. in Orange, May 14, 1847; m. Sept. 27, 1874, Lucy J. Bowen.
   He is a farmer; res. at Unique, Humbolt Co., Ia.

1066. iii. GEORGE W.[8], b. in Orange, Feb. 12, 1851; m. Nov. 24, 1886, Rose Reed Smith of Davenport, Ia.
   He is a farmer; res. Bradgate, Humbolt Co., Ia.

  iv. EUGENE[8], b. in Groton, Vt., Dec. 6, 1856; d. 29, Jan., 1875.

1067. v. JOSEPHINE[8] (twin), b. in Groton, Dec. 6, 1856; m. Oct. 20, 1878, Chas. W. Bowen; res. Bradgate, Iowa.

Children of SUSANNA[7], (1816) [537] (David[6], Stephen[5], William[4], Capt. Abraham[3], Sergt. Abraham[2], Robert[1]) and Henry Graff; res. Leicester, Mass.

1068. i. MARY ELIZA GRAFF, b. July 25, 1847; m. Oct. 28, 1869, Joseph Drabble; res. Leicester, Mass
  ii. GEORGE E. GRAFF, b. Dec. 12, 1849; d. 4 Sept., 1851.
  iii. ABBY ANN GRAFF, b. April 12, 1852; d. 12 Oct., 1854.
  iv. CHARLES H. GRAFF, b. Aug. 7, 1854; m. Laura Burrell, of Worcester, Mass.; she d. 5 July, 1891; res. Providence, R. I.
  v. ALBERT J. GRAFF, b. Jan. 7, 1857; res. Worcester, Mass.; unm.

Children of JOHN Q.[7], (1820) [538] (David[6], Stephen[5], William[4], Capt. Abraham[3], Sergt. Abraham[2], Robert[1]) and Eliza J. (Wood) Adams; res. Groton, Vt.

1069. i. DELIA M.[8], b. in Plainfield, Vt., May 6, 1849; m. Apr. 22, 1873, George D. Corry; res. Lowell, Mass.
1070. ii. JANE B.[8], b. in Groton, Vt., Jan. 30, 1853; m. (1) Jan. 11, 1870, Wm. Merrill Welch; he d. 23 Aug., 1887; m. (2) Mar. 19, 1895, George G. Welch; res. Helmville, Deer Lodge Co., Mont.

iii. ZELMA E.[8], b. in in Groton, 1860 ; m. May, 1886, George Rose. She d. 26 May, 1888, age 27 years ; no issue.
iv. FLORENCE E.[8], b. in Groton, 1867-8]; d. in Rutland. Ia., 14 Feb., 1883, age 15 years.

Children of JUDITH[7], (1828) [**539**] (David[6], Stephen[5], William[4], Capt. Abraham[3], Sergt. Abraham[2], Robert[1]) and Frank G. Lufkin; res. Worcester, Mass.
i. JOHN J. LUFKIN, b. Mar. 19, 1848.
ii. CLARISSA MARIA LUFKIN, b. May 30, 1850.

Children of ISRAEL[7], (1815) [**540**] (Israel[6], Stephen[5], William[4], Capt. Abraham[3], Sergt. Abraham[2], Robert[1]) and Maggie (McDonald) Adams; res. New Orleans, La.
i. THOMAS DORMAN[8], b. in New Orleans, June 2, 1838; m. Jan. 2, 1860, Arlotta Verondi of Melbourne, Aust.; res. Melbourne, Aust.
ii. STEPHEN[8], b. in New Orleans.
iii. WILLIAM[8], b. in New Orleans.
iv. CHARLES[8], b. in New Orleans.

Children of JOHN[7], (1817) [**541**] (Israel[6], Stephen[5], William[4], Capt. Abraham[3], Sergt. Abraham[2], Robert[1]) and Mary (Jones) Adams; res. New Orleans, La.
i. JACOB[8], b. in New Orleans.
ii. HENRY[8], b. in New Orleans.
iii. HANNAH[8], b. in New Orleans.

Children of SUSAN HAYWARD[7], (1814) [**542**] and Nathaniel T. Cofran; res. Goshen, N. H.
i. ADELIA COFRAN, b. in Goshen ; d. young.
ii. OPHELIA COFRAN, b. in Goshen ; m. John Baker. She d. in Newport, N. H., 1892.
iii. SUSAN E. COFRAN, b. in Goshen; m. Shepherd L. Bowers. She d. in Newport, 1890.
iv. BARZILLA H. COFRAN, b. 1842.
He was a soldier in Co. F, 16th N. H. Reg. of Volunteers ; d. in Goshen, 26 Jan, 1877, age 35 years.

Children of HANNAH PARSONS⁷, (1814) [543] (Enoch⁶, Stephen⁵, William⁴, Capt. Abraham³, Sergt. Abraham², Robert¹) and Benjamin Lane; res. E. Sangerfield, Me.
  i. BENJAMIN W. LANE, b. Mar. 17, 1845 ; d. 21 Sept,, 1846.
  ii. JULIA LANE, b. Nov. 1, 1847 ; m. June 6, 1875, Joseph B. Hutchinson, b. in Sangerfield, Dec. 12, 1843.
  iii. SAMUEL LANE, b. Dec. 8, 1850 ; m. Mary Alice Bradford ; res. Houlton, Me.
  iv. ELIZABETH SPRINGALL LANE, b. Feb. 1, 1853 ; d. 27 June, 1857.
  v. ANN LANE, b. Feb. 9, 1858 ; d. 18 Apr., 1859.
  vi. HANNAH LANE, b. May 11, 1860; m. Nov. 27. 1884, Albion D. Gray, a teacher in Philadephia, Pa., b. Mar. 21, 1860; d. 24 Feb., 1896.

Child of SUSANNA⁷, (1816) [544] (Enoch⁶, Stephen⁵, William⁴, Capt. Abraham³, Sergt. Abraham², Robert¹) and Enos G. Flanders; res. E. Sangerfield, Me.
  i. ENOCH A. FLANDERS, b. in Sangerfield, Aug. 31, 1843 ; m. Feb. 9, 1873, Helen C. Whidden of Canterbury, N. H., b. Aug. 8, 1845.

Children of REV. CHARLES WHEELER, D. D., LL. D., (1784) [545] and Charity Anna (Nelson) Wheeler; res. Prunytown, W. Va.
  i. CHARLES WHEELER, b. Sept. 14, 1814 ; d. 1822.
  ii. REBECCA BLAINE WHEELER, b. Feb. 20, 1816 ; m. Feb. 20, 1856, William Johnson. She d. in Bridgeport, W. Va., 24, Jan., 1897.
  iii. A SON. b. Jan. 5, 1818 ; d. 5 Feb., following.
  iv. NELSON ADAMS WHEELER, b. Mar. 12, 1819 ; was murdered by Indians, 1842.
  v. SAMUEL PIERCE WHEELER, b. Aug. 20, 1822 ; d. Sept., 1828.
  vi. CATHARINE ANN WHEELER, b, May 16, 1825 ; m. Oct. 27, 1842, John W. Reynolds ; res. Clarksburg, W. Va.; d. 11 Mar., 1897.
  vii. MARIA ANTOINETTE WEELER, b. May 31, 1828 ; m. Mar. 9, 1858, John R. Boggess; res. Lumberport and Clarksburg, West Virginia. She d. 5 Jan., 1874.
  viii. SAMUEL PERKINS WHEELER, b. June 20, 1832 ; d. unm. 1 July, 1873.
  ix. CHARLES WHEELER, b. Apr. 10, 1833 ; m. 1859, Mattie Bassell. He d. 1862.
  x. ADONIRAM J. WHEELER, b. Aug. 16, 1839 ; d. Oct., 1839.

MARY A. BARNES.

Children of MARY[7], (1785) [**546**] (Dr. Samuel[6], Capt. Benjamin[5], William[4], Capt. Abraham[3], Sergt. Abraham[2], Robert[1]) and James Wilson; res. Beaver, Beaver Co., Pa.

1071.   i. ELIZA WILSON, b. in Beaver, Pa., Mar. 14, 1807; m. July 30, 1827, Rev. Jonathan Holt, D. D., a Methodist Episcopal clergyman of the Pittsburg Conference, b. in Fayette Co., Pa., Nov. 19, 1800; d. in W. Milford, W. Va., 19 June, 1879. She d. in Weston, W. Va., 29 July, 1835.

1072.   ii. DR. ROBERT ADAMS WILSON, b. in Beaver, Jan. 31, 1809; m. May 18, 1840, at Wheeling, Va., Sarah Ann (James) Brown, widow of Wm. V. Brown, b. in Falmouth, Va., May 15, 1812; d. in New York, 6 Feb., 1897, age 85 years.

Dr. Wilson practiced medicine several years in Weston, Virginia, but on account of failing health removed to Pittsburg, Pa., and engaged in the manufacture of tonic, cathartic and anti-dyspeptic pills, invented by him and still sold by druggists. He was Asst. Surgeon of the 165th Penn. Reg. in 1864. He d. 28 Sept., 1864. His wife was active in charitable work among the soldiers.

1073.   iii. SAMUEL BEATTY WILSON, b. in Beaver, Oct. 25, 1811; m. Oct. 25, 1836, Julia Ann Lyon, dau. of James Lyon, a prominent merchant and lawyer of Beaver, b. Aug. 11, 1812; d. in Washington, D. C., 3 July, 1892. He is living 1899, at Washington, D. C.

    iv. CLARINDA WILSON, b. in Beaver, 1812; d. young.

1074.   v. THOMAS McKEAN WILSON, b. in Beaver, Aug. 20, 1813; m. Jan. 2, 1838, Elizabeth Henderson Murdock. He d. at Moberly, Randolph, Co., Mo., 8 July, 1881.

1075.   vi. MARY ANN OLIVIA WILSON, b. in Beaver, Feb. 15, 1815; m. Jan. 1, 1846, Dr. Newton Bennett Barnes. She d. in Weston, W. Va., 9 Jan., 1898.

She is said to have been noted for her culture, superior intelligence, and devoted piety. Her death was marked and lamented by special resolutions of the Woman's Christian Temperance Union.

    vii. MARTHA SOPHRONIA WILSON, b. in Beaver, 1819-1820; m. 1845-6, Hon. Lewis Maxwell of Weston, Va., formerly Member of Congress. She d. in Weston, W. Va., 1847; no issue.

Children of DR. MILO[7], (1790–1) [**547**] (Dr. Samuel[6], Capt. Benjamin[5], William[4], Capt. Abraham[3], Sergt. Abraham[2], Robert[1]) and Maria (Johnson) Adams; res. Beaver, Beaver Co., Pa.

1076.   i. ELIZA ANN[8], b. in Beaver, Jan. 16, 1815; m. Mar. 16, 1836, Hon. John Allison, M. C., b. Aug. 5, 1812; d. at Washington, D. C., while Register of the U. S. Treasury, 23, Mar., 1878; res. Greenville, Pa. She d. 4 May, 1884.

262 ROBERT ADAMS [Eighth Generation.

1077. ii. OSCAR EDMUND[8], b. in Beaver, Oct. 26, 1818 ; m. Jan. 13, 1846, Helen M. Plaston of McKillsport, Pa., b. May 25, 1829 ; d. 13 Jan., 1899. He res. in Bolivar and Bridgewater, Pa., until about 1863, when he settled in Oil City, where he d. 23 Dec., 1886.
1078. iii. MYRA HALL[8], b. in Beaver, Sept. 18, 1820; m. Mar. 17, 1842, Leonard S. Johns, son of John and Susanna (Shryock) Johns, b. Feb. 3, 1805 ; d. 9 May, 1871 ; res. Pittsbugh, Pa. She is living 1899.

Children of DR. MILO[7], (1790-1) and Cynthia B. (Darragh) Adams.

iv. CAPT. ROBERT DARRAGH[8], b. in Beaver, Oct. 9, 1827 ; m. 1857, Emma Walker of Chicago, Ill.
He set. in Chicago in 1852; enlisted in the Army and became a captain in the 57th Regt. of Illinois Vols.; was wounded at Pittsburg Landing, and killed in the battle of Shiloh, Apr. 7, 1862 ; no issue.
v. SAMUEL[8], b. in Beaver, Oct. 20, 1828 ; res. Beaver, Pa.; living unm. 1898.
vi. SHEPLEY HOLMES[8], b. in Sharon, Pa., Nov. 23, 1830 ; d. 27 Apr., 1832.
1079. vii. CAPT. MILO ROMULUS[8], b. in Sharon, Feb. 6, 1833 ; m. Sept. 10, 1868, Emma Weyland of Somerset, Pa.
He was at first a surveyor. At the breaking out of the Civil War he organized a company for the army, and was made the Captain of Co. F, 10th Pennsylvania Reserves ; he participated in several battles, notably at Drainsville, Gaines Mills, Mechanicville, White Oak Swamp, and Charles City Cross Roads, being wounded in the left lung in the latter and taken prisoner and confined in Libby Prison. After his exchange he was made a commissioner of the 24th Congressional District of Pennsylvania, and became Clerk of the Legislature. He is now employed at the Capitol in Washington, D. C.
viii. DEBORAH MARTHA[8], b. in Sharon, May 6, 1835 ; d. Sept., 1836.
*1080. ix. VICTORIA[8], b. in Pittsburg, Pa., May 6, 1837 ; m. July 8, 1857, Jacob Weyand of Beaver. She d. in Beaver, 10 Oct., 1892.
x. MARTHA FLORA[8], b. in Pittsburg, Aug. 1, 1839 ; d. Apr., 1840.
1081. xi. ISADORE M.[8], b. in Adamsville, Pa., Feb. 14, 1842; m. 1875, James S. McKelvey of Pittsburg ; res. Alleghany, Pa.
1082. xii. CYNTHIA DARRAGH[8], b. in Beaver, Mar. 12, 1844; m. July 22, 1866, Col. Alex. W. Taylor, son of Wm. and Mary Ann Taylor, b. Mar. 31, 1836 ; res. Beaver, Pa. She d. 1 Oct., 1879.

Children of SOPHRONIA[7], (1791-2) [548] (Dr. Samuel[6], Capt. Benjamin[5], William[4], Capt. Abraham[3], Sergt. Abraham[2], Robert[1]) and John T. Miller; res. Beaver Co., Ohio.

i. CLARINDA A. MILLER, b. May 15, 1826 ; d. 9 Apr., 1841.
ii. THORNTON MILLER, b. Jan. 13, 1828 ; d. 2 Apr., 1829.
iii. MARY JULIET MILLER, b. July 23, 1829 ; d. 22 July, 1830.
iv. ELIZA DICKEY MILLER, b. July 7, 1832 ; m. July 7, 1853, John E. P. Dorsey ; living in New York.

Children of ELVIRA W.⁷, (1804) [**549**] (Dr. Samuel⁶, Capt. Benjamin⁵, William⁴, Capt. Abraham³, Sergt. Abraham², Robert¹) and Hon. John Dickey ; res. Brighton, Beaver Co., Pa.

1083. i. HON. OLIVER JAMES DICKEY, b. Apr. 6, 1823 ; m. Nov. 3, 1857, Elizabeth Shenk ; she d. 24 Oct., 1879.
He was a lawyer and Member of Congress ; d. in Lancaster, Pa., 21 Apr., 1876.

ii. SAMUEL ADAMS DICKEY, b. Jan. 1, 1825 ; res. Bismark, Dakota ; unm.

1084. iii. SOCRATES ADAMS DICKEY, b. Mar. 15, 1827 ; m. June 25, 1855, Diana Wolf, dau. of Geo. Wolf, b. Sept., 1832 ; res. Fallston, Beaver Co., Pa.

1085. iv. ELIZABETH DICKEY, b. in Sharon, Pa., Apr. 1, 1829 ; m. Apr. 26, 1855, Eli Reno, b. May 31, 1818 ; d. 17 Nov., 1881 ; res. New Brighton, Beaver Co., Pa. Is a woman of great mental activity and has rendered valuable assistance in this work.

v. JULIETTE DICKEY, b. in Beaver, Pa., Aug. 23, 1831 ; d. 1 Feb., 1833.

1086. vi. ELVIRA DICKEY, b. in Beaver, Jan. 5, 1834 ; m. April 21, 1857, Daniel O. Patterson, b. Apr. 9, 1832. She d. 14 July, 1886.

1087. vii. SOPHRONIA DICKEY, b. in Sharon, Jan. 18, 1837 ; m. (1) Jan. 18, 1859, Andrew Marquis, b. Dec. 22, 1832 ; d. 10 Dec., 1864; m. (2) Dec. 6, 1876, John Shoemaker. She d. 23 Dec., 1898.

1088. viii. MAJ. CHARLES JOHN DICKEY, b. in Sharon, Nov. 1, 1839 ; m. Apr. 10, 1883, at Indianapolis, Ind., Lavalette Davidson, b. Mar. 4, 1847.
He enlisted as a private in the 10th Pennsylvania Reserves ; became Sergeant in May, 1861; joined the Reg. Army in July ; was commissioned as Captain Nov. 5, 1864; was transferred and became a Major in 1888 for meritorious service. After 24 years he was placed on the retired list, and died suddenly of apoplexy in Nov., 1893, highly esteemed for his nobleness of character.

ix. ROBERT DICKEY, b. in Sharon, Aug. 31, 1843 ; res. Denver, Col., unm.

1089. x. THADDEUS STEVENS DICKEY, b. in Sharon, July 22, 1847 ; m. Oct. 1, 1874, Susan E. Metzger of Lancaster, Pa.; res. Minneapolis, Minn.

Children of ELIZABETH P.⁷, (1807) [**550**] (Dr. Samuel⁶, Capt. Benjamin⁵, William⁴, Capt. Abraham³, Sergt. Abraham², Robert¹) and Ele W. Beall; res. Beaver, Beaver Co., Pa.

1090. i. MERCY P. BEALL, b. in Pennsylvania, May 6, 1830; m. Dec. 31, 1850, J. B. Dansman; deceased; res. Bountiful, Utah.
      She is an artist.

1091. ii. SOCRATES A. BEALL, b. Dec. 15, 1832; m. Aug. 24, 1854, Mary A. Boyle, b. Mar. 7, 1835; res. Golden Lake, Mississippi Co., Ark.

     iii. MILO A. BEALL, b. June 28, 1835; d. 11 Sept., 1867.

     iv. MARION R. BEALL, b. Feb. 2, 1839; d. 13 Aug., 1840.

     v. A SON, b. Apr. 4, 1842; d. same day.

1092. vi. JESSIE E. BEALL, b. Jan. 8, 1844; m. at Sharon, Pa., Jan. 18, 1864; Maj. Emory S. Foster; res. St. Louis, Mo.

1093. vii. ELE W. BEALL, b. June 6, 1847; m. Nov. 18, 1872, Camilla Townsley; res. Kansas.

     viii. NORMAN C. BEALL, b. Apr. 14, 1850.
      He is in an asylum, St. Louis, Mo.

Children of SAMUEL PLUMER⁷, (1812) [**551**] (Dr. Samuel⁶, Capt. Benjamin⁵, William⁴, Capt. Abraham³, Sergt. Abraham², Robert¹) and Ellen B. (Barker) Adams; res. Beaver Falls, Pa.

1094. i. EDGAR B.⁸, b. in Beaver, Pa., Apr. 9, 1838; m. Dec. 23, 1863, Barbara P. Trumbull of Salem, O., d. 23 July, 1887; res. 1898, Charity Island, Cassville, Huron Co., Mich.

     ii. EMMA⁸, b. in Beaver, July 27, 1840; d. 17 July, 1842.

1095. iii. CAPT. HORATIO NELSON⁸, b. in Beaver, Aug. 24, 1842; m. Oct. 14, 1867, America Cornwell.
      Capt. Adams served 3 years in the Army; was 12 years a resident of Louisville, Ky.; was collector of tolls on the Louisville and Portland Canal, and Assistant Superintendent. On the 13th birthday of his eldest daughter, he took a party for an excursion in his yacht America, and was caught in a collision with the New Orleans boat Guthrie, and killed, 7 May, 1884. He was highly esteemed by those who knew him, and his death was deeply regretted.

1096. iv. COL. MILTON B.⁸, b. in Beaver, April 11, 1845; m. May 1, 1878, Anna Waters Lewis, dau. of Ira and L. A. Lewis, b. at Oswego, N. Y., Mar. 1, 1855.
      He was a graduate of West Point Academy, 1865, and was stationed at Burlington, Vt., in charge of U. S. engineering corps; now at Nashville, Tenn.

1097. v. ELMA⁸, b. in Beaver, Feb. 17, 1848; m. Nov. 13, 1873, Thomas Tanner; res. Louisville, Ky.

Eighth Generation.] OF NEWBURY, MASS. 265

1098.   vi. SAMUEL PLUMER[8], b. in Beaver, Dec. 9, 1850; m. in Louisville, Ky., Aug. 21, 1877, Fanny C. Powers of Tennessee, dau. of D. J. Powers, b. Feb. 11, 1857; res. Milwaukee, Wis.
   vii. LOLA[8], b. in Beaver, July 26, 1852; d. 10 Apr., 1854.
   viii. MARY[8], b. in Beaver, Nov. 7, 1855; living unm., Sharon, Pa.

Children of MARY HARRIMAN PLUMER[7], (1799) [552] and John McCalmont; res. Franklin, Venango Co., Pa.

   i. PATTY ADAMS McCALMONT, b. Apr. 19, 1819; m. Aug. 24, 1841, Rev. Almeron G. Miller. She d. at Jackson, La., 19 Oct., 1855. Sons: Hon. John McCalmont Miller, Los Angeles, Cal.; Geo. P. Miller and Hon. Eugene G. Miller of Spokane, Wash.
   ii. JOHN CONRAD McCALMONT, b. June 15, 1821; d. 2 Jan., 1849.
   iii. SUMUEL PLUMER McCALMONT, b. Sept. 12, 1823; m. 1859, Harriet Osborn, dau. of Platt S. Osborn of Sherman, Chautauqua Co., N. Y.

   He studied law, and was admitted to the bar, Nov. 25, 1847; was in California 1850-53, since which time he has continued the practice of his profession in Franklin for more than forty years; was elected to the Legislature in 1855, and twice re-elected; since 1874 he has attained prominence in temperance work and the Prohibition party. His wife is an active contributor to genealogical and other literature.
   iv. JULIETTE H. McCALMONT, b. Sept. 2, 1826; d. unm. 27 Oct., 1862.
   v. MARGARET B. McCALMONT, b. Feb. 6, 1830,; d. unm. 25 Feb., 1896.

Child of ABRAHAM[7], (1800) [553] (Benjamin[6], Capt. Benjamin[5], Abraham[4], Capt. Abraham[3], Sergt. Abraham[2], Robert[1]) and Ruth Ann (Lofty) Adams; res. Georgetown, Mass.

1099.   i. LIZZIE[8], b. in Georgetown, Nov. 27, 1848; m. Sept. 18, 1870, Clarence Davis of Boston, Mass.; res. Cambridge, Mass.

Children of LOUISA[7], (1801) [554] (Benjamin[6], Capt. Benjamin[5], Abraham[4], Capt. Abraham[3], Sergt. Abraham[2], Robert[1]) and Col. John Kimball; res. Rowley, Mass.

   i. JOHN A. KIMBALL, b. Dec. 7, 1824; d. 23 Dec., 1824.
   ii. LOUISA M. KIMBALL, b. Nov. 28, 1825; d. 2 Aug., 1869.
   iii. CAROLINE A. KIMBALL, b. Jan. 10, 1828; m. June 10, 1849, Eben Hobson; res. Georgetown, Mass. d. Dec. 1904.

iv. GEORGE A. KIMBALL, b. Jan. 8, 1839; m. Mar. 7, 1860, Anna E. Todd of Rowley ; res. Georgetown, Mass.
v. ABBIE B. KIMBALL, b. Feb. 24, 1832; m. Oct. 7, 1849, Daniel W. Palmer; res. Georgetown, Mass.
vi. SARAH A. KIMBALL, b. Nov. 27, 1834 ; d. 12 Feb., 1840.
vii. CHARLES A. KIMBALL, b. Apr. 4, 1837 ; m. Jan. 1, 1860, Annie E. Gage ; res. Haverhill, Mass.
viii. SARAH A. KIMBALL, b. Dec. 11, 1840; m. Jan. 7, 1869, Robert Adams Coker, b. in Georgetown, Mass., Mar. 15, 1840.
ix. BENJAMIN A. KIMBALL, b. Mar. 22, 1844; d. 4 Oct., 1869.

Child of BENJAMIN PERLEY[7], (1806) [555] (Benjamin[6], Capt. Benjamin[5], Abraham[4], Capt. Abraham[3], Sergt. Abraham[2], Robert[1]) and Abbie L. (Stimson) Adams; res. Topsfield, Mass.

i. MARY ANN[8], b. in Topsfield, 1843; m. Charles A. Whittemore of Melrose, Mass.; res. Chula Vista, San Diego Co., Cal.; no issue.
ii. BENJAMIN P.[8], b. in Topsfield, 1845; d. unm. 1883.

Children of CHARLES HENRY[7], (1809) [556] (Benjamin[6], Capt. Benjamin[5], Abraham[4], Capt. Abraham[3], Sergt. Abraham[2], Robert[1]) and Eliza (Moore) Adams; res. Georgetown, Mass.

1100. i. ELLEN E[8], b. in Georgetown, July 12, 1835; m. Dec. 6, 1853, Augustus M. Spofford of Danvers, Mass.; res. Danvers, Mass.
1101. ii. CHARLES HENRY[8], b. in Georgetown, July 3, 1837; m. May 26, 1858, Elizabeth Proctor Hawkes, dau. of Timothy and Mary Ann (Smith) Hawks, b. Dec. 27, 1840. He d. 3 Sept., 1879 ; res. Lynn, Mass.
iii. JOHN K.[8], b. in Georgetown, June 18, 1846 ; d. 17 June, 1870.
iv. SARAH L.[8], b. in Georgetown, Nov. 29, 1848 ; d. 1 June, 1877.

Child of GEORGE WASHINGTON[7], (1815-6) [557] (Benjamin[6], Capt. Benjamin[5], Abraham[4], Capt. Abraham[3], Sergt. Abraham[2], Robert[1]) and Sarah J. (Perley) Adams; res. So. Georgetown, Mass.

i. CHARLES PIPER[8], b. in Georgetown, Nov. 8, 1859; res. Georgetown, Mass., unm.

Child of SARAH SPOFFORD⁷, (1821) [**558**] (Benjamin⁶, Capt. Benjamin⁵, Abraham⁴, Capt. Abraham³, Sergt. Abraham², Robert¹) and Charles S. Piper; res. Somerville, Mass.

    i. ANNA D. PIPER, b. Oct. 4, 1853; m. Charles West; res. Somerville, Mass.

        She was chosen president of the Heptorian Club of Somerville, at its formation in 1894, and still holds the position in 1899. It is a Ladies' Club of 350 members devoted to literary pursuits.

Children of CAROLINE SAWYER⁷, (1819) [**559**] (Col. Samuel⁶, Elder David⁵, Samuel⁴, Capt. Abraham³, Sergt. Abraham², Robert¹) and Albert S. Nesmith; res. Brooklyn, N. Y.

    i. CHARLES ADAMS NESMITH, b. Nov. 3, 1841; d. 12 Apr., 1843.
    ii. NORMAN ALBERT NESMTH, b. Oct. 20, 1843; d. 6 Nov., 1865.
    iii. CLARENCE EUGENE NESMITH, b. Jan. 6, 1846; d. 20 Sept., 1874.
        He was in the Army.
    iv. LOUIS ALBERT NESMITH, b. July 26, 1848; m. Maria Manderson. He was in the Army; d. 1 Nov., 1880.
    v. CAROLINE LOUISA NESMITH, b. Dec. 14, 1852; m. (1) May 21, 1872, Charles Anderson; m. (2) Aug. 17, 1892, Antonio Guimaraes; res. Orange, N. J.
    vi. MARY JOSEPHINE NESMITH, b. Sept. 28, 1854; res. New York City.
    vii. CHARLES ARTHUR NESMITH, b. Nov. 17, 1856; d. 11 June, 1863.
    viii. FRANCES MARION NESMITH, b. Dec. 11, 1857; res. Washington, D. C.
    ix. VICTORIA ROSALIE NESMITH, b. Jan. 20, 1860; m. July 15, 1884, C. Winsor Whitten; res. Wakefield, Mass.

Children of LOUISA⁷, (1822) [**560**] (Col. Samuel⁶, Elder David⁵, Samuel⁴, Capt. Abraham³, Sergt. Abraham², Robert¹) and Rev. Charles S. Porter; res. Plymouth and Boston, Mass.

    i. JANE ELIZABETH PORTER, b. June 5, 1848; m. Oct. 19, 1871, Frank K. Clarkson; res. W. Medford, Mass.
    ii. CHARLES DANE PORTER, b. Sept. 8, 1857; unm.
    iii. IRVING ADAMS PORTER, b. Mar. 17, 1860; m. June 11, 1884, Alice S. Parker, dau. of David A. Parker of Goffstown, N. H.; res. W. Medford, Mass.

Children of GEORGE FITZ⁷, (1824) [561] (Col. Samuel⁶, Elder David⁵, Samuel⁴, Capt. Abraham³, Sergt. Abraham², Robert¹) and Elizabeth W. (Whitney) Adams; res. Derry, N. H.

    i. HELEN LOUISE⁸, b. in Derry, Dec. 10, 1847; m. Feb. 10, 1874, J. Q. A. Jeffers of Haverhill, Mass.; res. Haverhill, Mass.; no issue.
1105. ii. LUCY ELIZABETH⁸, b. in Derry, Sept. 9, 1850; m. Jan. 1, 1870, George A. Proctor, son of John and Abigail (Choate) Proctor, b. July 2, 1845; res. S. Boston.
    iii. SARAH FITZ⁸, b. in Derry, June 22, 1852; unm.
    iv. GEORGE NEWELL⁸, b. in Derry, Dec. 27, 1853; m. June 22, 1891, Carrie Combs of Kansas City; he res. Manchester, N. H. He d. 6 Apr., 1896; no issue.
    v. FRANK WELLMAN⁸, b. in Derry, Aug. 28, 1859; d. 1 Feb., 1867.
    vi. PROF. CHARLES E.⁸, b. in Derry, June 23, 1861; m. Nov. 27, 1888, Ida Swain, dau. of Joseph and Maria Swain of Nantucket, Mass.
    He graduated from Pinkerton Academy, 1879, and from Bridge-water Normal School in 1886. After one year in the Leominster High School, became teacher of physics and chemistry in the Salem Normal School in Sept., 1887; no issue.
    vii. MARY WHITNEY⁸, b. in Derry, Sept. 4, 1863; d. same day.
    viii. MARION WHITNEY⁸, b. Jan. 7, 1867; d. 3 Feb., 1877.

Children of GEORGE WILLIAM⁷, (1818) [562] (Col. Gibbins⁶, Stephen⁵, Samuel⁴, Capt. Abraham³, Sergt. Abraham², Robert¹) and Mary (Thurlow) Adams; res. Byfield, Mass.

    i. MARY⁸, d. in infancy.
1106. ii. GEORGE WILLIAM⁸, JR., b. Feb. 2, 1855; m. Sept. 19, 1875, Lizzie Maria Dow, dau. of Amos and Maria (Morrison) Dow, b. in Salem, N. H., Nov. 10, 1853; res. "Highfields," So. Byfield, Mass.

Children of ADELINE⁷, (1823) [563] (Stephen⁶, Capt. Stephen⁵, Samuel⁴, Capt. Abraham³, Sergt. Abraham², Robert¹) and Isaac W. Wheelwright; res. Byfield, Mass.

    i. SARAH V. WHEELWRIGHT, b. Apr. 20, 1859; m. Aug. 13, 1883, Joseph N. Dummer; res. Rowley, Mass.
    ii. JOSEPH WHEELWRIGHT, b. Oct. 2, 1860; m. Jan. 18, 1884, Alice R. Upton of Salem, Mass.
    iii. MARTHA ADAMS WHEELWRIGHT, b. Feb. 17, 1862; d. 20 Aug., 1874.

iv. ELLEN AUGUSTA WHEELWRIGHT, b. Oct. 27, 1864; m. Sept. 21, 1890, Edward R. Sanford.
v. JANE COOMBS WHEELWRIGHT, b. Jan. 21, 1868; m. (1) July, 11, 1888, Elmer L. Cummings.; he d. 28 Oct., 1889 ; m. (2) Feb. 18, 1892, Rev. David C. Torrey. *d. Feb. 23, 1908*

Children of ALBERT S.[7], (1825) [564] (Stephen[6], Capt. Stephen[5], Samuel[4], Capt. Abraham[3], Sergt. Abraham[2], Robert[1]) and Abigail N. (Dummer) Adams; res. Hydepark, Mass.

1107.
i. HENRY DUMMER[8], b. Newport, N. H., Sept. 3, 1851 ; m. Oct. 29-30, 1878, Mabel Weld of Elgin, Ill., b. in Solon, Me., Nov. 29, 1859. He is a painter in Jamestown, N. Dak.
ii. ABBIE CLIFTON[8], b. in Newport, Jan. 30, 1855 ; m. Sept. 21, 1890, *d. Jan. 2, 1922* Joshua N. Foss of Rowley, Mass.; deceased ; res. Rowley, Mass.
iii. CHARLES WALTER[8], b. in Newport, Oct. 25, 1857 ; d. 16 Mar., 1859.
iv. ALBERT OTIS[8], b. in Rowley, Mass., Feb. 13, 1860 ; d. 24 Sept., 1863.
v. WILLIS LONGFELLOW[8], b. in Amesbury, Mass., July 7, 1867 ; m. May 20, 1890, Emma Bain of Buffalo, N. Y. *Emma B. d. Dec. 29, 19* He is an electrician and constructing engineer; res. Niagara Falls, N. Y.

Children of CAROLINE L.[7], (1831) [565] (Stephen[6], Capt. Stephen[5], Samuel[4], Capt. Abraham[3], Sergt. Abraham[2], Robert[1]) and Frederick W. Blake; res. Malden, Mass.

i. MARY ANNA BLAKE, b. Jan. 6, 1857 ; m. Feb. 15, 1879, John M. Jewett.
ii. SUSAN PARKER BLAKE, b. Dec. 1, 1858; m. July 2, 1885, Rev. James H. Childs.
iii. CARRIE LOUISA BLAKE, b. May 10, 1863.
Teacher ; unm.

Children of LEONARD[7], (1840) [566] (Stephen[6], Capt. Stephen[5], Samuel[4], Capt. Abraham[3], Sergt. Abraham[2], Robert[1]) and Adeline E. (Wallis) Adams; res. So. Byfield, Mass.

i. STEPHEN DENISON[8], b. in Byfield, Jan. 30, 1869. *m. Mary who d. Jan.* Salesman ; res. Boston, Mass.
ii. RUFUS DODGE[8], b. in Byfield, Aug. 11, 1870; m. June 9, 1898, *Aroline d. N.* Aroline F. Whittredge of Lynn, Mass.; res. Salem, Mass.
iii. WALLACE LONGFELLOW[8], b. in Byfield, Sept. 25, 1872; res. Byfield, Mass.; ~~un~~m. *Geneva*

1. Marjorie, dau. of Wallace,
11. Barbara, " " b. m. Elm
E. Bailey, Dec. 3, 1944

ROBERT ADAMS   [Eighth Generation.

    iv. EDITH MAY[8], b. in Byfield, Oct. 15, 1874; m. July 5, 1898, *d. May 10. 1918.* Maurice Lacroix of Geneva, Switz.; res. Byfield (Meadowmere), Mass.
    v. MAYBETH[8] (twin), b. in Byfield, Oct. 15, 1874; deceased.
    vi. LEON ALBERT[8], b. in Byfield, Jan. 7, 1877.
        He is a printer; res. Byfield, Mass.

Children of SARAH JANE[7], (1823) [**567**] (Sewall[6], Capt. Stephen[5], Samuel[4], Capt. Abraham[3], Sergt. Abraham[2], Robert[1]) and Charles Henry Hale; res. Newburyport, Mass.

    i. SARAH ANN HALE, b. June 11, 1847; m. Oct. 18, 1871, Moses Bartlett Little, b. Jan. 27, 1849; d. 25 Jan., 1892.
        She is matron of Anne Jaques Hospital, Newburyport, Mass.
    ii. JOSEPHINE MARIA HALE, b. June 8, 1848; unm.
    iii. ELIZA ADAMS HALE, b. Nov. 21, 1854; m. May 18, 1881, George Wheeler Ordway, b. Jan. 5, 1856; res. Providence, R. I.
    iv. HENRY SEWALL HALE, b. May 30, 1801; m. Dec. 6, 1887, Lizzie Broughton Wiggins; res. Newburyport, Mass.

Children of JAMES AUGUSTUS[7], (1830) [**568**] (Sewall[6], Capt. Stephen[5], Samuel[4], Capt. Abraham[3], Sergt. Abraham[2], Robert[1]) and Hannah J. (Adams) Adams; res. Newburyport, Mass.

    i. WILLIAM AUGUSTUS[8], b. in Newburyport, Aug. 6, 1854; d. in 4 mos.
    ii. HELEN AUGUSTA[8], b. in Newburyport, Nov. 17, 1857; d. 8 Mar., 1870.
    iii. EMMA LUCRETIA[8], b. in Newburyport, Nov. 13, 1859; m. June 1, 1882, Walter Stillman Martin, b. Mar. 8, 1862; no issue.
    iv. ANNIE SEWALL[8], b. in Newburyport, Jan. 22, 1861; m. Sept. 15, 1898, Frank Weare Field.; res. Newburyport, Mass.
    v. HENRY ILSLEY[8], b. in Newburyport, Apr. 22, 1863; d. 22 Feb., 1865.

Child of JAMES AUGUSTUS[7], (1830) and Harriet Augusta (Coffin) Adams.

    vi. CARRIE COFFIN[8], b. in Newburyport, July 25, 1874; d. 8 June, 1875.

Children of *HENRY SEWALL⁷, (1831) [569] (Sewall⁶, Capt. Stephen⁵, Samuel⁴, Capt. Abraham³, Sergt. Abraham², Robert¹) and Hannah M. (Little) Adams; res. Boston, Mass.

  i. AGNES LITTLE⁸, b. in Boston, Sept. 4, 1854; m. Oct. 10, 1887, Wm. Russell Comer, son of John H. Comer, b. in Boston, Sept. 7, 1854; res. Winthrop, Mass.
  ii. EMILY JUDSON⁸, b. in Chelsea, Mass., Sept. 4, 1857; unm. *d. Sept. 8, 19*
1108. iii. NORMAN ILSLEY⁸, b. in Hydepark, Mass., Feb. 16, 1864; m. Nov. 19, 1884, Mabel E. George, dau. of Cyrus A. and Lydia J. George, b. in Boston, May 16, 1868; res. Winthrop, Mass.
  iv. HENRIETTA SEWALL⁸, b. in Hydepark, Aug. 1, 1867; unm. *d. July 4, 19*
  v. HOWARD SHIRLEY⁸, b. in Hydepark, Apr. 14, 1870; m. Oct. 21, 1892, Anne Juliett Webber, dau. of David G. and Mary E. Webber, b. Dec. 17, 1868; res. Winthrop, Mass.
  vi. WESLEY IRVING⁸, b. in Hydepark, Dec. 29, 1871; d. 15 Apr., 1881.

---

*Mr. H. Sewall Adams entered the post-office at Newburyport in 1846, remaining until 1853. He then entered the Boston office under Postmaster G. W. Gordon. When E. C. Bailey succeeded Mr. Gordon, Mr. Adams was appointed his secretary. He held this position until 1857, when Postmaster Nahum Capen appointed him assistant cashier. In 1862 he was appointed to the office of "Cashier" by J. G. Palfrey, P. M., which position he has ever since retained. He was a member of the Massachusetts House of Representatives in 1871-1872.

Children of CAPT. JOHN QUINCY⁷, (1834) [570] (Sewall⁶, Capt. Stephen⁵, Samuel⁴, Capt. Abraham³, Sergt. Abraham², Robert¹) and Harriet Augusta (Forsyth) Adams; res. Chelsea, Mass.

1109. i. WILLIAM RICHARDSON⁸, b. in Chelsea, Aug. 26, 1863; m. (1) Apr. 1, 1886, A. Jennett McConnell; m. (2) Feb. 21, 1893, Addie Kent Smyth.
  ii. GEORGE FORSYTH⁸, b. in Chelsea, Nov. 19, 1870; d. 17 Jan., 1871.

Children of MARY E.⁷, (1830) [571] (John⁶, Joseph⁵, Rev. Joseph⁴, Capt. Abraham³, Sergt. Abraham², Robert¹) and Wm. H. Bartlett; res. New York City.

  i. JOHN FREDERICK BARTLETT, b. in Lowell, Mass., May 28, 1865; m. at Brooklyn, N. Y., April 14, 1887, Isabel Vance Warmley, dau. of Joseph Warmley of Brooklyn; she d. 20 Apr., 1888. He d. at Kingsbridge, N. Y., 30 May, 1887; no issue.
  ii. MARIA JOSEPHINE BARTLETT, b. in W. Deer Park, N. Y., Feb. 8, 1869; d. in infancy.

iii. EUGENE B. BARTLETT, b. in W. Deer Park, Dec. 17, 1871 ; d. in infancy.

Children of GEORGE W.^{7}, (1832) [**572**] (John^6, Joseph^5, Rev. Joseph^4, Capt. Abraham^3, Sergt. Abraham^2, Robert^1) and Emily E. (Butters) Adams; res. Lowell, Mass.

  i. EMMA MABEL^8, b. in Lowell, May 1, 1861; m. at Lowell, Sept., 1883, Joseph F. Carpenter ; res. Lowell, Mass.; no issue.
  ii. GEORGE F.^{8}, b. in Lowell, Mar. 6, 1864 ; m. Sept. 28, 1898, Florence Burkinshaw ;res. Lowell, Mass.; no issue.
1110. iii. ALBERT E.^{8}, b. in Lowell, Nov. 11, 1866 ; m. Sept., 1887, Bertha A. Webster of Lowell. He d. at Newton Center, Mass., 1 Aug., 1895.
1111. iv. CHARLES F.^{8}, b. in Dracut, Mass., Oct. 1, 1872 ; m. Nov. 29, 1893, Lila Nevens ; res. Lowell, Mass.

Children of CAROLINE C.^{7}, (1833) [**573**] (John^6, Joseph^5, Rev. Joseph^4, Capt. Abraham^3, Sergt. Abraham^2, Robert^1) and Wm. H. Bartlett; res. Lowell, Mass.

  i. GUELHEMENA I. BARTLETT, b. in Lowell, July 16, 1860 ; d. 18 Aug., 1860.
  ii. FREDERICK WM. BARTLETT, b. in Lowell, June 27, 1862 ; d. at W. Deer Park, N. Y., 10 Aug., 1864.

Children of JOHN HANCOCK^7, (1837) [**574**] (John^6, Joseph^5, Rev. Joseph^4, Capt. Abraham^3, Sergt. Abraham^2, Robert^1) and Emma (Davis) Adams; res. Lowell, Mass.

  i. CAROLINE^8, b. in Lowell, 1864 ; m. ——— Harris of Lowell, Mass. She d. in 1891, leaving children.
  ii. HENRY^8, b. in Lowell, 1869; he m. and has 4 children.
  iii. ANNE^8, b, in Lowell, 1872 ; she m. and had one child.

Child of MARIA THERESA^7, (1842) [**575**] (John^6, Joseph^5, Rev. Joseph^4, Capt. Abraham^3, Sergt. Abraham^2, Robert^1) and Edward G. Tuckerman ; res. New York City.

  i. HARRY G. TUCKERMAN, b. at Lowell, Mass., Feb. 22, 1864 ; m. April 15, 1886, at Brooklyn, N. Y., Minnie L. Kearr, dau. of David and Katherine Kearr of Brooklyn, N. Y.
   One child, Raymond E., b. Feb. 18, 1887.

Eighth Generation.] OF NEWBURY, MASS. 273

Child of GEORGE HENRY⁷, (1843) [576] (George⁶, Joseph⁵, Rev. Joseph⁴, Capt. Abraham³, Sergt. Abraham², Robert¹) and Sarah Leech (Macomber) Adams; res. Brookline, Mass.
    i. CAROLINE MARY⁸, b. in Brookline, Oct. 12, 1899.

Children of LUCY HEDDING⁷, (1826) [577] (Rev. John Folsom⁶, Lieut. John⁵, Rev. Joseph⁴, Capt. Abraham³, Sergt. Abraham², Robert¹) and Samuel Augustus Hatch; res. Greenland, N. H.
    i. IDA MARY HATCH, b. May 6, 1859 ; m. John Pottle ; res. Greenland, N. H.
    ii. JOHN WILLIAM HATCH, b. Dec. 21, 1862 ; m. Ada M. Paul; res. Kittery, Me.
    iii. CHARLOTTE ANNIE HATCH, b. Aug. 10, 1864; m. Ernest Holmes ; res. Portsmouth, N. H.
    iv. GEORGE AUGUSTUS HATCH, b. Feb. 21, 1868 ; d. 9 June, 1898, at Seattle, Wash., while returning from Alaska with a party of miners ; was unm.

Children of JOHN WILLIAM⁷, (1828) [578] (Rev. John Folsom⁶, Lieut. John⁵, Rev. Joseph⁴, Capt. Abraham³, Sergt. Abraham², Robert¹) and Sarah F. (Waterhouse) Adams; res. Springfield, Mass.

1112.   i. MAY⁸, b. in Lenoxville, Canada, June 19, 1866 ; m. Oct. 16, 1894, Edgar Jay Oatman; one son, b. Nov. 9, 1899.
1113.   ii. WALTER⁸, b. in Springfield, Mass., Sept. 25, 1867 ; m. Nov. 23, 1891, Mabel Cynthia Chapman ; res. Springfield, Mass.
    iii. JOHN COLLINS⁸, b. in Springfield, Dec. 8, 1869 ; d. 17 July, 1870.
    iv. WILLIE⁸, b. in Springfield, Dec. 15, 1869; d. 17 Feb., 1877.
    v. CHARLES⁸, b. in Springfield, Mar. 7, 1871 ; m. Nov. 12, 1895, Ella Belle Bostwick ; res. Springfield, Mass.; no issue.
    vi. NELLIE⁸, b. in Springfield, Oct. 10, 1873.

Children of MARTHA ANN⁷, (1822) [579] (David⁶, Lieut. John⁵, Rev. Joseph⁴, Capt. Abraham³, Sergt. Abraham², Robert¹) and Bradstreet Moody ; res. Newton, Mass.
    i. FRANKLIN H. MOODY, b. in Cambridge, Mass., Mar. 16, 1842 ; d. 25 May, 1842.

(18)

ROBERT ADAMS [Eighth Generation.

    ii. ELIZABETH BRADSTREET MOODY, b. in Cambridge, Apr. 5, 1844; d. next day.
   iii. THOMAS B. MOODY, b. in Cambridge, Sept. 3, 1845; d. 27 Oct., 1848.
   iv. ABBY MINOT MOODY, b. in Cambridge, Sept. 20, 1847; d. 30 June, 1849.
    v. MARTHA ADAMS MOODY, b. in Cambridge, July 26, 1849; living unm.
   vi. WILLIAM OWEN MOODY, b. in Cambridge, Dec. 9, 1850; m. Oct. 24, 1883, Florence Jennie Thompson; res. Oak Park, Chicago.
   vii. HARRY MINOT MOODY, b. in Cambridge, July 20, 1853; d. 17 June, 1856.
  viii. MERCER BROOKS MOODY, b. in Cambridge, Nov. 5, 1854; living.
   ix. BESSIE DELANO MOODY, b. in Newton, Feb. 26, 1865; m. Sept. 14,.1888, Geo. Taylor Allen.

Children of MARY ANN^7, (1825) [**580**] (David^6, Lieut. John^5, Rev. Joseph^4, Capt. Abraham^3, Sergt. Abraham^2, Robert^1) and Abbot R. Davis; res. Chelsea, Mass.

    i. ABBOT ADAMS DAVIS, b. July 12, 1852; d. 1853.
   ii. MARY ABBY DAVIS, b. May 13, 1855; res. Chelsea, Mass.; unm.
   iii. ABBOT A. DAVIS, b. Apr. 11, 1856; m. Nov. 12, 1882, Rachel Merritt; res. Cincinnati, O.
   iv. JOHN EDGAR DAVIS, b. Oct. 15, 1857; res. Chelsea, Mass.; unm.
    v. LUTHER FRANKLIN DAVIS, b. Oct. 15, 1860; d. 1 Sept., 1868.
   vi. PERCY SHERIFF DAVIS, b. June 4, 1866; res. Chelsea, Mass.; unm.
   vii. WILBUR MOODY DAVIS, b. Oct. 29, 1870; m. Francesca Ort; res. Chelsea, Mass.

Children of ABIGAIL CHAPMAN^7, (1828) [**581**] (David^6, Lieut. John^5, Rev. Joseph^4, Capt. Abraham^3, Sergt. Abraham^2, Robert^1) and Charles Henry Draper; res. E. Cambridge, Mass.

    i. CHARLES HENRY DRAPER, JR., b. Mar. 23, 1851; m. Louisa Smith; res. Brooklyn, N. Y.
   ii. GEO. EDWARD DRAPER, b. Oct. 30, 1853; d. Nov., 1895.

Children of SARAH PORTER^7, (1834) [**582**] Rev. Charles^6 D. D., Lieut. John^5, Rev. Joseph^4, Capt. Abraham^3, Sergt. Abraham^2, Robert^1) and William A. Barnes; res. Piedmont, Clallam Co., Wash.

Eighth Generation.] OF NEWBURY, MASS. 275

  i. CHARLES ADAMS BARNES, b. Aug. 12, 1859; d. unm. in Colombia, South America, 22 Jan., 1895.
  ii. PAUL BARNES, b. in Centerville, Ind., Feb. 1, 1862; living 1898, at Piedmont, Wash.; unm.
  iii. MARY ALICE BARNES, b. in Centerville, Nov. 22, 1864; m. June 30, 1890, William C. Eldridge; res. Washington, D. C.
  iv. PIERRE BARNES, b. in Indianapolis, Ind., Aug. 4, 1866; res. Seattle, Wash.; unm.
  v. ADAMS BARNES, b. in Washington, D. C., Aug. 30, 1872; res. Piedmont, Wash.; unm.
  vi. HORACE BARNES, b. in Washington, Oct. 14, 1878; res. Piedmont, Wash.; unm.

Children of COL. CHARLES HENRY[7], (1836) [583] (Rev. Charles[6], D. D., Lieut. John[5], Rev. Joseph[4], Capt. Abraham[3], Sergt. Abraham[2], Robert[1]) and Elvira (Hamilton) Adams; res. Rye, N. H.

1114. i. ALBERT HAMILTON[8], b. in Jacksonville, Ill., Sept. 14, 1863; m. Aug. 30, 1888, Carrie Allen, eldest dau. of John Allen of Elk Grove, Cook Co., Ill.
       He settled in Chicago in 1868; was graduated from Union College of Law, 1885, and is engaged in practice of Patent Law in Chicago; res. Oak Park, Ill.
  ii. CAROLINE PORTER[8], b. in Chicago, Sept. 26, 1868; m. Dec. 18, 1897, Prof. Herbert E. Griffith of Knox College; res. Galesburg, Ill.
  iii. HOWARD ORR[8], b. in Chicago, Nov. 9, 1872.
       He is a druggist, unm., at Spokane, Wash.

Children of CHARLOTTE A.[7], (1837) [584] (Rev. Charles[6], D. D., Lieut. John[5], Rev. Joseph[4], Capt. Abraham[3], Sergt. Abraham[2], Robert[1]) and Jacob Haynes; res. Bell Brook, Ohio.
  i. ELMER HAYNES, b. Nov. 17, 1861; d. young.
  ii. HERBERT HAYNES, b. Oct. 11, 1862; m. Aug. 14, 1889, Rose Mary Yonkey.
  iii. MAURICE PORTER HAYNES, b. Nov. 1, 1863; m. Aug. 28, 1890, Effie Carr.
  iv. GEORGE ADAMS HAYNES, b. 1865; d. young.
  v. ADELINE HAYNES, b. Dec. 11, 1868; m. Aug. 25, 1892, Gaius Glen Atkins.
  vi. ELOISE EMERY HAYNES, b. May 21, 1873; m. Jan. 15, 1894, Fred Hamilton Coombs.

vii. ROSALIE HAYNES, b. July 12, 1876.
viii. MARY EMMA CHENEY HAYNES, b. May 1, 1880.

Children of CAPT. GEORGE HUNTINGTON[7], (1846) [585] (Rev. Charles[6], D. D., Lieut. John[5], Rev. Joseph[4], Capt. Abraham[3], Sergt. Abraham[2], Robert[1]) and Augusta (Holmes) Adams; res. New York City.

    i. HUNTINGTON[8], b. in New York, Nov. 3, 1879.
        He is a student in Harvard University.
    ii. LAWRENCE HOLMES[8], b. in New York, Dec. 21, 1881; deceased.
    iii. CONSTANCE[8], b. in Cedarhurst, L. I., Sept. 6, 1888.

Child of FRANCIS MARIA[7], (1832) [586] (Joseph[6], Jr., Joseph[5], Rev. Benjamin[4], Capt. Abraham[3], Sergt. Abraham[2], Robert[1]) and Daniel W. Foster, res. Lynn, Mass.

    i. SUSAN M. FOSTER, b. July 15, 1854; res. Lynn, Mass.; unm.

Children of MARIA ELLEN[7], (1835) [587] (Joseph[6], Jr., Joseph[5], Rev. Benjamin[4], Capt. Abraham[3], Sergt. Abraham[2], Robert[1]) and George F. Breed; res. Lynn, Mass.

    i. HELEN GREENLEAF BREED, b. in Lynn, Apr. 15, 1859; d. 5 Sept., 1859.
    ii. MABEL BREED, b. in Lynn, June 12, 1864; res. Clinton, Mass., unm.

Child of REUBEN JOHNSON[7], (1839) [588] (Joseph[6], Jr., Joseph[5], Rev. Benjamin[4], Capt. Abraham[3], Sergt. Abraham[2], Robert[1]) and Jane (Knowlton) Adams.

    i. SUSAN[8], m. Rev. Geo. H. Kent; res. Stratham, N. H.

Child of GEORGE BENJAMIN[7], (1832) [591] (Benjamin Webb[6], Joseph[5], Rev. Benjamin[4], Capt. Abraham[3], Sergt. Abraham[2], Robert[1]) and Abby (Dobber) Adams; res. Marblehead, Mass.

    i. IRENE CLIFFORD[8], b. in Marblehead, Mar. 3, 1869; m. June 22, 1892, Chauncey G. Johnson. She rem. 1898, to Roxbury, Mass.; no issue.

Eighth Generation.] OF NEWBURY, MASS. 277

Children of JOSEPH NICHOLS⁷, (1834) [592] (Benjamin, Webb⁶, Joseph⁵, Rev. Benjamin⁴, Capt. Abraham³, Sergt. Abraham², Robert¹) and Susan Jane (Fairfield) Adams; res. Roslindale, Boston, Mass.

 i. IDA HELEN⁸, b. in Dorchester, June 9, 1859; res. Roslindale, Huntington Ave.; unm.
  She teaches in the Horace Mann School, Newbury St., Boston, Mass.
 ii. FANNIE CURRIER⁸, b. in Dorchester, Feb. 2, 1863; d. 20 Nov., 1882.
1115. iii. JOHN BENJAMIN F.⁸, b. in Dorchester, Oct. 20, 1868; m. May 16, 1893, Josephine Noonan; res. Mattapan, Mass.
 iv. MARY BURNHAM (adopted), b. July 6, 1877; res. Roslindale, Mass.; unm.

Child of HELEN ISADORA⁷, (1842) [593] (Benjamin Webb⁶, Joseph⁵, Rev. Benjamin⁴, Capt. Abraham³, Sergt. Abraham², Robert¹) and Alonzo Collins; res. Lakeport, N. H.

 i. NELSON BRADFORD COLLINS, b. in Dorchester, Mass., Aug. 24, 1872; res. Lakeport, N. H.; unm.

Children of JOHN QUINCY⁷, (1826) [594] (John Breed⁶, Nathan⁵, Capt. Nathan⁴, Capt. Abraham³, Sergt. Abraham², Robert¹) and Sarah Catherine (Clark) Adams; res. Boston, Mass., and Brooklyn, N. Y.

 i. GRACE CLARK⁸, m. Jan. 28, 1875, James Irving Raymond; res. Brooklyn, N. Y., and Stamford, Conn.
 ii. LILLIAN PRESTON⁸, m. June 19, 1894, John Sherlock; res. Boston, Mass.; no issue.
 iii. MAUD ADELINE⁸, m. Jan. 28, 1890, Charles W. Colton; res. New York.

Children of NATHAN PRESTON⁷, (1828) [595] (John Breed⁶, Nathan⁵, Capt. Nathan⁴, Capt. Abraham³, Sergt. Abraham², Robert¹) and Julia J. (Pasco) Adams; res. Broad Brook, Conn.

 i. ADELINE J.⁸, b. in Rockville, Conn., Sept. 30, 1850; d. at Broad Brook, Conn., 3 Nov., 1869.
 ii. ELLEN A⁸, b. in Rockville, July 4, 1852; d. 30 June, 1854.

iii. HENRY N.[8], b. in Broad Brook, Conn., Mar. 30, 1856; d. 30 Oct., 1858.
iv. EDITH E.[8], b. in Broad Brook, Oct. 21, 1859; res. with her mother in Chaplin, Conn.
v. LILIAN G.[8], b. in Broad Brook, Sept. 5, 1863; d. 3 Jan., 1878.
vi. MABEL A.[8], b. in Broad Brook, Aug. 26, 1867; d. in Windsor, Conn., 20 Dec., 1885.
vii. NATHAN P.[8], b. in Broad Brook, June 26, 1871; m. Apr. 26, 1897, Grace Howard of Los Angeles, Cal.; res. Riverside, Cal.

Children of MARY ADELINE[7], (1834) [**596**] (John Breed[6], Nathan[5], Capt. Nathan[4], Capt. Abraham[3], Sergt. Abraham[2], Robert[1]) and Andrew Lamphear; res. Abington, Conn.

i. ERWIN ANDREW LAMPHEAR, b. Sept. 24, 1863; m. (1) Feb. 21, 1884, Emily C. Burlingham of Hartford, Conn.; m. (2) Mar. 20, 1895, Annie L. Lucas and had one child, Ruth Warren, b. Aug. 30, 1896; res. Hartford, Conn.
ii. LOUIS A. LAMPHEAR, b. June 8, 1865; unm.; res. Brooklyn, N. Y.
iii. EVA M. LAMPHEAR, b. Sept. 16, 1872; unm.; res. Abington, Conn.

Children of JAMES ERWIN[7], (1839) [**597**] (John Breed[6], Nathan[5], Capt. Nathan[4], Capt. Abraham[3], Sergt. Abraham[2], Robert[1]) and Hannah (Williams) Adams; res. Brooklyn, N. Y.

i. FLORENCE A[8], b. in Brooklyn, Apr. 30, 1874.
ii. MARION[8], b. in Brooklyn, Dec. 1, 1880.

Child of GEORGE AUGUSTUS[7], (1841) [**598**] (Capt. George[6], Nathan[5], Capt. Nathan[4], Capt. Abraham[3], Sergt. Abraham[2], Robert[1]) and Ruth A. (Miller) Adams; res. Providence, R. I.

i. WILLIAM L.[8], b. in Eastford, Conn., Apr. 1, 1869; unm.

Children of ELIZABETH B.[7], (1844) [**599**] (Capt. George[6], Nathan[5], Capt. Nathan[4], Capt. Abraham[3], Sergt. Abraham[2], Robert[1]) and James E. Latham; res. Providence, R. I.

i. FRED J. LATHAM, b. in Eastford, Conn., Nov. 24, 1873; m. Oct. 14, 1897, Sarah Gates of Providence, R. I.
ii. LENA ADAMS LATHAM, b. in Eastford, Apr. 7, 1887.

Children of EVELINE AMELIA[7], (1850) [600] (Capt. George[6], Nathan[5], Capt. Nathan[4], Capt. Abraham[3], Sergt. Abraham[2], Robert[1]) and Samuel G. Pellett; res. Providence, R. I.

    i. HARRY A. PELLETT, b. Apr. 13, 1872; m. Sept. 14, [1897, Maud Latham of Windsor Locks, Conn.

    ii. MARY A. PELLETT, b. Nov. 20, 1875.

Children of WILLIAM[7], (1811) [601] (Enoch[6], Enoch[5], Henry[4], Capt. Abraham[3], Sergt. Abraham[2], Robert[1]) and Lucinda (Hall) Adams; res. So. Andover, Me.

1116.   i. JULIA ANN S.[8], b. in So. Andover, Apr. 23, 1839; m. Dec. 3, 1863, Hiram Dustin Abbott of So. Andover, Me.
    He was a mason and farmer, and became post master of So. Andover in 1880.

1117.   ii. JOSEPH EMORY[8], b. in So. Andover, Feb. 26, 1841; m. (1) Oct. 12, 1869, Ellen Olive Young of Bethel, Me.; d. in Bethel, 3 Nov., 1869; m. (2) Sept. 5, 1871, Irene Jane Sampson of Augusta, Me.; d. in Augusta, 31 Oct., 1872; m. (3) Nov. 20, 1873, Alba Sarah Tubbs of Mechanic Falls, Me.; divorced in 1875; m. (4) Nov. 1, 1887, Elsia Rhoda Sampson, a half sister of Irene Jane Sampson.
    He was a merchant in Augusta, but removed in 1888 to Vineland, N. J.

1118.   iii. CHARLES HALL[8], b. in So. Andover, June 24, 1844; m. Aug. 25, 1867, Marian Virginia Reed of Rumford, Me.; she d. 18 Dec., 1898.
    He was a contractor and builder in Mechanic Falls, Me.; in Fairfield, Me.; in Bethel, Me., and set. in Norway, Me., in 1894.

1119.   iv. WILLIAM HENRY[8], b. in So. Andover, Aug. 30, 1846; m. Dec. 23, 1874, Enna Maria Goodrich of So. Andover; she d. at Bryant's Pond, Me., 18 Jan. 1892; res. 1898, W. Paris, Me.

1120.   v. LUCINDA ELLA[8], b. in So. Andover, Aug. 31, 1848; m. Jan. 22, 1871, William Jones of Andover; res. So. Andover, Me. She d. 29 July, 1873.

1121.   vi. ENOCH[8], b. in So. Andover, Mar. 3, 1850; m. Dec. 18, 1880, Mrs. Mary Falkner Martin of Poland, Me.
    He is a carpenter; res. Poland, Me.

1122.   vii. LIZZIE EMMA[8], b. in So. Andover, May 20, 1852; m. Dec. 25, 1876, Chester Howard Lane of Sumner, Me.; res. Mechanic Falls, Me.

1123.   viii. MARY EDNA[8], b. in So. Andover, Oct. 2, 1855; m. Mar. 2, 1878, Andrew William Bridge; res. Mechanic Falls, Me.

1124.   ix. MATILDA McCLUNE[8], b. in So. Andover, Dec. 1, 1858; m. June 26, 1878, Calvin Curtis Yates; res. Mechanic Falls, Me. She d. 29 Mar., 1886.

Children of JULIA⁷, (1816) [602] (Enoch⁶, Enoch⁵, Henry⁴, Capt. Abraham³, Sergt. Abraham², Robert¹) and David B. Sawyer.

  i. EMELINE DAPHNA SAWYER, b. Nov. 17, 1842 ; m. June 19, 1862, Elijah Davenport of Sparta, Wis.; res. Sawyer Valley, Monroe Co., Wis.
  ii. MARTHA JANE SAWYER, b. July 20, 1845 ; m. May 8, 1869, Wm. Stinson Wyman ; res. Dakota.
  iii. AGNES JULIA SAWYER, b. Nov. 15, 1849 ; m. Feb. 10, 1874, John M. Ferguson of Chicago ; res. Hastings, Neb.

Children of EMILY⁷ (1817) [603] (Enoch⁶, Enoch⁵, Henry⁴, Capt. Abraham³, Sergt. Abraham², Robert¹) and Nelson Fickett; res. Wilson's Mills, Oxford Co., Me.

  i. JOHN N. FICKETT, b. Apr. 18, 1843 ; liv., unm.
  ii. LUCY A. A. FICKETT, b. Oct. 7, 1845 ; m. Dec., 1872, W. A. D. Jones of Dixfield, Me.; set in Littleton, N. H. She d. 30 June, 1892.
  iii. HARRIET S. FICKETT, b. July 17, 1847 ; m. Sept. 5, 1866, Thos. L. Flint of Wentworth, N. H. ; res. Bethel, Me. She d. Feb., 1875.
  iv. EMILY ADAMS FICKETT, b. Nov. 17, 1850 ; m. (1) Sept. 5, 1878, Stephen L. Williamson of New Sharon, Me.; m. (2) Mar. 18, 1890, Wm. H. Works ; res. New Sharon, Me.

Children of HARRIET⁷, (1826) [604] (Enoch⁶, Enoch⁵, Henry⁴, Capt. Abraham³, Sergt Abraham², Robert¹) and Simeon Shurtleff ; res. Wilson's Mills, Oxford Co., and Portland, Me.

  i. JENNIE L. SHURTLEFF, b. Jan. 15, 1839 ; res. Portland, Me.; unm.
  ii. DIANA SHAW SHURTLEFF, b. May 10, 1841 ; d. 10 Mar., 1844.
  iii. ALMIRA ADAMS SHURTLEFF, b. June 20, 1843 ; d. in Portland, Me., 13 Oct., 1856.

Children of MARY⁷, (1826) [606] (Enoch⁶, Enoch⁵, Henry⁴, Capt. Abraham³, Sergt. Abraham², Robert¹) and John S. Lovejoy ; res. Andover, Me.

  i. MAY HATTIE LOVEJOY, b. May 15, 1857 ; living, unm.
  ii. DAVIS GAGE LOVEJOY, b. Nov. 5, 1861 ; m. Jan. 4, 1890, at Bethel, Me., Nellie May Leach ; res. Bethel, Me.; one child, E. May Lovejoy, b. Aug. 17, 1893.

Eighth Generation.] OF NEWBURY, MASS. 281

 iii. ARTHUR LOVEJOY, b. Dec. 8, 1863; m. Feb. 22, 1898, at Newtonville, Mass., Annie MacMillan; res. Boston, Mass.
 iv. OWEN LOVEJOY, b. Nov. 9, 1866; living, unm.
 v. WALTER LOVEJOY, b. Aug. 5, 1869; living, unm.

Children of DR. ENOCH⁷, JR., (1829) [607] (Enoch⁶, Enoch⁵, Henry⁴, Capt. Abraham³, Sergt. Abraham², Robert¹) and Mary H. (Case) Adams; res. Litchfield, Kennebec Co., Me.

1125. i. ENOCH C.⁸, b. in Litchfield, May 13, 1852; m. 1879, Emma A. Huff. *7d June 6*
   He graduated from Bates College in 1876; is principal of the High School in West Newton, Mass. *d. Feb 17 1921*
1126. ii. DR. M. VINTON⁸, b. in Litchfield, May 25, 1853; m. 1877, Aroline Plumer.
   He graduated from the Medical Department of Pennsylvania University in 1877; set. in Brunswick, Me.; d. 3 Oct., 1896.
 iii. DR. WENDALL H.⁸, b. in Litchfield, June, 1854; m. 1882, Lena M. Walcott.
   He graduated from Bates College in 1876; received his degree of M. D., from Bowdoin College, 1881; set. in Kingston, Mass.; no issue.
 iv. ESTELLA⁸, b. in Litchfield, May, 1855; d. 1856.
1127. v. HERMAN H.⁸, b. in Litchfield, Aug. 25, 1856; m. (1) Sept., 1876, Hattie M. Taylor, dau. of Crowell C. Taylor, b. Oct., 1856; d. Jan. 1885; m. (2) 1886, Effie Philbrick, dau. of Jonathan Philbrick of Mt. Vernon, Me., b Jan., 1864. He settled in Belgrade, Me., 1876.
 vi. CECIL NUMA⁸, b. in Litchfield, May, 1857; d. 1859.
1128. vii. MARY LENORA⁸, b. in Litchfield, Aug. 7, 1859; m. July 1, 1885, Prof. Bradford O. McIntire, son of Amos and Harriet McIntire of York, Me., b. April 23, 1856. He graduated from Wesleyan University in 1883; taught at Kent's Hill, Me., till 1890, when he became professor of English Literature in Dickinson College, Carlisle, Pa.; he m. (2) Dec., 1897, Mary Florence Park of Jersey City, N. J. Mary Lenora d. suddenly, 10 Sept., 1874.
 viii. FRANK N.⁸, b. in Litchfield, June 14, 1862; m. June 27, 1888, Elnora J. True, dau. of Jacob K. True, b. Nov. 15, 1867; res. Litchfield, Me.; no issue.
1129. ix. LULU G.⁸, b. in Litchfield, June 20, 1865; m. 1894, Prof. Lyon L. Norton; res. Mt. Herman, Northfield, Mass.
1130. x. META LENA⁸, b. in Litchfield, Oct. 1, 1872; m. 1894, Maynard Maxim, Principal of Business Department of High School, Holyoke, Mass.

Children of JOHN EMERY⁷, (1805) [608] (Col. John Emery⁶, Enoch⁵, Henry⁴, Capt. Abraham³, Sergt. Abraham², Robert¹) and Belinda (Bell) Adams; res. Warrensville, Cuyahoga Co., Ohio.

1131. i. SARAH MOODY⁸, b. in Warrensville, June 7, 1830; m. April 8, 1852, Jared Hurd, son of Robert Hurd of E. Haddam, Conn., b. Nov. 24, 1822; res. Glenville, Ohio.
1132. ii. JOHN EMERY⁸, JR., b. in Warrensville, Sept. 5, 1833; m. Dec. 1, 1859, Jemima Powell, dau. of Henry and Cynthia (Crooks) Powell, b. in Portage Co., O., Oct. 8, 1828; d. 1 July, 1899, age 70 years. He set. in Solon, Johnson Co., Iowa, in March, 1873.
1133. iii. HARRIET B.⁸, b. in Warrensville, Mar. 31, 1836; m. Sept. 11, 1856, Wm. M. Warren, son of Moses Warren, who rem. from Ackworth, N. H., to Ohio in 1815; b. in 1832; res. W. Liberty, Iowa.
1134. iv. ALANTHA M.⁸, b. in Warrensville, May 19, 1841; m. Oct. 5, 1864, Cyrus P. Bell, son of Prosper and Emiline Bell, b. Sept. 2, 1836; d. 22 Oct., 1898; res. Stafford, Genesee Co., N. Y.
1135. v. LILLIS D⁸, b. in Warrensville, May 5, 1844; m. May 3, 1866, Dr. John L. Bean, son of John Mason Bean, formerly of Jay, Me., b. in Warrensville, O., Mar. 13, 1842; he graduated from the Cleveland Homeopathic Medical College in 1868; res. Bedford, O.
She was educated in Oberlin College.
1136. vi. MARY B.⁸, b. in Warrensville, July 9, 1845; m. Mar. 9, 1870, Demetriss Judd, son of O. B. and Amelia Judd, b. July 27, 1836; res. Paullina, O'Brien Co., Iowa.
vii. LEONIA SOPHIA⁸, b. in Warrensville, Oct. 4, 1847; m. Nov. 22, 1870, Cryners La Rue; res. Cleveland, O.; one dau., Lin Berenice.

Children of LYDIA BARTLETT⁷, (1809) [609] (Col. John Emery⁶, Enoch⁵, Henry⁴, Capt. Abraham³, Sergt. Abraham², Robert¹) and P. Clark Brown; res. Solon, Johnson Co., Iowa.

i. ALBIN BROWN, b. 1829, d. unm. 1857.
ii. WILLIS A. BROWN, b. 1831; m. Mrs. Emma Wright Du Boise; res. Solon, Ia.
iii. SARAH BROWN, b. 1833; m. Jan., 1855, Geo. W. Kinney; he d. 1895-6; res. Des Moines, Ia. She d. Feb., 1863.
iv. MATILDA BROWN, b. 1838; m. 1866, John Davis of Coos Co., Ore.; res. Plato, Ia. She d. 1 June, 1870.

Child of EBENEZER MOODY,⁷ (1811) [610] (Col. John Emery⁶, Enoch⁵, Henry⁴, Capt. Abraham³, Sergt. Abraham², Robert¹) and Sally (Gleason) Adams; res. Solon, Johnson Co., Iowa.

1187. i. DECATUR C.[8], b. in Warrensville, O., Mar. 7, 1837; m. in Geneva, Ill., 1865, Lydia Passmore.
He was a M. E. clergyman in Iowa, and a merchant in Mansfield, Mo.

Children of EBENEZER MOODY[7], (1811) and Henrietta (Lynn) Adams.

ii. FRANK[8], b. in Solon, Ia., Oct. 3, 1845; d. 28 Feb., 1858.
iii. MILO[8], b. in Solon, May 16, 1847; d. 28 Aug., 1858.
1138. iv. JOHN LYNN[8], b. in Solon, Mar. 9, 1852; m. 1876, Isabella Keen, b. Jan. 21, 1856.
He is a farmer; res. Solon, Ia.
1139. v. LILLIE[8], b. in Solon, Apr. 14, 1856; m. 1876, Herbert S. Fairall, an editor of Iowa City, Ia., and Superior, Wis.

Children of ENOCH[7], (1813) [611] (Col. John Emery[6], Enoch[5], Henry[4], Capt. Abraham[3], Sergt. Abraham[2], Robert[1]) and Lorinda (Auter) Adams; res. Cleveland, Cuyahoga Co., Ohio.

1140. i. HELEN E.[8], b. in Warrensville, O., Feb. 14, 1841-2; m. 1886. Abner D. Ruckel, a manufacturer of pottery, White Hall, Ill.
1141. ii. GEORGIE[8], b. in Akron, O., Apr. 30, 1844; m. June 28, 1882, Dwight W. Rockwell; res. Elyria, O., 1882-1887; now Cleveland, Ohio.
iii. WILLIAM FRANK[8], b. in Akron, 1847; d. 1848.
1142. iv. IDA E.[8], b. in Cuyahoga Falls, Mar. 4, 1849; m. Dec. 18, 1873, Orville Robertson of Cleveland, O.
v. CARRIE BELL[8], b. in Cuyahoga Falls, Nov. 4, 1853.
She is a graduate of Cleveland Homeopathic Medical College, and practices her profession in Cleveland, O.

Children of MOSES[7], (1815) [612] (Col. John Emery[6] (Enoch[5], Henry[4], Capt. Abraham[3], Sergt. Abraham[2], Robert[1]) and Sarah J. (Keislar) Adams; res. Solon, Iowa.

1143. i. CORA[8], b. in Solon, Nov. 28, 1857; m. Feb. 22, 1883, Joseph Walker; res. Iowa City, Ia.
1144. ii. MARY[8], b. in Solon, Dec. 16, 1861; m. Feb. 13, 1884. Frederick M. Warren; res. West Liberty, Iowa.
iii. JOHN QUINCY[8], b. in Solon, Aug. 6, 1864; res. Solon, Ia.; unm.
iv. MYRON DOW[8], b. in Solon, Sept. 12, 1866; res. Solon, Ia.; unm.
v. OLIVER M.[8], b. in Solon, Feb. 14, 1869; res. Solon, Ia.; unm.

vi. HARRIET E.[8], b. in Solon, Feb. 13, 1871 ; m. Feb. 15, 1899, Cassius Clay Moffit.
   She is a teacher ; res. Solon, Ia.

Children of FRANCIS CUSHMAN[7], (1820) [613] (Col. John Emery[6], Enoch[5], Henry[4], Capt. Abraham[3], Sergt. Abraham[2], Robert[1]) and Elizabeth (Edwards) Adams; res. Iowa City, Iowa.

   i. FRANCIS M.[8], b. in Hazel Green, Wis., Feb. 6, 1857.
   ii. FRED[8], b. in Hazel Green, July 12, 1858.
   iii. S. MATILDA[8], b. in Hazel Green, July 28, 1860 ; m. Oct. 16, 1889, Enoch H. Hope ; res. Oasis, Johnson Co., Ia.; no issue.
   iv. M. CATHERINE[8], b. in Iowa City, Ia., Apr. 4, 1862.
   v. WILLIAM E.[8], b. in Solon, Ia., Dec. 15, 1863 ; m. May, 1899, —— ——— ; res. Oklahoma.
   vi. LILLIE S.[8], b. in Iowa City, Oct. 7, 1867.

Children of MATILDA[7], (1826) [614] (Col. John Emery[6], Enoch[5], Henry[4], Capt. Abraham[3], Sergt. Abraham[2], Robert[1]) and Daniel F. McCune; res. Solon, Johnson Co., Ia.

   i. FRANK McCUNE, b. Aug., 1858 ; d. Jan., 1864.
   ii. JENNIE BELL McCUNE, b. April, 1860 ; d. Sept., 1861.

Children of JAMES MONROE[7], (1828) [615] (Col. John Emery[6], Enoch[5], Henry[4], Capt. Abraham[3], Sergt. Abraham[2], Robert[1]) and Sophia (Dudley) Adams; res. Solon, Johnson Co., Iowa.

1145. i. ADA P.[8], b. in Solon, June, 1857 ; m. Oct., 1878, Albert Hemingway; res. Plato, Cedar Co., Iowa.
1146. ii. LYDIA E.[8], b. in Solon, Nov. 18, 1858; m. 1879, Audry Hemingway; res. Plato, Ia.
1147. iii. EVA C.[8], b. in Solon, Oct. 9, 1860 ; m. 1886, Edward Askey.; res. Marysville, Mo.
   iv. HENRIETTA[8], b. in Solon, 1862; m. Sept. 23, 1891, Evert Bowman ; res. Solon, Ia.; no issue.
1148. v. JENNIE B.[8], b. in Solon, Feb., 1864 ; m. 1888, Harry Gaymon ; res. Oasis, Johnson County, Ia.
   vi. EMERY D.[8], b. in Solon, Aug., 1865 ; m. Dec., 1889, Annie Johnson. He is an insurance agent in Iowa City, Ia.; no issue.

Eighth Generation.] OF NEWBURY, MASS. 285

    vii. EUGENE M.[8], b. in Solon, Nov., 1868; res. White Lake, So. Dak.
   viii. EBEN W.[8], b. in Solon, Aug., 1864; res. White Lake, So. Dak.; unm.
    ix. HARRY T.[8], b. in Solon, July, 1876; res. White Lake, So. Dak.; unm.

Children of DAVID FARNUM[7], (1813) [616] (Dr. Joseph[6], Enoch[5], Henry[4], Capt. Abraham[3], Sergt. Abraham[2], Robert[1]) and Dorcas V. (Glines) Adams; res. Caribou, Aristook Co., Me.

1149.   i. DAVID WESTON[8], b. in Caribou, Jan. 18, 1835; m. (1) 1856, Sarah J. Virgin of Rumford; m. (2) April 17, 1861, Amanda Maria Brown of Livermore, Me.

        He was a farmer and hotel-keeper in Caribou, Me.; he served as a soldier in the Civil War, was wounded, and received a pension. He d. Sept., 1891.

      ii. JOSEPH CHANDLER[8], b. in Caribou, Nov. 25, 1840; d. 14 Oct., 1841.
     iii. MARIA GOODNO[8], b. in Caribou, Dec. 14, 1844; m. Nov. 17, 1890, Thomas C. Emerson of Pelham, Me.; res. Caribou, Me.; no issue.
1150.   iv. MARTHA BOLSTER[8], b. in Caribou, Sept. 20, 1850; m. (1) 1870, Lysanda Sawin; m. (2) about 1890, Edw. H. Townshend; res. Sherman, Me.

Children of ERASMUS DARWIN[7], (1814) [617] (Dr. Joseph[6], Enoch[5], Henry[4], Capt. Abraham[3], Sergt. Abraham[2], Robert[1]) and Catherine (Sturgis) Adams; res. Cedar Falls, Ia., and McAlister, Ind. Ter.

       i. MARTHA JANE[8], b. in Michigan, Apr. 15, 1843; d. 11 Aug., 1843.
1151.   ii. JOHN STURGIS[8], b. in Iowa, June 14, 1844; m. Apr. 7, 1872, Phebe Buechley, dau. of Dr. John Abraham Buechley, b. in Berlin, Somerset Co., Pa., Nov. 11, 1849.

        He is a carriage manufacturer and carpenter; was for ten years in the harvesting machine business as an expert on binders, and a general agent for Iowa; spent ten years in southern California; res. Waterloo, Ia.

1152. iii. HENRY FARNUM[8], b. in Cedar Falls, Oct. 3, 1846; m. Mar. 20, 1872, Harriet M. Clark, dau. of Timothy B. Clark of Waterbury, Conn.

        He is an expert book-keeper and short-hand reporter, also a musician and manager of Clark & Adams Lumber Co., Williams, Arizona Ter.

1153. iv. AMOS DARWIN⁸, b. Cedar Falls, Sept. 9, 1848; m. July 6, 1881, Catharine A. Dunning, who was a teacher from Clinton Co., N. Y., b. Sept. 23, 1846.

Although crippled for life by an accident in his childhood, he is a successful man of business ; removed from Newtonia, Mo., to Prescott, Arizona, in 1875, where he is a lumber merchant and mill owner.

1154. v. ARDILLACY STURGIS⁸, b. in Cedar Falls, Aug. 17, 1864 ; m. Aug. 6, 1890, Ernest W. Schreiner, a merchant; res. McAlister, Ind. Ter.

Children of MARIA BARTLETT⁷, (1817) [618] (Dr. Joseph⁶, Enoch⁵, Henry⁴, Capt. Abraham³, Sergt. Abraham², Robert¹) and Dr. David H. Goodno; res. Washington, D. C.

    i. CHARLES EDWARD GOODNO, b. July 6, 1843 ; m. Mar. 26, 1878, Annie Lake.

       He is a government clerk in the department of justice, Washington, D. C.

    ii. GEORGE ADAMS GOODNO, b. in Hallowell, 1848 ; d. 1870.

Children of WARREN MANN⁷, (1819) [619] (Dr. Joseph⁶, Enoch⁵, Henry⁴, Capt. Abraham³, Sergt. Abraham², Robert¹) and Adrian (Washburn) Adams; res. So. Rumford, Me.

    i. ELMAH DARWIN⁸, b. in Rumford, March 18, 1847; d. 28 Feb., 1850.

    ii. CHARLES HENRY⁸, b. in Rumford, Jan. 5, 1849; m. Sept. 1, 1886, Vesta A. Merrill.

       He is a farmer in Rumford, Me.; no issue.

1155. iii. CLARA FRANCES⁸, b. in Rumford, July 7, 1851 ; m. Jan. 19, 1871, Virgil E. Fuller.

    iv. EMMA MATILDA⁸, b. in Rumford, May 11, 1861 ; d. 21 Feb., 1862.

Children of DR. HENRY MILGROVE⁷, (1823) [620] (Dr. Joseph⁶, Enoch⁵, Henry⁴, Capt. Abraham³, Sergt. Abraham², Robert¹) and Cordelia (Hill) Adams; res. Hallowell, Me., and Cedar Falls, Ia.

    i. EDWARD HENRY⁸, b. in Hallowell, Apr. 27, 1851 ; d. 23 Mar., 1852.

    ii. FRANKLIN⁸, b. in Hallowell, July 26, 1852 ; d. 17 Mar., 1869.

1156. iii. DELIA HILL⁸, b. in Hallowell, Feb. 28, 1854 ; m. 1875, John L. Eichholtz of Blunt, Hughes Co., Dak.; res. Blunt, So. Dak.

1157. iv. MARY WILLIS⁸, b. in Cedar Falls, Ia., Nov. 19, 1857; m. Aug. 23, 1879, William T. Gibson of Luverne, Minn.; dealer in agricultural implements ; res. Luverne, Minn.

Eighth Generation.] OF NEWBURY, MASS. 287

v. FREDERICK HENRY⁸, b. in Cedar Falls, Apr. 15, 1859 ; m. June, 1883, Olive Beck ; res. Yankton, Dak.; d. 13 Mar., 1890.
He was a photographer.

Children of MARTHA HALL⁷, (1825) [**621**] (Dr. Joseph⁶, Enoch⁵, Henry⁴, Capt. Abraham³, Sergt. Abraham², Robert¹) and Hon. William W. Bolster; res. Dixfield, Oxford Co., Me.

    i. CLARA MARIA BOLSTER, b. Jan. 10, 1850 ; m. July 18, 1868, Albion Thorne, an attorney, and settled in Dell Rapids, Minnehaha Co., So. Dak.
    ii. BION BOLSTER, b. Dec. 25, 1851.
    iii. MARY JOSEPHINE BOLSTER, b. Apr. 13, 1854 ; m. July 31, 1876, Rev. Lauriston Reynolds. She set. at Yarmouth, Me., and d. 27 June, 1894.
    iv. ALVAN JOSEPH BOLSTER, b. Dec. 25, 1855 ; d. 12 Dec., 1885.
He was an attorney in Sioux City, Ia.
    v. WILLIAM HENRY BOLSTER, b. July 17, 1860; d. 15 Nov., 1861.
    vi. GEORGE FREDERICK BOLSTER, b. July 30, 1866 ; d. 21 Sept., 1866.

Children of ADAM WILLIS⁷, (1818) [**622**] (Moses⁶, Enoch⁵, Henry⁴, Capt. Abraham³, Sergt. Abraham², Robert¹) and Ann M. (Bean) Adams; res. Haverhill, Mass.

    i. ALVIA B.⁸, b. in Rumford, Me., Apr. 18, 1847 ; d. 13 July, 1861.
    ii. LEWIS E.⁸, b. in Rumford, Jan. 11, 1849 ; m. 1875, Annie N. Sargent, dau. of Amos Sargent of Haverhill ; res. Haverhill, Mass.; no issue.
    iii. HELENA M.⁸, b. in Rumford, Feb. 20, 1862 ; d. 2 Apr., 1864.
    iv. JOHN WILLIS⁸, b. in Rumford, Apr. 3, 1865 ; m. Mar. 26, 1894, Helen M. Pressey, dau. of Wm. Pressey of Bradford, N. H.; res. Haverhill, Mass.; no issue.

Children of AUGUSTUS HALL⁷, (1827) [**623**] (Moses⁶, Enoch⁵, Henry⁴, Capt. Abraham³, Sergt. Abraham², Robert¹) and Mary A. (Harriman) Adams; res. Haverhill, Mass.

1158. i. EMMA ISABEL⁸, b. in Haverhill, Feb. 11, 1856 ; m. Apr. 17, 1879, Edward Leonard Noyes, son of Edward and Elmira (Noyes) Noyes of Hampstead, N. H. ; he d. 29 Dec., 1881 ; res. Haverhill, Mass. no issue.
    ii. CARRIE LILLIAN⁸, b. in Haverhill, Nov. 22, 1858 ; m. May 26, 1880, Wm. Munroe Nichols, son of John Nichols of Haverhill, b. July 17, 1845 ; d. 22 Sept., 1895 ; res. Haverhill, Mass.; no issue.

Children of JOHN QUINCY[7], (1829) [**624**] (Moses[6], Enoch[5], Henry[4], Capt. Abraham[3], Sergt. Abraham[2], Robert[1]) and Susan E. (McIntire) Adams; res. Andover, Me.

1159. i. LEWIS EMERY[8]. b. in Andover, Feb. 5, 1858; m. Apr. 1, 1887, Emma Davis, dau. of Sampson Davis. He settled in Haverhill, Mass., 1883.
He is a furniture merchant.
1160. ii. FRANK DRESSER[8], b. in Andover, July 31, 1859 ; m. 1887, Minnie Bemis of Waltham, Mass.
He is a dealer in real estate, Waltham, Mass.
       iii. GEORGE HENRY[8], b. in Andover, June 7, 1865 ; d. 22 Mar., 1887.

Children of ISAAC[7], (1792) [**625**] (Samuel[6], Jr., Col. Samuel[5], Samuel[4], Isaac[3], Sergt. Abraham[2], Robert[1]) and Margaret Bishop Adams; res. Groveland, Mass.

1161. i. HARRIET NEWHALL[8], b. in Salem, Mass., Apr. 25, 1818 ; m. June 4, 1840, Healey Morse of Danvers, Mass., son of Caleb Morse and Mary Healey, b. in Salisbury, N. H., Mar. 18, 1802 ; d. 13 Nov., 1882 ; res. Penacook, N. H.; living 1899.
1162. ii. CHARLES H.[8], b. in Groveland, Mar., 1820; m. July 26, 1845, Mary Lank of Danvers, Mass.; she d. 26 July, 1867. He d. in Lynn, Mass., 1884.
1163. iii. MARY KIMBALL[8], b. in Groveland, Mar., 1820 ; m. Charles Chubb, son of Jabez and Lydia (Peabody) Chubb of Norway, Me. She d. in the hospital at Worcester, Mass., 1 Dec., 1865.
1164. iv. ENOCH[8], b. in Groveland, Aug. 9, 1824 ; m. Aug. 20, 1846, Caroline A. Perkins.
He went away to California soon after his marriage ; returned and d. in Ipswich, Mass., 7 Jan., 1852, aged 27 years; she m. 2nd Feb. 16, 1857, Charles Smith, b. in England, Nov. 7, 1831. He was a soldier in the 1st Massachusetts Regiment ; enlisted Feb. 23, 1864, and served 17 months ; res. Georgetown, Mass.
       v. ASA F.[8], b. in W. Newbury, Mass., Feb. 18, 1827 ; m. Mary J. Kimball of Bradford, Mass.; living 1899 in Concord, Mass.
He was a shoemaker ; d. in Plymouth, Mass., 8 Feb., 1877 ; no issue.
       vi. ANDREW JACKSON[8], b. in Groveland, Oct., 1829 ; d. in Sept., 1844, age 15 years.
       vii. ISAAC NEWCOMB[8], b. in Newburyport, Mass., Nov., 1832.
He enlisted Apr. 19, 1861, in Co. A, 1st Battalion of Massachusetts Rifles, afterward the 19th Massachusetts Reg.; was wounded in the battle of Antietam, Sept. 17, 1862, and d. Sept. 21 ; was buried in the National Cemetery at Antietam.

CAPT. JOHN GREGORY B. ADAMS.

Eighth Generation.] OF NEWBURY, MASS 289

  viii. MARTHA L.[8], b. in Groveland, Feb. 23, 1835; m. Apr. 14, 1888, Henry H. Heath; res. Haverhill, Mass.; he d. 5 July, 1898; no issue.

1165. ix. EMILY A.[8], b. in Groveland, Aug. 19, 1837; m. 1854, Samuel T. Perry; he was a soldier in the 22d Mass. Regt., and in the 2d Mass. Heavy Art.; he d. 5 Nov., 1871. She d. Mar., 1897.

  x. ELIZA J.[8], b. in Groveland, Oct., 1839; d. 24 Nov., 1839.

1166. xi. CAPT. JOHN GREGORY B.[8], b. in Groveland, Oct. 6, 1841; m. Apr. 6, 1866, Mary E. Dodge, dau. of Benjamin and Almira Dodge of Danvers, Mass.

   He enlisted as a private, 1861, in Maj. Ben. Perley Poor's Rifle Battalion, afterward the 19th Massachusetts Regt., and served through the war by re-enlistment; took part in every battle in which his regiment was engaged; saved the colors of his regiment at Fredericksburg after eight color-bearers had fallen; was wounded in [the battle of Gettysburg, and was captured with his regiment at Petersburg, June 22, 1864, remaining a prisoner for nine months in several of the southern prison-pens; from long service as a Lieutenant he became a Captain for faithful and meritorious conduct, and since the war has filled a number of important and honorable positions; was postmaster of Lynn from 1877 to 1885; was first member of Gen. Lander Post, No. 5, G. A. R., Lynn, and has served three terms as its Commander, being elected first in July, 1868; was commander of the Department of Massachusetts in 1879, and Commander-in-Chief 1893-1894; was Deputy Superintendent of the Concord Reformatory, and has been President of the Association of Survivors of Rebel Prisons, also President of the Trustees of the Soldiers' Home; he was elected Sergeant-at-Arms of the Commonwealth in 1885, and has continued as such for the last fifteen years.

Children of MARY[7], (1795) [626] (Samuel[6], Jr., Col. Samuel[5], Samuel[4], Isaac[3], Sergt. Abraham[2], Robert[1]) and Aaron L. Clark; res. Georgetown, Mass.

  i. SAMUEL EUSTIS CLARK, b. in Bradford, Mass., 1823; m. 1865, Hannah M. Creasy of Newburyport. He d. 1888.

  ii. JOSEPH MORTON CLARK, b. in Bradford, 1824; m. (1) Oct. 11, 1850, Ruby F. Dresser of Albany, Me.; she d. 1851; m (2) Nov. 16, 1852, Sarah Dresser of Georgetown, Mass.

  iii. ORRIN WESTON CLARK, b. in Boston, 1827; m. (1) 1851, Mary W. Emerton of Newburyport; m. (2) 1855, Mary A. Stockman; she d. 1857. He d. in 1879.

  iv. HENRY HENDERSON CLARK, b. in New Rowley, Mass., 1831; m. (1) 1851, Fanny P. Burnham of North Bridgeton, Me.; she d. 1857; m. (2) 1862, Lydia M. Butterfield of Hiram, Me. He d. in Malden, Mass., 1885.

Children of SALLY⁷, (1798) [627] (Samuel⁶, Jr., Col. Samuel⁵, Samuel⁴, Isaac³, Sergt. Abraham², Robert¹), and Jacob Dresser; res. Albany, Me.

    i. ADELINE D. DRESSER, b. Mar. 11, 1824; m. Nov. 25, 1847, James B. Fullerton of Wolfboro, N. H. She d. 27 July, 18—.

    ii. RUBY F. DRESSER, b. May 19, 1825; m. Oct. 11, 1850, Joseph Morton Clark of Georgetown, Mass. She d. 29 Nov., 1851.

    iii. JOHN TYLER DRESSER, b. Feb. 24, 1827; d. unm. 11 Feb., 1850.

    iv. NANCY FROST DRESSER, b. Nov. 18, 1828; d. 29 Sept., 1847.

    v. SARAH DRESSER, b. Aug. 14, 1830; m. Nov. 16, 1852, Joseph Morton Clark; res. Georgetown, Mass.

    vi. HANNAH O. DRESSER, b. Mar. 5, 1834; m. Oct., 1854, Addison Lovejoy; he d. 16 Sept., 1881. She res. in Georgetown, Mass., but removed to So. Paris, Me.

    vii. PARKER DRESSER, b. Feb. 11, 1832; m. Oct., 1855, Mary Wardwell; res. Albany, Me.

    viii. JACOB DRESSER, JR., b. June 21, 1836; m. Sept., 1859, Sylvia Becklar; res. Berlin, N. H.

    ix. GEORGE DRESSER, b. Feb. 12, 1838; m. July 28, 1860, Jane Becklar; res. Lyndon, Vt.

Children of ENOCH⁷, (1799) [628] (Samuel⁶, Jr., Col. Samuel⁵, Samuel⁴, Isaac³, Sergt. Abraham², Robert¹) and Mary A. (Willey) Adams; res. Groveland, Mass.

1167. i. SALLY D.⁸, b. in E. Bradford, Mass., Aug. 20, 1826; m. May, 1849, Henry B. Huntress of Groveland, Mass., son of George Huntress; res. 1898, So. Lawrence, Mass.

1168. ii. ROBERT W.⁸, b. in E. Bradford, Oct. 16, 1828; m. 1849, Hannah P. Chase of Groveland; res. Groveland.

1169. iii. PATIENCE F.⁸, b. in Groveland, Apr. 18, 1830; m. 1852, George H. Chase of Groveland.

    iv. MOSES⁸, b. in New Rowley, Mass., 1832; d. soon.

1170. v. ENOCH F.⁸, b. in E. Bradford, July, 1837; m. Nov. 23, 1864, Olive A. Palmer. He d. in Groveland, 1 Apr., 1898.

1171. vi. ANN MARY⁸, b. in Groveland, June, 1840; m. 1861, Chas. H. Smith, a soldier; res. Groveland, Mass., 1899.

    vii. SAMUEL W.⁸, b. in E. Bradford, 1842-3; d. 30 Mar., 1859, age 16 yrs.

    viii. AARON L. C.⁸, b. in Groveland, Nov. 1844-5; m. 1877, Henrietta Dennis of Beverly, Mass. He d. in Groveland, 1878.

Children of SAMUEL[7], (1802) [**629**] (Samuel[6], Jr., Col. Samuel[5], Samuel[4], Isaac[3], Sergt. Abraham[2], Robert[1]) and Sally B. (Clark) Adams; res. E. Bradford and Haverhill, Mass.

1172. i. HANNAH H.[8], b. in E. Bradford, June 17, 1826; m. Oct. 8, 1844, William J. Creasy of Newburyport. She d. in Newburyport, 27 June, 1883.

1173. ii. SARAH E.[8], b. in E. Bradford, April 26, 1828; m. Jan. 1, 1848, Oren Carleton of Plaistow, N. H.; res. with youngest sister, Mrs. Gardner, at Haverhill, Mass. She d. 20 Apr., 1896.

1174. iii. LUCY J.[8], b. in E. Bradford, Aug. 3, 1830; m. Nov. 27, 1851, Warner W. Tilton of Haverhill, Mass. She d. in Haverhill, 19 [26] Jan. 1884.

1175. iv. SELWYN POOR[8], b. in E. Bradford, Sept. 13, 1832; m. May 11, 1853-4, Matilda L. Freeman of York, Me.
He served as a soldier in the 35th Mass. Regt. for 3 years, and was a painter in Newburyport; d. 1 Nov., 1895.

  v. LAURA ANN[8], b. in Haverhill, Aug. 7, 1834; m. Mar. 18, 1865, Henry Taber of Lowell, Mass. She d. 1 Feb., 1888; no issue.

1176. vi. REBECCA B.[8], b. in Haverhill, Dec. 29, 1836; m. (1) May 2, 1859, Farnham P. Woodcock of Haverhill, son of Franklin and Hannah (Plumer) Woodcock; d. 15 Aug., 1872; m. (2) June 1, 1882, John Livingstone of Worcester, Mass., b. Feb. 25, 1829; res. Boylston Centre, Mass.

  vii. WILLIAM H.[8], b. in Haverhill, Mar. 12, 1839.
He enlisted in the 19th Mass. Regt. in 1861, and d. of fever in the hospital at Philadelphia, 25 Nov., 1862; buried in Haverhill, Mass.

1177. viii. ELLEN F.[8], b. in Haverhill, Jan. 8, 1843; m. Apr. 6, 1863, Geo. S. Smith of Merideth, N. H.; he d. 1898. She d. in Haverhill, 1 Mar., 1894.

  ix. ALMA R.[8], b. in Haverhill, Sept. 21, 1843; m. Jan. 8, 1865, S. Porter Gardner, president of First Nat'l Bank, Haverhill, b. 1844. She d. 20 Feb., 1898; no issue.

Children of HANNAH[7], (1805) [**630**] (Samuel[6], Jr., Col. Samuel[5], Samuel[4], Isaac[3], Sergt. Abraham[2], Robert[1]) and Stephen Horr; res. North Waterford, Me.

  i. ANN MARIA HORR, b. Dec. 15, 1829; m. Sept. 19, 1848, Asahel Allen; res. E. Stoneham, Me.

  ii. REBECCA H. HORR, b. Sept. 12, 1831; m. Dec. 19, 1852, James M. Burckes; res. Somerville, Mass.

  iii. MARY E. HORR, b. Jan. 24, 1833; res. Stoneham, Me.; unm.

  iv. STEPHEN CALVIN HORR, b. Nov. 27, 1835; m. Nov. 24, 1867, Henrietta French of Albany, Me.

He graduated from Bowdoin College, 1867, and went to Michigan the same year, where he engaged in teaching, but returned to Westbrook and d. 25 Apr., 1875.

    v. HANNAH FRANCES HORR, b. Feb. 6, 1838; m. Feb. 6, 1865, Horatio C. Woodworth; he d. 30 Apr., 1882; res. Somerville, Mass. She d. 3 Jan., 1899.

    vi. DR. JACOB L. HORR, b. Dec. 19, 1841; m. (1) Sept. 11, 1872, Louisa P. Lombard; she d. 2 July, 1877; m. (2) Aug. 28, 1879, Adeline A. Babb.

He was educated at Bridgeton Academy, and took his degree of M. D. from the Maine School of Medicine, Bowdoin College, in June, 1869; set. in Westbrook, Me.

    vii. SARAH A. HORR, b. Feb. 22, 1844; res. Somerville, Mass.; unm.

    viii. SOPHIA L. HORR, b. May 8, 1846; res. Somerville, Mass.; unm.

    ix. REV. SAMUEL ISAAC HORR, b. Sept. 30, 1848.

He went to Michigan at an early age and there studied, and entered the ministry of the M. E. Church, Sept. 30, 1848; res. Pipestone, Berrien Co., Mich.

Children of MOSES^7, (1810) [**631**] (Samuel^6, Jr., Col. Samuel^5, Samuel^4, Isaac^3, Sergt. Abraham^2, Robert^1) and Sarah (Colby) Adams; res. Groveland, Mass.

    i. GEORGE H.^{8}, b. in Groveland, Jan. 28, 1835; m. July 26, 1859, Mary L. B. Mitchell of So. Framingham, Mass. She d. June, 1877; res. homestead, Groveland, Mass.; no issue.

1178. ii. AMELIA ANN^8, b. in Groveland, July 16, 1837; m. Feb. 23, 1858, Charles R. Weston, son of Flint Weston of Georgetown, Mass., b. Jan. 6, 1833; res. Georgetown, Mass.

1179. iii. CHARLES SAMUEL^8, b. in Groveland, July 29, 1842; m. Apr. 3, 1866, Ellen E. Simpson of Alna, Lincoln Co., Me.; set. in Hickory Barren, Greene Co., Mo.

Children of SILENCE JONES^7, (1813) [**632**] (David^6, Capt. David^5, Capt. Isaac^4, Jr., Isaac^3, Sergt. Abraham^2, Robert^1) and Julius C. Sherwin; res. New Ipswich, N. H.

    i. GEORGE H. SHERWIN, b. in Rindge, N. H., Nov. 25, 1843; d. in St. Louis, Mo., 26 Sept., 1867.

    ii. MARY M. SHERWIN, b. in Groton, Mass., Oct. 11, 1844; m. George H. Nims; res. Keene, N. H.

    iii. ELLEN A. SHERWIN, b. in Rindge, Mar. 25, 1847; m. William O. Simonds; res. Fayette, Ia.—a son at West Point.

AMELIA ANN WESTON.

Eighth Generation.] OF NEWBURY, MASS. 293

    iv. KATE A. SHERWIN, b. in Rindge, Mar. 26, 1849 ; m. John Stevens; res. Beloit, Kan.
    v. ANNIE M. SHERWIN, b. in Rindge, Aug. 2, 1851 ; m. Charles M. Cummings ; res. Keene, N. H.

Children of EDWIN SPOFFORD[7], (1815) [**633**] (David[6], Capt. David[5], Capt. Isaac[4], Jr., Isaac[3], Sergt. Abraham[2], Robert[1]) and Cynthia Ann (Whitbeck) Adams; res. Brooklyn, N. Y.

    i. MARY ELIZABETH[8], b. in Albany, N. Y., Nov. 1, 1845.
        She is a graduate of the Packer Collegiate Institute, and a teacher in Brooklyn, N. Y.
    ii. CATHERINE WHITBECK[8], b. in Albany, May 10, 1847 ; m. Apr. 15, 1875, John Ward of Brooklyn. She grad. from the Packer Collegiate Institute.

Children of EDWIN SPOFFORD[7], (1815) and Frances F. (Colby) Adams.

    iii. FANNY ANN[8], b. in Brooklyn, Mar. 21, 1868 ; d. 22 Oct., 1871.
    iv. CHARLES EDWIN[8], b. in Brooklyn, Mar. 20, 1874 ; d. in infancy.

Children of HON. MOSES SAWIN[7], (1826) [**634**] (David[6], Capt. David[5], Capt. Isaac[4], Jr., Isaac[3], Sergt. Abraham[2], Robert[1]) and Lizzie (Damon) Adams; res. Cannon City, Col.

    i. GEORGE E.[8], b. in Leavenworth, Kan., Aug. 17, 1859 ; d. 1863.
    ii. FRANK E.[8], b. in Leavenworth, Dec. 29, 1866; unm.

Children of MARY PARKER[7], (1826) [**635**] (Isaac[6], Capt. David[5], Capt. Isaac[4], Isaac[3], Sergt. Abraham[2], Robert[1]) and Horace Lyman Peckham; res. Townshend, Mass.

    i. CHANDLER ADAMS PECKHAM, b. Aug. 16, 1861 ; d. 16 Oct., 1863.
    ii. HORACE LYMAN PECKHAM, JR., b. Apr. 10, 1865 ; drowned 19 July, 1883.
    iii. CHARLES WM. PECKHAM, b. Oct. 23, 1866 ; m. Susie J. Sargent of Malden, Mass.; res. Boston, Mass.

Children of ISAAC MILTON[7], (1841) [**636**] (Isaac[6], Capt. David[5], Capt. Isaac[4], Jr., Isaac[3], Sergt. Abraham[2], Robert[1]) and Emeline (Twitchell) Adams; res. Minneapolis, Minn.

i. STELLA GERTRUDE[8], b. in Boston, Mass., Dec. 11, 1864.
ii. CHARLES EDWARD[8], b. in Boston, Oct. 1, 1867.
iii. WILLIAM HENRY MURRAY[8], b. in Boston, Mar. 27, 1869.
iv. MABEL[8], b. in Gowanda, N. Y., May, 1873.
v. PAUL[8], b. in Gowanda, Aug. 28, 1876.
vi. HELEN[8], b. in Gowanda, Jan. 15, 1880.

Children of STEPHEN SEARLE[7], (1842) [**637**] (Isaac[6], Capt. David[5], Capt. Isaac[4], Jr., Isaac[3], Sergt. Abraham[2], Robert[1]) and Hannah (Goodell) Adams; res. Sioux City, Iowa.

i. JOHN SEARLE[8], b. in McCook, Dak., Dec. 31, 1885.
ii. STEPHEN JAMES[8], b. in McCook, Oct. 11, 1887.

Children of ELIPHALET[7], (1804) [**638**] (Isaac[6], Capt. Samuel[5], Capt. Isaac[4], Jr., Isaac[3], Sergt. Abraham[2], Robert[1]) and Mary (Peabody) Adams; res. Gilead, Me.

1180. i. THOMAS AUGUSTUS[8], b. in Gilead, Oct. 4, 1829; m. Nov. 17, 1856, Mary A. Flanders.
He is the station agent of the Grand Trunk Railway at Gorham, N. H., and post-master.
ii. AUGUSTA[8], b. in Gilead, Feb. 17, 1831; d. unm. 22 Aug., 1893.
iii. AURELIA[8] (twin), b. in Gilead, Feb. 17, 1831; d. in Gorham, Me.; unm. Mar., 1899.
1181. iv. HENRY H.[8], b. in Gilead, Dec. 19, 1839; m. Dec. 22, 1863, Augusta A. Martin; res. Richmond, Me.
1182. v. EDWARD PAYSON[8], b. in Gilead, May 24, 1842; m. May 7, 1868, Emma E. Williams.
He is a telegraph operator; res. Rutherford, Cal.
vi. MARY PEABODY[8], b. in Gilead, Dec. 3, 1845; d. unm. 17 Oct., 1859.

Children of PROF. SAMUEL[7], (1806) [**639**] (Isaac[6], Col. Samuel[5], Capt. Isaac[4], Jr., Isaac[3], Sergt. Abraham[2], Robert[1]) and Mary J. (Moulton) Adams; res. Jacksonville, Ill.

1183. i. MARIETTA[8], b. in Brunswick, Me., Aug. 6, 1837; m. Sept. 28, 1865, Robert K. Whiteley, a civil engineer of Wheeling, W. Va.; set. in Brainerd, Minn.; res. Brainerd, Minn.

ii. COL. FRANKLIN⁸, b. in Jacksonville, Ill., May 25, 1843.
He graduated from Illinois College in 1860, and served four years in the Union Army ; he was employed as a civil engineer in the construction of the Union Pacific Railroad, and while thus employed, far from his home, he contracted a malady which resulted in his death on the 24th of Nov., 1868, at his father's home in Jacksonville.

1184. iii. EMILY⁸, b. in Jacksonville, Dec. 28, 1846 ; m. June 26, 1873, Dr. Alfred Richmond, of Rochester, Vt. ; set. in Edmund, N. Dak.
She graduated at Illinois College, and was a teacher of music and German in the college ; res. Redlands, Cal.

1185. iv. CLARA MOULTON⁸, b. in Jacksonville, Oct. 31, 1850 ; m. Mar. 12, 1874, Julian Post Lippincott, an attorney of Jacksonville, Ill., b. Oct. 27, 1847 ; res. Jacksonville, Ill.

Children of DEBORAH⁷, (1808) [**640**] (Isaac⁶, Capt. Samuel⁵, Capt. Isaac⁴, Jr., Isaac³, Sergt. Abraham², Robert¹) and Thomas Peabody ; res. Gilead, Me.

i. SAMUEL ADAMS PEAPODY, b. Mar. 23, 1836.
He enlisted in Jan., 1862, in Co. I, of the 5th Maine Regt., and served for three years, the latter part of the time in the Invalid Corps ; returned in broken health, and d. at White Salmon, Klickitat Co., Wash., 25 Mar., 1885.

ii. MARIETTA PEABODY, b. Aug. 9, 1837 ; d. unm. at Gilead, 11 July, 1861.

iii. OLIVE ADAMS PEABODY, b. May 13, 1839 ; m. May 16, 1868, Edward L. Miller ; res. Burlington, Kan.

iv. THOMAS SPENCER PEABODY, b. Mar. 25, 1841.
He enlisted in Co. I, 5th Maine Regt., Apr., 1861 ; was taken prisoner with four others, Dec. 14, 1863, and d. a prisoner at Andersonville, 20 June, 1864.

v. DEBORAH JANE PEABODY, b. May 25, 1845 ; m. Nov. 9, 1867, Isaac P. Burbank ; no issue.

vi. GEORGE WASHINGTON PEABODY, b. Nov. 25, 1847.
He enlisted in Feb., 1864, when 16 years of age, in Co. B. 32d Maine Regt., and served in the trenches before Petersburg, Va. He d. in the hospital at Washington, D. C., 25 Nov., 1864 ; was buried in Gilead, Me.

Children of APHIA⁷, (1811) [**641**] (Isaac⁶, Capt. Samuel⁵, Capt. Isaac⁴, Jr., Isaac³, Sergt. Abraham², Robert¹) and Caleb S. Peabody ; res. Gorham, Me.

i. ISAAC A. PEABODY, b. Nov. 9, 1838 ; d. 7 Sept., 1843.

1186. ii. JOHN TARBEL PEABODY, b. June 9, 1841 ; m. Nov. 25, 1866, Frances W. Bartlett ; res. Gorham, Me.

iii. ISAAC A. PEABODY, b. Sept. 17, 1844 ; res. Gorham, Me.; unm.

Child of ISAAC⁷, (1813) [**642**] (Isaac⁶, Capt. Samuel⁵, Capt. Isaac⁴, Jr., Isaac³, Sergt. Abraham², Robert¹) and Lucia K. (Bartlett) Adams; res. Rockton, Ill.

    i. ELLA C.⁸, b. Sept. 3, 1848; d. 9 Sept., 1864.

Children of DEA. ISRAEL⁷, (1815) [**643**] (Isaac⁶, Capt. Samuel⁵, Capt. Isaac⁴, Jr., Isaac³, Sergt. Abraham², Robert¹) and Betsey E. (Stearns) Adams; res. Manhattan, Kan.

1187. i. DARIUS⁸, b. in Gilead, Me., Dec. 23, 1844; m. Feb. 6, 1868, Clara J. Low of Fairfield, Me.
        He was a merchant; d. in Manhattan, Kan., 24 July, 1892.
  ii. SARAH ELIZABETH⁸, b. in Gilead, Sept. 16, 1848, d. 15 Mar., 1851.
  iii. CHARLES ARTHUR⁸, b. in Gilead, July 29, 1852; d. 4 Aug., 1863.
  iv. CHARLES ISRAEL⁸, b. in Gilead, Mar. 11, 1855; d. 5 Aug., 1862.

Children of OLIVE⁷, (1818) [**644**] (Isaac⁶, Capt. Samuel⁵, Capt. Isaac⁴, Jr., Isaac³, Sergt. Abraham², Robert¹) and David Blake; res. Gilead, Me.

  i. ELLEN MARIA BLAKE, b. Feb. 13, 1844; m. Abial Chandler.
  ii. DAVID NEWTON BLAKE, b. July 7, 1845; m. Eunice Fifield; res. Bethel, Me.
  iii. MARY OLIVE BLAKE, b. Sept. 29, 1846; d. 29 Jan., 1862.
  iv. HANNAH E. BLAKE, b. Dec. 26, 1849; m. James N. Hodgdon; res. Bethel, Me.; no issue.
  v. ISAAC A. BLAKE, b. Oct. 21, 1849; m. Marcia Soule. He is an engineer; res. Portland, Me.
  vi. A SON, b. June 23, 1851; d. 13 July, 1851.
  vii. ELIPHALET A. BLAKE, b. Apr. 26, 1852; an engineer; unm.; res. Island Pond, Vt.
  viii. BENJAMIN F. BLAKE, b. Sept. 3, 1853; a farmer; unm.; res. Gilead, Me.
  ix. ADONIRAM J. BLAKE, b. May 10, 1855; a farmer; unm.; res. Gilead, Me.
  x. LILLIAN A. BLAKE, b. Mar. 11, 1857; unm.; res. Gilead, Me.

Children of ISRAEL⁷, (1818) [**645**] (Samuel⁶, Capt. Samuel⁵, Capt. Israel⁴ Israel³, Sergt. Abraham², Robert¹) and Harriet A. (Boynton) Adams; res. Watertown, N. Y.

  i. SAMUEL G.⁸, b. in Rodman, N. Y., 1858; d. 1860.
  ii. HATTIE⁸, b. in Rodman, 1861; m. Wm. B. Wheeler; res. Watertown, N. Y.; no issue.

HELEN BELLOWS FISK.

Children of BETSEY ADAMS BURNHAM, (1817) [**646**] (Mary⁶, Capt. Samuel⁵, Capt. Israel⁴, Israel³, Sergt. Abraham², Robert¹) and Valentine L. Stiles; res. Gorham, Me.

    i. HELEN ELIZABETH STILES, b. Nov. 16, 1842 ; m. (1) Aug. 30, 1877, John Bellows, Esq., of Exeter, N. H.; he d. 14 Dec., 1888, at Boston ; m. (2) Dec. 24, 1889, Charles Wesley Fisk of Logansport, Ind. He d. 14 Dec., 1896 ; res. Logansport, Ind.; no issue.

    ii. FLORA ANNETTA STILES, b. Sept. 15, 1844 ; m. May 13, 1865, John Green Wight of Gorham, N. H.; res. New York City.

    iii. EUGENE BURNHAM STILES, b. Aug. 23, 1846 ; d. 1 Dec., 1887.

    iv. ZILPHA ANNA STILES, b. Sept. 1, 1848 ; d. 23 Apr., 1879.

    v. CLIFFORD PRESTON STILES, b. Sept. 23, 1850 ; d. 13 Sept.' 1893.

    vi. MARY ELLA STILES, b. Sept. 24, 1853.
        She is a teacher in Somerville, Mass.

    vii. STELLA IDA STILES, b. Dec. 27, 1855.

Child of ENOS HOLMES⁷, (1827) [**647**] (Jonathan⁶, Capt. Samuel⁵, Capt. Isaac⁴, Jr., Isaac³, Sergt. Abraham², Robert¹,) and Clementine (Ward) Adams; res. Lowell, Mass.

    i. ENOS ALBERT⁸, b. in Lowell, Oct. 28, 1867.
        He was a carpenter ; d. unm. 7 Jan., 1892.

Children of ENOS HOLMES⁷, (1827) and Lizzie (Albee) Adams.

    ii. MARK ALBEE⁸, b. in Lowell, July 18, 1871 ; m. Sept 1, 1898, Etta Blanche Fife, dau. of Elmore R., and Martha A. (Given) Fife, b. in Lowell, July 28, 1867 ; res. Lowell, Mass.

    iii. MABEL HARRIET⁸, b. in Lowell, Oct. 10, 1874 ; res. Lowell, Mass.

Children of DARIUS⁷, (1831) [**648**] (Jonathan⁶, Capt. Samuel⁵, Capt. Isaac⁴, Jr., Isaac³, Sergt. Abraham², Robert¹) and Gracie A. (Huey) Adams; res. Lowell, Mass.

1188. i. EMMA JANE⁸, b. in Springfield, Vt., Sept. 19, 1855 ; m. June 30, 1873, Franklin A. Cook of Springfield, son of Aurelius J. and Sarah (Parker) Cook, b. in Cornish, N. H., Sept. 8, 1852. She d. 13 Aug. 1883. He m. 2d, July 11, 1886, Susie Smart ; res. Springfield, Vt.

1189. ii. FRANK HUEY⁸, b. in Springfield, June 6, 1858 ; m. Feb. 8, 1879, Lucy J. Barton of Lowell, Mass., b. July 23, 1856 ; res. Lowell, Mass.

1190. iii. ARTHUR DANIEL⁸, b. in Springfield, Dec. 14, 1859 ; m. Jan. 10, 1884, Anna Sargent Gilbert, b. Oct. 16, 1858 ; res. Springfield, O.
1191. iv. CHARLES ANDERSON⁸, b. in Springfield, Feb. 20, 1867; m. Nov. 26, 1889, Emma Mattie Brittan of Guilford, N. H., dau. of Thomas and Elvira (Folsom) Brittan, b. in Wolfsboro, N. H., Mar. 27, 1862 ; res. Boston, Mass.

Children of CHARLES ANDERSON⁷, (1855) [649] (Jonathan⁶, Capt. Samuel⁵, Capt. Isaac⁴, Jr., Isaac³, Sergt. Abraham², Robert¹) and Annette (Sawyer) Adams; res. Lowell, Mass.

    i. ELLEN MARIE⁸, b. in Lowell, Mar. 10, 1858 ; d. 10 Feb., 1863.
1192. ii. KATHERINE BLANCHE⁸, b. in Lowell, Apr. 21, 1862; m. Dec. 25, 1886, Lester Thomas Crook.

Child of ELLEN LOUISA⁷, (1839) [650] (Jonathan⁶, Capt. Samuel⁵, Capt. Isaac⁴, Jr., Isaac³, Sergt. Abraham², Robert¹) and Rev. J. F. Simmons; res. Woodstock, Vt.

    i. CLARENCE ADAMS SIMMONS, b. in Webster, Mass., Sept. 13, 1882.

Children of GEORGE DANIEL⁷, (1843) [651] (Jonathan⁶, Capt. Samuel⁵, Capt. Isaac⁴, Jr., Isaac³, Sergt. Abraham², Robert¹) and Dora (Hussey) Adams; res. Wellesley Hills, Mass.

    i. WILLIAM HUSSEY⁸, b. in Lowell, Mass., July 13, 1870.
        Supt. of bleachery, Providence, R. I.; present res. Lawrence, Mass.; unm.
    ii. ELIZABETH STARBUCK⁸, b. in Lowell, Oct. 14, 1873 ; res. Wellesley Hills, Mass.; unm.
    iii. JAMES DOUGLASS⁸, b. in Worcester, May 2, 1875 ; res. Worcester, unm.
    iv. ROBERT SUMNER⁸, b. in Worcester, Dec. 31, 1877 ; d. Aug., 1878.
    v. DANIEL⁸, b. in Lowell, Oct. 25, 1883.
    vi. HENRY COFFIN⁸, b. in Newburyport, Mass., Dec. 23, 1885.
    vii. CHRISTOPHER HUSSEY⁸, b. in Newburyport, Dec. 8, 1887.

Children of COLEMAN SEARL⁷, (1826) [652] (Joseph Searl⁶, Israel⁵, Jr., Israel⁴, Isaac³, Sergt. Abraham², Robert¹) and Mary E. (Winchester) Adams; res. Framingham, Mass.

Eighth Generation.] OF NEWBURY, MASS.

  i. HON. WALTER[8], b. in Portland, Me., May 5, 1848; m. May 25, 1885, Constance Winchester of Philadelphia, dau. of Thos. Weld Winchester, b. Dec. 22, 1851.
  He graduated from Harvard College, 1870, admitted to the bar, May, 1873; an attorney in So. Framingham, Mass., and Associate Judge of District Court since 1880; was a member of the Legislature in 1894 and 1896; no issue.
  ii. JOSEPH S.[8], b. in Boston, Mass., Jan. 6, 1851. He is an insurance agent; res. in Framingham, Mass.; unm.
  iii. MARION S.[8], b. in Boston, April 27, 1853; res. Framingham, Mass.; unm.

Child of JOSEPH[7], (1838) [653] (Charles[6], Israel[5], Jr., Israel[4], Isaac[3], Sergt. Abraham[2], Robert[1]) and Georgiana (Kelly) Adams; res. W. Rumney, N. H.

  i. MARTHA G.[8], b. in W. Rumney, Aug. 17, 1870; m. Oct. 5, 1892, Wilber L. Prescott, son of Henry Gates and Adelia (Smith) Prescott, b. July 8, 1869; res. Laconia, N. H.; no issue.

Children of ISRAEL GILMAN[7], (1846) [654] (Charles[6], Israel[5], Jr., Israel[4], Isaac[3], Sergt. Abraham[2], Robert[1]) and Ruby Anna (Elliot) Adams; res. Londonderry, N. H.

  i. WESLEY[8], b. in Nelson, N. H., July 2, 1872; res. Londonderry, N. H.; unm.
  ii. ROY B.[8], b. in Nelson, Sept. 16, 1879; res. Londonderry, N. H.; unm.

Child of JOHN QUINCY[7], (1844) [655] (George W.[6], Israel[5], Jr., Israel[4], Isaac[3], Sergt. Abraham[2], Robert[1]) and Ella (Hunkins) Adams; res. Haverhill, Mass. *Eleanor, widow of John d. died*
  i. HERBERT C.[8], b. in Haverhill. *b. Sept. 4, 1879 Mar. 10, 19..*
  He is a student of engineering and science in Dartmouth College.
m. Sylvia E. Turner,

Children of REV. FRANK E.[7], (1847) [656] (George W.[6], Israel[5], Jr., Israel[4], Isaac[3], Sergt. Abraham[2], Robert[1]) and Mary E. (Parker) Adams; res. Hill, etc., N. H. *lives in Elmira, N. Y.*
  i. HERMAN PARKER[8], b. in Hill, June 8, 1877.
  He enlisted in the autumn of 1898, in the 2d Oregon Regt., and was killed in a battle near Manila, P. I., in Mar., 1899.

1. ... Children of Herbert & Sylvia
11. Eleanor E. L. Adams 2?, 1908.
111. Alice L. L. S/pt. 26, 1910.
1v. B...... ..... 5, 1915.

300   ROBERT ADAMS   [Eighth Generation.

    ii. EDITH LOUISA⁹, b. in Hill, Dec. 30, 1878. *Lives in Wash. D. C.*
        She is a student in the State Normal School, Potsdam, N. Y., and was assisted by her brother, Herman P.
    iii. ROBERT MORRILL⁸, b. in Hill, June 28, 1882. *Van Gorden graduated from Yale*
        He is a student in the High School at Canton, N. Y.
    iv. CLIFFORD LA BARRON⁸, b. in Hill, July 14, 1889. *taught in Philippines by now Prof. at Cornell Univ.*
        ~~He is a student.~~ *in Civil Service Wash. D. C. married, has two children*

Children of SYBIL⁷, (1797) [657] (Israel 3d⁶, Israel⁵, Israel⁴, Sarah³, Sergt. Abraham², Robert¹) and Ebenezer Stratton; res. *Ithaca,* Rindge, N. H.

    i. MIRINDA STRATTON, b. Jan. 13, 1827; d. 15 Dec., 1842.
    ii. WILLIAM STRATTON, b. Oct. 28, 1829.
    iii. AUGUSTA STRATTON, b. Apr. 27, 1831; d. 6 Oct., 1873.
    iv. SAMUEL A. STRATTON, b. July 9, 1832; res. Grafton, N. H.
    v. MARIA MARTHA STRATTON, b. Jan. 23, 1835.

Children of ALBERT⁷, (1807) [658] (Israel 3d⁶, Israel⁵, Israel⁴, Sarah³, Sergt. Abraham², Robert¹) and Mary (Pollard) Adams; res. Rindge, N. H.

1193. i. CAPT.-GEORGE A.⁸, b. in Rindge, June 7, 1837; m. (1) Mar. 21, 1860, Hattie M. Phillips of Homer, N. Y.; she d. 26 May, 1861, leaving a son, in Royalston, Mass.; m. (2) May, 1862, Arvilla A. Brown.
        He enlisted 1862, in the 15th N. Y. Regt., from Homer, N. Y.; was wounded at Gettysburg, and d. 25 July, 1863; a son d. Mar., 1865; wid. in Kinsley, Kan.
    ii. ISRAEL⁸, b. in Rindge, Jan. 2, 1839; d. 28 Oct., 1841.
    iii. WILLIAM⁸, b. in Rindge, Oct. 5, 1840; d. 10 Sept., 1856.
1194. iv. JOHN BROOKS⁸, b. in Ringe, Aug. 12, 1842; m. May 23, 1872, Mary J. Woodbury of Winchendon, Mass.; res. Hancock, N. H., since Apr., 1890.
1195. v. FRANCIS A.⁸, b. in Rindge, Apr. 9, 1844; m. (1) Nov., 1863, Emma C. Bruce; she d. 24 Sept., 1873; m. (2) Tillie Corckin; res Royalston, Mass.
    vi. MARY B.⁸, b. in Rindge, Feb. 4, 1847; m. Jan. 17, 1863, Leonard F. Sawyer; res. Jaffrey, N. H.
1196. vii. DR. ORANGE H.⁸, b. in Rindge, Jan. 1, 1856; m. Nov. 21, 1881, Jessie Ballou of Franklin, Mass.; res. Vineland, N. J.

Children of ARAD[7], (1812) [**659**] (Israel 3d[6], Israel[5], Israel[4], Sarah[3], Sergt. Abraham[2], Robert[1]) and Ruba (Hall) Adams; res. Jaffrey, N. H.

    i. MARIA RUBA[8], b. in Jaffrey, June 25, 1840.
        She is a teacher in Jaffrey, N. H.; unm.
    ii. MARY ELIZABETH[8], b. in Jaffrey, Mar. 8, 1843 ; d. 14 Jan., 1856.

Children of LOUISA[7], (1815) [**660**] (Israel 3d[6], Israel[5], Israel[4], Sarah[3], Sergt. Abraham[2], Robert[1]) and Marshall A. Hale; res. Rindge, N. H.

    i. HENRY MARSHALL HALE, b. Feb. 22, 1846.
    ii. FRANCIS EDWIN HALE, b. Aug. 3, 1849.

Children of COL. JOSEPH HENRY[7], (1790) [**661**] (Lieut. and Maj. John[6], Capt. John[5], Israel[4], Sarah[3], Sergt. Abraham[2], Robert[1]) and Sarah Brown (White) Adams; res. Boston, Mass.

1197.   i. JOSEPH HENRY[8], b. in Boston, Jan. 2, 1818 ; m. (1) Feb. 29, 1852, Adelia De Leon ; m. (2) Anna Wilhelma Linch.
        He graduated from Harvard College in 1837 ; was a civil engineer ; surveyed the Eastern R. R. from Boston to Portland ; later he became Examiner in Chief of Interference in the Patent Office at Washington, D. C.; d. 17 Nov., 1886.
    ii. CAROLINE MATILDA[8], b. in Boston, Apr. 4, 1819 ; m. Apr. 25, 1843, Charles Royal Bond. She d. 26 Feb., 1893 ; a daughter, Elizabeth, m. A. Forbes Freeman of Boston, b. in Liverpool, N. S., in 1839 ; d. suddenly at his summer home in Brookline, Mass., 20 Oct., 1899.
    iii. SARAH FRANCES[8], b. in Boston, Sept. 18, 1820 ; m. Apr. 26, 1846, Dr. Wm. Johnson Dale. She d. 22 Nov.. 1887, leaving 2 or 3 children.
    iv. EDWARD F.[8], b. in Andover, Mass., Sept. 25, 1822 ; m. Matilda Ward Merrill or Merritt.
        He was an insurance agent in Haverhill, Mass.; d. suddenly o apoplexy, 4 Feb., 1891.
1198.   v. JOHN[8], b. in Andover, Sept. 5, 1825 ; m. Apr., 1852, Mary Hill. He d. Sept., 1869.
    vi. FREDERICK[8], b. in Andover, Feb. 21, 1828 ; d. 1847.
    vii. JULIA MARIA[8], b. in Andover, June 7, 1833 ; m. Sept. 23, 1868, James E. Gale of Haverhill, Mass. She d. in Haverhill, 8 Apr., 1888 ; no issue.

Children of HANNAH[7], (1791) [**662**] (Lieut. and Maj. John[6], Capt. John[5], Israel[4], Sarah[3], Sergt. Abraham[2], Robert[1]) and Daniel Appleton; res. Boston, Mass., and New York City.

    i. WILLIAM HENRY APPLETON, b. in Haverhill, Jan. 27, 1814; m. Apr. 16, 1844, Mary Moody Worthen, dau. of Ezra Worthen of Lowell, Mass. He d. in New York, 19 Oct., 1899.

    ii. MARIA LOUISA APPLETON, b. in Boston, Mar. 31, 1815; m. James E. Cooley of New York.

    iii. JOHN ADAMS APPLETON, b. in Boston, Jan. 9, 1817; m. Sept. 15, 1847, Serena P. Dole, dau. of Ebenezer Dole of Gloucester, Mass.

    iv. CHARLES HORATIO APPLETON, b. in Boston, May 1, 1819; d. 24 Jan., 1820.

    v. GEORGE SWETT APPLETON, b. in Boston, Aug. 11, 1821; m. Mar. 27, 1847, Caroline Osgood, dau. of Robert H. Osgood of Salem, Mass.

    vi. DANIEL SIDNEY APPLETON, b. in Boston, Apr. 9, 1824; m. Mar. 25, 1858, Melvina W. Marshall, dau. of Chas. H. Marshall of New York; she d. 30 Nov., 1873.

    vii. SAMUEL FRANCIS APPLETON, b. in Boston, Sept. 26, 1826.

    viii. SARAH EMELINE APPLETON, b. in New York, July 27, 1829; m. Leopold Bossange of Paris. She d. 3 Feb., 1861.

Children of CHARLOTTE[7], (1796) [**663**] (Lieut. and Maj. John[6], Capt. John[5], Israel[4], Sarah[3], Sergt. Abraham[2], Robert[1]) and Lieut. Isaac Osgood; res. No. Andover, Mass.

    i. REBECCA PICKMAN OSGOOD, b. Feb. 8, 1823; d. 20 Oct., 1863.

    ii. ISAAC FALKNER OSGOOD, b. Aug. 12, 1824; m. June 27, 1872, Lora Malvina White. He d. 24 Dec., 1893.

    iii. JOHN ADAMS OSGOOD, b. Aug. 29, 1826; d. unm. 23 Feb., 1897.

    iv. FRANCIS GAYTON OSGOOD, b. Dec. 28, 1829; d. 1 Aug., 1859.

    v. CHARLOTTE EMELINE OSGOOD, b. Dec. 20, 1831; m. May 5, 1853, Hon. Moses Tyler Stevens, M. C.; res. No. Andover, Mass. Children:

        1. Mary Osgood Stevens, b. May 29, 1854.

        2. Nathaniel Stevens, b. Sept. 11, 1857.

        3. Samuel Dale Stevens, b. June 16, 1859.

        4. Charlotte Adams Stevens, b. Nov. 22, 1860; d. 12 Aug., 1862.

        5. Virginia Stevens, b. Aug. 22, 1862.

        6. James Stevens, b. Nov. 26, 1863; d. 29 Nov., 1863.

        7. Helen Stevens, b. Aug. 15, 1866.

        8. Moses Tyler Stevens, Jr., b. Apr. 15, 1871.

Children of MARTHA[7], (1801) [663¼] (Lieut. and Maj. John[6], Capt. John[5], Israel[4], Sarah[3], Sergt. Abraham[2], Robert[1]) and Rev. John Chauncey; res. Charlton, Mass.
- i. MARY LOUISA CHAUNCEY, b. June 21, 1832.
- ii. ISABELLA GRAHAM CHAUNCEY, b. May 13, 1833.
- iii. JOHN ADAMS CHAUNCEY, b. Aug. 11, 1834; d. 24 Sept., 1840.
- iv. WM. ALLEN CHAUNCEY (twin), b. Aug. 11, 1834; d. 13 Apr., 1839.
- v. MARTHA ELIZABETH CHAUNCEY, b. Feb. 13, 1837; d. 14 Sept., 1867.
- vi. HARRIET MELISSA CHAUNCEY, b. Dec. 7, 1840.
- vii. JOHN EVARTS CHAUNCEY, b. Nov. 7, 1843.

Children of SARAH ANN[7], (1806) [663½] (Lieut. and Maj. John[6], Capt. John[5], Israel[4], Sarah[3], Sergt. Abraham[2], Robert[1]) and Rev. Asa D. Smith, D. D.; res. Hanover, N. H.
- i. MARY WILLIAMS SMITH, b. Sept. 26, 1837; d. 1 Apr., 1840.
- ii. WILLIAM THAYER SMITH, b. Mar. 30, 1839.
- iii. GEO. WHEELER SMITH, b. July 3, 1840; d. 21 July, 1840.
- iv. SARAH LOUISA SMITH, b. May 26, 1841.
- v. ALBERT DODGE SMITH, b. Aug. 3, 1842.
- vi. HARRIET MUNSON SMITH, b. May 10, 1844.
- vii. HENRY LEAVITT SMITH, b. Feb. 19, 1848.

Children of JULIA MARIA[7], (1809) [664] (David[6], David[5], Israel[4], Sarah[3], Sergt. Abraham[2], Robert[1]) and Leaverett W. Spofford; res. W. Boxford, Mass.
- i. LEAVERETT WINSLOW SPOFFORD, JR., b. Nov. 1, 1844; m. Jan., 1897, May Johnson of Augusta, Me.
    He is a book-keeper; res. Haverhill, Mass., no issue.
- ii. JULIA ANN SPOFFORD, b. Mar. 21, 1846; m. June 20, 1870, Charles Aiken.
    They have had one child, Annie May, b. Aug. 23, 1871; d. 20 Mar., 1892; res. Georgetown, Mass.

Children of SAMUEL JACKSON[7], (1810) [665] (Robert[6], David[5], Israel[4], Sarah[3], Sergt. Abraham[2], Robert[1]) and Phebe E. (Stevens) Adams; res. Richmond, Ashtabula Co., O.
- i. SYBIL[8], d. young.
- ii. GEORGE W.[8], rem. to the west and died.

Child of SAMUEL JACKSON[7] (1810) and Polly (James) Adams.

    iii. FRANK[8], res. Richmond, O.

Children of BENJAMIN FRANKLIN[7], (1811) [**666**] (Robbert[6], David[5], Israel[4], Sarah[3], Sergt. Abraham[2], Robert[1]) and Hannah (Greeley) Adams; res. Le Roy, Genesee Co., N. Y.

1199. i. AUGUSTA[8], b. in Le Roy, May 3, 1835 ; m. 1870, Albert W. Flinn, of Nashua, N. H. She d. Feb., 1873.
1200. ii. CHARLES CLINTON[8], b. in LeRoy, May 27, 1838; m. at Keeseville, N. Y., Aug. 25, 1863, Sarah Maria Morris, dau. of Charles and Sarah Maria (Smith) Morris, b. Mar. 22, 1838.
        He was formerly a merchant in Warren, O.; is now a dealer in real estate, N. Y. Life Building, Kansas City, Mo.; res. Argentine, Kan.
    iii. ELLA[8], b. in Le Roy, Dec., 1841 ; res. Nashua, N. H., unm.
1201. iv. HENRY KEELER[8], b. in Le Roy, July 28, 1845 ; m. July 19, 1884, Mary Jane Farrah, b. Apr. 21, 1857 ; res. Richmond, Ashtabula Co., O.

Child of CLARISSA JANE[7], (1816) [**667**] (Robert[6], David[5], Israel[4], Sarah[3], Sergt. Abraham[2], Robert[1]) and Alonzo Helmer.

    i. NEWTON B. HELMER, b. Feb. 9, 1840 ; m. Aug. 7, 1861, Florence A. Nims ; d. 5 Aug., 1866. He d. in Omaha, Neb., 22 Nov., 1888.

Children of PRESCOTT JONES[7], (1817) [**668**] (Robert[6], David[5], Israel[4], Sarah[3], Sergt. Abraham[2], Robert[1]) and Artemesia (Whitford) Adams; res. Factoryville, St. Joseph Co., Mich.

1202. i. GEORGE HERMAN[8], b. in Edinboro, Pa., May 26, 1844; m. (1) July 4, 1864, Jane McNett; m. (2) Eva Sweet; res. Vanderbilt, Otsego Co., Mich.
1203. ii. ALFRED LE ROY[8], b. in Factoryville, Mich., Mar. 7, 1849 ; m. May 7, 1869, Ardilla Davidson ; res. Athens, Calhoun Co., Mich.
1204. iii. OSCAR DE WITT[8], b. in Factoryville, Sept. 12, 1851 ; m. Oct. 5, 1876, Louisa Butler ; res. Sherman, Wexford Co., Mich.
1205. iv. ELLA FLORENCE[8], b. in Factoryville, Feb. 8, 1854–5; m. May, 1871, Geo. W. Pepple ; res. Athens, Mich.
1206. v. EUGENE ELMER[8], b. in Factoryville, Aug. 2, 1858 ; m. Sept. 20, 1889, Mattie House; res. Factoryville, Mich.

Children of MARY J.[7], (1814) [**669**] (Hezekiah[6], John[5], John[4], John[3], Sergt. Abraham[2], Robert[1]) and Simeon B. Drake; res. New London, N. H.

1207. i.   SIMEON H. DRAKE, b. May 1, 1838; m. Mar., 1866, Celia Henderson.
1208. ii. ABBIE M. DRAKE, b. Apr. 30, 1841; m. May, 1860, Michael Womeldorph. She d. 29 Dec., 1875.
1209. iii. RILLIE DRAKE, b. June 28, 1844; m. Nov. 3, 1860, Martin Rotner.
1210. iv. FRED M. DRAKE, b. Oct. 28, 1848; m. Feb. 20, 1869, Eleanor Rotner.
1211. v.   LIBBIE M. DRAKE, b. Jan. 13, 1853; m. Apr. 18, 1872, Russell Tucker. She d. 23 Dec., 1891.

Children of NANCY S.[7], (1815) [**670**] (Hezekiah[6], John[5], John[4], John[3], Sergt. Abraham[2], Robert[1]) and Allen Haskins.

 i.   MARY J. HASKINS, b. in New London, 1834; m. (1) 1854, R. B. Nelson, d. 1855; m. (2) 1860, H. G. Carleton.
 ii. SARAH M. HASKINS, b. in Andover, N. H., 1835; m. 1864, P. H. Whitcomb.
 iii. NANCY A. HASKINS, b. in Andover, 1839.
 iv. ELLEN G. HASKINS, b. in Andover, 1845; d. same year.

Child of NANCY S.[7], (1815) and David Cooper.

 i.   CARRIE H. COOPER, b. in Washington, N. H., 1859.

Children of CYRILLA SARGENT (1826) [**671**] and George W. F. Hayes; res. New London, N. H.

 i.   WILLIAM M. HAYES, b. Sept. 8, 1850; m. Oct., 1875, Nellie Larden. He d. 23 Feb., 1878; 1 child, Ellen Cyrilla, b. Nov. 30, 1876.
 ii. JAMES F. HAYES, b. Dec. 29, 1858; m. Dec. 20, 1885, Annie M. Pingree; 1 child, Wm. Chas., b. Nov. 7, 1890.
 iii. CHARLES R. HAYES, b. Nov. 3, 1861; m. Sept., 1889, Eva V. Everett.
 iv. GEORGE HAYES, b. Apr. 10, 1866; m. Feb. 18, 1873, Alice E. Messer.
 v.   ARCHIE HAYES, b. Mar. 20, 1871.

Children of AZRO⁷, (1822) [**672**] (Asa⁶, Benjamin⁵, John⁴, John³, Sergt. Abraham², Robert¹) and Mary C. (Hawes) Adams; res. Chelsea, Vt.

1212.
  i. SARAH H.⁸, b. in Chelsea, Feb. 9, 1853; m. (1) Mar. 5, 1876, Willard D. Grant; he d. 9 Feb., 1893; m. (2) June 5, 1894, Edward A. George; res. Barre City, Vt.

  ii. CHARLES H.⁸, b. in Chelsea, May 5, 1856; d. in Roxbury, Vt., unm., 7 Apr., 1888.

Children of BENJAMIN H.⁷, (1810) [**673**] (Benjamin⁶, Benjamin⁵, John⁴, John³, Sergt. Abraham², Robert¹) and Melvina M. (Cushman) Adams; res. Waitsfield, Vt.

  i. CATHERINE⁸, b. in Waitsfield, Nov. 11, 1839; d. 3 June, 1842.

1213.
  ii. BENJAMIN H. 2d⁸, b. in Waitsfield, Feb. 17, 1843; m. Apr. 28, 1868, Eunice A. Scribner, b. in Corinth, Vt., Nov. 30, 1845.

He enlisted Aug. 13, 1862, as a member of Co. D, 12th Regt., of Vermont Volunteers; was discharged July 13, 1863; enlisted again Aug. 5, 1864, in the 2d Vt. Light Battery; was transferred at Port Huron, La., in Jan., 1865, to the 1st Co. of Heavy Art., and discharged July 29, 1865; res. 1899, Chelsea, Vt.

  iii. WALTER F.⁸, b. in Waitsfield, Nov. 22, 1844; m. (1) Nov. 24, 1868, Julia Campbell, b. in Washington, N. H., Nov. 17, 1848, d. 26 June, 1872; no issue; m. (2) Feb. 19, 1878, Julia Hanson, b. in Washington, N. H., Dec. 17, 1846; no issue.

He enlisted Aug. 17, 1864, in the 2d Vermont Light Battery; was discharged July 29, 1865; res. Chelsea, Vt.

1214.
  iv. CATHERINE I.⁸; b. in Waitsfield, Oct. 18, 1846; m. June 20, 1864, Joseph H. Griffin, b. in Boston, June 17, 1839; res. Chelsea, Vt.

1215.
  v. MARCELLA F.⁸, b. in Waitsfield, July 20, 1848; m. July 3, 1875, Judd Scott, Jr.; res. Scottsmore, P. Q.

Children of MARY E.⁷, (1814) [**675**] (Solomon⁶, Jr., Solomon⁵, John⁴, John³, Sergt. Abraham², Robert¹) and Ija Gay; res. New London, N. H.

1216.
  i. MARCIA MARIA GAY, b. July 15, 1835; m. Oct. 8, 1854, John C. Worth.

1217.
  ii. HENRY WM. GAY, b. June 18, 1837; m. May 24, 1870, Julia M. Harrington.

  iii. MARY ABBY GAY, b. Jan. 21, 1839; m. Apr., 1867, Charles T. Thissell. She d. 27 Sept., 1871.

  iv. CHARLES HALL GAY, b. Sept. 22, 1844; m. Oct. 8, 1870, Fanny A. Butlers; res. Stockton, Cal.

1218.
  v. EVA MELVINA GAY, b. Nov. 29, 1853; m. Feb. 11, 1880, Frank H. Skinner; res. Corinth, Me.

Children of DENNIS H.⁷, (1819) [**676**] (Solomon⁶, Jr., Solomon⁵, John⁴, John³, Sergt. Abraham², Robert¹) and Betsey A. (Everett) Adams; res. New London, and Sutton, N. H.

  i. JULIA A⁸, b. in New London, Sept. 2, 1852; d. in Sutton, 24 Jan., 1865.

1219. ii. AUGUSTA M.⁸, b. in New London, May 21, 1856; m. at Sutton, N. H., May 12, 1872, John G. Hazen of Sutton, b. Dec. 28, 1844; res. No. Sutton, N. H.

Child of DENNIS H.⁷, (1819) and Betsey A. Clough (Upton) Adams.

1220. iii. WILLIAM H. H.⁸, b. in Pennacook, N. H., Oct. 23, 1866; m. (1) Apr. 13, 1887, Fanny A. Cate, of Belmont, N. H., b. Apr. 2, 1870; m. (2) May 30, 1894, Laura A. (Brown) Melcher, b. July 22, 1864.

Children of JOSEPH COLLINS⁷, (1824) [**677**] (Solomon⁶, Jr., Solomon⁵, John⁴, John³, Sergt. Abraham², Robert¹) and Ann Elizabeth (Wiggins) Adams; res. New London, N. H.

1221. i. ELMER ELLSWORTH⁸, b. in New London, Mar. 30, 1862; m. Nov. 6, 1895, Minnie Richardson of New London.
   He is post-master of New London.

  ii. HERMAN SOLOMON⁸, b. in New London, Feb. 3, 1871; m. Sept. 12, 1895, Flora M. Everett of Manchester, N. H.
   He is an insurance agent and town clerk of New London.

Children of NORMAN B.⁷, (1828) [**678**] (Solomon⁶, Jr., Solomon⁵, John⁴, John³, Sergt. Abraham², Robert¹) and Hannah A. J. (Sargent) Adams; res. New London, N. H.

1222. i. MARY ELIZABETH⁸, b. in New London, May 10, 1854; m. June 30, 1874, William C. Nye; res. Scytheville, now Elkins, N. H.

  ii. LORA SUSAN⁸, b. in New London, March 9, 1858; m. James Walker; res. No. Sutton, N. H.

  iii. CHARLES GARDNER⁸, b. in Scytheville, N. H., May 1, 1865; m. Apr. 5, 1890, Fannie Daggett, b. 1862; no issue.
   He is a stage-driver in N. Sutton or New London.

  iv. MINNIE ABIA GRACE⁸, b. in New London, Dec. 20, 1872; d. 14 Nov., 1874.

Child of SYLVANUS⁷, (1825) [**679**] (Peter⁶, Solomon⁵, John⁴, John³, Sergt. Abraham², Robert¹) and Martha S. (Hoyt) Adams; res. W. Rumney, N. H.

  i. ASA W.⁸, b. Apr., 1848.
   He is said to have been twice married.

Children of SYLVANUS[7], (1825) and Aldena D. (Matthews) Adams.
- ii. DELLA IMOGENE[8], b. 1866, d. 1868.
- iii. LEON LEWIS[8], b. 1870.
    He is a station-agent at W. Rumney, N. H., but declines to give any record.
- iv. LILLIAN BLANCHE[8], b. 1874.

Children of JOHN Q.[7], (1830) [**680**] (Peter[6], Solomon[5], John[4], John[3], Sergt. Abraham[2], Robert[1]) and —— Adams; res. Nashua, N. H.
  There are said to have been two children, one of whom was:
- i. ADDIE M. COLBY[8], b. in Nashua, Jan. 27, 1858; m. May 16, 1878, John William Phelps, b. Jan. 23, 1852.
    She was brought up by her Aunt Colby, and her children were:
    1. Mira Addie Phelps, b. Mar. 14, 1879.
    2. Minnie Alice Phelps, b. Nov. 11, 1885.

Child of DANIEL HAMILTON[7], (1836) [**681**] (Daniel Noyes[6], Solomon[5], John[4], John[3], Sergt. Abraham[2], Robert[1]) and Orinda T. (Kingsley) Adams; res. W. Springfield, N. H.
- i. DANIEL W.[8], b. in Springfield, May 15, 1866; m. Mar., 1892, Alice Eaton; res. Brockton, Mass.

Child of HELEN FRANCES[7], (1855) [**682**] (Daniel Noyes[6], Solomon[5], John[4], John[3], Sergt. Abraham[2], Robert[1]) and Waldo S. Chase; res. Springfield, N. H.
- i. DANIEL ADAMS CHASE; res. Hartford, Vt.

Children of GEORGE W. SAWYER[7], [**683**] and Nancy Ann Ryder; res. Manchester, N. H.
- i. ARIS LOIS SAWYER, b. Apr. 26, 1869; m. 1888, Thomas F. Doyle; res. Manchester, N. H.
- ii. GEORGE HENRY SAWYER, b. Mar. 10, 1872; d. 1 Feb., 1873.
- iii. JENNIE BLANCHE SAWYER, b. Jan. 17, 1874; m. Oct. 20, 1898, Willard Morris Smith; res. Manchester, N. H.
- iv. LEON EUGENE SAWYER, b. Feb. 7, 1876; res. Manchester, N. H.; unm.

Eighth Generation.]   OF NEWBURY, MASS.   309

Children of ANNA⁷, (1820) [**684**] (Moses⁶, Moses⁵, John⁴, John³, Sergt. Abraham², Robert¹) and Martin Packard; res. Brockton, Mass.

    i. SARAH AGNES PACKARD, b. Jan. 12, 1841; m. Jan. 23, 1859, John Brown Parker, son of Aaron L. Parker, b. in W. Boxford; enlisted in Co. F, 58th Mass. Vols., Feb. 18, 1864; discharged in May, 1865; res. Brockton, Mass.
        She is an active member of the Fletcher Webster Woman's Relief Corps of Brockton, occupying official positions.
    ii. MOSES À PACKARD, b. Feb. 27, 1843; m. Feb. 28, 1868. Abbie Dunbar of Brockton.
        He enlisted Sept., 1862, in Co. G, 45th Mass. Vols.; was discharged in July, 1863; is now a manufacturer and real estate dealer in Brockton, Mass.
    iii. HELEN J. PACKARD, b. Oct. 12, 1845; m. (1) Gardner Reynolds; m. (2) Chas. W. Dodge; res. Brockton, Mass.
    iv. GEORGE M. PACKARD, b. May 29, 1847; d. 28 Sept., 1849.
    v. WALTER M. PACKARD, b. Feb. 23, 1851; d. 22 Aug., 1851.

Children of DOLLY P.⁷, (1825) [**685**] (Moses⁶, Moses⁵, John⁴, John³, Sergt. Abraham², Robert¹) and Asa Tribon; res. Brockton, Mass.

    i. GEORGIANA M. TRIBON, b. Apr. 15, 1856; d. 1 Jan., 1860.
    ii. LIZZIE M. TRIBON, b. Oct. 25, 1858; d. 10 June, 1860.
    iii. JOHN TRIBON, b. Sept 30, 1861; m. Carrie M. Ransom; res. Brockton, Mass.
    iv. GEORGE M. TRIBON (twin), b. Sept. 20, 1861; d. Nov., 1861.

Child of MARY E.⁷, (1838) [**686**] (Moses⁶, Moses⁵, John⁴, John³, Sergt. Abraham², Robert¹) and David N. Chandler; res. Grafton, N. H.

    i. GEORGE A. CHANDLER, b. Oct. 22, 1866; m. Nov. 29, 1893, Mary J. Severance; res. Grafton, N. H.; one dau., Louisa Elizabeth Chandler, b. July 27, 1895.

Children of NANCY ALBINA⁷, (1827) [**687**] (Hon. Cyrus⁶, Moses⁵, John⁴, John³, Sergt. Abraham², Robert¹) and Peter Kimball; res. Grafton, N. H.

    i. MARY ALBINA KIMBALL, b. June 6, 1852; m. Feb. 20, 1879, Dr. Edw. M. Tucker of Canaan, N. H.; res. Canaan, N. H.
    ii. CYRUS KIMBALL, b. Apr. 30, 1855; d. 20 Aug., 1856.

iii. CARRIE AMELIA KIMBALL, b. Jan. 8, 1857; m. Jan. 14, 1880, Wm. E. Swentzel of Kansas City, Mo.; res. Kansas City, Mo.
iv. CYRUS A. KIMBALL, b. Apr. 6, 1861; m. June 6, 1889, Frances R. Beckford of Canaan, N. H.; res. Canaan, N. H.
v. GEO. BENJ. KIMBALL, b. Jan. 28, 1865; res. Grafton, N. H.; unm.
vi. HARRY CHEEVER KIMBALL, b. May 26, 1872; d. 26 Jan., 1876.

Children of JOHN LEWIS[7], (1826) [**688**] (Moses[6], Jonathan[5], John[4], John[3], Sergt. Abraham[2], Robert[1]) and Frances A. (Broughton) Adams; res. Tunbridge, Vt.

1223.   i. WALTER M.[8], b. in Tunbridge, May 23, 1852; m. Sept. 8, 1872, Adella E. Whipple of E. Douglass, Mass.; res. Detroit, Mich.
ii. MARY FRANCES[8], b. in Darien, Erie Co., N. Y., June 30, 1854; m. Dec. 19, 1883, William E. Waugh, b. in Hawick, Scotland, Mar. 1, 1854; res. Milwaukee, Wis.; no issue.

Child of JOHN LEWIS[7], (1826) and Eliza (Estee) Adams.
iii. GEORGE HENRY[8], b. in Tunbridge, Jan. 3, 1865; m. —— Davis of W. Lebanon, N. H. He d. in Brattleboro, Vt., Mar., 1893.

Children of MARTHA[7], (1830) [**689**] (Moses[6], Jonathan[5], John[4], John[3], Sergt. Abraham[2], Robert[1]) and Henry Morse Sanborn; res. Tunbridge, Vt.

1224.   i. MARY EUNICE SANBORN, b. in Tunbridge, May 18, 1853; m. Dennison J. Slack of Tunbridge.
ii. MARTHA F. SANBORN, b. Apr. 25, 1855; d. 25 May, 1855.
1225.   iii. CLARA EMMA SANBORN, b. Feb. 27, 1860; m. Feb. 6, 1884, Willis W. Whitney.

Child of LUNA[7], (1836) [**690**] (Seth[6], Jonathan[5], John[4], John[3], Sergt. Abraham[2], Robert[1]) and Alvah J. Dutton; res. W. Randolph, Vt.
i. CLARENCE L. DUTTON, b. May 20, 1877; res. Fitchburg, Mass.; unm.

Child of ARTHUR C.[7], (1842) [**691**] (Seth[6], Jonathan[5], John[4], John[3], Sergt. Abraham[2], Robert[1]) and Rosa (Lee) Adams; res. Tunbridge, Vt.
i. SARAH J.[8], b. in Tunbridge, Jan. 8, 1866; m. June 21, 1892, Edmond J. Busbee, principal of the High School at Weymouth, Mass.

Children of GEORGE W.⁷, (1828) [**692**] (Jonathan Tenny⁶, Jonathan⁵, John⁴, John³, Sergt. Abraham², Robert¹) and Anna Eliza (Anderson) Adams; res. Darien, Erie Co., and Corfu, Genesee Co., N. Y.

    i. FLORENCE ELLA⁸, b. in Alden, N. Y., Dec. 29, 1855 ; d. in Corfu, 19 May, 1865-6.
1226.   ii. GEORGIANA GRACE⁸, b. in Corfu, N. Y., May 12, 1868; m. Feb. 10, 1897, Geo. Cleveland, farmer ; res. Corfu, N. Y.
    iii. NINA EDITH⁸, b. in Corfu, Feb. 25, 1872 ; m. June 24, 1896, Wm. M. Hume of Corfu, N. Y., milk dealer; res. Buffalo, N. Y.
    iv. LE ROY ERNEST⁸, b. in Corfu, May 13, 1875 ; is a green-house gardner; res. Corfu, N. Y.; unm.

Children of DANIEL⁷, (1830) [**693**] Jonathan Tenny⁶, Jonathan⁵, John⁴, John³, Sergt. Abraham², Robert¹) and Julia M. (Cummings) Adams.

    i. JOHN AUSTIN⁸, b. in Ovid, Branch Co., Mich., Mar. 9, 1858 ; farmer ; res. (P. O.), Ferry, Mich.; unm.
1227.   ii. CHARLES DANIEL⁸, b. in Ovid, Nov. 12, 1860 ; m. Jan. 29, 1881, Emily M. Putney of Ferry, Mich., b. Sept. 21, 1861 ; rem. and set., 1864, in Ferry, Oceana Co.. Mich.; he is Sunday School Supt. in United Brethren Church.
    iii. LINCOLN F.⁸, b. in Otto, Mich., July 12, 1866 ; d. May, 1867.
1228.   iv. GEORGE T.⁸, b. in Otto, Mar. 19, 1868 ; m. (1) Dec. 24, 1892, Jennie Parmenter, b. 1874, d. 7 Apr., 1893 ; m. (2) July 4, 1894, Mary Law of Scottsville, Mason Co., Mich.; res. Scottsville, Mason Co., Mich.
    v. JOE M.⁸, b. in Otto, Oct. 9, 1871 ; m. Aug. 15, 1896, Jessie O'Connell ; res. Scottsville, Mich.; no issue.
1229.   vi. LURA⁸, b. in Otto, Oct. 24, 1877 ; m. Feb. 15, 1896, Wm. O'Connell, b. 1872.
    vii. NETTIE J.⁸, b. in Otto, Aug. 13, 1879 ; d. Sept., 1885.
    viii. O. K.⁸, b. in Otto, May 16, 1882 ; res. Ferry, Mich.

Children of JOHN S.⁷, (1831) [**694**] (Jonathan Tenny⁶, Jonathan⁵, John⁴, John³, Sergt. Abraham², Robert¹) and Ann Maria (Reynolds) Adams; res. Ovid, Clinton Co., Mich.

    i. CHARLES⁸, b. in Michigan, m. and settled in Sedro, Skagit Co., Wash.; has a son and four daughters.
    ii. EVA⁸, b. in Michigan.
        She married and settled in Mears, Oceana Co., Mich., where she died, leaving a daughter, now in Sedro, Wash.

Children of JOSEPH S.[7], (1836) [**695**] (Jonathan Tenny[6], Jonathan[5], John[4], John[3], Sergt. Abraham[2], Robert[1]) and Elizabeth (Churchill) Adams; res. Scottsville, Macon Co., Mich.

 i. RALPH[8], b. in Michigan; married and settled in Scottsville.
 ii. SAMUEL[8], b. in Michigan, and died.
 iii. CARRIE[8], an invalid.
 iv. HOMER[8], married and had four children; his wife died.
 v. JESSIE[8], married.
 vi. FREDERICK[8], res. in Scottsville.
 vii. JAMES[8].
  Repeated requests have been made for this record in vain.

Children of NATHAN[7], (1838-9) [**696**] (Jonathan Tenny[6], Jonathan[5], John[4], John[3], Sergt. Abraham[2], Robert[1]) and Emily C. (Parsons) Adams; res. Shelby, Mich.

 i. WILBUR DENNIS[8], b. in Shelby, Aug. 3, 1866; m. June 30, 1896, Leona Bell Mallison of Ferry, Mich., a graduate of the State Normal School and a teacher.
  He is a farmer in Shelby, Mich.; no issue.

1230. ii. ARTHUR J.[8], b. in Shelby, July 10, 1868; m. Apr. 23, 1895, Libbie S. Backum of Shelby, Mich.
  He is a farmer and teacher; res. Shelby, Mich.

1231. iii. ELIZABETH JENETTE[8], b. in Shelby, July 10, 1872; m. June 24, 1894, John H. Walcott of Shelby.

 iv. J. T.[8] (twin), b. in Shelby, July 10, 1872; m. Aug. 4, 1898, Frances Farrah.
 v. EDITH A.[8], b. in Shelby, Jan. 24, 1874; d. 2 Aug., 1874.

Children of HANNAH LORETTA[7], (1841) [**697**] (Jonathan Tenny[6], Jonathan[5], John[4], John[3], Sergt. Abraham[2], Robert[1]) and John Randall; res. Shelby, Mich.

 i. FRANK RANDALL, b. Apr. 6, 1866; m. Elna Whipple; res. Shelby, Mich.
 ii. WILLIE RANDALL, b. Oct., 1871; d. 1874.

Children of PHEBE ANN[7], (1845) [**698**] (Jonathan Tenny[6], Jonathan[5], John[4], John[3], Sergt. Abraham[2], Robert[1]) and Rev. Ambrose Bears; res. Shelby, Mich.

i. MILO BEARS, b. Sept. 10, 1865 ; d. 3 May, 1890.
ii. SYLVIA BEARS, b. Sept. 6, 1867; m. Jan. 24, 1889, Fred Chalker of Ferry, Mich.
iii. MELVA BEARS, b. July 23, 1869 ; res. Shelby, Mich.; unm.
iv. SETH BEARS, b. June 29, 1871 ; res. Shelby, Mich.; unm.

Children of HARRIET ELIZA[7], (1849) [**699**] (Jonathan Tenny[6], Jonathan[5], John[4], John[3], Sergt. Abraham[2], Robert[1]) and Lawrence Colburn; res. Shelby, Mich.

i. ELVA COLBURN, b. May 24, 1863 ; m. Dec. 25, 1890, Myron Joslin.
ii. ELNA COLBURN, b. July 2, 1871 ; res. Shelby, Mich.; unm.
iii. PHEBE ANN COLBURN, b. May 10, 1875 ; res. Shelby, Mich.; unm.
iv. ELON L. COLBURN, b. June 28, 1878.
v. MABEL COLBURN, b. Oct. 12, 1882.
vi. SYLVIA COLBURN, b. July 11, 1886.
vii. LEE L. COLBURN, b. June 27, 1888.

Children of GEORGE S.[7], (1841) [**700**] (George W.[6], Jonathan[5], John[4], John[3], Sergt. Abraham[2], Robert[1]) and Belle J. (West) Adams; res. Chelsea, Vt.

i. CORA E.[8], b. in Strafford, Vt., Aug. 17, 1870 ; m. Robert Lyon ; res. Chelsea, Vt.
ii. DAVID G.[8], b. in Strafford, Apr. 18, 1876.

Children of FRANK A.[7], (1847) [**701**] (George W.[6], Jonathan[5], John[4], John[3], Sergt. Abraham[2], Robert[1]) and Carrie E. (Davis) Adams; res. Hanover, N. H.

i. GEORGE SAMUEL[8], b. in Etna, N. H., July 4, 1879.
ii. ETHEL MAUD[8], b. in Hanover, N. H., Sept. 17, 1881.
iii. FRANK LESLIE[8], b. in Hanover, Sept. 3, 1887.

Children of CHARITY[7], (1801) [**702**] (Israel[6], Israel 3d[5], Matthew[4], Dr. Matthew[3], Sergt. Abraham[2], Robert[1]) and John Palfrey; res. W. Bridgewater, Mass.

i. CHARITY PALFREY, m. Alonzo Stevens. She d. in Haverhill, Mass.
ii. FRANK PALFREY.
   He enlisted in the regular army, and d. in Washington, D. C.
iii. GEORGIANA WALPOLE PALFREY, m. (1) Henry Huntington, who died in six weeks ; m. (2) Charles Beals. She d. in East Bridgewater, Mass.

Children of ELIZABETH[7], (1804) [704] (Israel[6], Israel 3d[5], Matthew[4], Dr. Matthew[3], Sergt. Abraham[2], Robert[1]) and Dca. Timothy Morse; res. Hopkinton, N. H., and Lowell, Mass.

 i. SARAH MARIA MORSE, b. 1830; d. 1832.

 ii. HORACE FLANDERS MORSE, b. Mar. 17, 1832; m. (1) 1856, Maria H. Salter, of Bellerica, Mass.; one child was born and died in infancy; m. (2) May 8, 1865, Regina Barnard Phillips of New Orleans, La.

  He was educated at Greenwich Academy, R. I., and the Biblical Institute, Concord, N. H., set. in the ministry of the N. E. M. E. Conference; enlisted in Aug., 1861, in the 3d Regt. Mass. Vols., serving first as Lieutenant, then as Captain; was breveted Major, and transferred to the 6th Mass. Cavalry, and served through the war. At its close he set. in business in New Orleans, and d. there, 16 May, 1870.

 iii. REV. FRANKLIN CURRIER MORSE, b. Feb. 23, 1835; m. June 26, 1861, Ellen J. Tuttle of Bristol, Conn.; living.

  He graduated from Wesleyan University, 1861, and settled in the ministry of the N. E. M. E. Conference. He enlisted in the 37th Regt. Mass. Vols., 1862, and served as chaplain through the war, returning to the ministry, he removed to Kansas in 1868, where he died 14 Jan., 1871.

 iv. LEILA MERTON MORSE, b. Nov. 17, 1840; res. Springfield, Mass.; unm.

Children of THOMAS B.[7], (1806) [705] (Israel[6], Israel 3d[5], Matthew[4], Dr. Matthew[3], Sergt. Abraham[2], Robert[1]) and Mary (Perry) Adams; res. Bradford, N. H.

 i. ISRAEL[8], b. in Henniker, N. H., Nov. 20, 1838; d. 5 Feb., 1839.

1232. ii. MARY E.[8], b. in Henniker, Nov. 26, 1839; m. Solomon C. Bumford; res. Bradford, N. H.

1233. iii. EBEN H.[8], b. in Henniker, Mar. 6, 1840; m. Aug. 2, 1878, Mrs. ELLEN M. (Atkins) Bumford, dau. of Job and Anna C. Atkins; res. Hillsboro, N. H.

 iv. THOMAS B[8], b. in Henniker, Mar. 4, 1842.

  He enlisted in the 4th N. H. Vols., and d. at Fort Independence, Boston, Harbor, 13 Feb., 1862, age 19 yrs. 11 mos. and 9 days.

 v. RICHARD S.[8], b. in Henniker, Aug. 28, 1845; d. 14 Aug., 1847.

1234. vi. ISRAEL[8], b. in Henniker, May 20, 1848; m. Mar. 8, 1878, Hepsebeth Bagley, dau. of David F. and Mahala Bagley, of Bradford, b. in Hillsboro, Feb. 25, 1857.

  He is a carpenter; res. Hillsboro and Washington, N. H.

Eighth Generation.] OF NEWBURY, MASS. 315

    vii. FRANCES A.[8], b. in Henniker, Mar. 18, 1850 ; m. Charles Booth ; res. Sunnapee, N. H.; no issue.
1235. viii. ELLA A.[8], b. in Henniker, Sept. 14, 1852 ; m. Fred Purington ; res. Bradford, N, H.

Children of EBENEZER H.[7], (1809) [706] (Israel[6], Israel 3d[5], Matthew[4], Dr. Matthew[3], Sergt. Abraham[2], Robert[1]) and Charlotte (Purington) Adams; res. Goshen, N. H.

1236. i. MARTHA A.[8], b. in Henniker, N. H., Nov. 30, 1838; m. Jan. 18, 1866, Lorenzo B. Colburn, son of Oren and Sarah (Cole) Colburn, b. in Morgan, Vt., d. in Hanover, N. H., 6 July, 1873 ; res. Lebanon, N. H.
1237. ii. IMRI P.[8], b. in Goshen, Aug. 3, 1841 ; m. Feb.. 12, 1872, Ella L. Laughlin, dau. of David and Elizabeth (Chandler) Laughlin ; res. Goshen, N. H. He d. 8 Feb., 1890.
   iii. AURORA C.[8], b. in Goshen, July 31, 1844 ; res. Lebanon, N. H., 1899 ; unm.

Children of AMANDA[7], (1811) [707] (Israel[6], Israel 3d[5], Matthew[4], Dr. Matthew[3], Sergt. Abraham[2], Robert[1]) and Rev. Azel P. Brigham; res. Henniker, and Lebanon, N. H.

   i. CAROLINE AUGUSTA BRIGHAM, b. in Henniker, Oct. 6, 1835 ; m. Jan. 1, 1857, George W. C. Dudley, son of Nathaniel W. Dudley, b. in Hanover, N. H., Apr. 14, 1834 ; res. Lebanon, N. H.
   ii. EMELINE AMANDA BRIGHAM, b. in Henniker, May 7, 1843 ; res. Lebanon, N. H., 1899 ; unm.

Children of AUGUSTA[7], (1811) [708] (Israel[6], Israel 3d[5], Matthew[4], Dr. Matthew[3], Sergt. Abraham[2], Robert[1]) and Rev. Richard M. Smith; res. Scituate, Mass.

   i. SARAH AUGUSTA SMITH, b. in Richmond Co., Ky., Apr. 26, 1844 ; d. in Providence, R. I., unm., 2 Jan., 1855.
1238. ii. RICHARD WATSON SMITH, b. in Richmond Co., May 16, 1846 ; m. (1) Sept. 6, 1871, Georgiana Skillings, b. Sept. 12, 1843, d. 26 July, 1883; m. (2) Apr. 19, 1894, Emily Phebe Wilbur ; res. Providence, R. I.
   iii. ABBY SMITH, b. in Scituate, Mass., Dec. 18, 1849 ; m. July, 1872, Isaac N. Clements of Cazenovia, N. Y.; res. Bridgewater, Mass. She d. 9 July, 1876 ; no issue.

Child of JOHN⁷, (1815) [710] (Israel⁶, Israel, 3d⁵, Matthew⁴, Dr. Matthew³, Sergt. Abraham², Robert¹) and Nancy (Davis) Adams; res. Hornellsville, N. Y.

1239. i. ROANA CUTTER⁸, b. in Hornellsville, July 8, 1843; m. June 25, 1864, Wm. Emerson Way of Lempster, N. H.; res. Lempster and Charleston, N. H.

Children of JUDITH FOLLENSBEE⁷, (1799) [711] (John⁶, John⁵, Matthew⁴, Dr. Matthew³, Sergt. Abraham², Robert¹) and Moses D. Wadleigh; res. Bradford, N H.

  i. FRANKLIN WADLEIGH, b. in Bradford; d. in infancy.
 ii. GEORGE ADAMS WADLEIGH, b. in Bradford, June 14, 1824; m. (1) Ruth Maria Booth, d. 1852; m. (2) June 20, 1855, Mary Tappan Lovejoy of Cambridge, Mass; she d. 15 May, 1896.
      He was a merchant in Boston; d. May, 1884.
iii. SARAH L. WADLEIGH, b. in Bradford, Mar. 23, 1826; m. Sept. 25, 1849, Dr. Samuel Woodbury Jones of Bradford, N. H., he d. 1879. She d. in Manchester, N. H., 29 Nov., 1879.
 iv. HARRIET E. WADLEIGH, b. in Bradford, Sept. 4, 1831; m. Jan. 24, 1856, Nathaniel W. Cumner of Wayne, Me.; res. Manchester, N. H.; he d. 13 Aug., 1888. She d. Jan., 1895.
  v. MARTHA J. WADLEIGH, b. in Bradford, and d. in infancy.
 vi. EMILY H. WADLEIGH, b. in Bradford, Mar. 24, 1838; m. June 1. 1881, John B. Handy of Wayne, Me.; res. Manchester, N. H.

Children of BENJAMIN, F.⁷, (1801) [712] (John⁶, John⁵, Matthew⁴, Dr. Matthew³, Sergt. Abraham², Robert¹) and Nancy N. (White) Adams; res. Sutton, N. H.

        i. JAMES HENRY⁸, b. in Bradford, N. H., July 28, 1834; d. 5 Nov., 1858.
       ii. JOHN FRANKLIN⁸, b. in Bradford, Aug. 11, 1836; d. 18 Oct., 1846.
1240. iii. JACOB KIMBALL⁸, b. in Bradford, Nov. 30, 1838; m. Dec. 8, 1865, Hattie A. Hurd of Newport, N. H., b. Oct. 23, 1846; res. Warner, N. H.
            He was selectman in 1885 and '86; Representative in the Legislature, 1889.
1241. iv. MARY AMANDA⁸, b. in Bradford, Feb. 25, 1844; m. Nov. 19, 1869. Dr. James M. Rix of Littleton, N. H., son of Hale and Adeline (Mar) Rix, b. Dec. 30, 1834, a graduate of Bellevue Medical Hospital, 1868; res. Warner, N. H.
1242.   v. JOHN FRANKLIN⁸. b. in Sutton, N. H., Mar. 19, 1848; m. (1) 1870, Nettie C. Hollis of Manchester, N. H.; m. (2) June 29, 1896, Fanny Clark of Warner, N. H.; res. Franklin Falls, N. H.

Eighth Generation.] OF NEWBURY, MASS. 317

Children of JOHN⁷, (1803) [713] (John⁶, John⁵, Matthew⁴, Dr. Matthew³, Sergt. Abraham², Robert¹) and Mary Elizabeth (Horton) Adams; res. Warner, N. H.

    i. MARGARET HORTON⁸, b. in Milton, Mass., Sept. 13, 1834 ; m. Sept. 1, 1868, Alonzo C. Carroll, of Croyden, N. H., son of John and Rachel Carroll, b. Nov. 24, 1826. She was his 2d wife ; res. Warner, N. H. He d. Apr., 1894 ; no issue.

    ii. LLOYD H.⁸, b. in Sutton, N. H., May 17, 1846 ; m. July 4, 1866, Elizabeth A. McAlpine of Warner, N. H., dau. of C. G. and Harriet (Osgood) McAlpine of Swanton, Vt., b. Aug. 15, 1847 ; she m. 2d Fred Smith of Swanton, Vt., and d. in Apr., 1894.

    He was a Justice of the Peace, moderator of town meeting, and a prominent citizen of Warner ; was post-master under President Cleveland, and d. in Warner, 9 Mar., 1893 ; no issue.

Children of SUSAN K.⁷, (1807) [714] (John⁶, John⁵, Matthew⁴, Dr. Matthew³, Sergt. Abraham², Robert¹) and John Andrew; res. Bradford, N. H.

    i. ELIZA JANE ANDREW, b. in Bradford, Jan. 22, 1833, m. Sept. 23, 1853, Wm. H. Dole of Concord, N. H.; res. Melrose, Mass.

    ii. JOHN A. ANDREW, b. in Bradford, Jan. 8, 1835 ; m. Dec. 9, 1874, Caroline Stickney Lovejoy of Cambridge, Mass.

    He is a wholesale grocer in Boston ; res. Chestnut Hill, Newton, Mass.; no issue.

    iii. SAMUEL G. ANDREW, b. in Bradford, Nov. 13, 1839 ; m. Oct. 11, 1876, Mrs. Sarah J. Larkin of Boston ; res. Melrose, Mass.; no issue.

    iv. JAMES FRANKLIN ANDREW, b. in Bradford, Dec. 1, 1841 ; m. Feb. 22, 1887, Frances Lambirth of Boston ; res. Dorchester, Mass. no issue.

    v. WILLIAM AUGUSTUS ANDREW, b. in Bradford, May 20, 1844, m. Mar. 27, 1878, Nellie Agnes Bass of W. Randolph, Vt.; res. Dorchester, Mass.

    vi. HARRIET N, ANDREW, b. in Bradford, May 8, 1847.
    She is an artist ; res. Boston, Mass.; unm.

Children of ELIZA JANE⁷, (1809) [715] (John⁶, John⁵, Matthew⁴, Dr. Matthew³, Sergt. Abraham², Robert¹) and David A. Bunton; res. Manchester, N. H.

    i. JOHN ADAMS BUNTON, b. Aug. 5, 1832; d. 5 Oct., 1841.
    ii. SARAH ADAMS BUNTON, b. Oct. 30, 1834 ; d. 27 Aug., 1841.
    iii. HARRIET NEWELL BUNTON, b. Sept. 3, 1837 ; d. 17 May, 1838.

ROBERT ADAMS   [Eighth Generation.

- iv. WILLIAM HENRY BUNTON, b. Mar. 5, 1840 ; d. 12 Aug., 1840.
- v. JOHN A. BUNTON, b. Oct. 27, 1842 ; d. 18 July, 1844.
- vi. WILLIAM AUGUSTUS BUNTON, b. in Manchester, June 7. 1846, m. Sept. 9, 1873, Jennie L. Richardson of Cambridge, Mass., b. May 18, 1848. He d. June, 1893 ; no issue.
- vii. GEORGE W. BUNTON, b. in Manchester, Sept. 29, 1850 ; m. Dec. 18, 1877, Elena S. Brown of Charlestown, Mass., b. Jan. 2, 1851 ; res. Cambridge, Mass.

Children of GEORGE W.^{7}, (1813) [**716**] (John^6, John^5, Matthew^4, Dr. Matthew^3, Sergt. Abraham^2, Robert^1) and Nancy (Bean) Adams; res. Manchester, N. H.

- i. SARAH BUNTON^8, b. in Sutton, N. H., Sept. 21, 1841 ; m. Sept. 18, 1866, Edwin R. Sias; he d. 30 Mar., 1886; res. Manchester, N. H.; no issue. She is a widow.
- 1243. ii. JOHN ANDREW^8, b. in Sutton, Nov. 8; 1843; m. Feb. 15, 1866, Mary Alma Bailey of Manchester.
  He is a grocer ; res. Manchester, N. H.
- iii. ELLEN MARIA^8, b. in Manchester, N. H., Sept. 1, 1851 ; d. 8 Sept., 1853.
- iv. GEORGE H.^{8}, b. in Manchester, Jan. 3, 1854 ; d. 26 July, 1874.

Child of HORTENSIA^7, (1830) [**717**] (Henry^6, John^5, Matthew^4, Dr. Matthew^3, Sergt. Abraham^2, Robert^1) and Alonzo Nelson; res. Sutton, N. H.

- i. ADELBERT W. NELSON ; res. Sutton, N. H.; unm.

Child of ADELAIDE^7, (1833) [**718**] (Henry^6, John^5, Matthew^4, Dr. Matthew^3, Sergt. Abraham^2, Robert^1) and David W. Bagley; res. Bradford, N. H.

- i. MARIA ADEL BAGLEY, b. Mar. 31, 1861 ; m. Geo. Burrell of Claremont, N. H.

Children of JOSEPH HENRY^7, (1836) [**719**] (Henry^6, John^5, Matthew^4, Dr. Matthew^3, Sergt. Abraham^2, Robert^1) and Judith Sargent (Currier) Adams; res. Contoocook, N. H.

- i. LILLIA P.^{8}, b. in Hopkinton, N. H., July 27, 1863 ; d. 14 Aug., 1863.
- ii. LEALA H.^{8}, b. in Hopkinton, Sept. 20, 1866 ; m. Mar. 22, 1888, John N. Bacon; res. Contoocook, N. H.; no issue.

iii. CLAUD D.⁸, b. in Hopkinton, May 26, 1869; m. July 24, 1898, Cora B. Getchell; res. Contoocook, N. H.
iv. LINDSEY W.⁸, b. in Hopkinton, Aug. 6, 1872; res. Contoocook, N. H.; unm.

Children of THOMAS JEFFERSON⁷, (1807) [720] (Matthew⁶, Benjamin⁵, Matthew⁴, Dr. Matthew³, Sergt. Abraham², Robert¹) and Rachel (Rowe) Adams; res. Bradford, N. H.

1244. i. ISRAEL⁸, b. in Bradford, Jan. 13, 1832; m. Sept. 4, 1855, Lydia M. Nelson; she d. 22 Dec., 1898, age 66 yrs., 11 mos. 22 days. He d. in Sutton, N. H., 3 Apr., 1890, age 58 yrs., 2 mos. 15 days; res. at Sutton Mills, N. H.

1245. ii. MOSES⁸, b. in Bradford, Apr. 22, 1833; m. (1) May 3, 1858, Mary Jane Perry, dau. of David and Fanny (Fish) Perry; she d. 23 Apr., 1881; m. (2) Mar. 18, 1883, Sarah A. Furnside of Andover, Mass. He was a tanner and courier; settled in Salem, Mass., 1886; was placed in the Asylum at Concord, N. H., in 1893.

iii. PHEBE⁸, b. in Bradford, Apr. 18, 1838; m. (1) Almon S. Howlett of Bradford; m. (2) ——— Grow; res. Bradford, N. H.

iv. HENRY GILBERT⁸, b. in Bradford, Apr. 21, 1841; m. Addie Leach of Newbury, N. H. He d. in Bradford, 9 Aug., 1877; no issue.

1246. v. ORIN⁸, b. in Bradford, Mar. 6, 1844; m. Addie Johnson; res. Newbury, N. H.

1247. vi. SARAH⁸, b. in Bradford, Jan. 21, 1848; m. (1) ——— White; m. (2) Horace F. Perry of Newport, N. H. She d. in Hillsboro, N. H., 1892.

Children of JOHN LANGDON⁷, (1807) [721] (Matthew⁶, Benjamin⁵, Matthew⁴, Dr. Matthew³, Sergt. Abraham², Robert¹) and Jane (Felch) Adams; res. Newbury, and Sutton, N. H.

1248. i. BETSEY J.⁸, b. in Newbury, N. H., Jan. 20, 1833; m. Sept. 16, 1851, Ira P. Whittier of Sutton, N. .H, son of John Osgood Whittier; res. Henniker, N. H.

1249. ii. MOSES J.⁸, b. in Newbury, July 9, 1834; m. Oct. 24, 1854, Anna E. Kidder of Newport, N. H.
He is a carpenter; res. York Beach, Me.

1250. iii. ABIGAIL A.⁸, b. in Newbury, Jan. 15, 1836; m. Ralph Brown of Newport, N. H.; he d. 5 Apr., 1886. She d. in Hillsboro, N. H., 4 Nov., 1890.

iv. JOHN FELCH⁸, b. in Newbury, Mar. 27, 1838; d. in Galveston, Tex., 27 Oct., 1859.

1251. v. ALMIRA L.⁸, b. in Newbury, Nov. 3, 1839; m. Elbridge Eaton; res. Preston, Ia.

    vi. MATTHEW[8], b. in Newbury, Mar. 10, 1842 ; m. 1862. Selmer F. Adams of Newport, N. H. He m. again, has two children, Maud and Paul ; wife, dau. of a Methodist minister.
He was clerk of the Court at Denver, Col.
    vii. SUSAN[8], b. in Sutton, N. H., Apr. 21, 1844 ; d. 3 July, 1846.
    viii. DAVID MARKS[8], b. in Sutton, May 23, 1846; d. on the Mississippi river, 15 Aug., 1864.

1252. ix. MARY D.[8], b. in Sutton, June 26, 1848 ; m. Charles Morrill, res. Concord, N. H.

1253. x. SYLVESTER FELCH[8], b. in Sutton, June 4, 1850 ; m. Addie Morey. He is a carpenter ; res. Everett, Wash.

1254. xi. SUSAN E.[8], b. in Sutton, Jan. 26, 1852 ; m. Nov. 17, 1869, Geo. F. Sleeper, a printer of Danbury, N. H.; res. Concord, N. H.

1255. xii. HANNAH MATILDA[8], b. in Sutton, April 12, 1855; m. Dec. 24, 1873, James Hawthorn ; res. Laconia, N. H.

Children of ENOCH CHENEY[7], (1809) [**722**] (Matthew[6], Benjamin[5], Matthew[4], Dr. Matthew[3], Sergt. Abraham[2], Robert[1]) and Elizabeth B. (Nourse) Adams; res. New London, N. H.

1256. i. DR. FRANK B.[8], b. Oct. 15, 1854 ; m. Dec. 25, 1878, Mary S. Bryant of Newbury, Vt. He settled in Plymouth, Mich.

1257. ii. CYRUS W.[8], b. Sept. 20, 1860 ; m. Mar. 16, 1882, Ella Pettengill of Andover, N. H.; res. Bethlehem, N. H.

Children of REBECCA[7], (1811) [**723**] (Rev. Theophilus B.[6], Benjamin[5], Matthew[4], Dr. Matthew[3], Sergt. Abraham[2], Robert[1]) and Ephraim Collins.
    i. LAURA W. COLLINS, b. May 4, 1835 ; d. 1855.
    ii. ENOCH COLLINS, b. June, 1837 ; m. Julia Hartman of Philadelphia. He d. in Austin, Nev., Oct., 1896.
    iii. JOSEPH A. COLLINS, b. Oct., 1838 ; m. Mary Emma Fowler.
    iv. HORACE B. COLLINS, b. Apr., 1843 ; d. age about 1 year.
    v. SARAH R. COLLINS, b. Mar. 15, 1845 ; m. Nov. 15, 1868, Albert P. Sawyer of Salisbury, N. H.; res. Newburyport, Mass.
    vi. JOHN H. COLLINS, b. Mar. 10, 1847 ; m. Margaret Fowler of Seabrook, N. H. He d. Nov., 1872.
    vii. FRED E. COLLINS, b. Feb. 14, 1854 ; m. Margaret Osgood ; res. Newburyport, Mass.

Children THEOPHILUS B.[7], JR., (1814) [**724**] (Rev. Theophilus B.[6], Benjamin[5], Matthew[4], Dr. Matthew[3], Sergt. Abraham[2], Robert[1]) and Fanny (Courier) Adams; res. Nashua, N. H.

Eighth Generation.] OF NEWBURY, MASS. 321

  i. ELLEN J.⁸, b. in Unity, N. H., Aug. 11, 1838 ; m. 1870, John L. Cummings of Ashburnham, Mass.; he d. June, 1891. She d. 3 July, 1891 ; no issue.
  ii. FANNY⁸, b. in Unity, Aug. 19, 1839 ; d. same day.
  iii. JOHN M.⁸, b. in Hillsboro, N. H., May 20, 1843; m. June 2, 1862, Sarah Jackman of Nashua, N. H.; res. Nashua, N. H.; no issue.
1258. iv. THEOPHILUS B.⁸, b. in Nashua, N. H., June 1, 1845 ; m. (1) Jan. 16, 1862, Margaret J. Sharp; m. (2) Nov., 1867, Mary O. Southard of Scranton, Pa.; res. Nashua, N. H.
  v. EMMA A.⁸, b. in Nashua, Sept. 23, 1846 ; m. 1870, Charles Farrow of Nashua. She d. 16 Sept., 1871 ; no issue.
1259. vi. GEORGIANA F.⁸, b. in Nashua, Apr. 9, 1848 ; m. 1866, Frank A. Barney of Nashua. She d. 11 Feb., 1874.
1260. vii. GEORGE F.⁸, b. in Nashua, Apr. 16, 1853 ; m. July 2, 1874, Emma Rolph.
   He is Supt. of Repairs of Boston & Maine R. R., Nashua, N. H.

  Children of JOSEPH M.⁷, (1816) [725] (Rev. Theophilus B.⁶, Benjamin⁵, Matthew⁴, Dr. Matthew³, Sergt. Abraham², Robert¹) and Abigail A. (Weed) Adams; res. Nashua, N. H.
  i. ABBA⁸, m. George Tower; res. So. Boston, Mass.
  ii. JOSEPH M.⁸, JR.; set. in Cambridge, Mass.
  iii. ADELBERT A.⁸
  iv. JUDITH R.⁸; m. Samuel Knapp ; res. Somerville, Mass.
  v. CLARA⁸; m. twice.
  vi. LAURA⁸.
   No records obtainable.

  Children of HARRISON H.⁷, (1823) [726] (Rev. Theophilus B.⁶, Benjamin⁵, Matthew⁴, Dr. Matthew³, Sergt. Abraham², Robert¹) and Lydia Ann (Osgood) Adams; res. Newburyport, Mass.
1261. 1. MARTHA ADELAIDE⁸, b. in Newburyport, Oct. 9, 1850; m. (1) 1872, Oliver D. Wright, of Seabrook ; he d. 10 Jan., 1878 ; m. (2) Nov. 14, 1886, Wm. Bartlett Morss; he d. 9 Aug., 1897; res. Newburyport, Mass.
  ii. ORRISA ANN⁸, b. in Newburyport, Sept. 9, 1855, d. 10 Jan , 1859.
  iii. HARRISON PARKER⁸, b. in Newburyport, Mar. 7, 1864.
   He is a moulder ; unm.; res. Worcester, Mass.
(21)

Children of BENJAMIN F.⁷, (1818) [727] (Jeremiah⁶, Benjamin⁵, Matthew⁴, Dr. Matthew³, Sergt. Abraham², Robert¹) and Lucinda (Allen) Adams; res. Royalton, Crawford Co., Pa.

    i. CLARA M.⁸, b. in Milford, Mass., May 13, 1844; d. 26 July, 1862.
    ii. SUSAN A.⁸, b. in Milford, Aug. 15, 1840; m. Nov. 15, 1877, George W. Botsford, b. Dec. 8, 1842; res. Warsaw, Wyoming Co., N. Y.
    iii. URSULA C.⁸, b. in Milford, Aug. 25, 1852; d. 4 Sept., 1852.

Children of MARY⁷, (1806) [728] (Capt. Tappan⁶, Abraham⁵, Abraham⁴, Dr. Matthew³, Sergt. Abraham², Robert¹) and Luke Shepard; res. Boscawen, N. H.

    i. FRANKLIN ADAMS SHEPARD, b. Nov. 4, 1827; m. Dec. 25, 1852, Hannah Call. He d. 14 Apr., 1885.
    ii. JAMES CULLIS SHEPARD, b. Oct. 29, 1829; m. Apr. 24, 1851, Frances C. Shepard.
    iii. MARY ANN SHEPARD, b. Sept. 15, 1833; m. Sept. 13, 1855, Frederick Gilman. She d. 6 Apr., 1892.

Children of FRANCIS⁷, (1826) [729] (Eli⁶, Enoch⁵, Richard⁴, Richard³, Sergt. Abraham², Robert¹) and Lydia (Colby) Adams; res. Warner, N. H.

    i. FRANCIS⁸, b. in Warner.
    ii. LAURA JANE⁸, b. in Warner.

Children of GILSON⁷, (1815) [730] (Russell⁶, Enoch⁵, Richard⁴, Richard³, Sergt. Abraham², Robert¹) and Harriet N. (Janes) Adams; res. Denmark, Oxford Co., Me.

1262. i. EDGAR G.⁸, b. in Denmark, Mar. 3, 1847; m. Dec. 17, 1872, **Maria E. Gordon** of Fryeburg, Me.

        He enlisted in Co. E, 12th Maine Regt., Aug., 1862, and served till Aug., 1865; was with Gen. Banks at Port Hudson, and in the Red River Expedition, taking part in a number of battles. After the war, he served as a stationary engineer in Boston, at Togus, Me., E. Pepperell, Mass., and in other places; d, in Buffalo, N. Y., 9 Mar., 1892.

    ii. EDWIN B.⁸, b. in Denmark, Sept. 14, 1848; d. 21 Apr., 1849.

Eighth Generation.] OF NEWBURY, MASS. 323

Children of GILSON⁷, (1815) and Abbie H. (Quincy) Adams.
- iii. GEORGE EDWIN⁸, b. in Denmark, Apr. 10, 1856 ; d. 9 June, 1861.
- iv. HORACE G.⁸, b. in Denmark, July 15, 1857; res. Fryeburg Center, Me., in 1883.
- v. HENRY⁸, b. in Denmark, Dec. 8, 1859 ; d. 13 Sept., 1864.
- vi. FRANK NELSON⁸, b. in Denmark, July 2, 1862 ; d. 13 Sept., 1864.

Children of HARRISON⁷, (1817) [731] (Russell⁶, Enoch⁵, Richard⁴, Richard³, Sergt. Abraham², Robert¹) and Margaret (Morse) Adams; res. Haverhill, Mass.

1263. i. GEORGE H.⁸, b. in Haverhill, June 21, 1845 ; m. Nov. 25, 1868, Abbie J. Shaw of Sanbornton, N. H., dau. of Parson C. and Martha Shaw ; res. Hill, N. H.
1264. ii. CHARLES F.⁸, b. in Hill, N. H., Oct. 2, 1857 ; m. June 19, 1880, Henrietta B. Morrill of Hill, dau. of Harrison and Olive Morrill ; res. Hill, N. H.

Children of JAMES R.⁷, (1821) [732] (Russell⁶, Enoch⁵, Richard⁴, Richard³, Sergt. Abraham², Robert¹) and Emily (Young) Adams; res. Hill, N. H.

1265. i. J. WARREN⁸, b. in Hill, June 17, 1845 ; m. Sarah A. Dickinson ; res. Elgin, Ill.; she d. 10 Apr., 1874.
1266. ii. ELLEN A.⁸, b. in Hill, Nov. 13, 1847 ; m. Geo. F. Chase. She d. 21 Apr., 1886.
- iii. SUSAN E.⁸, b. in Hill, June 14, 1854 ; unm.
- iv. MARTHA M.⁸, b. in Hill, June 13, 1856 ; unm.
- v. INFANT SON, b. in Hill, July 16, 1858 ; d. 17 July, 1858.
- vi. GEORGE F.⁸, b. in Hill, Mar. 22, 1863; d. 6 Jan., 1865.

Children of ENOCH⁷, (1823) [733] (Russell⁶, Enoch⁵, Richard⁴, Richard³, Sergt. Abraham², Robert¹) and Sylvia A. (Babcock) Adams; res. Belmont, N. H.

- i. WILLIE B.⁸, b. in Hill, N. H., Mar. 8, 1857 ; d. 11 Mar., 1857.
- ii. FRANCIS E.⁸, b. in Hill, Apr. 3, 1858 ; d. 2 Sept., 1861.
- iii. ARDELLA E.⁸, b. in Hill, Mar. 2, 1861 ; m. May 12, 1883, John R. Dearborn ; res. Belmont, N. H.
- iv. NELLIE M.⁸, b. in Hill, Oct. 27, 1863 ; res. Belmont, N. H.; unm.
- v. HERBERT C.⁸, b. in Hill, Nov. 12, 1866 ; m. June 14, 1893, Florentina E. Moulton ; res. Belmont, N. H. dau. of Edmu S. Moulton Belmont, N.
- vi. Margaret E. May 28, 1870

324   ROBERT ADAMS   [Eighth Generation.

Child of OBADIAH F.⁷, (1824) [**734**] (Russell⁶, Enoch⁵, Richard⁴, Richard³, Sergt. Abraham², Robert¹) and Louisa (Burke) Adams; res. Boston, Mass.
> i. CHARLES F.⁸, b. in Jamaica Plain, Mass., 1857. He is a civil engineer in Boston.

Child of EMILY⁷, (1817) [**735**] (Richard⁶, Enoch⁵, Richard⁴, Richard³, Sergt. Abraham², Robert¹) and Joseph B. Spiller; res. Haverhill, Mass.
> i. ABBIE W. SPILLER⁸, b. Dec. 5, 1846; m. July 9, 1872, Wm. F. Griffin; he d. 6 Jan., 1896.
>> She is a teacher of Christian Science; res. 315 Huntington Ave., Boston; 3 children.

Children of DORCAS⁷, (1821) [**736**] (Richard⁶, Enoch⁵, Richard⁴, Richard³, Sergt. Abraham², Robert¹) and Jonas Tyrrell; res. Hill, N. H.
> i. HENRY TYRRELL, b. Apr. 25, 1843; d. 29 Dec., 1865.
> ii. ABBY TYRRELL, b. Dec. 26, 1844; m. June 9, 1862, Harry Huntoon, a farmer; res, Danbury, N. H.
> iii. VICTORIA TYRRELL, b. July 16, 1850; m. June 6, 1871, Frank E. Mason of Franklin Falls, N. H.
> iv. GEORGE TYRRELL, b. July 12, 1856; d. Dec., 1860.
> v. NELLIE TYRRELL, b. Oct. 22, 1859; m. Oct. 4, 1876, John Allen, a stone-cutter; res. Manchester, N. H.

Children of ELIZABETH⁷, (1824) [**737**] (Richard⁶, Enoch⁵, Richard⁴, Richard³, Sergt. Abraham², Robert¹) and Daniel Tyrrell; res. Hill, N. H.
> i. ALVIN F. TYRRELL, b. May 14, 1845.
>> He enlisted in the 8th Regt. N. H. Vols., Dec. 17, 1861; d. at Manchester, N. H., 26 Jan., 1862.
> ii. STEPHEN A. TYRRELL, b. July 10, 1860; m. Jan. 1, 1891, Idella Couch, and has Leona, b. Oct. 23, 1891; res. Hill, N. H.
> iii. HATTIE TYRRELL, b. Nov. 20, 1861; m. Jan. 24, 1880, John W. Bartlett, and has Ella R., b. May 23, 1881; res. Hill, N. H.

Children of HENRY⁷, (1826) [**738**] (Richard⁶, Enoch⁵, Richard⁴, Richard³, Sergt. Abraham², Robert¹) and Sarah True (Judkins) Adams; res. Stockton, Cal.

1267. i. HENRY EASTLAND[8], b. in Sacramento, Cal., May 19, 1863; m. May 11, 1887, Etta May Chalmers, b. in Burlington, Ia., May 17, 1866-7.
He is superintendent of the Stockton Gas and Electric Company.
  ii. SARAH TRUE[8], b. in Sacramento, Sept. 16, 1865; m. Sept. 7, 1888, Lawrence W. Read, b. in Sacramento, Mar. 4, 1859; res. Alameda, Cal.; no issue.
  iii. FRANK PIERCE[8], b. in Napa, Cal., Oct. 9, 1868.
He is unm. and is superintendent of the Electric Works of Stockton.

Children of HENRY[7], (1826) and Edith S. (Spiller) Adams.

  iv. IRWIN DUNBAR[8], b. in Stockton, Sept. 9, 1878; res. Stockton, Cal.; unm.
  v. EDITH CAPP[8], b. in Stockton, Dec. 24, 1879; res. Stockton, Cal.; unm.
  vi. VERA[8], b. in Stockton, Feb. 5, 1881; d. 10 Dec., 1881.

Children of HENRY[7] (1826) and Louise (Brown) Adams.

  vii. HOWARD WEBSTER[8], b. in Stockton, Oct. 14, 1889.
  viii. RUSSELL BROWN[8], b, in Stockton, June 13, 1891.

Children of PHEBE JANE[7], (1827) [**739**] (Richard[6], Enoch[5], Richard[4], Richard[3], Sergt. Abraham[2], Robert[1]) and Daniel Lovering; res. Sanbornton, N. H.

  i. HELEN F. LOVERING, b. Oct. 31, 1857; m. Feb. 6, 1876, Lorenzo Ash; res. Franklin, N. H.; no issue.
  ii. SARAH A. LOVERING, b. Nov. 12, 1860; m. Nov. 20, 1880, Geo. G. Kincaid; 4 children.
  iii. ADDIE M. LOVERING, b. Jan. 3, 1866; m. Apr. 5, 1887, John W. Danforth. She d. in Bristol, N. H., 19 Mar., 1889; no issue.
  iv. GUSSIE A. LOVERING, b. Mar. 18, 1868; m. Dec. 19, 1888, Geo. W. Holt; res. E. Andover, N. H.; no issue.
  v. FRANK E. LOVERING, b. Oct. 28, 1871.

Child of STEPHEN C.[7] (1831) [**740**] (Richard[6], Enoch[5], Richard[4], Richard[3], Sergt. Abraham[2], Robert[1]) and Elizabeth B. (Currier) Adams; res. Haverhill, Mass.

1268. i. CHARLES B.[8], b. in Haverhill, Mass., Oct. 6, 1859; m. June 11, 1884, Lucy M. Horton; res. Somerville, Mass.
Employe of Brown, Darrell & Co., Boston.

Children of PAUL⁷, (1830) [**741**] (Asa⁶, Paul⁵, Richard⁴, Richard³, Sergt. Abraham², Robert¹) and Mary Jane (Tenny) Adams; res. Newburyport, Mass.

    i. FRANK SPOFFORD⁸, b. in Newburyport, Mar. 2, 1859; d. 13 July 1859.
    ii. CARROLL SPOFFORD⁸, b. in Newburyport, May, 1860; d. 28 July, 1860.

Child of PAUL⁷, (1830) and Martha R. (Russell) Adams.

    iii. PAULINE L.⁸, b. in Newburyport, June, 1882.

Children of HAZEN MICHAEL⁷, (1832) [**742**] (Asa⁶, Paul⁵, Richard⁴, Richard³, Sergt. Abraham², Robert¹) and Lucy A. (Ilsley) Adams; res. Newburyport, Mass.

    i. SUSAN ILSLEY⁸, b. in Newburyport, Feb. 21, 1860; unm. *d. Mar. 18, 1937*
    ii. SARAH COFFIN⁸, b. in Newburyport, June 28, 1865; unm.

Child of NANCY⁷, (1835) [**743**] (Asa⁶, Paul⁵, Richard⁴, Richard³, Sergt. Abraham², Robert¹) and Richard Knight; res. Newburyport, Mass.

    i. LIZZIE SUMNER KNIGHT, b. Sept. 30, 1857.

Children of ASA⁷, (1838) [**744**] (Asa⁶, Paul⁵, Richard⁴, Richard³, Sergt. Abraham², Robert¹) and Eliza A. (Tenney) Adams; res. Newburyport, Mass.

    i. EMILY JOHNSON⁸, b. in Newburyport, Oct. 20, 1859; d. 9 July, 1862.
    ii. MABEL L.⁸, b. in Newburyport, Apr. 11, 1869.

Child of JOSEPH LITTLE⁷, (1842) [**745**] (Asa⁶, Paul⁵, Richard⁴, Richard³, Sergt. Abraham², Robert¹) and Elizabeth A. (Woods) Adams; res. Newburyport, Mass.

    i. HAROLD WOODS⁸, b. in Newburyport, Dec. 29, 1889. *d. Jan. 4, 1919*

[Eighth Generation.] OF NEWBURY, MASS.

Children of MOSES CYRUS[7], (1844) [**746**] (Seneca[6], Paul[5], Richard[4], Richard[3], Sergt. Abraham[2], Robert[1]) and Mary (Dodge) Adams; res. Newburyport, Mass.

    i. ALBERT CYRUS[8], b. in Newburyport, Aug. 11, 1871 ; clerk ; res. Somerville, Mass.

    ii. JOHN ROLFE[8], b. in Newburyport, July 19, 1872 ; bank messenger, Newburyport. *d. Oct. 26, 1935*

    iii. FRANK ATHERTON[8], b. in Newburyport, July 11, 1874.

Children of LUCY JANE[7], (1843) [**747**] (Thomas Hall[6], Paul[5], Richard[4], Richard[3], Sergt. Abraham[2], Robert[1]) and Charles W. Rogers ; res. Ipswich, Mass.

    i. WILLIAM HALE ROGERS, b. Oct. 1, 1862 ; m. Nov. 7, 1897, Belle Goodhue.

    ii. LIZZIE MARY ROGERS, b. Dec. 29, 1864 ; m. Jan. 13, 1886, Granville Janes.

    iii. CHARLES THOMAS ROGERS, b. Oct. 11, 1866 ; m. Feb. 2, 1887, Mary Daniels.

    iv. FANNIE W. ROGERS, b. Aug. 25, 1874 ; m. Fred Russell. *Woodwan*

Child of EDWIN HALL[7], (1849) [**748**] (Thomas Hall[6], Paul[5], Richard[4], Richard[3], Sergt. Abraham[2], Robert[1]) and Olive Abbie (Howe) Adams; res. Rowley, Mass.

    i. MARY ABBIE[8], b. in Rowley, July 7, 1872 ; unm. *d. Aug. 15, 1945.*

Child of EDWIN HALL[7], (1849) and Ina J. (Saunders) Adams.

    ii. STELLA COLSON[8], b. in Rowley, Nov. 13, 1883. *m. Stanley McCormick, Oct. 11, 1913.*

Children of EDWARD LEWIS OSGOOD[7], (1827) [**749**] (Dr. Clement Jackson[6], Simeon[5], Richard[4], Richard[3], Sergt. Abraham[2], Robert[1]) and Lydia Jane (Walker) Adams; res. Portland, Me.

    i. CHARLES C.[8], b. in Portland, Aug. 25, 1860 ; res. Portland, Me.; unm.

        He is an insurance agent.

    ii. JAMES R.[8], b. in Portland, Oct. 3, 1867 ; m. Jan. 17, 1897, Geneva M. Tucker, dau. of Harding and Etta M. (Blake) Tucker, b. Oct. 7, 1868 ; res. Portland, Me.; no issue.

    iii. MARY C.[8], b. in Portland, Feb. 23, 1870 ; m. Oct. 20, 1897, Thomas J. Haskell, son of Thomas L. and Lizzie E. (Mullen) Haskell, b. July 20, 1872 ; res. Portland, Me.; no issue.

Children of SUSAN OSGOOD⁷, (1832) [750] (Dr. Clement Jackson⁶, Simeon⁵, Richard⁴, Richard³, Sergt. Abraham², Robert¹) and Alonzo B. Walker; res. Portland, Me.
- i. ANNIE OSGOOD WALKER, b. Nov 3, 1861; m. Apr. 16, 1890, Frank W. Palmer, b. May 2, 1858; one child, Majorie Irene, b. Nov. 8, 1891; res. Portland, Me.
- ii. JAMES ADAMS WALKER, b. Sept. 12, 1867; unm.
- iii. SUSIE CARROLL WALKER, b. Sept. 3, 1869; unm.
- iv. KATHERINE HAVILAND WALKER, b. Nov. 23, 1873; unm.

Children or CAROLINE MARGARET⁷, (1829) [751] (Simeon⁶, Simeon⁵, Richard⁴, Richard³, Sergt. Abraham², Robert¹) and William Tibbetts.
- i. GEORGE W. TIBBETTS, b. Jan. 14, 1850; d. 24 Jan., 1857.
- ii. VETTA C. TIBBETTS, b. June 1, 1851; m. June 12, 1878, William J. Knowlton; res. Portland, Me.
- iii. ALVA H. TIBBETTS, b, Apr. 24, 1853; d. 3 Aug., 1855.
- iv. CARRIE E. TIBBETTS, b. July 6, 1855; d. 6 June, 1856.

Children of MARY ELIZABETH⁷, (1832) [752] (Simeon⁶, Simeon⁵, Richard⁴, Richard³, Sergt. Abraham², Robert¹) and Stephen S. Wedgwood; res. Newport, Me.
- i. GEORGE WEDGWOOD, b. Apr. 26, 1854; d. 1 Mar., 1865.
- ii. ROSSI C. WEDGWOOD, b. Feb. 23, 1867; m. Apr. 28, 1891, Theo. P. Hope. Shed. 9 July, 1891.

Children of JOHN QUINCY⁷, (1835) [753] (Simeon⁶, Simeon⁵, Richard⁴, Richard³, Sergt. Abraham², Robert¹) and Helen M. (Burgess) Adams; res. Palmyra, Me.

1269. i. CARRIE E.⁸, b. in Corinna, Me., Aug. 3, 1859; m. Aug. 30, 1877, Charles G. Brackett. She d. in Bangor, Me., 10 July, 1885.
1270. ii. FRANK E.⁸, b. in Corinna, Oct. 16, 1861; m. May, 1888, Abbie M. Judkins of Newport, Me.; res. Newport, Me.
1271. iii. HOMER J.⁸, b. in Corinna, Dec. 11, 1863; m. June 16, 1888, Myra E. Dyer of Etna, Me.; res. Palmyra, Me.

Children of ELLEN LUCRETIA⁷, (1839) [754] (Simeon⁶, Simeon⁵, Richard⁴, Richard³, Sergt. Abraham², Robert¹) and George W. Pillsbury.

i. RALPH B. PILLSBURY, b. in Newport, Me., Dec. 13, 1857 ; res. Unity, Me.; unm.
ii. GEORGE B. PILLSBURY, JR., b. in Palmyra, Me., Apr. 1, 1859; m. Sept. 29, 1896, Lela M. Burt of Ticonderoga, N. Y.; ˌres. Charlestown, Mass.
iii. WALLACE S. PILLSBURY, b. in Palmyra, Mar. 3, 1861 ; m. Sept. 8, 1883, Helen E. Lewis of Springfield, Me.; res. Ft. Fairfield, Me.

Children of DR. SIMEON ADAMS EVANS, (1837) [755] and Louisa H. Illsley; res. Hopkinton and Conway, N. H.

i. HENRY CLINTON EVANS, b. Nov. 22, 1866 ; m. Sept. 16, 1888, Mary Helen Bell of Spencer, Mass.; res. Leicester, Mass.
ii. LOUIS ILSLEY EVANS, b. Sept. 8, 1868 ; d. 8 June, 1892.

Children of DR. SIMEON ADAMS EVANS, (1837) and Susan A. Hill.

iii. GEORGE HILL EVANS, b. May 6, 1872.
iv. JOHN ADAMS EVANS, b. Jan. 31, 1874.
v. MARY LOUISA EVANS, b. May 3, 1877.

Children of MARY LITTLE EVANS, (1842) [756] and Joseph T. Laird; res. Freehold, N. J.

i. MARION LAIRD, b. Jan. 1, 1874. Graduated from Vassar College.
ii. JOSEPH T. LAIRD, JR , b. Sept. 12, 1875.
iii. ELEANOR LAIRD, b. May 29, 1878.
iv. SAMUEL E. LAIRD, b. Dec. 17, 1882 ; d. 16 Sept., 1884.

Child of CLINTON BUSWELL EVANS, (1848) [757] and Emma Rose Townsend; res. Chicago, Ill.

i. MARION ROSE EVANS, b. Mar. 30, 1891.

Children of GILES AARON[7], (1822) [758] (Richard[6], Asa[5], Richard[4], Richard[3], Sergt. Abraham[2], Robert[1]) and Sarah E. (Jackson) Adams; res. Newburyport, Mass.

1272. i. ELLEN HARRIET[8], b. in Newbury, June 22, 1851; m. Apr. 22, 1877, Richard Tenny Noyes ; res. Newbury, Mass. *d. Mar. 13, 1937*
1273. ii. SARAH AGNES[8], b. in Newburyport, Jan. 8, 1854; m. Sept. 10, 1885, Edward F. Little ; res. Newbury, Mass.

iii. ALICE MORSE[8], b. in Newburyport, Nov. 5, 1856; d. 17 Jan., 1862.
iv. RICHARD GILES[8], b. in Newburyport, Dec. 30, 1858.
He is a carpenter; unm.; res. Newburyport, Mass. d. Nov. 6, 1945
v. NETTIE MORSE[8], b. in Newburyport, Aug. 26, 1861; d. 14 Feb., 1865.
1274. vi. CAROLINE LITTLE[8]; b. in Newburyport, Sept. 2, 1864; m. Nov. 2, 1887, Herbert A. Gillett; res. Newburyport, Mass. d. Dec. 19, 1931
vii. ELIZABETH CARR[8], b. in Newburyport, July 16, 1867; music teacher; unm. d. Oct. 4, 1943
viii. HERBERT LAWRENCE[8], b. in Newburyport, Mar. 23, 1872; d. of consumption, 17 Aug., 1891.

Children of MARY LITTLE[7], (1823) [**759**] (Richard[6], Asa[5], Richard[4], Richard[3], Sergt. Abraham[2], Robert[1]) and Joseph Noyes Rolfe; res. Newbury, Mass.

i. MOSES HENRY ROLFE, b. May 8, 1848.
ii. ABBIE LITTLE ROLFE, b. Dec. 21, 1849; d. 23 June, 1860.
iii. JOHN CALVIN ROLFE, b. Aug. 29, 1851.
iv. CHARLES GREENLEAF ROLFE, b. Aug. 27, 1853; d. 1 Sept., 1857.
v. HELEN NOYES ROLFE, b. Oct. 2, 1855.
vi. CHARLES JOSEPH ROLFE, b. Aug. 31, 1858.
vii. WILLARD GREENLEAF ROLFE, b. July 1, 1860.
viii. EDWARD ROLFE, b. June 8, 1862; d. 9 June, 1862.
ix. ABBY LITTLE ROLFE, b. Aug. 11, 1863.
x. WALTER LAMBERT ROLFE, b. Aug. 23, 1866; d. 31 Aug., 1869.

Children of ASA[7], (1824) [**760**] (Richard[6], Asa[5], Richard[4], Richard[3], Sergt. Abraham[2], Robert[1]) and Mary C. (Coleman) Adams; res. Newbury, Mass.

i. ANNIE FELLOWS[8], b. in Newbury, Apr. 5, 1858; d. 24 Oct., 1862.
1275. ii. GEORGE MOULTON[8], b. in Newbury, Apr. 25, 1861; m. Sept. 15, 1881, Hattie M. Stickney; farmer; res. homestead, Newbury.
iii. DANIEL COLEMAN[8], b. in Newbury, Mar. 16, 1863; d. Aug., 1865.

Children of ELIZABETH NOYES[7], (1831) [**761**] (Richard[6], Asa[5], Richard[4], Richard[3], Sergt. Abraham[2], Robert[1]) and Anthony Knapp; res. Newburyport, Mass.

i. ANNIE FLORENCE KNAPP, b. July 27, 1861; unm.

Eighth Generation.] OF NEWBURY, MASS 331

    ii. HENRY ANTHONY KNAPP, b. July 4, 1863; m. Ruth Lancey; res. Newbury, Mass.
    iii. SARAH RICHARDSON KNAPP, b. June 25, 1867; m. Fred Clark; res. Somerville, Mass.
    iv. MARGARET GERTRUDE KNAPP, b. July 13, 1872; m. Charles Knight; res. Newbury, Mass.

Children of MARGARET EMERY[7], (1833) [**762**] (Richard[6], Asa[5], Richard[4], Richard[3], Sergt. Abraham[2], Robert[1]) and George Washington Knight; res. Newbury, Mass.

    i. JOHN LITTLE KNIGHT, b. Jan. 15, 1859; m. Nov. 3, 1882, Mary Ellen Adams, dau. of Xenophon and Sarah H. (Knight) Adams. He d. 1 Mar., 1898.
    ii. GEORGE EDWARD KNIGHT, b. Sept., 1862; d. young.
    iii. LIZZIE HOYT KNIGHT, b. Feb., 1864; d. Feb., 1865.
    iv. ABBY FLORENCE KNIGHT, b. Sept. 13, 1869; res. Newburyport, Mass.; unm.

Children of SUSAN PIKE[7], (1838) [**763**] (Richard[6], Asa[5], Richard[4], Richard[3], Sergt. Abraham[2], Robert[1]) and Col. Charles L. Ayers; res. Newburyport, Mass.

    i. CHARLES WM. AYERS, b. Sept. 30, 1863; m. Georgie Bagley of Amesbury, Mass.; res. Newburyport, Mass.
    ii. EDW. RUSSELL AYERS, b. Feb. 20, 1867; m. Helen Johnston; res. Newburyport, Mass.
    iii. GEO. CUSTER AYERS, b. Nov. 17, 1876; d. 18 Nov., 1876.

Children of ISAAC WATTS[7], (1827) [**764**] (Nathan[6], Ebenezer[5], Richard[4], Richard[3], Sergt. Abraham[2], Robert[1]) and Elizabeth T. (Chase) Adams; res. Newburyport, Mass.

    There were 5 children, all of whom died at an early age.

Children of ISAAC WATTS[7], (1827) and Ann Maria (Goodwin) Adams.

    i. EDWIN GRAFTON[8], b. in Newburyport, Sept. 14, 1863; res. W. Newbury, Mass.; unm.
    ii. WILLIAM SHERMAN[8], b. in Newburyport, Oct., 1864; res. W. Newbury, Mass.; unm. *d. Apr. 22, 1944*

332   ROBERT ADAMS   [Eighth Generation.

    iii. ANNIE KNIGHT[8], b. in Newburyport, Apr. 29, 1868 ; d. 11 Sept., 1868.

    iv. FREDDIE WATTS[8], b. in Newburyport, June 12, 1869 ; d. 24 June, 1869.

Children of CAPT. DENNIS[7], (1830) *d. May 4, 1909.* [**765**] (Nathan[6], Ebenezer[5], Richard[4], Richard[3], Sergt. Abraham[2], Robert[1]) and Mary M. (Jacques) Adams; res. Judson, Sullivan Co., Mo.

1276. i. CHARLES W.[8], b. in Sullivan Co., Mo., Nov. 11, 1859 ; m. Apr. 27, 1881, Virtue E. Lucas ; P. O., Clear Springs, Texas Co., Mo.

    ii. MARY HELEN[8], b. in Missouri, Dec. 31, 1861 ; m. Sept. 17, 1887, John M. Taylor ; P. O., Slack, Little Horn Mt., Wyo.; no issue.

1277. iii. NATHAN E.[8], b. in Missouri, Feb. 22, 1864 ; m. Dec. 1, 1885, Rebecca J. Wyrick ; res. Clear Springs, Mo.

1278. iv. DENNIS EZRA[8], b. in Missouri, Nov. 5, 1866 ; m. Feb. 15, 1891, Violet E. Coon; res. (Hulton) Rosebud, Custer Co., Mont.

1279. v. ANNIE S.[8], b. in Missouri, Oct. 13, 1868 ; m. Nov. 21, 1886, Wm. M. Somerville ; res. Clear Springs, Mo.

    vi. JOHN Q.[8], b. in Missouri, Mar. 21, 1870 ; m. Mar. 22, 1896, Clara L. Ames ; res. Judson, Mo.

    vii. MOSES N.[8], b. in Missouri, Nov. 16, 1872.

    viii. MILES T.[8], b. in Missouri, July 27, 1875.

    ix. EMILY M.[8], b. in Missouri, Oct. 4, 1877 ; m. Dec. 26, 1898, Edw. Royels ; res. Hulton, Mont.

Children of GREEN[7], (1831) [**766**] (Nathan[6], Ebenezer[5], Richard[4], Richard[3], Sergt. Abraham[2], Robert[1]) and Emily (Stewart) Adams; res. Newbury, Mass.

    i. LOUISA SAXONY[8], b. in Newbury, Dec. 16, 1864; res. Newbury, Mass.; unm.

    ii. SUSIE STEWART[8], b. in Newbury, July, 1868 ; m. 1884, Charles Kidder of Athol, Mass.; res. Athol, Mass.

Children of LOUISA[7], (1833) [**767**] (Nathan[6], Ebenezer[5], Richard[4], Richard[3], Sergt. Abraham[2], Robert[1]) and Capt. Edwin Janvrin ; res. Newburyport, Mass.

    i. FREDERICK SARGENT[8], b. in Newburyport, May 8, 1855; d. unm., 6 Apr., 1884.

    ii. EDWIN GRAFTON[8], b. in Newburyport, Sept. 10, 1857 ; d. 22 June, 1861.

Eighth Generation.] OF NEWBURY, MASS.

iii. HELEN LOUISA⁸, b. in Newburyport, Sept. 4, 1866 ; d. Oct., 1887.
iv. EDWIN GRAYSON⁸, b. in Newburyport, Sept. 11, 1872 ; living, 1898 ; unm.

Children of CAROLINE⁷, (1835) [**768**] (Nathan⁶, Ebenezer⁵, Richard⁴, Richard³, Sergt. Abraham², Robert¹) and Charles Ordway; res. Newburyport, Mass.
  i. GEO. ABBOT ORDWAY, b. Oct., 1857; m. Mary Titcomb ; res. W. Newbury, Mass.
  ii. ETTA CLIFTON ORDWAY, b. Dec., 1860 ; m. Apr., 1886, Rufus N. Ellwell of Exeter, N. H. She d. 4 July, 1886.

Children of ADELAIDE⁷, (1844) [**769**] (Nathan⁶, Ebenezer⁵, Richard⁴, Richard³, Sergt. Abraham², Robert¹) and Stephen S. Huse; res. Newton Junction, N. H.
  i. CARRIE EMMA HUSE, b. May, 1870 ; d. in Amesbury, Mass., at 22 months of age.
  ii. REV. STEPHEN S. HUSE, b. Dec., 1872.
      He has been approbated to preach.
  iii. ALBERT FRANKLIN HUSE, b. Apr. 12, 1875 ; m. Nannie Bridges of Newton, N. H.
  iv. ERNEST LESLIE HUSE, b. Jan. 18, 1880.
  v. OSCAR EARL HUSE, b. Nov. 25, 1883.

Children of PHILIP TYLER⁷, (1842) [**770**] (Philip D.⁶, Ebenezer⁵, Richard⁴, Richard³, Sergt. Abraham², Robert¹) and Emma (Wright) Adams; res. Essex, Mass.
  i. PROF. BURTON ALDEN⁸, b. in Essex, Mass., May 9, 1875.
     He is a teacher of Technology in the University at Tongaloo, Hinds Co., Miss.
  ii. RUBIE MARION⁸, b. in Newbury, July 20, 1877. *m. Arthur D. Sto[...]*
      She is a teacher in Essex, Mass.
  iii. BERNICE WRIGHT⁸, b. in Newbury, Nov. 8, 1889; d. 17 Sept., 1890. *Jan. 2, 1[...]*

Child of JOHN CALVIN⁷, (1844) [**771**] (Philip D.⁶, Ebenezer⁵, Richard⁴, Richard³, Sergt. Abraham², Robert¹) and Hattie S. (Davis) Adams; res. Marblehead, Mass.

1280, i. ARTHUR SUMNER⁸, b. in Marblehead, Feb. 14, 1868; m. Carrie Bell Haynes of Marblehead, dau. of Robert and Rachel Haynes, b. July 29, 1871; res. Marblehead, Mass.
He is a freight agent.

Children of MARTHA BELL⁷, (1846) [772] (Philip D.⁶, Ebenezer⁵, Richard⁴, Richard³, Sergt. Abraham², Robert¹) and Cadwell Bowlen; res. Newburyport, Mass.

  i. WILLIAM CADWELL BOWLEN, b. May 12, 1869; m. Sept. 15, 1891, Abby P. Jackman; res. Chicago, Ill.; artist.
  ii. ISABEL ADAMS BOWLEN, b Apr., 1871; m. May 16, 1894, Lewis Stiles; res. Stratton Centre, N. H.
  iii. HELEN BOWLEN, b. Jan., 1875; res. Newburyport, Mass.; unm.

Child of CHARLES ALBERT⁷, (1848) [773] (Philip D.⁶, Ebenezer⁵, Richard⁴, Richard³, Sergt. Abraham², Robert¹) and Susan E. (Sanborn) Adams; res. Newburyport, Mass.

  i. CHARLES STEWART⁸, b. in E. Salisbury, Mass., Mar. 11, 1877.

Children of GEORGE EDWARD⁷, (1824) [774] (George⁶, George⁵, John⁴, Richard³, Sergt. Abraham², Robert¹) and Susan B. (Folsom) Adams; res. Newbury, Mass.

  i. GEORGE⁸, b. in Newbury, Sept. 15, 1852; m. Jan. 26, 1878, Eunice Noyes Knight; no issue. *d. June 8, 19*
  He was a farmer in Newbury (old town); d. 7 Jan., 1897.
  ii. SUSANNA F.⁸, b. in Newbury, Dec. 14, 1854; d. 1 Dec., 1860.
  iii. ANNA G.⁸, b. in Newbury, Aug. 31, 1862; living unm.
  iv. SARAH W.⁸, b. in Newbury, Jan. 26, 1865; m. Mar. 28, 1884, Wilbur D. Taylor, of Lisbon, N. H.; res. Newbury, Mass.
  v. CHARLES EDWARD⁸, b. in Newbury, May 1, 1869.
  He is a farmer, unm.; res. Rowley, Mass., 1894.

Child of ZILPAH⁷, (1840) [775] (Moody⁶, George⁵, John⁴, Richard³, Sergt. Abraham², Robert¹) and James J. Thomas; res. Boston, Mass.

  i. ALICE ZILPAH THOMAS, b. 1868, m. June 26, 1893, David J. Lindsay; res. Richmond, Va.

Children of EZRA⁷, (1842) [776] (Moody⁶, George⁵, John⁴, Richard³, Sergt. Abraham², Robert¹) and Fanny M. (Russell) Acams; res. Worcester, Mass.
- i. FRANK L.⁸, b. in Salem, Mass., May 30, 1869.
- ii. GEORGE WILLIAM⁸, b. in Salem.
- iii. FANNIE.

Children of SARAH LITTLE⁷, (1831) [777] (Freeborn⁶, George⁵, John⁴, Richard³, Sergt. Abraham², Robert¹) and George Henry Thurston; res. Lexington, Mass.
- i. CALEB ADAMS THURSTON, b. in So. Boston, Apr. 26, 1854; m. June 11, 1879, Emma Antoinette ———.
- ii. HARRIET FRANCES THURSTON, b. in So. Boston, Apr. 15, 1855; m. Sept. 29, 1879, George Albert Cottrell; res. Jamaica Plain, Mass.
- iii. ELIZABETH JANE THURSTON, b. in So. Boston, Oct. 14, 1856; d. 18 Oct., 1864.
- iv. GEORGE HENRY THURSTON, b. in So. Boston, Jan. 19, 1858; d. 11 Dec., 1864.
- v. BABY THURSTON, b. in Lexington, July 31, 1859; d. same day.
- vi. GEORGIANA THURSTON, b. in Lexington, Sept. 4, 1860; d. 6 Jan., 1874.
- vii. HENRIETTA THURSTON (twin), b. in Lexington, Sept. 4. 1860; d. same day.
- viii. SARAH EVELINE THURSTON, b. in Lexington, Nov. 10, 1863; m. Oct. 1, 1884, James H. R. Cowley; res. Lexington, Mass.
- ix. RUTH ESTELLE THURSTON, b. in Lexington, Nov. 10, 1864; d. 22 Mar., 1876.
- x. HELEN IRENE THURSTON, b. in Lexington, Dec. 27, 1867; d. 8 Nov., 1868.

Children of GARDINER⁷, (1833) [778] (Freeborn⁶, George⁵, John⁴, Richard³, Sergt. Abraham², Robert¹) and Frances Melvina (Leeds) Adams; res. Chelsea, Mass.
- i. ELIZABETH GARDINER⁸, b. in Somerville, Mass., July 5, 1855; m. Feb., 1890, William H. Hinckley; res. Washington, D. C.
- ii. CARRIE FRANCES⁸, b. in Charlestown, Mass., May 24, 1858; res. Chelsea, Mass.; unm.

Children of CHARLES[7], (1841) [779] (Freeborn[6], George[5], John[4], Richard[3], Sergt. Abraham[2], Robert[1]) and Mary Ellen (Leeds) Adams; res. Somerville, Mass.

   i. MARY ALLETTA[8], b. in Somerville, June 30, 1863; d. 6 Oct., 1877.
   ii. CHARLES WARREN[8], b. in Somerville, Dec. 2, 1865; m. Feb. 17, 1888, Mildred Southard, dau. of Paul Minot and Eunice (Monroe) Southard of Corinna, Me., b. Jan. 23, 1868; clerk with Bigelow & Co., Boston, Mass.; no issue.
   iii. CHESTER FREEBORN[8], b. in Somerville, Nov. 17, 1878.
       He graduated from the Somerville High School in 1897.

Child of WARREN[7], (1842) [780] (Isaac[6], Simon[5], John[4], Richard[3], Sergt. Abraham[2], Robert[1]) and Jane (Withum) Adams; res Newburyport, Mass.

   i. NETTIE MARION[8], b. in Newburyport, Apr. 7, 1875; m. Oct. 4, 1896, Benjamin W. Hersey. *1 son Bert*

Children of SIMON AUGUSTUS[7], (1836) [781] (Jesse[6], Simon[5], John[4], Richard[3], Sergt. Abraham[2], Robert[1]) and Elizabeth (Brown) Adams; res. Newbury, Mass.

1281.
   i. WALTER LESLIE[8], b. in Newbury, Sept. 3, 1867; m. Dec. 25, 1893, Florence H. Ogden, dau. of J. R. Ogden.
       He is an electrician; res. Norwich, Conn., since 1892.
   ii. JESSIE MAY[8], b. in Newbury, Mar. 11, 1872; unm.; res. Newburyport, Mass. *d. June 13, 1902.*
   iii. ERNEST CLIFTON[8], b. in Newbury, Aug. 27, 1874; res. Norwich, Conn.; unm. *D. Aug 9-1949*
   iv. FRANK WILSON[8], b. in Newbury, Jan. 12, 1878; res. Newbury, Mass.; unm. *Bessie Wilder Nov. 17, 1909*
   v. EMMA FRANCES[8], b. in Newbury, Oct. 27, 1880; res. Newbury, Mass.; unm. *Fred Angus, Sept. 5, 1906.*
   vi. NELLIE AVSTICE[8], b. in Newbury, Mar. 4, 1883; res. Newbury, Mass.; unm.

Children of CHARLES WILLIAM[7], (1847) [782] (William[6], John[5], John[4], Richard[3], Sergt. Abraham[2], Robert[1]) and Virginia (Fairfield) Adams; res. Newburyport, Mass.

   i. MARY INA[8], b. in Newbury, Mass., Oct. 22, 1872; m. Sept. 2, 1896, Moses Edward Wright.
   ii. WILLIAM ELMER[8], b. in Newbury, Oct. 6, 1874; unm.
   iii. VIRGINIA MAUD[8], b. in Newbury, Mar. 7, 1879.

[handwritten top] × Emily Mabel Adams Jewett died 26 May, 1946.

Children of LEWIS AUSTIN⁷, (1839) [**783**] (John Coffin⁶, John⁵, John⁴, Richard³, Sergt. Abraham², Robert¹) and Emily M. (Hutchinson) Adams; res. Rowley, Mass.

    i. WILFRED PRESTON⁸, b. in Rowley, Apr. 27, 1867; *[hw: m. Edith M. John Feb 26 1903]*
× ii. EMILY MABEL⁸, b. in Rowley, Nov. 12, 1870; *[hw: m. Amos Everett Jewett]*
    iii. FANNY HOBSON⁸, b. in Rowley, June 17, 1873; *[hw: m. John W. Hale, Aug.]*
    iv. ALICE NOYES⁸, b. in Rowley, June 24, 1876; unm. *[hw: d. May 14, 1957 d. Rowley]*
    v. EDITH MYRA⁸, b. in Rowley, Dec. 25, 1877; d. 10 May, 1897. *[hw: Edith M. wife of W.P. died Sept. 26, 1... Wilfred P. d. Mar. 14, 19..]*

[hw left margin: Frannie H. Hale d. Apr. 4, 1941 in Orange, Calif.]

Children of MARGARET COFFIN⁷, (1840) [**784**] (John Coffin⁶, John⁵, John⁴, Richard³, Sergt. Abraham², Robert¹) and Daniel Adams Brown; res. Newbury, Mass. *[hw: Margaret C. d. Jan. 13; d. Oct. 30, 1901]*

[hw: Died June 16, 1953]
    i. MARY FLORENCE BROWN, b. Dec. 31, 1869.
    ii. JUSTIN ADAMS BROWN, b. Apr. 12, 1871. *[hw: m. Abbie Leigh Apr]*
    iii. DANIEL BURTON BROWN, b. Mar. 16, 1873. *[hw: m. Hannah Lay June 14]*
    iv. PERCY TRUE BROWN, b. Dec. 17, 1874.
    v. ETHEL ASHTON BROWN, b. Jan. 20, 1877. *[hw: m. William Knight Sept 2]*
    vi. FRED CARROLL BROWN, b. Mar. 14, 1879.
    vii. MARGARET LUNT BROWN, b. July 10, 1884. *[hw: m. Silas Little, Sept 6]*

Children of JAMES KNIGHT⁷, (1851) [**785**] (John Coffin⁶, John⁵, John⁴, Richard³, Sergt. Abraham², Robert¹) and Lizzie A. (Goodwin) Adams; res. Newbury, Mass. *[hw: d. Nov. 4, 1937; dau. of Sam'l and Nancy (Russell) Goodwin. d. Mar. 12, 192.]*

    i. GRACE GARLAND⁸, b. in Newbury, Apr. 23, 1870; unm. *[hw: d. Oct. 10, 193.]*
    ii. GERTRUDE RUSSELL⁸, b. in Newbury, Dec. 17, 1872; d. 8 Jan., 1877.
    iii. ETTA DANFORTH⁸, b. in Newbury, Oct. 2, 1874; ; d. 20 Jan., 1877.
    iv. EDITH FOSS⁸, b. in Newbury, Apr. 11, 1877; d. in infancy. *[hw: Apr 23, 1877]*
    v. JOHN RAYMOND⁸, b in Newbury, Sept. 17, 1878; unm.
    vi. NEWELL⁸, b. in Newbury, May 15, 1881. *[hw: Alice (Little) Wa. July 28, 192]*
    vii. RALPH⁸, b. in Newbury, July 20, 1883; d. 19 Aug., 1883.
    viii. PRESTON GOODWIN⁸, b. in Newbury, Oct. 16, 1884. *[hw: m. J. Anna]*
    ix. HARRY CARLTON⁸, b. in Newbury, Feb. 26, 1886. *[hw: m. Jessie Rogers and]*
    x. LOUISA GERTRUDE⁸, b. in Newbury, Sept. 10, 1891. *[hw: Lillia (Kyle) Wil..]*

[hw: Died July 14, 1952. m. May 4, 1926 Fred C. Gowdy]

Children of DAVID JEWETT⁷, (1820) [**786**] (Capt. Richard⁶, *[hw: Apr 11,]* Moses⁵, Moses⁴, Richard³, Sergt. Abraham², Robert¹) and Sarah Chase (Pettengill) Adams; res. Newburyport, Mass.

(22)

[hw bottom left: Abbie (Leigh) Brown d. Oct. 3, 1945. Alice C. W. Adams wife]

[hw bottom right: Jessie A. d. Apr. 23, 1917. Harry C. m. (2) Lillian E. (Lyle) Wilson Apr. 11, 192.]

i. WILLIAM WALLACE⁸, b. in Newburyport, June 3, 1842; d. unm., 8 Aug., 1890.
  ii. DAVID JEWETT⁸, b. in Newburyport, Sept. 10, 1844; m. Kate ———. He d. 7 Feb., 1847; no issue.
 iii. MARY ANN⁸, b. in Newburyport, Feb. 8, 1847; d. 1 Apr., 1856.
  iv. EBEN PETTENGILL⁸, b. in Newburyport, Feb. 26, 1853; d. 23 Aug., 1853.

Children of RICHARD⁷, (1822) [**787**] (Capt. Richard⁶, Moses⁵, Moses⁴, Richard³, Sergt. Abraham², Robert¹) and Lydia (Moody) Adams; res. Charlestown, Mass.

   i. LYDIA M.⁸, b. in Charlestown, Jan. 16, 1845; d. 28 Jan. following.
  ii. SARAH COOK⁸, b. in Charlestown, Aug. 30, 1846; m. June, 1863, Geo. O. Burgess. She d. Aug., 1888; no issue. *Geo. O. Burgess d. Aug. 15/12*
1282. iii. RICHARD HENRY⁸, b. in Charlestown, Dec. 26, 1855; m. Nov. 15, 1881, Annie Cunningham of Newton, Mass., dau. of Luther T. and Abbie (Beyer) Cunningham, b. Feb. 10, 1855.
       He is a cabinet-maker; res. Newton, Upper Falls, Mass.

Children of JOHN Q.⁷, (1824) [**788**] (Capt. Richard⁶, Moses⁵, Moses⁴, Richard³, Sergt. Abraham², Robert¹) and Eliza Ann (Hager) Adams; res. Newburyport, Mass.

1283. i. JOHN Q.⁸, JR., b. in Newburyport, May 5, 1848; m. Nov. 17, 1868, Mary T. Young; res. Newburyport, Mass.
       ii. CHARLES HENRY⁸, b. in Newburyport, Mar. 31, 1850; living unm. *d. Feb 19/12*
1284. iii. GEORGE F.⁸, b. in Newburyport, Apr. 11, 1852; m. Mar. 9, 1869. Elizabeth G. Mitchell. *d. June/2, 1924*

Children of EDWIN⁷, (1825) [**789**] (Capt. Richard⁶, Moses⁵, Moses⁴, Richard³, Sergt. Abraham², Robert¹) and Louisa J. (Murphy) Adams; res. Newburyport, Mass.

   i. MARY ALICE⁸, b. in Newburyport, Mass., Oct. 30, 1854; d. 8 Mar., 1869.
  ii. ROBERT E.⁸, b. in Newburyport, June 4, 1858; m. Carrie F. Ayers He set. in Lowell, Mass.; no issue.
 iii. ERNEST H.⁸, b. in Newburyport, Mar. 9, 1860; res. Newburyport, Mass.; unm. *d. Mar 3, 1926*
  iv. FOREST H.⁸ (twin), b. in Newburyport, Mar. 9, 1860; d. 24 Dec., 1862.

[Eighth Generation.] OF NEWBURY, MASS.

Children of EDWIN⁷, (1825) and Hannah Jane (Young) Adams.

    v. LIZZIE L.⁸, b. in Newburyport, July 26, 1864 ; d. Aug., 1865.
    vi. FRED⁸, b. in Newburyport, Aug. 15, 1866; m. Jan. 1, 1891, Addie *d. Ma* Louisa Hobbs of Yarmouth, N. S. *had son Earl L.*
    vii. FOREST EDWIN⁸, b. in Newburyport, Mar. 11, 1869 ; d. 28 July, 1869.
    viii. ETTA M.⁸, b. in Newburyport, Mar. 12, 1871 ; d. 8 Mar., 1875.
    ix. CHARLES J.⁸, b. in Newburyport, June 29, 1872 ; d. 14 Aug., 1872.
    x. JAMES⁸, b. in Newburyport, May 30, 1874.

Children of XENOPHON⁷, (1838) [790] (Capt. Richard⁶, Moses⁵, Moses⁴, Richard³, Sergt. Abraham², Robert¹) and Sarah H. *d. July 18* (Knight) Adams; res. Newburyport, Mass.

1285. i. MARY ELLEN⁸, b. in Newburyport, Sept. 11, 1861 ; m. Nov. 3, 1882, John L. Knight. He d. 1 Mar., 1898. *She m. (2) Elvyn D. Moby*
    ii. XENOPHON⁸, b. in Newburyport, Dec. 1, 1865 ; d. 27 Feb., 1869. *Dec. 19*
    iii. WILLIAM BROWN⁸, b. in Newburyport, Mar. 13, 1868. *d. Mar.* He was accidently shot, and d. 27 Oct., 1895.
1286. iv. MARIA CHRISTINE⁸, b. in Newburyport, Oct. 11, 1871 ; m. June 28, 1893, Frank W. Reynolds ; res. Somerville, Mass.
    v. LILLIAN KNIGHT⁸, b. in Newburyport, July 22, 1874 ; d. 18 Dec., 1884.
    vi. XENOPHON⁸, JR., b. in Newburyport, Sept. 18, 1876. *d. Dec. 9, 192*
    vii. CHARLES LAWRENCE⁸, b. in Newburyport, Dec. 29, 1880. *d. Nov. 25,*

Children of MOSES COOK⁷, (1840) [791] (Capt. Richard⁶, Moses⁵, Moses⁴, Richard³, Sergt. Abraham², Robert¹) and Lizzie J. (Disney) Adams; res. Newburyport, Mass.

    i. LIZZIE DISNEY⁸, b. in Newburyport, Sept. 14, 1862; m. Dec. 24, 1884, Fred A. Nield. *had one son Arthur Nield, o*
1287. ii. CARRIE STONE⁸, b. in Newburyport, Dec. 29, 1864 ; m. Dec. 29, *Shreve* 1881, Frank Perkins. She d. 8 Jan., 1887.
    iii. ~~LIZZIE~~ COFFIN⁸, b. in Newburyport, Dec. 21, 1867 ; unm. *Geo. E. Sti* *Susan*   *d. Jan. 16, 1925*

Children of MOSES⁷, (1837) [792] (Moses⁶, Moses⁵, Moses⁴, Richard³, Sergt. Abraham², Robert¹) and Ellen (Mears) Adams; res. Essex, Mass.

    i. STELLA W.⁸, b. in Essex, Nov. 14, 1864 ; d. 12 Aug., 1865.
    ii. NELLIE W.⁸, b. in Essex, Nov. 6, 1866 ; d. 25 July, 1871.

1288. iii. LIZZIE B.[8], b. in Essex, Apr. 2, 1873; m. Aug. 16, 1894, Fred M. Burnham, son of Alphonso and Josephine Burnham of Gloucester, Mass., b. in Gloucester, June 14, 1869; res. Essex, Mass.

Children of MARY P.[7], (1844) [**793**] (Woodbridge[6], Moses[5], Moses[4], Richard[3], Sergt. Abraham[2], Robert[1]) and James G. Robinson; res. Providence, R. I.

    i. ALICE MAUD ROBINSON, b. in Lynn, Mass., June 30, 1873; res. Providence, R. I.
    ii. JAMES W. ROBINSON, b. in Lynn, June 17, 1878; living unm.

Children of JOHN PEABODY[7], (1847) [**794**] (Woodbridge[6], Moses[5], Moses[4], Richard[3], Sergt. Abraham[2], Robert[1]) and Helen M. (Todd) Adams; res. Auburndale, Mass.

    i. JOHN IRVING[8], b. in Ipswich, Mass., Sept. 7, 1877.
    ii. JENNIE H.[8], b. in Auburndale, July 6, 1879.
    iii. GEORGE ROYAL[8], b. in Auburndale, Oct. 1, 1883.
    iv. GRACE K.[8], b. in Auburndale, Sept. 5, 1884.
    v. HAROLD C.[8], b. in Auburndale, Dec. 29, 1885.

Children of JAMES[7], (1817) [**795**] (John[6], Ens. James[5], Dea. Edmund[4], Richard[3], Sergt. Abraham[2], Robert[1]) and Lois Ann (Hall) Adams; res. Londonderry, N. H.

    i. ABBIE O.[8], b. in Londonderry, Oct. 15, 1855; living unm.; res. Manchester, N. H.
    ii. ALFRED JAMES[8], b. in Londonderry, Oct. 10, 1862; d. 7 Nov., 1867.

Children of CHARLES[7], (1819) [**796**] (John[6], Ens. James[5], Dea. Edmund[4], Richard[3], Sergt. Abraham[2], Robert[1]) and Mary (Hall) Adams; res. Derry, N. H.

1289. i. LOUISA BRADLEY[8], b. in Derry, Sept. 19, 1848; m. May 25, 1873, Rufus Crombie; he d. in Marietta, Ga., 3 Mar. [1874; res. Derry, N. H.
    ii. MARY ELIZABETH[8], b. in Derry, Dec. 22, 1852; m. Jan. 17, 1882, Orison G. Reed. She d. 18 May, 1889.

Child of HORACE⁷, (1821) [**797**] (John⁶, Ens. James⁵, Dea. Edmund⁴, Richard³, . Sergt. Abraham², Robert¹) and Margaret (Richardson) Adams; res. Hampstead, N. H.

    i. JOHN⁸, b. in Hampstead, Feb. 22, 1857; res. Hampstead, N. H.; unm.

Children of HORACE⁷, (1821) and Lucy Ann (Anderson) Adams.

    ii. LUCY J.⁸, b. in Hampstead, Nov. 23, 1861 ; d. 19 Mar., 1864.
1290. iii. CHARLES F.⁸, b. in Hampstead, Feb. 23, 1864 ; m. Nov. 27, 1881, Ella Page ; res. Hampstead, N. H.
    iv. GEORGE⁸, b. in Hampstead, Mar. 28, 1873; res. Haverhill, Mass.; unm.

Children of ELIZA⁷, (1823) [**798**] (John⁶, Ens. James⁵, Edmund⁴, Richard³, Sergt. Abraham², Robert¹) and James Pettengill.

    i. GEORGE C. PETTENGILL, b. Dec. 10, 1848 ; d. in Londonderry, N. H., 1 Feb., 1870.
    ii. ANNA E. PETTENGILL, b. Feb. 24, 1853 ; d. 1871, age 18 yrs. 3 mos. 4 days.
    iii. DR. JAMES B. PETTENGILL, b. May 10, 1858 ; m. 1882, Ada E. Bartlett, of Limerick, Me.
        He graduated from Pembrook Academy, 1880 ; studied medicine with Dr. Daniel S. Adams of Manchester, and attended lectures at Burlington, University of Vermont, and Dartmouth College ; set. in Amherst, N. H., in Jan., 1884 ; is an Odd Fellow and a Mason.
    iv. HERBERT PETTENGILL, b. May 10, 1860; was drowned 17 July, 1870.

Children of NATHAN⁷, (1825) [**799**] (John⁶, Ens. James⁵, Dea. Edmund⁴, Richard³, Sergt. Abraham², Robert¹) and Jane E. (Boyce) Adams; res. Bedford, N. H.

    i. LUCELIA E.⁸, b. in Londonderry, N. H., Dec. 26, 1845 ; m. Dec. 13, 1871, Wm. H. Gage ; res. No. Londonderry, N. H.
    ii. ROVENA⁸, b. in Londonderry, Feb. 10, 1850 ; m. June 15, 1882, John W. Yeaton ; res. W. Newton, Mass.
    iii. GEORGE⁸, b. in Londonderry, Jan. 2, 1852 ; d. 31 Aug., 1874.

iv. FRANK⁸, b. in Londonderry, Nov. 2, 1854; m. June 9, 1875, Anna Whidden; one child, Rowena L., b. Apr. 2, 1881; d. 15 Aug., 1881. He is an engineer of the Old Colony R. R.; res. Fitchburg, Mass.
v. CHARLES⁸, b. in Londonderry, Mar. 13, 1860; m. Oct. 22, 1885, M. M. Woods; res. No. Londonderry, N. H.; no issue.
vi. GERTRUDE⁸, b. in Bedford, N. H., Jan. 15, 1870; d. 19 Nov., 1883.

Child of JANE⁷, (1845) [**800**] (Benjamin⁶, Ens. James⁵, Dea. Edmund⁴, Richard³, Sergt. Abraham², Robert¹) and W. Preston Melvin; res. Derry, N. H.

i. MARY MELVIN, b. in Derry, July 4, 1882.

Children of ANNA ELIZABETH⁷, (1844) [**801**] (David⁶, Ens. James⁵, Dea. Edmund⁴, Richard³, Sergt. Abraham², Robert¹) and Myron D. Tracey; res. Warren's Corner, Niagara Co., N. Y.

i. CORA M. TRACEY, b. Aug. 20, 1872; m. Feb. 25, 1897, Zerembe Folger.
ii. MARY ADELLA TRACEY, b. Jan. 26, 1876; unm.
iii. GEORGE A. TRACEY, b. Oct. 29, 1879; unm.

Children of REV. LUCIEN HARPER⁷, (1829) [**802**] (Edmund⁶, Ens. James⁵, Dea. Edmund⁴, Richard³, Sergt. Abraham², Robert¹) and N. Dora (Francis) Adams; res. Derry, N. H.

i. LUCIEN B.⁸, b. in Derry, Feb. 6, 1869; d. 5 Apr., 1869.
ii. HELEN AUGUSTA⁸, b. in Antioch, Asia, Aug. 3, 1871. She was graduated from the State Normal School at Bridgewater, Mass., 1893, and is a teacher at N. Adams, Mass.; unm.
iii. EDWARD FRANCIS⁸, b. in Antioch, June 8, 1874; res. Derry, N. H.; unm.
iv. WALTER SIDNEY⁸, b. in Antioch, Dec. 20, 1876. He is a professor in a college in Chicago, Ill.; unm.
v. GEORGE H.⁸, b. in Antioch, Feb. 21, 1881; d. 30 Dec., 1883.

Child of DANIEL M.⁷, (1833) [**803**] (Edmund⁶, Ens. James⁵, Dea. Edmund⁴, Richard³, Sergt. Abraham², Robert¹) and Helen A. (True) Adams; res. Derry, N. H.

i. RUFUS⁸, b. in Derry, June 26, 1857; d. 15 Jan., 1860.

Children of DANIEL M⁷, (1833) and Ollie A. (Thomas) Adams.

    ii. HELEN FRANCES⁸, b. in Topeka, Kan., Jan. 30, 1868.
          She is unm. and a clerk in office of the Santa Fe R. R. Co., at St. Louis, Mo.
    iii. KATHERINE JANE⁸, b. in Topeka, Feb. 22, 1870 ; res. Topeka, Kan.; unm.
    iv. DANIEL M.⁸, JR., b. in Topeka, Mar. 4, 1872.
          He is a clerk in the Pension office at Topeka; uum.

Child of ROSWELL 2D⁷, (1794) [804] (Asahel⁶, Zadoc⁵, Jacob⁴, Sergt. Jacob³, Jacob², Robert¹) and Lucy (Sikes) Adams; res. Suffield, Conn.

1291. i. NORMAN R.⁸, b. in Suffield, May 7, 1821 ; m. Nov. 8, 1843, Chloe Remington, b. Sept. 17, 1823 ; d. 22 Nov., 1894, age 71 yrs. 2 mos. He d. in Suffield, 5 Feb., 1866.

Children of ALVIN⁷, (1792) [805] (Noadiah⁶, Zadoc⁵, Jacob⁴, Sergt. Jacob³, Jacob², Robert¹) and Hannah (Ainsworth) Adams; res. Suffield, Conn.

1292. i. MARY BEDORTHA⁸, b. in Suffield, Dec. 6, 1817; m. Jan. 1, 1843, Sullivan P. Lamberton, carpenter and member of Co. G, 1st Conn. Artillery. b. Feb. 13, 1816 ; d. 7 Apr., 1865.
    ii. JULIA N.⁸, b. in Suffield, Dec. 4, 1819; res. Westfield, Mass.; d. unm.
1293. iii. AMASA A.⁸, b. in Suffield, Mar. 4, 1822; m. Dec. 26, 1847, Cyndonia Kibbe of N. Somers, Conn.
          He is a carpenter and contractor; res. Springfield, Mass.
    iv. ESTHER CATHERINE⁸, b. in Suffield, July 8, 1824 ; m. Dec. 17, 1843, Andrew Campbell, cigar maker of Westfield, Mass. She d. in Westfield, Mass., 10 Jan., 1884.
    v. AMELIA⁸, b. in Suffield, Aug. 29, 1826 ; d. same day.
    vi. MARCIA⁸, b. in Suffield, Aug. 25, 1828 ; m. Apr. 8, 1852, Marcus Dean, carpenter. They settled in Springfield, Mass.

Children of HARVEY⁷, (1793) [806] (Noadiah⁶, Zadoc⁵, Jacob⁴, Sergt. Jacob³, Jacob², Robert¹) and Mary (Porter) Adams; res. Agawam, formerly West Springfield, Mass.

    i. LUCIUS E.⁸, b. in W. Springfield, Sept. 16, 1820 ; d. in Agawam, unm., 22 May, 1883.

1294. ii. LOUISA[8], b. in W. Springfield, Oct. 30, 1822; m. Oct. 5, 1843 Job Fowler of Agawam, b. Feb. 2, 1816; d. 7 June, 1895. She d. in Suffield, Conn., 29 Jan., 1872.

1295. iii. JOHN P.[8], b. in W. Springfield, Oct. 26, 1825; m. Apr. 20, 1857, Susanna B. Bashore, dau. of John and Elizabeth Bashore; she was the first white child born in Lima, Ohio; was b. Mar. 10, 1824.
He was a merchant in Lima, Ohio.

1296. iv. ALBERT[8], b. in W. Springfield, Mar. 30, 1828; m. Jan. 17, 1854, Elizabeth Bogardus, dau. of Peter and Mary (Smith) Bogardus of Hudson, N. Y., b. May 26, 1829. He d. in Springfield, Mass., 18 Dec., 1880.

v. ELIJAH P.[8], b. in W. Springfield, Feb. 23, 1830; m. Feb. 23, 1873, Rebecca Eliza Parker, b. Sept. 15, 1844; res. Springfield, Mass., 1899; no issue.

1297. vi. JOSEPH B.[8], b. in W. Springfield, Sept. 10, 1834; m. (1) Mar. 6, 1862, Eliza Ann Doss; m. (2) May 7, 1871, Mary Ann Sprague.
He settled in Blairsville, Posey Co., Ind., in Jan., 1854, and engaged in teaching—his calling for 41 years, having taught 85 schools and 2,591 pupils. He is now a farmer; P. O. Hepburn, Posey Co., Ind.

1298. vii. BENJAMIN F.[8], b. in W. Springfield, Sept. 11, 1841; m. (1) Oct., 1864, Lurana Cox, dau. of David Cox of Posey Co., Ind.; m. (2) Dec. 25, 1884, Alice Montgomery, dau. of Elias Montgomery, b. in Warren Co., O., Mar. 11, 1860; m. (3) June 10, 1896, at Marysville, O., Virginia (Jennie) P. Creal, dau. of Thomas H. and Mary (Phelps) Creal, an early Virginia family.
He was a teacher in Evansville and in Posey Co., Ind.; enlisted July, 1861, in the 25th Regt. Ind. Vols.; was discharged Oct., 1862; resumed teaching until 1885, when he received an appointment in the Post Office at Cincinnati, Ohio. He is now a letter carrier; res. Golden Ave., Cincinnati, Ohio.

Children of LUCIUS[7], (1795) [**807**] (Noadiah[6], Zadoc[5], Jacob[4], Sergt. Jacob[3], Jacob[2], Robert[1]) and Julia (Norton) Adams; res. Springfield, Mass.

1299. i. ALVIN[8], b. in Springfield, Apr. 21, 1819; m. June 1, 1845, Emily A. Sherwin of Newfane, Vt. She d. 6 Nov., 1849; res. Springfield, Mass.

ii. HENRY L.[8], b. in Springfield, 1825; d. in Petersham, Mass., 20 Dec., 1889.

Children of DIANTHE[7], (1790) [**808**] (Zadoc[6], Jr., Zadoc[5], Jacob[4], Sergt. Jacob[3], Jacob[2], Robert[1]) and Calvin Sikes; res. Suffield, Conn.

Eighth Generation.] OF NEWBURY, MASS. 345

　　i. DIANTHE SIKES, m. —— Hume ; res. Long Meadow, Mass.
　　ii. CLARISSA SIKES, m. John Parker, who d. in Missouri.
　　iii. CAROLINE SIKES, m. —— Churchill.
　　iv. REBECCA DESIRE SIKES ; m. —— Thomas.
　　v. MARTHA SIKES.
　　vi. CALVIN SIKES, JR.
　　vii. CALVIN SIKES, JR.
　　viii. SIMON SIKES.
　　ix. REUBEN SIKES.
　　x. THEODORE SIKES.
　　xi. JOSEPH SIKES ; m. Mary Moore.
　　xii. LUCINDA SIKES.

Children of ALMIRA[7], (1796) [**809**] (Ebenezer[6], Zadoc[5], Jacob[4], Sergt. Jacob[3], Jacob[2], Robert[1]) and Zenas Sikes; res. Suffield, Conn.

　　i. CYRUS A. SIKES, b. Oct. 26, 1817 ; m. 1841, Mary Ann Cooper. He d. 1844.
　　ii. LEWIS Z. SIKES, b. Dec. 19, 1819 ; m. Mar., 1842, Margaret Sikes.
　　iii. JULIUS F. SIKES, b. May 24, 1824 ; m. Nov. 23, 1848, Jane E. King, dau. of Julius and Emily (Adams) King ; res. Suffield (Mapleton), Conn.; living 1898.

Children of ALMIRA[7], (1796) and Edwin Bement.

　　i. MARY S. BEMENT, b. Dec. 25, 1829 ; m. Apr., 1852, Edward Francis King ; he d. June, 1878. She d. Dec., 1877.
　　ii. DAVID K. BEMENT, b. Feb. 5, 1831 ; d. age 5 years.
　　iii. EDWIN BEMENT, JR., b. Nov. 13, 1833.
　　　　He enlisted in Aug., 1863, in the 16th Conn. Regt. of Volunteers, and was killed in the battle of Antietam.
　　iv. HANNAH BEMENT, b. Apr. 19, 1835 ; m. Apr., 1859, Jerome W. Merritt. She d. in Suffield, 11 May, 1868.
　　v. HIRAM BEMENT, b. May 8, 1837 ; m. (1) June, 1867, Celia King ; she d. Jan., 1872 ; m. (2) Oct. 4, 1882, Ellen Eager ; res. Suffield, Conn.
　　vi. DOREMUS D. BEMENT, b. Mar. 21, 1839 ; res. Suffield ; unm.

Children of JARVIS[7], (1798) [**810**](Ebenezer[6], Zadoc[5], Jacob[4], Sergt. Jacob[3], Jacob[2], Robert[1]) and Hannah D. (Williams) Adams; res. Hartford, Conn.

i. ALONZO⁸, b. perhaps in Suffield, Conn., 1827-8.
   He is reported as married, and resident on Long Island.
ii. CICERO⁸.
   He is said to have been a Captain in the Southern Army, and to have died at sea; unm.

Children of RUTH⁷, (1799) [**811**] (Ebenezer⁶, Zadoc⁵, Jacob⁴, Sergt. Jacob³, Jacob², Robert¹) and Stoddard Parker; res. Springfield, Mass.

1300. i. FRANCIS J. PARKER, b. in Springfield, Mass., Apr. 2, 1822; m. Oct. 3, 1847, Mary D. Puffer; res. San Francisco, Cal.
1301. ii. RENSLOW S. PARKER, b. Nov. 29, 1823; m. (1) Sarah Cole; m. (2) Mrs. Maria A. Lester; res. 3413 Vernon Ave., Chicago, Ill.
1302. iii. EBEN G. PARKER, b. June 27, 1825; m. Oct. 10, 1847, Mary A. Chapin. He d. 27 Sept., 1855.
   iv. MARY A. PARKER, b. Mar. 10, 1826; d. 19 Mar., 1843.
1303. v. MIRANDA C. PARKER, b. Nov. 16, 1828; m. Oct. 10, 1847, Palmer S. Vinton. She d. in Chicago, Ill., Dec., 1889.
   vi. MATILDA ANN PARKER, b. Sept. 30, 1830; d. 28 Feb., 1843.
   vii. MARIA LOEVY PARKER, b. Oct. 22, 1832; m. Dec. 23, 1857, Edwin R. Colton. She d. Mar., 1861.
   viii. MARTHA S. PARKER, b. July 25, 1835; d. 3 June, 1836.
1304. ix. JANE LEROY PARKER, b. Mar. 16, 1837; m. Feb. 23, 1860, in Springfield, Mass., James F. Gillette, son of James and Martha (Granger) Gillette of Suffield, b. Apr. 7, 1832; d. 17 Sept., 1894; res. 2908 Michigan Ave., Chicago, Ill.
   x. REBECCA G. A. PARKER, b. Aug. 3, 1839; d. 31 Jan., 1843.
   xi. JOSEPH W. PARKER, b. May 23, 1841; d. 25 Aug., 1850.

Children of LYDIA⁷, (1802-3) [**812**] (Ebenezer⁶, Zadoc⁵, Jacob⁴, Sergt. Jacob³, Jacob², Robert¹) and David Tyler; res. Agawam, Mass.

i. JULIA ANN TYLER, b. June 15, 1822; m. Silas Cook; res. Agawam, Mass.; d. 15 Apr., 1850.
ii. JAMES TYLER, b. July 10, 1825; m. Sarah Tucker; res. Agawam, Mass.
iii. LYDIA MARIA TYLER, b. July 31, 1827; m. John Quackenbush; res. Beloit, Wis.
iv. MARY LOUISA TYLER, b. Apr. 22, 1829; m. Silas Cook (his 2nd wife); res. Agawam, Mass.

Children of CYNTHIA⁷, (1805) **[813]** (Ebenezer⁶, Zadoc⁵, Jacob⁴, Sergt. Jabob³, Jacob², Robert¹) and Oren Parker; res. Suffield, Conn.

    i. SOPHRONIA PARKER, b. Dec. 2, 1830 ; m. Jan. 9, 1853, Louis K. Adams, son of Calvin and Lucy (King) Adams. She d. 26 Oct. 1886.
    ii. OREN NEWTON PARKER, b. Mar. 17, 1835; d. 21 Dec , 1837.
    iii. CHARLES EARL PARKER, b. May 5, 1841 ; d. 10 Oct., 1871.
    iv. REBECCA E. PARKER, b. Sept. 15, 1844; m. Feb. 23, 1873, Elijah P. Adams, son of Harvey and Mary (Porter) Adams ; res. Springfield, Mass.; no issue.

Child of NEWTON SKINNER⁷, (1808) **[814]** (Ebenezer⁶, Zadoc⁵, Jacob⁴, Sergt. Jacob³, Jacob², Robert¹) and Catherine (Bundle) Adams; res. New York City, N. Y.

    i. CHRISTINA⁸, b. in New York.

Children of HANNAH⁷, (1810) **[815]** (Ebenezer⁶, Zadoc⁵, Jacob⁴, Sergt. Jacob³, Jacob², Robert¹) and Cornelius R. Doremus.

    i. CYNTHIA ALMIRA DOREMUS, b. Aug. 24, 1833; d. 19 Jan., 1837.
    ii. ANN ELIZABETH DOREMUS, b. June 29, 1835 ; m. Dec. 5, 1855, Nelson J. Wright, b. July 27, 1834; d. 4 Apr., 1870 ; res. Springfield, Mass.
    iii. MARTHA SOPHRONIA DOREMUS, b. Nov. 8, 1838 ; d. 8 Nov., 1838.

Children of HANNAH⁷, (1810) and John Van Delinda.

    i. CORNELIUS D. VAN DELINDA, b. May 6, 1845 ; m. Nov. 23, 1870, Mary I. Easton ; res. Springfield, Mass.
    ii. KATE E. VAN DELINDA, b. Feb. 3, 1849 ; res. Springfield, Mass.; unm.

Children of EDWARD⁷, (1801) **[816]** (Arah⁶, Zadoc⁵, Jacob⁴, Sergt. Jacob³, Jacob², Robert¹) and Sally (Worthington) Adams; res. South Wilbraham, now Hampden, Mass.

1305.   i. BETSEY⁸, b. in So. Wilbraham, Sept. 20, 1823 ; m. Nov. 30, 1843, Austin Dwight Bliss of Monson, Mass. They rem. to Rockton, Ill., in Oct., 1855. He. m. 2nd, July 3, 1866, Mrs. Helen Estes, and bad a daughter, Lillian Bliss, b. May 1, 1873 ; m. June 24, 1896, Clifford Atkinson of Shirland, Ill. Betsey d. in Rockton, 23 May, 1865.

 ii. JOHN EDWARD⁸, b. in So. Wilbraham, Dec. 7, 1825; d. 13 Sept., 1827.

1306. iii. FRANCES ANN⁸, b. in Hampden, Jan. 21, 1828 ; m. Sept. 28, 1850, Calvin Clark ; he rem. to Iowa, and m. 2nd ——— Ormsby. Frances Ann d. [12 Aug., 1853] 11 Sept., 1852, age 34 years.

1307. iv. LYDIA ROGERS⁸, b. in Hampden, Dec. 27, 1829 ; m. Sept. 17, 1849, George Lincoln Bathrick ; he d. 26 May, 1878 ; res. Springfield, Mass.

1308. v. EDWARD⁸, JR., b. in Hampden, Jan. 15, 1832 ; m. June, 1855, Margaret Mixter ; she d. in Palmer, Mass., 24 Feb., 1867 ; was buried in Hampden.
   He is a carpenter ; res. W. Hartford, Conn., since 1863.

 vi. SYLVESTER⁸, b. in Hampden, Aug. 14, 1834; m. a German lady in New York ; made a trip to Germany ; parted ; rem. West ; no issue.

 vii. FLORILLA⁸, b. in Hampden, Apr. 17, 1837 ; m. Nov., 1860, Luman Eno of Somers, Conn. She d. 23 June, 1864 ; no issue.

Child of EDWARD⁷, (1801) and Julia A. (Webster) Adams.

1309. viii. JOHN QUINCY⁸, b. in Hampden, Dec. 10, 1847 ; m. May 22, 1872, Delia F. Lee ; she has been librarian of the Free Public Library since its establishment in 1891.
   He has been the town clerk and treasurer of Hampden since 1889.

Children of ELIZA⁷, (1804) [**817**] (Arah⁶, Zadoc⁵, Jacob⁴, Sergt. Jacob³, Jacob², Robert¹) and Roderic Fuller; res. Westfield, Mass.

1310. i. ELIZABETH GRAY FULLER, b. Jan. 14, 1830 ; m. July 4, 1847, Ransford Worthington of Enfield, Conn., b. 1827 ; d. 2 Aug., 1892, age 65 years ; res. Westfield, Mass.

 ii. MARY ANN FULLER, b. Mar. 7, 1831 ; m. 1851, Comfort Bell. She d. 2 Aug., 1865.

 iii. DELOS A. FULLER, b. July 2, 1832 ; m. Jan. 1, 1859, Lucinda Stevens of Westfield, Mass. She d. Aug., 1898.

 iv. GEORGE R. FULLER, b. May 18, 1834 ; d. 6 Aug., 1834.

 v. FANNY R. FULLER, b. Nov. 26, 1836 ; m. 1858, Alonzo Clark ; res. Westfield, Mass.

 vi. JAY B. FULLER, b. Sept. 26, 1841 ; m. 1862, Ellen Haley ; she d. 8 Oct., 1884. He d. 26 Apr., 1870 ; no issue.

Eighth Generation.] OF NEWBURY, MASS. 349

Children of JOHN[7], (1809) [**818**] (Arah[6], Zadoc[5], Jacob[4], Sergt. Jacob[3], Jacob[2], Robert[1]) and Betsey (Snow) Adams; res. Suffield, Conn.

1311.   i. BELINDA SHARLON[8], b. in Suffield, Sept. 7, 1832; m. Nov. 24, 1853, Chas. A. Roberts; he d. 29 Oct., 1872; res. Meriden, Conn.

       ii. ABEL SNOW[8], b. in Suffield, Nov., 1834; res. Hartford, Conn.; unm.

1312. iii. MASSENA CLARK[8], b. in Suffield, Sept. 20, 1840 ; m. Elizabeth Sherwood. He d. in Hartford, Conn., 21 May, 1894, age 53 years.

Children of RHODOLPHUS SNOW, (1803) [**818½**] and Mary Ann King; res. Suffield, Conn.

       i. ALBERT RHODOLPHUS SNOW, b. May 5, 1831 ; m. Oct. 17, 1860, Huldah M. Warren of Hamden, Conn.; res. Hamden, Conn. Children :
- 1. Lillian Alice Snow, b. in Hamden, Nov. 25, 1862 ; m. Apr. 8; 1884, Wm. E. Dickerman.
- 2. Lydia Maria Snow, b. in Hamden, Mar. 5, 1867 ; m. Apr. 18, 1988, Fred'k C. Reynolds of Westville, Conn.
- 3. Clara May Snow, b. in Hamden, May 12, 1871 ; d. 20 Sept., 1872.
- 4. Albert Otis Snow, b. in Hamden, May 21, 1877 ; m. May 23, 1899, May H. Riley.

      ii. MARY ELECTA SNOW, b. Aug. 16, 1833 ; m. Apr. 29, 1857, Dwight J. Osborn of Windsor Locks, Conn.

    iii. HENRY ROBERT SNOW, b. Feb. 22, 1835 ; m. Jan. 2, 1865, Julia Root of Berlin, Conn.; she d. 5 Apr., 1891, age 54 years. He d. in Meriden, Conn., 7 Jan., 1894.

    iv. SARAH ELIZABETH SNOW, b. Jan. 26, 1837 ; m. Seth Liswell of Feeding Hills, Mass ; he d. in the Civil War.

     v. FRANCIS BYRON SNOW, b. July 29, 1841 ; m. Almenia Chapman of Hamden, Conn ; res. Meriden, Conn.

    vi. OTIS DWIGHT SNOW, b. June 6, 1849 ; m. May 29, 1882, Selena Lazell of Meriden, Conn. He d. 12 Oct., 1890 ; no issue.

Child of LOUIS K.[7], (1822) [**819**] (Calvin[6], Zebulon[5], Jr., Zebulon[4], David[3], Jacob[2], Robert[1]) and Sophronia (Parker) Adams; res. Shoshone, Lincoln Co., Idaho.

       i. CLARENCE ELLIOT[8], b. in Suffield, Conn., Jan. 19, 1854 ; d. 17 May, 1870; buried in Agawam, Mass.

Children of MARIA LUCY DEWEY, (1823) [**820**] and John Mills Woolley; res. Salt Lake City, Utah.

- i. JOHN DEWEY WOOLLEY, b. Dec. 30, 1846 ; d. 14 May, 1849.
- ii. ASHBEL DEWEY WOOLLEY, b. June 1, 1850 ; m. Dec. 12, 1878, Ida Ann Bird, b. Dec. 15, 1851.
- iii. HARRIET ARABEL WOOLLEY.
- iv. FRANK ALBERT WOOLLEY, b. May 2, 1856; m. May 14, 1880, Eliza Kimball. He d. 23 Jan., 1890.
- v. WM. DEWEY WOOLLEY, b. Feb. 25, 1858.
- vi. VILATE ANABEL WOOLLEY, b. Aug. 21, 1860.
- vii. MARION DEWEY WOOLLEY, b. June 28, 1862 ; d. 19 Dec., 1888.

Children of ALBERT CORNING DEWEY, (1825) [**821**] and Sarah Burton; res. Salt Lake City, Utah.

- i. ALBERT ASHBEL DEWEY, b. in Nassau Valley, Nev., June 17, 1857; m. Laura Decker.
- ii. MARY ELLEN DEWEY, b. in Salt Lake City, Utah, Apr. 21, 1859 ; m. Nov. 16, 1881, Henry E. Heath, b. in Salt Lake City, July 30, 1857.
- iii. ANABEL DEWEY, b. in Salt Lake City, Dec. 26, 1861 ; d. 21 Nov., 1863.
- iv. THEODORE DEWEY, b. in Salt Lake City, Apr. 28, 1863.
- v. ROBERT BURTON DEWEY, b. in Salt Lake City, May 7, 1867 ; d. 14 June, 1869.

Children of ALBERT DEWEY, (1825) and Elizabeth Ann Wright.

- vi. ASENATH JOSEPHINE DEWEY, b. in Salt Lake City, Apr. 20, 1868.
- vii. HOMER ROBERTS DEWEY, b. in Salt Lake City, Jan. 17, 1873 ; d. 16 Apr., 1880.

Children of BENJAMIN FRANKLIN DEWEY, (1829) [**822**] and Eliza Smithson; res. Salt Lake City, Utah.

- i. BENJAMIN FRANKLIN DEWEY, JR., b. in San Bernardino, Cal., Feb. 14, 1856; unm.
- ii. LOIS ELIZA DEWEY, b. Dec. 19, 1857; m. Evan Milton Crane.
- iii. ELLA LUCINDA DEWEY, b. in Salt Lake City, Mar. 30, 1860 ; d. 7 Apr., 1862.

Eighth Generation.] OF NEWBURY, MASS. 351

    iv. HARRIET MARIA DEWEY, b. in Salt Lake City, Apr. 12, 1862 ; d. 19 Sept., 1863.
    v. ELIZABETH DEWEY, b. Mar. 12, 1864 ; m. Charles Thompson of Los Angeles, Cal.
    vi. GEORGE DEWEY, b. Feb. 11, 1868 ; unm.

Children of BENJAMIN FRANKLIN DEWEY, (1829) and Diza Paralle Russell.

    vii. MARGARET MAY DEWEY, b. in Salt Lake City, May 5, 1874 ; m. Samuel Athay of Paris, Idaho.
    viii. LOUIS ADAMS DEWEY, b. in Salt Lake City, Sept. 27, 1896.

Children of JOHN HENRY DEWEY, (1832) [**823**] and Ann Lamoreaux ; res. Salt Lake City, Utah.

    i. ANNETTE DEWEY, b. May 19, 1856 ; m. Jan. 25, 1882, Thos. K. Stevens.
    ii. MARY LUELLA DEWEY, b. Aug. 28, 1857 ; became blind.
    iii. EMILY DEWEY, b. July 16, 1859.
    iv. JOHN HENRY DEWEY, JR., b. Sept. 22, 1861; m. Oct. 6, 1896, Annie C. Smith, b. June 28, 1873.
    v. CAROLINE L. DEWEY, b. Sept. 13, 1863; m. June 29, 1883, Arthur A. Moulton.
    vi. ABIGAIL DEWEY, b. July 31, 1866 ; m. June 19, 1890, Oscar James Bourne.
    vii. WILLIAM GEORGE DEWEY, b. Dec. 26, 1868 ; d. by accident, 31 Aug., 1888.
    viii. CHAS. ADAMS DEWEY, b. Sept. 6, 1871.
        Was an expert electrician ; engaged in mining and was killed by a snow slide, Feb., 1899.
    ix. ISABELLE DEWEY, b. Apr. 22, 1874.

Children of ELIZA ANGELINE[7], (1806) [**825**] (Calvin[6], Capt. Gideon[5], Daniel[4], Daniel[3], Jacob[2], Robert[1]) and Chester Ives Bidwell ; res. Verona, N. Y., and Galesville, Wis.

    i. CHARLES C. BIDWELL, b. Feb. 20, 1828 ; m. Sept. 7, 1852, Mary Gilbert.
    ii. SARAH BIDWELL, b. in Rome, N. Y., June 1, 1830 ; m. Jan. 1, 1850, A. J. Doty.
    iii. GEORGE W. BIDWELL, b. in Rome, Aug. 10, 1832 ; m. (1) Feb. 18, 1858, Caroline Burt ; m. (2) Mar. 4, 1869, Dora Cook.

352   ROBERT ADAMS   [Eighth Generation.

iv. HELEN BIDWELL, b. in Parish, N. Y., Apr. 6, 1835 ; m. Dec. 29, 1861, Daniel Kennedy ; res. Galesville, Wis.
v. PORTER BIDWELL, b. in Parish, June 21, 1837 ; m. Mar. 4, 1867, Jennie Cleveland.
He is an inventor ; res. McGregor, Ia.
vi. CHESTER BIDWELL, b. Feb. 7, 1839; was a soldier, and d. at Federal Hill, Baltimore, Md., 31 Oct., 1862.
vii. WILLIAM BIDWELL, b. Oct, 18, 1841 ; d. at Galesville, Wis., 20 Apr., 1870.
viii. HERMAN BIDWELL, b. at Rome, N. Y., Mar. 2, 1851 ; m. Nov. 9, 1875, Luraney Curtis.

Children of GIDEON[7], (1808) [**826**] (Calvin[6], Capt. Gideon[5], Daniel[4], Daniel[3], Jacob[2], Robert[1]) and Orinda (Haskins) Adams; res. Manston, Wis.

i. THEODORE M.[8]
ii. CALVIN[8].
iii. GUIDON[8].
Many efforts to find this family have proved fruitless.

Children of SARAH CLINTON[7], (1813) [**827**] (Calvin[6], Capt. Gideon[5], Daniel[4], Daniel[3], Jacob[2], Robert[1]) and William S. Wilder.

i. GEORGE WILDER, b. Mar. 4, 1836 ; d. in Nebraska, 22 Oct., 1858.
ii. THEODORE B. WILDER, b. Dec. 29, 1837 ; m. Aug., 1867, Frances Durand.
He left Oberlin College and enlisted in Co. C, 7th Ohio Regt.; was wounded at Cedar Mountain, and remained in the hospital at Alexandria 5 months; returned to college and graduated and became professor at Ripon, Wis. He d. 9 Mar., 1870, and his widow and son went out as missionaries to China in 1894.
iii. ANGELINE E. WILDER, b. Dec. 8, 1839 ; m. Apr. 20, 1859, Chas. Williams ; res. Chester, O.
iv. HUBERT WILDER, b. Mar. 28, 1844 ; d. 7 Oct., 1868.
v. MARTHA WILDER, b. June 27, 1847 ; m. Feb. 6, 1866, John C. Linderman ; res. Alameda, Cal.
vi. ABEL WILDER, b. Aug., 1848 ; d. 28 Nov., 1872.
vii. WILLIAM D. WILDER, b. Nov. 16, 1854 ; m. Jan., 1877, Alma Radcliffe ; res. Mulberry Corners, O.

JAMES HENRY ADAMS.

Eighth Generation.] OF NEWBURY, MASS. 353

Children of ELIZA ANGELINE⁷, (1814) [828] (Horace⁶, Capt. Gideon⁵, Daniel⁴, Daniel³, Jacob² Robert¹) and Philander Soper; res. Verona, N. Y.

    i. HORACE WYLIE SOPER, b. May 18, 1842; m. May 12, 1880, Georgia Jackman ; res. Chicago, Ill. He.d. 11 Oct., 1898.
    ii. WILLARD HANFORD SOPER, b. April 6, 1846 ; m. Dec. 22, 1870, Emma Jane Wilson ; res. Verona, Oneida Co., N. Y.
    iii. CLINTON PHILANDER SOPER, b. Mar. 24, 1851 ; m. Nov. 23, 1881, Emma Burr ; res. Bloomington, Ill.

Children of WINFRED SCOTT⁷, (1819) [829] (Horace⁶, Capt. Gideon⁵, Daniel⁴, Daniel³, Jacob², Robert¹) and Elouisa (Miller) Adams; res. Phelps, N. Y.

    i. SARAH LAMOINE⁸, b. in Lee, N. Y., May 8, 1842; m. Sept. 5, 1866, Albert Buckingham of Marshall, N. Y.; he d. 20 July, 1887 ; res. Phelps, N. Y.
    ii. ELLA MILLER⁸, b. in Rome, N. Y., Jan. 31, 1847; m. Jan. 1, 1868, Samuel R. Allen ; res. Deansville, Oneida Co., N. Y.
    iii. HORACE WINFIELD S.⁸, b. in Augusta, N. Y., Feb. 2, 1854 ; m. Feb. 16, 1876, Clemmis L. Brown ; res. Clifton Spa., N. Y.

Child of SARAH⁷, (1823) [830] (Horace⁶, Capt. Gideon⁵, Daniel⁴, Daniel³, Jacob², Robert¹) and Joshua R. Lawton ; res. Great Barrington, Mass.

    i. CORA ANGELINE LAWTON, b. in Great Barrington, July 13, 1856 ; m. Nov. 28, 1883, Wm. E. Barnes of Pittsfield, Mass.; res. Boston, Mass.

Children of CLINTON⁷, (1828) [832] (Horace⁶, Capt. Gideon⁵, Daniel⁴, Daniel³, Jacob², Robert¹) and Mary (Savery) Adams; res. Valley Mills, Madison Co., N. Y.

    i. ELBERT CLINTON⁸, b. in Valley Mills, Mar. 26, 1869; m. July 18, 1893, Jennie M. Ayers of Oneida, N. Y.; res. Oneida, N. Y.; no issue.
    ii. LYNDON E.⁸, b. in Valley Mills, Mar. 21, 1871 ; m. Nov. 12, 1892, Nettie E. Mott, dau. of Philander Mott, b. in Phelps, N. Y.; res. Oak Ridge Sta., Pa.; no issue.
    iii. FRANK WALTER⁸, b. in Valley Mills, July 18, 1874.
    iv. ESTELLA MAY⁸, b. in Valley Mills, Jan. 29, 1878.

Children of HENRY L.[7], (1830) **[833]** (Horace[6], Capt. Gideon[5], Daniel[4], Daniel[3], Jacob[2], Robert[1]) and Mary A. (Noble) Adams; res. Rome, N. Y.

1813. i. HATTIE ALICE[8], b. in Rome, May 1, 1859; m. Nov. 3, 1881, Dr. Arthur A Gillette.
       ii. MARY LYNDON[8], b. in Rome, June 12, 1861; d. 20 Nov., 1861.
1814. iii. HORACE WYLIE[8], b. in Rome, Nov. 18, 1862; m. Mar. 19, 1885, Julia C. Wilson.
       iv. GEORGE D.[8], b. in Rome, Nov. 11, 1864; unm.
       v. LESTER N.[8], b. in Rome, Sept. 11, 1866; d. 24 Jan., 1873.

Child of AMANDA[7], (1833) **[834]** (Horace[6], Capt. Gideon[5], Daniel[4], Daniel[3], Jacob[2], Robert[1]) and William Baker.

   i. ALICE BAKER; m. —— Smith; res. Saticoy, Cal.

Children of AMANDA E.[7], (1823) **[835]** (Harvey[6], Capt. Gideon[5], Daniel[4], Daniel[3], Jacob[2], Robert[1]) and George Spencer; res. Fergus, Saginaw Co., Mich.

   i. ARABELL SPENCER, b. Aug. 21, 1843.
  ii. GEORGE H. SPENCER, b. May 19, 1846.
 iii. FREELOVE SPENCER, b. Apr 13, 1848.
  iv. BENJAMIN SPENCER, b. Nov. 17, 1850; d. 1859.
   v. CHARLES SPENCER, b. July 4, 1855; d. 1871.
  vi. JOHN SPENCER, b. July 8, 1859.
 vii. ESTHER SPENCER, b. May 30, 1862; d. 1863.

Child of RHODA[7], (1827) **[836]** (Harvey[6], Capt. Gideon[5], Daniel[4], Daniel[3], Jacob[2], Robert[1]) and Henry Lincoln; res. Bancroft, Mich.

   i. —— ——; m. Pone Kent; res. Bancroft, Mich.

Children of GEORGE HADLEY[7], (1830) **[837]** (Harvey[6], Capt. Gideon[5], Daniel[4], Daniel[3], Jacob[2], Robert[1]) and Mary E. (Higgins) Adams; res. Brooklyn, N. Y.

   i. HARVEY H.[8], b. in Hallowell, Me., 1856; d. 16 Apr., 1896.
  ii. MARY L.[8], b. in Indianapolis, Ind., 1860; d. 1880, age 20 years.
 iii. CHARLES G.[8], b. in Indianapolis, 1862; m. Anna W. Work; she rem. to Paris, Fr. He d. in Brooklyn, N. Y., 1 Oct., 1893.

Eighth Generation.] OF NEWBURY, MASS. 355

Child of MARY J.⁷, (1832) [**838**] (Harvey⁶, Capt. Gideon⁵, Daniel⁴, Daniel³, Jacob², Robert¹) and Albert Fay; res. Bancroft, Mich.
    i. WILLARD FAY, b. Oct. 30, 1860 ; m. 1881, Elnora Schauppe ; res. Fergus, Mich.; no issue.

Children of HELEN L.⁷, (1836) [**839**] (Harvey⁶, Capt. Gideon⁵, Daniel⁴, Daniel³, Jacob², Robert¹) and Charles H. Goodspeed; res. Bancroft, Mich.
    i. FRANK E. GOODSPEED, b. Dec. 5, 1865.
    ii. GEORGE W. GOODSPEED, b. Oct. 28, 1868.
    iii. LENA BELL GOODSPEED, b. Dec. 22, 1871; d. 1882.
    iv. ARTHUR G. GOODSPEED, b. June 7, 1875.

Children of LEWIS ALANSON⁷, (1810) [**840**] (Eliphalet⁶, Jr., Eliphalet⁵, Freegrace⁴, Abraham³, Jacob², Robert¹) and Elizabeth (Fawcett) Adams; res. Drayton, Ont.

1315. i. WILLIAM ELIPHALET⁸, b. in Acton, Ont., Nov. 7, 1837 ; m. Feb. 18, 1863, Isabelle Gordon of Drayton, b. Sept. 21, 1843.
    He is a carpenter ; res. Drayton, Ont.
1316. ii. MELINDA MARIA⁸, b. in Acton, Jan. 27, 1839; m. Dec. 22, 1862, George M. Smith ; res. South Lansing, Mich.
    iii. JOSEPH HENRY⁸, b. in Acton, Jan. 24, 1842 ; d. 14 Jan., 1861.
1317. iv. ALMIRA JANE⁸, b. in Acton, Apr. 20, 1844 ; m. Jan. 12, 1860, James Roe of Hawrick, Ont. He d. 30 Sept., 1898.
1318. v. VINCENT RICE⁸, b. in Acton, Sept. 16, 1846 ; m. Oct. 7, 1869, Arletta Ann Crane, dau. of Rev. Isaac Crane, b. Jan. 12, 1851 ; res. Drayton, Ont. He d. 7 Sept., 1896.
1319. vi. THOMAZING AUGUSTA⁸, b. in Drayton, Feb. 12, 1849 ; m. 1868, Edward A. Noice ; he married again; res. Guelph, Ont. She d. 28 Nov., 1875.
1320. vii. JOHN QUINCY⁸, b. in Drayton, Dec. 5, 1851; m. Oct. 5, 1876, Sarah Ellen Dales ; she d. 5 Dec., 1893, age 41 years.
    He was a merchant in Drayton, Ont., was elected shire-reeve of Drayton in 1893, and re-elected by acclamation in 1894 ; d. 22 Oct., 1894.
1321. viii. LUCAS RUFUS⁸, b. in Drayton, Sept. 22, 1853 ; m. May 2, 1882, Melissa Proctor. He d. 25 June, 1889.
1322. ix. LEWIS RANSOM⁸, b. in Drayton, Dec. 23, 1856 ; m. Feb. 25, 1885, Mary Ann Close.

Children of EZRA[7], (1814) [**841**] (Eliphalet[6], Jr., Eliphalet[5], Freegrace[4], Abraham[3], Jacob[2], Robert[1]) and Jerusha (Worden) Adams; res. Acton, Ont.

1323. i. ISRAEL JOSIAH[8], b. in Acton, June 25, 1844; m. Mar., 1870-1, —— Reinshaw. He d. 15 June, 1881.
  ii. SALINA[8], b. May 13, 1850; d. young.
  iii. ABNER AMASA[8], b. June 24, 1859, d. 25 Aug., 1870.

Children of WELLINGTON[7], (1822) [**843**] (Eliphalet[6], Jr., Eliphalet[5], Freegrace[4], Lieut. Abraham[3], Jacob[2], Robert[1]) and Ellen (Clemenshaw) Adams; res. Minto, Ont.

1324. i. MARY EMELINE[8], b. in Minto, Feb. 26, 1852; m. Nov. 23, 1869, Wellington Wilson. She d. 31 July, 1877.
  ii. ELIZABETH ANN[8], b. in Minto, June 23, 1853; d. 8 May, 1862.
1325. iii. EZRA[8], b. in Minto, May 6, 1855; m. Dec. 30, 1875, Margaret Jane Anderson.
  iv. ELLEN MARIA[8], b. in Minto, May 13, 1857; m. Nov. 13, 1877. Wellington Wilson.
  v. AMY ELIZA[8], b. in Minto, Jan. 10, 1859; d. June, 1884.
  vi. ESTHER NARCISSE[8], b. in Minto, Dec. 1, 1860; d. 25 Apr., 1862.

Children of EMELINE MARIA[7], (1820) [**843½**] (Rufus[6], Eliphalet[5], Freegrace[4], Capt. Abraham[3], Jacob[2], Robert[1]) and Rev. Francis Coleman.

  i. ALBERT E. COLEMAN, b. July 20, 1847; m. (1) Agnes Paton; m. (2) Mary Norton of New York.
  ii. FRANCIS COLEMAN; d. young.
  iii. PROF. ARTHUR P. COLEMAN, b. April 4, 1852.
    He studied at the Freiburg School of Mines and also at Breslau, Germany, and is State Geologist of Canada; res. Toronto, Ont.
  iv. LUCIUS R. COLEMAN, b. Feb. 17 1854; m. at Marley, Alberta, N. W. Ter., Oct., 1896, Ella Hough, dau. of Rev. John Hough of Ontario.
  v. RUFUS ADAMS COLEMAN, b. Apr. 26, 1856; m. Dec. 28, 1882, Clara E. Fleury of Aurora, Ont.

Children of BETSEY or ELIZABETH ALMIRA[7], (1815) [**845**] (Rev. Ezra[6], Eliphalet[5], Freegrace[4], Abraham[3], Jacob[2], Robert[1]) and Rev. Thomas Hurlburt.

Eighth Generation.] OF NEWBURY, MASS. 357

 i. JOHN ADAMS HURLBURT, b. at Muncytown, U. C., Dec. 13, 1833; m. Mary Adams.
 ii. RHODA ISABEL HURLBURT, b. at Saugeeng, U. C., Oct. 22, 1838; m. Thomas Crispin.
 iii. ASAHEL THOMAS HURLBURT, b. at Esquising, U. C., Aug. 12, 1838.
 iv.. ANNA ELIZABETH HURLBURT, b. at LaPic, Lake Superior, May 27, 1840; m. Rev. Ezra A. Stafford.
 v. HEMAN SYLVESTER HURLBURT, b. at Orillia, U. C., Sept. 26, 1843.
 vi. HORACE GEO. HURLBURT, b. in Ind. Ter., Mar. 16, 1847.
 vii. ALMIRA MARIA HURLBURT, b. in Cass Co., Mo., Sept. 15, 1849; m. —— King.
 viii. ALICE.
 ix. LUCY.
 x. FRANKLIN.

Children of HENRY PROCTOR', (1823) [**846**] (Rev. Ezra⁶, Eliphalet⁵, Freegrace⁴, Lieut. Abraham³, Sergt. Abraham², Robert¹) and Huldah (Griffin) Adams; res. Hanover, Ont.

1326. i. ELIZA M.⁸, b. in Westport, Mo., Nov. 4, 1846; m. June 16, 1871, Rev. John Saunders. B. A., of Drayton, Ont., b. Feb. 10, 1839; ordained 1871, in the Wesleyan Truth Church. She d. in Drayton, Ont., 11 Dec., 1865.
1327. ii. EZRA P.⁸, b. in Westport, Oct. 29, 1848; m. Oct. 11, 1875, Margaret Flewelling. He set. in Fergus Falls, Minn., in 1888.
 iii. JOHN A.⁸, b. in Durham, Grey Co., Ont., Feb. 23, 1850; d. soon.
1328. iv. JAMES HENRY⁸, b. in Durham, Aug. 16, 1855; m. June 23, 1878, Lizzie M. Boyd, eldest dau. of Thomas and Mary Boyd.
  He settled in Hanover, Ont., with his father's family in 1856; became a manufacturer of woolen goods in 1876; and later engaged in the banking business at Hanover in company with Samuel McNully. He is now resident manager of The Merchants Bank of Canada, at Hanover, Ont.

Children of HENRY PROCTOR', (1823) and Emily (Griffin) Adams.

1329. v. HULDAH⁸, b. in Hanover, Ont., Jan. 8, 1858; m. Nov. 15, 1882, Andrew Thomas Carr, son of John Carr of Prince Edwards Island She set. 1891, in Centralia, Wash.
1330. vi. GEORGE E.⁸, b. in Hanover, Oct. 16, 1859; m. Sept. 4, 1889, Alice Elizabeth Garrett of Hanover, Ont.; res. Edinboro, N. Dak.

1331. vii. KELLY G.⁸, b. in Hanover, Oct. 25, 1861 ; m. Dec. 13, 1887, Annie Murphy of Nebo, N. D.; res. Cavalier, Pembina Co., N. Dak.
1332. viii. WILLIAM E.⁸, b. in Hanover, Sept. 15, 1863 ; m. July 31, 1894, Rachel Jamieson of Brucefield, Ont. He settled in Hannah, Cavalier Co., N. Dak., 1897.
1333. ix. JOHN Q.⁸, b. in Hanover, Apr. 2, 1865; m. Aug. 3, 1892, Mary Gibson. He settled in Fergus, Minn., in 1895.
x. COLEMAN B⁸, b. in Hanover, July 14, 1867; res. Nevada, Mo.; unm.
xi. MARY E.⁸, b. in Hanover, Aug. 6, 1869 ; res. Minneapolis, Minn.; unm.
1334. xii. EMILY A.⁸, b. in Hanover, Aug. 4, 1871; m. Sept. 9, 1891, Thomas E. Morgan, b. Jan. 20, 1869; res. Drayton, Pembina Co., N. Dak.
1335. xiii. ISA AGNES⁸, b. in Hanover, Mar. 20, 1873 ; m. Apr. 9, 1896, William Renwick, b. Feb. 24, 1868 ; res. Bruce, N. Dak.
xiv. CHARLES W.⁸, b. in Hanover, Oct. 18, 1875 ; res. Bruce, N. Dak.; unm.
xv. HOWARD L.⁸, b. in Hanover, Nov. 7, 1877 ; res. Bruce, N. Dak.; unm.

Child of DR. WILLIAM CASE⁷, (1823) **[847]** (Rev. Ezra⁶, Eliphalet⁵, Freegrace⁴, Lieut. Abraham³, Jacob², Robert¹) and Matilda (Osman) Adams; res. Toronto, Ont.

i. LILLIE O.⁸, b. in Toronto, Ont., July 2, 1861 ; res. Toronto, Ont.; unm.
She is well and favorably known as an artist and china painter.

Children of ELIZA ROXANA⁷, (1828) **[849]** (Rev. Ezra⁶, Eliphalet⁵, Freegrace⁴, Lieut. Abraham³, Jacob², Robert¹) and Rev. Matthew Swann ; res. Fergus, Ont.

i. ELECTA MARIA SWANN, b. Dec. 9, 1848 ; d. 26 Sept., 1850.
ii. EMMA ELIZA SWANN, b. Sept. 8, 1850 ; m. Feb. 12, 1873, Thomas Reid.
iii. REV. FRANCIS SWANN, b. Oct. 1, 1853; m. Oct. 1, 1879, Carrie Crow ; res. Ripley, Ont.
iv. EZRA SWANN, b. Aug. 8, 1855.
v. MARGARET SWANN, b. Oct. 14, 1857; m. May 5, 1888, Rev. Samuel Sellers; res. Woodstock, Ont.
vi. MATTHEW SWANN, b. Aug. 8, 1859 ; d. 17 Aug., 1859.
vii. WM. OSBOURNE SWANN, b. July 26, 1860 ; d. in infancy.
viii. THOMAS SWANN, b. Nov. 26, 1861 ; d. Feb., 1862.

DR. JOHN FRANKLIN ADAMS.

Eighth Generation.] OF NEWBURY, MASS. 359

    ix. MARY IDA SWANN, b. Dec. 25, 1862 ; res. Fergus, Ont.
    x. GEORGE ADAMS SWANN, b. July 3, 1864 ; m. Apr. 3, 1890, Annie Hough; res. Toronto, Ont.
    xi. ISA MATILDA ROXANA SWANN, b. Nov. 6, 1866 ; m. Oct., 1891, George Fear ; res. Toronto, Ont.
    xii. JOHN HENRY SWANN, b. July 6, 1868 ; m. 1890, Ella Andrews ; res. Bruce Mines, Ont.
    xiii. ANNIE MORLEY SWANN, b. Nov. 2, 1870 ; d. 29 Jan., 1871.

Children of GEORGE WASHINGTON[7], (1830) [**850**] (Rev. Ezra[6], Eliphalet[5], Freegrace[4], Lieut. Abraham[3], Jacob[2], Robert[1]) and Isabelle Jane (Lowes) Adams ; res. Acton, Ont., and Grand Rapids, Mich.

    i. JOHN ELMER[8], b. in Acton, Oct. 6, 1853 ; d. 12 Nov., 1853.
    ii. WILLIAM ELMER[8], b. in Drayton, Ont., Mar. 16, 1855 ; d. in Hanover, Ont., 8 Nov., 1856.
    iii. JAMES ALFRED[8], b. in Hanover, Ont., June 5, 1858 ; d. in Grand Rapids, Mich., 9 Mar., 1886.
    iv. EMMA JANE[8], b. in Hanover, Mar. 2, 1862 ; res. Grand Rapids, Mich.; unm.
    v. ABNER JAY[8], b. in Hanover, Nov. 1, 1864 ; living 1900 ; unm.

Children of ELECTA ANN[7], (1834) [**851**] (Rev. Ezra[6], Eliphalet[5], Freegrace[4], Lieut. Abraham[3], Jacob[2], Robert[1]) and Rev. James E. Dyer ; res. Toronto, Ont.

    i. MARY MATILDA DYER, b. in Millbank, Ont., Aug. 7, 1862 ; m. Dr. Wm. H. Hodgson of Lockport, N. Y.
    ii. DR. JAMES ADAMS DYER, b. in Stewarttown, Ont., Nov. 29, 1863 ; m. June 9, 1896, Sarah Ellen Grimstone ; dental surgeon ; res. Wilson, N. Y.
    iii. EDWARD LINCOLN DYER, b. in London, Ont., Aug. 9, 1866 ; m. June 3, 1896, Lena Dye of Chicago ; druggist ; res. Waukegan, Ill.

Children of SARAH ROWENA[7], (1835) [**852**] (Rev. Ezra[6], Eliphalet[5], Freegrace[4], Lieut. Abraham[3], Jacob[2], Robert[1]) and Rev. Thomas Culbert.

    i. MELZEINA GEORGIANA CULBERT, b. Apr. 26, 1855 ; d. June, 1856.

ii. ELECTA ALWILDA CULBERT, b. Jan. 27, 1858 ; m. Rev. Wm. Herbert Hawkins.
iii. DR. EDGAR ETHELBERT CULBERT, b. Nov. 28, 1859; m. Winnie Burns; res. Toronto, Ont.

Children of DR. JOHN GLENNINGS CURTIS⁷, (1839) [853] (Rev. Ezra⁶, Eliphalet⁵, Freegrace⁴, Lieut. Abraham³, Jacob², Robert¹) and Sarah A. (Fawcett) Adams; res. Toronto, Ont.

i. AMY LOVINA⁸, b. in Drayton, Ont., Jan. 16, 1863 ; m. Jan. 16, 1883, Rev. David A. Moir, B. D.; res. Walkerton, Ont.

1336. ii. JOHN FRANKLIN⁸, D. D. S., L. D. S., b. in Drayton, Sept. 23, 1864 ; m. (1) June 4, 1890, Edith Bishop Young; she d. 17 May, 1891 ; m. (2) Mar. 22, 1894, Ada E. R. Hoggan.
He is a dentist ; res. Toronto, Ont.

iii. EZRA HERBERT⁸, M. D., D. D. S., b. in Drayton, Sept. 19, 1866.
He was educated in the public schools of Toronto, attaining to one of the higher scholarships in the Toronto Collegiate Institute ; studied dentistry in the Loyal College of Dental Surgeons; graduated from the Pennsylvania Dental College of Philadelphia in 1887, and from the medical course in Toronto University in 1890, receiving the degree of M. D., C. M.; is a member of the College of Physicians and Surgeons of Ontario ; past commodore of Muskoka Lakes Association; medical director of the Y. M. C. A. Gymnasium ; editor of the department of Public Health, and Surgery of the Canadian Journal of Medicine and Surgery ; Past Grand President of the Sons of Canada ; a Mason, Odd Fellow and member of other fraternal societies ; a Liberal in politics ; a Methodist in religion, and has been favorably mentioned for political honors. He is a practicing physician and surgeon at 44 Queen Street, East Toronto, Ont.

iv. ELEANOR JANE⁸, b. in Drayton, July 1, 1868 ; living 1900; unm.

v. MATILDA MARIA⁸, b. in Toronto, Sept. 1, 1870; m. May 23, 1894, Dr. George S. Martin; res. Toronto Junc., Ont.; no issue.

1336½. vi. SARAH ELECTA⁸, b. in Toronto, Sept. 15, 1872 ; m. Oct. 24, 1894, Arthur Murdock Matthews, b. Aug. 28, 1870, of the firm of Matthews Bros. & Co.; res. Toronto, Ont.

vii WILLIAM FAWCETT⁸, D. D S., b in Toronto, Nov. 27, 1874.
He is a graduate in dentistry of the Royal College of Dentists and Surgeons, Toronto, and a student of Art in Trinity College.

viii. LOUISA ADELAIDE⁸, b. in Toronto, Feb. 12, 1882.

ix. GEORGE ARTHUR MAURICE⁸, b. in Toronto, Feb. 24, 1884.

DR. EZRA HERBERT ADAMS.

Eighth Generation.] OF NEWBURY, MASS. 361

Children of CHARLES FREDERICK⁷, (1827) [**854**] (Rev. Zenas⁶, Eliphalet⁵, Freegrace⁴, Lieut. Abraham³, Jacob², Robert¹) and Ann (Maywood) Adams; res. E. Tawas, Mich.

1337.   i. CHARLOTTE ARMOUR⁸, b. in Millbank, Ont., May 2, 1856; m. July 3, 1877, George Ellery Oakes of E. Tawas, Mich.
       ii. ALBERT FELLOWS⁸, b. in Millbank, Mar. 17, 1857; d. in E. Tawas, Mich., 20 Mar., 1875.
      iii. CHARLES ZENAS⁸, b. in Lynnville, Morgan Co., Ill., Sept. 18, 1859; d. 22 July, 1860.

Children of MARY⁷, (1828) [**855**] (Rev. Zenas⁶, Eliphalet⁵, Freegrace⁴, Lieut. Abraham³, Jacob², Robert¹) and Rev. William Glass; res. St. Clair, Mich.

       i. ADAM GLASS, b. in Newport, Mich., Dec. 12, 1850; d. in Newport, now Marine City, Mich., 26 Sept., 1852.
      ii. ISAAC GLASS, b. in Newport, Aug. 24, 1852; d. in St. Clair, 13 Feb., 1876.
     iii. WILLIAM GLASS, b. in Erin, Ont., July 11, 1854; res. 1899, Cooperstown, N. Dak.; unm.
      iv. MARY CHARLOTTE GLASS, b. in Wellesley, Ont., Nov. 7, 1855; res. St. Clair, Mich.; unm.
1338. v. FRANCIS ADAMS GLASS, b. in Acton, Ont., Mar. 24, 1857; m. 1882-3, Marietta Augusta Adams, dau. of Wilbur Fisk and Nancy (Christie) Adams. He d. in Colorado Springs, Col., 4 Apr., 1891.
      vi. ALEX. JOSEPH GLASS, b. in Acton, May 23, 1859; res. Basin, Mont.; unm.
     vii. JOHN NOBLE GLASS, b. in Oxford Mills, Ont., Aug. 21, 1860; m. June 17, 1897, Rebecca Edgar; res. Montana.
1339. viii. ANN ELIZABETH GLASS, b. in Hawick, Ont., Aug. 14, 1862; m. Oct. 27, 1886, Harry Giles Pickett; res. Helena, Mont.
      ix. JAMES GLASS, b. in Hawick, Apr. 1, 1864; m. Apr. 19, 1898, C. Elizabeth Taylor; res. Basin, Mont.

Children of WILBUR FISK⁷, (1834) [**856**] (Rev. Zenas⁶, Eliphalet⁵, Freegrace⁴, Lieut. Abraham³, Jacob², Robert¹) and Nancy (Christie) Adams; res. St. Clair, St. Clair Co., Mich.

       i. ESTHER MARIA⁸, b. in Acton, Ont., Sept 17, 1858; m. at Norway, Mich., Feb. 29, 1882, Frederick Gage; no issue.
      ii. MARIETTE AUGUSTA⁸, b. in Acton, Nov. 8, 1860; m. 1882-3, Francis A. Glass, son of Rev. William and Mary (Adams) Glass, b. Mar. 24, 1857.

iii. FREDERICK JOSEPH[8], b. in Owen Sound, Ont., Feb. 4, 1870 ; res. Omaha, Neb.
iv. WILBUR FISK[8], b. in Owen Sound, Aug. 18, 1875 ; res. Omaha, Neb.

Children of LUCINDA RUTH[7], (1838) **[857]** (Rev. Zenas[6], Eliphalet[5], Freegrace[4], Lieut. Abraham[3], Jacob[2], Robert[1]) and Rev. Thomas Lottridge Wilkinson ; res Hanover, Ont.

i. VIOLA VICTORIA WILKINSON, b. in B lton, P. Q., Mar. 5, 1868.
    She is a graduate of the Conservatory of Music, Toronto, Ont.
ii. BERTHA LUCINDA WILKINSON, b. near St. Catharine, July 1, 1869 ; d. at Parkdale, Toronto, 24 Sept., 1885.
iii. JOHN HENRY WILKINSON, b. in Bartonville, Ont., July 17, 1870 ; d. 9 Sept., 1870.
iv. MARY EVELYN WILKINSON, b. in Bartonville, Jan. 21, 1872.
    She is a teacher of music.
v. THOS. ALEX. WILKINSON, b. in Aurora, Ont., Apr. 8, 1874.
    He is a graduate of the School of Science, Toronto, Ont.
vi. CHAS. EDWIN WILKINSON, b. in Nassagawna, Ont., Nov. 5, 1878; d. 13 Sept., 1885.
vii. FLORENCE GERTRUDE WILKINSON, b. in Fergus, Ont , Dec. 5, 1879 ; d. 7 Sept., 1885.

Children of HARRIET ELECTA[7], (1839) **[858]** (Rev. Zenas[6], Eliphalet[5], Freegrace[4], Lieut. Abraham[3], Jacob[2], Robert[1]) and Rev. Daniel Stewart Kenney ; res. Van Buren, Crawford Co., Ark.

i. HERBERT A. KENNEY, b. in Acton, Ont., Feb. 25, 1861; m. Dec. 4, 1888, Emma E. Feller, b. in Jackson Co., Mo., Dec. 4, 1868; d. near Van Buren, Ark., 20 Aug., 1895 ; res. Van Buren, Ark.
ii. GEORGE ERNEST KENNEY, b. in Saginaw, Mich., Feb. 19, 1863 ; m. Apr. 7, 1897, Clara V. Stecky of Greeley, Col.; res. Greeley, Col.
iii. STEWART F. KENNEY, b. in Ypsilanti, Mich., Mar. 15, 1865 ; m. Mar. 5, 1890, Laura L. Stevenson, dau. of James and Elizabeth Stevenson of Crawford Co., Ark.; res. Van Buren, Ark.
iv. MARY GERTRUDE KENNEY, b. in Buena Vista, Boyd Co., Ky., July 12, 1867; unm.

Children of ABIGAIL LUCRETIA[7], (1844) **[859]** (Rev. Zenas[6], Eliphalet[5], Freegrace[4], Lieut. Abraham[3], Jacob[2], Robert[1]) and Rev. Daniel Steward Kenney ; res. Van Buren, Crawford Co., Ark.

i. ARTHUR NEWMAN KENNEY, b. in Harrison, Jewell Co., Kan., Aug. 3, 1872 ; m. Apr. 14, 1895, Ida M. Stevenson, dau. of James and Elizabeth Stevenson, b. May 27, 1874; res. Van Buren, Ark.
ii. EDGAR LE ROY KENNEY, b. in Harrison, Jan. 7, 1874 ; d. 27 Nov., 1878.
iii. JOHN NELSON KENNEY, b in Harrison, Oct. 18, 1875; d. 12 Dec. 1878.
iv. WINNIE M. KENNEY, b. in Harrison, Feb. 27, 1878; m. Feb. 27, 1896, S. E. Winfrey ; res. Crawford Co., Ark.
v. BERTHA L. KENNEY, b. in Van Buren, Oct. 6, 1887.

Child of LAURA KING, (1808) [860] and Josiah Powers; res. W. Brattleboro, Vt.

1340.   1. AMANDRIN CLARK POWERS, b. in Troy, N. Y., July 19, 1835; m. Mar. 12, 1862, at Lynden, Minn., Phedora Cady Heaton, dau. of Tertius and Fatima (Perkins) Heaton, b. in Moretown, Vt., July 29, 1844; res. Clearwater, Minn.

Children of LEVI KING, (1814) [861] and Mary Elizabeth Hicklin.

1341.   i. CARLOS MARCELLUS KING, b. in Marshall Co., Ky., June 3, 1850 ; m. Nov. 19, 1884, in Livingston Co., Ky., Letitia Rhodes, dau. of Henry and Brunetta (Spencer) Rhodes, b. near Tell City, Indiana, Sept. 20, 1862 ; res. Carrsville, Ky.
ii. JULIAN LEVI KING, b. in Crittenden Co., Ky., Dec. 17, 1851 ; res. Carrsville, Livingston Co., Ky.
1342.   iii. WM. RUFUS KING, b. in Crittenden Co., Ky., Sept. 30, 1853 ; m. Nov. 9, 1884, in Livingston Co., Ky., Norah Anne Hall, dau. of De Wilton Posey and Sarah Jane (Dixon) Hall, b. in Mt. Washington, Ky., Oct. 9, 1866 ; res. Carrsville, Ky.
iv. LAURA KING, b. in Livingston Co., Ky., Apr. 7, 1856 ; res. Carrsville, Ky.
v. MARY EMMA KING, b. in Livingston Co., Ky., Sept. 2, 1858 ; res. Carrsville, Ky.
1343.   vi. JULIETTE KING, b. in Livingston Co., Ky., Mar. 26, 1861 ; m. Oct. 30, 1883, in Livingston Co., Ky., Jacob Soul Love, son of Arthur and Paulina (Franklin) Love, b. in Jasper Co , Mo., Dec. 20, 1859 ; res. Carrsville, Ky.
1344.   vii. SALLIE CLARENTINE KING, b. in Livingston Co., Ky., June 1, 1865; m. Nov. 28, 1886, in Livingston Co., Ky., Joseph Dodge Morris, son of Leroy and Minerva (Dodge) Morris, b. in Livingston Co., Dec. 12, 1853 ; d. at Carrsville, Ky., 9 Aug., 1892.
viii. ANNIE RUTH KING, b. in Livingston Co., Ky., Oct. 5, 1867 ; d. in Livingston Co., Ky., 27 Aug., 1871.

364   ROBERT ADAMS   [Eighth Generation.

Children of HOLLIS KING, (1818) [**862**] and Jane Elizabeth Derby; res. Marlboro, Vt.

1345.   i. CARLOS EDGAR KING, b. in Marlboro, Vt., June 29, 1852; m. Jan. 5, 1877, at Peterboro, N. H., Nettie Alfarata Whittaker, dau. of Edward and Sarah (Eaton) Whittaker, b. in So. Gardner, Mass., Feb. 13, 1859. He d. in Somerville, Mass., 28 Nov., 1887.
        ii. NELSON KING, b. in Marlboro, Vt., Mar., 1857; d. in Marlboro, Vt., 30 Aug., 1861.
        iii. CLARA FRANCES KING, b. in Marlboro, Vt., Sept. 6, 1859; m. May 1, 1880, at Peterboro, N. H., Fred John Upton, son of John Adelbert and Emily Jane (Farnsworth) Upton, b. in Dublin, N. H., July 12, 1861; res. Winchendon, Mass.; no issue.

Children of CLARA KING, (1823) [**863**] and Josiah Powers.

    i. ELBRIDGE MATTHEWS POWERS, b. in Troy, N. Y., Jan. 8, 1849; d. in Troy, N. Y., 31 Dec., 1851.
    ii. CHARLES ELBRIDGE POWERS, b. in Troy, N. Y., July 21, 1852; d. in Troy, N. Y., 30 Nov., 1858.
    iii. LAURA ALICE POWERS, b. in Troy, N. Y., Apr. 2, 1860; res. W. Brattleboro, Vt.
    iv. CARLOS KING POWERS, b. in W. Brattleboro, Vt., June 15, 1864; d. in W. Brattleboro, Vt., 25 Sept., 1871; buried in Marlboro, Vt.

Children of ELIZABETH KING, (1812) [**863¼**] and Newton Thomas Procter; res. Whitcomb, Franklin Co., Ind.

    i. JOHN MOSS PROCTER, b. in Cincinnati, O., Oct. 25, 1828; m. Sept. 18, 1851, Elizabeth Shockley. He d. in Palestine, Ind., 18 Sept., 1867, buried in Whitcomb, Ind. Four children, eldest, Indiana, m. Mr. Spradling; res. Brookville, Ind.
    ii. GEORGE M. PROCTER, b. in Cincinnati, Jan. 19, 1831; d. in Cuba, Ind., 19 May, 1850, buried in Cincinnati, O.
    iii. CHARLES KING PROCTER, b. in Cincinnati, Nov. 1, 1833; m. at Wynn, Ind., Nov. 1, 1854, Mary Elizabeth Holliday, dau. of Samuel and Mary (Isgreeg) Holliday, b. in Cincinnati, Dec. 3, 1833, d. in Chicago, Ill., 17 Apr., 1894. He d. in Chicago, Ill., 13 June, 1888. Children:
        1. Edward Procter, b. in Cincinnati, Dec. 16, 1857, d. in Wynn, Ind., 20 Feb., 1858.
        2. Jennie Procter, b. in Whitcomb, Ind., June 30, 1863; m. in Chicago, May 21, 1885, William Busby, son of John and Charlotte (Curtis) Busby, b. in Oxfordshire, Eng., Nov. 3, 1846; res. Chicago, Ill.; no issue.

Eighth Generation.] OF NEWBURY, MASS. 365

  3. William Sherman Procter, b. in Cincinnati, Nov. 29, 1865 ; m. in Chicago, Jan. 17, 1887, Lilly Harp, dau. of Wm. and Mary Harp, b. in Pennsylvania, Jan. 17, 1870 ; res. Chicago, Ill.; no issue.
  4. Charles Procter, b. in Cincinnati, Dec. 24, 1867 ; d in Cincinnati, O , 11 Feb., 1868; buried in Wynn, Ind.
  5. Nellie Pearl Procter, b. in Chicago, June 23, 1874 ; d. in Chicago; Ill., 14 July. 1874; buried in Wynn, Ind.
  6. Infant, b. in Chicago, Nov. 11, 1878 ; d. same day.

 iv. NEWTON M. PROCTER, b. in Cincinnati, Oct. 24, 1836 ; d. in Cincinnati, O., 2 Nov., 1837.

 v. JUSTIN KING PROCTER, b. in Cincinnati, Oct. 21, 1838 ; m. at Brookville, Ind., June 12, 1864, Mary Boxwell, dau. of John and Elizabeth (Hardy) Boxwell, b. in Franklin Co., Ind., May 9, 1846. ; res. Connersville. Ind. Children b. in Brookville, Ind. :
  1. Ida Murtain Procter, b. May 19, 1866.
  2. Edward King Procter, b. May 10, 1870.
  3. Bessie M. Procter, b. Nov. 11, 1878.

 vi. ABRAM PROCTER, b. in Cincinnati, July 21, 1841 ; m. at Oxford, O., Mar. 30, 1870, Susan Jane Anderson. He d. in Brookville, Ind., 17 Oct., 1877, buried in Whitcomb ; Ind.; no issue.

 vii. ANN ELIZA PROCTER, b. in Cincinnati, July 26, 1844 , d. in Cincinnati, O., 9 June, 1845.

 viii. MARY ELIZABETH PROCTER, b. in Cincinnati, Sept. 13, 1846 ; m. Dec. 24, 1870, in Brookville, Ind., James A. Hawkins ; res. Richmond, Ind. Three children, all dead.

 ix. FRANCES ANNIE PROCTER, b. in Kentucky. Oct. 31, 1849 ; m. Jan. 2, 1867, in Whitcomb, Ind., Nathan B. Knotts, son of Arnold and Phebe (French) Knotts, b. Feb. 10, 1838 ; res. Elwood, Ind. Their children are:
  1 Mary Elizabeth Knotts, b. Sept. 25, 1867.
  2. Wm. Arnold Knotts, b. Mar. 13, 1868.
  3. Chas. Newton Knotts, b. Mar. 31, 1870.
  4. Abbie Jane Knotts, b. Jan. 31, 1874.
  5. Orrie Winfred Knotts, b. Aug. 19, 1877.
  6. Clenice Arnold Knotts, b. Aug. 14, 1879.
  7. Wever Ellsworth Knotts, b. Aug. 14, 1881.
  8. Grace M. Knotts, b. Feb. 12, 1883.
  9. Nathan LeRoy Knotts, b. Mar. 17, 1887.
  They have seven grandchildren.

 x. NATHAN MERCHANT PROCTER, b. in Cincinnati, O., July 12, 1852 ; m. May 16, 1894, in Cincinnati, Mrs. Catherine (Fearey) Smith, dau. of Thomas and Elizabeth (Stevenson) Fearey, b. in

Whitcomb, Ind., Jan. 16, 1860; res. Whitcomb, Ind. Children, b. in Whitcomb:

1. Esther Elizabeth Procter, b. July 27, 1897; d. in Whitcomb, Ind., 28 Aug., 1898.
2. Catherine Fearey Procter, b. Jan. 26, 1900.

Children of CHARLES COOK KING, (1816) [863½] and Martha Chumley; res. Cincinnati, Ohio.

i. ELIZABETH CATHERINE KING, b. in Shelbyville, Ky., Jan. 7, 1838; m. in Cincinnati, Oct. 18, 1855, Curtis Oliver Edwards, son of James Westcott and Catherine (Rockenfield) Edwards, b. in Cincinnati, Aug. 6, 1832; d. in Chicago, 28 Mar., 1894; res. Chicago, Ill. Children:

1. Willie Edwards, b. July 22, 1856; d. in Cincinnati, O., 26 July, 1856.
2. Chas. Westcott Edwards, b. in Cincinnati, Sept. 11, 1857; m. in Cincinnati, Mar. 18, 1885, Elizabeth Ann Williams, dau. of Thomas and Jane Williams, b. in Cincinnati, Jan. 13, 1865; one child, Jane Elizabeth, b. in Cincinnati, Jan. 15, 1886.
3. Martha Edwards, b. in Cincinnati, Dec. 12, 1859; d. in Cincinnati, O., 20 Apr., 1869.
4. George Lyford Edwards, b. in Cincinnati, Nov. 13, 1861; m. in Houston, Texas, Dec. 1, 1899, Clarissa Howall, dau. of William and Lydia Ann (Bloxham) Howall, b. in Linden, Ia., Nov. 30, 1865.
5. John Milton Edwards, b. in Cincinnati, Jan. 4, 1864; m. in Chicago, Mar. 26, 1892, Mary Hughes, dau. of Peter Price and Anna (Pugh) Hughes, b. in Caerwys, Wales, Apr. 22, 1873; res. Chicago. Children: Charles Streble, b. in Cincinnati, Feb. 1, 1893, and John Milton, b. in Chicago, July 4, 1897.
6. Frank Oliver Edwards, b in Cincinnati, Jan. 29, 1866; m. Aug. 14, 1893, in Milwaukee, Wis., Jessie Duffey, dau. of John and Mary Elizabeth Duffey, b. in Cincinnati, Jan. 10, 1878.
7. Jessie Alma Edwards, b. in Cincinnati, Oct. 24, 1867; d. in Cincinnati, 26 Jan., 1869.
8. Alice King Edwards, b. in Cincinnati, Feb. 11, 1870; d. in Cincinnati, 1 Oct., 1870.
9. Calvin Kingsley Edwards, b. in Cincinnati, May 23, 1871; d. 10 June, 1872.
10. Curtis Oliver Edwards, b. in Hartwell, Ohio, Sept. 29, 1872.

Eighth Generation.] OF NEWBURY, MASS 367

    11. Elizabeth Catherine Edwards, b. in Hartwell, Ohio, Oct. 24, 1873, m. Oct. 10, 1892, in Chicago, Frank Miller, son of Thomas and Mary (Smith) Miller, b. in St. Johns, Mich., Jan. 29, 1858; res Chicago. They have: Oliver Frank, b. in Chicago, July 24, 1893; d. 9 Apr., 1894; Edith, b. in Chicago, Oct. 26, 1894, and Howard Thomas, b. in Chicago, Oct. 23, 1896.
    12. Richard Rust Edwards, b. in Hartwell, Ohio, Apr. 1, 1875.
    13. Grace Edwards, b. in Hartwell, Ohio, Jan. 19, 1879.

ii. CHARLES NEWTON KING, b. in Cincinnati, Dec. 3, 1839; d. in Columbus, Ky., 17 June, 1865; buried in Cincinnati, Ohio.

iii. MARTHA KING, b. in Cincinnati, Feb. 13, 1841; m. Nov. 1, 1861, James Cummins, son of John and Mary Cummins. She d. 9 Oct., 1872. They had one child, Ida Cummins, b. in Cincinnati, Mar. 24, 1864; she m. Oliver Morris Ellsworth of Dayton, Ohio, b. July 11, 1858, in Morrow, Ohio, and has four children, viz.: Robert Cummins Ellsworth, b. in Dayton, June 20, 1887; Harry Morris Ellsworth, b. in Dayton, Nov. 28, 1889; Walker Erwine Ellsworth, b. in W. Carrollton, Ohio, Apr. 8, 1892; Catherine Ellsworth, b. in W. Carrollton, May 5, 1899.

iv. ANNIE KING, b. in Cincinnati, Nov. 8, 1842; d. in Cincinnati, 10 Jan., 1886.

v. HENRIETTA CLAY KING, b. in Cincinnati, Oct. 8, 1844; m. Feb. 26, 1863, in Cincinnati, Wesley Addison Crouch, son of John Dair and Maria Ann (Markwood) Crouch, b. in Dayton, O., Dec. 29, 1842; res. Chicago, Ill. Children:
    1. Charles Cook Crouch, b. in Cincinnati, Dec. 8, 1863; d. in Indianapolis, Ind., 28 Sept., 1864.
    2. Wesley Addison Crouch, Jr., b. in Shelbyville, Ind., July 9, 1865; m. in Saginaw, Mich., Apr. 27, 1887, Margaret Kempt, and has one child, Zelma Crouch, b. in Saginaw, Sept. 7, 1888; res. Detroit, Mich.
    3. Geo. Fletcher Crouch, b. in Shelbyville, Sept. 12, 1868, d. in Cincinnati, 20 June, 1888.
    4. Alice May Crouch, b. in Mt. Vernon, Ohio, July 21, 1871.

vi. WILLIAM HARRISON KING, b. in Cincinnati, Apr. 11, 1849, m. in Cincinnati, Jan. 8, 1872, Sarah Levy, dau. of Bernard and Rosa (Cohn) Levy, b. in New York City, Oct. 21, 1852; res. Cincinnati, O. Children, b. in Cincinnati, O.:
    1. Curtis Edward King, b. Nov. 12, 1878.
    2. Pearl Grace King, b. Dec. 23, 1880.
    3. Stella Margaret King, b. Sept. 28, 1882.
    4. Wm. Harrison King, b. Aug. 31, 1884.
    5. Chas. Cook King (twin), b. Aug. 31, 1884; d. Sept. 3, 1884.

vii. GEORGE ELEAZOR KING, b. in Cincinnati, Dec. 9, 1851; m. Dec. 15, 1870, in Cincinnati, Ella Floyd Copes, dau. of Wm. Robert and Maria Louisa (Ferrell) Copes, b. in Bambridge, O., Feb. 13, 1851 ; res. Cincinnati, O. Children, b. in Cincinnati:

    1. Chas. Newton King, b. Sept. 15, 1871.
    2. Clifford Dimetry King, b. Aug. 26, 1872 ; m. Jan. 6, 1894, in Cincinnati, Fannie Miller, dau. of Chas. and Lena (Bernhardt) Miller, b. in Cincinnati, May 31, 1874. They have a son, Clifford Dimetry King, Jr., b. in Cincinnati, Dec. 11, 1895; res. Chicago.
    3. Frank Copes King, b. May 28, 1874 ; m. Nov. 9, 1897, in Lexington, Ky., Anna Valeria Ward, dau. of Thomas James and Katherine (Ryder) Ward, b. in Glasgow, Scotland, Aug. 7, 1876; res. Cincinnati; one child, Andrew Ryder King, b. in Cincinnati, Nov. 11, 1898.

viii. JOHN MORSE KING, b. in Cincinnati, Apr. 30, 1854 ; res. Cincinnati ; unm.

ix. CURTIS EDWARD KING, b. in Cincinnati, Mar. 22, 1856, d. 24 Sept., 1878.

Child of CHARLES COOK KING, (1816) and Catherine (Baumann) Hubbell.

x. CHARLES E. KING, b. in Cincinnati, Dec. 31, 1872 ; m. in Cincinnati, Oct. 1, 1892, Antoinette Netzer, dau. of Anthony and Margaret (Sommers) Netzer, b. in Cincinnati, Dec. 28, 1873 ; res. Reading Road, Cincinnati. Children, b. in Cincinnati:

    1. Russell Bryan King, b. Sept. 7, 1893.
    2. Clinton Burton King, b. Mar. 7, 1895.
    3. Myrtle Margaret King, b. Dec. 19, 1896.

Children of ELLIS KING POWERS, (1824) [**864**] and Caroline Bullock; res. New York City.

i. MARY BULLOCK POWERS, b. in New York City, Feb. 1, 1876.
ii. ELLIS BULLOCK POWERS, b. in New York City, Sept. 20, 1878.

Child of HANNAH MARANDA POWERS, (1825) [**865**] and Ira Willard Gale; res. Ludlow, Vt.

i. GEORGE POWERS GALE, b. in Ludlow, May 24, 1868 ; m. July 23, 1887, at Saratoga, N. Y., Catharine Agnes Hynes, dau. of John and Mary (Welch) Hynes, b. in Rutland, Vt., Oct. 12, 1864 ; one child, Hollis Powers Gale, b. in Ludlow, Vt., Sept. 30, 1888 ; res. Boston, Mass.

Eighth Generation.] OF NEWBURY, MASS. 369

Children of JOSEPH HENRY HAMILTON, (1824) [**866**] and Abbie Adams Mather; res. Marlboro, Vt.

1346. i. LESLIE HENRY HAMILTON, b. in Marlboro, Vt., Dec. 6, 1852; m. Aug. 10, 1887, at Sage Creek Ranch, Fergus Co., Mont., Lizzie Gertrude Montgomery, b. in Waterbury, Vt., Oct. 26, 1861; res. Great Falls, Mont.

1347. ii. CARLETON MATHER HAMILTON, b. in Marlboro, Vt., Apr. 19, 1854; m. Aug. 18, 1879, at W. Brattleboro, Vt., Ella Halladay, dau. of Elliot and Nancy (Miller) Halladay, b. in Marlboro, Vt., July 26, 1856; res. Marlboro, Vt.

 iii. EDGAR EMERSON HAMILTON, b. in Marlboro, Vt., Apr. 1, 1856; d. in Marlboro, Vt., 27 June, 1862.

1348. iv. JOSEPH WRIGHT HAMILTON, b. in Marlboro, Vt., Sept. 21, 1857; m. May 10, 1882, at Marlboro, Vt., Alice Winchester, dau. of George and Sarah Janette (Higley) Winchester, b. in Marlboro, Aug. 10, 1862; res. W. Brattleboro, Vt.

1349. v. ABBIE MATHER HAMILTON, b. in Marlboro, Vt., Apr. 5, 1859; m. July 31, 1880, at W. Brattleboro, Vt., Joseph Gilbert Stafford, son of Samuel and Almeda (Gallup) Stafford, b. in Halifax, Vt., Jan. 28, 1856; res. Brattleboro, Vt.

Children of JOSEPH HENRY HAMILTON, (1824) and Abbie Cross.

 vi. EDGAR ANGEL HAMILTON, b. in Marlboro, Vt., Oct. 24, 1863; m. Mar. 22, 1892, in W. Marlboro, Vt., Belle Moore Hughes, dau. of John Robert and Catherine (Moore) Hughes, b. in Marlboro, Vt., Aug. 15, 1862; res. Stanford, Mont.; no issue.

1350. vii. ROLAND PETER HAMILTON, b. in Marlboro, Vt., July 16, 1865; m. Sept. 15, 1892, in Brattleboro, Vt., Minnie Johnson, dau. of Lewis Joseph and Eunice Asenath (Holmes) Johnson, b. in Weston, Ill., Oct. 25, 1868; res. Utica, Mont.

 viii. HARRY KIRK HAMILTON, b. in Marlboro, Vt., Dec. 27, 1869; m. Jan. 1, 1900, in W. Brattleboro, Mary Esther Johnson, dau. of Lewis Joseph and Eunice Asenath (Holmes) Johnson, b. in Vernon, Vt., Aug. 18, 1871; res. W. Brattleboro, Vt.

Children of JULIA ANNA HAMILTON, (1826) [**867**] and Laban Jones; res. Dover, Vt.

1351. i. ELWIN HAMILTON JONES, b. in Dover, Vt., Aug. 24, 1850; m. (1) Sept. 1, 1872, in E. Dover, Vt., Lilla Elsie Sherman, dau. of Edwin Fisher and Sophia Russell (Merrifield) Sherman, b. in Dover, Vt., Apr. 15, 1854; d. in E. Dover, Vt., 5 June, 1873; m.

(2) Feb. 23, 1875, in E. Dover, Vt., Ella Sophia Johnson, dau. of Chester and Mary Ann (Holden) Johnson, b. in Wardsboro, Vt., June 28, 1852 ; res. E. Dover, Vt.

1352. ii. CARLOS KING JONES, b. in Dover, Vt., Aug. 22, 1852; m. June 11, 1879, in Brattleboro, Vt., Jessie Maud Adams, dau. of Winthrop Hart and Mary Ann (Eames) Adams, b. in Dover, Vt., May 17, 1862; res. Brattleboro. Vt.

iii. CLINTON AVERY JONES, b. in Dover, Vt., Apr., 1854; d. 11 Dec., 1856.

1353. iv. ROSE JULIA JONES, b. in Dover, Vt., Apr. 15, 1857 ; m. Aug. 26, 1886, at Canon City, Colo., Morris Pierson Robbins, son of George Washington and Abby Edith (Lewis) Robbins, b. in Newfane, Vt., Mar. 24, 1856 ; res. Pueblo, Colo.

1354. v. PERCY LABAN JONES, b. in Dover, Vt., Jan. 28, 1862 ; m. Nov. 26, 1885, at Dover, Vt., Ida Nell Thorn, dau. of Rufus Chase and Jane Eliza (Jackson) Thorn, b. in Newfane, Vt., Sept. 4, 1866 ; res. Beulah, Colo.

Children of RUFUS KING CALDWELL, (1829) [868] and Almeda Harriet Bascom; res. West Northfield, Mass.

1355. i. EXSIE ALMEDA CALDWELL, b. in W. Northfield, Mass., Dec. 12, 1866; m. Mar. 3, 1888, at Bernardston, Mass., Mahlon Charles Weeks, son of John and Caroline (Shafer) Weeks, b. in W. Northfield, Mass., Feb. 24, 1864 ; res. W. Northfield, Mass.

1356. ii. MARY KING CALDWELL, b. in W. Northfield, Mass., June 24, 1869 ; m. Oct. 7, 1893, at W. Northfield, Mass., William George Morgan, son of George Henry and Nancy (Chatfield) Morgan, b. in Lockport, N. Y., Jan. 23, 1870 ; res. Lockport, N. Y.

Children of HARRIET LUCINDA CALDWELL, (1831) [869] and Elijah Pierce Burton; res. Corydon, Ia.

1357. i. WILLIAM CALDWELL BURTON, b. in Wardsboro, Vt., Oct. 22, 1856 ; m. Dec. 30, 1886, at Chicago, Ill., Helen Maria Howe, dau. of Orlando Cutter and Maria (Wheelock) Howe, b. near Spirit Lake, Ia., Oct. 8, 1859. He d. in New York, Ia., 28 Feb., 1897.

1358. ii. MINNIE (MARY) MARIA BURTON, b. in Wardsboro, Vt., June 24, 1858 ; m. Sept. 8, 1881, at New York, Ia., Isaac Garinger Davis, son of Friend and Margaret (Crow) Davis, b. in Batavia, Ia., Dec. 23, 1855 ; res. Corydon, Ia.

1359. iii. ALMON PIERCE BURTON, b. in Chesterfield, Ill., Nov. 17, 1863; m. May 3, 1893, at Shelbina, Mo., Mariana Cross McMurry, dau. of William Wesley and Mary Elizabeth (Williams) McMurry, b. in Shelbyville, Mo., Jan. 7, 1868 ; res. Corydon, Ia.

Eighth Generation.] OF NEWBURY, MASS. 371

 iv. ALICE ELLEN BURTON, b. in New York, Ia., Aug. 2, 1868; res. Chicago, Ill.

Children of HANNAH MARIA CALDWELL, (1833) [870] and Henry Baxter Parker; res. Northfield, Mass.

1360. i. ARTHUR HENRY PARKER, b. in W. Northfield, Mass., Mar. 4, 1860; m. (1) Apr. 20, 1886, at Worcester, Mass., Alice Edson Stone, dau. of James Munroe and Hannah Abby (Loring) Stone, b. in Holden, Mass., Apr. 28, 1865; d. in Worcester, Mass., 9 Dec., 1890; buried in Holden, Mass.; m. (2) June 5, 1894, at Worcester, Mass., Eva Maria Wilson, dau. of Charles Wm. and Lucy Maria (Bacon) Wilson, b. in Worcester, Mass., June 7, 1869; res. Worcester, Mass.

 ii. IDA MARIA PARKER, b. in Northfield, Mass., Feb. 27, 1862; d. unm. in Northfield, Mass., 22 Feb., 1885.

1361. iii. WILLIS KING PARKER, b. in Northfield, Mass., Aug. 21, 1863; m. Dec. 23, 1885, in Orange, Mass., Jennie Clara Delvy, dau. of Jonathan and Nancy Olivia (Battle) Delvy, b. in Warwick, Mass., Aug. 25, 1864. He d. in Orange, Mass., 14 Jan., 1890.

 iv. ELLA MAY PARKER, b. in Northfield, Mass., Mar. 23, 1866; m. May 27, 1897, at Bellows Falls, Vt., Chas. Williston Paine, son of Chas. Thomas and Mary (Atkins) Rich Paine, b. in Truro, Mass., Nov. 14, 1853. res. Worcester, Mass.; no issue.

1362. v. CORA MATILDA PARKER, b. in Northfield, Mass., Aug. 10, 1868; m. Apr. 30, 1890, at Brattleboro, Vt., Ozro Daniel Adams, son of Elijah Watkins and Hannah (Benson) Adams, b. in Sherburne, Vt., Jan. 25, 1861; res. Northfield (Farms), Mass.

1363. vi. CHARLES ALBERT PARKER, b. in Northfield, Mass., July 15, 1874; n. Mar. 31, 1896, at Bernardston, Mass., Fannie May Kelly, dau. of Enos and Sarah (Lair) Kelly, b. in Iowa Falls, Ia., May 27, 1869; res. Northfield, Mass.

 vii. LEON PERCY PARKER, b. in Northfield, Mass., Dec. 29, 1878; d. in Northfield, Mass., 20 Feb., 1879.

Children of SUSAN MANDANA CALDWELL (1835) [871] and Dwight Solomon Priest; res. W. Northfield, Mass., and Shenandoah, Ia.

 i. JEANNETTE SUSAN PRIEST, b. in W. Northfield, Mass., Aug. 24, 1859; res. Shenandoah, Ia.

1364. ii. EDWARD DWIGHT PRIEST, b. in Northfield, Mass., Nov. 9, 1861; m. Feb. 27, 1894, at Lynn, Mass., Lena Videtto, dau. of James and Hannah (Saunders) Vidito, b. in Nictaux, N. S., July 5, 1862; res. Schenectady, N. Y.

iii. ALICE LUCINDA PRIEST, b. in W. Northfield, Mass., Mar. 28, 1866; res. Shenandoah, Ia.
iv. WALTER CALDWELL PRIEST, b. in So. Vernon, Vt., Apr. 11, 1873; d. in So. Vernon, 15 Nov., 1875; buried in W. Northfield, Mass.

Children of JULIA ANN CALDWELL, (1837) [**872**] and Charles Thomas Willard; res. Philadelphia, Pa., and New Haven, Conn.

i. MABEL CALDWELL WILLARD, b. in Philadelphia, Pa., July 3. 1862; res. Shenandoah, Iowa.
ii. WALTER CHARLES THOMAS WILLARD, b. in W. Northfield, Mass., Oct. 14, 1866; d. unm. in New Haven, Conn., 11 Apr., 1891; buried in W. Northfield, Mass.

Children of JOHN WESLEY CALDWELL, (1841) [**873**] and Jane Ann Ferris; res. New York City.

1365. i. WESLEY FERRIS CALDWELL, b. in New York City, Aug. 5. 1867; m. May 28, 1889, in New York City, Nettie B. Irwin; res. Brooklyn, N. Y.
ii. LOUISE CALDWELL, died in infancy in New York City.
iii. SON, died in infancy in New York City.

Child of JOSEPH MERRITT KING, (1828) [**874**] and Frances A. (Taylor) Raymond; res. Red Oak, Ia.

i. JOSEPH MERRITT KING, JR., b. in Red Oak, Ia., May 3, 1886.

Child of JUSTIN LEAVITT KING, (1829) [**875**] and Martha Ann Twichell; res. W. Brattleboro, Vt.

i. HARRIET ASENATH KING, b. in New York City, Dec. 3, 1865; res. Athol, Mass.

Children of SARAH ELVIRA KING, (1833) [**876**] and James Edward Priest; res. W. Northfield, Mass., and Brattleboro, Vt.

i. EVERETT EDWARD PRIEST, b. in W. Northfield, Mass., June 15, 1863; d. at W. Northfield, Mass., 7 Dec., 1875.
ii. MARY ELVIRA PRIEST, b. in W. Northfield, Mass., July 21, 1865, d. at W. Northfield, Mass., 18 Nov., 1875.

[Eighth Generation.] OF NEWBURY, MASS. 373

    iii. FRANK JAMES PRIEST, b. in W. Northfield, Mass., Nov. 5, 1866, d. at W. Northfield, Mass., 17 Nov., 1875.
    iv. MERRITT KING PRIEST, b. in W. Northfield, Mass., Apr. 7, 1870 ; d. at W. Northfield, Mass., 2 Dec., 1875.

Children of FREDERICK AUGUSTUS L.[7], (1816) [**877**] (Capt. Milton[6], Freegrace[5], Jr., Freegrace[4], Lieut. Abraham[3], Jacob[2], Robert[1]) and Lodice (Mather) Adams; res. Springfield, Mass.

    i. JOHN Q.[8], b. in Chicopee Falls, Mass., Dec. 13, 1841 ; unm. and no residence.
    ii. CHARLES F[8], b. in Chicopee Falls, May 4, 1844 ; d. 6 Aug., 1845.
1366. iii. CHARLES FRANCIS[8], b. in Chicopee Falls, June 3, 1846 ; m. Sept. 13, 1876, Annie Baldwin, dau. of D. C. Baldwin, of Toledo, O.
        He is cashier of the Second National Bank of Toledo, O.; set. in Toledo in Sept., 1865.

Children of PHILENA[7], (1821) [**878**] (Capt Milton[6], Freegrace[5], Jr., Freegrace[4], Lieut. Abraham[3], Jacob[2], Robert[1]) and Edwin L. Drake.

    i. ARTHUR M. DRAKE; d. at 7 years of age.
    ii; GEO. L. DRAKE ; d. 19 Sept., 1856.

Children of OLIVE MATHER[7], (1823) [**879**] (Capt. Milton[6], Freegrace[5], Jr., Freegrace[4], Lieut. Abraham[3], Jacob[2], Robert[1]) and James S. Bryant; res. Chicopee Falls, Mass.

    i. CAPT. HENRY BRYANT, b. Sept. 21, 1847 ; res. Hartford, Conn.
    ii. JAMES S. BRYANT, b. Sept. 9, 1855 ; unm.

Child of EMELINE[7], (1838) [**880**] (Capt. Milton[6], Freegrace[5], Jr., Freegrace[4], Lieut. Abraham[3], Jacob[2], Robert[1]) and David Kellogg; res. Springfield, Mass.

    i. LENIE O. KELLOGG, b, Dec. 6, 1867 ; d. 9 May, 1871.

Children of ANNIE CORDELIA[7], (1830) [**881**] (Martin[6], Freegrace[5], Jr., Freegrace[4], Lieut. Abraham[3], Jacob[2], Robert[1]) and Frank B. Cadwell; res. Chicopee, Mass.

374   ROBERT ADAMS   [Eighth Generation.

    i. FRANK MARCELLUS CADWELL; d. at 5 years of age.
    ii. GEORGE EDW. CADWELL ; d. age 6 years.
    iii. WILLIE EUGENE CADWELL ; d. age 4 weeks.
    iv. NELLIE FRANCES CADWELL ; d. age 3 yrs. 9 mos.

Children of KATE SOPHIA⁷, (1847) [**882**] (Elihu⁶, Freegrace⁶, Jr., Freegrace⁵, Lieut. Abraham³, Jacob², Robert¹) and John W. Trafton; res. W. Somerville, Mass.

    i. MARK TRAFTON, b. Sept. 18, 1871 ; an employe of a Boston bank.
    ii. ROY DENNETT TRAFTON, b. May 17, 1873 ; d. 26 Aug., 1874.

Children of ADELAIDE FINETTE ALVERSON, (1843) [**883**] and Charles Henry Lee; res. Clinton, Iowa.

    i. EDWARD HENRY LEE, b. in Janesville, Wis., Dec. 2, 1860 ; m. Dec. 28, 1884, at Clarion, Ia., Anna Lora Wilber, dau. of Thomas and Lucy (Pettit) Wilber, b. Oct. 7, 1865. He d. in Eagle Grove, Ia., 18 Jan., 1887, leaving one child, Charles Thomas, b. Feb. 7, 1886.
    ii. WM. ALVERSON LEE, b. in Heart Prairie, Wis., May 29, 1863 ; m. Dec. 1, 1892, at Des Moines, Ia., Bertha Guinter, dau. of Joseph and Mary (Bellows) Guinter, b. May 4, 1870. He d. at Clinton, Ia., 25 Oct., 1898, leaving 2 children, b. in Des Moines, Ia., Lloyd and Roy C.
    iii. MINNIE MAY LEE, b. in Clinton, Apr. 11, 1866 ; m. Sept. 15, 1886, Fortes Ellinwood, son of Benj. F. and Emily (Garner) Ellinwood, b. in Welland, Ont., Sept. 28, 1861 ; 3 children, Adelbert Lee, b. Jan. 17, 1888, Hazel Eliza, b. Feb. 19, 1889, and Gracie A.; res. Clinton, Ia.
    iv. MAUDE CORINNA LEE, b. in Clinton, Aug. 23, 1878 ; m. Apr. 16, 1898, Chas. Wm. Lake, son of John and Jane (Tippett) Lake, b. Sept. 8, 1875.

Children of EMELINE ELIZA ALVERSON, (1845) [**884**] and John Taylor; res. Clinton, Ia.

    i. CHAS. J. TAYLOR, b. Dec. 5, 1874 ; d. in Clinton, 13 June, 1883.
    ii. HERBERT ROY TAYLOR, b. Feb. 7, 1876.
    iii. FRED BERNARD TAYLOR, b. July 23, 1877.
    iv. FLORENCE RUBY TAYLOR, b. Nov. 7, 1882.
    v. GERTRUDE EMMA TAYLOR, b. July 13, 1884.

Child of LAURA VINETT ALVERSON, (1847) [**885**] and Henry Dake; res. Whitewater, Wis.

    i. NETTIE DAKE, b. in Whitewater, Wis., Aug. 18, 1866; m. May 11, 1887, at La Cross, Wis., Harry Bell, son of John and Henrietta (Haller) Bell.

Children of LAURA VINETT ALVERSON, (1847) and Charles Fales; res. La Cross, Wis.

    i. HARRY FALES, b. July 9, 1877.
    ii. ILO FALES, b. Aug. 28, 1883.

Children of LORETTA NILES, (1836) [**886**] and George Henry Gilbert; res. Hartford, Conn.

    i. MARY ELLEN GILBERT, b. Mar. 1856; d. 30 July, 1874.
    ii. CHARLES HENRY GILBERT, b. May 23, 1858; d. 15 June, 1860.
    iii. GEO. ADDISON GILBERT, b. July 7, 1859.
    iv. ALMA LORETTE GILBERT, b. Dec. 5, 1865.
    v. EFFIE JULIA GILBERT, b. Mar. 5, 1869.

Child of SAMUEL A.^{7}, (1839) [**887**] (Abraham^6, Jr., Abraham^5, Samuel^4, Lieut. Abraham^3, Jacob^2, Robert^1) and Minnie (Heath) Adams; res. Loyal, Clark Co., Wis.

    i. CYNTHIA^8, b. 1873; m. Edw. Young; res. Loyal, Wis.

Children of EMILY E.^{7}, (1840) [**888**] (Abraham^6, Jr., Abraham^5, Samuel^4, Lieut. Abraham^3, Jacob^2, Robert^1) and David Rogers; res. Loyal, Clark Co., Wis.

    i. WYMAN ROGERS, b. 1862; d. Dec., 1897.
    ii. NORMAN ROGERS; res. York. Jackson, Co., Wis.
    iii. NOEL ROGERS; res. York, Jackson Co., Wis.
    iv. EMMA ROGERS, b. 1873; m. Edward Bailey.
    v. WILLIE ROGERS, b. 1875; unm.
    vi. FRANKIE ROGERS, b. 1877; unm.
    vii. ELSIE ROGERS, b. 1880.

Children of EMEROY C.[7], (1845) [889] (Abraham[6], Jr., Abraham[5], Samuel[4], Lieut. Abraham[3], Jacob[2], Robert[1]) and Henry D. Ransier; res. Menomonie, Dunn Co., Wis.

    i. DE LISLE RANSIER, b. 1868; m. Mary Norrish; res. Superior, Douglas Co., Wis.
    ii. HELEN RANSIER, b.1871; m. Clarence Depew; res. Aunsburg, Dunn Co., Wis.
    iii. SARAH RANSIER; m. James Kildow; res. Menomonie, Wis.
    iv. CHARLES RANSIER, b. 1879; unm.
    v. MAUD RANSIER, b. 1882.

Children of NOBLE D.[7], (1850) [890] (Abraham[6], Jr., Abraham[5], Samuel[4], Lieut. Abraham[3], Jacob[2] Robert[1]) and Agnes (Carter) Adams; res. Mukwonago, Waukesha Co., Wis.

    i. EARL[8], b. 1882.
    ii. ELMER[8], b. 1884.
    iii. STELLA[8], b. 1888.

Children of DAVID Q.[7], (1852) [891] (Abraham[6], Jr., Abraham[5], Samuel[4], Lieut. Abraham[3], Jacob[2], Robert[1]) and Laura (Baker) Adams; res St. Paul, Minn.

    i. GRACE[8], b. 1883.
    ii. EDITH[8], b. 1892.

Children of FRANKIE E.[7], (1855) [892] (Abraham[6], Jr., Abraham[5], Samuel[4], Lieut. Abraham[3], Jacob[2], Robert[1]) and Charles A. George; res. Menomonie, Wis.

    i. NOBLE GEORGE, b. 1879.
    ii. HARRY GEORGE, b. 1880.
    iii. BERT GEORGE, b. 1882.
    iv LOU GEORGE, b. 1884.

Child of W. DELISLE[7] (1861).[894] (Abraham[6], Jr., Abraham[5], Samuel[4], Lieut. Abraham[3], Jacob[2], Robert[1]) and Mabel E. (Irvine) Adams; res. Menomonie, Wis.

    i. GRACE[8], b. in Menomonie, Wis., 1895.

Children of ALMIRA S.[7], (1850) [**895**] (William Spurr[6], Abraham[5], Samuel[4], Lieut Abraham[3], Jacob[2], Robert[1]) and Jerry W. Briggs; res. Oakfield, Wis.

    i. MAUD I. BRIGGS, b. in Nebraska, Aug. 29, 1881.
    ii. ARTHUR A BRIGGS, b. in Nebraska, Dec. 12. 1882.
    iii. CHARLES J. BRIGGS, b. in Oakfield, July 23 1883.
    iv. HARRIET BRIGGS, b. in Oakfield, Mar. 14, 1886.
    v. LYNN W. BRIGGS, b. in Oakfield, Apr. 28, 1888.

Children of WILSON M.[7], (1852) [**896**] (William Spurr[6], Abraham[5], Samuel[4], Lieut. Abraham[3], Jacob[2], Robert[1]) and Adeline E· (White) Adams; res. Upson, Iron Co., Wis.

    i. ROYAL W.[8], b. in Greenbush, Wis., Dec. 26, 1882.
    ii. ESTELLA MYRA[8], b. in Greenbush, Sept. 16, 1885.

Children of DAYTON A.[7], (1855) [**897**] (William Spurr[6], Abraham[5], Samuel[4], Lieut. Abraham[3], Jacob[2], Robert[1]) and Josephine (Thayer) Adams; res. Empire, Wis.

    i. FLORA R.[8], b. in Stevens Point, Wis., Nov. 25, 1887.
    ii. KATHERINE M.[8], b. in Stevens Point, Dec. 15, 1890.

Children of WILBUR C.[7], (1855) [**898**] (William Spurr[6], Abraham[5], Samuel[4], Lieut. Abraham[3], Jacob[2], Robert[1]) and Emeline (Hopkins) Adams; res. Empire, Wis.

    i. CARROLL RUTHFORD[8], b. in Empire, Mar. 31, 1876.
    ii. ELWYN EVERETT[8], b. in Empire, Aug. 8, 1883.
    iii. JESSIE D.[8], b. in Empire, Oct. 21, 1887.

Child of ELLSWORTH C.[7], (1861) [**899**] (William Spurr[6], Abraham[5], Samuel[4], Lieut. Abraham[3], Jacob[2], Robert[1]) and Laura D. (Palmer) Adams; res. Joel, Polk Co., Wis.

    i. ESTELLA ALMIRA[8], b. in Joel, Jan. 29, 1894.

Children of FRANCES ELIZA[7], (1841) [**900**] (Samuel[6], Horace[5], Samuel[4], Lieut. Abraham[3], Jacob[2], Robert[1]) and Orson C. Martin; res. Shoreham, Vt.

    i. SAMUEL I. MARTIN, b. in Benson, Vt., Dec. 25, 1869.
    ii. MARY G. MARTIN, b. in Benson, Oct. 16, 1873.

Children of HENRY J.[7], (1843) [**901**] (Samuel[6], Horace[5], Samuel[4], Lieut. Abraham[3], Jacob[2], Robert[1]) and Hannah L. (Martin) Adams; res. West Haven, Vt.

    i. SAMUEL[8], b. in West Haven, Apr. 18, 1872.
        He graduated from Brown University, June, 1897.
    ii. HATTIE M.[8], b. in West Haven, Nov. 6, 1875; m. Feb. 22, 1900, Francis Eugene Lockwood of Springfield, Vt.; res. Springfield, Vt. She graduated from Vermont Academy, Saxtons River, Vt., 1896.
    iii. HARRY J.[8], b. in West Haven, Jan. 7, 1878.
        He is a student in Vermont Academy.

Children of EMILY A. FORBES, (1851) [**902**] and Richard W. Kempshall; res. Peoria, Ill.

    i. CLARA A. KEMPSHALL, b. Feb. 8, 1877.
    ii. IDA FORBES KEMPSHALL, b. Dec. 26, 1878; d. 9 July, 1880.

Children of EMILY O. GOODRICH, (1848) [**903**] and Herbert S. Reed; res. Topeka, Kan.

    i. GERTRUDE G. REED, b. in Topeka, Mar. 21, 1883.
    ii. STANLEY G. REED, b. in Topeka, Aug. 17, 1884.
    iii. FANNY G. REED, b. in Topeka, Oct. 13, 1887; d. 5 Sept., 1897.

Children of FLOYD IRWIN GOODRICH, (1854) [**904**] and Ida A. (Marsh) Goodrich; res. Concord, Mich.

    i. CLARE M. GOODRICH, b. July 5, 1878.
    ii. LULU A. GOODRICH, b. Nov. 5, 1883; d. 19 July, 1884.

Child of ELIZABETH MARIA GOODRICH, (1856) [**905**] and William J. Grills.

    i. BENJAMIN G. GRILLS, b. in Marion, O., May 1, 1890.

Eighth Generation.] OF NEWBURY, MASS. 379

Child of RALPH⁷, (1812) [**906**] (Seth⁶, Jr., Seth⁵, Moses⁴, John³, Jacob², Robert¹) and Frances A. (Leonard) Adams; res. W. Springfield, Mass.

1367. i. ELIZA⁸, b. in W. Springfield, Oct. 17, 1843 ; m. Sept. 22, 1869, Rev. George Olcott King, son of John Newton and Margaret King, b. in Suffield, Conn., Apr. 11, 1841 ; graduated from Brown University, 1866, and from Rochester Theo. Sem., 1869.

He has been a pastor in Jamestown, N. Y.; Cincinnati, O., Cleveland and Springfield, O., and Fredonia, N. Y.

Children of DESDEMONIA⁷, (1805) [**907**] (Levi⁶, Seth⁵, Moses⁴, John³, Jacob², Robert¹) and Daniel M. Lee; res. Highland, Oakland Co., Mich.

i. HENRY NELSON LEE, b. Nov. 6, 1826 ; m. Mary Dunham. He d. 20 Apr., 1844.
ii. GEORGE ROGERS LEE, b. Jan. 9, 1828-9 ; m. Martha Jane Parks ; res. Fenton, Mich.
iii. JAMES H. LEE, b. June 6, 1831 ; d 20 Apr., 1844.
iv. ELBERT NORMAN LEE, b. Sept. 11, 1833; m. (1) Lucy Goss; m. (2) Eliza Woolman. He d. 9 Aug., 1893.
v. DANIEL SPENCER LEE, b. May 23, 1837 ; m. Sarah Putnam ; res. Highland, Mich.
vi. FRANCIS CAULKINS LEE, b. Nov. 3, 1840 ; m. Maria Monroe ; res. Blencoe, Monona, Co., Ia.
vii. WILLIAM MINER LEE, b. Feb. 28, 1842 ; m. Sarah Williams ; res. Luzerne, Osceola Co , Mich.
viii. FANNY ELIZABETH LEE, b. May 22, 1845 ; m. Delos Tenny; res. Hilton, N. Y.
ix. HARRIET ELVIRA LEE, b. Nov. 9, 1848 ; m. Jan. 25, 1877, Windham Hewett ; res. Highland, Mich.
x. CHARLES MENZO LEE, b. May 18, 1851 ; d. 3 Mar., 1855.

Children of HIRAM E.⁷, (1811) [**908**] (Levi⁶, Seth⁵, Moses⁴, John³, Jacob², Robert¹) and Marietta (Hodge) Adams; res. Warsaw, N. Y.

i. LUCY J.⁸, b. in Warsaw, June 23, 1843 ; a milliner in Warsaw, N. Y.; unm.
ii. WEALTHY M.⁸. b. in Warsaw, July 23, 1845 ; d. at 6 weeks of age

Children of ELIZABETH WORTHINGTON[7], (1813) [909] (Levi[6], Seth[5], Moses[4], John[3], Jacob[2], Robert[1]) and Chauncey C. Buxton; res. Warsaw, N. Y.

 i. HELEN E. BUXTON, b. Dec. 22, 1838 ; m. Oct., 1860, Hon. Harlow L. Comstock; he d. in Canandaigua, N. Y., 24 Sept., 1883. She d. 3 June, 1862, leaving one child, Helen E. Comstock, b. Jan. 24, 1862 ; she m. Dec. 7, 1882, John S. Rockwell of the Erie Co. Savings-Bank of Buffalo, N. Y. They have two children, Harlow L., b. Sept. 22, 1883, and Kenneth D., b. Dec 17, 1889.
 ii. HARRIET L. BUXTON, b. May 5, 1841 ; d. 8 Jan., 1859.
 iii. WILLIAM C. BUXTON, b. Aug. 9, 1843 ; d. 28 Oct., 1879.
 iv. CHARLES H. BUXTON, b. Sept. 1, 1848; d. 9 Sept. following.
 v. JOHN A. BUXTON, b. Sept. 14, 1850 ; res. Pearl Creek, N. Y., unm.
 vi. MARION C. BUXTON, b. Jan. 28, 1853 ; d. 25 Feb., 1859.
 vii. GEORGE T. BUXTON, b. Oct. 16, 1855; res. Warsaw, N. Y.
 viii. JULIA P. BUXTON, b Oct , 1859; d. soon.

Children of HENRY LEWIS[7], (1809) [910] (Gaius[6], Seth[5], Moses[4], John[3], Jacob[2], Robert[1]) and Lucy (Sherman) Adams; res, Springfield, Bradford Co., Pa.

 i. HENRY L.[8], Jr., b. in Springfield, Oct. 24, 1832; m. at Tamaqua, Pa., July 21, 1868, Mary Mackey; res. Columbia X Roads, Pa.; no issue.
 ii. J. ALONZO[8], b. in Springfield, July 30, 1834 ; m. at Gillett, Pa., 1881, Fanny Humiston ; res. Rheims, Steuben Co., N. Y.; no issue.
1368. iii. THADDEUS SOLOMON[8], b. in Springfield, June 7, 1836 ; m. at Logansport, Ind., Oct. 7, 1865, Jennie Wilson, b. Sept. 12, 1849; she m. 2d, Thomas Cochran of Indianapolis, Ind.
  He was a soldier under Gen. Mead; was wounded at Antietam; set. in Kokomo, Howard Co., Ind., and d. 16 Apr., 1884.
1379. iv. JULIUS T.[8], b in Springfield, Nov. 22, 1840 ; m. Dec. 23, 1884, Lucy Preston ; res. Springfield, Pa.
 v. BENJAMIN FRANK[8], b. in Springfield, Apr. 28, 1842; m. Sept. 16, 1869, Hannah E. Newburg ; P. O. address, Columbia X Roads, Pa.; no issue.
 vi. EDWIN W.[8], b. in Troy, Pa., Mar. 19, 1849 ; m. Apr. 6, 1880, Watie Parmenter; res. Elmira, N. Y.

Children of JAMES KENT[7], (1811) [911] (Gaius[6], Seth[5], Moses[4] John[3], Jacob[2], Robert[1]) and Melinda (Potter) Adams; res. Troy, Bradford Co., Pa.

Eighth Generation.] OF NEWBURY, MASS 381

  i. OSCAR POTTER⁸, b in Troy, Feb. 25, 1835 ; m. Mar. 30, 1860, Jane Willis ; one child ; d. young ; res. Troy, Pa.
  ii. NORTON KENT⁸, b. in Troy, Apr. 10, 1836.
   He was a soldier in the Confederate army, and d. unm., at Mobile, Ala , 20 June, 1872.
  iii. ELIZA JANE⁸, b. in Troy, Aug. 15, 1837 ; m. Nov. 21, 1883, Rev. Thomas Mitchell, son of Thomas and Mary (Harding) Mitchell, b. in Easton, Pa., Dec. 15, 1817 ; he first married Maria Whipple of Mohoopang, Pa.; she d. 27 Feb., 1859 ; he was ordained in the Baptist ministry at Rowe, Pa., Oct. 27, 1841 ; res. Troy, Pa.; no issue.
1370. iv. MARTHA MARIA⁸, b. in Troy, Oct. 2, 1839 ; m. Mar. 10, 1860, Rev. Thomas Mitchell. She d in Colorado Spa., Colo., 13 July, 1879.
  v. JAMES OTIS⁸, b. in Troy, June 28, 1843.
   He is a harness maker ; unm.; res. Southampton, N. Y.
1371. vi. HARRIET ELIZABETH⁸, b. in Troy, Mar. 25, 1845 ; m. Mar. 29, 1869, George F. Brown; set. in Poultney, Vt., rem. to Rutland, Vt., 1881.

Children of JAMES KENT⁷, (1811) and Eliza (Mosher) Adams.

  vii. CLARA⁸, b. in Troy, Aug. 25, 1851 ; d. Sept., 1852.
  viii. KATE⁸, b. in Troy, May 6, 1853 ; m. Oct. 8, 1875, Platt Coonley, cashier ; res. Coxsackie, N. Y.; no issue.
  ix. WILLIAM WILSON⁸, b. in Troy, Dec. 19, 1854.
   He is a florist; unm.; res. E. Orange, N. J.
  x. EMMA JULIA⁸, b. in Troy, July 24, 1859 ; a teacher ; unm.; res. Coxsackie, N. Y.
  xi. MARY JENETTE⁸, b. in Troy, Apr. 17, 1864; unm.; res. Elmira, N. Y.

Children of HARRIET⁷, (1818) [912] (Gaius⁶, Seth⁵, Moses⁴, John³, Jacob², Robert¹) and Sidney Struble; res. Ionia, Mich.

  i. CYNTHIA MARY STRUBLE, b. Jan. 19, 1846 ; m. Dec. 8, 1864, Harlan P. Edwards ; he d. 27 Mar., 1871. She d. 1 Feb., 1885.
  ii. LAMBERT BELA STRUBLE, b. Dec. 27, 1847 ; m. July 2, 1874, Cora M. Williams.
  iii. EMMA JULIA STRUBLE, b. May 30, 1850.
  iv. EDWARD SIDNEY STRUBLE, b. May 12, 1852 ; m. July 19, 1877, Clara L. Alvord.
  v. PHEBE JENETTE STRUBLE, b. Jan. 31, 1855.

Children of JOEL[7], (1824) [913] (Gaius[6], Seth[5], Moses[4], John[3], Jacob[2], Robert[1]) and Joanna (Strange) Adams; res. Troy, Bradford Co., Pa.

 i. JULIA MARTHA[8], b. in Springfield. Pa. Dec. 24, 1853; living unm. in Troy, Pa.
 ii. FANNIE LOUISA[8], b. in Springfield, June 6, 1861; m. Feb. 9, 1898, Willis Baker.

Children of LUCRETIA[7], (1826) [914] (Gaius[6], Seth[5], Moses[4], John[3], Jacob[2], Robert[1]) and Ambrose Brown; res. Springfield, Bradford Co., Pa.

1372. i. SALLY MINOR BROWN, b. Jan. 30, 1847; m. Apr. 8, 1880, Emerson Harris; res. E. Smithfield, Pa.
1373. ii. WILLARD AMBROSE BROWN, b. Dec. 14, 1848; m. Jan. 29, 1884, Thersea Harkness; res. Leona, Springfield P. O., Pa.
1374. iii. CYNTHIA JANET BROWN, b. Feb. 3, 1852; m. Feb. 3, 1874, Judson Phillips; res. Springfield Center, Pa.
 iv. FRANCES E. BROWN, b. Feb. 22, 1855; res. Leona, Bradford Co., Pa.; unm.

Child of JERE[7], (1831) [915] (Gaius[6], Seth[5], Moses[4], John[3], Jacob[2], Robert[1]) and Maria (Scott) Adams; res. Agawam, Mass.

 i. SCOTT[8], b. in Agawam, Mar. 27, 1874.

Child of BENJAMIN DICKINSON[7], (1809) [916] (Enos[6], Seth[5], Moses[4], John[3], Jacob[2], Robert[1]) and Sarah Ann (Getchell) Adams; res. Bennington, Vt.

 i. ORIN DICKINSON[8], b. in Bennington, Aug. 19, 1839; m. Fanny J. Bradish, of Pittstown, N. Y; no issue; living 1900.

Children of BENJAMIN DICKINSON[7], (1809) and Lydia Ann (Wardsworth) Adams.

1375. ii. JOSEPH ASHLEY[8], b. in Bennington, Mar. 4, 1853; m. Mar. 4, 1874, Franc Alesia Mattison, dau. of Charles S. and Julia D. Mattison of New Centerville, Oswego Co., N. Y.
  He was a painter; d. at New Berlin, N. Y., 28 Dec., 1893; buried in Bennington.

Eighth Generation.] OF NEWBURY, MASS. 383

1376. iii. CHARLES[8], b. in Bennington, Dec. 9, 1855 ; m. (1) Oct. 14, 1879, Eliza S. Gleason, dau. of Elma and Abbie J. Gleason of Bennington ; she d. 15 Apr., 1882 ; m. (2) Mar. 19, 1885, Adelaide Luella Mattison, a sister of Franc Aleisa Mattison ; res. Bennington, Vt.

Child of JULIA ANN[7], (1817) [917] (Enos[6], Seth[5], Moses[4], John[3], Jacob[2], Robert[1]) and Sireno P. Peck; res. Bennington, Vt.

  i. JULIETTE ELIZABETH PECK, b. Sept., 1858 ; d. 2 July, 1859.

Child of LAURIETTE ASHLEY[7], (1821) [918] (Enos[6], Seth[5], Moses[4], John[3], Jacob[2], Robert[1]) and Sireno P. Peck.

  i. LAURIETTE ADAMS PECK, b. in Bennington, June 30, 1851; m. June 16, 1886, John Henry Norton, son of Harry and Lucy Norton of Bennington.

Children of NELSON[7], (1817) [919] (Jere[6], Seth[5], Moses[4], John[3], Jacob[2], Robert[1]) and Mary (Wilbor) Adams; res. Troy, Pa.

  i. JOHN QUINCY[8], b. in Troy, Aug. 14, 1851 ; res. Troy; unm.
1377. ii. HELEN LOUISA[8], b. in Troy, Nov. 30, 1859 ; m. June, 1886, James W. Ballard ; one child, Mildred Florence, b. June 6, 1888.

Children of LUCINDA MARIA[7], (1821) [920] (Jere[6], Seth[5], Moses[4], John[3], Jacob[2], Robert[1]) and Frederick Orwan ; res. Troy, Pa.

  i. WILLIAM BALDWIN ORWAN, b. June 27, 1841 ; m. 1872, Catherine Ballard ; res. Bath, N. Y.
  ii. JULIA FLORENCE ORWAN, b. Oct. 28, 1843 ; m. (1) Mar. 15, 1864, Edw. P. Perrine of Bath, N. Y.; m. (2) Oct. 20, 1869, Giles Fonda Viele, res. Troy, Pa.

Children of CLARISSA JANE[7], (1829) [921] (Joel[6], Seth[5], Moses[4], John[3], Jacob[2], Robert[1]) and Ransom Marean; res. Rochester, N. Y.

  i. VIOLETTA MAREAN, d. young.
  ii. LOUIS PLINY MAREAN, b. Dec. 6, 1851 ; m. Nellie Bell ; she d. 1884.
     He studied medicine and settled in practice at New Richmond, Wis., where he d. 11 July, 1882 ; no issue.

iii. WILLIS ADAMS MAREAN, b. in Woodhull, Steuben Co., N. Y., May 24, 1853; m. Dec. 19, 1891, Charlotte Terese Hemeranger.

He began carpenter work at 14 years of age; studied in Middlebury Academy, Wyoming, N. Y., and completed the course In mathematics and geometry at the State Normal School, Geneseo, N. Y., 1872-3, carrying on the building business during the time; studied architecture with Prof. A. Colon of New York City in 1875-6, and engaged in the practice of his profession at Rochester, N. Y. He removed to Denver, Col., in 1880, and formed a partnership with Frank E. Edbrooks, which continued till 1895, and originated plans for many of the large public buildings of Colorado, Brown Palace Hotel, the Cooper Building, Masonic Temple, etc. He is now head of the firm of Marean & Norton; is a Knights Templar, Scottish Right Mason, member of the sons of the Revolution, Artists Club, and the Denver Chapter of American Institute of Architects.

Children of MARTHA⁷, (1831) [**922**] (Joel⁶, Seth⁵, Moses⁴, John³, Jacob², Robert¹) and John W. Winder; res. Uvaldo, Uvaldo Co., Tex.

    i. LEWIS ADAMS WINDER, b. in Cincinnati, O., July 27, 1858; d. unm., 15 Apr., 1883.

1378. ii. ALBERT THOMAS WINDER, b. in Cincinnati, June 30, 1862; m. Sept. 7, 1892, at Elgin, Ill., Mary Eva Swan, dau. of Theodore F. and Amanda (Du Bois) Swan, b. in Elgin, Sept. 23, 1869.
      He set. in Alpine, Texas, 1883.

Child of MARIA⁷, (1835) [**923**] (Joel⁶, Seth⁵, Moses⁴, John³, Jacob², Robert¹) and Simeon Anson Goodwin; res. prob. Lawrenceville, Pa.

    i. MAY GOODWIN, m. Dr. Hartwell Lyon; res. 3910 Russell Ave., St. Louis, Mo.

Child of CHARLOTTE⁷, (1836) [**924**] (Joel⁶, Seth⁵, Moses⁴, John³, Jacob², Robert¹) and Ward Harry Merchant; res. Lawrenceville, Pa.

    i. CLIFFORD MERCHANT, b. Sept. 14, 1878; d. 9 Mar., 1879.

Children of ENOS SETH⁷, (1837) [**925**] (Joel⁶, Seth⁵, Moses⁴, John³, Jacob², Robert¹) and Hannah J. (Nicholson) Adams; res. Cincinnati, Ohio.

WILLIS ADAMS MARRAN.

Eighth Generation.] OF NEWBURY, MASS. 385

    i. NELLIE M.[8], m. Frank E. Hart.
    ii. HENRY NICHOLSON[8], m. Ida May Hall.
    iii. FLORENCE MAY[8], m. Charles Hulbert.
    iv. CLARA MAREAN[8].

Children of FIDELIA[7], (1840) [**926**] (Joel[6], Seth[5], Moses[4], John[3], Jacob[2], Robert[1]) and James Edwin Sweetland ; res. Lawrenceville, Tiago, Co., Pa.

    i. GRACE ELIZABETH SWEETLAND, b. June 19, 1870 ; d. at Lawrenceville, 30 Jan., 1880.
    ii. ARTHUR ADAMS SWEETLAND, b. Mar. 22, 1872 ; unm ; res. Hazelhurst, Pa.
    iii. EDWIN SWEETLAND, b. Feb. 2, 1874 ; d. 28 Sept. 1874, age 6 mos.
    iv. JOEL ADAMS SWEETLAND, b. Jan. 1, 1876 ; d. 28 Nov. 1881.

Child of ELBERT J.[7], (1844) [**927**] (Joel[6], Seth[5], Moses[4], John[3], Jacob[2], Robert[1]) and Mary E. (Simms) Adams; res. Jacksonville, Ill.

1379. i. WINONA M.[8], b. in Jacksonville, Dec. 20, 1868 ; m. June 5, 1888, George C. Clement ; res. Roodhouse, Green Co., Ill.

Children of ELBERT J.[7] (1844) and Susan C. (Cassell) Adams.

1380 ii. ANNA B.[8], b. in Jacksonville, Feb. 18, 1873; m. Oct. 31, 1895, G. Ross Chambers of Jacksonville ; res. Citronville, Ala.
    iii. SUSAN PEARL[8], b. in Jacksonville, Jan. 5, 1876 ; m. June 22, 1899, C. A. Johnson of Jacksonville ; res. Jacksonville, Ill.

Children of LUCY[7], (1845) [**928**] (Joel[6], Seth[5], Moses[4], John[3], Jacob[2], Robert[1]) and Wesley C. Chapin ; res. Whitehall, Ill.

    i. FLORENCE CHAPIN, b. Mar. 11, 1867 ; d. 24 Apr., 1872.
    ii. STELLA CHAPIN, b. Jan. 14, 1874; m. Oct. 23, 1895, Henry E. Bell, Superintendent of Public Schools for Green Co., Ill.; res. Whitehall, Ill.
    iii. LIVONIA CHAPIN, b. May 26, 1878 ; d. July, 1878.

(25)

386 . ROBERT ADAMS [Eighth Generation.

Children of GAMALIEL KING⁷, (1817) [**929**] (Thaddeus⁶, Jr., Thaddeus⁵, Moses⁴, John³, Jacob², Robert¹) and Lucina M. (Barton) Adams; res. East Hampton, Mass.

    i. LYMAN K.⁸, b. in East Hampton, July 9, 1851; d. unm. 22 Apr., 1887.
1381. ii. SADIE J.⁸, b. in East Hampton, Jan. 15, 1859; m. (1) 1882, Herbert L. Canterbury; m. (2) 1889, John W. Ropp of East Hampton, Mass.; res. Greenfield, Mass.
    iii. MARY ESTHER, b. in East Hampton, Aug. 24, 1866; m. Oct. 19, 1892, Hugh Fitzgerald; res. East Hampton, Mass.; no issue.

Children of ALFRED⁷, (1820) [**930**] (Thaddeus⁶, Jr., Thaddeus⁵, Moses⁴, John³, Jacob², Robert¹) and Maria (Davis) Adams; res. Springfield, Mass.

    i. SARAH M.⁸, b. in Springfield, Aug. 3, 1851; d. same day.
    ii. JOHN WATSON⁸, b. in Springfield, Mar. 27, 1854; d. 25 Mar., 1857.
    iii. CHARLES⁸, b. in Springfield, Sept. 5, 1859; d. 10 Sept., 1859.
1382. iv. FRED A.⁸, b. in Northampton, Mass., Oct. 19, 1860; m. Nellie Stearns, dau. of Dwight Stearns of Hinsdale, N. H.
    He is station agent at So. Vernon, Vt.

Children of ELIZA ANN⁷, (1830) [**931**] (Thaddeus⁶, Jr., Thaddeus⁵, Moses⁴, John³, Jacob², Robert¹) and Leander Brigham; res. Montague, Mass.

    i. MARY BRIGHAM, b. in Northampton, Nov. 18, 1852; m. Philip McCue; res. Millers Falls, Mass.
    ii. JULIA BRIGHAM, b. in Northampton, Oct. 20, 1854; res. Greenfield, Mass.
    iii. HATTIE BRIGHAM, b. in Northampton, Aug. 10, 1857; res. Montague.
    iv. EDGAR BRIGHAM, b. in Montague, July 9, 1867.

Children of MARIETTE⁷, (1837) [**932**] (Martin⁶, Thaddeus⁵, Moses⁴, John³, Jacob², Robert¹) and Leander L. Rhodes; res. West Hampton, Mass.

    i. LYMAN A. RHODES, b. Dec. 1, 1857; res. Gove, Gove Co., Kan.; unm.
    ii. LILLA B. RHODES, b. July 27, 1860.
    She is a nurse; unm.; res. Northampton, Mass.

Eighth Generation.] OF NEWBURY, MASS. 387

   iii. CARRIE M. RHODES, b. Aug. 8, 1863 ; m. Sept., 1888, Allen M. Coit of Huntington, Mass.

   iv. ALICE E. RHODES, b. Jan. 7, 1866 ; m. Nov. 23, 1886, P. A. Connery of Holyoke, Mass.

Children of PHINEAS M.⁷, (1817) [**933**] (Abraham⁶, Capt Oliver⁵, Simeon⁴, John³, Jacob², Robert¹) and Olive (Austin) Adams; res. Royalton, N. Y.

   i. GEORGE A⁸, b. in Royalton, Aug. 12, 1839.
       He enlisted in the 1st. Regt., Missouri Cavalry ; d. at St. Louis, Mo., 22 Sept., 1861.

   ii. BEDA ELIZABETH⁸, b. in Royalton, Jan. 10, 1841 ; m. Edwin Messenger ; res. Geddes, N. Y.

1383. iii. MARY ANN⁸, b. in Royalton, Sept. 5, 1843 ; m. June 25, 1861, John Salisbury, d. 30 July, 1899; res. Kansas City, Mo.

   iv. IDA MELVINA⁸, b. in Royalton, Jan. 10, 1846; m. Edwin Gordon.

   v. CORNELIUS⁸, b. in Royalton, Apr. 30, 1848 ; d. 24 Aug., 1851, age 3 yrs. 5 mos. 14 days.

Children of HULDAH TAYLOR⁷, (1821) [**934**] (Abraham⁶, Capt. Oliver⁵, Simeon⁴, John³, Jacob², Robert¹) and Lorin King; res. Lockport and Buffalo, N. Y.

   i. ELLEN E. KING, b. Jan. 12, 1844 ; m. Nov. 6, 1865, B. Frank Dunn of Lockport, N. Y.; res. Lockport, N. Y.

   ii. MARY E. KING, b. Aug. 9, 1845 ; m. Sept. 20, 1865, Ephraim Weaver, d. 5 Dec., 1889 ; res. Buffalo, N. Y.

   iii. MARTHA A. KING, b. Feb. 24, 1847 ; m. Nov. 21, 1869, W. B. M. Donald.

Children of RUFUS⁷, (1824) [**935**] (Abraham⁶, Capt. Oliver⁵, Simeon⁴, John³, Jacob², Robert¹) and Caretta (Kimball) Adams; res. Pana, Christian Co., Ill.

   i. DELIA ELIZABETH⁸, b. in Royalton, N. Y., Sept. 17, 1855 ; res Pana, Ill.; unm.

   ii. CHARLES FAYETTE⁸, b. in Royalton, July 28, 1857 ; res. Pana, Ill.; unm.

   iii. DORA ISABELLE⁸, b. in Royalton, Apr. 11, 1859 ; d. 5 Oct., 1865.

   iv. OMER C.⁸, b. in Bunker Hill, Ill., Dec. 16, 1860 ; res. Pana, Ill.; unm.

1384. v. OSCAR RUFUS⁸, b. in Bunker Hill, Apr. 2, 1863 ; m. Feb. 17, 1886, Nancy Caroline Allen ; res. Oconee, Shelby Co., Ill.

Children of HANNAH JANE⁷, (1829) [**936**] (Abraham⁶, Capt. Oliver⁵, Capt. Simeon⁴, John³, Jacob², Robert¹) and Henry S. Harrington; res. Orangeport, Niagara Co., N. Y.

1385.   i.   LOUIS K. HARRINGTON, b. Sept. 1, 1853 ; m. about 1884, Florie E. Freeman ; res. Buffalo, N. Y.

1386.   ii.   DR. FRANK A. HARRINGTON, b. Oct. 19, 1854 ; m. July, 1898, Carrie Ortolam.
> He graduated from Harvard University in class of 1884, and received the degree of A. M. in 1886, and likewise the degree of M. D. from Harvard Medical School ; res. Buffalo, N. Y.

     iii.   JOHN H. HARRINGTON, b. Sept. 9, 1858 ; m. 1888, Maude Claggett; res. Kansas City, Mo.; no issue.

1387.   iv.   *CHARLES M. HARRINGTON, b. Oct. 22, 1860 ; m. Apr. 21, 1891, Mary Bassett.
> He graduated from Harvard University in the class of 1885, and is an attorney in Buffalo, N. Y.

1388.   v.   ALBERT P. HARRINGTON, b. June 2, 1864 ; m. Oct. 17, 1888, Florie A. Pease ; res. Orangeport, N. Y.

     vi.   CARRIE A. HARRINGTON, b. Aug. 3, 1871 ; d. in Buffalo, N. Y., 19 Apr., 1890, age 19 years ; buried in Orangeport, N. Y.

Children of OLIVER L⁷, (1532) [**937**] (Abraham⁶, Capt. Oliver⁵, Simeon⁴, John³, Jacob², Robert¹) and Mary Elizabeth (Storer) Adams; res. Ransomville, Niagara Co., N. Y.

1389.   i.   GEORGE G.⁸, b. in Ransomville, Mar. 22, 1859 ; m. Mar. 16, 1886, Matilda Lehman. He was killed on R. R. crossing in Buffalo, 20 Aug., 1895; res. Ransomville, N. Y.

1390.   ii.   BEDA J.⁸, b. in Ransomville, Apr. 5, 1860 ; m. Mar., 1886, Julius Hoyt, b. Jan. 2, 1851 ; res. Wrights Corners, Niagara Co., N. Y.

1391.   iii.   JOHN A.⁸, b. in Ransomville, Jan. 24, 1862 ; m. May 29, 1890, Jane N. Lawton ; res. Ransomville, N. Y.

1392.   iv.   REUBEN O.⁸, b. in Clinton Co., Mich., July 28, 1863 ; m. Apr. 9, 1890, Sarah Lawton, b. Mar. 13, 1862, dau. of Geo. Lawton ; res. Buffalo, N. Y.

     v.   MARY E.⁸, b. in Ransomville, July 6, 1865 ; d. in Brooklyn, N. Y., 1 Oct., 1893.

     vi.   HARRIET B.⁸, b. in Ransomville, Dec. 28, 1868; m. Dec. 24, 1895, Wm. Arms.

1393.   vii.   HERBERT C.⁸, b. in Ransomville, Feb. 10, 1871 ; m. Mar. 18, 1897, Rosa Craine.

     viii.   BENJAMIN⁸, b. in Ransomville, Apr. 10, 1873 ; d. 28 Oct., 1876.

     ix.   BENJAMIN⁸, b. in Ransomville, Aug. 17, 1876.

Children of LUCIUS F.⁷, (1835) [**938**] (Abraham⁶, Capt. Oliver⁵, Simeon⁴, John³, Jacob², Robert¹) and Sophia (Merritt) Adams; res. Lockport, N. Y.

 i. ELIZABETH ANN⁸, b. in Orangeport, N. Y., May 15, 1871 ; living; unm.
 ii. MARTHA ESTHER⁸, b. in Orangeport, May 5, 1875.

Children of CHARLES F.⁷, (1838) [**939**] (Abraham⁶, Capt. Oliver⁵, Simeon⁴, John³, Jacob², Robert¹) and Sarah Caroline (Brown) Adams; res. Morgan Park, Chicago, Ill.

 i. NELLIE ANNA⁸, b. in Wetaug, Pulaski Co., Ill., May 29, 1868; m. May 29, 1889, Charles H. Kerr. She d. 9 Apr., 1891 ; res. Chicago, Ill.
 ii. GRACE GERTRUDE⁸, b. in Chicago, Feb. 28, 1878 ; res. Morgan Park, Chicago, Ill.; unm.

Children of GAD MATHER⁷, (1840) [**940**] (Abraham⁶, Capt. Oliver⁵, Simeon⁴, John³, Jacob², Robert¹) and Josephine (Benson) Adams; res. Lockport, N. Y.

1394. i. MARY BEDA⁸, b. in Pana, Ill., Feb. 10, 1865 ; m. Dec. 24, 1894, William Wilson ; res. Appleton, Niagara Co., N. Y.
1395. ii. EUGENE M.⁸, b. in Pana, June 30, 1868; m. Dec. 31, 1891, Cornie Chaplin, b. Sept. 5, 1874.
  He was educated in Cornell University, and is a teacher in Snohomish, Wash.
 iii. CORA B.⁸, b. in Pana, Apr. 5, 1870.
  She is a teacher in Snohomish.
 iv. LOTTIE MABEL⁸, b. in Chicago, Apr. 10, 1876 ; teacher.

Children of SARAH BRAGG⁷, (1829) [**941**] (Oliver⁶, Jr., Capt. Oliver⁵, Simeon⁴, John³, Jacob², Robert¹) and Wilson Harris; res. Cleveland, O.

 i. ADDIE THERESA HARRIS, b. Aug. 3, 1853.
 ii. NORMAN HARRIS, b. Jan. 16, 1858 ; res. Cleveland, O.; unm.
 iii. HERMAN A. HARRIS, b. Feb. 12, 1863; res. Cleveland, O.; unm.
 iv. EDITH M. HARRIS, b. Apr. 2, 1865 ; d. 11 Aug., 1894.

Children of WILLIAM BRADLEY⁷, (1831) [**942**] (Oliver⁶, Jr., Capt. Oliver⁵, Simeon⁴, John³, Jacob², Robert¹) and Polly Ann (Winchester) Adams; res. Hinsdale, N. H.

1396. i. OLIVER WINCHESTER⁸, b. in Hinsdale, Sept. 30, 1870 ; m. Mar. 31, 1897, Clara Jane Burnette, dau. of Jonathan and Elona M. (Ayers) Burnette, b. in So. Hadley, Mass., Nov. 15, 1871.

        He graduated from the Albany Business College in 1890, and is a clerk in the Holyoke Gas Works.

  ii. WILLIAM CLAUD⁸, b. in Hinsdale, Jan. 11, 1872.

  iii. CARRIE ELLA⁸, b. in Hinsdale, Nov. 4, 1873.

  iv. BENJAMIN FRANKLIN⁸, b. in Hinsdale, July 10, 1875.

        He graduated from Dartmouth College, 1897; studied medicine and surgery in the College of Physicians and Surgeons of New York; res. Hinsdale, N. H.

Children of HENRY⁷, (1832) [**943**] (Oliver⁶, Jr., Capt. Oliver⁵, Simeon⁴, John³, Jacob², Robert¹) and Helen M. (Hastings) Adams; res. Hinsdale, N. H.

  i. FREDERICK H.⁸, b. in Hinsdale, Oct. 19, 1859; d. 31 July, 1865.

  ii. NELLY M.⁸, b. in Hinsdale, Feb. 22, 1861 ; d. 17 Aug., 1865.

  iii. LUCY T.⁸, b. in Hinsdale, Mar. 28, 1863 ; res. Hinsdale, N. H.; unm.

  iv. MILLER O.⁸, b. in Hinsdale, June 17, 1866 ; d. 21 July, 1878.

Children of HENRY⁷, (1832) and Eva S. (Pettee) Adams.

1397. v. GEORGE WILLARD⁸, b. in Hinsdale, July 13, 1869 ; m. June 28, 1893, Louisa Park of E. Deerfield, Mass., b. July 8, 1873 ; res. Greenfield, Mass.

  vi. ALICE E.⁸, b. in Hinsdale, Oct. 1, 1871; unm.

1398. vii. ANNIE F.⁸, (twin), b. in Hinsdale, Oct. 1, 1871 ; m. May 2, 1896, Cecil Cheney of Jamaica, Vt., b. Jan. 7, 1869; res. Brattleboro, Vt.

  viii. IDA E.⁸, b. in Hinsdale, Oct. 1, 1873 ; m. 1897, E A. Iverson of Boston.

  ix. OLIVE E.⁸, b. in Hinsdale, May 7, 1877 ; d. 2 Aug., 1878.

  x. EDITH M.⁸, b. in Hinsdale, Apr. 16, 1881.

Children of CAROLINE FRANCES⁷, (1836) [**944**] (Oliver⁶, Jr., Capt. Oliver⁵, Simeon⁴, John³, Jacob², Robert¹) and Solon N. Alexander; res. Bellows Falls, Vt.

  i. HARRY OLIN ALEXANDER, b. May 28, 1861 ; res. Boston, Mass.; unm.

Eighth Generation.] OF NEWBURY, MASS. 391

    ii. HUGH ALEXANDER, b. Feb. 5, 1863-4 ; m. Henriette Bonnette ; lawyer ; set. in Concordia, Kan.
    iii. SOLON N—— ALEXANDER, b. Nov. 30, 1869.
        He was drowned in the Connecticut river, 16 Apr., 1895.

Children of EMELINE GRATIA', (1842) [945] (Oliver^6, Jr., Capt. Oliver^5, Simeon^4, John^3, Jacob^2, Robert^1) and Noyes Wilson Fisk; res. Springfield, Mass.

    i. GRACE M. FISK, b. May 30, 1863 ; d. 26 Aug., 1864.
    ii. HARRY GEORGE FISK, b. May 5, 1873.
        He graduated in 1896 from the Massachusetts Institute of Technology ; res. Springfield, Mass.

Children of SIMEON HOUGHTON', (1822) [946] (Capt.|Ira^6, Capt. Simeon^5, Simeon^4, John^3, Jacob^2, Robert^1) and Lucinda Ethel (Knight) Adams; res. W. Marlboro, Vt.

    i. LOUISA JENETTE^8, b. in Marlboro, Vt., July 29, 1849 ; m. Nov. 29, 1867, David Adams, son of Simeon and Mary Ann W. (Sargent) Adams.
1399. ii. MARY ELIZABETH^8, b. in Marlboro, Jan. 16, 1852 ; m. Sept. 1867-8, Charles E. Mather.
    iii. EMMA MELVINA^8, b. in Marlboro, Oct. 14, 1854 ; m. Dec. 29, 1885, Clarence Halliday of Marlboro ; no issue.
    iv. GEORGE EMERSON^8, b in Marlboro, July 20, 1857 ; m. Jan. 4, 1887, Carrie M. Frost; res. Brattleboro, Vt.; no issue.
    v. FRANK HERBERT^8, b. in Marlboro, May 20, 1860; res. Marlboro; unm.
1400. vi. ALICE L.^{8}, b. in Marlboro, Mar. 8, 1863 ; m. 1884, Julian Whittaker; res. (Brookside) Newfane, Vt.
    vii. CLARENCE^8, b. in Marlboro, Nov. 24, 1867; res. W. Marlboro, Vt.
    viii. WILLIAM H.^{8}, b. in Marlboro, Dec. 16, 1871 ; res. W. Marlboro, Vt.

Children of IRA', JR., (1826) [947] (Capt. Ira^6, Capt. Simeon^5, Simeon^4, John^3, Jacob^2, Robert^1) and Eliza (Winchester) Adams; res. Marlboro, Vt.

1401. i. MINERVA E.^{8}, b. in Marlboro, Nov. 5, 1850 ; m. Dec. 31, 1872, Edwin P. Adams, son of Leander Clark Adams, b. Oct. 18, 1848. She d. 21 Oct., 1880.

1402. ii. MARTIN IRA⁸, b. in Marlboro, Mar. 5, 1854; m. Oct. 24, 1882, Ida Harriman, dau. of John and Mary Harriman, b. in Liberty, Me., Feb. 12, 1862; res. Dorchester, Mass.
1403. iii. NELLIE CLARA⁸, b. in Marlboro, Mar. 14, 1858; m. Mar. 17, 1884, Harry Clark, son of Albert and Sarah Clark. She d. 1896.
       iv. LUCY ANNETTE⁸, b. in Marlboro, Nov. 23, 1861; res. Cambridge, Mass.; unm.
       v. LE ROY HIRAM⁸, b. in Marlboro, Oct. 7, 1866; d. 7 Sept., 1868.
       vi. ELLIOT ALBERT⁸, b. in Marlboro, Aug. 3, 1869; d. 13 June, 1871.

Children of CHARLES MORTON⁷, (1835) [948] (Capt. Ira⁶, Capt. Simeon⁵, Simeon⁴, John³, Jacob², Robert¹) and Marilla L. (Howe) Adams; res. Guilford, Vt.

   i. INFANT⁸, d. 3 Nov., 1858.
   ii. LESLIE E⁸. b. in Guilford, Jan. 26, 1863.
       He was killed on the railroad, 19 Feb., 1893.
   iii. LULU M.⁸, b. in Guilford, Mar. 5, 1867; m. Frank Wellman; res. Guilford, Vt.

Children of ANNETTE MINERVA⁷, (1837) [949] (Capt. Ira⁶, Capt. Simeon⁵, Simeon⁴, John³ Jacob², Robert¹) and Daniel G. Leonard; res. Wilmington, Vt.

   i. CLAUDE GREEN LEONARD, b. in W. Dover, Vt., May 14, 1864; m. Feb. 21, 1886, Eleanor P. Rice; res. Springfield, Vt.
   ii. FLORRIE MAUD LEONARD, b. in W. Dover, Mar. 7, 1868; m. Jan. 15, 1888, Wm. E. Corse; res. Springfield, Vt.
   iii. MABEL GRACE LEONARD, b. in W. Dover, Feb. 21, 1872; res. with her mother; unm.
   iv. CHARLES HUGHES LEONARD, b. in W. Dover, July 14, 1874; res. White River Junction, Vt.; unm.

Children of LYMAN WHITNEY OLDS, (1824) [950] and Sarah M. Curry; res. Muscatine, Iowa.

   i. EMMA OLDS, b. June 16, 1849; m. Sept. 8, 1875, Ferdinand Reppert; res. Muscatine, Ia. Children:
       1. Lyell Reppert, b. Oct. 16, 1877; a student of medicine in Iowa State University.
       2. Ella Olds Reppert, b. Oct. 26, 1885.
   ii. GEORGE OLDS, b. Feb. 2, 1853; d. 20 Aug., 1854.

Eighth Generation.] OF NEWBURY, MASS. 393

 iii. FRANK OLDS, b. July 20, 1860 ; d. 10 Aug., 1860.
 iv. ELLA OLDS, b. Feb. 13, 1863 ; m. Apr. 14, 1880, Robert F. Payne; res. Warsaw, Ky. Children :
   1. Bettie Payne, b. May 18, 1883 ; mem. of Hamilton College, Lexington, Ky.
   2. Lyman W. Olds Payne, b. Aug. 8, 1889.

Child of SARAH[7], (1832) [**951**] (Simeon[6], Capt. Simeon[5], Simeon[4], John[3], Jacob[2], Robert[1]) and Cotton M. Houghton; res. Marlboro, Vt.

 i. GEORGE HOUGHTON, b. in Marlboro, July 5, 1855 ; m. June 24, 1891, Jennie B. Boyd of Dummerston, Vt.; farmer ; res. Guilford, Vt.

Children of HENRY[7], (1833) [**952**] (Simeon[6], Capt. Simeon[5], Simeon[4], John[3], Jacob[2], Robert[1]) and Lucy Ann (Winchester) Adams; res. Marlboro, Vt.

1404. i. LIZZIE ANN[8], b. in Marlboro, Sept. 23, 1858 ; m. Mar. 12, 1877, Freeman Scott, son of Martin and Fanny H. (Larabee) Scott, b. May 24, 1854 ; res. Marlboro, Vt.
1405. ii. JOHN C.[8], b. in Marlboro, Aug. 9, 1861 ; m. Jan. 19, 1892, Lestina E. Thurber, dau. of Emerson and Sarah (Ballou) Thurber, b. Jan. 22, 1871 ; res. Brattleboro, Vt.
 iii. MARY[8], b. in Marlboro, Nov. 9, 1864 ; d. Aug., 1878-80.

Children of HENRY[7], (1833) and Ellen L. (Fowler) Adams.

 iv. LOTTIE LEE[8], b. in Marlboro, Mar. 28, 1876 ; m. Jan. 13, 1898, Clarence Worden ; res. New York ; no issue.
 v. LOUISA M.[8], b. in Marlboro, Feb 17, 1883 ; unm.

Children of HANNAH[7], (1836) [**953**] (Simeon[6], Capt. Simeon[5], Simeon[4], John[3], Jacob[2] Robert[1]) and David Mather; res. Marlboro, Vt.

 i. LUCIUS MATHER, b. Jan. 27, 1861 ; d. 8 Sept., 1877.
 ii. LUCY MATHER, d. young.
 iii. ERVIN MATHER, b. Oct. 6, 1864 ; res. Marlboro, Vt.

iv. HERBERT MATHER, b. Feb. 16, 1866 ; m. June 12, 1888, Clara Winchester, dau. of Wells Winchester, b. Feb., 1866 ; res. Marlboro, Vt.
v. LUCY MATHER, b. Sept. 29, 1869; m. Dec. 2, 1890, George Reed ; res. Brattleboro, Vt.
vi. FREDDIE MATHER, b. June 1, 1873 ; d. Sept., 1873.

Children of LUCY^7, (1838) [954] (Simeon^6, Capt. Simeon^5, Simeon^4, John^3, Jacob^2, Robert^1) and George C. Higley; res. Marlboro, Vt.

i. LUCIUS HIGLEY, b. July 28, 1858 ; d. 15 Jan., 1860.
ii. JENNEVIA HIGLEY, b. Nov. 20, 1862; d. 29 Feb., 1864.
iii. LARKIN E. HIGLEY, b. Sept. 10, 1863; m. —— Nelson ; res. Wyoming or Washington.
iv. MINNIE E. HIGLEY, b. Mar. 30, 1879 ; m. Aug. 28, 1899, Cotton A. Mather; res. No. Springfield, Mass.

Children of LUTHER^7, (1840) [955] (Simeon^6, Capt. Simeon^5, Simeon^4, John^3, Jacob^2, Robert^1) and Emeline Susan (Winchester) Adams; res. W. Halifax, Vt.

1406. i. EVENA L.^{8}, b. in West Halifax, Feb. 6, 1862 ; m. Feb. 22, 1883, Charles H. Parmelee; res. Wilmington, Vt. She d. 25 Feb. 1893.
ii. MERWIN L.^{8}, b. in W. Halifax, Feb. 6, 1865.
iii. ALICE S.^{8}, b. in W. Halifax, July 28, 1867.
1407. iv. MARION S.^{8}, b. in W. Halifax, Apr. 2, 1871 ; m. June 12, 1895, Wm. B. McClellan.
She graduated from the State Normal School at Castleton, 1891 ; res. No. Hatfield, Mass.
v. ELLA A.^{8}, b. in W. Halifax, Dec. 28, 1874.
vi. ERUNIA^8, b. in W. Halifax, Jan. 23, 1877.

Children of MARY ANN^7, (1842) [956] (Simeon^6, Capt. Simeon^5, Simeon^4, John^3, Jacob^2, Robert^1) and Elliot J. Higley; res. Guilford, Vt.

i. ETTA G. HIGLEY, b. Jan. 24, 1865; res. Guilford, Vt.; unm.
ii. WILLIE HIGLEY, b. Nov. 28, 1869 ; m. Oct. 26, 1897, Nellie Brackett.

Children of SIMEON[7], (1844) [**957**] (Simeon[6], Capt. Simeon[5], Simeon[4], John[3], Jacob[2], Robert[1]) and Mary Jane Squire (Fulton) Adams; res. W. Rindge, N. H.

    i. SARAH GERTRUDE[8], b. in Marlboro, Vt., Mar. 20, 1869.
1408. ii. EDWARD EFFINGHAM[8], b. in Marlboro, Jan. 11, 1872 ; m. at W. Rindge, Dec. 27, 1893, Rosana Moore ; res. Fitchburg, Mass.
    iii. WILLIAM ALLARD S.[8], b. in Brattleboro, Vt., June 3, 1874.
    iv. PEARL CHARLOTTE[8], b. in W. Brattleboro, Aug. 9, 1876; m. Nov. 23, 1899, Horatio C. Goulding ; res. Worcester, Mass.
    v. LAURA JANE[8], b. in Brattleboro, Dec. 2, 1878.
    vi. WINNIE MAY[8], b. in Guilford, Vt., Nov. 7, 1882.
    vii. WARNER SIMEON[8] (twin), b. in Guilford, Nov. 7, 1882.
    viii. CHARLES FRANCIS[8], b. in Guilford, Nov. 15, 1886.
    ix. ESTHER HARRIET[8], b. in Worcester, Mass., Oct. 27, 1889.

Children of DAVID[7], (1850) [**958**] (Simeon[6], Capt. Simeon[5], Simeon[4], John[3] Jacob[2], Robert[1]) and Louisa Jenette (Adams) Adams; res. Marlboro, Vt.

    i. MINNIE L.[8], b. in Marlboro, Sept. 21, 1868 ; m. William H. Ames of Brattleboro, Vt.; res. Brattleboro, Vt.
    ii. ROLLIN D.[8], b. in Marlboro, Mar. 2, 1873.
    iii. WALTER C [8], b. in Marlboro, Dec. 21, 1878.
    iv. CHARLES A.[8], b. in Marlboro, Feb. 16, 1882 ; d. 21 Feb., 1883.
    v. ARTHUR S.[8], b. in Marlboro, Oct. 9, 1884.

Children of HENRY LEROY[7], (1842) [**959**] (Timothy Mather[6], Capt. Simeon[5], Simeon[4], John[3], Jacob[2], Robert[1]) and Ellen M. (Dunklee) Adams; res. Marlboro, Vt.

    i. EVA R.[8], b. in Marlboro, Sept. 25, 1872.
    ii. ARTHUR P.[8], b. in Marlboro, Aug. 22, 1876 ; d. 14 Apr., 1881.
    iii. BERTHA H.[8], b. in Marlboro, Mar. 12, 1879.

Children of LE ROY F.[7], (1846) [**960**] (Lucius Franklin[6], Capt. Simeon[5], Simeon[4], John[3], Jacob[2], Robert[1]) and Ella (Crosby) Adams; res. Brattleboro, Vt.

    i. WALTER CROSBY[8], b. in Brattleboro, Jan. 4, 1877.
    ii. FREDERICK C.[8], b. in Brattleboro, Jan. 31, 1879.

iii. GEORGE EDWARD⁸, b. in Brattleboro, Dec. 8, 1880.
iv. PARKER SUMNER⁸, b. in Brattleboro, Nov. 8, 1882.
v. RUTH LOVISA⁸, b. in Brattleboro, Mar. 19, 1886.
vi. CROSBY⁸, b. in Brattleboro, June 3, 1888.
vii. ELLA CROSBY⁸, b. in Brattleboro, Jan. 23, 1890.

Children of LOREN M⁷., (1847) [**961**] (Lucius Franklin⁶, Capt. Simeon⁵, Simeon⁴, John³, Jacob², Robert¹) and Cora M. (Jillson) Adams; res. Guilford, Vt.

i. LESLIE LOREN⁸, b. in Brattleboro, Vt., Jan. 19, 1882.
ii. FOREST ELMER⁸, b. in Whitingham, Vt., July 3, 1883; d. 25 Sept., 1883.
iii. CARRIE LUCY⁸, b. in Stuart, Neb., June 15, 1885.
iv. LILLIAN C.⁸, b. in Stuart, Mar. 16, 1887.
v. ERNEST EDGAR⁸, b. in Whitingham, Aug. 15, 1890.
vi. ALICE ANNA⁸, b. in Whitingham, July 28, 1893.
vii. STELLA CORA⁸, b. in Whitingham, Jan. 4, 1895.
viii. ELNA VIOLA⁸, b. in Whitingham, July 29, 1896.
ix. WALTER CLYDE⁸, b. in Whitingham, Feb. 6, 1898.

Child of LUCIUS W.⁷, (1859) [**962**] (Lucius Franklin⁶, Capt. Simeon⁵, Simeon⁴, John³, Jacob², Robert¹) and Ola E. (Clough) Adams; res. Brattleboro, Vt.

i. RAYMOND LUCIUS⁸, b. in Brattleboro, May 24, 1891.

Children of NELLIE J.⁷, (1854) [**963**] (Lucius Franklin⁶, Capt. Simeon⁵, Simeon⁴, John³, Jacob², Robert¹) and Charles H. Smith; res. Minneapolis, Minn.

i. CLARA MAY SMITH, b. Sept. 29, 1877; d. 6 May, 1892.
ii. FLORENCE ELLA SMITH, b. Dec. 7, 1879.
iii. HARRY ADAMS SMITH, b. Jan. 15, 1882.
iv. HELEN MAUD SMITH, b. Sept. 23, 1883.
v. EDWIN CHAS. SMITH, b. Aug. 12, 1886; d. 23 Jan., 1898.

Child of ELIAS⁷, (1828) [**964**] (George⁶, Job⁵, Joel⁴, John³, Jacob², Robert¹) and Cornelia Elizabeth (Hall) Adams; res. Theresa, N. Y.

MATTHEW MCKELVEY.   FRED L. MCKELVEY.
MARY WOOLSEY MCKELVEY AND GRANDSON,
RAYMOND MCKELVEY.
ELIZABETH MCKELVEY LAIRD.   DR. J. T. LAIRD.

1409. i. DR. GEORGE FRANCIS[8], b. in Theresa, Jan. 28, 1863; m. Sept. 9, 1891, in Pulaski, N. Y., Beulah Witt Muzzy, dau. of Lawson Reed and Allie (Witt) Muzzy of Pulaski, N. Y.

He was educated in the Theresa High School, and Potsdam Normal School; studied medicine, and received his diploma at the Hahnaman Medical College and Hospital, Chicago, Ill., in 1888; practiced for seven years in Pulaski, N. Y.; was appointed in 1895, Assistant Physician in the Massachusetts Insane Hospital at Westboro, Mass.; resigned in 1898, and accepted a position in the Homeopathic Hospital at Gowanda, N. Y.

Children of MATTHEW McKELVEY, (1833) [965] (Nancy[6], Bildad[5], Joel[4], John[3], Jacob[2], Robert[1]) and Mary Woolsey; res. Sandusky and Tiffin, O.

i. LIZZIE McKELVEY, b. in Sandusky, Dec. 7, 1830; m. at Tiffin, Sept. 27, 1888, John Thomas Laird, son of Matthew and Margaret (McCalmont) Laird, b. Sept. 27, 1850; he is a dentist, but resides on a farm in Greenfield, O.; no issue.

ii. FRED L. McKELVEY, b. in Sandusky, May 1, 1866; m. in Tiffin, Oct. 25, 1888, Helena Lowe; she d. 7 Apr., 1896, leaving one child, Raymond, b. Apr. 18, 1890.

He was a merchant for several years; is now in the printing business at Tiffin with his father.

Children of JOHN McKELVEY, (1835) [966] (Nancy[6], Bildad[5], Joel[4], John[3], Jacob[2], Robert[1]) and Jane Rowland Huntington; res. Sandusky, O.

i. JANET HUNTINGTON McKELVEY, b. in Sandusky, Apr. 2, 1862; m. July 24, 1886, Rev. Clarence F. Swift, son of Henry O. and Angeline (Haynes) Swift, b. in Oberlin, O., July 27, 1861.

From the Sandusky High School she entered Oberlin College in 1879, and graduated with honor in 1883; she received a gold medal for the best essay in a prize oratorical contest in that year. In March, 1886, she received a prize of two hundred dollars awarded by the Prafg Company of Boston, for the best essay on Christmas cards, there being about six hundred contestants, and has attained a literary reputation for other productions. Mr. Swift was pastor of a Congregationalist church at Smyrna, N. Y., for a time; then for seven years pastor of the N. E. Congregational church at Saratoga Spa. In Dec., 1894, he removed to Lansing, Mich., and took charge of the Plymouth Congregational church for five years. He is now pastor of the Park Avenue Congregational church, Minneapolis, Minn. They have two children, b. in Saratoga Springs: Dorothy Rowland, b. Nov. 22, 1890, and Helen McK., b. Sept. 30, 1892.

ii. JOHN JAY McKELVEY, b. May 24, 1863; m. July 12, 1887, Mary Clark Mattocks, dau. of Daniel J. and Laura (Clarke) Mattocks of Cleveland, b. Nov. 28, 1862, a graduate of Oberlin College in the class of 1885.

>He graduated from the Sandusky High School, 1880, and from Oberlin College in 1884; studied at the Law School of Harvard University, and was graduated with the degree of L. L. B. (*cum laude*) in June, 1887, and also received the degree of Master of Arts from the University; was one of the founders, and the first editor-in-chief of the "Harvard Law Review." While a student he published for the use of students a small book on Common Law Pleading, which he subsequently revised, and which is now used in the leading Law Schools of the country. He has published a text-book on Evidence, and has been in the practice of law in New York for twelve years, being counsel for a number of large and important firms. His residence "Bonnie Brae," is on the Hudson at Spuyten Duyvil. They have three children: Mary Alice, b. May 20, 1889; Constance, b. Feb. 19, 1891, and Ruth, b. Apr. 8, 1893.

iii. ALICE ROWLAND McKELVEY, b. Apr. 25, 1867; m. June 15, 1892, James Melville Milne, son of Wm. Gordon Melville and Catherine (Kennedy) Milne, b. in Sandusky, Jan. 22, 1861, educated in chemistry and pharmacy at Michigan University and a druggist in Sandusky, O.; is adjutant of the 6th Ohio Regt., serving the government in 1898.

>She graduated from the Sandusky High School in 1885, and studied for a time in Oberlin College. They have three children: Jane Huntington Milne, b. Aug. 22, 1893; Francis Rowland Milne, b. May 1, 1896, and Martha McK. Milne, b. Apr. 12, 1898.

iv. JENNIE ADAMS McKELVEY, b. Jan. 22, 1873; d. 8 Apr., 1876.

v. CHARLES SUMNER McKELVEY, b. Jan. 3, 1875; d. 17 Aug., 1875.

vi. RALPH HUNTINGTON McKELVEY, b. Dec. 7, 1877.

>He was the class historian of the High School in Sandusky, 1896; has taken three years of classical studies in the Ohio State University and in Oberlin College, and will graduate at Stanford University, California, in 1900.

Child of LOUISA ANDREWS, (1827) [967] and Orin Downs.

i. GEORGE DOWNS, b. Oct. 1, 1848; m. Nellie Robinson; res. Idaho.

Children of LOUISA ANDREWS, (1827) and John Eaton.

i. CANDACE EATON, b. Sept. 22, 1854; m. Amasa Burns; res. Vancouver, Wash.

CLARENCE F. SWIFT, A. M., D. D., AND WIFE, JANET HUNTINGTON MCKELVEY, A. M., AND THEIR CHILDREN, DOROTHY ROWLAND AND HELEN MCKELVEY.

Eighth Generation.] OF NEWBURY, MASS. 399

    ii. EVA EATON, b. Dec. 17, 1856; m. John Tranmer; res. Tekama, Neb.
    iii. LEWIS EATON, b. Apr. 12, 1862.

Children of EDWIN ANDREWS, (1828) [**968**] and Lydia Olmstead; res. Sphinx Corners, Barrien Co., Mich.
    i. DELLA ANDREWS, d. in infancy.
    ii. LILLY ANDREWS, d. in infancy.
    iii. LUTHER ANDREWS, b. Apr. 3, 1862; res. Benton Harbor, Mich.
    iv. CURTIS ANDREWS, b. Oct. 24, 1866; res. Sphinx Corners, Mich.

Children of EMILY ANDREWS, (1830) [**969**] and Curtis Printiss.
    i. ELLA PRINTISS, b. Oct. 31, 1854; m. Charles Hollenbeck; res. Tekonsha, Calhoun Co., Mich.
    ii. CARRIE PRINTISS, b. July 28, 1856.
    iii. GEORGE PRINTISS, b. Nov. 10, 1858; m. Mattie Starts; res. Burr Oak, Mich.
    iv. HATTIE PRINTISS, b. Nov 13, 1860; m. Thomas Sanford; res. Girard, Mich.
    v. CARL PRINTISS, b. 1863; d. in infancy.
    vi. MAY PRINTISS, b. July 26, 1865; d. 7 Mar., 1869.

Child of LUCINA ANDREWS, (1833) [**970**] and Abraham Phillips.
    i. ADDIE PHILLIPS, b. Dec. 2, 1857; m. Feb. 22, 1879, Sidney Smith; res. Union City, Mich.

Child of LUCINDA ANDREWS, (1833) and John Newcomb.
    i. GEORGE LEWIS NEWCOMB, b. Aug. 1, 1866; res. Union City, Mich.

Children of FRANKLIN B.[7], (1828) [**971**] (Horace Hale[6], Bildad[5], Joel[4], John[3], Jacob[2], Robert[1]) and Lucinda (Fletcher) Adams; res. Lawton, Mich.

i. HORACE HALE[8], b. in Porter, Van Buren Co., Sept. 27, 1857; d. 8 Apr., 1860.
ii. CLARA LUCINDA[8], b. in Van Buren Co., Jan. 28, 1859; m. Aug. 1, 1879, Dudley L. Thornton, son of Dudley Thornton; res. near Lawton, Van Buren Co., Mich., and have a fine fruit farm.

Children of FRANKLIN B.[7], (1828) and Anna (Fletcher) Adams.

iii. FRANKLIN K.[8], b. in Van Buren Co., Oct. 9, 1882.
iv. HORACE HALE[8], b. in Van Buren Co., July 21, 1884.

Children of URI M.[7], (1832) [972] (Horace Hale[6], Bildad[5], Joel[4], John[3], Jacob[2], Robert[1]) and Jane (McKain) Adams; res. Lawton, Mich.

i. EFFIE MAY[8], b. in Van Buren Co., Mich., Feb. 28, 1866; m. May 17, 1891, George Adams, son of Geo. and Mary (Stewart) Alford, b. Jan. 28, 1858, and adopted by Franklin B. Adams; res. Marcellus, Cass Co., Mich.
ii. HORACE CHESTER[8], b. in Van Buren Co., Sept. 10, 1868.
iii. ARCHIE L.[8], b. in Van Buren Co., July 10, 1871; m. Jan. 21, 1897, Lillie Douglass, dau. of John and Nancy Douglass.
iv. MARY CALISTA[8], b. in Van Buren Co., Nov. 21, 1875.
v. MASON CLARENCE[8], b. in Van Buren Co., Dec. 25, 1877.
vi. ROSS URI[8], b. in Van Buren Co., June 2, 1883.

Children of SARAH LUCINA[7], (1835) [973] (Horace Hale[6], Bildad[5], Joel[4], John[3], Jacob[2], Robert[1]) and Dorry Fletcher; res. Lawton, Mich.

i. JULIAN FLETCHER, b. in Van Buren Co., Oct. 11, 1857; d. in infancy.
ii. JULIUS FLETCHER (twin), b. Oct 11, 1857; m. Sept. 11, 1881, Sophia E. Stutes; res. near Lawton, Mich.

Children of EMILY LORANIA[7], (1839) [974] (Horace Hale[6], Bildad[5], Joel[4], John[3], Jacob[2], Robert[1]) and Isaac Leonard Bates; res. Andover, Brown Co., So. Dak.

i. FRANKLIN ADAMS BATES, b. in Van Buren Co., Mich., Sept. 6, 1867; m. Sept. 13, 1898, Laura Perkins of E. Paw Paw, Ill.
He is mail-route agent between Lincoln, Neb., and Edgemont, So. Dak.; res. Lincoln, Neb.

ii. SARAH SOPHIA BATES, b. near Schoolcraft, Mich., Sept. 18, 1869; m. Dec. 8, 1895, Jason D. Feller.
   She was a graduate of the State Normal School, Madison, So. Dak., and for several years a teacher; res. Scotland township, Day Co., S. Dak.

iii. WINNIE LEONORA BATES, b. near Schoolcraft, June 14, 1876; m. Apr. 7, 1896, Wm. H. Austiss of Porter, Mich.
   She graduated with honor in June, 1895, at Burlington, Iowa, and was a teacher of music; res. Andover P. O., Brown Co., So. Dak.

Child of MARY CALISTA[7], (1842) [**975**] (Horace Hale[6], Bildad[5], Joel[4], John[3], Jacob[2], Robert[1]) and D. F. Smith; res. Chicago, Ill.

i. HORACE HERBERT SMITH, b. June 8, 1868.
   He is city editor of the *Butte Miner*, Butte, Mont.

Children of HORACE H.[7], (1819) [**976**] (Alden[6], Joel[5], Jr., Joel[4], John[3], Jacob[2], Robert[1]) and Lucy (Willard) Adams; res. Antwerp, Jefferson Co., N. Y.

1410. i. CELIA CORBIN[8], b. in Antwerp, Aug. 29, 1845; m. Jan. 1, 1863, Huron Wescott, son of Ashabel Wescott, b. in Sacket's Harbor, N. Y., 1840; res. Watertown, N. Y.

ii. ELLA ELIZABETH[8], b. in Antwerp, Apr. 2, 1849; d. at Carthage, N. Y., 25 April, 1868, age 23 years.

iii. FRANCES JOSEPHINE[8], b. in Antwerp, July 17, 1850; d. in Philadelphia, N. Y., 15 June, 1854.

iv. MARY HELEN[8], b. in Antwerp, Dec. 9, 1852; d. in Carthage, 28 Aug., 1876, age 23 years.

1411. v. CORA ESTELLE[8], b. in Philadelphia, N. Y., Sept. 3, 1857; m. George Salter. She d. in Carthage, 10 May, 1881, age 23 years.

Children of LUCY MARIA[7], (1829) [**977**] (Alden[6], Joel[5], Jr., Joel[4], John[3], Jacob[2] Robert[1]) and Henry Stebbins; res. Antwerp, Jefferson Co., N. Y.

i. CHARLES H. STEBBINS, b. in Antwerp, Feb. 27, 1850; res. Chicago, Ill. He has a son Horace, b. Apr. 14, 1884.

ii. MILLEY STEBBINS, b. in Antwerp, June 14, 1852.

Children of GEORGE HEALD', (1827) [978] and Maria Shaffee; res. Birmingham, Erie Co., Ohio.

- i. CHARLES A. HEALD, b. Apr. 20, 1851; m. Oct. 10, 1880, Florence Robinson of Napanoch, Ulster Co., N. Y.; she d. 16 Apr., 1885.
- ii. GEORGE C. HEALD, b. July 19, 1863; m. Feb. 18, 1888, Mattie Brooks of Vermillion, Ohio.

Children of CLARK HEALD, (1830) [979] and Catharine Gilmore.

- i. MARY E. HEALD, b. 1867.
- ii. ARTHUR D. HEALD, b. 1869.
- iii. FRANK C. HEALD, b. 1871.
- iv. ALONZO A. HEALD, b. 1874; d. 1889.
- v. FRANCES I. HEALD, b. 1876.
- vi. HORATIO HEALD, b. 1879.
- vii. GROVER C. HEALD, b. 1882; d. 1883.
- viii. CLARK HEALD, b. 1884.
- ix. ALICE HEALD, b. 1887.

Child of CHARLES S. HEALD, (1833) [980] and Emily Middleton.

- i. KATE HEALD, b. 1865.

Children of ALONZO K. HEALD', (1835) [981] and Julia Heath; res. Farley, Dubuque Co., Ia.

- i. EVA ADELLE HEALD, b. in York, Ia., Feb. 14, 1861; d. Mar., 1867.
- ii. AMANDA MAY HEALD, b. in York, June 29, 1862; d. 13, Sept., 1863.
- iii. CORA HEALD, b. in York, Nov. 23, 1864; m. Mar. 12, 1889, John Pitman. She d. 3 Jan., 1898.
- iv. BURTON DAVID HEALD, b. in Farley, Ia., Feb. 21, 1867; m. Aug. 29, 1889, Tillie Smith.
- v. MINNIE M. HEALD, b. in Farley, July 3, 1872; d. Aug., 1873.
- vi. WINNIE B. HEALD (twin), b. in Farley, July 3, 1872.
- vii. GLEN DALE HEALD, b. Jan. 26, 1878.
- viii. GENEVIEVE DAISY HEALD (twin), b. in Farley, Jan. 26, 1878; m. Oct. 26, 1899, Burt M. Lasher.

JOHN JAY MCKELVEY, A. M., LL. B., AND WIFE, MARY CLARK MATTOCKS, A. B.

Child of AMOS S. HEALD, (1839) [**982**] and Amanda Brown.
  i. EUGENE S. HEALD, b. 1868 ; m. 1890, Ada Comfort.
  ii. TOLA J. HEALD, b. 1870 ; m. 1896, Etta Comfort.

Child of FRANK A. HEALD, (1844) [**983**] and Rachel German.
  i. BESSIE HEALD, d. 1873.
    A son by Aramantha Needham d. in infancy.

Children of CHARLES CURRIER, (1800) [**984**] and Anna Hale; res. Newbury, Mass.

    i. GORHAM CURRIER, b. Oct. 19, 1823; d. in San Francisco, 15 Sept., 1868; unm.
    ii. WASHINGTON CURRIER, b. Feb. 22, 1830; d. 6 Mar., 1830.
    iii. SON, b. Nov. 16, 1830; d. 17 Nov., 1830.
    iv. DAUGHTER, b. Feb. 13, 1832; d. same day.
    v. CLARISSA ANN CURRIER, b. Dec. 31, 1832; living, 1899. Supplied this record.
    vi. SARAH JANE H. CURRIER, b. Sept. 6, 1834; m. Sept. 6, 1857, Enoch Pierce Stickney.
    vii. A STILL-BORN.
    viii. LUCY HALE CURRIER, b. Dec. 27, 1836; d. unm. 26 Jan., 1897.
    ix. CHARLES OTIS CURRIER, b. Mar. 21, 1839; d. unm. 22 Sept., 1886.
    x. FRANCES ELLEN CURRIER, b. Oct. 14, 1840; d. unm. 5 Feb., 1891.
    xi. CALEB CUSHING CURRIER, b. Nov. 21, 1842; d. 25 Sept., 1850.
    xii. SARISSA CURRIER, b. Sept. 12, 1844; m. June 26, 1867, Chas. Henry Colby; res. Newburyport, Mass.

Children of PHILIP[6], (1805) [**985**] (Henry[7], Henry[6], Robert[5], Abraham[4], Robert[3], Sergt. Abraham[2], Robert[1]) and Mary (Goodwin) Adams; res. Newburyport, Mass.

    i. PHILIP HENRY[9], b. in Newburyport, Mar. 4, 1829; m. Nancy ———, of Texas; res. Florence, Texas. *d. Nov. 1923*
    ii. SAMUEL GOODWIN[9], b. in Newburyport, Mar. 31, 1830; m. Cordelia ———; res. Lexington, Ky.
1412. iii. GEORGE EDWARD[9], b. in Newburyport, Apr. 27, 1832; m. (1) Nov. 28, 1855, Caroline J. Ordway; she d. 29 Jan., 1866, age 31 years; m. (2) Dec. 17, 1867, Rebecca Jane Ordway (cousin of Caroline J.); res. Newburyport, Mass.; she d. ~~13 Feb., 1871~~, age ~~39~~ years. He d. 12 Feb., 1871. *aged 39 yrs.* " " *12 July 1907* " *68* "
    He was a merchant in Georgetown, Mass., in the firm of Adams & Goodwin.

Children of JOEL[8], (1810) [**986**] (Joseph[7], Henry[6], Robert[5], Abraham[4], Robert[3], Sergt. Abraham[2], Robert[1]) and Irene (Felch) Adams; res. Newbury, Mass.

1413. i. GEORGE FRANKLIN[9], b. Apr. 29, 1833; m. June 27, 1856, Sarah J. Lunt. He d. 11, Feb., 1858, age 25 years.

Ninth Generation.] OF NEWBURY, MASS. 405

  ii. CHARLES HENRY⁹, b. Nov. 24, 1834; unm.; res. New Jersey.
  iii. HORACE CLINTON⁹, b. June 18, 1838 ; d. June, 1839.
  iv. IRENE FELCH⁹, b. Mar. 14, 1841 ; d. 31 Aug., 1857.
  v. HENRY PLUMER⁹, b. Mar. 31, 1843 ; d. 2 Sept., 1875.
  vi. EDWARD PAYSON⁹, b. Nov. 17, 1845 ; unm.; res. Haverhill, Mass.
1414. vii. HORACE CLINTON⁹, b. Apr. 6, 1848 ; m. 1872-3, Amelia Mitch of Haverhill, Mass.; res. Haverhill, Mass.

Children of OBED⁸, (1810) [**987**] (Joseph⁷, Henry⁶, Robert⁵, Abraham⁴, Robert³, Sergt. Abraham², Robert¹) and Laura A. (Lakeman) Adams; res. Ipswich, Mass.

  i. CAROLINE⁹, b. in Ipswich, Dec., 1847 ; d. 5 Apr., 1848.
  ii. LAURA F.⁹, b. in Ipswich, May 17, 1849 ; m. 1872, Frank C. Miller ; res. Roxbury, Mass.; no issue.

Children of NANCY JENNIE⁸, (1854) [**988**] (Joseph⁷, Henry⁶, Robert⁵, Abraham⁴, Robert³, Sergt. Abraham², Robert¹) and Edward Osgood; res. Newburyport, Mass.

  i. JENNIE EDWARDS OSGOOD, b. Oct. 11, 1878.
  ii. EDWARD ADAMS OSGOOD, b. May 9, 1881.
  iii. MABEL STOREY OSGOOD, b. Oct. 20, 1885.

Children of CHARLES⁸, (1821) [**989**] (Abraham⁷, Henry⁶, Robert⁵, Abraham⁴, Robert³, Sergt. Abraham², Robert¹) and Adalaide (Clement) Adams; res. Kenduskeag, Penobscot Co., Me.

  i. ROSILLA⁹, b. in Kenduskeag, Dec. 9, 1844 ; d. 3 May, 1849.
1415. ii. CLARA CLEMENT⁹, b. in Kenduskeag, Feb. 27, 1847 ; m. Jan. 16, 1868, Wm. Henry H. Bradbury, son of Ebenezer and Mary T. Bradbury of Newburyport, b. Feb. 24, 1840 ; res. Hammonton, N. J.

Children of CHARLES⁸, (1821) and Matilda P. (Woodcock) Adams.

  iii. ELLA MARIA⁹, b. in Newbury, May 21, 1853 ; res. Concord, Mass., unm.
1416. iv. ADALINE FRANCES⁹, b. in Newbury, Dec. 10, 1854 ; m. May 2, 1890, Elias Pike Bartlett ; res. Amesbury, Mass.

ROBERT ADAMS   [Ninth Generation.

- v. HARRIET STOWE[9], b. in Newbury, Nov. 5, 1856; m. Marcellus Hemmenway; res. Concord, Mass.
- vi. CHARLES CARROLL[9], b. in Newbury, Dec. 13, 1861; m. Mary Davis of Washington, D. C.; res. Redlands, San Bernardo Co., Cal.

Children of HARRIET[8], (1812) [**990**] (Abraham[7], Henry[6], Robert[5], Abraham[4], Robert[3], Sergt. Abraham[2], Robert) and Daniel D. Nealey; res. Exeter, N. H.

- i. JULIA ADAMS NEALEY, b. Jan. 15, 1844; m. John Pound; res. Dover, N. H.; no issue.
- ii. ALBERTO NEALEY, b. June 20, 1845.
    He married and resided for many years in Blue Rapids, Kan., where he died, leaving one child now deceased. He d. 13 Dec., 1895.
- iii. ALONZO NEALEY, b. Feb. 11, 1847; d. 30 Nov., 1849.
- iv. ALWILDA NEALEY, b. Sept. 24, 1848; d. 5 Oct., 1848.
- v. LORENZO NEALEY, b. Nov. 2, 1849.
- vi. EDWIN NEALEY, b. Mar. 28, 1853; d. 19 Aug., 1854.
- vii. MARY P. NEALEY, b. Aug. 26, 1855; d. 8 Feb., 1859.
- viii. HARRIET NEALEY, b. July 10, 1858.

Children of HENRY PETTENGILL[8], (1801) [**991**] and Abigail Palmer Dole; res. Georgetown, Mass.

- i. MARTHA ANN PETTENGILL, b. June 22, 1827; d. Nov., 1832.
- ii. MARTHA ANN PETTENGILL, b. Dec. 10, 1833; m. May 16, 1859, Charles Holmes of Ipswich. She d. 11 Apr., 1864.
- iii. LOVEY ADAMS PETTENGILL, b. June 16, 1836; d. in infancy.
- iv. HANNAH COLEMAN PETTENGILL, b. Apr. 17, 1838; living unm.
- v. GEORGE HENRY PETTENGILL, b. May 18, 1840.

Children of ELIZABETH COLLEY PETTENGILL[8], (1812) [**992**] and Daniel Knight Hale; res. Newbury, Mass.

- i. LUCY KIMBALL HALE, b. Mar. 9, 1839; m. June 20. 1860, Joseph Knight Danforth; he d. 22 Nov., 1864; res. Newbury, Mass.
- ii. SARAH CURTIS HALE, b. Aug. 30, 1840; m. Feb. 12, 1861, Joseph Little, Jr.; res. Newbury, Mass.
- iii. GEORGIANA BALCH HALE, b. Apr. 20, 1842; m. Feb. 12, 1864, Paul Moody Ilsley.

MARY ALICE.   RUTH.   CONSTANCE.

CHILDREN OF JOHN JAY MCKELVEY AND WIFE, MARY CLARK MATTOCKS.

- iv. MARY ELIZABETH HALE, b. Nov. 27, 1844 ; m. May 14, 1868, Nathaniel Moody Ilsley ; he was a soldier in the 35th Mass. Regt., was wounded, losing an eye.
- v. ABBIE FRANCES HALE, b. Apr. [9] 20, 1849 ; m. Jan, 15, 1873, Moses Henry Rolfe.
- vi. STEPHEN PETTENGILL HALE, b. Mar. 7, 1851.
  Farmer ; res. Newbury, Mass.; unm.
- vii. ADELINE KNIGHT HALE; b. in Newburyport, Aug. 29, 1852 ; res. Newbury, Mass.; unm.
- viii. ANN REBECCA HALE, b. in Newburyport, May 12, 1855; m. Dec. 19, 1881, Edward E. Bartlett.

Children of JANE N.^{8}, (1828) [**993**] (Joseph^7, Daniel^6, Robert^5, Abraham^4, Robert^3, Sergt. Abraham^2, Robert^1) and Ezekiel R. Todd ; res. Rowley, Mass.

- i. HELEN ADAMS TODD, b. Dec. 27, 1849 ; m. [Sept. 10 ?] Oct. 21, 1876, John Peabody Adams, son of Woodbridge and Mary Peabody Adams; res. Auburndale, Mass.
- ii. HARRIET ADAMS TODD, b. Oct. 9, 1866; m. Feb. 25, 1894, Wm. Johnson Merriam ; res. Milwaukee, Wis. Children :
  1. Russell Adams Merriam, b. Dec. 29, 1895.
  2. Grace Merriam, b. Feb. 11, 1897.
  3. Elizabeth Merriam, b. Oct. 28, 1898.

Children of CALEB CUSHING^8, (1833) [**994**] (Joseph^7, Daniel^6, Robert^5, Abraham^4, Robert^3, Sergt. Abraham^2, Robert^1) and Sarah F. (Jewett) Adams; res. Brooklyn, N. Y.

- i. ELIZABETH STONE^9, b. in Brooklyn, June 4, 1858 ; d. 17 Apr., 1860.
- 1417. ii. IDA^9, b. in Brooklyn, Mar. 31, 1862 ; m. June 2, 1883, Charles Francis Tarbell, son of Chas. Lee and Martha Emeline (Fiske) Tarbell, b. in Lincoln, Mass., May 6, 1850, d. in Lincoln, Mass., 31 Oct., 1891 ; res. Milton, Mass.
- 1418. iii. GEORGE SHRIEVE^9, b. in Brooklyn, Sept. 15, 1864 ; m. Jan. 10, 1889, Katherine L. Bradley ; res. Brooklyn, N. Y.
- 1419. iv. SARAH JEWETT^9, b. in Brooklyn, Feb. 25, 1867 ; m. Jan. 27, 1888, Wm. Augustus Hall ; res. Bellows Falls, Vt.
- 1419½. v. CUSHING^9, b. in Brooklyn, July 8, 1870; m. May 18, 1898, Jenette Hale Eastman, dau. of Geo. W. and Jenette (Webster) Hale, b. in Minneapolis, Minn., Nov. 2, 1868, d. in Bellows Falls, Vt., 4 Apr., 1900 ; res. Bellows Falls, Vt.
- vi. DANIEL^9, b. in Brooklyn, June 30, 1871 ; unm.; res. Philadelphia, Pa.

Children of JOSEPH WEBSTER⁸, (1835) [**995**] (Joseph⁷, Daniel⁶, Robert⁵, Abraham⁴, Robert³, Sergt. Abraham², Robert¹) and Mary (Cook) Adams; res. Newbury, Mass.

    i. CHARLES CUSHING⁹, b. in Newbury, Feb. 21, 1860; m. Sept. 7, 1881, Elizabeth Jane Wells. He is a fisherman; res. Newbury, Mass.
    ii. ARTHUR COOK⁹, b. in Newbury, Mar. 1, 1867; d. 20 Apr., 1867.
    iii. DANIEL PALMER⁹, b. in Newbury, Mar. 1, 1867; d. 1 May, 1867.
    iv. MARY ABBY⁹, b. in Newbury, July 16, 1869.
    v. CLARA C.⁹, b. in Newbury, Aug. 30, 1871.

Children of HON. JOHN POPKIN⁸, (1839) [**996**] (Joseph⁷, Daniel⁶, Robert⁵, Abraham⁴, Robert³, Sergt. Abraham², Robert¹) and Grace (Chapman) Adams; res. Brooklyn, N. Y.

    i. JOHN POPKIN⁹, b. in Brooklyn, Sept. 13, 1879; mem. of Amherst Col., class of 1901.
    ii. CHARLES HOLMES⁹, b. in Brooklyn, May 13, 1881; d. 16 Feb., 1885.
    iii. RICHARD SPOFFORD⁹, b. in Brooklyn, May 16, 1885; d. 18 Nov., 1886.

Children of MARY AUGUSTA⁸, (1815) [**997**] (Aaron⁷, Isaac⁶, Benjamin⁵, Abraham⁴, Robert³, Sergt. Abraham², Robert¹) and John Henry Dennis; res. Dorchester, Mass.

    i. GEORGE W. DENNIS, b. Feb. 27, 1834; m. Apr., 1868, Mrs. Augautte B. ———, dau. of Benjamin C. and Mary C. Gould, b. in Lowell, Mass., Mar. 15, 1828; res. Sunbright, Tenn.
    ii. HENRY WALES DENNIS, b. Jan. 13, 1836; m. May 16, 1859, Abby Lonti Paddock, dau. of Horace and Mary L. (Paine) Paddock, b. in Troy, Vt., Aug. 25, 1836.
        He was a member of Co. D., First Mass, Cavalry, and one of the firm of Lecman, Dennis & Co., furniture, New York City; res. 354 State St., Brooklyn, N. Y.
    iii. MARY CATHERINE DENNIS, b. July 30, 1838; m. Jan. 29, 1867, Isaac Smith Clark, son of Gilbert and Polly (Smith) Clark, b. in Wareham, Mass., May 13, 1835.
        He was a member of Co. G, 4th Mass. Regt.; res. Chelsea, Mass.
    iv. CHARLOTTE LOUISA DENNIS, b. Sept. 16, 1840; res. Dorchester, Mass.; unm.
    v. THEODORE CHARLES DENNIS, b. Dec. 6, 1842; m. Nov. 2, 1866, Cornelia P. Pressey.

He was a member of the 1st Regt., Mass. Inf.; participated in the battle at Balls Bluff; mail carrier; res. 31 Humphrey Sq., Dorchester, Mass.

- vi. AGNES MARIA DENNIS, b. July 16, 1845; d. unm.
- vii. ANNA ELIZABETH DENNIS, b. Feb. 19, 1848; d. unm.
- viii. EDWIN FRANK DENNIS, b. Nov. 17, 1849; res. Brooklyn.
- ix. FANNY FERA DENNIS, b. Jan. 29, 1854; res. Dorchester, Mass.

Child of ELIZA THERESA[8], (1819) [998] (Aaron[7], Isaac[6], Benjamin[5], Abraham[4], Robert[3], Sergt. Abraham[2], Robert[1]) and Geo. Washington Somerby; res. Boston, Mass.

- i. HANNAH ELIZABETH SOMERBY, b. Apr. 23, 1843; m. Dec. 6, 1860, Stephen S. Van Wart; res. Boston, Mass.

Child of MARTHA AGNES[8], (1821) [999] (Aaron[7], Isaac[6], Benjamin[5], Abraham[4], Robert[3], Sergt. Abraham[2], Robert[1]) and Samuel Merrill; res. Boston, Mass.

- i. SAMUEL AUGUSTUS MERRILL, b. July 4, 1847; m. May 2, 1870, Lucy M. Wann.
  He is cashier of the Mechanics National Bank, 378 Wash. St., Boston.

Child of BENJAMIN[8], (1830) [1000] (Benjamin[7], Isaac[6], Benjamin[5], Abraham[4], Robert[3], Sergt. Abraham[2], Robert[1]) and Ann Stone (Walker) Adams; res. Milford, Mass.

1420.   i. SARAH ANN[9], b. in Upton, Mass., Dec. 20, 1850; m. Nov. 29, 1871, Frederic Warren Hawes of Wrentham, Mass.

Child of WEBSTER[8], (1834) [1001] (Benjamin[7], Isaac[6], Benjamin[5], Abraham[4], Robert[3], Sergt. Abraham[2], Robert[1]) and Emily (Blanchard) Adams; res. Chelsea, Mass.

- i. CHARLES WEBSTER[9].

Children of FRANCIS DODDRIDGE[8], (1835) [1002] (Abraham Doddridge[7], Isaac[6], Benjamin[5], Abraham[4], Robert[3], Sergt. Abraham[2], Robert[1]) and Mary Jane (Arnold) Adams; res. Townsend, Mass.

- i. FRANK ARNOLD[9], b. in Townsend, 1858; went to Sandusky, O., 1884; not heard from.
- ii. CLARA[9], b. in Townsend, 1859; d. 1864.

Child of FRANCIS DODDRIDGE[8], and Sarah E. (Davis) Adams.

    iii. MELVIN THURSTON[9], b. in Townsend, Aug. 17, 1877; res. Townsend, Mass.

Child of WILLIAM RUSSELL[8], (1838) [**1003**] (Abraham Doddridge[7], Isaac[6], Benjamin[5], Abraham[4], Robert[3], Sergt. Abraham[2], Robert[1]) and Lavinia J. (Phillips) Adams; res. Haverhill, Mass.

    i. CLARA RUSSELL[9], b. in Haverhill, Apr. 15, 1880.

Child of SMITH[8], (1828) [**1004**] (Charles[7], Smith[6], Charles[5], Abraham[4], Robert[3], Sergt. Abraham[2], Robert[1]) and Mary S. (Stevens) Adams; res. Bangor, Me.

1421.   i. LAURA JANE[9], b. in Bangor, Mar. 2, 1850; m. (1) July 1, 1866, Augustus H. Sutherland, son of Benjamin F. and Marcia (Merrill) Sutherland, b. Nov. 14, 1846; m. (2) Feb. 17, 1872, Nahum D. Lander, son of Freeman and Ann (Piper) Lander, b. Jan. 8, 1853.

Children of SMITH[8], (1828) and Ellen Jane (Wilson) Adams.

    ii. SMITH[9], b. in St. Johns, N. B., May 19, 1865; d. 19 Aug., 1866.
1422.   iii. SMITH[9], b. in Milltown, Me., Dec. 22, 1866; m. Jan. 6, 1892, Eliza Hand, dau. of Richard and Margaret (Wilson) Hand, b. June 9, 1865; res. Milltown, Me.
    iv. CHARLES[9], b. in Milltown, Oct. 25, 1869.
    v. GEORGE[9], b. in Milltown, Aug. 12, 1871.
    vi. ROBERT[9], b. in Milltown, Aug. 22, 1876.

Children of SARAH ELIZABETH[8], (1832) [**1005**] (Charles[7], Smith[6], Charles[5], Abraham[4], Robert[3], Sergt. Abraham[2], Robert[1]) and Thomas Jefferson Spinney; res. Portsmouth, N. H.

    i. EMMA STONE SPINNEY, b. Sept. 5, 1854; d. 15 May, 1863.
1423.   ii. CHARLES EDWIN SPINNEY, b. Oct. 14, 1857; m. Nellie M. Chandler, b. July 14, 1861; d. 16 July, 1896. He d. in Bridgewater, Mass., 23 Feb., 1890.
    iii. SARAH ELIZA SPINNEY, b. May 25, 1860; m. George L. Bemis; he d. 1899. She d. 26 Feb., 1898.

Child of MARY SWETT[8], (1843) [1006] (Charles[7], Smith[6], Charles[5], Abraham[4], Robert[3], Sergt. Abraham[2], Robert[1]) and Joseph Haslam; res. Newburyport, Mass.

1424. i. ALICE BROWNING HASLAM, b. Nov. 5, 1868; m. (1) Apr. 27, 1884, William D. Ford; m. (2) Jan. 24, 1892, Warren M. Thurlow. She d. 6 Sept., 1895.

Children of AMOS HENRY[8], (1849) [1007] (Charles[7], Smith[6], Charles[5], Abraham[4], Robert[3], Sergt. Abraham[2], Robert[1]) and Cynthia C. (Dunn) Adams; res. Newburyport, Mass.

  i. ETTA MANSFIELD[9], b. in Newburyport, July 7, 1871; m. Apr., 1898, Albert Stevens.
  ii. LENA SMITH[9], b. in Newburyport, Jan. 24, 1874; m. Feb. 24, 1891, Geo. E. Morse, son of Joseph and Betsey (Follensbee) Morse, b. Sept. 9, 1866.
  iii. HOWARD RUSSELL[9], b. Apr. 28, 1876; d. 14 July, 1877.
  iv. WEBSTER DERBY[9], b. Aug. 1, 1877; m. Dec. 5, 1898, Mary E. Page. *Geo. Page, b. Aug 7, 1910*

Children of HANNAH or ANNA WEYMOUTH[8], (1828) [1008] (Moses[7], James[6], Moses[5], John[4], Robert[3], Sergt. Abraham[2], Robert[1]) and John H. Riggs; res. Portland, Me.

  i. ELLEN FRANCES RIGGS, b. Oct. 20, 1854; d. in Portland, 1856.
  ii. KATE PLUMMER RIGGS, b. Aug. 5, 1856; m. June 21, 1876, Edwin A. Gray; one child, Ethel Weymouth Gray; res. Portland, Me.
  iii. JAMES HENRY RIGGS, b. May 2, 1858; m. Oct. 23, 1879, Sarah E. James; two children; res. Portland, Me.
  iv. CLINTON RIGGS, b. May 4, 1860; d. in Portland, about 1864.
  v. GEORGIANA RIGGS, b. Aug 5, 1864; m. John Conant; no issue; res. Somerville, Mass.

Children of JAMES A.[6], (1831) [1009] (Moses[7], James[6], Moses[5], John[4], Robert[3], Sergt. Abraham[2], Robert[1]) and Clarissa Ann (Robinson) Adams; res. Woodfords, Portland, Me.

  i. ALFRED WALKER[9], b. June 27, 1861; d. in Portland, 26 Sept., 1861.
  ii. ANNA WEYMOUTH[9], b. Jan. 5, 1864; m. July 17, 1889, James Wm. Harper, son of James and Ellen (Holden) Harper, b. in Boston, Jan. 19, 1855; no issue; res. Portland, Me.

Children of SUSAN NOYES⁸, (1837) **[1010]** (Moses⁷, James⁶, Moses⁵, John⁴, Robert³, Sergt. Abraham², Robert¹) and Francis A. De Bremon.

    i. ADELAIDE DE BREMON, b. July 12, 1856.
    ii. MOSES DE BREMON, b. Jan. 22, 1857.

Children of CHARLES HENRY⁸, (1839) **[1011]** (Moses⁷, James⁶, Moses⁵, John⁴, Robert³, Sergt. Abraham², Robert¹) and Helen Pierce (Skillings) Adams; rer. Portland, Cumberland Co., Me.

    i. CHARLES ELLSWORTH⁹, d. in Portland, 5 Nov., 1873.
    ii. FREDERIC A.⁹, b. Oct. 6 [9?], 1867 ; d. Portland, 4 Nov., 1873.
    iii. ELIZABETH H.⁹, b. Oct. 7, 1869 ; m. Sept. 7, 1892, Joseph N. Harvey, son of Aaron and Elizabeth (Goodwin) Harvey, b. in Westbrook, Me., 1864; res. Winthrop, Mass.; no issue.
    iv. HENRY WILLIAM⁹, b. Nov. 7, 1881.
    v. EDWARD PRINCE⁹, b. Sept. 9, 1889.

Children of BENJAMIN BRADLEY⁸, (1831) **[1012]** (John⁷, Israel⁶, Moses⁵, John⁴, Robert³, Sergt. Abraham², Robert¹) and Elizabeth Ann (Welch) Adams; res. Minonk, Woodford Co., Ill., and Kearney, Neb.

    i. CHARLES DE LEON⁹, b. in Elmira, Ill., Sept. 4, 1857 ; d. in Macon Co., Mo., 1858.
    ii. DWIGHT DEAN⁹, b. in Macon Co., Mo., Aug. 20, 1858 ; d. at Roswell, New Mexico, 28 July, 1884.
1425. iii. ELIZABETH ELLEN⁹, b. in Green River, Ill., Apr. 8, 1861 ; m. May 25, 1880, Tjark F. Memmen of Benson, Woodford Co., Ill.; res. Kearney, Buffalo Co., Neb.
1426. iv. MARY ANN⁹, b. in Minonk, July 24, 1863 ; m. Nov. 28, 1883, James Selleck of Minonk, Ill.; res. Kearney, Neb.

Children of DANIEL SEWALL⁸, (1842) **[1013]** (John⁷, Israel⁶, Moses⁵, John⁴, Robert³, Sergt. Abraham², Robert¹) and Mattie (Welch) Adams; res. Corvalis, Benton Co., Ore.

1427. i. RALPH NORTON⁹, b. in Minonk, Ill., July 18, 1867 ; m. Aug. 18, 1892, at Rich Hill, Mo., Lillian Maud Hall.
1428. ii. NEWTON ROMEYN⁹, b. in Minonk, Feb. 5, 1872 ; m. Oct. 11, 1892, at Washburn, Ill., Blanche Mae Arnold of Washington, D. C.
    iii. GRACE ETHEL⁹, b. in Minonk, Mar. 12, 1875; unm.

Children of HATTIE EUNICE⁸, (1851) [1014] (John⁷, Israel⁶, Moses⁵, John⁴, Robert³, Sergt. Abraham², Robert¹) and Howard Early; res. Kewanee, Henry Co., Ill.
- i. JOHN ERNEST EARLY, b. Apr. 30, 1880.
- ii. RAYMOND EARLY, b. June 15, 1881.
- iii. VERNON EARLY, b. Dec. 15, 1884.
- iv. JESSIE RUTH EARLY, b. Mar. 6, 1887.
- v. WALTER LEON EARLY, b. Feb. 18, 1893.

Children of JULIA B. PRINCE, (1821) [1015] and Harrison G. Cole.
- i. CHARLES H. COLE, b. Sept. 18, 1841; m. Sept., 1866, Mary Gabriel of Athens, O.
- ii. FREDERICK G. COLE, b. Jan. 22, 1844; d. 28 Oct., 1847.
- iii. FRANK C. COLE, b. Nov. 30, 1846.
- iv. GEO. A. COLE, b. July 4, 1848; d. 22 June, 1876.
- v. EDWARD F. COLE, b. Aug. 4, 1849.
- vi. HENRY P. COLE, b. Mar. 10, 1851; m. Oct. 10, 1877, Elizabeth C. Sanderson, of Boston.
- vii. WILLIAM 1. COLE, b. Jan. 8, 1854.
- viii. JOHN F. COLE, b. Mar. 31, 1855; d. 12 Mar., 1879.

Child of HENRY G. PRINCE, (1835) [1016] and Sarah G. Frazier; res. Oakland, Cal.
- i. CHAS. A. PRINCE, b. Dec. 27, 1868.

Children of ELLEN R. PRINCE, (1837) [1017] and Chas. L. Bugbee; res. San Francisco, Cal.
- i. ALICE UNDERWOOD BUGBEE, b. Mar. 3, 1866.
- ii. LOUIS A. BUGBEE.

Children of EDWARD B. PRINCE, (1841) [1018] and Florence A. Knight; res. Cape Elizabeth, Me.
- i. ELLEN R. PRINCE, b. Aug. 27, 1865.
- ii. CLARENCE K. PRINCE, b. Sept. 9, 1868.
- iii. BURTON A. PRINCE.

414   ROBERT ADAMS   [Ninth Generation.

Child of GEORGE WILLIAM⁸, (1853) [1019] (Benjamin Whiting⁷, Isaac⁶, Moses⁵, John⁴, Robert³, Sergt. Abraham², Robert¹) and Eudora Hannah (Burton) Adams; res. Cumberland, Cumberland Co., Me.

    i. LILLIAN GERTRUDE⁹, b. Jan. 24, 1875.

Children of GEORGE MOSES⁸, (1834) [1020] (Silas Merrill⁷, Moses⁶, Jr., Moses⁵, John⁴, Robert³, Sergt. Abraham², Robert¹) and Hannah Rosina (Adams) Adams; res. Deering District, Portland, Me.

1429. i. SILAS BRADLEY⁹, b. in Portland, Oct. 17, 1863; m. Oct. 5, 1886, Aurilla Emma Patterson, dau. of Capt. Elias and Myra (Hitchborn) Patterson, b. in Stockton, Me., Sept., 1864; res. 68 Ocean St., Portland, Me.

  ii. MARTHA PREBLE⁹, b. in Portland, Feb. 15, 1865; d. 22 Sept., 1886.

1430. iii. FREDERICK WALDEMAR⁹, b. in Portland, Jan. 7, 1869; m. in Somerville, Mass., Edith Caroline Patridge, dau. of Frank and Mary (Skilling) Patridge, b. in Portland, Nov. 27, 1869; res. Somerville, Mass.

  iv. OLIVE CHARLOTTE⁹, b. in Portland, Jan. 3, 1871; res. 289 Ocean St., Portland, Me.; unm.

  v. MOSES PARKER⁹, b. in Portland, June 12, 1873; res. Portland, Me.; unm.

  vi. HENRY CHARLES⁹, b. in Portland, May 18, 1875; res. Portland, Me.; unm.

  vii. GEORGE PALMER⁹, b. in Portland, Oct. 25, 1877; res. Portland, Me., unm.

  viii. JOHN HOWARD⁹, b. in Portland, Nov. 10, 1879; res. Portland, Me., unm.

Children of ELLA ELETHEA⁸, (1842) [1021] (Moses Woodman⁷, Moses⁶, Jr., Moses⁵, John⁴, Robert³, Sergt. Abraham², Robert¹) and Lorenzo Warren Eldridge, res. Atkinson, Henry Co., and Chicago, Ill.

  i. ARTHUR WARREN ELDRIDGE, b. May 17, 1864; unm.

  ii. FRANCES ELLA ELDRIDGE, b. in Chicago, Jan. 7, 1870; d. 11 June, 1881.

Children of ELLA ELETHEA[8], (1842) and Albert Henry Simonton.
  i. HARRY PATTISON SIMONTON, b. Sept. 5, 1874.
  ii. ROY ADAMS SIMONTON, b. Apr. 12, 1876.

Children of MARY FRANCES[8], (1846) [1022] (Moses Woodman[7], Moses[6], Jr., Moses[5], John[4], Robert[3], Sergt. Abraham[2], Robert[1]) and Henry Boyce; res. Salem, Mass.
  i. JOHN A. WOODMAN BOYCE, b. in Salem, July 13, 1874; deceased.
  ii. MARY ELLA BOYCE, b. in Chicago, Feb. 19, 1877.
  iii. ASA ADAMS BOYCE, b. in Chicago, June 8, 1881.

Children of FRANCES ALLEN HAGGETT[8], (1849) [1023] and Charles P. Waldron; res. Portland, Me.
  i. MARTHA PREBLE WALDRON, b. in Portland, May 26, 1874.
  ii. ANN MARIA WALDRON, b. in Bath, Me., 1876.
  iii. MARION ISABELLE WALDRON, b. in Portland, June 17, 1887.

Children of SARAH FRANCES PARKER[8], (1839) [1024] and Samuel K. Worthen; res. Bristol, N. H.
  i. ALBERT P. WORTHEN, b. Sept. 8, 1861; m. Aug. 16, 1892, Harriet L. Reed of Weymouth, Mass.; she d. 18 Dec., 1893.
    He is an attorney, Niles Block, School St., Boston, Mass.
  ii. SAMUEL E. WORTHEN, b. June 1, 1868; living unm.
  iii. HADLEY B. WORTHEN, b. Mar. 19, 1871; living unm.

Children of DR. FRANK HOWARD PARKER[8], (1855) [1025] and Marion E. King; res. Malden, Mass.
  i. HOWARD KING PARKER, b. Sept. 24, 1886.
  ii. RALPH ROBINSON PARKER, b. Oct. 23, 1888.

Children of WILLIAM P.[8], (1827) [1026] (Aaron[7], Joshua[6], Benjamin[5], John[4], Robert[3] Sergt. Abraham[2], Robert[1]) and Sarah E. T. (Thompson) Adams; res. Wolfboro, N. H.

ROBERT ADAMS [Ninth Generation.

    i. ELIZA J.⁹, b. in Dover, N. H., Oct. 17, 1853 ; m. May 20, 1871, Charles G. Hasty; res. Wolfboro, N. H.
    ii. FRANK B.⁹, b. in Fairfield, Me., May 16, 1856 ; m. Nov., 1878, Mary Hayes ; res. Dover, N. H.
    iii. MARY A.⁹, b. in Wolfboro, Dec. 1, 1858 ; m. Apr. 15, 1879, Frank Edgerly ; res. Wolfboro, N. H.
    iv. FLORA P.⁹, b. in Biddeford, Me., July 15, 1866 ; m. June 29, 1886, John Dorr ; res. Concord, N. H.
    v. WILLIE A.⁹, b. in Wolfboro, Nov. 7, 1871 ; m. June 29, 1895, Eveline Lane ; res. Concord, N. H.

Children of GEORGE N.⁸, (1836) [1027] (Aaron⁷, Joshua⁶, Benjamin⁵, John⁴, Robert³, Sergt. Abraham², Robert¹) and Elizabeth B. (Foss) Adams; res. Wheeling, Livingston Co., Mo.

    i. EDDIE L.⁹, b. in Biddeford, Me., June 5, 1866.
1431. ii. MINNIE F. A.⁹, b. in Biddeford, Me., July 14, 1868 ; m. Sept. 8, 1886, Fred S. Wood of Wheeling, Mo.; res. Wheeling, Mo.
    iii. JAMES C.⁹, b in Wheeling, Feb. 17, 1871.

Children of SARAH A.⁸, (1838) [1028] (Aaron⁷, Joshua⁶, Benjamin⁵, John⁴, Robert³, Sergt. Abraham², Robert¹) and George W. Fogg ; res. Monmouth, Kennebec Co., Me.

1432. i. FANNIE FOGG, b. Dec. 19, 1867 ; m. Apr. 11, 1889, L. Chandler Berry, son of Charles H. and Deborah (Chandler) Berry of No. Monmouth, Me., b. Sept. 25, 1854. She d. 11 Aug., 1892.
    ii. GEORGIA A. FOGG, b. Aug. 15, 1869 ; m. Aug. 15, 1894, L. Chandler Berry ; res. No. Monmouth, Me.
    iii. BENJAMIN F. FOGG, b. Sept. 14, 1873 ; living unm.
    iv. ARTHUR J. FOGG, b. Sept. 11, 1881 ; living unm.

Children of CHARLES HENRY⁸, (1822) [1029] (Charles M.⁷, Joshua⁶, Benjamin⁵, John⁴, Robert³, Sergt. Abraham², Robert¹) and Mary G. (Fuller) Adams; res. Portland, Me.

    i. ELLA MARY⁹, b. in Portland, May 26, 1853 ; res. 15 Thomas St., Portland, Me.; unm.
    ii. CHARLES EDWIN⁹, b. in Portland, Dec. 18, 1855 ; res. New York, unm.
    iii. FRED WILLIAM⁹, b. in Portland, May 12, 1857 ; res. New York, unm.

ALICE ROWLAND McKELVEY, WIFE OF JAMES E. MELVILLE MILNE, AND THEIR CHILDREN, JANE HUNTINGTON, FRANCIS ROWLAND AND MARTHA McKELVEY.

Ninth Generation.] OF NEWBURY, MASS. 417

Children of ALMIRA[8], (18—) [1030] (Charles M.[7], Joshua[6], Benjamin[5], John[4], Robert[3], Sergt. Abraham[2], Robert[1]) and Dr. Byron Porter; res. Newport, Me.

    i. DR. CHARLES BYRON PORTER; m. Georgie Pulsifer; res. Oldtown or Orono, Me.
    ii. WOODBURY PORTER; m. Jennie Coffin; no issue.
    iii. DR. WM. PORTER.
        Dentist; Spring St., Deering District, Portland, Me.; no issue.

Children of JOHN QUINCY[8], (——) [1031] (Charles M[7], Joshua[6], Benjamin[5], John[4], Robert[3], Sergt. Abraham[2], Robert[1]) and Abby ——— Adams; res. Dix Island, Me.

    i. OSCAR[9].
    ii. WILLIAM[9].
    iii. ALBERT[9].
    iv. MINNIE[9], m. Amos Stevens.

Children of GEORGE E.[8], (——) [1032] (Charles M.[7], Joshua[6], Benjamin[5], John[4], Robert[3], Sergt. Abraham[2], Robert[1]) and Angie Jenison (Dixon) Adams; res. Dixmont, Penobscot Co., Me.

    i. CHARLES[9].
    ii. EVERETT[9].

Children of NELLIE[8], (——) [1033] (Charles M[7], Joshua[6], Benjamin[5], John[4], Robert[3], Sergt. Abraham[2], Robert[1]) and E. Woodward Whittemore; res. Fairfield, Me.

    i. JAMES O. WHITTEMORE.
        He is an editor and publisher in Bucksport, Me.

Children of ESTHER ELIZABETH[8], (1826) [1034] (Joshua[7], Jr., Joshua[6], Benjamin[5], John[4], Robert[3], Sergt. Abraham[2], Robert[1]) and Corydon Bacheller; res. Solon, Me.

    i. NORRIS C. BACHELLER, b. Sept. 26, 1856; m. Aug. 13, 1893, Olive A. Bean, dau. of Sylvanus and Susan (Austin) Bean, b. Sept. 13, 1865.
        He was postmaster of LaCrosse, Wis., in 1893; is a prominent Democratic citizen.

ii. FRED ELMER W. BACHELLER, b. Dec. 1861 ; d. in infancy.
iii. EMILY ELIZABETH BACHELLER, b. May 8, 1863; m. July 30, 1890, F. N. Smith, b. Aug. 10, 1856 ; res. Helena, Mont.

Child of LIEUT. ISAAC ROGERS[6], (1829) [**1035**] (Joshua[7], Jr., Joshua[6], Benjamin[5], John[4], Robert[3], Sergt. Abraham[2], Robert[1]) and Louisana Maynard (Hender) Adams; res. Wilton, Me.

1433. 1. ABBY LUELLA[9], b in Wilton. Jan. 23, 1855 ; m. (1) July 3, 1870, Volney Everard Young of Weymouth, Mass., b. in Buckfield, Me.; m. (2) Sept. 17, 1888, Frank Warren Low of Roxbury, Mass.; no issue.

Children of SERGT. JOSHUA RICHMOND[8], (1833) [**1036**] (Joshua[7], Jr., Joshua[6], Benjamin[5], John[4], Robert[3], Sergt. Abraham[2], Robert[1]) and Melvina Susan (Whitney) Adams ; res. Eustis, P. O., Stratton, Franklin, Co., Me.

i. MABEL V.[9], b. in Wilton, Me., Jan. 17, 1861 ; m. Allen W. Dunnell of Eustis, Me.
ii. BLANCHE E.[9], b. in Wilton, Mar. 25, 1864.
iii. SUSIE A.[9], b. in New Vineyard, Me., Sept. 25, 1874 ; d. 27 May, 1899.

Children of JOHN ALDEN SMITH, (1830) [**1037**] and Amy Elizabeth Wiggins; res. Boulder, Col.

i. CHILD ; d. in infancy.
ii. EMMA CARR SMITH, b. Oct. 4, 1856 ; m. Sept. 1875, William H. Thompson of Boulder, Col.

Children of MARY R. SMITH[8], (1849) [**1038**] and Isaac Walker; res. Pembroke, N. H.

i. RALPH ISAAC WALKER, b. Aug. 13, 1868 ; d. 21 Aug., 1869.
ii. MARY BLANCHE WALKER, b. May 22, 1870 ; m. Dec. 4, 1895, Dr. Edmund Hill ; res. Suncook, N. H.
iii. ARTHUR PARSONS WALKER, b. Sept. 17, 1872.
iv. FLORENCE JUDITH WALKER, b. June 25, 1880.

Children of BENJAMIN⁸, (1820) [**1039**] (Isaac⁷, Samuel⁶, Benjamin⁵, John⁴, Robert³, Sergt. Abraham², Robert¹) and Abbey (Hatch) Adams; res. E. Deering, Portland, Me.

    i. ABBEY SARAH⁹, b. in Gray; d. in Gray.
    ii. MARY ELLEN⁹, b. in Gray, Oct., 1846; d. in Portland, 29 Jan., 1870, age 23 yrs. 3 mos.
    iii. ANNIE KING⁹, b. in Gray, Sept., 1848; living at E. Deering, Portland, Me.; unm.
    iv. THOMAS HATCH⁹, b. in Gray; m. Sarah Bates of Chelsea, Mass.; He d. in Gray, Me.
    v. ELLA FRANCES⁹, m. July 14, 1875, in Portland, Fred A. Robinson; res. Denver, Col.
1434. vi. GEORGE WILLIS⁹, b. in Gray, Apr. 16, 1854; m. (1) July 8, 1879, in Portland, Hattie M. Cole, b. 1858; d. at Portland, 10 Apr., 1884; m (2) Jan. 6, 1892, Linda Frances Swett, dau. of Ferdinand M. and Irene F. (Kenney) Swett, b. in E. Deering, Jan. 19, 1859; living 1900; E. Deering, Portland, Me.
    vii. JESSIE FREMONT⁹, b. in Deering, Apr. 15, 1858. She was a teacher; d. in Gray, Me.; unm.
    viii. ISAAC CLARENCE⁹, b. 1859; d. in Portland, Me., unm., 27 Oct., 1877; age 18 years.
    ix. EFFIE⁹, d. young.

Children of JOHN SMITH⁸, (1825) [**1040**] (Isaac⁷, Samuel⁶, Benjamin⁵, John⁴, Robert³, Sergt. Abraham², Robert¹) and Sarah H. (Purington) Adams; res. Gray, Cumberland, Co., Me.

    i. CHARLES B.⁹, b. in Gray, Mar. 4, 1849; d. 2 Apr., 1850.
1435. ii. CHARLES S.⁹, b. in Gray, Apr. 7, 1851; m. Dec. 25, 1872, Almeda E. Skillings.
    iii. FRED L.⁹, b. in Gray, Nov. 6, 1856; m. Etta Lawrence.

Children of MARY ELIZABETH⁸, (1827) [**1041**] (Isaac⁷, Samuel⁶, Benjamin⁵, John⁴, Robert³, Sergt. Abraham², Robert¹) and William Elder; res. Gray, Cumberland Co., Me.

    i. EDDIE H. ELDER, b. Oct. 5, 1851; d. 29 Oct., 1861.
    ii. KATIE ALICE ELDER, b. Oct. 30, 1853; d. 3 Oct., 1854.

Child of HELEN⁸, (1830) [**1042**] (Isaac⁷, Samuel⁶, Benjamin⁵, John⁴, Robert³, Sergt. Abraham², Robert¹) and Stephen Huston; res. Gray, Cumberland Co., Me.

    i. EDGAR ISAAC HUSTON, b. in Gray, Nov. 19, 1860; living 1900; unm.

Child of ISAAC H.⁸, (1835) [1043] (Isaac⁷, Samuel⁶, Benjamin⁵, John⁴, Robert³, Sergt. Abraham², Robert¹) and Libbie (Field) Adams; res. Vale, Malhuer, Co., Ore.

    i. ERNEST E.⁹, b. in Reno, Nevada, Feb. 2, 1870 ; res. Vale, Ore.; unm.

Children of ROBERT ADAMS ALLEN, (1820) [1044] and Sarah E. Smith.

    i. AGNES LUCETTA ALLEN, b. Dec. 6, 1846 ; m. (1) Sept. 10, 1865, Whitman Lesley ; m. (2) Andrew Johnson of New York. Children: Kate and Maude Lesley.
    ii. ABBIE DORCAS ALLEN, b. June 13, 1848 ; m. June 13, 1865, Edw. Cobb. Children: Willard H. Cobb and Will Allen Cobb, b. Nov. 28, 1874.
    iii. KATE EDDA ALLEN, b. Aug. 29, 1850 ; m. Aug. 29, 1872, Geo. D. Skillings.
    iv. JOHN HUGH ALLEN, b. Jan. 16, 1854 ; m. Jennie Proctor. Children: Edith May and Geo. Proctor Allen.
    v. HANNAH ELIZABETH ALLEN, b. Feb. 28, 1856.
    vi. JOSEPH BENJAMIN ALLEN, b. Sept. 16, 1860 ; m. Annie Burnelle.
    vii. GEO. BAILEY ALLEN, b. Sept. 16, 1862.
    viii. ROBERT LESLEY ALLEN, b. Nov. 6, 1863 ; m. Georgie Gee.
    ix. WALLACE LINCOLN ALLEN, b. Jan 3, 1865 ; d. 15 May, 1873.
    x. CHAS. SMITH ALLEN, b. Jan. 1866 ; m. Minnie Field of Gray, Me.

Children of LORENZO BENSON⁸, (1836) [1046] (Silas Hall⁷, Samuel⁶, Benjamin⁵, John⁴, Robert³, Sergt. Abraham², Robert¹) and Clara Alice (Forsyth) Adams; res. Gray, Me., and Millbury, Mass.

1436. i. VIOLA BERTHA⁹, b. in Gray, Oct. 22, 1865 ; m. at Millbury, Sept. 9, 1886, Fred Kent Mackenzie, b. in Cambridge, Mass., Jan. 14, 1860 ; res. Shrewsbury, Mass.
1437. ii. SILAS HALL⁹, b. in Millbury, June 20, 1867 ; m. at Worcester, Mass., Mar., 1894, Mary Ann Evans, b. in England.
1438. iii. MARY ISABELLE⁹, b. in Sutton, Mass., June 19, 1868 ; m. at Charlton, Mass., June 7, 1892, Obed Wilbur, b. in Prince Edwards Island ; res. Millville, N. J.
    iv. HENRIETTE WOOD⁹, b. in Millbury, Nov. 28, 1869.

JAMES E. MELVILLE MILNE,
FIRST LIEUT. AND ADJT. OF THE SIXTH O. V. I., SPANISH WAR.

v. SELDEN C.⁹, b. in Millbury, May 12, 1876; res. Worcester, Mass.; unm.
vi. LULU⁹, b. in Millbury, Aug. 8, 1877; d. 26 Oct., 1877.

Children of SILAS LOWELL⁸, (1838) [1047] (Silas Hall⁷, Samuel⁶, Benjamin⁵, John⁴, Robert³, Sergt. Abraham², Robert¹) and Katherine Allen (Adams) Adams; res. W. Gray, Cumberland Co., Me.

    i. WILL HORTON⁹, b. in Gray (Corners), Sept. 30, 1861; m. Jan. 30, 1893, at Canton, Me., Elizabeth Mary Ryder, dau. of Charles D. and Eliza J. (Manning) Ryder, b. in Gray, Sept. 29, 1872; res. Portland, Me.; no issue.
    He is a clerk with Maine Steamship Co., Franklin Wharf.
    ii. FRANK FORRESTALL⁹, b. in W. Gray, May 12, 1876; res. Gray, Me.; unm.

Children of HANNAH SUSAN⁸, (1842) [1048] (Silas Hall⁷, Samuel⁶, Benjamin⁵, John⁴, Robert³, Sergt. Abraham², Robert¹) and John Walter Gray; res. Worcester, Mass.

    i. WALTER A. GRAY, b. in Worcester. Aug. 6, 1878; a salesman in Worcester; unm.
    ii. ERNEST GRAY, b. in Worcester, June 18, 1880; a salesman in Worcester; unm.

Children of JOHN⁸, (1844) [1049] (Silas Hall⁷, Samuel⁶, Benjamin⁵, John⁴, Robert³, Sergt. Abraham², Robert¹) and Eleanor J. (Wheeler) Adams; res. Worcester, Mass.

    i. NORRIS WHEELER⁹, b. Feb. 21, 1876; res. Worcester, Mass.; unm.
    ii. ALLEN LONGFELLOW⁹, b. Mar. 26, 1882.

Child of JOSHUA⁸,(——) [1050] (Samuel⁷, Samuel⁶, Benjamin⁵, John⁴, Robert³, Sergt. Abraham², Robert¹) and Maria A. (Brown) Adams; res. Portland, Cumberland Co., Me.

    i. FLORENCE B.⁹, b. in Portland, 1867; m. June 16, 1898, Charles H. Adams, son of Alfred and Catherine (Welch) Adams, b. in Portland, 1867; res. Portland, Me.

Child of ANDREW JACKSON⁸, (——) [**1051**] (Samuel⁷, Samuel⁶, Benjamin⁵, John⁴, Robert³, Sergt. Abraham², Robert¹) and —— ——; res. Falmouth, Cumberland Co., Me.
  i. LAURA E.⁹, m. [pub. Jan. 28, 1877] David F. Murdock; res. Portland, Me.

Child of CELIA ANNA⁸, (1851) [**1052**] (Isaiah⁷, Samuel⁶, Benjamin⁵, John⁴, Robert³, Sergt. Abraham²,'Robert¹) and Daniel M. Means; res. Merrimac, Mass.
  i. PHILIP CORYDON MEANS, b. in W. Amesbury, Mass., Oct. 11, 1872.
    He was graduated from Harvard Medical College, 1897, and settled as a practicing physician in Milford, Mass.

Child of CAPT. JACOB ADAMS COBB, (1818) [**1053**] and Sarah Matilda Hyde; res. Brooklyn, N. Y.
  i. MAGRETTA COBB, b. in Staten Island, N. Y., Oct. 16, 1842; d. 26 June, 1843.
  ii. SARAH MARIA COBB, b. in Brooklyn, Dec. 31, 1843; res. 15 Willoughby Ave., Brooklyn, N. Y.; unm.
  iii. CHAS. J. McGILL COBB, b. in Brooklyn, Apr. 14, 1846; res. Brooklyn.
  iv. HIRAM COBB 2D, b. in Brooklyn, Apr. 13, 1848; d. 13 Dec., 1852.
  v. WILLIAM H. COBB, b. in Portland, Me., Dec., 1855-6; d. 1872.

Children of CYNTHIA MARIA COBB, (1834) [**1054**] and Daniel Webster Ames; res. Portland, Me.
  i. CHARLES COBB AMES, b. Apr. 25, 1864; m. Sadie F. Conery of Deer Isle, Me.; res. So. Portland, Me.; one child, Grace W., b. Aug., 1887.
  ii. HATTIE YEATON AMES, b. Feb. 8, 1868; m. Aug. 24, 1891, Fred S. Smith; res. Portland, Me.; one child, Helen Ames Smith, b. Jan. 12, 1893.
  iii. MIRIAM ELLEN AMES, b. Jan. 11, 1872.

Children of COL. THOMAS A. ROBERTS, (1817) [**1055**] and Mary A. Frates; res. Portland, Me.
  i. CHARLES W. ROBERTS, b. Feb. 21, 1843; m. Oct. 4, 1864, Elizabeth Willington Clark, dau. of Freeman S. and Eleanor P. Clark, b. in Portland, Dec. 5, 1843; res. Portland, Me. Children:

1. Eleanor Clark Roberts, b. June 29, 1865 ; m. Mar. 1, 1887, Howard N. Leighton.
2. Herbert A. Roberts, b. May, 1870 ; m. June 24, 1891, Mildred J. Green, dau. of Wm. H. and Lizzie R. Green, b. in Portland, Sept. 12, 1869 ; res. Portland, Me.

ii. THOMAS FRATES ROBERTS, b. Apr. 25, 1844; m. Apr. 9, 1873, Sarah Warner, living 1900, 169 Oxford St. He d. in Portland, 10 Jan., 1897. Children.
1. Mary L. Roberts, b. Sept. 6, 1873.
2. Lucy F. Roberts, b. Nov. 16, 1874.

iii. GEO. HENRY ROBERTS, b. May 24, 1845; m. Aug. 4, 1870, Julia A. Coffey. He d. in Portland, 16 Jan., 1885. Children:
1. Thos. A. Roberts, b. Dec. 22, 1871.
2. Susan E. Roberts, b. Mar. 20, 1874.
3. Charles A. Roberts, b. Sept. 8, 1878.

iv. EDW. ROBERTS, b. Mar. 13, 1847; d. 8 Jan., 1849.
v. FREDERIC A. ROBERTS, b. Apr., 1848 ; d. 11 Aug., 1848.

Children of JAMES S. ROBERTS, (1822) [1056] and Abbie A Lord; res. Portland, Me.

i. HARRIET ISABELLA ROBERTS, b. Aug. 12, 1843.
ii. JAMES STETSON ROBERTS, b. Aug. 29, 1845 ; d. in Portland, 7 Feb., 1848.

Children of WILLIAM H. ROBERTS, (1826) [1057] and Irene B. Lane; res. Portland, Me.

i. EDWIN EUGENE ROBERTS, b. May 1, 1851 ; d. in the West.
ii. FREDERIC WM. ROBERTS, b. Mar. 12, 1853 ; m. Mar. 22, 1889, Clara L. Smith, b. in Hodgdon, Me.; res. Portland, Me.; no issue.

Children of SARAH W. ROBERTS, (1834) [1058] and George A. Merry; res. Cape Elizabeth, Me.

i. ALBERT MERRY, b. in Portland, Aug. 20, 1852.
ii. OSCAR MERRY, b. in Portland, Jan. 4, 1854.

Children of SARAH ELIZABETH[8], (1836) [1059] (John Watson[7], Benjamin Watson[6], Benjamin[5], John[4], Robert[3], Sergt. Abraham[2], Robert[1]) and Edward H. Phinney; res. Waltham, Mass.

i. EDWARD HALLETT PHINNEY, b. in Milford, Mass., Aug., 1872; d. soon.
　　　ii. EDWARD ADAMS PHINNEY, b. in Milford, Aug., 1873; d. May 1874.
　　　iii. MABEL INEZ PHINNEY, b. in Milford, July 7, 1875; res. Waltham, Mass.; unm.

Children of JOHN MERRIAM^8, (1834) [1060] (John Hall^7, Jacob^6, Stephen^5, William^4, Capt. Abraham^3, Sergt. Abraham^2, Robert^1) and Hattie (Bigelow) Adams; res. W. Lebanon, N. Y.

　　　i. JOHN ALBERT^9, b. in Minnesota, Feb. 15, 1862; was killed by the Indians, 4 Sept., 1861; the mother was held a prisoner by the Indians for 14 days and then released.
　　　ii. GEORGE NELSON^9, b. in Minnesota, Oct. 4, 1864; was a news-boy on the train, and was killed in a railroad accident at Pine City, Minn., 12 Aug., 1880.
　　　iii. CHARLES M.^{9}, b. in Anoka, Minn., Sept. 25, 1866.
　　　iv. FRANK S.^{9}, b. in Anoka, Mar. 14, 1869; m. Dec. 24, 1889, Ida May Braman, b. Mar. 2, 1870; d. 3 Dec., 1892, and left a dau. Ida M., b. Dec. 24, 1890, who was adopted by her grandfather.

Children of AARON^8, (1838) [1061] (Stephen^7, David^6, Stephen^5, William^4, Capt. Abraham^3, Sergt. Abraham^2, Robert^1) and Mary C. (Sigman) Adams; res. Salina, Saline Co., Kan.

1439.　i. GEORGE WILLIS^9, b. in Chanute, Kan., Nov. 29, 1870; m. Feb. 15, 1896, Harriet Elizabeth Dackins, dau. of John and Lorinda Dackins; res. Gypsum City, Kan.
　　　ii. LILLIAN ANGELINE^9, b. in Chanute, July 31, 1873.
　　　iii. CHARLES STEVENS^9, b. in Chanute, Apr. 12, 1875; d. soon.
　　　iv. MAMIE GRACE^9, b in Salina, Oct. 25, 1876.
　　　v. ANNIE GERTRUDE^9 (twin), b. in Salina, Oct. 25, 1876.

Children of MARIA^8, (1841) [1062] (Stephen^7, David^6, Stephen^5, William^4, Capt. Abraham^3, Sergt. Abraham^2, Robert^1) and John L. Wheelock; res. Spencer, Mass.

　　　i. WALTER ADAMS WHEELOCK, b. in Leicester, Mass., Feb. 22, 1871; d. 16 Mar., 1888.
　　　ii. WINNIFRED AGNES WHEELOCK, b. in Leicester, May 22, 1872; a teacher; unm.
　　　iii. MALINDA GERTRUDE WHEELOCK, b. Mar. 19, 1875; m. Dec. 13, 1899, Solon Mowry Gilbert, son of Wm. and Rosa Gilbert of W. Auburn, Mass.; res. Worcester, Mass.

Children of JANE EMILY[8], (1844) [1063] (Stephen[7], David[6], Stephen[5], William[4], Capt. Abraham[3], Sergt. Abraham[2], Robert[1]) and George M. Berkeley; res. Worcester, Mass.

    i. DAISY A. BERKELEY, b. in Dixon, Ill., Sept. 30, 1871.
    ii. IMO M. BERKELEY, b. in Dixon, Feb. 23, 1873; d. 4 Jan., 1894.
    iii. MAUDE L. BERKELEY, b. in Dixon, May 11, 1877.

Children of GEORGE[8], ( ) [1064] (David[7], David[6], Stephen[5], William[4], Capt. Abraham[3], Sergt. Abraham[2], Robert[1]) and Charlotte (James) Adams; res. Leicester, Mass.

    i. LEWIS WILLIAM[9], b. in Leicester, July, 17, 1863.
    ii. GEORGE E.[9], b. in Leicester, Oct. 20, 1866.

Children of CHARLES WOOD[8], (1847) [1065] (Moses[7], David[6], Stephen[5], William[4], Capt. Abraham[3], Sergt. Abraham[2], Robert[1]) and Lucy J. (Bowen) Adams; res. Unique, Humbolt Co., Ia.

    i. ERNEST EUGENE[9], b. in Humbolt Co., June 11, 1876; unm.
    ii. INFANT (twin), b. in Humbolt Co., June 11, 1876; d. same day.
    iii ALBERTUS MILTON[9], b. in Humbolt Co, Aug. 15, 1878; unm.
    iv. HARRY JUDSON[9], b. in Humbolt Co., Jan. 3, 1882.
    v. EDITH ELSIE[9], b. in Humbolt Co., June 9, 1890.

Children of GEORGE W.[8], (1851) [1066] (Moses[7], David[6], Stephen[5], William[4], Capt. Abraham[3], Sergt. Abraham[2], Robert[1]) and Rose Reed (Smith) Adams; res. Bradgate, Humbolt Co., Ia.

    i. ARCHIE[9], b. May 5, 1888.
    ii. LEOLA[9], b. Mar. 28, 1890.
    iii. ROY[9], b. Dec. 15, 1891.

Children of JOSEPHINE[8], (1856) [1067] (Moses[7], David[6], Stephen[5], William[4], Capt. Abraham[3], Sergt. Abraham[2], Robert[1]) and Charles W. Bowen; res. Bradgate, Humbolt Co., Ia.

    i. CLARENCE A. BOWEN, b. Sept. 8, 1879.
    ii. WILLIAM E. BOWEN, b. Dec. 2, 1880.

iii. LUCY M. BOWEN, b. May 13, 1885.
iv. BESSIE B. BOWEN, b. Aug. 23, 1888.
v. NELLIE B. BOWEN, b. June 4, 1891.

Children of MARY ELIZA GRAFF[8], (1847) [1068] and Joseph Drabble; res. Leicester, Mass.

i. ARTHUR ALBERT DRABBLE, b. May 29, 1873; m. Apr. 15, 1896, Nellie H. Cole of Worcester, Mass.; res. Lynn, Mass.
ii. ABBIE MABEL DRABBLE, b. Apr. 7, 1876; m. Jan. 12, 1897, Geo. B. Magoon; res. Lynn, Mass.
iii. GEORGE J. DRABBLE, b. Mar. 1, 1880; res. Leicester, Mass.

Children of DELIA M.[8], (1849) [1069] (John Q.[8], David[6], Stephen[5], William[4], Capt. Abraham[3], Sergt. Abraham[2], Robert[1]) and George D. Corey; res. Lowell, Mass.

i. MABEL B. COREY, b. May 4, 1875.
ii. EDITH M A. COREY, b. May 16, 1878.
iii. MILTON R. COREY, b. Oct. 24, 1879.

Children of JANE B.[8], (1853) [1070] (John Q.[7], David[6], Stephen[5], William[4], Capt. Abraham[3], Sergt. Abraham[2], Robert[1]) and Wm. Merrill Welch; res. Helenville, Deer Lodge Co., Mont.

i. LIZZIE J. WELCH; m. J. F. Fellows of Westville, Vt.
ii. WALTER WELCH.
iii. ORANGE H. WELCH.
iv. HAYNES WELCH.
v. CHARLES WELCH.
vi. RONEY WELCH.
vii. MARK WELCH.
viii. ZELMA WELCH.
ix. BARTLETT WELCH.

Children of ELIZA WILSON, (1807) [1071] and Rev. Jonathan Holt, D. D.; res. Weston, W. Va.

i. MARY LOUISE HOLT, b. in Beaver, Pa., Dec 3, 1828; m. Sept. 18, 1849, in Weston, W. Va., Benja. W. Byrne, Esq., an attorney of Sutton, now a prominent man of Charleston, W. Va.

ii. HON. HOMER ALONCIOUS HOLT, b. in Parkersburg, W. Va., Apr. 27, 1831; m. Jan. 27, 1857, at Sutton, Va., Mary Ann Byrne. He d. at his home in Lewisburg, W. Va., 7 Jan., 1898.

He was a soldier of the Confederacy; was elected a judge in the Circuit Court in 1872, in which capacity he served with honor and ability for 16 years. He was appointed to the Supreme Court in 1890, and served six years. Although reserved and retiring he is pronounced one of the ablest judges of the Supreme Court, who left the impress of his wisdom and learning in the state constitution which he assisted in framing. His son, John Homer Holt, is the nominee for governor of West Virginia, 1900, on the Democratic ticket.

iii. SUSAN ELIZA HOLT, b. in Weston, W. Va., Jan. 13, 1834; m. Sept. 11, 1855, Dr. Thos. Bland Camden of Sutton, W. Va., b. Aug. 16, 1829; graduated from Jefferson Medical College, Philadelphia; was Superintendent of the West Virginia Insane Asylum, 1871 to 1881; afterward settled in Parkersburg, W. Va., where Mrs. Camden still resides. She has assisted in compiling these records.

Children of DR. ROBERT ADAMS WILSON, (1809) [1072] and Sarah Ann J. (Brown) Wilson; res. Pittsburg, Pa.

i. MARY REBECCA WILSON, b. in Pittsburg, Feb. 10, 1841; m. Aug. 28, 1862, Lorenzo Dow Smith. She d. in Cincinnati, O., 27 May, 1893, leaving one son and three daughters.

ii. OREGON WILSON, b. in Pittsburg, May 12, 1843.

He was an artist and portrait painter, educated in New York and Europe, and painted the portraits of many prominent men. He enlisted in the army, first, as Aide to Col. Rowley of the 13th Pennsylvania Infantry, and again in the 10th Pennsylvania Reserves, and was honorably discharged. He d. unm. at Santa Barbara, Cal., 27 Sept., 1873; was buried in Alleghany Cemetery, Pittsburg, Pa.

iii. DR. MILO ADAMS WILSON, b. in Pittsburg, July 4, 1845; m. Sept. 30, 1875, Ada Canda of Brooklyn, N. Y.

He enlisted as Drum Major in the 63d Pennsylvania Volunteers, Col. Hayes, and afterward as Hospital Steward of Knapp's Battery, Pennsylvania Volunteers. He studied medicine and served as post surgeon in the forts at Newbern and Charleston, S. C., and later practiced his profession in New York. He resided for a time at Denver, Col., but returned to New York, and d. 6 July, 1882; was interred in Greenwood Cemetery. His widow and a dau., Natalie C., survive him.

iv. THEODORE DEHON WILSON, b. in Pittsburg, Sept. 18, 1849. He is unm. and is employed as a clerk in the Naval Office, Custom House, New York, the only surviving member of his family.

v. VIRGINIA BEATRICE WILSON, b. in Pittsburg, June 25, 1852; d. in New York, 22 Feb., 1875; unm.; was interred in Alleghany Cemetery, Pittsburg, Pa.

Children of SAMUEL BEATY WILSON, (1811) [1073] and Julia Ann (Lyon) Wilson; res. Washington, D. C.

  i. ELECTA MARIA WILSON. b. Sept. 30, 1837; m. Jan. 1, 1856, Geo. McKee of Pittsburg, Pa., and d. 18 Jan., 1858, leaving one son.
  ii. JAMES LYON WILSON, b. Mar. 8, 1839.
      He enlisted in Co. F, 10th Pennsylvania Reserves, and was killed in the first battle at Fredericksburg, Va.
  iii. ELIZA WILSON, b. Apr. 12, 1842; d. 12 Dec., 1842.
  iv. ROBERT ADAMS WILSON, b. Sept. 15, 1843; m. Margaret J. Dravo, dau. of Capt. John F. Dravo, an iron merchant of Pittsburg and Beaver, Pa. Robert A. Wilson d. Jan., 1881.
  v. ERASTUS SMITH WILSON, b. Sept. 10, 1845; d. 21 Aug., 1847.
  vi. ATLAS E. WILSON, b. Mar. 4, 1848; d. 23 July, 1848.
  vii. LOUISA CATHERINE WILSON (twin), b. Mar. 4, 1848; living, unm., in Washington, D. C.
  viii. HARRIET MARIA WILSON, b. Jan. 5, 1850; d. 1864.

Children of THOMAS McKEAN WILSON, (1813) [1074] and Elizabeth Henderson Murdock; res. Moberly, Randolph Co., Mo.

  i. MARY WILSON; m. Rev. J. L. Polk of Fagg's Manor, Pa.
  ii. ALEX. MURDOCK WILSON.
      He was 2d Lieut. of Co. G, 140th Pennsylvania Volunteers; killed in the battle of Gettysburg, 2 July, 1863.
  iii. ELIZA WILSON; m. J. A. Wray; he d. Aug., 1894; res. 525 Fisk Ave., Moberly, Mo.
  iv. ANNIE WILSON; m. W. B. Stewart of Canonsburg, Pa.
  v. ROBERT ADAMS WILSON; m. Mary Porter Hollins of Nashville, Tenn.
  vi. JOHN GOW WILSON; res. Moberly, Mo.; unm.
  vii. LOUIS WILSON; d. in Canonsburg, Pa., at 2½ years of age.
  viii. VIRGINIA MURDOCK WILSON; m. J. Q. Mason; res. Tacoma, Wash.
  ix. LOUIS MAXWELL WILSON; res. Tacoma, Wash.; unm.
  x. JAMES WILSON; d. in Canonsburg, Pa., age 9 months.
  xi. EDWIN STANTON WILSON; m. Margaret Bryan; res. Mexico, Mo.

Children of MARY ANN O. WILSON, (1815) [1075] and Dr. Newton Bennett Barnes; res. Weston, W. Va.

i. SOPHRONIA M. BARNES, b. at Weston, Oct. 14, 1846; d. in Weston, 9 Feb., 1881.
ii. HARRIET M. BARNES, b. in Weston; m. Jan. 23, 1872, Marshall T. Frame, an attorney of Sutton, W. Va. They had:
  1. Newton Bennett Frame, b. in Sutton, W. Va., June 29, 1874.
  2. Mary Plumer Frame, b in Weston, Oct. 2, 1880.
  3. Chas. Duffield Frame, b. in Weston, July 21, 1882.
  4. Thos. Adams Frame, b. in Wheeling, W. Va., Oct. 28, 1884.
iii. MARY MATILDA BARNES, b. in Weston; m. Rev. Theodore N. Eaton of the M. E. Church. They had:
  1. Paul Eaton.
  2. Oliver Knight Eaton.
  3. Nina Eaton.
iv. PAULINA WILSON BARNES, b. in Weston, Sept. 20, 1852; m. Apr. 29, 1879, Chas. O'Hara, merchant. They had:
  1. Charles Albert O'Hara, b. in Weston, Oct. 8, 1884.
  2. Roscoe O'Hara, b. in Weston, Aug. 18, 1888.
v. JOHN ADAMS BARNES, b. in Weston, Nov. 2, 1854; m. June 3, 1884, Mary Emma Bodley of Wheeling; res. Weston, W. Va.; a general merchant. They had:
  1. Maude Wilson Barnes, b. in Weston, Mar. 5, 1889.
  2. Mary Anna Barnes, b. in Weston, Nov. 2, 1893.

Children of ELIZA ANN[8], (1815) [**1076**] (Dr. Milo[7], Dr. Samuel[6], Capt. Benjamin[5], William[4], Capt. Abraham[3], Sergt. Abraham[2], Robert[1]) and Hon. John Allison; res. Greenville, Pa.

i. MARY JOHNSON ALLISON, b. Dec. 6, 1836; m. Apr. 19, 1860, Chas. M. Merrick of New Brighton, Pa. She d. 12 June, 1894.
ii. JAMES ALLISON, b. July 7, 1840; m. Mar. 9, 1864, Pricilla Stewart of New Brighton. He d. 30 Sept., 1894.
iii. LOUISA ALLISON. b. Jan. 10, 1843; m. Aug. 17, 1869, George O. Keck; res. Greenville, Pa.
iv. ANNA C. ALLISON, b. May 10, 1845; m. Oct. 16, 1875, Wm. H. Beil; res. Greenville, Pa.
v. ELIZA ANN ALLISON, b. Feb. 15, 1848; m. Aug. 15, 1872, W. O. Tillotson of Greenville, Pa.
vi. MIRA JOHNS ALLISON, b. Sept. 4, 1850; d. 19 June, 1855.
vii. JOHN H. ALLISON, b. June 4, 1853; m. Feb. 22, 1885, Martha Roe; res. Butler, Mo.

Children of OSCAR EDMUND[8], (1818) **[1077]** (Dr. Milo[7], Dr. Samuel[6], Capt. Benjamin[5], William[4], Capt. Abraham[3], Sergt. Abraham[2], Robert[1]) and Helen M. (Easton) Adams; res. Oil City, Venango Co., Pa.

  i. MILO R.[9], b. in Bridgewater, Pa., Apr. 9, 1847; m. Oct. 26, 1871, Nettie Culbertson. They have two children, Fannie and Forest.

1440. ii. MARY T.[9], b. in Bridgewater, May 25, 1848; m. June 13, 1872, Francis McKinney.

1441. iii. CYNTHIA B.[9], b. in Bolivar, Pa., Jan. 26, 1850; m. Jan. 19, 1876, Frederick Zerald Trax; res. Meadville, Pa.

  iv. DAVID E[9], b. in Bolivar, July 18, 1852; m. in 1877, Lucinda Wilson. Children:
    1. Harry.
    2. Zerald I.
    3. Oscar E.
    4. Frank M.

  v. MYRA H.[9], b. in Bolivar, Feb. 27, 1854; m. Sept., 1895, Benjamin Plumer. Two children, deceased.

  vi; OSCAR E.[9], b. in Bolivar, Apr. 20, 1855; m. Apr., 1876, Lillie Rectenus. Six children:
    1. Edmund.
    2. Tray.
    3. Helen.
    4. Laura.
    5. John.
    6. Frank.

  vii. ELIZA A.[9], b. in Bolivar, Dec. 25, 1856; d. 18 Apr., 1857.

  viii. ELVIRA D.[9], b. in Bolivar, Jan. 1, 1859; d. May, 1859.

  ix. FANNIE L.[9], b. in Bolivar, Jan. 30, 1860; d. 24 Dec., 1865.

  x. SAMUEL P.[9], b. in New Era, Pa., Sept. 17, 1861; m. Nancy Davis. Two children, Clara and Myra.

  xi. ROBERT A.[9], b. in Oil City, Pa., Oct. 1, 1863; d. 24 Dec., 1864.

  xii. ARNOLD P.[9], b. in Oil City, Nov. 5, 1865; m. 1887, Elizabeth King. Four daughters.
    1. Margaret.
    2. Theo.
    3. Mary.
    4. Cynthia.

  xiii. JAMES E.[9], b. in Oil City, Jan. 28, 1867.

  xiv. JOHN A.[9], b. in Oil City, Mar. 30, 1869; d. 6 Apr., 1898.

Ninth Generation.] OF NEWBURY, MASS. 431

Children of MIRA HALL,[8] (1820) [1078] (Dr. Milo[7], Dr. Samuel[6], Capt. Benjamin[5], William[4], Capt. Abraham[3], Sergt. Abraham[2], Robert[1]) and Leonard S. Johns; res. Pittsburg, Pa.

1442. i. CLARENCE MARSHALL JOHNS, b. Mar. 7, 1843 ; m. Sept. 30, 1869, Martha S. Robinson.
1443. ii. LEONARD EDGAR JOHNS, b. Jan. 1, 1846 ; m. Mar. 16, 1872, Valeria M. Whiteley, dau. of Gen. R. H. K. Whiteley and Hester, his wife ; insurance agent, Pittsburg, Pa.
    iii. BLANCHE JOHNS, b. Feb. 2, 1842 ; d. unm. 5 Apr., 1874.
1444. iv. CORA IDA JOHNS, b. May 5, 1854 ; m. June 13, 1876, Rev. H. O. Gibbons, D. D. of Philadelphia.
    v. EUGENE WILLIS JOHNS, b. Sept 23, 1847 ; d. 1854.
    vi. ERNEST STANLEY JOHNS, b. Oct. 29, 1849 ; d. 1854.
    vii. IMOGENE JOHNS, b. Oct. 21, 1856 ; d. unm. 16 Feb., 1876.
    viii. ESTELLA JOHNS, b. Apr. 24, 1859 ; unm.
1445. ix. HERBERT ADAMS JOHNS, b. Feb. 5, 1864 ; m. Dec. 31, 1891 Rebecca Torrens.

Children of CAPT. MILO ROMULUS,[8] (1833) [1079] (Dr. Milo[7], Dr. Samuel[6], Capt. Benjamin[5], William[4], Capt. Abraham[3], Sergt. Abraham[2], Robert[1]) and Emma (Weyand) Adams; res. Washington, D. C.

    i. JESSIE STAFFORD[9], b. Apr. 6, 1872 ; m. William S. Anderson ; res. Washington, D. C.
    ii. BERTHA HART[9], b. Dec. 19, 1875.
    iii. CYNTHIA DARRAGH[9], b. Mar. 19, 1880.

Children of VICTORIA[8], (1837) [1080] (Dr. Milo[7], Dr. Samuel[6], Capt. Benjamin[5], William[4], Capt. Abraham[3], Sergt. Abraham[2], Robert[1]) and Jacob Weyand ; res. Beaver, Pa.

    i. EMMA WEYAND, b. in Carrolton, O., Mar. 28, 1858 ; m. at Beaver, Pa., Dec. 17, 1884, Harry W. Reens ; res. Beaver Falls, Pa.
    ii. SON, b. and d. 1859.
    iii. SON (twin), b. and d. 1859.
    iv. MILO A. WEYAND, b. Oct., 186·' ; d. 4 Jan., 1863.
    v. EDWIN S. WEYAND, b. in W. Bridgewater, Pa., Oct. 27, 1862 ; m. at Marion, O., Apr. 15, 1896, Wilhelmina Thompson. They have 4 children ; res. Beaver, Pa.

Children of ISADORE M.[8], (1842) [1081] (Dr. Milo[7], Dr. Samuel[6], Capt. Benjamin[5], William[4], Capt. Abraham[3], Sergt. Abraham[2], Robert[1]) and James S. McKelvey; res. Alleghany, Pa.
   i. EUGENE ADAMS McKELVEY; in school.
  ii. MARION DISK McKELVEY; in school.

Children of CYNTHIA DARRAGH[8], (1844) [1082] (Dr. Milo[7], Dr. Samuel[6], Capt. Benjamin[5], William[4], Capt. Abraham[3], Sergt. Abraham[2], Robert[1]) and Col. Alexander W. Taylor; res. Beaver, Pa.
   i. LAURA M. TAYLOR, b. in Beaver, Apr. 22, 1867; m. July 15, 1886, Dr. Lewis M. Cobble. Four children: Nellie, Olive, Charles N., and George A.; res. Midway, Tenn.
  ii. OLIVE TAYLOR, b. in Beaver, June 1, 1869; unm.; res. Beaver, Pa.
 iii. DR. CHARLES STOW TAYLOR, b. in Norwalk, O., June 11, 1872; m. Nov., 1898, Willie M. Dorris of Tracy City. He is a dentist in Tracy City, Tenn.; one dau., Dorris Taylor.

Children of HON. OLIVER JAMES DICKEY[8], (1823) [1083] and Elizabeth Shenk; res. Lancaster, Pa.
   i. MARY ELVIRA DICKEY, b. in Lancaster, Sept. 10, 1858; m. Richard E. Cochran of York, Pa. She d. 30 Aug., 1887; no issue.
  ii. ELIZABETH DICKEY, b. in Lancaster, June 17, 1860; d. unm. 24 Oct., 1879.
 iii. JOHN DICKEY, b. in Lancaster, May 20, 1865; m. Ada Retalik.
  iv. ANNA DICKEY, b. in Lancaster, Nov. 3, 1872; m. Oct. 18, 1893, Wm. H. Keller. Children:
       1. Daniel S., b. Aug. 15, 1894.
       2. Elizabeth Dickey, b. Dec. 4, 1895.
       3. Oliver James, b. Feb. 9, 1898.

Children of SOCRATES ADAMS DICKEY, (1827) [1084] and Diana Wolfe; res. Fallston, Beaver Co., Pa.
   i. JOHN B. DICKEY, b. Dec. 30, 1857; m. Margareta L. Philips, b. May 1, 1865.
  ii. GEO. E. DICKEY, b. Oct. 20, 1859; m. Maggie Laurimore.
 iii. H. ANNA DICKEY, b. Oct. 16, 1861; m. Robert Forbes.
  iv. ERNEST DICKEY, b. Oct. 25, 1863.

Ninth Generation.]   OF NEWBURY, MASS.   433

  v. SOCRATES DICKEY, b. Aug. 21, 1866 ; m. ———- Thompson.
  vi. ALASKA DICKEY, b. May 8, 1868.
  vii. MARK DICKEY, b. May 8, 1870.
  viii. MINNIE F. DICKEY, b. June 4, 1874.

Child of ELIZABETH DICKEY, (1829) [**1085**] and Eli Reno; res. New Brighton, Pa.

  i. ELVIRA SOPHIA RENO, b. Sept. 8, 1856 ; d. 29 Sept., 1878.

Child of ELVIRA DICKEY, (1834) [**1086**] and Daniel O'C. Patterson; res. Beaver Falls, Pa.

  i. JOHN DICKEY PATTERSON, b. Feb. 12, 1858.
  ii. ELIZA PATTERSON, b. Oct. 28, 1859 ; d. 9 Dec., 1863.
  iii. GRACE PATTERSON, b. Mar. 5, 1868.
  iv. JAMES O'CONNELL PATTERSON.
  v. ELVIRA PATTERSON, b. Apr. 21, 1872.

Children of SOPHRONIA DICKEY, (1837) [**1087**] and Andrew Marquis.

  i. ELVIRA MARQUIS, b. Oct. 18, 1859 ; m. Henry Ellwood.
  ii. LYDIA MARQUIS, b. Oct. 4, 1861 ; m. Robert Donald Brothers.
  iii. CHARLES F. MARQUIS, b. Sept. 15, 1862 ; m. ——— Hurd of Oneida, N. Y.
  iv. MERTHYNE MARQUIS, b. Dec. 29, 1863 ; d. 12 June, 1866.

Child of MAJ. CHARLES JOHN DICKEY, (1839) [**1088**] and Lavalette Davidson.

  i. A SON, b. 1885.

Children of THADDEUS STEVENS DICKEY, (1847) [**1089**] and Sue E. Metzger; res. Lancaster, Pa., and Minneapolis, Minn.

  i. ELVA E. DICKEY, b. Nov. 10, 1875 ; res. Minneapolis, Minn.
  ii. MAUDE DICKEY, b. Mar. 4, 1877 ; d. 22 Aug., 1877.
  iii. THADDEUS R. DICKEY, b. May 2, 1879 ; d. 10 July, 1880.
  iv. SUE M. DICKEY, b. Nov. 22, 1882.
(28)

Children of MERCY P. BEALL, (1830) [**1090**] and J. B. Bausman; res. Bountiful, Utah.
   i. FRANK BAUSMAN, b. Nov. 1, 1851.
   ii. LILLIE BAUSMAN (twin), b. Nov. 1, 1851 ; d. at New Lisbon, O., 4 Oct., 1853.
   iii. JULIE BAUSMAN, b. Sept. 22, 1853.
   iv. HARRY BAUSMAN, b. May 15, 1856 ; d. in Iowa, 12 June, 1856.

Children of SOCRATES A. BEALL, (1832) [**1091**] and Mary A. Boyle; res. Golden Lake, Mississippi Co., Ark.
   i. DANNIE BEALL, b. Oct. 18, 1855.
   ii. MERCY BEALL, b. Sept. 15, 1857.
   iii. DAVIE BEALL, b. Sept. 15, 1860.
   iv. LIZZIE BEALL, b. Mar. 18, 1862.
   v. MILO BEALL, b. Oct. 6, 1867 ; d. 5 Oct., 1868.
   vi. JESSIE BEALL, b. Oct. 5, 1869 ; d. 5 Sept., 1871.
   vii. J. B. BEALL, b. Mar. 14, 1872.

Child of JESSIE E BEALL, (1844) [**1092**] and Maj. Emory S. Foster; res. St. Louis, Mo.
   i. JESSIE FOSTER, b. in Missouri, Jan. 13, 1865.

Child of ELE W. BEALL, (1847) [**1093**] and Camilla Townsley; res. Kansas.
   i. CAMILLA BEALL, b. in Minneapolis, Minn., Apr. 24, 1875.

Children of EDGAR B.[8], (1838) [**1094**] (Samuel Plumer[7], Dr. Samuel[6], Capt. Benjamin[5], William[4], Capt. Abraham[3], Sergt. Abraham[2], Robert[1]) and Barbara (Trumble) Adams; res. Caseville, Huron Co., Mich.
   i. IDA[9], b. in Salem, O., Sept. 28, 1864 ; unm.; res. Salem, O.
   ii. GEORGE T.[9], b. in Salem, Oct., 1867 ; d. in infancy.

Children of CAPT. HORATIO NELSON⁸, (1842) [1095] (Samuel Plumer⁷, Dr. Samuel⁶, Capt. Benjamin⁵, William⁴, Capt. Abraham³, Sergt. Abraham², Robert¹) and America (Cornwell) Adams; res. Louisville, Ky.

 i. MARIE PANSEE⁹, b. in Salem, O., May 7, 1871; m. Samuel Dalrymple; res. Alexandria, Ind.
 ii. ELLEN LEOTA⁹, b. in Louisville, Dec. 29, 1876.

Children of COL. MILTON B.⁸, (1845) [1096] (Samuel Plumer⁷, Dr. Samuel⁶, Capt. Benjamin⁵, William⁴, Capt. Abraham³, Sergt. Abraham², Robert¹) and Anna Waters (Lewis) Adams; res. Nashville, Tenn.

 i. CARL NELSON⁹, b. in Cleveland, O., Feb. 22, 1879.
  He is a member of Michigan University.
 ii. LEWIS MILTON⁹, b. in Erie, Pa., May 22, 1882.
  He is in West Point Military Academy.

Child of ELMA⁸, (1848) [1097] (Samuel Plumer⁷, Dr. Samuel⁶, Capt. Benjamin⁵, William⁴, Capt. Abraham³, Sergt. Abraham², Robert¹) and Thomas Tanner; res. Louisville, Ky.

 i. ADAMS PLUMER TANNER, b. in Sharon, Pa., July 10, 1876.
  He is a graduate of the Case School of Science, Cleveland, O., and is a mechanical engineer; res. Pittsburg, Pa.

Children of SAMUEL PLUMER,⁸ (1850) [1098] (Samuel Plumer⁷, Dr. Samuel⁶, Capt. Benjamin⁵, William⁴, Capt Abraham³, Sergt. Abraham², Robert¹) and Fanny Catherine (Powers) Adams; res. Milwaukee, Wis.

 i. OLA MAY⁹, b. in Louisville, Ky., Nov. 12, 1877; m. Oct. 11, Chas. McPharren, Mayor of Caddo, Indian Territory.
 ii. ELMA LUCILLE⁹, b. in Calhoun, Tenn., Jan. 26, 1880.
 iii. FANNIE CATHERINE⁹, b. in Erie, Pa., July 11, 1882.
 iv. LEALA⁹, b. in Burlington, Vt., Apr 30, 1891.

Children of LIZZIE⁸, (1848) [1099] (Abraham⁷, Benjamin⁶, Capt. Benjamin⁵, Abraham⁴, Capt. Abraham³, Sergt. Abraham², Robert¹) and Clarence Davis; res. Cambridge, Mass.

[Ninth Generation.

i. LIZZIE FREDERIKA DAVIS, b. in Georgetown, Mass., Aug. 15, 1871.
ii. CLARA EVELINE DAVIS, b. in Cambridge, Nov. 8, 1882; d. 27 July, 1883.
iii. JOHN CLARENCE DAVIS, b. in Cambridge, July 14, 1887.

Children of ELLEN E.[8], (1835) [**1100**] (Charles Henry[7], Benjamin[6], Capt. Benjamin[5], Abraham[4], Capt. Abraham[3], Sergt. Abraham[2], Robert[1]) and Augustus M. Spofford; res. Danvers, Mass.

i. FRANK MALVIN SPOFFORD, b. Oct. 13, 1854; m. Oct. 27, 1880, Clara Todd; res. Danvers, Mass.
ii. CHARLES AUGUSTUS SPOFFORD, b. Apr., 1865; res. Danvers, Mass.; unm.

Child of CHARLES HENRY[8], (1837) [**1101**] (Charles Henry[7], Benjamin[6], Capt. Benjamin[5], Abraham[4], Capt. Abraham[3], Sergt. Abraham[2], Robert[1]) and Elizabeth P. (Hawkes) Adams; res. Lynn, Mass.

i. ALICE PUTNAM[9], b. in Danvers, Mass., June 18, 1860; m. Nov. 23, 1892, Geo. F. Banford, son of Sidney and Abbie W. Banford, b. June 6, 1862; res. Lynn, Mass; no issue.

Children of LUCY ELIZABETH[8], (1850) [**1105**] (Geo. Fitz[7], Col. Samuel[6], Elder David[5], Samuel[4], Capt. Abraham[3], Sergt. Abraham[2], Robert[1]) and George A. Proctor; res. Hopkinton, Mass.

i. GEORGE ADAMS PROCTOR, b. in Derry, N. H., Sept. 21, 1870; m. Mar. 14, 1894, Daisy Danforth; res. formerly Manchester, N. H.
ii. ABIGAIL CHOATE PROCTOR, b. in So. Boston, Dec. 26, 1879; unm.
iii. JOHN CHOATE PROCTOR, b. about 1896.

Children of GEORGE WILLIAM[8], JR., (1855) [**1106**] (George William[7], Col. Gibbins[6], Stephen[5], Samuel[4], Capt. Abraham[3], Sergt. Abraham[2], Robert[1]) and Lizzie Maria (Dow) Adams; res. So. Byfield, Mass.

i. RAYMOND MORRISON DOW[9], b. in Byfield, Oct. 30, 1876.
He is a student of theology, Episcopal School, Cambridge.
ii. EVA MARGUERITE[9], b. in Byfield, May 21, 1884.

Children of HENRY DUMMER[8], (1851) [1107] (Albert S.[7], Stephen[6], Capt. Stephen[5], Samuel[4], Capt. Abraham[3], Sergt. Abraham[2], Robert[1]) and Mabel (Weld) Adams; res. Jamestown, N. Dak.

    i. LE ROY WESLEY[9], b. Nov. 30, 1879; d. 18 Jan., 1880.
    ii. INFANT DAUGHTER[9], b. Sept. 9, 1882; d. 12 Sept., 1882.

Child of NORMAN ILSLEY[8], (1864) [1108] (Henry Sewall[7], Sewall[6], Capt. Stephen[5], Samuel[4], Capt. Abraham[3], Sergt. Abraham[2], Robert[1]) and Mabel E. (George) Adams; res. Winthrop, Mass.

    i. NORMAN ILSLEY[9], b. in Winthrop, Sept. 20, 1895.

Child of WILLIAM RICHARDSON[8], (1863) [1109] (Capt. John Quincy[7], Sewall[6], Capt. Stephen[5], Samuel[4], Capt. Abraham[3], Sergt. Abraham[2], Robert[1]) and A. Jenette (McConnell) Adams; res. (Beachmont) Revere, Mass.

    i. HATTIE MAY[9], b. in E. Boston, Mass.

Child of WILLIAM RICHARDSON[8], (1863) and Addie Kent (Smythe) Adams.

    ii. HESTER FORSYTHE[9], b. in Chelsea, Ma .

Children of ALBERT E.[8], (1866) [1110] (George W.[7], John[6], Joseph[5], Rev. Joseph[4], Capt. Abraham[3], Sergt. Abraham[2], Robert[1]) and Bertha A. (Webster) Adams; res. Newton, Mass.

    i. GEORGE W.[9], b. Sept. 1. 1889.
    ii. FRANK L.[9], b. Mar. 30, 1891.

Child of CHARLES F.[8], (1872) [1111] (George W.[7], John[6], Joseph[5], Rev. Joseph[4], Capt. Abraham[3], Sergt. Abraham[2], Robert[1]) and Lilla (Nevens) Adams; res. Lowell, Mass.

    i. ESTHER[9], b. in Lowell, Dec. 29, 1897.

Children of WALTER[8], (1867) [**1113**] (John William[7], Rev. John Folsom[6], Lieut. John[5], Rev. Joseph[4], Capt. Abraham[3], Sergt. Abraham[2], Robert[1]) and Mabel Cynthia (Chapman) Adams; res. Springfield, Mass.

    i. ETHEL LURA[9], b. in Springfield, June 29, 1894.
    ii. RUTH MARION[9], b. in Springfield, Apr. 10, 1897.

Child of ALBERT HAMILTON[8], (1863) [**1114**] (Col. Charles Henry[7], Rev. Charles[6], D. D., Lieut. John[5], Rev. Joseph[4], Capt. Abraham[3], Sergt. Abraham[2], Robert[1]) and Carrie (Allen) Adams; res. Chicago, Ill.

    i. HOWARD ALLEN[9], b. in Oak Park, Ill., Mar. 9, 1893.

Children of JOHN BENJAMIN F.[8], (1868) [**1115**] (Joseph Nichols[7], Benjamin Webb[6], Joseph[5], Rev. Benjamin[4], Capt. Abraham[3], Sergt. Abraham[2], Robert[1]) and Josephine (Noonan) Adams; res. Mattapan, Mass.

    i. JOHN FAIRFIELD[9], b. in Roslindale, Mass., Aug. 26, 1895.
    ii. ROBERT NICHOLS[9], b. in Roslindale, Dec. 3, 1896.
    iii. BENJAMIN WEBB[9], b. in Mattapan, Mass., Apr. 22, 1898.

Child of JULIA ANN S.[8], (1839) [**1116**] (William[7], Enoch[6], Enoch[5], Henry[4], Capt. Abraham[3], Sergt. Abraham[2], Robert[1]) and Hiram Dustin Abbott; res. So. Andover, Me.

    i. HERMAN D. ABBOTT, b. in So. Andover, Nov. 2, 1868.
        He is an employe in a shoe factory at Haverhill, Mass.; unm. in 1898.

Child of JOSEPH EMERY[8], (1841) [**1117**] (William[7], Enoch[6], Enoch[5], Henry[4], Capt. Abraham[3], Sergt. Abraham[2], Robert[1]) and Irene Jane (Sampson) Adams; res. Augusta, Me.

1446. i. GRACE IRENE[9], b. in Augusta, Me., Oct. 20, 1872; m. Dec. 24, 1891, Wm. Albert Gilbert of Camden, Pa.; set. in Camden, Pa.; rem. 1895, to Chicago, Ill.

Child of JOSEPH EMERY⁸, (1841) and Alba Sarah (Tubbs) Adams; res. Mechanic Falls, Me.

1447. ii. NELLIE ALBA⁹, b. in Mechanic Falls, Dec. 6, 1874; m. Dec. 6, 1893, Edwin G. Skillings of Norway, Me.

Child of JOSEPH EMERY⁸, (1841) and Elsie Rhoda (Sampson) Adams; res. Vineland, N. J.

iii. CLARA EVELYN⁹, b. in Vineland, May 21, 1895.

Children of CHARLES HALL⁸, (1844) [1118] (William⁷, Enoch⁶, Enoch⁵, Henry⁴, Capt. Abraham³, Sergt. Abraham², Robert¹) and Marion Virginia (Reed) Adams; res. Norway, Me.

1448. i. CHARLES CLIFFORD⁹. b. in So. Andover, Me., Sept. 15, 1868; m. (1) Apr. 27, 1890, Irene May Curtis of W. Paris, Me.; divorced; m. (2) July 3, 1896, Mamie Moffat of Gorham, Me.
He left Maine as a member of the 1st Maine Regt., May 27, 1898.

1449. ii. ABBIE EVELYN⁹, b. in Mechanic Falls, Me., Oct. 20, 1876; m. Feb. 28, 1894, Walter Shepard Chandler of Bethel, Me.; res. Norway, Me.

iii. MARION VIRGINIA⁹, b. in Fairfield, Me., Dec. 24, 1883; d. 20 Apr., 1884.

Child of WILLIAM HENRY⁸, (1846) [1119] (William⁷, Enoch⁶, Enoch⁵, Henry⁴, Capt. Abraham³, Sergt. Abraham², Robert¹) and Enna Maria (Goodrich) Adams; res. W. Paris, Me.

i. EVA MAY⁹, b. in So. Andover, May 12, 1882.

Children of LUCINDA ELLA⁸, (1848) [1120] (William⁷, Enoch⁶, Enoch⁵, Henry⁴, Capt. Abraham³, Sergt. Abraham², Robert¹) and William Jones; res. So. Andover, Me.

i. MANER ALBA JONES, b. Mar. 26, 1872; d. 3 Nov., 1890.
ii. WILLIE SCOTT JONES, b. June 16, 1873; d. 18 Oct., 1873.

Children of ENOCH⁸, (1850) [1121] (William⁷, Enoch⁶, Enoch⁵, Henry⁴, Capt. Abraham³, Sergt. Abraham², Robert¹) and Mary Falkner (Martin) Adams; res. Poland, Me.

i. RALPH ENOCH⁹, b. in Poland, Aug. 1, 1881.
ii. ROY POWERS⁹, b. in Poland, Nov. 1, 1882.
iii. HAROLD MERLE⁹, b. in Poland, July 15, 1888.

Children of LIZZIE EMMA[8], (1852) [1122] (William[7], Enoch[6], Enoch[5], Henry[4], Capt. Abraham[3], Sergt. Abraham[2], Robert[1]) and Chester Howard Lane; res. W. Paris, Me.

    i. JOHN WILLIAM LANE, b. Mar. 4, 1878 ; d. 11 Apr., 1878.
    ii. CHESTER HOWARD LANE, b. July 2, 1880.
    iii. LOLA ADAMS LANE, b. Feb. 4, 1886.

Children of MARY EDNA[8], (1855) [1123] (William[7], Enoch[6], Enoch[5], Henry[4], Capt. Abraham[3], Sergt. Abraham[2], Robert[1]) and Andrew Wm. Bridge; res. Mechanic Falls, Me.

    i. LOTTIE MAY BRIDGE, b. Jan. 2, 1879 ; d. 28 Feb., 1879.
    ii. ANDREW WILLIAM BRIDGE, b. Nov. 15, 1880; d. 7 Mar., 1881.
    iii. INA MILDRED BRIDGE, b. Aug. 23, 1883 ; d. 3 May, 1884.
    iv. HARRY SIGOURNEY BRIDGE. b. Mar. 13, 1885.
    v. EVIS HAZLE BRIDGE, b. Nov. 16, 1886.
    vi. VINTON ANDREW BRIDGE, b. Oct. 18, 1889.
    vii. MARY ADAMS BRIDGE, b. Apr. 23, 1895.

Children of MATILDA McCLUNE[8], (1858) [1124] (William[7], Enoch[6], Enoch[5], Henry[4], Capt. Abraham[3], Sergt. Abraham[2], Robert[1]) and Calvin Curtis Yates; res. Mechanic Falls, Me.

    i. LENA LUCINDA YATES. b. Oct. 6, 1879 ; d. 13 Nov., 1894.
    ii. EVA ADAMS YATES, b. in Lawrence, Mass., Mar. 31, 1883.
    iii. OLEN VINCENT YATES, b. in Mechanic Falls, Me., Sept. 23, 1885.

Children of ENOCH C.[8], (1852) [1125] (Dr. Enoch[7], Jr., Enoch[6], Enoch[5], Henry[4], Capt. Abraham[3], Sergt. Abraham[2], Robert[1]) and Emma A. (Huff) Adams; res. W. Newton, Mass. *d. June 6, 1933*

    i. MARY D.[9], b. in Beverly, Mass., July 2, 1881.
    ii. EDITH H.[9], b. in Beverly, Nov., 1882.
    iii. SCHUYLER[9], b. in New Britain, Conn., June, 1893. *d. Aug. 10, 1921*
    iv. KATHERINE[9], b. in New Britain, June, 1897.

Two of these children living 1933 Mrs. Hubert L. Carter, Mrs. Melville H. Haskell

Child of DR. M. VINTON[7], (1853) [1126] (Dr. Enoch[7], Jr., Enoch[6], Enoch[5], Henry[4], Capt. Abraham[3], Sergt. Abraham[2], Robert[1]) and Aroline (Plumer) Adams; res. Brunswick, Me.

    i. WATMOUGH S. A.[9], b. in Brunswick.

Child of HERMAN H.⁸, (1856) [**1127**] (Dr. Enoch⁷, Jr., Enoch⁶, Enoch⁵, Henry⁴, Capt. Abraham³, Sergt. Abraham², Robert¹) and Hattie M. (Taylor) Adams; res. Belgrade, Me.

 i. J. R. or J. P., b. in Belgrade, Feb., 1879.

Child of HERMAN H.⁹, (1856) and Effie (Philbrick) Adams.

 ii. MARY LULU, b. in Belgrade, Jan., 1887.

Children of MARY LENORA⁸, (1859) [**1128**] (Dr. Enoch⁷, Jr., Enoch⁶, Enoch⁵, Henry⁴, Capt. Abraham³, Sergt. Abraham², Robert¹) and Prof. Bradford O. McIntire; res. Kent's Hill, Me.

 i. LEON ADAMS McINTIRE, b. June 19, 1887.
 ii. MARJORIE McINTIRE, b. Oct., 1889.
 iii. JOHN VINTON McINTIRE, b. Dec. 24, 1891.

Children of LULU G.⁸, (1865) [**1129**] (Dr. Enoch⁷, Jr., Enoch⁶, Enoch⁵, Henry⁴, Capt. Abraham³, Sergt. Abraham², Robert¹) and Prof. Lyon L. Norton; res. Mt. Herman, Northfield, Mass.

 i. MARY NORTON, b. Aug. 23, 1886.
 ii. STEPHEN ADAMS NORTON, b. Dec. 17, 1897.

Child of META LENA⁸, (1872) [**1130**] (Dr. Enoch⁷, Jr., Enoch⁶, Enoch⁵, Henry⁴, Capt. Abraham³, Sergt. Abraham², Robert¹) and Maynard Maxim; res. Holyoke, Mass.

 i. METATENA MAXIM, b. Nov. 6, 1896.

Children of SARAH MOODY⁸, (1830) [**1131**] (John Emery⁷, Col. John Emery⁶, Enoch⁵, Henry⁴, Capt. Abraham³, Sergt. Abraham², Robert¹) and Jared Hurd; res. Glenville, Cuyahoga Co., O.

 i. MARY BRAINARD HURD, b. Dec. 18, 1852; m. Feb. 13, 1878, William Mandenhall; res. Collinwood, Cuyahoga Co., O.
 ii. DR. CHARLES EMERY HURD, b. June 19, 1859; m. Dec. 11, 1884, Evelyn P. Kelly; res. Cleveland. O., P. O., "Sta. C."
  He is a dentist and Professor of Prosthetic Dentistry in the Dental College of Western Reserve University; no issue.

Children of JOHN EMERY⁸, (1833) [**1132**] (John Emery⁷, Col. John Emery⁶, Enoch⁵, Henry⁴, Capt. Abraham³, Sergt. Abraham², Robert¹) and Jemima (Powell) Adams; res. Solon, Johnson Co., Iowa.

1450.   i. CORA J.⁹, b. in Warensville, O., Sept. 27, 1860; m. Oct. 8, 1884, Jared Brown, b. near Solon, July 5, 1861; res. Solon, Ia.
    ii. CADIS F.⁹, b. in Warrensville, May 10, 1862; d. 15 Aug., 1866.
    iii. EMERY D.⁹, b. in Belmont, O., Aug. 28, 1864; d. 9 Sept., 1865.
1451.   iv. ETHIE L.⁹, b. in Van Buren, O., Jan. 4, 1868; m. Nov. 14, 1889, Alonzo Brown, b. in Solon, Oct. 15, 1850, cousin of Jared, above; res. Solon, Ia.
1452.   v. HARRY DELVA⁹, b. in Van Buren, Nov. 22, 1870; m. Nov. 14, 1894, Virginia Bacon; res. Solon, Ia.
    vi. BERDIE⁹, b. near Solon, Ia., Apr. 25, 1874; d. 21 May, 1874.

Children of HARRIET B.⁸, (1836) [**1133**] (John Emery⁷, Col. John Emery⁶, Enoch⁵, Henry⁴, Capt. Abraham³, Sergt. Abraham², Robert¹) and William M. Warren; res. Cleveland, O., and West Liberty, Iowa.

    i. FREDERICK M. WARREN, b. Apr. 5, 1858; m. Feb. 13, 1884, Mary Adams, dau. of Moses and Sarah J. (Keisler) Adams; res. W. Liberty, Ia. Children:
        1. Ernest M. Warren, b. Nov. 27, 1884.
        2. William Warren, b. 1886.
        3. Roland Warren, b. 1889.
        4. Cora L. Warren, b. Aug. 24, 1893.
    ii. ADDIE L. WARREN, b. May 1, 1866; d. 24 Aug., 1883.
    iii.* WILLIAM ADAMS WARREN, b. Aug. 25, 1868; m. Sept. 8, 1898, Nellie A. Moore; res. W. Liberty, Ia.

Children of ALANTHA M.⁸, (1841) [**1134**] (John Emery⁷, Col. John Emery⁶, Enoch⁵, Henry⁴, Capt. Abraham³, Sergt. Abraham², Robert¹) and Cyrus P. Bell; res. Stafford, Genesee Co., N. Y.

    i. CLARA BELL, b. Aug. 5, 1865.
        She graduated from Normal School, 1890.
    ii. HARRIET BELL, b. Jan. 29, 1868.
        She graduated from the Genesee Normal School in 1890, and is now a teacher.
    iii. HOWARD BELL (twin), b. Jan. 29, 1868; unm.
    iv. FLORENCE BELL, b. Dec. 2, 1869; unm.

Children of LILLIS D⁶, (1844) [**1135**] (John Emery⁷, Col. John Emery⁶, Enoch⁵, Henry⁴, Capt. Abraham³, Sergt. Abraham², Robert¹) and Dr. John L. Bean; res. Bedford, Cuyahoga Co., O.

    i. GEORGIE EMMA BEAN, b. Mar. 1, 1867; d. Oct., 1875.
    ii. DR. HOWARD H. BEAN, b. Feb. 17, 1871.
        He graduated from Hiram College, and from the Cleveland Homeopathic Medical College and set. in Fremont, O.; unm.
    iii. JOHN CORWIN BEAN, b. Jan. 12, 1874.
        He was educated at Hiram College.
    iv. SHERWOOD ADAMS BEAN, b. May 8, 1878.
        He was educated in Buchtel College, Akron, O., and is studying law in Medina, O.
    v. CLARENCE DALE BEAN, b. Feb. 28, 1881.
        He is a graduate of the Bedford High School, class of 1899, and and is a professional musician.

Children of MARY B.⁶, (1845) [**1136**] (John Emery⁷, Col. John Emery⁶, Enoch⁵, Henry⁴, Capt. Abraham³, Sergt. Abraham², Robert¹) and Demetriss Judd; res. Paullina, O'Brien Co., Ia.

    i. LILLIAN A. JUDD, b. in Ohio, Jan. 27, 1871; m. Mar. 19, 1890, Cassius C. Moffit, son of Alexander and Martha Moffit, b. Aug. 4, 1864; d. at Paullina, Ia., 8 Jan., 1897.
    ii. FRANK D. JUDD, b. in Mechanicsville, Ia., Feb. 22, 1874; res. Paullina, Ia.
    iii. MAE BELL JUDD, b. in Mechanicsville, July 31, 1876.
    iv. HARRIET M. JUDD, b. in Mechanicsville, Feb. 4, 1879.
    v. HOWARD G. JUDD, b. in Mechanicsville, Mar. 23, 1881.

Child of DECATUR C.⁸, (1837) [**1137**] (Eben Moody⁷, Col. John Emery⁶, Enoch⁵, Henry⁴, Capt. Abraham³, Sergt. Abraham², Robert¹) and Lydia (Passmore) Adams; res. Mansfield, Wright Co., Mo.

    i. EBEN H.⁹, b. Mar., 1871; d. 5 May, 1889.

Children of JOHN LYNN⁸, (1852) [**1138**] (Eben Moody⁷, Col. John Emery⁶, Enoch⁵, Henry⁴, Capt. Abraham³, Sergt. Abraham², Robert¹) and Isabelle (Keen) Adams; res. Solon, Johnson Co., Ia.

i. GEORGIA⁹, b. in Solon, Nov. 27, 1877.
ii. RICHARD K.⁹, b in Solon, Jan. 23, 1882.
iii. ROBERT PERRY⁹, b. in Solon, July 29, 1886.

Children of LILLIE⁸, (1856) [1139] (Eben Moody⁷, Col. John Emery⁶, Enoch⁵, Henry⁴, Capt. Abraham³, Sergt. Abraham², Robert¹) and Herbert S. Farrell; res. Iowa City, Ia.

i. SNOWDON FARRELL, b. May 4, 1878.
ii. HENRIETTA FARRELL, b. Dec. 2, 1879.

Child of HELEN E.⁸, (1842) [1140] (Enoch⁷, Col. John Emery⁶, Enoch⁵, Henry⁴, Capt. Abraham³, Sergt. Abraham², Robert¹) and Abner D. Ruchel; res. Whitehall, Ill.

i. CARROLL RUCHEL, b. Apr. 9, 1872; m. Oct. 8, 1894, Nora Mutinger; res. Whitehall, Ill.

Child of GEORGIE⁸, (1844) [1141] (Enoch⁷, Col. John Emery⁶, Enoch⁵, Henry⁴, Capt. Abraham³, Sergt. Abraham², Robert¹) and Dwight W. Rockwell; res. 97 Rosedale Ave., Cleveland, O.

i. HELEN BELL ROCKWELL, b. July 20, 1890.

Children of IDA E.⁸, (1849) [1142] (Enoch⁷, Col. John Emery⁶, Enoch⁵, Henry⁴, Capt. Abraham³, Sergt. Abraham², Robert¹) and Orville Robertson; res. E. Liverpool, O.

i. BESSIE L. ROBERTSON, b. in Akron, O., Apr. 14, 1874; m. June 24, 1896, John Sargent; res. Cleveland, O.
ii. FREDERICK ROBERTSON, b. in Cleveland, O., Dec. 24, 1880.

Children of CORA⁸, (1857) [1143] (Moses⁷, Col. John Emery⁶, Enoch⁵, Henry⁴, Capt. Abraham³, Sergt. Abraham², Robert¹) and Joseph Walker; res. Iowa City, Ia.

i. FRED M. WALKER, b. Nov. 26, 1884; d. 6 Apr., 1893.
ii. BERNICE WALKER, b. Aug. 25, 1889; d. 13 Dec., 1891.
iii. MYRON WALKER, b. Sept. 5, 1892.
iv. RALPH WALKER, b. Apr. 22, 1896.

Ninth Generation.] OF NEWBURY, MASS. 445

Children of MARY[8], (1861) [1144] (Moses[7], Col. John Emery[6], Enoch[5], Henry[4], Capt. Abraham[3], Sergt. Abraham[2], Robert[1]) and Fred M. Warren; res. W. Liberty, Ia.
    i. ERNEST MOSES WARREN, b. Nov. 29, 1884.
    ii. WILLIAM JOSEPH WARREN, b. Dec. 25, 1886.
    iii. ROLAND WARREN, b. May 9, 1891.
    iv. CORA LUCILE WARREN, b. Aug. 24, 1893.

Children of ADA P.[8], (1857) [1145] (James Monroe[7], Col. John Emery[6], Enoch[5], Henry[4], Capt. Abraham[3], Sergt. Abraham[2], Robert[1]) and Albert Hemingway; res. Plato, Cedar Co., Ia.
    i. ELWOOD N. HEMINGWAY, b. May 4, 1880.
    ii. MONROE A. HEMINGWAY, b. Nov. 6, 1882.
    iii. GRANT HARRY HEMINGWAY, b. Nov. 18, 1884.
    iv. LINNIE HEMINGWAY, b Sept. 17, 1886.
    v. ABBIE GRACE HEMINGWAY, b. Apr. 12, 1888.
    vi. EMERY HEMINGWAY, b. Sept. 7, 1891.
    vii. MAY HEMINGWAY, b. 1894.
    viii. EVA HEMINGWAY, b. Aug. 11, 1896 ; d. 24 Jan., 1897.

Children of LYDIA E.[8], (1858) [1146] (James Monroe[7], Col. John Emery[6], Enoch[5], Henry[4], Capt. Abraham[3], Sergt. Abraham[2], Robert[1]) and Audry Hemingway; res. Plato, Cedar Co., Ia.
    i. IRENE M. HEMINGWAY, b. Jan. 5, 1879 ; d. 7 June, 1891.
    ii. MABEL S. HEMINGWAY, b. June 3, 1881 ; d. 29, Sept , 1883.

Children of EVA C.[8], (1860) [1147] (James Monroe[7], Col. John Emery[6], Enoch[5], Henry[4], Capt. Abraham[3], Sergt. Abraham[2], Robert[1]) and Edward Askey; res. Maryville, De Kalb Co., Mo.
    i. HAZEL S. ASKEY, b. 1888.
    ii. LEE ASKEY, b. 1889.
    iii. ELLIS M. ASKEY, b. 1891.
    iv. ADA B. ASKEY, b. 1893.
    v. TONY ASKEY, b. 1894 ; d. soon.

Child of JENNIE B.⁸, (1864) [**1148**] (James Monroe⁷, Col. John Emery⁶, Enoch⁵, Henry⁴, Capt. Abraham³, Sergt. Abraham², Robert¹) and Harry Gaymon; res. Oasis, Johnson Co., Ia.
    i. ETHEL GAYMON, b. 1891.

Child of DAVID WESTON⁸, (1835) [**1149**] (David Farnham⁷, Dr. Joseph⁶, Enoch⁵, Henry⁴, Capt. Abraham³, Sergt. Abraham², Robert¹) and Sarah J. (Virgin) Adams; res. Caribou, Aroostook Co., Me.
    i. FRANKIE⁹, b. in Caribou; d. young.

Children of DAVID WESTON⁸, (1835) and Amanda Maria (Brown) Adams.

1453.   ii. CHARLES LINCOLN⁹, b. in Caribou, Aug. 14, 1863; m. Nov. 24, 1892, Annie Eunice Bailey.
        He is a dry-goods merchant; res. New Haven, Conn.
  iii. ADELBERT WESTON⁹, b. in Caribou, Aug. 3, 1868.
        He is salesman; res. Lynn, Mass.
  iv. FLORUS FARNUM⁹, b. in Caribou, Jan. 21, 1871; a book-keeper in Boston, Mass.

Children of MARTHA BOLSTER⁸, (1850) [**1150**] (David Farnum⁷, Dr. Joseph⁶, Enoch⁵, Henry⁴, Capt. Abraham³, Sergt. Abraham², Robert¹) and Lysander Sawin; res. Sherman, Aroostook Co., Me.
    i. OLIVE BLANCHE SAWIN; d. age 3 years.
    ii. JOSEPHINE HORTENSE SAWIN.
        she is a violinist, and teacher.
    iii. BERT HART SAWIN; an ingenious boy.

Children of JOHN STURGIS⁸, (1844) [**1151**] (Erasmus Darwin⁷, Dr. Joseph⁶, Enoch⁵, Henry⁴, Capt. Abraham³, Sergt. Abraham², Robert¹) and Phebe Beckley Adams; res. Waterloo, Blackhawk Co., Ia.

1454.   i. JESSIE⁹, b. in Waterloo, Mar. 3, 1873; m. Mar. 18, 1891, Geo. B. Mock; res. Los Angeles, Cal.

ii. JENNIE⁹ (twin), b. in Waterloo, Mar. 3, 1873.
iii. KATIE STURGIS⁹, b. in Waterloo, June 13, 1876 ; d. in San Diego, Cal., 4 Dec., 1889.
iv. ERASMUS DARWIN⁹, b. in Waterloo, Aug. 10, 1877.
v. JOHN ABRAHAM⁹, b. in Waterloo, Nov. 5, 1881.
vi. ANNA MAY⁹, b. in Waterloo, Aug. 30, 1884.

Children of HENRY FARNUM⁸, (1846) [1152] (Erasmus Darwin⁷, Dr. Joseph⁶, Enoch⁵, Henry⁴, Capt. Abraham³, Sergt. Abraham², Robert¹) and Harriet M. (Clark) Adams; res. Newtonia, Mo., and Prescott, Ariz.

i. HERBERT C.⁹, b. in Newtonia, July 29, 1875.
ii. AMOS DARWIN⁹, b. in Newtonia, Sept. 15, 1877.
iii. CHARLES H.⁹, b. in Newtonia, July 23, 1879.
iv. MABEL H.⁹, b. in Newtonia, July 16, 1881.

Children of AMOS DARWIN⁸, (1848) [1153] (Erasmus Darwin⁷, Dr. Joseph⁶, Enoch⁵, Henry⁴, Capt. Abraham³, Sergt. Abraham², Robert¹) and Catherine A. (Dunning) Adams; res. Prescott, Ariz.

i. HELEN RANSOM⁹, b. in Prescott, Nov. 17, 1873.
ii. ALICE DUNNING⁹, b. in Prescott, Aug. 11, 1886.
iii. HENRY FARNUM⁹, b. in Prescott, Aug. 25, 1889.
iv. ARTHUR STURGIS⁹, b. in Prescott, Sept. 26, 1890.

Children of ARDILACY STURGIS⁸, (1864) [1154] (Erasmus Darwin⁷, Dr. Joseph⁶, Enoch⁵, Henry⁴, Capt. Abraham³, Sergt. Abraham², Robert¹) and Ernest W. Schreiner; res. McAlister, Ind. Ter.

i. GERTRUDE ADAMS SCHREINER, b. Aug. 15, 1891.
ii. ERNEST WILLIAM SCHREINER, b. Aug. 30, 1893.
iii. CARL S. SCHREINER, b. Oct. 2, 1896.

Children of CLARA FRANCES⁸, (1851) [1155] (Warren Mann⁷, Dr. Joseph⁶, Enoch⁵, Henry⁴, Capt. Abraham³, Sergt. Abraham², Robert¹) and Virgil E. Fuller; res. Rumford, Me.

i. DELIA FRANCES FULLER, b. Sept. 2, 1871 ; d. 6 Jan., 1876.
ii. HATTIE ELLIOT FULLER, b. Dec. 28, 1873; d. 12 Mar., 1893.
iii. NETTIE PEABODY FULLER (twin), b. Dec. 28, 1873; m. Jan. 7, 1892, Wm. H. Freeman ; res. Rumford, Me.
iv. HERBERT EUGENE FULLER, b. Jan. 31, 1876 ; d. 18 June, 1894.
v. MARY ADRIAN FULLER, b. Nov. 2, 1884.

Children of DELIA HILL[8], (1854) [1156] (Dr. Henry Milgrove[7], Dr. Joseph[6], Enoch[5], Henry[4], Capt. Abraham[3], Sergt. Abraham[2], Robert[1]) and John L. Eichholtz; res. Blunt, Hughes Co., So. Dak.

i. MABEL CLARA EICHHOLTZ, b. Aug. 17, 1876 ; d. 1 Sept., 1891.
ii. LIZZIE MARY EICHHOLTZ, b. Sept. 5, 1882.

Children of MARY WILLIS[8], (1857) [1157] (Dr. Henry Milgrove[7], Dr. Joseph[6], Enoch[5], Henry[4], Capt. Abraham[3], Sergt. Abraham[2], Robert[1]) and William T. Gibson; res. Luverne, Rock Co., Minn.

i. THOMAS LYNN GIBSON.
ii. WILLIAM HENRY GIBSON.

Children of EMMA ISABEL[8], (1856) [1158] (Augustus Hollowell[7], Moses[6], Enoch[5], Henry[4], Capt Abraham[3], Sergt. Abraham[2], Robert[1]) and Edward Leonard Noyes; res. Hampton, N. H.

i. HARRY ADAMS NOYES, b. Sept. 17, 1880.
ii. CARRIE ALVIRA NOYES, b. Mar. 20, 1882.

Children of LEWIS EMERY[8], (1858) [1159] (John Quincy[7], William[6], Enoch[5], Henry[4], Capt. Abraham[3], Sergt. Abraham[2], Robert[1]) and Emma (Davis) Adams; res. Haverhill, Mass.

i. GEORGE AUGUSTUS[9], b. in Haverhill, June 12, 1889.
ii. FRANK ELMORE[9], b. in Haverhill, July 31, 1891.

Children of FRANK DRESSER⁸, (1859) [**1160**] (John Quincy⁷, William⁶, Enoch⁵, Henry⁴, Capt. Abraham³, Sergt. Abraham², Robert¹) and Minnie (Bemis) Adams; res. Waltham, Mass.

    i. HELEN⁹, b. in Waltham.
    ii. MABEL⁹, b. in Waltham.
    iii. GRACE⁹, b. in Waltham.

Children of HARRIET NEWHALL⁸, (1818) [**1161**] (Isaac⁷, Samuel⁶, Jr., Col. Samuel⁵, Samuel⁴, Isaac³, Sergt. Abraham², Robert¹) and Healey Morse; res. Penacook, N. H.

    i. FRANCIS HEALEY MORSE, b. in Danvers, Mass., Apr. 11, 1841; m. at Boscawen, N. H., Dec. 14, 1875, Armenia J. Whitney of Boscawen, N. H.
1455. ii. HARRIET AUGUSTA MORSE, b. in Danvers, Mar. 25, 1844; m. at Penacook, N. H., Mar. 11, 1868, Frederick J. Gage; res. Boston, Mass.
1456. iii. GEORGE A. MORSE, b. in Danvers, Sept. 21, 1847; m. at Boscawen, N. H. Dec. 7, 1871, Ella G. Kimball of Boscawen, N. H.; res. Penacook, N. H.
    iv. ALBERT H. MORSE, b. in Salisbury, N. H., Oct. 23, 1849; d. at Penacook, N. H., 4 July, 1875.
    v. JAMES MADISON MORSE, b. in Salisbury, Mar. 11, 1853; m. at Lebanon, N. H., Sept. 23, 1879, Martha A. Hardy of Lebanon.
    vi. MARY E MORSE, b. in Penacook, Aug. 22, 1858; res. Penacook, N. H.; unm.

Children of CHARLES H.⁸, (1820) [**1162**] (Isaac⁷, Samuel⁶, Jr., Col. Samuel⁵, Samuel⁴, Isaac³, Sergt. Abraham², Robert¹) and Mary (Lank) Adams; res. Salem, Mass.

1457. i. HON. CHARLES FRANCIS⁹, b. in Salem, Dec. 25, 1848; m. Mar. 20, 1873, Mary Elizabeth Cone.
        He is an engineer, an Odd Fellow, and an alderman; res. Lynn, Mass.
1458. ii. MARY ALICE⁹, b. in Salem, Sept. 13, 1853; m. Jan. 21, 1885, Walter F. Peck, son of Freeman S. Peck; res. Salem, Mass.

Children of MARY KIMBALL⁸, (1822) [**1163**] (Isaac⁷, Samuel⁶, Jr., Col. Samuel⁵, Samuel⁴, Isaac³, Sergt. Abraham², Robert¹) and Charles Chubb; res. Lynn, Mass.

i. LIZZIE P. CHUBB, b. Aug., 1845.
   She was adopted by James Rogers, Groveland, Mass., and died of consumption.
ii. CHARLES L. CHUBB, b. Feb. 2, 1847 ; m. Ann ——
   He was a soldier in the civil war ; res. E. Dover, Vt.
iii. OLIVER CHUBB, b. Jan., 1852 ; d. young.
iv. ANETTA A. CHUBB, b. Nov. 5, 1855 ; m. Apr. 17, 1872, Increase C. Brown ; res. Haverhill, Mass.

Child of ENOCH⁸, (1824) [**1164**] Isaac⁷, Samuel⁶, Jr., Col. Samuel⁵, Samuel⁴, Isaac³, Sergt. Abraham², Robert¹) and Caroline A. (Perkins) Adams: res. Georgetown, Mass.

i. LOWELLA STANWOOD⁹, b. in Georgetown, July 26, 1847; m. Mar. 19, 1866, Samuel Thurlow Poor, a grocer of Haverhill, Mass.

Children of EMILY A.⁸, (1837) [**1165**] (Isaac⁷, Samuel⁶, Jr., Col. Samuel⁵, Samuel⁴, Isaac³, Sergt. Abraham², Robert¹) and Samuel T. Perry ; res. Groveland, Mass.

i. HATTIE M. PERRY, b. 1857 ; m. 1877, Charles Abbott ; res. Braggville, Mass.
ii. ANNIE PERRY, b. Oct., 1861 ; m. 1881, Albert Abbott ; res. Stoneham, Mass.
iii. LEWIS G. PERRY, b. 1864 ; m. 1884, Etta Colby ; res. Haverhill, Mass.

Children of CAPT. JOHN GREGORY B.⁸, (1841) [**1166**] (Isaac⁷, Samuel⁶, Jr., Col. Samuel⁵, Samuel⁴, Isaac³, Sergt. Abraham², Robert¹) and Mary E. (Dodge) Adams; res. Lynn, Mass.

i. WILLIAM MUMFORD⁹, b. Aug. 28, 1869 ; d. 2 Feb., 1871.
ii. MARTHA LENA⁹, b. Feb. 17, 1875 ; d. 19 Sept., 1875.

Children of SALLY D.⁸, (1826) [**1167**] (Enoch⁷, Samuel⁶, Jr., Col. Samuel⁵, Samuel⁴, Isaac³, Sergt. Abraham², Robert¹) and Henry B. Huntress; res. Groveland, Mass.

i. ARABELLA J. HUNTRESS⁹, b. in Groveland, May 29, 1850 ; m. July, 1870, Eugene Brown, now deceased.
ii. CLARA A. HUNTRESS⁹, b. in Groveland, Dec. 6, 1853 ; m. Edward Reynolds; he d. 1889.
iii. HENRY LEWIS HUNTRESS, b. in Groveland, Aug. 3, 1857 ; m. Feb. 11, 1893, Carrie T. Pike of Salisbury, Mass.

Children of ROBERT W.⁸, (1829) [1168] (Enoch⁷, Samuel⁶, Jr., Col. Samuel⁵, Samuel⁴, Isaac³, Sergt. Abraham², Robert¹) and Hannah P. (Chase) Adams; res. Groveland, Mass.

    i. LIZZIE L.⁹, b. in Groveland, Mar. 22, 1853; d. unm. 7 Aug., 1895.
    ii. JOSEPH G.⁹, b. in Groveland, Dec. 28, 1855; m, Jan. 20, 1872, Annie P. Jones; 4 children; res. Salem, Mass.

1459. iii. EDWARD F.⁹, b. in Groveland, 1857; m. Mary Parker, dau. of Simon Parker; res. Groveland, Mass.

Children of PATIENCE T.⁸, (1830) [1169.] (Enoch⁷, Samuel⁶, Jr., Col. Samuel⁵, Samuel⁴, Isaac³, Sergt. Abraham², Robert¹) and George H. Chase; res. Groveland, Mass.

    i. SARAH J. CHASE, b. 1853; d. 6 July, 1870, age 16 years.
    ii. CHARLES W. CHASE, b. Jan., 1855, d. 12 Apr., 1858.
    iii. CHARLES M. CHASE, b. Apr. 16, 1858; m. 1881, Agnes Ann Woodburn.
    iv. WALTER M. CHASE, b. Apr. 26, 1861-3; d. 7 May, 1877.
    v. WILLARD S. CHASE (twin), b. Apr. 26, 1861-3; d. 15 Feb., 1881.

Children of ENOCH F.⁸, (1835) [1170] (Enoch⁷, Samuel⁶, Jr., Col. Samuel⁵, Samuel⁴, Isaac³, Sergt. Abraham², Robert¹) and Olive A. (Palmer) Adams; res. Groveland, Mass.

    i. FRANK ALBERT⁹, b. in Groveland, 1865; d. 18 Aug., 1866.
    ii. MABEL⁹, b. in Groveland, Apr. 5, 1869; m. Nov. 2, 1889, Jerry Silk of W. Newbury.
    iii. HERBERT LE ROY⁹, b. in Groveland, Aug. 9, 1871; res. Groveland, Mass., unm.
    iv. CHARLES⁹, b. in Groveland, Apr. 12, 1873; m. Apr 11-3, 1894, Mary Harrigan of So. Groveland, Mass.; no issue.

Children of ANN MARY⁸, (1839) [1171] (Enoch⁷, Samuel⁶, Jr., Col. Samuel⁵, Samuel⁴, Isaac³, Sergt. Abraham², Robert¹) and Charles Smith; res. Groveland, Mass.

    i. ELMER SMITH, b. in Groveland, July 22, 1865; m. June 2, 1891, Isaac Hardy; res. Groveland, Mass.
    ii. MARY SMITH, b. in Groveland, Mar. 5, 1869; m. Aug. 22, 1889, Geo. F. Wilson.

Children of HANNAH H.⁸, (1826) [1172] (Samuel⁷, Samuel⁶, Jr., Col. Samuel⁵, Samuel⁴, Isaac³, Sergt. Abraham², Robert¹) and William J. Creasy; res. Newburyport, Mass.

   i. WILLIAM AUGUSTUS CREASY, b. Aug. 1, 1845 ; d. 8 Aug., 1847.
   ii. WILLIAM WESTON CREASY, b. Nov. 16, 1848 ; m. Nov. 24, 1872, Mary Ellen Brookins. He d. 11 Oct., 1890.
   iii. MARY LIZZIE CREASY, b. May 26, 1853 ; m. Oct. 8, 1874, Robert R. Kimball of Boston; he d. 6 June, 1876. She d. 7 June, 1876 ; buried in one grave.

Child of SARAH E.⁸, (1828) [1173] (Samuel⁷, Samuel⁶, Jr., Col. Samuel⁵, Samuel⁴, Isaac³, Sergt. Abraham², Robert¹) and Oren Carlton; res. Plaistow, N. H.

   i. EMMA FRANCES CARLETON, b. Oct. 20, 1848; m. Dec. 19, 1872, Geo. W. Sherborn of Georgetown, Mass.; res. So. Lawrence, Mass.

Children of LUCY J.⁸, (1830) [1174] (Samuel⁷, Samuel⁶, Jr., Col. Samuel⁵, Samuel⁴, Isaac³, Sergt. Abraham², Robert¹) and Warner W. Tilton; res. Haverhill, Mass.

   i. CLARENCE EDGAR TILTON, b. Nov. 4, 1852 ; d. 26 Feb., 1863.
   ii. HELEN LILLIAN TILTON, b. Mar. 10, 1856 ; m. Nov. 26, 1874, C. Scott Sargent of Groveland, Mass.; b. Feb. 27, 1850 ; no issue.
   iii. AGNES MABEL TILTON, b. Aug. 31, 1866 ; m. June 13, 1887, F. E. Nason of Haverhill ; res. Haverhill, Mass.

Children of SELWYN P⁸, (1832) [1175] (Samuel⁷, Samuel⁶, Jr., Col. Samuel⁵, Samuel⁴, Isaac³, Sergt. Abraham², Robert¹) and Matilda L. (Freeman) Adams; res. Newburyport, Mass.

1460.   i. IDA FRANCIS⁹, b. in Cape Neddick, Me., Feb. 14, 1855 ; m. Oct. 7, 1880, James P. Reed of Newburyport, Mass. She d. 8 Aug., 1895.
1461.   ii. SELWYN M.⁹, b. in Newburyport, Aug. 12, 1858 ; m. July 5, 1883, Belle B. Emerton.
   iii. WILLIAM FREEMAN⁹, b. in Newburyport, Feb. 13, 1873 ; res. Newburyport, Mass.; unm.

Child of REBECCA B.⁸, (1836) [1176] (Samuel⁷, Samuel⁶, Jr., Col. Samuel⁵, Samuel⁴, Isaac³, Sergt. Abraham², Robert¹) and Farnham P. Woodcock; res. Haverhill, Mass.

   i. ERNEST FRANKLIN WOODCOCK, b. July 26, 1860 ; m. Sept. 1, 1881, Emma L. Lewis ; res. Worcester, Mass.

Children of ELLEN F.[8], (1843) (**1177**) (Samuel[7], Samuel[6], Jr., Col. Samuel[5], Samuel[4], Isaac[3], Sergt. |Abraham[2], Robert[1]) and George Sullivan Smith; res. Haverhill, Mass.

    i. WILLIAM HENRY SMITH, b. Feb. 17, 1869; d. 7 Oct. 1872.
    ii. GEORGE HOWARD SMITH, b. Feb. 11, 1873; m. Mar. 28, 1894, Inez Izetta Hoyt of Haverhill.
    iii. RUSSELL HOWARD SMITH, b. June 21, 1875.
    iv. DOROTHY SMITH, b. Nov. 13, 1877.

Child of AMELIA ANN[8], (1837) [**1178**] (Moses[7], Samuel[6], Jr., Col. Samuel[5], Samuel[4], Isaac[3], Sergt. Abraham[2], Robert[1]) and Charles R. Weston; res. Groveland, Mass.

1462.   i. IDA LOUISE WESTON, b. in Groveland, May 22, 1859; m. Nov. 24, 1881, Bainbridge [Morse of Georgetown, Mass., son of John G. and Martha (Buckminster) Morse of Georgetown, b. Mar. 9, 1858. He is a clothing merchant, 56 Merrimac St.; res. Haverhill, Mass.

Children of CHARLES SAMUEL[8], (1842) [**1179**] (Moses[7], Samuel[6], Jr., Col. Samuel[5], Samuel[4], Isaac[3], Sergt. Abraham[2], Robert[1]) and Ellen E. (Simpson) Adams; res. Hickory Barrens, Green Co., Mo.

    i. CULLIE ROOT[9], b. in Lyons, Ia., May 17, 1867; d. 30 Oct., 1889.
    ii. FANNIE AMELIA[9], b. in Lyons, Sept. 15, 1869; d. 3 Dec., 1870.
    iii. HOWARD EDWIN[9], b. in Groveland, Mass., July 12, 1877; res. Hickory Barrens, Mo.; unm.
    iv. LENA SIMPSON[9], b. in Groveland, May 25, 1879; living unm.
    v. LOWELL HENRY[9], b. in No. Springfield, Mo., Oct. 8, 1881.
    vi. LAWRENCE WARD[9] (twin), b. Oct. 8, 1881; d. 4 Mar., 1884.

Children of THOMAS AUGUSTUS[8], (1829) [**1180**] (Eliphalet[7], Isaac[6], Capt. Samuel[5], Capt. Isaac[4], Jr., Isaac[3], Sergt. Abraham[2], Robert[1]) |and Mary E. (Flanders) Adams; res. Gorham, N. H.

    i. CHARLES F.[9], b. in Gorham, May 24, 1862; m. Jan. 16, 1893, Belle Houghton of Chicago.
    He is a merchant; set. 1895 in Anaconda, Mont.; no issue.

ii. EDITH M.⁹, b. in Gorham, Oct. 7, 1866 ; m. Aug. 20, 1889, Prof. Charles R. Richardson, son of Isaac E. Richardson, b. in Hartford. Me., Dec. 7, 1855 ; graduated from Colby University, 1883 ; was President of Dakota State Normal School for four years, and later Professor of Mathematics and Astronomy in Olivet College, Michigan; now engaged in mining and real estate ; set. in Anaconda, Mont., 1896; no issue.

Child of HENRY H.⁸, (1839) [1181] (Eliphalet⁷, Isaac⁶, Capt. Samuel⁵, Capt. Isaac⁴, Jr., Isaac³, Sergt. Abraham², Robert¹) and Augusta A. (Martin) Adams; res. Richmond, Me.

1463. i. DURWARD C.⁹, b. in N. Stratford, N. H., Dec. 30, 1865; m. Sept. 9, 1891, Gladys Hopkins, b. Dec. 30, 1868 ; res. Richmond, Me.

Children of EDWARD PAYSON⁸, (1842) [1182] (Eliphalet⁷, Isaac⁶, Capt. Samuel⁵, Capt. Isaac⁴, Jr., Isaac³, Sergt. Abraham², Robert¹) and Emma E. (Williams) Adams; res. Rutherford, Cal.

i. EDWARD L.⁹, b. in Gorham, N. H., Apr. 6, 1869 ; d. 16 Aug., 1869.
ii. MARY P.⁹, b. in Corrinne, Boxelder Co., Utah, Nov. 21, 1874 ; res. Rutherford.

Children of MARIETTA⁸, (1837) [1183] (Prof. Samuel⁷, Isaac⁶, Capt. Samuel⁵, Capt. Isaac⁴, Jr., Isaac³, Sergt. Abraham², Robert¹) and Robert (Kirkwood) Whiteley; res. Brainerd, Minn.

1464. i. ROBERT HENRY KIRKWOOD WHITELEY, b. June 6, 1866 ; m. Oct. 4, 1893, Alice C. Everts.
  He is an editor of the *Detroit Tribune*. He graduated from Illinois College in 1887, and became associated with the press of Minneapolis, Minn.; was the political editor of the *Minneapolis Tribune*, and first city editor of the *Minneapolis Times*, started in 1889. He removed to Detroit, Mich., in May, 1891 ; was for two years night editor of the *Tribune,* and has been the managing editor since that time.
ii. KATE ADAMS WHITELEY, b. Oct. 21, 1867.
iii. FRANK ADAMS WHITELEY, b. Jan. 9, 1871.
  Superintendent of schools, Excelsior, Minn.
iv. MARY WHITELEY, b. Mar. 14, 1872.
v. HESTER ELIZABETH WHITELEY, b. Sept. 29, 1873.
vi. SAMUEL ADAMS WHITELEY, b. Aug. 17, 1875 ; d. 22 Aug., 1877.
vii. EUGENE EDGERTON WHITELEY, b. May 26, 1878.

Ninth Generation.] OF NEWBURY, MASS. 455

Children of EMILY[8], (1846) **[1184]** (Prof. Samuel[7], Issac[6], Capt. Samuel[5], Capt. Isaac[4], Jr., Isaac[3], Sergt. Abraham[2], Robert[1]) and Dr. Alfred Richmond; res. Redlands, Cal.
  i. CARL ADAMS RICHMOND, b. Apr. 30. 1874.
  ii. FRANK ADAMS RICHMOND, b. Dec. 6, 1876.
  iii. RUTH RICHMOND, b. Oct. 3, 1884.

Children of CLARA MOULTON[8], (1850) **[1185]** (Prof Samuel[7], Isaac[6], Capt. Samuel[5], Capt. Isaac[4], Jr., Isaac[3], Sergt. Abraham[2], Robert[1]) and Julian Post Lippincott; res. Jacksonville, Ill.
  i. ALICE LIPPINCOTT, b. Dec. 21, 1874; unm.
  ii. WINTHROP GILMAN LIPPINCOTT, b. May 23, 1880; d. 27 May, 1881.
  iii. WILLIAM ADAMS LIPPINCOTT, b. July 3, 1882.
  iv. LUCIA LOUISA LIPPINCOTT, b. Jan. 29, 1891.

Children of JOHN TARBEL PEABODY[8], (1838) **[1186]** and Frances W. Bartlett; res. Gorham, Me.
  i. ALICE RUTH PEABODY, b. Feb. 8, 1868; m. Dec. 28, 1887, Thomas Wight.
  ii. GRACE APHIA PEABODY, b. Dec. 25, 1869.
  iii. CLARA BROWN PEABODY, b. Aug. 10, 1873; m. Feb. 5, 1896, Vincent Wm. Crosby; res. Boston, Mass.

Children of DARIUS[8], (1844) **[1187]** (Dea. Israel[7], Isaac[6], Capt. Samuel[5], Capt. Isaac[4], Jr., Isaac[3], Sergt. Abraham[2], Robert[1]) and Clara J. (Low) Adams; res. Manhattan, Kan.
  i. HORACE IVORY[9], b. in Bethel, Me., May 29, 1870.
      He is a clerk.
  ii. EMMA ELIZABETH[9], b. in Manhattan, Kan., Mar. 17, 1874.

Child of EMMA JANE[8], (1855) **[1188]** (Darius[7], Jonathan[6], Capt. Samuel[5], Capt. Isaac[4], Jr., Isaac[3], Sergt. Abraham[2], Robert[1]) and Franklin Augustus Cook; res. Springfield, Vt.
  i. ALVAH JASON COOK, b. Apr. 5, 1874; res. New York.

Child of FRANK HUEY[8], (1858) **[1189]** (Darius[7], Jonathan[6], Capt. Samuel[5], Capt. Isaac[4], Jr., Isaac[3], Sergt. Abraham[2], Robert[1]) and Lucy J. (Barton) Adams; res. Lowell, Mass.

    i. MAY EMMA[9], b. in Lowell, July 15, 1879.

Children of ARTHUR DANIEL[8], (1859) **[1190]** (Darius[7], Jonathan[6], Capt. Samuel[5], Capt. Isaac[4], Jr., Isaac[3], Sergt. Abraham[2], Robert[1]) and Anna Sargent (Gilbert) Adams.

    i. ARTHUR GILBERT[9], b. Jan. 20, 1885.
    ii. GEORGE HOWARD[9], b. Aug. 19, 1886.
    iii. GRACE ELLEN[9], b. Apr. 5, 1895.
    iv. ELIZABETH W.[9], b. Jan. 25, 1898

Child of CHARLES ANDERSON[8], (1867) **[1191]** (Darius[7], Jonathan[6], Capt. Samuel[5], Capt. Isaac[4], Jr., Isaac[3], Sergt. Abraham[2], Robert[1]) and Emma Mattie (Britton) Adams; res. Boston, Mass.

    i. THEODORE[9], b. in Milford, N. H., Mar. 29, 1891.

Child of KATHERINE BLANCHE[8], (1862) **[1192]** (Chas. Anderson[7], Jonathan[6], Capt. Samuel[5], Capt. Isaac[4], Jr., Isaac[3], Sergt. Abraham[2], Robert[1]) and Lester Thomas Crook; res. Lowell, Mass.

    i. STEWART ADAMS CROOK, b. Apr. 5, 1888.

Child of CAPT. GEORGE A.[8], (1837) **[1193]** (Albert[7], Israel[6], 3d, Israel[5], Israel[4], Sarah[3], Sergt. Abraham[2], Robert[1]) and Hattie M. (Phillips) Adams; res. Homer, Cortland Co., N. Y.

    i. DAVID HALL[9], b. in Homer, May, 1861 ; res. W. Boylston, Mass.

Children of JOHN BROOKS[8], (1842) **[1194]** (Albert[7], Israel[6], 3d, Israel[5], Israel[4], Sarah[3], Sergt. Abraham[2], Robert[1]) and Mary J. (Woodbury) Adams; res. Hancock, N. H.

    i. GEORGE ARTHUR[9], b. in Winchendon, Mass., Feb. 5, 1873.

ii. FRED ALBERT[9], b. in Jaffrey, N. H., July 6, 1875.
iii. J. HENRY[9], b. in Rindge, N. H., June 15, 1878.
iv. EDWIN MYRON[9], b. in Swansey, N. H., Aug. 7, 1882.
v. ERNEST LEON[9], b. in Swansey, Jan. 5, 1885.
vi. CHARLES EVERETT[9], b. in Swansey, July 9, 1887.
vii. RALPH WOOD[9], b. in Hancock, N. H., Oct. 5, 1891.

Children of FRANCIS A.[8], (1844) **[1195]** (Albert[7], Israel[6], 3d, Israel[5], Israel[4], Sarah[3], Sergt. Abraham[2], Robert[1]) and Emma C. (Bruce) Adams; res. Royalston, Mass.

i. NELLIE EMMA[9], b. Sept., 1865; res. Athol, Mass.
ii. FLORENCE MARION[9], b. Dec., 1866; res. Greenfield, Mass.
iii. WALTER FRANCIS[9], b. May, 1868; res. Fitzwilliam Depot, N. H.

Children of DR. ORANGE H.[8], (1856) **[1196]** (Albert[7], Israel[6], 3d, Israel[5], Israel[4], Sarah[3], Sergt. Abraham[2], Robert[1]) and Jessie (Ballou) Adams; res. Vineland, N. J.

i. ALICE M.[9], b. Dec., 1885.
ii. GERTRUDE[9], b. Nov., 1888.

Children of JOSEPH HENRY[8], (1818) **[1197]** (Col. Joseph Henry[7], Lieut. and Maj. John[6], Capt. John[5], Israel[4], Sarah[3], Sergt. Abraham[2], Robert[1]) and ——— Adams; res. Boston, Mass.

i. JOSEPH HENRY[9], JR., b. in Boston, 1857.
   He was graduated from Harvard College in 1881, and is a practicing attorney in New York City.
ii. MARION S.[9], b. in Boston; m. ——— Page; res. Kingston, Mass.

Child of JOHN[8], (1825) **[1198]** (Col. Joseph Henry[7], Lieut. and Maj. John[6], Capt. John[5], Israel[4], Sarah[3], Sergt. Abraham[2], Robert[1]) and Mary (Hill) Adams; res. Haverhill, Mass.

1465. i. JOHN FREDERICK[9], b. in Boston, Jan. 8, 1853; m. June 6, 1876, Anne B. Kelley, dau. of Amos S. Kelley of Haverhill, Mass.
   He is an insurance agent; res. Haverhill, Mass.

Child of AUGUSTA[8], (1835) **[1199]** (Benjamin Franklin[7], Robert[6], David[5], Israel[4], Sarah[3], Sergt. Abraham[2], Robert[1]) and Albert W. Flinn; res. Nashua, N. H.

i. ALBERT ADAMS FLINN, b. July 27, 1870; res. Nashua, N. H.

Children of CHARLES CLINTON[6], (1838) [1200] (Benjamin Franklin[7], Robert[6], David[5], Israel[4], Sarah[3], Sergt. Abraham[2], Robert[1]) and Sarah M. (Morris) Adams; res. Argentine, Kan.

    i. JENNIE MARIA[9], b. in Warren, O., Apr. 2, 1866; m. Jan. 2, 1892, Henry M. Richards; res. Spokane, Wash.

1466. ii. MARY[9], b. in Warren, Aug. 26, 1869; m. Oct. 10, 1891, Chas. C. Paige; res. Warren. She d. 29 Sept., 1896.

Children of HENRY KEELER[8], (1845) [1201] (Benjamin Franklin[7], Robert[6], David[5], Israel[4], Sarah[3], Sergt. Abraham[2], Robert[1]) and Mary Jane (Farrah) Adams; res. Richmond, Ashtabula Co., O.

    i. PHEBE[9], b. in Richmond, Jan. 27, 1886.
    ii. MYRTIE E.[9], b. in Richmond, Jan. 27, 1891.

Children of GEORGE HERMAN[8], (1844) [1202] (Prescott Jones[7], Robert[6], David[5], Israel[4], Sarah[3], Sergt. Abraham[2], Robert[1]) and Jane (McNett) Adams; res. Vanderbilt, Otsego Co., Mich.

    i. ARCHER[9], b. in Vanderbilt, Jan. 1, 1866.
    ii. BERTRAND[9], b. in Vanderbilt, Jan. 17, 1867.
    iii. LEONARD[9], b. in Vanderbilt, Oct. 3, 1868.
    iv. MARIA[9], b. in Vanderbilt, Jan. 1, 1869.

Children of ALFRED LE ROY[8], (1849) [1203] (Prescott Jones[7], Robert[6], David[5], Israel[4], Sarah[3], Sergt. Abraham,[2] Robert[1]) and Ardilla (Davidson) Adams; res. Athens, Calhoun Co., Mich.

    i. NELSON[9], b. May 7, 1873.
    ii. ERNEST[9], b. Nov. 29, 1877; m. Dec. 23, 1897, —— ——

Child of OSCAR DE WITT[8], (1851) [1204] (Prescott Jones[7], Robert[6], David[5], Israel[4], Sarah[3], Sergt. Abraham[2], Robert[1]) and Louisa (Butler) Adams; res. Sherman, Wetford Co., Mich.

    i. PARSHALL E.[9], b. in Sherman, June 22, 1879.

Children of ELLA FLORENCE[8], (1855) [1205] (Prescott Jones[7], Robert[6], David[5], Israel[4], Sarah[3], Sergt. Abraham[2], Robert[1]) and George W. Pepple; res. Athens, Calhoun Co., Mich.
- i. MYRTIE PEPPLE, b. Aug. 6, 1872; m. Earle Bullard; res. Ashtabula, O.
- ii. HERMAN PEPPLE, b. Aug. 24, 1873; m. Sept. 18, 1899, Elizabeth Harrigan; res. Ashtabula, O.

Child of EUGENE ELMER[8], (1858) [1206] (Prescott Jones[7], Robert[6], David[5], Israel[4], Sarah[3], Sergt. Abraham[2], Robert[1]) and Mattie (House) Adams; res. Factoryville, Mich.
- i. HELEN[9], b. in Factoryville, Aug. 31, 1892.

Children of SIMEON H. DRAKE, (1838) [1207] and Celia Henderson; res. New London, N. H.
- i. WILLIE DRAKE, b. July 7, 1868.
- ii. CLARENCE DRAKE, b. July 8, 1870.
- iii. JENNIE DRAKE, b. Sept. 15, 1876.

Children of ABBIE M. DRAKE, (1841) [1208] and Michael Womeldorf; res. New London, N. H.
- i. CLARA WOMELDORF, b. Sept. 17, 1862.
- ii. JOHN WOMELDORF, b, Nov. 19, 1867.
- iii. SHANGON H. WOMELDORF, b. June 27, 1873.

Children of RILLIE DRAKE, (1844) [1209] and Martin Rotner; res. New London, N. H.
- i. LILLIE ROTNER, b. May 11, 1861.
- ii. JENNIE ROTNER, b. July 12, 1873.

Children of FRED M. DRAKE, (1848) [1210] and Eleanor Rotner; res. New London, N. H.
- i. JACOB DRAKE, b. May 27, 1870.
- ii. JAMES DRAKE, b. Jan. 28, 1872.
- iii. SIMEON DRAKE, b. Sept. 30, 1873.
- iv. CLARENCE DRAKE, b. Nov. 25, 1875.

Children of LIBBIE M. DRAKE, (1853) [1211] and Russell Tucker; res, New London, N. H.

    i. HARVEY TUCKER, b. May, 1873.
    ii. MINNIE TUCKER, b. July, 1876.

Children of SARAH H.[8], (1853) [1212] (Azro[7], Asa[6], Benjamin[5], John[4], John[3], Sergt. Abraham[2], Robert[1]) and Willard D. Grant; res. Barre City, V.t.

    i. FRED A. GRANT. b. Dec. 16, 1876; unm.
    ii. CHARLES D. GRANT, b. Sept. 12, 1878 ; unm.

Children of BENJAMIN H.[8], 2ND, (1843) [1213] (Benjamin H.[7], Benjamin[6], Benjamin[5], John[4], John[3], Sergt. Abraham[2], Robert[1]) and Eunice A. (Scribner) Adams; res. Chelsea, Vt.

1467.   i. BENJAMIN H.[9], 3D, b. in Tunbridge, Vt., June 21, 1869; m. Sept. 14, 1892, Cora J. Ackerman of Chelsea, Vt., dau. of Jonathan and Minerva (Johnson) Ackerman, b. May 10, 1866 ; res. Chelsea, Vt.
    ii. ALMA F.[9], b. in Tunbridge, Mar. 7, 1871 ; m. Dec. 28, 1898, Evarts P. Brown of Vershire, Vt., son of Asa A. and Viola B. (Philbrook) Brown, b. Jan. 19, 1868 ; res. Vershire, Vt.; no issue.
1468.   iii. JULIA O.[9], b. in Chelsea, Feb. 22, 1873; m. June 28, 1894, Frank E. Bixby of Chelsea, son of Orcott and Rosetta Bixby, b. Nov. 9, 1868; res. in Chelsea.

Children of CATHERINE I.[8], (1846) [1214] (Benjamin H.[7], Benjamin[6], Benjamin[5], John[4], John[3], Sergt. Abraham[2], Robert[1]) and Joseph H. Griffin; res. Chelsea, Vt.

    i. FRANK E. GRIFFIN, b. in Chelsea, Apr. 5, 1867 ; m. Oct. 15, 1890, Emma L. Taylor of Chelsea, Vt. He d. 22 Dec., 1891.
    ii. JULIAN H. GRIFFIN, b. in Washington, Vt., July 26, 1872 ; m. May 18, 1897, Margaret Downs of Hancock, Vt. He d. 21 Aug., 1897.
    iii. NED A. GRIFFIN, b. in Washington, May 23, 1878; unm.
    iv. GEO. F. GRIFFIN, b. in Chelsea, Vt., Dec. 9, 1885.

Children of MARCELLA F.[8], (1848) [1215] (Benjamin H.[7], Benjamin[6], Benjamin[5], John[4], John[3], Sergt. Abraham[2], Robert[1]) and Jedd Scott; res. Scottsmore, P. Q.

i. JULIA MAUD SCOTT, b. Dec. 24, 1876.
ii. GRACE I. SCOTT, b. Aug. 21, 1881.
iii. CASPER A. SCOTT, b. Aug. 9, 1883.
iv. GOLDA R. SCOTT, b. Feb. 19, 1890.

Children of MARCIA MARIA GAY, (1835) [**1216**] and John C. Worth; res. New London, N. H., and California.

i. MARY E. WORTH, b. Dec. 4, 1855 ; m. Chas. Bickford of Stockton, Cal. Children, Ulmer and Earle.
ii. ADDIE INIS WORTH, b. Oct. 24, 1859 ; m. Fred Howett of Stockton, Cal.
iii. STEPHEN HENRY WORTH, b. Jan., 1861.
iv. ABBIE GERTIE WORTH, b. June 24, 1876.

Child of HENRY WM. GAY, (1837) [**1217**] and Julia M. Harrington; res. Corinth, Me.

i. MAURICE C. GAY, b. Nov. 21, 1880.

Child of EVA MELVINA GAY, (1853) [**1218**] and Frank H. Skinner; res. Corinth, Me.

i. FRED GAY SKINNER, b. Sept. 12, 1882.

Children of AUGUSTA M.[6], (1856) [**1219**] (Dennis H.[7], Solomon[6], Jr., Solomon[5], John[4], John[3], Sergt. Abraham[2], Robert[1]) and John G. Hazen; res. No. Sutton, N. H.

i. HERBERT W. HAZEN, b. Feb. 4, 1873 ; m. Jan. 5, 1897, Jennie T. Fellows of Wilmot, N. H., b. Apr. 21, 1878.
ii. MINNIE L. HAZEN, b. July 15, 1874 ; m. Mar. 22, 1891, Sidney J. Thurber of Unity, N. H., b. Oct. 24, 1868.
iii. ERNEST H. HAZEN, b. Oct. 6, 1882.
iv. LUNIE E. HAZEN, b. June 9, 1886.
v. MYRTIE HAZEN, b. Dec. 27, 1897 ; d. same day.

Child of WILLIAM H. H.[8], (1866) [**1220**] (Dennis H.[7], Solomon[6], Jr., Solomon[5], John[4], John[3], Sergt. Abraham[2], Robert[1]) and Fanny A. (Cate) Adams; res. Hopkinton, N. H.

i. ERNEST H.[9], b. in Belmont, N. H., Feb. 10, 1889 ; d. 12 Feb., 1890.

Child of WILLIAM H. H.[8], (1866) and Laura A. B. (Melcher) Adams.

 ii. HOWARD D.[9], b. in Hopkinton, Apr. 10, 1895.

Child of ELMER ELLSWORTH[8], (1862) [1221] (Joseph Collins[7], Solomon[6], Jr., Solomon[5], John[4], John[3], Sergt. Abraham[2], Robert[1]) and Minnie (Richardson) Adams; res. New London, N. H.

 i. MYRON RICHARDSON[9], b. in New London, June 13, 1897.

Children of MARY ELIZABETH[8], (1854) [1222] (Norman B.[7], Solomon[6], Jr., Solomon[5], John[4], John[3], Sergt. Abraham[2], Robert[1]) and William C. Nye; res. Scytheville, now Elkins, N. H.

 i. MAUD E. NYE, b. in Scytheville, Sept. 17, 1875; m. Feb. 5, 1893, Frank W. Pressey.
 ii. BELL M. NYE, b. in Scytheville, Apr. 2, 1878.
 iii. EARL H. N. NYE, b. in New London, N. H., July 4, 1880.
 iv. CHARLES A. NYE, b. in New London, June 20, 1882.
 v. EMIL S NYE, b. in Sutton, N. H., Sept. 14, 1883.
 vi. HAZEL B. NYE, b. in Scytheville, Aug. 7, 1888; d, 16 Aug., 1891.
 vii. MAE B. NYE, b. in Scytheville, Mar. 15, 1891.

Children of WALTER M.[8], (1852) [1223] (John Lewis[7], Moses[6], Jonathan[5], John[4], John[3], Sergt. Abraham[2], Robert[1]) and Adella E. (Whipple) Adams; res. Detroit, Mich.

 i. EDNA MAY[9], b. in So. Framingham, Mass., Dec. 1, 1874; m. June 22, 1898, Wm. A. Richards; no issue.
 ii. ETHEL LUCETTA[9], b. in So. Framingham, Nov. 12, 1876; m. Sept. 14, 1898, James Brown.
 iii. LEWIS ANDREW[9], b. in Detroit, Mich., Feb. 16, 1882.
 iv. WALTER CLIFFORD[9], b. in Detroit, June 26, 1884.
 v. WILLIAM WAUGH[9], b. in Detroit, June 26, 1887.

Children of MARY EUNICE SANBORN, (1853) [1224] and Dennison J. Slack; res. Tunbridge, Vt.

 i. HENRY MORSE SLACK, b. May 5, 1873.
 ii. BERT BENNETT SLACK, b. June 30, 1875; d. 30 Jan., 1886.

Ninth Generation.]   OF NEWBURY, MASS.   463

Children of CLARA EMMA SANBORN, (1860) [1225] and Willis W. Whitney.
    i. ALEX. H. WHITNEY, b. Dec. 13, 1886.
    ii. CARROLL C. WHITNEY, b. Nov. 3, 1888.

Children of GEORGIANA GRACE[8], (1868) [1226] (George W.[7], Jonathan Tenny[6], Jonathan[5], John[4], John[3], Sergt. Abraham[2], Robert[1]) and George Cleveland; res. Corfu, Genesee Co., N. Y.
    i. ALBERTA GRACE CLEVELAND, b. Sept. 30, 1897.
    ii. ERNEST CLEVELAND, b. Sept. 19, 1899.

Child of CHARLES DAVID[8], (1860) [1227] (Daniel[7], Jonathan Tenny[6], Jonathan[5], John[4], John[3], Sergt. Abraham[2], Robert[1]) and Emily M. (Putney) Adams; res. Ferry, Mich.
    i. LESTER D.[9], b. in Otto, Mich., Aug. 9, 1891.

Children of GEORGE T.[8], (1868) [1228] (Daniel[7], Jonathan Tenny[6], Jonathan[5], John[4], John[3], Sergt. Abraham[2], Robert[1]) and Mary (Law) Adams; res. Otto, Oceana Co., Mich.
    i. LEWIS D.[9], b. in Scottville, Mich., Apr. 17, 1894.
    ii. HAZEL[9], b. in Scottville, Nov. 4, 1895.
    iii. JAMES[9], b. in Otto, July 3, 1897; d. 11 Sept., 1898.

Child of LURA[8], (1877) [1229] (Daniel[7], Jonathan Tenny[6], Jonathan[5], John[4], John[3], Sergt. Abraham[2], Robert[1]) and William O'Connell; res. Otto, Oceana Co., Mich.
    i. DANIEL R. O'CONNELL, b. in Otto, June 19, 1897.

Children of ARTHUR J.[8], (1868) [1230] (Nathan[7], Jonathan Tenny[6], Jonathan[5], John[4], John[3], Sergt. Abraham[2], Robert[1]) and Libbie S. (Backum) Adams; res. Shelby, Mich.
    i. GLADYS GAY[9], b. in Shelby, Feb. 18, 1896.
    ii. EMILY[9], b. in Shelby, Feb. 15, 1899.

Children of ELIZABETH JENETTE[8], (1872) [1231] (Nathan[7], Jonathan Tenny[6], Jonathan[5], John[4], John[3], Sergt. Abraham[2], Robert[1]) and John H. Walcott; res. Shelby, Mich.
- i. LENA WALCOTT, b. June 22, 1896.
- ii. HOWARD NATHAN WALCOTT, b. Nov. 11, 1897.
- iii. IRENE WALCOTT, b. Jan. 1, 1899.

Children of MARY E[8], (1839) [1232] (Thomas B.[7], Israel[6], Israel[5], Matthew[4], Dr. Matthew[3], Sergt. Abraham[2], Robert[1]) and Solomon C. Bumford; res. Bradford, N. H.
- i. MARY E. BUMFORD.
- ii. NELLIE F. BUMFORD.
- iii. ANNIE B. BUMFORD.

Children of EBEN H.[8], (1840) [1233] (Thomas B.[7], Israel[6], Israel[5], Matthew[4], Dr. Matthew[3], Sergt. Abraham[2], Robert) and Ellen M. A. (Bumford) Adams; res. Hillsboro, N. H.

1469.
- i. JULIA A.[9], b. in Bradford, N. H., Sept. 20, 1878; m. Nov. 17, 1895, William E. Gibson; res. Hillsboro, N. H.
- ii. EVA E.[9], b. in Hillsboro, June 28, 1881; m. July 2, 1899, James R. Hudson; res. Hillsboro, N. H.
- iii WALTER E.[9], b. in Hillsboro, July 26, 1887.

Children of ISRAEL[8], (1848) [1234] (Thomas B.[7], Israel[6], Israel[5], Matthew[4], Dr. Matthew[3], Sergt. Abraham[2], Robert[1]) and Hepsebeth (Bagley) Adams; res. Washington, N. H.
- i. LURA M[9], b. in Hillsboro, N. H., Sept. 12, 1881.
- ii. ROY W.[9], b. in Hillsboro, Aug. 29, 1886.
- iii. WARREN F.[9], b. in Hillsboro, Nov. 2, 1893.

Child of ELLA A.[8], (1852) [1235] (Thomas B.[7], Israel[6], Israel[5], Matthew[4], Dr. Matthew[3], Sergt. Abraham[2], Robert[1]) and Fred Purington; res. Bradford, N. H.
- i. ALLIE PURINGTON.

Ninth Generation.] OF NEWBURY, MASS. 465

Child of MARTHA A.⁸, (1838) [1236] (Ebenezer H.⁷, Israel⁶, Israel⁵, Matthew⁴, Dr. Matthew³, Sergt. Abraham², Robert¹) and Lorenzo B. Colburn; res. Hanover, N. H.
- i. ALICE M. COLBURN, b. in Hanover, Dec. 17, 1870; living, unm.

Children of IMRI P.⁸, (1841) [1237] (Ebenezer H.⁷, Israel⁶, Israel⁵, 3d, Matthew⁴, Dr. Matthew³, Sergt. Abraham², Robert¹) and Ella L. (Laughlin) Adams; res. Goshen, N. H.
- i. ELIZABETH C.⁹, b. in Goshen, Mar 4, 1875; m. Sept. 1, 1898, William H. Royce; res. Mill Village, N. H.
- ii. ISABEL E.⁹, b. in Goshen, Aug. 26, 1877.
  She is a teacher.

Children of RICHARD W. SMITH⁸, (1841) [1238] and Georgiana Skillings; res. Providence, R. I.
- i. RICHARD EDWIN SMITH, b. July 22, 1872; m. Sept. 6, 1893, Marion Chase Brownell; 2 children.
- ii. MARGARET AUGUSTA SMITH, b. April 20, 1874; d. July, 1874.
- iii. MARGARET GERTRUDE SMITH, b. Sept. 10, 1878.
- iv. WILLIAM PERCY SMITH, b. June 14, 1881.
- v. GEORGIANA SMITH, b. Apr. 11, 1883.

Children of ROANA CUTTER⁸, (1843) [1239] (John⁷, Israel⁶, Israel⁵, 3d, Matthew⁴, Dr. Matthew³, Sergt. Abraham², Robert¹) and William E. Way; res. Charlestown, N. H.
- i. CATHERINE RUTH WAY, b. May 20, 1866; d. 20 Nov., 1886.
- ii. JOHN RICHARDS WAY, b. Oct. 26, 1870; d. 5 Jan., 1872.
- iii. LOIS EMOGENE WAY, b. Apr. 3, 1872; d. 9 Aug., 1872.
- iv. WILL GARDNER WAY, b. Aug. 25, 1878.

Children of JACOB KIMBALL⁸, (1838) [1240] (Benjamin F.⁷, John⁶, John⁵, Matthew⁴, Dr. Matthew³, Sergt. Abraham², Robert¹) and Hattie A (Hurd) Adams; res. Warner, N. H.

1470. i. FLORA BELL⁹, b. in Sutton, N. H., Nov. 9, 1866; m. July 15, 1887, Wilson B. Flanders, son of Walter M. and Sarah P. Flanders of Warner, N. H.; res. Charlestown, Mass.

1471.
ii. BENJAMIN F.⁹, b. in Sutton, July 5, 1868 ; m. Nov. 29, 1893, Catherine Moreau, dau. of Entoine and Emelie Morean, b. in Germain, P. Q., June 11, 1872 ; res. Sutton. N. H.
iii. HATTIE MAY⁹, b. in Sutton, Apr. 30, 1870 ; m. May 26, 1894, Alvin A. Jepson, son of James H. and Naomi Jepson of Warner, N. H., b. July 26, 1871 ; res. Waterloo, N. H.
iv. CLARENCE W.⁹, b. in Sutton, Aug. 30, 1873 ; m. June 7, 1898, Luella M. Chace, dau. of Edgar and Emma Chace of Warner, N. H., b. Nov. 2, 1878 ; res. Welch Glade, Webster Co., W. Va.
v. GEORGE W.⁹, b. in Sutton, Nov. 10, 1879 ; res. Sutton, N. H.; unm.

Child of MARY AMANDA⁸, (1844) [1241] (Benjamin F.⁷, John⁶, John⁵, Matthew⁴, Dr. Matthew³, Sergt. Abraham², Robert¹) and Dr. James M. Rix; res. Warner, N. H.

i. LEE ARTHUR A. RIX, b. Aug. 17, 1878 ; res. Warner, N. H.; unm.

Children of JOHN F.⁸, (1840) [1242] (Benjamin F.⁷, John⁶, John⁵, Matthew⁴, Dr. Matthew³, Sergt. Abraham², Robert¹) and Nettie C. (Hollis) Adams; res. Franklin Falls, N. H.

i. FLORENCE N.⁹, b. in Manchester, N. H., Jan. 24, 1872; res. Manchester, N. H.; unm.
ii. MIRA B.⁹, b. in Croyden, N. H.; Apr. 27, 1875 ; unm.

Child of JOHN ANDREW⁸, (1843) [1243] (George W.⁷, John⁶, John⁵, Matthew⁴, Dr. Matthew³, Sergt. Abraham², Robert¹) and Mary Alma (Bailey) Adams; res, Manchester, N. H.

i. EDWARD SHEPHERD⁹, b. in Manchester, Feb. 20, 1873 ; res. Manchester, N. H.; unm.

Children of ISRAEL⁶, (1832) [1244] (Thomas Jefferson⁷, Matthew⁶, Benjamin⁵, Matthew⁴, Dr. Matthew³, Sergt. Abraham², Robert¹) and Lydia M. (Nelson) Adams; res. Newbury, and Sutton, N. H.

i. FRED B.⁹, b. in Newbury June 13, 1859 ; m. Oct. 23, 1883, Córa D. Rowell ; set. in Sutton, N. H., 1886; no issue.
ii. ELNORA E.⁹, b. in Newbury, Sept. 12, 1864; d. 22 Sept., 1878.

Children of MOSES[8], (1833) [1245] (Thomas Jefferson[7], Matthew[6], Benjamin[5], Matthew[4], Dr. Mathew[3], Sergt. Abraham[2], Robert[1]) and Mary Jane (Perry) Adams; res. Salem, Mass.

    i. CHARLES H.[9], b. in New London, N. H., Sept. 21, 1859; m. Jan. 20, 1882, Martha Tilton of Newport, N. H.; set. in Camden, Me.

    ii. ADA FRANCES[9], b. in Warner, N. H., Sept. 24, 1862; book-keeper; unm.; res. Salem, Mass.

Children of ORIN[8], (1844) [1246] (Thomas Jefferson[7], Matthew[6], Benjamin[5], Matthew[4], Dr. Matthew[3], Sergt. Abraham[2], Robert[1]) and Addie (Johnson) Adams; res. Newbury, N. H.

    i. GEORGE[9].

    ii. GALE[9].

Child of SARAH[8], (1848) [1247] (Thomas Jefferson[7], Matthew[6], Benjamin[5], Matthew[4], Dr. Matthew[3], Sergt. Abraham[2], Robert[1]) and ——— White.

    i. GEORGE WHITE; m. ——— Warner.

Children of SARAH[8], (1848) and Horace F. Perry; res. Newport, N. H.

    i. TYRA F. PERRY; m. ——— Cutter; res. Antrim Branch, N. H.

    ii. BERTIE PERRY.

Children of BETSEY J.[8], (1833) [1248] (John Langdon[7], Matthew[6], Benjamin[5], Matthew[4], Dr. Matthew[3], Sergt. Abraham[2], Robert[1]) and Ira P. Whittier; res. So. Newbury, N. H.

    i. IRA CERENDO WHITTIER, b. in Sutton, N. H., Apr. 13, 1853; d. 2 Feb., 1857.

    ii. AMOS C. WHITTIER, b. Mar. 1, 1858; m. Sept. 11, 1880, Alice Hadley of Enfield, N. H.; res. Sunapee, N. H.

    iii. JOHN E. WHITTIER, b. Dec. 21, 1860; m. May 1, 1889, Katie Dimond of Warner; res. Henniker, N. H.

    iv. MOSES FELCH WHITTIER, b. Feb. 27, 1864; m. June 6, 1888, Jennie Nelson of Warner; res. Henniker, N. H.

Children of MOSES J.[8], (1834) [**1249**] (John Langdon[7], Matthew[6], Benjamin[5], Matthew[4], Dr. Matthew[3], Sergt. Abraham[2], Robert[1]) and Annie E. (Kidder) Adams; res. York Beach, Me.
    i. ADA G.[9], b. in Newport, N. H., Aug. 13, 1855; m. Feb. 1, 1877, Geo. A. Proctor; res. York Beach, Me.
    ii. GEORGE F.[9], b. in Concord, N. H., May 15, 1857; d. 1 Dec., 1870.
    iii. KATIE J.[9], b. in Sunapee, N. H., Nov. 10, 1859; m. Sept. 10, 1880, Chancey Marshall; res. York Beach, Me.
    iv. HATTIE J.[9], b. in Sunapee, Dec. 14, 1861; m. Sept. 16, 1884, C. A. Gates. She d. 22 Apr., 1891.
    v. JOHN Q.[9], b. in New London, N. H., June 7, 1868; res. York Beach, Me.; unm.
    vi. JENNIE P.[9], b. in New London, Feb. 7, 1871; m. Nov. 10, 1897.
    vii. FRED C.[9], b. in New London, Oct. 5, 1873; d. 23 June, 1898.

Children of ABIGAIL A.[8], (1836) [**1250**] (John Langdon[7], Matthew[6], Benjamin[5], Matthew[4], Dr. Matthew[3], Sergt. Abraham[2], Robert[1]) and Ralph Brown; res. Contocook, N. H.
    i. WILLIE RALPH BROWN, b. Jan. 11, 1858; res. Wilmot, N. H.
    ii. FLORA ETTA BROWN, b. June 19, 1866; res. Newport, N. H.

Children of ALMIRA L.[8], (1839) [**1251**] (John Langdon[7], Matthew[6], Benjamin[5], Matthew[4], Dr. Matthew[3], Sergt. Abraham[2], Robert[1]) and Elbridge Eaton; res. Creston, Ia.
    i. CHARLES L. EATON, b. in Bradford, N. H., Aug. 8, 1859.
    ii. NELLIE J. EATON, b. in Newbury, N. H., Oct. 18, 1861.
    iii. EMMA A. EATON, b. in Black River Falls, Wis., Mar. 14, 1868.
    iv. JOHN A. EATON, b. Black River Falls, Sept. 29, 1874.

Children of MARY D.[8], (1848) [**1252**] (John Langdon[7], Matthew[6], Benjamin[5], Matthew[4], Dr. Matthew[3], Sergt. Abraham[2], Robert[1]) and Charles Morrill; res. Concord, N. H.
    i. LUTHER H. MORRILL, b. June 16, 1867.
    ii. OTIS MORRILL, b. June 27, 1876.

Child of SYLVESTER FELCH[8], (1850) [**1253**] (John Langdon[7], Matthew[6], Benjamin[5], Matthew[4], Dr. Matthew[3], Sergt. Abraham[2], Robert[1]) and Addie (Morey) Adams; res. Everett, Snohomish Co., Wash.
    i. MYRTIE MAY[9], b. in Wilmot, N. H., Apr. 2, 1874; m. —— Whittier; res. New London, N. H.

Children of SUSAN E.[8], (1852) [1254] (John Langdon[7], Matthew[6], Benjamin[5], Matthew[4], Dr. Matthew[3], Sergt. Abraham[2], Robert[1]) and George F. Sleeper; res. Concord, N. H.
i. LURA DELL SLEEPER, b. in Concord, Aug. 3, 1872.
ii. ALICE ETHELWYN SLEEPER, b. in Concord, Sept. 18, 1874.
iii. GEORGE ANDREW SLEEPER, b. in Concord, Nov. 17, 1876.
iv. MINNIE MAY SLEEPER, b. in Concord, Nov. 9, 1880; d. 10 Sept., 1897.

Children of HANNAH MATILDA[8], (1855) [1255] (John Langdon[7], Matthew[6], Benjamin[5], Matthew[4], Dr. Matthew[3], Sergt. Abraham[2], Robert[1]) and James Hawthorn; res. Laconia, N. H.
i. WILLIAM JOHN HAWTHORN, b. Mar. 19, 1875; d. 3 Dec., 1876.
ii. DAVID MACK HAWTHORN, b. Jan. 8, 1878.
iii. SUSIE MAE HAWTHORN, b. Jan. 4, 1882.
iv. JAMES HENRY HAWTHORN, b. June 1, 1884.
v. JOHN LANGDON HAWTHORN, b. Dec. 15, 1886.
All born in Franklin Falls, N. H.

Children of DR. FRANK B.[8], (1854) [1256] (Enoch Cheney[7], Matthew[6], Benjamin[5], Matthew[4], Dr. Matthew[3], Sergt. Abraham[2], Robert[1]) and Mary S. (Bryant) Adams; res. Plymouth, Mich.
i. EVA BRYANT[9], b. Oct. 8, 1887.
ii. KATHERINE[9], b. Feb. 22, 1890.

Children of CYRUS W.[8], (1860) [1257] (Enoch Cheney[7], Matthew[6], Benjamin[5], Matthew[4], Dr. Matthew[3], Sergt. Abraham[2], Robert[1]) and Ella (Pettengill) Adams; res. Bethlehem, N. H.
i. LIZZIE MAY[9], b. May 1, 1883.
ii. GRACE MILDRED[9], b. May 29, 1885.

Child of THEOPHILUS B[8], (1845) [1258] (Theophilus B.[7], Rev. Theophilus B.[6], Benjamin[5], Matthew[4], Dr. Matthew[3], Sergt. Abraham[2], Robert[1]) and Margaret J. (Sharp) Adams; res. Nashua, N. H.
i. WILLIAM[9], b. in Nashua, Dec., 1866; d. young.

Child of Theophilus B.⁸ (1845) and Mary C. (Southard) Adams.

 ii. CHARLES T.⁹, b. in Nashua, Nov., 1868; d. young.

Child of GEORGIANA F.⁸, (1848) [1259] (Theophilus B.⁷, Rev. Theophilus B.⁶, Benjamin⁵, Matthew⁴, Dr. Matthew³, Sergt. Abraham², Robert¹) and Frank A. Barney; res. Nashua, N. H.

 i. ALICE M. BARNEY, b. in Nashua.

Children of GEORGE F.⁸, (1853) [1260] (Theophilus B.⁷, Rev. Theophilus B.⁶, Benjamin⁵, Matthew⁴, Dr. Matthew³, Sergt. Abraham², Robert¹) and Emma (Rolph) Adams; res. Nashua, N. H.

 i. EDDIE L.⁹, b. in Nashua, Sept. 4, 1876.
 ii. EMMA LIZZIE⁹, b. in Nashua, May 3, 1880.

Child of MARTHA ADELAIDE⁸, (1850) [1261] (Harrison H.⁷, Rev. Theophilus B.⁶, Benjamin⁵, Matthew⁴, Dr. Matthew³, Sergt. Abraham², Robert¹) and Oliver D. Wright; res. Newburyport, Mass.

 i. WALTER B. WRIGHT, b. 1873; m. Oct. 26, 1896, Mary Bell Smith of Ipswich, Mass.; res. Beverly, Mass.; 2 children: Henry P. and Jessie D.

Children of EDGAR G.⁸, (1847) [1262] (Gilson⁷, Russell⁶, Enoch⁵, Richard⁴, Richard³, Sergt. Abraham², Robert¹) and Maria E. (Gordon) Adams; res. Togus, Me.

 i. EMMA⁹, b. in Togus, June 23, 1874; d. 27 May, 1878.
 ii. LOUISA M.⁹, b. in Togus, Apr. 25, 1876; d. 25 May. 1878.
 iii. HATTIE G.⁹, b. in Togus, Jan. 14, 1878; res. Fryeburg, Me.; unm.
 iv. JOSIAH G.⁹, b. in Togus, Apr. 7, 1882; unm.

Child of GEORGE H.⁸, (1845) [1263] (Harrison⁷, Russell⁶, Enoch⁵, Richard⁴, Richard³, Sergt. Abraham², Robert¹) and Abbie J. (Shaw) Adams; res. Hill, N. H.

 i. ERVIN P.⁹, b. in Hill, N. H. Sept. 21, 1876; d. 23 Dec., 1878.

Children of CHARLES F.⁸, (1857) [**1264**] (Harrison⁷, Russell⁶, Enoch⁵, Richard⁴, Richard³, Sergt. Abraham², Robert¹) and Henrietta B. (Morrill) Adams; res. Hill, N. H.

    i. HEBER M.⁹, b. in Hill, N. H., June 17, 1881.
    ii. GEORGE E.⁹, b. in Hill, July 26, 1888.
    iii. CARL H.⁹, b. in Hill, Dec. 24, 1891.

Child of J. WARREN⁸, (1845) [**1265**] (James R.⁷, Russell⁶, Enoch⁵, Richard⁴, Richard³, Sergt. Abraham², Robert¹) and Sarah A. (Dickinson) Adams; res. Elgin, Kane Co., Ill.

    i. FRED A.⁹, b. in Hill, N. H., Dec. 11, 1873; res. Hill, N. H.; unm.

Child of ELLEN A.⁸, (1847) [**1266**] (James R.⁷, Russell⁶, Enoch⁵, Richard⁴, Richard³, Sergt. Abraham², Robert¹) and Geo. F. Chase.

    i. FLORENCE M. CHASE, b. July 24, 1872; res. Hill, N. H.; unm.

Children of HENRY EASTLAKE⁸, (1863) [**1267**] (Henry⁷, Richard⁶, Enoch⁵, Richard⁴, Richard³, Sergt. Abraham², Robert¹) and Etta May (Chalmers) Adams; res. Stockton, Cal.

    i. FRANK CHALMERS⁹, b. in Stockton, Nov. 15, 1888.
    ii. JANET TRUE⁹, b. in Stockton, Feb. 15, 1890.
    iii. HENRIETTA⁹, b. in Stockton, June 16, 1895; d. 25 Mar., 1897.

Child of CHARLES B.⁸, (1859) [**1268**] (Stephen C.⁷, Richard⁶, Enoch⁵, Richard⁴, Richard³, Sergt. Abraham², Robert¹) and Lucy M. (Horton) Adams; res. Somerville, Mass.

    i. FLORENCE E.⁹, b. in Somerville, June 11, 1889.

Child of CARRIE E.⁸, (1856) [**1269**] (John Quincy⁷, Simeon⁶, Simeon⁵, Richard⁴, Richard³, Sergt. Abraham², Robert¹) and Charles G. Brackett; res. Bangor, Me.

    i. EDITH M. BRACKETT, b. in Palmyra, Me., Oct. 5, 1883; d. 5 May, 1885.

Child of FRANK E.⁸, (1861) [**1270**] (John Quincy⁷, Simeon⁶, Simeon⁵, Richard⁴, Richard³, Sergt. Abraham², Robert¹) and Abby M. (Judkins) Adams; res. Newport, Me.

  i. ALFRED S.⁹, b. in Newport, Dec. 2, 1890.

Children of HOMER J.⁸, (1863) [**1271**] (John Quincy⁷, Simeon⁶, Simeon⁵, Richard⁴, Richard³, Sergt. Abraham², Robert¹) and Myra E. (Dyer) Adams; res. Palmyra, Me.

  i. CARRIE E⁹, b. April 20, 1889.
  ii. LEON E.⁹, b. Oct. 20, 1891.

Child of ELLEN HARRIET⁸, (1851) [**1272**] (Giles Aaron⁷, Richard⁶, Asa⁵, Richard⁴, Richard³, Sergt. Abraham², Robert¹) and Richard Tenny Noyes; res. Newbury, Mass.

  i. HOWARD ADAMS NOYES, b. May 7, 1879.

Child of SARAH AGNES⁸, (1854) [**1273**] (Giles Aaron⁷, Richard⁶, Asa⁵, Richard⁴, Richard³, Sergt. Abraham², Robert¹) and Edward F. Little; res. Newbury, Mass.

  i. AGNES LAWRENCE LITTLE, b. Sept. 27, 1896.

Children of CAROLINE LITTLE⁸, (1864) [**1274**] (Giles Aaron⁷, Richard⁶, Asa⁵, Richard⁴, Richard³, Sergt. Abraham², Robert¹) and Herbert A. Gillett; res. Newburyport, Mass.

  i. RUSSELL WILEY GILLETT, b. Sept. 15, 1889.
  ii. LAWRENCE ARNOLD GILLETT, b. Mar. 1, 1897.

Children of GEORGE MOULTON⁸, (1861) [**1275**] (Asa⁷, Richard⁶, Asa⁵, Richard⁴, Richard³, Sergt. Abraham², Robert¹) and Hattie M. (Stickney) Adams; res. Newbury, Mass.

  i. WINTHROP CLARK⁹, b. in Newbury, Nov. 24, 1881.
  ii. HAROLD COLEMAM⁹, b. in Newbury, June 10, 1883.
  iii. LAWRENCE KINMAN⁹, b. in Newbury, Sept. 22, 1885.
  iv. GEORGE ELLIOTT⁹, b. in Newbury, July 15, 1887.
  v. WM. BROWN⁹, b. in Newbury, May 29, 1889.

vi. RICHARD ELLSWORTH[9], b. in Newbury, Sept. 19, 1890 ; d. 15 Aug., 1891.
vii. ERNEST STICKNEY[9], b. in Newbury, Jan. 25, 1892 ; d. 16 Apr., 1894.
viii. ROLAND[9], b. in Newbury, Nov. 15, 1892 ; d. 14 Dec., 1892.
ix. ELEANOR[9], b. in Newbury, Dec. 27, 1893.
x. MILDRED[9], b. in Newbury, May 1, 1895.
xi. JOHN COLBY[9], b. in Newbury, May 11, 1896.

Child of CHARLES W.[8], (1859) **[1276]** (Capt. Dennis[7], Nathan[6], Ebenezer[5], Richard[4], Richard[3], Sergt. Abraham[2], Robert[1]) and Virtue E. (Lucas) Adams; res. Clear Springs, Mo.

i. ALTA G.[9], b. in Missouri, Jan. 19, 1891.

Children of NATHAN E.[8], (1864) **[1277]** (Capt. Dennis[7], Nathan[6], Ebenezer[5], Richard[4], Richard[3], Sergt. Abraham[2], Robert[1]) and Rebecca J. (Wyrick) Adams; res. Clear Springs, Mo.

i. MARY M.[9], b. in Clear Springs, July 12, 1887.
ii. HELEN L.[9], b. in Clear Springs, Mar. 10, 1889.
iii. DENNIS E.[9], b. in Clear Springs, Dec. 9, 1890.
iv. WILLIAM R.[9], b. in Clear Springs, May 29, 1893.

Child of DENNIS EZRA[8], (1866) **[1278]** (Capt. Dennis[7], Nathan[6], Ebenezer[5], Richard[4], Richard[3], Sergt. Abraham[2], Robert[1]) and Violet E. (Coon) Adams; res. Hulton, Mont.

i. INEZ G.[9], b. Sept. 22, 1897.

Children of ANNIE S.[8], (1868) **[1279]** (Capt. Dennis[7], Nathan[6], Ebenezer[5], Richard[4], Richard[3], Sergt. Abraham[2], Robert[1]) and William M. Somerville; res. Clear Springs, Mo.

i. ALPHA M. SOMERVILLE, b. June 24, 1888.
ii. RUBA M. SOMERVILLE, b. Jan. 5, 1890.
iii. ELSIE R. SOMERVILLE, b. Sept. 22, 1891.
iv. SHERMAN S. SOMERVILLE, b. Mar. 10, 1896.

Children of ARTHUR SUMNER[8], (1868) **[1280]** (John Calvin[7], Philip D.[6], Ebenezer[5], Richard[4], Richard[3], Sergt. Abraham[2], Robert[1]) and Carry Bell (Haynes) Adams; res. Marblehead, Mass.

i. EDNA PALMER[9], b. in Marblehead, Mar. 11, 1890.
ii. JOHN SUMNER[9], b. in Marblehead, Apr., 1897.

474   ROBERT ADAMS   [Ninth Generation.

Child of WALTER LESLIE⁸, (1867) [1281] (Simeon Augustus⁷, Jesse⁶, Simeon⁵, John⁴, Richard³, Sergt. Abraham², Robert¹) and Florence H. (Ogden) Adams; res. Norwich, Conn.

    i. WALTER LESLIE⁹, b. in Norwich, June 31, 1896. *m. Gladys Coburg of Middletown, N. Y. Apr. 14, 1928. 1 son born Walter Leslie 3rd. Duke College*

Children of RICHARD HENRY⁸, (1855) [1282] (Richard⁷, Capt. Richard⁶, Moses⁵, Moses⁴, Richard³, Sergt. Abraham², Robert¹) and Annie (Cunningham) Adams; res. Newton Upper Falls, Mass.

    i. MYRTIE⁹, b. in Newton Upper Falls, May 6, 1883.
    ii. FLORENCE EMMA⁹, b. in Newton Upper Falls, Mar. 22, 1891.

Children of JOHN Q.⁸, JR., (1848) [1283] (John Q.⁷, Capt. Richard⁶, Moses⁵, Moses⁴, Richard³, Sergt. Abraham², Robert¹) and Mary T. (Young) Adams; res. Newburyport, Mass.

    i. JOHN EVERETT⁹, b. in Newburyport, Mar. 8, 1869; d. 19 Mar., 1889.
    ii. SARAH BURGESS⁹, b. in Newburyport, Jan. 7, 1871.
    iii. BLANCH LILIAN⁹, b. in Newburyport, Mar. 14, 1873. *m. Arpton J. Woodward Dec. 18, 1901*
    iv. HERBERT CLIFTON⁹, b. in Newburyport, May 7, 1881; d. 6 Dec., 1883.

Children of GEORGE F.⁸, (1852) [1284] (John Q.⁷, Capt. Richard⁶, Moses⁵, Moses⁴, Richard³, Sergt. Abraham², Robert¹) and Elizabeth G. (Mitchell) Adams; res. Newburyport, Mass.

    i. GEORGE F.⁹, JR., b. in Newburyport, May 1, 1870; m. Feb. 21, 1891, Lizzie G. Robbins.
    ii. CHARLES H.⁹, b. in Newburyport, Dec. 12, 1871; m. Dec. 2, 1893, Hannah E. Fleming. *d. Oct. 9, 1943*
    iii. LOTTIE E.⁹, b. in Newburyport, Nov. 15, 1874; m. July 2, 1893, Fred D. Russell.
    iv. WARREN OTIS⁹, b. in Newburyport, May 19, 1877; d. 21 July, 1880.
    v. FLORENCE⁹, b. in Newburyport, Jan. 3, 1881.
    vi. WARREN O.⁹, b. in Newburyport; d. Jan. 26, 1884.
    vii. MABEL G.⁹, b. in Newburyport, Mar. 15, 1892.

[Ninth Generation.] OF NEWBURY, MASS. 475

Child of MARY ELLEN[8], (1861) [1285] (Xenophon[7], Capt. Richard[6], Moses[5], Moses[4], Richard[3], Sergt. Abraham[2], Robert[1]) and John L. Knight; res. Newburyport, Mass.

i. LILLIAN HOYT KNIGHT, b. Feb. 22, 1885.

m. Walter Knapp
d. Dec. 9, 1941/43

Child of MARIA CHRISTIAN[8], (1871) [1286] (Xenophon[7], Capt. Richard[6], Moses[5], Moses[4], Richard[3], Sergt. Abraham[2], Robert[1]) and Frank W. Reynolds; res. Somerville, Mass.

i. MARION ADAMS REYNOLDS, b. Oct. 25, 1897.

Child of CARRIE STONE[8], (1864) [1287] (Moses Cook[7], Capt. Richard[6], Moses[5], Moses[4], Richard[3], Sergt. Abraham[2], Robert[1]) and Frank Perkins; res. Newbury, Mass.

i. MAUD PERKINS, b. July 25, 1885.

died June 13, 1916

Child of LIZZIE B.[8], (1873) [1288] (Moses[7], Moses[6], Moses[5], Moses[4], Richard[3], Sergt. Abraham[2], Robert[1]) and Fred M. Burnham; res. Essex, Mass.

i. MASON A. BURNHAM, b. Mar. 22, 1897.

Child of LOUISA BRADLEY[8], (1848) [1289] (Charles[7], John[6], Ensign James[5], Edmund[4], Richard[3], Sergt. Abraham[2], Robert[1]) and Rufus Crombie; res. Derry, N. H.

i. LOUISE R. CROMBIE, b. May 5, 1874; m. Sept. 3, 1896, Geo. F. Bampton; res. Derry, N. H.

Children of CHARLES F.[8], (1864) [1290] (Horace[7], John[6], Ensign James[5], Edmund[4], Richard[3], Sergt. Abraham[2], Robert[1]) and Ella (Page) Adams; res. Hampstead, N. H.

i. CHARLES WILLIE[9], b. in Hampstead, Apr. 17, 1882.
ii. NELLIE FRANK[9], b. in Hampstead, Dec. 22, 1885.
iii. LUCY ALMIRA[9], b. in Hampstead, Feb. 22, 1888.
iv. HORACE[9], b. in Atkinson, N. H., Mar. 4, 1890.
v. HELEN MARION[9], b. in Atkinson, Jan. 7, 1893.
vi. FLORENCE[9], b. in Hampstead, Dec. 21, 1895.
vii. CARRIE H.[9], b. in Hampstead, July 3, 1899.

Children of NORMAN R.⁸, (1821) [**1291**] (Roswell⁷, Asahel⁶, Zadoc⁵, Jacob⁴, Sergt. Jacob³, Jacob², Robert¹) and Chloe (Remington) Adams; res. Suffield, Conn.

1472. i. ADDISON L.⁹, b. in Agawam, Mass., Dec. 22, 1844; m. July 10, 1869, Minerva E. Fish of Granby, b. Mar. 18, 1846; res. Suffield, Conn.
    ii. ROSWELL⁹, b. in Agawam, [June 17, 1845?] May 20, 1846; unm.; res. Suffield, Conn.
    iii. SUSAN E.⁹, b. in Agawam, Nov. 30, 1848; m. Mar. 12, 1880, Franklin Smith; res. Suffield, Conn.; no issue.
1473. iv. GEORGE W.⁹, b. in Agawam, Nov. 8, 1850; m. (1) Jan. 19, 1873, Hattie A. Moore, b. Apr. 30, 1849; d. 5 Dec., 1875; m. (2) Nov. 30, 1876, Flora E. Thompson, b. July 25, 1858; res. Suffield (Mapleton), Conn.
1474. v. MARIE J.⁹, b. in Agawam, Sept. 14, 1852; m. Apr. 16, 1874, Chas. H. Fowler; res. Thompsonville, Conn.
    vi. HELEN H.⁹, b. in Suffield, Apr. 19, 1855; m. Joseph D. Kelson of Bridgeport, Conn.; res. Wallingford, Conn.; no issue.

Children of MARY BEDORTHA⁸, (1817) [**1292**] (Alvin⁷, Noadiah⁶, Zadoc⁵, Jacob⁴, Sergt. Jacob³, Jacob², Robert¹) and Sullivan P. Lamberton; res. Suffield, Conn.

    i. EDWARD CLARENCE LAMBERTON, b. May 21, 1844; d. 22 May, 1844.
    ii. CHARLES EDWARD LAMBERTON, b. Sept. 17, 1845; d. 29 Aug., 1847.
    iii. ADELINE ISABELLE LAMBERTON, b. Sept. 11, 1847; m. Silas Lester. She d. 21 Mar., 1871.
    iv. MARY EMILY LAMBERTON, b. July 23, 1849; unm.
    v. WILBUR FISK LAMBERTON, b. Sept. 20, 1851; did he m. Ellen J. Sikes, dau. of John Sykes?
    vi. CARRIE ANNETTA LAMBERTON, b. Dec. 28, 1853; m. James Quackenbush; res. Beloit, Wis.
    vii. HENRY ALVIN LAMBERTON, b. Aug. 7, 1856; d. 1 Feb., 1880.
    viii. JULIA ANN LAMBERTON, b. Jan 18, 1858; m. Arthur Rice; res. No. Granby, Conn.

Child of AMASA A⁸, (1822) [**1293**] (Alvin⁷, Noadiah⁶, Zadoc⁵, Jacob⁴, Sergt. Jacob³, Jacob², Robert¹) and Cyndonia (Kibbe) Adams; res. Springfield, Mass.

    i. JOSEPHINE⁹, b. in Springfield, Oct. 4, 1852; d. 26 Nov., 1864.

Children of LOUISA[8], (1822) [**1294**] (Harvey[7], Noadiah[6], Zadoc[5], Jacob[4], Sergt. Jacob[3], Jacob[2], Robert[1]) and Job Fowler; res. Suffield, Conn.

    i. LOUIS ADAMS FOWLER, b. Apr. 3, 1848 ; m. (1) Catherine Young ; she d. 15 Mar., 1873 ; m. (2) Sadie Rithman.
       He is a contractor and builder ; res. Baltimore, Md.

    ii. CHARLES HARVEY FOWLER, b. Apr. 16, 1853 ; m. Apr. 16, 1874, Marie J. Adams, dau. of Norman R. and Chloe (Remington) Adams, b. Sept. 14, 1852 ; res. Thompsonville, Conn.

    iii. WILLIAM ELIJAH FOWLER, b. May 10, 1855; m. (1) Flora Willey of Agawam ; m. (2) Mary McFethers ; res. West Springfield (Merrick), Mass.
       He is a railroad engineer.

Children of JOHN P.[8], (1825) [**1295**] (Harvey[7], Noadiah[6], Zadoc[5], Jacob[4], Sergt. Jacob[3], Jacob[2], Robert[1]) and Susanna B. (Bashore) Adams; res. Lima, Ohio.

    i. IDA L.[9], b. in Lima, Mar. 5, 1858 ; m. Feb. 14, 1887, D. Y. Grieb of Chattanoga, Tenn.; res. Missionary Ridge, Ga.; P. O. Suburba, Tenn.

    ii. MILLY[9], b. in Lima, Dec. 16, 1859 ; unm.

    iii. DICKIE[9] (twin), b. in Lima, Dec. 16, 1859 ; d. 20 May, 1873.

Child of ALBERT[8], (1828) [**1296**] (Harvey[7], Noadiah[6], Zadoc[5], Jacob[4], Sergt. Jacob[3], Jacob[2], Robert[1]) and Elizabeth (Bogardus) Adams; res. Springfield, Mass.

1475.   i. NELLIE M.[9], b. in Springfield, June 1, 1856; m. Apr. 24, 1879, James A. Bryan.

Children of JOSEPH B.[8], (1834) [**1297**] (Harvey[7], Noadiah[6], Zadoc[5], Jacob[4], Sergt. Jacob[3], Jacob[2] Robert[1]) and Eliza Ann (Doss) Adams; res. Blairsville, Posey Co., Ind.

    i. CHARLES HARVEY[9], b. in Wadesville, Ind., Aug. 19, 1864 ; d. 16 Mar., 1867.

    ii. ELLA[9], b. in Wadesville, May 25, 1867 ; m. (1) Mar., 1891, Willie Kincheloe of New Haven, Ill.; he d. 1893 ; m. (2) about 1895, —— York ; res. New Haven, Gallatin Co., Ill.; no issue.

Child of JOSEPH B.⁸, (1834) and Mary Ann (Sprague) Adams.

1476. iii. ADDIE LOUISA⁹, b. in Wadesville, July 19, 1872; m. Aug. 26, 1891, Hovey Kincheloe of Harmony, Posey Co., Ind.

Children of BENJAMIN F.⁸, (1841) [**1298**] (Harvey⁷, Noadiah⁶, Zadoc⁵, Jacob⁴, Sergt. Jacob³, Jacob², Robert¹) and Lurana (Cox) Adams; res. Cincinnati, Ohio.

 i. FLORA A.⁹, b. in Posey Co., Ind., May 3, 1866.
 ii. CLARA D.⁹, b. in Posey Co., Sept. 2, 1868; m. 1890, Josiah Wade of Posey Co., Ind.
  They had one child, Flora E. Wade, when the mother became insane, and is in an asylum at Evansville, Ind.
 iii. HARVEY J.⁹, b. in Posey Co., Feb. 21, 1875; m. Feb. 23, 1898, Aldine Robinson of Cincinnati, Ohio.
 iv. DAVID M.⁹, b. in Posey Co., Mar. 6, 1878.
 v. TINY M.⁹ (twin), b. in Posey Co., Mar. 6, 1878; d. in 4 months.

Children of BENJAMIN F.⁸, (1841) and Alice (Montgomery) Adams.

 vi. EVA⁹, b. in Ohio, Dec. 12, 1885.
 vii. BENNIE⁹, b. in Ohio, Mar. 5, 1889.

Children of ALVIN⁸, (1819) [**1299**] (Lucius⁷, Noadiah⁶, Zadoc⁵, Jacob⁴, Sergt. Jacob³, Jacob², Robert¹) and Emily A. (Sherwin) Adams; res. Springfield, Mass.

 i. ALVIN⁹.
 ii. EMILY⁹.
 iii. FRANCES⁹.
 iv. EMILY S.⁹; d. 23 Jan., 1850.
  No representative of this family can be found.

Child of FRANCIS J. PARKER, (1822) [**1300**] and Mary D. Puffer; res. San Francisco, Cal.

 i. CHARLES M. T. PARKER, b. Aug. 4, 1861; res. San Francisco, Cal.

Children of RENSLOW S. PARKER, (1823) [**1301**] and Sarah Cole; res. Chicago, Ill.

    i. EDWARD PARKER. d. in Denver, Col.
    ii. HENRY PARKER, res. Evanston, Ill.
    iii. ELVIRA PARKER, m. Samuel J. Sherer; res. Chicago.

Child of EBEN G. PARKER, (1825) [**1302**] and Mary A. Chapin.

    i. HOWARD PARKER.

Children of MIRANDA C. PARKER, (1828) [**1303**] and Palmer S. Vinton.

    i. EUGENE VINTON.
    ii. ADA VINTON, m. Henry A. Dean; res. New York.

Children of JANE LE ROY PARKER, (1837) [**1304**] and James F. Gillette; res. Chicago, Ill.

    i. MARTHA PARKER GILLETTE, b. Aug. 29, 1861; d. 24 May, 1890.
    ii. ALBERT KENT GILLETTE, b. Feb. 5, 1863; d. 13 Nov., 1863.
    iii. MARY ASHTON GILLETTE, b. Jan. 15, 1868; m. Oct. 28, 1897, Charles Wesley Dempster; res. Chicago, Ill.
    iv. HOWARD FRANK GILLETTE, b. Apr. 9, 1872; res. 2908 Michigan Ave., Chicago, Ill.

Children of BETSEY[6], (1823) [**1305**] (Edward[7], Arah[6], Zadoc[5], Jacob[4], Sergt. Jacob[3], Jacob[2], Robert[1]) and Austin Dwight Bliss; res. Monson, Mass., and Rockton, Ill.

    i. MARY ANN BLISS, b. in Monson, Oct. 22, 1845; m. Addison Hart; res. Clinton, Ia.; d. there; one child d. young.
    ii. GEORGE W. BLISS, b. in Monson, June 19, 1847; m. Mar. 11, 1873, at W. Chesterfield, Mass., Alice M. Eddy, b. in Williamsville, Mass., Apr. 8, 1850; res 131 State St., Northampton, Mass.
    iii. JENNIE BLISS, b. in Rockton, Ill., Nov. 21, 1856; d. in Rockton, 21 June, 1875.
    iv. EDW. ADAMS BLISS, b. in Rockton, Mar. 29, 1858; m. Sept. 22, 1881, Mary Kimball of Rockton, Ill., b. Sept. 20, 1864; res. Nashville, Mo.
    v. EMMA BLISS, b. in Rockton, June 11, 1862; d. in Amboy, Ill., 5 Aug., 1877.

480   ROBERT ADAMS   [Ninth Generation.

Child of FRANCIS ANN⁸, (1828) [1306] (Edward⁷, Arah⁶ Zadoc⁵, Jacob⁴, Sergt. Jacob³, Jacob², Robert¹) and Calvin Clark; res. Hampden, Mass.

    i. WILLIE W. CLARK, b. in Hampden, July 13, 1852; d. 17 Sept., 1852.

Children of LYDIA ROGERS⁸, (1829) [1307] (Edward⁷, Arah⁶, Zadoc⁵, Jacob⁴, Sergt. Jacob³, Jacob², Robert¹) and George Lincoln Bathrick; res. Whitinville and Springfield, Mass.

    i. GEORGE FRANKLIN BATHRICK, b. July 12, 1850; m. Sept. 12, 1872, Annetta Skinner of N. Dana, Mass.
    ii. DWIGHT WORTHINGTON BATHRICK, b. Apr. 15, 1855; m. Mar. 6, 1878, Ella Sherman of Whitin, Mass.
    iii. ELIZABETH FRANCES BATHRICK, b. Apr. 7, 1859; d. 9 Oct., 1859.
    iv. JUDSON HAYWARD BATHRICK, b. Jan. 1, 1863; living; unm.
    v. EDWARD ADAMS BATHRICK, b. Aug. 15, 1866; m. July 4, 1894; Mary F. May of Plymouth.

Child of EDWARD⁸, JR., (1832) [1308] (Edward⁷, Arah⁶, Zadoc⁵, Jacob⁴, Sergt. Jacob³, Jacob², Robert¹) and Margaret (Mixter) Adams; res. W. Hartford, Conn.

1477.   i. FRANK SYLVESTER⁹, b. in Hampden, Mass., Apr. 16, 1857; m. Nov. 24, 1881, Nellie Woodford of Hartford.
        He is an employe of the Machine Works, W. Hartford, Conn.

Children of JOHN QUINCY⁸, (1847) [1309] (Edward⁷, Arah⁶, Zadoc⁵, Jacob⁴, Sergt. Jacob³, Jacob², Robert¹) and Delia F. (Lee) Adams; res. Hampden, Mass.

    i. JOHN EDWARD⁹, b. in Hampden, May 9, 1876.
        He is a student in Wesleyan University, Middletown, Conn.
    ii. HERBERT WEBSTER⁹, b. in Hampden, Mar. 4, 1879.
        He is an employe of the Organ Works, Springfield, Mass.
    iii. EMORY ELI⁹, b. in Hampden, Apr. 14, 1886.
        He is a student at home.

Children of ELIZABETH GRAY FULLER, (1830) [1310] and Ransford Worthington; res. Springfield, Mass.

i. JANE ELIZABETH WORTHINGTON, b. July 15, 1848 ; m. 1878, Wm. Chiswick.
ii. ANIZETTA WORTHINGTON, b. Oct. 15, 1851; m. 1870, Robert Miller.
iii. GERALDINE WORTHINGTON, b. May 20, 1856; m. 1887, Frank Fowler. She d. 18 Aug., 1896.
iv. CORA WORTHINGTON, b. June 24, 1861 ; d. 2 Nov., 1862.
v. CORA L. WORTHINGTON, b. June 11, 1865 ; m. 1886, Reuben Humphebill.
vi. ALGERON WORTHINGTON, b. Mar. 16, 1867 ; m. 1894, Mary A. Mahony.
vii. FRANK J. WORTHINGTON, b. May 24, 1869 ; m. Dec. 28, 1896, Rosetta Howarth.

Child of BELINDA SHARLON[8], (1832) [**1311**] (John[7], Arah[6], Zadoc[5], Jacob[4], Sergt. Jacob[3], Jacob[2], Robert[1]) and Charles A. Roberts; res. Meriden, Conn.
i. ARTHUR HENRY ROBERTS, b. May 19, 1858 ; d. 29 Feb., 1864.

Children of MASSENA CLARK[8], (1840) [**1312**] (John[7], Arah[6], Zadoc[5], Jacob[4], Sergt. Jacob[3], Jacob[2], Robert[1]) and Elizabeth (Sherwood) Adams; res. Hartford, Conn.
i. CHARLES F.[9], b. 1868 ; d. in Hartford, 10 Feb., 1892.
ii. WALTER SHERWOOD[9], b. 1872; d. in Hartford, 13 Sept., 1893, age 21 years.
iii. ELIZABETH[9].

Children of HATTIE ALICE[8], (1859) [**1313**] (Henry L.[7], Horace[6], Capt. Gideon[5], Daniel[4], Daniel[3], Jacob[2], Robert[1]) and Dr. Arthur A. Gillette; res. Rome, N. Y.
i. ALICE MARY GILLETTE, b. Nov. 3, 1883 ; d. 1 Aug., 1893.
ii. ALFRED A. H. WYLIE GILLETTE, b. Aug. 8, 1898.

Children of HORACE WYLIE[8], (1862) [**1314**] (Henry L.[7], Horace[6], Capt. Gideon[5], Daniel[4], Daniel[3], Jacob[2], Robert[1]) and Julia C. (Wilson) Adams; res. Rome, N. Y.
i. HENRY B.[9], b. in Rome, Feb. 22, 1888.
ii. RUTH[9], b. in Rome, July 8, 1892.

Children of WILLIAM ELIPHALET⁸, (1837) [**1315**] (Lewis Alonson⁷, Eliphalet⁶, Jr., Eliphalet⁵, Freegrace⁴, Abraham³, Jacob², Robert¹) and Isabelle (Gordon) Adams; res. Drayton, Ont.

1478. i. MIRION (Minnie)⁹, b. in Drayton, Jan. 5, 1866 ; m. Dec. 1, 1890, Geo. Wesley Cook ; res. Grand Rapids, Mich.
1479. ii. LAURA THERESA, b. in Drayton, Aug. 22, 1867-8 ; m. Mar. 27, 1893, Chas. James Hodgins, b. in Granton, Ont., July 24, 1868; res. Cleveland, Ohio.
   iii. WILLIAM HENRY⁹, b. in Drayton, Feb. 22, 1870.
       He was a brakeman, and was killed in a railroad accident in Michigan, July 1, 1897.
   iv. ELSIE EFFIE⁹, b. in Drayton, Aug. 24, 1874 ; res. Drayton, unm.
   v. THOMAS H. G.⁹, b. in Drayton, Sept. 27, 1877; d. 29 Sept., 1877.
   vi. CLIFFORD NEWMAN⁹, b. in Drayton, July 11, 1879 ; res. Grand Rapids, Mich ; clerk, unm.
   vii. CARMINA⁹, b. in Drayton, Mar. 10, 1885 ; res. Drayton, Ont.
   viii. JOHN CARROLL⁹, b. in Drayton, June 28, 1886 ; d. 23 Oct., 1886.

Children of MALINDA MARIA⁸, (1839) [**1316**] (Lewis Alonson⁷, Eliphalet⁶, Jr., Eliphalet⁵, Freegrace⁴, Abraham³, Jacob², Robert¹) and George M. Smith; res. Lansing, Mich.

   i. LIZZIE A. SMITH, b. Dec. 12, 1866 ; m. Fred Lewis.
   ii. WILLIAM HENRY SMITH, b. Aug. 6, 1872 ; d. 15 Sept., 1873.

Children of ALMIRA JANE⁸, (1844) [**1317**] (Lewis Alanson⁷, Eliphalet⁶, Jr., Eliphalet⁵, Freegrace⁴, Abraham³, Jacob², Robert¹) and James Roe; res. Gorric, Ont.

   i. LIZZIE JANE ROE, b. Aug. 22, 1862.
       She is a teacher of music ; unm.
   ii. LAURA T. ROE, b. Feb. 28, 1865 ; m. Dec. 19, 1888, J. A. Strong, a farmer ; res. Gorric, Ont.
   ii. JAMES LEWIS ROE, b. Feb. 23, 1867 ; m. Oct. 8, 1891, Lizzie Diebel ; a farmer.
   iv. MARY ROE, b. Nov. 18-20, 1869.
   v. MARY E. ROE, b. Dec. 10, 1870 ; m. July 7, 1898, John A. Strong, a liveryman ; res. Gorric, Ont.
   vi. LETETIA ROE, b. Mar. 2, 1874.
   vii. WILLIE J. ROE, b. Aug. 20, 1876.

- viii. WESLEY R. ROE, b. Apr, 19, 1879.
- ix. AUGUSTA A. ROE, b. Aug. 17, 1882.
- x. BLAKE A. ROE, b. Nov. 1, 1884; d. 19 May, 1885.

Children of VINCENT RICE[5], (1846) [1318] (Lewis Alanson[7], Eliphalet[6], Jr., Eliphalet[5], Freegrace[4], Abraham[3], Jacob[2], Robert[1]) and Arletta Ann (Crane) Adams; res. Drayton, Ont.

- i. JOSEPH MORLEY[9], b. in Drayton, Jan. 1, 1871; unm.; res. Drayton, Ont.
- ii. ISAAC ALANSON[9], b. in Drayton, July 7, 1872.
- iii. GEORGE AMBROSE[9], b. in Drayton, July 22, 1874; d. 24 May, 1876.
- iv. EMMA AUGUSTA[9], b. in Drayton, Mar. 31, 1876; d. 19 Jan., 1895.
- v. EZRA HENRY[9], b. in Drayton, July 16, 1878.
- vi. CHARITY ELIZABETH[9], b. in Drayton, June 28, 1880.
- vii. VINCENT ELIPHALET[9], b. in Drayton, Jan. 8, 1883; d. 22 Jan., 1895.
- viii. ARLETTA A. M.[9], b. in Drayton, Feb. 12, 1885.
- ix. VICTORIA MABEL[9], b. in Drayton, July 9, 1887.
- x. PEARL W.[9], b. in Drayton, Oct. 6, 1889.
- xi. PERCY W.[9] (twin), b. in Drayton, Oct. 6, 1889; d. 13 Nov., 1894.
- xii. EVA MILDRED[9], b. in Drayton, Oct. 6, 1892; d. 31, Dec., 1894.

Children of THOMAZING AUGUSTA[8], (1849) [1319] (Lewis Alanson[7], Eliphalet[6], Jr., Eliphalet[5], Freegrace[4], Abraham[3], Jacob[2], Robert[1]) and Edward A. Noice; res. Guelph, Ont.

- i. FREDERICK VINCENT NOICE, b. Aug. 20, 1869; res. Yukon country.
- ii. HERBERT E. S. NOICE, b. Sept. 22, 1871; res. Yukon country.
- iii. E. JOHN Q. NOICE, b. Aug. 31, 1874; d. 18 Dec., 1888.

Children of JOHN QUINCY[8], (1851) [1320] (Lewis Alanson[7], Eliphalet[6], Jr., Eliphalet[5], Freegrace[4], Abraham[3], Jacob[2], Robert[1]) and Sarah Ellen (Dales) Adams; res. Drayton, Ont.

- i. JOSEPH MASON[9], b. in Drayton, May 18, 1878.
  He is a druggist in Toronto, Ont.
- ii. JAMES FRANKLIN[9], b. in Drayton, Dec. 6, 1879.
- iii. EMERSON BLAKE[9], b. in Drayton, June 4, 1885; res. Portage, La Prairie, Mank.

Children of LUCAS RUFUS⁸, (1853) [**1321**] (Lewis Alanson⁷, Eliphalet⁶, Jr., Eliphalet⁵, Freegrace⁴, Abraham³, Jacob², Robert¹) and Melissa (Proctor) Adams; res. Drayton, Ont.
   i. HOWARD RYERSON⁹, b. in Drayton, May 2, 1884.
   ii. GARFIELD PROCTOR⁹, b. in Drayton, July 25, 1886.
   iii. LENELLA PEARL⁹, b. in Drayton, July 29, 1888.

Children of LEWIS RANSOM⁸, (1856) [**1322**] (Lewis Alanson⁷, Eliphalet⁶, Jr., Eliphalet⁵, Freegrace⁴, Abraham³, Jacob², Robert¹) and Mary Ann (Close) Adams; res. Drayton, Ont.
   i. EDNA E.⁹, b. in Drayton, Feb. 3, 1886 ; d. 25 Aug., 1886.
   ii. EDITH MAY⁹, b. in Drayton, Apr. 6, 1887.
   iii. MYRTLE ALMIRA⁹, b. in Drayton, Aug. 30, 1890 ; d. 23 Apr., 1891.
   iv. JOHN QUINCY⁹, b. in Drayton, Apr. 16, 1893.

Children of MARY EMELINE⁸, (1852) [**1324**] (Wellington⁷, Eliphalet⁶, Jr., Eliphalet⁵, Freegrace⁴, Abraham³, Jacob², Robert¹) and Wellington Wilson; res. Minto, Ont.
   i. CAROLINE WILSON.
   ii. FRANCIS WILSON.
   iii. WILLIAM WILSON.

Children of EZRA⁸, (1855) [**1325**] (Wellington⁷, Eliphalet⁶, Jr., Eilphalet⁵, Freegrace⁴, Lieut. Abraham³, Jacob², Robert¹) and Margaret Jane (Anderson) Adams; res. Minto, Ont.
   i. WELLINGTON⁹, b. in Minto, July 3, 1877
   ii. MARY ELLEN⁹, b. in Minto, Feb. 23, 1879.
   iii. ELIZABETH⁹, b. in Minto, Aug. 21, 1880.
   iv. WILLIAM⁹, b. in Minto, July 19, 1882.
   v. EDITH MAY⁹, b. in Minto, Jan. 12, 1889.

Children of ELIZA M.⁸, (1846) [**1326**] (Henry Proctor⁷, Rev. Ezra⁶, Eliphalet⁵, Freegrace⁴, Abraham³, Jacob², Robert¹) and Rev. John Saunders; res. Georgetown, Ont.
   i. EMILY LETITIA SAUNDERS, b. Mar. 20, 1872 ; m. Sept. 28, 1898, J. Edgar Slaght.

ii. S. HENRY ADAMS SAUNDERS, b. Feb. 6, 1874.
iii. JOHN EZRA SAUNDERS, b. Oct. 20, 1876 ; m. about 1896,—— ——
iv. JAMES ALBERT SAUNDERS, b. Nov. 10, 1878.
v. LILLIAN MAY SAUNDERS, b. Feb. 7, 1884.
vi. GEORGE ALEX. SAUNDERS, b. Feb. 26, 1887.

Children of EZRA P.[8], (1848) [**1327**] (Henry Proctor[7], Rev. Ezra[6], Eliphalet[5], Freegrace[4], Abraham[3], Jacob[2], Robert[1]) and Margaret (Flewelling) Adams; res. Fergus Falls, Minn.

i. EMILY ELIZABETH[9], b. in Minneapolis, Minn., Dec. 17, 1876 ; d. 22 Oct., 1877.
ii. WILLIAM HENRY[9], b. in Baldwin, Wis., Dec. 7, 1878; res. Fergus Falls, Minn.; unm. 1899.
iii. BESSIE METCALF[9], b. in Baldwin, Mar. 31, 1881.
iv. MABEL ELIZA[9], b. in Baldwin, June 3, 1883.
v. HULDAH REBECCA[9], b. in Baltic, S. Dak., Apr. 4, 1885.
vi. ETHEL MARGARET[9], b. in Fergus Falls, Minn., Feb. 22, 1890.

Children of JAMES HENRY[8], (1855) [**1328**] (Henry Proctor[7], Rev. Ezra[6], Eliphalet[5], Freegrace[4], Abraham[3], Jacob[2], Robert[1]) and Lizzie M. (Boyd) Adams; res. Hanover, Ont.

i. HENRY PROCTOR[9], b. in Hanover, May 2, 1879 ; d. 17 Mar., 1880.
ii. THOMAS BOYD[9], b. in Hanover, Nov. 29, 1880 ; d. 20 Mar., 1889.
iii. WILLIAM EZRA[9], b. in Hanover, Nov. 3, 1882.
iv. PHEBE LOUISA[9], b. in Hanover, Jan. 13, 1885.
v. MARY VICTORIA[9], b in Hanover, July 8, 1887.
vi. ANNIE MAMETA[9], b. in Hanover, Aug. 18, 1889.
vii. JAMES FRANKLIN[9], b. in Hanover, May 21, 1893.
viii. COLEMAN BOYD[9], b. in Hanover, June 13, 1895.

Children of HULDAH[8], (1858) [**1329**] (Henry Proctor[7], Rev. Ezra[6], Eliphalet[5], Freegrace[4], Abraham[3], Jacob[2], Robert[1]) and Andrew Thomas Carr; res. Centralia, Wash.

i. ELIZABETH ADAMS CARR, b. June 11, 1884.
ii. GERTRUDE M. CARR, b. Nov. 14, 1892-3.

Children of GEORGE E.[8], (1859) [**1330**] (Henry Proctor[7], Rev. Ezra[6], Eliphalet[5], Freegrace[4], Abraham[3], Jacob[2], Robert[1]) and Alice Elizabeth (Garrett) Adams; res. Edinburg, N. Dak.
- i. ALFRED EDMUND[9], b. in Edinburg, July 30, 1890.
- ii. WILLIAM QUINCY[9], b. in Edinburg, Sept. 6, 1893.
- iii. GEORGE GRIFFIN[9], b. in Edinburg, Sept. 21, 1895.
- iv. HENRY PROCTOR[9], b. in Edinburg, Mar. 3, 1898.

Child of KELLY G.[8], (1861) [**1331**] (Henry Proctor[7], Rev. Ezra[6], Eilphalet[5], Freegrace[4], Abraham[3], Jacob[2], Robert[1]) and Annie (Murphy) Adams; res. Cavalier, Pembina Co., N. Dak.
- i. HERBY CARTER[9], b. in Cavalier, July 28, 1895.

Child of WILLIAM E.[8], (1863) [**1332**] (Henry Proctor[7], Rev. Ezra[6], Eliphalet[5], Freegrace[4], Abraham[3], Jacob[2], Robert[1]) and Rachel (Jamieson) Adams; res. Hannah, Cavalier Co., N. Dak.
- i. HOWARD WILBUR[9], b. in Edinburg, N. Dak., Sept. 7, 1894.

Child of JOHN Q.[8], (1865) [**1333**] (Henry Proctor[7], Rev. Ezra[6], Eliphalet[5], Freegrace[4], Abraham[3], Jacob[2], Robert[1]) and Mary (Gibson) Adams; res. Fargo, Minn.
- i. FRANK GIBSON[9], b. in Fargo, Apr. 26, 1899.

Child of EMILY A.[8], (1871) [**1334**] (Henry Proctor[7], Rev. Ezra[6], Eliphalet[5], Freegrace[4], Abraham[3], Jacob[2], Robert[1]) and Thomas E. Morgan; res. Drayton, N. Dak.
- i. ISA PROCTOR MORGAN, b. Sept. 19, 1893.

Child of ISA AGNES[8], (1873) [**1335**] (Henry Proctor[7], Rev. Ezra[6], Eliphalet[5], Freegrace[4], Abraham[3], Jacob[2], Robert[1]) and William Renwick; res. Bruce, Pembina Co., N. Dak.
- i. CHARLES HENRY RENWICK, b. Feb. 11, 1899.

Ninth Generation.]   OF NEWBURY, MASS.   487

Child of DR. JOHN FRANKLIN⁸, (1864) [**1336**] (Dr. John Glennings C.⁷, Rev. Ezra⁶, Eliphalet⁵, Freegrace⁴, Lieut. Abraham³, Jacob², Robert¹) and Edith Bishop (Young) Adams; res. Toronto, Ont.

    i. EDITH FRANCES⁹, b. in Toronto, May 11, 1891.

Children of DR. JOHN FRANKLIN⁸, (1864) and Ada E. R. (Hoggan) Adams.

    ii. AMY DORA⁹, b. in Toronto, Dec. 26, 1894.
    iii. JOHN HOGGAN⁹, b. in Toronto, Mar. 2, 1897 ; d. 31█Mar., 1899.
    iv. JAMES HERBERT F.⁹, b. in Toronto, Mar. 16, 1899.

Children of SARAH ELECTA⁸, (1872) [**1336½**] (Dr. John Glennings C.⁷, Rev. Ezra⁶, Eliphalet⁵, Freegrace⁴, Lieut. Abraham³, Jacob², Robert¹) and Arthur Murdock Matthews; res. Toronto, Ont.

    i. KENNETH ADAMS MATTHEWS, b. Sept. 26, 1896.
    ii. HAROLD MOOR MATTHEWS, b. Aug. 27, 1897.
    iii. WM. ARTHUR MATTHEWS, b. Apr. 1, 1899.

Children of CHARLOTTE ARMOUR⁸, (1856) [**1337**] (Charles Frederick⁷, Rev. Zenas⁶, Eliphalet⁵, Freegrace⁴, Lieut. Abraham³, Jacob², Robert¹) and George Ellery Oakes; res. E. Tawas, Mich.

    i. FLORENCE BELL OAKES, b. in Detroit, Mich., Apr. 29, 1878 ; unm.
    ii. JAY ADAMS OAKES, b. in E. Tawas, Dec. 2, 1881.
    iii. ORA PRATT OAKES, b. in Detroit, May 2, 1884.
    iv. BOYD ERNEST OAKES, b. in E. Tawas, July 28, 1886; d. next day.
    v. ELLERY ARMOUR OAKES, b. in E. Tawas, May 31, 1894.

Children of FRANCIS ADAMS GLASS⁸, (1857) [**1338**] and Marietta Augusta Adams; res. Colorado Spa., Col., and Basin, Mont.

    i. FRANCIS ALEX. GLASS.

ii. MAY AUGUSTA GLASS.
iii. LAWRENCE GLASS ; d. in infancy.
iv. FREDERICK GLASS ; d. in infancy.
v. ORA ANNA GLASS.

Children of ANN ELIZABETH GLASS, (1862) [1339] and Harry Giles Pickett; res. Helena, Mont.

i. KENNETH WM. PICKETT, b. in North Dakota, Nov. 20, 1888.
ii. RUTH PICKETT, b. in Helena, Aug. 3, 1890.

Child of AMANDRIN CLARK POWERS, (1835) [1340] and Phedora Cady Heaton; res. Clearwater, Minn.

i. CLARA FATIMA POWERS, b. in Lynden, Minn., Jan. 24, 1863 ; m. in Lynden, Minn., Feb. 1, 1881, Albert Lincoln Slattery, son of Albert and Emma Amanda (Rathbun) Slattery, b. in Minneapolis, Minn., Oct. 1, 1860 ; res. Lynum, Minn. Children:
   1. Amandrin Clark Slattery, b. in Lynum, Minn., Nov. 5, 1881.
   2. Alfred Jay Slattery, b. in Lynum, Minn., July 2, 1883; d. in Lynum, Minn., 14 June, 1896.
   3. Nora Belle Slattery, b. in Lynum, Minn., Jan. 27, 1885.
   4. Grace Emma Slattery, b. in Lynum, Minn., Oct. 1, 1888.
   5. Jesse Ellis Slattery, b. in Lynum, Minn., June 3, 1892.
   6. Laura Alice Slattery, b. in Lynum, Minn., Sept. 9, 1896.
   7. George Dewey Slattery, b. in Lynum, Minn., June 4, 1898.
   8. Helen Clara Slattery, b. in Lynum, Minn., Sept. 12, 1899.

Children of CARLOS MARCELLUS KING, (1850) [1341] and Letitia Rhodes; res. Carrsville, Ky.

i. ETHEL FLORENCE KING, b. in Livingston Co., Ky., Sept. 25, 1885.
ii. KATIE SPENCER KING, b. in Livingston Co., Ky., Nov. 14, 1890.

Children of WILLIAM RUFUS KING, (1853) [1342] and Norah Anne Hall; res. Carrsville, Livingston Co., Ky.

i. HOLLIS ARTHUR KING, b. in Livingston Co., Ky., Dec. 2, 1885.
ii. HALLIE DEE KING, b. in Livingston Co., Ky., Oct. 2, 1894.
iii. LOIS LEVI KING, b. in Livingston Co., Ky., Dec. 6, 1896.

Ninth Generation.] OF NEWBURY, MASS. 489

Children of JULIETTE KING, (1861) [1343] and Jacob Soul Love; res. Carrsville, Livingston Co., Ky.
  i. LILLIAN ERNESTINE LOVE, b. in Livingston Co., Ky., Dec. 5, 1884.
  ii. CLARA ETTIE LOVE, b. in Livingston Co., Ky., Nov. 23, 1886.
  iii. WILBUR KING LOVE, b. in Livingston Co., Ky., Mar. 14, 1889.
  iv. ALLEN LOVE, b. in Livingston Co., Ky., May 13, 1891.
  v. MARY LOVE, b. in Carrsville, Ky., July 27, 1895.
  vi. WILLIE ALICE LOVE, b. in Livingston Co., Ky., Oct. 20, 1898.

Children of SALLIE CLARENTINE KING, (1865) [1344] and Joseph Dodge Morris; res. Carrsville, Livingston Co., Ky.
  i. RUBY KATHERINE MORRIS, b. in Livingston Co., Ky., Dec. 21, 1887.
  ii. NELLIE EDITH MORRIS, b. Livingston Co., Ky., Oct. 4, 1889.

Children of CARLOS EDGAR KING, (1852) [1345] and Nettie Alfarata Whittaker.
  i. LILLIAN CLARA KING, b. in Dublin, N. H., Aug. 9, 1879; res. Somerville, Mass.
  ii. LOTTIE SARAH KING, b. in So. Boston, Mass., Aug. 22, 1881; m. May 28, 1898, at Somerville, Mass., Clarence Heber Kent, son of George Washington and Victoria Adelia (Hodgton) Kent, b. in Charlestown, Mass., July 8, 1875; res. Somerville, Mass.
  iii. FLORENCE NETTIE KING, b. in Somerville, Mass., May 24, 1883.

Children of LESLIE HENRY HAMILTON, (1852) [1346] and Lizzie Gertrude Montgomery; res. Great Falls, Mont.
  i. JULIA BELLE HAMILTON, b. in Sage Creek Ranch, Mont., Feb. 11, 1889.
  ii. HENRY MONTGOMERY HAMILTON, b. in Sage Creek Ranch, Dec. 1, 1890.
  iii. ABBIE MATHER HAMILTON, b. in Great Falls, July 9, 1892.
  iv. HARLEY ALEXANDER HAMILTON, b. in Great Falls, Mar. 18, 1895.
  v. LESLIE HENRY HAMILTON, b. in Great Falls, Oct. 13, 1897.

Children of CARLETON MATHER HAMILTON, (1854) [1347] and Ella Halladay; res. Marlboro, Vt.
   i. SARAH ABBIE HAMILTON, b. in Marlboro, Vt., Mar. 17, 1884.
   ii. MERRILL HALLADAY HAMILTON, b. in Marlboro, Vt., June 2, 1897,

Children of JOSEPH WRIGHT HAMILTON, (1857) [1348] and Alice Winchester; res. W. Brattleboro, Vt.
   i. GEORGE HENRY HAMILTON, b. in Marlboro, Vt., Oct. 10, 1883.
   ii. ARTHUR JOSEPH HAMILTON, b. in Marlboro, Aug. 16, 1886.
   iii. RAY ELLIOT HAMILTON, b. in Brattleboro, Sept. 19, 1890.

Children of ABBIE MATHER HAMILTON, (1859) [1349] and Joseph Gilbert Stafford; res. Brattleboro, Vt.
   i. DANA HAMILTON STAFFORD, b. in Halifax, Vt., Mar. 13, 1881,
   ii. HECTOR LESLIE STAFFORD, b. in W. Brattleboro, Apr. 26, 1882.
   iii. VERNOR FAY STAFFORD, b. in Brattleboro, Sept. 9, 1888; d. in Brattleboro, Vt., 1 May, 1890.

Children of ROLAND PETER HAMILTON, (1865) [1350] and Minnie Johnson; res. Utica, Mont.
   i. LEWIS JOHNSON HAMILTON, b. in Utica, Aug. 23, 1893.
   ii. SON, b. in W. Brattleboro, Vt., Apr. 2, 1900.

Children of ELWIN HAMILTON JONES, (1850) [1351] and Ella Sophia Johnson; res. E. Dover, Vt.
   i. MABEL ROSE JONES, b. in Dover, Vt., Jan. 13, 1876; m. in Dover, Vt., Dec. 25, 1895, Gilbert Alva Allen, son of Winslow James and Cynthia Louisa (Farnum) Allen, b. in Wardsboro, Vt., Mar. 2, 1867; res. W. Dover, Vt. Child:
      1. Ruth Eleanor Allen, b. in E. Dover, Vt., Nov. 6, 1896.
   ii. ELROY ELWIN JONES, b. in Dover, Vt., Sept. 7, 1883.

Ninth Generation.] OF NEWBURY, MASS. 491

Children of CARLOS KING JONES, (1852) [1352] and Jessie Maud Adams; res. Brattleboro, Vt.

    i. AIMEE IONE JONES, b. in Brattleboro, Vt., Mar. 23, 1880 ; m. in Brattleboro, Vt., Nov. 8, 1899, Louis Henry Henkell, son of Charles and Anna (Lillis) Henkell, b. in Brattleboro, Oct. 20, 1870 ; res. Brattleboro, Vt.
    ii. GUY CARLOS JONES, b. in Atlanta, Ga., Apr. 25, 1885.

Children of ROSE JULIA JONES, (1857) [1353] and Morris Pierson Robbins; res. Pueblo, Col.

    i. RALPH MORRIS ROBBINS, b. in Monarch, Col., Jan. 3, 1888.
    ii. RUTH JULIA ROBBINS, b. in Monarch, Mar. 9, 1890.
    iii. ESTHER LEWIS ROBBINS, b. in Pueblo, Dec. 12, 1891.
    iv. ROSE ELIZABETH ROBBINS, b. in Pueblo, Apr. 23, 1894.

Children of PERCY LABAN JONES (1862) [1354] and Ida Nell Thorn; res. Beulah, Col.

    i. PERCY LABAN JONES, b. in Canon City, Col., Nov. 8, 1887.
    ii. PAUL WILSON JONES, b. in Canon City, Mar. 15, 1889.
    iii. JULIA HAMILTON JONES, b. in Beulah, Jan. 8, 1892.
    iv. FLOYD CARLOS JONES, b. in Beulah, June 15, 1895.

Children of EXSIE ALMEDA CALDWELL, (1866) [1355] and Mahlon Charles Weeks; res. W. Northfield, Mass.

    i. RAYMOND CALDWELL WEEKS, b. in W. Northfield, Mass., Sept. 9, 1890.
    ii. RALPH KING WEEKS, b. in W. Northfield, Mass., Sept. 4, 1892.
    iii. MARION ALMEDA WEEKS, b. in W. Northfield, Mass., Nov. 15, 1894.
    iv. RUTH LUCINDA WEEKS, b. in W. Northfield, Mass., Jan. 5, 1897.
    v. MARGARET VICTORIA WEEKS, b. in W. Northfield, Mass., Aug. 29, 1899.

Children of MARY KING CALDWELL, (1869) [1356] and William Geo. Morgan; res. Lockport, N. Y.

    i. LILLIAN EXSIE MORGAN, b. in Springfield, Mass., July 30, 1894.

ii. RUFUS GEORGE MORGAN, b. in Auburn, Me., Aug. 29, 1895.
iii. ROBERT WILLIAM MORGAN, b. in New Haven, Conn., Oct. 30, 1897.
iv. JAMES PHILIP MORGAN, b. in Lockport, N. Y., Sept. 7, 1899.

Children of WILLIAM CALDWELL BURTON, (1856) [1357] and Helen Maria Howe; res. New York, Iowa.
i. GEORGE HOWE BURTON, b. in Canon City. Col., Dec. 29, 1888; d. at Medicine Lodge, Kan., 25 Jan., 1890.
ii. WILLIAM ERNEST BURTON, b. in New York, Ia., June 1, 1891.

Children of MINNIE MARIA BURTON, (1858) [1358] and Isaac Garinger Davis; res. Corydon, Iowa.
i. HARRIET RACHEL DAVIS, b. in New York, Iowa, July 7, 1882.
ii. ERNEST FRIEND DAVIS, b. in New York, Iowa, Nov. 1, 1884.
iii. A SON, b. in New York, Iowa, Dec. 18, 1886; d. in New York, Iowa, 26 Jan., 1887.
iv. HELEN CALDWELL DAVIS, b. in New York, Iowa, Apr. 2, 1890.
v. LESLIE BURTON DAVIS, b. in New York, Iowa, July 25, 1893.

Child of ALMON PIERCE BURTON, (1863) [1359] and Mariana Cross McMurry; res. Corydon, Iowa.
i. WESLEY McMURRY BURTON, b. in Corydon, Apr. 3, 1897.

Child of ARTHUR HENRY PARKER, (1860) [1360] and Alice Edson Stone; res. Worcester, Mass.
i. ALICE RUTH PARKER, b. in Worcester, Mass., Nov. 28, 1890.

Children of ARTHUR HENRY PARKER, (1860) and Eva Maria Wilson.
ii. HERBERT WILLIS PARKER, b. in Worcester, Mass., Dec. 21, 1896; d. same day.
iii. EDITH MABEL PARKER, b. in Worcester, Mass., Sept. 26, 1898.

Children of WILLIS KING PARKER, (1863) **[1361]** and Jennie Clara Delvy; res. Orange, Mass.
> i. LEON WILLIS PARKER, b. in Orange, Mass., Sept. 16, 1886.
> ii. HARRY KING PARKER, b. in Orange, Mass., Sept. 15, 1888.

Child of CORA MATILDA PARKER, (1868) **[1362]** and Ozro Daniel Adams; res. Northfield (Farms), Mass.
> i. FLORENCE HANNAH ADAMS, b. in Putney, Vt., Apr. 11, 1891.

Children of CHARLES ALBERT PARKER, (1874) **[1363]** and Fannie May Kelly; res. Northfield, Mass.
> i. WALTER RAYMOND PARKER, b. in Northfield, Mass., Jan. 14, 1899.
> ii. HELEN MAY PARKER, b. in Northfield, Mass., Jan. 20, 1900.

Children of EDWARD DWIGHT PRIEST, (1861) **[1364]** and Lena Videtto; res. Schenectady, N. Y.
> i. EDWARD PRIEST, b. in Schenectady, Aug. 22, 1896; d. in Schenectady, 25 Aug., 1896; buried in W. Northfield, Mass.
> ii. MARCIA SUSAN PRIEST, b. in Schenectady, Aug. 30, 1897.
> iii. ELEANOR PRIEST, b. in Schenectady, Apr. 19, 1899.

Children of WESLEY FERRIS CALDWELL, (1867) **[1365]** and Nettie B. Irwin; res. Brooklyn, N. Y.
> i. WESLEY STUART CALDWELL, b. in Brooklyn, Dec. 29, 1890.
> ii. RUTH MAGDALINE CALDWELL.
> iii. WILLIAM CALDWELL, b. Sept., 1895.

Children of CHARLES FRANCIS[8], (1846) **[1366]** (Frederick Augustus L.[7], Capt. Milton[6], Freegrace[5], Jr., Fregrace[4], Abraham[3], Jacob[2], Robert[1]) and Annie (Baldwin) Adams; res. Toledo, O.
> i. FREDERICK BALDWIN[9], b. in Toledo, Feb. 4, 1878.
> ii. ANNIE HELEN[9], b. in Toledo, Dec. 14, 1879.
> iii. CHARLES EDWARD[9], b. in Toledo, Oct. 29, 1881.

Child of ELIZA[8], (1843) [**1367**] (Ralph[7], Seth[6], Jr., Seth[5], Moses[4], John[3], Jacob[2], Robert[1]) and Rev. George Olcott King; res. Fredonia. N. Y.

    i. PRESTON A. KING, b. in Agawam, Mass., Aug. 10, 1870; d. 13 Dec., 1870.

Children of THADDEUS SOLOMON[8], (1836) [**1368**] (Henry Lewis[7], Gaius[6], Seth[5], Moses[4], John[3], Jacob[2], Robert[1]) and Jennie (Wilson) Adams; res. Kokomo, Howard Co., Ind.

1480.   i. CLARENCE EVERAGE[9], b. in Fulton, Ind., Dec. 1, 1868 ; m. Aug. 2, 1888, Matilda Longerich, dau. of Prof. Edward Longerich of Indianapolis, Ind.

       He graduated from the Normal School of Kokomo, Ind., 1884, and set. in Chicago, 1887, and is the dry-goods buyer of Haskell & Co.

1481.   ii. CLAUDE CHARLES[9], b. in Kokomo, Nov. 14, 1871 ; m. Sept. 30, 1889, Dora Adking ; res. Richmond, Ind.

    iii. ALONZO GAY[9], b. in Kokomo, Aug. 13, 1873; unm.; res. Indianapolis, Ind.

    iv. LULU[9], b. in Kokomo, Apr. 25, 1878 ; unm.

    v. FELECIA C.[9], b. in Kokomo, June 12, 1883 ; unm.

Children of JULIUS T.[8], (1840) [**1369**] (Henry Lewis[7], Gaius[6], Seth[5], Moses[4], John[3], Jacob[2], Robert[1]) and Lucy (Preston) Adams; res. Springfield, Pa.

    i. FRANC[9], b. in Springfield, Sept. 16, 1886.

    ii. CLARA[9], b. in Springfield, June 22, 1889.

    iii. HENRY L.[9], b. in Springfield, Mar. 31, 1895.

Children of MARTHA MARIA[8], (1839) [**1370**] (James Kent[7], Gaius[6], Seth[5], Moses[4], John[3], Jacob[2], Robert[1]) and Rev. Thomas Mitchell; res. Troy, Bradford Co., Pa.

    i. CHILD ; d. in infancy.

    ii. CHILD ; d. in infancy.

    iii. CHILD ; d. in infancy.

    iv. HENRY KENT MITCHELL, b. June 27, 1869 ; m. Sept. 16, 1896, Martha Redington.

       He is a member of the law firm of Rockwell & Mitchell, Troy, Pa.

    v. FRANK ADAMS MITCHELL, b. Apr. 17, 1879.

       He entered Bucknell University, 1899.

Child of HARRIET ELIZABETH[8], (1845) [1371] (James Kent[7], Gaius[6], Seth[5], Moses[4], John[3], Jacob[2], Robert[1]) and George F. Brown; res. Rutland, Vt.

  i. FRANK J. BROWN, b. Jan., 1870; m. Nov. 28, 1898, Mattie Dye of Rutland, Vt.
  He is a jeweler in Rutland, Vt.

Child of SALLY MINOR BROWN, (1847) [1372] and Emerson Harris; res. E. Smithfield, Pa.

  i. MARY HARRIS, b. Jan. 19, 1882; d. 24 Feb., 1892.

Child of WILLARD AMBROSE BROWN, (1848) [1373] and Theresa Harkness; res. Leona, Springfield P. O., Pa.

  i. GRACE BROWN, b. Sept. 23, 1886.

Children of CYNTHIA JANET BROWN, (1852) [1374] and Judson Phillips; res. Springfield Center, Pa.

  i. FRANCES PHILLIPS, b. Jan. 29, 1876; m. 1895, Wm. Brace. She d. Jan., 1896.
  ii. MARTHA PHILLIPS, b. Dec., 1891.

Children of JOSEPH ASHLEY[8], (1853) [1375] (Benjamin Dickinson[7], Enos[6], Seth[5], Moses[4], John[3], Jacob[2], Robert[1]) and Franc Alesia (Mattison) Adams; res. Bennington, Vt.

  i. GEORGE ASHLEY[9], b. in Bennington, Dec. 14, 1874; d. 22 Jan., 1878.
  ii. CHARLOTTE FRANCES[9], b. in Bennington, Dec. 11, 1877; m. Jan. 4, 1899, —— ——
  iii. LAURIETTE BLANCHE[9], b. in Bennington, Sept. 16, 1880.
  iv. FRANK GEORGE[9], b. in Columbus, N. Y., Jan. 16, 1884.
  v. WINNIFRED ASHLEY[9], b. in New Berlin, N. Y., Sept. 14, 1888.

Child of CHARLES[8], (1855) [1376] (Benjamin Dickinson[7], Enos[6], Seth[5], Moses[4], John[3], Jacob[2], Robert[1]) and Adelaide L. (Mattison) Adams; res. Bennington, Vt.

  i. CHARLES WAYNE[9], b. in Bennington, Sept. 27, 1890.

Child of HELEN LOUISA⁸, (1859) [1377] (Nelson⁷, Jere⁶, Seth⁵, Moses⁴, John³, Jacob², Robert¹) and James W. Ballard; res. Troy, Pa.
    i. MILDRED FLORENCE BALLARD, b. June 6, 1888.

Children of ALBERT THOMAS WINDER, (1862) [1378] and Mary Eva Swan; res. Alpine, Texas.
    i. WM. ALBERT WINDER, b. in Elgin, Ill., Dec. 11, 1893.
    ii. LOUISE WINDER, b. in Alpine, Sept. 1, 1897.

Child of WINONA M.⁸, (1868) [1379] (Elbert J.⁷, Joel⁶, Seth⁵, Moses⁴, John³, Jacob², Robert¹) and George C. Clement; res. Roodhouse, Green Co., Ill.
    i. MABEL CLEMENT, b. June 24, 1890.

Child of ANNA B.⁸, (1873) [1380] (Elbert J.⁷, Joel⁶, Seth⁵, Moses⁴, John³, Jacob², Robert¹) and G. Ross Chambers; res. Citronolle, Ala.
    i. ROLAND CHAMBERS, b. July 26, 1896.

Children of SADIE J.⁸, (1859) [1381] (Gamaliel K.⁷, Thaddeus⁶, Jr., Thaddeus⁵, Moses⁴, John³, Jacob², Robert¹) and Herbert L. Canterbury; res. East Hampton, Mass.
    i. NINA MAY CANTERBURY, b. Dec. 24, 1883; d. in infancy.
    ii. FLOSSIE CANTERBURY, b. July 15, 1885; d. in infancy.

Child of SADIE J.⁸, (1859) and John W. Ropp; res. Greenfield, Mass.
    i. HAROLD ROPP, b. July 31, 1894.

Child of FRED A.⁸, (1860) [1382] (Alfred⁷, Thaddeus⁶, Jr., Thaddeus⁵, Moses⁴, John³, Jacob², Robert¹) and Nellie (Stearns) Adams; res. So. Vernon, Vt.
    i. MARION M.⁹, b. in Springfield, Mass., July 2, 1883.

Ninth Generation.] OF NEWBURY, MASS.

Children of MARY ANN⁸, (1843) **[1383]** (Phineas M.⁷, Abraham⁶, Capt. Oliver⁵, Simeon⁴, John³, Jacob², Robert¹) and John Salisbury; res. Kansas City, Mo.

    i. FLORA OLIVE SALISBURY, b. Aug. 8, 1863; d. 29 Jan., 1870.
    ii. EFFIE MARY SALISBURY, b. 1864; m. 1887, Wm. Franklin Forsyth; res. Kansas City, Mo.; no issue.

Children of OSCAR RUFUS⁸, (1863) **[1384]** (Rufus⁷, Abraham⁶, Capt. Oliver⁵, Simeon⁴, John³, Jacob², Robert¹) and Nancy Caroline (Allen) Adams; res. Oconee, Shelby Co., Ill.

    i. IRA RUFUS⁹, b. in Pana, Ill., Dec. 26, 1886.
    ii. OSCAR RAY⁹, b. in Oconee, Ill., Apr. 1, 1888.
    iii. ASA SAMUEL⁹, b. in Oconee, Oct. 12, 1889.
    iv. LEE ELMER⁹, b. in Oconee, May 3, 1891; d. 5 June, 1895.
    v. DELLA⁹, b. in Oconee, Dec. 10, 1892; d. 25 Mar., 1893.
    vi. DORA⁹ (twin), b. in Oconee, Dec. 10, 1892.
    vii. CORA⁹, b. in Oconee, Nov. 28, 1894; d. 29 May, 1895.
    viii. EVA⁹, b. in Oconee, Sept. 9, 1897; d. 9 Jan., 1898.

Child of LOUIS K. HARRINGTON, (1853) **[1385]** and Florie E. Freeman; res. Buffalo, N. Y.

    i. HAROLD HARRINGTON, b. 1884-5.

Child of DR. FRANK A. HARRINGTON, (1854) **[1386]** and Carrie Ortolam; res Buffalo, N. Y.

    i. FRANCIS L. HARRINGTON, b. Mar., 1899.

Children of CHARLES M. HARRINGTON, (1860) **[1387]** and Mary Bassett; res. Buffalo, N. Y.

    i. HENRY B. HARRINGTON, b. Feb. 22, 1892.
    ii. RALPH M. HARRINGTON, b. Dec. 21, 1893.
    iii. GEORGE L. HARRINGTON, b. Feb. 17, 1896.

Children of ALBERT P. HARRINGTON, (1864) **[1388]** and Florie A. Pease; res. Orangeport, Niagara Co., N. Y.

    i. HELEN L. HARRINGTON, b. 1890.
    ii. DOROTHY E. HARRINGTON, b. 1893.
    iii. CARRIE F. HARRINGTON, b. 1895.

Children of GEORGE G.⁸, (1859) [**1389**] (Oliver L.⁷, Abraham⁶, Capt. Oliver⁵, Simeon⁴, John³, Jacob², Robert¹) and Matilda (Lehman) Adams; res. Ransomville, N. Y.

    i. ELSIE⁹, b. in Ransomville, Dec. 22, 1866.
    ii. HARRY⁹, b. in Ransomville, Oct. 20, 1888.
    iii. SILLY⁹, b. in Ransomville, Aug. 14, 1890.
    iv. GEORGE⁹, b. in Ransomville, Apr. 15, 1892.

Children of BEDA J.⁸, (1860) [**1390**] (Oliver L.⁷, Abraham⁶, Capt. Oliver⁵, Simeon⁴, John³, Jacob², Robert¹) and Julius Hoyt; res. Wrights Crossing, Niagara Co., N. Y.

    i. ALICE HOYT, b. Mar. 15, 1890.
    ii. MINNIE HOYT, b. May 8, 1892.

Child of JOHN A.⁸, (1862) [**1391**] (Oliver L.⁷, Abraham⁶, Capt. Oliver⁵, Simeon⁴, John³, Jacob², Robert¹) and Jane N. (Lawton) Adams.

    i. BERTHA⁹, b. May 11, 1892.

Children of REUBEN O.⁸, (1863) [**1392**] (Oliver L.⁷, Abraham⁶, Capt. Oliver⁵, Simeon⁴, John³, Jacob², Robert¹) and Sarah (Lawton) Adams; res. Buffalo, N. Y.

    i. RUBY A.⁹, b. in Buffalo, Feb. 3, 1891; d. 26 Sept., 1891.
    ii. CHARLES L.⁹, b. in Buffalo, Aug. 22, 1892.

Child of MARY BEDA⁸, (1865) [**1394**] (Gad Mather⁷, Abraham⁶, Capt. Oliver⁵, Simeon⁴, John³, Jacob², Robert¹) and William Wilson; res. Appleton, Niagara Co., N. Y.

    i. EUGENE WILSON, b. Oct. 13, 1896.

Child of EUGENE M.⁸, (1868) [**1395**] (Gad Mather⁷, Abraham⁶, Capt. Oliver⁵, Simeon⁴, John³, Jacob², Robert¹) and Cornie (Chaplin) Adams; res. Snohomish, Snohomish Co., Wash.

    i. LEON⁹, b. Aug. 7, 1895.

Ninth Generation.]   OF NEWBURY, MASS.   499

Child of OLIVER WINCHESTER⁸, (1870) [1396] (William Bradley⁷, Oliver⁶, Jr., Capt. Oliver⁵, Capt. Simeon⁴, John³, Jacob², Robert¹) and Clara Jane (Burnette) Adams; res. Holyoke, Mass.
   i. CHRISTINE ELAINE⁹, b. in Holyoke, Apr. 18, 1898.

Child of GEORGE WILLARD⁸, (1869) [1397] (Henry⁷, Oliver⁶, Jr., Capt. Oliver⁵, Simeon⁴, John³, Jacob², Robert¹) and Louisa (Park) Adams; res. Greenfield, Mass.
   i. CLYDE RAYMOND⁹, b. Mar. 25, 1898.

Child of ANNIE F.⁸, (1871) [1398] (Henry⁷, Oliver⁶, Jr., Capt. Oliver⁵, Simeon⁴, John³, Jacob², Robert¹) and Cecil Cheney; res. Brattleboro, Vt.
   i. FLORENCE JARALDA CHENEY, b. Mar. 2, 1897.

Children of MARY ELIZABETH⁸, (1852) [1399] (Simeon Houghton⁷, Capt. Ira⁶, Capt. Simeon⁵, Simeon⁴, John³, Jacob², Robert¹) and Charles E. Mather.
   i. HENRY MATHER, b. Sept. 22, 1869; m. Sept. 8, 1896, Fanny Carver.
   ii. ROSA MATHER, b. 1879; m. 1898, Ernest Winter.
   iii. FRANK MATHER, b. 1884.

Children of ALICE L.⁸, (1863) [1400] (Simeon Houghton⁷, Capt. Ira⁶, Capt. Simeon⁵, Simeon⁴, John³, Jacob², Robert¹) and Julian Whittaker; res. Newfane, Vt.
   i. ERWIN WHITTAKER.
   ii. HARRY WHITTAKER.

Children of MINERVA E.⁸, (1850) [1401] (Ira⁷, Jr., Capt. Ira⁶, Capt. Simeon⁵, Simeon⁴, John³, Jacob², Robert¹) and Edwin P. Adams; res. Marlboro, Vt.
   i. ROY L. ADAMS, b. Sept. 23, 1875; m. Aug. 23, 1898, Florence A. Snow.
   ii. MERLE H. ADAMS, b. May 10, 1880; d. 11 Apr., 1881.

Children of MARTIN IRA⁸, (1854) [1402] (Ira⁷, Jr., Capt. Ira⁶, Capt. Simeon⁵, Simeon⁴, John³, Jacob², Robert¹) and Ida (Harriman) Adams; res. Westmoreland, N. H.
    i. HAROLD E.⁹, b. July 23, 1884; d. 28 Aug., 1884.
    ii. LEON⁹, b. in Westmoreland, Jan. 12, 1891.

Child of NELLIE CLARA⁸, (1858) [1403] (Ira⁷, Jr., Capt. Ira⁶, Capt. Simeon⁵, Simeon⁴, John³, Jacob², Robert¹) and Harry Clark; res. Malden, Mass.
    i. RALPH CLARK, b. Mar. 15, 1893.

Children of LIZZIE ANN⁸, (1858) [1404] (Henry⁷, Simeon⁶, Capt. Simeon⁵, Simeon⁴, John³, Jacob², Robert¹) and Freeman Scott; res. Brattleboro, Vt.
    i. MINNIE ANN SCOTT, b. Feb. 13, 1878.
    ii. ARTHUR WAYNE SCOTT, b. Apr. 12, 1883.
    iii. HORACE LESLIE SCOTT, b. Apr. 15, 1885.

Children of JOHN C.⁸, (1861) [1405] (Henry⁷, Simeon⁶, Capt. Simeon⁵, Simeon⁴, John³, Jacob², Robert¹) and Lestina E. (Thurber) Adams; res. Brattleboro, Vt.
    i. MARGARET⁹, b. in Brattleboro, Feb. 15, 1893.
    ii. PAULINE⁹, b. in Brattleboro, Aug. 18, 1897.

Children of EVENA L.⁸, (1862) [1406] (Luther⁷, Simeon⁶, Capt. Simeon⁵, Simeon⁴, John³, Jacob², Robert¹) and Charles H. Parmelee, res. Washington, Vt.
    i. DONALD A. PARMELEE, b. Nov. 3, 1886; d. 15 Dec., 1887.
    ii. EVA KATHLEEN PARMELEE, b. Feb. 25, 1893.

Child of MARION S.⁸, (1871) [1407] (Luther⁷, Simeon⁶, Capt. Simeon⁵, Simeon⁴, John³, Jacob², Robert¹) and William B. McClellan; res. No. Hatfield, Mass.
    i. ADAMS NEWTON McCLELLAN, b. July 8, 1896.

Child of EDWARD EFFINGHAM[8], (1872) [**1408**] (Simeon[7], Simeon[6], Capt. Simeon[5], Simeon[4], John[3], Jacob[2], Robert[1]) and Rosana (Moore) Adams; res. Fitchburg, Mass.

    i. WILLIAM VINCENT[9], b. in W. Rindge, N. H., Oct. 24, 1895.

Child of DR. GEORGE FRANCIS[8], (1863) [**1409**] (Elias[7], George[6], Job[5], Joel[4], John[3], Jacob[2], Robert[1]) and Beula Witt (Muzzy) Adams; res. Gowanda, N. Y.

    i. DOROTHY CORNELIA[9], b. in Pulaski, N. Y., Nov. 24, 1893.

Children of CELIA CORBIN[8], (1845) [**1410**] (Horace H.[7], Alden[6], Joel[5], Jr., Joel[4], John[3], Jacob[2], Robert[1]) and Huron Wescott; res. Watertown, N. Y.

    i. FRED ALDEN WESCOTT, b. in Philadelphia, N. Y., July 18, 1865; m. Aug. 3, 1887, Minnie O'Neil of Carthage, N. Y.; no issue. res. Benson Mines, St. Lawrence Co., N. Y.
    ii. CHARLES HORACE WESCOTT, b. in Carthage, N. Y., July 17, 1872; m. Apr. 24, 1899, Mary H. Derby of Felts Mills, N. Y.
    iii. ELLA MAUD WESCOTT, b. in Carthage, Jan. 4, 1875.

Child of CORA ESTELLE[8], (1857) [**1411**] (Horace H.[7], Alden[6], Joel[5], Jr., Joel[4], John[3], Jacob[2], Robert[1]) and George Salter; res. Carthage, Jefferson Co., N. Y.

    i. MARY HELEN SALTER, b. in Carthage, July 25, 1877.

Children of GEORGE EDWARD⁹, (1832) [1412] (Philip⁸, Henry⁷, Henry⁶, Robert⁵, Abraham⁴, Robert³, Sergt. Abraham², Robert¹) and Caroline J. (Ordway) Adams; res. Newburyport, Mass.

  i. GEORGE EDWARD¹⁰, JR., b. in Newburyport, Apr. 22, 1857 ; d. 17 July, 1857.
  ii. SOPHIA ORDWAY¹⁰, b. in Newburyport, July 25, 1858 ; d. 21 Mar., 1874.
1482. iii. SUSAN THURLOW¹⁰, b. in Newburyport, Feb. 9, 1862 ; m. Oct. 7, 1885, Frank I. Barrett ; res. Shawomet, R. I.
1483. iv. GEORGE KNIGHT¹⁰, b. in Newbury, Mar. 16, 1863 ; m. (1) Mar. 27, 1887, Esther A. Turner; she d. 20 Sept., 1887 ; m. (2) Nov. 14 1888, Nettie H. Hale, dau. of F. H. and Susan D. Hale ; set in Fitchburg, Mass., 1888.
  v. ULYSES SIDNEY¹⁰, b. in Lynn, Mass., Aug. 24, 1864 ; res. Fitchburg, Mass.; unm.

Child of GEORGE EDWARD⁹, (1832) and Rebecca Jane (Ordway) Adams.

  v. CAROLINE ORDWAY¹⁰, b. Sept. 30, 1870; res. Bradford, Mass.; ~~unm.~~ *Stoddard*

Child of GEORGE FRANKLIN⁹, (1833) [1413] (Joel⁸, Joseph⁷, Henry⁶, Robert⁵, Abraham⁴, Robert³, Sergt. Abraham², Robert¹) and Sarah J. (Lunt) Adams; res. Newbury, Mass.

  i. FRANKLIN W.¹⁰, b. in Newburyport, Aug. 19, 1856.

Children of HORACE CLINTON⁹, (1848) [1414] (Joel⁸, Joseph⁷, Henry⁶, Robert⁵, Abraham⁴, Robert³, Sergt. Abraham², Robert¹) and Amelia (Mitch) Adams; res. Haverhill, Mass.

  i. GEORGE¹⁰ ; deceased.
  ii. MARY¹⁰.
  iii. ARTHUR¹⁰.
  iv. ALICE¹⁰.
  v. CHARLES¹⁰.

Children of CLARA CLEMENT⁹, (1847) [1415] (Charles⁸, Abraham⁷, Henry⁶, Robert⁵, Abraham⁴, Robert³, Sergt. Abraham², Robert¹) and William Henry H. Bradbury; res. Hammonton, N. J.

    i. GEORGIE ANNA BRADBURY, b. in Vineland, N. J., Aug. 28, 1868.
    ii. WYMOND HENRY BRADBURY, b. in Elwood, N. J., Dec. 1, 1869.
    iii. CLARA ADELINE BRADBURY, b. in Philadelphia, Pa., Aug. 22, 1871; d. 18 Feb., 1876.
    iv. ELLA ADAMS BRADBURY, b. in Philadelphia, Nov. 20, 1874; d. 28 May, 1876.
    v. CHARLES KIMBALL BRADBURY, b. in Philadelphia, Apr. 28, 1877.
    vi. HOWARD MELVILLE BRADBURY, b. in Philadelphia, Nov. 7, 1881.
    vii. WILLIAM IRVING BRADBURY, b. in Hammonton, July 28, 1886.

Child of ADELINE FRANCES⁹, (1854) [1416] (Charles⁸, Abraham⁷, Henry⁶, Robert⁵, Abraham⁴, Robert³, Sergt. Abraham², Robert¹) and Elias Pike Bartlett; res. Amesbury, Mass.

    i. THEODORE WOODCOCK BARTLETT, b. Oct. 4, 1890.

Children of IDA⁹, (1862) [1417] (Caleb Cushing⁸, Joseph⁷, Daniel⁶, Robert⁵, Abraham⁴, Robert³, Sergt. Abraham², Robert¹) and Charles F. Tarbell; res. Milton, Mass.

    i. SARAH ADAMS TARBELL, b. in Providence, R. I., Nov. 16, 1884.
    ii. GEORGE GROSVENOR TARBELL, b. in Woonsocket, R. I., Dec. 8, 1886.

Child of GEORGE SHRIEVE⁹, (1864) [1418] (Caleb Cushing⁸, Joseph⁷, Daniel⁶, Robert⁵, Abraham⁴, Robert³, Sergt. Abraham², Robert¹) and Katherine L. (Bradley) Adams; res. Brooklyn, N. Y.

    i. KATHERINE LOUISE¹⁰, b. in Brooklyn, June 21, 1890.

Child of SARAH JEWETT⁹, (1867) [1419] (Caleb Cushing⁸, Joseph⁷, Daniel⁶, Robert⁵, Abraham⁴, Robert³, Sergt. Abraham², Robert¹) and William A. Hall; res. Bellows Falls, Vt.

    i. MELVIN ADAMS HALL, b. Apr. 14, 1889.

Child of CUSHING⁹, (1870) [1419½] (Caleb Cushing⁸, Joseph⁷, Daniel⁶, Robert⁵, Abraham⁴, Robert³, Sergt. Abraham², Robert¹) and Janette Hale (Eastman) Adams; res. Bellows Falls, Vt.

    i. CUSHING¹⁰, JR., b. in Bellows Falls, Mar. 30, 1900; d. same day.

Child of SARAH ANN⁹, (1850) [1420] (Benjamin⁸, Benjamin⁷, Isaac⁶, Benjamin⁵, Abraham⁴, Robert³, Sergt. Abraham², Robert¹) and Frederick Warren Hawes; res. Milford, Mass.

    i. SUSAN MAY HAWES, b. in Milford, May 22, 1873 ; m. Nov. 29, 1891, Fred Clifton Woodes, a son of Wilbur H. Woodes; res. Lynn, Mass.

Children of LAURA JANE⁹, (1850) [1421] (Smith⁸, Charles⁷, Smith⁶, Charles⁵, Abraham⁴, Robert³, Sergt. Abraham², Robert¹) and Augustus H. Sutherland; res. Greene, Androscoggin Co., Me.

    i. CHARLES A. SUTHERLAND. b. Dec. 29, 1867 ; m. Maggie Helen.
    ii. MINNIE M. SUTHERLAND, b. Apr. 24, 1870; m. (1) Apr. 24, 1886, Benjamin F. Rogers of Skowhegan, Me.; m. (2) Nov. 20, 1894, Charles C. Davis.

Children of LAURA JANE⁹, (1850) and Nahum D. Lander; res. Auburn, Me.

    i. MERTIE K. LANDER, b. June 28, 1873 ; d. 4 Mar., 1896.
    ii. ETHEL B. LANDER, b. Sept. 3, 1874.
    iii. LAURA B. LANDER, b. Sept. 26, 1875.
    iv. FRANK N. LANDER, b. May 10, 1877.
    v. LUCY A. LANDER, b. Apr. 24, 1879 ; d. 15 Mar., 1881.
    vi. NELLIE F. LANDER, b. Apr. 4, 1881 ; d. 11 Mar., 1888.
    vii. EDITH ESTELLE LANDER, b. June 18, 1885.
    viii. SMITH A. LANDER, b. July 25, 1887.
    ix. FREEMAN A. LANDER, b. July 1, 1891.
    x. MAUD ELLA LANDER, b. Nov. 18, 1897.

Children of SMITH[9], (1866) [1422] (Smith[8], Charles[7], Smith[6], Charles[5], Abraham[4], Robert[3], Sergt. Abraham[2], Robert[1]) and Eliza (Hand) Adams; res. Milltown, Me.
  i. ESTELLE S.[10], b. Dec. 25, 1892.
  ii. COZE EVELYN[10], b. Aug. 27, 1896; d. 27 Feb., 1899.

Child of CHARLES EDWIN SPINNEY, (1854) [1423] and Nellie M. Chandler.
  i. CHARLES ADAMS SPINNEY.

Child of ALICE BROWNING HASLAM, (1868) [1424] and William D. Ford.
  i. EDITH MARY FORD, b. Feb. 8, 1885.

Children of ELIZABETH ELLEN[9], (1861) [1425] (Benjamin Bradley[8], John[7], Israel[6], Moses[5], John[4], Robert[3], Sergt. Abraham[2], Robert[1]) and Tjark F. Memmen; res. Kearney, Buffalo Co., Neb.
  i. HENRY OLIVER MEMMEN, b. in Minonk, Ill., Dec. 16, 1883.
  ii. MAE MARIE MEMMEN, b. in Minonk, Mar. 15, 1886.
  iii. DWIGHT DEAN MEMMEN, b. in Kearney, Nov. 20, 1887.
  iv. LITTA JEANE MEMMEN, b. in Kearney, Apr. 25, 1892.

Children of MARY ANN[9], (1863) [1426] (Benjamin Bradley[8], John[7], Israel[6], Moses[5], John[4], Robert[3], Sergt. Abraham[2], Robert[1]) and James Selleck; res. Kearney, Buffalo Co., Neb.
  i. DELLA DEAN SELLECK, b. in Minonk, Ill., Feb. 13, 1885.
  ii. FREDERICK SELLECK, b. in Nebraska, Sept. 4, 1888.
  iii. HERBERT HIRAM SELLECK, b. in Nebraska, Apr. 23, 1891.
  iv. ROY MILTON SELLECK, b. in Nebraska, Apr. 17, 1893.

Children of RALPH NORTON[9], (1867) [1427] (Daniel Sewall[8], John[7], Israel[6], Moses[5], John[4], Robert[3], Sergt. Abraham[2], Robert[1]) and Lillian Maude (Hall) Adams; res. Corvallis, Benton Co., Ore.
  i. RALPH SEWALL[10], b. in Corvallis, Jan. 25, 1894.
  ii. JESSIE RUTH[10], b. in Corvallis, Sept. 18, 1895.
  iii. HARRY ROMEYN[10], b. in Corvallis, Sept. 27, 1899.

Children of NEWTON ROMEYN[9], (1872) [**1428**] (Daniel Sewall[8], John[7], Israel[6], Moses[5], John[4], Robert[3], Sergt. Abraham[2], Robert[1]) and Blanche Mae (Arnold) Adams; res. Corvallis, Benton Co., Ore.

    i. OLIVE ALENE[10], b. in Washburn, Ill., July 7, 1893.
    ii. GORDON KENNETH[10], b. in Corvallis, Mar. 23, 1895.
    iii. ETHEL LILLIAN[10], b. in Corvallis, Feb. 25, 1898.

Children of SILAS BRADLEY[9], (1863) [**1429**] (Geo. Moses[8], Silas Merrill[7], Moses[6], Jr., Moses[5], John[4], Robert[3], Sergt. Abraham[2], Robert[1]) and Aurilla Emma (Patterson) Adams; res. Deering, Portland, Me.

    i. ELEANOR WILSON[10], b. in Deering, July 27, 1888.
    ii. WALDEMAR PATTERSON[10] b. in Deering, July 11, 1891.

Child of FREDERICK WALDEMAR[9], (1869) [**1430**] (George Moses[8], Silas Merrill[7], Moses[6], Jr., Moses[5], John[4], Robert[3], Sergt. Abraham[2], Robert[1]) and Edith Caroline (Patridge) Adams; res. Somerville, Mass.

    i. WARREN LINCOLN[10], b. Sept. 23, 1895.

Children of MINNIE F. A.[9], (1868) [**1431**] (George N.[8], Aaron[7], Joshua[6], Benjamin[5], John[4], Robert[3], Sergt. Abraham[2], Robert[1]) and Frederick S. Wood; res. Wheeling, Livingston Co., Missouri.

    i. CORNELIUS A. WOOD, b. in Wheeling, Aug. 27, 1887.
    ii. GEORGE F. WOOD, b. in Wheeling, Apr. 3, 1890.

Children of FANNY FOGG[9], (1867) [**1432**] and L. Chandler Berry; res. Monmouth, Me.

    i. GEORGIE ELLA BERRY, b. Feb. 14, 1890.
    ii. FANNY DEBORAH BERRY, b. Mar. 3, 1892.

Child of ABBY LUELLA[9], (1855) [1433] (Lieut. Isaac Rogers[8], Joshua[7], Jr., Joshua[6], Benjamin[5], John[4], Robert[3], Sergt. Abraham[2], Robert[1]) and Volney Everard Young; res. Weymouth, Mass.

1. JAMES ELMORE YOUNG, b. in Weymouth, Dec. 4, 1871; m. at Chicago, Ill., Oct. 4, 1893, Ella Eugenia McGettrick, b. in East Boston, Mass., May 10, 1876. They have one child, Marion Adams Young, b. in Boston, Mass., Sept. 1, 1898.

Children of GEORGE WILLIS[9], (1854) [1434] (Benjamin[8], Isaac[7], Samuel[6], Benjamin[5], John[4], Robert[3], Sergt. Abraham[2], Robert[1]) and Hattie M. (Cole) Adams; res. Portland, Cumberland Co., Me.

i. ELLA F.[10], b. in Portland, May, 1882; d. 25 Sept., 1882, age 4 months.
ii. ELLEN BRAZIER[10], b. in Portland, Mar. 28, 1884.

Children of GEORGE WILLIS[9], (1854) and Linda Frances (Swett) Adams.

iii. FERDINAND SWETT[10], b. in Portland, Dec. 6, 1892.
iv. LEON WILLIS[10], b. in Portland, Sept. 13, 1894.

Children of CHARLES S[9], (1851) [1435] (John Smith[8], Isaac[7], Samuel[6], Benjamin[5], John[4], Robert[3], Sergt. Abraham[2], Robert[1]) and Almeda E. (Skillings) Adams, res. Gray, Cumberland Co., Me.

i. EFFIE LILLIAN[10], b. Jan. 22, 1874.
ii. HARRY O.[10], b. Apr. 2, 1879.
iii. HARVEY[10], b. May 27, 1881.
iv. JOHN PERLEY[10], b. Jan. 5, 1892.
v. FOREST EUGENE[10], b. Mar. 22, 1895.

Children of VIOLA BERTHA[9], (1865) [1436] (Lorenzo Benson[8], Silas Hall[7], Samuel[6], Benjamin[5], John[4], Robert[3], Sergt. Abraham[2], Robert[1]) and Fred Kent Mackenzie; res. Shrewsbury, Mass.

i. PHILIP NEWTON MACKENZIE, b. in Worcester, Mass., Jan. 10, 1887; d. 15 Oct., 1895.
ii. FRANK MOSELEY MACKENZIE, b. in Worcester, May 28. 1888.
iii. ARTHUR LORENZO MACKENZIE, b. in Worcester, Aug. 4, 1889; d. 12 Oct., 1895.
iv. ETHEL LOUISA MACKENZIE, b. in Worcester, July 6, 1891; d. 26 Sept., 1895.
v. RALPH BLAKE MACKENZIE, b. in Worcester, Oct. 19, 1892.

Child of SILAS HALL^9, (1867) [**1437**] (Lorenzo Benson^8, Silas Hall^7, Samuel^6, Benjamin^5, John^4, Robert^3, Sergt. Abraham^2, Robert^1) and Mary Ann (Evans) Adams; res. Worcester, Mass.

i. DE FORREST^{10}, b. in Worcester, Apr. 19, 1897.

Children of MARY ISABELLE^9, (1868) [**1438**] (Lorenzo Benson^8, Silas Hall^7, Samuel^6, Benjamin^5, Jonn^4, Robert^3, Sergt. Abraham^2, Robert^1) and Obed Wilbur; res. Millville, N. J.

i. HARRY ADDISON WILBUR, b. in Charlton, Mass., Apr. 10, 1893.
ii. GLADYS ALFREDA WILBUR, b. in Millville, Nov., 1898.

Children of GEORGE WILLIS^9, (1870) [**1439**] (Aaron^8, Stephen^7, David^6, Stephen^5, William^4, Capt. Abraham^3, Sergt. Abraham^2, Robert^1) and Harriet Elizabeth (Dackins) Adams; res. Gypsum City, Salina Co., Kan.

i. FLORENCE MAY^{10}, b. in Manhattan, Kan., Aug. 1, 1897.
ii. GEORGE EARLE^{10}, b. in Bridgport, Kan., July 17, 1899.

Children of MARY T.^{9}, (1848) [**1440**] (Oscar Edmund^8, Dr. Milo^7, Dr. Samuel^6, Capt. Benjamin^5, William^4, Capt. Abraham^3, Sergt. Abraham^2, Robert^1) and Francis McKinney; res. Oil City, Pa.

i. MACIE McKINNEY, d. in infancy.
ii. CLAUDE A. McKINNEY, b. Feb. 19, 1874.
iii. HELEN McKINNEY, d. in infancy.

Children of CYNTHIA B.[9], (1850) [1441] (Oscar Edmund[8], Dr. Milo[7], Dr. Samuel[6], Capt. Benjamin[5], William[4], Capt. Abraham[3], Sergt. Abraham[2], Robert[1]) and Frederick Zerald Trax; res. Meadville, Pa.

    i. F. ZERALD TRAX, b. June 22, 1878.
    ii. HARLAND A. TRAX, b. Feb. 11, 1880.
    iii. HELEN ELIZABETH TRAX, b. July 12, 1883.
    iv. MARY EDNA TRAX, b. Aug. 11, 1891.

Children of CLARENCE MARSHALL JOHNS, (1843) [1442] and Martha S. Robinson; res. Pittsburg, Pa.

    i. WILLIAM ROBINSON JOHNS, b. Aug. 7, 1870.
    ii. MARY BISHOP JOHNS, b. July 9, 1872.

Children of LEONARD EDGAR JOHNS, (1846) [1443] and Valeria Marshall Whiteley; res. Pittsburg, Pa.

    i. LEONARD SHRYOCK JOHNS, b. Apr. 24, 1873.
    ii. HESTER WHITELEY JOHNS, b. Apr. 4, 1875.
    iii. MIRA ADAMS JOHNS, b. in Clarion, Pa., Mar. 28, 1878.
    iv. ROBERT KIRKWOOD JOHNS, b. Aug. 10, 1881; d. in infancy.
    v. RICHARD LEA JOHNS, b. Feb. 20, 1883; d. in infancy.
    vi. HERBERT ADAMS JOHNS, b. Dec. 31, 1885; d. in infancy.
    vii. ARTHUR WHITELEY JOHNS, b. Dec. 31, 1885; d. in infancy.
    viii. LOUIS EDGAR JOHNS, b. Sept. 27, 1886.
    ix. HENRY KIRKWOOD JOHNS, b. 1889.
        All born in Pittsburg except Mira A.

Children of CORA IDA JOHNS, (1854) [1444] and Rev. H. O. Gibbons; res. Philadelphia, Pa.

    i. CARRIE OLIPHANT GIBBONS, b. in Annapolis, Md., Apr. 7, 1877; d. in infancy.
    ii. HENRY GIBBONS, b. in Philadelphia, Sept. 27, 1878.
    iii. HERBERT ADAMS GIBBONS, b. Apr. 9, 1879.
    iv. MIRA VERNON GIBBONS, b. Feb. 11, 1881; d. in infancy.
    v. CORA LOUISE GIBBONS, b. Feb. 13, 1883.
    vi. OLIPHANT GIBBONS, b. Jan. 22, 1885.

Children of HERBERT ADAMS JOHNS, (1864) [1445] and Rebecca Torrens; res. Pittsburg and Carnegie, Pa.
1. HAROLD CHESTER JOHNS, b. Dec. 4, 1892.
ii. HERBERT GREEN JOHNS, b. Sept. 9, 1897.
iii. STANLEY ADAMS JOHNS, b. Apr. 18, 1899.

Children of GRACE IRENE^9, (1872) [1446] (Joseph Emery^8, William^7, Enoch^6, Enoch^5, Henry^4, Capt. Abraham^3, Sergt. Abraham^2, Robert^1) and William Adams Gilbert; res. Chicago, Ill.
i. PROCTOR SAMPSON GILBERT, b. in Camden, Pa., July 19, 1894; d. 30 Sept., 1894.
ii. EARL ADAMS GILBERT. b. in Chicago, Oct. 22, 1895.

Child of NELLIE ALBA^9, (1874) [1447] (Joseph Emery^8, William^7, Enoch^6, Enoch^5, Henry^4, Capt. Abraham^3, Sergt. Abraham^2, Robert^1) and Edwin G. Skillings; res. Norway, Me.
i. ARTHUR LIONEL SKILLINGS, b. July, 1896.

Children of CHARLES CLIFFORD^9, (1868) [1448] (Charles Hall^8, William^7, Enoch^6, Enoch^5, Henry^4, Capt. Abraham^3, Sergt. Abraham^2, Robert^1) and Irene May (Curtis) Adams.
i. MARION IRENE^{10}, b. in Norway, Me., Dec. 9, 1890.
ii. EARL VERNA^{10}, b. in Norway, Apr. 16, 1892.
iii. THELMA^{10}, b. in Norway, June 7, 1898.

Children of ABBIE EVELYN^9, (1876) [1449] (Charles Hall^8, William^7, Enoch^6, Enoch^5, Henry^4, Capt. Abraham^3, Sergt. Abraham^2, Robert^1) and Walter Shepard Chandler; res. Norway, Me.
i. HAROLD WALTER CHANDLER, b. Dec. 21, 1895.
ii. FRANCIS ADAMS CHANDLER, b. Mar. 10, 1897.
iii. EVELYN ABBIE CHANDLER, b. May 22, 1898.

Children of CORA J.[9], (1860) [**1450**] (John Emery[8], Jr., John Emery[7], Col. John Emery[6], Enoch[5], Henry[4], Capt. Abraham[3], Sergt. Abraham[2], Robert[1]) and Jared Brown; res. Solon, Johnson Co., Ia.

    i. LAURA BROWN, b. Jan. 18, 1886.
    ii. E. BROWN, b. Sept. 5, 1887.
    iii. JULIUS BROWN, b. Oct. 28, 1888.
    iv. CLARA BROWN, b. Sept. 12, 1891.
    v. MARJORIE BROWN, b. Mar. 11, 1898.

Children of ETHIE L,[9], (1868) [**1451**] (John Emery[8], Jr., John Emery[7], Col. John Emery[6], Enoch[5], Henry[4], Capt. Abraham[3], Sergt. Abraham[2], Robert[1]) and Alonzo Brown; res. Solon, Johnson Co., Ia.

    i. ARLO E. BROWN, b. Sept. 12, 1895.
    ii. VERNON BROWN, b. Feb. 12, 1897.

Children of HARRY DELVA[9], (1870) [**1452**] (John Emery[8], Jr., John Emery[7], Col. John Emery[6], Enoch[5], Henry[4], Capt. Abraham[3], Sergt. Abraham[2], Robert[1]) and Virginia (Bacon) Adams.

    i. DOROTHY BELINDA[10], b. in Solon, Ia., Dec. 30, 1895.
    ii. FLORENCE[10], b. in Solon, Dec. 31, 1896.
    iii. JOHN EMERY[10], b. in Solon, June 5, 1898.

Child of CHARLES LINCOLN[9], (1863) [**1453**] (David Weston[8], David Farnum[7], Dr. Joseph[6], Enoch[5], Henry[4], Capt. Abraham[3], Sergt. Abraham[2], Robert[1]) and Annie Eunice (Bailey) Adams; res. New Haven, Conn.

    i. SHERMAN WESTON[10], b. in New Haven, Feb. 24, 1894.

Children of JESSIE[9], (1873) [**1454**] (John Sturgis[8], Erasmus Darwin[7], Dr. Joseph[6], Enoch[5], Henry[4], Capt. Abraham[3], Sergt. Abraham[2], Robert[1]) and George B. Mock; res. Los Angeles, Cal.

i. GEORGE B. MOCK, b. in Los Angeles, Mar. 21, 1892; was killed on electric railway, 12 Jan., 1899.
ii. JESSIE MOCK, b. in Los Angeles, May 11, 1893.
iii. PHEBE MOCK, b. in Waterloo, Ia., Oct. 17, 1896; d. in McAlester, Ind. Ter., 6 Jan., 1898.

Children of HARRIET AUGUSTA MORSE, (1844) **[1455]** and Frederick J. Gage; res. Boston (Roxbury Dist.), Mass.
i. BLANCHE GAGE, b. in Penacook, N. H., Nov. 24, 1869.
ii. CHARLOTTE H. GAGE, b. in Boston, Feb. 23, 1873.
iii. FRED H. GAGE, b. in Boston, Oct. 20, 1874.

Child of GEORGE A. MORSE, (1847) **[1456]** and Ella G. (Kimball) Adams; res. Penacook, N. H.
i. HARLEY G. MORSE, b. in Penacook. Sept. 15, 1875.

Children of HON. CHARLES FRANCIS[9], (1848) **[1457]** (Charles H.[8], Isaac[7], Samuel[6], Jr., Col. Samuel[5], Samuel[4], Isaac[3], Sergt. Abraham[2], Robert[1]) and Mary Elizabeth (Cone) Adams; res. Lynn, Mass.
i. CHARLES FRANCIS[10], JR., b. Aug. 13, 1874; m. Sept. 5, 1899, Goldie Randall.
ii. ALICE MAY[10], b. Mar. 30, 1877; d. 11 Jan., 1880.

Children of MARY ALICE[9], (1853) **[1458]** (Charles H.[8], Isaac[7], Samuel[6], Jr., Col. Samuel[5], Samuel[4], Isaac[3], Sergt. Abraham[2], Robert[1]) and Walter F. Peck; res. Salem, Mass.
i. HELEN CHESLEY PECK, b. Aug. 25, 1886.
ii. JOHN ADAMS PECK, b. Aug. 7, 1888.

Children of EDWARD F.[9], (1857) **[1459]** (Robert W.[8], Enoch[7], Samuel[6], Jr., Col. Samuel[5], Samuel[4], Isaac[3], Sergt. Abraham[2], Robert[1]) and Mary (Parker) Adams; res. Groveland, Mass.
i. FLORENCE[10], b. in Groveland, 1885.
ii. HAROLD[10], b. in Groveland, 1894.
iii. ROBERT PARKER[10], b. in Groveland, Aug. 12, 1896.

Children of IDA FRANCES[9], (1855) [1460] (Selwyn P.[8], Samuel[7], Samuel[6], Jr., Col. Samuel[5], Samuel[4], Isaac[3], Sergt. Abraham[2], Robert[1]) and James P. Reed; res. Newburyport, Mass.

    i. ETHEL M. REED, b. May 30, 1888.
    ii. FRED A. REED, b. June 7, 1890 ; d. 17 Sept., 1892.

Children of SELWYN M.[9], (1858) [1461] (Selwyn P.[8], Samuel[7], Samuel[6], Jr., Col. Samuel[5], Samuel[4], Isaac[3], Sergt. Abraham[2], Robert[1]) and Belle B. (Emerton) Adams; res. Newburyport, Mass.

    i. FRANK WOOD[10], b. in Newburyport, Sept. 2, 1884. *d. Sept. 1, 1930 m. Helen*
    ii. EDITH MARION[10], b. in Newburyport, Mar. 20, 1892.

Child of IDA LOUISA WESTON, (1859) [1462] and Bainbridge Morse; res. Haverhill, Mass.

    i. GRETA WESTON MORSE, b. in Haverhill, Sept. 13, 1885.

Children of DURWARD C.[9], (1865) [1463] [Henry H.[8], Eliphalet[7], Isaac[6], Capt. Samuel[5], Isaac[4], Isaac[3], Sergt. Abraham[2], Robert[1]) and Gladys (Hopkins) Adams; res. Richmond, Sagadahoc Co., Me.

    i. ELEANOR B.[10], b. in Richmond, Oct. 17, 1892.
    ii. EVA[10], b. in Richmond, Nov. 18, 1894.

Children of ROBERT HENRY K. WHITELEY, (1866) [1464] and Alice E. Eberts; res. Detroit, Mich.

    i. HELEN LE BARON WHITELEY, b. Feb. 2, 1895.
    ii. KATHERINE KIRKWOOD WHITELEY, b. Dec. 12, 1898.

Children of JOHN FREDERICK[9], (1853) [1465] (John[8], Col. Joseph Henry[7], Lieut. and Maj. John[6], Capt. John[5], Israel[4], Sarah[3], Sergt. Abraham[2], Robert[1]) and Anne B. (Kelley) Adams; res. Haverhill, Mass.

i. HENRY SHAW[10], b. June 9, 1877.
ii. ELIZABETH RAND[10], b. Jan. 21, 1879.
iii. JULIA MARGUERITE[10], b. Sept. 17, 1881.
iv. JOHN AMOS[10], b. Jan. 10, 1883.
v. WARD[10], b. July 21, 1884 ; d. 7 Nov., 1884.
vi. FAITH K.[10], b. Dec. 5, 1885.
vii. EDWARD FREDERICK[10], b. Dec. 26, 1887.
viii. CHARLES ARTHUR[10], b. May 5, 1881 ; d. 1 Nov., 1896.
ix. ANNIE[10], b. Oct. 6, 1893; d. 25 Nov., 1896.

Children of MARY[9], (1869) [**1466**] (Charles Clinton[8], Benjamin Franklin[7], Robert[6], David[5], Israel[4], Sarah[3], Sergt. Abraham[2], Robert[1]) and Charles C. Paige; res. Warren, O.

i. DAVID R. PAIGE, b. Dec. 31, 1892.
ii. SARAH PAIGE, b. Aug. 16, 1894.

Children of BENJAMIN H.[9], 3D, (1869) [**1467**] (Benjamin H.[8], 2d, Benjamin H.[7], Benjamin[6], Benjamin[5], John[4], John[3], Sergt. Abraham[2], Robert[1]) and Cora J. (Ackerman) Adams; res. Chelsea, Vt.

i. BENJAMIN HACKET[10], b. in Chelsea, Oct. 2, 1892.
ii. WILLIAM HENRI[10], b. in Chelsea, May 9, 1899.

Child of JULIA O.[9], (1873) [**1468**] (Benjamin H.[8], 2D, Benjamin H.[7], Benjamin[6], Benjamin[5], John[4], John[3], Sergt. Abraham[2], Robert[1]) and Frank E. Bixby; res. Chelsea, Vt.

i. GERALD A. BIXBY, b. Jan. 26, 1897.

Children of JULIA A.[9], (1878) [**1469**] (Eben H.[8], Thomas B.[7], Israel[6], Israel[5], Matthew[4], Dr. Matthew[3], Sergt. Abraham[2], Robert[1]) and William E. Gibson; res. Hillsboro, N. H.

i. HARRY S. GIBSON, b. July 2, 1896.
ii. FOREST E. GIBSON, b. Mar. 10, 1898.

Children of FLORA BELL[9], (1866) [1470] (Jacob K.[8], Benjamin F.[7], John[6], John[5], Matthew[4], Dr. Matthew[3], Sergt. Abraham[2], Robert[1]) and Wilson B. Flanders; res. Charlestown, Mass.

    i. NINA MAY FLANDERS, b. Feb. 10, 1889; d. 1 May, 1891.
    ii. MAURICE WINIFRED FLANDERS, b. Apr. 21, 1892.

Children of BENJAMIN F.[9], (1868) [1471] (Jacob K.[8], Benjamin F.[7], John[6], John[5], Matthew[4], Dr. Matthew[3], Sergt. Abraham[2], Robert[1]) and Catherine ((Morean) Adams; res. Sutton, N. H.

    i. JACOB K[10], b. Nov. 27, 1895.
    ii. HARRY B. F.[10], b. Mar. 9, 1899.

Children of ADDISON L.[9], (1844) [1472] (Norman R.[8], Roswell[7], Asahel[6], Zadoc[5], Jacob[4], Sergt. Jacob[3], Jacob[2], Robert[1]) and Minerva E. (Fish) Adams; res. Suffield, Conn.

1484.   i. HELEN ADELE[10], b. in Suffield, Dec. 22, 1871; m. Sept. 14, 1892, Maurice L. Barden; res. Suffield, Conn.
1485.   ii. GILBERT ADDISON[10], b. in Suffield, Nov. 15, 1873; m. Dec. 8, 1894, Adele I. Cotton.
    iii. CHLOE M.[10], b. in Suffield, Apr. 27, 1875.
    iv. GEORGE DEXTER[10], b. in Suffield, Aug. 30, 1878.

Child of GEORGE W.[9], (1850) [1473] (Norman R.[8], Roswell[7], Asahel[6], Zadoc[5], Jacob[4], Sergt. Jacob[3], Jacob[2], Robert[1]) and Hattie A. (Moore) Adams; res. Suffield, Conn.

    i. JENNIE E.[10], b. in Suffield, June 24, 1873; prob. m. Arthur Rowley of Agawam, Mass.

Children of GEORGE W.[9], (1850) and Flora E. (Thompson) Adams.

    ii. HATTIE E.[10], b. in Suffield, June 24, 1879.
    iii. LIZZIE M.[10], b. in Suffield, Jan. 11, 1883.

Children of MARIE J.[9], (1852) [1474] (Norman R.[8], Roswell[7], Asahel[6], Zadoc[5], Jacob[4], Sergt. Jacob[3], Jacob[2], Robert[1]) and Charles H. Fowler; res. Thompsonville, Conn.

    i. CHARLES J. FOWLER, b. June 5, 1875.
        He graduated from the Thompsonville High School in June, 1894, and worked his way through Yale College in the class of 1898.
    ii. JAMES H. FOWLER, b. May 23, 1887.

Children of NELLIE M.[9], (1856) [1475] (Albert[8], Harvey[7], Noadiah[6], Zadoc[5], Jacob[4], Sergt. Jacob[3], Jacob[2], Robert[1]) and James A. Bryan; res. Springfield, Mass.

    i. CLARK A. BRYAN, b. in Great Barrington, Mass., Oct. 30, 1880.
    ii. ANNA BRYAN, b. in Great Barrington, Nov. 15, 1881.
    iii. FRANCES S. BRYAN, b. in Great Barrington, June 8, 1883.
    iv. JAMES A. BRYAN, b. in Great Barrington, Jan. 31, 1886.
    v. RUTH W. BRYAN, b. in Great Barrington, Nov. 30, 1887.
    vi. IRAD R. BRYAN, b. in Springfield, Mass., July 26, 1889; d. 21 July, 1894.
    vii. HELEN BRYAN, b. at Springfield, Sept. 8, 1891.
    viii. WILLIAM BRYAN, b. in Springfield, Mar. 19, 1896; d. 28 July, 1896.

Children of ADDIE LOUISA[9], (1872) [1476] (Joseph B.[8], Harvey[7], Noadiah[6], Zadoc[5], Jacob[4], Sergt. Jacob[3], Jacob[2], Robert[1]) and Hovey Kincheloe; res. Harmony, Posey Co., Ind.

    i. HARL KINCHELOE, b. June 2, 1893.
    ii. EMILY MADGE KINCHELOE, b. Dec. 26, 1895.
    iii. AMY KINCHELOE, b. Oct. 17, 1898.

Children of FRANK SYLVESTER[9], (1857) [1477] (Edward[8], Jr., Edward[7], Arah[6], Zadoc[5], Jacob[4], Sergt. Jacob[3], Jacob[2], Robert[1]) and Nellie (Woodford) Adams; res. Hartford, Conn.

    i. ALICE WOODFORD[10], b. in Hampden, Mass., Sept. 21, 1882; d. 21 Jan., 1890.
    ii. CLARK EDWARD[10], b. Nov. 19, 1883; d. 17 Aug., 1884.
    iii. EVA JANE[10], b. Feb. 26, 1885; d. 24 Aug., 1885.
    iv. LILLIAN MAUD[10], b. in Hartford, Mar. 18, 1891.

Tenth Generation.]   OF NEWBURY, MASS.   517

Child of MINNIE[9], (1866) [1478] (William Eliphalet[8], Lewis Alanson[7], Eliphalet[6], Jr., Eliphalet[5], Freegrace[4], Abraham[3], Jacob[2], Robert[1]) and George Wesley Cook; res. Grand Rapids, Mich.

   i. GEORGE NEWMAN COOK, b. in Toronto, Ont., Aug. 10, 1892.

Children of LAURA THERESA[9], (1868) [1479] (William Eliphalet[8], Lewis Alanson[7], Eliphalet[6], Jr., Eliphalet[5], Freegrace[4], Abraham[3], Jacob[2], Robert[1]) and Charles James Hodgins; res. Cleveland, O.

   i. SIDNEY G. HODGINS, b. in Cleveland, Feb. 15, 1894.
   ii. ROY C. HODGINS, b. in Cleveland, Apr. 12, 1896.

Child of CLARENCE EVERAGE[9], (1868) [1480] (Thaddeus Solomon[8], Henry Lewis[7], Gaius[6], Seth[5], Moses[4], John[3], Jacob[2], Robert[1]) and Matilda (Longerich) Adams; res. Chicago, Ill.

   i. FREDERICK CHARLES, b. in Indianapolis, Ind., May 27, 1889.

Children of CLAUDE CHARLES[9], (1871) [1481] (Thaddeus Solomon[8], Henry Lewis[7], Gaius[6], Seth[5], Moses[4], John[3], Jacob[2], Robert[1]) and Dora (Adking) Adams; res. Richmond, Ind.

   i. FELECIA ROSE[10], b. in Richmond, Aug. 18, 1890.
   ii. LELIA O.[10], b. in Richmond.

Children of Rufus D. and Aroline.

I. Elizabeth Hamilton[9], b. Feb. 1, 1899
II. Rosamond, b.
m. Adelbert P. Lodbout, Sept. 16, 19__

ROBERT ADAMS [Eleventh Generation.

Children of SUSAN THURLOW[10], (1862) [1482] (George Edward[9], Philip[8], Henry[7], Henry[6], Robert[5], Abraham[4], Robert[3], Sergt. Abraham[2], Robert[1]) and Frank I. Barrett; res. Shawomet, R. I.
  i. MARY A. BARRETT, b. Aug. 20, 1886.
  ii. RICHARD BARRETT, b. Oct. 15, 1890.
  iii. HOWARD BARRETT, b. Sept., 1894.

Children of GEORGE KIMBALL[10], (1863) [1483] (George Edward[9], Philip[8], Henry[7], Henry[6], Robert[5], Abraham[4], Robert[3], Sergt. Abraham[2], Robert[1]) and Nettie H. (Hale) Adams; res. Fitchburg, Mass.
  i. ESTHER MABEL[11], b. in Fitchburg, Oct. 7, 1889.
  ii. ETHEL HALE[11], b. in Fitchburg, Apr. 23, 1891.
  iii. EDWARD AUGUSTUS[11], b. in Fitchburg, Sept. 29, 1893.
  iv. ALICE ORDWAY[11], b. in Fitchburg, Dec. 3, 1895.
  v. MILDRED LOUISA[11], b. in Fitchburg, Dec. 13, 1897.

Children of HELEN ADELE[10], (1871) [1484] (Addison L.[9], Norman R.[8], Roswell[7], Asahel[6], Zadoc[5], Jacob[4], Sergt. Jacob[3], Jacob[2], Robert[1]) and Maurice L. Barden.
  i. ALTA AZALIA BARDEN, b. Nov. 19, 1893; d. 13 Mar., 1895.
  ii. ALVAH ADAMS BARDEN, b. June 2, 1896.

Children of GILBERT ADDISON[10], (1873) [1485] (Addison L.[9], Norman R.[8], Roswell[7], Asahel[6], Zadoc[5], Jacob[4], Sergt. Jacob[3], Jacob[2], Robert[1]) and Adel I. (Colton) Adams.
  i. ADA ADEL[11], b. Feb. 24, 1895; d. 16 Aug., 1897.
  ii. STANLEY ADDISON[11], b. July 3, 1898.

INDEX I.

NAMES OF MALES WITH NAME OF FATHER.

	Page.
Aaron[6], (1796) Daniel	82
" [7], (1793) Isaac	108
" [7], (1795) Joshua	119
" [7], (1819) Israel	161
" [8], (1838) Stephen	257
" Bray[8], (1842) Aaron B.	241
" Isaiah[8], (1855) Isaiah	255
" L. C.[8], (1844) Enoch	290
Abel Snow[8], (1834) John	349
Abner Amasa[8], (1859) Ezra	356
" Jay[8], (1864) Geo. Washington	359
Abraham[2], (Sergt.) (1639) Robert	4
" [3], (Capt.) (1676) Sergt. Abraham	7
" [3], (Lieut.) (1687) Jacob	9
" [4], (1696) Robert	10
" [4], (1713) Dr. Matthew	15
" [4], (1715) Capt. Abraham	12
" [4], (1715) Lieut. Abraham	17
" [5], (1748) Abraham	37
" [5], (1769) Samuel	46
" [6], (1746) Robert	49
" [6], (1750) Benjamin	50
" [6], (1776) Capt. Benjamin	60
" [6], —— Abraham	79
" [6], Jr. (1808) Abraham	95
" [6], (1793) Capt. Oliver	99
" [7], (1791) Henry	105
" [7], —— Abraham	107
" [7], (1800) Benjamin	125
" Doddridge[7], (1810) Isaac	109
Adam Willis[7], (1810) Moses	141
Addison L.[9], (1844) Norman R.	476
Adelbert A.[8], —— Joseph M	321
" Weston[9], (1868) David Weston	446
Albert[7], (1807) Israel	151
" [7], (1841) Benjamin	185
" [8], —— Charles M.	250
" [8], (1828) Harvey	344
" [9], —— John Quincy	417
" Cyrus[8], (1871) Moses Cyrus	327
" E.[8], (1866) George W.	272
" F.[7], (1829) Nathan	177
" Fellows[8], (1857) Chas Frederick	361

	Page.
Albert Howard[8], (1842) Benjamin	240
" Hamilton[8], (1863) Col. Chas. Henry	275
" Martin[8], (Hon.) (1843) Moses	258
" S.[7], (1825) Stephen	128
Albetus Milton[9], (1878) Chas. Wood	425
Alden[6], (1796) Joel, Jr.	103
Alfred[6], (1794) Thaddeus	98
" [7], (1820) Thaddeus, Jr.	218
" Edmund[9], (1890) George E.	486
" Le Roy[8], (1849) Prescott Jones	304
" S.[9], (1890) Frank E.	472
" Walker[9], (1861) James A.	411
Allen Longfellow[9], (1882) John	421
Alonzo[8], —— Jarvis	346
" Gay[9], (1873) Thad. Solomon	494
" J.[9], (1834) Henry Lewis	380
Alpheus[7], (1818) Rev. Theophilus B.	166
Alvin[7], (1792) Noadiah	187
" [7], (1825) Eli	167
" [8], (1819) Lucius	344
" [9], —— Alvin	478
Amasa A.[8], (1822) Alvin	343
Amos[5], (1768) Dea. Edmund	41
" [6], (1768) Charles	51
" [8], (1829) Edmund	89
" Bray[7], (1796) Smith	110
" Darwin[8], (1848) Erasmus Darwin	286
" " [9], (1877) Henry Farnum	447
" Henry[8], (1849) Charles	243
Andrew M.[7], (1833) Moody	180
" Jackson[8], —— Samuel	254
" " [8], (1829) Isaac	288
Arah[6], (1775) Zadoc	90
Arad[7], (1812) Israel	151
Archie[8], (1888) George W.	425
" L.[8], (1871) Uri M.	400
Archer[9], (1866) Geo. Herman	458
Arnold P.[9], (1865) Oscar Edmund	430
Artemas L.[7], (1821) Samuel	147
Arthur[10], —— Horace Clinton	502
" C.[7], (1842) Seth	159
" Daniel[8], (1859) Darius	298
" Gilbert[9], (1885) Arthur Daniel	456
" J.[8], (1868) Nathan	312

INDEX I.

	Page.
Arthur P.[8], (1876) Henry Le Roy	395
" Sumner[8], (1868) John Calvin	334
" S.[8], (1884) David	395
" Sturgis[9], (1890) Amos Darwin	447
Asa[5], (1772) Richard	40
" [6], (1781) Benjamin	74
" [6], (1801) Paul	81
" [7], Jr., (1838) Asa	172
" [7], (1824) Richard	176
" F.[8], (1827) Isaac	288
" Pratt[8], (1844) John	245
" Samuel[9], (1859) Oscar Rufus	497
" W.[8], (1848) Sylvanus	307
Asahel[6], (Capt.) (1762) Zadoc	89
" [7], (1803) Zadoc, Jr	188
Ashbel[5], (1739) Jacob	42
Ashley[7], (1833) Martin	218
Augustine[6], —— Solomon	75
Augustus Hall[7], (1827) Moses	141
Azro[7], (1822) Asa	154
Bela Kent[7], (1813) Gaius	215
Bemis[9], (1889) Benjamin F	478
Benjamin[4], (Rev.) (1719) Capt. Abraham	12
" [4], (1724) John	14
" [4], (1718) Sergt. Jacob	17
" [5], (1723) Abraham	20
" [5], (1745) John	24
" [5], (Capt.) (1735) William	26
" [5], (Capt.) (1746) Abraham	27
" [5], (Dr.) (1758) Rev. Benjamin	30
" [5], (1751) John	35
" [5], (1752) Matthew	36
" [5], (1782) Dea. Edmund	42
" [5], (1772) Benjamin	43
" [6], Jr., (1784) Benjamin	50
" [6], (1773) Capt. Benjamin	60
" [6], (1781) Joseph	63
" [6], (1787) Benjamin	74
" [6], (1773) Benjamin	78
" [6], (1795) Ens. James	88
" [6], (1724) Edmund	89
" [7], (1807) Isaac	108
" [7], —— Israel	117
" [7], (1793) Joshua	119
" [7], (1803) Benjamin	163
" [7], (1803) Matthew	164
" [8], (1830) Benjamin	240
" [8], —— Benjamin	249
" [8], (1820) Isaac	252
" [8], (1876) Oliver L	388
" Bradley[8], (1831) John	245
" Dickinson[7], (1809) Enos	215
" F.[6], (1799) Lieut. John	65
Benjamin F.[7], (1782) Samuel	107
" F.[7], (1801) John	162
" F.[7], (1818) Jeremiah	166
" F.[8], (1841) Harvey	344
" F.[9], (1868) Jacob Kimball	466
" Foster[7], (1824) Benjamin	187
" Frank[8], (1842) Henry Lewis	380
" Franklin[7], (1811) Robert	153
" " [7], (1803) Levi	214
" " [8], (1875) Wm. Bradley	390
" H.[7], (1810) Benjamin	154
" H.[8], 2d, Benjamin H	306
" H.[9], 3d., (1869) Benjamin H., 2d	460
" Hackett[10], (1892) Benjamin H., 3d	514
" P.[8], (1845) Benjamin Perley	266
" Perley[7], (1806) Benjamin	125
" Tenney[7], (1842) Capt. Richard	183
" Watson[6], (1778) Benjamin	58
" Webb[6], (1809) Joseph	66
" " [9], (1898) John Benjamin F	438
Bertrand[9], (1867) Geo. Herman	458
Bildad[5], (1765) Lieut. Joel	48
" [8], (1880) Bildad	103
Bradley[6], (1807) Capt. Oliver	100
" [7], —— Israel	117
" Jewett[7], (1830) Isaac	118
Burton Alden[8], (Prof.) (1875) Philip Tyler	333
Caleb[6], (1754) Benjamin	50
" [6], (1787) Joseph	63
" Cushing[8], (1833) Joseph	238
" Greenleaf[5], (1852) Rev. Joseph	29
" Miller[7], (1835) Horace	195
Calvin[6], (1790) Zebulon, Jr	90
" [6], (1780) Capt. Gideon	90
" [8], —— Gideon	352
" Lyman[7], (1816) Calvin	190
Carl H.[9], (1891) Charles F	471
" Nelson[9], (1879) Col. Milton B	435
Carroll Rutherford[8], (1876) Wilbur C	377
" Spofford[8], (1860) Paul	326
Carver Parker[7], (1826) Rev. Theophilus B	166
Chandler Braman[7], (1829) Isaac	145
Charles[5], (1729) Abraham	20
" [6], (Rev. D. D.) (1808) Lieut. John	65
" [6], (1812) Israel, Jr	72
" [6], (1824) John	86

	Page.
Charles[7], (1802) Amos	109
" [7], (1805) Smith	110
" [7], (1817) Benjamin	163
" [7], (1841) Freeborn	180
" [7], (1819) John	185
" [8], (1821) Abraham	235
" [8], —— Benjamin	249
" [8], —— Israel	259
" [8], (1855) Benjamin Dickinson	383
" [8], (1871) John William	273
" [8], —— John S.	311
" [8], (1860) Nathan	342
" [9], —— George E.	417
" [9], (1869) Smith	410
" [9], (1873) Enoch F.	451
" [10], —— Horace Clinton	502
" A.[8], (1882) David	395
" Aaron[8], (1834) Charles	242
" Albert[7], (1848) Philip D.	178
" Anderson[7], (1837) Jonathan	149
" " [8], (1867) Darius	298
" Arthur[8], (1852) Dea. Israel	296
" B.[8], (1859) Stephen C.	325
" C.[8], (1860) Edward Lewis Osgood	327
" Carroll[7], (1829) Dr. Clement Jackson	174
" Carroll[9], (1861) Charles	406
" Clifford[9], (1868) Charles Hall	439
" Clinton[8], (1838) Benjamin Franklin	304
" Cushing[8], (1860) Joseph Webster	408
" Daniel[8], (1842) Isaiah	255
" " [8], (1860) Daniel	311
" De Leon[9], (1857) Benjamin Bradley	412
" E.[8], (Prof.) (1861) George Fitz.	268
" Edward[7], (1829) Capt. Richard	183
" " [7], (1842) Joseph, Jr.	135
" " [8], (1869) Geo. Edward.	333
" " [8], (1870) Benj. Whiting	247
" " [8], (1867) Isaac Milton.	294
" " [9], (1881) Chas. Francis	493
" Edwin[9], (1855) Chas. Henry	416
" Ellsworth[9], (1873) Chas. Henry	412
" Everett[9], (1887) John Brooks.	457
" F.[7], (1838) Abraham	220
" F.[8], (1857) Harrison	323
" F.[8], (1864) Horace	341
" F.[8], (1872) George W.	272
" F.[8], (1857) Obadiah F.	324
" F.[9], (1862) Thos. Augustus	453
" F.[9], (1868) Massena Clark	481

	Page.
Charles Fayette[8], (1857) Rufus	387
" Frederick[6], (1794) Joseph	64
" " [7], (1827) Rev. Zenas.	199
" " Jr.[7], (1824) Charles Frederick	131
" Francis[8], (1846) Frederick Augustus L.	373
" Francis[8], (1886) Simeon	395
" " [9], (Hon.) (1848) Charles Henry	449
" Francis[10], Jr., (1870) Hon. Chas. Francis.	512
" G.[8], (1862) George Hadley	354
" Gardner[8], (1866) Norman B.	307
" H.[7], (1851) George W.	150
" H.[8], (1839) Moses	244
" H.[8], (1820) Isaac	288
" H.[8], (1856) Azro	306
" H.[9], (1859) Moses	467
" H.[9], (1871) George F.	474
" H.[9], (1879) Henry Farnum	447
" Hall[8], (1844) William	279
" Harvey[9], (1864) Joseph B.	477
" Henry[7], (1836) (Col) Rev. Charles, D. D.	133
" Henry[7], (1809) Benjamin	126
" " [8], (1822) Charles M.	250
" " [8], (1837) Chas. Henry	266
" " [8], (1849) Warren Mann.	286
" " [8], (1850) John Q.	338
" " [9], (1834) Joel	405
" Israel[7], (1823) Isaac	145
" " [8], (1855) Dea. Israel	296
" Charles L.[9], (1892) Reuben O.	498
", Lawrence[8], (1880) Xenophon.	339
" Lincoln[9], (1863) David Weston	446
" M.[7], (1796) Joshua	119
" M.[9], (1866) John Merriam	424
" Morton[7], (1835) Capt. Ira.	223
" Morris[8], (1836) Joshua, Jr.	251
" P.[8], (1859) Geo. Washington	266
" S.[9], (1851) John Smith	419
" Stewart[8], (1877) Chas. Albert.	332
" Samuel[8], (1843) Moses	292
" W.[6], (1818) Ebenezer	84
" W.[8], (1875) Henry Proctor	358
" Warren[8], (1865) Charles	336
" Wayne[9], (1890) Charles	495
" Webster[9], —— Webster	409
" Wesley[7], (1844) Charles	150
" William[7], (1847) William	181
" Willis[9], (1882) Charles F.	475
" Zenas[8], (1859) Chas. Frederick	361
Chester Freeborn[8], (1878) Charles	336

INDEX I.

Christopher C.[7], (1813) Israel 161
" Hussey[8], (1887) George Daniel 298
Cicero[8], — Jarvis 346
Clarence[6], (1867) Simeon Houghton... 391
" Elliot[8], (1854) Louis K....... 349
" Everage[9], (1868) Thaddeus Solomon..... 494
" W.[9], (1873) Jacob Kimball.... 466
Clark[6], (1807) Capt. Simeon 100
" [7], — Eli 210
" Hiram[7], (1848) Clark 225
Claud Charles[9], (1871) Thaddeus Solomon........ 494
" D.[8], (1869) Joseph Henry........ 319
Clement Jackson[6], (1795) Simeon 82
" " [7], (1833) Dr. Stephen 174
Clifford Newman[9], (1879) Wm. Eliphalet.................... 482
" La B.[8], (1889) Rev. Frank E.. 300
Clinton[7], (1828) Horace................. 195
Clyde Raymond[9], (1898) Geo. Willard. 499
Coleman B.[8], (1867) Henry Proctor.... 358
" Boyd[9], (1895) James Henry.. 485
Cornelius[8], (1848) Phineas M.......... 387
Crosby[8], (1888) Le Roy F............... 396
Cullie Root[9], (1867) Chas. Samuel..... 453
Cushing[9] (1870) Caleb Cushing........ 407
Cyrus [6], (Hon.) (1745) Moses.......... 76
" A.[7], (1837) George W............ 160
" F.[7], (1857) Clark................. 225
" W.[8], (1860) Enoch Cheney...... 320
Daniel[3], (1682) Jacob.... 9
" [4], Jr., (1726) Daniel............. 17
" [4], (1734) Richard................ 16
" [5], (1739) Abraham :............. 20
" [5], (1754) Capt. Isaac 32
" [5], (1760) Abraham.... 37
" [5], (1760) Richard 39
" [6], (1756) Robert.............. 49
" [6], (1756) Benjamin.............. 50
" [6], — Israel 72
" [6], (1775) Daniel 73
" [7], (Col.) (1787) Daniel........... 106
" [7], (1807) Eliphalet 145
" [7], (1823) Jacob 148
" [7], (1837) Peter.................. 156
" [7], (1830) Jonathan Tenney 159
" [7], (1819) Russell................ 168
" [7], (Dr.) (1846) David............. 186
" [8], (1883) Geo. Daniel............ 298
" [9], (1871) Caleb Cushing 407
" Coleman[8], (1863) Asa..... 330
" Dole[7], (1830) George.............. 179

Daniel Hamilton[7], (1836) Daniel Noyes 156
" Marsh[7], (1833) Edmund........ 186
" Marsh[8], Jr, (1872) Daniel M... 343
" Palmer[8], (1823) Joseph......... 238
" Noyes[6], (1803) Solomon 75
" Sewall[8], (1842) John 245
" W.[8], (1866) Daniel Hamilton .. 308
" Webster[8], (1845) Charles....... 243
Darius[5], (1744) Capt. Isaac 32
" [7], (1805) Isaac.. 146
" [7], (1831) Johathan.............. 149
" [8], (1844) Dea. Israel............. 296
" S.[7], (1833) David 185
David[4], (1720) Isaac.................... 13
" [5], (Eld.) (1754) Samuel.......... 28
" [5], (Capt.) (1747) Capt. Isaac..... 32
" [5], (1742) Israel 34
" [5], (1754) Abraham 37
" [5], (1773) Capt. Simeon......... 47
" [6], (1773) Benjamin............ 58
" [6], (1772) Stephen............. 59
" [6], (1782) Eld. David 61
" [6], (1798) Lieut. John......... 65
" [6], (1782) Capt. David......... 70
" [6], (1796) Capt. Samuel 71
" [6], (1762) Capt. Stephen....... 79
" [6], (1797) Ens. James......... 88
" [6], (1797) Abraham 95
" [7], (1809) David................. 122
" [7], (1850) Simeon................. 225
" E.[9], (1852) Oscar Edmund....... 430
" Farnum[7], (1813) Dr. Joseph..... 140
" G.[8], (1876) George S 313
" H.[7], (Rev.) (1835) George W..... 160
" Hall[9], (1861) Capt. George A 456
" Jackson[7], (1823) Robert......... 153
" Jewett[7], (1820) Capt. Richard... 183
" " [8], (1844) David Jewett... 338
" Marks[6], (1846) John Langdon... 320
" M.[9], (1878) Benjamin F......... 478
" P.[7], (1812) Joshua............... 120
" Q.[7], (1852) Abraham, Jr......... 209
" Weston[8], (1835) David Farn'm.. 285
" Wood[7], (1823) David 144
Dayton A.[7], (1855) Wm. Spurr 311
Decatur C.[8], (1837) Ebenezer Moody.. 283
De Forest[10], (1897) Silas Hall.......... 508
Delisle W.[7], (1861) Abraham, Jr...... 209
Dennis H.[7], (1819) Solomon, Jr....... 155
" [7], (Capt.) (1830) Nathan........ 177
" Ezra[8], (1866) Capt. Dennis..... 333
" E.[9], (1890) Nathan E........... 473
Dickey[9], (1859) John P 477
Dudley[5], (1781) Moses 41

	Page.
Durward C.[9], (1865) Henry H	459
Dwight[7,!]—— Horace	206
" Dean[9], (1858) Benja. Bradley	412
Earl[8], (1882) Noble D	376
" Verna[10], (1892) Chas. Clifford	510
Eben[6], (1817) Ebenezer	84
" E.[7], (1840) Charles	150
" H.[8], (1840) Thomas B	314
" H.[9], (1871) Decatur O.	443
" W.[8], (1864) James Monroe	285
Ebenezer[5], (1776) Richard	40
" [6], (1771) Zadoc	89
" [6], (1802) Simeon	83
" H.[7], (1809) Israel	161
" Moody[7], (1811) Col. John Emery	139
Eddie L.[9], (1866) George N	416
" [9], (1876) George F	470
Edgar B.[8], (1838) Samuel Plumer	264
" G.[8], (1847) Gilson	322
Edmund[4], (Dea.) (1740) Richard	16
" [5], (1777) Dea. Edmund	42
" [6], (1802) Ens. James	88
Edward[7], (1801) Arah	189
" [8], Jr., (1832) Edward	348
" Augustus[11], (1893) Geo. Kimball	518
" Effingham[8], (1872) Simeon	395
" F.[8], (1822) Col. Joseph Henry	301
" [9], (1857) Robert W	451
" Frederick[10], (1887) John Frederick	514
" Francis[8], (1874) Rev. Lucien H	342
" Huntington[7], (1842) Rev. Charles, D. D	134
" Lewis O.[7], (1827) Dr. Clement Jackson	174
" Payson[8], (1842) Eliphalet	294
" " [9], (1846) Joel	405
" Prince[9], (1889) Chas. Henry	412
" Shepherd[9], (1873) John Andrew	466
" Silas[8], (1844) Moses Woodman	248
Edwin[7], (1825) Capt. Richard	183
" Grafton[8], (1863) Isaac Webb	337
" Hall[7], (1849) Thos. Hall	173
" Myron[9], (1882) John Brooks	457
" Robert[7], (1827) Isaac	118
" S.[7], (1806) Daniel	152
" Spofford[7], (1815) David	144
Elbert Clinton[8], (1869) Clinton	353
" J.[7], (1844) Joel	217
Eli[5], (1780) Samuel	46

	Page.
Eli[6], (1784) Enoch	80
" [6], (1810) Abraham	95
Elias[6], —— Job	102
" [7], (1828) George	228
" Bartlett[7], (1823) Moses	141
Elihu[6], (1798) Freegrace, Jr	94
Elijah[5], (1760) David	44
" French[7], (1836) Benja. Webb	136
" P.[8], (1830) Harvey	344
Elliot[6], (1801) Joel, Jr	103
Eliphalet[5], (1756) Freegrace	44
" [6], (1775) Capt. Samuel	70
" [6], Jr., (1779) Eliphalet	91
" [7], (1804) Isaac	146
Elmer[8], (1884) Noble D	376
" Ellsworth[8], (1862) Joseph Collins	307
Ellsworth C.[7], (1861) Wm. Spurr	211
Elwyn Everett[8], (1883) Wilbur C	377
Emerson Blake[9], (1885) John Quincy	483
Emery D.[8], (1865) James Monroe	284
Emory Eli[9], (1886) John Quincy	480
Enoch[4], (1724) Richard	15
" [5], (1752) Henry	31
" [5], (1750) Abraham	37
" [5], (1755) Richard	39
" [6], (1783) Stephen	59
" [6], Jr., (1779) Enoch	67
" [6], (1779) Daniel	80
" [7], (Dr.) (1829) Enoch	138
" [7], (1813) Col. John Emery	139
" [7], (1799) Samuel, Jr	142
" [7], (1823) Russell	168
" [8], (1824) Isaac	288
" [8], (1850) William	279
" C.[8], (1852) Dr. Enoch	281
" Cheney[7], (1809) Matthew	264
" Elliot[7], (1810) Abraham B	167
" F.[8], (1837) Enoch	290
" G.[7], (1833) Richard	169
Enos[6], (1785) Seth	97
" [7], (1816) Enos	215
" Albert[8], (1867) Enos Holmes	297
" Holmes[7], (1829) Jonathan	149
" Seth[7], (1833) Joel	216
Erasmus Darwin[7], (1814) Dr. Joseph	140
" [9], (1877) John Sturgis	447
Ernest[9], (1877) Alfred Le Roy	458
" C.[7], (1859) Abraham, Jr	209
" Clifton[8], (1874) Simeon Augustus	336
" E.[9], (1870) Isaac H	420
" Edgar[8], (1890) Loren M	396
" Eugene[9], (1876) Chas. Wood	425

	Page.
Ernest H.[9], (1860) Edwin	338
" Leon[9], (1885) John Brooks	457
" Stickney[9], (1892) Geo. Moulton	473
Ervin P.[9], (1876) George H	470
Eugene[8], (1856) Moses	258
" C.[7], (1837) Abraham, Jr	209
" Elmer[8], (1858) Prescott Jones	304
" M.[8], (1868) James Monroe	285
Ezra[5], (1773) Moses	41
" [6], (Rev.) (1788) Eliphalet	92
" [7], (1842) Moody	180
" [7], (1814) Eliphalet, Jr	196
" [8], (1855) Wellington	356
" Henry[9], (1878) Vincent Rice	483
" Herbert[8], (Dr.) (1866) Dr. John G. C.	360
" P.[8], (1848) Henry Proctor	357
Everett[9], —— George E	417
Ezekiel[5], (1757) Freegrace	44
" [6], (1805) Freegrace, Jr	94
Ferdinand Swett[10], (1892) Geo. Willis.	507
Florus Farnum[9], (1871) David Weston	446
Forest Eugene[10], (1895) Charles S	507
" H.[8], (1860) Edwin	388
Francis[7], (1826) Eli	167
" [8], —— Francis	322
" A.[8], (1844) Albert	300
" Cushman[7], (1820) Capt. John Emery	139
" Cutler[8], (1896) Moses Woodburn	247
" Doddridge[8], (1835) Abraham Doddridge	241
Frank[8], (1845) Ebenezer Moody	283
" [8], —— Samuel Jackson	304
" [8], (1854) Nathan	342
" A.[7], (1847) George W	160
" Arnold[9], (1858) Francis A	409
" Atherton[8], (1874) Moses Cyrus	327
" B.[8], (Dr.) (1854) Enoch Cheney	320
" B.[9], (1856) William P	416
" Chalmers[9], (1888) Henry Eastlake	471
" Doddridge[7], (1832) Philip D	178
" Dresser[8], (1859) John Quincy	288
" E.[7], (Rev.) (1847) George W	150
" E.[8], (1861) John Quincy	328
" E.[8], (1866) Hon. Moses Sawin	293
" Elmore[9], (1891) Lewis Emery	448
" Forestall[9], (1876) Silas Lowell	421
" George[9], (1884) Joseph Ashley.	
" Gibson[9], (1829) John Q	486
" Hale[7], (1857) John Coffin	182
" Huey[8], (1858) Darius	297

	Page.
Frank Herbert[8], (1860) Simeon Houghton	391
" L.[8], (1869) Ezra	335
" L.[9], (1891) Albert E	437
" Leslie[8], (1887) Frank A	313
" N.[8], (1862) Dr. Enoch, Jr	281
" Nelson[8], (1862) Gilson	323
" Pierce[7], (1848) Moody	180
" " [8], (1868) Henry	325
" S.[9], (1869) John Merriam	424
" Spofford[8], (1859) Paul	326
" Sylvester[9], (1857) Edward, Jr	480
" Walter[8], (1874) Clinton	353
" Wilson[8], (1878) Simeon Augustus	336
" Wood[10], (1884) Selwyn M	513
Franklin[8], (1852) Dr. Hon. Milgrove	286
" [8], (Col.) (1843) Prof. Samuel	205
" B.[7], (1828) Horace Hale	230
" K.[8], (1882) Franklin B	400
" W.[10], (1856) Geo. Franklin	502
Fred[8], (1866) Edwin	339
" A.[8], (1860) Alfred	386
" A.[9], (1873) J. Warren	471
" Albert[9], (1875) John Brooks	457
" B.[9], (1859) Israel	466
" C.[9], (1873) Moses	468
" L.[9], (1856) John Smith	419
" William[9], (1857) Chas. Henry	416
Frederick[6], (1815) John	86
" [8], —— Joseph S	312
" A.[9], (1867) Chas. Henry	412
" Augustus L.[7], (1816) Capt. Milton	204
" Baldwin[9], (1878) Chas. Francis	493
" C.[8], (1879) Le Roye F	395
" Charles[10], (1889) Clarence Everage	517
" H.[8], (1859) Henry	390
" Henry[8], (1859) Dr. Henry Milgrove	287
" Joseph[8], (1870) Wilbur Fisk	362
" Waldemar[9], (1869) Geo. Moses	414
Freeborn[5], (Dr.) (1774) John	40
" [6], (1806) George	85
" [7], Jr., (1829) Freeborn	180
Freegrace[4], (1723) Lieut. Abraham	18
" [5], Jr., (1765) Freegrace	45
Gad Mather[7], (1845) Abraham	230
Gaius[6], (1781) Seth	97
Gale[9], —— Orin	467
Gamaliel[7], (1814) Zadoc, Jr	188

INDEX I.

	Page.
Gamaliel King[7], (1817) Thaddeus, Jr..	217
Gardiner[7], (1833) Freeborn	180
Garfield Proctor[9], (1886) Lucas Rufus.	484
George[5], (1768) John	40
" 6, (1792) Joseph	64
" 6, (Capt.) (1807) Nathan	67
" 6, (1798) George	85
" 6, (1790) Job	102
" 7, —— Capt. Jacob	121
" 7, —— Hiram	219
" 8, —— David	257
" 8, (1852) Geo. Edward	334
" 8, (1873) Horace	341
" 8, (1852) Nathan	341
" 9, (1871) Smith	410
" 9, —— Orin	467
" 9, (1892) Geo. G	498
" 10, —— Horace Clinton	502
" A.[8], (Capt.) (837) Albert	300
" A.[8], (1839) Phineas M	387
" Ambrose[9], (1874) Vincent Rice	483
" Arthur Maurice[8], (1884) Dr. John G. C	360
" Arthur[9], (1873) John Brooks..	456
" Ashley[9], (1874) Jos. Ashley	495
" Augustus[7], (1841) Capt. George	137
" 9, (1889) Louis Emery	448
" Benjamin[7], (1832) Benjamin Webb	136
" D.[8], (1864) Henry L	354
" Daniel[7], (1843) Jonathan	149
" Dexter[10], (1878) Addison L	515
" E.[8], —— Charles M	250
" E.[8], (1859) Hon. Moses Sawin..	293
" E.[8], (1859) Henry Proctor	357
" E.[9], (1866) George	425
" E.[9], (1888) Charles F	471
" Earl[10], (1899) Geo. Willis	508
" Edward[7], (1824) George	179
" " 8, (1880) Le Roy F	396
" " 9, (1832) Philip	404
" Edwin[8], (1856) Gilson	323
" Elliot[9], (1887) Geo. Moulton	472
" Emerson[8], (1857) Simeon Houghton	301
" F.[8], (1852) John Q	338
" F.[8], (1853) Theophilus B., Jr	321
" F.[8], (1864) George W	272
" F.[9], Jr., (1870) George F	474
" Fitz[7], (1824) Col. Samuel	126
" Forsyth[8], (1870) Capt. John Q	271
" Francis[7], (Dr.) (1863) Elias	397
" Franklin[8], (1830) Geo. Hall	257
" " 9, (1833) Joel	404

	Page.
George G.[8], (1859) Oliver L	388
" Griffin[9], (1895) George E	486
" H.[7], (1843) Moses	183
" H.[8], (1835) Moses	292
" H.[8], (1845) Harrison	323
" H.[8], (1854) George W	318
" Hadley[7], (1830) Harvey	195
" Henry[7], (1843) George	131
" " 8, (1835) Moses	292
" " 8, (1865) John Quincy	288
" " 8, (1865) John Lewis	310
" Herbert[7], (1840) Capt. Ira	223
" Herman[8], (1844) Prescott Jones	304
" Howard[9], (1886) Arthur Daniel	456
" Huntington[9], (Capt.) (1844) Rev. Charles, D. D	134
" Knight[10], (1863) Geo. Edward..	502
" M.[7] (1858) George W	150
" Moses[8], (1834) Silas Merrill	247
" Moulton[8], (1861) Asa	330
" N.[8], (1836) Aaron	249
" Nelson[9], (1864) John Merriam.	424
" Newell[8], (1853) George Fitz	268
" Palmer[9], (1877) Geo. Moses	414
" Pettengill[8], (1845) Aaron Bray	241
" Royal[8], (1883) John Peabody..	340
" S.[7], (1841) George W	160
" S.[7], (1844) Samuel	212
" Samuel[8], (1879) Frank A	313
" Shrieve[9], (1864) Caleb Cushing	407
" Smith[7], (1810) Amos	109
" Spafford[7], (1827) Jonathan	149
" T.[8], (1868) David	311
" W.[9], (1815) Israel, jr	72
" W.[6], (1809) Jonathan	77
" W.[6], (1832) John	130
" W.[7], (1813) John	162
" W.[8], (1851) Moses	258
" W.[8], —— Samuel Jackson	303
" W.[9], (1850) Norman R	476
" W.[9], (1879) Jacob Kimball	466
" W.[9], (1889) Albert E	437
" Walter[7], (1827) Simeon	174
" Weymouth[7], (1828) Jona. Tenney	159
" Willis[9], (1854) Benjamin	419
" " 9, (1870) Aaron	424
" Washington[7], (1815) Benjamin	126
" " 7, (1830) Rev. Ezra	198
" " 8, —— Samuel	254
" William[7], (1818) Col. Gibbons	127
" " Jr.[8], (1855) Geo. Wm	268
" " 8, —— Ezra	335

George William⁸, (1853) Benj. Whiting	245
" " Mosher⁸, (1839) Joshua, jr.	251
" " Willard⁸, (1869) Henry	390
Gibbins⁶, (Col.) (1787) Capt. Stephen	62
Gideon⁴, (1716) Daniel	17
" ⁵, (Capt.) (1754) David	44
" ⁷, (1808) Calvin	192
Gilbert Addison¹⁰, (1873) Addison L.	515
Giles⁶, (1799) Daniel	82
" Aaron⁷, (1822) Richard	176
Gilson⁷, (1815) Russell	168
Gordon Kenneth¹⁰, (1895) Newton Romeyn	506
Green⁵, (1781) John	40
" ⁷, (1831) Nathan	177
Guidon⁸, —— Gideon	352
Harold¹⁰, (1894) Edward F.	512
" C.⁸, (1885) John Peabody	340
" Coleman⁹, (1883) Geo. Moulton	472
" Merle⁹, (1888) Enoch	439
" Woods⁸, (1889) Joseph Little	326
Harrison⁷, (1817) Russell	168
" H.⁷, (1827) Rev. Theophilus B.	166
" Parker⁸, (1864) Harrison H.	321
Harry⁹, (1888) George G.	498
" B. F.¹⁰, (1899) Benjamin F.	515
" Carleton⁸, (1886) James Knight	337
" Delva⁹, (1870) John Emery	442
" J.⁸, (1878) Henry J.	378
" Judson⁷, (1882) Chas. Wood	425
" O.¹⁰, (1879) Charles S.	507
" Romeyn¹⁰, (1899) Ralph Norton	505
" T.⁸, (1876) James Monroe	286
Harvey⁶, (1799) Capt. Gideon	91
" ⁷, (1793) Noadiah	187
" ¹⁰, (1885) Charles S.	507
" F.⁷, (1825) Harvey	195
" H.⁸, (1856) Geo. Hadley	354
" J.⁹, (1875) Benjamin F.	478
Hazen Michael⁷, (1832) Asa	171
Heber M.⁹, (1881) Charles F.	471
Henry⁴, (1722) Capt. Abraham	12
" ⁶, (1741) Robert	49
" ⁶, (1766) Stephen	58
" ⁶, (1783) Joseph	63
" ⁶, (1790) Enoch	67
" ⁶, (1787) John	77
" ⁶, (1800) Freegrace, Jr	94
" ⁷. (1774) Henry	105
" ⁷, (1801) Jacob	121
" ⁷, (1826) Richard	169
" ⁷, (1832) Oliver J.	221
Henry⁷, (1833) Simeon	224
" ⁸, —— John	259
" ⁸, (1869) John Hancock	272
" B.⁹, (1885) Horace Wylie	481
" Carter⁹, (1895) Kelly G.	486
" Charles⁹, (1875) Geo. Moses	414
" Coffin⁸, (1885) George Daniel	298
" Dummer⁸, (1831) Albert S.	269
" Eastlake⁸, (1863) Henry	325
" F.⁷, (1807) Thos. Fosdick	129
" Farnum⁸, (1846) Erasmus Darwin	285
" Farnum⁹, (1889) Amos Darwin	447
" Gilbert⁸, (1841) Thos. Jefferson	319
" ⁸, (1873) Benjamin Whiting	247
" H.⁸, (1839) Eliphalet	294
" Harmon⁷, (1843) John Breed	137
" J.⁹, (1843) Samuel	212
" (J.)⁹, (1878) John Brooks	457
" Keeler⁸, (1845) Benjamin F.	304
" L.⁷, (1830) Horace	195
" L.⁸, (1825) Lucius	344
" L.⁸, (1832) Henry Lewis	380
" Henry L.⁹, (1895) Julius T.	494
" Le Roy⁷, (1842) Timo. Mather	225
" Lewis⁷, (1809) Gaius	215
" Milgrove⁷, (1823) Dr. Joseph	140
" Nicholson⁸, —— Enos Seth	385
" Plumer⁹, (1843) Joel	405
" Proctor⁷, (1822) Rev. Ezra	198
" " ⁹, (1879) James Henry	485
" " ⁹, (1898) George E.	486
" Sewall⁷, (1831) Sewall	129
" Shaw¹⁰, (1877) John Frederick	514
" William⁷, (1809) Zadoc, Jr.	188
" ⁹, (1881) Charles Henry	412
Herbert C.⁸, —— John Quincy	299
" C.⁸, (1866) Enoch	323
" C.⁸, (1871) Oliver L.	388
" C.⁹, (1871) Henry Farnum	497
" Lawrence⁸,(1872) Giles Aaron	330
" Le Roy⁹, (1871) Enoch P.	451
" Webster⁹, (1879) John Quincy	480
Herman H.⁸, (1850) Dr. Enoch	281
" Parker⁸, (1877) Rev. Frank E.	299
" Solomon⁸, (1871) Joseph Collins	307
Hezekiah⁶, (1786) Corp. John	74
Hiram⁶, (1808) Thaddeus	99
" ⁷, (1802) Levi	213
" E.⁷, (1811) Levi	214
Homer⁸, —— Joseph S.	312
" J.⁸, (1863) John Quincy	328
Horace⁶, (1784) Samuel	46

INDEX I.

	Page
Horace[6], (1790) Capt. Gideon	91
" [6], (1807) Freegrace, Jr	94
" 7, (1821) John	185
" 7, (1844) Martin	218
" [8], (1836) Benjamin	240
" [9], (1890) Charles F.	475
" Chester[8], (1868) Uri M	400
" Clinton[9], (1848) Joel	405
" G[8], (1857) Gilson	323
" Hale[7], (1805) Bildad	103
" " 7, (1819) Allen	231
" " [8], (1884) Franklin B.	400
" Walter[7], (Dr.) —— Charles Frederick	131
" Winfield S., (1854) Winfred Scott	353
" Wylie[7], (1816) Horace	194
" " [8], (1862) Henry L	354
Horatio Nelson[8], (Capt.) (1842) Samuel Plumer	264
Howard[8], (1838) Benjamin	240
" Allen[9], (1893) Albert Hamilton	438
" D.[9], (1895) William H. H	462
" Edwin[9], (1877) Chas. Samuel	453
" L.[8], (1877) Henry Proctor	358
" Orr[8], (1872) Col. Chas. Henry	275
" Ryerson[9], (1884) Lucas Rufus	484
" Shirley[8], (1870) Henry Sewall	271
" Webster[8], (1889) Henry	325
" Wilbur[9], (1894) William E	486
Hugh Mather[7], (1858) Timothy Mather	225
Huntington[8], (1879) Capt. George Buntington	276
Imri P.[8], (1841) Ebenezer H	315
Ira[6], (Capt.) (1798) Capt. Simeon	100
" 7, Jr., (1826) Capt. Ira	223
" Rufus[9], (1886) Oscar Rufus	497
Irwin Dunbar[8], (1878) Henry	325
Isaac[2], (1647) Robert	5
" 3, (1678) Sergt. Abraham	7
" 4, (Capt.) (1713) Isaac	13
" 5, (1745) Capt. Isaac	32
" 5, (Dr.) (1777) John	40
" 6, (1761) Benjamin	50
" 6, (1774) Corp. Moses	56
" 6, (1793) Capt. David	70
" 6, (1776) Capt. Samuel	70
" 6, (1773) Israel, Jr	71
" 6, (Dr.) (1767) Capt. John	73
" [8], (1807) Simon	85
" 7, (1788) Caleb	107
" 7, (1794) Samuel	120
" 7, (1793) Samuel, Jr	142

	Page
Isaac[7], (1813) Isaac	147
" Alanson[9], (1872) Vincent Rice	483
" Clarence[9], (1859) Benjamin	419
" Deering[7], (1815) Isaac	118
" H.[8], (1835) Isaac	253
" Milton[7], (1841) Isaac	145
" Newcomb[8], (1832) Isaac	288
" Rogers[8], (Lieut.) (1829) Josh'a, Jr	250
" Watts[7], (1827) Nathan	176
Isaiah[7], (1811) Samuel	120
Israel[8], (1688) Sergt. Abraham	8
" 4, (1716) Isaac	13
" 4, (1707) Sarah	13
" 5, (Capt.) (1735) Robert	22
" 5, (1761) Capt. Isaac	33
" 5, Jr., (1748) Israel	33
" 5, (1733) Israel	34
" 5, (1746) Matthew	36
" 6, (1792) Capt. Moses	56
" 6, (1776) Stephen	59
" 6, (1790) Capt. Samuel	71
" 6, (1768) Israel	72
" 7, (1815) Israel	122
" 7, (Dea.) (1815) Isaac	147
" 7, (1818) Samuel	147
" 7, (1802) Israel	160
" [8], (1848) Thomas B	314
" [8], (1832) Thomas Jefferson	319
" Gilman[7], (1846) Charles	150
" Josiah[8], (1844) Ezra	356
Jacob[2], (1651) Robert	5
" 3, (Sergt.) (1631) Jacob	9
" 4, (1713) Robert	11
" 4, (1703) Sergt. Jacob	16
" 5, Jr., (1743) Jacob	25
" 5, (1759) Capt. Isaac	33
" 5, (1785) Dea. Edmund	42
" 6, (1764) Charles	51
" 6, (Capt.) (1772) Benjamin	57
" 6, (1761) Stephen	58
" 6, (1791) Capt. Samuel	71
" 7, (1808) Joshua	119
" [8], —— John	259
" K.[10], (1895) Benjamin F	515
" Kimball[8], (1838) Benjamin F	316
James[5], (Ens.) (1765) Dea. Edmund	41
" 6, (1765) Corp. Moses	56
" 6, (1768) David	73
" 6, —— Joseph	78
" 7, (1817) John	185
" 7, (Dr.) —— Eli	210
" [8], —— Joseph S	312
" [8], (1874) Edwin	339
" 9, (1897) George T	463

	Page.
James A.[8], (1831) Moses..	244
" Alfred[8], (1858) Geo. Washington.	359
" Augustus[7], (1830) Sewall	129
" C.[9], (1871) George N	416
" Douglass[8], (1875) Geo. Daniel..	298
" E.[9], (1867) Oscar Edmund	430
" Edwin[7], (1839) John Breed	137
" Franklin[9], (1879) John Quincy.	483
" " [9], (1893) James Henry.	485
" Henry[8], (1831) Joshua, Jr	250
" " [8], (1855) Henry Proctor..	357
" " [8], (1834) Benjamin F	316
" Herbert F.[9], (1899) Dr. John Franklin	487
" Kent[7], (1811) Gaius	215
" Knight[7], (1851) John Coffin	182
" M.[8], (1827) Charles M	250
" Monroe[7], (1828) Col. John Emery	139
" Otis[8], (1843) James Kent	381
" R.[7], (1821) Russell	168
" R.[8], (1867) Edward Lewis O	327
" Riley[7], (1834) Dr. Clement Jackson	174
Jarvis[7], (1798) Ebenezer	189
Jedediah[5], (1761) John	35
Jefferson[6], —— Nathan	68
Jeffrey Thornton[7], (Dr.) (1831) Joseph Thornton	131
Jere[6], (1793) Seth	98
" [7], (1831) Gaius	215
Jeremiah[6], (1793) Benjamin	78
" [7], (1807) Rev. Theophilus B.	165
Jesse[5], (1750) Abraham	28
" [5], (1764) John	40
" [6], (1789) Capt. Benjamin	61
" [6], (1805) Simon	85
Job[6], (1765) Lieut. Joel	48
" [6], —— Job	102
Joel[4], (Lieut.) (1729) John	19
" [5], Jr., (1767) Lieut. Joel	48
" [6], (1801) Seth	98
" [6], (1811) Joel, Jr	103
" [7], (1824) Gaius	215
" [8], (1810) Joseph	235
Jonathan[4], (1713) Jacob	17
" [5], (1767) John	36
" [5], (1762) Moses	47
" [6], (1801) Capt. Samuel	71
" Tenney[6], (1805) Jonathan	76
John[2], —— Robert	4
" [3], (1684) Sergt. Abraham	7
" [3], (1694) Jacob	9

	Page.
John[4], (1705) Robert	10
" [4], (1721) John	14
" [4], (1732) Richard	15
" [4], (1706) Sergt. Jacob	17
" [5], (Lieut.) (1758) Rev. Joseph	29
" [5], (1748) Henry	31
" [5], (Capt.) (1735) Israel	34
" [5], (Corp.) (1749) John	35
" [5], (1749) Matthew	36
" [5], (1778) John	40
" [6], (1744) John	42
" [5], (1750) Moses	47
" [6], (1786) Joseph	63
" [6], (1784) Israel, Jr	71
" [6], (Lieut. and Maj.) (1766) Capt. John	73
" [6], (1796) Jonathan	76
" [6], —— Israel	77
" [6], (1776) John	77
" [6], (1793) Ens. James	88
" [6], (1810) Edmund	89
" [6], (1796) Bildad	102
" [7], (1794) Israel	117
" [7], (1817) Israel	122
" [7], (1815) Israel	161
" [7], (1803) John	162
" [7], (1827) Henry	163
" [7], (1809) Arab	190
" [8], —— Benjamin	249
" [8], (1844) Silas Hall	254
" [8], (1825) Col. Joseph Henry	301
" [8], (1857) Horace	341
" A.[8], (1862) Oliver L	388
" A.[9], (1869) Oscar Edmund	430
" Abraham[9], (1881) John Sturgis	447
" Albert[9], (1862) John Merriam	424
" Andrew[8], (1843) George W	317
" Amos[10], (1883) John Frederick	514
" Augustus[7], (1818) Amos	109
" Austin[8], (1858) Daniel	311
" Benjamin F.[8], (1868) Joseph Nichols	277
" Bodily[7], (1865) Benjamin	163
" Breed[6], (1793) Nathan	66
" Brooks[8], (1842) Albert	300
" C.[8], (1861) Henry	393
" Coffin[6], (1812) John	86
" Colby[9], (1896) George Moulton	473
" Calvin[7], (1844) Philip D	178
" Edward[8], (1825) Edward	348
" " [9], (1876) John Quincy	480
" Emery[6], (Col.) (1780) Enoch	67
" " [7], (1805) Col. John Emery	138
" " [8], Jr., (1833) John Emery.	282

INDEX I.   529

	Page.
John Emery[10], (1898) Harry Delva....	511
" Everett[9], (1869) John Q., Jr	474
" F.[6], (Rev.) (1790) Lieut. John...	65
" F.[7], (1831) David.................	132
" Fairfield[9], (1895) John Benjamin	438
" Felch[8], (1838) John Langdon....	319
" Fenno[7], (1789) Samuel...........	108
" Franklin[8], (1848) Benjamin F...	316
" " [8], (Dr.) (1864) Dr. John G. C.......................	360
" Frederick[9], (1853) John	457
" Glennings Curtis[7], (Dr.) (1839) Rev. Ezra.................	199
" Gregory B.[8], (Capt.) (1841) Isaac	289
" Hall[7], (1796) Jacob	121
" Hancock[7], (1837) John...........	130
" Henry[8], (1818) Col. Joseph Henry	301
" Hoggan[9], (1897) Dr. John Franklin...	487
" Howard[9], (1879) George Moses..	414
" Irving[8], (1877) John Peabody...	340
" Jones[9], (1805) Paul.............	81
" K.[8], (1846) Chas. Henry.........	266
" Langdon[7], (1807) Matthew......	164
" Lewis[7], (1826) Moses...........	158
" Lynn[8], (1852) Ebenezer Moody.	283
" M.[8], (1843) Theophilas B., Jr....	321
" Marsh[6], (Capt.) (1779) David....	73
" " [7], Jr., (1815) Capt. John Marsh.......	152
" Merriam[8], (1834) John Hall.....	257
" Mosher[8], (Capt.) (1836) Joshua Jr	251
" Noyes[7], (1854) John Coffin......	182
" Osgood[7], (1811) Lieut. and Maj. John.................	152
" P.[8], (1825) Harvey...............	344
" Peabody[7], (1847) Woodbridge..	184
" Perley[10], (1892) Charles S........	507
" Popkin[6], (1812) Moses..........	87
" " [8], (Hon.) (1837) Joseph...	238
" " [9], (1879) Hon. John Popkin	408
" Q.[7], (1820) David....	122
" " [7], (1824) Capt. Richard......	183
" " [7], (1830) Peter....	156
" " [7], (1839) Harvey..............	196
" " [7], (1845) George W...........	160
" " [8], (1841) Fred'k Augustus L..	373
" " [8], (1865) Henry Proctor......	358
" " [8], (1870) Capt. Dennis........	332
" " [8], Jr., (1848) John Q..........	338
" " [9], (1868) Moses J..............	468
" Quincy[7], (1825) Joseph, Jr......	135

	Page.
John Quincy[7], (1826) John Breed....	136
" " [7], (1827) Rufus	197
" " [7], (1829) William........	142
" " [7], (Capt.) (1834) Sewall..	129
" " [7], (1835) Simeon....... ..	174
" " [7], (1844) George W......	150
" " [8], (1836) John.............	245
" " [8], (1847) Edward.........	348
" " [8], (1851) Lewis Alanson.	355
" " [8], (1864) Moses..........	283
" " [8], (1851) Nelson.........	383
" " [9], (1893) Lewis Ransom.	484
" Raymond[8], (1878) James Knight	337
" Rolfe[7], (1842) Seneca.............	172
" " [8], (1872) Moses Cyrus......	327
" S.[7], (1831) Jonathan Tenney ...	159
" Searle[6], (1885) Stephen Searle..	294
" Smith[8], (1825) Isaac.............	253
" Spofford[6], (1791) Capt. David....	70
" Stowell[8], —— Isaac............	239
" Sturgis[8], (1844) Erasmus Darwin	285
" Sumner[9], (1897) Arthur Sumner	473
" Watson[7], (1806) Benj. Watson..	121
" Wesley[7], (1814) Enoch	138
" Wm.[7], (1828) Rev. John Folsom	132
" Willis[8], (1865) Adam Willis	287
" Woodman[6], (1785) Eld. David...	61
" Wright[7], (1816) Samuel.........	147
Joseph[4], (Rev.) (1719) Capt. Abraham.	12
" 4, —— Dr. Matthew	15
" 4, (Rev.) (1715) Lieut. Abraham	18
" [5], (1748) Abraham.............	28
" [5], (1748) Samuel...............	28
" [5], (1750) Rev. Joseph...........	29
" [5], (1769) Rev. Benjamin........	30
" [5], (1762) Capt. Nathan..........	31
" [5], (1755) Matthew....	36
" [5], (1743) Abraham...............	37
" [6], (1738) Robert.........	49
" [6], (1775) Capt. Joshua..........	56
" [6], (1771) Capt. Benjamin.......	60
" [6], (1779) Joseph................	63
" [6], (1794) Lieut. John......... ..	65
" [6], Jr., (1800) Joseph.............	66
" [6], (Dr.) (1788) Enoch............	68
" [6], —— Nathan................	68
" [6], (1783) John...........	77
" [6], (1779) Abraham....	79
" [6], (1803) Ezra	87
" [7], (1783) Henry....	105
" [7], (1799) Daniel.................	106
" [7], (1838) Charles.................	150
" Ashley[8], (1853) Benjamin Dickinson................	382

(34)

530 INDEX I.

Joseph Augustus[7], (1818) Rev. John F. 132
" B.[8], (1834) Harvey 344
" Bedortha[7], (1803) Noadiah 188
" Chandler[8], (1840) David
    Farnum................ 285
" Collins[7], (1824) Solomon, Jr.... 155
" E.[7], (1818) Thaddeus, Jr........ 218
" Edwin[7], (1833) Stephen......... 128
" Emory[8], (1841) William 279
" Fellows[7], (1836) Rev. Zenas ... 200
" G.[9], (1855) Robert W.... 451
" Henry[7], (Col.) (1790) Lt. and
    Maj. John................. 151
" Henry[7], (1836) Henry............ 163
"   " [8], (1842) Lewis Alanson.. 355
"   " [9], (1857) Joseph Henry.. 457
" Little[7], (1842) Asa.............. 172
" M.[7], (1816) Rev. Theophilas B.. 166
" M.[8], (1871) David.............. 311
" M., Jr.[8], —— Joseph M 321
" Mason[9], (1878) John Quincy... 483
" Mitchell[7], (1807) Benjamin..... 163
" Morley[9], (1891) Vincent Rice .. 483
" Nichols[7], (1834) Benj. Webb... 136
" S.[7], (1836) Jonathan Tenney... 159
" S.[8], (1851) Coleman Searle..... 299
" Searle[6],'(1785) Israel, Jr........ 72
" Thornton[6], —— Joseph........ 64
" Warren[7], (1828) Joseph, Jr..... 135
" Webb[8], (1835) Joseph........ 238
" Winchell[5], (1748) John......... 42
Joshua[5], (Capt.) (1735) John......... 23
" [6], (1766) Benjamin............. 57
" [6], (1763) Israel................. 72
" [7], Jr., (1801) Joshua............ 119
" [8], —— Benjamin........:..... 249
" [8], —— Samuel................ 254
" Richmond[8], Sergt. (1833)
    Joshua, Jr................. 251
Josiah[5], (Adjt.) (1757) Samuel......... 28
" G.[9], (1882) Edgar G............. 470
J. T.[8], (1872) Nathan 312
Julius T.[8], (1840) Henry Lewis... ... 380
Justin[7], —— Hiram................. 219
" Noyes[7], (1842) John Coffin..... 182
Kelly G.[8], (1861) Henry Proctor....... 358
Lawrence Holmes[8], (1881) Capt. Geo.
    Huntington................ 276
" Kinman[9], (1885) George
    Moulton................... 472
" Ward[9], (1881) Chas. Samuel 453
Leon[9], (1895) Eugene M............. ... 498
" [9], (1891) Martin Ira.... 500
" Alfred[8], (1877) Leonard... 270

Leon E[9], (1891) Homer J.............. 472
" Lewis[8], (1870) Sylvanus.......... 308
" Willis[10], (1894) George Willis.... 507
Leonard[7], (1840) Stephen.............. 128
" [9], (1868) George Herman..... 458
" Jarvis[7], —— Jos. Thornton.. 131
Le Roy Ernest[8], (1875) George W...... 311
" F.[7], (1846) Lucius Franklin.... 226
Leslie E.[8], (1863) Charles Morton...... 392
" Lorin[8], (1882) Loren M......... 396
Lester D.[9], (1891) Charles David 463
Levi[6], (1774) Seth..................... 97
Lewis[6], —— Seth..................... 98
" Alanson[7], (1810) Eliphalet...... 196
" Andrew[7], (1882) Walter M...... 462
" Austin[7], (1839) John Coffin...... 182
" D.[9], (1894) George T............. 463
" E.[8], (1849) Adam Willis......... 287
" Emery[8], (1858) John Quincy..... 288
" Milton[9], (1882) Capt. Milton B.. 435
" Ransom[8], (1856) Lewis Alanson.. 355
" William[9], (1863) George.......... 425
Lindsley[7], (1821) Henry.................. 163
" W.[8], (1872) Joseph Henry.... 319
Liphe[5], (1736) Robert.................. 22
Lloyd H.[8], (1846) John................. 317
Lorenzo Benson[8], (1836) Silas Hall.... 254
Lorin[7], (1809) Levi..................... 214
" M.[7], (1847) Lucius Franklin..... 226
Louis K.[7], (1822) Calvin 190
Lowell Henry[9], (1881) Chas. Samuel.. 453
Lucas Rufus[8], (1853) Lewis Alanson.. 355
Lucien Harper[7], (Rev.) (1829) Edmund 186
Lucius[7], (1795) Noadiah................ 188
" E.[8], (1820) Harvey.............. 343
" F.[8], (1816) Capt. Simeon 100
" F[7], (1835) Abraham.......... ... 220
" Rufus[7], (1825) Rufus............ 197
" W.[7], (1859) Lucius Franklin.... 226
Luther[6], (1794) Jonathan............... 99
" [7], (1840) Simeon................ 224
Lyman K.[8], (1851) Gamaliel King.... 386
Lyndon E.[8], (1871) Clinton............. 353
Mark Alba[7], (1871) Enos Holmes..····· 297
" Trafton[7], (1835) Dr. Joseph..... 140
Martin[6], (1794) Freegrace 93
" [6], (1802) Thaddeus.............. 98
" Ira[8], (1854) Ira, Jr............... 392
" Marcellus[7], (1831) Martin...... 205
Mason Clarence[8], (1877) Uri M........ 400
Massena Clark[8], (1840) John.... 349
Matthew[3], (Dr.) (1686) Sergt. Abraham 7
" [4], (1709) Dr. Matthew........ 15
" [6], (1778) Benjamin............ 78

INDEX I.

	Page.
Matthew[8], (1842) John Langdon	320
Melvin[8], (1831) Benjamin	240
" Thurston[9], (1877) Francis Doddridge	410
Merwin L.[8], (1865) Luther	394
Miles T.[8], (1875) Capt. Dennis	332
Miller O.[8], (1866) Henry	390
Milo[7], (Dr.) (1790) Dr. Samuel	124
" [8], (1847) Ebenezer Moody	283
" R.[9], (1847) Oscar Edmund	430
" Romulus[6], (Capt.) (1833) Dr. Milo	262
Milton[6], (Capt.) (1792) Freegrace	93
" B.[7], (1799) Dr. Samuel	124
" B.[8], (Col.) (1845) Samuel Plumer	264
Minor[7], (1804) Levi	214
" [7], (1818) Ebenezer	189
Moody[5], (1762) John	40
" [6], (1784) Capt. David	70
" [6], (1791) Daniel	81
" [6], (1802) George	85
Mortimer[7], (1842) Abraham, Jr.	209
Moses[4], (1737) Richard	16
" [4], (1722) John	18
" [5], (Corp.) (1737) John	23
" [5], (1765) John	35
" [5], (1770) Moses	41
" [5], Jr., (1754) Moses	47
" [6], Jr., (1776) Corp. Moses	57
" [6], (1793) Enoch	67
" [6], Jr., (1792) Moses	75
" [6], (1795) Jonathan	76
" [6], —— Joseph	78
" [6], (1804) Moses	87
" [7], (1805) James	117
" [7], (1814) David	122
" [7], (1815) Col. John Emery	139
" [7], (1810) Samuel Jr	142
" [7], (1819) Israel	161
" [7], (1837) Nathan	177
" [7], (1837) Moses	183
" [8], (1833) Thomas Jefferson	319
" Andrew[8], (1845) Moses Woodman	248
" Cook[7], (1840) Capt. Richard	183
" Cyrus[7], (1844) Seneca	172
" J.[8], (1834) John Langdon	319
" N.[7], (1841) Moses Noyes	178
" N.[8], (1872) Capt. Dennis	332
" Noyes[6], (1807) Ebenezer	84
" Parker[9], (1873) Geo. Moses	414
" Sawin[7], (Hon.) (1826) David	144
" Woodman[7], (1847) Moses, Jr.	118
Myron Dow[5], (1866) Moses	283
" Richardson[9], (1897) Elmer Ellsworth	462

	Page.
Nathan[4], (Capt.) (1721) Capt. Abraham	12
" [5], (1760) Rev. Joseph	29
" [5], (1769) Rev. Benjamin	30
" [5], (1761) Capt. Nathan	31
" [5], (1755) Henry	31
" [6], (1803) Lieut. John	65
" [6], (1801) Ebenezer	84
" [7], (1825) John	185
" [7], (1838) Jonathan Tenney	159
" E.[8], (1864) Capt. Dennis	332
" L.[7], (1841) Nathan	177
" P.[8], (1871) Nathan Preston	278
" Preston[7], (1828) John Breed	136
Nathaniel[5], (1749) Rev. Benjamin	30
" [5], (Lieut.) (1748) Enoch	39
" [6], —— Benjamin	58
" [7], (1806) Arah	190
" Folsom[6], (1782) Dr. Caleb G.	64
Nelson[7], (1817) Jere	215
" [9], (1873) Alfred Le Roy	458
Newell[8], (1881) James Knight	337
Newton Romeyn[9], (1872) Daniel Sewall	412
" Skinner[7], (1808) Ebenezer	189
Noadiah[5], (1763) Zadoc	89
" [7], (1800) Noadiah	188
Noble D.[7], (1850) Abraham, Jr.	209
Norman B.[7], (1828) Solomon, Jr	155
" Ilsley[8], (1864) Henry Sewall	271
" " [9], (1895) Norman Ilsley	457
" R.[6], (1821) Roswell, 2d	343
Norris Wheeler[9], (1876) John	421
Norton Kent[8], (1836) James Kent	381
Obadiah F.[7], (1824) Russell	168
Obed[8], (1810) Joseph	235
Oliver[5], (Capt.) (1769) Capt. Simeon	47
" [6], Jr., (1799) Capt. Oliver	99
" L.[7], (1831) Abraham	220
" M.[8], (1869) Moses	283
" Miller[7], (1834) Oliver, Jr.	221
" Winchester[8], (1870) Wm. Bradley	390
Omer C.[8], (1860) Rufus	387
Orange H.[8], (Dr.) (1856) Albert	300
Orin[8], (1844) Thomas Jefferson	319
" Dickinson[8], (1839) Benj. Dickinson	382
Oscar[9], —— John Quincy	417
" DeWitt[8], (1851) Prescott Jones	304
" E.[9], (1855) Oscar Edmund	430
" Edmund[8], (1818) Dr. Milo	262
" Potter[8], (1835) James Kent	381
" Ray[9], (1888) Oscar Rufus	497
" Rufus[8], (1863) Rufus	387
Otis[7], (1830) John	185
Parker[6], —— Joseph	78

INDEX I.

	Page.
Parker Sumner[8], (1882) Le Roy F.	396
Parshall E.[9], (1879) Oscar De Witt	458
Paul[5], (1763) Henry	31
" [5], (1758) Richard	39
" [6], Jr., (1814) Paul	81
" [7], (1830) Asa	171
" [8], (1876) Isaac Milton	294
Peter[6], (1800) Solomon	75
Philip[8], (1865) Henry	234
" D.[6], (1814) Gaius	84
" Henry[7], (1829) Philip	404
" Tyler[7], (1842) Philip D	178
Phineas[5], (Rev.) (1742) Abraham	72
" [5], (1779) Benjamin	43
" [6], Jr., (1773) Rev. Phineas	60
" M.[7], (1817) Abraham	220
" R.[6], (1798) Eliphalet	92
Prescott Jones[7], (1817) Robert	153
Preston Goodwin[8], (1884) James Knight	337
Ralph[7], (1812) Seth, Jr	213
" [8], —— Joseph S.	312
" Enoch[9], (1881) Enoch	439
" Norton[9], (1867) Daniel Sewall	412
" Sewall[10], (1894) Ralph Norton	505
" Wood[9], (1891) John Brooks	457
Ransom[7], (1812) Eliphalet, Jr	196
Raymond Lucius[8], (1891) Lucius W	396
" Morrison D.[9], (1876) George Wm., Jr.	436
Reuben Johnson[7], (1839) Joseph, Jr	135
" O.[8], (1863) Oliver L	388
Richard[3], (1693) Sergt. Abraham	8
" [4], (1726) Richard	15
" [5], (1790) Enoch	80
" [5], (1796) Asa	84
" [6], (Capt.) (1795) Moses	86
" [7], (1822) Capt. Richard	183
" Calvin[7], (1835) Richard	176
" Ellsworth[9], (1890) Geo. Moulton	473
" F.[7], (1819) Richard	168
" Giles[8], (1858) Giles Aaron	330
" Henry[8], (1855) Richard	338
" K.[9], (1882) John Lynn	444
Robert[3], (1674) Sergt. Abraham	6
" [4], (1702) Robert	10
" [5], (1717) Abraham	20
" [5], (1750) Robert	22
" [6], (1787) Liphe	55
" [6], (1775) Robert	55
" [6], (1783) David	74
" [7], (1792) Samuel	120
" [8], —— Jacob	252

	Page.
Robert[9], (1876) Smith	410
" Darrah[8], (Capt.) (1827) Dr. Milo	262
" E.[8], (1858) Edwin	338
" Merrill[8], (1882) Rev. Frank E.	300
" Nichols[9], (1896) John Benjamin F.	438
" Parker[10], (1896) Edward F.	512
" Perry[9], (1886) John Lynn	444
" W.[8], (1828) Enoch	290
Rodolphus[7], (1798) Capt. Asahel	187
Rollin[7], —— Eli	210
" D.[8], (1873) David	395
Ross Uri[8], (1883) Uri M	400
Roswell[7], (1794) Capt. Asahel	187
" [9], (1861) Norman R	476
Roy[9], (1891) George W	425
" B.[8], (1879) Israel Gilman	299
" Powers[9], (1882) Enoch	439
" W.[9], (1886) Israel	464
Royal W.[8], (1882) Wilson M.	377
Rufus[5], (1785) Capt. Simeon	48
" [6], (1783) Eliphalet	92
" [7], (1829) Richard	176
" [7], (1824) Abraham	220
" [8], (1757) Daniel M.	342
" Dodge[8], (1870) Leonard	269
Russell[6], (1788) Enoch	80
" Brown[8], (1891) Henry	325
Samuel[4], (1717) Capt. Abraham	12
" [4], (1710) Isaac	13
" [4], (1736) Lieut. Abraham	18
" [5], (Dr.) —— William	27
" [5], (1752) Samuel	28
" [5], (Col.) (1736) Samuel	32
" [5], (Capt.) (1750) Capt. Isaac	32
" [5], (1774) Samuel	46
" [6], (1759) Benjamin	50
" [6], (1769) Benjamin	57
" [6], (Dr.) (1767) Capt. Benjamin	59
" [6], (Hon.) (1784) Capt. Benjamin	61
" [6], (Col.) (1779) Elder David	61
" [6], (1788) Capt. Stephen	62
" [6], —— Nathan	68
" [6], Jr., (1768) Col. Samuel	69
" [6], (1782) Capt. Samuel	70
" [6], (1765) Israel	72
" [6], (1818) Horace	96
" 7, Jr., (1807) Samuel	120
" 7, (1823) David	122
" 7, (1811) Benjamin	126
" 7, (1802) Samuel, Jr	142
" 7, (1846) Simeon	225
" 7, (Prof.) (1806) Isaac	146
" [8], (1828) Dr. Milo	262

	Page.
Samuel[8], (1872) Henry J.	318
" A.[6], (1839) Abraham, Jr	209
" F.[8], (1842) Isaiah	255
" Goodhue[7], (1800) Benjamin	163
" Goodwin[9], (1830) Philip	404
" Jackson[7], (1810) Robert	152
" Newell[6], (1819) Capt. Simeon	100
" P.[8], (1779) Henry	234
" P.[9], (1861) Oscar Edmund	430
" Plumer[7], (1812) Dr. Samuel	124
" " [8], (1850) Samuel Plumer	265
" Swan[7], (1826) Jonathan	149
Schuyler[9], (1893) Enoch C.	440
Scott[8], (1874) Jere	382
Selden C.[9], (1876) Lorenzo Benson	421
Selwyn M.[9], (1858) Selwyn Poor	452
" Poor[8], (1832) Samuel	291
Seneca[6], (1808) Paul	81
Seth[5], (1746) Moses	46
" [6], (1803) Jonathan	76
" [6], Jr., (1772) Seth	97
Sewall[6], (1798) Capt. Stephen	62
Sherman Weston[10], (1894) Charles Lincoln	511
Silas[5], (Capt.) (1741) Robert	22
" [7], (1829) Asa	191
" [7], (1836) Wait	217
" Bradley[9], (1863) George Moses	414
" Hall[7], (1804) Samuel	120
" " [9], (1867) Lorenzo Benson	420
" Lowell[8], (1838) Silas Hall	254
" Merrill[7], (1809) Moses, Jr	118
" Wilmot[7], (1803) Calvin	192
Simeon[4], (Capt.) (1724) John	18
" [5], (1765) Richard	39
" [5], (Capt.) (1776) Capt. Simeon	47
" [6], (1797) Simeon	82
" [6], (1803) Capt. Simeon	100
" [7], (1844) Simeon	225
" Houghton[7], (1822) Capt. Ira	223
Simon[5], (1770) John	40
" Augustus[7], (1836) Jesse	181
Smith[6], (1771) Charles	51
" [7], (1811) Smith	110
" [8], (1828) Charles	242
" [9], (1866) Smith	410
Socrates[7], (Dr. 1801) Dr. Samuel	124
Solomon[5], (1759) John	35
" [6], Jr., (1780) Solomon	75
Stanley Addison[11], (1898) Gilbert Addison	518
Stephen[4], (1721) Daniel	17
" [5], (1728) William	25

	Page.
Stephen[5], (Capt.) (1760) Samuel	29
" [5], (Capt.) (1742) Abraham	37
" [5], (1768) Zebulon	43
" [6], (1792) Capt. Stephen	62
" [6], (1784) Capt. Stephen	79
" [6], (Dr.) (1804) Simeon	83
" [7], (1807) David	121
" [8], —— Israel	259
" C.[7], (1831) Richard	169
" Denison[8], (1869) Leonard	269
" James[8], (1887) Stephen Searle	294
" Little[7], (1837) Dr. Stephen	175
" Searle[7], (1842) Isaac	145
Sylvanus[7], (1825) Peter	156
Sylvester[8], (1834) Edward	348
" Felch[8], (1850) John Langdon	320
Tappan[5], (Capt.) (1786) Abraham	79
Thaddeus[5], (1759) Moses	47
" [6], Jr., (1792) Thaddeus	98
" Solomon[8], (1836) Henry Lewis	380
Theodore[7], (1797) Zadoc, Jr.	188
" [9], (1891) Charles Anderson	456
" M.[8], —— Gideon	352
Theophilus B.[8], (Rev.) (1789) Benjamin B.[7], Jr., (1814) Rev. Theophilus B	78 166
" B.[8], (1845) Theophilus B. Jr.	321
Thomas[5], (1752) Capt. Isaac	32
" [6], —— Corp. John	74
" [7], —— Abraham	107
" [7], (1814) Benjamin	163
" Augustus[8], (1829) Eliphalet	294
" B.[8], (1842) Thomas B.	314
" Bailey[7], (1806) Israel	160
" Do-man[8], (1838) Israel	259
" Fosdick[6], (1776) Joseph	63
" Hall[6], (1817) Paul	81
" Hatch[9], —— Benjamin	419
" Jefferson[7], (1807) Matthew	164
Timothy Mather[6], (1811) Capt. Simeon	100
Ulyses Sidney[10], (1864) Geo. Edward	502
Uri M.[7], (1852) Horace Hale	230
Vincent[6], (1785) Eliphalet	92
" Eliphalet[9], (1883) Vincent Rice	483
" Rice[8], (1846) Lewis Alanson	355
Vinton M., (Dr.) (1853) Dr. Enoch	281
Wait[6], (1786) Thaddeus	98
Waldemar Patterson[10], (1891) Silas Bradley	506
Wallace Longfellow[8], (1872) Leonard	269
Walter[8], (1867) John William	273

Walter[8], (Hon.) (1848) Coleman Searle 299
" C.[8], (1878) David 395
" Clifford[8], (1884) Walter M 462
" Clyde[6], (1898) Loren M 396
" Crosby[8], (1877) Le Roy F 395
" E.[9], (1887) Eben. H. 464
" F.[7], (1840) Martin 218
" F.[8], (1844) Benjamin H 306
" Francis[9], (1868) Francis A 487
" Leslie[8], (1867) Simon Augustus 336
" " [9], (1896) Walter Leslie... 474
" M.[8], (1852) John Lewis 310
" Scott[7], (1851) Moses Noyes..... 178
" Sherwood[9], (1872) Massena
    Clark 487
Warner Simeon[8], (1882) Simeon 395
Warren[7], (1842) Isaac 180
" Albern[7], (1815) Henry 162
" F.[9], (1893) Israel 464
" Lincoln[10], (1895) Frederick
    Waldemar 506
" Mann[7], (1819) Dr. Joseph...... 140
" (J.)[7], (1845) James R 323
Washington[6], (1816) Moses 87
" [8], (1830) Abraham 236
Watmough S. A., —— Dr. M. Vinton. 440
Webster[8], (1834) Benjamin 240
" Derby[9], (1877) Amos Henry.. 411
Wellington[7], (1822) Eliphalet, Jr...... 196
" [9], (1877) Ezra 484
Wendall H.[8], (Dr.) (1854) Dr. Enoch... 281
Wesley[8], (1872) Israel Gilson......... 299
" Irving[8], (1871) Henry Sewall... 271
Wilbur C.[7], (1855) Wm. Spurr........ 211
" Dennis[8], (1866) Nathan........ 312
" Fisk[7], (1834) Rev. Zenas....... 199
" " [8], (1875) William F...... 362
Wilfred Preston[8], (1867) Lewis Austin 337
Will Horton[9], (1861) Silas Lowell..... 421
William[4], (1706) Capt. Abraham 11
" [6], (1801) Enoch 68
" [6], (1801) John 86
" [7], —— Capt. Jacob 121
" [7], (1811) Enoch 138
" [7], (1827) William........... 141
" [8], —— Israel 259
" [8], (1840) Albert............. 300
" [9], —— John Quincy......... 417
" [9], (1882) Ezra 484
" A.[7], (1811) Matthew 164
" Allard S.[8], (1874) Simeon..... 395
" Augustus[8], (1854) James
    Augustus 270
" B.[7], (1803) Smith............ 110

William Bradley[7], (1831) Oliver, Jr.... 221
" Brown[8], (1868) Zenophon..... 339
" " [9], (1889) Geo. Moulton. 472
" Case[7], (Dr.) (1823) Rev. Ezra.. 198
" Claud[8], (1872) Wm. Bradley... 390
" E.[8], (1863) Henry Proctor.... 358
" Edwards[7], (1833) Capt.
    Richard 183
" Eliphalet[8], (1837) Lewis
    Alanson 355
" Elmer[8], (1855) George
    Washington 359
" Elmer[8], (1874) Chas. William.. 336
" Ezra[9], (1882) James Henry.... 485
" Fawcett[8], (Dr.) (1874)
    Dr. John G. C. 360
" Freeman[9], (1873) Selwyn P.... 452
" H.[8], (1839) Samuel............ 291
" H.[8], (1871) Simeon Houghton.. 391
" H. H.[8], (1866) Dennis H. 307
" H. Harrison[8], (1841) John
    Watson 256
" Henry[7], (1805) Amos.......... 109
" " [8], (1827) William Bray.. 242
" " [8], (1846) William....... 279
" " [9], (1870) Wm. Eliphalet. 482
" Murray[8], (1869) Isaac
    Milton 294
" " [9], (1878) Ezra P......... 485
" Henri[10], (1899) Benj. H., 3rd .. 514
" Hussey[8], (1870) Geo. Daniel... 298
" L.[8], (1869) George Augustus .. 278
" Lewis[6], (1809) Nathan....... 67
" " [7], (1837) Capt. George... 137
" Moody[7], (1818) Moody.......... 144
" P.[8], (1827) Aaron............. 249
" Quincy[9], (1893) George E..... 486
" R.[9], (1893) Nathan E.......... 473
" Richardson[8], (1863) Capt.
    John Quincy 271
" Russell[8], (1838) Abraham
    Doddridge 241
" Sherman[8], (1864) Isaac Watts. 331
" Spurr[6], (1819) Abraham....... 96
" Vincent[9], (1895) Edward
    Effingham 501
" Wallace[8], (1842) David Jewett 338
" Waugh[8], (1857) Walter M...... 462
" Wilson[8], (1854) James Kent... 381
Willie[8], (1869) John William.......... 273
" A.[9], (1871) William P......... 416
Willis Longfellow[8], (1867) Albert S... 269
Wilson M.[7], (1852) William Spurr..... 210
Winfred Scott[7], (1819) Horace........ 194

	Page.
Winnifred Ashley[9], (1888) Joseph Ashley	495
Winthrop Clark[9], (1881) George Moulton	472
Woodbridge[6], (1819) Moses	87
Xenophon[7], (1838) Capt. Richard	183
" [8], (1876) Xenophon	337
Zadoc[5], (1736) Jacob	42
Zadoc[6], Jr., (1765) Zadoc	89
Zebedee[6], —— Solomon	75
Zebulon[4], (1713) Daniel	17
" [5], (1744) Jacob	25
" [5], Jr., (1765) Zebulon	43
Zenas[6], (Rev.) (1792) Eliphalet	92
" [7], (1820) Eliphalet, Jr.	196

INDEX II.

FEMALE NAMES WITH NAME OF FATHER.

	Page.
Abigail⁴, (1722) Isaac	13
" ⁵, (1721) Abraham	20
" ⁵, (1750) Israel	33
" ⁵, (1752) Moses	47
" ⁶, (1753) Robert	49
" ⁶, (1752) Benjamin	50
" ⁶, —— Solomon	75
" ⁶, (1803) Daniel	82
" ⁷, (1802) Samuel	120
" A.⁸, (1836) John Langdon	319
" Chapman⁷, (1828) David	182
" Frances⁸, (1840) Isaac	253
" Lucretia⁷, (1844) Rev. Zenas	200
Abba⁸, —— Joseph M	331
Abbie Clifton⁸, (1855) Albert S	269
" Evelyn⁹, (1876) Chas. Hall	439
" Merrill⁸, (Dr.) (1842) Joshua, Jr	251
" O⁸, (1855) James	340
Abby⁶, (1787) Capt. Gideon	91
" C.⁷, (1845) Moody	180
" Luella⁹, (1885) Lieut. Isaac R	418
Ada Adel¹¹, (1895) Gilbert Addison	518
" G.⁹, (1855) Moses J	468
" P.⁸, (1857) James Monroe	284
Addie Louisa⁷, (1872) Joseph B	478
" M. C.⁸, (1858) John Q	308
Adaline Frances⁹, (1854) Charles	405
Adelaide⁷, (1844) Nathan	177
Adeline⁷, (1823) Stephen	127
" ⁷, (1836) Peter	156
" ⁷, (1824) Matthew	165
" J.⁸, (1850) Nathan Preston	277
Agnes⁴, (1710) Sergt. Jacob	17
" Little⁸, (1854) Henry Sewall	271
" Maria⁷, (1842) Rev. Zenas	200
Alantha M.⁸, (1841) John Emery	282
Alice⁷, (1768) Henry	105
" ¹⁰, —— Horace Clinton	502
" Anna⁸, (1893) Loren M	396
" Dunning⁹, (1886) Amos Darwin	447
" E.⁸, (1871) Henry	390
" L.⁸, (1863) Simeon Houghton	391
" Morse⁸, (1856) Giles Aaron	330
" M.⁹, (1885) Dr. Orange H	457
" Noyes⁸, (1876) Lewis Austin	337

	Page.
Alice Ordway¹¹, (1895) Geo. Kimball	518
" Putnam⁹, (1860) Chas. Henry	436
" S.⁸, (1867) Luther	394
" Woodford¹⁰, (1882) Frn'k Sylve'r	516
Almira⁷, (1808) Smith	110
" ⁷, (1824) Enoch	138
" ⁷, (1796) Ebenezer	189
" S.⁷, (1850) Wm. Spurr	210
" ⁸, —— Charles M	250
" Jane⁸, (1844) Lewis Alanson	355
" L.⁸, (1839) John Langdon	319
Alta G.⁹, (1891) Charles W	473
Alma F.⁹, (1871) Benjamin H., 2d	460
Alvira⁷, (1807) Levi	214
" B.⁸, (1847) Adam Willis	287
Amanda⁷, (1811) Israel	161
" ⁷, (1833) Horace	195
" E.⁷, (1823) Harvey	195
Amelia⁶, (1762) Stephen	58
" Ann⁸, (1837) Moses	292
Amy Dora⁹, (1894) Dr. John Franklin	487
" Eliza⁸, (1859) Wellington	356
" Lovina⁸, (1863) Dr. John G. C.	360
" Mary⁷, (1822) Rev. John Folsom	132
Ann Mary⁸, (1840) Enoch	290
Anna⁴, (1734) Lieut. Abraham	18
" ⁴, (1727) John	19
" ⁵, (1745) Robert	22
" ⁵, (1763) Freegrace	45
" ⁶, (1776) Liphe	54
" ⁶, (1780) Capt. Silas	55
" ⁶, (1791) Moses	75
" ⁶, (1810) Freegrace, Jr	94
" ⁶, (1801) Capt. Oliver	100
" ⁷, (1820) Moses, Jr	157
" Elizabeth⁷, (1844) David	186
" B.⁸, (1873) Elbert J	385
" Boardman⁸, (1817) Aaron	239
" G.⁸, (1862) Geo. Edward	334
" May⁹, (1884) John Sturgis	447
" Weymouth⁹, (1864) James A	411
Annetta Minerva⁷, (1837) Capt. Ira	223
Angelina K.⁷, (1832) Isaac	118
" Kimball⁸, (1861) Benjamin Whiting	247

INDEX II.

	Page.
Anne⁴, (1705) Capt. Abraham	11
" ⁵, (1733) William	26
" ⁵, (1766) Rev. Benjamin	30
" ⁵, (1747) Henry	31
" ⁵, (1770) Samuel	46
" ⁸, (1872) John Hancock	272
" Cordelia⁷, (1830) Martin	205
Annie F.⁸, (1871) Henry	390
" Fellows⁸, (1850) Asa	330
" Gertrude⁹, (1876) Aaron	424
" Helen⁹, (1879) Chas. Francis	423
" King⁹, (1848) Benjamin	419
" Mameta⁹, (1889) James Henry	485
" S.⁸, (1868) Capt. Dennis	332
" Sewall⁸, (1861) James Augustus	270
Aphia⁷, (1811) Isaac	146
Arabella⁷, (1792) Zadoc, Jr	188
Arethusa⁷, —— Israel	117
Ardella E.⁸, (1861) Enoch	323
Ardillacy Sturgis⁸, (1864) Erasmus Darwin	286
Aterista M.⁷, (1870) Horace	206
Augusta⁷, (1811) Israel	161
" Minerva⁷, (1830) Rufus	197
" M.⁸, (1856) Dennis H	307
" ⁸, (1831) Eliphalet	294
" ⁸, (1835) Benjamin Franklin	304
Aurelia⁸, (1831) Eliphalet	294
Aurora C.⁸, (1844) Ebenezer H	315
Beda Elizabeth⁸, (1841) Phineas M	387
" J.⁸, (1860) Oliver L	388
Belinda⁶, (1808) Moses	76
" Sharlon⁶, (1832) John	349
Bertha⁹, (1892) John A	498
" H.⁸, (1879) Henry Le Roy	395
" Hart⁹, (1875) Capt. Milo R	431
Bessie Metcalf⁹, (1881) Ezra P	485
Betty⁶, (1775) Benjamin	58
Betsey⁶, (1792) Eld. David	62
" ⁶, (1798) Nathan	67
" ⁶, (1778) Corp. John	74
" ⁶, (1775) Capt. Stephen	79
" ⁶, (1805) Joel, Jr	103
" ⁷, (1798) Noadiah	188
" ⁸, (1823) Edward	347
" Almira⁷, (1815) Rev. Ezra	198
" C.⁷, (1825) William	141
" J.⁸, (1833) John Langdon	319
Blanche E.⁹, (1864) Sergt. Joshua Richmond	418
" Lilian⁹, (1873) John Q., Jr	474
Candace⁶, (1803) Bildad	103
Carmina⁹, (1885) William Eliphalet	482
Caroline⁶, (1799) Paul	81
Caroline⁷, (1835) Nathan	177
" ⁸, (1864) John Hancock	272
" Cartwright⁷, (1833) John	130
" E.⁷, (1824) Asa	154
" Elizabeth⁷, (1826) Samuel	147
" " ⁷, (1846) Seneca	173
" " ⁸, (1811) Henry	234
" Frances⁷, (1836) Oliver, Jr	221
" Kezia⁷, (1804) Isaac	108
" L.⁷, (1831) Stephen	128
" Little⁸, (1864) Giles Aaron	330
" Mary⁸, (1899) Geo. Henry	273
" Matilda⁸, (1819) Col. Joseph Henry	301
" Ordway¹⁰, (1870) Geo. Edw	502
" Porter⁶, (1868) Col. Charles Henry	275
" Walter⁷, —— Benjamin	130
Carrie Bell⁸, (1853) Enoch	283
" Coffin⁸, (1874) James Augustus	270
" E.⁸, (1859) John Quincy	328
" E.⁹, (1889) Homer J	472
" Ella⁸, (1873) Wm. Bradley	390
" Frances⁸, (1858) Gardiner	335
" H.⁹, (1890) Charles F	475
" Lillian⁸, (1858) Augustus Hall	287
" Lucy⁸, (1885) Loren M	396
" Stone⁸, (1864) Moses Cook	339
Cassandra⁷, (1817) Israel	161
Catherine⁶, (1805) Ebenezer	84
" I.⁸, (1846) Benjamin H	306
" Noyes⁷, (1785) Samuel	108
" " ⁷, (1848) John Coffin	182
" Sawin⁷, (1819) David	144
" Whitbeck⁸, (1847) Edwin Spofford	293
Celia Anna⁸, (1851) Isaiah	255
" Corbin⁸, (1845) Horace H	401
Charity⁷, (1801) Israel	160
Charlotte⁶, (1787) Capt. Silas	55
" ⁶, (1782) Capt. Gideon	90
" ⁷, (1796) Lieut. and Maj. John	151
" ⁷, (1795) Zadoc, Jr	188
" ⁷, (1830) Rev. Zenas	199
" ⁷, (1836) Joel	216
" Armour⁸, (1856) Chas. Frederick	361
" Augusta⁸, (1834) John Watson	256
" Frances⁹, (1877), Joseph Ashley	495
" Louisa⁸, —— Moses Woodman	248

	Page.
Chloe[6], (1815) Solomon	75
" Angeline[6], (1816) Abraham	95
" M.[10], (1875) Addison L	515
Christina[7], (1826) Jacob	148
" [8], —— Newton Skinner	347
Christine Elaine[9], (1898) Oliver Winchester	499
Clara[8], —— Joseph M.	321
" [9], (1889) Julius T.	494
" C.[9], (1871) Joseph Webster	408
" Clement[9], (1847) Charles	405
" D.[9], (1868) Benjamin F	478
" Evelyn[9], (1895) Joseph Emery	439
" Frances[8], (1857) Warren Mann	286
" Lucinda[8], (1850) Franklin B	400
" M.[8], (1844) Benjamin F	322
" Marean[8], —— Enos Seth	385
" Moulton[8], (1850) Prof. Samuel	295
" Newell[7], (1853) Samuel N	226
Clarinda[7], (1795) Dr. Samuel	124
Clarissa[6], (1791) Simeon	82
" [7], (1802) Israel	151
" [8], (1802) Henry	234
" Jane[7], (1816) Robert	153
" " [7], (1829) Joel	216
Constance[8], (1888) Capt. Geo. Huntington	276
Cora[8], (1857) Moses	283
" B.[8], (1870) Gad Mather	389
" E.[8], (1870) George S.	313
" Estelle[8], (1857) Horace H	401
" Gertrude[7], (1846) George	131
" J.[9], (1860) John Emery	442
Cynthia[7], (1805) Ebenezer	189
" [8], (1873) Samuel A	375
" B.[9], (1850) Oscar Edmund	430
" Darragh[8], (1844) Dr. Milo	262
" " [9], (1880) Capt. Milo R.	431
" Kent[7], (1815) Gaius	215
Deborah[6], (1837) Israel, Jr	71
" [7], (1808) Isaac	146
" [8], (1814) Col. Daniel	237
Delia Elizabeth[8], (1855) Rufus	387
" Hill[8], (1854) Dr. Henry Milgrove	286
" M.[8], (1849) John Q	258
Desdemonia[7], (1805) Levi	214
Dianthe[7], (1790) Zadoc, Jr	188
Dolly[6], (1776) Dr. Caleb G	64
" [6], (1784) Enoch	67
" B.[7], (1825) Moses, Jr	157
" Farrington[7], (1831) Enoch	128
Dora[9], (1892) Oscar Rufus	497
" Isabelle[8], (1859) Rufus	387
Dorcas[5], (1731) Jacob	42

	Page.
Dorcas[5], (1788) Samuel	46
" [6], (1797) Enoch	80
" [6], (1769) Zadoc	89
" [7], (1821) Richard	168
Dorothy[8], (1691) Sergt. Abraham	8
" [8], (1679) Jacob	9
" [4], (1718) Robert	11
" [7], (1821) Rev. Theophilus B.	166
" Cornelia[9], (1893) Dr. George Francis	501
" Belinda[10], (1895) Harry Delva.	511
" Merrill[7], (1817) Isaac	118
Edith[8], (1892) David Q	376
" A.[8], (1874) Nathan	312
" Capp[8], (1879) Henry	325
" E.[8], (1859) Nathan Preston	278
" Elsie[9], (1890) Charles Wood	425
" Frances[9], (1891) Dr. John Franklin	487
" H.[9], (1882) Enoch C	440
" Louisa[8], (1878) Rev. Frank E	300
" M.[8], (1881) Henry	390
" M.[9], (1866) Thomas Augustus	454
" Marion[10], (1892) Selwyn M	513
" May[8], (1892) Leonard	270
" " [9], (1887) Lewis Ransom	484
" " [9], (1889) Ezra	484
" Myra[8], (1877) Lewis Austin	337
Edna[5], (1778) Moses	41
" [6], (1798) Daniel	82
" May[9], (1874) Walter M	462
" Palmer[9], (1890) Arthur Sumner	473
Effie Lillian[10], (1874) Charles S	507
" May[8], (1866) Uri M	400
Eleanor[6], (1792) Daniel	82
" [9], (1893) Gad Mather	473
" B.[10], (1892) Durward C	513
" Jane[8], (1868) Dr. John G. C.	360
" Wilson[10], (1888) Silas Bradley.	506
Electa[6], (1790) Eliphalet	92
" Ann[7], (1834) Rev. Ezra	198
Eliza[6], (1805) Lieut. John	65
" [6], —— Isaac, Jr	72
" [6], —— Solomon	75
" [6], (1803) Ebenezer	84
" [6], (1808) Ezra	87
" [7], (1805) Amos	109
" [7], (1815) Eliphalet	145
" [7], (1817) Jacob	148
" [7], (1823) John	185
" [7], (1804) Arah	190
" [7], (1803) Seth, Jr	213
" [7], (1830) George	228
" [8], (1843) Ralph	379

INDEX II.

	Page.
Eliza[8], (1825) Aarón	249
" Ann[8], (1815) Dr. Milo	261
" Angeline[7], (1806) Calvin	192
" " [7], (1814) Horace	194
" Ilsley[7], (1872) Charles W.	179
" " [7], (1825) Sewall	129
" J.[9], (1853) William P.	416
" Jane[7], (1809) John	162
" Jane[8], (1830) John Watson	256
" " [8], (1837) James Kent	381
" M.[8], (1846) Henry Proctor	357
" Matilda[7], —— Benjamin F.	133
" Roxana[7], (1828) Rev. Ezra	198
" Theresa[8], (1819) Aaron	239
Elizabeth[2], (1641) Robert	5
" [3], (1686) Jacob	9
" [4], (1717) John	14
" [4], (1728) Dr Matthew	15
" [4], (1715) Sergt. Jacob	17
" [4], (1724) Daniel	17
" [5], (1741) Abraham	20
" [5], (1731) William	26
" [5], (1760) Rev. Benjamin	30
" [5], (1759) Israel	33
" [5], 1737) Israel	34
" [5], (1756) John	35
" [5], (1759) Matthew	36
" [5], (1790) Richard	39
" [6], (1766) John	40
" [5], (1761) Moses	41
" [5], (1747) Jacob	42
" [5], (1782) Samuel	46
" [5], (1763) Lieut. Joel	48
" [6], (1786) Nathan	68
" [6], (1761) Israel	72
" [6], (1780) Benjamin	78
" [6], (1792) Enoch	80
" [6], (1810) Simeon	83
" [6], (1778) Seth	97
" [7], (1791) Daniel	106
" [7], (1812) Isaac	109
" [7], (1821) Enoch	123
" [7], (1834) Peter	156
" [7], (1804) Israel	160
" [7], (1824) Richard	168
" [7], (1848) Moses Noyes	178
" [9], —— Massena Clark	481
" [9], (1880) Ezra	484
" Ann[8], (1871) Lucius F.	389
" B.[7], (1844) Capt. George	137
" C.[9], (1875) Imri P.	465
" Carr[8], (1867) Giles Aaron	330
" Cartwright[7], (1811) Thomas Fosdick	129

	Page.
Elizabeth Ellen[8], (1839) John	245
" " [9], (1861) Benjamin Bradley	412
" Ford[7], (1343) Benj. Webb	136
" Gardiner[8], (1855) Gardiner	325
" H.[9], (1869) Charles Henry	412
" Jenette[7],(1834) Jona.Tenncy	159
" " [8], (1872) Nathan	312
" Noyes[7], (1836) Richard	176
" P.[7], (1807) Dr. Samuel	124
" Rand[10], (1872) John Fr'd'k	514
" Stannard[8], (1833) Wm. Bray	242
" W.[9], (1898) Arthur Daniel	456
" Woodbury[7], (1815) Moody	144
" Worthington[7], (1813) Levi	214
Ella[8], (1841) Benjamin Franklin	304
" [9], (1867) Joseph B	477
" A.[8], (1852) Thomas B.	315
" A.[8], (1874) Luther	394
" C.[8], (1849) Isaac	296
" Crosby[8], (1890) Le Roy F.	396
" Elethea[8], (1842) Moses Woodman	248
" Elizabeth[8], (1849) Horace H.	401
" Florence[8], (1854) Prescott Jones	304
" " [8], (1856) Benj. Whiting	247
" Frances[9], (1875) Benjamin	419
" Maria[9], (1853) Charles	405
" Mary[9], (1853) Charles Henry	416
" Miller[8], (1847) Winfred Scott	353
Ellen A.[8], (1847) James R.	323
" Brazier[10], (1884) George Willis	507
" E., (1835) Charles Henry	266
" F.[8], (1893) Samuel	291
" Grace Derby[7], —— Joseph Thornton	131
" Harriet[8], (1851) Giles Aaron	329
" J.[8], (1838) Theophilus B., Jr.	321
" Leota[9], (1876) Capt. Horatio Nelson	435
" Louisa[7], (1839) Jonathan	149
" Maria[8], (1857) Wellington	356
Elma[8], (1848) Samuel Plumer	264
Elna Viola[8], (1896) Loren M	396
Elnora E.[9], (1864) Israel	466
Elsie[9], (1866) George G.	498
" Effie[9], (1874) Wm. Eliphalet	482
Elvira[6], (1810) John	86
" F.[8], (1841) Aaron	249
" W.[7], (1804) Dr. Samuel	124
Emeline[7], (1818) Capt. Milton	204
" [7], (1821) Matthew	165
" [7], (1838) Capt. Milton	205
" Maria[7], (1822) Rufus	197
" Matilda[7], (1823) Chas. Fr'd'k.	131

INDEX II.

Emeline Osgood[7], (1808) Lt. and Maj.
    John 152
"   S.[7], (1830) Russell 168
Emeroy C.[7], (1845) Abraham, Jr 209
Emily[6], (1794) Solomon 75
"   [6], (1806) Zebulon, Jr 90
"   [6], (1809) Bildad 103
"   [7], (1817) Enoch 138
,"   [7], (1817) Richard 168
"   [7], (1830) Joel 216
"   [8], (1846) Prof. Samuel 205
"   [9], (1899) Luther, Jr 463
"   [9], — Alvin 478
"   A[8], (1837) Isaac 289
"   A.[9], (1871) Henry Proctor 358
"   E.[7], (1840) Abraham, Jr 209
"   Eliza[7], (1840) Daniel Noyes 156
"   Gratia[7], (1842) Oliver, Jr 222
"   J.[8], (1847) John Watson 256
"   Johnson[8], (1859) Asa 326
"   Judson[8], (1857) Henry Sewall ... 271
"   Lorania[7], (1839) Horace Hale ... 230
"   M.[8], (1877) Capt. Dennis 332
"   Mabel[8], (1870) Lewis Austin 337
"   Sophia[7], (1813) Amos 109
Emma[7], — Abraham 107
"   A.[8], (1846) Theophilus B., Jr 321
"   Ellen[7], (1851) Jesse 181
"   Frances[7], (1844) George 131
"   " [8], (1880) Simeon
    Augustus 336
"   Isabel[8], (1856) Augustus Hall ... 287
"   Jane[8], (1855) Darius 297
"   " [8], (1842) Geo. Washington .. 359
"   Julia[8], (1859) James Kent 381
"   Lizzie[9], (1880) George F 470
"   Lucille[9], (1880) Samuel Plumer .. 435
"   Lucretia[8], (1859) Jas. Augustus. 270
"   Mabel[8], (1861) George W 272
"   Matilda, (1861) Warren Mann .. 286
"   Melvina[8], (1854) Simeon
    Houghton 391
Erixene Chase[8], (1858) Benj. Whiting. 247
Erunia[8], (1877) Luther 394
Estella Almira[8], (1894) Ellsworth C... 377
"   May[8], (1878) Clinton. 353
"   Myra[8], (1885) Wilson M 377
Estelle S.[10], (1892) Smith 505
Esther[6], (1770) Israel 72
"   [7], (1779) Henry 105
"   [7], (1832) Rev. Zenas 199
"   [9], (1897) Charles F 437
"   Catharine[9], (1824) Alvin 343
"   Elizabeth[7], (1826) Joshua, Jr .. 250

Esther Hall[7], (1827) Abraham 223
"   Harriet[8], (1889) Simeon 395
"   Lee[8], (1841) Charles 243
"   Mabel[11], (1889) Geo. Kimball .. 518
"   Maria[8], (1858) Wilbur F 361
Ethie L.[9], (1868) John Emery 442
Ethel Hale[11], (1891) George Kimball .. 518
"   Lillian[10], (1898) Newton
    Romeyn 506
"   Lucetta[9], (1876) Walter M 462
"   Lura[9], (1894) Walter 438
"   Margaret[9], (1890) Ezra P 485
"   Maud[8], (1881) Frank A 313
Etta M.[8], (1871) Edwin 339
"   Mansfield[9], (1871) Amos Henry .. 411
Eunice[4], (1719) Dr. Matthew 15
"   [5], (1732) Robert 22
"   [5], (1768) Moses 41
"   [6], (1763) Benjamin 50
"   [6], (1775) Liphe 54
"   [6], (1793) Jonathan 99
"   [8], (1827) Moses 244
Eva[8], — John S 311
"   [9], (1855) Benjamin F 478
"   [10], (1894) Durward C 513
"   Bryant[9], (1887) Dr. Frank B 469
"   C.[8], (1860) Joseph Monroe 284
"   E.[9], (1881) Eben H 464
"   May[9], (1882) William Henry 439
"   Maryette[9], (1884) Geo. Wm., Jr ... 436
"   R.[8], (1872) Henry Le Roy 395
Evelyn Amelia[9], (1851) Capt. George.. 137
Evena L.[8], (1862) Luther 394
Faith K.[10], (1885) John Frederick 514
Fannie[8], — Ezra 338
"   Catharine[9], (1882) Samuel
    Plumer 435
"   Currier[8], (1863) Joseph Nichols 277
"   Louisa[8], (1867) Joel.. 382
Fanny[6], (1814) Horace 96
"   Almira[6], (1813) Joseph 66
"   Hobson[8], (1873) Lewis Austin 337
Felecia C.[9], (1883) Thaddeus Solomon 494
"   Rose[10], (1890) Claude Charles .. 517
Fidelia[7], (1840) Joel 216
Flora A.[9], (1866) Benjamin F 478
"   Bell[9], (1866) Jacob Kimball 465
"   P.[9], (1866) William P 416
"   R.[8], (1887) Dayton A 377
Florilla[8], (1837) Edward 348
Florence[9], (1881) George F 474
"   [9], (1895) Charles F 475
"   [10], (1885) Edward F. 512
"   [10], (1896) Harry Delva 511

	Page.
Florence A.[8], (1874) James Erwin	278
" B.[9], (1867) Joshua	421
" E.[8], (1867) John Q	259
" E.[9], (1889) Charles B	471
" Ella[8], (1855) George W	311
" Emma[9], (1891) Richard H.	474
" Marion[9], (1866) Francis A	457
" May[8], —— Enos Seth	385
" " [10], (1897) George Willis	508
" N.[9], (1872) John F	466
Franc[9], (1886) Julius T	494
Frances[7], —— Eli	210
" [8], —— David P	252
" A.[8], (1850) Thomas B	315
" Ann[8], (1828) Edward	348
" Eliza[7], (1844) Samuel	212
" Ellen[8], (1863) Benjamin Whiting	247
" Josephine[8], (1850) Horace Hale	401
" Maria[7], (1832) Joseph, Jr.	135
" Pickering[7], (1835) Benjamin	130
Frankie E.[7], (1855) Abraham, Jr	209
Georgiana F.[8], (1853) Theophilus B.,Jr.	321
" Grace[8], (1868) George W	311
Georgie[8], (1844) Enoch	283
Gertrude[8], (1870) Nathan	342
" [7], (1888) Dr. Orange H	457
" Russell[8], (1872) James Knight	337
Gladys Gay[9], (1896) Arthur, Jr	463
Grace[8], (1889) David Q	376
" [8], (1875) W. Delisle	376
" [9], —— Frank Dresser	449
" Clark[8], (1875) John Quincy	277
" Ellen[9], (1865) Arthur Daniel	456
" Ethel[9], (1875) Daniel Sewall	442
" Garland[8], (1870) James Knight	337
" Gertrude[8], (1878) Charles F	389
" Irene[9], (1872) Joseph Emery	438
" K.[8], (1884) John Peabody	340
" Mildred[9], (1885) Cyrus W	469
Hannah[2], (1650) Robert	5
" [4], (1709) Isaac	13
" [4], (1727) John	14
" [4], (1722) Richard	15
" [5], (1746) David	33
" [5], (1741) Abraham	37
" [5], (1768) Richard	39
" [5], (1759) Daniel	40
" [5], (1764) Moses	41
" [5], (1775) Dea. Edmund	42
" [5], (1737) John	42
" [5], (1775) Capt. Simeon	47
" [6], (1788) Eld. David	62

	Page.
Hannah[6], (1775) Israel, Jr	71
" [6], (1784) Israel	72
" [6], (1760) Capt. John	73
" [6], (1803) Moses	76
" [6], (1786) Benjamin	78
" [6], —— Joseph	78
" [6], (1780) Capt. Stephen	79
" [6], (1779) Abraham	79
" [6], (1795) Paul	81
" [8], (1799) Ens. James	88
" [6], (1809) Capt. Simeon	100
" [7], (1800) Henry	105
" [7], (1798) Smith	110
" [7], (1798) Jacob	121
" [7], (1805) Samuel, Jr	142
" [7], (1811) Eliphalet	145
" [7], (1791) Lieut. and Maj. John	151
" [7], (1810) Ebenezer	189
" [7], (1836) Simeon	224
" Augusta[7], (1840) Oliver, Jr.	222
" C.[7], (1813) Matthew	164
" H.[8], (1826) Samuel	291
" Ilsley[7], (1827) Asa	171
" Jane[7], (1829) Abraham	220
" Lord[7], (1807) Daniel	107
" Loretta[7], (1841) Jona. Tenney	159
" Matilda[8], (1853) John Langdon	320
" P.[8], (1832) Aaron	249
" Parsons[7], (1814) Enoch	123
" Rosina[8], (1840) John	245
" Susan[8], (1841) Silas Hall	254
" Swett[7], (1799) Israel	117
" Weymouth[8], (1828) Moses	244
Harriet[6], (1798) Moses	86
" [6], (1800) Zebulon	90
" [6] (1804) Thaddeus	99
" [7], (1795) Isaac	108
" [7], (1796) Samuel	108
" [7], (1817) Enoch	138
" [7], (1817) Matthew	164
" [7], (1818) Gaius	215
" [8], (1822) Abraham	235
" A.[7], —— James	117
" B.[8], (1836) John Emery	282
" B.[8], (1868) Oliver L	388
" Dutton[8], (1836) Charles	242
" E.[8], (1871) Moses	284
" Electa[7], (1839) Rex. Zenas	200
" Eliza[7], (1849) Jonathan Tenney	160
" Elizabeth[8], (1845) James Kent	381
" Maria[7], (1834) Jonathan	149
" N.[7], (1815) John	162

INDEX II.

Name	Page
Harriet Newhall[8], (1818) Isaac	278
" R.[7], (1815) Jeremiah	166
" Stowe[9], (1856) Charles	466
" Winchester[7], (1862) Timo. Mather	225
Hattie[8], (1861) Israel	296
" Alice[8], (1859) Henry L	354
" E.[10], (1879) George W	515
" Eunice[8], (1851) John	245
" G.[9], (1878) Edgar G	470
" J.[9], (1861) Moses J	468
" M.[8], (1875) Henry J	378
" May[9], (1870) Jacob Kimball	466
Hazel[9], (1895) George T	463
Helen[8], (1830) Isaac	253
" [8], (1880) Isaac Milton	294
" [9], — Frank Dresser	449
" [9], (1892) Eugene Elmer	459
" Adele[10], (1871) Addison L	515
" Augusta[8], (1857) James Augustus	270
" Augustus[8], (1871) Rev. Lucien H	342
" E.[8], (1841) Enoch	283
" Frances[7], (1855) Daniel Noyes	156
" " [7], (1856) Philip D	178
" " [8], (1868) Daniel M	343
" H.[9], (1855) Norman R	476
" Isadore[7], (1839) George	130
" " [7], (1842) Benjamin Webb	136
" L.[7], (1836) Harvey	196
" L.[9], (1889) Nathan E	473
" Louisa[8], (1847) George Fitz	268
" " [8], (1859) Nelson	383
" M.[7], (1843) Horace	206
" Marian[9], (1893) Charles F	475
" S.[7], (1847) Abraham, Jr	209
Helena M.[8], (1862) Adam Willis	287
Henrietta[9], (1895) Henry Eastlake	471
" A.[8], (1862) James Monroe	284
" Sewall[8], (1867) Henry Sewall	271
" Wood[9], (1869) Lorenzo Benson	420
Hepzibah[9], (1780) Corp. John	74
Hester Forsythe[9], — William Richmond	437
Hetty Perley[7], (1804) Benjamin	126
Huldah[5], (1763) Daniel	44
" [8], (1858) Henry Proctor	357
" Rebecca[9], (1885) Ezra P	485
" Taylor[7], (1821) Daniel	44
Ida[9], (1862) Caleb Cushing	407
" [9], (1864) Edgar B	434
" E.[8], (1849) Enoch	283
" E.[8], (1873) Henry	590
Ida Frances[9], (1856) Selwyn P	452
" Helen[8], (1859) Joseph Nichols	277
" L.[9], (1858) John P	497
" Melvina[8], (1846) Phineas M	387
Inez G.[9], (1897) Dennis Ezra	473
Irene[6], — Corp. John, Jr	74
" Clifford[8], (1869) Geo. Benjamin	276
" Felch[9], (1841) Joel	405
Isa Agnes[8], (1873) Henry Proctor	358
Isabel E.[9], (1877) Imri P	465
Isabella[7], (1828) Jacob	148
Isadore M.[8], (1842) Dr. Milo	262
Isanna[8], (1800) George	85
Jane[6], (1733) John	23
" [6], (1757) John	35
" [6], (1763) Samuel	29
" [6], (1773) Asa Edmund	41
" [6], (1797) Paul	81
" [7], (1808) Amos	109
" [7], (1845) Benjamin	185
" [7], (1821) George	228
" [8], (1814) Benjamin	249
" B.[8], (1853) John Q	258
" Emily[8], (1844) Stephen	257
" Maria[7], (1826) Rev. Ezra	198
" N.[8], (1828) Joseph	238
Janet True[9], (1890) Henry Eastlake	411
Jemima[5], (1770) Freegrace	45
" [7], (1820) Rev. Theophilus B	166
" [7], (1823) Peter	156
Jennie[9], (1873) John Sturgis	447
" B.[8], (1864) James Monroe	284
" E.[10], (1813) George W	515
" H.[8], (1879) John Peabody	340
" Josephine[7], (1858) Daniel Noyes	156
" Maria[7], (1866) Charles Clinton	458
" P.[9], (1871) Moses J	468
Jenny[6], (1784) Corp. John, Jr	74
Jerusha[6], (1787) Paul	81
Jessie[9], (1873) John Sturgis	446
" D.[8], (1887) Wilbur C	377
" Fremont[9], (1858) Benjamin	419
" May[8], (1872) Simon Augustus	336
" Ruth[10], (1895) Ralph Norton	505
" Stafford[9], (1872) Capt. Milo R	431
Joanna[2], (1633) Robert	4
" [4], (1720) Lieut. Abraham	18
" [8], (1800) Simon	85
Josephine[8], (1856) Moses	258
" [9], (1852) Amasa A	476
Judith[4], (1716) Dr. Matthew	15
" [5], — William	27
" [6], (1770) Capt. Stephen	79
" [6], (1775) Benjamin	78

	Page.
Judith[6], (1787) Enoch	80
" [6], (1801) Ezra	87
" [7], (1770) Henry	105
" [7], (1824) Rev. Theophilus B	166
" A.[7], (1814) Mathew	164
" Follansbee[7], (1799) John	162
" R.[8], —— Joseph M	321
Julia[6], (1801) Nathan	68
" [6], (1816) Horace	96
" [7], (1816) Enoch	138
" [7], (1823) Enoch	123
" A.[8], (1852) Dennis H	307
" A.[9], (1878) Eben H	464
" Ann[7], (1817) Enos	215
" " S.[8], (1839) William	279
" Elizabeth[7], (1825) Jere	216
" Maria[7], (1809) Daniel	152
" " [8], (1833) Col. John Henry	301
" Marguerite[10], (1881) John Frederick	514
" Martha[8], (1853) Joel	382
" N.[8], (1819) Alvin	343
" O.[9], (1873) Benjamin H., 2d	460
Juliette[7], (1797) Dr. Samuel	124
" [8], (1851) Benjamin Whiting	247
" Rogers[7], (1848) Samuel Newell	226
Juliana[5], (1753) Freegrace	44
" [6], (1764) Stephen	58
Kate[6], (1853) James Kent	381
" Sophia[7], (1849) Elihu	205
Katie J.[9], (1861) Moses J	468
" Sturgis[9], (1874) John Sturgis	447
Katherine[6], (1764) Capt. Benjamin	59
" [9], (1890) Dr. Frank B	469
" [9], (1892) Enoch C	440
" Allen[8], (1837) Isaac	253
" Louise[10], (1890) Geo. Shrieve	503
" M.[8], (1890) Wilson M	377
" Jane[7], (1799) Samuel	120
" " [8], (1870) Daniel M	343
Laura Ann[8], (1834) Samuel	291
" E.[9], (1877) Andrew Jackson	422
" F.[9], (1849) Obed	405
" Jane[8], —— Francis	322
" " [8], (1878) Simeon	395
" Livermore[7], (1820) Rev. John Folsom	132
" Theresa[9], (1867) Wm. Eliphalet	482
Lauriette Ashley[7], (1821) Enos	215
" Blanche[9], (1880) Joseph Ashley	495
Leala[9], (1891) Samuel Plumer	435
" H.[8], (1866) Joseph Henry	318
Lelia O.[10], —— Claude Samuel	517

	Page.
Lena Simpson[9], (1879) Chas. Samuel	453
" Smith[9], (1874) Amos Henry	411
Lenella Pearl[9], (1888) Lucas Rufus	484
Leola[9], (1890) George W	425
Lilian G.[8], (1863) Nathan Preston	278
Lillian Angeline[9], (1873) Aaron	424
" Blanche[8], (1874) Sylvanus	308
" C.[8], (1887) Loren M	396
" Gertrude[9], (1875) Geo. William	414
" Knight[8], (1874) Xenophon	339
" Maud[10], (1891) Frank Sylvester	516
" Preston[8], (1894) John Quincy	277
Lillie[8], (1856) Ebenezer Moody	283
" O.[8], (1861) Dr. William Case	358
Lillis D.[8], (1844) John Emery	282
Lizzie[7], —— John Popkin	184
" [8], (1848) Abraham	265
" Ann[8], (1858) Henry	393
" B.[8], (1873) Moses	340
" Coffin[8], (867) Moses Cook	339
" Disney[8], (1862) Moses Cook	339
" Emma[8], (1852) William	279
" L.[8], (1864) Edwin	339
" L.[9], (1853) Robert W	451
" M.[10], (1883) George W	515
" May[9], (1883) Cyrus W	469
Lois[6], (1754) John	35
" [6], (1805) Dr. Benjamin	66
" [6], —— Solomon	75
" [6], (1799) Ebenezer	84
Lora Susan[6], (1858) Norman B	307
Lottie E.[9], (1874) George F	474
" Lee[8], (1876) Henry	393
" Mabel[8], (1876) Gad Mather	389
Louisa[6], (1799) Capt. Samuel	71
" [6], (1813) Capt. Simeon	100
" [7], (1801) Benjamin	125
" [7], (1822) Col. Samuel	126
" [7], (1815) Israel	151
" [7], (1803) Lieut. and Maj. John	152
" [7], (1800) Rev. Theophilus B	165
" [7], (1828) Rev. Theophilus B	166
" [7], (1833) Nathan	177
" [8], (1822) Harvey	344
" Adelaide[8], (1882) Dr. John G. C.	360
" Ann[7], —— Benjamin	130
" Bradley[8], (1848) Charles	340
" Gertrude[8], (1891) Jos. Knight	337
" Jenette[8], (1849) Simeon Houghton	391
" M.[8], (1883) Henry	393
" Nichols[6], (1804) Joseph	66
" Saxony[8], 1864) Green	332
" Sewall[7], (1807) Israel	117

	Page.
Louisa Sophia[8], (1847) John Emery	282
Love[7], (1779) Daniel	106
Lovisa[6], (1739) Freegrace	45
" [6], (1805) Abraham	95
Lowella Stanwood[9], (1847) Enoch	450
Lucelia E.[8], (1845) Nathan	341
Lucina[5], (1762) Lieut. Joel	48
Lucinda[6], (1776) Samuel	46
" [6], (1787) Eliphalet	92
" [7], (1800) Zadoc, Jr	188
" [7], (1808) Eliphalet, Jr	196
" [7], (1819) Matthew	164
" Ella[8], (1848) William	279
" Maria[7], (1821) Jere	216
" Ruth[7], (1838) Rev. Zenas	200
Lucretia[6], (1813) Simeon	83
" [7], (1826) Gaius	215
" Little[7], (1829) Asa	171
Lucy[4], (1731) John	19
" [5], (1757) Moses	47
" [6], (1785) Capt. Silas	55
" [6], (1785) Capt. Samuel	70
" [6], (1779) Seth	97
" [6], (1792) Capt. Oliver	99
" [6], (1805) Capt. Simeon	100
" [7], —— Caleb	107
" [7], (1806) Eliphalet	145
" [7], (1810) Isaac	146
" [7], (1821) Jacob	148
" [7], (1845) Joel	217
" [7], (1833) Capt. Ira	223
" [7], (1878) Simeon	224
" A.[7], (1822) Samuel	147
" Almira[9], (1888) Charles F	435
" Anna[7], (1827) Oliver, Jr	221
" Ann S.[7], (1819) Isaac	118
" Annette[8], (1861) Ira, Jr	392
" Billings[8], (1813) Horace	96
" Elizabeth[8], (1850) George Fitz	268
" Hedding[7], (1826) Rev. John Folsom	132
" J.[8], (1830) Samuel	291
" J.[8], (1843) Hiram E	379
" J.[8], (1861) Horace	341
" Jane[7], (1843) Thomas Hall	173
" Maria[7], (1829) Alden	231
" Mather[7], (1851) Samuel Newell	226
" Miller[7], (1823) Abraham	220
" T.[8], (1863) Henry	390
Lulu[9], (1877) Lorenzo Benson	421
" [9], (1878) Thaddeus Solomon	494
" G.[8], (1868) Dr. Enoch, Jr	281
" M.[8], (1867) Charles Morton	392
Luna[7], (1836) Seth	158

	Page.
Lura[6], (1808) Joel, Jr	103
" [8], (1877) Daniel	311
" M.[8], (1881) Israel	464
Luthera Theresa[7], (1838) Oliver, Jr	222
Lydia[5], (1719) Abraham	20
" [5], (1758) Abraham	37
" [7], (1806) Joshua	119
" [7], (1802) Ebenezer	189
" Bartlett[7], (1809) Col. John Emery	139
" E.[8], (1858) James Monroe	284
" Rogers[8], (1829) Edward	348
" S.[7], (1802) Henry	105
Mabel[8], (1873) Isaac Milton	294
" [9], —— Frank Dresser	449
" [9], (1869) Enoch F	451
" A.[8], (1867) Nathan Preston	278
" Eliza[9], (1883) Ezra P	485
" G.[9], (1892) George F	474
" H.[9], (1881) Henry Farnum	447
" Harriet[9], (1874) Enos Holmes	297
" L.[8], (1860) Asa	326
" V.[9], (1861) Sergt. Joshua Richmond	418
Malinda[8], (1802) Abraham	95
Mamie Grace[9], (1876) Aaron	424
Marcella F.[8], (1848) Benjamin H	306
Marcia[7], —— John Popkin	184
" [8], (1828) Alvin	343
Margaret[6], (1803) John	86
" [6], (1817) Edward	89
" [7], (1820) Gaius	215
" [9], (1893) John C	500
" Coffin[7], (1840) John Coffin	182
" E.[7], (1821) Robert	153
" Emery[7], (1833) Richard	176
" Horton[8], (1834) John	317
Maria[7], (1790) Capt. Stephen	64 [?]
" [6], (1794) Bildad	102
" [7], (1835) Joel	216
" [8], (1841) Stephen	257
" [9], (1869) George Herman	458
" Bartlett[7], (1817) Dr. Joseph	140
" Christine[8], (1871) Xenophon	339
" Goodno[8], (1844) David Farnum	285
" Ruby[8], (1841) Arad	301
" Theresa[7], (1842) John	130
Marie J.[9], (1852) Norman R	476
" Pansee[9], (1871) Capt. Horatio Nelson	435
Marietta[8], (1837) Prof. Samuel	294
Mariette[7]. (1837) Martin	218
" Augusta[8], (1860) Wilbur Fisk	361
Marion[8], (1881) James Erwin	278

	Page.
Marion Irene[10], (1890) Charles Clifford	510
" M.[9], (1883) Fred A	496
" S.[8], (1853) Coleman Searle	299
" S.[8], (1871) Luther	394
" S.[9], —— Joseph Henry	457
" Virginia[9], (1883) Charles Hall	439
" Whiting[8], (1867) George Fitz	268
Martha[5], —— Matthew	36
" [6], (1782) Charles	51
" [6], (1801) Lieut. John	65
" [6], —— David	74
" [7], (1842) Stephen	128
" [7], (1801) Lieut. and Maj. John	152
" [7], (1833) Moses	158
" [7], (1818) Eliphalet, Jr	196
" [7], (1831) Joel	216
" [8], (1832) Abraham	236
" A.[8], (1838) Ebenezer H	315
" Adelaide[8], (1850) Harrison H	321
" Agnes[8], (1821) Aaron	239
" Ann[8], (1829) William Bray	242
" Anna[7], (1822) David	132
" Bell[7], (1846) Philip D	178
" Bolster[8], (1850) David Farnum	285
" Esther[8], (1875) Lucius F	303
" G.[8], (1870) Joseph	299
" Hall[7], (1825) Dr. Joseph	140
" L.[8], (1835) Isaac	289
" M.[8], (1856) James R	323
" Maria[7], (1839) James Kent	381
" " [7], (1825) Robert	153
" Preble[7], (1815) Moses, Jr	119
" " [9], (1865) George Moses	414
" Webb[6], (1796) Joseph	66
Mary[2], (1643) Robert	5
" [3], (1672) Sergt. Abraham	6
" [4], (1700) Robert	10
" [4], (1707) Capt. Abraham	12
" [4], (1722) John	14
" [4], (1718) Richard	15
" [4], (1716) Sergt. Jacob	17
" [4], (1719) Daniel	17
" [5], (1727) Abraham	20
" [5], (1738) Abraham	27
" [5], (1750) Samuel	28
" [5], (1747) Rev. Joseph	29
" [5], (1745) Capt. Isaac	32
" [5], (1753) Israel	33
" [5], (1748) David	33
" [5], (1763) John	35
" [5], (1752) Abraham	37
" [5], (1740) Jacob	42
" [5], (1748) David	44
" [6], (1778) Charles	51

	Page.
Mary[6], (1781) Eld. David	61
" [6], (1782) Joseph	63
" [6], (1796) Enoch	68
" [6], —— Nathan	68
" [6], (1787) Capt. Samuel	71
" [6], —— Solomon	75
" [6], (1782) Benjamin	78
" [6], —— Joseph	78
" [6], (1807) Paul	81
" [6], (1807) Simeon	83
" [6], (1803) Moses	86
" [6], (1810) Ezra	87
" [6], (1805) Ens. James	88
" [7], (1795) Daniel	106
" [7], —— Abraham	107
" [7], (1803) Isaac	108
" [7], (1800) Amos	109
" [7], (1810) Robert	113
" [7], (1801) Joseph	116
" [7], —— James	117
" [7], (1785) Dr. Samuel	133
" [7], (1826) Enoch	138
" [7], (1795) Samuel, Jr	142
" [7], (1820) Jacob	148
" [7], (1806) Capt. Tappan	167
" [7], (1828) Rev. Zenas	199
" [7], (1801) Seth, Jr	213
" [8], (1855) Samuel Plumer	265
" [8], (1861) Moses	283
" [8], (1864) Henry	393
" [9], (1869) Charles Clinton	458
" A.[7], (1840) Moses	183
" A.[8], (1834) Aaron	249
" A.[9], (1858) William P	416
" Abbie[8], (1872) Edwin Hall	327
" Abby[9], (1869) Joseph Webster	488
" Adeline[7], (1834) John Breed	137
" Alice[8], (1854) Edwin	338
" Alice[9], (1853) Charles H	449
" Alletta[8], (1863) Charles	336
" Amanda[8], (1844) Benjamin F	316
" Ann[6], (1792) Lieut. John	65
" " [6], (1807) Joseph	66
" " [7], (1812) Zadoc, Jr	188
" " [7], (1813) Eliphalet	145
" " [7], (1825) David	132
" " [7], (1852) Charles	150
" " [7], (1842) Simeon	224
" " [8], (1832) John Watson	256
" " [8], (1843) Benjamin Perley	266
" " [8], (1843) Phineas M	387
" " [8], (1847) David Jewett	338
" " [9], (1819) Jere	216
" " [9], (1863) Benjamin Bradley	412

(35)

INDEX II.

Mary Anna⁷, (1839) Capt. George...... 137
" Augusta⁸, (1815) Aaron.......... 239
" B.⁶, (1790) Nathan................ 66
" B.⁸, (1847) Albert................ 300
" B.⁸, (1875) John Emery.......... 282
" Beda⁸, (1865) Gad Mather........ 389
" Bedortha⁸, (1817) Alvin.......... 343
" Burnham⁸, (1877) Joseph Nichols 277
" C.⁸, (1870) Edward Lewis O...... 327
" Calista⁷, (1842) Horace Hale..... 230
" " ⁸, (1872) Uri M............ 400
" D.⁷, (1818) Moses, Jr............. 119
" D.⁸, (1848) John Langdon........ 320
" D.⁹, (1891) Enoch C.............. 440
" E.⁷, (1814) Solomon, Jr.......... 155
" E.⁷, (1838) Moses, Jr............ 157
" E.⁷, (1837) Stephen............... 128
" E.⁷, (1830) John.................. 130
" E.⁸, (1839) Thomas B............ 314
" E.⁸, (1865) Oliver L............. 388
" E.⁸, (1869) Henry Proctor........ 358
" Edna⁷, (1866) Charles M.......... 179
" " ⁸, (1855) William............ 279
" Electa⁷, (1823) Rufus............. 197
" Eliza⁹, —— Benjamin F.......... 133
" Elizabeth⁷, (1835) Moody........ 180
" " ⁸, (1827) Isaac.......... 253
" " ⁸, (1843) Arad........... 301
" " ⁸, (1845) Edwin Spofford................ 292
" " ⁸, (1852) Charles....... 340
" " ⁸, (1852) Simeon Houghton......... 391
" " ⁸, (1854) Norman B ... 307
" Ellen⁷, (1835) Capt. Richard..... 183
" " ⁷, (1835) Joseph, Jr........ 135
" " ⁷, (1834) Philip D........... 178
" " ⁸, (1861) Xenophon......... 339
" " ⁹, (1846) Benjamin 419
" Emeline⁸, (1802) Wellington..... 356
" Esther⁸, (1866) Gamaliel King... 386
" Frances⁸, (1854) John Lewis. .. 308
" " ⁸, —— Charles M........ 250
" " ⁸, (1846) Moses Woodman................. 248
" H.⁷, (1800) Smith 110
" Helen⁷, (1852) Horace Hale 401
" " ⁸, (1861) Capt. Dennis...... 332
" Holt⁷, (1793) Lieut. and Maj. John 151
" Ina⁸, (1872) Charles William..... 336
" Isabelle⁷, (1837) George........ .. 130
" " ⁸, (1868) Lorenzo Benson 420
" J.⁷, (1814) Hezekiah 154

Mary J.⁷, (1832) Harvey................ 196
" Jane⁷, (1831) Benjamin Webb... 136
" " ⁷, (1846) John Coffin........ 182
" Janette⁸, (1864) James Kent.... 381
" Jones⁷, (1820) David 144
" Kimball⁸, (1820) Isaac............ 288
" L.⁷, (1813) Jeremiah 166
" L.⁸, (1821) Joseph................ 238
" L.⁸, (1860) George Hadley........ 354
" Little⁷, (1808) Robert............ 113
" " ⁷, (1823) Richard........... 176
" Lulu⁹, (1887) Herman H......... 441
" M.⁹, (1887) Nathan E 473
" Noyes⁸, (1847) John.............. 245
" P.⁷, (1844) Woodbridge 184
" P.⁹, (1874) Edward Payson 454
" Parker⁷, (1826) Isaac............. 145
" Peabody⁸, (1845) Eliphalet....... 294
" Pettengill⁷, —— Israel.......... 107
" Susan⁷, (1828) Isaac 118
" Swett⁸, (1843) Charles............. 243
" T.⁹, (1848) Oscar Edmund........ 430
" Victoria⁹, (1887) James Henry.. 485
" Willis⁶, (1857) Dr. Henry Milgrove................. ... 286
Matilda⁶, (1802) Abraham.............. 95
" ⁷, (1799) Zadoc, Jr............. 188
" ⁷, (1826) Col. John Emery...... 139
" Maria⁸, (1870) Dr. John G. C.. 360
" McClune⁸, (1858) William..... 279
Maud Adeline⁸, (1890) John Quincy... 277
May⁸, (1866) John William 273
" Emma⁹, (1879) Frank Huey...... 456
Mehitable⁵, (1734) Abraham...... ... 20
" ⁵, (1764) Henry.............. 31
" ⁶, (1789) Thaddeus........... 98
Melinda Maria⁸, (1839) Lewis Alanson 355
Mercy⁴, (1708) Sergt. Jacob 17
" ⁵, (1756) Capt. Isaac 33
" ⁶, (1776) Benjamin............. 43
" ⁶, (1779) Capt. David............. 69
Meta Lena⁸, (1872) Dr. Enoch, Jr. .. 281
Mildred⁹, (1895) George Moulton...... 473
" Louisa¹¹, (1847) Geo. Kimball.. 518
Milly⁹, (1859) John P................. 477
Minerva⁶, (1797) Thaddeus............ 98
" ⁶, (1821) Capt. Simeon......... 100
" E.⁸, (1850) Ira, Jr.............. 391
Minnie⁹, —— John Quincy............ 417
" A. G.⁸, (1872) Norman B........ 307
" F.⁹, (1868) George N 416
" L.⁸, (1860) David................ 395
Mira⁶, (1797) Ezra.................... 87
Miranda Smith⁷, (1816) Solomon, Jr .. 155

	Page.
Miriam⁶, (1798) Jonathan	99
" 7, (1816) Capt. Jacob	120
" W.⁷, (1803) Joshua	119
Mirion⁹, (1866) Wm. Eliphalet	482
Molly⁵, (1738) William	27
" ⁶, (1750) Robert	49
Mournful⁴, (1726) Lieut. Abraham	18
Myra⁶, (1811) Moses	76
" B.⁹, (1875) John F	466
" H.⁹, (1854) Oscar Edmund	430
" Hall⁸, (1820) Dr. Milo	262
" Jane⁶, (1828) Moody	144
Myrtie⁹, (1883) Richard Henry	474
" E.⁹, (1891) Henry Keeler	458
" May⁹, (1874) Sylvester Felch	468
Nancy⁵, (1769) Benjamin	43
" ⁶, (1801) Nathan	67
" ⁶, (1796) George	85
" ⁶, (1798) Bildad	102
" 7, (1827) Robert	153
" 7, (1835) Asa	171
' Albina⁷, (1827) Hon. Cyrus	157
" Jennie⁸, (1854) Joseph	235
" S.⁷, (1815) Hezekiah	154
Naomi⁶, (1788) Capt. David	70
" 7, (1832) Peter	156
Nellie⁶, —— Charles M	250
" ⁸, (1873) John William	273
" Alba⁹, (1874) Joseph Emery	439
" Anna⁸, (1868) Charles F	389
" Austice⁸, (1883) Simon Augustus	336
' Clara⁸, (1858) Ira, Jr	392
" E.⁸, (1863) Enoch	323
" Emma⁹, (1865) Francis A	457
" Frank⁹, (1885) Charles F	475
" J.⁷, (1854) Lucius Franklin	226
" M.⁸, (1861) Henry	390
" M.⁹, (1856) Albert	477
" W.⁸, (1868) Moses	339
Nettie Marion⁸, (1875) Warren	336
Nina Edith⁸, (1872) George W	311
Ocenia M.⁷, (1858) Charles	150
Ola May⁹, (1877) Samuel Plumer	435
Olive⁷, (1818) Isaac	147
" Alene¹⁰, (1893) Newton Romeyn	506
" Charlotte⁹, (1871) George Moses	414
" Mather⁷, (1823) Capt. Milton	205
Orissa Ann⁸, (1855) Harrison H	321
Orpha⁶, (1780) Zadoc	90
Pamelia, —— Nathan	68
Patience⁵, (1770) Deacon Edmund	41
" F.⁸, (1830) Enoch	290
Patty⁶, (1779) Capt. Benjamin	60

	Page.
Patty⁶, (1782) Corp. John, Jr	74
Pauline⁹, (1897) John C	560
" L.⁸, (1882) Paul	326
Pearl Charlotte⁸, (1876) Simeon	395
Persis⁶, —— Seth	97
Phebe⁶, (1795) Enoch	80
" ⁶, (1777) Capt. David	69
" ⁶, (1781) Eliphalet	91
" 7, (1772) Henry	105
" ⁸, (1838) Thomas Jefferson	319
" ⁹, (1886) Henry Keeler	458
" Ann⁷, (1845) Jonathan Tenney	159
" E.⁷, (1848) Moses	184
" Jane⁷, (1827) Richard	169
" Jewett⁶, (1794) Moses	86
" Louisa⁹, (1885) James Henry	485
Philina⁶, (1800) Capt. Simeon	100
" 7, (1821) Capt. Milton	204
Polly⁵, (1761) Abraham	28
" ⁶, (1781) David	73
" ⁶, (1782) Capt. Israel	54
" ⁶, (1784) Benjamin	74
" ⁶, (1785) Capt. Stephen	62
" ⁶, (1785) Thaddeus	98
" ⁶, (1795) Capt. Oliver	99
" ⁶, (1795) Bildad	102
" ⁶, (1799) Corp. John, Jr	74
" 7, (1778) Henry	105
" 7, —— Abraham	107
Priscilla⁶, (1772) Rev. Phineas	60
" ⁸, —— Jacob	252
Prudence⁵, (1738) Abraham	36
Rachel⁴, (1725) Sergt. Jacob	17
" ⁵, (1761) Zadoc	89
Rapsima⁹, (1792) Jonathan	76
Rebecca³, (1680) Jacob	9
" 4, (1698) Robert	10
" 5, (1730) Robert	22
" 5, (1751) David	44
" 5, (1757) Rev. Benjamin	30
" 6, (1775) Charles	51
" 6, (1780) Johathan	76
" 6, (1797) Capt. Gideon	91
" 6, (1812) Paul	81
" 6, (1815) Simeon	83
" 7, (1806) Matthew	164
" 7, (1811) Rev. Theophilus	165
" B.⁸, (1836) Samuel	291
" Fessenden⁷, (1846) Benj. Webb	136
" Little⁷, (1840) Dr. Stephen	175
" P.⁶, (1816) Ens. James	88
Rhoda⁶, (1786) Capt. Gideon	91
" ⁶, (1799) Thaddeus	98
" 7, (1827) Harvey	195

548   INDEX II.

	Page.
Roana Cutter[7], (1820) Israel	161
" " [8], (1804) John	316
Roby, (1825) Horace	194
Rosaltha Minerva[7], (1846) Timothy Mather	225
Rovena[8], (1850) Nathan	341
Rubie Marion[8], (1877) Philip Tyler	333
Ruth[5], (1763) Moses	41
" [6], (1771) Israel, Jr	71
" [6], (1774) Zadoc	90
" [6], (1793) Paul	81
" [6], (1805) Ezra	87
" [7], (1799) Ebenezer	189
" [7], (1829) Peter	156
" [9], (1892) Horace Wylie	481
" Lovisa[8], (1886) Le Roy F.	396
" Marion[9], (1897) Walter	438
" Noyes[7], (1809) Isaac	117
Sabrina[6], —— Corp. Moses	56
Sadie J.[8], (1859) Gamaliel King	386
Sally[6], (1780) Capt. Benjamin	61
" [6], (1795) Eld. David	62
" [6], (1796) Capt. Stephen	62
" [6], (1803) Nathan	67
" [6], (1774) Capt. David	69
" [6], (1779) Capt. Samuel	70
" [6], —— Benjamin	74
" [6], (1783) Thaddeus	98
" [6], (1803) Capt. Oliver	100
" [7], (1795) Capt. Jacob	120
" [7], (1778) Samuel, Jr	142
" Crowell[7], —— Abraham	107
" D.[8], (1826) Enoch	290
Sarah[8], (1681) Sergt. Abraham	7
" [4], (1713) Capt. Abraham	12
" [4], (1714) John	14
" [4], (1711) Dr. Matthew	15
" [5], (1743) Abraham	20
" [5], (1739) Robert	22
" [5], (1743) William	72
" [5], (1761) Rev. Benjamin	30
" [5], (1757) Henry	31
" [5], (1733) Samuel	31
" [5], (1744) Israel	34
" [5], (1753) John	35
" [5], (1745) Matthew	36
" [5], (1756) Abraham	37
" [5], (1763) Richard	39
" [5], (1768) Lieut. Joel	48
" [6], (1777) Liphe	54
" [6], (1782) Enoch	67
" [6], —— Nathan	68
" [6], (1773) Israel	72
" [6], (1794) Daniel	82

	Page.
Sarah[6], (1800) Simeon	82
" [6], (1801) Moses	86
" [6], (1814) Ens. James	88
" [6], (1807) Bildad	103
" [7], (1776) Henry	105
" [7], (1812) Amos	109
" [7], (1810) Joshua	119
" [7], (1809) Eliphalet	145
" [7], (1819) Capt. Richard	182
" [7], (1842) Woodbridge	184
" [7], (1823) Horace	194
" [7], (1844) Martin	218
" [7], (1832) Simeon	224
" [8], (1848) Thomas Jefferson	319
" [8], —— David	257
" A[8]., (1838) Aaron	249
" Agnes[8], (1854) Giles Aaron	329
" Ann[6], (1820) John	86
" " [7], (1806) Lieut. and Maj. John	152
" " [7], (1844) John Coffin	182
" " [9], (1850) Benjamin	409
" Bragg[7], (1829) Oliver, Jr	221
" Bartlett[6], (1764) Capt. Stephen	79
" Bunton[8], (1841) George W	318
" Burgess[9], (1871) John Q., Jr	474
" Clinton[7], (1813) Calvin	192
" Coffin[8], (1868) Hazen Michael	326
" Cook[8], (1846) Richard	338
" E.[7], (1833) Moses	183
" E.[8], (1826) Samuel	291
" Electa[8], (1872) Dr. John G. C.	360
" Elizabeth[7], (1838) Jesse	181
" " [8], —— Charles M	250
" " [8], (1832) Charles	242
" " [8], (1836) John Watson	256
" Fitz[8], (1852) George Fitz	268
" Frances[8], (1820) Col. Joseph Henry	301
" Gertrude[6], (1869) Simeon	395
" H.[8], (1853) Azro	306
" J.[6], (1820) Moses	87
" J.[8], (1866) Arthur C	310
" Jane[7], (1823) Sewall	128
" " [8], (1821) Isaac	253
" Jewett[9], (1867) Caleb Cushing	407
" L.[8], (1848) Charles Henry	266
" Lamoine[6], (1842) Winfred Scott	353
" Little[7], (1831) Freeborn	180
" Louisa[8], (1833) John	245
" Lucina[7], (1835) Horace Hale	230
" M.[7], (1828) Asa	154
" Maria[8], (1838) Moses Woodman	248
" Moody[7], (1809) Col. John Emery	139

	Page.
Sarah Moody[8], (1830) John Emery	282
" Porter[7], (1834) Rev. Charles, D. D	133
" Rowena[7], (1835) Rev. Ezra	199
" Sophia[7], (1834) Isaac	145
" Spofford[7], (1821) Benjamin	126
" True[8], (1865) Henry	325
" W.[8], (1865) George Edward	334
" Welch[7], (1800) Isaac	108
Silence Jones[7], (1813) David	143
Silly[9], (1890) George G	498
Sophia[6], (1799) Abraham	95
" Ordway[10], (1858) George Edward	502
Sophronia[7], (1791) Dr. Samuel	124
" 7, (1813) Ebenezer	189
Stella[6], (1892) Noble D	376
" B.[7], (1851) Clark	225
" Colson[8], (1883) Edwin Hall	327
" Cora[8], (1895) Loren M	396
" Gertrude[8], (1864) Isaac Milton	294
Susan[5], (1811) Dea. Edmund	42
" 6, (1794) Nathan	67
" 6, —— Solomon	75
" 7, (1791) Caleb	107
" 7, (1800) Joseph	116
" 7, (1798) Israel	151
" 7, (1823) Benjamin	155
" 8, —— Reuben Johnson	276
" Amelia[6], (1792) Jacob	121
" Augusta[7], (1833) Daniel Noyes	156
" C.[7], (1814) Matthew	164
" E.[8], (1852) John Langdon	320
" E.[8], (1854) James R	323
" E.[9], (1848) Norman R	476
" Ilsley[8], (1860) Hazen Michael	326
" Jarvis[7], —— Joseph Thornton	131
" Kimball[7], (1807) John	162
" M.[8], (1849) Benjamin F	322
" Noyes[8], (1837) Moses	244
" Pearl[8], (1876) Elbert J	385
" Pike[7], (1838) Richard	176
" Thurlow[10], (1862) Geo. Edward	502

	Page.
Susanna[4], (1729) Richard	15
" 5, (1731) John	23
" 5, (1740) William	27
" 5, (1746) Abraham	37
" 5, (1772) John	40
" 6, (1766) Moses	41
" 5, (1763) Zebulon	43
" 5, (1753) David	44
" 5, (1778) Capt. Simeon	48
" 6, (1779) Stephen	59
" 6, (1768) Abraham	79
" 6, (1803) Zebulon, Jr	90
" 6, (1796) Freegrace, Jr	94
" 6, (1798) Capt. Oliver	99
" 6, (1811) Bildad	103
" 7, —— Abraham	107
" 7, (1816) Enoch	123
Susie A.[9], (1874) Sergt. Joshua Richmond	418
" Stewart[8], (1868) Green	332
Sybil[7], (1797) Israel	150
Sylvia[6], (1791) Daniel	81
Temperance[5], (1768) Freegrace	45
Thelma[10], (1898) Charles Clifford	510
Thomazing Augusta[8], (1849) Lewis Alanson	355
Tirzey[7], —— Hiram	219
Tryphena[5], (1748) Moses	47
Ursula C.[7], (1825) Jeremiah	167
" C.[8], (1852) Benjamin F	322
Victoria[8], (1837) Dr. Milo	262
Viola Bertha[9], (1865) Lorenzo Benson	420
Virginia Maud[8], (1879) Chas. William	336
Wealthy M.[8], (1845) Hiram E	379
Winnie May[8], (1882) Simeon	395
Winnifred Ashley[9], (1888) Jos. Ashley	495
Winona M.[8], (1868) Elbert J	385
Zebina[6], (1794) Zebulon, Jr	90
Zelma E.[8], (1860) John Q	259
Zilpha[5], (1786) Moses	41
" 6, (1812) Ezra	88
" 6, (1844) Moses	87
" 7, (1840) Moses	180

INDEX III.

OTHER THAN ADAMS NAMES.

	Page.		Page.
Aans	214	Baker	100, 195, 209, 223, 259, 354, 382
Abbott	279, 438, 450	Baldwin	158, 373
Ackerman	179, 460	Ball	43, 101
Ackley	238	Ballard	383, 496
Adking	494	Ballou	171, 300
Aiken	303	Bampton	475
Ainsworth	187	Bancroft	35
Albee	149	Banford	436
Alexander	201, 221, 390	Barbour	113
Allard	227	Barden	515, 518
Allen	5, 42, 47, 57, 112, 120, 166, 187, 253, 274, 275, 291, 324, 353, 387, 420, 490.	Bariston	182
		Barker	124
Allison	261, 429	Barnard	75
Alverson	45, 94, 206	Barney	321, 470
Alvord	381	Barnes	61, 133, 261, 274, 353, 428, 429
Ames	46, 255, 332, 388, 395	Barnum	98, 217
Anderson	159, 185, 267, 356, 365, 431	Barrager	208
Andrew	317	Barrett	100, 147, 222, 502, 518
Andrews	8, 103, 110, 116, 147, 162, 229, 359, 399.	Barstow	27
		Bartlett	15, 37, 51, 95, 130, 147, 166, 182, 236, 271, 272, 295, 324, 341, 405, 407, 503.
Appleton	97, 151, 302		
Arms	388	Barton	54, 217, 247, 297
Arnold	241, 412	Bascom	202, 213
Ash	325	Bashore	344
Ashley	204	Bass	317
Askey	284, 445	Bassell	260
Athay	351	Bassett	388
Atkins	118, 275	Batchelder	31, 70, 250
Atkinson	7, 8, 49, 348	Bathrick	348, 480
Atwater	217, 219	Bates	230, 400, 419
Atwood	172	Battell	111
Austin	9, 17, 148, 220	Bausman	264, 434
Austiss	401	Baxter	33, 193
Auter	139	Beach	99, 218
Avery	90, 155, 169	Beall	124, 195, 264, 434
Ayer	27, 60, 176	Beals	313
Ayers	331, 338, 353	Bean	77, 86, 88, 141, 162, 282, 417, 443
Babcock	168	Bears	159, 313
Bacheller	417	Beatty	124
Backum	312	Beck	287
Bacon	69, 318, 442	Beckford	310
Bagley	78, 163, 314, 318, 331	Becklar	290
Bailey	77, 241, 246, 253, 318, 446	Bedortha	89
Bain	269	Bell	138, 282, 329, 348, 383, 385, 427, 442
Baion	17	Bellows	297

INDEX III.

Name	Page
Bement	89, 188, 189, 345
Bemis	288, 410
Bennett	158
Benson	220
Berkley	257, 425
Berry	166, 253, 416, 506
Bickford	74, 461
Bidwell	192, 351
Bigelow	257
Billings	46, 96
Bird	350
Bishop	142
Bixby	460, 514
Black	120
Blackman	50
Blake	21, 39, 82, 108, 128, 146, 269, 296
Blakeley	148
Blaisdell	35
Blanchard	69, 240
Bliss	143, 158, 347, 479
Blossom	256
Bodley	429
Bodwell	33
Bogardus	344
Boggess	260
Bohannon	211
Bolster	138, 140, 287
Bolton	179
Bond	301
Bonnette	391
Booth	315, 316
Bossange	302
Bostwick	273
Bosworth	98, 139
Botsford	322
Bourne	187, 351
Bowen	258, 425
Bowers	259
Bowlen	178, 334
Bowman	66, 135, 284
Boxwell	365
Boyce	185, 248, 415
Boyd	357, 393
Boyden	144
Boyle	264, 434
Boynton	22, 105, 147, 233
Brace	495
Brackett	21, 328, 394, 471
Bradbury	82, 173, 405, 503
Bradford	255, 260
Bradish	382
Bradley	407
Bragg	219
Brainerd	249
Braman	424
Brancher	230
Brewster	191
Breed	135, 276, 300
Brickett	36, 37, 243
Bridge	279
Bridges	333
Briggs	377
Brigham	161, 218, 315, 386
Broadhead	193
Brocklebank	14, 35, 36, 76, 158
Bronson	43
Brooks	402
Brookins	452
Brothers	433
Brown	8, 12, 25, 93, 97, 98, 105, 139, 149, 164, 169, 180, 181, 182, 194, 209, 215, 220, 231, 251, 254, 261, 282, 318, 319, 337, 353, 381, 382, 442, 450, 460, 462, 468, 495, 511
Brownbeck	82
Brownell	465
Bruce	135, 276, 300
Bryan	428, 477, 516
Bryant	205, 320, 373
Buck	136
Buckingham	353
Buechley	285
Buel	69
Buffum	184
Bugbee	246, 413
Bullard	30, 459
Bullock	202
Bumford	314, 464
Bundle	189
Bunton	162, 317
Burbank	6, 13, 135, 148, 295
Burgess	174, 338
Burke	168
Burcker	291
Burkinshaw	272
Burley	64
Burtingham	278
Burnelle	420
Burnette	195, 390
Burnham	71, 148, 289, 340, 475
Burns	360, 398
Burpee	35
Burr	353
Burrage	20
Burrell	258, 318
Burrill	134, 221
Burt	329, 351
Burton	191, 205, 370, 492
Busby	364

Bush	42, 97
Bushee	310
Butler	304
Butterfield	289
Butters	130, 306
Buxton	214, 380
Byrne	426, 427
Cadwell	192, 205
Caldwell	93, 202, 370, 373, 493
Call	321
Calute	196
Camden	427
Campbell	306, 343
Canda	427
Canedy	227
Canterbury	386, 496
Carleton	34, 69, 170, 201, 452
Carr	42, 117, 246, 275, 357, 485
Carpenter	272
Carroll	317
Carter	207, 208, 209
Carver	499
Case	138
Cass	72
Cassell	217
Cate	307
Cawley	21
Chace	466
Chaffee	214
Chalker	313
Chalmers	325
Chambers	195, 385, 496
Chamberlain	54, 252
Chandler	157, 296, 309, 410, 439, 510
Chapin	98, 217, 346, 385
Chaplin	389
Chapman	71, 98, 158, 238, 273, 349
Chase	25, 41, 60, 68, 152, 156, 164, 176, 227, 290, 308, 323, 451, 471
Chauncey	152, 303
Cheever	110, 233
Cheney	78, 240, 251, 390, 499
Cheswick	481
Childs	93, 269
Chipman	109, 214
Christie	199
Chubb	288, 449
Chumley	201
Churchill	159, 233
Chute	15, 38
Cilley	173
Claflin	87
Claggett	388
Clapp	66, 135, 217
Currier	25, 105, 110, 113, 160, 163, 165, 169, 233, 404

Clark	45, 53, 69, 70, 104, 110, 119, 122, 125, 136, 142, 171, 232, 236, 285, 289, 290, 316, 331, 348, 392, 408, 422, 480, 500
Clarkson	267
Clayton	219
Clement	167, 235, 385, 496
Clements	315
Clemenshaw	196
Cleveland	311, 352, 463
Close	355
Clough	227
Cobb	112, 120, 255, 420, 422
Cobble	432
Cochran	432
Codman	108, 240
Coffey	423
Coffin	84, 129, 417
Cofran	123
Coit	387
Coker	110, 242, 266
Colburn	74, 153, 156, 160, 313, 315, 465
Colby	52, 114, 142, 144, 165, 167, 404, 450
Cole	246, 413, 419, 426
Coleman	12, 38, 176, 197, 356
Collamore	249
Colley	49, 118
Collins	75, 76, 136, 165, 277, 320
Colton	94, 277
Comer	271
Comfort	403
Comstock	380
Conant	411
Combs	112, 268
Cone	449
Connery	387
Cook	86, 98, 114, 116, 217, 238, 297, 346, 455, 482, 517
Cooley	215, 302
Coombs	275
Coon	332
Coonley	381
Cooper	8, 154, 155, 305, 345
Copes	367
Corbett	95, 208, 209
Corey	426
Cornell	193
Corning	88
Cornwell	264
Corry	258
Corse	392
Cotton	515
Cottrell	335
Couch	324
Cowley	335

INDEX III.

	Page.
Cox	344
Craine	388
Crandall	98
Crane	350, 355
Creal	344
Creasy	20, 52, 289, 291, 452
Crispin	357
Crocker	250
Crockett	68
Crombie	340, 475
Crook	298, 456
Crosby	226, 455
Cross	55, 148, 160, 192, 202
Crouch	366
Crow	358
Culbert	199, 359
Culbertson	430
Cummins	367
Cummings	126, 159, 269, 293, 321
Cumner	316
Cunningham	338
Curtis	92, 131, 219, 352, 439
Curry	71, 224
Cushman	154
Cutler	46, 149
Cutts	161
Cutter	118
Dackins	424
Daggett	307
Dake	209, 375
Dale	301
Dales	355
Dalrymple	435
Damon	144
Danforth	184, 325, 406, 436
Daniels	87, 327
Darragh	124
Davenport	280
Davidson	46, 263, 304
Davis, 51, 55, 57. 110, 130, 132, 152, 160, 161 170, 172, 178, 193, 218, 241, 265, 274, 282 288, 310, 370, 406, 430, 435, 492, 504	
Day	37, 60
Dean	343
Dearborn	84, 172, 176, 323
De Bremon	244, 412
Decker	98, 350
De Leon	301
Delinda	189
Delvy	371
Deming	205
Dempster	479
Dennis	81, 133, 172, 239, 290, 408
Denison	223

	Page.
Depew	376
Derby	201
Dewey	90, 191, 350
Dibble	99
Dickerman	349
Dickinson	97, 170, 323
Dickey	124, 263, 432, 433
Diebel	482
Dilloway	148
Dimond	467
Dingley	56
Dingman	218
Disney	84, 183
Dixon	250
Dobber	136
Dobson	240
Dodd	113
Dodge	22, 172, 289, 309
Dole	37, 38, 49, 85, 237, 302, 317
Donald	387
Doolittle	222
Dore	236
Doremus	189, 347
Dorman	25, 174
Dorr	416
Dorris	432
Doss	344
Doty	351
Douglass	400
Dow	78, 111, 268
Downs	229, 398, 460
Doyle	308
Drabble	258, 426
Drake	154, 204, 305, 373, 459
Draper	132, 274
Dravo	428
Dresser	67, 137, 141, 142, 289, 290, 449
Dwinal	120
Dubois	282
Dudley	139, 161, 315
Duffey	366
Duillis	107
Dummer	11, 128, 268
Dunbar	80, 118, 309
Dunham	118, 246, 379
Dunklee	225
Dunlap	131
Dunn	243, 387
Dunnell	418
Dunning	286
Dunton	156
Durand	352
Durrie	14
Dutton	158, 310

INDEX III.

	Page.
Dye	359, 495
Dyer	198, 328, 359
Eager	345
Earley	245, 413
Eastman	67, 80, 167, 407
Easton	192, 262, 347
Eaton	229, 239, 308, 319, 398, 429, 468
Ebbage	92
Eddy	479
Edgar	361
Edgerly	416
Edgerton	102
Edwards	139, 366, 381
Eicholtz	286, 448
Elder	253, 419
Eldridge	248, 275, 414
Ellinwood	374
Elliot	52, 150
Ellis	206, 213, 242
Ellwell	333
Ellwood	433
Elmer	93, 99
Elwell	87
Emerson	51, 72, 285
Emerton	289, 452
Emery	12
English	127
Eno	348
Estes	347
Evans	83, 175, 227, 329, 420
Everett	105, 155, 305, 307
Everts	121, 454
Fairall	283
Fairbox	116
Fairfield	136, 181
Farman	46
Fales	375
Falkner	73
Farmer	156
Farnam	13, 14, 67
Farrar	304, 312
Farrell	444
Farrington	67
Farrow	321
Fawcett	196, 199
Fay	195, 196, 355
Fear	359
Feary	365
Felch	164, 235
Feller	362, 401
Fellows	92, 461
Fenno	50, 108
Ferguson	280
Ferris	203

	Page.
Fenton	63, 147
Field	211, 212, 253, 270, 420
Fields	91
Fife	297
Fifield	80, 296
Finch	40
Fish	96, 211, 476
Fisher	212
Fisk	222, 297, 391
Fitz	61
Fitzgerald	386
Flagg	156
Flanders	35, 123, 152, 167, 260, 294, 465, 515
Fleming	474
Flether	143, 230, 400
Fleury	356
Flinn	304, 457
Flint	280
Fluent	82
Fogg	249, 416
Folger	342
Follensbee	36
Folsom	29, 76, 141, 179
Forbes	97, 121, 212, 432
Ford	66, 411, 505
Forken	231
Forsythe	129, 254, 497
Fosdick	29
Foss	119, 249, 252, 269
Foster	88, 89, 135, 207, 264, 278, 434
Fowler, 19, 168, 193, 224, 234, 320, 344, 476, 477, 481, 516.	
Fox	186
Frame	429
Francis	186
Franklin	161
Frates	255
Frazier	246
Freeman	193, 291, 388, 448
Freeze	20
French	66, 291
Freewelling	357
Frickett	138, 280
Frisbie	231
Frost	18, 24, 112, 172, 391
Fuller	181, 190, 227, 245, 250, 286, 348, 447
Fullerton	23, 53, 290
Fulton	225
Furber	132
Furnside	319
Fussellneaux	208
Gabriel	413
Gage	160, 266, 341, 361, 449, 512
Gale	202, 221, 301

INDEX III.

Name	Page
Gammage	168
Gardner	291
Garrett	357
Gates	192, 278, 468
Gay	155, 240, 306, 461
Gaylord	127
Gaymon	284, 446
Gee	420
Georstine	70
George	83, 209, 271, 306, 376
German	231
Gerrish	12, 85
Getchell	215, 319
Gibbs	95, 207, 210
Gibbons	431, 509
Gibson	286, 358, 448, 464, 514
Gifford	113
Gilbert	207, 298, 351, 375, 424, 438, 510
Gile	60
Gillett	9, 232, 330, 346, 354, 472, 479, 481
Gillingham	164
Gilman	322
Gilmore	231
Glass	199, 361, 487
Gleason	139, 383
Glines	140
Goodell	145
Goodhue	168...78, 327
Goodno	140
Goodnough	222
Goodnow	226
Goodrich	5, 8, 15, 96, 97, 207, 213, 279, 378
Goodspeed	91, 195, 196, 355
Goodwin	33, 105, 176, 177, 182, 216, 234, 235, 384
Gordon	163, 171, 232, 355, 387
Goss	379
Gotham	130
Gott	220
Gould	126, 250, 408
Goulding	395
Gowell	56
Gowdy	147
Graff	122, 258
Granger	4, 6, 47, 81, 171
Grant	306, 460
Graves	23, 55, 102, 115, 217
Gray	90, 254, 256, 260, 411, 421
Greeley	52, 153
Green	151, 236, 423
Greenleaf	12, 68, 178
Greenwood	83
Gregg	96, 211
Griffin	41, 92, 198, 306, 320, 460

Name	Page
Griffis	88, 185
Griffith	85, 275
Grieb	477
Grills	213, 378
Grimstone	359
Grinnell	95, 208
Griswold	214
Grover	117, 244
Grow	319
Growther	110
Guild	134
Guimaraes	267
Guinter	374
Gunn	188
Gurley	193
Gurney	233, 234
Guthrie	231
Hackett	74
Hadley	108, 195, 467
Hager	183
Haggett	119, 248
Hale, 10, 37, 38, 48, 49, 52, 55, 69, 88, 113, 128, 143, 151, 186, 231, 237, 270, 406, 502.	
Haley	348
Hall, 53, 58, 68, 117, 138, 151, 185, 228, 231, 240, 363, 385, 407, 412, 503.	
Halladay	45, 48, 101, 226, 369
Hamilton, 93, 120, 133, 202, 250, 369, 489, 490	
Hanchett	6, 44
Hand	410
Handy	316
Hanson	111, 236, 306
Hardy	7, 14, 34, 449, 451
Harkness	382
Harmon	9
Harp	365
Harper	48, 411
Harrigan	451, 459
Harriman	26, 69, 164, 243, 392
Harrington	108, 141, 220, 306, 388, 497
Harris, 82, 205, 206, 221, 223, 272, 382, 389, 495	
Hart	385, 479
Harthorn	77
Hartshorn	113, 115
Hartman	320
Hartwell	14
Harvey	65, 78, 137, 165, 412
Haskell	56, 77, 327
Haskins	154, 192, 305
Haslum	241, 243, 411
Hastings	221
Hasty	416
Hatch	63, 92, 132, 252, 273
Hawes	154, 409, 504

INDEX III.

	Page.
Hawkes	266
Hawkins	360, 365
Hawthorn	320, 469
Hayden	9, 45, 248
Hayes	75, 154, 305, 416
Hayner	134
Haynes	48, 236, 275, 334
Hayward	59, 122
Hazeltine	250
Hazen	7, 14, 34, 307, 461
Heald	103, 231, 402, 403
Healy	288
Heath	188, 209, 231, 289, 350
Heaton	363
Helmer	153, 304
Hemeranger	384
Hemingway	284, 445
Hemmingway	406
Hendee	250
Henderson	305
Herron	150
Hersey	336
Hervey	128
Hewett	379
Hibbard	141
Hidden	31, 51
Higgins	95, 109, 181, 195, 207, 210, 249
Higley	104, 224, 232, 394
Hill	96, 100, 140, 147, 153, 175, 243, 301, 418
Hills	11, 20
Hillard	104
Hilpert	171
Hinckley	335
Hinckline	200
Hines	222
Hoague	110, 111
Hobbs	339
Hobson	83, 265
Hodgdon	296, 359
Hodge	214
Hodgins	482, 517
Hogg	107
Hoggan	360
Holcomb	194
Holdridge	14
Hollenbeck	399
Holliday	364, 391
Hollins	428
Hollis	316
Hollister	100
Holmes	134, 273, 406
Holt	34, 261, 325, 426
Hooker	110

	Page.
Hope	284, 328
Hopkins	17, 211, 454
Hopson	78, 164
Horr	142, 291
Horton	162, 325
Hosmer	88
Hough	356, 359
Houghton	100, 153, 224, 232, 233, 393, 453
House	27, 101, 148, 170, 173, 223, 226, 304
Howard	51, 92, 93, 127, 278
Howall	366
Howarth	481
Howe	370
Howett	461
Howlett	319
Hoyt	29, 62, 88, 156, 164, 192, 388, 453, 498
Hubbard	92, 99, 219
Hudson	245, 464
Huey	149
Huff	281
Hughes	196, 366, 369
Hulbert	385
Hulett	226
Hume	311, 345
Humiston	380
Humphebill	481
Humphrey	111
Hunkins	88, 150
Hunt	52, 92
Huntington	229, 313
Huntley	132
Huntoon	324
Huntress	290, 450
Hurd	282, 316, 433, 441
Hurlburt	198, 356
Huse	127, 177, 333
Hussey	149
Huston	253
Hutchinson	7, 55, 74, 182, 256, 260
Hyde	255
Hynes	368
Ilsley	37, 39, 62, 81, 171, 175, 234, 406, 407
Ingraham	124, 219
Ingalls	135
Irvine	209
Irwin	372
Jack	116
Jackman	10, 15, 26, 176, 208, 327, 334, 353
Jackson	13, 68, 73, 74
James	152, 257, 411
Jamieson	358
Janes	327
Janvrin	177, 332
Jaques	10, 20, 22, 27, 36, 49, 51, 115, 177, 178

INDEX III.

Name	Pages
Jarvis	64
Jasper	222
Jenkins	27
Jennings	81, 240
Jepson	466
Jewett	41, 82, 233, 238, 269
Jeffers	268
Jillson	226
Johns	262, 431, 509, 510
Johnson	37, 55, 78, 86, 111, 114, 124, 148, 164, 192, 217, 247, 260, 276, 284, 303, 319, 369, 370, 385, 420
Johnston	331
Jones	67, 135, 148, 168, 202, 279, 280, 451, 490, 491
Joslin	313
Joslyn	89
Jove	119
Judd	282, 443
Judkins	169, 328
Judson	207
Kearr	272
Keck	429
Keen	283
Keisler	139
Keller	432
Kelley	78, 441, 457
Kellogg	45, 94, 205, 208, 373
Kelly	150, 165, 171
Kelson	476
Kemp	71
Kempshall	213, 378
Kempt	367
Kendall	17, 43, 90, 191
Kendrick	20
Keniston	39
Kennedy	352
Kenney	200, 362
Kent	18, 44, 46, 54, 68, 85, 97, 113, 240, 276, 354, 489
Kenyon	46
Kerr	389
Keyes	209
Knapp	22, 55, 85, 176, 321, 330
Knight	7, 20, 22, 49, 51, 112, 113, 114, 171, 176, 183, 223, 246, 326, 331, 334, 339, 475
Knott	150
Knotts	365
Knowles	84
Knowlton	78, 135, 328
Kibbe	343
Kidder	319, 332
Kilborn	14, 91, 196
Kildow	376
Kimball	16, 33, 48, 73, 77, 106, 114, 125, 127, 135, 157, 220, 242, 265, 288, 309, 350, 440, 452, 479, 488, 489
Kincaid	325
Kincheloe	477, 478, 516
King	17, 45, 90, 92, 122, 189, 190, 200, 211, 214, 220, 228, 249, 345, 363, 364, 366, 372, 379, 387
Kingsbury	188
Kingsley	156
Kinney	103, 282
Kinsey	228
La Croix	270
La Grasse	13
Laird	175, 329, 397
Lake	286, 374
Lakeman	235
Lamb	210
Lamberton	343, 476
Lambirth	317
Lamoreaux	191
Lamphere	137, 278
Lancey	331
Lander	105, 236, 504
Lane	17, 46, 47, 60, 65, 123, 256, 260, 279, 416, 440
Lanford	81
Lank	288
Larden	305
Larkin	317
Larned	70
Larrabee	96
La Rue	282
Lasher	402
Latham	137, 278, 279
Laughlin	315
Laurimore	432
Law	256, 311
Lawrence	70, 419
Lawton	194, 353, 388
Lazell	349
Leach	52, 64, 107, 280, 319
Learnard	250
Leavitt	109, 152
Le Barron	95, 208
Lee	110, 159, 207, 214, 241, 348, 374, 379
Leeds	180
Leggett	103
Lehman	288
Leighton	252, 423
Leonard	18, 45, 108, 180, 188, 213, 223
Lesley	420
Leslie	206
Lester	190, 346, 476

	Page.
Letts	195
Levy	367
Lewis	56, 98, 159, 208, 264, 329, 452
Libby	246
Lillie	160
Linch	301
Lincoln	134, 195, 354
Linderman	352
Lindsay	334
Lippincott	295, 455
Liswell	349
Little	15, 22, 37, 39, 49, 51, 55, 81, 84, 129, 177, 178, 258, 270, 329, 406, 472.
Livereaux	196
Livermore	121
Livingstone	80, 170, 291
Lockwood	378
Lofty	125
Lombard	11, 292
Long	112
Longerich	494
Longfellow	7, 40, 41, 62
Longley	107, 239
Loomis	91, 191, 193, 194, 279
Lord	49, 151, 175, 195, 256
Lothrop	120
Love	94, 363, 489
Lovejoy	138, 280, 290, 316, 317
Lovell	229
Lovering	126, 169, 325
Low	296, 418
Lowe	397
Lowes	198
Lucas	278, 332
Luce	251
Lucy	113, 243
Lufkin	122, 259
Lunt	40, 86, 111, 148, 404
Lynde	225
Lyndon	91
Lyon	139, 261, 313
Mackenzie	420, 507, 508
Mackey	380
MacMillan	281
Macomber	131
Madden	136
Magoun	426
Mahony	481
Mallett	56, 116
Mallison	312
Mandenhall	441
Manderson	267
Manley	219
Manning	179

	Page.
Mansfield	242, 243
Marden	170
Marean	216, 383, 466
Marquis	263, 433
Marsh	34, 41, 88, 213
Marshall	184, 302, 468
Marston	65, 83, 132
Martin	51, 200, 270, 279, 294, 360, 378
Mason	109, 169, 324, 428
Mather	47, 93, 99, 202, 219, 221, 223, 224, 231, 391, 393, 394, 499.
Matthews	22, 156, 360, 487
Matthewson	196
Mattison	382, 383
Mattocks	398
Maxim	281, 441
Maxom	77
Maxwell	261
May	480
Maywood	199
McAlpine	317
McCallum	198
McCalmont	125, 265
McCarthy	30, 109
McClellan	394, 500
McConnell	271
McCready	145
McCue	386
McCune	139, 284
McDonald	119, 122
McDaniels	52
McGraw	62
McGettrick	507
McKain	230
McKee	428
McKelvey	102, 229, 262, 397, 432
McKinney	430, 508
McKnight	189
McIntire	142, 281, 441
McLaren	227
McLaughlin	210
McMurray	370
McNett	304
McPharren	435
Means	255, 422
Mears	183
Melcher	112, 307
Melvin	185
Memmen	412, 505
Merriam	194, 407
Merrick	429
Merchant	216, 384
Merrill	7, 10, 21, 23, 37, 38, 53, 68, 160, 170, 239, 286, 301, 409.

INDEX III.

Merritt............41, 96, 105, 212, 274, 345
Merry................................256, 423
Messenger 387
Messer................................ 305
Metcalf................................ 132
Metzger............................... 263
Middleton............................. 231
Mighill................................ 182
Miller, 47, 59, 124, 137, 186, 194, 206, 248, 263
   265, 295, 367, 368, 405, 481.
Milne.................................. 398
Minot.................................. 112
Mitchell.............256, 292, 238, 381, 494
Mixer.................................. 94
Mixter................................. 348
Mock..............................446, 511
Moffat................................. 439
Moffit...............................284, 443
Moir................................... 360
Monroe.............................136, 379
Montgomery.......................344, 369
Moody................51, 67, 132, 183, 273
Moon.................................. 161
Moor................................... 36
Moore...............41, 126, 395, 442, 476
Morden................................ 103
Morean................................ 466
Morey...............................160, 320
Morgan............................358, 370, 486, 491
Morrisey............................... 257
Morrill..................171, 320, 323, 468
Morris...........................304, 363, 489
Morrison.............................. 120
Morse, 10, 20, 40, 49, 51, 52, 53, 79, 106, 110
   111, 144, 160, 167, 168, 236, 288, 314, 321
   411, 449, 453, 512, 513.
Morss................................. 237
Mosher................................ 119
Moses.................................. 52
Motley................................ 108
Mott................................... 353
Moulthrop.............................. 89
Moulton........................118, 146, 323, 351
Munger................................. 97
Munaker............................... 145
Munn................................... 94
Munsy........................117, 145, 244
Murdock.................254, 261, 422
Murphy...........................183, 358
Muzzy................................. 397
Nason.................................. 452
Nealey.............................235, 406
Needham..............................231
Nelson.....61, 123, 163, 241, 305, 319, 394, 467

Nesmith...........................126, 267
Netzer................................. 368
Nevens................................ 272
Newbury............................... 380
Newcomb.............................. 399
Newell................................ 228
Newman................................ 49
Newton................................ 212
Nield.................................. 339
Nichols............................12, 287
Nicholson............................. 216
Nickerson............................. 116
Nightingale........................... 240
Niles............................93, 94, 207
Nims.................................. 292
Noble.................................. 195
Nobles................................. 192
Noice.............................355, 483
Noonan................................ 277
Norman................................ 69
Norrish................................ 376
Northen................................ 31
Northend............................... 68
Norton...........9, 188, 281, 356, 383, 441
Nourse................................ 164
Noyes, 7, 11, 15, 16, 21, 38, 49, 52, 53, 54, 83
   86, 110, 117, 118, 154, 181, 236, 246 287, 329
   448, 472.
Nye..........................45, 93, 307, 462
Oakes.............................361 487
Oatman................................ 273
O'Connell.........................311, 463
Ogden................................. 336
O'Hara................................ 429
Olds.........................6, 100, 224, 226, 392
Olmstead.............................. 229
Ordway...................34, 177, 270, 333, 404
Ormsby................................ 348
Orne................................... 30
Ort.................................... 274
Ortolam............................... 388
Orwan.............................216, 383
Osborn............................265, 349
Osgood, 34, 69, 82, 86, 151, 166, 184, 219, 235
   302, 320.
Osman................................ 198
Ostrander............................. 194
Otis..........................48, 101, 103
Owen..........................89, 119, 252
Oxnard................................ 130
Packard................136, 157, 256, 309
Paddock............................... 408
Page..................142, 179, 240, 341, 411
Paige............................458, 514

	Page.
Paine	371
Palfrey	160, 313
Palmer	16, 211, 290, 328, 366
Parish	38
Park	281, 389, 390
Parks	379
Parker, 62, 119, 126, 150, 189, 190, 203, 248, 267 309, 344, 345, 346, 347, 371, 415, 451, 478 479, 492	
Parmalee	90
Parmelee	394, 500
Parmenter	311, 380
Parshley	206
Parson	159
Parsons	95, 216
Pascoe	136
Passmore	283
Paton	356
Patridge	414
Patterson	205, 224, 228, 263, 414, 433, 450
Paul	273
Payne	393
Payson	12
Pearson	7, 39, 49, 105, 113, 128, 187
Pease	388
Peaslee	25
Peck	96, 215, 383, 449, 512
Peckham	145, 194, 293
Pellett	187, 279
Pennell	113
Peabody	87, 146, 295, 455
Pepper	42, 88
Pepple	304, 459
Perham	227, 232
Perkins, 27, 35, 81, 114, 126, 158, 172, 175, 176 245, 288, 339, 400, 475.	
Perley	35, 60, 76, 126, 157
Perrine	383
Perry	160, 202, 289, 319, 450, 467
Pettengill, 4, 8, 21, 106, 114, 183, 185, 237, 320 341, 406.	
Pettee	221
Pettet	208
Peters	31
Peterson	241
Phelps	5, 8, 183, 308
Philbrick	182, 281
Phillips, 119, 230, 241, 300, 314, 382, 399, 432 495.	
Phinney	256, 423
Pierce	10, 31, 39, 87, 94
Pierson	119
Pickett	361, 488
Pike	8, 10, 237, 450

	Page.
Pillsbury	174, 329
Pingree	305
Piper	126
Pitman	402
Plumb	47, 204
Plumer, 35, 47, 59, 60, 80, 85, 86, 105, 125, 181 236, 281, 430.	
Plummer	37
Poland	183
Polk	428
Pollard	183
Pomeroy	191, 226
Pond	50
Poole	180
Poor	6, 12, 37, 55, 107, 235, 236, 238
Porter	30, 32, 53, 65, 126, 187, 250, 267, 417
Post	110
Pote	53, 54
Potter	143, 215
Pottle	273
Powell	282
Power	125
Powers	93, 200, 201, 265, 363, 364, 368, 488
Pound	406
Pratt	94, 104, 117
Prescott	67, 112, 249, 299
Pressey	154, 287, 408, 462
Preston	66, 380
Pride	245
Priest	203, 371, 372, 493
Prime	184
Prince	108, 117, 246, 413
Printiss	230, 399
Procter	201, 202, 364
Proctor	92, 208, 268, 355, 364, 420, 436, 468
Puffer	346
Pulsifer	49, 417
Purchase	18
Purington	253, 315, 464
Purrington	161
Putnam	71, 166, 227, 379
Putney	311
Quackenbush	346, 476
Quimby	156, 171
Quincy	168
Rackley	76
Radcliffe	352
Rainsford	109
Raleigh	194
Randall	159, 512
Ransier	209, 376
Ransom	309
Rawlins	15
Raymond	143, 203, 277

INDEX III.

Name	Page
Read	213, 325
Rectenus	430
Redfield	62, 127
Redington	494
Reed	237, 279, 340, 378, 394, 452, 513
Reens	431
Reid	358
Reinshaw	356
Remington	343
Reno	263, 433
Renwick	358, 486
Reynolds	159, 260, 287, 309, 339, 349, 450, 475.
Rhodes	218, 363, 386
Rice	44, 204, 392, 476
Richards	458, 462
Richardson	185, 189, 307, 318, 454
Richmond	223, 295, 455
Rider	112
Riggs	52, 244, 411
Riley	349
Rix	316, 466
Robbins	94, 110, 146, 207, 370, 474, 491
Roberts	120, 171, 255, 349, 422, 423, 481
Robertson	193, 283, 444
Robinson	99, 125, 171, 179, 184, 221, 244, 346, 402, 419, 431, 478.
Rockwell	283, 380, 444
Rockwood	121
Roe	355, 429, 482
Rogers	51, 100, 112, 128, 173, 187, 209, 327, 450, 504.
Rolfe	21, 81, 176, 330, 407
Rollins	159
Rolph	321
Root	189, 349
Ropp	386, 496
Rose	259
Rotner	315, 459
Rounds	148
Rouse	208
Rowe	9, 36, 164
Rowell	466
Rowley	184, 515
Royals	342
Royce	465
Ruckel	283, 444
Russell	39, 41, 112, 130, 141, 171, 180, 191, 244, 327, 474.
Ryder	421
Salisbury	387, 497
Salter	314, 401, 501
Sampson	279
Sanborn	65, 158, 175, 178, 310
Sanders	52
Sanderson	413
Sanford	174, 269, 399
Sanger	113, 149, 157, 280
Sargent	59, 74, 75, 100, 106, 154, 155, 162, 165, 206, 238, 287, 293, 444, 452.
Saunders	52, 357, 484
Savary	17, 69, 195
Sawin	70, 285, 446
Sawyer	52, 75, 116, 138, 320
Sayders	215
Schauppe	355
Schreiner	286, 447
Scott	143, 215, 222, 306, 393, 460, 500
Scribner	306
Searle	13, 33, 38
Secomb	10
Sedgewick	91, 192
Selecman	211
Selleck	412, 505
Sellers	358
Severance	49, 309
Sewall	7
Sexton	203
Shaffer	231
Shannon	186
Sharp	321
Shattuck	144
Shaw	112, 323
Shepard	167, 321
Sherborn	452
Sheriff	65
Sherlock	277
Sherman	112, 215, 369, 480
Sherwin	143, 292, 344
Sherwood	349
Shockley	364
Short	51, 53, 106, 110, 174, 243
Shumaker	226
Shurtliff	98, 138, 280
Shute	113
Sias	318
Sigman	257
Sikes	6, 9, 17, 18, 187, 188, 189, 191, 345, 476.
Silk	451
Simonds	292
Simons	214
Simmons	149
Simms	217
Simonton	415
Simpson	292
Skillings	56, 57, 244, 315, 419, 420, 439, 510
Skillinger	253

INDEX III.

Skinner 184, 306, 461, 480
Slack 310, 462
Slaght 484
Slattery 488
Sleeper 320, 469
Small 86
Smead 96, 212
Smith.. 50, 51, 57, 68, 91, 106, 109, 119, 120
　127, 141, 151, 152, 153, 161, 169, 170, 193
　204, 222, 226, 227, 230, 248, 251, 253, 258
　274, 290, 291, 303, 308, 315, 351, 354, 355
　401, 402, 418, 422, 423, 427, 451, 453, 465
　470, 476, 482.
Smithson 191
Smythe 165
Snow 90, 190, 349, 499
Somerby 12, 239, 409
Somerville 332, 473
Soper 194, 353
Soule 296
Southard 321, 336
Spencer 45, 195, 204, 354
Spiller 168, 169, 324
Spinney 242, 243, 410, 505
Spofford..... 7, 27, 28, 32, 70, 144, 152, 266
　303, 436.
Sprague 134, 344
Springall 123
Spurr 46
St. Marie 252
Stafford 239, 359, 369, 490
Stanwood 110, 112
Stark 133
Starr 210
Starts 399
Stearns 99, 101, 147, 156, 386
Stebbins 195, 231, 461
Stecky 362
Steele 62, 127, 145, 249
Stevens .. 34, 68, 69, 143, 152, 167, 169, 232
　233, 242, 292, 302, 313, 348, 351, 411.
Stevenson 250, 362, 363
Stewart 177, 428, 429
Stickney 14, 32, 330, 404
Stiles 148, 297, 334
Still 182
Stilman 90
Stimson 125
Stimpson 38
Stinson 68, 74, 75, 76, 142, 257
Stockman 234
Stone 252, 371
Storer 211, 220
Story 177

Stowell 107
Strange 215
Stratton 143, 150
Straw 66, 255
Strickland 67
Strong 222, 482
Struble 215, 381
Stuart 4, 11, 25, 253, 254
Studley 135
Sturgis 140
Stutes 400
Sutherland 56, 410, 504
Swain 268
Swan 71, 87, 384
Swann 198, 358
Sweet 254
Sweetland 216, 385
Swentzell 310
Swett 56, 419
Swift 397
Switcher 52
Sylvester 112
Taber 291
Tandy 72
Tanner 264, 435
Tappan 83, 85
Tarbell 407, 503
Tarbox 116
Taylor, 6, 179, 207, 220, 222, 240, 262, 281, 332
　334, 361, 374, 432, 460.
Tenney 86, 171, 172, 182, 379
Thayer 104, 211, 223
Thissell 306
Thomas 100, 104, 113, 180, 186, 222, 345
Thompson, 23, 53, 193, 249, 274, 418, 431, 476
Thorne 287, 370
Thornton 400
Thresher 8
Thurber 204, 393, 461
Thurlow, 6, 10, 15, 37, 38, 39, 40, 41, 83, 84,
　86, 127, 411.
Thurston 16, 34, 38, 80, 109, 147, 180, 335
Tibbetts 174, 328
Tillotson 429
Tilton 85, 179, 247, 291, 452, 467
Titcomb 21, 62, 68, 86, 114, 117, 128
Todd 184, 238, 266, 407, 436
Tomblin 232
Topliff 189
Torrens 431
Torrey 269
Tower 171, 321
Towne 108
Townsend 175

INDEX III.

Name	Page
Townsley	264
Tracey	186, 342
Trafton	205, 374
Tranmer	397
Trax	430, 509
Tribon	157, 309
True	24, 56, 80, 186, 281
Trumball	12, 264
Tubbs	279
Tucker	104, 169, 171, 305, 309, 327, 346, 460
Tuckerman	130, 272
Turner	502
Tuttle	314
Twichell	203
Twitchell	70, 145
Tyler	33, 38, 189, 220, 346
Tyrrell	168, 169, 324
Underwood	18, 22
Upton	155, 268, 364
Vance	145
Van Delinda	347
Van Skiver	71
Van Wart	409
Varney	58, 194
Veasey	179
Verondi	259
Vidito	371
Viele	383
Vincent	143
Vinton	346
Virgin	285
Wade	136, 478
Wadleigh	162, 316
Wadsworth	215
Wait	94, 212
Waite	206
Walcott	281, 312, 464
Waldron	248, 415
Walker	148, 174, 235, 240, 251, 262, 283, 307, 328, 418, 444.
Wallace	69, 82
Wallis	128
Walter	63, 64
Ward	91, 149, 293, 368
Wardwell	78, 140, 290
Wareham	5, 9
Warfield	133
Warmley	271
Wann	409
Warner	9, 423, 467
Warren	76, 222, 239, 282, 283, 349, 442, 445
Warriner	97
Washburn	70, 140, 225
Waterhouse	29
Watson	24, 86
Wattles	215
Watts	111
Waugh	310
Way	316, 465
Weare	21
Weaver	387
Webb	30
Webber	271
Webster	75, 156, 185, 189, 272
Wedgwood	174, 328
Weed	166
Weeks	52, 370, 491
Welch	245, 258, 426
Weld	269
Wellman	392
Wells	72, 111, 234, 237, 408
Westcott	401, 501
West	56, 131, 160, 267
Weston	292, 456
Weyand	262, 431
Weyland	262
Weymouth	36, 56
Wheeler	59, 79, 123, 158, 227, 254, 260, 296
Wheelock	257, 424
Wheelwright	127, 268
Whidden	59, 260, 342
Whipple	310, 312
Whitbeck	144
Whitcomb	305
White	14, 93, 101, 151, 162, 210, 220, 226, 302, 319.
Whiteley	294, 431, 454, 513
Whitford	153
Whitney	51, 100, 126, 149, 212, 223, 251, 310, 449, 463.
Whitridge	269
Whittaker	364, 391, 499
Whittemore	250, 252, 266, 417
Whitten	267
Whittier	75, 319, 467, 468
Wiggan	82
Wiggin	133
Wiggins	29, 65, 132, 133, 155, 251, 270
Wight	70, 141, 297, 455
Wilber	374
Wilbor	214
Wilbur	248, 315, 420, 508
Wilcox	101
Wilder	192, 352
Wildes	131
Wiley	178
Wilkinson	200, 362
Williamson	280

	Page.		Page.
Williams	75, 137, 189, 236, 294, 352, 366, 379, 381.	Woodford	480
Willard	101, 203, 231, 372	Woodman	8, 14, 27, 28
Willis	68, 104, 136, 141, 142, 381, 477	Woodward	80, 101, 102, 170
Wilson	123, 189, 242, 261, 353, 354, 356, 371, 380, 389, 427, 428, 430, 451, 484, 498.	Woodworth	188, 199, 292
Winchell	17	Woolcott	6
Winchester	48, 71, 100, 104, 149, 221, 223, 224, 231, 299, 369, 394.	Wooley	350
		Woolman	379
Winder	384, 496	Woolsey	229
Winfrey	363	Worden	196, 232, 393
Winslow	21, 102	Work	354
Winter	95, 216, 499	Wormstead	83
Winters	213	Worthen	79, 248, 302, 415
Winthrop	130	Worth	306, 461
Wise	184	Worthington	189, 348, 480, 481
Withington	67, 139	Wray	428
Withum	180	Wright	70, 97, 99, 178, 191, 214, 321, 336, 347, 470.
Wolf	263	Wylie	91
Womeldorph	302, 459	Wyman	280
Wood	13, 87, 102, 116, 122, 184, 416, 506	Wyrick	332
Woodes	504	Yates	279, 440
Woods	172, 342	Yeaton	341
Woodburn	451	Yonkey	275
Woodbury	300	Young	80, 112, 163, 168, 169, 170, 172, 183, 279, 338, 360, 418, 477, 507.
Woodcock	235, 291, 452	Younglove	6

www.ingramcontent.com/pod-product-compliance
Lightning Source LLC
Chambersburg PA
CBHW071131300426
44113CB00009B/945